ECONOMICS

FOURTH EDITION

Joseph E. Stiglitz
COLUMBIA UNIVERSITY

Carl E. Walsh
UNIVERSITY OF CALIFORNIA, SANTA CRUZ

ECONOMICS

FOURTH EDITION

W. W. Norton & Company
New York · London

W. W. Norton & Company has been independent since its founding in 1923, when William Warder Norton and Mary D. Herter Norton first published lectures delivered at the People's Institute, the adult education division of New York City's Cooper Union. The Nortons soon expanded their program beyond the Institute, publishing books by celebrated academics from America and abroad. By mid-century, the two major pillars of Norton's publishing program—trade books and college texts—were firmly established. In the 1950s, the Norton family transferred control of the company to its employees, and today—with a staff of four hundred and a comparable number of trade, college, and professional titles published each year—W. W. Norton & Company stands as the largest and oldest publishing house owned wholly by its employees.

Copyright © 2006, 2002, 1997, 1993 by W. W. Norton & Company, Inc.

All rights reserved
Printed in the United States of America

Manufacturing by RR Donnelley
Book design by Rubina Yeh
Editor: Jack Repcheck
Director of Manufacturing—College: Roy Tedoff
Project Editor: Lory A. Frenkel
Manuscript Editor: Alice Falk
Editorial Assistants: Sarah Solomon, Mik Awake
Photo Researcher: Kelly Mitchell

Library of Congress Cataloging-in Publication Data
Stiglitz, Joseph E.
    Economics / Joseph E. Stiglitz, Carl E. Walsh.—4th ed.
      p. cm.
    Includes index.
    ISBN 0-393-92622-2
    1. Economics. I. Walsh, Carl E. II. Title

    HB171.5.S884   2005
330—dc22

2005055518

W. W. Norton & Company, Inc., 500 Fifth Avenue, New York, N. Y. 10110
www.wwnorton.com
W. W. Norton & Company Ltd., Castle House, 75/76 Wells Street, London W1T 3QT

1 2 3 4 5 6 7 8 9 0

ABOUT THE AUTHORS

Joseph E. Stiglitz is professor of economics, business, and international and public affairs at Columbia University. Before joining the Columbia faculty, he held appointments at Yale, Oxford, Princeton, and Stanford. Internationally recognized as one of the leading economists of his generation, Professor Stiglitz has made important contributions to virtually all of the major subfields of economics, in particular the economics of information, one of the key topics highlighted in this text. He was a co-recipient of the Nobel Prize in Economic Science in 2001, and earlier in his career received the American Economic Association's John Bates Clark Medal, which is given every two years to the most outstanding economist under the age of forty. Professor Stiglitz is the author and editor of hundreds of scholarly articles and books, including the best-selling undergraduate textbook *Economics of the Public Sector* (Norton) and, with Anthony Atkinson, the classic graduate textbook *Lectures in Public Economics*. He is the author of two influential popular books as well: *Globalization and Its Discontents* and *The Roaring Nineties*. In addition, he was the founding editor of the *Journal of Economic Perspectives*. Professor Stiglitz has also played a prominent role at the highest levels of economic policy making. He was a member and chairman of President Clinton's Council of Economic Advisers and later served as Senior Vice President and Chief Economist of the World Bank.

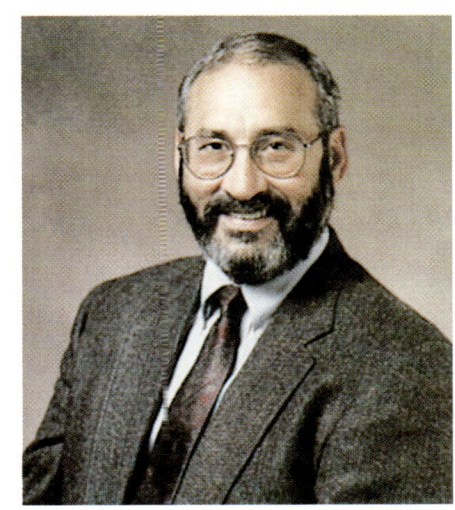

Carl E. Walsh is professor of economics at the University of California, Santa Cruz, where he teaches principles of economics. He previously held faculty appointments at Princeton and the University of Auckland, New Zealand, and has been a visiting professor at Stanford. He is widely known for his research in monetary economics and is the author of a leading graduate text, *Monetary Theory and Policy* (MIT Press). Before joining the Santa Cruz faculty, Professor Walsh was senior economist at the Federal Reserve Bank of San Francisco, where he continues to serve as a visiting scholar. He has also been a visiting scholar at the Federal Reserve Banks of Kansas City, Philadelphia, and at the Board of Governors. He has taught courses in monetary economics to the research department and staff economists at the central banks of Hong Kong, Norway, Portugal, Spain, and the United Kingdom, and at the International Monetary Fund. He is a past member of the board of editors of the *American Economic Review* and is currently an associate editor of the *Journal of Money, Credit, and Banking* and the *Journal of Economics and Business*. He is also on the editorial board of the *Journal of Macroeconomics*.

CONTENTS IN BRIEF

PART 1 INTRODUCTION 1

Chapter 1 Modern Economics • 3
Chapter 2 Thinking Like an Economist • 25

PART 2 PERFECT MARKETS 51

Chapter 3 Demand, Supply, and Price • 53
Chapter 4 Using Demand and Supply • 77
Chapter 5 The Consumption Decision • 101
Chapter 6 The Firm's Costs • 131
Chapter 7 The Competitive Firm • 155
Chapter 8 Labor Markets • 175
Chapter 9 Capital Markets • 191
Chapter 10 The Efficiency of Competitive Markets • 215

PART 3 IMPERFECT MARKETS 237

Chapter 11 Introduction to Imperfect Markets • 239
Chapter 12 Monopoly, Monopolistic Competition, and Oligopoly • 261
Chapter 13 Government Policies Toward Competition • 289
Chapter 14 Strategic Behavior • 311
Chapter 15 Imperfect Information in the Product Market • 333
Chapter 16 Imperfections in the Labor Market • 355

PART 4 ISSUES IN PUBLIC POLICY 373

Chapter 17 The Public Sector • 375
Chapter 18 Environmental Economics • 405
Chapter 19 International Trade and Trade Policy • 423
Chapter 20 Technological Change • 453

PART 5 INTRODUCTION TO MACROECONOMICS 471

Chapter 21 Macroeconomics and the Economic Perspective • 473
Chapter 22 Measuring Output and Unemployment • 485
Chapter 23 The Cost of Living and Inflation • 509

PART 6   FULL-EMPLOYMENT MACROECONOMICS   523

Chapter 24   The Full-Employment Model • 525
Chapter 25   Government Finance at Full Employment • 547
Chapter 26   The Open Economy at Full Employment • 567
Chapter 27   Growth and Productivity • 585
Chapter 28   Money, the Price Level, and the Federal Reserve • 605

PART 7   MACROECONOMIC FLUCTUATIONS   635

Chapter 29   Introduction to Macroeconomic Fluctuations • 637
Chapter 30   Aggregate Expenditures and Income • 661
Chapter 31   Aggregate Demand and Inflation • 689
Chapter 32   The Federal Reserve and Interest Rates • 715
Chapter 33   The Role of Macroeconomic Policy • 727

PART 8   THE GLOBAL ECONOMY   755

Chapter 34   The International Financial System • 757
Chapter 35   Policy in the Open Economy • 779
Chapter 36   Development and Transition • 793

PART 9   FURTHER TOPICS IN MACROECONOMICS   817

Chapter 37   Inflation and Unemployment • 819
Chapter 38   Controversies in Macroeconomic Policy • 837
Chapter 39   A Student's Guide to Investing • 865

CONTENTS

PREFACE   xxxv

PART 1   INTRODUCTION   1

CHAPTER 1   MODERN ECONOMICS   3
    INTERNET CONNECTION: Tracking the Digital
        Economy   6
    What Is Economics?   6
        Trade-offs   7
        Incentives   8
    THINKING LIKE AN ECONOMIST: Incentives and
        the Price of AOL   9
        Exchange   10
    INTERNET CONNECTION: Auction Sites   11
        Information   13
        Distribution   14
    The Three Major Markets   15
        Keeping Track of Tricky Terms   16
    Microeconomics and Macroeconomics: The Two
        Branches of Economics   17
    The Science of Economics   18
        Discovering and Interpreting Relationships   18
        Causation and Correlation   19
    Why Economists Disagree   19
    REVIEW AND PRACTICE   21

CHAPTER 2 — THINKING LIKE AN ECONOMIST 25

The Basic Competitive Model 25
- Rational Consumers and Profit-Maximizing Firms 26
- Competitive Markets 27

e-INSIGHT: Markets, Exchange, and e-Commerce 27
- Efficiency and Distribution in the Basic Competitive Model 28
- The Basic Competitive Model as a Benchmark 28

Incentives and Information: Prices, Property Rights, and Profits 29
- Incentives Versus Equality 31
- When Property Rights Fail 31

Alternatives to the Price System 32

Opportunity Sets and Trade-Offs 34
- Budget and Time Constraints 34
- The Production Possibilities Curve 35

Costs 37
- Opportunity Costs 38

THINKING LIKE AN ECONOMIST: Trade-Offs 39

INTERNET CONNECTION: Internet Resources for Economists 40

CASE IN POINT: The Opportunity Cost of Attending College 40
- Sunk Costs 42
- Marginal Costs 43

INTERNET CONNECTION: The Economists' Voice 43

REVIEW AND PRACTICE 45

APPENDIX: Reading Graphs 47
- Slope 48
- Interpreting Curves 49

PART 2 — PERFECT MARKETS 51

CHAPTER 3 — DEMAND, SUPPLY, AND PRICE 53

The Role of Prices 53

Demand 54
- The Individual Demand Curve 54
- The Market Demand Curve 55
- Shifts in Demand Curves 57

Sources of Shifts in Demand Curves 57
CASE IN POINT: Gasoline Prices and the Demand for SUVs 59
Shifts in a Demand Curve Versus Movements along a Demand Curve 60
FUNDAMENTALS OF DEMAND, SUPPLY, AND PRICE 1: Demand Declines as Price Rises 61
Supply 61
e-INSIGHT: The Demand for Computers and Information Technology 62
Market Supply 64
Shifts in Supply Curves 65
Sources of Shifts in Supply Curves 65
Shifts in a Supply Curve Versus Movements along a Supply Curve 67
FUNDAMENTALS OF DEMAND, SUPPLY, AND PRICE 2: Supply Increases as Price Rises 67
Law of Supply and Demand 67
Using Demand and Supply Curves 69
Consensus on the Determination of Prices 70
FUNDAMENTALS OF DEMAND, SUPPLY, AND PRICE 3: The Market Clears at the Equilibrium Price 71
Price, Value, and Cost 70
INTERNET CONNECTION: The Demand and Supply in the Oil Market 71
REVIEW AND PRACTICE 72

CHAPTER 4 USING DEMAND AND SUPPLY 77

The Price Elasticity of Demand 77
Price Elasticity and Revenues 79
The Determinants of the Elasticity of Demand 80
The Price Elasticity of Supply 82
INTERNATIONAL PERSPECTIVE: Comparing Reactions to the Oil Price Shock of 2000 83
Using Demand and Supply Elasticities 85
Shortages and Surpluses 88
Interfering with the Law of Supply and Demand 90
THINKING LIKE AN ECONOMIST: Incentives and the Window Tax 90
Price Ceilings 91
CASE IN POINT: Rent Control in New York City 93

Price Floors 93
INTERNET CONNECTION: Flawed Deregulation 94
Alternative Solutions 94
REVIEW AND PRACTICE 96
APPENDIX: Elasticity and Slope 98

CHAPTER 5 — THE CONSUMPTION DECISION 101

The Basic Problem of Consumer Choice 101
The Budget Constraint 102
Choosing a Point on the Budget Constraint: Individual Preferences 104
What Happens to Consumption When Income Changes? 105

CASE IN POINT: The Fate of the BTU Tax 107
INTERNET CONNECTION: What We Consume 109

A Closer Look at the Demand Curve 109
Deriving Demand Curves 110
The Importance of Distinguishing Between Income and Substitution Effects 111

THINKING LIKE AN ECONOMIST: Incentives, Income Effects, and Substitution Effects 112

Utility and the Description of Preferences 113
Consumer Surplus 117

Looking Beyond the Basic Model 118
How Well Do the Underlying Assumptions Match Reality? 118
Behavioral Economics 119

REVIEW AND PRACTICE 122
APPENDIX: Indifference Curves and the Consumption Decision 124
Using Indifference Curves to Illustrate Consumer Choices 124

Indifference Curves and Marginal Rates of Substitution 126

Using Indifference Curves to Illustrate Choices 127
Using Indifference Curves to Derive Demand Curves 128
Substitution and Income Effects 128

CHAPTER 6 — THE FIRM'S COSTS 131

Profits, Costs, and Factors of Production 132
Production with One Variable Input 132
Types of Costs and Cost Curves 135

Short-Run and Long-Run Cost Curves   141
Short-Run Cost Curves   *142*
Long-Run Cost Curves   *142*
INTERNET CONNECTION: Economic Definitions   146
Production with Many Factors   146
Cost Minimization   *147*
The Principle of Substitution   *147*
CASE IN POINT: The Principle of Substitution and Global Warming   148
Economies of Scope   150
REVIEW AND PRACTICE   **151**

CHAPTER 7   THE COMPETITIVE FIRM   155

Revenue   155
Costs   156
INTERNET CONNECTION: Firms' Profit-and-Loss Statements   157
Basic Conditions of Competitive Supply   158
Entry, Exit, and Market Supply   160
Sunk Costs and Exit   *161*
The Firm's Supply Curve   *162*
The Market Supply Curve   *163*
Long-Run Versus Short-Run Supply   164
e-INSIGHT: The 2001 Recession: Cutbacks Versus Shutdowns   165
Accounting Profits and Economic Profits   166
Opportunity Costs   *166*
Economic Rent   *168*
CASE IN POINT: Entering the Painting Business and Opportunity Costs   169
The Theory of the Competitive Firm   171
REVIEW AND PRACTICE   **172**

CHAPTER 8   LABOR MARKETS   175

The Labor Supply Decision   175
INTERNET CONNECTION: Labor Force Data   176
The Choice Between Leisure and Consumption   *176*
Labor Force Participation   *179*
THINKING LIKE AN ECONOMIST: Trade-Offs   179
Firms and the Demand for Labor   181
Factor Demand   *182*

From the Firm's Factor Demand to the Market's Factor Demand   184
Labor Supply, Demand, and the Equilibrium Wage   184
REVIEW AND PRACTICE   186
APPENDIX: Indifference Curves and the Labor Supply Decision   188
Deciding Whether to Work   188

CHAPTER 9   CAPITAL MARKETS   191

Supply in the Capital Market   191
The Household Decision to Save   192
THINKING LIKE AN ECONOMIST: Wealth Distribution and Interest Rates   197
INTERNET CONNECTION: Household Saving   198
CASE IN POINT: Why is the U.S. Saving Rate So Low?   198
Demand in the Capital Market   200
A Behavioral Perspective on Saving   202
Education and Human Capital   203
e-INSIGHT: Financing the New Economy   205
Education and Economic Trade-Offs   206
The Basic Competitive Model   206
REVIEW AND PRACTICE   207
APPENDIX A: Indifference Curves and the Saving Decision   209
Deciding How Much to Save   209
Changing the Interest Rate   210
APPENDIX B: Calculating Present Discounted Value   211

CHAPTER 10   THE EFFICIENCY OF COMPETITIVE MARKETS   215

Competitive Markets and Economic Efficiency   216
Consumer and Producer Surplus   217
FUNDAMENTALS OF COMPETITIVE MARKETS 1: Households and Firms are Price Takers   218
FUNDAMENTALS OF COMPETITIVE MARKETS 2: The Equilibrium Price Maximizes Consumer Plus Producer Surplus   219
INTERNET CONNECTION: Digital Economist   219
Taxes and Efficiency   220
Efficiency   221
Pareto Efficiency   222

Conditions for the Pareto Efficiency of the Market Economy 222
THINKING LIKE AN ECONOMIST: Exchange and Distribution 224
Competitive Markets and Pareto Efficiency 225
FUNDAMENTALS OF COMPETITIVE MARKETS 3: The Competitive Market Economy is Pareto Efficient 225
Competitive Markets and Income Distribution 225
General Equilibrium Analysis 227
The Basic Competitive Equilibrium Model 227
THINKING LIKE AN ECONOMIST: Indirect Trade-Offs and Air Safety for Children 228
CASE IN POINT: The Labor Market and the Widening Wage Gap 230
CASE IN POINT: The Minimum Wage and General Equilibrium 231
General Equilibrium Over Time 232
When Partial Equilibrium Analysis Will Do 234
Looking Beyond the Basic Model 234
REVIEW AND PRACTICE 235

PART 3 IMPERFECT MARKETS 237

CHAPTER 11 INTRODUCTION TO IMPERFECT MARKETS 239

Extending the Basic Competitive Model 240
FUNDAMENTALS OF IMPERFECT MARKETS 1: Imperfect Markets Lead to Market Failures 242
Imperfect Competition and Market Structure 242
Price and Quantity with Imperfect Competition 244
Government Policies 245
INTERNET CONNECTION: The Federal Trade Commission 245
INTERNATIONAL PERSPECTIVE: Trade and Competition 246
FUNDAMENTALS OF IMPERFECT MARKETS 2: Imperfect Competition 246
Imperfect Information 247
The Information Problem 247
How Big a Problem? 247

How Prices Convey Information 248
Markets for Information 249
e-INSIGHT: Information, Competition, and the Internet 249
Government Policies 250
FUNDAMENTALS OF IMPERFECT MARKETS 3: Imperfect Information 251
Externalities 252
Government Policies Toward Externalities 252
THINKING LIKE AN ECONOMIST: Incentives and the Environment 253
FUNDAMENTALS OF IMPERFECT MARKETS 4: Externalities 254
Public Goods 254
FUNDAMENTALS OF IMPERFECT MARKETS 5: Public Goods 255
Looking Ahead 256
REVIEW AND PRACTICE 257

CHAPTER 12 MONOPOLY, MONOPOLISTIC COMPETITION, AND OLIGOPOLY 261

Monopoly Output 261
An Example: The ABC-ment Company 264
Monopoly Profits 265
Price Discrimination 266
Economies of Scale and Natural Monopolies 267
INTERNATIONAL PERSPECTIVE: South Africa, AIDS, and Price Discrimination 268
Assessing the Degree of Competition 270
Number of Firms in the Industry 270
Product Differentiation 271
e-INSIGHT: Network Externalities, the New Economy, and Monopoly Power 272
Equilibrium with Monopolistic Competition 273
Oligopolies 274
Collusion 275
Restrictive Practices 279
Entry Deterrence 281
INTERNET CONNECTION: Keeping Track of Oligopolies 281

THINKING LIKE AN ECONOMIST: Trade-Offs, American Airlines, and Predation 283
The Importance of Imperfections in Competition 284
REVIEW AND PRACTICE 285

CHAPTER 13 GOVERNMENT POLICIES TOWARD COMPETITION 289

The Drawbacks of Monopolies and Limited Competition 289
Restricted Output 289
Managerial Slack 291
Reduced Research and Development 291
Rent Seeking 292
Further Drawbacks of Limited Competition 292
e-INSIGHT: Using the Internet to Enhance Price Discrimination 293
Policies Toward Natural Monopolies 293
Public Ownership 294
Regulation 295
Encouraging Competition 296
INTERNATIONAL PERSPECTIVE: The Darker Side of Privatization 296
CASE IN POINT: California Electricity Deregulation 298
Antitrust Policies 299
Limiting Market Domination 300
Defining Markets 301
INTERNET CONNECTION: U.S. Department of Justice and Antitrust Laws 301
THINKING LIKE AN ECONOMIST: Incentives and the Remedy to the Microsoft Monopoly Problem 302
Curbing Restrictive Practices 304
Enforcing the Antitrust Laws 305
CASE IN POINT: Coke and Pepsi Play Merger 306
REVIEW AND PRACTICE 308

CHAPTER 14 STRATEGIC BEHAVIOR 311

Review of the Prisoner's Dilemma 312
Dominant Strategies 313

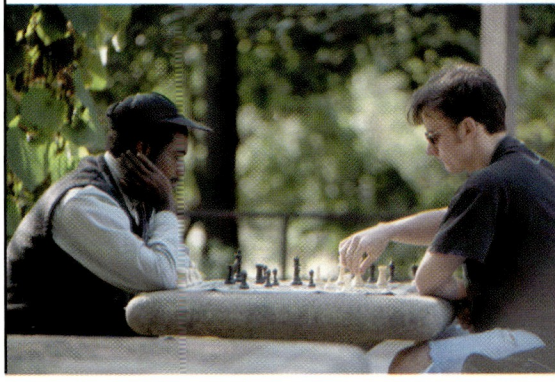

Nash Equilibrium 313
Strategic Behavior in More General Games 316
   Games With Only One Dominant Strategy 316
   INTERNATIONAL PERSPECTIVE: Beggar-Thy-Neighbor Tariff Policies 317
   Games Without Dominant Strategies 318
INTERNET CONNECTION: The Zero-Sum Game Solver 319
Repeated Games 320
   Reputations 321
   Tit for Tat 321
INTERNET CONNECTION: The Prisoner's Dilemma 321
   Institutions 322
CASE IN POINT: Banking Panics 322
Sequential Moves 324
   THINKING LIKE AN ECONOMIST: Information and Thinking Strategically 326
Time Inconsistency 326
   Commitment 327
REVIEW AND PRACTICE 329

CHAPTER 15   IMPERFECT INFORMATION IN THE PRODUCT MARKET   333

The Market for Lemons and Adverse Selection 333
   Signaling 335
   Judging Quality by Price 336
The Incentive Problem 337
   Market Solutions 337
   Contract Solutions 338
   Reputation Solutions 339
   The Market for Health Insurance 340
CASE IN POINT: Buying Health Insurance 341
The Search Problem 342
THINKING LIKE AN ECONOMIST: Incentive and Information Problems in the Housing Market 343
e-INSIGHT: Information Technology and Middlemen 344
INTERNET CONNECTION: Job Search 345
   Search and Imperfect Competition 345
   Search and the Labor Market 346

    Search and Information Intermediaries   *346*
Advertising   *347*
    Advertising and Competition   *348*
    Advertising and Profits   *348*
The Importance of Imperfect Information   *350*
REVIEW AND PRACTICE   **351**

CHAPTER 16   IMPERFECTIONS IN THE LABOR MARKET   355

Labor Unions   *355*
    A Brief History   *356*
    INTERNET CONNECTION: Unions on the Internet   358
    Economic Effects   *359*
    Limits on Union Power   *360*
Wage Differentials   *362*
    Discrimination   *363*
Motivating Workers   *364*
    Piece Rates and Incentives   *365*
    Efficiency Wages   *366*
    CASE IN POINT: Minimum Wages   367
    Other Incentives   *368*
    Compensating Workers   *368*
e-INSIGHT: Labor Markets and the Internet   369
REVIEW AND PRACTICE   **371**

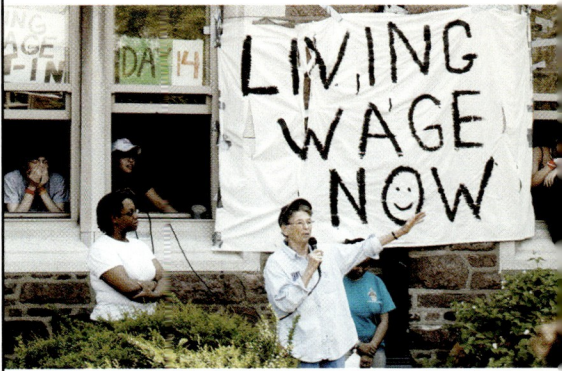

PART 4   ISSUES IN PUBLIC POLICY   373

CHAPTER 17   THE PUBLIC SECTOR   375

Why Does the Government Intervene in the Economy?   *377*
    INTERNATIONAL PERSPECTIVE: The Size of Government in Different Countries   377
    Equity-Efficiency Trade-Offs   *380*
    e-INSIGHT: The New Economy and Inequality   381
The U.S. Tax System in Practice   *381*

Characteristics of a Good Tax System 382
The Scope of the U.S. Tax System 383
Grading the U.S. Tax System 383
Transfers 386
Welfare 387
Housing 388
Social Insurance 389
Designing Government Programs 390
Government Failures 391
Incentives and Constraints 392
Budgeting and Spending Procedures 393
Imperfections of Information 393
Collective Decision Making 394
Current and Recent Controversies in the Economics of the Public Sector 395
Dealing With the Deficit 395
Social Security 396
Health Care 398
INTERNET CONNECTION: Policy Analysis 400
REVIEW AND PRACTICE 401

CHAPTER 18 ENVIRONMENTAL ECONOMICS 405

Negative Externalities and Oversupply 405
Policy Responses to Problems in the Environment 407
Property Rights Responses 407
INTERNATIONAL PERSPECTIVE: Global Warming 408
THINKING LIKE AN ECONOMIST: Environmental and Economic Trade-Offs 410
Regulation 410
Taxes and Subsidies 412
The Marketable Permit Response 413
CASE IN POINT: Reducing Acid Rain 414
Weighing the Alternative Approaches 415
Natural Resources 416
INTERNET CONNECTION: The National Center for Environmental Economics 416
e-INSIGHT: Information and the Environment 418
Merit Goods and the Environment 418
REVIEW AND PRACTICE 419

CHAPTER 19 INTERNATIONAL TRADE AND TRADE POLICY 423

Trade Between Countries 423
   Interdependence in the Product Market 424
   Interdependence in the Labor Market 424
   Interdependence in the Capital Market 425
   Multilateral Trade 425
Comparative Advantage 426
INTERNET CONNECTION: David Ricardo 427
   Production Possibilities Curves and Comparative Advantage 427
   Comparative Advantage and Specialization 428
e-INSIGHT: The United States' Comparative Advantage in the Internet Age 429
   What Determines Comparative Advantage? 430
The Perceived Costs of International Interdependence 432
THINKING LIKE AN ECONOMIST: Exchange and the Globalization Controversy 432
Trade Policies 434
   Commercial Policy 434
   Tariffs 435
   Quotas 436
   Voluntary Export Restraints 436
   Other Nontariff Barriers 437
   "Fair Trade" Laws 437
INTERNATIONAL PERSPECTIVE: Surrogate Countries and Canadian Golf Carts 438
Political and Economic Rationale for Protection 439
   Displaced Firms and Workers 440
   Beggar-Thy-Neighbor Policies 441
   Wages in Affected Sectors 442
   Increased Competition 442
THINKING LIKE AN ECONOMIST: Distribution and Trade Liberalization 443
   The Infant Industry Argument 443
e-INSIGHT: Trade Liberalization in Information Technology and Financial Services 444
   Strategic Trade Theory 445
International Cooperation 445
   GATT and the WTO 445

The Growing Protest Against the WTO   446
CASE IN POINT: The Banana War   447
Regional Trading Blocs   448
INTERNET CONNECTION: The World Trade Organization   449
REVIEW AND PRACTICE   450

CHAPTER 20   TECHNOLOGICAL CHANGE   453

Links Between Technological Change and Imperfect Competition   454
e-INSIGHT: The New Economy and Innovation   455
Patents and the Production of Ideas   455
THINKING LIKE AN ECONOMIST: Intellectual Property Rights and Distribution   456
The Trade-Off Between Short-term Efficiency and Innovation   457
CASE IN POINT: Eli Whitney and the Cotton Gin   460
R & D as a Fixed Cost   460
Learning by Doing   461
Access to Capital Markets   462
Schumpeterian Competition   463
Basic Research as a Public Good   464
Government Promotion of Technological Progress   465
Subsidies   465
Protection   466
Relaxing Antitrust Policies   466
INTERNET CONNECTION: Competitiveness   468
Technological Change and Economic Growth   468
REVIEW AND PRACTICE   469

PART 5   INTRODUCTION TO MACROECONOMICS   471

CHAPTER 21   MACROECONOMICS AND THE ECONOMIC PERSPECTIVE   473

The Commitment to Full Employment and Growth   474
Getting the Country Moving Again   477
Stagflation   477
The Conquest of Inflation   478

Government Deficits and Trade Deficits 479
Getting the Economy Moving (Again) 479
New Challenges 480
The Three Key Goals of Macroeconomic Performance 481
A Look Ahead 482
REVIEW AND PRACTICE 483

CHAPTER 22 MEASURING OUTPUT AND UNEMPLOYMENT 485

Measuring Output and Growth 485
Gross Domestic Product 486
Measuring GDP: The Value of Output 489
INTERNET CONNECTION: The Bureau of Economic Analysis 489
CASE IN POINT: Is Software a Final Good or an Intermediate Good? 491
Potential GDP 494
INTERNATIONAL PERSPECTIVE: What Gets Measured in the GDP? 495
Problems in Measuring Output 496
Measuring the Standard of Living 497
A Green GDP 497
Unemployment 498
Unemployment Statistics 499
Forms of Unemployment 500
Output Gaps and the Natural Rate of Unemployment 503
Flows and Stocks 505
REVIEW AND PRACTICE 506

CHAPTER 23 THE COST OF LIVING AND INFLATION 509

The Costs of Inflation 509
Who Suffers from Inflation 510
The Economy 511
The Costs of Deflation 512
CASE IN POINT: Hyperinflation in Germany in the 1920s 512
Measuring Inflation 514
INTERNET CONNECTION: Improving Our Measure of the CPI 516
CASE IN POINT: The Price Index Makes a Difference 516

Alternative Measures of Inflation 517
INTERNET CONNECTION: The Inflation Calculator 517
e-INSIGHT: Measuring the Price and Quantity of Software 518
The American Experience with Inflation 519
REVIEW AND PRACTICE 521

PART 6 FULL-EMPLOYMENT MACROECONOMICS 523

CHAPTER 24 THE FULL-EMPLOYMENT MODEL 525

Macroeconomic Equilibrium 526
The Labor Market 527
 Shifts in the Demand and Supply of Labor 529
CASE IN POINT: Mass Migration in the Nineteenth Century 531
e-INSIGHT: Labor Markets and the Internet 532
The Product Market 532
 Potential GDP 533
 Demand and Equilibrium Output 534
The Capital Market 536
 Household Saving 536
 Investment 537
 Equilibrium in the Capital Market 538
The General Equilibrium Model 540
 Using the General Equilibrium Model 541
REVIEW AND PRACTICE 543

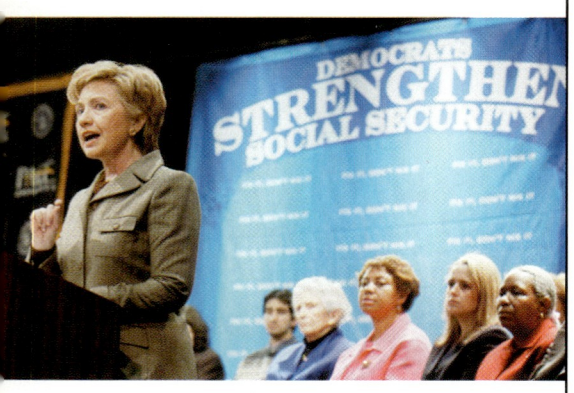

CHAPTER 25 GOVERNMENT FINANCE AT FULL EMPLOYMENT 547

The Composition of Spending and Taxes 548
Extending the Basic Full-Employment Model 548
Adding the Government 549
 The Government and the Capital Market 549
 Leakages and Injections 554
INTERNATIONAL PERSPECTIVE: Deficits in Other Countries 555
THINKING LIKE AN ECONOMIST: Distribution, Deficits and Intergenerational Transfers 556

Evaluating Government Deficits and Surpluses 557
Government Deficits and Surpluses: Our Recent Experiences 558
Factors Affecting the Federal Budget 561
Risk Factors for the Federal Budget 562
REVIEW AND PRACTICE 563

CHAPTER 26 THE OPEN ECONOMY AT FULL EMPLOYMENT 567

The Open Economy 568
The Capital Market in the Open Economy 568
The Basic Trade Identity 572
INTERNET CONNECTION: U.S. Trade Data 573
CASE IN POINT: The Trade Deficit 574
e-INSIGHT: High-Tech Exports and Imports 576
Exchange Rates 577
THINKING LIKE AN ECONOMIST: Net Exports and the Exchange Rate 579
Is the Trade Deficit a Problem? 580
REVIEW AND PRACTICE 583

CHAPTER 27 GROWTH AND PRODUCTIVITY 585

Rising Standards of Living 586
Explaining Productivity 589
INTERNET CONNECTION: How Fast Is Modern Economic Growth? 590
The Capital Stock and the Role of Saving and Investment 590
The Quality of the Labor Force 592
The Reallocation of Resources from Low- to High-Productivity Sectors 592
Technological Change and the Role of Ideas 593
Total Factor Productivity: Measuring the Sources of Growth 596
CASE IN POINT: Calculating Total Factor Productivity in the 1990s 597
e-INSIGHT: Computers and Increased Productivity Growth 598
FUNDAMENTALS OF GROWTH: Growth in the Economy's Labor Force, Growth in the Economy's Capital Stock, Technological Change 599

Are There Limits to Economic Growth? 600
THINKING LIKE AN ECONOMIST: Trade-Offs and the Costs of Economic Growth 601
REVIEW AND PRACTICE 602

CHAPTER 28 MONEY, THE PRICE LEVEL, AND THE FEDERAL RESERVE 605

Prices and Inflation 606
Money Demand 607
Money Supply 609
The Price Level 609
INTERNET CONNECTION: How Much Cash Do We Hold? 610
The Financial System in Modern Economies 612
CASE IN POINT: When Atlanta Printed Money 614
Creating Money in Modern Economies 615
Money Is What Money Does 615
Measuring the Money Supply 617
Money and Credit 618
CASE IN POINT: "Boggs Bills" and the Meaning of Money 619
The Money Supply and the Bank's Balance Sheet 620
THINKING LIKE AN ECONOMIST: Exchange, Money, and the Internet 620
How Banks Create Money 622
e-INSIGHT: Electronic Cash 623
The Federal Reserve 626
How the Fed Affects the Money Supply 628
INTERNET CONNECTION: The Federal Reserve Banks and International Central Banks 629
The Stability of the U.S. Banking System 630
Reducing the Threat of Bank Runs 631
REVIEW AND PRACTICE 633

PART 7 MACROECONOMIC FLUCTUATIONS 635

CHAPTER 29 INTRODUCTION TO MACROECONOMIC FLUCTUATIONS 637

Economic Fluctuations 638
INTERNET CONNECTION: Dating Business Cycle Peaks and Troughs 642
CASE IN POINT: Estimating the Output Costs of a Recession 642
THINKING LIKE AN ECONOMIST: Employment Fluctuations and Trade-Offs 643
Why Economies Experience Fluctuations 643
  Nominal Versus Real Wages 645
  The Slow Adjustment of Nominal Wages 645
  The Slow Adjustment of Prices 645
THINKING LIKE AN ECONOMIST: Information and Measuring the Business Cycle 647
Understanding Macroeconomic Fluctuations: Key Concepts 648
Sticky Wages 649
FUNDAMENTALS OF FLUCTUATIONS 1: Sticky Wages 649
Sticky Prices 649
e-INSIGHT: Cyclical and Structural Productivity 650
FUNDAMENTALS OF FLUCTUATIONS 2: Sticky Prices 651
  Inflation and Adjustment 652
FUNDAMENTALS OF FLUCTUATIONS 3: Short-Run Inflation-Unemployment Trade-Off 653
  Inflation, Monetary Policy, and Spending 653
FUNDAMENTALS OF FLUCTUATIONS 4: Inflation, Monetary Policy, and Spending 655
CASE IN POINT: Inflation Targeting 655
  Linking the Four Key Concepts 656
REVIEW AND PRACTICE 657

CHAPTER 30 AGGREGATE EXPENDITURES AND INCOME 661

Income-Expenditure Analysis 661
   The National Income-Output Identity 663
   Equilibrium Output 663
   Shifts in the Aggregate Expenditures Schedule 664
   Mathematical Formulation 665
A Look Forward 666
Consumption 667
   Disposable Income 667
   Expectations of Future Income 671
   Wealth 671
Investment 672
   Investment and the Real Interest Rate 673
   Inventory Investment 674
   Macroeconomic Implications of Investment 675
Government Purchases 676
Net Exports 676
   Exports 678
   Imports 678
   Macroeconomic Implications 679
   Putting International Trade into the Equation 680
Calculating Equilibrium Output 681
Aggregate Expenditures and the Real Interest Rate 683
THINKING LIKE AN ECONOMIST: Incentives and the Real After-Tax Rate of Interest 684
REVIEW AND PRACTICE 685

CHAPTER 31 AGGREGATE DEMAND AND INFLATION 689

The Real Interest Rate and the Capital Market 690
The Aggregate Demand–Inflation Curve 691
   The Fed's Policy Rule 692
   What Can Shift the ADI Curve? 694
INTERNATIONAL PERSPECTIVE: How Do Other Central Banks React to Inflation? 696
   Other Factors That Can Shift the ADI Curve 696
Using the ADI Curve 697
   Output Effects of a Shift in the ADI Curve 698
CASE IN POINT: The Volcker Disinflation 700

An Expansionary Shift in the ADI Curve 701
CASE IN POINT: The Kennedy Tax Cut 701
THINKING LIKE AN ECONOMIST: Tough Trade-Offs 703
Macroeconomic Policy and Shifts in the ADI Curve 703
Shifts in the Inflation Adjustment Curve 704
Changes in Energy Prices 704
CASE IN POINT: Oil Price Shocks of the 1970s 705
A Shift in Potential GDP 705
CASE IN POINT: The 1990s 707
e-INSIGHT: Productivity Growth and the Punch Bowl 708
INTERNET CONNECTION: The FOMC 710
REVIEW AND PRACTICE 711

CHAPTER 32 THE FEDERAL RESERVE AND INTEREST RATES 715

The Federal Funds Market 715
A Day at the Trading Desk 716
The Demand for Reserves 718
The Supply of Reserves 719
Open Market Operations 719
Equilibrium in the Federal Funds Market 720
Monetary Policy Operating Procedures 721
Inflation, Money Supply, and the Nominal Rate of Interest 722
REVIEW AND PRACTICE 724

CHAPTER 33 THE ROLE OF MACROECONOMIC POLICY 727

Inflation-Unemployment Trade-Offs 728
The Old Inflation-Unemployment Trade-Off 728
The New Trade-Off: Output Stability–Inflation Stability 429
Fiscal Policy 729
Automatic Stabilizers 729
Discretionary Policy Actions 731
INTERNET CONNECTION: The Economic Report of the President 732
The Full-Employment Deficit 733

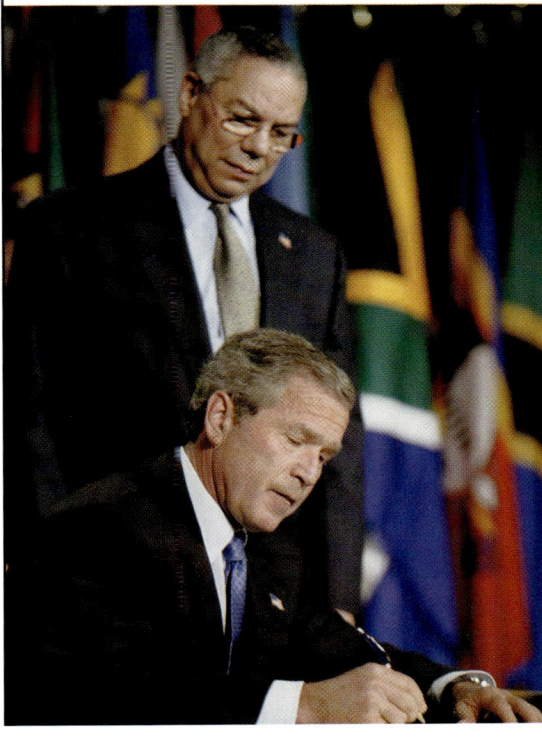

INTERNATIONAL PERSPECTIVE: Fiscal Transfers 734
Monetary Policy 736
  Behind the ADI Curve—The Role of Monetary Policy 736
INTERNET CONNECTION: The Beige Book 738
CASE IN POINT: Announcing the Fed's Decisions 738
Real Interest Rates and Nominal Interest Rates 739
The Central Bank Policy Rule 740
THINKING LIKE AN ECONOMIST: Real Values Matter for Incentives 742
CASE IN POINT: The Interest Rate Cut of January 3, 2001 743
CASE IN POINT: September 11, 2001 743
e-INSIGHT: The Dot-Com Bubble and Macroeconomic Stability 744
The Position of the Policy Rule 745
The Slope of the Policy Rule 748
Interactions Between Monetary and Fiscal Policies 749
REVIEW AND PRACTICE 752

PART 8 THE GLOBAL ECONOMY 755

CHAPTER 34 THE INTERNATIONAL FINANCIAL SYSTEM 757

Determining the Exchange Rate 758
  Supply and Demand in the Foreign Exchange Market 759
THINKING LIKE AN ECONOMIST: Incentives and the Real Exchange Rate 764
Exchange Rate Management 766
INTERNATIONAL PERSPECTIVE: Global Financial Crises 770
Flexible Exchange Rate Systems 771
CASE IN POINT: Currency Boards and Dollarization 772
REVIEW AND PRACTICE 775

CHAPTER 35 POLICY IN THE OPEN ECONOMY 779

The ADI Curve and the Open Economy   780
   Inflation, the Interest Rate, and the Exchange Rate   780
   The Exchange Rate and Aggregate Expenditures   781
The Exchange Rate and Inflation   783
   Imported Inputs   783
   THINKING LIKE AN ECONOMIST: Interest Parity and Incentives   784
   Consumer Price Inflation and the Exchange Rate   784
INTERNET CONNECTION: Foreign Exchange Rates   785
Comparing Monetary and Fiscal Policies in the Open Economy   785
   Monetary Policy with Flexible Exchange Rates   785
e-INSIGHT: New Technology and the Integration of World Financial Markets   786
   Fiscal Policy with Flexible Exchange Rates   787
INTERNATIONAL PERSPECTIVE: Is a Strong Dollar Good for the United States?   788
Policy Coordination   789
REVIEW AND PRACTICE   790

CHAPTER 36 DEVELOPMENT AND TRANSITION 793

Development   794
INTERNET CONNECTION: The World Bank's Development Goals   796
   Life in a Less-Developed Country   797
   The Success of East Asia   799
   Alternative Development Strategies   802
   Globalization and Development   803
CASE IN POINT: A Historical Perspective on Globalization   804
e-INSIGHT: Indian Engineers in Silicon Valley and Silicon Valley's Capital in India   806
   The Prognosis for Development   807
Economies in Transition   808
   The Communist Economic System   808
   The Move Toward a Market Economy   810
REVIEW AND PRACTICE   814

PART 9 FURTHER TOPICS IN MACROECONOMICS 817

CHAPTER 37 INFLATION AND UNEMPLOYMENT 819

Short-Run Inflation Adjustment 820
  The Role of Expectations: Shifts in the Short-Run Inflation Adjustment Curve 824
  THINKING LIKE AN ECONOMIST: Distributional Effects of Inflation and Unemployment 826
  CASE IN POINT: Nobel Views on Inflation and Unemployment 827
  INTERNET CONNECTION: Winners of the Nobel Prize in Economics 829
Shifts in the Natural Rate 829
  CASE IN POINT: The Baby Boomers and the Natural Rate 829
Shifts in Potential GDP 830
Inflation Shocks 830
  FUNDAMENTALS OF INFLATION: Cyclical Unemployment, Expectations, Inflation Shocks 831
Combining the Aggregate Demand–Inflation and Inflation Adjustment Curves 832
REVIEW AND PRACTICE 834

CHAPTER 38 CONTROVERSIES IN MACROECONOMIC POLICY 837

Do Deficits Matter? 838
  Deficits and the Traditional View 839
  Economic Consequences of Deficits and Surpluses 840
  How Future Generations Are Affected by Government Debt 840
  Alternative Views 841
The Goals of Macroeconomic Policy 842
  The Noninterventionist Perspective 844
  THINKING LIKE AN ECONOMIST: Trade-Offs and Choices 845
  The Interventionist Perspective 847
Should the Federal Reserve Target Inflation? 848
  Inflation Targeting and Policy Trade-Offs 849

CASE IN POINT: Fed Policy Statements—Balancing Policy Goals   851
INTERNET CONNECTION: Banks and Inflation Targeting   852
Consequences of Inflation Targeting   853
INTERNATIONAL PERSPECTIVE: Central Bank Mandates   855
Demand Versus Supply Disturbances and Policy Trade-Offs   857
e-INSIGHT: e-Time and Macroeconomic Policy   858
REVIEW AND PRACTICE   860
APPENDIX: Price Level Targeting   862

CHAPTER 39 A STUDENT'S GUIDE TO INVESTING   865

Investment Alternatives   866
Bank Deposits   866
Housing   866
INTERNET CONNECTION: Calculating Interest Rates   867
Bonds   867
Shares of Stock   868
Mutual Funds   869
Desirable Attributes of Investments   870
Expected Returns   870
INTERNET CONNECTION: Index Funds   870
e-INSIGHT: Investing in the New Economy   872
CASE IN POINT: PG&E Employees Learn Why Diversification Is Important   872
Risk   874
Tax Considerations   876
Liquidity   877
Expectations and the Market for Assets   878
THINKING LIKE AN ECONOMIST: The Distribution of Wealth and Ownership of Assets   879
Forming Expectations   880
Efficient Market Theory   881
Efficiency and the Stock Market   882
Efficient Markets or Random Noise?   884
Strategies for Intelligent Investing   885
REVIEW AND PRACTICE   887

GLOSSARY   A-1

CREDITS   A-13

INDEX   A-15

PREFACE

The study of economics has always been fascinating, yet it is difficult to remember a more exciting or important time in the discipline. Think of today's major economic issues—the huge American trade and budget deficits, global warming, the debate between proponents of conservation and energy exploration, ensuring adequate health care, ending global poverty, reforming Social Security, outsourcing, rethinking the nature of competition and regulation in the Internet age, and copyright protection in a digital, "downloadable" world. The list goes on and on. To understand these issues, the core insights of economics are invaluable.

Exciting new theoretical advances are allowing economists to better understand how individuals, families, and businesses make decisions about what to buy, what to sell, how much to save, and how to invest their savings. These advances affect the way governments design policies to protect the environment, promote educational opportunities, and deal with the changes in our economy brought about by innovations in information technologies and the increasingly global economic marketplace in which we all participate.

There has never been a time in which the need to be informed about economic issues has been more acute. Nor is it any less critical for students to acquire the tools that will enable them to think critically about the economic decisions they face in their personal lives and the issues they must decide on as engaged citizens. Even something as basic to the study of economics as the concept of trade-offs helps provide students with a tool that can inform the way they think about issues at the personal, local, state, national, and even global level. Whereas the Principles of Economics course has always been popular among business students, now most students realize that *everyone* needs to be conversant with the fundamentals of economics. We have written our book, and revised it for the Fourth Edition, keeping this very important concept of the politically engaged student in mind.

Preparing the Fourth Edition of this textbook has provided us with the opportunity to make several fundamental improvements over the previous edition. We still emphasize the five core concepts of modern economics, which are the importance of **trade-offs, incentives, exchange, information, and distribution.** Yet, economic research is continuously yielding new, interesting, and important insights, and we believe that these exciting new developments should be conveyed to students in introductory courses. While the textbook has always offered the most integrated coverage of information economics, in this new edition we introduce students to some of the results from new research in behavioral economics. We have also made several changes to the organization of the book that will give instructors increased flexibility in structuring their courses.

Mission Statement for the Fourth Edition

Our text has always strived for two goals: One, to be transparently accessible and interesting, dare we say a "good read," for the student reader; and two, to not shy away from teaching students the latest exciting insights of the discipline, to teach them the substance of economics as a field of study. Many books seem to take the stance that students cannot "handle" the new topics—we believe that it is just a matter of explaining the ideas simply and clearly.

To achieve these goals, the four main objectives of previous editions continued to guide us. These objectives are to provide students with a clear presentation of the basic competitive model, to present macroeconomics in its modern form consistent with the way active researchers and economists in policy-making institutions analyze the economy, to structure the textbook in ways that are conducive to good teaching and to student learning, and to ensure that the textbook reflects the contemporary scene, stressing the core insights economics provides for understanding the ever-changing economy.

Changes to the Fourth Edition—Microeconomics

The hallmark of this textbook, its emphasis on information, imperfect markets, innovation, and technology, remain in the new edition. New material on behavioral economics has been incorporated into the chapters on consumer choice and capital markets.

KEY CHANGES FOR THE FOURTH EDITION:

For the Fourth Edition, we worked hard to streamline the text. Chapters in earlier editions that many students found too long or too dense have been significantly restructured. In some cases, material has been divided into separate chapters, making chapters shorter on average and more focused.

Important changes made to the microeconomic sections include:

- Shortening the introductory section, Part 1, to provide a greater focus on the core concepts of economics.

- Splitting the material on the labor and capital markets under perfect competition into two separate chapters. This helps make the presentation more student-friendly as well as giving instructors increased flexibility in deciding what material to include in their courses.

- Reorganizing Part 3 to provide a more cohesive discussion of imperfect markets and public policy issues. Because strategic behavior is at the heart of the economist's approach to imperfect competition, the chapter on strategic behavior has been moved into Part 3 (Chapter 14).

- Part 4, now titled Issues in Public Policy, is more closely organized around the theme of public policy, rather than simply including a set of "topics." Part 4 includes chapters on the public sector (Chapter 17), environmental policy (Chapter 18), and international trade and trade policy (Chapter 19).

Changes to the Fourth Edition—Macroeconomics

The new edition maintains the modern approach to macroeconomics, one that recognizes that the Federal Reserve and other central banks implement monetary policy through interest rates rather than through the explicit control of the money supply. By providing a more realistic treatment of monetary policy, the modern approach also allows students to understand and discuss the types of policy actions they read about in newspapers. While the general approach developed in the Third Edition is maintained, our treatment of macroeconomics in the new edition aims to streamline the presentation, moving more advanced material into the "Topics" chapters.

KEY CHANGES FOR THE FOURTH EDITION:

Important changes made to the macroeconomic sections include:

- The opening chapter of the macroeconomics material has been updated to reflect new developments since the Third Edition.

- The discussion of price indices and the measurement of inflation are now treated in a separate chapter (Chapter 23).

- Part 6, on Full-Employment Macroeconomics, has been reorganized. Separate chapters are now devoted to government finance (Chapter 25) and the open economy (Chapter 26). This allows these two important topics to be treated individually, allowing instructors greater choice in deciding how to organize their course, as well as reducing the number of new concepts introduced in each chapter.

- The important material on government deficits and surpluses has been combined in Chapter 25 rather than split between Part 6 and Part 8 as in the previous edition.

- The material on money, prices, and the Federal Reserve has been moved to the end of Part 6 (Chapter 28). This improves the flow of the full-employment section, with Chapter 24 providing the basic framework for the determination of real output, real wages, and the real interest rate, Chapter 25 adding the government, Chapter 26 extending the results to the case of the open economy, and Chapter 27 providing a discussion of economic growth. The material on money and prices then follows in Chapter 28.

- Part 7 on Macroeconomic Fluctuations has been extensively rewritten to improve the exposition. Many users of the Third Edition felt that too much material was introduced in the chapters on the aggregate demand–inflation relationship and the short-run inflation adjustment relationship. To address this concern, we have moved the extended discussion of inflation and unemployment into Part 9 (Further Topics in Macroeconomics). Part 7 begins with an overview (Chapter 29), covers the basics of aggregate expenditures (Chapter 30), and then develops the aggregate demand–inflation relationship in Chapter 31.

- The material on the international economy has been consolidated into a new Part 8, with chapters dealing with the international financial system (Chapter 34), policy in the open economy (Chapter 35), and economic development and transition (Chapter 36).

In making these changes, we have continued to be motivated by the desire to write a modern, student-friendly textbook that reflects the way economists approach their subject today.

The Organization of the Text

The text is organized to work for both students and instructors. For students, we utilize the five core concepts of trade-offs, incentives, exchange, information, and distribution throughout the text, in both the chapters on microeconomics and those on macroeconomics. These concepts anchor the wide range of topics we cover, linking all the topics to a core set of basic principles to which students can always refer. We also provide a firm grounding in basic concepts first, but we do not stop there. We also ensure that students are able to understand the tremendous insights offered by the basic economic model of competitive markets and its limitations. This prepares the student for understanding the lessons offered by modern economics for study of imperfect competition, information, growth, and economic fluctuations. We show how these insights help one understand economic phenomena that classical economics cannot. By exposing students to modern economics—from the economics of information and innovation to behavioral economics—the text helps them obtain a sense of the richness of the discipline and its value for understanding the world around them.

The text is designed to offer solid coverage of traditional topics, combined with a flexible structure that allows it to be tailored to fit with the individual needs of the instructor. In covering both microeconomics and macroeconomics, the basic material of competitive markets and the full-employment economy are presented first. Then, the sections dealing with imperfect markets and fluctuations each begin with an overview chapter that allows students to gain insight into the basic institutions and key issues that are addressed in more detail in subsequent chapters. This structure also allows an instructor who does not wish to devote too much time to a topic such as imperfect information to still give students a sense of the its importance and the lessons economists have learned about this important topic. Finally, both the microeconomics and macroeconomics sections end with topics chapters that offer additional flexibility for the instructor in fine-tuning the readings from the text to the context of his or her course structure, while a new and expanded treatment of the international economy is contained in the macroeconomics section.

Learning Tools

We have developed a clutch of Learning Tools that will help our student readers relate to the principles being described and also better retain the information.

1 RIVETING BOXES THAT HIGHLIGHT THE NEW ECONOMY BEING CREATED BY THE INTERNET AND INFORMATION REVOLUTION

From Google, to eBay, Expedia, StubHub, Napster, and online poker, the manifestations of the New Economy are changing the way we live, work, shop, travel, and spend our leisure time. Though the fundamentals of economics will not change, how those fundamentals are utilized is changing, at an ever-quickening pace. Stiglitz/Walsh Fourth Edition recognizes this fact.

e-INSIGHT BOXES apply economic principles to new developments in information technology and the Internet.

INTERNET CONNECTION BOXES provide useful links to Web resources and home pages.

2 ADDITIONAL TOOLS TO HEIGHTEN STUDENT UNDERSTANDING

THINKING LIKE AN ECONOMIST boxes reinforce the core ideas emphasized throughout the book: Trade-offs, Incentives, Exchange, Information, and Distribution.

CASE IN POINT vignettes highlight real-world applications in each chapter.

INTERNATIONAL PERSPECTIVE boxes present applications to international issues.

FUNDAMENTALS OF . . . sections distill the essence of particularly important and tricky topics.

WRAP-UPS provide a short summary of the key points presented in a section.

ECONOMICS, FOURTH EDITION e-BOOK

Same Great Content, Half the Price   The e-book version of *Economics, Fourth Edition*, offers the full content of the print version, at half the price.

In addition, a variety of features make the Norton e-book a powerful tool for study and review.

- **Zoomable images** allow students to get a closer look at the figures and photographs.
- **Clear text**, designed specifically for screen use, makes reading easy.
- A **search function** facilitates study and review.
- A **print function** permits individual pages to be printed as needed.
- **Sticky notes** allow students to add their own notes to the text.

Online and cross-platform software works on both Macs and PCs and allows students to access their e-book from home, school, or anywhere with an Internet connection. Visit NortonEbooks.com for more information.

Ancillary Package

A variety of valuable supplements are available to students and teachers who use the textbook.

SmartWork Homework Management System   Developed in coordination with Science Technologies, SmartWork is an innovative online homework management system. SmartWork requires active learning from students and provides smart, interactive feedback. Instructors can choose from three types of ready-made assignments:

- *Interactive Graphing Exercises* allow students to manipulate points, lines, and curves, see the implications instantly, and then answer questions about them.
- *Audio Graphs* guide students step-by-step through a slide show presenting core concepts. On screen, students see economic equations worked out and graphs manipulated while hearing an audio presentation of the lesson.
- *Conceptual Quizzes* pair questions with thought-provoking feedback. Students are asked to reconsider their answers after they respond to each question.

With SmartWork's intuitive interface, instructors can also customize Norton's ready-made assignments or write their own exercises with remarkable ease. Access to SmartWork is free to all students who purchase a new textbook or e-book.

Student Web Site   This free companion Web site offers students powerful review materials. Practice quizzes feature diagnostic feedback indicating which sections in the chapter the student should review. The student Web site also provides chapter reviews, a glossary, and a daily economics newsfeed.

NORTON MEDIA LIBRARY

This instructor's CD-ROM includes PowerPoint lecture slides (corresponding to the lecture modules in the *Instructor's Manual*) as well as all the graphs and tables from the book. New **lecture-launcher audio/visual slide shows** provide brief segments on each chapter's material as it relates to imperfect markets or the new economy.

NORTON RESOURCE LIBARY

The Norton Resource Library provides comprehensive instructor resources in one centralized online location. In the library, instructors can download ready-to-use, one-stop solutions for online courses, such as WebCT e-packs and BlackBoard course cartridges, or can tailor these pre-made course packs to suit their own needs. The library's exceptional resources include PowerPoint lecture slides, graphs and tables from the book, and a computerized test-item file.

TRANSPARENCIES

A set of color transparencies is available to qualified adopters.

STUDY GUIDE

BY LAWRENCE W. MARTIN, *MICHIGAN STATE UNIVERSITY*
PRINCIPLES OF MICROECONOMICS 0-393-92826-8 • PAPER
PRINCIPLES OF MACROECONOMICS 0-393-92827-6 • PAPER

This innovative study guide reinforces the key concepts of each chapter through reviews, practice exams, and problem sets designed to help students apply what they've learned. "Doing Economics" sections are structured around a series of "Tool Kits" in which students learn a problem-solving technique through its step-by-step application. Each "Tool Kit" is followed by worked examples and practice problems that apply the relevant technique.

INSTRUCTOR'S MANUAL

BY GERALD McINTYRE, *OCCIDENTAL COLLEGE*
PRINCIPLES OF MICROECONOMICS 0-393-92805-5 • PAPER
PRINCIPLES OF MACROECONOMICS 0-393-92821-7 • PAPER

For each chapter of the textbook the *Instructor's Manual* contains lecture advice, lecture modules, lecture applications, problem sets, and solutions. The extensive lecture modules can be used with a set of PowerPoint slides that Gerald McIntyre has prepared. These lecture notes are far more extensive than what other publishers offer, and will be extremely valuable to the first time instructor.

TEST-ITEM FILE

BY DAVID GILLETTE, *TRUMAN STATE UNIVERSITY*
PRINCIPLES OF MICROECONOMICS 0-393-92840-3 • PAPER
PRINCIPLES OF MACROECONOMICS 0-393-10727-2 • PAPER

The Fourth Edition *Test-Item File* includes over 4,000 questions, a 15 percent increase over the previous edition. In addition, each chapter includes a subset of questions covering the boxed inserts (such as e-Insights), which professors can use in their exams, thereby encouraging students to read these discussions.

Acknowledgments

The book's first three editions were improved immeasurable by the input of numerous reviewers. In particular, we thank Robert T. Averitt, Smith College; Mohsen Bahmani-Oskoose, University of Wisconsin, Milwaukee; Richard Barret, University of Montana; H. Scott Bierman, Carleton College; John Payne Bigelow, University of Missouri; Howard Bodenhorn, Lafayette College; Bruce R. Bolnick, Northeastern University; Adhip Chaudhuri, Georgetown University; Michael D. Curley, Kennesaw State College; John Devereus, University of Miami; Stephen Erfle, Dickinson College; Rudy Fichtenbaum, Wright State University; Kevin Forbes, Catholic University; K. K. Fung, Memphis State; Christopher Georges, Hamilton College; Ronald D. Gilbert, Texas Tech University; Robert E. Graf, Jr., United States Military Academy; Glenn W. Harrison, University of South Carolina; Marc Hayford, Loyola University; Yutaka Horiba, Tulane University; Charles How, University of Colorado; Sheng Cheng Hu, Purdue University; Glenn Hubbard, Columbia University; Nancy Jianakopolos, Colorado State University; Allen C, Kelley, Duke University; Lori Kletzer, University of California, Santa Cruz; Michael M. Knetter, Dartmouth College; Kevin Lang, Boston University; William Lastrapes, University of Georgia; John Leahy, Boston University; Eric Leeper, Indiana University; Colin Linsley, St. John Fisher College; Stefan Lutz, Purdue University; Mark J. Machina, University of California, San Diego; Burton G. Malkiel, Princeton University; Lawrence Martin, Michigan State University; Thomas Mayer, University of California, Davis; Craig J. McCann, University of South Carolina; Henry N. McCarl, University of Alabama, Birmingham; John McDermott, University of South Carolina; Marshall H. Medoff, University of California, Irving; Peter Mieszkowski, Rice University; Myra Moore, University of Georgia; W. Douglas Morgan, University of California, Santa Barbara; John S. Murphy, Canisius College; Michael Nelson, University of Akron; William Nielson, Texas A & M University; Neil B. Niman, University of New Hampshire; David H. Papell, University of Houston; Douglas Pearce, North Carolina State University; Jerrold Peterson, University of Minnesota, Duluth; James E. Price, Syracuse University; Daniel M. Raff, Harvard Business School; Christina D. Romer, University of California, Berkeley; Richard Rosenberg, Pennsylvania State University; Rosemary Rossiter, Ohio University; David F. Ruccio, University of Notre Dame; Christopher J. Ruhm, Boston University; Suzanna A. Scotchmer, University of California, Berkeley; Richard Selden, University of Virginia; Andrei Shleifer, Harvard University; Nirvikar Singh, University of California, Santa Cruz; John L. Solow, University of Iowa; George Spiva, University of Tennessee, Mark Sproul, University of California, Los Angeles; Frank P. Stafford, University of Michigan; Raghu Sundaram, University of Rochester; Hal R. Varian, University of California, Berkeley; Franklin V. Walker, State University of New York at Albany; James M. Walker, Indiana University; Andrew Weiss, Boston University; Mark Wohar, University of Nebraska, Omaha; and Gilbert R. Yochum, Old Dominion University.

Many additional reviewers provided suggestions that help guide us in preparing the Fourth Edition. Our thanks to John Nader, Grand Valley State University; Timothy A. Duy, University of Oregon; Richard Fox, Madonna University; Dale Cloninger, University of Houston, Clear Lake; Gavin Wright, Stanford University;

Richard Stahnke, Hamilton College; Maristella Botticini, Boston University; Chris Niggle, University of Redlands; Santanu Roy, Southern Methodist University; Roger White, Franklin and Marshall College; Geoffrey Carliner, Boston University; Robert L. Pennington, University of Central Florida; Roger A. McCain, Drexel University; Nancy A. Jianakoplos, Colorado State University; Sudeshna C. Bandyopadhyay, West Virginia University; Jennifer Thacher, University of New Mexico; Alan Gummerson, Florida International University; Nejat Anbarci, Florida International University; Samuel Allen, University of California, Davis; Robert G. Bise, Orange Coast College; Sarah L. Stafford, College of William and Mary; Catherine Krause, University of New Mexico; Ariel Belasen, Binghamton University; Alina Luca, Drexel University; S. Abu Turab Rizvi, University of Vermont; Nivedita Mukherji, Oakland University; Faik A. Koray, Louisiana State University; Mehdi Haririan, Bloomsburg University; F. G. Hank Hilton, Loyola College; Michael Margolis, Oberlin College; Joseph K. Cavanaugh, Wright State University; Lisa Gundersen, Iowa State University; Eva Toth Szalvai, Bowling Green State University; Maya Federman, Pitzer College; Annie Fang Yang, University of Minnesota, Twin Cities; Molly Espey, Clemson University; Nora Underwood, University of California, Davis; Mary Schranz, University of Wisconsin, Madison; Scott Cunningham, University of Georgia; Ehsan Ahmed, James Madison University; Lee van Scyoc, University of Wisconsin, Oshkosh; Parker Wheatley, Carleton College; Daniel Rubenson, Southern Oregon University; Elliott Parker, University of Nevada, Reno; Peter Murrell, University of Maryland; Abdulhamid Sukar, Cameron University; Philip S. Heap, James Madison University; Erik D. Craft, University of Richmond; Sharmila King, University of the Pacific; Linus Yamane, Pitzer College; Cathleen Leue, University of Oregon; Daniel Monchuk, University of Southern Mississippi; Rik W. Hafer, Southern Illinois University, Edwardsville; and Ben Young, University of Missouri, Kansas City.

A particular note of appreciation is due Mary Schranz, University of Wisconsin, Madison, who provided detailed, thoughtful, and extremely helpful comments on draft chapters of the macroeconomics material. Her insights significantly improved the end product.

The major changes in the Fourth Edition and the improvements they represent are due in no small measure to the constant encouragement, advice, and enthusiasm of our editor, Jack Repcheck. Jack provided the perfect blend of critical feedback and positive reinforcement to encourage us at each stage of the process to strive towards our goals of accessibility and modernity, and to incorporate the latest insights from the forefront of economics in a manner that is accessible to students getting their first introduction to economics.

We would also like to thank and acknowledge the entire team at Norton who made working on the Fourth Edition such a pleasure: Lory Frenkel, Matt Arnold, Mik Awake, Sarah Solomon, Rubina Yeh, Kelly Mitchell, Roy Tedoff, John McAusland, Alice Falk, and Barbara Hults.

A special note of thanks continues to be owed Judy Walsh. Judy's knowledge of economics and her willingness to discuss ideas, make suggestions, offer examples and encouragement have all helped contribute greatly to the improvements made to the Fourth Edition.

Alternative Course Outline

In the Fourth Edition, we have further improved the flexibility of the book, allowing it to be easily adapted to courses of varying length and objectives. **Part 4, Issues in Public Policy** and **Part 9, Further Topics in Macroeconomics**, contain chapters that can be covered at the end of a course, time permitting, or integrated with the core discussions of microeconomics and macroeconomics. **Part 8, The Global Economy**, provides instructors with the option of constructing a more internationally focused introductory course, covering international trade, finance, and development. Alternatively, instructors can selectively choose from among these topics and include them in a more traditional organized course. The following outlines, which represent only a small subset of those that might be devised, reflect the flexibility the Fourth Edition offers.

OUTLINE FOR A ONE-SEMESTER COURSE IN MICROECONOMICS AND MACROECONOMICS

CHAPTER	TITLE
1	Modern Economics
2	Thinking Like an Economist
3	Demand, Supply, and Price
4	Using Demand and Supply
5	The Consumption Decision
6	The Firm's Costs
7	The Competitive Firm
8	Labor Markets
9	Capital Markets
10	The Efficiency of Competitive Markets
11	Introduction to Imperfect Markets
12	Monopoly, Monopolistic Competition, and Oligopoly
13	Government Policies Toward Competition
21	Macroeconomics and the Economic Perspective
22	Measuring Economic Output and Unemployment
23	The Cost of Living and Inflation
24	The Full-Employment Model
25	Government Finance at Full-Employment
26	Money, the Price Level, and the Federal Reserve
29	Introduction to Economic Fluctuations
31	Aggregate Demand and Inflation
32	The Federal Reserve and Interest Rates
33	The Role of Macroeconomic Policy

OUTLINE FOR A SHORT COURSE IN MICROECONOMICS AND MACROECONOMICS

CHAPTER	TITLE
1	Modern Economics
2	Thinking Like an Economist
3	Demand, Supply, and Price
4	Using Demand and Supply
5	The Consumption Decision
6	The Firm's Costs
7	The Competitive Firm
10	The Efficiency of Competitive Markets
11	Introduction to Imperfect Markets
21	Macroeconomics and the Economic Perspective
22	Measuring Economic Output and Unemployment
23	The Cost of Living and Inflation
24	The Full-Employment Model
25	Government Finance at Full Employment
28	Money, the Price Level, and the Federal Reserve
29	Introduction to Macroeconomic Fluctuations
31	Aggregate Demand and Inflation
32	The Federal Reserve and Interest Rates

OUTLINE FOR A ONE-SEMESTER COURSE IN MICROECONOMICS

CHAPTER	TITLE
1	Modern Economics
2	Thinking Like an Economist
3	Demand, Supply, and Price
4	Using Demand and Supply
5	The Consumption Decision
6	The Firm's Costs
7	The Competitive Firm
8	Labor Markets
9	Capital Markets
10	The Efficiency of Competitive Markets
11	Introduction to Imperfect Markets
12	Monopoly, Monopolistic Competition, and Oligopoly
13	Government Policies Toward Competition
14	Strategic Behavior
15	Imperfect Information in the Product Market
16	Imperfections in the Labor Market

Plus any of the optional chapters comprising Part 4.

17	The Public Sector	
18	Environmental Economics	
19	International Trade and Trade Policy	
20	Technological Change	
39	A Student's Guide to Investing	

OUTLINE FOR A SHORT COURSE IN MICROECONOMICS

CHAPTER	TITLE
1	Modern Economics
2	Thinking Like an Economist
3	Demand, Supply, and Price
4	Using Demand and Supply
5	The Consumption Decision
6	The Firm's Costs
7	The Competitive Firm
8	Labor Markets
9	Capital Markets
10	The Efficiency of Competitive Markets
11	Introduction to Imperfect Markets
12	Monopoly, Monopolistic Competition, and Oligopoly
13	Government Policies Toward Competition
17	The Public Sector

OUTLINE FOR A ONE-SEMESTER COURSE IN MACROECONOMICS

CHAPTER	TITLE
21	Macroeconomics and the Economic Perspective

Core macroeconomics presentation

22	Measuring Economic Output and Unemployment
23	The Cost of Living and Inflation
24	The Full-Employment Model
25	Government Finance at Full Employment
26	The Open Economy at Full Employment
27	Growth and Productivity
28	Money, the Price Level, and the Federal Reserve
29	Introduction to Economic Fluctuations
30	Aggregate Expenditures and Income

31	Aggregate Demand and Inflation
32	The Federal Reserve and Interest Rates
33	The Role of Macroeconomic Policy

Plus any of the optional chapters comprising Parts 8 and 9

34	The International Financial System
35	Policy in the Open Economy
36	Economic Development and Transition
37	Inflation and Unemployment
38	Controversies in Macroeconomics
39	A Student's Guide to Investing

OUTLINE FOR A SHORT COURSE IN MACROECONOMICS

CHAPTER	TITLE
21	Macroeconomics and the Economic Perspective

Core macroeconomics presentation

22	Measuring Economic Output and Unemployment
23	The Cost of Living and Inflation
24	The Full-Employment Model
25	Government Finance at Full Employment
27	Growth and Productivity
28	Money, the Price Level, and the Federal Reserve
29	Introduction to Macroeconomic Fluctuations
31	Aggregate Demand and Inflation
32	The Federal Reserve and Interest Rates
33	The Role of Macroeconomic Policy

Part 1

INTRODUCTION

Learning Goals

In this chapter, you will learn

1. What economics is, and what the key concepts that define core ideas in economics are

2. What markets are, and which are the principal markets that make up the economy

3. Why economics is called a science, and why it is that economists often disagree

Chapter 1

MODERN ECONOMICS

The past decade has seen tremendous changes in the world economy. Many of these changes are linked to new technological advances that have transformed what the global economy produces, the ways in which many goods and services are produced, where they are produced, and how goods and services are transferred from the firms that produce them to the households, governments, and other firms that buy them. New technologies are transforming everything, from how airlines sell tickets to how automobiles are produced, from how we buy books to how we communicate with one another.

Like the industrial revolution of the eighteenth and nineteenth centuries that transformed first Britain and then other countries from agricultural to manufacturing-based economies, the information revolution of the late twentieth and early twenty-first centuries promises to transform almost all aspects of our daily lives. In 1999, in recognition of the growing importance of new, high-tech firms, Microsoft and Intel—the producer of the Windows computer operating system and the major producer of the microprocessors at the heart of personal computers respectively—were added to the Dow-Jones Industrial Average, the most widely followed index of prices on U.S. stock markets. Though the booming stock market of the late 1990s that was driven in part by enthusiasm for new technologies came to an end in 2000, innovation continues to be a critical force in the economy.

But the old economy is still alive and kicking. Four of the five largest United States corporations in *Fortune* magazine's top 500 list for 2003 were traditional industrial firms—General Motors, Exxon, Ford, and General Electric. IBM at number 8 and Verizon Communications at number 10 were the only information or "tech" firms in the top 10. Hewlett-Packard was number 14 and Dell Computers was 36, but Microsoft managed to make it no higher than number 47.

So the old economy and the new economy coexist side by side. But it is not just the emergence of new software and Internet companies that represents the effects of new technologies. The way all firms do business is being changed, and their customers are being affected too. Assembly lines now rely on robots aided and controlled by computers. Car repair shops with grease-stained floors have been replaced by clean, quiet garages where computers diagnose a car's problems. The way we buy things is also changing. Whether an individual purchases a car, book, or CD over the Web; books a hotel or plane reservation; or even applies to a college through the Internet, the relationship between people and firms is evolving. New technologies are changing the way courses are taught, too—textbooks like this one have Web sites that provide students with help, with interactive exercises, and with links to news, policy debates, and the latest economic information. The address of the home page for this text is www.wwnorton.com/stiglitzwalsh4.

With such far-reaching changes, what insights and understanding does the study of economics have to offer? After all, the field usually looks to Adam Smith, an eighteenth-century Scottish professor of moral philosophy, as its founder. Smith published his most famous book, *The Wealth of Nations,* in 1776, a time when today's industrial economies were still overwhelmingly agriculture-based. It might seem unlikely that a theory developed to understand the factors that determine the price of wheat would have much to say about today's modern economy.

But, in fact, study of economics continues to provide a critical understanding of today's global economy. As Carl Shapiro and Hal Varian of the University of California, Berkeley, put it, "Technology changes. Economic laws do not."[1] The way we produce things, what we produce, and how goods are exchanged have altered tremendously since Smith wrote. Yet the same fundamental laws of economics that explained agricultural prices in the eighteenth century can help us understand how economies function in the twenty-first century The foundation laid by Adam Smith and built upon by generations of economists has yielded insights that will continue to offer guidance to anyone wishing to make sense of the modern economy.

Over the past two hundred years, economists have refined and expanded our understanding of economic behavior. By incorporating the role of information and technological change, they are now able to explain much more than was possible just twenty years ago, offering new insights into topics that range from why car dealers build fancy showrooms to how the factors important for encouraging the production of new ideas differ from those that encourage the production of new cars.

But what are these insights? What do economists study? And what can we learn from looking at things from the perspective of economics? How can economics help us understand why we need to worry about the extinction of salmon but not of sheep, why auto manufacturers advertise but wheat farmers don't, why countries that rely on uncoordinated markets have done better than countries that rely on government planners, and why letting a single firm dominate an industry is bad?

The headlines from some recent news stories involving the computer industry and the Internet illustrate some of the key issues that a study of economics can help illuminate.

- **"Bill to Curb Online Piracy Is Challenged as Too Broad,"** *New York Times,* June 24, 2004. A bill recently introduced in the U.S. Senate aims to restrict

---

[1]Carl Shapiro and Hal R. Varian, *Information Rules: A Strategic Guide to the Network Economy* (Boston: Harvard Business School Press, 1999), p. 2.

the illegal online sharing of music and other files. This proposed legislation represents just the latest development in the running battle between the companies that own the rights to the music and consumers who want to freely share music files. After all, it doesn't cost the music company any more to have a file shared by a thousand people than it does to have it shared by two. So why, many ask, should they have to pay for music files? The advent of digital music has made it possible for listeners to exchange copies indistinguishable from the originals. But if the producers of the music cannot earn a profit, they have less incentive to seek out and record new artists. Property rights—in this case, the legal right of the music company to charge for the use of its property—play an important role in market economics, and disputes over property rights aren't new. But the new information technologies have made trading this property much easier and raised new questions. As we will see, economics can tell us a great deal about the issues involved in these disputes.

- **"Internet Drug Trade Proves Bitter Pill for Canada,"** *Financial Times,* April 21, 2004. The Internet has changed the nature of the market for goods such as prescription drugs. Buyers in Florida can as easily have their prescriptions filled by a pharmacy based in California, or Canada, as by one in Florida. But why has this led to shortages of some popular prescription drugs in Canada? What will be the likely consequences for drug prices in Canada and the United States?
- **"Intel Cancels 2 Chip Projects,"** *San Jose Mercury News,* May 8, 2004. After spending as much as $2 billion on a new line of computer chips called the Itanium, Intel pulled the plug on the project. As the company decided whether to go ahead with the project, was the money already invested a factor? Firms are always concerned about costs, but economics gives critical insights that help us understand which costs are important and whether some costs, such as the $2 billion Intel had already sunk into the Itanium project, aren't.
- **"Ebay Bids and Buys Baazee,"** *The Economic Times,* June 23, 2004. According to a story on economictimes.indiatimes.com, the online auction company eBay purchased Baazee.com, an Indian online shopping company, for $50 million. The purchase extends eBay's network throughout Asia, adding to its current ventures in Hong Kong, Singapore, and China. By linking online buyers and sellers globally, eBay will enable a consumer in Sioux City, Iowa, to trade with someone in Bangalore, India.
- **"Oracle's Bid for PeopleSoft to Be Tested in Court,"** *New York Times,* June 7, 2004. In early 2004, the software giant Oracle announced that it was making a hostile bid to buy PeopleSoft, another software company. The U.S. Justice Department initially filed a lawsuit to block this takeover, arguing that it would reduce competition in the market for business software. Oracle was eventually allowed to take over PeopleSoft, but why does the government try to ensure that there is competition? What are the advantages of competition? What tools does the government use to promote competition?
- **"FASB Holds Meeting on Expensing Stock Options,"** *San Jose Mercury News,* June 24, 2004. Many tech companies, particularly those located in California's Silicon Valley, have used stock options to reward their employees.

Internet Connection

TRACKING THE DIGITAL ECONOMY

Since 1998, the U.S. Department of Commerce has issued an annual report on the digital economy. You can find the latest report at www.esa.doc.gov/reports.cfm.

This mechanism grants the employee the opportunity to purchase shares in the company at a set price. If the company does well and its shares go up in value, the employee can sell the stock for a profit—a prospect that creates an incentive to work hard and help the company succeed. The Federal Accounting Standards Board (FASB) proposed new accounting rules requiring firms that offer stock options to report these as an expense, thereby reducing the firm's reported profits. The FASB argues that to do so would present investors with a more accurate picture of the firm's profits, enabling investors to make better decisions about buying stock in the company.

News headlines frequently focus on economic issues, and these six point to some of the key topics that economists study: the role of incentives and information, globalization and exchange, competition and government regulation, costs and business decisions. The study of economics will give you new insights into the news stories you see in the paper, it will give you insights into the world of business, and it will help you understand the world of economics you participate in every day.

What Is Economics?

Headlines can illustrate many of the important issues with which economics deals, but now a definition of our subject is in order. *Economics* studies how individuals, firms, government, and other organizations within our society make *choices,* and how these choices determine society's use of its resources. Why did consumers choose to buy small, energy-efficient cars in the 1970s and large sports utility vehicles in the 1990s? What determines how many individuals work in health care industries and how many work in the computer industry? Why did the income gap between rich and poor rise in the 1980s? To understand how choices are made and how these choices affect the use of society's resources, we must examine five concepts that play an important role: trade-offs, incentives, exchange, information, and distribution.

1. Choice involves **trade-offs**—deciding to spend more on one thing leaves less to spend on something else; devoting more time to studying economics leaves less time to study physics.

2. In making choices, individuals respond to **incentives.** If the price of Zen MP3 players falls relative to the price of iPods, there is a greater incentive to buy a Zen. If the salaries for engineers rise relative to the salaries of people with an MBA, there is an increased incentive to choose to study for an engineering degree rather than a business degree.
3. When we **exchange** with others, our range of choices becomes larger.
4. Making intelligent choices requires that we have, and utilize, **information.**
5. Finally, the choices we make—about how much education to get, what occupation to enter, and what goods and service to buy—determine the **distribution** of wealth and income in our society.

These five concepts define the core ideas that are critical to understanding economics. They also guide the way economists think about issues and problems. Learning to "think like an economist" means learning how to discover the trade-offs and incentives faced, the implications of exchange, the role of information, and the consequences for distribution. These key concepts are emphasized throughout the text in "Thinking Like an Economist" boxes.

TRADE-OFFS

Each of us is constantly making choices—students decide to study at the library rather than in the dorm, to have pizza rather than sushi, to go to college rather than work full-time. Societies, too, make choices—to preserve open spaces rather than provide more housing, to produce computers and import televisions rather than produce televisions and import computers, to cut taxes rather than increase government expenditures. In some cases, individuals or governments explicitly make these choices. You decided to study economics rather than some other subject. The government decides each year whether to cut taxes or to increase spending. In other cases, however, the choices were the result of the uncoordinated actions of millions of individuals. Neither the government nor any one individual decided that the United States would import cars from Japan and export wheat to India. But in each case, choice involves trade-offs—to get more of one thing involves having less of something else. We are forced to make trade-offs because of **scarcity.**

Scarcity figures prominently in economics; choices matter because resources are scarce. For most of us, our limited income forces us to make choices. We cannot afford everything we might want. Spending more on rent leaves less available for clothes and entertainment. Getting a sunroof on a new car may mean forgoing leather seats to stay within a fixed budget. Limited income is not the only reason we are forced to make trade-offs. Time is also a scarce resource, and even the wealthiest individual must decide what expensive toy to play with each day. When we take time into account, we realize scarcity is a fact of life for everyone.

One of the most important points on which economists agree concerns the critical role of scarcity. We can summarize this point as follows: *There is no free lunch. Having more of one thing requires giving up something else. Scarcity means that* trade-offs *are a basic fact of life.*

INCENTIVES

It is one thing to say we all face trade-offs in the choices we make. It is quite another to understand how individuals and firms make choices and how those choices might change as economic circumstances change. If new technologies are developed, will firms decide to increase or decrease the amount of labor they employ? If the price of gasoline rises, will individuals decide to buy different types of automobiles?

When faced with a choice, people evaluate the pros and cons of the different options. In deciding what to eat for dinner tonight, you and your roommates might weigh the advantages and disadvantages of having a frozen pizza again over going out for sushi. Similarly, a firm evaluates the pros and cons of its alternatives in terms of the effects different choices will have on its profits. For example, a retail chain deciding on the location for a new store must weigh the relative advantages of different locations. One location might have more foot traffic but also higher rent. Another location might be less desirable but have lower rent.

When decision makers systematically weigh the pros and cons of the alternatives they face, we can predict how they will respond to changing economic conditions. Higher gas prices raise the cost of driving, but the cost of driving a fuel-efficient car rises less than the cost of driving a sports utility vehicle. Therefore, households weighing a car purchase have a greater incentive to choose the fuel-efficient car. If a firm starts selling more of its goods through the Internet, it will rely less on foot traffic into its retail store. This shift reduces its incentive to pay a high rent for a good location.

Economists analyze choices by focusing on incentives. In an economic context, incentives are benefits (including reduced costs) that motivate a decision maker in favor of a particular choice. Many things can affect incentives, but among the most important are *prices*. If the price of gasoline rises, people have a greater incentive to drive less. If the price of MP3 players falls, people have a greater incentive to buy one. When the price of a good rises, firms are induced to produce more of that good, in order to increase their profits. If a resource used in production, such as labor or equipment, becomes more expensive, firms have an incentive to find new methods of production that economize on that resource. Incentives also are affected by the return people expect to earn from different activities. If the income of college graduates rises relative to that of people with only a high school diploma, people have a greater incentive to attend college.

When economists study the behavior of people or firms, they look at the incentives being faced. Sometimes these incentives are straightforward. Increasing the number of courses required to major in biology reduces the incentive to pick that major. In other circumstances, they may not be so obvious. For example, building safer cars may create incentives to drive faster. Identifying the incentives, and disincentives, to take different actions is one of the first things economists do when they want to understand the choices individuals or firms make.

Decision makers respond to incentives; for understanding choices, incentives matter.

Trade-offs and Incentives in Practice: Online Music Sharing Since 1999, when Napster introduced the first file-sharing program that allowed users to swap music files over the Internet, the practice has been embroiled in controversy. On one side is the music industry, which views the sharing of music files as an illegal activity, and on the other side are the companies producing the software that allows file sharing and the millions of music lovers who do not want to pay for music. The debates now also encompass the movie industry, as digitized movies can be shared as easily as music files. The legal battle between MGM and Grokster, a distributor of peer-to-peer file-sharing software, reached the United States Supreme Court in 2005.

Incentives are at the heart of the case against file sharing. Record companies make money by selling CDs. They, or the artists who create the music, hold copyrights that give them the right to charge others for its use. Copyrighted material, which includes books like this text as well as music, cannot be distributed or sold without the permission of the copyright holder. In that way, the holder of the copyright—the book publisher, author, artist, composer, or record company—is able to limit access to the material and charge a fee for its use. When music could only be copied by physically duplicating a tape recording or burning a CD, it was costly to make illegal copies. While people might burn a CD to use in the car or give to a friend, this type of sharing was relatively minor, and something the music industry tolerated.

The advent of digital music changed the situation dramatically. Now, a music file can be shared with millions of other listeners. In 1999, Napster introduced a file-sharing service that focused exclusively on music. In the process, Napster helped to popularize the MP3 format; by February 2001 the service had over 26 million users worldwide. Napster also quickly attracted the attention of the record companies, who sued Napster for distributing copyrighted music without paying royalties to the copyright holders. In 2001, Napster settled the lawsuit, agreeing to pay $26 million to the music copyright holders. Faced with paying this huge fee, Napster declared bankruptcy in 2002. It has recently converted itself to a subscription service for downloading music legally.

Thinking Like an Economist
INCENTIVES AND THE PRICE OF AOL

Today, most online services such as AOL charge their customers a fixed monthly fee for Internet access. In the earlier days of the Internet, the access charge was commonly based on how many minutes the member was connected to the Internet. In 1997, AOL announced that it would change its pricing policy and move to a flat monthly fee with unlimited minutes of connect time. AOL's servers were quickly overwhelmed and members found it almost impossible to log on. Why? Because charges were no longer based on the number of minutes a member was logged on, many customers never logged off. Once connected, they simply left AOL running, tying up its modem capacity. When members had to pay on a per-minute basis, they had an incentive to log off when the service was not being used. The flat fee left no incentive to economize on connect time. Thinking about incentives would have shown AOL that it needed to greatly increase its modem capacity *before* announcing the new pricing plan.

Napster's place has been taken by services such as Grokster and Morpheus that offer peer-to-peer (p2p) file sharing. In their legal battles with the music industry, these services have argued that they should not be held liable simply becuse their products might be used to duplicate copyrighted materials illegally. However, in July 2005, the U.S. Supreme Court ruled that the services could be found liable because they knowingly promoted products that were designed to infringe on the rights of copyright holders and did nothing to disourage this illegal activity.

So how does all this relate to the concept of incentives? First, free music clearly creates an incentive for music lovers to download songs rather than pay for them by buying a CD. This is at the heart of the music industry's opposition to p2p file sharing. Second, if record companies cannot charge for their music because it can be downloaded for free, they have less of an incentive to record new music. According to the record industry, by reducing the incentive to produce new music, file sharing will ultimately reduce the opportunities for new musicians to record with major record labels.

While the effects of free, online file sharing on incentives are clear, the magnitude of those effects is open to debate. The music industry points to a decline in CD sales, from 942.5 million CDs in 2000 to 766.9 in 2004, as evidence that the availability of free downloads has hurt their business. However, critics of the music industry argue that this decline in sales is simply a reflection of the economic slowdown and rise in unemployment that began in 2001. Some studies have argued that the availability of free music downloads might actually increase CD sales. Listening to music online can actually increase interest in new music and individuals who are able to listen to music online before buying an album may actually be more likely to purchase CDs. A study by economists at the University of North Carolina and the Harvard Business School was unable to find any effect of online access to music on subsequent CD sales.

Whatever the ultimate outcome of this battle might be, incentives are essential to understanding the issues. The incentive to avoid paying for music provided by low-cost or free access reduces the incentive of record companies to discover, record, and promote new musical talents.

EXCHANGE

Somehow, decisions that are made—by individuals, households, firms, and government as they face trade-offs and respond to incen
tives—together determine how the economy's limited resources, including its land, labor, machines, oil, and other natural resources, are used. The key to understanding how this happens lies in the role of *voluntary* exchange in *markets*.

Long before the rise of modern industrial societies, the benefits of exchange were well understood. Coastal societies with access to fishing resources, for example, would trade some of their fish to inland societies in return for meat and furs. The coastal group sought meat and furs that were worth more to them than the fish they gave up; the inland group likewise exchanged meat and furs for fish. Both groups benefited from voluntary exchange.

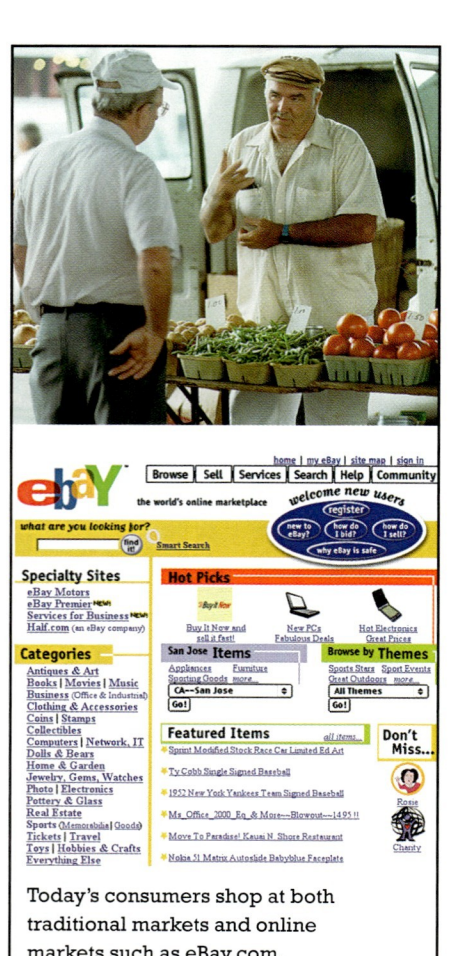

Today's consumers shop at both traditional markets and online markets such as eBay.com.

Internet Connection
AUCTION SITES

An auction is one form of market that used to require potential buyers to be physically present in a single location. Now, auctions are held over the Internet and can involve participants from around the world. Some sites, such as eBay (www.ebay.com), offer just about everything for sale. Other sites specialize. For instance, Heritage Coins (www.heritagecoins.com) provides an auction site for rare coins. Even the U.S. government has gotten into the act. The U.S. Treasury does not actually auction items online, but it uses the Web to publicize the locations at which confiscated property will be auctioned (www.treas.gov/auctions/customs).

In modern societies, millions of exchanges take place. Few individuals produce any of the goods and services they themselves want to consume. Instead, teachers, police officers, lawyers, and construction workers sell their labor services to a school district, a city, a client, or a homebuilder and then exchange the income they earn for all the various goods and services they wish to consume that are produced by others. An important insight in economics is the recognition that *both* parties in a voluntary exchange gain. Whether it takes place between two individuals, between an individual and a firm, or between residents of two different countries, exchange can improve the well-being of both parties.

Economists describe any situation in which exchange takes place as a *market*. For thousands of years, societies have established physical locations such as village markets or periodic trading fairs where people have brought their products, haggled over terms of exchange, and reaped the benefits of trade. The economic concept of markets covers any situation in which exchange takes place, though this exchange may not necessarily resemble a traditional village market or a modern stock exchange. In department stores and shopping malls, customers rarely haggle over the price. When manufacturers purchase the materials they need for production, they give in exchange money, not other goods. Most goods, from cameras to clothes, are not sold directly from producers to consumers. Instead they are sold from producers to distributors, from distributors to retailers, and from retailers to consumers. All of these transactions are embraced by the concept of markets and a **market economy.**

In a market economy like that of the United States, most exchanges take place through markets, and these exchanges are guided by the prices of the goods and services involved. The goods and services that are scarcer, or require more resources for their production, come at a higher price. Automobiles are more expensive than paper cups; lawyers charge more than janitors. As a result, markets enable consumers and firms to make choices that reflect scarcity, and therefore lead to efficient uses of resources.

Market economies thus rely primarily on market exchanges to resolve the most basic economic questions: What and how much is produced? How is it produced? For whom is it produced? And who makes the economic decisions? Individuals and firms make the decisions. Individuals make decisions that reflect their own desires as they respond to the incentives they face. Firms make decisions that maximize their profits, and to do so they strive to produce the goods that consumers want at the lowest possible cost. This process determines what is produced, how it is produced, and for whom. As firms compete in the quest for profits, consumers benefit, both from the kinds of goods produced and from the prices at which they are supplied. On the whole, markets ensure that society's resources are used efficiently.

In some areas, however, markets lead to outcomes that society may find inadequate. There may be too much pollution, too much inequality, and too little concern about education, health, and safety. When the market is not perceived to be working well, people often turn to government. An economy such as in the United States is often called a *mixed economy*—one that relies primarily but not exclusively on the free interaction of producers and consumers to determine what is produced, how, and for whom. In some areas, the government makes the decisions, in others it imposes regulations that affect the incentives firms and households face; and in many areas, both the *private sector* (households and businesses) and the *public sector* (local, state, and federal governments) are involved (education is a good example).

Governments play a critical role in all market economies. For example, governments provide the legal structure within which private firms and individuals operate. No one would open a store if others could simply steal things off the shelf with impunity; the store owner needs to know there is a legal system that he can use to prosecute theft. No bank would lend money to a family to buy a home if it could not legally require the family to repay the loan. Governments also regulate businesses in many ways. There are regulations to ensure firms do not discriminate by race or sex, do not mislead consumers, and are careful about the safety of their workers. In some industries, such as education and mail service, the government is a major supplier of services. In other industries, such as the defense industry, government is the major purchaser. The government also supplies goods and services that the private sector does not, such as the national defense, roads, and currency. Government programs provide for the elderly through Social Security (which pays income to retired individuals) and Medicare (which funds the medical needs of the aged). The government helps those who have suffered economic dislocation, through unemployment insurance for those temporarily unemployed and disability insurance for those who are no longer able to work. The government also provides a safety net of support for the poor, particularly children, through various welfare programs.

One can easily imagine the government controlling the economy more directly. In countries where decision making is centralized and concentrated in the government, government bureaucrats might decide what and how much a factory should produce and set the wages that should be paid. At least until recently, governments in countries such as the former Soviet Union and China attempted to control practically all major decisions regarding resource allocation. Even in Europe, not long ago many governments ran oil companies, coal mines, and the telephone system. Increasingly, however, governments have sold these enterprises to the private sector, a process called *privatization.*

Market economies in which individuals and firms make the decisions about what to produce and how much to pay have proven adept at developing new technologies and products. It is hard to imagine government bureaucrats developing MP3 players or iMacs in neon colors. Markets also generally ensure that resources are used efficiently.

Exchange in markets is a key to understanding how resources are allocated, what is produced, and who earns what.

INFORMATION

Making informed choices requires information. After all, it is hard to weigh the costs and benefits of alternative choices if you do not know what they are! A firm that is contemplating the purchase of a new software system needs to know not only the costs of the various alternatives but also the capabilities and limitations of each. Information is, in many ways, like other goods and services. Firms and individuals are willing to purchase information, and specialized institutions develop to sell it. In many areas, separate organizations are designed solely to provide information to consumers. *Consumer Reports* is a prime example. The Internet also now serves as a major source of independent information for buyers. But there are some fundamental ways in which information differs from other goods. A car seller will let you test-drive a vehicle, but a seller of information cannot let you see the information before you buy. Once you have seen the information, you have no incentive to pay for it. Another way information differs from other goods is that unlike a can of soda or a bagel, information can be freely shared. When I tell you something, it does not subtract from what I know (though it may subtract from the profits I might earn from that information).

In some key areas of the economy, the role of information is so critical that it affects the nature of the market. In the used-car market, buyers and sellers negotiating over the price of a vehicle may have quite different information about its quality. The seller may have better information about the quality of the car but also has an incentive to misrepresent its condition, since better-quality cars command higher prices. As a result, the buyer will be reluctant to trust claims that the car is in perfect shape.

When consumers lack adequate information to make informed choices, governments frequently intervene to require that firms provide information. In the United States, we are all familiar with the mandatory nutritional information placed on food products. The Securities and Exchange Commission (SEC) that oversees American stock markets compels firms to meet certain reporting requirements before their stock can be listed on exchanges such as the New York Stock Exchange. Such reporting helps ensure that private investors have reliable information on which to base their investment decisions. Often, however, these regulations do not work adequately, as the Enron scandal in 2001 clearly illustrates. The oil trading company Enron had cooked its books to overstate its profitability in its mandated reports. One outcome of Enron's subsequent financial collapse was the introduction of new regulations designed to improve the reliability of the information that companies must provide to the public. Governments also regulate the safety of products. In the United States, the Food and Drug Administration (FDA) must approve new pharmaceuticals before they can be sold. The need for such oversight was driven home in 2005 when the drug manufacturer Merck had to pull its pain relief drug Vioxx off the market after studies suggested it increased the risk of heart attacks and strokes. Critics of the FDA argued that the agency is not adequately monitoring the safety of drugs once they are approved, and proposals have been made to establish a new government review board whose job it will be to decide when new information warrants removing a drug from the market.

Even in the absence of regulation, firms have incentives to signal to buyers that their products are of high quality. One way they do this is to offer guarantees that a producer of low-quality goods could not afford to offer.

Imperfect information also can interfere with incentives. Employers want to create incentives for employees to work hard. One way to do this is to base pay on a measure of how productive each worker is. Often, however, it is difficult to measure a worker's productivity. Under such conditions, it is difficult to link pay to performance. For example, a major debate in the United States concerns tying teacher salaries to performance. Because it is hard to measure teaching performance, the pay of most teachers is based primarily on how long they have been teaching.

Information, or its absence, plays a key role in determining the shape of markets and the ability of private markets to ensure that the economy's scarce resources are used efficiently.

DISTRIBUTION

The market economy determines not only what goods are produced and how they are produced but also for whom they are produced. Many people find unacceptable the way the market distributes goods among households. "While recognizing the efficacy of capitalism to produce wealth, there remains considerable unease among some segments about the way markets distribute that wealth and about the effects of raw competition on society."[2] Like bidders at an auction, what market participants are willing and able to pay depends on their income. Incomes differ markedly across occupations. Some groups of individuals—including those without skills that are valued by the market—may receive such a low income that they cannot feed and educate their children without outside assistance. Government provides the assistance by taking steps to increase income equality.

Steps that soften the distributional impact of markets may blunt economic incentives. While welfare payments provide an important safety net for the poor, the taxation required to finance them may discourage people from working and saving. If the government takes one out of every two or three dollars that an individual earns, that individual may not be inclined to work as much. And if the government takes one out of every two or three dollars a person earns from interest on savings, the person may decide to spend more and save less. Thus, efforts by the government to redistribute income may come at the cost of reduced economic efficiency.

---

[2] Alan Greenspan, speech at the Federal Reserve Bank of Kansas City Jackson-Hole Conference, August 25, 2000.

The primary reliance on private decision making in the United States reflects economists' beliefs that this reliance is appropriate and necessary for economic efficiency. However, economists also believe that certain interventions by government are desirable. Like the appropriate balance between public and private sectors, the appropriate balance between concerns about equality (often referred to as *equity concerns*) and efficiency is a central issue of modern economies. As elsewhere, trade-offs must be made.

Wrap-Up

FIVE CORE IDEAS

1. *Trade-offs:* resources are scarce, so trade-offs are a basic fact of life.
2. *Incentives:* in making choices, decision makers respond to incentives.
3. *Exchange:* people benefit from voluntary exchange, and in market economies, market exchanges lead to the efficient use of resources.
4. *Information:* the structure that markets take and how well they can function depend critically on the information available to decision makers.
5. *Distribution:* markets determine how the goods and services produced by the economy are allocated to members of society.

The Three Major Markets

The market economy revolves around exchange between individuals (or households) who buy goods and services from firms, and firms, which take *inputs*, the various materials of production, and produce *outputs*, the goods and services that they sell. In thinking about a market economy, economists focus their attention on three broad categories of markets in which individuals and firms interact. The markets in which firms sell their outputs to households are referred to collectively as the **product market.** Many firms also sell goods to other firms; the output of the first firm becomes the input of the second. These transactions too are said to occur in the product market.

On the input side, firms need (besides the materials they buy in the product market) some combination of labor and machinery to produce their output. They purchase the services of workers in the **labor market.** They raise funds to buy inputs in the **capital market.** Traditionally, economists also have highlighted the importance of a third input, land, but in modern industrial economies land is of secondary importance. For most purposes, it suffices to focus attention on the three major markets—product, labor, and capital—and this text will follow that pattern.

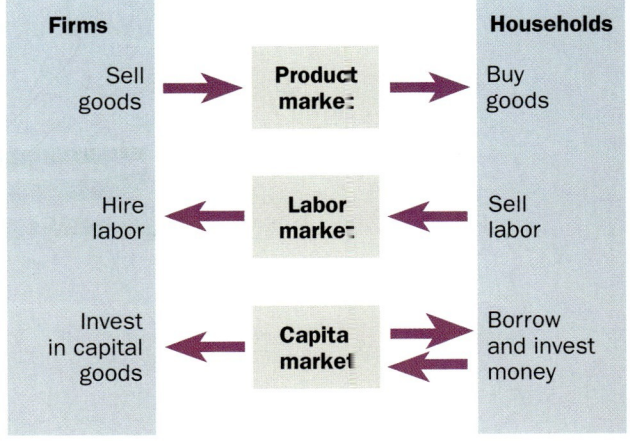

Figure 1.1

THE THREE MARKETS

To economists, people wear different hats. They are usually consumers in the product market, workers in the labor market, and borrowers or lenders in the capital market.

As Figure 1.1 shows, individuals participate in all three markets. When individuals buy goods and services, they act as *consumers* in the product market. When people act as *workers,* economists say they "sell their labor services" in the labor market. When people buy shares of stock in a firm, deposit money in a savings account, or lend money to a business, they are participating in the capital market as *investors.*

KEEPING TRACK OF TRICKY TERMS

Terms in economics often are similar to terms in ordinary usage, but they can have special meanings. The terms *markets* and *capital* illustrate this problem.

Though the term *market* is used to conjure up an image of a busy *marketplace,* there is no formal marketplace for most goods and services. There are buyers and sellers, and economists analyze the outcomes *as if* there were a single marketplace in which all transactions occur. For example, economists analyze the "market for books," even though the buyers and sellers in the market for books interact in thousands of individual bookstores and online selling locations.

Moreover, economists often talk about the "market for labor" as if all workers were identical. But workers differ in countless ways. In some cases, these differences are important. We might then talk about the "market for skilled workers" or the "market for computer engineers." In other cases—such as when we are talking about the overall state of the economy and focusing on the overall unemployment rate (the proportion of workers who are looking for jobs but cannot find them)—these differences can be ignored.

When newspapers refer to the *capital market,* they mean the bond traders and stockbrokers and the companies they work for on Wall Street and in other financial districts. When economists use the term *capital market,* they have in mind a broader concept that includes all the institutions concerned with raising funds (and, as we will see later, sharing and insuring risk), including banks and insurance companies.

The term *capital* is used in still another way—to refer to the machines and buildings used in production. To distinguish this particular usage, in this book we refer to machines and buildings as **capital goods.** The term *capital markets* thus refers to the markets in which funds are raised, borrowed, and lent. *Capital goods markets* refers to the markets in which capital goods are bought and sold.

Wrap-Up

THE THREE MAJOR MARKETS

1. *The product market:* the markets in which firms sell the goods they produce.
2. *The labor market:* the market in which households sell labor services and firms buy labor services.
3. *The capital market:* the market in which funds are borrowed and lent.

Microeconomics and Macroeconomics: The Two Branches of Economics

Economists have developed two different ways to look at the economy. The detailed study of the decisions of firms and households, and of prices and production in specific industries, is called **microeconomics.** Microeconomics (*micro* is derived from the Greek word meaning "small") focuses on the behavior of the units—the firms, households, and individuals—that make up the economy. It is concerned with how the individual units make decisions and what affects those decisions.

By contrast, **macroeconomics** (*macro* is derived from the Greek word meaning "large") looks at the behavior of the economy as a whole, in particular the behavior of such aggregate measures as the overall rates of unemployment, inflation, and economic growth and the balance of trade. The aggregate numbers do not tell us what any one firm or household is doing. They tell us what is happening in total, or on average. In a dynamic economy, there are always some industries expanding and others contracting. For instance, the economic expansion of the late 1990s saw rapid growth in Internet-related industries, while oil firms in Texas contracted. But there are times when overall growth in an economy slows and times when the level of economic activity actually declines, not just in an isolated industry but seemingly across all or almost all industries.

In macroeconomics, we also look at the behavior of the general level of prices, interest rates, and exchange rates. Why do prices of almost all goods and services seem to rise at rapid rates during some periods, while at other times they remain stable? Why do interest rates fluctuate? And what determines the value of the dollar relative to other currencies?

In approaching these questions, it is important to remember that the behavior of the economy as a whole is dependent on the decisions made by the millions of households and firms in the economy, as well as the decisions made by the government. Micro and macro perspectives are simply two ways of looking at the same thing. Microeconomics is the bottom-up view of the economy; macroeconomics is the top-down view.

Wrap-Up

THE BRANCHES OF ECONOMICS

Microeconomics: focuses on the decisions of households and firms and the detailed study of prices and production in specific industries.

Macroeconomics: focuses on the behavior of the economy as a whole and the behavior of aggregate variables such as overall employment, output, economic growth, the price level, and inflation.

The Science of Economics

Economics is a *social science*. It studies the social problem of choice from a scientific viewpoint, which means that it is built on a systematic exploration of the problem of choice. This systematic exploration involves both the formulation of theories and the examination of data.

A **theory** consists of a set of assumptions (or hypotheses) and conclusions derived from those assumptions. Theories are logical exercises: *if* the assumptions are correct, *then* the results follow. If all college graduates have a better chance of getting jobs and Ellen is a college graduate, then Ellen has a better chance of getting a job than a nongraduate. Economists make predictions with their theories. They might use their theory to predict what would happen if a tax is increased or if imports of foreign cars are limited. The predictions of a theory are of the form "If a tax is increased and if the market is competitive, then output will decrease and prices will increase."

In developing their theories, economists use *models*. To understand how models are used in economics, consider a modern car manufacturer trying to design a new automobile. It is extremely expensive to construct a new car. Rather than creating a separate, fully developed car for every conception of what engineers or designers would like the new car to be, the company uses models. The designers might use a plastic model to study the general shape of the vehicle and to assess reactions to the car's aesthetics. The engineers might use a computer model to study air resistance, from which they can calculate fuel consumption.

Just as engineers construct different models to study particular features of a car, economists construct different models of the economy—in words or equations—to depict particular features of the economy. An economic model might describe a general relationship ("When incomes rise, the number of cars purchased increases"), describe a quantitative relationship ("When incomes rise by 10 percent, the number of cars purchased rises, on average, by 12 percent"), or make a general prediction ("An increase in the tax on gasoline will decrease the demand for cars").

DISCOVERING AND INTERPRETING RELATIONSHIPS

A *variable* is any item that can be measured and that changes. Prices, wages, interest rates, and quantities bought and sold are variables. What interests economists is the connection between variables. When economists see what appears to be a systematic relationship among variables, they ask, Could it have arisen by chance or is there indeed a relationship? This is the question of **correlation**.

Economists use statistical tests to measure and test correlations. Consider the problem of deciding whether a coin is biased. If you flip the coin 10 times and get 6 heads and 4 tails, is the coin a fair one? Or is it weighted toward heads? Statistical tests will show that the result of 6 heads and 4 tails easily could have happened by chance, so the evidence does not prove that the coin is weighted. It also does not prove that the coin is *not* weighted. The evidence is not strong enough for either conclusion. But if you flip the coin 100 times and get 80 heads, statistical tests will tell you that the possibility of this happening by blind chance with a fair coin is extremely small. The evidence supports the assertion that the coin is weighted.

A similar logic can be used on correlations among economic variables. People with more education tend to earn higher wages. Is the connection merely chance? Statistical tests support the existence of a systematic relationship between education and wages.

CAUSATION AND CORRELATION

Economists want to accomplish more than just asserting that different variables are indeed correlated. They would like to conclude that changes in one variable *cause* the changes in another variable. This distinction between correlation and **causation** is important. If one variable "causes" the other, then changing the first variable necessarily will change the other. If the relationship is just a correlation, this may not be true.

During the 1970s, imports of Japanese cars into the United States increased while sales of U.S.-produced cars decreased. The two variables were negatively correlated. But did increased Japanese car sales *cause* the decrease in sales of American-made cars? Perhaps both were responding to a common factor that was the true cause of both the rise in Japanese car sales and the decline in sales of American cars. In fact, that is what was happening—the huge increase in oil prices after 1973 caused consumers to shift their purchases away from gas-guzzling American cars and toward more fuel-efficient Japanese cars.

Why Economists Disagree

Economists are frequently called on to make judgments on matters of public policy. Should the government cut taxes? How should Social Security be reformed? Should Internet commerce be taxed? In these public policy discussions, economists often disagree. These disagreements arise for two reasons. First, economists can differ in their views on the consequences of a proposed policy. Second, they can differ in how they evaluate those consequences.

When economists describe the economy and construct models that predict how the economy will be affected by different policies, they are engaged in what is called **positive economics.** When they evaluate alternative policies, weighing the various benefits and costs, they are engaged in **normative economics.**

Consider the positive and normative aspects of a proposal to restrict imports of textiles produced in developing countries. Positive economics would describe the consequences: the increased prices American consumers would have to pay for clothes, the increased sales of American textiles, the increased employment and profits of U.S. textile manufacturers, and the reduced employment among textile workers in developing countries. Economists might disagree over the consequences of restricting imports because they disagree over the magnitude of the effects, perhaps agreeing that prices to consumers would rise but disagreeing over the size of that rise.

In the end, though, the policy question is, *Should there be restraints on textile imports?* This is a normative question. Normative economics would weigh these various effects—the losses to consumers, the gains to U.S. textile workers, the increased profits—to reach an overall judgment. Normative economics develops frameworks within which these complicated judgments can be systematically made. Good normative economics also tries to be explicit about precisely which values or objectives it is incorporating. It tries to couch its statements in the form "If these are your values, then this is the best policy."

Economists, like members of any other profession, often have different values. Two economists might agree that a particular tax change would increase saving but would benefit the wealthy more than the poor. However, they might reach different conclusions about the desirability of that tax change. One might oppose it because it increases income inequality; the other might support it because it promotes saving. They differ in the values they place on the effects of the policy change, so they reach different conclusions even when they agree on the positive analysis of the proposed policy.

While economists may often seem to differ greatly among themselves, in fact they agree more than they disagree. When they do disagree, economists try to be clear about the source of their disagreement: (1) to what extent does it arise out of differences in models, (2) to what extent does it arise out of differences in estimates of quantitative relationships, and (3) to what extent does it arise out of differences in values? Clarifying the source of and reasons for disagreement can be a very productive way of learning more about an issue.

Review and Practice

SUMMARY

1. Economics is the study of how individuals, firms, and governments within our society make choices. Choices, and therefore trade-offs are unavoidable because desired goods, services, and resources are inevitably scarce.
2. Economists study how individuals, firms, and governments within our society make choices by focusing on incentives. People respond to changes in incentives by altering the decisions they make.
3. Exchange occurs in markets. Voluntary exchange can benefit both parties.
4. Making choices requires information. Limited or imperfect information can interfere with incentives and affect the ability of the private market to ensure an efficient use of society's scarce resources.
5. The incomes people receive are determined by the market economy. Concerns over the equitable distribution of wealth and income in the economy lead to government programs that increase income equality.
6. The United States has a mixed economy, one in which there is a mix of public and private decision making. The economy relies primarily on the private interaction of individuals and firms to determine how resources are allocated, but government plays a large role as well. A central question for any mixed economy is the balance between the private and public sectors.
7. The term *market* is used to describe any situation where exchange takes place. In the U.S. market economy, individuals, firms, and government interact in product markets, labor markets, and capital markets.
8. The two major branches of economics are microeconomics and macroeconomics. Microeconomics focuses on the behavior of the firms, households, and individuals that make up the economy. Macroeconomics focuses on the behavior of the economy as a whole.
9. Economists use models to study how the economy works and to make predictions about what will happen if something is changed. A model can be expressed in words or equations and is designed to mirror the essential characteristics of the particular phenomena under study.
10. A correlation exists when two variables tend to change together in a predictable way. However, the simple existence of a correlation does not prove that one factor causes the other to change. Additional outside factors may be influencing both.
11. Positive economics is the study of how the economy works. Disagreements in positive economics center on the appropriate model of the economy or market and the quantitative magnitudes characterizing the models.
12. Normative economics deals with the desirability of various actions. Disagreements in normative economics center on differences in the values placed on the various costs and benefits of different actions.

KEY TERMS

trade-offs
incentives
exchange
information
distribution
scarcity
market economy
product market
labor market
capital market
capital goods
microeconomics
macroeconomics
theory
correlation
causation
positive economics
normative economics

REVIEW QUESTIONS

1. Why are trade-offs unavoidable? Why are incentives important in understanding choices?
2. After a voluntary exchange, why are both parties better off?
3. As a commodity, how does information differ from standard goods? How do information imperfections affect markets?

4. Why might there be a trade-off between equity and efficiency?
5. What is a mixed economy? Describe some of the roles government might play, or not play, in a mixed economy.
6. Name the three main economic markets, and describe how an individual might participate in each one as a buyer or a seller.
7. Give two examples of economic issues that are primarily microeconomic and two examples that are primarily macroeconomic. What is the general difference between microeconomics and macroeconomics?
8. What is a model? Why do economists use models?
9. Give two examples of variables that you would expect to be positively correlated. For each example, explain whether a causal relationship exists between the two variables.

PROBLEMS

1. How does each of the following affect the incentive to go to college?
   (a) An increase in tuition costs
   (b) A fall in the interest rate on student loans
   (c) A rise in wages for unskilled jobs
   (d) An increase in incomes of college graduates
2. Characterize the following events as microeconomic, macroeconomic, or both.
   (a) Unemployment increases this month.
   (b) A drug company invents and begins to market a new medicine.
   (c) A bank lends money to a large company but turns down a small business.
   (d) Interest rates decline for all borrowers.
   (e) A union negotiates for higher pay and better health insurance.
   (f) The price of oil increases.
3. Characterize the following events as part of the labor market, the capital market, or the product market.
   (a) An investor tries to decide which company to invest in.
   (b) With practice, the workers on an assembly line become more efficient.
   (c) The opening up of economies in eastern Europe offers new markets for American products.
   (d) A big company that is losing money decides to offer its workers special incentives to retire early, hoping to reduce its costs.
   (e) A consumer roams around a shopping mall looking for birthday gifts.
   (f) The federal government uses a surplus to pay off some of its debt.
4. The back of a bag of cat litter claims, "Cats that use cat litter live three years longer than cats that don't." Do you think that cat litter actually causes an increased life expectancy for cats, or can you think of some other factors to explain this correlation? What evidence might you collect to test your explanation?
5. Life expectancy in Sweden is almost eighty years; life expectancy in India is close to sixty years. Does this prove that if an Indian moved to Sweden, he would live longer? That is, does this prove that living in Sweden causes an increase in life expectancy, or can you think of some other factors to explain these facts? What evidence might you collect to test your explanation?
6. During 2004, some economists argued that the Federal Reserve should undertake policies to slow the economic expansion in the United States in order to ensure low inflation. Other economists opposed such policies, arguing that the dangers of inflation were exaggerated and attempts by the Federal Reserve to slow the economy would lead to higher unemployment. Is this a disagreement about positive economics, or about normative economics? Explain.

Learning goals

In this chapter, you will learn

1. What economists mean by the "basic competitive model"

2. The role played by incentives, property rights, prices, and the profit motive in a market economy

3. About alternatives to the market system for allocating resources

4. About some of the basic tools that economists use to study how people make choices

Chapter 2

THINKING LIKE AN ECONOMIST

Economists have a distinctive way of thinking about issues, and the best way to learn economics is to understand how to think like an economist. Thinking like an economist involves focusing on trade-offs, incentives, exchange, information, and distribution—the five key concepts introduced in Chapter 1—and more. Economists focus on the choices individuals and business make when they are faced with scarcity. These choices can involve a decision to eat at home rather than to go to a restaurant, to go to college rather than take a job right out of high school, to locate a plant overseas rather than in the United States, or any of a thousand other alternatives. The choices made by individuals and business involve trade-offs and are affected by the incentives they face, the opportunities for exchange that are available, the information at hand, and the initial distribution of wealth. To understand choices, economists start with a simple model of how individuals and firms interact with one another in markets to carry out exchanges. This simple model is introduced in this chapter and developed further in Part Two.

The Basic Competitive Model

Every day, millions of people take part in thousands of exchanges in hundreds of different markets. Somehow, out of all these exchanges, computers are produced and end up in student dorm rooms, food is grown and ends up on the dinner tables of households, and electricity is delivered to millions of homes and offices at a flick of a switch. In an economy like that of the United States, markets play a critical role in ensuring that workers find jobs, things get produced, and firms sell their products. Exchange and the role of markets are important, but what makes them work? How can you be sure that your local grocery store will have bread in the morning or that your favorite café will have milk and espresso for your morning latte? And how can you be sure that the grocery store won't charge you $20 for that loaf of bread or that your espresso won't cost $10?

The answer can be given in one word—**competition.** When firms compete with one another for customers, they will offer customers the desired products at the lowest possible price. Consumers also compete with one another. Only a limited number of goods are available, and they come at a price. Consumers who are willing to pay that price can enjoy the goods, but others are left empty-handed. This picture of competitive markets, which economists call the **basic competitive model,** provides the point of departure for studying the economy. It consists of three parts: assumptions about how consumers behave, assumptions about how firms behave, and assumptions about the markets in which these consumers and firms interact. Consumers are assumed to be *rational,* firms are assumed to be *profit maximizing,* and the markets in which they interact are assumed to be highly *competitive.* The model ignores the government, because we first need to see how an economy without a government might function before we can understand the role of the government.

RATIONAL CONSUMERS AND PROFIT-MAXIMIZING FIRMS

Scarcity, which we encountered in Chapter 1, implies that individuals and firms face trade-offs and must make choices. Underlying much of economic analysis is the basic assumption of **rational choice:** that is, people weigh the costs and benefits of each possibility whenever they must make a choice. This assumption, in turn, is based on the expectation that individuals and firms will act consistently, with a reasonably well-defined notion of what they like and what their objectives are, and with a reasonable understanding of how to attain those objectives.

In the case of individuals, the rationality assumption is taken to mean that they make choices and decisions in pursuit of their own *self-interest*. Of course, different people will have different goals and desires. Sarah may want to drive a Porsche, own a yacht, and have a large house; to attain those objectives, she knows she needs to work long hours and sacrifice time with her family. Andrew is willing to accept a lower income in return for longer vacations and more leisure time throughout the year.

Economists make no judgment about whether Sarah's preferences are "better" or "worse" than Andrew's. They do not even spend much time asking why different individuals have different views on these matters, or why tastes change over time. These are important issues, but they are more the province of psychology and sociology. Economists are concerned with the consequences of these different preferences. What decisions can they expect Sarah and Andrew to make when each is rationally pursuing her or his respective interests?

In the case of firms, the rationality assumption is taken to mean that firms operate to maximize their profits.

COMPETITIVE MARKETS

To complete the model, economists make assumptions about the places where self-interested consumers and profit-maximizing firms meet: markets. Economists begin by focusing on the case of many buyers and sellers, all buying and selling the same thing. Picture a crowded farmers' market with everyone buying and selling just one good. Let's say we are in Florida, and the booths are full of oranges.

Each of the farmers would like to raise her prices. That way, if she can still sell her oranges, her profits go up. Yet with a large number of sellers, each is forced to charge close to the same price, since any farmer who charged much more would lose business to the farmer next door. Profit-maximizing firms are in the same position. In an extreme case, if a firm charged any more than the going price, it would lose *all* its sales. Economists label this case **perfect competition.** In perfect competition, each firm is a **price taker,** which simply means that it has no influence on the market price. The firm takes the market price as given because it cannot raise its price without losing all sales, and at the market price it can sell as much as it wishes. Even a decision to sell ten times as much would have a negligible effect on the total quantity marketed or on the price prevailing in the market. Markets for agricultural goods would be, in the absence of government intervention, perfectly competitive. There are so many wheat farmers, for instance, that each farmer believes he can grow and sell as much wheat as he wishes without affecting the price of wheat.

e-Insight
MARKETS, EXCHANGE, AND E-COMMERCE

In traditional societies, markets are places where people get together to exchange goods. They are active, bustling places, full of life. In the modern economy, goods and services are being exchanged *as if* there were a well-defined marketplace. The Internet has created a new kind of marketplace where people all over the world can exchange goods and services without ever getting together.

In traditional economies, prices for similar goods in different marketplaces could differ markedly. Traders would buy goods in a marketplace where they were cheap and then transport them to where the price was higher, making a handsome profit in doing so. These merchants helped make markets work better. Much of their high income could be thought of as a return on their information—on knowing where to buy cheap and sell dear. And by moving goods from places where they were valued less to places where they were valued more, the traders performed an important social function.

The Internet has enabled all of this to be done far more efficiently, at lower cost, with more complete information. Markets all over the world can be joined instantaneously, creating a global marketplace. Now any buyer (not just a merchant) can find the place where the good is selling at the lowest price, and any seller can find the place where the good is selling at the highest price.

Some have worried that the role of the middleman, of merchants, will disappear. But there is more to trade than just information about price. Many goods differ in a variety of dimensions, such as quality and durability. E-markets work best for well-defined goods, for which these issues are not relevant—goods such as wheat or steel, or products like this textbook.

(Later in the book, we will encounter markets with limited or no competition, like monopolies, in which firms can raise prices without losing all their sales.)

On the other side of our farmers' market are rational individuals, each of whom would like to pay as little as possible for oranges. But no consumer can pay less than the going price, because the seller sees another buyer in the crowd who *will* pay it. Thus, the consumers also have to compete against each other for the limited number of oranges in the market, and as a result each takes the market price as given.

While a farmers' market provides one illustration of what economists mean by a market, most markets do not take this form. Today buyers and sellers are more likely to interact over the Internet than at a farmers' market. But the same basic principles apply. When there are lots of buyers and sellers, each will take the price as given in deciding how much to buy or sell.

EFFICIENCY AND DISTRIBUTION IN THE BASIC COMPETITIVE MODEL

The basic competitive model, assuming it accurately represents actual markets, has one very strong implication: the economy will be efficient. Scarce resources will not be wasted. It will not be possible to produce more of one good without producing less of another, and it will not be possible to make any person better off without making someone else worse off. These results are obtained in the absence of any government activity.

Competitive markets also determine the distribution of goods—who gets to consume how much of the goods that are available. High levels of competition for the services of an individual with a rare and valuable skill will result in a very high income for that individual. On the other hand, competition among suppliers of unskilled labor may result in these workers earning very low wages, so low that even long workdays fail to win them a decent standard of living. This disparity raises the question of the fairness of competitive distribution. Though efficiency is a desirable property of any economic system, fairness is a separate issue that must be considered. Later in this book we will discuss how economists and policymakers approach the inequalities that inevitably emerge from the workings of the competitive market.

THE BASIC COMPETITIVE MODEL AS A BENCHMARK

Virtually all economists recognize that the competitive model is not a *perfect* representation of actual economies, but most economists still use it as a convenient benchmark—as we will throughout this book. After all, as you learned in Chapter 1, an economic *model* is never a complete and accurate description—it is not meant to be—but instead is designed to highlight critical aspects of the economy that provide insight and help us understand particular features of it. We will point out important differences between the predictions of the basic competitive model and observed outcomes, and in Part Three, we will show how this model can be extended to offer new insights into markets and situations that the basic competitive model cannot fully address. Differences between the predictions of the basic competitive model and observed outcomes can help guide us to other models that provide a better understanding of particular markets and circumstances. While the basic competitive model may not provide a *perfect* description of some markets, most economists believe that it gives us tremendous insights into a wide range of economic issues; for that reason, it is the foundation on which economists build.

Wrap-Up

INGREDIENTS IN THE BASIC COMPETITIVE MODEL

1. Rational, self-interested consumers
2. Rational, profit-maximizing firms
3. Competitive markets with price-taking behavior

Incentives and Information: Prices, Property Rights, and Profits

For market economies to work efficiently, firms and individuals must be informed and have incentives to act on available information. Indeed, incentives can be viewed as at the heart of economics. Without incentives, why would individuals go to work in the morning? Who would undertake the risks of bringing out new products? Who would put aside savings for a rainy day? There is an old expression about the importance of having someone "mind the store." But without incentives, why would anyone bother?

Market economies provide information and incentives through *prices, profits,* and *property rights.* Prices provide information about the relative scarcity of different goods. The **price system** ensures that goods go to those individuals and firms that are most willing and able to pay for them. Prices convey information to consumers about scarcity, and consumers respond by adjusting their consumption. Similarly, prices convey information to firms about how individuals value different goods.

The desire for profits motivates firms to respond to the information provided by prices. By most efficiently producing what consumers want, in ways that least use scarce resources, they increase their profits. Similarly, rational individuals' pursuit of self-interest induces them to respond to prices: they buy goods that are more expensive—in a sense, relatively more scarce—only if those goods provide commensurately greater benefits. If a good such as oil becomes scarcer, its price rises. In order to make rational decisions about how much heating oil to use, consumers do not need to know why the price of oil has risen. Perhaps a particularly cold winter has increased demand. Or perhaps troubles in the Middle East have decreased supply. In either case, the higher price signals consumers to reduce their purchases of oil products. If the price of home heating oil rises, that increase signals oil refineries to produce more heating oil. Prices provide the information that individuals and firms need to make rational decisions.

For the profit motive to be effective, there must be **private property,** with its attendant **property rights.** Under a system of private property, firms and individuals are able to own and use (or sell if they choose) factories, land, and buildings. Without private property, firms would not have an incentive to invest in new factories or new technologies, hire employees, produce goods and services that consumers want to buy, and earn profits. Even if the profits to be earned from building a new factory are huge, no firm will begin construction without the confidence that the factory cannot just be taken away. Firms need to be able to keep at least some of their profits to use as they see fit. Similarly, households need to be able to keep at least some of the return on their investments. (The return on their investment is simply what they receive back in excess of what they invested.) Property rights include both the right of the owner to use property as she sees fit and the right to sell it.

These two attributes of property rights give individuals the incentive to use property under their control efficiently. The owner of a piece of land tries to figure out the most profitable use of the land—for example, whether to build a store or a restaurant. If he makes a mistake and opens a restaurant when he should have opened a store, he bears the consequences: the loss in income. The profits he earns if he makes the right decisions—and the losses he bears if he makes the wrong ones—give him an incentive to think carefully about the decision and do the requisite research. The owner of a store tries to make sure that her customers get the kind of merchandise and the quality of service they want. She has an incentive to establish a good reputation, which will enable her to do more business and earn more profits.

The store owner will also want to maintain her property—not just the land but also the store—because doing so will enable her to get a better price when the time comes to sell her business to someone else. Similarly, the owner of a house has an incentive to maintain *his* property, so that he can sell it for more when he wishes to move. Again, the profit motive combines with private property to provide incentives.

Wrap-Up

HOW THE PROFIT MOTIVE DRIVES THE MARKET SYSTEM

In market economies, incentives are supplied to individuals and firms by prices, profits, and property rights.

INCENTIVES VERSUS EQUALITY

While incentives are at the heart of market economies, they come with a cost: inequality. Any system of incentives must tie compensation to performance. Whether through variations in luck or ability, the performances of individuals will differ. In many cases, the reason for high performance is unclear. The successful salesperson may point to his superior skill and effort, while his colleague may view him as lucky.

If pay is tied to performance, inequalities are inevitable. And the more closely compensation is tied to performance, the greater the inequality. The fact that greater incentives lead to greater resulting inequality is called the *incentive-equality trade-off*. If society provides greater incentives, total income is likely to be higher, but the gap between incomes will also probably be greater.

Society thus faces a basic question: How much would incentives be diminished by an increase in tax rates to finance a better welfare system and thus reduce inequality? And what would be the results of those reduced incentives?

WHEN PROPERTY RIGHTS FAIL

Prices, profits, and property rights are the three essential ingredients of market economies. Their importance is underscored by those cases in which property rights and prices are interfered with. Each example below highlights a general point. Whenever society fails to define the owner of its resources and does not allow the highest bidder to use them, inefficiencies result. Resources will be wasted or not used in the most productive way.

Ill-Defined Property Rights: The Grand Banks Fish are a valuable resource. Not long ago, the area between Newfoundland and Maine, called the Grand Banks, was teeming with fish. Not surprisingly, it was also teeming with fishermen, who saw scooping out the fish from the sea as an easy livelihood. Since there were no property rights, everyone tried to catch as many fish as they could. A self-interested fisherman would rationally reason that if he did not catch the fish, someone else would. The result was a tragedy: the Grand Banks was so badly overfished that commercial fishing became unprofitable.

Overfishing is just one example of what is called the **tragedy of the commons.** In the 1830s, an Oxford University economist named William Forster Lloyd explained why the commons—the pasture land in England that was not privately owned—was overgrazed. Because this land was freely available to all, each herder had an incentive to increase the size of his herd. As a result, the commons was overused until it was too damaged to support any grazing. When property rights are difficult to define, the tragedy of the commons is often addressed through international agreements. For example, Canada and the United States now have a treaty limiting the amount of fish that their fisherman can take from the Grand Banks, and in 1979 the Northwest Atlantic Fisheries Organization (NAFO) was established to manage fish stocks.

Restricted Property Rights In California, the government allocates water rights among various groups. Because water is scarce in California, these rights are very valuable. But they come with a restriction: they are not transferable. Water rights allow farmers to purchase water at much lower rates than the price charged to nonfarm households. What thirsty urban consumers would be willing to pay for additional water exceeds the profits from many of the crops the water is being used to grow. If water rights were transferable, farmers would have a strong incentive to sell them to California cities. Farmers could then switch away from water-intensive crops such as rice to crops that need less water. By selling their water rights, the farmers would be better off—the value of the water exceeds the value of the crops they are growing; urban residents would also be better off, because lower-price water would be available to them. A restriction on property rights—in this case, the restriction on the farmers' ability to sell—has led to inefficiencies.

Entitlements as Property Rights Property rights do not always entail full ownership or control. A *legal entitlement,* such as the right to occupy an apartment for life at a rent that is controlled, common in some large cities, is viewed by economists as a property right. Individuals do not own and thus cannot sell the apartment, but under normal circumstances they cannot be evicted.

These partial and restricted property rights result in many inefficiencies. Because someone in a rent-controlled apartment cannot (legally) sell the right to live in her apartment, as she gets older she may have limited incentives to maintain its condition, let alone improve it.

Incentives, prices, profits, and property rights are central features of any economy, and highlight an important area of consensus among economists: *Providing appropriate incentives is a fundamental economic problem. In modern market economies, profits provide incentives for firms to produce the goods individuals want, and wages provide incentives for individuals to work. Property rights also provide people with important incentives, not only to invest and to save but also to put their assets to the best possible use.*

Alternatives to the Price System

The price system is only one way of allocating resources, and a comparison with other systems will help clarify the advantages of markets. When individuals get less of a good than they would like at the terms being offered, the good is said to be *rationed.* Different **rationing systems** are different ways of deciding who gets society's scarce resources.

Rationing by Queues Rather than supplying goods to those willing and able to pay the most for them, a society could give them instead to those most willing to wait in line. This system is called *rationing by queues,* after the British term for lines. Tickets are often allocated by queues, whether they are for movies, sporting events, or rock concerts. A price is set, and it will not change no matter how many people line up to buy at that price. (The high price that scalpers can get for hot tickets is a good indication of how much more than the ticket price (*some*) people would be willing to pay.[1])

Rationing by queues is thought by many to be a more desirable way of supplying medical services than the price system. Why, it is argued, should the rich—who are most able to pay for medical services—be the ones to get better or more medical care? Using this reasoning, Britain provides free medical care to everyone on its soil. To see a doctor there, all you have to do is wait in line. Rationing medicine by queues turns the allocation problem around: since the value of time for low-wage workers is lower, they are more willing to wait, and therefore they get a disproportionate share of (government-supplied) medical services.

In general, rationing by queues is an inefficient way of distributing resources, because the time spent in line is a wasted resource. There are usually ways of achieving the same goal within a price system that can make everyone better off. To return to the medical example, if some individuals were allowed to pay for doctors' services instead of waiting in line, more doctors could be hired with the proceeds, and the lines for those unable or unwilling to pay could actually be reduced.

Rationing by Lotteries *Lotteries* allocate goods by a random process, such as picking a name from a hat. University dormitory rooms are usually assigned by lottery. So are seats in popular courses; when more students want to enroll in a section of a principles of economics course than the size of the section allows, there may be a lottery to determine admission. Like queue systems, lotteries are thought to be fair because everyone has an equal chance. However, they are also inefficient, because the scarce resources do not go to the individual or firm who is willing and able to pay (and therefore values them) the most.

Rationing by Coupons Most governments in wartime use *coupon rationing*. People are allowed so many gallons of gasoline, so many pounds of sugar, and so much flour each month. To get the good, consumers must pay the market price *and* produce a coupon.

Coupon systems take two forms, depending on whether coupons are tradable or not. Coupons that are not tradable give rise to the same inefficiency that occurs with most of the other nonprice systems—goods do not in general go to the individuals who are willing and able to pay the most. Moreover, the inability to legally trade coupons creates strong incentives for the establishment of a *black market,* an illegal market in which the goods or the coupons for goods are traded.

---

[1] So why are concert tickets rationed by queues rather than by price? The musicians and concert promoters could increase their profits by raising the ticket price, but consider the situation of a popular musician who is concerned with both concert income and income from CD sales. Allocating tickets by queue favors those with the most free time and helps ensure that tickets go to the musician's core fans—particularly those who are younger, who have less money to spend. These fans may be the most likely to buy CDs, and CD sales depend heavily on word-of-mouth advertising. So by ensuring that her core fans are not priced out of concerts, a musician may actually end up increasing her profits.

Opportunity Sets and Trade-offs

Market economic systems leave to individuals and firms the question of what to consume and what to produce. How are these decisions made?

For a rational individual or firm, the first step in the economic analysis of any choice is to identify what is possible—what economists call the **opportunity set,** which is simply the group of available options. If you want a sandwich and have only tuna fish and cheese in the refrigerator, then your opportunity set consists of a tuna fish sandwich, a cheese sandwich, a tuna and cheese sandwich, or no sandwich. A ham sandwich is out of the question. Defining the limitations facing an individual or firm is a critical step in any analysis of choice. You can spend time yearning after the ham sandwich, or anything else outside the opportunity set, but when it comes to making decisions, only what is within the opportunity set is relevant.

So the first step in analyzing choice is to identify what is within the opportunity set.

BUDGET AND TIME CONSTRAINTS

Constraints limit choice and define the opportunity set. In most economic situations, the constraints that limit a person's choices—that is, those constraints that actually are relevant—are time and money. Opportunity sets whose constraints are imposed by money are referred to as **budget constraints;** opportunity sets whose constraints are prescribed by time are called **time constraints.** A billionaire may feel his choices are limited not by money but by time, while the limits for an unemployed worker are set by lack of money rather than lack of time.

The budget constraint defines a typical opportunity set. Consider the budget constraint of Michelle, who has decided to spend $120 on either CDs or DVDs. A CD costs $10, a DVD $20. So Michelle can buy 12 CDs *or* 6 DVDs; or 8 CDs and 2 DVDs; or 4 CDs and 4 DVDs. The various possibilities are set forth in Table 2.1. They are also depicted graphically in Figure 2.1.[2] Along the vertical axis, we measure the number of CDs purchased, and along the horizontal axis, we measure the number of DVDs. The line marked B_1B_2 is Michelle's budget constraint. The extreme cases, in which Michelle buys only DVDs or only CDs, are represented by the points B_1 and B_2, respectively. The dots between these two points, along the budget constraint, represent the other possible combinations. The cost of each combination of CDs and DVDs must add up to $120. If Michelle decides to buy more DVDs, she will have to settle for fewer CDs. The point actually chosen by Michelle is labeled *E,* where she purchases 6 CDs (for $60) and 3 DVDs (for $60).

Michelle's budget constraint is the line that defines the outer limits of her opportunity set. But the whole opportunity set is larger. It also includes all points below the budget constraint—in the figure, the shaded area. The budget constraint shows the maximum number of DVDs Michelle can buy for each number of CDs purchased, and vice versa. Michelle is always happiest when she chooses a point on her budget constraint rather than below it. To see why, compare the points *E* and *D*. At point *E,*

TABLE 2.1

MICHELLE'S OPPORTUNITY SET

DVDs	CDs
6	0
5	2
4	4
3	6
2	8
1	10
0	12

[2]See the chapter appendix for help in reading graphs. Economists have found graphs to be extremely useful and they will be employed throughout this book. It is important that you learn to read and understand them.

she has more of both goods than at point D. She would be even happier at point F, where she has still more DVDs and CDs, but that point, by definition, is unattainable.

Figure 2.2 depicts a time constraint. The most common time constraint simply says that the sum of what an individual spends her time on each day—including sleep—must add up to 24 hours. The figure plots the hours spent watching television on the horizontal axis and the hours spent on all other activities on the vertical axis. People—no matter how rich or poor—have only 24 hours a day to spend on different activities. The time constraint is quite similar to the budget constraint. A person cannot spend more than 24 hours or fewer than zero hours a day watching TV. The more time she spends watching television, the less time she has available for all other activities. If she wants to watch more TV, she must make a trade-off and reduce her time spent in some other activity.

Figure 2.1

MICHELLE'S BUDGET CONSTRAINT

The budget constraint identifies the limits of Michelle's opportunity set between CDs and DVDs. Points B_1 and B_2 are extreme options, where she chooses all of one or the other. Her actual choice corresponds to point E. Choices from the shaded area are possible but less attractive than choices actually on the budget constraint.

THE PRODUCTION POSSIBILITIES CURVE

Business firms and whole societies face constraints. They too must make choices limited to opportunity sets. The amount of goods a firm or society can produce, given a fixed amount of land, labor, and other inputs, is referred to as its **production possibilities.**

A commonly used example considers a society in which all economic production is divided into two categories, military spending and civilian spending. Of course, each of these two kinds of spending has many different elements, but for the moment, we'll focus only on the two broad categories. For the sake of simplicity, Figure 2.3 refers to military spending as "guns" and civilian spending as "butter." The production of guns is given along the vertical axis, the production of butter along the horizontal. The possible combinations of military and civilian spending—of guns and butter—is the opportunity set. Table 2.2 sets out some of the possible combinations—which 90 million guns and 40 million tons of butter, or 40 million guns and 90 million tons of butter. These possibilities are depicted in the figure. In production decisions, the boundary of the opportunity set—the maximum amount of guns that can be produced for each amount of butter and vice versa—is called the **production possibilities curve.**

When we compare the individual's opportunity set and that of society, we notice one major difference. The individual's budget constraint is a straight line, while the production possibilities curve bows outward. There is a good reason for this. An individual typically faces fixed *trade-offs*: if Michelle spends $20 more on DVDs (that is, she buys one more DVD), she has $20 less to spend on CDs (she can buy two fewer CDs).

In contrast, the trade-offs faced by society are not fixed. If a society produces only a few guns, it will use those resources—the workers and machines—that are best equipped for gun making. But as society tries to produce more and more guns, doing so becomes more difficult; it will increasingly depend on resources that are less good at producing guns.

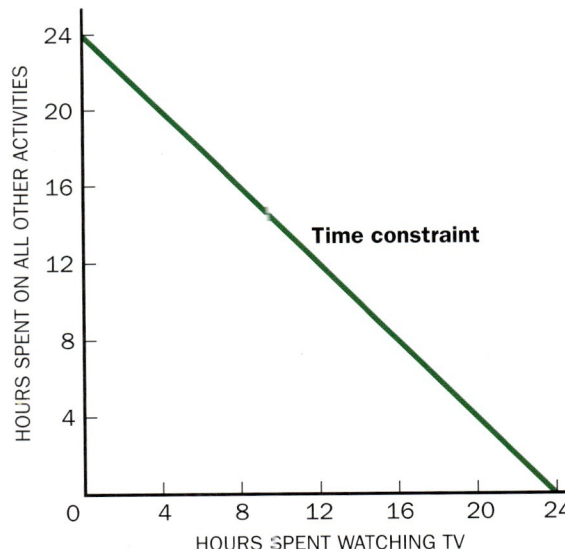

Figure 2.2

AN OPPORTUNITY SET FOR WATCHING TV AND OTHER ACTIVITIES

This opportunity set is limited by a time constraint, which shows the trade-off a person faces between spending time watching television and spending it on other activities.

TABLE 2.2

PRODUCTION POSSIBILITIES FOR THE ECONOMY

Guns (millions)	Butter (millions of tons)
100	0
90	40
70	70
40	90
0	100

It will be drawing these resources out of the production of other goods, in this case, butter. Thus, when the economy increases its production of guns from 40 million a year (point A) to 70 million (B), butter production falls by 20 million tons, from 90 million tons to 70 million tons. But if production of guns is increased further, to 90 million (C), an increase of only 20 million, butter production has to decrease by 30 million tons, to only 40 million tons. For each increase in the number of guns, the reduction in the number of tons of butter produced gets larger. That is why the production possibilities curve is curved.

In another example, assume that a firm owns land that can be used for growing wheat but not corn, and land that can grow corn but not wheat. In this case, the only way to increase wheat production is to move workers from the cornfields to the wheat fields. As more and more workers are put into the wheat fields, production of wheat goes up, but each successive worker increases production less. The first workers might pick the largest and most destructive weeds. Additional workers lead to better weeding, and better weeding leads to higher output. But the additional weeds removed are smaller and less destructive, so output is increased by a correspondingly smaller amount. This is an example of the general principle of **diminishing returns.** Adding successive units of any input such as fertilizer, labor, or machines to a fixed amount of other inputs—seeds or land—increases the output, or amount produced, but by less and less.

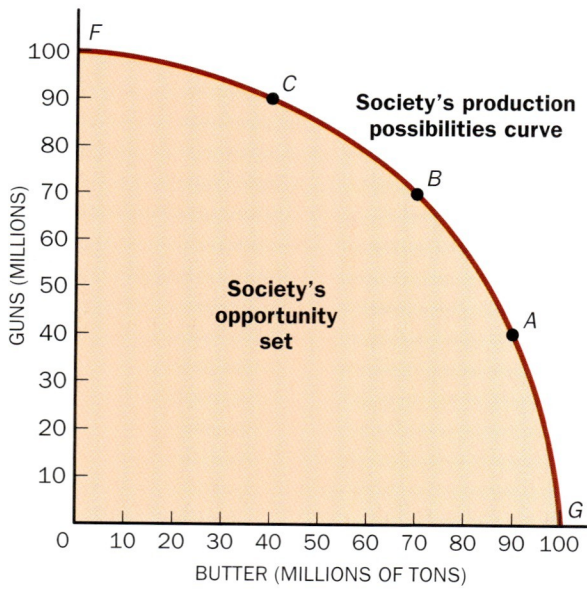

Figure 2.3

THE GUNS AND BUTTER TRADE-OFF

A production possibilities curve can show society's opportunity set. This one describes the trade-off between military spending ("guns") and civilian spending ("butter"). Points F and G show the extreme choices, where the economy produces all guns or all butter. Notice that unlike the budget and time constraint lines, the production possibilities line curves, reflecting diminishing returns.

Diminishing returns is an important concept in economics. The phenomenon occurs in many situations. You have probably discovered that you usually get more out of the first hour of studying than the tenth, and that studying a few hours may bring big payoffs when you are preparing for an exam; but if you stay up all night to cram, your concentration is likely to decrease, and you may be so tired in the morning that you actually do worse on the exam than if you had quit studying sooner. Having one of your roommates help you fix dinner cuts the preparation time; but if all your roommates try to help, they may end up just getting in each other's way. In Chapter 6, where we examine the factors that affect the costs of producing goods and services, the notion of diminishing returns will help us understand why a rise in price is necessary to induce firms to increase the amount they produce.

Table 2.3 shows the output of the corn- and wheat fields as labor is increased in each. Assume the firm has 6,000 workers to divide between wheat production and corn production. Thus, the second and fourth columns together give the firm's production possibilities, which are depicted in Figure 2.4.

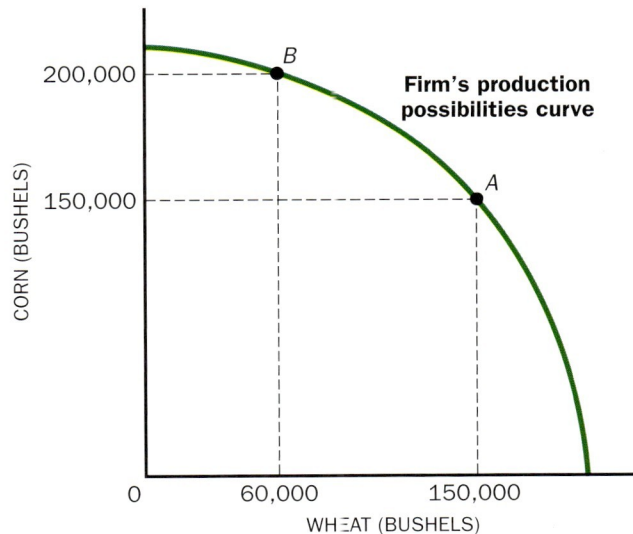

Figure 2.4

THE WHEAT AND CORN TRADE-OFF

This production possibilities curve shows that as wheat production increases, it becomes necessary to give up larger and larger amounts of corn. Or to put the same point a different way, as corn production falls, the resulting increase in wheat production gets smaller.

Costs

Making trade-offs always involves weighing costs and benefits. What you gain is the benefit; what you give up is the cost. Often, the benefits depend on an individual's personal preferences—some people would gladly skip a tennis game to go play golf, and others would just as gladly make the opposite choice. Economists generally do not try to explain why people have different preferences; instead, when it comes to understanding the choices individuals make, economists focus on costs. An opportunity set, like the budget constraint, the time constraint, or the production possibilities curve, specifies the cost of one option in terms of another. If the individual,

TABLE 2.3

DIMINISHING RETURNS

Labor in cornfield (no. of workers)	Corn output (bushels)	Labor in wheat field (no. of workers)	Wheat output (bushels)
1,000	60,000	5,000	200,000
2,000	110,000	4,000	180,000
3,000	150,000	3,000	150,000
4,000	180,000	2,000	110,000
5,000	200,000	1,000	60,000

the firm, or society is operating on the constraint or curve, then it is possible to get more of one thing only by sacrificing some of another. The "cost" of one more unit of one good is how much you have to give up of the other.

Economists think about costs in terms of trade-offs within opportunity sets. Let's go back to Michelle choosing between CDs and DVDs in Figure 2.1. The trade-off is given by the **relative price,** the ratio of the prices of CDs and DVDs. In our example, a CD costs $10, and a DVD $20. The relative price is $20/$10 = 2. For every DVD Michelle gives up, she can buy 2 CDs. Likewise, societies and firms face trade-offs along the production possibilities curve, like the one shown in Figure 2.3. There, point A is the choice where 40 million guns and 90 million tons of butter are produced. The trade-off can be calculated by comparing points A and B. Society can have 30 million more guns by giving up 20 million tons of butter.

Trade-offs are necessary because resources are scarce. If you want something, you have to pay for it—you have to give up something. If you want to go to the library tomorrow night, you have to give up going to the movies. If a sawmill wants to make more two-by-four beams from its stock of wood, it will not be able to make as many one-by-four boards.

OPPORTUNITY COSTS

If someone were to ask you right now what it costs to go to a movie, you would probably answer, "Ten dollars," or whatever you last paid for a ticket. But the concept of trade-offs suggests that a *full* answer is not that simple. To begin with, the cost is not the $10 but what that $10 could otherwise buy. Furthermore, your time is a scarce resource that must be figured into the calculation. Both the money and the time represent opportunities forgone in favor of going to the movie, or what economists refer to as the **opportunity cost** of the movie. To apply a resource to one use means that it cannot be put to any other use. Thus, we should consider the next-best, alternative use of any resource when we think about putting it to any particular use. This next-best use is the formal measurement of opportunity cost.

Some examples will help clarify the idea of opportunity cost. Consider a college student, Sarah, who works during the summer. She has a chance to go surfing in Costa Rica with friends, but to do so she has to quit her summer job two weeks early. The friends have found a cheap airfare and place to stay, and they tell Sarah the trip will cost only $1,000. To the economist, $1,000 is not the total cost of the trip for Sarah. Since she would have continued working in her summer job for an extra two weeks if she did not go to Costa Rica, the income she would have earned is part of the opportunity cost of her time. This forgone income must be added to the airfare and hotel costs in calculating the total economic cost of the surfing trip.

Now consider a business firm that has bought a building for its headquarters that is bigger than necessary. If the firm could receive $3 per month in rent for each square foot of space that is not needed, then that is the opportunity cost of leaving the space idle.

Thinking Like an Economist
TRADE-OFFS

Whenever you see an opportunity set, a budget or time constraint, or a production possibilities curve, think *trade-off*. The variables on the two axes identify the objects of the trade-offs, whether those are CDs and DVDs, guns and butter, or something else. The line or curve drawn from one axis to the other provides quantities for the trade-off. The opportunity set shows the choices that are available. The budget constraint illustrates the trade-offs that must be made because of limited money to spend, while the time constraint reflects the limited time we all have. The production possibilities curve gives the trade-offs faced in deciding what to produce when the amount of land, labor, and other inputs is limited. All three focus attention on the necessity of making trade-offs.

Many people think economists study only situations that involve money and budget constraints, but often time constraints are very important in defining trade-offs. Political elections provide a good example of the importance of time constraints. As the 2004 presidential election campaign entered its final stages, each candidate faced tough choices because of the time constraint. The election date was fixed leaving only so much time available for campaigning. Ohio was one of the critical states for both John Kerry and George W. Bush, and both candidates visited it frequently in the months leading up to the election. But time spent in Ohio was time that could not be spent in the other toss-up states. Each candidate had to decide how best to allocate the time remaining before the election.

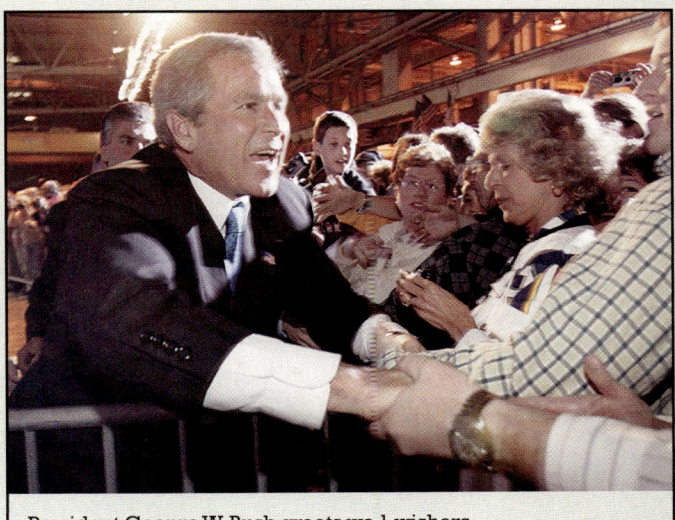

President George W. Bush greets well-wishers.

Economists find it useful to distinguish between budget constraints and time constraints, but often we study trade-offs that involve both time *and* money. Choosing how to spend your Saturday evening usually involves both. You might decide to go to a movie that lasts for 2 hours and costs $10 or go to a concert that lasts 4 hours and costs $40. Both your budget and time constraints are important for defining your opportunity set.

The analysis can be applied to the government as well. The federal government owns a vast amount of wilderness. In deciding whether it is worthwhile to convert some of the land into a national park, the government needs to take into account the opportunity cost of the land. The land might be used for growing timber or for grazing sheep. Whatever the value of the land in its next-best use, this is the economic cost of the national park. The fact that the government does not have to buy the land does not mean that the land should be treated as a free good.

Thus, in the economist's view, when rational firms and individuals make decisions—whether to undertake one investment project rather than another, whether to buy one product rather than another—they take into account *all* of the costs (the full opportunity costs), not just the direct expenditures.

Internet Connection

INTERNET RESOURCES FOR ECONOMISTS

A guide to Internet resources for economists can be found at http://rfe.wustl.edu. The American Economic Association sponsors this guide. It lists more than 1,200 resources in sixty-nine sections and subsections that are of interest to professional economists as well as those simply interested in economics.

Case in Point

THE OPPORTUNITY COST OF ATTENDING COLLEGE

Opportunity cost is a key concept in economics. It is the correct measure of the cost of everything we do. As a college student, what is your opportunity cost of attending college? If you (or your parents) are asking how much your college costs, you probably think of the tuition, room and board, and books as major costs. But a consideration of the opportunity cost suggests that such a list includes both too much and too little.

Since you would need a place to live, and you would certainly need to eat, even if you were not in school, these costs do not represent part of the opportunity cost of attending college. Only if your college charges higher rent than you would otherwise pay would your dorm costs be part of your opportunity cost.

To correctly evaluate opportunity cost, you need to think about what you would be doing if you had decided not to continue in school. The economist's mind immediately turns to the job you might have had if you had not enrolled in college and the income you could have earned. That amount will vary from student to student; but in 2004, eighteen- to twenty-four-year-olds with a high school diploma who were working full-time earned just under $15,000 per year.[3] This *forgone income* must be added to the direct costs such as tuition to obtain the opportunity cost of attending school. For most students, this forgone income is a major component of the opportunity cost of college.

Test your understanding: Use the concept of opportunity cost to explain why great college basketball players often fail to complete four years of college.

Opportunity Cost and International Trade The concepts of opportunity cost and exchange play a pivotal role in helping to understand why economists argue that all countries can gain from international trade. Consider the case of two fictional countries, which we will call North and South. North is highly developed with skilled workers and modern capital equipment. South is much poorer; its workers are generally unskilled and have little capital equipment to aid them in production. For simplicity, assume further that these two countries produce only two goods,

[3]U.S. Census Bureau, Annual Demographic Survey, Table PINC-04, March 2004 (http://pubdb3.census.gov/macro/032004/perinc/new04_001.htm).

computers and textiles. The developed country is more productive than the less-developed country at producing both computers and textiles. Despite the fact that North can produce either good more efficiently than South can, economists argue that it will still pay for the two countries to trade, and opportunity cost provides the key to understanding why.

Let's make our example more concrete by assuming that in North, 100 hours of labor can produce either 5 computers or 100 shirts. In South, 100 hours of labor can produce only 1 computer or 50 shirts. These numbers reflect our assumption that North is more productive in producing both computers and textiles (in this case, shirts). These numbers are listed in the top half of Table 2.4. We describe this situation by saying that North has an **absolute advantage** in producing both computers and textiles. But the key insight to understanding international trade is that trade patterns are not based on absolute advantage. Instead, they are based on a comparison of the opportunity cost in each country of producing the two goods. In North, the opportunity cost of producing 100 shirts is 5 computers; shifting 100 hours of labor into textile production to produce the 100 extra shirts would reduce computer production by 5 computers. In contrast, the opportunity cost of producing 100 shirts in South is only 2 computers; shifting 200 hours of labor into textile production to produce the extra 100 shirts would reduce computer production by 2 computers. The opportunity cost of producing more shirts is lower in South than it is in North. We describe this by saying South has a **comparative advantage** in producing textiles. South is *relatively* more efficient in producing shirts than North is.

While South has a comparative advantage in producing shirts, North has a comparative advantage in producing computers; it is relatively more efficient in producing computers. To see this, consider the opportunity cost in North of producing 1 more computer. To produce an additional computer, North must shift 20 hours of labor out of textile production and into computer production, reducing shirt production by 20 shirts. The opportunity cost of the computer in North is 20 shirts. To produce an additional computer, South must shift 100 hours of labor out of textile production and into computer production, reducing shirt production by 50. The opportunity cost of a computer is higher in South (50 shirts) than it is in North (20 shirts). North has a comparative advantage in computer production.

The bottom half of Table 2.4 shows the opportunity cost of producing computers (expressed in terms of shirts) and the opportunity cost of producing shirts (expressed in terms of computers) for each country. While North has an absolute advantage in producing both goods, its comparative advantage lies in producing computers. South's comparative advantage lies in producing shirts.

Because South has a comparative advantage in shirt production and North has a comparative advantage in computer production, both countries can benefit by trading. By shifting 100 hours of labor from computer production to shirt production, South produces 1 less computer and 50 more shirts. By shifting 20 hours of labor from shirt production into computer production, North produces 1 more computer and 20 fewer shirts. By this move toward specialization in each country, total computer production has remained unchanged (1 less produced in South, 1 more produced in North), but total shirt production has risen by 30 shirts (50 more in South, 20 fewer in North). These extra shirts represent (in our example), the gains to specialization. Because the opportunity cost of a computer in North is 20 shirts,

TABLE 2.4

LABOR PRODUCTIVITY IN PRODUCING COMPUTERS AND SHIRTS

	North	South
Computers produced with 100 hours of labor	5	1
Shirts produced with 100 hours of labor	100	50

OPPORTUNITY COST OF PRODUCING COMPUTERS AND SHIRTS

	North	South
Opportunity cost of a computer (in terms of shirts)	20	50
Opportunity cost of 100 shirts (in terms of computers)	5	2

North will be willing to accept no less than 20 shirts from South in exchange for 1 computer. If South were to offer fewer than 20 shirts for a computer, North would be better off producing its own shirts. Because the opportunity cost of a computer in South is 50 shirts, South will be willing to pay no more than 50 shirts to obtain a computer from North. As long as the price for a computer lies between 20 and 50 shirts per computer, both countries can gain if North shifts labor into computer production, South shifts labor into textile production, and the two then engage in trade. For example, if the price of a computer is 30 shirts, South can buy 1 computer from North (leaving South with the same number of computers as it had previously) and it will still have 20 shirts left over to better clothe its own residents. Meanwhile, North reduced its own shirt production by 20 shirts, but was able to obtain 30 shirts in exchange for the extra computer it produced. So North is also better off. North will benefit by exporting computers to South, and South will benefit by exporting textiles to North.

By recognizing the important role of opportunity cost, we can understand why both North and South gain from specializing in production and engaging in international trade. Despite the economists' argument that free trade can benefit both countries, many people oppose moves to promote international trade. Their arguments, and the role of various government policies that affect international trade, will be the subject of Chapter 19.

SUNK COSTS

Economic cost includes costs, as we have just seen, that noneconomists often exclude, but it also ignores costs that noneconomists include. If an expenditure has already been made and cannot be recovered no matter what choice is made, a rational person would ignore it. Such expenditures are called **sunk costs.**

To understand sunk costs, let's go back to the movies, assuming now that you have spent $10 to buy a movie ticket. You were skeptical about whether the movie was worth $10. Half an hour into the movie, your worst suspicions are realized: the movie is a disaster. Should you leave the movie theater? In making that decision, the $10 should be ignored. It is a sunk cost; your money is gone whether you stay or leave. The only relevant choice now is how to spend the next 60 minutes of your time: watch a terrible movie or go do something else.

Or assume you have just purchased a fancy laptop computer for $2,000. But the next week, the manufacturer announces a new computer with twice the power for $1,000; you can trade in your old computer for the new one by paying an additional $400. You are angry. You feel you have just paid $2,000 for a computer that is now almost worthless, and you have gotten little use out of it. You decide not to buy the new computer for another year, until you have gotten at least some return for your investment. Again, an economist would say that you are not approaching the question rationally. The past decision is a sunk cost. The only question you should ask yourself is whether the extra power of the fancier computer is worth the additional $400. If it is, buy it. If not, don't.

MARGINAL COSTS

The third aspect of cost that economists emphasize is the extra costs of doing something, what they call the **marginal costs.** These are weighed against the (additional) **marginal benefits** of doing it. The most difficult decisions we make are not whether to do something or not. They are whether to do a little more or a little less of something. Few of us waste much time deciding whether or not to work. We have to work; the decision is whether to work a few more or a few less hours. A country does not consider whether or not to have an army; it decides whether to have a larger or smaller army.

Polly is considering flying to Colorado for a ski weekend. She has three days off from work. The airfare is $200, the hotel room costs $100 a night, and the ski ticket costs $35 a day. Food costs the same as at home. She is trying to decide whether to go for two or three days. The *marginal* cost of the third day is $135, the hotel cost plus the cost of the ski ticket. There are no additional transportation costs involved in staying the third day. She needs to compare the marginal cost with the additional enjoyment she will have from the third day.

Internet Connection

THE ECONOMISTS' VOICE

One way to start thinking like an economist is to read what economists have to say about current events. The Economists' Voice at www.bepress.com/ev/ provides articles about current economic issues.

People, consciously or not, think about the trade-offs at the margin in most of their decisions. Economists, however, bring them into the foreground. Like opportunity costs and sunk costs, marginal analysis is one of the critical concepts that enable economists to think systematically about the costs of alternative choices.

This kind of marginal analysis has come to play an increasingly important role in policy discussions. For instance, the key issue in various environmental regulations and safety standards is not whether there should be such regulations, but how tight they should be. Higher standards have both marginal benefits and marginal costs. From an economic standpoint, justification of higher standards hinges on whether the marginal benefits outweigh the marginal costs. Consider, for instance, auto safety. For the past three decades, the government has taken an active role in ensuring auto safety. It sets standards that all automobiles must meet. For example, an automobile must be able to withstand a side collision of a particular velocity. One of the most difficult problems the government faces is deciding what those standards should be. It recently considered tightening standards for withstanding side collisions on trucks. The government calculated that the higher standards would result on average in 79 fewer deaths per year. It calculated that meeting the higher standards would increase the cost of each vehicle by $81. (In addition, the heavier trucks would use more fuel.) In deciding whether to impose the higher standard, it used marginal analysis. It looked at the *additional* lives saved and at the *additional* costs.

Wrap-Up

BASIC STEPS OF RATIONAL CHOICE

Identify the opportunity sets.
Define the trade-offs.
Calculate the costs correctly, ignoring sunk costs, taking into account opportunity costs and marginal costs.

Review and Practice

SUMMARY

1. The basic competitive model consists of rational, self-interested individuals and profit-maximizing firms, interacting in competitive markets.
2. The profit motive and private property provide incentives for rational individuals and firms to work hard and efficiently. Ill-defined or restricted property rights can lead to inefficient behavior.
3. Society often faces choices between efficiency, which requires incentives that enable people or firms to receive different benefits depending on their performance, and equality, which entails people receiving more or less equal benefits.
4. The price system in a market economy is one way of allocating goods and services. Other methods include rationing by queue, by lottery, and by coupon.
5. An opportunity set illustrates what choices are possible. Budget constraints and time constraints define individuals' opportunity sets. Both show the trade-offs of how much of one thing a person must give up to get more of another.
6. A production possibilities curve defines a firm or society's opportunity set, representing the possible combinations of goods that the firm or society can produce. If a firm or society is producing below its production possibilities curve, it is said to be inefficient, since it could produce more of either good without producing less of the other.
7. The opportunity cost is the cost of using any resource. It is measured by looking at the next-best use to which that resource could be put.
8. A sunk cost is a past expenditure that cannot be recovered, no matter what choice is made in the present. Thus, rational decision makers ignore them.
9. Most economic decisions concentrate on choices at the margin, where the marginal (or extra) cost of a course of action is compared with its extra benefits.

KEY TERMS

competition
basic competitive model
rational choice
perfect competition
price taker
price system
private property
property rights
tragedy of the commons
rationing systems
opportunity set
budget constraints
time constraints
production possibilities
production possibilities curve
diminishing returns
relative price
opportunity cost
sunk costs
marginal costs
marginal benefits

REVIEW QUESTIONS

1. What are the essential elements of the basic competitive model?
2. Consider a lake in a state park where everyone is allowed to fish as much as they want. What outcome do you predict? Might this problem be averted if the lake were privately owned and fishing licenses were sold?
3. Why might government policy to make the distribution of income more equitable lead to less efficiency?
4. List advantages and disadvantages of rationing by queue, by lottery, and by coupon. If the government permitted a black market to develop, might some of the disadvantages of these systems be reduced?
5. What are some of the opportunity costs of going to college? What are some of the opportunity costs a state should consider when deciding whether to widen a highway?
6. Give two examples of a sunk cost, and explain why they should be irrelevant to current decisions.
7. How is marginal analysis relevant in the decision about which car to purchase? After deciding the kind of car to purchase, how is marginal analysis relevant?

PROBLEMS

1. Imagine that many businesses are located beside a river, into which they discharge industrial waste. There is a city downstream, which uses the river as a water supply and for recreation. If property rights to the river are ill-defined, what problems may occur?
2. Suppose an underground reservoir of oil may reside under properties owned by several different individuals. As each well is drilled, it reduces the amount of oil that others can take out. Compare how quickly the oil is likely to be extracted in this situation with how quickly it would be extracted if one person owned the property rights to drill for the entire pool of oil.
3. In some states, hunting licenses are allocated by lottery; if you want a license, you send in your name to enter the lottery. If the purpose of the system is to ensure that those who want to hunt the most get a chance to do so, what are the flaws of this system? How would the situation improve if people who won licenses were allowed to sell them to others?
4. Imagine that during time of war, the government imposes coupon rationing. What are the advantages of allowing people to buy and sell their coupons? What are the disadvantages?
5. Kathy, a college student, has $20 a week to spend; she spends it either on junk food at $2.50 a snack, or on gasoline at $2 per gallon. Draw Kathy's opportunity set. What is the trade-off between junk food and gasoline? Now draw each new budget constraint she would face if
   (a) a kind relative started sending her an additional $10 per week;
   (b) the price of a junk food snack fell to $2;
   (c) the price of gasoline rose to $2.50 per gallon.
   In each case, how does the trade-off between junk food and gasoline change?
6. Why is the opportunity cost of going to medical school likely to be greater than the opportunity cost of going to college? Why is the opportunity cost of a woman with a college education having a child greater than the opportunity cost of a woman with just a high school education having a child?
7. Bob likes to divide his recreational time between going to movies and listening to compact discs. He has 20 hours a week available for recreation; a movie takes two hours, and a CD takes one hour to listen to. Draw his "time-budget constraint" line. Bob also has a limited amount of income to spend on recreation. He has $60 a week to spend on recreational activities; a movie costs $10, and a CD costs $15. (He never likes to listen to the same CD twice.) Draw his budget constraint line. What is his opportunity set?

Appendix: Reading Graphs

Whether the old saying that a picture is worth a thousand words under- or overestimates the value of a picture, economists find graphs extremely useful.

For instance, look at Figure 2.5; it is a redrawn version of Figure 2.1, showing the budget constraint—the various combinations of CDs and DVDs that an individual, Michelle, can buy. More generally, a graph shows the relationship between two variables: here, the number of CDs and the number of DVDs that can be purchased. The budget constraint gives the maximum number of DVDs that she can purchase, given the number of CDs that she has bought.

In a graph, one variable (here, DVDs) is put on the horizontal axis and the other variable on the vertical axis. We read a point such as E by looking across to the vertical axis and seeing that it corresponds to 6 CDs, and by looking down to the horizontal axis and seeing that is corresponds to 3 DVDs. Similarly, we read point A by looking across to the vertical axis and seeing that it corresponds to 8 CDs, and by looking down to the horizontal axis and seeing that it corresponds to 2 DVDs.

In the figure, each of the points from the table has been plotted, and then a curve has been drawn through those points. The "curve" turns out to be a straight line in this case, but we still use the more general term. The advantage of the curve over the individual points is that with it, we can read off from the graph points on the budget constraint that are not in the table.

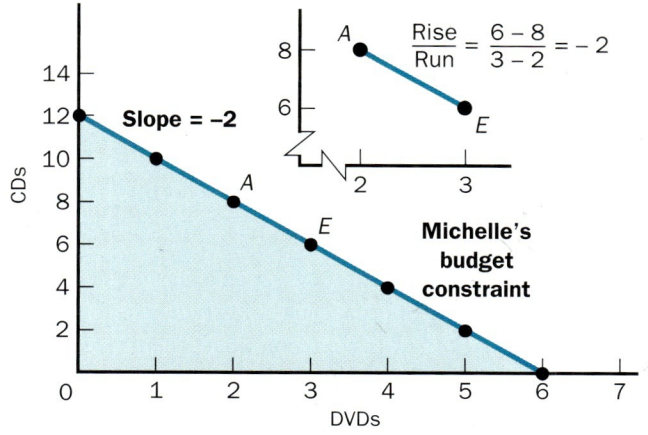

Figure 2.5
READING A GRAPH: THE BUDGET CONSTRAINT

Graphs can be used to show the relationship between two variables. This one shows the relationship between the variable on the vertical axis (the number of CDs) and the variable on the horizontal axis (the number of DVDs). The slope of the curve—here, the budget constraint—gives the change in the number of CDs Michelle can purchase if she buys another DVD. The slope of the budget constraint is negative. A small portion of the graph has been blown up to illustrate how to calculate the curve's slope. (The jagged sections of the axes near the blown-up graph's origin indicate that the distance from the origin to the first value on each axis is not drawn to scale.)

Sometimes, of course, not every point on the graph is economically meaningful. You cannot buy half a DVD or half a CD. For the most part, we ignore these considerations when drawing our graphs; we simply pretend that any point on the budget constraint is actually possible.

SLOPE

In any diagram, the amount by which the value along the vertical axis increases from a change in a unit along the horizontal axis is called the *slope,* just like the slope of a mountain. Slope is sometimes described as "rise over run," meaning that the slope of a line can be calculated by dividing the change on the vertical axis (the "rise") by the change on the horizontal axis (the "run").

Look at Figure 2.5. As we move from E to A, increasing the number of CDs by 2, the number of DVDs purchased falls from 3 to 2. For every two additional CDs bought, the feasible number of DVDs that can be purchased falls by 1. So the slope of the line is

$$\frac{\text{rise}}{\text{run}} = \frac{6-8}{3-2} = \frac{-2}{1} = -2.$$

When, as in Figure 2.5, the variable on the vertical axis falls when the variable on the horizontal axis increases, the curve, or line, is said to be *negatively sloped.* A budget constraint is always negatively sloped. But when we describe the slope of a budget constraint, we frequently omit the term "negative." We say the slope is 2, knowing that since we are describing the slope of a budget constraint, we should more formally say that the slope is negative 2. Alternatively, we sometimes say that the slope has an absolute value of 2.

Figure 2.6 shows the case of a curve that is *positively sloped.* The variable along the vertical axis, income, increases as schooling increases, giving the line its upward tilt from left to right.

In later discussions, we will encounter two special cases. A line that is very steep has a very large slope; that is, the increase in the vertical axis for every unit increase in the horizontal axis is very large. The extreme case is a perfectly vertical line, and we say then that the slope is infinite (Figure 2.7, panel A). At the other extreme is a flat, horizontal line; since there is no increase in the vertical axis no matter how large the change along the horizontal, we say that the slope of such a curve is zero (panel B).

Figures 2.5 and 2.6 both show straight lines. Everywhere along the straight line, the slope is the same. This is not true in Figure 2.8, which repeats the production possibilities curve shown originally in Figure 2.3. Panel B of the figure blows up the area around point E. From the figure, you can see that if the output of butter increases by 1 ton, the output of guns decreases by 1 million guns. Thus, the slope is

$$\frac{\text{rise}}{\text{run}} = \frac{69-70}{71-70} = -1.$$

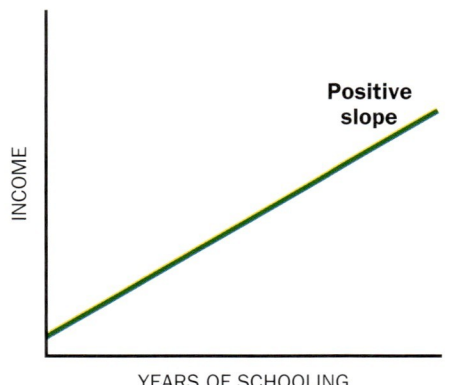

Figure 2.6

POSITIVELY SLOPED CURVE

Incomes increase with the number of years of schooling.

Now look at point A, where the economy is producing more butter. The area around A has been blown up in panel C. Here, we see that when we increase butter by 1 more unit, the reduction in guns is greater than before. The slope at A (again, millions of fewer guns produced per extra ton of butter) is

$$\frac{\text{rise}}{\text{run}} = \frac{38-40}{91-90} = -2.$$

With curves such as the production possibilities curve, the slope differs as we move along the curve.

INTERPRETING CURVES

Look at Figure 2.9. Which of the two curves has a steeper slope? The one on the left appears to have a slope that has a larger absolute value. But look carefully at the axes. Notice that in panel A, the vertical axis is stretched relative to panel B. The same distance that represents 20 CDs in panel B represents only 10 CDs in panel A.

Figure 2.7
LIMITING CASES

In panel A, the slope of a vertical line is infinite. In panel B, the slope of a horizontal line is zero.

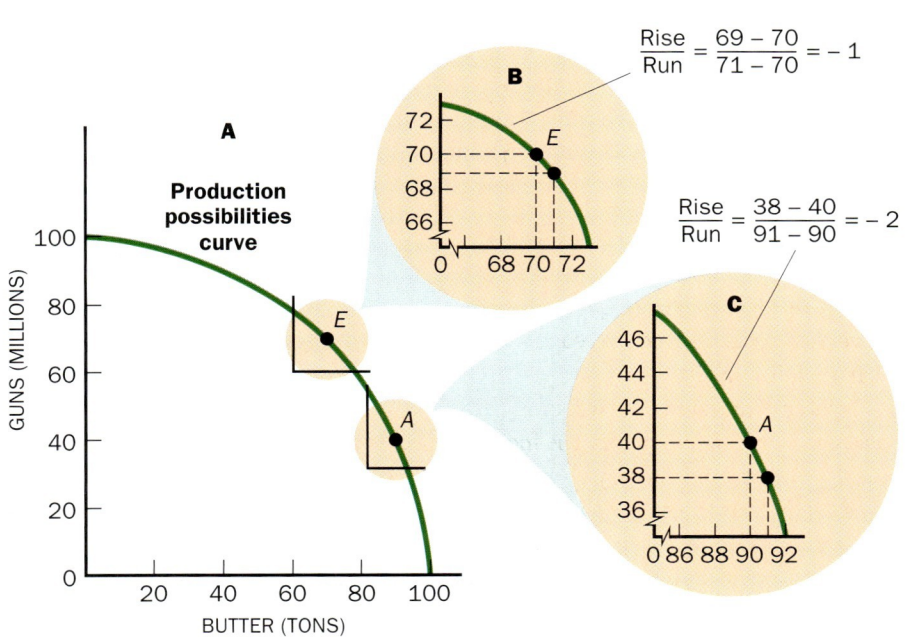

FIGURE 2.8

THE GUNS AND BUTTER TRADE-OFF

Panel A shows a trade-off between military spending ("guns") and civilian spending ("butter"), where society chooses point E. Panel B is an enlargement of the area around E, which focuses on the slope there, which also measures the marginal trade-offs society faces near that point. Similarly, panel C is an enlargement of the area around A and shows the marginal trade-offs society faces near that point.

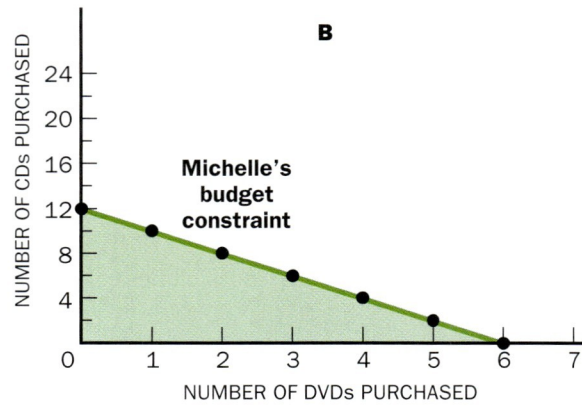

Figure 2.9
SCALING AND SLOPE

Which of these two lines has the steeper slope? The units along the vertical axis have changed. The two curves have exactly the same slope.

In fact, both panels represent the same budget constraint. They have exactly the same slope.

This kind of cautionary tale is also important in looking at graphs of data. Compare, for instance, panels A and B of Figure 2.10. Both graphs show the level of passenger car production from 1980 to 1990. Which one exhibits more variability? Which looks more stable? Panel B appears to show that car production does not change much over time. But again, a closer look reveals that the axis has been stretched in panel A. The two curves are based on exactly the same data, and there is really no difference between them.

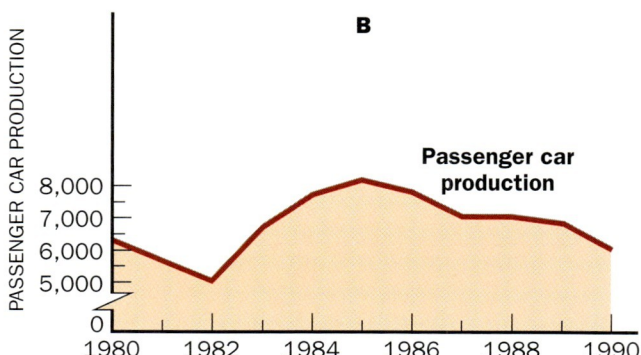

Figure 2.10
SCALING AND GRAPHS OF DATA

Which of these two curves shows greater variability in the output of cars over time? The two curves plot the same data. The vertical scale has again been changed.
SOURCE: *Ward's Automotive Reports* (1991).

50 **CHAPTER 2** THINKING LIKE AN ECONOMIST

Part 2
PERFECT MARKETS

Learning goals

In this chapter, you will learn

1. What a demand curve is, why demand curves normally slope downward, and what other factors, besides price, affect the quantity demanded

2. What a supply curve is, why supply curves normally slope upward, and what other factors, besides price, affect the quantity supplied

3. How the demand and supply curves can be used to determine the equilibrium price of a good

4. How shifts in the demand and supply curve affect the equilibrium price

Chapter 3

DEMAND, SUPPLY, AND PRICE

Choice in the face of scarcity is the fundamental concern of economics. But if scarcity is such a concern for economists, why is it that whenever I go to my local grocery store it has all the tomatoes I want to buy? Tomatoes might be more expensive one week and less expensive the next but they are always available. In what sense are tomatoes scarce? The same is true for most goods most of the time; as long as I am willing to pay the market price, I can buy the good. A key economic insight is that when the forces of supply and demand operate freely, the price of a good measures its scarcity. If bad weather destroys part of the tomato crop, tomatoes *are* more scarce, and their price will rise to reflect that condition. But price does more than simply measure scarcity. Prices also convey critical economic information. When the price of a resource—such as land, labor, or capital—used by a firm is high, the company has a greater incentive to economize on its use. When the price of a good that the firm produces is high, the company has a greater incentive to produce more of that good, and its customers have an incentive to economize on its use. Thus, prices provide our economy with incentives to use scarce resources efficiently, and a major objective of economists is to understand the forces that determine prices. This chapter describes how prices are determined in competitive market economies.

The Role of Prices

The **price** of a good or service is what must be given in exchange for the good. Usually we identify the price of something with how much it costs in dollars. But price can include other factors—for example, if you have to wait to buy something, the total price includes the value of your time spent in line. For most of our discussion, however, we will keep things simple and just think of the price as the number of dollars paid to obtain a good or service.

Prices are the way participants in the economy communicate with one another. Assume a drought hits the country, drastically reducing the supply of corn. Households will need to lower their consumption of corn or there will not be enough to go around. But how will they know this? Suppose newspapers across the country ran an article informing people they would have to eat less corn because of a drought. What incentive would they have to pay attention to it? How would each family know how much it ought to reduce its consumption? Alternatively, consider the effect of an increase in the price of corn. The higher price conveys all the relevant information. It simultaneously tells families corn is scarce and provides incentives for them to consume less of it. Consumers do not need to know anything about why corn is scarce, nor do they need to be told how much to reduce their consumption of it.

Price changes and differences present interesting problems and puzzles. In the early 2000s, while the price of an average house in Los Angeles went up by 76 percent, the price of a house in Milwaukee, Wisconsin, increased by only 32 percent. Why? During the same period, the price of computers fell dramatically, while the price of bread rose, but at a much slower rate than the price of housing in Los Angeles. Why? The "price" of labor is just the wage or salary that is paid. Why does a physician earn three times as much as a college professor, though the college professor may have performed better in the college courses they took together? Why is the price of water, without which we cannot live, very low in most cases, but the price of diamonds very high? The simple answer to all these questions is that in market economies like that of the United States, price is determined by supply and demand. Changes in prices are determined by changes in supply and demand.

Understanding the causes of changes in prices and being able to predict their occurrence are not just matters of academic interest. One of the events that precipitated the French Revolution was the rise in the price of bread, for which the people blamed the government. And gas price increases were a topic of political debate in the 2004 U.S. presidential election.

Demand

Economists use the concept of **demand** to describe the quantity of a good or service that a household or firm chooses to buy at a given price. It is important to understand that economists are concerned not just with what people desire but with what they choose to buy given the spending limits imposed by their budget constraint and given the prices of various goods. In analyzing demand, the first question economists ask is how the quantity of a good purchased by an individual changes as the price changes, when everything else is kept constant.

THE INDIVIDUAL DEMAND CURVE

Think about what happens as the price of candy bars changes. At a price of $5.00, you might never buy one. At $3.00, you might buy one as a special treat. At $1.25, you might buy a few, and if the price declined to $0.50, you might buy a lot. The table in Figure 3.1 summarizes the weekly demand of one individual, Roger, for candy bars at these different prices. We can see that the lower the price, the larger the quantity demanded. We can also draw a graph that shows the quantity Roger demands at each price. The quantity demanded is measured along the horizontal axis, and the price is measured along the vertical axis. The graph in Figure 3.1 plots the points.

A smooth curve can be drawn to connect the points. This curve is called the **demand curve.** The demand curve gives the quantity demanded at each price. Thus, if we want to know how many candy bars a week Roger will demand at a price of $1.00, we simply look along the vertical axis at the price $1.00, find the corresponding point A along the demand curve, and then read down the horizontal axis. At a price of $1.00, Roger buys 6 candy bars each week. Alternatively, if we want to know at what price he will buy just 3 candy bars, we look along the horizontal axis at the quantity 3, find the corresponding point B along the demand curve, and then read across to the vertical axis. Roger will buy 3 candy bars at a price of $1.50.

As the price of candy bars increases, the quantity demanded decreases. This can be seen from the numbers in the table in Figure 3.1 and in the shape of the demand curve, which slopes downward from left to right. This relationship is typical of demand curves and makes common sense: the cheaper a good is (the lower down we look on the vertical axis), the more of it a person will buy (the farther right on the horizontal axis); the more expensive, the less a person will buy.

Figure 3.1

AN INDIVIDUAL'S DEMAND CURVE

This demand curve shows the quantity of candy bars that Roger consumes at each price. Notice that quantity demanded increases as the price falls, and the demand curve slopes down.

Wrap-Up

DEMAND CURVE

The demand curve gives the quantity of the good demanded at each price.

THE MARKET DEMAND CURVE

Suppose there was a simple economy made up of two people, Roger and Jane. Figure 3.2 illustrates how to add up the demand curves of these two individuals to obtain a demand curve for the market as a whole. We "add" the demand curves horizontally by taking, at each price, the quantities demanded by Roger and by Jane and adding the two together. Thus, in the figure, at the price of $0.75, Roger demands 9 candy bars and Jane demands 11, so that the total market demand is 20 candy bars. The same principles apply no matter how many people there are in the economy. The **market demand curve** gives the total quantity of the good that will be demanded at each price. The table in Figure 3.3 summarizes the information for our example of candy

Figure 3.2

DERIVING THE MARKET DEMAND CURVE

The market demand curve is constructed by adding up, at each price, the total of the quantities consumed by each individual. The curve here shows what market demand would be if there were only two consumers. Actual market demand, as depicted in Figure 3.3, is much larger because there are many consumers.

bars; it gives the total quantity of candy bars demanded by everybody in the economy at various prices. If we had a table like the one in Figure 3.1 for each person in the economy, we would construct Figure 3.3 by adding up, at each price, the total quantity of candy bars purchased. Figure 3.3 tells us, for instance, that at a price of $3.00 per candy bar, the total market demand for candy bars is 1 million candy bars, and that lowering the price to $2.00 increases market demand to 3 million candy bars.

Figure 3.3 also depicts the same information in a graph. As in Figure 3.1, price lies along the vertical axis, but now the horizontal axis measures the quantity demanded by everyone in the economy. Joining the points in the figure together, we get the market demand curve. If we want to know what the total demand for candy bars will be when the price is $1.50 per candy bar, we look on the vertical axis at the price $1.50, find the corresponding point A along the demand curve, and read down to the horizontal axis; at that price, total demand is 4 million candy bars. If we want to know what the price of candy bars will be when the demand equals 20 million, we find 20 million along the horizontal axis, look up to find the corresponding point B along the market demand curve, and read across to the vertical axis; the price at which 20 million candy bars are demanded is $0.75.

Notice that just as when the price of candy bars increases, the individual's demand decreases, so too when the price of candy bars increases, market demand decreases. At successively higher prices, more and more individuals exit the market. Thus, the market demand curve also slopes downward from left to right. This general rule holds both because each individual's demand curve is downward sloping and because as the price is increased, some individuals will decide to stop buying altogether. In Figure 3.1, for example, Roger *exits the market*—consumes a quantity of zero—at the price of $5.00, at which his demand curve hits the vertical axis.

Figure 3.3

THE MARKET DEMAND CURVE

The market demand curve shows the quantity of the good demanded by all consumers in the market at each price. The market demand curve is downward sloping, for two reasons: at a higher price, each consumer buys less, and at high-enough prices, some consumers decide not to buy at all—they exit the market.

SHIFTS IN DEMAND CURVES

When the price of a good increases, the demand for that good decreases—when everything else is held constant. But in the real world, everything is not held constant. Any changes other than in the price of the good in question shift the (whole) demand curve—that is, they alter the amount that will be demanded at each price. How the demand curve for candy has shifted as Americans have become more weight conscious provides a good example. Figure 3.4 shows hypothetical demand curves for candy bars in 1960 and in 2000. We can see from the figure that the demand for candy bars at a price of $0.75 has decreased from 20 million candy bars (point E_{1960}) to 10 million (point E_{2000}), as people have reduced their taste for candy.

SOURCES OF SHIFTS IN DEMAND CURVES

Two of the factors that shift the demand curve—changes in income and in the price of other goods—are specifically economic factors. As an individual's income increases, she normally purchases more of any good. Thus, rising incomes shift the demand curve to the right, as illustrated in Figure 3.5. At each price, more of the good is consumed.

Changes in the price of other goods, particularly closely related goods, will also shift the demand curve for a good. For example, when the price of margarine increases, some individuals will substitute butter. Two goods are **substitutes** if an increase in the price of one *increases* the demand for the other. Butter and margarine are thus substitutes. When people choose between butter and margarine, one important factor is the relative price, that is, the ratio of the price of butter to the price of margarine. An increase in the price of butter and a decrease in the price of margarine increase the relative price of butter. Thus, both induce individuals to substitute margarine for butter.

Candy bars and granola bars can also be considered substitutes, as the two goods satisfy a similar need. Thus, an increase in the price of granola bars makes candy bars relatively more attractive, and hence leads to a rightward shift in the demand curve for candy bars. (At each price, the demand for candy is greater.)

Sometimes, however, an increase in a price of other goods has just the opposite effect. Consider an individual who takes sugar in his coffee. In deciding on how much coffee to demand, he is concerned with the price of a cup of coffee *with* sugar. If sugar becomes more expensive, he will demand less coffee. For this person, sugar and coffee are **complements;** an increase in the price of one *decreases* the demand for the other. A price increase for sugar shifts the

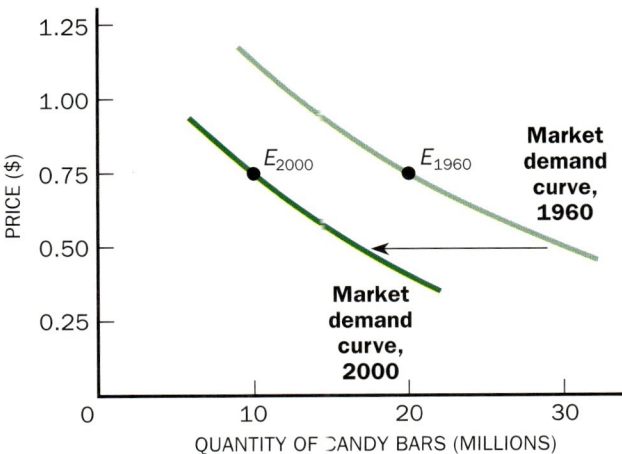

Figure 3.4

SHIFTS IN THE DEMAND CURVE

A leftward shift in the demand curve means that a lesser amount will be demanded at every given market price.

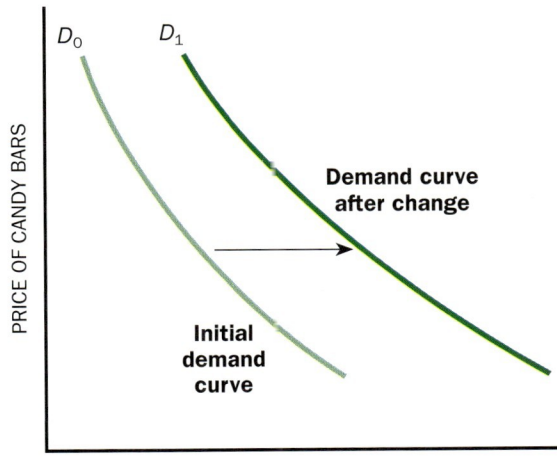

Figure 3.5

A RIGHTWARD SHIFT IN THE DEMAND CURVE

If, at each price, there is an increase in the quantity demanded, then the demand curve will shift to the right, as depicted. An increase in income, an increase in the price of a substitute, or a decrease in the price of a complement can cause a rightward shift in the demand curve.

demand curve for coffee to the left: at each price, the demand for coffee is less. Similarly a *decrease* in the price of sugar shifts the demand curve for coffee to the right.

Market demand curves can also be shifted by noneconomic factors. The major ones are changes in tastes, cultural factors, and changes in the composition of the population. The candy example discussed earlier reflected a change in tastes. Other taste changes in recent years in the United States include shifts in food choices as a result of new health information or (often short-lived) fads associated with diets. Health concerns led to a shift from high-cholesterol to low-cholesterol foods, and the Atkins diet produced a temporary shift away from high-carbohydrate foods such as bread. Cultural factors also affect demand curves. During the late twentieth century, increasing numbers of women entered the workforce as attitudes toward married middle-class women working outside the home shifted; and with this change, the demand curves for child care services shifted.

Population changes that shift demand curves are often related to age. Young families with babies purchase disposable diapers. The demand for new houses and apartments is closely related to the number of new households, which in turn depends on the number of individuals of marriageable age. The U.S. population has been growing older, on average, both because life expectancies are increasing and because birthrates fell somewhat after the baby boom that followed World War II. So there has been a shift in demand away from diapers and new houses. Economists working for particular firms and industries spend considerable energy ascertaining such **demographic effects** on the demand for the goods their firms sell.

Sometimes demand curves shift as the result of new information. The shifts in demand for alcohol and meat—and even more strongly for cigarettes—are related to improved consumer information about health risks.

Changes in the cost and available of credit can also shift demand curves—for goods such as cars and houses that people typically buy with the help of loans. When interest rates rise and borrowing money becomes more expensive, the demand curves for cars and houses shift; at each price, the quantity demanded is less.

Finally, what people expect to happen in the future can shift demand curves. If people think they may become unemployed, they will reduce their spending. In this case, economists say that their demand curves depend on expectations.

Wrap-Up

SOURCES OF SHIFTS IN MARKET DEMAND CURVES

A change in income
A change in the price of a substitute
A change in the price of a complement
A change in the composition of the population
A change in tastes or cultural attitudes
A change in information
A change in the availability of credit
A change in expectations

Case in Point

GASOLINE PRICES AND THE DEMAND FOR SUVS

When demand for several products is intertwined, conditions affecting the price of one will affect the demand for the other. Changes in gasoline prices in the United States, for example, have affected the types of cars Americans buy.

Gasoline prices soared twice in the 1970s, once when the Organization of Petroleum Exporting Countries (OPEC) shut off the flow of oil to the United States in 1973 and again when the overthrow of the shah of Iran in 1979 led to a disruption in oil supplies. The price of gasoline at the pump rose from $0.35 a gallon in 1971 to $1.35 a gallon by 1981 (see Figure 3.6). In response to the price increases, Americans had to cut back demand. But how could they conserve on gasoline? The distance from home to office was not going to shrink, and people had to get to their jobs. One solution was for American drivers to replace their old cars with smaller cars that offered more miles to the gallon.

Analysts classify car sales according to car size, and usually the smaller the car, the better the gas mileage. Just after the first rise in gas prices, about 2.5 million large cars, 2.8 million compacts, and 2.3 million subcompacts were bought each year. By 1985, the proportions had shifted dramatically. About 1.5 million large cars were sold that year, representing a significant decline from the mid-1970s. The number of subcompacts sold was relatively unchanged at 2.2 million, but the number of compacts sold soared to 3.7 million.

The demand curve for any good (like cars) assumes that the price of complementary goods (like gasoline) is fixed. The rise in gasoline prices caused the demand curve for small cars to shift out to the right and the demand curve for large cars to shift back to the left.

By the late 1980s, the price of gasoline had fallen significantly from its peak in 1981, but in the 1990s, gasoline prices again rose markedly. However, the prices of other goods were also rising over the thirty-five-year period shown in the figure. When

Low gas prices in 1990s and early 2000s led to higher demand for SUVs.

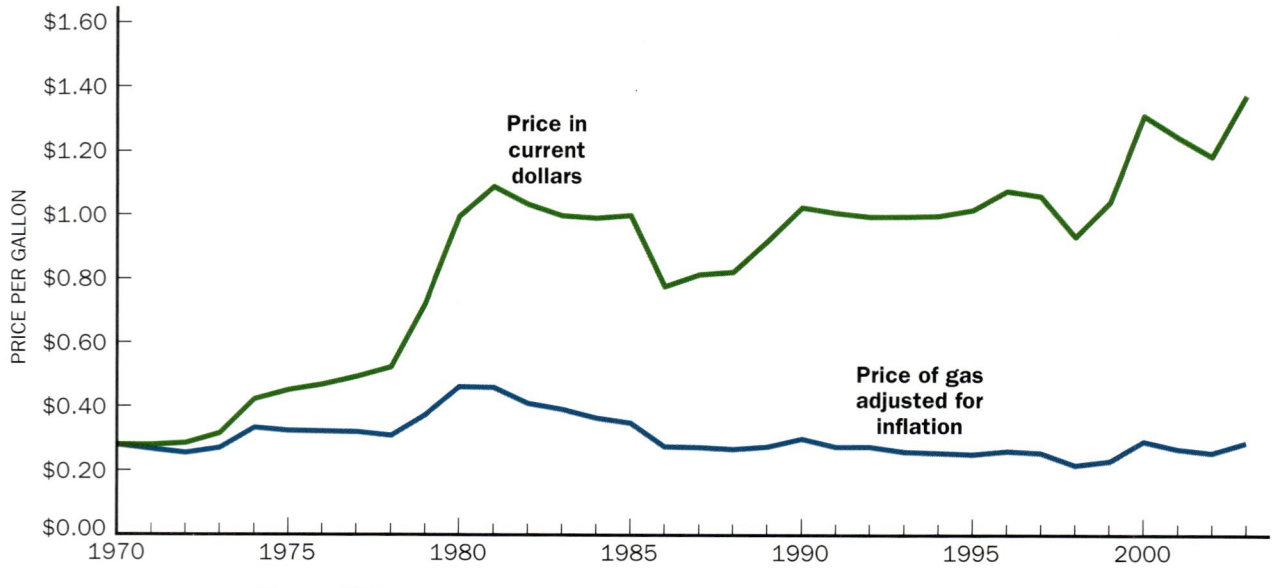

Figure 3.6
U.S. GASOLINE PRICES

Adjusted for inflation, gasoline prices over the past decade have been about the same as they were before the price increases of the 1970s.

SOURCE: Department of Energy, *Annual Energy Review 2003*, September 7, 2004 (www.eia.doe.gov/emeu/aer/petro.html).

gas prices are adjusted for inflation, the real price of gasoline—the price of gas *relative* to the prices of other goods—was lower in the 1990s than it had been *before* the big price increases of the 1970s (Figure 3.6). As a consequence, the demand curve for large cars shifted back to the right. This time, the change in demand was reflected in booming sales of sports utility vehicles, or SUVs. The registrations of light-duty trucks (which include SUVs, minivans, and pickups) jumped from less than 20 percent of all vehicles in 1980 to 46 percent in 1996.[1]

SHIFTS IN A DEMAND CURVE VERSUS MOVEMENTS ALONG A DEMAND CURVE

The distinction between changes that result from a *shift* in the demand curve and changes that result from a *movement along* the demand curve is crucial to understanding economics. A movement along a demand curve is simply the change in the quantity demanded as the price changes. Figure 3.7A illustrates a movement along the demand curve from point A to point B; *given a demand curve,* at lower prices, more is consumed. Figure 3.7B illustrates a shift in the demand curve to the right; *at a given price,* more is consumed.

[1] P. S. Hu, S. D. Davis, and R. L. Schmoyer, *Registrations and Vehicle Miles of Travel for Light-Duty Vehicles, 1985–1995* (publication ORNL-6936) (Oakridge, Tenn.: Center for Transportation Analysis, February 1998), p. 1.

In practice, both effects are often present. Thus, in panel C of Figure 3.7, the movement from point A to point C—where the quantity demanded has been increased from Q_0 to Q_2—consists of two parts: a change in quantity demanded resulting from a shift in the demand curve (the increase in quantity from Q_0 to Q_1), and a movement along the demand curve due to a change in the price (the increase in quantity from Q_1 to Q_2).

The distinction will be important for understanding how quantities and prices are determined once we combine our analysis of demand with an analysis of supply. For example, along a given demand curve for gasoline, a rise in the price of gasoline causes a reduction in the quantity demanded. In contrast, the introduction of a new rapid transit system in a city would shift the demand curve for gasoline to the left; in this example, at each price of gasoline, the quantity demanded would be less because alternative transportation services are available.

WRAP UP

SHIFTS VERSUS MOVEMENTS ALONG DEMAND CURVES

A change in price, given a demand curve, is reflected in a movement along the given demand curve.

A shift in the demand curve causes the quantity demanded to change, at a given price.

FUNDAMENTALS OF DEMAND, SUPPLY, AND PRICE 1

DEMAND DECLINES AS PRICE RISES

As the price of a good increases, the quantity demanded falls. Changes in factors other than price—such as incomes, consumer tastes, or the prices of other substitutes or complements—shift the demand curve.

Supply

Economists use the concept of **supply** to describe the quantity of a good or service that a household or firm would like to sell at a particular price. Supply in economics refers to such seemingly

Figure 3.7
MOVEMENT ALONG THE DEMAND CURVE VERSUS SHIFT IN THE DEMAND CURVE

Panel A shows an increase in quantity demanded caused by a lower price—a movement along a given demand curve. Panel B illustrates an increase in quantity demanded caused by a shift in the entire demand curve, so that a greater quantity is demanded at every market price. Panel C shows a combination of a shift in the demand curve (the movement from point A to B) and a movement along the demand curve (the movement from B to C).

e-Insight
THE DEMAND FOR COMPUTERS AND INFORMATION TECHNOLOGY

The demand for computers and other information technology investments rose markedly during the 1980s and 1990s. Panel A shows an index of real investment in computers and related equipment; the index is scaled so that it equals 100 in the year 2000. Real investment has grown an average of 29 percent over the period shown (1990–2003). This growth in the demand for computers occurred for a simple reason: the effective price of computers fell enormously. Even though the average price of a personal computer remained relatively stable, today's computer delivers much

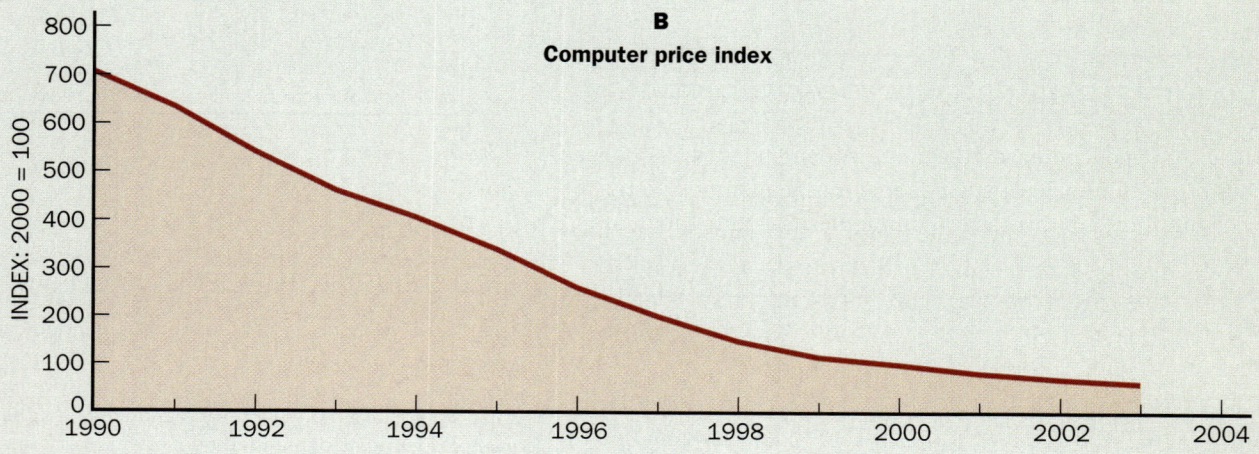

higher performance at that price. Adjusting for this change in quality, between 1990 and 2003 the price of computers is estimated to have fallen an average of 17 percent per year (see panel B). At the lower price, we see a higher quantity demanded.

A major reason for the decline in computer prices is technological innovations that have lowered the cost of producing computers. Firms able to take advantage of these technological improvements have increased their profits, as their costs have fallen faster than the prices of the computers they sell. Other firms have been less successful, and the fall in prices has forced them to leave the market.

The demand for computers rose markedly during the 1980s and 1990s.

disparate choices as the number of candy bars a firm wants to sell and the number of hours a worker is willing to work. As with demand, the first question economists ask is, How does the quantity supplied change when price changes, if everything else is kept the same?

Figure 3.8 shows the number of candy bars that a candy company would like to sell, or supply to the market, at each price. If the price of a candy bar is only 75 cents, the firm does not find it profitable to produce and sell any candy bars. At a higher price, however, the firm can make a profit. If the price is $2.00, the firm wants to sell 85,000 candy bars. At an even higher price—for example, $5.00 per candy bar—it wants to sell even more candy bars, 100,000.

Figure 3.8 also depicts these points in a graph. The curve drawn by connecting the points is called the firm's **supply curve.** It shows the quantity that the candy company will supply at each price, when all other factors are held constant. For this curve, like the demand curve, we put the price on the horizontal axis. Thus, we can read point A on the curve as indicating that at a price of $1.50, the firm would like to supply 70,000 candy bars.

In direct contrast to the demand curve, the typical supply curve slopes upward from left to right; at higher prices, firms will supply more. This is because higher prices yield suppliers higher profits—giving them an incentive to produce more.

Figure 3.8

ONE FIRM'S SUPPLY CURVE

The supply curve shows the quantity of a good a firm is willing to produce at each price. Normally a firm is willing to produce more as the price increases, which is why the supply curve slopes upward.

Figure 3.9
THE MARKET SUPPLY CURVE

The market supply curve shows the quantity of a good all firms in the market are willing to supply at each price. The market supply curve is normally upward sloping, both because each firm is willing to supply more of the good at a higher price and because higher prices entice new firms to produce.

MARKET SUPPLY

The *market supply* of a good is the total quantity that all the firms in the economy are willing to supply at a given price. Similarly, the market supply of labor is the total quantity of labor that all the households in the economy are willing to supply at a given wage. Figure 3.9 tells us, for instance, that at a price of $2.00, firms will supply 70 million candy bars, while at a price of $0.50, they will supply only 5 million.

Figure 3.9 also shows the same information graphically. The curve joining the points in the figure is the **market supply curve.** The market supply curve gives the total quantity of a good that firms are willing to produce at each price. Thus, we read point A on the market supply curve as showing that at a price of $0.75, the firms in the economy would like to sell 20 million candy bars.

As the price of candy bars increases, the quantity supplied increases, other things being equal. The market supply curve slopes upward from left to right for two reasons: at higher prices, each firm in the market is willing to produce more; and at higher prices, more firms are willing to enter the market to produce the good.

The market supply curve is calculated from the supply curves of the different firms in the same way that the market demand curve is calculated from the demand curves of the different households: at each price, we add horizontally the quantities that each of the firms is willing to produce.

Wrap-Up

SUPPLY CURVE

The supply curve gives the quantity of the good supplied at each price.

SHIFTS IN SUPPLY CURVES

Just as demand curves can shift, supply curves too can shift, so that the quantity supplied at each price increases or decreases. Suppose a drought hits the breadbasket states of mid-America. Figure 3.10 illustrates the situation. The supply curve for wheat shifts to the left, which means that at each price of wheat, the quantity firms are willing to supply is smaller.

SOURCES OF SHIFTS IN SUPPLY CURVES

There are several sources of shifts in market supply curves, just as we saw for market demand curves. One is changing prices of the inputs used to produce a good. Figure 3.11 shows that as corn becomes less expensive, the supply curve for cornflakes shifts to the right. Producing cornflakes costs less, so at every price, firms are willing to supply

Figure 3.10

SHIFTING THE SUPPLY CURVE TO THE LEFT

A drought or other disaster (among other possible factors) will cause the supply curve to shift to the left, so that at each price, a smaller quantity is supplied.

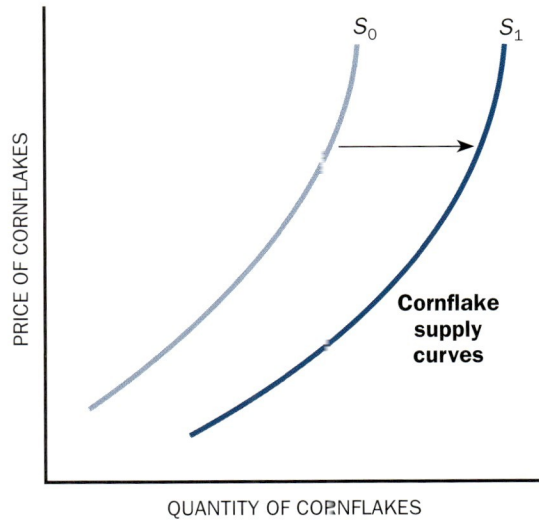

Figure 3.11

SHIFTING THE SUPPLY CURVE TO THE RIGHT

An improvement in technology or a reduction in input prices (among other possible factors) will cause the supply curve to shift to the right, so that at each price, a larger quantity is supplied.

a greater quantity. That is why the quantity supplied along the curve S_1 is greater than the quantity supplied, at the same price, along the curve S_0.

Another source of shifts is changes in technology. The technological improvements in the computer industry over the past two decades have led to a rightward shift in the market supply curve. Yet another source of shifts is nature. The supply curve for agricultural goods may shift to the right or left depending on weather conditions, insect infestations, or animal diseases.

Firms often borrow to obtain inputs needed for production, and a rise in interest rates will increase the cost of borrowing. This increase too will induce a leftward shift in the supply curve. Finally, changed expectations can also lead to a shift in the supply curve. If firms believe that a new technology for making cars will become available in two years, they will discourage investment today, leading to a temporary leftward shift in the supply curve.

> ## Wrap-Up
>
> ## SOURCES OF SHIFTS IN MARKET SUPPLY CURVES
>
> A change in the prices of inputs
> A change in technology

 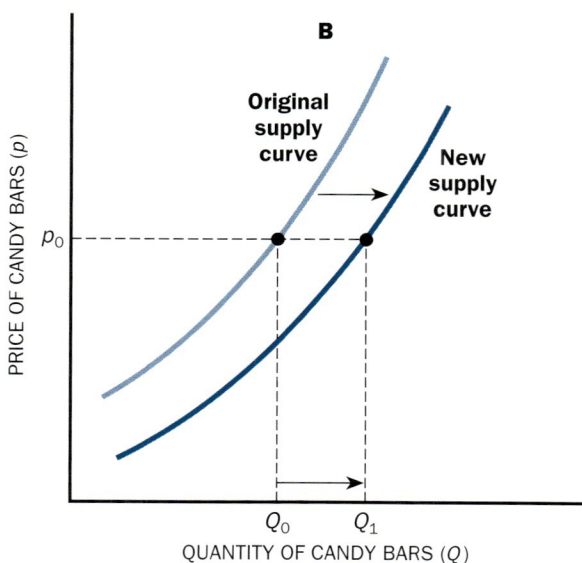

Figure 3.12

MOVEMENT ALONG THE SUPPLY CURVE VERSUS SHIFT IN THE SUPPLY CURVE

Panel A shows an increase in quantity supplied caused by a higher price—a movement along a given supply curve. Panel B illustrates an increase in quantity supplied caused by a shift in the entire supply curve, so that a greater quantity is supplied at every market price.

A change in the natural environment
A change in the availability of credit
A change in expectations

SHIFTS IN A SUPPLY CURVE VERSUS MOVEMENTS ALONG A SUPPLY CURVE

Distinguishing between a movement *along* a curve and a *shift* in the curve itself is just as important for supply curves as it is for demand curves. In Figure 3.12A, the price of candy bars has gone up, with a corresponding increase in quantity supplied. Thus, there has been a movement along the supply curve.

By contrast, in Figure 3.12B, the supply curve has shifted to the right, perhaps because a new production technique has made it cheaper to produce candy bars. Now, even though the price does not change, the quantity supplied increases. The quantity supplied in the market can increase either because the price of the good has increased, so that for a *given supply curve,* the quantity produced is higher; or because the supply curve has shifted, so that at a *given price,* the quantity supplied has increased.

FUNDAMENTALS OF DEMAND, SUPPLY, AND PRICE 2

SUPPLY INCREASES AS PRICE RISES

As the price of a good increases, the quantity firms are willing to supply rises. Changes in factors other than price—such as the costs of production or changes in technology—shift the supply curve.

Law of Supply and Demand

This chapter began with the assertion that supply and demand work together to determine the market price in competitive markets. Figure 3.13 puts a market supply curve and a market demand curve on the same graph to show how this happens. The price actually paid and received in the market will be determined by the intersection of the two curves. This point is labeled E_0, for equilibrium, and the corresponding price ($0.75) and quantity (20 million) are called, respectively, the **equilibrium price** and the **equilibrium quantity.**

Since the term **equilibrium** will recur throughout the book, it is important to understand the concept clearly. Equilibrium describes a situation where there are no forces (reasons) for change. No one has an incentive to change the result—the price or quantity consumed or produced, in the case of supply and demand.

Physicists also speak of equilibrium in describing a weight hanging from a spring. Two forces are working on the weight. Gravity is pulling it down; the spring is pulling

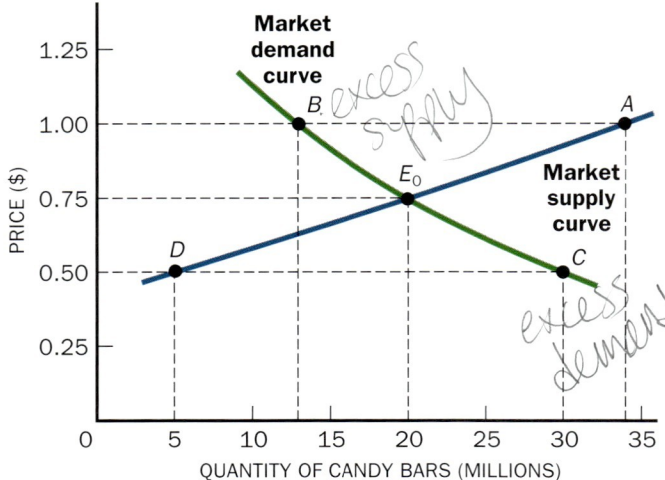

Figure 3.13

SUPPLY AND DEMAND EQUILIBRIUM

Equilibrium occurs at the intersection of the demand and supply curves, at point E_0. At any price above E_0, the quantity supplied will exceed the quantity demanded, the market will be out of equilibrium, and there will be excess supply. At any price below E_0, the quantity demanded will exceed the quantity supplied, the market will be out of equilibrium, and there will be excess demand.

it up. When the weight is at rest, it is in equilibrium, with the two forces just offsetting each other. If someone pulls the weight down a little bit, the force of the spring will be greater than the force of gravity, and the weight will spring up. In the absence of any further interventions, the weight will bob back and forth and eventually return to its equilibrium position.

An economic equilibrium is established in the same way. At the equilibrium price, consumers get precisely the quantity of the good they are willing to buy at that price, and producers sell precisely the quantity they are willing to sell at that price. The market clears. To emphasize this condition, economists sometimes refer to the equilibrium price as the **market clearing price**. In equilibrium, neither producers nor consumers have any incentive to change.

But consider the price of $1.00 in Figure 3.13. There is no equilibrium quantity here. First find $1.00 on the vertical axis. Now look across to find point A on the supply curve, and read down to the horizontal axis; point A tells you that a price of $1.00, firms want to supply 34 million candy bars. Now look at point B on the demand curve. Point B shows that at a price of $1.00 consumers want to buy only 13 million candy bars. Like the weight bobbing on a spring however, this market will work its way back to equilibrium in the following way. At a price of $1.00, there is **excess supply.** As producers discover that they cannot sell as much as they would like at this price, some of them will lower their prices slightly, hoping to take business from other producers. When one producer lowers prices, his competitors will have to respond, for fear that they will end up unable to sell their goods. As prices come down, consumers will also buy more, and so on until the market reaches the equilibrium price and quantity.

Similarly, assume that the price is lower than $0.75, say $0.50. At the lower price, there is **excess demand:** individuals want to buy 30 million candy bars (point C), while firms want to produce only 5 million (point D). Consumers unable to purchase all they want will offer to pay a bit more; other consumers, afraid of having to do without, will match these higher bids or exceed them. As prices start to increase, suppliers will also have a greater incentive to produce more. Again the market will tend toward the equilibrium point.

To repeat for emphasis: at equilibrium, no purchaser and no supplier has an incentive to change the price or quantity. In competitive market economies, actual prices tend to be the equilibrium prices at which demand equals supply. This is called the **law of supply and demand.** Note: this law does not mean that at every moment of time the price is precisely at the intersection of the demand and supply curves. Like the weight on a spring described above, the market may bounce around a little bit when it is in the process of adjusting. What the law of supply and demand does say is that when a market is out of equilibrium, there are predictable forces for change.

USING DEMAND AND SUPPLY CURVES

The concepts of demand and supply curves—and market equilibrium as the intersection of demand and supply curves—constitute the economist's basic model of demand and supply. This model has proved to be extremely useful. It helps explain why the price of a given commodity is high, and that of some other commodity is low. It also helps *predict* the consequences of certain changes. Its predictions can then be tested against what actually happens. One of the reasons that the model is so useful is that it gives reasonably accurate predictions.

Figure 3.14 repeats the demand and supply curve for candy bars. But assume now that sugar becomes more expensive. As a result, at each price the amount of candy firms are willing to supply is reduced. The supply curve shifts to the left, as in panel A. There will be a new equilibrium, at a higher price and a lower quantity of candy consumed.

Alternatively, assume that Americans become more health conscious, and as a result, at each price fewer candy bars are consumed: the demand curve shifts to the left, as shown in panel B. Again, there will be a new equilibrium, at a lower price and a lower quantity of candy consumed.

This illustrates how changes in observed prices can be related either to shifts in the demand curve or to shifts in the supply curve. To take a different example, when the war in Kuwait interrupted the supply of oil from the Middle East in 1990, the supply curve shifted. The model predicted the result: an increase in the price of oil. This increase was the natural outcome of the law of supply and demand.

Figure 3.14

USING SUPPLY AND DEMAND CURVES TO PREDICT PRICE CHANGES

Initially the market for candy bars is in equilibrium at E_0. An increase in the cost of sugar shifts the supply curve to the left, as shown in panel A. At the new equilibrium, E_1, the price is higher and the quantity consumed is lower. A shift in taste away from candy results in a leftward shift in the demand curve as shown in panel B. At the new equilibrium, E_1, the price and the quantity consumed are lower.

CONSENSUS ON THE DETERMINATION OF PRICES

The law of supply and demand plays such a prominent role in economics that there is a joke about teaching a parrot to be an economist simply by training it to say "supply and demand." That prices are determined by the law of supply and demand is one of the most long-standing and widely accepted ideas of economists. *In competitive markets, prices are determined by the law of supply and demand. Shifts in the demand and supply curves lead to changes in the equilibrium price. Similar principles apply to the labor and capital markets. The price for labor is the wage, and the price for capital is the interest rate; thus in later chapters we can use the same principles of demand and supply developed in this chapter to study labor and capital markets.*

FUNDAMENTALS OF DEMAND, SUPPLY, AND PRICE 3

THE MARKET CLEARS AT THE EQUILIBRIUM PRICE

The price at which the quantity demanded and the quantity supplied are equal is the equilibrium price. At the equilibrium price, consumers are able to obtain the quantity they wish to purchase and firms are able to sell the quantity they wish to produce. When the market clears, there are no shortages or surpluses. The law of supply and demand allows us to predict how price and quantity will change in response to shifts in the demand and supply curves.

Price, Value, and Cost

To an economist, price is what is given in exchange for a good or service. Price, in this sense, is determined by the forces of supply and demand. Adam Smith, often thought of as the founder of modern economics, called our notion of price "value in exchange," and contrasted it to the notion of "value in use":

> The things which have the greatest value in use have frequently little or no value in exchange; and on the contrary, those which have the greatest value in exchange have frequently little or no value in use. Nothing is more useful than water: but it will purchase scarce any thing; scarce any thing can be had in exchange for it. A diamond, on the contrary, has scarce any value in use; but a very great quantity of other goods may frequently be had in exchange for it.[2]

The law of supply and demand can help to explain the diamond-water paradox and many similar examples where "value in use" is very different from "value in

---

[2]*The Wealth of Nations* (1776), Book One, Chapter IV.

Internet Connection

THE DEMAND AND SUPPLY IN THE OIL MARKET

The U.S. Energy Information Administration (EIA) has a slide presentation at www.eia.doe.gov/emeu/25opec/anniversary.html that illustrates some of the major ways that the energy price increases during the 1970s affected the types of cars Americans bought and how they heated their homes.

exchange." Figure 3.15 presents a demand and a supply curve for water. Individuals are willing to pay a high price for the water they need to live, as illustrated by point *A* on the demand curve. But above some quantity, *B*, people will pay almost nothing more for additional water. In most of the inhabited parts of the world, water is readily available, so it is supplied in plentiful quantities at low prices. Thus, the supply curve of water intersects the demand curve to the right of *B*, as in the figure—hence, the low equilibrium price. (Of course, in the desert the water supply may be very limited and the price, as a result, very high.)

To an economist, the observations that the price of diamonds is high and the price of water is low are statements about supply and demand conditions. They say nothing about whether diamonds are "more important" or "better" than water. In Adam Smith's terms, they are not statements about value in use.

Price is related to the *marginal* value of an object: that is, the value of an additional unit of the object. Water has a low price not because the *total* value of water is low—it is obviously high, since we could not live without it—but because the marginal value, what we would be willing to pay to be able to drink one more glass of water a year, is low.

Just as economists take care to distinguish between the words "price" and "value," so they also distinguish the *price* of an object (what it sells for) from its *cost* (the expense of making the object). This is another crucial distinction in economics. The costs of producing a good affect the price at which firms are willing to supply that good. An increase in the costs of production will normally cause prices to rise. And in the competitive model, *in equilibrium,* the price of an object will normally equal its (marginal) cost of production (including the amount needed to pay a firm's owner to stay in business rather than seek some other form of employment). But there are important cases—as we will see in later chapters—where price does not equal cost.

As we think about the relationship of price and cost, it is interesting to consider the case of a good in fixed supply, such as land. Normally, land is something that cannot be produced, so its cost of production can be considered infinite (though sometimes land can be produced, as when Chicago filled in part of Lake Michigan to expand its lake shore). Yet there is still an equilibrium price of land—where the demand for land is equal to its (fixed) supply.

Figure 3.15

SUPPLY AND DEMAND FOR WATER

Point *A* shows that people are willing to pay a relatively high price for the first few units of water. But to the right of *B*, people have plenty of water already and are not willing to pay much for an additional amount. The price of water will be determined at the point where the supply curve crosses the demand curve. In most cases, the resulting price is extremely low.

PRICE, VALUE, AND COST

Review and Practice

SUMMARY

1. An individual's demand curve gives the quantity demanded of a good at each possible price. It normally slopes down, which means that the person demands a greater quantity of the good at lower prices and a lesser quantity at higher prices.
2. The market demand curve gives the total quantity of a good demanded by all individuals in an economy at each price. As the price rises, demand falls, both because each person demands less of the good and because some people exit the market.
3. A firm's supply curve gives the amount of a good the firm is willing to supply at each price. It is normally upward sloping, which means that firms supply a greater quantity of the good at higher prices and a lesser quantity at lower prices.
4. The market supply curve gives the total quantity of a good that all firms in the economy are willing to produce at each price. As the price rises, supply rises, both because each firm supplies more of the good and because some additional firms enter the market.
5. The law of supply and demand says that in competitive markets, the equilibrium price is that price at which quantity demanded equals quantity supplied. It is represented on a graph by the intersection of the demand and supply curves.
6. A demand curve shows *only* the relationship between quantity demanded and price. Changes in tastes, in demographic factors, in income, in the prices of other goods, in information, in the availability of credit, or in expectations are reflected in a shift of the entire demand curve.
7. A supply curve shows *only* the relationship between quantity supplied and price. Changes in factors such as technology, the prices of inputs, the natural environment, expectations, or the availability of credit are reflected in a shift of the entire supply curve.
8. It is important to distinguish movements along a demand curve from shifts in the demand curve, and movements along a supply curve from shifts in the supply curve.

KEY TERMS

price
demand
demand curve
market demand curve
substitutes
complements
demographic effects
supply
supply curve
market supply curve
equilibrium price
equilibrium quantity
equilibrium
market clearing price
excess supply
excess demand
law of supply and demand

REVIEW QUESTIONS

1. Why does an individual's demand curve normally slope down? Why does a market demand curve normally slope down?
2. Why does a firm's supply curve normally slope up? Why does a market supply curve normally slope up?
3. What is the significance of the point where supply and demand curves intersect?
4. Explain why, if the price of a good is above the equilibrium price, the forces of supply and demand will tend to push the price toward equilibrium. Explain why, if the price of the good is below the equilibrium price, the market will tend to adjust toward equilibrium.
5. Name some factors that could shift the demand curve out to the right.
6. Name some factors that could shift the supply curve in to the left.

PROBLEMS

1. Imagine a company lunchroom that sells pizza by the slice. Using the following data, plot the points and graph

the demand and supply curves. What is the equilibrium price and quantity? Find a price at which excess demand would exist and a price at which excess supply would exist, and plot them on your diagram.

Price per slice	Demand (number of slices)	Supply (number of slices)
$1	420	0
$2	210	100
$3	140	140
$4	105	160
$5	84	170

2. Suppose a severe drought hits the sugarcane crop. Predict how this will affect the equilibrium price and quantity in the market for sugar and the market for honey. Draw supply and demand diagrams to illustrate your answers.
3. Imagine that a new invention allows each mine worker to mine twice as much coal. Predict how this will affect the equilibrium price and quantity in the market for coal and the market for heating oil. Draw supply and demand diagrams to illustrate your answers.
4. Americans' tastes have shifted away from beef and toward chicken. Predict how this change has affected the equilibrium price and quantity in the market for beef, the market for chicken, and the market for roadside hamburger stands. Draw supply and demand diagrams to illustrate your answers.
5. During the 1970s, the postwar baby boomers reached working age, and it became more acceptable for married women with children to work. Predict how this increase in the number of workers is likely to affect the equilibrium wage and quantity of employment. Draw supply and demand curves to illustrate your answers.
6. In 2001, Europeans became very concerned about what is called mad cow disease, and thus about the dangers posed by eating contaminated meat. What would this concern do to the demand curve for beef? to the demand curves for chicken and fish? to the equilibrium price of beef, chicken, and fish?

   Mad cow disease is spread by feeding cows food that contains parts from infected animals. Presumably the reason why cows are fed this food is that doing so is cheaper than relying exclusively on grain. What is the consequence for the supply curve of beef of restricting feed to grain? What are the consequences for the price of beef (a) if the new restrictions fail to restore confidence in beef and (b) if the new restrictions succeed in restoring confidence so that the demand curve returns to its original position?

   At about the same time in Europe, there was an outbreak of hoof-and-mouth disease; to stop the spread of the disease, large numbers of cattle were killed. What does this do to the supply curve of beef? to the equilibrium price of beef?
7. Many advanced industrialized countries subsidize farmers. Assume that the effect of the subsidy is to shift the supply curve of agricultural products by farmers in the advanced industrialized countries to the right. Why might less-developed countries be unhappy with such policies?
8. Farm output is extremely sensitive to the weather. In 1988, the midwestern region of the United States experienced one of the worst droughts ever recorded; corn production fell by 35 percent, wheat production by more than 10 percent, and oat and barley production by more than 40 percent. What do you suppose happened to the prices of these commodities?

   These grains are an input into the production of cattle. The higher cost of grain led many ranchers to slaughter their cattle earlier. What do you think happened to the price of beef in the short run? In the intermediate run?

   Why did the drought in the Midwest lead to increased prices for vegetables and fruits?
9. Suppose that there are 1,000 one-bedroom apartments in a small town and that this number is fixed. The table gives the quantity demand in the market for one-bedroom apartments.

Price (Rent per month)	Demand (Apartment units)
$500	1,600
$600	1,400
$700	1,200
$800	1,000
$900	800
$1,000	600
$1,200	400

(a) What is the equilibrium rental for a one-bedroom apartment?
(b) Suppose 200 new one-bedroom apartments are constructed. What happens to the equilibrium rent?
(c) Suppose more people move into the town, increasing the demand for one-bedroom apartments by 200 units at each price. What is the new equilibrium price? (Assume the supply remains fixed at 1,200 units.)

10. Suppose a town decides to give a $100 subsidy to each renter to help with rent payments. Thus if initially the rent had been $1,000, with the $100 subsidy the out-of-pocket cost to the renter of a one-bedroom apartment is only $900. Using the data from Problem 9, answer each of the following questions.
(a) Using the data from Problem 9, draw the demand curve before the subsidy. How does this subsidy affect the demand for one-bedroom apartments? Draw the new demand curve after the subsidy is introduced.
(b) If the supply of apartments is fixed at 1,200 units, what is the equilibrium price *before* the subsidy? What is the equilibrium price *after* the subsidy?
(c) At the new equilibrium price, what is the out-of-pocket cost to a renter for a one-bedroom apartment?
(d) Have renters benefited from the town's rent subsidy? Have apartment owners (suppliers)?

Learning Goals

In this chapter, you will learn

1. What is meant by the concept of elasticity
2. How elasticity helps explain the effects on prices and quantities of shifts in demand and supply
3. How government policies such as rent control or agricultural price supports that interfere with market outcomes lead to shortages and surpluses

Chapter 4

USING DEMAND AND SUPPLY

Why are doctors, on average, paid more than lawyers? And why are lawyers paid more than schoolteachers? Why does your economics professor probably make more than your literature professor? And why has the wage gap between college graduates and those with only a high school education widened in recent years? The concepts of demand and supply developed in the previous chapter can help us answer these questions. Moreover, these concepts help us predict what will happen if the government increases the tax on cigarettes or the tax on gasoline. But economists are usually interested in more specific predictions. They want to know how much the tax on gasoline would need to be raised if the goal is to lower gasoline consumption by, say, 10 percent, or how much a frost in Florida that reduces the orange crop will increase the price of orange juice.

In this chapter, we develop some of the concepts needed to make these sorts of predictions. In addition, we examine what happens when governments intervene with the workings of competitive markets. High rents and expensive food may seem to block poor people's access to adequate housing and nutrition, farmers may feel that the prices of their crops are too low, and textile workers may object to competing with laborers producing similar goods in low-wage countries. Political pressures are constantly brought to bear on government to intervene on behalf of groups that feel disadvantaged by the workings of the market. In the second part of this chapter, we track some of the consequences of these political interventions.

The Price Elasticity of Demand

To predict the effects of a tax on gasoline on how much people drive or of a frost on the price of orange juice, we must start by asking what substitutes exist for the good in question. If the price of orange juice rises, consumers have an incentive to buy less orange juice and to buy apple juice, cranberry juice, or any one of a number of other drinks instead. If a new tax pushes up the price of gasoline, drivers likewise have an incentive to reduce their consumption of gas; but doing so may be difficult for those who have to drive to work in cars with conventional engines. Some may be able to ride the bus, but many will be hard-pressed to find an alternative means of transportation. And switching to an electric or hybrid vehicle can be costly.

As these examples illustrate, substitutes exist for almost every good or service, but substitution will be more difficult for some goods and services than for others. When substitution is difficult, an increase in the price of a good will not cause the quantity demanded to decrease by much, and a decrease in the price will not cause the quantity demanded to increase much. In terms of the demand curves we discussed in Chapter 3, the demand curve for a good with few substitutes will be relatively steep: changes in price do not cause very large changes in the quantity demanded.

When substitution is easy, as in the case of orange juice, an increase in price may lead to a large decrease in the quantity demanded. Ice cream is another example of a good with many close substitutes. A price increase for ice cream means that frozen yogurt, gelato, and similar products become relatively less expensive, and the demand for ice cream would thus significantly decrease. The demand curve for a good with many substitutes will be relatively flat: changes in price cause large changes in the quantity demanded.

For many purposes, economists need to be precise about how steep or how flat the demand curve is. They therefore use the concept of the **price elasticity of demand** (for short, the price elasticity or the elasticity of demand), which is defined as the percentage change in the quantity demanded divided by the percentage change in price. In mathematical terms,

$$\text{elasticity of demand} = \frac{\text{percentage change in quantity demanded}}{\text{percentage change in price}}.$$

If the quantity demanded changes 8 percent in response to a 2 percent change in price, then the elasticity of demand is 4.

(Price elasticities of demand are really *negative* numbers; that is, when the price increases, quantities demanded are reduced. But the convention is to simply give the elasticity's absolute value with the understanding that it is negative.)

It is easiest to calculate the elasticity of demand when there is just a 1 percent change in price. Then the elasticity of demand is just the percentage change in the quantity demanded. In the telescoped portion of Figure 4.1A, we see that increasing the price of orange juice from $2.00 a gallon to $2.02—a 1 percent increase in price—reduces the demand from 100 million gallons to 98 million, a 2 percent decline. So the price elasticity of demand for ice cream is 2.

By contrast, assume that the price of gas increases from $2.00 a gallon to $2.02 (again a 1 percent increase in price), as shown in the telescoped portion of Figure 4.1B. This reduces demand from 100 million gallons per year to 99.8 million. Demand has gone down by 0.2 percent, so the price elasticity of demand is therefore 0.2. Larger values for price elasticity indicate that demand is more sensitive to changes in price. Smaller values indicate that demand is less sensitive to price changes.

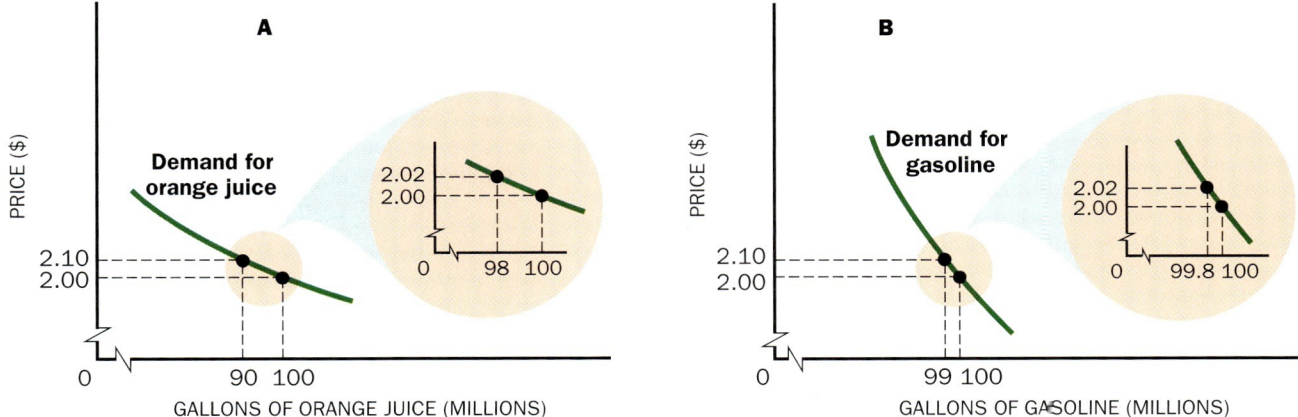

Figure 4.1

ELASTIC VERSUS INELASTIC DEMAND CURVES

Panel A shows a hypothetical demand curve for orange juice. Note that the quantity demanded changes greatly with fairly small price changes, indicating that demand for orange juice is elastic. The telescoped portion of the demand curve shows that a 1 percent rise in price leads to a 2 percent fall in quantity demanded. Panel B shows a hypothetical demand curve for gasoline. Note that the quantity demanded changes very little, regardless of changes in price, indicating that demand for gas is inelastic. The telescoped portion of the demand curve shows that a 1 percent rise in price leads to a 0.2 percent fall in quantity demanded.

PRICE ELASTICITY AND REVENUES

The revenue received by a firm in selling a good is its price times the quantity sold. We can write this definition in a simple equation. Letting R denote revenues, p price, and Q quantity:

$$R = pQ.$$

Thus when price goes up by 1 percent, the effect on revenues depends on the magnitude of the decrease in quantity. If quantity decreases by more than 1 percent, then total revenues decrease; by less than 1 percent, they increase.

We can express this result in terms of the concept of price elasticity. When the elasticity of demand is greater than 1, the change in quantity more than offsets the change in prices; we say that the demand for that good is **relatively elastic,** or *sensitive* to price changes, and revenues decrease as price increases and increase as price decreases. For example, the demand for different brands of personal computers is judged to be relatively elastic.

In the case in which the price elasticity is 1, the decrease in the quantity demanded just offsets the increase in the price, so price increases have no effect on revenues. This is called **unitary elasticity.** Many basic food products and entertainment activities, such as going to the movies, are considered to have unitary elasticities of demand. If the price elasticity is less than 1, then a 1 percent increase in the price of a good will reduce the quantity demanded by less than 1 percent. Since demand falls little when elasticities are in this range, between 0 and 1, price increases for such goods will increase revenues. And price decreases will decrease revenues. We say the demand for these goods is **relatively inelastic,** or *insensitive* to price changes.

Business firms must pay attention to the price elasticity of demand for their products. Suppose a cement producer, the only one in town, is considering a 1 percent increase in price. The firm hires an economist to estimate the elasticity of demand so that it will know what will happen to sales after the increase. The economist tells the firm that its demand elasticity is 2. This means that if the price of cement rises by 1 percent, the quantity sold will decline by 2 percent.

The firm's executives will not be pleased by the findings. To see why, assume that initially the price of cement was $1,000 per ton, and 100,000 tons were sold. To calculate revenues, you multiply the price times the quantity sold. So initially revenues were $1,000 × 100,000 = $100 million. With a 1 percent increase, the price will be $1,010. If the elasticity of demand is 2, then a 1 percent price increase results in a 2 percent decrease in the quantity sold: sales drop to 98,000 tons. Revenues are down to $98.98 million ($1,010 × 98,000), a fall of just slightly over 1 percent. Because of the high elasticity, this cement firm's price *increase* leads to a *decrease* in revenues.

The price elasticity of demand works the same way for price decreases. Suppose the cement producer decided to lower the price of cement 1 percent, to $990. With an elasticity of demand of 2, sales would then increase 2 percent, to 102,000 tons. Thus, revenues would *increase* to $100,980,000 ($990 × 102,000)—that is, by a bit less than 1 percent.

There are two extreme cases that deserve attention. One is that of a flat demand curve, a curve that is perfectly horizontal. We say that such a demand curve is perfectly elastic, or has **infinite elasticity,** since even a slight increase in the price results in demand dropping to zero. The demand curve facing a firm that produces computer memory chips is perfectly elastic; if the manufacturer tried to charge a slightly higher price for its chips, sales would fall to zero as buyers would simply buy their memory chips elsewhere. The other extreme case is that of a demand curve that is perfectly vertical. We say that such a demand curve is perfectly inelastic, or has **zero elasticity,** since whatever the price, demand remains the same. The rabid sports fan's demand for a Super Bowl ticket may in effect be perfectly inelastic; no matter how much it costs, the fan will buy a ticket. Table 4.1 summarizes the different cases that we have discussed, together with some illustrative examples of goods with differing elasticities of demand.

The Determinants of the Elasticity of Demand

In our earlier discussion, we noted one of the important determinants of the elasticity of demand: the availability of substitutes. There are, in turn, two important determinants of the degree of substitutability: the relative price of the good consumed and the length of time it takes to make an adjustment.

When the price of a commodity is low, and its consumption is high, a variety of substitutes exist. Figure 4.2 illustrates the case for aluminum. When the price of aluminum is low, it is used as a food wrap (aluminum foil), in containers for canned

Figure 4.2

CHANGING ELASTICITY ALONG A DEMAND CURVE

Near point A, where the price is high, the demand curve is quite steep and inelastic. In the area of the demand curve near B, the demand curve is very flat and elastic.

Table 4.1

PRICE ELASTICITY OF DEMAND

Elasticity	Description	Effect on Quantity Demanded of 1% Increase in Price	Effect on Revenues of 1% Increase in Price	Examples
Zero	Perfectly inelastic (vertical demand curve)	Zero	Increased by 1%	Superbowl Tickets
Between 0 and 1	Inelastic	Reduced by less than 1%	Increased by less than 1%	gasoline
1	Unitary elasticity	Reduced by 1%	Unchanged	
Greater than 1	Elastic	Reduced by more 1%	Reduced; the greater the elasticity, the more revenue is reduced	Brands of PCs
Infinite	Perfectly elastic (horizontal demand curve)	Reduced to zero	Reduced to zero	Brands of memory chips

goods, and in airplane frames because it is lightweight. As the price increases, customers seek out substitutes. At first, substitutes are easy to find, and the demand for the product is greatly reduced. For example, plastic wrap frequently can be used instead of aluminum foil. As the price rises still further, tin replaces aluminum for cans. At very high prices, say near point A, aluminum is used only where its properties are essential, such as in airplane frames. At this point, it may take a *huge* price increase before some other material becomes an economical substitute.

A second important determinant of the elasticity of demand is time. Because it is always easier to find substitutes and to make other adjustments when a longer time is available to make them, the elasticity of demand is normally larger in the *long run*—in the period in which all adjustments can be made—than it is in the *short run*, when at least some adjustments cannot be made. Figure 4.3 illustrates the difference in shape between short-run and long-run demand curves for gasoline.

The sharp increase in oil prices in the 1970s beautifully exemplifies this point. The short-run price elasticity of gasoline was 0.2 (a 1 percent increase in price led to only a 0.2 percent decrease in quantity demanded), while the long-run elasticity was 0.7 or more; the short-run elasticity of fuel oil was 0.2, and the long-run elasticity was 1.2. In the short run, consumers were stuck with their old gas-guzzling cars, their drafty houses, and their old fuel-wasting habits. In the long run, however, consumers bought smaller cars, became used to houses kept at slightly lower

Figure 4.3

ELASTICITY OF DEMAND OVER TIME

Demand curves tend to be inelastic in the short run, where there is little time to adapt to price changes, but more elastic in the long run.

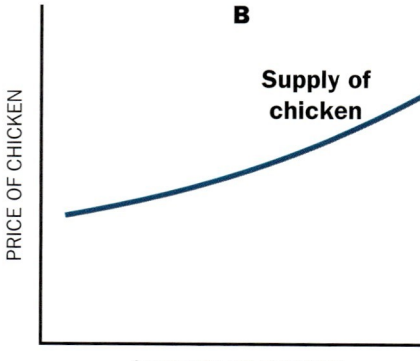

Figure 4.4

DIFFERING ELASTICITIES OF SUPPLY

Panel A shows a supply curve for oil. It is inelastic: the quantity supplied increases only a small amount with a rise in price. Panel B shows a supply curve for chicken. It is elastic: the quantity supplied increases substantially with a rise in price.

temperatures, installed better insulation in their homes, and turned to alternative energy sources. The long-run demand curve was therefore much more elastic (flat) than the short-run curve. Indeed, the long-run elasticity turned out to be much larger than anticipated.

The duration of "the long run" will vary from product to product. In some cases, adjustments can occur rapidly; in other cases, they are very gradual. As old gas-guzzlers wore out, they were replaced with fuel-efficient compact cars. As furnaces broke, they were replaced with more efficient ones. New homes are now constructed with better insulation, so that gradually, over time, the fraction of houses that are well insulated is increasing.

Some of these changes are reversible: in the 1990s, in response to low gas prices, fuel-efficient cars were replaced by gas-guzzling sport utility vehicles (SUVs). But when higher prices induce innovations—for example, manufacturers of cars discover ways of increasing mileage per gallon—then the benefits of those innovations remain even when prices subsequently fall.

The Price Elasticity of Supply

Supply curves normally slope upward. Like demand curves, they are steep in some cases and flat in others. The degree of steepness reflects sensitivity to price changes. A steep supply curve, like the one for oil in Figure 4.4A, indicates that a large change in price generates only a small change in the quantity firms want to supply. A flatter curve, like the one for chicken in Figure 4.4B, indicates that a small change in price generates a large change in supply. Economists have developed a precise way of representing the sensitivity of supply to prices in a way that parallels the one already introduced for demand. The **price elasticity of supply** is defined as the percentage change in quantity supplied divided by the percentage change in price (or the percentage change in quantity supplied corresponding to a price change of 1 percent):

$$\text{Elasticity of supply} = \frac{\text{percentage change in quantity supplied}}{\text{percentage change in price}}.$$

The elasticity of supply of oil is low—an increase in the price of oil will not have a significant effect on the total supply. The elasticity of supply of chicken is high, as President Richard Nixon found out when he imposed price controls in August 1971. When the price of chicken was forced almost 10 percent below the market equilibrium price, farmers found that producing and selling chickens at that price was simply unprofitable; there was a large decrease in the quantity supplied, and huge shortages resulted.

As is the case with demand, if a 1 percent increase in price results in more than a 1 percent increase in supply, we say the supply curve is elastic. If a 1 percent increase in price results in less than a 1 percent increase in supply, the supply curve is inelastic. In the extreme case of a vertical supply curve—where the amount supplied does not depend at all on price—the curve is said to be perfectly inelastic, or to have *zero*

International Perspective
COMPARING REACTIONS TO THE OIL PRICE SHOCK OF 2000

When gasoline prices soared in the fall of 2000, in response to the increase in oil prices, people in Great Britain and other countries in Europe took to the streets. Truckers blocked roads and entrances to refineries. There was a massive political outcry. One might have thought, given Americans' greater dependence on oil (Americans use far more gasoline per capita) and given the far smaller *percentage* increase in prices in Europe (since taxes constitute a far larger fraction of the total price), that the outcry would have been louder in the United States. But this brings home an important point: the consequences of the massive price increase depend not only on the level of consumption but also on consumers' ability to absorb the price increase. Europeans already had cut their use of oil down to low levels, because prices of gasoline were already so high. Hence, the cost to them of a further increase in price may be far greater than to individuals who can easily find ways of conserving on the use of oil.

For instance, Americans can easily conserve on gasoline by switching from high-consuming sports utility vehicles, many of which get as few as 15 miles to the gallon, to efficient diesel cars, which can get 50 miles or more to the gallon. Americans can conserve on fuel oil by keeping the temperature in their homes at 68 degrees rather than 72 degrees. But what are Europeans to do, when they already drive small, fuel-efficient cars and already keep their homes at colder temperatures?

These ideas can be related to demand curves. The elasticity of demand is the percentage reduction in the demand resulting from a 1 percent increase in the price. When the price is very low, the demand curve is very elastic; that is, the elasticity of demand is high because there are many ways of conserving on the good (here, oil). When the price is very high, the demand curve is very inelastic; that is, the elasticity of demand is very low because all of the obvious methods of conservation have already been employed.

Truckers in Newcastle, England, protested high prices for fuel in September 2000.

Figure 4.5

CHANGING ELASTICITY ALONG A SUPPLY CURVE

When output is low and many machines are idle, a small change in price can lead to a large increase in quantity produced, so the supply curve is flat and elastic. When output is high and all machines are working close to their limit, it takes a very large price change to induce even a small change in output; the supply curve is steep and inelastic.

elasticity; and in the extreme case of a horizontal supply curve, the curve is said to be perfectly elastic, or to have *infinite* elasticity.

Table 4.2 summarizes the different cases for the price elasticity of supply. Paintings by Rembrandt, who died in 1669, and new songs by John Lennon, who died in 1980, have a zero elasticity of supply because no more original Rembrandts can be produced or Lennon songs written. The supply elasticity of labor is estimated to be low; a 1 percent increase in wages leads to a less than 1 percent increase in the total supply of labor. The elasticity of some agricultural crops, such as spinach, is estimated to be greater than 1 because resources (mainly land) used for growing spinach can relatively easily be switched to growing other crops if the price of spinach falls. Finally, the supply of a music CD is close to being infinitely elastic. While producing a greater number of different CDs may require that new artists be developed, new songs be written, and new recording studios be built, a CD, once recorded, can easily be copied at little additional cost.

Just as the demand elasticity varies at different points of the demand curve, so too the supply elasticity varies at different points on the supply curve. Figure 4.5 shows a typical supply curve in manufacturing—perhaps a semiconductor manufacturer. At very low prices, the semiconductor plant is just producing enough to cover its operating costs. Some plants may shut down. Under these circumstances, a small increase in the price of semiconductors elicits a large increase in supply. The supply curve is relatively flat (elastic). But eventually, the plant will reach full capacity, as the company uses three shifts of workers a day to run it around the clock. At this point, it may be very hard to increase supply further, so

Table 4.2

PRICE ELASTICITY OF SUPPLY

Elasticity	Description	Effect on Quantity Supplied of 1% Increase in Price	Examples
Zero	Perfectly inelastic (vertical supply curve)	Zero	Works by Rembrandt
Between 0 and 1	Inelastic	Increased by less than 1%	Labor
1	Unitary elasticity	Increased by 1%	
Greater than 1	Elastic	Increased by more than 1%	Spinach
Infinite	Perfectly elastic (horizontal supply curve)	Infinite increase	A CD recording

the supply curve becomes close to vertical (inelastic). That is, however much the price increases, the supply will not change very much.

Short Run Versus Long Run Economists distinguish between the responsiveness of supply to price in the short run and in the long run, just as they do with demand. Here, too, the long-run elasticity is greater than the short-run elasticity. We define the short-run supply curve as the supply response *given the current stock of machines* and *buildings*. The long-run supply curve assumes that firms can adjust the stock of machines and buildings.

Farm crops are a typical example of a good whose supply in the short run is not very sensitive to changes in price; that is, the supply curve is steep (inelastic). After farmers have done their spring planting, they are committed to a certain level of production. If the price of their crop goes up, they cannot go back and plant more. If the price falls, they are stuck with the crop they have. In this case, the supply curve is relatively close to vertical, as illustrated by the steeper curve in Figure 4.6.

The long-run supply curve for many crops, in contrast, is very flat (elastic). A relatively small change in price can lead to a large change in the quantity supplied. A small increase in the price of soybeans relative to the price of corn may induce many farmers to shift their planting from corn and other crops to soybeans, generating a large increase in the quantity of soybeans. This is illustrated in Figure 4.6 by the flatter curve.

Figure 4.6
ELASTICITY OF SUPPLY OVER TIME

Supply curves may be inelastic in the short run and very elastic in the long run, as in the case of agricultural crops like soybeans.

Wrap-Up

ELASTICITY

Price elasticity of demand: the percentage change in the quantity of a good demanded as a result of a 1 percent increase (change) in the price charged. When elasticity is low, price changes have little effect on demand. When elasticity is high, price changes have a large effect on demand.

Price elasticity of supply: the percentage change in the quantity of a good supplied as a result of a 1 percent increase (change) in the price charged. When elasticity is low, price changes have little effect on supply. When elasticity is high, price changes have a large effect on supply.

Using Demand and Supply Elasticities

When the demand curve for a good such as beef shifts to the right—when, for instance, beef becomes more popular so that at each price the demand is greater—there is an increase in both the equilibrium price of beef and the quantity demanded, or consumed. Similarly, when the supply curve for a good such as corn shifts to the left—because, for instance, of a drought that hurt the year's crop so that at each price farmers supply

Figure 4.7

ELASTICITY OF DEMAND AND SUPPLY CURVES: THE NORMAL CASES

Normally, shifts in the demand curve will be reflected in changes in both price and quantity, as seen in panels A and B. When the supply curve is highly elastic, shifts in the demand curve will result mainly in changes in quantities; if it is relatively inelastic, shifts in the demand curve will result mainly in price changes. Likewise, shifts in the supply curve will be reflected in changes in both price and quantity, as seen in panels C and D. If the demand curve is highly elastic, shifts in the supply curve will result mainly in changes in quantities; if it is relatively inelastic, shifts in the supply curve will result mainly in price changes.

less—there is an increase in the equilibrium price of corn and a decrease in quantity. Knowing that the shifts in the demand or supply curve will lead to an adjustment in both price *and* quantity is helpful, but it is even more useful to know whether most of the impact of a change will be on price or on quantity. To make this determination, we have to consider the price elasticity of both the demand and supply curves.

Figure 4.7 illustrates the typical range of outcomes. If the supply curve is highly elastic (approaching the horizontal, as in panel A), shifts in the demand curve will be reflected more in changes in quantity than in price. If the supply curve is *relatively* inelastic (approaching the vertical, as in panel B), shifts in the demand curve will be reflected more in changes in price than in quantity. If the demand curve is highly elastic (approaching the horizontal, as in panel C), shifts in the supply curve will be reflected more in changes in quantity than in price. Finally, if the demand curve is *relatively* inelastic (approaching the vertical, as in panel D), shifts in the supply curve will be reflected more in changes in price than in quantity.

The extreme cases can be easily seen by extending the graphs in Figure 4.7. If one tilts the supply curve in panel A to be completely flat (perfectly elastic), a shift in the demand curve will have no effect on price. If one tilts the supply curve in panel B to be vertical (perfectly inelastic), a shift in the demand curve will have no effect on quantity.

Long-Run Versus Short-Run Adjustments Because demand and supply curves are likely to be less elastic (more vertical) in the short run than in the long run, shifts in the demand and supply curves are more likely to be reflected in price changes in the short run and in quantity changes in the long run. In fact, price increases in the short run signal firms to increase their production. Therefore, short-run price increases can be thought of as responsible for the output increases that occur in the long run.

Tax Policy and the Law of Supply and Demand For many questions of public policy, understanding the law of supply and demand is vital. One of the important ways economists use this law is in projecting the effect of taxes. Assume that the tax on a pack of cigarettes is increased by 10 cents, that the tax is imposed on cigarette manufacturers, and that all the companies try to pass on the cost increase to consumers by raising the price of a pack by 10 cents. At the higher price, fewer cigarettes will be consumed; the precise decrease depends on the price elasticity of demand. As demand falls, firms must reduce their price if demand is to equal supply; the size of the reduction depends on the price elasticity of supply. The new equilibrium is depicted in Figure 4.8A.

For firms to produce the same amount as before, they must receive 10 cents more per pack (which they pass on to the government). Thus, the supply curve is shifted up by 10 cents. Since the demand for cigarettes is relatively inelastic, this shift will result in a large increase in price and a relatively small decrease in quantity demanded.

When a tax on producers results in consumers' paying a higher price, economists say the tax is "passed on" or "shifted" to consumers. That the consumer bears the tax (even though it is collected from the producers) does not mean that the producers are "powerful" or have conspired together. It simply reflects the system of supply and demand. Note, too, that the price does not rise the full 10 cents. Producers receive slightly lower after-tax prices and therefore bear a small fraction of the tax burden.

A tax imposed on a good for which the demand is very elastic leads to a different result. Assume, for instance, that the government decides to tax cheddar cheese (but not other cheeses). Since many cheeses are similar to cheddar,

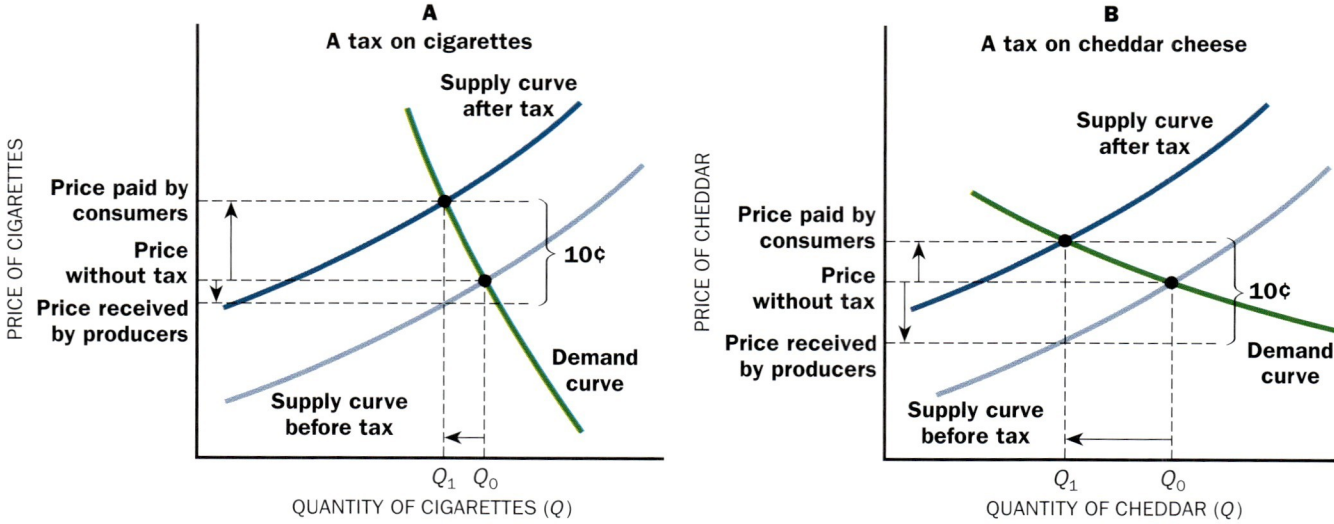

Figure 4.8

PASSING ALONG A TAX TO CONSUMERS

A tax on the output of an industry shifts the supply curve up by the amount of the tax. Panel A shows that if the demand curve is relatively inelastic, as it is for cigarettes, then most of the tax will be passed on to consumers in higher prices. Panel B shows that if the demand curve is relatively elastic, as it is for cheddar cheese, then most of the tax cannot be passed along to consumers in higher prices, and must instead be absorbed by producers.

the demand curve for cheddar cheese is very elastic. In this case, as Figure 4.8B makes clear, most of the tax is absorbed by the producer, who receives (after the tax is paid) a lower price. Production of cheddar cheese is reduced drastically as a consequence.

Shortages and Surpluses

In general, the law of supply and demand works so well in a developed modern economy that everyone can take it for granted. A buyer willing to pay the "market price"—the prevailing price of the good, determined by the intersection of demand and supply—can obtain almost any good or service. Similarly, if a seller of a good or service is willing to charge no more than the market price, she can always sell what she wants to.

When the price is set so that demand equals supply—so that any individual can get as much as he wants at that price, and any supplier can sell the amount she wants at that price—economists say that the market clears. But when the market does not clear, there are shortages or surpluses. To an economist, a **shortage** means that people would like to buy something but simply cannot find it for sale at the going price. A **surplus** means that sellers would like to sell their product, but they cannot sell as much of it as they would like at the going price. These cases that seem to illustrate the market's failure to work in fact often underscore most forcefully the importance of the law of supply and demand. The problem is that the "going price" is not the market equilibrium price.

Shortages and surpluses can be seen in the standard supply and demand diagrams shown in Figure 4.9. In both panels A and B, the market equilibrium price is p^*. In panel A, the going price, p_1, is below p^*. At this price, demand exceeds supply; you can see this by reading down to the horizontal axis. Demand is Q_d; supply is Q_s. The gap between the two points is the "shortage." The shortage forces consumers to scramble to get the limited supply available at the going price.

In panel B, the going price, p_1, is above p^*. At this price, demand is less than supply. Again we denote the demand by Q_d and the supply by Q_s. There is a surplus in the market of $Q_s - Q_d$. Now sellers are scrambling to find buyers.

At various times and for various goods, markets have not cleared. There have been shortages of apartments in New York; farm surpluses have plagued both western Europe and the United States; in 1973, a shortage of gasoline led to cars waiting in long lines at U.S. gas stations. Unemployment is a type of surplus, when people who want to work find that they cannot sell their labor services at the going wage.

In some markets, like the markets for agricultural goods, the adjustment of prices to shifts in the demand and supply curves tends to be very rapid. In other cases, such as in the housing market, the adjustments tend to be sluggish. When price adjustments are sluggish, shortages or surpluses may appear as prices adjust. Houses tend not to sell quickly, for instance, during periods of decreased demand, as that lower demand translates only slowly into lower housing prices.

 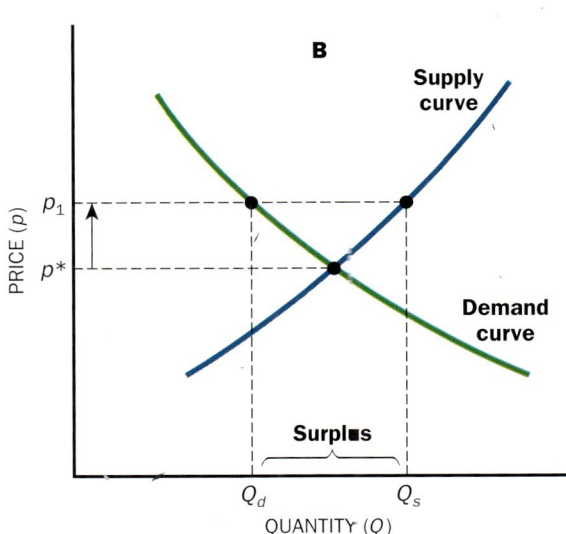

Figure 4.9
SHORTAGES AND SURPLUSES

In panel A, the actual price p_1 is below the market-clearing price p^*. At a price of p_1, quantity demanded exceeds quantity supplied, and a shortage exists. In panel B, the actual price p_1 is above the equilibrium price of p^*. In this case quantity supplied exceeds quantity demanded, and there is a surplus, or glut, in the market.

Even when the market is not adjusting quickly toward equilibrium, the analysis of market equilibrium is useful. It indicates the direction of the changes—if the equilibrium price exceeds the current price, prices will tend to rise. Moreover, the rate at which prices fall or rise is often related to the gap, at the going price, between the quantity demanded and the quantity supplied.

Interfering with the Law of Supply and Demand

The law of supply and demand, which governs how prices are determined, can produce results that some individuals or groups do not like. For example, a reduction in supply may lead to a higher equilibrium price for oil. The higher price reflects the law of supply and demand; the price increase gives firms and consumers an incentive to reduce their consumption of products, like gasoline, that are derived from oil. That such consequences are predictable does not make them welcome. Truck drivers, many of whom own and operate their own rigs, will be forced to spend more on fuel; in the short run, their demand is likely to be very inelastic (they can't suddenly improve their mileage or shorten the distance between their destinations). Some may be forced into bankruptcy. Low demand for unskilled labor may lead to very low wages for unskilled workers. An increase in the demand for apartments in

---

Thinking Like an Economist
INCENTIVES AND THE WINDOW TAX

The city of Bath in England predates the Roman occupation of the British Isles. Because naturally heated springs are located at its site, the Romans built baths there. During the late eighteenth and early nineteenth centuries, the city became a popular watering hole for the well-to-do.

One of the city's striking features is the beautiful brick used to build many of the buildings. But a visitor's attention is also caught by the number of houses with windows that appear to have been bricked up. The story behind them illustrates how taxation affects incentives and people's behavior.

In the eighteenth century, Bath imposed taxes on houses, windows, and male servants—a set of taxes called the *assessed taxes*. People with more windows (and more male servants) presumably had larger houses and were wealthier. Thus, a tax based on the number of windows was intended to force the wealthy to pay more than the poor.

The effect of the tax was to raise the cost of having a window. Anyone planning to build a new house would need to factor in that higher cost and could design their house with fewer windows. Those whose houses were already built might seem unable to avoid the tax—but individuals can be extremely inventive in finding ways to lower their consumption of goods whose price has risen. People living in houses could and did reduce their taxes by bricking up some of their windows. The reduced demand for windows caused by the tax explains the blank walls that replaced window frames in many homes in Bath.

New York City leads, in the short run (when supply is inelastic), to an increase in rents, a consequence again of the law of supply and demand—one that will please landlords and leave tenants angry.

In each of these cases, pressure from those who did not like the outcome of supply and demand has led government to act. The price of oil and natural gas was, at one time, regulated; minimum wage laws set a minimum limit on what employers can pay, even if the workers are willing to work for less; and rent control laws limit what landlords can charge. The concerns behind these interferences with the market are understandable, but the agitation for government action is based on two errors.

First, someone (or some group) was assigned responsibility for the change: the oil price rises were blamed on the oil companies, low wages on the employer, and rent increases on the landlord. As already explained, economists emphasize the role of anonymous market forces in determining these prices. After all, if landlords or oil companies are basically the same people today as they were last week, there must be some reason why they started charging different prices this week. To be sure, sometimes the price increase does result from producers' collusion. That was the case in 1973, when the oil-exporting countries got together to raise the price of oil. But far more often, the explanation lies in the market—as in 2004, when faster economic growth in the United States, Japan, and China led to an increase in the demand for oil that pushed up oil prices.

The second error is to forget that as powerful as governments may be, they can no more repeal the law of supply and demand than they can repeal the law of gravity. When they interfere with its workings, the forces of supply and demand will remain out of balance, with either excess supply or excess demand. Surpluses and shortages create problems of their own. Indeed, if shortages develop, individuals may find that instead of paying the high prices that triggered the government intervention, they cannot obtain the desired good at any price.

Two straightforward examples of government attempts to control the market are **price ceilings,** which impose a maximum price that can be charged for a product, and **price floors,** which impose a minimum price. Rent control laws are price ceilings, and minimum wage laws and agricultural price supports are price floors. A closer look at each will help highlight the perils of interfering with the law of supply and demand.

PRICE CEILINGS

Price ceilings—setting a maximum charge—are always tempting to governments because they seem an easy way to ensure that everyone will be able to afford a particular product. If the price ceiling is effective—that is, it is below the market clearing price—the result is to create shortages at the controlled price. People want to buy more of a good than producers want to sell. Those who can buy at the cheaper price benefit; producers and those unable to buy suffer.

Cities from San Francisco to New York have instituted controls on rents in the hopes of making housing more affordable. The effect of rent control laws—setting the maximum rent that a landlord can charge for a one-bedroom apartment, for example—is illustrated by Figure 4.10. In panel A, R^* is the market equilibrium rental rate, at which the demand for housing equals the supply. However, the local government is concerned that at R^*, many poor people cannot afford housing in the city; it therefore passes a law that caps rents at R_1. But at R_1, there is an excess demand for apartments. While the motives behind its action may well have been praiseworthy, the government has created an artificial scarcity.

The problems caused by rent control are likely to be worse in the long run than in the short run, because long-run supply curves are more elastic than short-run supply curves. In the short run, the quantity of apartments does not change much. But in the long run, the quantity of apartments can decline for several reasons. Apartments may be abandoned as they deteriorate; they can be converted to condominiums and sold instead of rented; and apartment owners may not wish to undertake new construction if they cannot charge enough in rent to cover their costs.

Figure 4.10B illustrates how the housing shortages under rent control will increase over time. Rent control results in all *existing* renters being better off, at least as long as the landlord stays in the business. But the quantity of available rental housing will decrease, leaving many would-be residents unable to find rental housing in the market. Since renters tend to be poorer than those who buy their homes, a shortage of rental housing will tend to hurt the poor most.

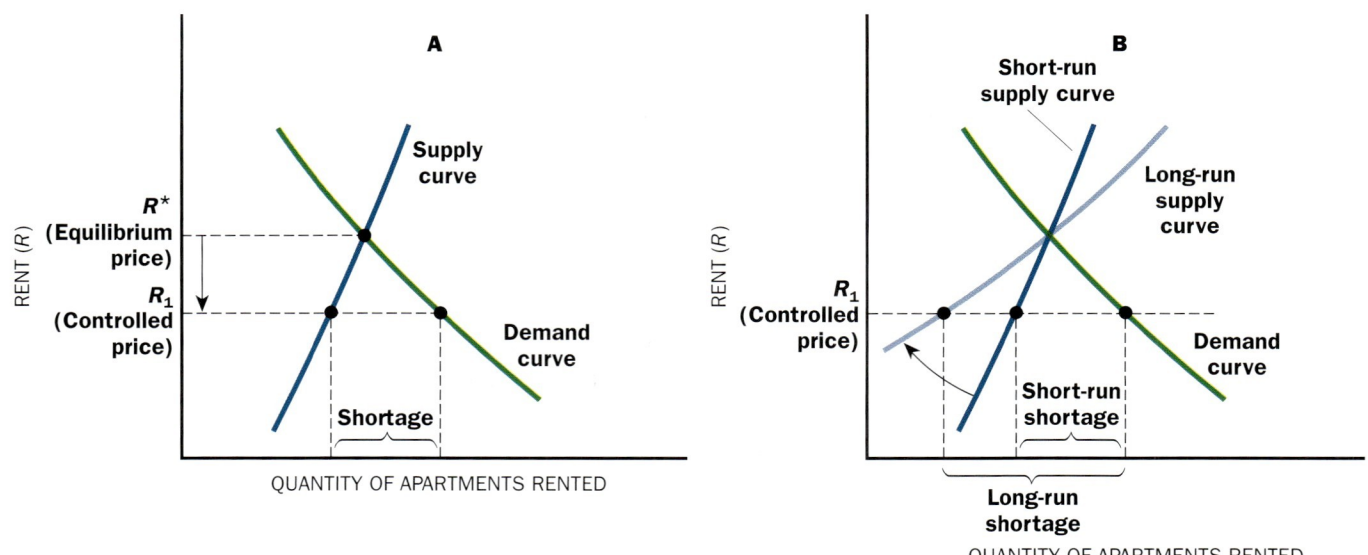

Figure 4.10

A PRICE CEILING: RENT CONTROL

Rent control laws limit the rents apartment owners may charge. If rents are held down to R_1, below the market-clearing level R^*, as in panel A, there will be excess demand for apartments. Panel B shows the long-run response. The supply of rental housing is more elastic in the long run, since landlords can refuse to build new apartment buildings or they can sell existing apartments as condominiums. The price ceiling eventually leads to the quantity supplied being even farther below the quantity demanded.

Case in Point

RENT CONTROL IN NEW YORK CITY

Rent control creates a housing shortage while, at the same time, it discourages the construction of new rental housing. In cities with rent control such as New York, vacancy rates for rental units are quite low, usually around 2 to 3 percent. In contrast, the vacancy rate normally averages around 7 percent in cities such as Chicago, San Diego, and Philadelphia that do not have rent control. With many people struggling to obtain one of the few available apartments, poor people tend to lose out. Some studies have indicated that rent control in Californian cities such as Santa Monica and Berkeley lead to increased gentrification as highly educated professionals hold on to rent-controlled apartments, forcing working-class families (and students, in the case of Berkeley) to look for housing in surrounding communities.

Rent control is widespread in New York City.

It is difficult for newcomers to find rental housing in New York, San Francisco, and other cities with rent control. Fewer apartments are available, and those that are tend to be very expensive. For example, a 1997 survey of rents found that the median rent for an advertised apartment in New York City was about two and a half times the median rent for all apartments in the city ($1,350 per month for advertised apartments versus $545 per month for all apartments). In contrast, in Philadelphia, a city that does not have rent control, the median rent for advertised apartments was only $2 more per month than the median for all apartments ($500 per month versus $498 per month). There were many more inexpensive and reasonably priced apartments available in Philadelphia than there were in New York City. The lack of affordable housing due to rent control forces individuals to share apartments or live farther away from where they work, thereby contributing to commuter congestion.[1]

PRICE FLOORS

Just as consumers try to get government to limit the prices they pay, so sellers would like the government to put a floor on the prices they receive: a minimum wage for workers and a minimum price on wheat and other agricultural products for farmers. Both groups appeal to fairness, arguing that the price they are receiving is inadequate to cover the effort (and other resources) they are contributing.

In many countries, farmers, because of their political influence, have succeeded in persuading government to impose a floor on the prices of numerous agricultural products—a price that is above the market equilibrium, as illustrated in

---

[1] William Tucker, "We All Pay for Others' Great Apartment Deals," *Newsday,* May 24, 1986; Tucker, "Moscow on the Hudson," *The American Spectator,* July 1986, pp. 19–21; Tucker, "How Rent Control Drives Out Affordable Housing," *Cato Policy Analysis* No. 274, May 21, 1997.

Internet Connection

FLAWED DEREGULATION

The California electricity market became a major national news story in 2001 as Californians suffered rolling blackouts, a major utility declared bankruptcy, and the state government spent as much as $70 million per day to purchase electricity. Rising demand, shrinking supply, and a price ceiling on what utilities could charge consumers produced electricity shortages. Information on the California electric industry may be found at the California Public Utilities Commission Web site: www.cpuc.ca.gov. The University of California Energy Institute provides data on daily demand and supply curves for electricity in California from 1998 to 2003 at www.ucei.berkeley.edu/ucei/datamine/datamine.htm.

Figure 4.11. The consequences should be obvious: supply exceeds demand. To sustain the price, government has had to purchase and stockpile huge amounts of agricultural goods. The cost of supporting the price at these above-market levels has been in the billions.

As government interferes with the law of supply and demand, it enters a labyrinth of problems. To reduce supplies, it has imposed production limitations. Such limitations not only are administratively cumbersome but also prevent the market from adapting quickly to changing conditions. Because quotas are based on past production, the appropriate adjustments cannot be made easily. Worse still, wheat farmers have to keep producing wheat to maintain their quota. But doing so prevents them from rotating their crops to protect the soil and the environment. To avoid the buildup of surpluses, exports are subsidized. But these subsidies have angered other countries, which view them as evidence of unfair competition. Our subsidies of wheat exports to Mexico have hurt our economic relations with Argentina. Even Mexico has viewed them with alarm, as they have interfered with Mexico's attempts to reform its agricultural sector.

ALTERNATIVE SOLUTIONS

The examples of government attempts to interfere with the workings of supply and demand yield an important cautionary moral: one ignores the workings of the law of supply and demand only at one's peril. This is not to say that the government should simply ignore the distress caused by large price and wage changes. But government must take care in addressing the problems; relying on price controls, including price ceilings and floors, is unlikely to be effective.

Later chapters will discuss ways in which the government can mitigate the sometimes painful consequences of the law of supply and demand—by making use of the power of the market rather than trying to fight against it. For example, if the government is concerned with low wages paid to unskilled workers, it can try to increase the demand for these workers. A shift to the right in the demand curve will increase their price—that is, the wages they receive. The government can either subsidize firms that hire unskilled workers or provide more training to these workers and thus increase their productivity.

If the government wants to increase the supply of housing to the poor, it can provide them with housing subsidies, which will elicit a greater supply. If the government wants drivers to conserve on the use of gasoline, it can impose a tax on gasoline. Noneconomists often object that these sorts of economic incentives have other distasteful consequences, and sometimes they do. But government policies will tend to be more effective, with fewer unfortunate side effects, when they take into account the law of supply and demand rather than ignoring its predictable economic consequences.

Figure 4.11
PRICE FLOORS

If the government imposes a price floor on, say, wheat—at a price in excess of the market equilibrium—there will be excess supply. Either the government will have to purchase the excess, to be stored or somehow disposed of, or it will have to limit production.

Review and Practice

SUMMARY

1. The price elasticity of demand describes how sensitive the quantity demanded of a good is to changes in the price of the good. When demand is inelastic, an increase in the price has little effect on the quantity demanded and the demand curve is steep; when demand is elastic, an increase in the price has a large effect on the quantity demanded and the curve is flat.
2. The price elasticity of supply describes how sensitive the quantity supplied of a good is to changes in the price of the good. If price changes do not induce much change in supply, the supply curve is very steep and is said to be inelastic. If the supply curve is very flat, indicating that price changes cause large changes in supply, supply is said to be elastic.
3. The extent to which a shift in the supply curve affects price or affects quantity depends on the shape of the demand curve. The more elastic the demand, the more a given shift in the supply curve will be reflected in changes in equilibrium quantities and the less it will be reflected in changes in equilibrium prices. The more inelastic the demand, the more a given shift in the supply curve will be reflected in changes in equilibrium prices and the less it will be reflected in changes in equilibrium quantities.
4. Likewise, the extent to which a shift in the demand curve affects price or affects quantity depends on the shape of the supply curve.
5. Demand and supply curves are likely to be more elastic in the long run than in the short run. Therefore a shift in the demand or supply curve is likely to have a larger price effect in the short run and a larger quantity effect in the long run.
6. Elasticities can be used to predict how much consumer prices will rise when a tax is imposed on a good. If the demand curve for a good is very inelastic, consumers in effect have to pay the tax. If the demand curve is very elastic, the quantities produced and the price received by producers are likely to decline considerably.
7. Government regulations may prevent a market from moving toward its equilibrium price, leading to shortages or surpluses. Price ceilings lead to excess demand. Price floors lead to excess supply.

KEY TERMS

price elasticity of demand
relatively elastic
unitary elasticity
relatively inelastic
infinite elasticity
zero elasticity
price elasticity of supply
shortage
surplus
price ceilings
price floors

REVIEW QUESTIONS

1. What is meant by the elasticity of demand and the elasticity of supply? Why do economists find these concepts useful?
2. Is the slope of a perfectly elastic demand or supply curve horizontal or is it vertical? Is the slope of a perfectly inelastic demand or supply curve horizontal or is it vertical? Explain.
3. If the elasticity of demand is 1, what happens to total revenue as the price increases? What if the demand for a product is very inelastic? What if it is very elastic?
4. Under what condition will a shift in the demand curve result mainly in a change in quantity? in price?
5. Under what condition will a shift in the supply curve result mainly in a change in price? in quantity?
6. Why do the elasticities of demand and supply tend to change from the short run to the long run?
7. Under what circumstances will a tax on a product be passed along to consumers?
8. Why do price ceilings tend to lead to shortages? Why do price floors tend to lead to surpluses?

PROBLEMS

1. Suppose the price elasticity of demand for gasoline is 0.2 in the short run and 0.7 in the long run. If the price of gasoline rises 28 percent, what effect on quantity demanded will this have in the short run? in the long run?

2. Imagine that the short-run price elasticity of supply for a farmer's corn is 0.3, while the long-run price elasticity is 2. If prices for corn fall 30 percent, what are the short-run and long-run changes in quantity supplied? What are the short- and long-run changes in quantity supplied if prices rise by 15 percent? What happens to the farmer's revenues in each of these situations?
3. Assume that the demand curve for hard liquor is highly inelastic and the supply curve for hard liquor is highly elastic. If the tastes of the drinking public shift away from hard liquor, will the effect be larger on price or on quantity? If the federal government decides to impose a tax on manufacturers of hard liquor, will the effect be larger on price or on quantity? What is the effect of an advertising program that succeeds in discouraging people from drinking? Draw diagrams to illustrate each of your answers.
4. Suppose a government wishes to ensure that its citizens can afford adequate housing. Consider three ways of pursuing that goal. One method is to pass a law requiring that all rents be cut by one-fourth. A second method offers a subsidy to all builders of homes. A third provides a subsidy directly to renters equal to one-fourth of the rent they pay. Predict what effect each of these proposals would have on the price and quantity of rental housing in the short run and the long run.
5. In 1990, the U.S. government imposed a 10 percent tax on certain luxuries such as pleasure boats. Sales of pleasure boats fell by nearly 90 percent in southern Florida as prospective buyers bought boats in the Bahamas to avoid paying the tax. What does this imply about the size of the elasticity of demand?
6. Assume the elasticity of demand for oil is 0.7 and the initial quantity demanded is 100 million barrels a day. What is the impact of a 10 percent increase in the price of oil on the quantity of oil demanded? What happens to total expenditures? Assume that the United States initially imports 50 million barrels a day and that production remains unchanged. What happens to the level of imports and to expenditures on imports?

Assume that in the long run the elasticity of demand increases to 1. How does this change your answers?

Appendix: Elasticity and Slope

The elasticity of a curve is not the same as its slope. The best way to see the distinction is to look at a *linear* demand curve. A linear demand curve is a straight line, as depicted in Figure 4.12. With a linear demand curve, a $1 change in price always leads to the same change in quantity demanded, whether we start from a price of $2 or a price of $10. Table 4.3 contains information on price and quantity demanded for such a curve, and we can use this information to calculate the elasticity of demand at different prices. When the price increases from $1 to $2, a 100 percent increase, demand falls by 5 units, from 45 to 40. This represents an 11 percent fall in demand. The elasticity of demand is 11 percent divided by 100 percent, or 0.11. A $1 increase in price from $5 to $6 represents a 20 percent price increase. Because the demand curve is linear, the $1 price increase again reduces demand by 5 units, from 20 to 15 units. This is a 20 percent change in the quantity demanded. The elasticity of demand is 20 percent divided by 20 percent, or 1. As the price goes higher, a $1 change represents a smaller percentage change in the price; moreover, quantity demanded drops, so the 5-unit

Figure 4.12

LINEAR DEMAND CURVE

The linear demand curve is a straight line; it is represented algebraically by the equation $Q = a - bp$. The slope of the demand curve is a constant. However, the elasticity varies with output. At low outputs (high prices), it is very high. At high outputs (low prices), it is very low.

Table 4.3

ELASTICITY AND A LINEAR DEMAND CURVE

Price	Quantity demanded	Change in price (%)	Change in quantity (%)	Elasticity
1	45			
		100	−11	0.11
2	40			
		50	−13	0.25
3	35			
		33	−14	0.43
4	30			
		25	−17	0.67
5	25			
		20	−20	1.00
6	20			
		17	−25	1.50
7	15			
		14	−33	2.33
8	10			
		13	−50	4.00
9	5			

fall represents a larger percentage change in demand. Thus, at higher prices, the elasticity—the percentage change in quantity divided by the percentage change in price—becomes larger.

At times, however, we can use information about the slope of the demand curve to draw a conclusion about elasticity. Figure 4.13 shows two demand curves going through the same point. Consider a 1 percentage point change in the price at the point of intersection. The quantity demanded changes more along the flatter demand curve. Because price and quantity were initially the same for the two curves, the percentage change in quantity is larger along the flatter one. We can conclude that at the point of intersection, the flatter demand curve (the one with the smaller slope) has the greater elasticity.

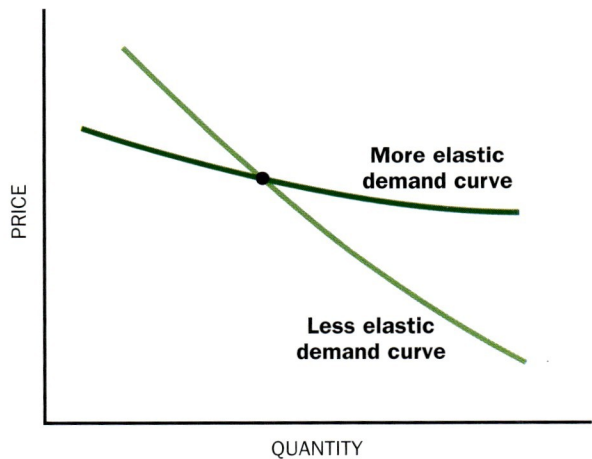

Figure 4.13
COMPARING ELASTICITIES

If two demand curves intersect, at the point of intersection the flatter demand curve has the greater price elasticity.

Learning Goals

In this chapter, you will learn

1. Where demand curves come from
2. Why demand curves are downward sloping
3. What factors cause demand curves to shift
4. What is meant by behavioral economics

Chapter 5

THE CONSUMPTION DECISION

How many economic decisions have you made today? Did you decide to ride the bus to campus rather than drive, buy a bagel for breakfast rather than a muffin, or eat in a local café rather than at home? Perhaps you decided to look for a new job or ask for more hours at your current one. You may have decided to take out another student loan, or apply for a bank loan to buy a car. Maybe you set aside some money to finance a trip this summer. If so, you then had to decide whether to put your savings into an account at a bank or to invest in the stock market.

These decisions—about spending, about working, about saving, and about investing—represent the basic economic choices all individuals face. In this chapter, we focus on spending decisions. By studying these decisions, we will gain a better understanding of the demand curves that were introduced in Chapter 3 and used in Chapter 4. While our main focus will be on the basic model used by economists to explain how consumers make their spending decisions, we will also see that in recent years, new insights from fields such as psychology have enriched our understanding of these choices.

The Basic Problem of Consumer Choice

The basic framework for analyzing economic decision making was introduced in Chapter 2. Consumers start by defining an opportunity set: they determine what is *possible* given the constraints they face. In most cases we will discuss, what consumers can purchase is constrained by their income. And for many decisions, the time available to consumers also constrains their choices. Once the opportunity set is defined, the consumer selects the most preferred option within it. Because opportunity sets

THE BUDGET CONSTRAINT

The individual's opportunity set is defined by the **budget constraint**. If, after taxes, a person's weekly paycheck comes to $300 and he has no other income, that sum is his budget constraint. Total expenditures on food, clothing, rent, entertainment, travel, and all other categories cannot exceed $300 per week. (For now we ignore the possibilities that individuals may borrow money, or save money, or change their budget constraints by working longer or shorter hours.)

The line *BC* in Figure 5.1A shows a simplified individual budget constraint. A student, Fran, has a total of $300 each month to spend on "fun" items. Figure 5.1 assumes that there are two goods, candy bars and compact discs. This simplification enables us to highlight the main points of the analysis.

Let's say that a candy bar costs $1, while a compact disc costs $15. If Fran spent all her income on candy bars, she could purchase 300 candy bars (point *B* on the budget constraint). If she spent all her income on CDs, she could buy 20 CDs (point *C* on the budget constraint). Fran can also choose any of the intermediate choices on line *BC*. For example, she could buy 10 CDs (for $150) and 150 candy bars (for $150), or 15 CDs ($225) and 75 candy bars ($75). Each combination of purchases along the budget constraint totals $300.

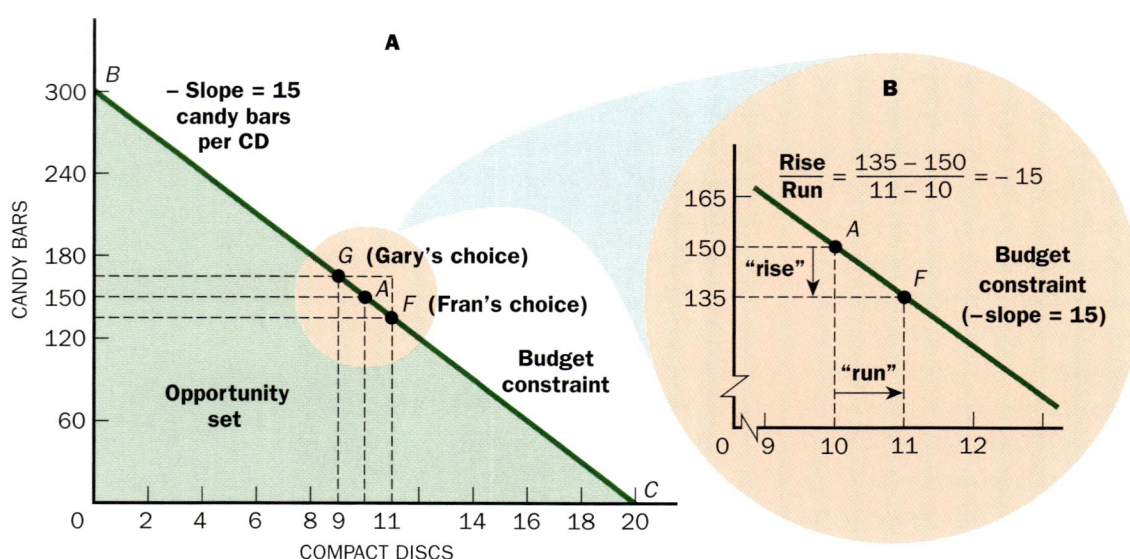

Figure 5.1

AN INDIVIDUAL'S BUDGET CONSTRAINT

Panel A is a budget constraint that shows the combinations of compact discs (at $15) and candy bars (at $1) that an individual could buy with $300. Fran chooses point *F*, with a relatively large number of CDs; Gary chooses point *G*, with a relatively large number of candy bars. Panel B shows that the trade-off of moving from 10 CDs to 11 (point *A* to *F*) is 15 candy bars.

As we learned in Chapter 2, a budget constraint diagram has two important features. First, although any point in the shaded area of Figure 5.1A is feasible, only the points on the line *BC* are really relevant, because Fran is not consuming her entire budget if she is inside her budget constraint. Second, by looking along the budget constraint, we can see her trade-offs—how many candy bars she has to give up to get 1 more CD, and vice versa. Look at points *F* and *A,* a part of the budget constraint that is blown up in panel B. At point *A,* Fran has 10 CDs; at *F,* she has 11. At *F,* she has 135 candy bars; at *A,* 150. To get 1 more CD, she has to give up 15 candy bars.

These are her trade-offs, and they are determined by the relative prices of the two goods. If one good costs twice as much as another and we went 1 more unit of the costly good, we have to give up 2 units of the cheaper good. If, as here, one good costs fifteen times as much as another, and we want 1 more unit of the costly good, we have to give up 15 units of the less costly good.

The **slope** of the budget constraint, which measures how steep it is, also tells us what the trade-off is. As we move 1 unit along the horizontal axis (from 10 to 11 CDs), the slope represents the size of the change along the vertical axis. It is the rise (the movement up or down on the vertical axis) divided by the run (the corresponding horizontal movement). The slope of this budget constraint is thus 15.[1] It tells us how much of one good, at a given price, we need to give up if we want 1 more unit of the other good: it tells us, in other words, what the trade-off is.

Note that the relative price of CDs to candy bars is 15; that is, a CD costs fifteen times as much as a candy bar. But we have just seen that the slope of the budget constraint is 15, and that the trade-off (the number of candy bars Fran has to give up to get 1 more CD) is 15. It is no accident that these three numbers—relative price, slope, and trade-off—are the same.

This two-product example was chosen because it is easy to illustrate with a graph. But the same logic applies to any number of products. Income can be spent on one item or a combination of items. The budget constraint defines what a certain amount of income can buy, a balance that depends on the prices of the items. Giving up some of one item would allow the purchase of more of another item or items.

Economists represent these choices by putting the purchases of the good to which they are paying attention, say CDs, on the horizontal axis and "all other goods" on the vertical axis. By definition, what is not spent on CDs is available to be spent on all other goods. Fran has $300 to spend altogether. A more realistic budget constraint for her is shown in Figure 5.2. The intersection of the budget constraint with the vertical axis, point *B*—where purchases of CDs are zero—is $300. If Fran spends nothing on CDs, she has $300 to spend on other goods. The budget constraint intersects the horizontal axis at 20 CDs (point *C*); if she spends all her income on CDs and CDs cost $15 each, she can buy 20. If Fran chooses a point such a *F,* she will buy 11 CDs, costing $165, and she will have $135 to spend on other goods ($300–$165). The distance 0*D* on the vertical axis measures what she spends on other goods; the distance *BD* measures what she spends on CDs.

---

[1] We ignore the negative sign. See the appendix to Chapter 2 for a more detailed explanation of the slope of a line.

CHOOSING A POINT ON THE BUDGET CONSTRAINT: INDIVIDUAL PREFERENCES

The budget constraint and a recognition of possible trade-offs are the starting points for the study of consumer behavior. The process of identifying the budget constraints and the trade-offs is the same for *any* two people. Any individual will choose *some* point along the budget constraint. But the point actually chosen depends on the individual's preferences: Fran, who likes to listen to music, might choose point F in Figure 5.1, while Gary, who loves candy, might choose G.

Few people will choose either of the extreme points on the budget constraint, B or C in Figure 5.1, where only one of the goods is consumed. The reason for this is that the more you have of a good—say, the more CDs you have relative to another good such as candy—the less valuable you will find an additional unit of that good relative to additional units of another good. At points near C, it seems safe to assume that to most individuals, an extra CD does not look as attractive as some candy bars. Certainly, at B, most people would be so full of candy bars that they would prefer an extra CD.

Where the individual's choice lies depends on how she values the two goods. Chapter 2 emphasized the idea that in making decisions, people look at the *margin:* they look at the extra costs and benefits. In this case, the choice at each point along the budget constraint is between 1 more CD and 15 more candy bars. If Gary and Fran choose different points along the budget constraint, it is because they value the marginal benefits (how much better off they feel with an *extra* CD) and the marginal costs (how much it hurts to give up 15 candy bars) differently. Gary chooses point G in Figure 5.1 because that is the point where, for him, the marginal benefit of an extra CD is just offset by what he has to give up to get the extra CD, which is 15 candy bars. When Fran, who loves listening to music, considers point G, she realizes that for her, at that point, CDs are more important and candy bars less important than they are for Gary. So she trades along the line until she feels that the marginal benefits of an extra CD and the marginal costs of 15 fewer candy bars are equal. This point, in our example, is F.

The same reasoning holds for a budget constraint like the one shown in Figure 5.2. Here, Gary and Fran are choosing between CDs and all other goods, measured in dollar terms. Again, the decision to buy an extra CD hinges on comparing the marginal benefit of an extra CD with the marginal cost—here, what has to be given up in other goods. With CDs priced at $15, choosing to buy a CD means giving up $15 of other goods. For Gary, the marginal benefit of an extra CD equals the cost, $15, when he has only 9 CDs and can therefore spend $165 on other goods. For Fran, who has more of a taste for CDs, the marginal benefit of an extra CD does not equal this marginal cost until she reaches 11 CDs, with $135 to spend elsewhere. Price thus serves as a quantitative measure of marginal benefit.

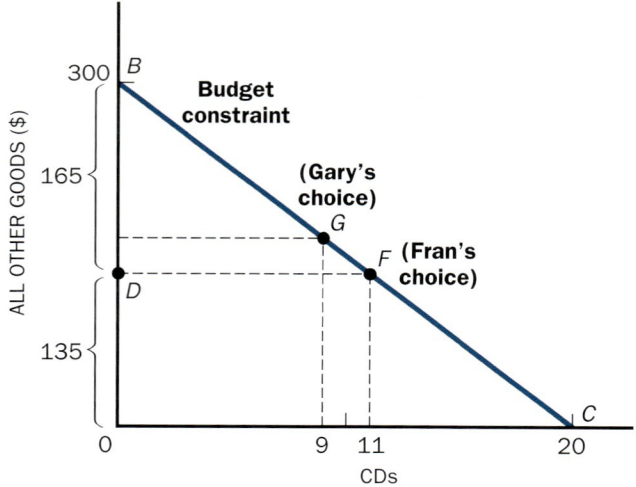

Figure 5.2

ALLOCATING A BUDGET BETWEEN A SINGLE GOOD AND ALL OTHERS

Some budget constraints show the choice between a particular good, in this case CDs, and all other goods. The other goods that might be purchased are collectively measured in money terms, as shown on the vertical axis.

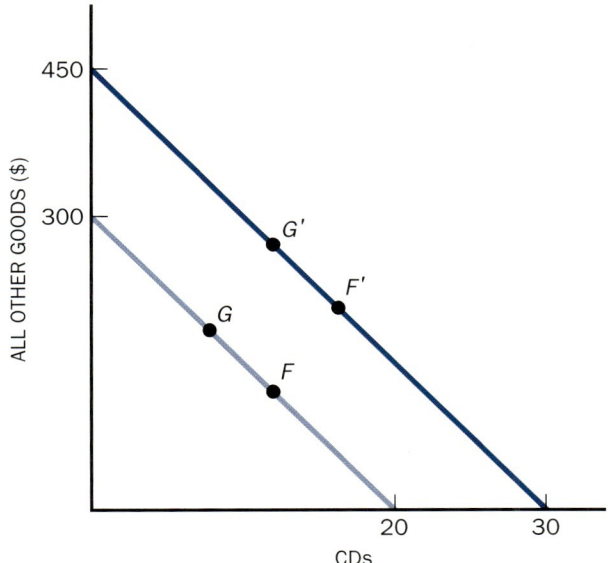

Figure 5.3
THE EFFECT ON CONSUMPTION WHEN INCOME CHANGES

If the amount Gary and Fran have to spend on CDs and other good rises from $300 to $450, the budget line shifts to the right. Because the price of CDs is still $15, the slope of the budget line does not change. The points Gary and Fran choose on the new budget line are G' and F'. With additional income, they both choose to buy more CDs *and* to spend more on other goods.

WHAT HAPPENS TO CONSUMPTION WHEN INCOME CHANGES?

When an individual's income increases, he has more to spend on consumption. Figure 5.3 shows the effect on the budget constraint of an increase in income. The original budget line is the same as that used in Figure 5.2: Gary and Fran have $300 to spend on CDs or other goods. If the total amount they have to spend increases to $450, the new budget line is farther to the right. Now, Gary and Fran could purchase 30 CDs if they spend the entire $450 on CDs, or they could spend it all on other goods. Because the price of a CD has not changed, the slope of the new budget line is the same as that of the old budget line. Changes in income shift the budget line but do not alter its slope.

The new choices of Gary and Fran are at points G' and F'. Because they have more to spend, Gary and Fran each decide to purchase more CDs *and* more of other goods. Their behavior is typical; when people's incomes increase, they will buy a little more of many goods, although the consumption of some goods will increase more than that of others, and different individuals will spend their extra income in different ways.

The **income elasticity of demand** (which parallels the price elasticity of demand presented in Chapter 4) measures how much consumption of a particular good increases with income:

$$\text{income elasticity of demand} = \frac{\text{percentage change in consumption}}{\text{percentage change in income}}.$$

The income elasticity of demand, in other words, is the percentage change in consumption that would result from a 1 percent increase in income. If the income elasticity of demand of a certain good is greater than 1, a 1 percent increase in an individual's income results in a more than 1 percent increase in expenditures on that good. That is, the amount he spends on that good increases more than proportionately with income. By definition, if the income elasticity of demand is less than 1, then a 1 percent increase in income results in a less than 1 percent increase in expenditures. Thus the share of income a consumer spends on that good decreases with a rise in income.

As people's incomes increase, the types of goods they choose to buy also change. In particular, they have more money to spend on goods other than those required just to survive. For instance, while they may spend some of the extra income to improve the quality of necessities they buy, such as food, more money goes toward movies, more expensive automobiles, vacations, and other luxuries. Accordingly, poor individuals spend a larger percentage of their income on food and housing and a smaller percentage of their income on perfume. In other words, the income elasticity of necessities is less than 1, and the income elasticity of luxuries is greater than 1.

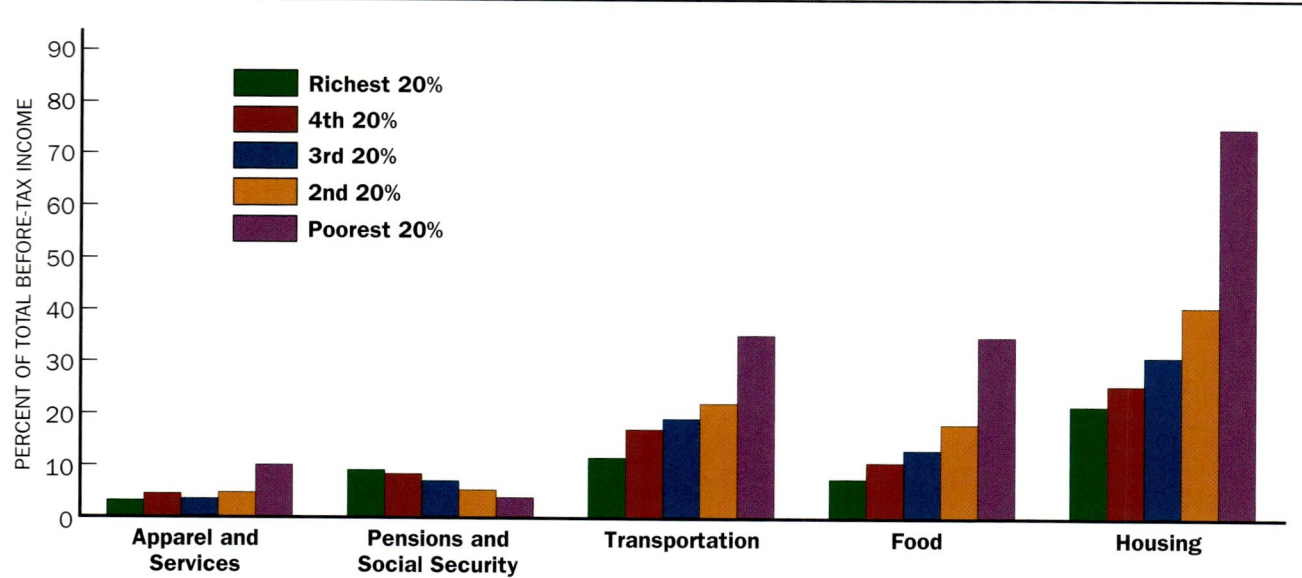

Figure 5.4

HOW HOUSEHOLDS OF DIFFERENT INCOMES SPEND THEIR MONEY

The poor spend far higher proportions of their income on basic necessities such as food and housing than do the rich.

SOURCE: U.S. Department of Labor, Bureau of Labor Statistics, *Consumer Expenditure Survey* (2002).

The consumption of some goods actually decreases as income increases and increases as income decreases; these are called **inferior goods.** In sharp contrast, the consumption of **normal goods** increases with income. In other words, goods for which the income elasticity is *negative* are, by definition, inferior, while all other goods are called normal. For instance, if Fran, who has been riding the bus to work, gets a large raise, she may find that she can afford a car. After buying the car, she will spend less on bus fare. Thus, in this particular sense, bus rides represent an inferior good.

Figure 5.4 shows how typical families at different income levels spend their income. We see that *on average,* the poorest 20 percent of the population spend almost 80 percent of their before-tax income on housing. Yet the richest 20 percent spend only a fifth of their income on housing. Similarly, the poorest 20 percent spend 38 percent of their before-tax income on food, while the richest 20 percent spend less than a tenth. The total spending of the poorest 20 percent on food and housing adds up to more than 100 percent of their income; this is possible only because of government subsidies.

Information like that contained in Figure 5.4 is of great practical importance. For example, it helps determine how a tax will affect different groups. Anybody who purchases food will be hurt by a tax on it. But if the poor spend a larger fraction of their income on food, as the figure suggests, they will bear a disproportionately large share of the tax.

Wrap-Up

INCOME ELASTICITY OF DEMAND

The *income elasticity of demand* for a good is the percentage change in consumption that would result from a 1 percent increase in income.

When income elasticity of demand is *greater than 1,* a 1 percent increase in an individual's income results in a more than 1 percent increase in expenditures on the good.

When income elasticity of demand is *less than 1,* a 1 percent increase in an individual's income results in a less than 1 percent increase in expenditures on the good.

Normal goods have a positive income elasticity of demand.

Inferior goods have a negative income elasticity of demand.

Case in Point

THE FATE OF THE BTU TAX

Some of the differences in choices along a budget constraint reflect nothing more than differences in tastes—Fran likes CDs more than Gary does. But some differences in choices are systematic, and many of these reflect differences in circumstances. Eleanor lives in New England and spends more on oil to heat her apartment than does Jim, who lives in Florida; Amy, who lives in Montana, 200 miles from the nearest town, buys more gas and spends more on cars than does Tom, who travels from home to work by subway in New York City.

Understanding such systematic determinants in how people spend their money helps us understand the markedly different responses in different regions of the country to government proposals to tax different goods. A case in point arose in 1993 after the Clinton administration took office with a pledge to reduce the huge federal deficit. Many policy analysts, both inside and outside government, favored a tax on energy. Most energy sources are relatively cheap in the United States compared to many other industrialized countries. Low energy prices lead Americans to consume high quantities of energy, thus increasing urban congestion, air pollution, and greenhouse gas emissions. A tax on energy would provide incentives to conserve energy—making such a tax an environmentally sound way of raising revenue.

The administration proposed a BTU tax—named after the British thermal unit, a standard measure of energy. The intent was to levy the tax on the basis of energy used, treating all energy sources alike. The tax proposal generated immediate opposition from heavy energy users. Americans living in the Northeast, who needed to heat their homes for much of the year, claimed that the tax would hit them unfairly. The aluminum industry, a heavy user of energy, strongly opposed it; so did other energy-intensive industries.

In an effort to make the tax more politically palatable—and increase its chance of passage through the Congress—policymakers whittled it down to a single-form-of-energy tax—on gasoline. The proposal turned into a 6.5 cents per gallon increase in the gasoline tax, from 14.1 cents to 20.6 cents per gallon. Americans in the West, who drive much longer distances in a typical day than people in other parts of the country, were up in arms. Politics dictated a reduction in the proposed gas tax. Congress finally passed, and the president signed, a mere 4.3 cents per gallon increase in the tax on gasoline, which raises only an added $5 billion a year in federal revenue.

Low energy prices in the United States lead Americans to consume high quantities of energy.

Internet Connection
WHAT WE CONSUME

The Bureau of Labor Statistics conducts regular surveys to discover what households spend their income on. Information from these Consumer Expenditure Surveys is available at www.bls.gov/cex/home.htm. If you follow the link to "Consumer Expenditures Annual Reports," you will discover that the average expenditure of the households surveyed in 2002 was $40,677, of which 7.6 percent was spent on food at home, 5.1 percent on food away from home, 32.7 percent on housing, and 1.0 percent on public transportation. How do your expenditures compare to those of a typical American household?

A Closer Look at the Demand Curve

In Chapter 3, we saw the principal characteristic of the demand curve: when prices rise, the quantity of a good demanded normally falls. Here, we take a closer look at why. Doing so will help us understand why some goods respond more strongly to price changes, that is, have a greater price elasticity.

Let us return to our earlier example of Fran buying CDs, shown in Figure 5.2. If the price of CDs rises from $15 to $20, Fran will face a new budget constraint. If she buys no CDs, she will still have $300 to spend on other goods; but if she decides to spend all of her income on CDs, she can buy only 15 rather than 20. Figure 5.5 shows Fran's original budget constraint in light green and her new budget constraint in dark green.

The increase in the price of CDs has one obvious and important effect: Fran cannot continue to buy the same number of CDs and the same amount of other goods as she did before. Earlier, Fran bought 11 CDs. If she again buys the same number of CDs, it will cost her $55 more, and she will have $55 less to spend on other goods. No matter what she does, Fran is worse off as a result of the price increase. It is *as if* she had less income to spend. When she has less income to spend, she reduces her expenditure on each good, including CDs. This part of the response to the higher price is called the **income effect.** An increase in income of about $55, or 18 percent ($55 out of $300), would offset the price increase.[2] Assume the income elasticity is approximately 1; that is, with income reduced by 18 percent, she would reduce purchases of CDs by 18 percent, which is about 2 CDs. This part of the reduction of the demand of CDs, from 11 to 9, is the income effect.

The magnitude of the income effect depends on two factors: how important the commodity is to the individual—that is, how large a fraction of the individual's income

Figure 5.5

EFFECT OF PRICE INCREASE

An increase in the price of CDs moves the budget constraint down as shown. Fran must cut back on the consumption of some goods. Here, using the black dots to mark her consumption points, we show her cutting back on the consumption of both CDs and other goods.

---

[2]Actually, it would slightly overcompensate. With the $55 increase, Fran could buy exactly the same bundle of goods as before, but as we will soon see, she will *choose* to reallocate her spending. The reallocation will make her better off.

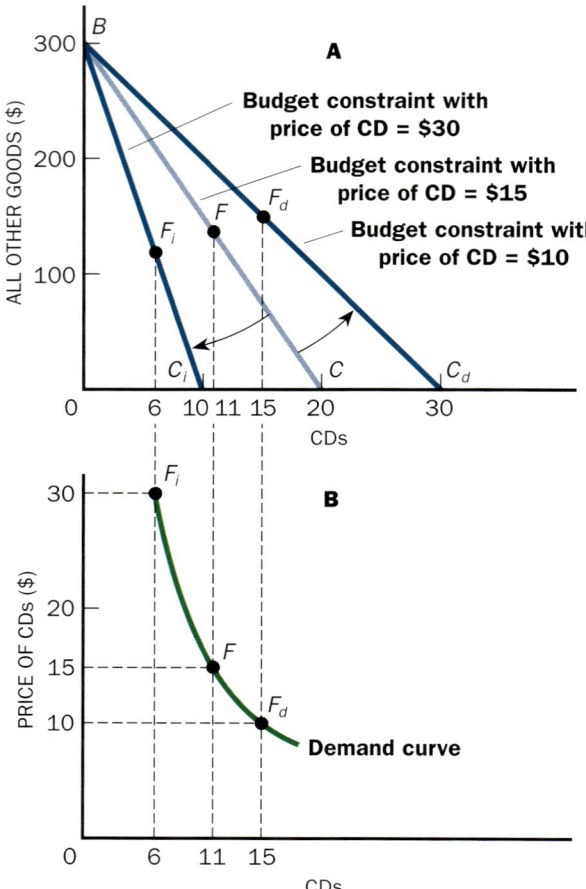

Figure 5.6

DERIVING DEMAND CURVES FROM SHIFTING BUDGET CONSTRAINTS

In panel A, the budget constraint rotates down to the left as the price of CDs increases, leading Fran to change consumption from F to F_i. The budget constraint rotates to the right when the price of CDs decreases, and Fran moves from F to F_d. Panel B shows the corresponding demand curve for CDs, illustrating how the rising prices lead to a decline in quantity consumed.

is spent on the good—and how large the income elasticity is. Since, in most cases, individuals spend a relatively small fraction of their income on any particular good, the income effect is relatively small. But sometimes the income effect of a price increase can be significant—in the case of housing, for example, a good on which most individuals spend between a fourth and a third of their income.

Let us return to Fran and the CDs. At the higher price, giving up one CD gets her more of other goods—more candy bars, more movies, more DVDs, more sweaters. The relative price of CDs, or the trade-off between CDs and other goods, has changed. At the higher price, she *substitutes* goods that are less expensive for the more expensive CDs. Not surprisingly, this effect is called the **substitution effect.** Its magnitude depends on how easily Fran can substitute other goods. If Fran can subscribe to an online music service that allows her to purchase songs and download them to her MP3 player, and the price of the subscription remains unchanged when the price of CDs rises, the substitution effect might be large. She might reduce the number of CDs she purchases to 2. But if Fran does not have an MP3 player, if her sole source of entertainment is listening to her music, and if she dislikes the music played by the local radio stations, the substitution effect may be small. Fran may cut her purchases of CDs far less sharply, only to 8.

DERIVING DEMAND CURVES

We can now see both how to derive the demand curve and why it has the shape it does. At each price, we draw the budget constraint and identify the point along the budget constraint that is chosen. In panel A of Figure 5.6, budget constraints are drawn for three different prices for CDs. If the price of a CD is $10, Fran purchases 15 CDs, indicated by point F_d. If the price rises to $15, the budget constraint shifts and Fran chooses to buy 11 CDs (point F). If the price is $30, Fran only buys 6 CDs (point F_i). As the price of CDs increases, Fran will purchase fewer CDs, as represented by points along successive budget constraints. Higher prices mean she is less well-off, and therefore she decreases her purchases of all goods, including CDs. This is the income effect. The higher price of CDs *relative to other goods* means she will substitute other goods for CDs. This is the substitution effect.

Panel B plots the number of CDs purchased at each price. This is Fran's demand curve for CDs, and it is derived directly from the information in panel A. Because Fran purchases more CDs as the price falls, the demand curve is downward sloping. The case illustrated in panel B is the normal case. As price falls, the quantity demanded increases through *both* the income effect and the substitution effect. For *inferior goods,* such as cheap cuts of meat and bus travel, the income effect goes in the opposite direction. As the price is lowered, the substitution effect leads to more consumption, but the income effect leads to less. The net effect can be either positive or negative. Generally, though, as individuals become better off, they typically reduce their consumption of these goods.

THE IMPORTANCE OF DISTINGUISHING BETWEEN INCOME AND SUBSTITUTION EFFECTS

Distinguishing between the income and substitution effects of a change in price is important for two reasons.

Understanding Responses to Price Changes First, the distinction improves our understanding of consumption responses to price changes. Thinking about the substitution effect helps us understand why some demand curves have a low price elasticity and others a high price elasticity. It also helps us understand why the price elasticity may well differ at different points along the demand curve. Recall from Chapter 4 that when an individual is consuming large amounts of one good, substitutes for it are easy to find, and a small increase in price leads to a large reduction in the quantity demanded; but as consumption falls, finding good substitutes becomes increasingly difficult.

Or consider the effect of an increase in the price of one good on the demand for *other* goods. There is always an income effect; the income effect, by itself, would lead to reduced consumption of all commodities. But the substitution effect leads to *increased* consumption of substitute commodities. Thus, an increase in the price of Coke will lead to increased demand for Pepsi at each price; the demand curve for Pepsi shifts to the right, because the substitution effect outweighs the slight income effect.

Understanding Inefficiencies Associated with Taxes A second reason to focus on income and substitution effects is to identify some of the inefficiencies associated with taxation. The purpose of a tax is to raise revenue so that the government can purchase goods; it represents a transfer of purchasing power from the household to the government. If the government is to obtain more resources, individuals have to consume less. Thus, any tax must have an income effect.

But beyond that, taxes often distort economic activity. The distortion caused by taxation is associated with the substitution effect. Take the window tax discussed in Chapter 4. Intended to raise revenue, it instead led people to cover up their windows—a major distortion of the tax. Most of the distortions associated with modern taxes are somewhat more subtle. Consider a tax on airline tickets or on telephone calls. Reducing consumption of things that are against society's interest can be a legitimate goal of taxation. But the government does not think flying or making telephone calls is a bad thing. The tax is levied simply to raise revenues. But it results in fewer air flights and telephone calls anyway—an unintentional consequence. Any tax leads to *some* reduction in consumption, through the income effect. But most taxes also change relative prices; so they have a substitution effect. It is the substitution effect that gives rise to the distortion. If the substitution effect is small, the distortion is small; if the substitution effect is large, the distortion is large.

Thinking Like an Economist

INCENTIVES, INCOME EFFECTS, AND SUBSTITUTION EFFECTS

Economists focus on incentives because they want to understand how choices are made. By using the concepts of income and substitution effects, economists are able to analyze the way that prices affect incentives, and therefore choices. The best way to understand income effects and substitution effects—and to begin thinking like an economist—is to use them, as the following example illustrates.

During the winter of 2001, the state of California was hit with an energy shortage, the result of both bad weather and market manipulation by energy traders such as Enron. Under a partial deregulation of the electrical market, the state's major electrical utilities were required to buy electricity on the open market and to sell to consumers at prices that were capped. As the cost of wholesale electricity rose sharply during 2001, the price the utilities had to pay for electricity soared above what they were allowed to charge their customers. Demand outstripped the available supply.

When demand exceeds supply, two solutions are possible—increase supply or reduce demand. In a deregulated market system, the price of electricity would have risen, and the higher prices would have provided consumers with the incentive to conserve. A higher price for electricity reduces demand through two channels. As electricity prices rise relative to the prices of other goods that households purchase, each household has an incentive to economize on electricity. This is the *substitution effect*. But there is an income effect as well. Because electricity is more expensive, the household's real income is reduced—it has to spend more to obtain the same set of consumer goods (including electricity). With a reduced real income, the household cuts back its spending on all types of goods, including electricity. This is the *income effect*.

Because higher energy costs may have a disproportionate impact on low-income families, politicians are often reluctant to let energy prices rise. The solution is not to cap prices—keeping prices low simply reduces the incentives to all households to conserve a scarce resource. Instead, suppose the added energy costs for each household average $200. The income effect can be eliminated, while still allowing the substitution effect to do its job in reducing demand, by giving each household a refund of $200. On average, households' real income no longer falls—the impact of higher electricity prices is offset by the refund of $200. But the substitution effect still operates. In spending its income, a household faces a higher relative price of electricity. It has an incentive to conserve on its use of electricity.

Wrap-Up

INCOME AND SUBSTITUTION EFFECTS AND THE SHAPE OF DEMAND CURVES

The *income effect* refers to a change in consumption arising from a change in the consumer's real income. When the price of a good you consume increases, your real income is reduced because you can no longer afford the same level of consumption. By the same logic, when the price of a good that you consume falls, your real income is increased.

The *substitution effect* refers to a change in consumption arising from a change in the relative prices of goods. When the price of a good you consume increases, that good becomes more expensive relative to other goods, inducing you to consume less of the expensive good and more of the other goods.

Normally, demand curves are downward sloping. As the price is lowered, consumers are better off and so consume more of the good (the income effect); and the lower *relative* price induces a further increase in consumption (the substitution effect).

Utility and the Description of Preferences

We have seen that people choose a point along their budget constraint by weighing the benefits of consuming more of one good against the costs—what they have to forgo of other goods. Economists refer to the benefits of consumption as the **utility** that individuals get from the combination of goods they consume. Presumably a person can tell you whether or not he prefers a certain combination of goods to another. Economists say that the preferred bundle of goods gives that individual a higher level of utility than the other bundle of goods he could have chosen. Similarly, economists say that the individual will choose the bundle of goods—within the budget constraint—that maximizes his utility.

In the nineteenth century, social scientists, including the British philosopher Jeremy Bentham, hoped that science would someday develop a machine that could actually measure utility. A scientist could simply hook up some electrodes to an individual's head and read off a unique measure of "happiness." Modern economists have several useful ways of measuring changes in how well-off a person is.

For our purposes, one simple approach will suffice: we ask how much an individual would be willing to pay to be in one situation rather than another. For example, if Joe likes chocolate ice cream more than vanilla, it stands to reason that he would be willing to pay more for a scoop of chocolate ice cream than for a scoop of vanilla. Or if Diane would rather live in California than in New Jersey, it stands to reason that she would be willing to pay more for the West Coast location.

Note that how much a person is willing to pay tells us nothing about the price actually paid. What Joe has to pay for chocolate ice cream depends on market prices; what he is willing to pay reflects his preferences. Willingness to pay is a useful measure of utility, often helpful for purposes such as thinking about how individuals allocate income along budget constraints. But the hopes of nineteenth-century economists, that we could find some way of measuring utility that would enable us to compare how much utility Fran got from a bundle of goods with how much utility Gary obtained, are now viewed as pipe dreams.

Using willingness to pay as our measure of utility, we can construct a diagram like Figure 5.7A, which shows the level of utility Mary receives from sweatshirts as the number of sweatshirts she buys increases. This information is also given in Table 5.1. Here we assume that Mary is willing to pay $400 for 5 sweatshirts, $456 for 6 sweatshirts, $508 for 7 sweatshirts, and so on.[3] Thus, 5 sweatshirts give her a

---

[3] If these dollar amounts seem high relative to typical market prices, keep in mind that they reflect Mary's willingness to pay for sweatshirts, which is our measure of the utility she derives from them. Market prices may be lower.

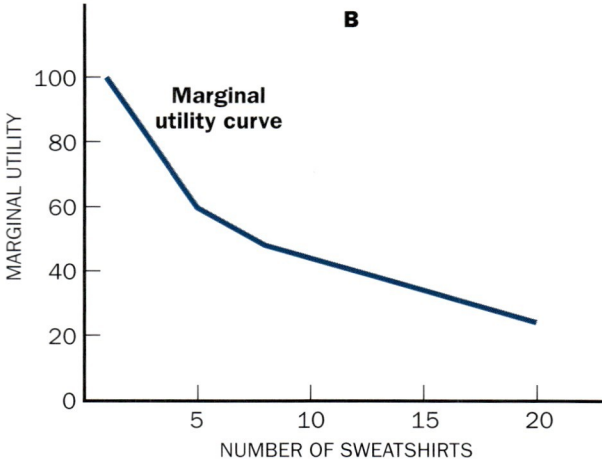

Figure 5.7
UTILITY AND MARGINAL UTILITY

Panel A shows that utility increases continually with consumption but tends to level off as consumption climbs higher. Panel B explicitly shows marginal utility; notice that it declines as consumption increases.

utility of 400, 6 a utility of 456, and 7 sweatshirts a utility of 508. Mary's willingness to pay increases with the number of sweatshirts, reflecting the fact that additional sweatshirts give her additional utility. The extra utility of an additional sweatshirt, measured here by the additional amount she is willing to pay, is the **marginal utility.** The numbers in the third column of Table 5.1 give the marginal (or extra) utility she received from her most recently purchased sweatshirt. When Mary owns 5 sweatshirts, an additional sweatshirt yields her an additional or marginal utility of 56 (456–400); when she owns 6 sweatshirts, an additional one gives her a marginal utility of only 52 (508–456). Figure 5.7B traces the marginal utilities of each of these increments.[4]

As an individual's bundle of goods includes more and more of a good, each successive increment increases her utility less. This is the law of **diminishing marginal utility.** The first sweatshirt is very desirable, and additional ones are attractive as well. But each sweatshirt does not increase utility by as much as the one before, and at some point, Mary may get almost no additional pleasure from adding to her sweatshirt wardrobe.

When Mary has a given budget and must choose between two goods that cost the same, say sweatshirts and pizza, each of which costs $15, she will make her choice so that the marginal utility of each good is the same. Table 5.1 shows Mary's willingness to pay (utility) for both sweatshirts and pizza. Suppose Mary has a $300 budget for sweatshirts and pizza. Look at what happens if she buys 20 sweatshirts with her money and no pizza. The marginal utility of the last sweatshirt is 24, and that of the first pizza is 36. If she switches $15 from sweatshirts to pizza, she loses a utility of 24 from the decreased sweatshirt, but gains 36 from her first pizza. It obviously pays for her to switch.

Now look at the situation when she has decreased her purchases of sweatshirts to 17 and increased purchases of pizza to 3. The marginal utility of the last sweatshirt

---

[4]Since marginal utility is the extra utility from an extra unit of consumption, it is measured by the slope of the utility curve in panel A.

is 30, and that of the last pizza is also 30. At this point, she will not want to switch anymore. If she buys another sweatshirt, she gains 28, but the *last* pizza, her 3rd, which she will have to give up, has a marginal utility of 30; she loses more than she gains. If she buys another pizza, she gains 28, but the last sweatshirt (her 17th) gave her a marginal utility of 30; again, she loses in net. We can thus see that with her budget, she is best off when the marginal utility of the two goods is the same.

The same general principle applies when the prices of two goods differ. Assume that a sweatshirt costs twice as much as a pizza. So long as the marginal utility of sweatshirts is more than twice that of pizzas, it still pays for Mary to switch to sweatshirts. To get one more sweatshirt, she has to give up two pizzas, and we reason, as before, that she will adjust her consumption until she gets to the point where the marginal utilities of the two goods, *per dollar spent,* are equal. This is a general rule: in choosing between two goods, consumers adjust choices to the point at which the marginal utilities are proportional to the prices. Thus, the last unit purchased of a good that costs twice as much as another must generate twice the marginal utility as the last unit purchased of the other good; the last unit purchased of a good that costs three times as much must generate three times the marginal utility as the last unit purchased of the other good; and so on.

Table 5.1

UTILITY AND MARGINAL UTILITY

Number of sweatshirts	Mary's willingness to pay (utility)	Marginal utility	Number of pizzas	Mary's willingness to pay (utility)	Marginal utility
0	0	100	0	0	36
1	100	90	1	36	32
2	190	80	2	64	30
3	270	70	3	98	28
4	340	60	4	126	26
5	400	56	5	152	24
6	456	52	6	176	22
7	508	48	7	198	20
8	556	46	8	218	18
9	602	44	9	236	16
10	646	42	10	252	14
11	688	40	11	266	12
12	728	38	12	272	10
13	766	36	13	288	8
14	802	34	14	296	
15	836	32			
16	868	30			
17	898	28			
18	926	26			
19	952	24			
20	976				

We can write this result simply as

$$\frac{MU_x}{P_x} = \frac{MU_y}{P_y},$$

where MU_x is the marginal utility of good x, MU_y is the marginal utility of good y, P_x is the price of good x, and P_y is the price of good y. The ratio of marginal utility to price should be the same for all goods. When this condition is met, Mary's consumption problem is solved—she has found the combination of the two goods that make her best off.

We have already seen that when the prices of sweatshirts and pizzas are the same, Mary is best off when she buys 17 sweatshirts and 3 pizzas. At that point, the marginal utility of the last sweatshirt purchased is the same as the marginal utility of the last pizza purchased. But let's suppose instead that a pizza costs only $7.50, while sweatshirts continue to cost $15. Using the information in Table 5.1, we can see the combination of 17 sweatshirts and 3 pizzas is no longer the best one for Mary when the prices of the two goods differ. She could give up 1 sweatshirt, which reduces her utility by 30. With the $15 she saved, she can buy 2 more pizzas, for a gain in utility of 54. On net, her utility has gone up by 24, so it pays her to give up that last sweatshirt and buy more pizzas. Does it pay to give up more sweatshirts? Yes. By giving up a second sweatshirt, she reduces her utility by 32, but she gains 46 from the 2 additional pizzas she can buy. Now look at Mary's situation if she buys 14 sweatshirts and 9 pizzas. By Mary giving up the last sweatshirt, her utility drops by 34, but by buying 2 more pizzas, going from 7 to 9, her utility gained 38. She is better off. Does it pay to reduce purchases of sweatshirts any more? No. Giving up 1 more sweatshirt leads to a loss in utility of 36 and the 2 extra pizzas only give a gain in utility of 30. She is best off with 14 sweatshirts and 9 pizzas. The marginal utility of the last sweatshirt is 36; the marginal utility of the last pizza is 18. Since sweatshirts cost twice as much as pizzas, the ratio of the marginal utility of each good to its price is the same, just as our formula said it should be.

In the example we have just analyzed, we relied on the simplifying assumption that Mary's willingness to pay for sweatshirts—her measure of utility—does not depend on how many pizzas, or other goods, she has. This is seldom the case. The utility, and hence marginal utility, of sweatshirts will depend on all her other possessions. Thus, even when the price of sweatshirts remains the same, if the price of other goods changes, she will change her consumption of those other goods *and* sweatshirts. Similarly, a change in Mary's income will affect the marginal utility of the goods she consumes.

Wrap-Up

MARGINAL UTILITY AND CONSUMER CHOICE

Consumers allocate their income among different goods so that the marginal utility associated with the last unit purchased, per dollar spent, is the same for all goods.

CONSUMER SURPLUS

In Chapter 1, we learned that one of the basic principles of economics is that people are better off as a result of voluntary trade. Now that we have developed the fundamental ideas of consumer choice, we can use the demand curve to show how we can measure some of the gains that arise from economic exchange.

Assume you go into a store to buy a can of soda. The store charges you $0.75. If you are particularly thirsty, you might be willing to pay as much as $1.25 for that can of soda. The difference between what you paid and what you would have been willing to pay is called **consumer surplus.** It provides a measure of how much you gained from the trade. In this example, you only had to pay $0.75 for something for which you would have been willing to pay $1.25; the difference, or $0.50, is your consumer surplus.

Earlier, we used the concept of marginal utility to determine Mary's choice of sweatshirts and pizzas. We can calculate from her demand curve the consumer surplus that goes to Mary when she buys pizza. Suppose a pizza costs $10 and Mary buys 13. From the information in Table 5.1, we can see that the 13th pizza gives her a marginal utility of 10 and costs $10. But the 12th pizza she purchased also only cost her $10, yet it yielded a marginal utility of 12. Mary is getting a bargain; she would have been willing to pay more for the earlier pizzas. She would have been willing to pay $12 for the 12th pizza. In fact, for her first pizza, she would have been willing to pay $36, for the second $32, and so on. She would have been willing to pay a total of $288 ($36 + $32 + $30 + $28 + $26 + $24 + $22 + $20 + $18 + $16 + $14 + $12 + $10) for the 13 pizzas. The difference between what she has to pay for 13 pizzas—$10 × 13 = $130—and what she would have been willing to pay, $288, is her consumer surplus. In this example, her surplus is $158.

Figure 5.8 shows Mary's demand curve for pizzas. If the price of pizzas is $36, she would purchase 1 pizza; if the price falls to $20, she would buy 8; and at a price of $10, she would buy 13. The total amount Mary would have been willing to pay for 13 pizzas is the total area under the demand curve between the vertical axis and 13, the combination of the blue and yellow areas. This area is the sum as detailed in the previous paragraph. The amount Mary actually has to pay is represented by the blue area—the price, $10, times the quantity, 13 pizzas. Her consumer surplus is the *difference,* the yellow area above the price line and below the demand curve, over the range of the quantity purchased.

There is always some consumer surplus so long as the consumer has to pay only a fixed price for all the items she purchases. The downward slope of demand curves means the previous units the consumer purchases are more valuable than the marginal units. She would have been willing to pay more for the earlier units than for the last unit, but she does not have to.

We can use the concept of consumer surplus to measure the effect on consumers of the type of agricultural price floor we analyzed in Chapter 4

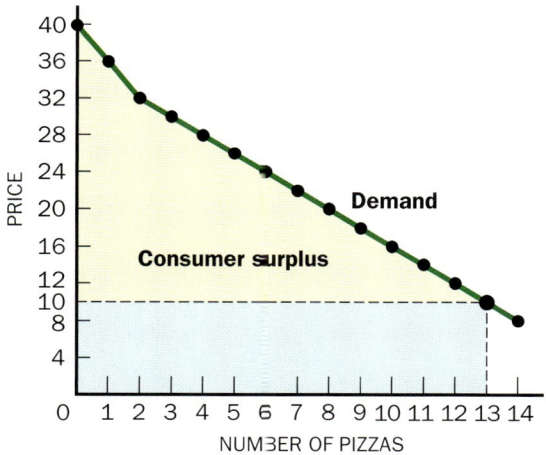

Figure 5.8
CONSUMER SURPLUS

The demand curve plots the amount Mary would be willing to pay for her 1st, 2nd, 3rd, and so on pizza. The total amount she is willing to pay for 13 pizzas is the area under the demand curve up to the 13th pizza. The amount she actually has to pay is the *blue shaded* area. The consumer surplus is the difference between the two the *yellow shaded* area above the line and below the demand curve, over the range of the quantity purchased.

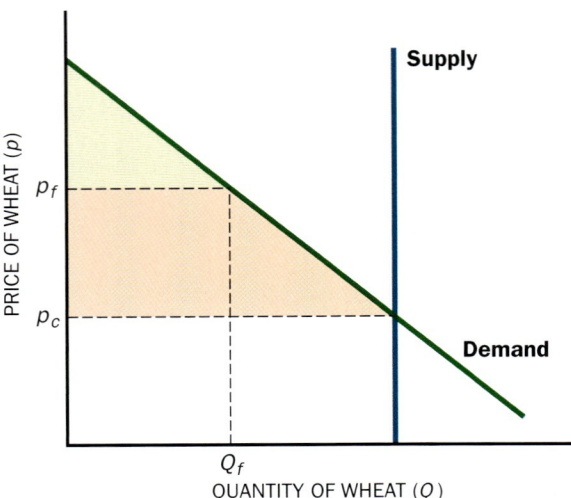

Figure 5.9

CONSUMER SURPLUS AND A PRICE FLOOR

The demand and supply of wheat are equal if the price is p_c. At this price, total consumer surplus is equal to the area between the demand curve, showing willingness to pay, and the market price, p_c. This is the sum of the yellow and orange areas. With a price floor at p_f, the quantity demanded is only Q_f. At the price p_f, consumer surplus is the yellow area. The orange area measures the fall in consumer surplus due to the price floor.

using demand and supply. Figure 5.9 shows the demand and supply curves for wheat. For the sake of simplicity, supply is drawn as a vertical line (inelastic supply). In the absence of a price floor, the equilibrium price will be p_c, and the consumer surplus is the total of the yellow and orange areas. If the government imposes a price floor, at p_f, then the quantity demanded is Q_f. Consumer surplus is equal to the yellow area, the area under the demand curve from the vertical axis to the quantity purchased. The price floor reduces consumer surplus. The orange area measures the cost to consumers of the price floor.

Wrap-Up

CONSUMER SURPLUS

Consumer surplus is the difference between what individuals would have been willing to spend to purchase a given amount of a good and what they actually had to spend. It is measured by the area under the demand curve, but above the price.

Consumer surplus provides a measure of the benefit to consumers of the market exchange for the good.

Looking Beyond the Basic Model

In the market economy, "For whom are goods produced?" has a simple answer: goods are produced for consumers. Thus to understand market economies, we must understand how consumers make choices. The model of budget constraints and individual preferences sketched in this chapter is the economist's basic approach to consumer choice, a powerful one whose insights carry well beyond this course. Still, it has been criticized, and in the past few decades, alternative models of consumer choice have been proposed. In the remainder of this chapter, we discuss four criticisms of the basic model before turning to recent work that goes under the name *behavioral economics*.

HOW WELL DO THE UNDERLYING ASSUMPTIONS MATCH REALITY?

The first criticism of the basic model of consumer choice is that it fails to reflect the actual thought processes of consumers. This line of criticism is like the claim of a pool player that the physicist's model of motion, which predicts with great precision how billiard balls will interact, is invalid because players do not work through the equations before taking a shot. The appropriate question is whether the economic model of consumer choice can be used to make accurate predictions. By and large, it can. Many businesses, for example, have found the model useful for predicting the demand for their products. And economists have used the model with remarkable success to predict consumer behavior in a variety of circumstances. Sometimes, however, it does not make reliable predictions, and we will consider some of these instances when we discuss behavioral economics.

The second criticism questions the model's assumption that individuals know what they like—that is, that they have *well-defined preferences*. Given a choice between two bundles of goods—one consisting of two T-shirts and three sweatshirts and the other containing one pair of jeans and two sweatshirts—they could tell you quickly which they preferred. Moveover, their answer would be the same tomorrow or next week. But in many cases, someone asked which of two things is preferred replies, "I don't know. Let me try them out." And what people like may change from day to day. In addition, their preferences may be affected by what others like. How else can we account for the short-lived fads so common in food and fashion as well as in other spheres?

The third criticism focuses on the model's assumption that individuals know the prices of each good in the market. In fact, people often lack this knowledge. And even when they know that bargains can be found, it is costly to search for them. While we can talk meaningfully about the price of a barrel of oil, what do we mean by the "price" of a couch, computer, or house? If we are lucky and stumble onto a good deal, we may find a leather couch for $600. If unlucky, even after looking all day, we may not find one for under $1,000. The ability to search on the Internet for prices at various stores before we go shopping has helped lower the costs of finding bargains and has made it easier for consumers to know the prices of goods.

The final criticism points out that sometimes the interactions of prices and preferences are more complicated than this chapter has depicted. In particular, people's attitudes toward a good can depend on its price. More expensive goods may be attractive simply because they have snob appeal. And when the quality of certain goods cannot easily be ascertained, people use price as their yardstick. Because, on average, better (more durable) products are more costly, a cheap item is assumed to be of poorer quality than its more expensive counterpart. In either case, demand curves will look quite different from those described in this chapter. Lowering the price for a good may actually lower its demand.

The need to extend or modify the basic economic model for some goods in some instances does not detract from its overall utility: in the vast majority of situations, it provides just the information that businesses and governments need to make important decisions. Even when it is less effective, the model provides a basic framework that enhances our understanding of the behavior of households. We will build on this framework in Part Three. And asking which of its underlying assumptions may be inappropriate whenever we apply it will help us search for a better model.

BEHAVIORAL ECONOMICS

In recent years, a growing number of economists have combined insights from psychology and economics to gain new understanding into how people make choices. Those engaged in this new field, called **behavioral economics,** reject the simple model of consumer choice that was developed in this chapter. Instead, they argue that a theory of consumer choice should be based on how people actually make decisions. Behavioral economists therefore draw on the findings of psychologists who conduct laboratory experiments to study that question. As a sign of the growing importance of this work, the 2002 Nobel Prize in Economics was shared by a psychologist, Daniel Kahneman, whose research has heavily influenced the new field.

Behavioral economics takes as its starting point a number of findings that appear to be inconsistent with the basic model of consumer choice we have developed in this chapter. A few of them, discussed below, illustrate the types of evidence on which behavioral economists focus.

Endowment Effects A large body of evidence suggests that the simple act of possessing something can alter a person's preferences. Consider the following experiment involving a group of college undergraduates, half of whom were given college coffee mugs that sold for $6.00 at the college bookstore. The students were then allowed to participate in a market in which mugs could be bought and sold. One might expect that those students with mugs who valued them least would end up selling them to those without mugs who valued them most. Since the coffee mugs had been distributed randomly, about half should trade hands. In fact, very few trades took place. The experimenters found that the median price demanded by mug sellers was $5.25, and the median amount buyers were willing to spend was around $2.25. Initially, there were no reasons to expect predictable differences in how students valued coffee mugs; but the mere fact of being given a mug seemed to make individuals value mugs more highly.

This phenomenon is called the *endowment effect*. In the standard model of consumer choice, individuals purchase those goods that they value more than the dollars they have to give up to make the purchase. But people are not expected to value more highly those items that they happen to possess. In another experiment, college students were given either a lottery ticket or $2.00. They were then allowed to exchange whichever they had received for the other; that is, a student who had been given a lottery ticket could turn it in and get $2.00, or a student who had received $2.00 could exchange it for a lottery ticket. Surprisingly, at least from the perspective of the standard model of consumer choice, very few students wanted to make the trade. Those who received lottery tickets seemed to prefer them to the cash; those who received the cash preferred it to the ticket. Since the two groups of students were otherwise similar, there was no reason to expect that those who happened to receive lottery tickets would value them more than did the students given cash.

Loss Aversion The standard model of consumer choice assumes that individuals' well-defined preferences for goods do not depend on whether they actually have those items. The endowment effect may reflect what psychologists have called *loss aversion*. Individuals seem to be particularly sensitive to losses. Once the students had mugs in their possession, they didn't want to give them up; thus they set the sale price above what they would have been willing to pay for a mug in the first place. Similarly, a person with $1,100 who then loses $100 feels worse than someone with $900 who then finds $100. Even though both ultimately have the same amount of money, their feelings about their situations are very different.

The Status Quo Bias Loss aversion and endowment effects lead to behavior that exhibits a bias in favor of the status quo. In the example just given, the status quo or reference point of the first person is the $1,100 he had, so he feels worse off when he has only $1,000. The reference level of the second person was $900, so she feels better off when she has $1,000. In the basic model of consumer choice outlined in this chapter, we assumed that individuals' utility depended on the absolute level of their consumption. If reference points are important, utility may instead depend on the difference between an individual's current consumption and a reference level of consumption. This reference level might be recent levels of consumption—a certain standard of living to which people become accustomed. Or it might be the consumption levels of an individual's peer group, an idea captured in the phrase "keeping up with the Joneses."

The tendency of individuals to accept whatever happens to be the default among a number of options illustrates the importance of the status quo. For example, many employers offer their employees the option of participating in a 401(k) savings plan, a way to set aside before-tax income for retirement. If the default is automatic participation, so that employees must actively decide to opt out of the plan, then most employees end up contributing. If the default is to not participate, requiring employees to sign up for the plan, the fraction of employees who participate is much lower. Ignoring status quo effects may undercut major public policy initiatives. In 2003, the U.S. federal government introduced a medical drug benefit as part of Medicare, the health insurance program for older Americans. To obtain discounts on prescription drugs, seniors had to sign up for a "drug discount card." The default option was to not sign up. According to a survey conducted by the Harvard School of Public Health and the Kaiser Family Foundation, only about 10 percent of eligible seniors had signed up by the middle of 2004. The status quo effect may have been one factor at work.

Implications These examples, and many others that behavioral economists have investigated, suggest the economist's simple model of choice is incomplete. But what is critical for an analysis of market economies is understanding how the behavior uncovered by psychologists and behavioral economists affects market demand curves. Do we need to change the basic ideas developed in this chapter about how consumers respond to changes in prices? Broadly speaking, the answer is clearly no. Individuals do respond to incentives—as the price of a good falls, we expect more consumers will purchase it. As price rises, less is demanded. The findings from behavioral economics do suggest, however, that preferences can depend on what individuals view as the status quo, and that consumers may display a greater reluctance to change than the basic economic model would predict. This reluctance to change, reflected in the endowment effect and the status quo effect, may reduce their sensitivity to incentives. These effects may help explain why economists often observe individuals passing up the opportunity to make exchanges that appear to be advantageous.

Behavioral economists have developed new insights into saving behavior, as well. We will consider some of them in Chapter 9, where we will discuss the factors that affect household decisions about how much to save.

Review and Practice

SUMMARY

1. The amount of one good a person must use to purchase another good is determined by the relative prices of the two goods, and is illustrated by the slope of the budget constraint.
2. As a good becomes more expensive relative to other goods, an individual will substitute other goods for the higher-priced good. This is the substitution effect.
3. As the price of a good rises, a person's buying power is reduced. The response to this lower "real" income is the income effect. Consumption of a normal good rises as incomes rise. Thus, usually, when price rises, both the substitution and income effects lead to decreased consumption of that good.
4. When substitution is easy, demand curves tend to be elastic, or flat. If substitution is difficult, demand curves tend to be inelastic, or steep.
5. Economists sometimes describe the benefits of consumption by referring to the utility that people get from a combination of goods. The extra utility of consuming one more unit of a good is referred to as the marginal utility of that good.
6. Consumers will allocate their income so that the marginal utility per dollar spent is the same for all goods.
7. Consumer surplus measures the difference between what a consumer would be willing to pay and what she has to pay (the market price).

KEY TERMS

slope
income elasticity of demand
inferior goods
normal goods
income effect
substitution effect
utility
marginal utility
diminishing marginal utility
consumer surplus
behavioral economics

REVIEW QUESTIONS

1. How is the slope of the budget constraint related to the relative prices of the goods on the horizontal and vertical axes?
2. How can the budget constraint appear the same even for individuals whose tastes and preferences differ dramatically?
3. Is the income elasticity of demand positive or negative for an inferior good?
4. If the price of a normal good increases, how will the income effect cause the quantity demanded of that good to change?
5. What is the substitution effect? Why do the substitution and income effects normally reinforce each other? Is this true for an inferior good?
6. Does a greater availability of substitutes make a demand curve more elastic or less elastic? Explain.
7. Why does marginal utility tend to diminish?
8. What is meant by consumer surplus?

PROBLEMS

1. A student has an entertainment budget of $200 per term and spends it on either concert tickets at $40 apiece or movie tickets at $10 apiece. Suppose movie tickets decrease in price, first falling to $5, then $2. Graph the three budget constraints, with movies on the horizontal axis. If the student's demand for movies, D, is represented by the function $D = 10 - 1.0p$, where p is the price, graph both the demand curve for movies and the point she will choose on the budget line corresponding to each price.
2. Choose two normal goods and draw a budget constraint illustrating the trade-off between them. Show how the budget line shifts if income increases. Arbitrarily choose a point on the first budget line as the point a particular consumer will select. Now find two points on the new budget line such that the new preferred choice of the consumer must fall between these points.
3. Compare one poor person, with an income of $10,000 per year, with a relatively wealthy person who has an income

of $60,000 per year. Imagine that the poor person drinks 15 bottles of wine per year at an average price of $10 per bottle, while the wealthy person drinks 50 bottles of wine per year at an average price of $20 per bottle. If a tax of $1 per bottle is imposed on wine, who pays more in taxes? Who pays the greater amount as a percentage of income? If a tax equal to 10 percent of the value of the wine is imposed, who pays more in taxes? Who pays the greater amount as a percentage of income?

4. The income elasticity for alcoholic beverages is 0.62. Consider two people with incomes of $20,000 and $40,000. If all alcohol is taxed at the same rate, by what percentage more will the tax paid by the $40,000 earner be greater than that paid by the $20,000 earner? Why might some people think this unfair?

5. The following table gives Sarah's willingness to pay for music CDs and movie DVDs. Calculate Sarah's marginal utility for CDs and DVDs by filling in the columns of the table labeled "marginal utility." Suppose the price of a CD is $10 and the price of a DVD is $30. How many CDs and how many DVDs should Sarah purchase if she has a fixed budget of $150 to spend on these two items? Suppose her budget for these two goods is only $80. How many CDs and how many DVDs should she purchase?

CDs	Willingness to pay	Marginal utility	DVDs	Willingness to pay	Marginal utility
0	0		0	0	
1	24		1	42	
2	46		2	78	
3	66		3	108	
4	84		4	132	
5	100		5	150	
6	114		6	162	
7	126		7	168	
8	136		8	168	
9	144				
10	150				
11	154				
12	156				
13	156				

Appendix: Indifference Curves and the Consumption Decision[5]

This chapter explained the consumption decision in terms of the budget constraint facing the individual and the individual's choice of her most preferred point on the budget constraint. Effects of changes in prices on the quantity demanded were analyzed in terms of income and substitution effects.

To help them more rigorously analyze choices and the consequences of changes in prices, economists have developed an extremely useful tool called **indifference curves.** Indifference curves give the combinations of goods among which an individual has no preference (that is, is indifferent) or which yield the same level of utility. This appendix shows how indifference curves can be used to derive the demand curve and to separate more precisely changes in consumption into income and substitution effects.

USING INDIFFERENCE CURVES TO ILLUSTRATE CONSUMER CHOICES

In this chapter solutions to consumer choice problems were characterized as having two stages: first, identify the opportunity set, and second, find the most preferred point in the opportunity set. The budget constraint defines the opportunity set for consumers with a given income to spend on goods. Figure 5.10 repeats the budget constraint for Fran, who must divide her income between candy bars and CDs. In the chapter, we simply said that Fran would choose the most preferred point along the budget constraint. If she likes CDs a lot, she might choose point B; if she has a stronger preference for candy, she might choose point A.

The concept of the indifference curve can help us see which of these points she chooses.

The indifference curve shows the various combinations of goods that make a person equally happy. For example, in Figure 5.11, the indifference curve I_0 gives all those combinations of candy bars and compact discs that Fran finds just as attractive as 150 candy bars and 10 CDs (point A on the curve). At B, for instance, she has 12 CDs but only 130 candy bars—not so much candy, but in her mind the extra CDs make up for the loss. The fact that B and A are on the same indifference curve means that Fran is indifferent to the choice between them. That is, if you asked her whether she preferred A to B or B to A, she would answer that she couldn't care less.

Indifference curves simply reflect preferences between pairs of goods. Unlike demand curves, they have nothing to do with budget constraints or prices. The different combinations of goods along the indifference curve cost different amounts of money. The indifference curves are drawn by asking an individual which he prefers: 10 candy bars and 2 CDs or 15 candy bars and 1 CD? or 11 candy bars and 2 CDs or 15 candy bars and 1 CD? or 12 candy bars and 2 CDs or 15 candy bars and 1 CD? When he answers, "Given those options, I am indifferent," the two points that represent those choices are on the same indifference curve.

---

[5]Skipping this appendix will not affect your understanding of later chapters.

Moving along the curve in one direction, Fran is willing to accept more CDs in exchange for fewer candy bars; moving in the other direction, she is willing to accept more candy bars in exchange for fewer CDs. Any point on the same indifference curve, by definition, makes her just as happy as any other—whether it is point A or C or an extreme point like D, where she has many candy bars and very few CDs, or F, where she has relatively few candy bars but more CDs.

However, if Fran were to receive the same number of candy bars but more CDs than at A—say 150 candy bars and 15 CDs (point E)—then she would be better off, on the principle that "more is better." The new indifference curve I_1 illustrates all those combinations of candy bars and CDs that make her just as well-off as the combination of 150 candy bars and 15 CDs.

Figure 5.11 shows two indifference curves for Fran. Because more is better, Fran (or any individual) will prefer a choice on the indifference curve that is higher than another curve. On the higher indifference curve, she can have more of both items. By definition, we can draw an indifference curve for *any* point in the space of an indifference curve diagram. Also by definition, indifference curves cannot cross, as Figure 5.12 makes clear. Assume that the indifference curves I_0 and I_1 cross at point A. That would mean that Fran is indifferent to a choice between A and all points on I_0, and between A and all points on I_1. In particular, she would be indifferent when choosing between A and B, between A and C, and accordingly between B and C. But B is clearly preferred to C; therefore, indifference curves cannot cross.

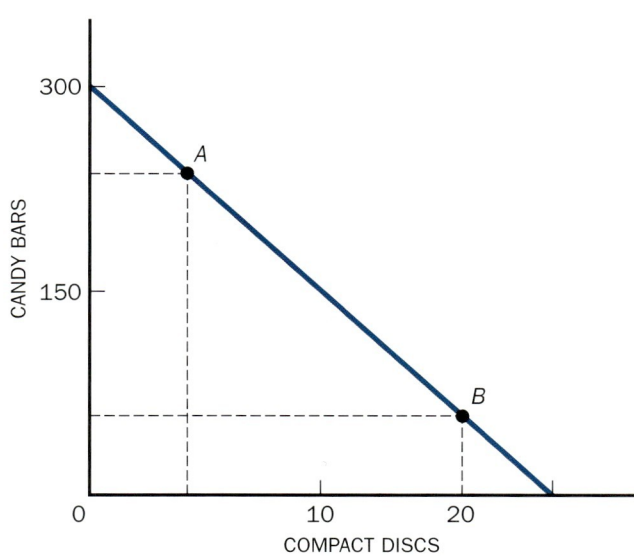

Figure 5.10

BUDGET CONSTRAINT

The budget constraint defines the opportunity set. Fran can choose any point on or below the budget constraint. If she has strong preferences for CDs, she might choose B; if she has strong preferences for candy bars, she might choose point A.

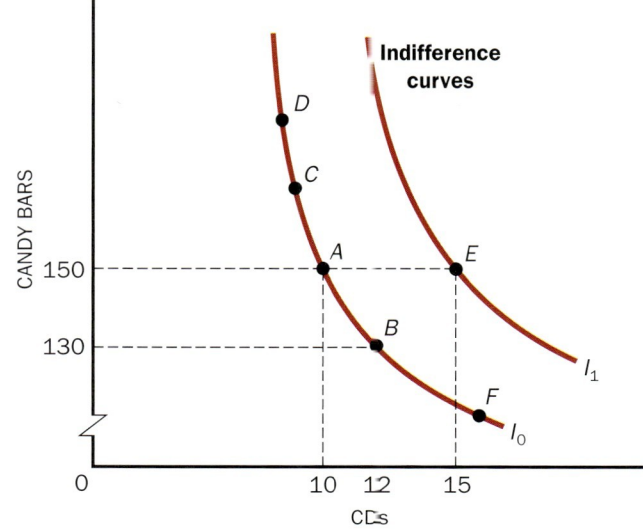

Figure 5.11

INDIFFERENCE CURVES

An indifference curve traces combinations of goods to which an individual is indifferent. Each reflects Fran's taste for CDs and for candy bars. She is just as well-off (has an identical amount of utility) at all points on the indifference curve I_0: A, B, C, D, or F.

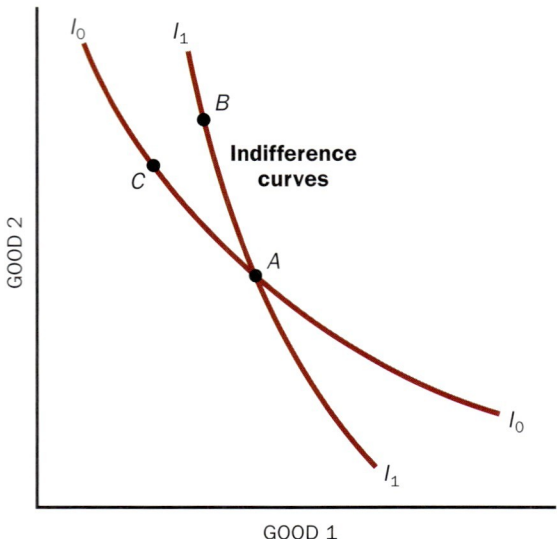

Figure 5.12

WHY INDIFFERENCE CURVES CANNOT CROSS

If two indifference curves crossed, a logical contradiction would occur. If curves crossed at point A, then Fran would be indifferent between A and B, between A and C, and therefore between B and C. But since B involves higher consumption of both goods than C, B is clearly preferred to C.

Indifference Curves and Marginal Rates of Substitution

The slope of the indifference curve measures the number of candy bars that the individual is willing to give up to get another compact disc. The technical term for the slope of an indifference curve is the **marginal rate of substitution.** The marginal rate of substitution tells us how much of one good an individual is *willing* to give up in return for one more unit of another. The concept is quite distinct from the amount a consumer *must* give up, which is determined by the budget constraint and relative prices.

If Fran's marginal rate of substitution of candy bars for CDs is 15 to 1, this means that if she is given 1 more CD, she is willing to give up 15 candy bars. If she only had to give up 12 candy bars, she would be happier. If she had to give up 20, she would say, "That's too much—having one more CD isn't worth giving up twenty candy bars." Of course, Gary could have quite different attitudes toward CDs and candy bars. His marginal rate of substitution might be 25 to 1. He would be willing to give up 25 candy bars to get 1 more CD.

The marginal rate of substitution rises and falls according to how much of an item an individual already has. For example, consider point F back in Figure 5.11, where Fran has many CDs and few candy bars. In this case, Fran already has bought all her favorite CDs; the marginal CD she buys now will be something she likes but not something she is wild over. In other words, because she already has a large number of CDs, having an additional one is less important. She would rather have some candy bars instead. Her marginal rate of substitution of candy bars for CDs at F is very low; for the sake of illustration, let's say that she would be willing to give up the marginal CD for only 10 candy bars. Her marginal rate of substitution is 10 to 1 (candy bars per CD).

The opposite holds true when Fran has lots of candy bars and few CDs. Since she is eating several candy bars almost every day, the chance to have more is not worth much to her. But since she has few CDs, she does not yet own all of her favorites. The marginal value of another candy bar is relatively low, while the marginal value of another CD is relatively high. Accordingly, in this situation, Fran might insist on getting 30 extra candy bars before she gives up 1 CD. Her marginal rate of substitution is 30 to 1 (candy bars per CD).

As we move along an indifference curve, we increase the amount of one good (like CDs) that an individual has. In Fran's case, she requires less and less of the other good (candy bars) to compensate her for each one-unit decrease in the quantity of the first good (CDs). This principle is known as the **diminishing marginal rate of substitution.** As a result of the principle of diminishing marginal rate of substitution, the slope of the indifference curve becomes flatter as we move from left to right along it.

Using Indifference Curves to Illustrate Choices

By definition, an individual does not care where he sits on any *given* indifference curve. But he would prefer to be on the highest indifference curve possible. What pins him down is his budget constraint. As Figure 5.13 illustrates, the highest indifference curve that a person can attain is the one that just touches the budget constraint—that is, the indifference curve that is *tangent* to the budget constraint. The point of tangency (labeled E) is the point the individual will choose. Consider any other point on the budget constraint, say A. The indifference curve through A is below the curve through E; the individual is better off at E than at A. But consider an indifference curve above I_0—for instance, I_1. Since every point on I_1 lies above the budget constraint, there is no point on I_1 that the individual can purchase given his income.

When a curve is tangent to a line, the curve and line have the same slope at the point of tangency. Thus, the slope of the indifference curve equals the slope of the budget constraint at the point of tangency. The slope of the indifference curve is the marginal rate of substitution; the slope of the budget constraint is the relative price. This two-dimensional diagram therefore illustrates a basic principle of consumer choice: *individuals choose the point where the marginal rate of substitution equals the relative price.*

This principle makes sense. If the relative price of CDs and candy bars is 15 (CDs cost $15 and candy bars cost $1) and Fran's marginal

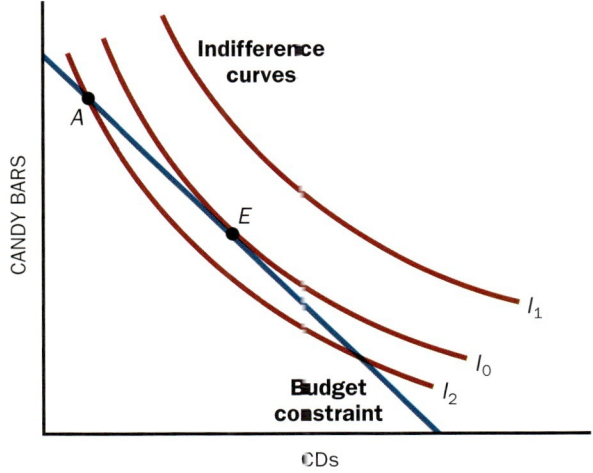

Figure 5.13

INDIFFERENCE CURVES AND THE BUDGET CONSTRAINT

The highest feasible indifference curve that can be reached is the one just tangent to the budget constraint, or indifference curve I_0 here. This individual's budget constraint does not permit her to reach I_1, nor would she want to choose point A, which would put her on I_2, since along I_2 she is worse off.

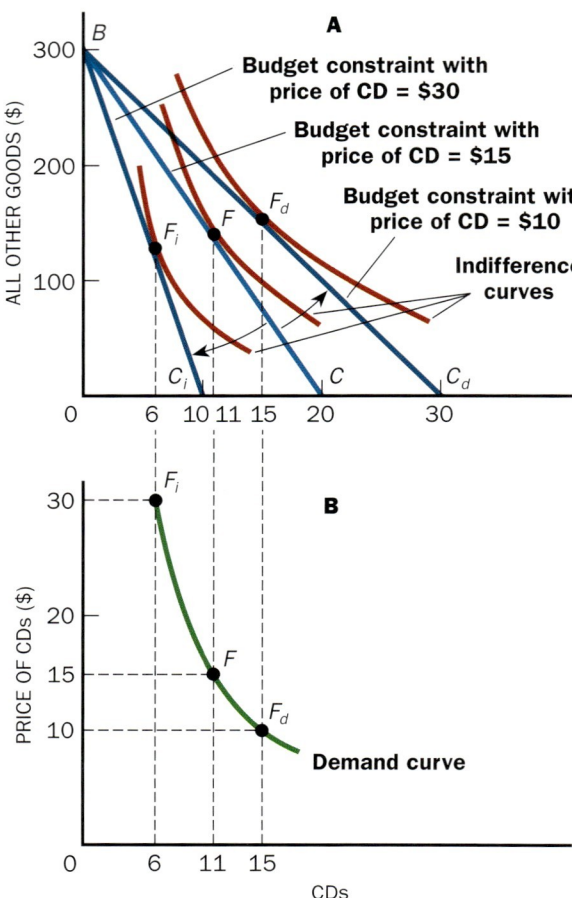

Figure 5.14

DERIVING DEMAND CURVES FROM SHIFTING BUDGET CONSTRAINTS

In panel A, the budget constraint rotates down to the left as the price of CDs increases, leading Fran to change consumption from F to F_i. The budget constraint rotates to the right when the price of CDs decreases, and Fran moves from F to F_d. Panel B shows the corresponding demand curve for CDs, illustrating how the rising prices lead to a decline in the quantity consumed.

rate of substitution is 20, Fran is willing to give up 20 candy bars to get 1 more CD, but only *has* to give up 15; it clearly pays her to buy more CDs and fewer candy bars. If her marginal rate of substitution is 10, she is willing to give up 1 CD for just 10 candy bars; but if she gives up 1 CD, she can get 15 candy bars. She will be better off buying more candy bars and fewer CDs. Thus, if the marginal rate of substitution exceeds the relative price, Fran is better off if she buys more CDs; if it is less, she is better off if she buys fewer CDs. When the marginal rate of substitution *equals* the relative price, it does not pay for her to either increase or decrease her purchases.

USING INDIFFERENCE CURVES TO DERIVE DEMAND CURVES

Indifference curves and budget constraints can be used to derive the demand curve, and thus to show what happens when prices increase. The analysis consists of two steps.

First, we identify what happens to the budget constraint as, say, the price of CDs increases. We did this earlier in Figure 5.6, but now we can add indifference curves to the analysis. In the budget constraint drawn in Figure 5.14A, we find CDs on the horizontal axis and all other goods on the vertical axis. If Fran buys no CDs, she has $300 to spend on all other goods. At a CD price of $15, she can buy up to 20 CDs, producing the budget line running from point B to C. As the price of CDs increases, the budget constraint rotates in and becomes steeper. If she buys no CDs, she still has $300 to spend on other goods. But if she buys only CDs, the number of CDs she can buy falls as their price rises. If the price of CDs falls, the budget constraint rotates out and becomes flatter.

For each budget constraint, we find the point of tangency between the indifference curve and the budget constraint, here labeled F_i, F, and F_d. This shows the point chosen along each budget constraint. Looking at the horizontal axis, we see, at each price, the quantity of CDs purchased. Panel B then plots these quantities for each price. At the price of $15, Fran chooses 11 CDs; at a price of $30, she chooses to buy only 6.

SUBSTITUTION AND INCOME EFFECTS

Indifference curves also permit a precise definition of the substitution and income effects. Figure 5.15 plots some of Jeremy's indifference curves between CDs and candy bars. Jeremy's original budget constraint is line BC and his indifference curve is I_0; the point of tangency, the point he chooses, is point E_0. Suppose the price of candy increases. Now he can buy fewer candy bars; but the number of CDs he can buy, were he to spend all of his income on CDs, is unchanged. Thus, his budget constraint becomes flatter; it is now line B_2C. While Jeremy originally chose point E_0 on the indifference curve I_0, now he chooses E_1 on the *lower* indifference curve I_1.

The price change has moved Jeremy's choice from E_0 to E_1 for two reasons: the substitution effect and the income effect. To see how this has happened, let's isolate the two effects. First, we focus on the substitution effect by asking what would happen to Jeremy's consumption if we changed relative prices but did not change how well-off he was. To keep him just as well-off as before the price change, we must keep him on the same indifference curve, I_0. Thus, the substitution effect is a movement along an indifference curve. As the price of candy rises, Jeremy, moving down the indifference curve, buys more CDs and fewer candy bars. The movement from E_0 to E_2 is the substitution effect. The budget constraint B_1C_1 represents the *new* prices, but it does not account for the income effect, by definition, since Jeremy is on the same indifference curve that he was on before.

To keep Jeremy on the same indifference curve when we increase the price of candy requires giving Jeremy more income. The line B_1C_1 is the budget constraint with the *new* prices that would leave Jeremy on the same indifference curve. Because prices are the same, the budget constraint B_1C_1 is parallel to B_2C. We now need to take away the income that left Jeremy on the same indifference curve. We keep prices the same (at the new levels), and we take away income until we arrive at the new budget constraint B_2C, and the corresponding new equilibrium E_1. The movement from E_2 to E_1 is called the income effect, since only income is changed. We have thus broken down the movement from the old equilibrium, E_0, to the new one, E_1, into the movement from E_0 to E_2, the substitution effect, and the movement from E_2 to E_1, the income effect.

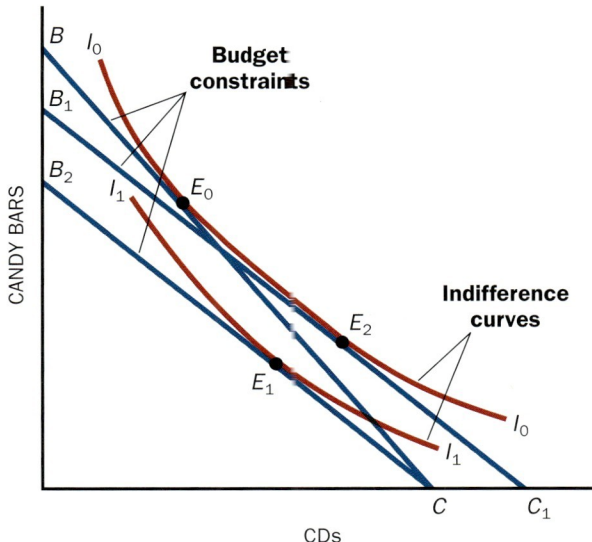

Figure 5.15

SUBSTITUTION AND INCOME EFFECTS WITH INDIFFERENCE CURVES

As the price of candy bars increases, the budget constraint rotates down. The change of Jeremy's choice from E_0 to E_1 can be broken down into an income and a substitution effect. The line B_1C shows the substitution effect, the change in the budget constraint that would occur if relative prices shifted but the level of utility remained the same. (Notice that Jeremy stays on the same indifference curve in this scenario.) The substitution effect alone causes a shift from E_0 to E_2. The shift in the budget constraint from B_1C_1 to B_2C shows the income effect, the change that results from changing the amount of income but leaving relative prices unchanged. The income effect alone causes a shift from E_2 to E_1.

Learning Goals

In this chapter, you will learn

1. The different types of costs a firm faces
2. The relationship between average and marginal costs
3. How costs differ in the short run and long run
4. How firms minimize cost when they have many factors of production

Chapter 6

THE FIRM'S COSTS

Imagine the situation facing a firm in the basic competitive model. There are many other firms that make the identical product, all trying to sell what they produce to well-informed consumers who respond to any price differences. Each firm must accept the price set by the forces of supply and demand in the market as a whole. In a competitive market, a firm will lose all its customers if it charges a price even slightly above the market price. And there is no point in lowering its price, since at the market price it can already sell as much as it wants to produce. Selling at a lower price would just reduce the firm's profits.

In a competitive market, each firm is a *price taker*. No individual firm is large enough to affect the price. A firm that produces standardized memory chips or an agricultural product such as milk or almonds does not have to decide what price to set—the market sets the price; the firm decides only how much to produce.

A key factor in that decision will be the costs of producing memory chips or milk. The firm's total costs are affected by its level of production, how much labor and capital it uses in production, and the prices (wages and interest) of these inputs. Whatever output level it chooses, a firm that tries to maximize profits will seek to minimize its costs of production. This chapter focuses on how firms minimize costs and how costs are affected by the level of production. In the following chapter, we will show how a firm chooses the level of production that maximizes its profits.

Even though we talk in terms of "production" and "goods," it is important to bear in mind that only one-third of the U.S. economy consists of industries that produce goods in the conventional sense—manufacturing, mining, construction, and agriculture. The other two-thirds of the economy produces primarily services, in industries such as transportation, education, health care, wholesale and retail trade, and finance. The principles laid out here, however, apply equally to these other sectors.

Profits, Costs, and Factors of Production

A business that over time continually incurs losses will cease to exist, because it will not have enough money to pay its bills. Businesses are under constant pressure to make money. The need to make as much money as possible—maximizing profits—provides a useful starting point for discussing the behavior of firms in competitive markets.

The definition of **profits** is simple. Profits are equal to the money the business receives from selling its products—its **revenues**—minus the costs of producing those products:

$$\text{profits} = \text{revenues} - \text{costs}.$$

If a computer memory chip manufacturer sells 1 million chips at $0.20 each, its revenues would be $200,000—$0.20 times the 1 million chips sold. The revenue a business receives is just the quantity of the product it sells multiplied by the actual price the firm received for the product that it sold. A firm's *costs* are defined as the total expenses of producing the good.

What the firm uses to produce the goods are called inputs or *factors of production*: labor, materials, and capital goods. The firm's total costs are simply the sum of the costs of these inputs. Labor costs are what the company pays for the workers it hires and the managers it employs to supervise them. The costs of materials include raw materials and intermediate goods. Intermediate goods are whatever supplies the company purchases from other firms—such as seeds, fertilizer, and gasoline for a farm; or iron ore, coal, coke, limestone, and electric power for a steel company. The costs of capital goods include the cost of machinery and structures such as buildings and factories.

All firms work to keep their costs as low as possible. For given prices and levels of output, a firm maximizes its profits by finding the least costly way of producing its output. Thus, profit-maximizing firms are also cost-minimizing firms. Within limits, firms can vary the mix of labor, materials, and capital goods they use; and they will do so until they find the lowest-cost method of producing a given quality and quantity of product.

PRODUCTION WITH ONE VARIABLE INPUT

The simplest way of understanding how firms find the lowest cost point is to look at a firm with only two factors of production, one fixed (such as the amount of land a farmer has or the number of plants a manufacturer has) and one that varies with the level of production (such as the number of workers the firm hires). Not surprisingly, inputs that vary with the level of production are said to be *variable*.

A wheat farmer with a fixed amount of land who uses only labor to produce his crop is our example. The more labor he applies to the farm (his own time, plus the time of workers that he hires), the greater the output. Labor is the single variable factor (input).

The relationship between the quantity of inputs used in production and the level of output is called the **production function**. Figure 6.1 shows the farmer's production function; the data supporting the figure are set forth in Table 6.1. The increase in output corresponding to a unit increase in any factor of production, labor in this case, is the **marginal product** of that factor. For example, when the number of hours worked per year rises from 8,000 to 9,000, output increases by 10,000 bushels, from 155,000 to 165,000. The marginal product of an extra 1,000 hours of labor is thus 10,000 bushels. The marginal product is given in the last column of the table. Diagrammatically, it is given by the slope of the production function. The slope of a curve is the change along the vertical axis (the increase in output) from a unit increase along the horizontal axis (the increase in labor input).

Diminishing Returns In the case of the wheat farmer, as more labor is added to a fixed amount of land, the marginal product of labor diminishes. This is another application of the concept of *diminishing returns,* which we originally encountered in Chapter 2. In the case of a firm's production function, diminishing returns implies that each additional unit of labor generates a smaller increase in output than the last. Increasing the number of hours worked from 7,000 to 8,000 raises output by 15,000 bushels, but increasing the hours worked from 8,000 to 9,000 raises output by only 10,000 bushels. Diminishing returns sets in with a vengeance at higher levels of input; moving from 10,000 to 11,000 hours worked adds nothing. Diagrammatically, diminishing returns are represented by the slope's flattening out as the amount of labor increases. It is clear that because of diminishing returns, increases in input lead to less than proportionate increases in output; doubling the input results in output that is less than twice as large.

Figure 6.1

PRODUCTION FUNCTION WITH DIMINISHING RETURNS TO AN INPUT

As the amount of the input (labor) increases, so does the output (wheat). But there are diminishing returns to labor: each increase in labor results in successively smaller increases in wheat output. Since the slope of the curve is the marginal product of labor, the slope on the graph flattens out as the amount of labor increases.

Table 6.1

LEVEL OF OUTPUT WITH DIFFERENT AMOUNTS OF LABOR

Number of hours worked	Amount of wheat produced (bushels)	Marginal Product (additional bushels produced by 1,000 additional hours of labor)
5,000	95,000	25,000
6,000	120,000	20,000
7,000	140,000	15,000
8,000	155,000	10,000
9,000	165,000	5,000
10,000	170,000	0
11,000	170,000	

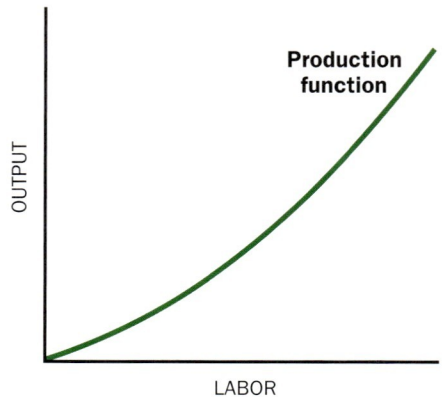

Figure 6.2

PRODUCTION FUNCTION WITH INCREASING RETURNS TO AN INPUT

As the amount of labor increases, so does output. But the returns to labor are increasing in this case; successive increases in labor result in successively larger increases in output. The slope on the graph therefore becomes steeper as the amount of labor increases.

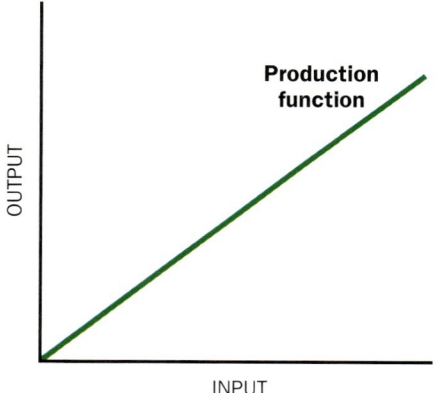

Figure 6.3

PRODUCTION FUNCTION WITH CONSTANT RETURNS TO AN INPUT

The marginal product of the input is constant, neither increasing nor diminishing as the firm expands production. The slope on the graph therefore does not change.

Wrap-Up

DIMINISHING RETURNS

As more and more of one input is added, *while other inputs remain unchanged,* the marginal product of the added input diminishes.

Increasing Returns Although a production function with diminishing returns is the most important case, other functions are possible. Figure 6.2 shows a production function where increasing an input (here, labor) raises output more than proportionately. A firm with this kind of production function has *increasing returns*. In the single-input case depicted, it is clear that the marginal product of the input increases with the amount produced; that is, adding one more worker increases output by more when the firm is producing a lot than it does when the firm is producing little.

Imagine a business that picks up garbage. If this business counts only one out of every five houses as customers, it will have a certain cost of production. But suppose the company can expand to picking up the garbage from two out of every five houses: while it will need more workers, the workers will be able to drive a shorter distance per customer and pick up more garbage faster. Thus, a doubling of output can result from a less than doubling of labor. Many examples of increasing returns, like garbage collection, involve providing service to more people in a given area. Telephone companies and electric utilities are two other familiar instances.

Constant Returns In between the cases of diminishing and increasing returns lies the case of *constant returns,* shown in Figure 6.3. Each additional unit of input increases output by the same amount, and the relationship between input and output is a straight line.

Even though we have discussed the cases of diminishing, increasing, and constant returns separately, it is important to recognize that most production functions can display all three types of returns at different levels of production. For example, at low levels of output, the addition of a unit of input may lead to a more than proportionate increase in output. As more and more of the input is added, however, diminishing returns eventually sets in. The use of fertilizer as an input into agriculture provides a good example, and one that has been well studied by agricultural economists. Imagine a large plot of land planted in corn. With the addition of only 5 pounds of nitrogen fertilizer per acre, the corn yield might be quite low, say 35 bushels per acre. Doubling the amount of fertilizer to 10 pounds per acre might more than double yields to 80 bushels per acre—an example of increasing returns. Doubling the use of fertilizer again to 20 pounds per acre increases yields to 160 bushels per acre. The impact is proportionately less than when fertilizer use was increased from 5 to 10 pounds per acre. Doubling the use of fertilizer from 10 to 20 pounds doubled the yield, a case of constant returns to scale. If the farmer again doubles the fertilizer applied, to 40 pounds per acre, yields again rise, say to 200 bushels per acre. Now yields less than double, so diminishing returns to fertilizer use have set in.

Figure 6.4

FIXED, VARIABLE, AND TOTAL COST CURVES

Panel A shows a firm's fixed cost; by definition, fixed costs do not depend on the level of output. Panel B shows a firm's variable costs, which rise with the level of production. The increasing slope of the curve indicates that it costs more and more to produce at the margin, which is a sign of diminishing returns. Panel C shows a total cost curve. It has the same slope as the variable cost curve but is higher by the amount of the fixed costs.

TYPES OF COSTS AND COST CURVES

The production function is important to the firm because the inputs determine the cost of production. These costs are key determinants of the firm's profits and its decisions about how much to produce.

Fixed and Variable Costs Some costs associated with inputs do not vary as the firm changes the level of production. For instance, the firm may need to hire someone to run the personnel office and someone to supervise the workers, and the cost of these inputs remain constant as production varies (within limits). These costs are called **fixed costs.** Whether the firm produces nothing or produces at maximum capacity, it antes up the same fixed costs. Figure 6.4 shows how costs depend on output. Panel A depicts fixed costs as a horizontal line—by definition, they do not depend on the level of output. As an example, consider a would-be farmer who has the opportunity to buy a farm and its equipment for $25,000. Her fixed costs are $25,000.

Variable costs correspond to inputs that vary with the level of production. Any cost that the firm can change during the time period under study is a variable cost. To the extent that the costs of such items as labor and materials can go up or down as output does, these are variable costs. If our farmer has only one input to vary, labor, then her variable cost would be, say, $15 per hour for each worker. The variable costs corresponding to levels of output listed in Table 6.1 are shown in Table 6.2 and plotted in Figure 6.4B. As output increases, so do variable costs, and therefore the curve slopes upward.

Total Costs Table 6.2 also includes a column labeled "Total cost." **Total costs** are defined as the sum of fixed and variable costs, so this column is obtained by adding the farmer's fixed costs of $25,000 to the variable costs. Thus, total costs = total variable costs + fixed costs.

The total cost curve, summarizing these points, is shown in Figure 6.4c.

Marginal Cost and the Marginal Cost Curve Having come this far in studying economics, you know that rational decision making depends on evaluating trade-offs in terms of *marginal* costs and *marginal* benefits. If you have the opportunity to work more hours at your part-time job, you need to evaluate the marginal cost—the other things you could do during those extra hours you will be working (like studying economics perhaps)—against the marginal benefit, here the extra income you will earn. Firms apply this same logic in their decision making: they focus on marginal costs and benefits. Thus, one of the most important cost concepts is **marginal costs,** which are defined as the extra cost corresponding to each additional unit of production.

In the case of the wheat farmer's costs (see Table 6.2), as he increases labor input from 7,000 hours to 8,000 hours, output increases from 140,000 bushels to 155,000 bushels. Thus, the *marginal product* of the extra 1,000 hours of labor is 15,000 bushels. If the wage is $15 per hour, the cost of increasing output by 15,000 bushels is $15,000 ($15 × 1,000 extra hours). The marginal cost of the extra 15,000 bushels is $15,000. To determine the marginal cost per bushel, we divide the change in cost (C) by the change in output (Q):

$$\frac{\Delta C}{\Delta Q} = \frac{\$15,000}{15,000} = \$1 \text{ per bushel}$$

The *marginal cost curve* traces out the marginal cost for each additional unit of output. To derive the marginal cost curve using a graph, we start with the total cost curve. The marginal cost is the change in total cost (movements along the vertical axis) resulting from each unit increase in output (movements along the horizontal axis). This is shown in panel A of Figure 6.5. Panel B of Figure 6.5 shows the same relationship in a different way. The slope of the line tangent to the total cost curve at Q_1

Table 6.2

COST OF PRODUCING WHEAT

Output (bushels)	Labor required (hours)	Total variable cost (at a wage of $15 per hour)	Total cost ($)	Marginal cost ($ per bushel)	Average cost ($ per bushel)	Average variable cost ($ per bushel)
95,000	5,000	75,000	100,000	—	1.05	0.79
120,000	6,000	90,000	115,000	0.60	0.96	0.75
140,000	7,000	105,000	130,000	0.75	0.93	0.75
155,000	8,000	120,000	145,000	1.00	0.94	0.77
165,000	9,000	135,000	160,000	1.50	0.97	0.82
170,000	10,000	150,000	175,000	3.00	1.03	0.88

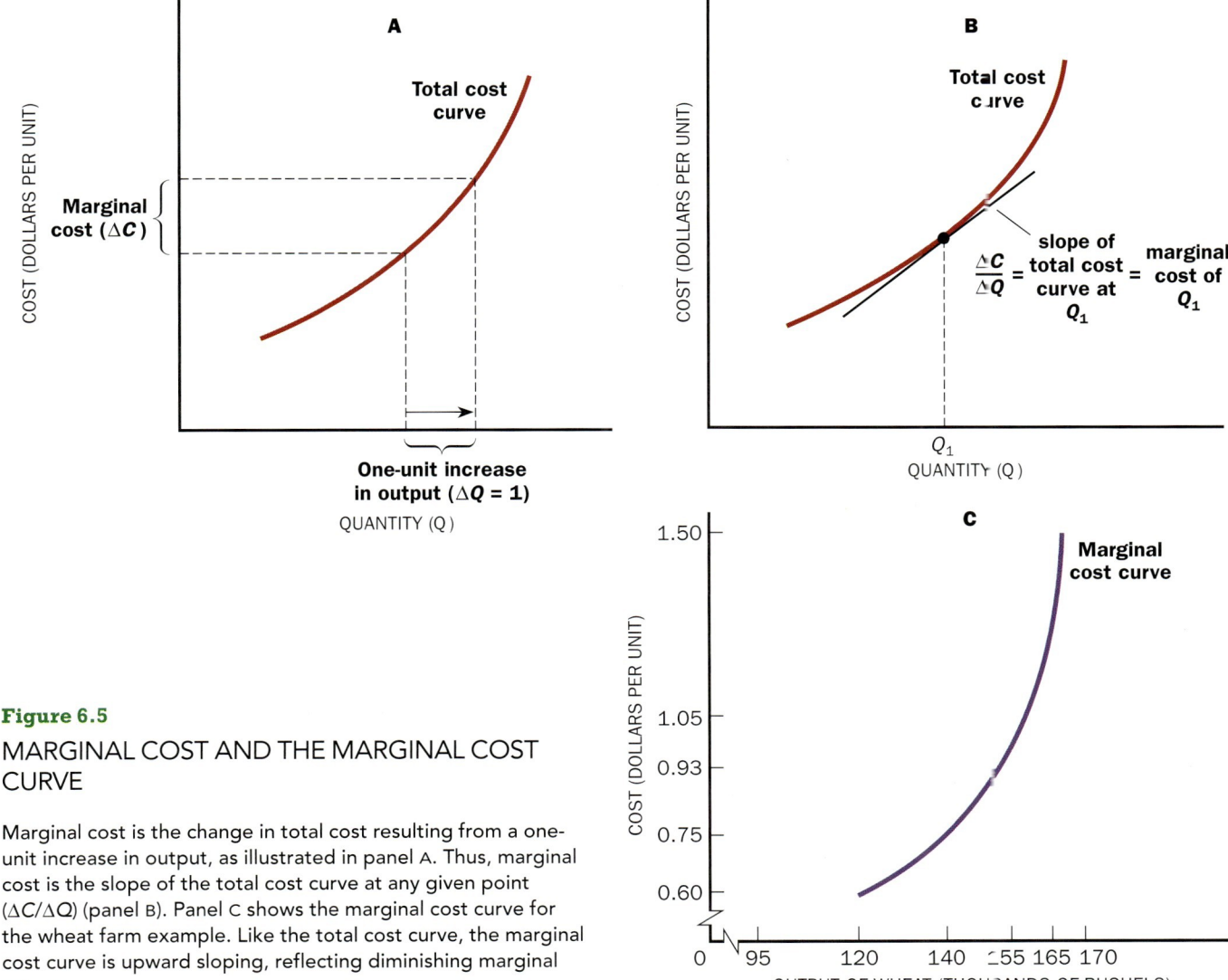

Figure 6.5

MARGINAL COST AND THE MARGINAL COST CURVE

Marginal cost is the change in total cost resulting from a one-unit increase in output, as illustrated in panel A. Thus, marginal cost is the slope of the total cost curve at any given point ($\Delta C/\Delta Q$) (panel B). Panel C shows the marginal cost curve for the wheat farm example. Like the total cost curve, the marginal cost curve is upward sloping, reflecting diminishing marginal returns.

gives the marginal cost of Q_1. Thus, the marginal cost curve represents the slope of the total cost curve at each quantity of output.

Panel C of Figure 6.5 shows the marginal cost curve for the wheat farm example. Note that the curve is upward sloping, like the total cost curve, which reflects the fact that as more is produced, it becomes harder and harder to increase output further. This is an application of the familiar principle of diminishing marginal returns. In our wheat farm example, suppose the farmer is considering increasing production by 1,000 bushels. If his current level of output is 140,000 bushels, the marginal cost of this increase will be $1,000. But if his current level of output is 155,000 bushels, increasing production by 1,000 units will entail a marginal cost of $1,500. At the higher level of output, the marginal cost is greater because of diminishing marginal returns to labor.

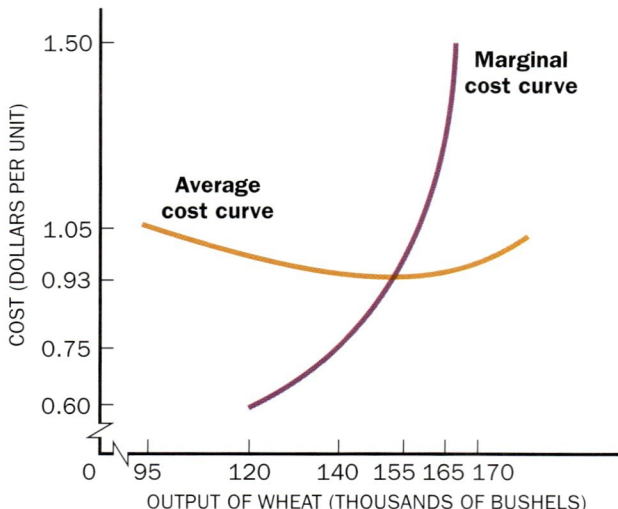

Figure 6.6

MARGINAL AND AVERAGE COST CURVES

This figure shows the marginal cost curve and average cost curve for the wheat farm example of Table 6.2. With diminishing returns to an input, marginal costs increase with the level of output, giving the marginal cost curve its typical, upward-sloping shape. Average costs initially fall with increased output, as fixed costs are spread over a larger amount of output, and then begin to rise as diminishing returns to the variable input become increasingly important. Thus, the average cost curve is typically U-shaped. With a U-shaped average cost curve, the marginal cost curve will cross the average cost curve at its minimum.

Average Cost and the Average Cost Curve A business firm also is concerned with its **average cost.** This is the total cost (TC) divided by output (Q), or

$$\text{average cost} = TC/Q.$$

The *average cost curve* gives average costs corresponding to different levels of output. Figure 6.6 shows the average cost curve for our wheat farm example (along with the marginal cost curve, for reasons indicated below). Working from the total cost curve (see Figure 6.4C and Table 6.2), we derive the average cost curve by dividing total costs (TC) by quantity (Q) at each level of output. Thus, since it takes 7,000 hours of labor to produce 140,000 bushels of wheat, and the wage is $15 per hour, the total cost is $105,000 + $25,000 (the fixed cost), for an average cost of $0.93 per bushel ($130,000/140,000 bushels). When output increases to 155,000 bushels, costs increase to $145,000, for an average cost of $0.94 per bushel.

The typical average cost curve is U-shaped, like the one in Figure 6.6. To understand why, we need to think about the two parts of total costs—fixed costs and variable costs. Just to start production usually requires a significant expense on inputs. These fixed costs do not vary with the level of output. As output increases, these costs are spread over more units of output, so the average cost of each unit of output that is due to the firm's fixed costs will fall. If these were the only costs the firm faced, average costs would decline as output increases.

Firms also face variable costs. Because of diminishing returns, beyond some level of output the firm requires more and more labor to produce each additional unit of output. Eventually, it may be almost impossible to increase output. This is why the production function in Figure 6.1 flattens out as output rises and the total cost curve in Figure 6.4C becomes steeper as output increases.

Just as we defined average costs as total costs divided by output, we define **average variable costs** as total variable costs divided by output:

$$\text{average variable costs} = \frac{\text{total variable costs}}{\text{output}}.$$

Average variable costs increase with output as the law of diminishing returns sets in strongly. The final column of Table 6.2 gives the average variable costs associated with producing wheat. At low levels of output, the falling average fixed costs dominate, and average total costs decline. But once a high-enough level of output is achieved, rising average variable costs start to dominate and average total costs increase. The result is the typical U-shape of the average cost curve, as shown in Figure 6.6.

Even if the average cost curve is U-shaped, the output at which average costs are lowest may be very great—so high that there is not enough demand to justify producing that much. As a consequence, the industry will produce at an output level below that at which average cost are lowest. When the average cost curve is U-shaped, average costs are declining at output levels that are less than the minimum average cost level of production. Thus an industry producing less than the output that results in minimum average costs will be operating in the region where average costs are declining. When economists say that an industry has declining average costs, they usually do not mean that average costs are declining at all levels of output. Instead, they typically mean that costs are declining at the output levels at which the industry is currently producing.

Relationship Between Average and Marginal Cost Curves The relationship between average costs and marginal costs is reflected in Figure 6.6. The marginal cost curve intersects the average cost curve at the bottom of the U—the *minimum* average cost. To understand why the marginal cost curve will *always* intersect the average cost curve at its lowest point, consider the relationship between average and marginal costs. As long as the marginal cost is below the average cost, producing an extra unit of output will pull down average costs. Thus, everywhere the marginal cost is below the average cost, the average cost curve is declining. If the marginal cost is above the average cost, then producing an extra unit of output will raise average costs. So everywhere that the marginal cost is above the average cost, the average cost curve must be rising.

Changing Input Prices and Cost Curves The cost curves shown thus far are based on the fixed prices of the inputs (factors) the firm uses. An increase in the price of a variable input like labor would shift the total, average, and marginal cost curves upward, as shown in Figure 6.7. An increase in fixed costs, such as an increase in the cost of the wheat farmer's land, shifts the total cost and average cost curves upward. Since fixed costs do not vary with output (by definition), a change in fixed costs does not affect the marginal cost curve.

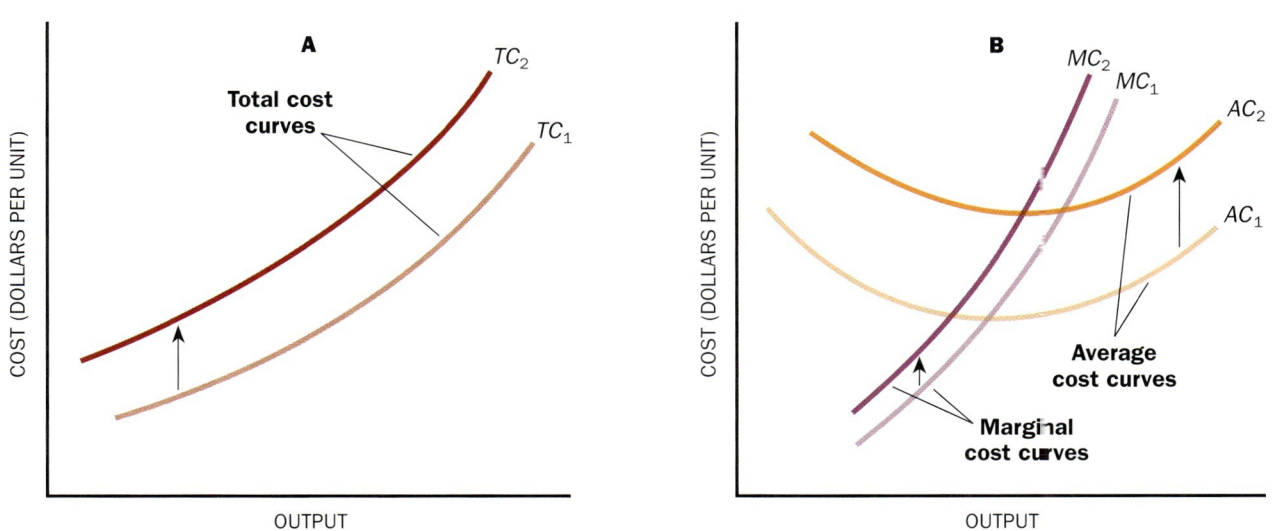

Figure 6.7
HOW CHANGING INPUT PRICES AFFECT COST CURVES

An increase in the price of a variable factor shifts the total, average, and marginal cost curves upward.

Table 6.3

DEBORAH'S COSTS IF SHE WORKS 10 HOURS DOING WEB CONSULTING

	Fixed Costs	Variable Costs	Total
Sunk costs			
Software	$125.00		$125.00
Laptop lease	$ 60.00		$ 60.00
Opportunity costs			
Forgone earnings		$50.00	$ 50.00
Total	$185.00	$50.00	$235.00
Revenue			$200.00
Profit			$ (35.00)

Example: Deborah's Web Consulting Business A simple example illustrates these various cost concepts and relates them to the notions of opportunity costs introduced in Chapter 2.

Deborah tutors for the computer science department at her college, earning $5 per hour. She works a total of 20 hours per week, which is the most she can devote to working while still maintaining good grades in her own courses. Recently, she decided to start her own business helping professors create Web pages for their classes. Deborah plans to charge $20 per hour for this service.

To get started, she had to purchase $125 worth of software, and she needed to obtain a faster laptop. A local computer store leased her the laptop she needs for $60 per month.

Tables 6.3 and 6.4 set out the costs Deborah faces in her first week of business if she works 10 hours for her new business (and continues to work 10 hours tutoring) and if she works 20 hours for her new business (and so quits tutoring completely).

Since Deborah has already purchased the software and leased the computer, these are fixed costs; they remain the same whether she decides to work 10 hours or 20 hours on her new business. These are also sunk costs; even if she decides to quit, she will be out the cost of the software and the first month's lease on the laptop.

What are her variable costs? Variable costs are costs that depend on the number of hours Deborah devotes to her Web business. For each additional hour she spends on her Web business, she works 1 hour less tutoring. The *opportunity cost* of each hour working in her new business is the $5 she could have made if she had instead spent the hour tutoring. So her variable costs consist of the $5 per hour she gives up by not tutoring.

We can now calculate Deborah's profits for the week. If she works 10 hours, her revenue is $200 (10 hours × $20 per hour). Her total costs are $125 + $60 + $50 = $235. She suffers a loss of $35. If she works 20 hours, her revenue rises to $400, while her total costs rise only to $125 + 60 + $100 = $285. She makes a profit of

Table 6.4

DEBORAH'S COSTS IF SHE WORKS 20 HOURS DOING WEB CONSULTING

	Fixed Costs	Variable Costs	Total
Sunk costs			
Software	$125.00		$125.00
Laptop lease	$ 60.00		$ 60.00
Opportunity costs			
Forgone earnings		$100.00	$100.00
Total	$185.00	$100.00	$285.00
Revenue			$400.00
Profit			$115.00

$400 – $285 = $115. So she would be better off working the entire 20 hours she has available for her new business and quitting her tutoring job completely. Note that since Deborah has $185 in sunk costs, she is better off consulting for 10 hours than closing up her business entirely. If she works 10 hours doing Web consulting, her revenues are $200, more than enough to cover her variable costs of $50.

Wrap-Up

COST CONCEPTS

Fixed costs:	Costs that do not depend on output, such as office space
Variable costs:	Costs that depend on output, such as labor costs
Total costs:	Total costs of producing output = fixed costs + variable costs
Marginal costs:	Extra cost of producing an extra unit
Average costs:	Total costs divided by output
Average variable costs:	Total variable costs divided by output

Short-Run and Long-Run Cost Curves

Up to this point, we have referred to the distinction between inputs that are fixed (their cost does not vary with quantity produced) and inputs that are variable (their cost does depend on quantity produced). We have sidestepped the fact that inputs, and costs, may be fixed for some period of time but can vary with production over a longer period. Take the inputs of labor and machines, for example. In the short run, the supply of machines may be fixed. Output is then increased only by increasing labor. In the longer run, the numbers of both machines and workers can be adjusted. The short-run cost curve, then, is the cost of production with a *given* stock of machines. The long-run cost curve is the cost of production when all factors are adjusted.[1]

SHORT-RUN COST CURVES

If we think of the number of machines as being fixed in the short run, and labor as the principal input that can be varied, our earlier analysis of production with a single variable factor provides a good description of short-run cost curves. Thus, short-run *average* cost curves are normally U-shaped.

LONG-RUN COST CURVES

Though short-run average cost curves for a given manufacturing facility are typically U-shaped, the firm's long-run average cost curve may have a quite different shape. As production grows, it will pay at some point to build a second plant, and then a third, a fourth, and so on. The curve labeled TC_1 in panel A of Figure 6.8 shows the total cost of producing different levels of output, assuming the firm has only one manufacturing plant. The panel also shows the total costs of producing different levels of output when the firm builds two plants; this cost curve is labeled TC_2. If production is very low, it is cheaper to produce using only a single plant (TC_1 is below TC_2), but as the level of production increases, it becomes more and more costly to try to handle all production in a single plant; total costs are lower if two plants are used, so TC_1 eventually rises above TC_2. The total cost curve when the firm builds three plants is shown by TC_3. How many plants should the company build? Clearly, the firm wishes to minimize the total cost of producing at any output level. If it produces less than Q_1, total costs are lowest if the firm has only one plant. Between Q_1 and Q_2, total costs are lowest if the firm has two plants. And if the firm produces more than Q_2, total costs are lowest if it uses three plants. Thus, the relevant *long-run* total cost curve when the firm is able to adjust the number of plants it has is the lower boundary of the three curves in the figure. The long-run total cost curve is the darker curve.

Panel B of Figure 6.8 shows the same result using average cost curves. If the firm minimizes the total costs of producing any particular output, it minimizes the average cost of producing that level of output. The figure shows the average cost curves corresponding to using one, two, or three plants. Once the company has

---

[1]The distinction between short-run and long-run costs corresponds to the distinction between short-run and long-run supply curves introduced in Chapter 3. Chapter 7 will make clear the relationship. It is an exaggeration to think that only capital goods are fixed in the short run while all of labor is variable. In some cases, capital goods may easily be varied; a firm can, for instance, rent cars. And in some cases, as when a company has long-term contracts with its workers, it may be very difficult to vary labor in the short run.

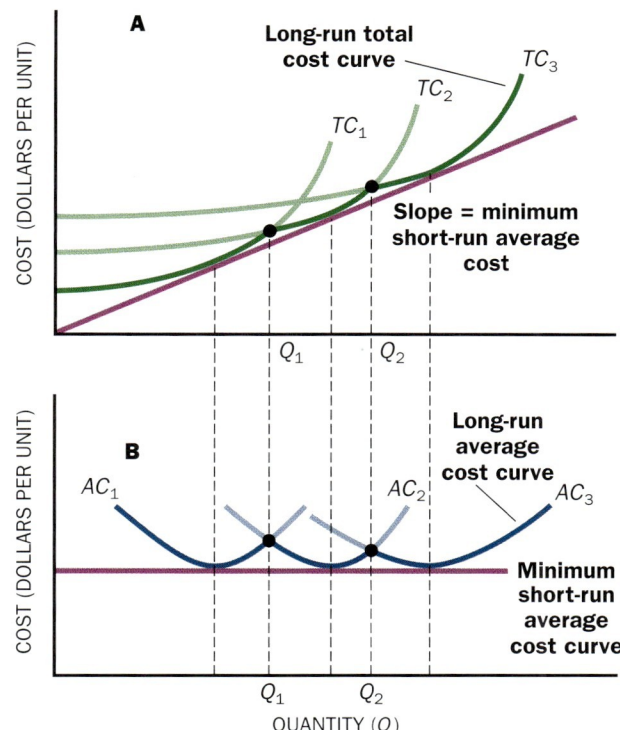

Figure 6.8
SHORT-RUN AND LONG-RUN COST CURVES

Panel A shows a series of short-run total cost curves, TC_1, TC_2, and TC_3, each representing a different level of fixed capital input. In the long run, a cost-minimizing firm can choose any of these, so the long-run total cost curve will be the lowest cost of producing any level of output, as shown by the darkened lower boundary of the curves. Panel B shows a series of short-run average cost curves, AC_1, AC_2, and AC_3, each representing a different level of fixed capital input. In the long run, a cost-minimizing firm can choose any of these, so the long-run average cost curve will be the darker lower boundary of the curves.

decided how much output it plans to produce, it will choose the number of plants that minimizes its average costs. Thus, if the firm plans to produce less than Q_1, it builds only one plant; AC_1 is less than AC_2 for all outputs less than Q_1. If the firm plans to produce between Q_1 and Q_2, it builds two plants, because in this interval, AC_2 is less than either AC_1 or AC_3. For outputs greater than Q_2, the firm builds three plants. The long-run average cost curve is the darker bumpy curve in Figure 6.8B.

The bumps in the long-run average cost curve arise because we have assumed the only alternatives in the long run that are available to the firm involve building one, two, or three plants. We have ignored the many other options a firm has. If the firm is operating one plant, it can expand by, say, adding a new assembly line rather than building a whole new plant. Or it can add new machines to its current plant. These types of adjustments would lead to a series of total cost curves between TC_1 and TC_2 in Figure 6.8A. When we take into account all the options a firm typically has to adjust its fixed costs, the bumps in the long-run average cost curve will become progressively smaller, enabling us to ignore them in most cases. Thus, when we draw a long-run average cost curve, we will typically ignore the bumps and draw a smooth curve.

But what does a smooth long-run average cost curve look like? Does it slope upward or downward? Or is it flat? A good way to answer these questions is to ask what happens to average costs if the firm doubles all its inputs. That is, it doubles the number of workers it employs and the number of plants it operates. If output also doubles when inputs are doubled, then average costs will remain unchanged. More generally, if all inputs are increased in proportion and output then increases by the same proportion, average costs will be constant. In this case, the long-run average cost curve is flat, and we say there are **constant returns to scale.** Under these conditions, changing the scale of production leaves average costs constant. Many economists argue that constant returns to scale are most prevalent in manufacturing; a firm can increase its production simply by replicating its plants. Similarly, the average cost of teaching introductory economics to 500 students is the same as it is for teaching it to 250 students. Just add another lecture hall and hire another lecturer. When long-run average cost is constant, then the marginal cost of additional output must be equal to the average cost (otherwise average costs would be changing); thus the long-run average cost curve and the long-run marginal cost curve are the same.

While constant returns to scale are common, other patterns are also possible. Suppose all inputs are increased in proportion but output increases proportionately less. For example, suppose all inputs are increased by 20 percent but output rises by only 15 percent. Costs will have risen more than output, and average costs therefore will have risen. This case is an example of **diminishing returns to scale.** If there are diminishing returns to scale, the long-run average cost curve slopes upward since long-run costs rise more than output as the firm expands production. With diminishing returns to scale, small is beautiful and big is bad. As the firm tries to grow, adding additional plants, management becomes more complex. It may have to add layer upon layer of managers, and each of these layers increases costs. When the firm is small, the owner can supervise all the workers. When the firm grows, the owner can no longer supervise everyone and will have to hire a new employee to help supervise. As the firm grows even larger, and more supervisors are hired, eventually the owner needs someone to help supervise the supervisors. Doubling the output of the firm may require not just doubling existing inputs but adding new layers of bureaucracy that can slow decision making in the firm, adding further to costs. Many small firms find they face these difficulties as they grow and that their average costs increase. Firms that attempt to grow quickly often just as quickly run into problems trying to contain costs, and many do not succeed. A recent example of a company that faltered after expanding rapidly is the Krispy Kreme Doughnut Corporation, which grew in the 1990s from a regional to a national chain. Because long-run average costs rise with output when there are diminishing returns to scale, the long-run marginal cost curve is above the long-run average cost curve.

There is one last case to consider. Suppose that increasing all inputs in proportion leads to a more than proportionate increase in output. Suppose, for example, that when all inputs are increased by 20 percent, output jumps by 25 percent. This is a case of **increasing returns to scale,** sometimes described as **economies of scale.** Big is beautiful in this case, since average costs decline as the scale of the firm is increased. Increasing returns to scale are common at low and moderate levels of production. As a company expands from one plant to ten plants, it still needs only one corporate headquarters building. Moreover, it has to pay the cost for the basic design of its plants only once. Companies with many outlets or stores, such as McDonald's or Wal-Mart, typically use a very small number of store designs, whether they are opening in Florida or Minnesota. Since these costs associated with running the firm—the overhead costs—do not increase in proportion to the increase in production, long-run average cost curves may be slightly downward sloping, as illustrated in Figure 6.9A.

For most firms, however, diminishing returns to scale eventually set in as production levels become very large. As the firm increases its size, adding additional plants, it starts to face increasing managerial problems; it may have to add layer upon layer of management, and each of these layers increases costs. Long-run average costs start to rise with output at high levels of output, as illustrated in Figure 6.9B.

Yet in some industries, increasing returns to scale are possible even for very large outputs. As the firm produces a higher output, it can take advantage of machines that are larger and more efficient than those used by smaller firms. Software companies may enjoy increasing returns to scale. Once the program code is written, the firms can expand production with very little additional costs—just the costs of blank CDs to hold the programs and the costs for distribution. At higher production levels, the initial costs of developing and writing the software are spread over a larger output, leading to declining average costs. If there are increasing returns to scale, the long-run average cost curve and the marginal cost curve will be downward sloping, as in Figure 6.9C.

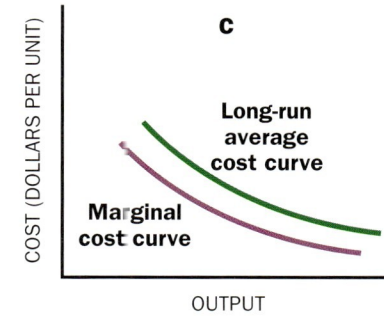

Figure 6.9
LONG-RUN AVERAGE COSTS

Panel A shows that with overhead costs, long-run average costs may be declining, but they flatten out as output increases. In panel B, with managerial costs increasing with the scale of the firm, eventually average and marginal costs may start to rise. Panel C shows that if there are increasing returns to scale, long-run costs may be continuously falling.

Internet Connection
ECONOMIC DEFINITIONS

Keeping straight the terms *average cost, marginal cost, variable cost, diminishing returns,* and *economics of scale* can be difficult. Investopedia provides an online dictionary of economic terms at www.investopedia.com/dictionary/. Another useful source of economic definitions is the classroom page maintained by the Short Run (www.theshortrun.com/main.html).

> **Wrap-Up**
>
> ### THE FIRM'S COSTS: KEY IDEAS
>
> 1. Profits are equal to total revenues minus total costs.
> 2. Marginal cost is the extra cost of producing one more unit of output. Marginal cost normally increases at higher levels of output as diminishing returns set in.
> 3. Average fixed costs decline as output increases, but average variable costs eventually rise. As a result, the average total cost curve is typically U-shaped.
> 4. The long-run average cost curve traces out the lower boundaries of the short-run average cost curve.
> 5. Returns to scale: There are economies of scale if doubling all inputs more than doubles output, and when there are economies of scale, the long-run average total cost curve slopes downward. There are diseconomies of scale if doubling all inputs less than doubles output, and when there are diseconomies of scale, the long-run average total cost curve slopes upward. There are constant returns to scale if doubling all inputs doubles output; in that case, the long-run average total cost curve is flat.
>
> *Relationships between the cost curves*
> 1. The marginal cost at output level Q is the slope of the total cost curve at output level Q.
> 2. The average cost curve is falling when the marginal cost is less than the average cost; the average cost curve is rising when the marginal cost is greater than the average cost. Consequently, the marginal cost curve always intersects the average cost curve at the point where average costs are at their minimum.

Production with Many Factors

The basic principles of the case with only two factors—one fixed, one variable—apply also to firms producing many products with many different inputs. The only fundamental difference is that the presence of many factors makes it possible to produce the same output in several different ways. To minimize cost, firms must therefore weigh the costs of different mixes of inputs.

COST MINIMIZATION

There are usually several ways a good can be produced, using different quantities of various inputs. Table 6.5 illustrates two alternative ways of making car frames, one a highly automated process requiring little labor and the other a less-automated process that uses more assembly-line workers. The table shows the daily wage and capital costs for each process. Each method produces the same quantity of output (say, 10,000 car frames per day). In this simple example, we assume all workers are identical (of equal skill) and hence get paid the same wage, and that all machines cost the same. As we can see from the table, the less-automated process clearly costs more at the given costs of labor ($20 per worker per hour) and machines (rental costs equal $1,000 per day).

Although this table provides only two stark alternatives, it should be clear that in some cases the alternative possibilities for production will form a continuum along which the input of one increases a bit, the input of another falls a bit, and output remains the same. In other words, the firm can smoothly substitute one input for another. For instance, in producing cars, different machines vary slightly in their degree of automation. The less labor required to run a machine, the more it tends to cost. When firms make their decisions about investment, they thus have a wide range of intermediate choices between the two described in the table.

THE PRINCIPLE OF SUBSTITUTION

In the case of multiple factors of production, the principle of cost minimization has a particularly important consequence: when the price of one input (say, labor) increases relative to that of other factors of production, firms will substitute cheaper inputs for the more costly factor. This is an illustration of the general *principle of substitution* we encountered in Chapter 3.

The principle of substitution can be illustrated using the information in Table 6.5. If the wage is $20 per hour and each machine costs $1,000, output can be produced at less cost by using the more-automated process. But suppose the price of

Table 6.5
COSTS OF PRODUCTION

Inputs	More-automated process	Less-automated process
Labor	50 man-hours @ $20 = $1,000	500 man-hours @ $20 = $10,000
Machines	5 machines @ $1,000 = $5,000	2 machines @ $1,000 = $ 2,000
Total	$6,000	$12,000

machines increases to $3,500 each. Then, the more-automated process will cost $17,500, while the less-automated process will cost $17,000. Both processes rise in cost, but the less-automated process rises less. It now becomes the less costly method. As a consequence, firms will switch from the more-automated process to the less-automated process. In this way, they are able to substitute away from the factor whose price has risen (machines, in this case).

An increase in the price of any input shifts the cost function up. The amount by which the cost function shifts up depends on several factors, including how much of the input was being used in the first place and how easy it is to substitute other inputs. If the production process uses a great deal of the input, then the shift will be large. If there is a large increase in the price of an input, and the firm cannot easily substitute other inputs, then the cost curve will shift up more than it would if substitution of other inputs were easy.

In some cases, substitution is quick and easy; in other cases, it may take time and be difficult. When the price of oil increased fourfold in 1973 and doubled again in 1979, firms found many ways to economize on the use of oil. For instance, companies switched from oil to natural gas (and in the case of electric power companies, often to coal) as a source of energy. More energy-efficient cars and trucks were constructed, often using lighter materials such as aluminum and plastics. These substitutions took time, but they did eventually occur.

The principle of substitution should serve as a warning to those who think they can raise prices without bearing any consequences. For example, Argentina has almost a world monopoly on linseed oil. At one time, linseed oil was universally used for making high-quality paints. Since there was no competition, Argentina decided that it would raise the price of linseed oil, assuming everyone would have to pay it. But as the price increased, paint manufacturers learned to substitute other natural oils that could do almost as well.

Raising the price of labor (wages) provides another example. Unions in the auto and steel industries successfully demanded higher wages for their members during the boom periods of the 1960s and 1970s, and firms paid the higher wages. But at the same time, the firms redoubled their efforts to mechanize their production and to become less dependent on their labor force. Over time, these efforts were successful and led to a decline in employment in those industries.

Case in Point

THE PRINCIPLE OF SUBSTITUTION AND GLOBAL WARMING

In the two hundred years since the beginning of the industrial revolution, the amount of carbon dioxide (CO_2) in the atmosphere has increased enormously, and concentrations continue to rise. There is growing agreement among scientists that the higher concentration of CO_2 and related gases (called greenhouse gases) will lead to global warming, with potentially significant impacts on the environment. Reflecting this consensus, the countries of the world signed an agreement in Rio de Janeiro in

Hydroelectric power being generated at the Grand Coulee Dam.

1992 to work toward limiting the growth of greenhouse gases; in a subsequent meeting in 1997, in Kyoto, Japan, an effort was made to strengthen the international commitment to greenhouse gas reductions. In order for it to take effect, the Kyoto agreement had to first be ratified by countries that account for at least 55 percent of the world's greenhouse gas emissions. While President Bill Clinton supported the aims of the Kyoto agreement, he did not submit it for approval to the Senate, where it faced certain defeat; and in 2001 President George W. Bush announced that he opposed the treaty, effectively ensuring that the United States would not ratify the agreement. It eventually did take effect in early 2005 after being ratified by Russia. The agreement commits industrialized nations to make significant cuts in emissions by 2012.

From an economic perspective, the principle of substitution is at the heart of the problem of greenhouse gas reductions. Slowing down the rate of increase in greenhouse gases entails using less energy, and substituting away from sources of energy that produce large amounts of greenhouse gases, like coal, toward sources of energy that produce less, like natural gas, or even none at all, like hydroelectric power. Increasing the cost of greenhouse gas–producing energy sources by, for example, imposing a tax on fuels in proportion to how much they contribute to greenhouse gases would create an incentive for firms to substitute alternative energy sources that produce fewer greenhouse gases.

Wrap-Up

THE PRINCIPLE OF SUBSTITUTION

An increase in the price of an input will lead the firm to substitute other inputs in its place.

Economies of Scope

Most firms produce more than one good. Deciding which goods to produce and in what quantities, as well as how to produce them, are central problems facing firm managers. The problems would be fairly straightforward were it not for some important interrelations among the products. The production of one product may affect the costs of producing another.

In some cases, products are produced naturally together; we say they are **joint products.** From crude oil, a petroleum refinery can produce gasoline, lubricating oils, and diesel fuel. If more crude oil is distilled into gasoline, more lubricating oil and diesel fuel will also be produced as by-products of the process.

If it is less expensive to produce a set of goods together than separately, economists say there are **economies of scope.** The concept of economies of scope helps us understand why certain activities are often undertaken by the same firm. Your mobile phone company probably also provides text-messaging services. A company like PeopleSoft, now part of Oracle, provides software for a variety of business needs, such as human resources, finance, information technology, procurement, marketing, services, and sales. It is less expensive for one company to produce all these software services together than it would be to produce each one separately.

Review and Practice

SUMMARY

1. A firm's production function specifies the level of output resulting from any combination of inputs. The increase in output corresponding to a unit increase in any input is the marginal product of that input.
2. Short-run marginal cost curves are generally upward sloping, because diminishing returns to a factor of production imply that it will take ever-increasing amounts of the input to produce a marginal unit of output.
3. The typical short-run average cost curve is U-shaped. When an average cost curve is U-shaped, the marginal and average cost curves will intersect at the minimum point of the average cost curve.
4. Economists often distinguish between short-run and long-run cost curves. In the short run, a firm is generally assumed not to be able to change its capital stock. In the long run, it can. Even if short-run average cost curves are U-shaped, long-run average cost curves can take on a variety of shapes, including flat and continuously declining as well as declining and then increasing.
5. When a number of different inputs can be varied, and the price of one input increases, the change in relative prices of inputs will encourage a firm to substitute relatively less expensive inputs; this is an application of the principle of substitution.
6. Economies of scope exist when it is less expensive to produce two products together than it would be to produce each one separately.

KEY TERMS

profits
revenues
production function
marginal product
fixed costs
variable costs
total costs
marginal costs
average costs
average variable costs
constant, diminishing, **or** increasing returns to scale (economies of scale)
joint products
economies of scope

REVIEW QUESTIONS

1. What is a production function? When there is a single (variable) input, why does output normally increase less than in proportion to input? What are the alternative shapes that the relationship between input and output takes? What is the relationship between these shapes and the shape of the cost function?
2. What is meant by these various concepts of cost: total, average, average variable, marginal, and fixed? What are the relationships between these costs? What are short-run and long-run costs? What is the relationship between them?
3. Why are short-run average cost curves frequently U-shaped? Assume that the average cost curve is U-shaped: What is the relationship between the average and marginal costs? What does the total cost curve look like?
4. What happens to average, marginal, and total costs when the price of an input rises?
5. If a firm has a number of variable inputs and the price of one of them rises, will the firm use more or will it use less of this input? Why?
6. What are diminishing, constant, and increasing returns to scale? When might you expect each to occur? What is the relationship between these properties of the production function and the shape of the long-run average and total cost curves?
7. What are economies of scope, and how do they affect what a firm chooses to produce?

PROBLEMS

1. Tom and Dick, who own the Tom, Dick, and Hairy Barbershop, need to decide how many barbers to hire.

The production function for their barbershop looks like this:

Number of barbers	Haircuts provided per day	Marginal product
0	0	
1	12	
2	36	
3	60	
4	72	
5	80	
6	84	

Calculate the marginal product of hiring additional barbers, and fill in the last column of the table. Over what range is the marginal product of labor increasing? constant? diminishing? Graph the production function. By looking at the graph, you should be able to tell at what point the average productivity of labor is highest. Calculate average productivity at each point to illustrate your answer.

2. The overhead costs of the Tom, Dick, and Hairy Barbershop are $160 per day, and the cost of paying a barber for a day is $80. With this information, and the information in Problem 1, make up a table with column headings in this order: Output, Labor required, Total variable cost, Total cost, Marginal cost, Average variable cost, and Average cost. If the price of a haircut is $10 and the shop sells 80 per day, what is its daily profit?

3. Using the information in Problems 1 and 2, draw the total cost curve for the Tom, Dick, and Hairy Barbershop on one graph. On a second graph, draw the marginal cost curve, the average cost curve, and the average variable cost curve. Do these curves have the shape you would expect? Do the minimum and average cost curves intersect at the point you expect?

4. Suppose a firm has the choice of two methods of producing: one method entails a fixed cost of $10 and a marginal cost of $2; the other entails a fixed cost of $20 and a marginal cost of $1. Draw the total and average cost curves for both methods. At what levels of output will the firm use the low-fixed-cost technology? At what levels of output will it use the high-fixed-cost technology?

5. The cost data below are from the Acme Pizza Company. Fill in the information on the firm's total costs, marginal costs, average total costs, and average variable costs. Draw the total cost curve on one graph. On another graph, draw the marginal cost, average cost, and average variable cost curves. Are there output levels that exhibit increasing returns to scale? Are there output levels that display decreasing returns to scale?

Pizzas	Fixed costs	Variable costs	Total costs	Marginal costs	Average total costs	Average variable costs
0	$1,000	$–				
200	$1,000	$360				
400	$1,000	$840				
600	$1,000	$1,440				
800	$1,000	$2,160				
1,000	$1,000	$3,000				
1,200	$1,000	$3,960				
1,400	$1,000	$5,040				
1,600	$1,000	$6,240				
1,800	$1,000	$7,560				
2,000	$1,000	$9,000				

Learning Goals

In this chapter, you will learn

1. What determines the level of output a firm will supply at any given price

2. What determines whether a firm enters or exits a market

3. How the market supply curve is derived and why it is upward sloping

4. How competition drives economic profits to zero, and how economic profits and accounting profits differ

Chapter 7

THE COMPETITIVE FIRM

Whether it is a flower seller at a local farmer's market, a memory chip manufacturer in China, or a huge corporation such as Microsoft, Citibank, or Intel, every firm is in business to make profits. In competitive markets, firms are price takers—they are too small to affect the market price of the goods they produce. They also take as given the prices they have to pay for the inputs they purchase. The chief decision such a firm needs to make is how much to produce. In this chapter, we develop the principles that govern this decision, which will be guided by the aim of maximizing the firm's profits. Chapter 6 looked at the cost curves of the firm. Because profits are the difference between the firm's revenues and its costs, we focus here on the firm's revenues. By comparing revenues and costs, we will be able to determine the level of output the firm will supply at any given price.

This chapter examines firms in highly competitive markets. Accordingly, economists sometimes refer to the principles developed here as the *theory of the competitive firm.*

Revenue

Consider the hypothetical example of the High Strung Violin Company, manufacturers of world-class violins. The company hires labor; it buys wood, utilities, and other materials; and it rents a building and machines. Its violins sell for $40,000 each. Last year the company sold 7 of them, for a gross revenue of $280,000. Table 7.1 gives a snapshot of the firm's financial health, its profit-and-loss statement for last year.

We see that High Strung's revenues were $280,000, and its costs were $175,000, so its profits were $105,000. If its costs had been $400,000 instead of $175,000, its profits would have been −$120,000. The firm would have made a negative profit—in other words, a loss.

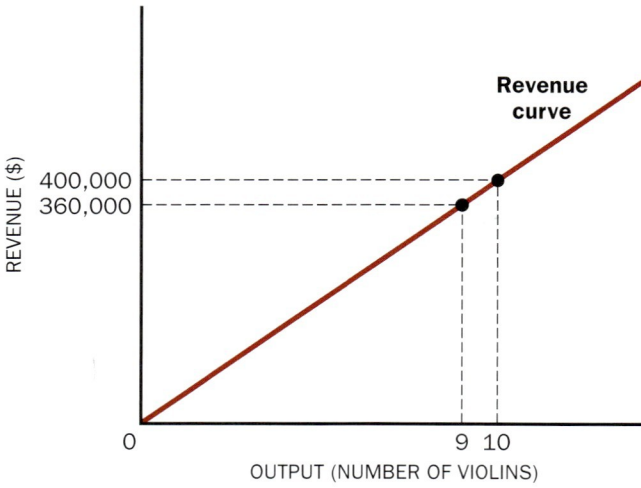

FIGURE 7.1

THE REVENUE CURVE

The revenue curve shows a firm's revenues at each level of output. For the firm in a competitive industry, price does not change as more is produced, so the revenue curve is a straight line with a constant slope. In this example, the revenue yielded by each additional violin is always $40,000.

The relationship between revenue and output is shown by the **revenue curve** in Figure 7.1. The horizontal axis measures the firm's output, while the vertical axis measures the revenues. When the price of a violin is $40,000 and the firm sells 9 violins, its revenue is $360,000; when it sells 10, revenue rises to $400,000.

The extra revenue that a firm receives from selling an extra unit is called its **marginal revenue.** Thus, $40,000 is the extra (or marginal) revenue from selling the tenth violin. It is no accident that the marginal revenue equals the price of the violin. A fundamental feature of competitive markets is that firms receive the same market price for each unit they sell, regardless of the number of units they sell. Thus, the extra revenue that firms in competitive markets receive from selling one more unit—the marginal revenue—is the same as the market price of the unit.

Costs

High Strung's costs increase as it expands its level of output. Total costs are given in column 1 of Table 7.2 and depicted diagrammatically in Figure 7.2A. Panel B shows the corresponding average and marginal costs. High Strung's average cost curve exhibits the typical U-shape that we associate with manufacturing firms.

Even before it builds its first violin, the company must spend $90,000. Space must be rented. Some employees will have to be hired. Equipment must be purchased. No matter how many or how few violins High Strung produces, its fixed costs will remain $90,000.

TABLE 7.1

PROFIT-AND-LOSS STATEMENT FOR THE HIGH STRUNG VIOLIN COMPANY

Gross revenue		$280,000
Costs		$175,000
Wages (including fringe benefits)	$150,000	
Purchases of wood and other materials	$ 15,000	
Utilities	$ 1,000	
Rent of building	$ 5,000	
Rent of machinery	$ 2,000	
Miscellaneous expenses	$ 2,000	
Profits		$105,000

Internet Connection

FIRMS' PROFIT-AND-LOSS STATEMENTS

Corporations issue annual reports each year, and these reports include their profit-and-loss statements. These statements are also called *income statements*. You can find the annual reports of many corporations on the Web. For example, you can find the Microsoft annual report at the Microsoft Web page, www.microsoft.com, under "Company Information: Investor Relations." Within the report, the income statement is found with the basic financial information. In 2003, Microsoft's net income was $10 billion on a total revenue of just over $32 billion. You can order copies of the annual reports from many corporations from the Public Register's Annual Report Service (PRARS), whose home page is www.prars.com.

The *extra* cost of producing an additional violin, the marginal cost, is shown in column 3. Marginal cost is always associated with the extra cost of producing a *particular* unit of output. The marginal cost of increasing production from 1 to 2 violins, for example, is $10,000. Each additional violin costs $10,000 more to produce until production reaches 6 violins. The extra (marginal) cost producing the seventh violin is $25,000 (perhaps another violin maker needs to be hired; or perhaps only limited quantities of the special wood the company uses in its violins are available, and finding enough of the wood for more than 6 violins is difficult and expensive). The marginal cost of producing the eighth violin is $40,000.

The High Strung Violin Company's average costs initially decline as its production increases, since the fixed costs can be divided among more units of production.

Table 7.2

HIGH STRUNG VIOLIN COMPANY'S COSTS OF PRODUCTION (THOUSANDS OF DOLLARS)

Output	(1) Total cost	(2) Average cost	(3) Marginal cost	(4) Total variable cost	(5) Average variable cost
0	90				
1	100	100.0	10	10	10.0
2	110	55.0	10	20	10.0
3	120	40.0	10	30	10.0
4	130	32.5	10	40	10.0
5	140	28.0	10	50	10.0
6	150	25.0	10	60	10.0
7	175	25.0	25	85	12.1
8	215	26.9	40	125	15.6
9	270	30.0	55	180	20.0
10	400	40.0	130	310	31.0

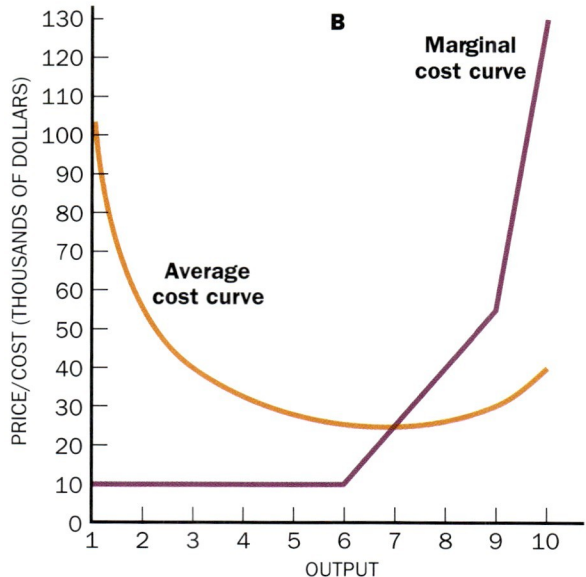

Figure 7.2
RELATING REVENUES AND COSTS

The firm's revenue and total cost curves can be diagrammed on the same graph, as in panel A. When total revenue exceeds total costs, the firm is making profits at that level of output. Profits, the difference between revenues and costs, are measured by the distance between the two curves; in this case, the highest level of profit is being made at a production level of 7 or 8. When total costs exceed total revenue, the firm is making losses at that level of output. When the two lines cross, the firm is making zero profits. The marginal and average cost curves for this company have their expected shape in panel B. Marginal costs are constant until a production level of 6, and then they begin to increase. The average cost curve is U-shaped.

But after 7 violins, average costs begin to increase, as the effect of the increasing average variable costs dominates the effect of the fixed costs.

Basic Conditions of Competitive Supply

In choosing how much to produce, a profit-maximizing firm will focus its decision at the margin. Because it has already incurred the fixed cost of getting into this market, its decision is generally not the stark one of whether or not to produce, but whether to produce one more unit of a good or one less. For a firm in a competitive market, making this choice is relatively easy: the company simply compares the marginal revenue it will receive by producing an extra unit—which is just the price of the good—with the extra cost of producing that unit, the marginal cost. As long as the marginal revenue exceeds the marginal cost, the firm will make additional profit by producing more. If marginal revenue is less than marginal cost, then producing an extra unit will cut profits, and the firm will reduce production. In short, the firm will produce to the point where the marginal cost equals marginal revenue, which in a competitive market is equal to price.

Figure 7.3 develops the graphical analysis underlying this principle. Panel A shows the firm's marginal cost curve. If the price of the good in a competitive market is p_1, the profit-maximizing output level will be Q_1. This is the level of output at which price and marginal cost are equal. An upward-sloping marginal cost curve clearly leads the firm to produce more as price increases.

The marginal cost curve is upward sloping, just as the supply curves in Chapter 3 were upward sloping. This too is no accident: a firm's marginal cost curve is actually the same as its supply curve. The marginal cost curve shows the additional cost of producing one more unit at different levels of output. A competitive firm chooses to produce at the level of output where the cost of producing an additional unit (that is, the marginal cost) is equal to the market price. We can thus read from the marginal cost curve what the firm's supply will be at any price: it will be the quantity of output at which marginal cost equals that price.

Before we turn to Figure 7.3B, look once more at Figure 7.2A, which shows total revenues as well as total costs of the High Strung Violin Company. We can see that profits—the gap between revenues and costs—are maximized at an output of either 7 or 8. If the price were just slightly lower than $40,000, profits would be maximized at 7, and if the price were just slightly higher than $40,000, profits would be maximized at 8.

The profit-maximizing level of output can also be seen in panel B of Figure 7.3, which shows the total revenue and total cost curves. Profits are the difference between revenues and costs. In panel B, profits are the distance between the total revenue curve and the total cost curve. The profit-maximizing firm will choose the

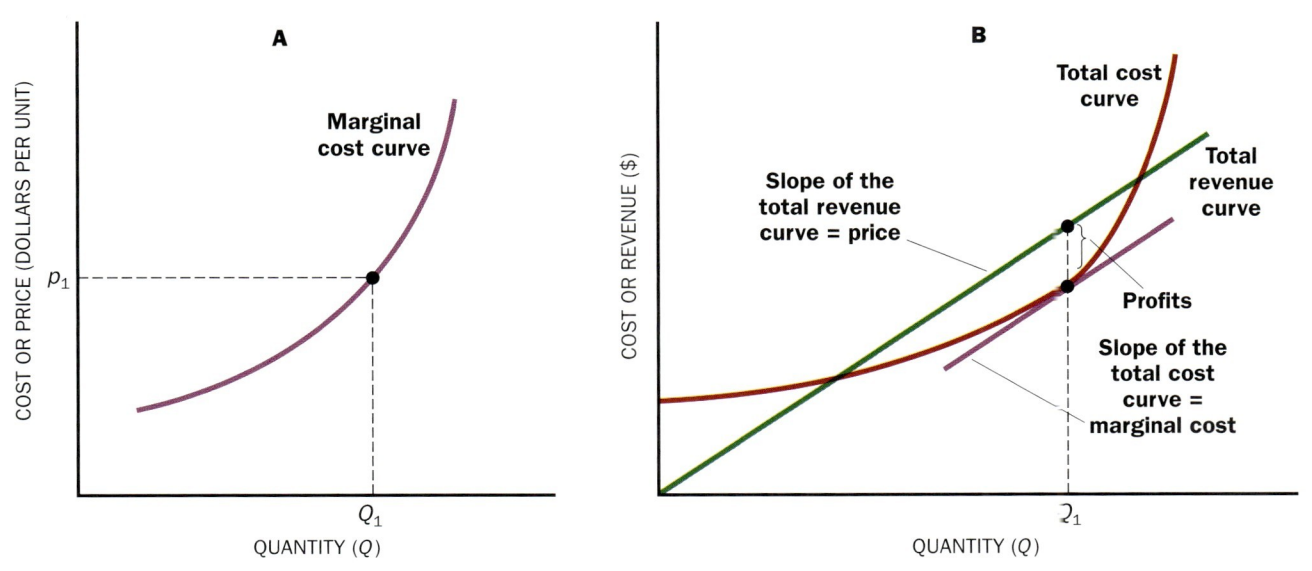

Figure 7.3
THE PROFIT-MAXIMIZING LEVEL OF OUTPUT

A competitive firm maximizes profits by setting output at the point where price equals marginal cost. In panel A, at the price of p_1, this quantity is Q_1. Panel B shows total revenue and total costs. Profits are maximized when the distance between the two curves is maximized, which is the point where the two lines are parallel (and thus have the same slope).

output where that distance is greatest. This occurs at Q_1. Below Q_1, price (the slope of the revenue curve), exceeds marginal costs (the slope of the total cost curve), so profits increase as output increases; above Q_1, price is less than marginal cost, so profits decrease as output increases.

> **Wrap-Up**
>
> **EQUILIBRIUM OUTPUT FOR COMPETITIVE FIRMS**
>
> In competitive markets, firms produce at the level where price equals marginal cost.

Entry, Exit, and Market Supply

We are now in a position to tackle the market supply curve. To do so, we need to know a little more about each firm's decision to produce. First, let's consider a firm that is currently not producing. Under what circumstances should it incur the fixed costs of entering the industry? This is a relatively easy problem: the company simply looks at the average cost curve and the price. *If price exceeds minimum average costs, it pays for the firm to enter.* A company that enters the industry can sell the goods for more than the cost of producing them, thus making a profit.

Book publishing and the restaurant business are two industries that are easy to enter. If book prices are above minimum average costs, new publishers will enter the market, as it is relatively easy to produce a book. Similarly, if prices of restaurant meals in an area exceed minimum average cost, new restaurants will open up or restaurant chains will expand with branches in new locations.

Figure 7.4A shows the U-shaped average cost curve. Minimum average cost is c_{min}. If the price is less than c_{min}, then there is no level of output at which the firm could produce and make a profit. If the price is above c_{min}, then the firm will produce at Q^*, the level of output at which price (p) equals marginal cost. At Q^*, marginal costs exceeds average costs. (This is always true at output levels greater than that at which average costs are minimal.) Profit per unit is the difference between price and average costs. Total profits are the product of profit per unit and the level of output (the shaded area in the figure).

Different companies may have different average cost curves. Some will have better management. Some will have a better location. Accordingly, firms will differ in their minimum average cost. As prices rise, additional firms will find it attractive to enter the market. Figure 7.4B shows the U-shaped average cost curves for three different firms. Firm 1's minimum average cost is AC_1, firm 2's minimum average cost is AC_2, and firm 3's minimum average cost is AC_3. Thus, firm 1 enters at the price p_1, firm 2 at the price p_2, and firm 3 at the price p_3.

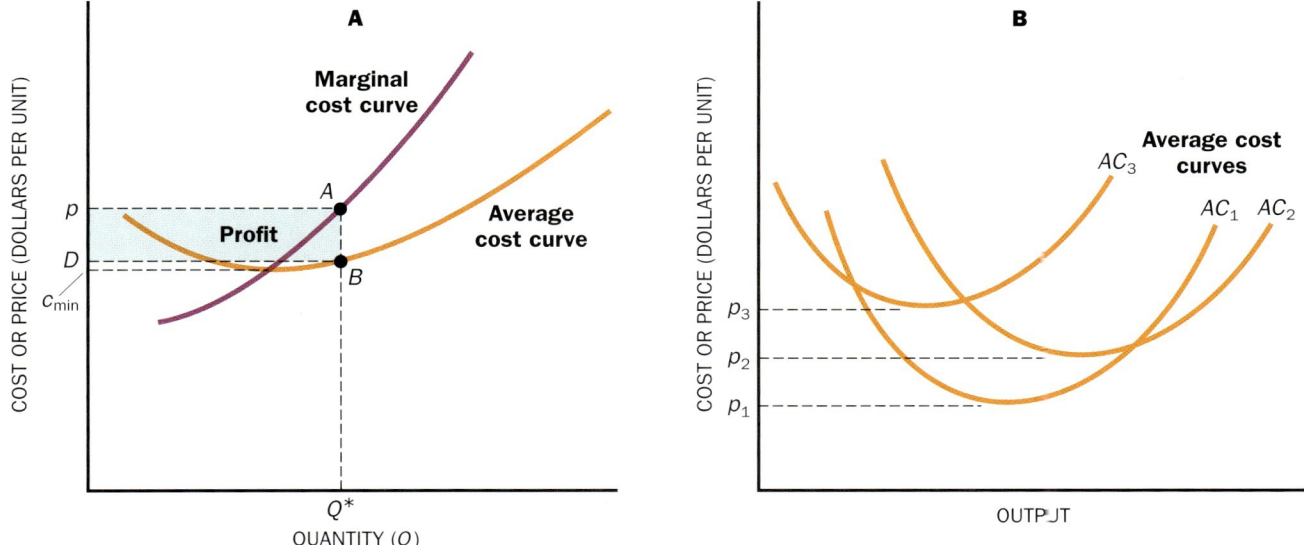

Figure 7.4

COST CURVES, PROFITS, AND ENTRY

Panel A shows that if price is above the minimum of the average cost curve, profits will exist. Profits are measured by the area formed by the shaded rectangle, the profit per unit (price minus average cost, corresponding to the distance AB) times the output, Q^*. Thus, profits are the shaded rectangle, $ABDp$. Panel B shows average cost curves for three different firms. At price p_1, only one firm will enter the market. As price rises to p_2 and then to p_3, first the firm whose cost curve is AC_2 and then the firm whose cost curve is AC_3 will enter the market.

SUNK COSTS AND EXIT

The converse of the decision of a firm to enter the market is the decision of a firm already producing to exit the market. *Sunk costs* are costs that are not recoverable, even if a firm goes out of business. The High Strung Violin Company, for example, may have had an extensive television advertising campaign. The cost of this campaign is a sunk cost. There is no way this expenditure can be recouped even if production ceases. If there were no sunk costs, the decision to enter and the decision to exit would be mirror images of each other. Firms would exit the market when their average costs rose above the good's price. But if some costs remain even after a firm exits the market, the question facing that firm is whether it is better off continuing to produce or exiting.

Let us assume for the sake of simplicity that all fixed costs are sunk costs. A firm with no fixed costs has an average cost curve that is the same as its average variable cost curve. It will shut down as soon as the price falls below minimum average costs—the cost at the bottom of its U-shaped variable cost curve. But a firm *with* fixed costs has a different decision to make. Figure 7.5A depicts both the average variable cost curve and the average cost curve for such a case. As in the case with no sunk costs, the firm shuts down when price is below minimum average *variable* costs (costs that vary with the level of output), p_1. But if the price is

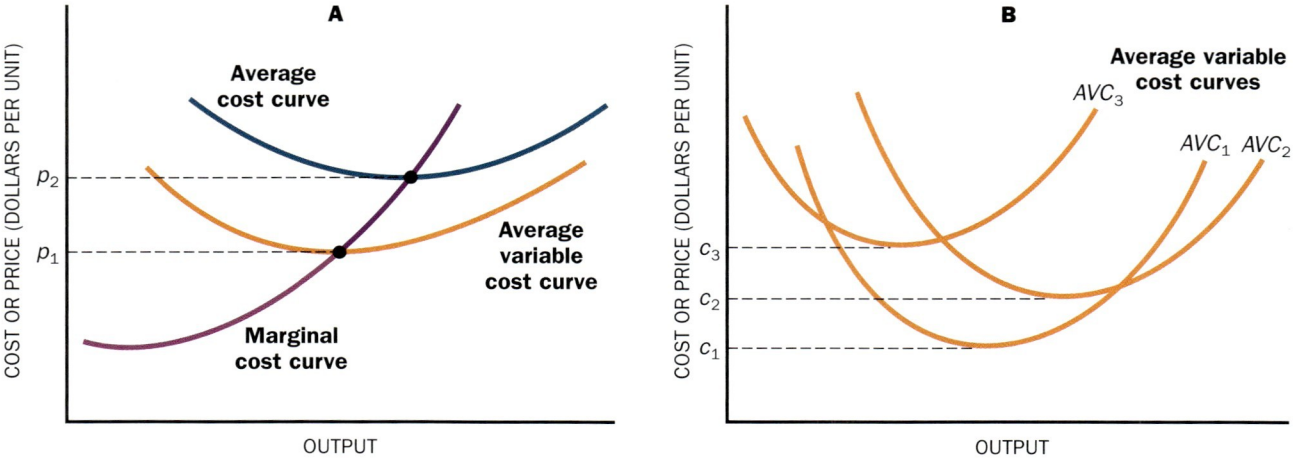

Figure 7.5

AVERAGE VARIABLE COSTS AND THE DECISION TO PRODUCE

Panel A shows a firm's average variable cost curves. In the short run, firms will produce as long as price exceeds average variable costs. Thus, for prices between p_1 and p_2, the firm will continue to produce, even though it is recording a loss (price is less than average cost). Panel B shows that firms with different average variable cost curves will decide to shut down at different price levels. As price falls below c_3, the minimum average variable cost for firm 3, firm 3 shuts down; as price falls still lower, below c_2, firm 2 shuts down. Finally, when price falls below c_1, firm 1 shuts down.

between average variable costs and average costs, the firm will continue to produce, even though it will show a loss. It continues to produce because it would show an even bigger loss if it ceased operating. Since price exceeds average variable costs, the revenues it obtains exceed the additional costs it incurs from producing.

Different firms in an industry will have different average variable costs, and so will find it desirable to exit the market at different prices. Figure 7.5B shows the average variable cost curves for three different firms. Their cost curves differ; some may, for instance, have newer equipment than others. As the price falls, the firm with the highest minimum average variable costs finds it is no longer able to make money at the going price, and decides not to operate. Thus, firm 3 (represented by the curve AVC_3) shuts down as soon as the price falls below c_3, firm 2 shuts down as soon as the price falls below c_2, and firm 1 shuts down as soon as the price falls below c_1.

THE FIRM'S SUPPLY CURVE

We can now draw the firm's supply curve. As Figure 7.6A shows, for a firm contemplating entry into the market, supply is zero up to a critical price, equal to the minimum average cost. Thus, for prices below $c_{min} = p$, the firm produces zero output. For prices greater than $c_{min} = p$, the firm produces up to the point where price equals

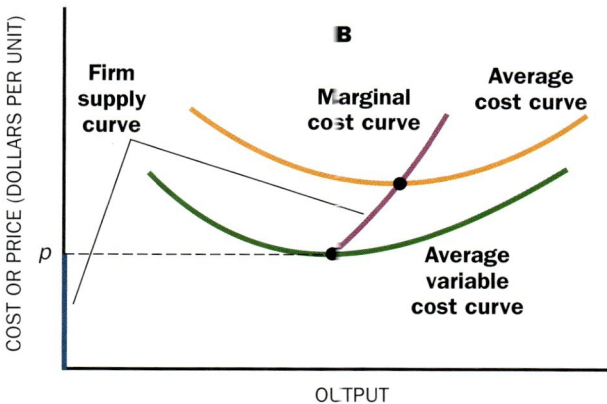

FIGURE 7.6

THE SUPPLY CURVE FOR A FIRM

Panel A shows that for a firm contemplating entry into the market, supply is zero up to a critical price, equal to the firm's minimum average cost, after which the firm's supply curve coincides with the marginal cost curve. Panel B shows a firm that has already entered the market, incurring positive sunk costs; this firm will produce as long as price exceeds the minimum of the average variable cost curve.

marginal cost, so the firm's supply curve coincides with the marginal cost curve. For a firm that has incurred sunk costs in entering the market (panel B), the supply curve coincides with the marginal cost curve so long as price exceeds the minimum value of average *variable* costs; when price is below the minimum value of average variable costs, the firm exits, so supply is again zero.

THE MARKET SUPPLY CURVE

With this information about the cost curves of individual firms, we can derive the overall market supply curve. Back in Chapter 3, the market supply curve was defined as the sum of the amounts that each firm was willing to supply at any given price. Figure 7.7 provides a graphical description of the supply curve for a market with two firms. More generally, if the price rises, the firms already in the market (firms 1 and 2) will find it profitable to increase their output, and new firms (with higher average variable cost curves) will find it profitable to enter the market. Because higher prices induce more firms to enter a competitive market, the market supply response to an increase in price is greater than if the number of firms were fixed. In the same way, as price falls, there are two market responses. The firms that still find it profitable to produce at the lower price will produce less, and the higher-cost firms will exit the market. In this way, the competitive market ensures that whatever the product, it is produced at the lowest possible price by the most efficient firms.

FIGURE 7.7

THE MARKET SUPPLY CURVE

The market supply curve is derived by horizontally adding up the supply curves for each of the firms. More generally, as price rises, each firm produces more and new firms enter the market.

Long-Run Versus Short-Run Supply

As we saw in Chapter 6, in the short run the typical firm will have a U-shaped average cost curve, and a rising marginal cost curve at output levels above the lowest point of the U. But its long-run marginal cost curve is flatter because adjustments to changes in market conditions take time, and some adjustments take longer than others. In the short run, a firm can add workers, work more shifts, and run the machines harder (or reduce the rate at which these things are done), but it is probably stuck with its existing plant and equipment. In the long run, it can acquire more buildings and more machines (or sell them). Thus, the long-run supply curve for a firm is more elastic (flatter) than the short-run supply curve, as shown in Figure 7.8.

The same difference, only more marked, is seen for the industry—again because the number of firms is not fixed. Even if each firm can operate only one plant, the industry's output can be increased by 5 percent by increasing the number of firms by 5 percent. The extra costs of increasing output by 5 percent are approximately the same as the average costs. Accordingly, the long-run market supply curve is roughly horizontal. Under these conditions, even if the demand curve for the product shifts drastically, the market will supply much more of the

FIGURE 7.8

ELASTICITY OF SHORT-RUN AND LONG-RUN SUPPLY CURVES FOR A FIRM

Because there is a greater chance for a firm to adjust to changes in price in the long run, the price elasticity of the supply curve is greater in the long run than in the short run.

Figure 7.9

MARKET EQUILIBRIUM IN THE SHORT RUN AND LONG RUN

In panel A, the market equilibrium is originally at a price p_0 and an output Q_0. In the short run, a shift in the demand curve from D_0 to D_1 raises the price to p_1 and quantity to Q_1. In the long run, the supply elasticity is greater, so the increase in price is smaller—price is only p_2—and quantity is greater, Q_2. If supply is perfectly elastic in the long run, as shown in panel B, shifts in demand will change only the quantity produced in the long run, not the market price.

e-Insight
THE 2001 RECESSION: CUTBACKS VERSUS SHUTDOWNS

In late 2000, the economy seemed to slow down, and by early 2001 some parts of the economy were actually contracting. Many dot-com firms that had opened in the late 1990s found themselves struggling. Some businesses shut down, while others cut back. How do we explain the difference?

Hit particularly badly were publishers of magazines, which depend heavily on advertisements for revenues. Ad revenues for one magazine that focused on the new economy, *The Industry Standard,* fell by more than 60 percent. Publishing firms cut back on employment, but even the most adversely affected in this sector did not shut down. Why? The reason was simple: though they were showing losses, their revenues exceeded their variable costs. Much of their costs were sunk costs that would not be recovered if they closed. It paid them to continue publishing, even if on a smaller scale.

On the other hand, many Internet companies (dot-coms) did shut down. Some that had depended on advertising revenue closed because although their variable costs were low, their revenues were even lower. They could not cover their variable costs.

The online grocery service Webvan closed its doors for good during the economic slowdown of 2001.

product at close to the same price, as additional plants are constructed and additional firms enter the market.

Thus, the market supply curve is much more elastic in the long run than in the short run. Indeed, in the *very* short run, a firm may find it impossible to hire more skilled labor or to increase its capacity. Its supply curve, and the market supply curve, would be nearly vertical. In the short run, machines and the number of firms are fixed, but labor and other inputs can be varied. Figure 7.9A shows the short-run supply curve. Contrast the short-run market supply curve with the long-run market supply curve: the short-run curve slopes up much more sharply. A shift in the demand curve has a larger effect on price and a smaller effect on quantity than it does in the long run. In the long run, the market supply curve may be horizontal. In that case, shifts in the demand curve have an effect *only* on quantity, as in panel B. Price remains at the level of minimum average costs; *competition leads to entry up to the point where there are zero profits.*

Again, it is worth asking, "How long is the long run?" The answer depends on the industry. It takes an electric power company years to change its capacity. For most other firms, buildings and equipment can be added if not within months, then certainly within a year or two. Recent improvements in technology, such as computer-aided design and manufacturing, have made it possible for many companies to change what they are producing more rapidly, and thus have reduced the length of the long run and made supply curves more elastic than they had been in the past.

> **Wrap-Up**
>
> ## ADJUSTMENTS IN THE SHORT RUN AND THE LONG RUN
>
> In the very short run, firms may be unable to adjust production at all; only the price changes.
>
> In the short run, firms may be able to hire more labor and adjust other variable inputs.
>
> In the long run, firms may be able to buy more machines, and firms may decide to enter or to exit.
>
> The times required for these adjustments may vary from industry to industry.

Accounting Profits and Economic Profits

This chapter has shown how firms enter and exit markets in pursuit of profits. The result of this process is that competition among firms drives profits to zero—in an apparent contradiction of the basic competitive model. If firms are profit maximizers, as we learned in Chapter 6, why would they ever choose to produce when there are no profits to be made? Moreover, how can it be true that profits are zero when firms in the real world routinely report making profits?

The answer to these questions is that accountants and economists think about profits differently in two important respects. The first is that economists take opportunity costs into account. The second has to do with the economic concept of rent. Both deserve a closer look.

OPPORTUNITY COSTS

To begin to see how opportunity costs affect the economist's view of profits, consider a small firm in which the owner has invested $100,000. Assume the owner receives a small salary and devotes sixty hours a week to running the enterprise. An economist would argue that the owner ought to calculate his opportunity costs related to his investment of time and money into the business. The opportunity cost of his time is the best wage available to him if he worked sixty hours a week at an alternate job. The opportunity cost of his capital is the return that the $100,000 invested in this enterprise would produce in another investment. These are the true costs of the owner's time and capital investment. To calculate the firm's profits as the economist sees them, these opportunity costs have to be subtracted out.

One can easily imagine a business whose accountant reports a profit equal to 3 percent of the capital investment. An economist would note that if the investment capital had been put in a bank account, it would have earned at least 5 percent. Thus, the economist would say the business is operating at a loss. Because they generally fail to take into account opportunity costs, reported profits often are frequently higher than true economic profits.

Taking opportunity costs into account is often not a simple matter; it is not always easy to determine the alternative uses of a firm's resources. Managerial time spent in expanding the firm in one direction, for example, might have been spent in controlling costs or expanding the firm in another direction. Land that is used for a golf course for the firm's employees might have been used for some other purpose, and the money saved could have more than covered golf club memberships for all employees who want them. In making decisions about resources like these, firms must constantly ask what price the resources might fetch in other uses.

Sometimes market data can provide appropriate prices for calculating opportunity costs. For example, the opportunity cost of giving huge offices to top executives can be gauged by the money those offices would bring if they were rented to some other company. But often the calculation involves imponderables, such as the opportunity cost of the vice president who cannot be fired and will not retire for five years.

What about the costs associated with an expenditure already made, say on a building that is no longer really needed by the firm? The relevant opportunity cost of this building is not the original purchase or lease price, but instead the value of the building in alternate uses, such as the rent that could be earned if the building were leased to other firms.

The fundamental point is that past expenditures cannot be used to calculate opportunity costs. Consider a computer manufacturer that has purchased a parcel of land for $1 million an acre. It turns out, however, that the company made a mistake: the land is worth only $100,000 an acre. The firm now must choose between two different plants for producing new computers, one of which uses much more of the land than the other. In figuring opportunity costs, should the property be valued at the purchase price of $1 million an acre, or at what it could be sold for—$100,000 an acre? The answer can help determine whether the firm chooses to conserve on land. From an economics viewpoint, the answer to this valuation problem should be obvious: the firm should evaluate costs according to its *current* opportunity costs. The fact that the company made a mistake in purchasing the land is irrelevant.

Yet individuals and firms frequently do compound their economic errors by continuing to focus on past expenditures. Business executives who were originally responsible for making a bad decision may be particularly reluctant to let bygones be bygones. Publicly declaring that the correct market price of land is $100,000 an acre, for example, would be tantamount to announcing that a major mistake had been made. Acknowledging such a mistake could jeopardize a business executive's future with the firm.

ECONOMIC RENT

A second difference between an economist's and an accountant's definition of profit concerns **economic rent.** Economic rent is the difference between the price that is actually paid and the price that would have to be paid in order for the good or service to be produced.

Economic rent has far broader applications than its historic use to refer to payments made by farmers to their landlords for the use of their land, but the example of rent for land use is still instructive. The critical characteristic of land in this context is that its supply is inelastic. Higher payments for land (higher rents) will not elicit a greater supply. Even if landlords received virtually nothing for their land, the same land would be available. Many other factors of production have the same inelastic character. Even at double the salary, Shaquille O'Neal would not "produce" more baskets for the Miami Heat. The extra payments for this kind of rare talent fall into the economist's definition of rent.

While the supersalaries of movie stars and professional athletes consist largely of economic rent, many workers with more mundane salaries also receive it. For example, suppose Jim has just finished his degree in education and has offers to teach high school from two school districts in California, one in Santa Cruz on the Pacific Ocean and one in San Jose, a forty-minute drive from the beach. Both districts offer Jim the same starting salary. If Jim loves to surf, he will take the job in Santa Cruz, where he can surf before and after work. In fact, he would have taken the job in Santa Cruz even at a slightly lower salary than was offered by the school in San Jose. The difference between what he actually is paid and his opportunity cost—the value of his next best-alternative—is economic rent.

The concept of opportunity cost explains our claim that the salaries of movie stars and top professional athletes are mainly economic rent. Before Brad Pitt became a famous and highly paid actor, he supported himself as a limo driver and by dressing as a giant chicken for an L.A. restaurant chain. He studied journalism in college but left before graduating. None of these occupations would have paid anything near what he earns as an actor. The value of his next-best opportunity is low, making almost all his income economic rent. The same is true of people like Kobe Bryant; his income in his next-best alternative to basketball is probably trivial compared to what he is paid by the Lakers. Anyone who is in a position to receive economic rents is fortunate indeed, because these "rents" are unrelated to effort. They are payments determined entirely by demand.

Firms earn economic rent to the extent that they are more efficient than other firms. We saw earlier that a firm is willing to produce at a price equal to its minimum average cost. Some firms might be more efficient than others, so their average cost curves are lower. Consider a market in which all firms except one have the same average cost curve, and the market price corresponds to the minimum average cost of these firms. The remaining firm is super-efficient, pushing its average costs far below those of the other firms. The company would have been willing to produce at a lower price, at its minimum average cost. What it receives in excess of what is required to induce it to enter the market are rents—returns on the firm's superior capabilities.

In some cases, supplies of inputs are inelastic in the short run but elastic in the long run. An example is payment for the use of a building. In the short run, the supply of buildings does not depend on the return, and hence payments for the use of the building are rents, in the economist's sense. But in the long run, the supply of buildings does depend on the return—investors will not construct new buildings unless they receive a return equal to what they could obtain elsewhere. So the "rent" received by the building's owner is not really a rent, in the sense in which economists use the term.

Thus, when economists say that competition drives profits to zero, they are focusing on the fact that in competitive equilibrium, price equals marginal cost for every firm producing. A company will not increase profits by expanding production, and firms outside the industry will not gain by entering it. We say that competition drives profits to zero at the margin.

Case in Point

ENTERING THE PAINTING BUSINESS AND OPPORTUNITY COSTS

Individuals often forget to include opportunity costs when they are making important decisions, as the following story illustrates.

House painting is a summer business, for days that are hot and long, using available low-skilled labor on vacation from high school and college. As a way of picking up some cash, Michael decided to start Presto Painters during the summer, after taking introductory economics.

Just getting started involved some substantial fixed costs. Michael ran the business out of his parents' home so he had no costs for office space. His fixed costs ended up looking like this:

Fixed costs	
Used van	$5,000
Paint and supplies	$2,000
Flyers and signs	$1,200
Business cards and estimate sheets	$ 500
Phone line and answering machine	$ 300
Total	$9,000

Michael went to work drumming up business. He took calls from potential customers and knocked on doors, made estimates of what he thought it would cost to paint someone's home, and then offered them a price. Of course, he was in direct competition with many other painters and had to meet the competition's price to get a job.

Michael found that the going rate for labor was $10 per hour. In the real world, labor is not the only variable input required for house painting—there are also the costs of buying additional paint and brushes—but for the sake of simplicity, let's assume that he started off the summer with all the paint he needed. Thus, his variable costs were related to the labor he needed to hire.

Variable costs are also related to the amount of time it takes to paint a house, which depends in part on the quality of the labor available. The variable costs for Presto Painters were as follows:

Houses painted	Hours of labor hired	Payroll cost
5	100	$ 1,000
10	300	$ 3,000
15	600	$ 6,000
20	1,000	$10,000
25	1,500	$15,000
30	2,100	$21,000

Number of homes	Total cost	Average cost	Marginal cost (per house)
0	$ 9,000		
5	$10,000	$2,000	$ 200
10	$12,000	$1,200	$ 400
15	$15,000	$1,000	$ 600
20	$19,000	$ 950	$ 800
25	$24,000	$ 960	$1,000
30	$30,000	$1,000	$1,200

Given this information, Michael could calculate cost curves for Presto Painters (see above).

Based on his marginal and average cost curves, Michael figured that if market conditions allowed him to charge $1,000 or more for a typical house, then he could make a profit by painting at least 25 houses. Roughly speaking, that is how his summer worked out; painting 25 houses for $1,000 apiece. Thus, he earned $1,000 in profits.

Or so he thought. Nowhere on this list of costs did Michael consider the opportunity cost of his time. He was not getting paid $10 an hour for painting houses; he was out there stirring up business, hiring and organizing workers, taking calls from customers, dealing with complaints.

Imagine that Michael had an alternate job possibility: waiting on tables. He could earn $6 per hour (including tips) and work 40-hour weeks during a 12-week summer vacation. Thus, he could have earned $2,880 during the summer with little stress or risk. If this opportunity cost is added to the fixed costs of running the business, then his apparent profit turns into a loss. Since Presto Painters did not cover Michael's opportunity cost *and* compensate him for the risk and aggravation of running his own business, he would have been financially better off sticking to the business of filling people's stomachs rather than painting their houses.

> **Wrap-Up**
>
> ## ACCOUNTANTS' VERSUS ECONOMISTS' PROFITS
>
> Accounting profits: revenues minus expenditures
>
> Economic profits: revenues minus rents minus economic costs (including opportunity costs of labor and capital)

The Theory of the Competitive Firm

We now have completed half of our description of the theory of the competitive firm. The firm takes as given the prices it pays for the inputs it uses, including the wages it pays workers and the costs of capital goods. From these figures, it can calculate the costs of producing different levels of output. Taking the prices it receives for the goods it sells as given, the firm chooses the level of output to maximize its profits—that is, it sets price equal to marginal cost. From this information, we can derive the supply curves that were used in Chapters 3 and 4. As prices increase, output increases; firms produce more, and more firms produce. Thus, supply curves are upward sloping.

But as the firm produces more, it will also demand more labor and more capital. Deriving firms' demand curves for labor and capital is our next task, which we take up in the following chapters.

Review and Practice

SUMMARY

1. A revenue curve shows the relationship between a firm's total output and its revenue. For a competitive firm, the marginal revenue it receives from selling an additional unit of output is the price of that unit.
2. A firm in a competitive market will choose the level of output at which the market price—the marginal revenue it receives from producing an extra unit—equals the marginal cost.
3. A firm will enter a market if the market price for a good exceeds its minimum average costs, since it can make a profit by selling the good for more than it costs to produce the good.
4. If the market price is below minimum average costs and a firm has no sunk costs, the firm will exit the market immediately. If the market price is below minimum average costs and a firm has sunk costs, it will continue to produce in the short run as long as the market price exceeds its minimum average variable costs.
5. For a firm contemplating entering a market, its supply is zero up to the point at which price equals minimum average costs. Above that price, the supply curve is the same as the marginal cost curve.
6. The market supply curve is constructed by adding up the supply curves of all firms in an industry. As prices rise, more firms are willing to produce, and each firm is willing to produce more, so that the market supply curve is normally upward sloping.
7. The economist's and the accountant's concepts of profits differ in how they treat opportunity costs and economic rents.

KEY TERMS

revenue curve
marginal revenue
economic rent

REVIEW QUESTIONS

1. In a competitive market, what rule determines the profit-maximizing level of output? What is the relationship between a firm's supply curve and its marginal cost curve?
2. What determines firms' decisions to enter a market? to exit a market? Explain the role of the average variable cost curve in determining whether firms will exit the market.
3. Why is the long-run supply curve more elastic than the short-run supply curve?
4. What is the relationship between the way accountants use the concept of profits and the way economists use that term?

PROBLEMS

1. The market price for painting a house in Centerville is $10,000. The Total Cover-up House-Painting Company has fixed costs of $4,000 for ladders, brushes, and so on, and the company's variable costs for house painting follow this pattern:

Output (houses painted)	2	3	4	5	6	7	8	9	10
Variable cost (in thousands of dollars)	26	32	36	42	50	60	72	86	102

   Calculate the company's total costs, and graph the revenue curve and the total cost curve. Do the curves have the shape you expect? Over what range of production is the company making profits?

2. Calculate and graph the marginal cost, the average costs, and the average variable costs for the Total Cover-up House-Painting Company. Given the market price, at what level of output will this firm maximize profits? What profit (or loss) is it making at that level? At what price will the firm no longer make a profit? Assume its fixed costs are sunk; there is no market for used ladders, brushes, etc. At what price will the company shut down?

3. Draw a U-shaped average cost curve. On your diagram, designate at what price levels you would expect entry and at what price levels you would expect exit if all the fixed costs are sunk. What if only half the fixed costs are sunk? Explain your reasoning.

4. José is a skilled electrician at a local company, a job that pays $50,000 per year, but he is considering quitting to start his own business. He talks it over with an account-

ant, who helps him to draw up the following chart with their best predictions about costs and revenues.

Predicted annual costs		Predicted annual revenues
Basic wage	$20,000	$75,000
Rent of space	$12,000	
Rent of equipment	$18,000	
Utilities	$ 2,000	
Miscellaneous	$ 5,000	

The basic wage does seem a bit low, the accountant admits, but she tells José to remember that as owner of the business, José will get to keep any profits as well. From an economist's point of view, is the accountant's list of costs complete? From an economist's point of view, what are José's expected profits?

Learning Goals

In this chapter, you will learn

1. What determines the number of hours an individual works
2. How income and substitution affect labor supply decisions in opposing ways
3. What determines a firm's demand for labor
4. How wages ensure that demand and supply balance in the labor market

CHAPTER 8

LABOR MARKETS

The previous three chapters examined demand and supply in the markets for goods and services. Choosing what goods to purchase and how much of them are among the most basic decisions of households. The amount of money available to spend depends on two other basic decisions: how much to work (and earn) and how much to save (or spend from savings). The decisions that people make about work determine the economy's supply of labor. Their decisions about saving determine the economy's supply of funds in the capital market. Understanding the factors that influence these decisions will give us insight into the supply side of the economy's labor and capital markets.

In this chapter, we focus on the labor market and the decisions that determine both the demand for labor and the supply of labor. We will find that the approach developed in Chapter 5 to understand how households decide about consuming can also offer insights into how they decide how much to work. We will also look into the factors that determine the firm's demand for labor. By bringing together the demand and supply sides of the labor market, we will see how wages are determined in a competitive market economy. Chapter 9 will then examine saving decisions and the capital market.

The Labor Supply Decision

At one time, going to college was a full-time job. Students were supported by their families or by scholarships and loans, with few students holding down jobs. Today, most college students work to help pay their tuition and living expenses. In addition to deciding which classes to take, students have to decide whether to work; and if they decide to work, they need to decide how many hours to work each week. Working more helps pay the bills, but it also takes time away from studies, perhaps

175

Internet Connection
LABOR FORCE DATA

The Bureau of Labor Statistics, part of the U.S. Department of Labor, is responsible for collecting much of the data that economists use to track developments in the labor supply. Its Web site can be found at www.bls.gov.

even delaying graduation. Understanding the forces that affect decisions about how much to work—how much labor to supply to the market—is central to understanding how labor markets function.

The increase in student employment is just one of many changes in the pattern of labor supply that have taken place over the past half century. The average workweek has declined from 39 hours in 1959 to just under 34 hours in 2004. At the same time, the fraction of women in the labor force has increased enormously. In 1950, just 34 percent of women over the age of sixteen were in the labor force. Today, that figure is close to 60 percent. Many of the changes in American society in recent decades are reflections of the decisions individuals make about how much labor to supply.

THE CHOICE BETWEEN LEISURE AND CONSUMPTION

Economists use the basic model of choice to help understand these patterns of labor supply. This is the model we used in Chapter 5 to examine the consumption decision. The decision about how much labor to supply is a choice between consumption (or income) and leisure. (*Leisure* to an economist means all the time an individual could potentially work for pay that is not actually spent working.) By giving up leisure, a person receives additional income, and this enables her to increase consumption. By working less and giving up some consumption, a person obtains more leisure. Her increase in income does not necessarily translate *immediately* into consumption; she has to decide whether to spend the extra income now or in the future. We will tackle that choice in Chapter 9. Here, we assume the person spends all her income.

Even though the typical job seems to entail set hours of work, people have many ways to influence how much labor they will supply. Many workers may not have discretion as to whether they will work full-time, but they have some choice in whether they will work overtime. In addition, many individuals moonlight, taking second jobs that provide them with additional income. Most of these jobs—for example, driving a taxi—provide considerable discretion in the number of hours worked. Hence, people still have choices even when they lack control of their work hours at their primary job. And because jobs differ in their normal workweek, a worker has some flexibility in choosing a job that allows her to work the number of hours she wishes. Finally, economists believe that social conventions concerning the "standard" workweek—the 40-hour week that has become the 35-hour week—respond over time to the attitudes (preferences) of workers.

We now apply the analysis of Chapter 5 to an individual's choice between work and leisure. Figure 8.1 shows the budget constraint of Steve, who earns an hourly wage of $7. Accordingly, for each hour less of leisure Steve enjoys—for each extra hour he works—he earns $7 more. That is, his consumption increases by $7. Underlying this budget constraint is his time constraint. He has only so many hours a day, say 16, to spend either working or at leisure. For each extra hour he works, he has 1 less hour of leisure. If he works 1 hour, his income is $7; if he works 2 hours, his income is $14; and so forth. If he works 16 hours—he has no leisure—his income is $7 × 16 = $112. The trade-off between income and leisure given by his budget constraint is $7 per hour.

Steve will choose a point on the budget constraint according to his own preferences, just as a consumer chooses between two goods (see Chapter 5). Let's suppose that he chooses point E_0. At E_0 he has 10 hours of leisure, which means that he works 6 hours out of the total available time of 16 hours. His income is $42 per day.

In deciding which of the points along the budget constraint to choose, Steve balances the marginal benefits of what he can buy with an additional hour's wage against the marginal costs—the value of the hour's worth of leisure that he will have to forgo. Steve and his brother, Jim, assess the marginal benefits and marginal costs differently. Steve chooses point E_0, while his brother chooses point E_1. Jim values the material things in life more and leisure less.

For Steve, at E_0, the marginal benefit of the extra concert tickets or other goods he can buy with the money he earns from working an extra hour just offsets the marginal costs of that hour—the extra leisure he has to give up. At points to the left of E_0, Steve has less leisure (so the marginal value of leisure is greater) and he has more goods (so the marginal value of the extra goods he can get is lower). The marginal benefit of working less exceeds the marginal costs, and so he works less—he moves toward point E_0. The converse arguments apply to Steve's thinking about points to the right of E_0.

We can apply the same kind of reasoning to see why the workaholic Jim chooses a point to the left of E_0. At E_0, Jim values goods more and leisure less. The marginal benefit of working more exceeds the marginal costs. At E_1, the marginal benefit of working an extra hour (the extra consumption) just offsets the marginal costs.

We can use this framework to derive a _labor supply curve_ that shows the quantity of labor supplied at different wages. Changes in wages have both an income effect and a substitution effect. An increase in wages makes individuals better off. When individuals are better off, they purchase more of all goods. One of the "goods" they will want more of is leisure, so they work less. This is the income effect. But an increase in wages also changes the trade-offs. By giving up one more hour of leisure, the individual can get more goods. Because of this, individuals are willing to work more. This is the substitution effect.

When we looked at the case of a typical good in Chapter 5, we saw that the income and substitution effects reinforce each other. A higher price

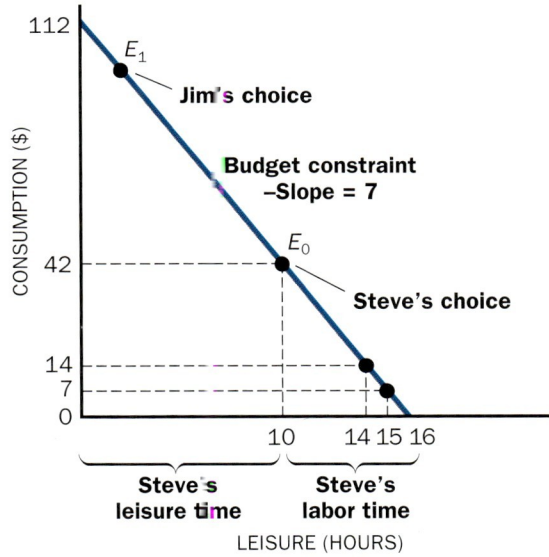

FIGURE 8.1

A BUDGET CONSTRAINT BETWEEN LEISURE AND INCOME

Individuals are willing to trade leisure for an increase in income, and thus in consumption. The budget constraint shows Steve choosing E_0, with 10 hours of daily leisure, 6 hours of work, and $42 in daily wages.

means that individuals are worse off—this income effect leads to reduced consumption of the good; and individuals substitute away from the good whose price has increased—the substitution effect also leads to reduced consumption of the good. *With labor supply, income and substitution effects work in opposite directions, so the net effect of an increase in wages is ambiguous.*

If your wage goes up by 5 percent and you cut back on your hours of work by 5 percent, your total wage income (the hourly wage multiplied by the number of hours you work) will be unchanged: you would have the same income while gaining some extra leisure time. Alternatively, you could work the same number of hours as before and enjoy a higher income. Here, the income effect acts to reduce labor supply. But the opportunity cost of leisure also rises when the wage increases, for the cost of enjoying an extra hour of leisure is the wage income you are giving up. At lower income levels, people generally prefer not to cut back their hours of work when their wage rises; instead, they increase their hours to take advantage of the opportunity to earn the higher wage (the substitution effect of the higher hourly wage dominates the income effect). Labor supply increases as the wage increases. This normal case of an upward-sloping labor supply curve is shown in Figure 8.2A. People choose to work more as their wage rises, trading off leisure for more income.

If income is already very high, however, people often prefer to work less and enjoy more leisure when their wage increases (the income effect dominates the substitution effect). For examples of individuals whose labor supply curve is backward-bending at high wage levels, think of those doctors, dentists, and other high-income professionals who work only a four-day week. This case is illustrated in Figure 8.2B.

If income and substitution effects just balance each other, then labor supply will be relatively unaffected by wage changes. The evidence is that at least for men, the labor supply curve elasticity—the percentage increase in hours worked as a result of a 1 percent increase in wages—is positive but small. For this reason, the average hours that men work has changed little over the past fifty years despite the huge increase in their wages. For women, the evidence suggests that a rise in wages increases labor supply.

So far, we have discussed the impact of a change in wages on labor supply while implicitly assuming that the prices of consumer goods remain unchanged. But in assessing the trade-off between leisure and consumption, an individual is concerned with the actual goods and services that can be purchased, not simply the number of dollars available to spend on consumption. If wages and the prices of all consumer goods double at the same time, then the trade-off between leisure and consumption has not changed. If Jim's wage rises from $7 per hour to $14 per hour, but the price of a compact disc goes up from $10.50 to $21.00, Jim must still give up an hour and a half of leisure to obtain one CD. What is important for labor supply decisions is the average dollar wage, called the **nominal wage,** corrected for changes in the prices of consumer goods. This corrected wage is called the **real wage.** Since 1980, the average nominal wage has risen by more than 100 percent, from $6.84 to $15.38 per hour. Yet the prices of the things we buy have also risen; in fact, the average real wage has remained constant over the past twenty years.

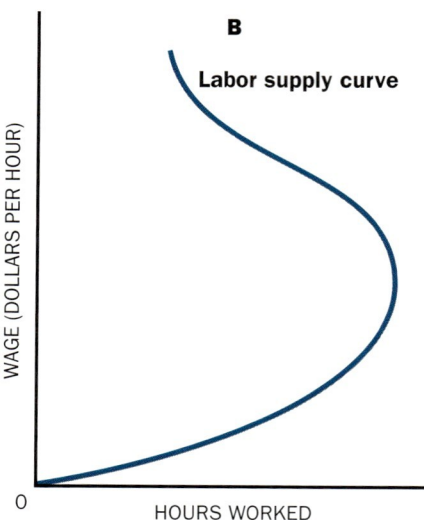

Figure 8.2

THE LABOR SUPPLY CURVE

Panel A shows the case where the substitution effect exceeds the income effect by just a bit, so increases in wages lead to only a small change in labor supply, and the labor supply curve is very steep. In panel B, the substitution effect dominates the income effect at low wages, so that the labor supply curve is upward sloping; and the income effect dominates the substitution effect at high wages, so that the labor supply is downward sloping over that range. Thus, the labor supply curve bends backward.

Wrap-Up

WAGE CHANGES AND LABOR SUPPLY

Labor supply decisions depend on the real wage—the nominal wage corrected for the price of consumer goods.

As real wages rise, individuals become better off. This income effect induces them to work less. Offsetting it is the substitution effect—the higher return to working provides an incentive to work longer hours. Either effect may dominate. Thus, the quantity of labor supplied may increase or decrease with wage increases.

LABOR FORCE PARTICIPATION

The decision about how much labor to supply can be divided into two parts: whether to work and, if so, how much to work. For men, the first question traditionally has had an obvious answer. Unless they were very wealthy, they had to work to support themselves (and their families). Accordingly, the wage at which they decided to work rather than not to work was very low. A change in wage still does not affect the decision of most men about whether to work. It influences only their decision about how many hours to work, and even that effect is small.

Thinking Like an Economist
TRADE-OFFS

The relevant trade-off for deciding how much labor to supply is that between consumption and leisure, as delineated in the budget constraint in Figure 8.1. To gain more consumption, you have to work more, and as a result you have to give up leisure. To gain more leisure time, you have to give up consumption as you work fewer hours and earn less money.

Like all trade-offs, this one reflects an opportunity cost, a concept we introduced in Chapter 2. In the present case, the opportunity cost of an extra hour of leisure is the consumption you have to give up by working one hour less. Similarly, the opportunity cost of an extra $25 of consumption is the leisure time you have to give up to earn the extra $25.

Because the opportunity cost of leisure is the forgone consumption, this opportunity cost depends on the wage you can earn. If your wage is $7 per hour, the opportunity cost of an hour of leisure is $7. If your wage is $25 per hour, the opportunity cost of an hour of leisure is $25. So the opportunity cost of leisure is greater for someone who earns a high wage than it is for someone who earns a lower wage.

Another key idea to remember is that economic decisions are determined by marginal trade-offs (see Chapter 2). If you want to consume more, the benefit of the *extra* consumption must be weighed against the (opportunity) cost of the *diminished* leisure. On the basis of individual preferences for consumption and leisure, the worker chooses the point on the budget constraint where the marginal benefits and costs are equal.

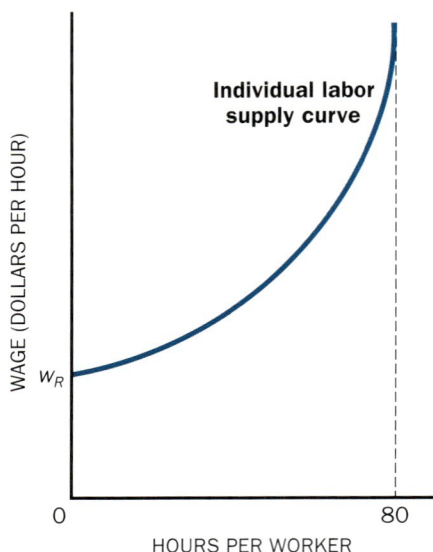

Figure 8.3

THE LABOR PARTICIPATION DECISION

The reservation wage W_R is the minimum wage at which an individual supplies labor.

The decision about *whether* to work is called the **labor force participation decision.** Figure 8.3 shows the labor supply curve for an individual—it shows how many hours that person is willing to supply at each real wage. The minimum wage at which the individual is willing to work, W_R, is called the **reservation wage.** Below the reservation wage, the individual does not participate in the labor force. For men, the reservation wage traditionally has been very low.

Today, most women also work for pay, but for them, unlike men, such employment is not traditional. Only a few decades ago, the social presumption was that middle-class women, if they worked at all, would drop out of the labor market after they began to bear children. And many mothers did not reenter the market even after their children were grown.

The increased quantity of labor supplied by women over the past fifty years can be viewed partly as a *movement* along the labor supply curve and partly as a *shift* in the curve. Job opportunities for women have burgeoned over the past thirty years, and relative wages have risen. Thus, the remuneration from working has increased, raising by the same amount the *opportunity cost* of being out of the labor force. For women already in the labor force, these wage increases have opposing income and substitution effects, just as they do for men. But for women who were not previously part of the labor force, only the substitution effect operates: if a woman was working zero hours, an increase in wages does not raise her income—there is no income effect. Therefore, the substitution effect acts to draw more women into the labor force.[1] The aggregate effect of increased wages on the quantity of labor supplied by women represents a movement along the labor supply curve.

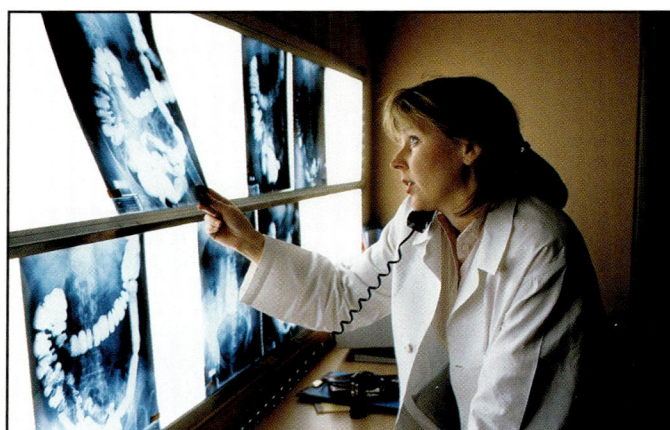

There has been a large increase in labor force participation by women over the past thirty years.

---

[1] It is important to note here that the labor force, as economists define it, includes not only those who have jobs but also those who are looking for jobs. It is also important to note that when we refer to "labor supply," we refer to "market" labor supply—that is, work for pay. Many people perform tasks at home that are comparable to those they perform at work; nonetheless, these are not included in the analysis of labor supply.

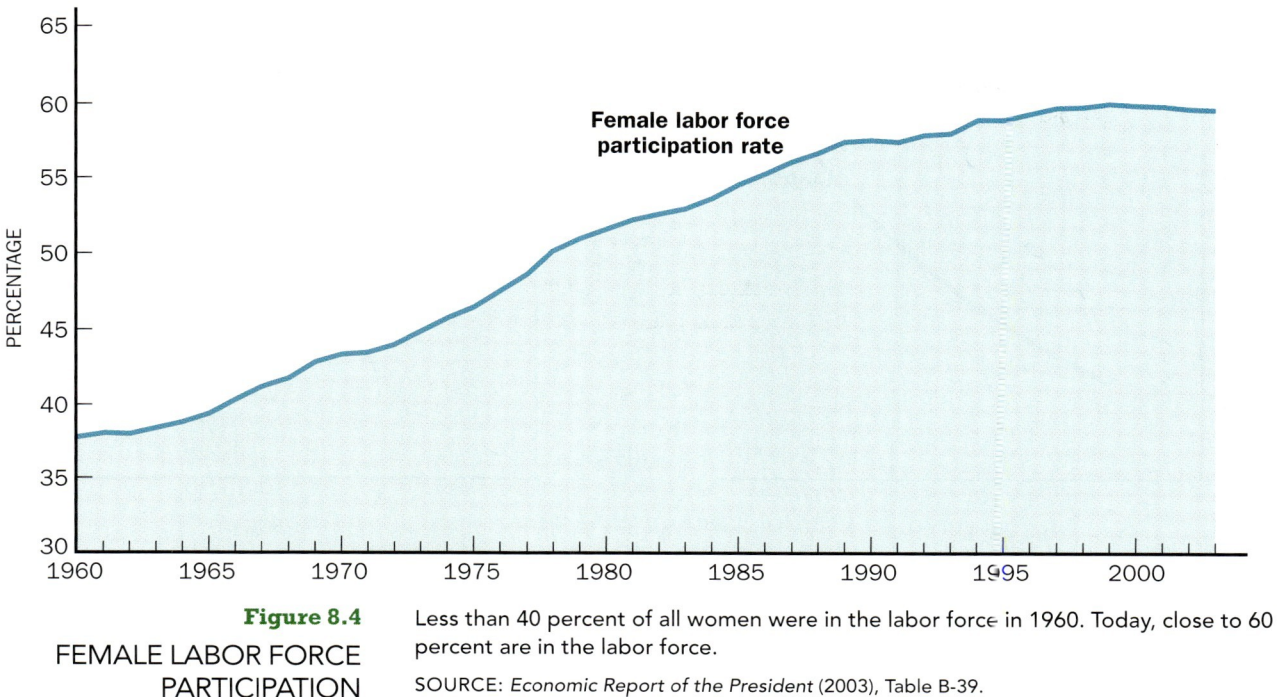

Figure 8.4
FEMALE LABOR FORCE PARTICIPATION

Less than 40 percent of all women were in the labor force in 1960. Today, close to 60 percent are in the labor force.

SOURCE: *Economic Report of the President* (2003), Table B-39.

The labor supply curve for women also has shifted, increasing the labor supply at each value of the wage. Two changes have shifted the labor supply curve to the right and contributed to the dramatic increase in labor force participation of women that is shown in Figure 8.4. Beginning around 1973, (real) wages stopped growing at the rate they had been increasing during the period following World War II. Individuals and families had come to expect regular increases in their material standards of living. When these increases stopped, they felt the loss. This development encouraged married women to take part-time or full-time jobs as a way of keeping the family income increasing or, in many cases, to prevent it from falling.

Attitudes about the role of women, both among women themselves and among employers, have changed significantly. Outright discrimination against women was barred by federal law in 1964; as more careers were open to them, entering the labor force became more attractive. Changed attitudes are also reflected in the dramatic increase in the enrollment of women in professional schools. Most women without small children participate in the labor market, and many with children leave the labor force only for relatively short periods of time. These changes contributed to the shift in the labor supply curve for women and, along with the effects of higher wages, led to the large increases in labor supply by women over the past thirty years.

Firms and the Demand for Labor

Having explored the supply side of the labor market, we now turn to the demand side. What factors influence firms' decisions about how much labor to hire? Once

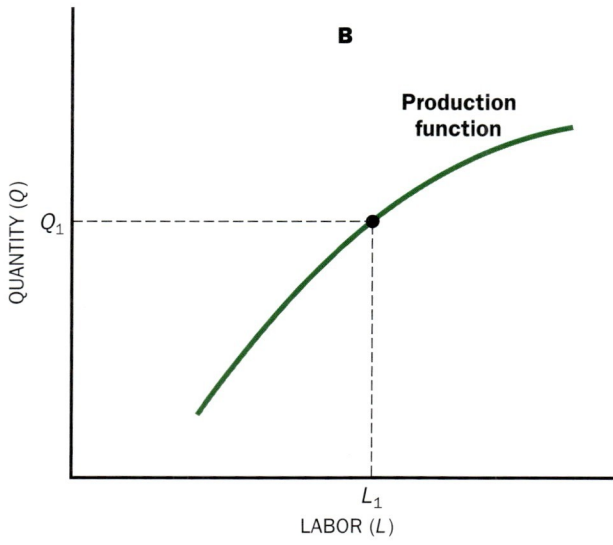

FIGURE 8.5
THE DEMAND FOR LABOR

The demand for labor can be calculated from the firm's supply curve and its production function. Panel A shows how the firm, given a market price p_1, chooses a level of output Q_1 from its supply curve. Panel B shows that to produce the output Q_1 requires L_1 units of labor. L_1 is the demand for labor.

we have examined these decisions, the basic law of supply and demand can be used to show how the wage is determined in the labor market. Labor is one of the primary inputs that firms use in producing output. So our discussion begins by considering what determines a firm's demand for inputs.

FACTOR DEMAND

In the process of deciding how much of each good to supply and determining the lowest-cost method of producing those goods, firms also decide how much of various inputs they will use. This is called **factor demand.** In Chapter 6, the analysis of costs was broken up into two cases, one in which there was a single variable input, or factor of production, and one in which there were several factors. We proceed along similar lines here. Labor is used as our main example of an input, but the same principles apply to any factor of production.

When there is only a single factor of production—here labor—then the decision about how much to produce is the same as the decision about how much labor to hire. As soon as we know the price of the good, we can calculate the supply (output) from the marginal cost curve. As soon as we know the output the firm plans to produce, we know the labor required simply by looking at the production function, which gives the labor input required to produce any level of output.

FIGURE 8.6

THE DEMAND CURVE FOR LABOR

The value of the marginal product of labor declines with the level of employment. Since labor is hired up to the point at which the wage equals the value of the marginal product, at wage w_1, employment is L_1, and at wage w_2, employment is L_2. The demand curve for labor thus traces out the values of the marginal product of labor at different levels of employment.

182 **CHAPTER 8** LABOR MARKETS

Thus, in Figure 8.5, at the price p_1, the output is Q_1 (panel A), and the labor required to produce that output (factor demand) is L_1 (panel B).

There is another way to derive the demand for a factor. If the firm hires one more worker, for example, the extra (or marginal) cost to the firm is her wage. The extra benefit of the worker is the additional revenue that the firm receives from selling the output she produces. This is equal to the price at which the good sells multiplied by the amount of extra output she produces. The extra output produced by the worker is the marginal product of labor—the amount of output produced by the last worker added by the firm. Thus the marginal benefit to the firm of adding an extra worker is the price of the firm's good multiplied by the marginal product of labor. If adding an extra employee at the local Jiffy Lube enables the owner to handle an extra 50 oil changes a month, and the price of each oil change is $25, then the marginal benefit to the owner of adding the worker is $40 times 50, or $1,250 per month. This dollar amount is called the **value of the marginal product of labor.** While the marginal product of labor is measured in units of output (e.g., 50 oil changes per month), the value of the marginal product is measured in dollars.

As long as the value of the marginal product of labor is greater than the marginal cost of hiring the extra worker, the firm can increase its profits by hiring an extra worker. In the Jiffy Lube example, as long as the added wage is less than $1,250 per month, it pays the owner to hire another worker. The firm hires labor up to the point at which the value of the marginal product (the marginal benefit to the firm) is equal to the price of labor, the wage (the marginal cost to the firm).

Using p for the price of the good, MPL for the marginal product of labor, and w for the wage of the worker, we can write this equilibrium condition as

$$\text{value of marginal product} = p \times MPL = w = \text{wage}.$$

From this equilibrium condition, we can derive the demand curve for labor. Figure 8.6 plots the value of the marginal product of labor for each level of labor. Since the marginal product of labor decreases as labor increases, the value of the marginal product also decreases. When the wage is w_1, the value of the marginal product of labor equals the wage with a level of labor at L_1. This is the firm's demand for labor at a wage w_1. Thus, the curve giving the value of the marginal product of labor at each level of employment *is* the demand curve for labor.

It is easy to use this diagram to see the effect of an increase in the price of the good the firm produces. In Figure 8.7, the higher price increases the value of the marginal product of labor at each level of employment, and it immediately follows that at each wage, the demand for labor increases. The demand curve for labor shifts to the right.

Thus, the demand for labor depends on both the wage and the price the firm receives for the goods it sells. In fact, the demand for labor depends only on the ratio of the two, as we will now see.

FIGURE 8.7

EFFECT OF PRICE CHANGE ON THE DEMAND CURVE FOR LABOR

An increase in the price received by a firm shifts the value of the marginal product of labor curve up, so that at each wage, the demand for labor is increased. At wage w_1, employment rises from L_1 to L_4; at wage w_2, employment rises from L_2 to L_3.

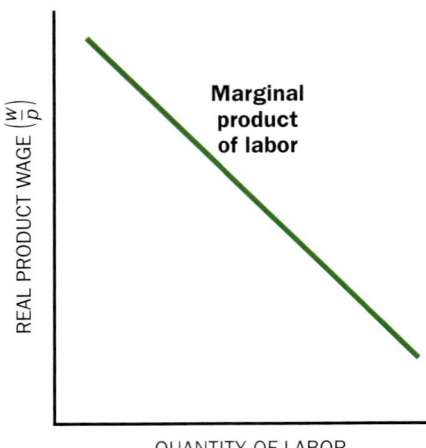

FIGURE 8.8

THE FIRM'S DEMAND CURVE FOR LABOR AND THE REAL PRODUCT WAGE

Firms hire labor up to the point at which the real product wage equals the marginal product of labor. As the real product wage increases, the demand for labor decreases.

If we divide both sides of the previous equation giving the equilibrium condition by the price, we obtain the condition

$$MPL = w/p.$$

The wage divided by the price of the good being produced is defined as the **real product wage.** It measures what firms pay workers in terms of the goods the worker produces rather than in dollar terms. Thus, the firm hires workers up to the point at which the real product wage equals the marginal product of labor.

This principle is illustrated in Figure 8.8, which shows the marginal product of labor. Because of diminishing returns, the marginal product diminishes as labor (and output) increases. As the real product wage increases, the demand for labor decreases.

Wrap-Up

FACTOR DEMAND

A factor of production will be demanded up to the point at which the value of the marginal product of that factor equals its price. In the case of labor, this is the same as saying that the marginal product of labor equals the real product wage.

FROM THE FIRM'S FACTOR DEMAND TO THE MARKET'S FACTOR DEMAND

Once we have derived the firm's demand curve for labor, we can derive the total market demand for labor. At a given set of prices, we simply add up the demand for labor by each firm at any particular wage rate. The total is the market demand at that wage. Since each firm reduces the amount of labor that it demands as the wage increases, the market demand curve is downward sloping.

Labor Supply, Demand, and the Equilibrium Wage

We have now discussed the factors that determine labor supply decisions and those that determine the demand for labor by firms. Households decide how much labor to supply to the marketplace, at each value of the wage. If the substitution effect dominates, higher real wages increase the quantity of labor supplied. Firms decide how much labor to demand at each value of the wage. At higher real wages, the quantity of labor that firms demand is lower. The labor market is in equilibrium when the wage has adjusted to balance labor supply and labor demand. When the labor market is in equilibrium, the demand for labor equals the supply of labor. No worker who wishes to get a job (for which he is qualified) at the going market wage will fail to get one. No firm that wants to hire a worker at the going wage will fail to find a qualified employee.

If demand and supply are not equal at the going market wage, the wage will adjust. If, at the going wage, the number of hours of labor that households wish to supply is greater than the number of hours of labor that firms wish to employ, those in the labor force without jobs will offer to work for less than the going wage. The process of competition will lead to lower wages, until eventually demand again equals supply. Likewise, if firms in the economy demand more labor at the going wage than is supplied, competition by firms to hire scarce labor services will bid the wage up until demand and supply are equal.

This basic model of the labor market makes clear predictions for the consequences of shifts in the demand and supply of labor. Consider first shifts in the supply curve of labor. Such shifts can occur because the total labor force grows, as the number of young people reaching working age exceeds the numbers of workers retiring, because of new immigrants, or because of social changes such as the entry of more women into the labor force. The U.S. labor force expanded rapidly in the 1970s, for example, as the baby boomers entered the labor force and more and more women worked outside the home. An increase in the labor force shifts the supply curve of labor to the right; at each real wage, the total number of labor hours that individuals wish to supply is greater. The equilibrium real wage falls. This fall in the price of labor indicates to firms that labor is less scarce than it was before, and firms should therefore economize less in the use of labor. Firms respond to the lower real wage by creating more jobs. Employment rises to absorb the increase in labor supply.

Consider now the effects of a shift in the demand curve for labor. Suppose technological progress makes workers more productive, raising the marginal product of labor. At each wage, firms now wish to hire more labor, and the labor demand curve shifts to the right. Real wages rise to restore equilibrium in the labor market.

Over the past quarter century, increases in the American labor force have shifted the labor supply curve to the right. At the same time, increases in worker productivity have shifted the labor demand curve to the right as well. The basic model predicts that the total quantity of labor employed will rise, but real wages may either fall (if supply shifts more than demand) or rise (if demand shifts more than supply). Average real wages in the United States in fact have fallen slightly over this period.

Review and Practice

SUMMARY

1. The decision about how to allocate time between work and leisure can be analyzed using the basic ideas of budget constraints and preferences. Individuals face a trade-off along a budget constraint between leisure and income. The amount of income a person can obtain by giving up leisure is determined by the wage rate.
2. In labor markets, the substitution and income effects of a change in wages work in opposite directions. An increase in wages makes people better-off, and they wish to enjoy more leisure as well as more consumption; this is the income effect. But an increase in wages raises the opportunity cost of leisure and encourages more work; this is the substitution effect. The overall effect of a rise in wages will depend on whether the substitution or income effect is actually larger.
3. An upward-sloping labor supply curve represents a case in which the substitution effect of higher wages outweighs the income effect. A relatively vertical labor supply curve represents a case in which the substitution and income effects of higher wages are nearly equal. A backward-bending labor supply curve represents a case in which the substitution effect dominates at low wages (labor supply increases as the wage increases), but the income effect dominates at high wages (labor supply decreases as the wage increases).
4. The basic model of choice between leisure and income also can be used to analyze decisions concerning labor force participation, including when to enter the labor force and when to retire.
5. The demand for labor arises from the firm's demand for the factors of production. To maximize profits, the firm will use labor up to the point at which the value of the marginal product of labor equals the wage. This means the marginal product will equal the *real* wage.
6. In this basic competitive model, the real wage adjusts in labor markets to balance supply and demand.

KEY TERMS

nominal wage
real wage
labor force participation decision
reservation wage
factor demand
value of the marginal product of labor
real product wage

REVIEW QUESTIONS

1. How do people make choices about the amount of time to work, given their personal tastes and real wages in the market?
2. How will the income effect of a fall in wages affect hours worked? How will the substitution effect of a fall in wages affect hours worked?
3. What does the labor supply curve look like if the income effect dominates the substitution effect? What will it look like if the substitution effect dominates the income effect?
4. How does a technological change that makes workers more productive affect the demand for labor at a given wage and price?
5. How does an increase in the price of a firm's output affect the firm's demand for labor at a given wage?
6. Why is the labor demand curve downward sloping?

PROBLEMS

1. Imagine that a wealthy relative dies and leaves you an inheritance in a trust fund that will provide you with $20,000 per year for the rest of your life. Draw a diagram to illustrate this shift in your budget constraint between leisure and consumption. After considering the ideas of income and substitution effects, decide whether this inheritance will cause you to work more or less.
2. Most individuals do not take a second job (moonlight), even if they can get one—say, as a taxi driver—even though their "basic job" may require them to work only 37 hours a week. Most moonlighting jobs pay less per hour than the worker's basic job. Draw a typical worker's budget constraint. Explain why the budget

constraint has a kink at 37 hours of work. Discuss the consequences of the kink in the budget constraint.

3. Under current economic conditions, let's say that an unskilled worker will be able to get a job at a wage of $6 per hour. Now assume the government decides that all people with a weekly income of less than $180 will be given a check from the government to bring them up to the $180 level. Draw one such worker's original budget constraint and the constraint with the welfare program. Will this welfare program be likely to cause a recipient who originally worked 30 hours to work less? How about a recipient who worked less than 30 hours? more than 30 hours? Explain how the government might reduce these negative effects by offering a wage subsidy that would increase the hourly wage to $7 per hour for each of the first 20 hours worked, and draw a revised budget constraint to illustrate.

4. There is a negative relationship between a woman's real wage and her family size. Two possible explanations have been put forth. One is that women with higher real wages *choose* to have smaller families. Explain why this might be so. The second explanation is that larger family sizes might cause women to receive lower wages, perhaps because they can accept only jobs that allow them the flexibility to stay home when their children are sick. What evidence might help you choose between these two explanations?

5. John is a college student who has decided that at current wage levels, it is not worthwhile getting a part-time job. Now suppose the wage increases. Explain how the substitution effect of the wage increase affects John's decision. Is there an income effect on John of the wage increase?

6. Over the past twenty years, the income gap between workers with college degrees and those without a college education has grown. Draw two supply and demand diagrams, one for workers with college degrees and one for workers without degrees. Now suppose new information technologies raise the marginal product of highly educated workers but do not affect the marginal product of less-educated workers. Use your supply and demand diagrams to illustrate what happens to the wage gap between the two types of workers.

7. Suppose an increase in educational opportunities increases the supply of college-educated workers and reduces the supply of workers without college educations. Using supply and demand diagrams, illustrate how this change would affect the gap between the wages of workers with and those without college educations.

Appendix: Indifference Curves and the Labor Supply Decision[2]

This appendix investigates the labor supply decision using the indifference curve approach applied in the appendix to Chapter 5 to the consumption decision.

Figure 8.9 shows Tom's budget constraint between leisure and consumption. The slope of the budget constraint is the wage. The figure also shows two indifference curves; each gives the combination of leisure and consumption choices toward which Tom is indifferent. As usual, since people prefer more of both consumption and leisure if that is possible, Tom will move to the highest indifference curve he can attain—the one that is just tangent to his budget constraint.

The slope of the indifference curve is the marginal rate of substitution between leisure and consumption. It measures the amount of extra consumption Tom requires to compensate him for forgoing one additional hour of leisure. At the point of tangency between the indifference curve and the budget constraint, point E, both have the same slope. That is, the marginal rate of substitution equals the wage at this point.

As in the appendix in Chapter 5, we can easily see why Tom chooses this point. Assume his marginal rate of substitution is $15 (dollars per hour), while his wage is $20 (dollars per hour). If he works an hour more—gives up an hour's worth of leisure—his consumption goes up by $20. But to compensate him for the forgone leisure, he requires only $15. Since he gets more than he requires by working, he clearly prefers to work more.

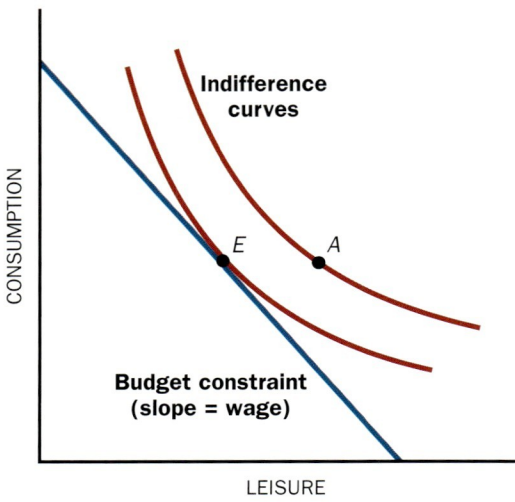

Figure 8.9
INDIFFERENCE CURVES AND LEISURE-INCOME CHOICES

An individual will choose the combination of leisure and income at E. Point A would be more desirable, but it is not feasible. Other points on the budget line or inside it are feasible, but they lie on lower indifference curves and are therefore not as desirable.

DECIDING WHETHER TO WORK

Figure 8.10 shows how to use indifference curves to analyze how people decide whether or not to work. Consider a low-wage individual facing a welfare system that provides a fixed level of benefits to those whose income is below a threshold. Benefits are cut off once income exceeds a certain level. The indifference curve I_0 is tangent to the budget constraint without welfare, and the point of tangency is E_0. The curve I_1 is the highest indifference curve consistent with the person receiving welfare.

The three possible cases are illustrated in panels A, B, and C. In panel A, the indifference curve through point E_0, I_0, is higher than the curve I_1. The individual chooses to work at E_0 and is unaffected by the welfare program. In panels B and C, the person works sufficiently little to be eligible for welfare; that is, I_1 is higher than I_0, and so he chooses point E_1. In panel B, the individual realizes that if he works more, he will lose his welfare benefits. He earns just (little) enough to be eligible for welfare. In panel C, the welfare system has only an income effect. If the welfare benefits are large enough, the individual may choose not to work at all.

---

[2] You will need to have read the appendix to Chapter 5 in order to follow this appendix.

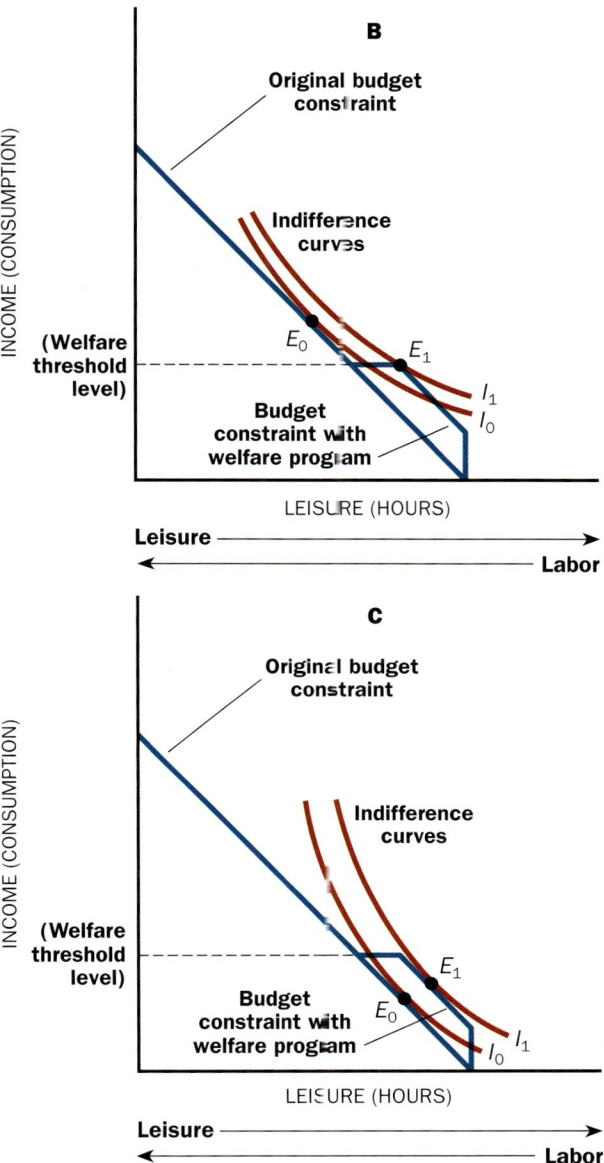

Figure 8.10
INDIFFERENCE CURVES AND WELFARE PROGRAMS

Panel A shows the case of an individual who chooses to work whether or not the welfare program exists. In panel B, before a welfare program is introduced, the individual is earning more than the welfare threshold. With the availability of welfare, this individual relies on welfare benefits to work less and move to a higher indifference curve. Panel C shows the case of someone who is earning less than the welfare threshold but would choose to work still less if the welfare program existed.

APPENDIX: INDIFFERENCE CURVES AND THE LABOR SUPPLY DECISION 189

Learning Goals

In this chapter, you will learn

1. How the basic tools introduced in Chapter 5 can be used to analyze decisions about saving and education

2. What economists mean by the time value of money

3. How income and substitution affect saving decisions in opposing ways

4. What determines the firm's demand for capital

5. How interest rates ensure that demand and supply balance in capital markets

6. Why education is an investment that leads to what economists call human capital

Chapter 9

CAPITAL MARKETS

At any given time, there are some people and companies who would like to borrow to enable them to spend more than their current income. John has his first job and knows he needs a car for transportation; Jill is borrowing money to buy a new home; Chad needs to purchase kitchen equipment, tables, and chairs to open his new restaurant; Intel needs to build a new chip-assembly plant. Others would like to save, spending less than their current income. Julie is putting money aside for her children's college education and for her retirement; Bill is putting aside money to make a down payment on a house.

The basic tools we have developed in previous chapters to explain how households and firms make decisions about which goods to buy, which to produce, how much to work, and how many workers to hire can also be used to explain saving and borrowing decisions. When households save, spending less than they earn in income, they provide funds for those who want to spend more than their income. When an individual household puts its savings in a bank or into the stock market, it might not think of itself as lending money, but that is exactly what it is doing. Firms that wish to buy new machines or build new factories or office buildings borrow the savings of the household sector. The **capital market**—or, as it is also called, the **loanable funds market**—is the market in which the funds made available when households save are directed to those who wish to borrow, whether to build a new home, to buy a new car, to build a new factory, or to install new machinery.

Supply in the Capital Market

To understand the supply of saving to the loanable funds market, we will focus on households; even though many individual households borrow, households as a group typically save. This is not always the case, though: in 1999 U.S. households actually dissaved, spending more than they earned in income. We will focus on firms as the major borrowers in the economy.

THE HOUSEHOLD DECISION TO SAVE

The assumption that individuals spend their money in a rational manner, thinking through the alternatives clearly, holds for decisions about saving as well as about spending and working. In making their saving decisions, individuals are making a choice about *when* to spend or consume. If they consume less today—that is, if they save more today—they can consume more tomorrow.

We use the budget constraint to analyze this decision. Instead of showing a choice between goods, the budget constraint now shows, as in Figure 9.1, a choice between spending in two time periods: here, "working years" and "retirement years." Consider the case of Joan. She faces the lifetime budget constraint depicted in the figure. The first period is represented on the horizontal axis, the second on the vertical axis. Her wages during her working life (the first period) are w. Thus, at one extreme, she could consume all of w in the first period (point C) and have nothing for her retirement. At the other extreme, she could consume nothing in the first period, save all of her income, and consume her savings, together with any accumulated interest she has earned on her savings, in the second period (point B). If we use r to denote the rate of interest, her consumption in the second period at point B is $w(1+r)$. In between these extremes lies a straight line that defines the rest of her choices. She can choose any combination of first- and second-period consumption on this line. This is Joan's two-period budget constraint.

By postponing consumption—that is, by saving—Joan can increase the total amount of goods that she can obtain, because she is paid interest on her savings. The cost, however, is that she must wait to enjoy the goods. But what is the relative price, the trade-off between future and current consumption? To put it another way, how much extra future consumption can she get if she gives up one unit of current consumption?

If Joan decides not to consume one more dollar today, she can take that dollar, put it in the bank, and get back at the end of the year that dollar plus interest. If the interest rate is 5 percent, then for every dollar of consumption that Joan gives up today, she can get $1.05 of consumption next year. The relative price (of consumption today relative to consumption tomorrow) is thus 1 plus the interest rate. Because Joan must give up more than $1.00 of consumption in the second period to get an additional $1.00 worth of consumption today, current consumption is more expensive than future consumption. The opportunity cost of current consumption is the future consumption that is forgone, and this cost depends on the rate of interest.

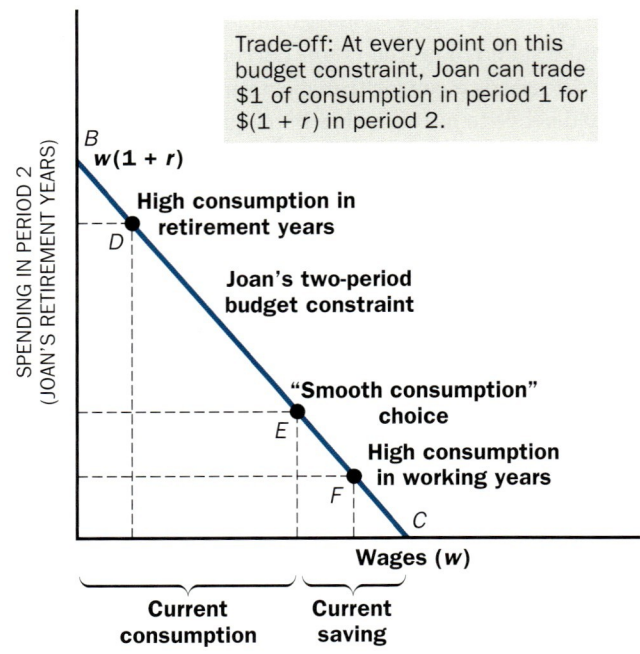

Figure 9.1
THE TWO-PERIOD BUDGET CONSTRAINT

The two-period budget constraint BC describes the possible combinations of current and future consumption available. Wages not spent in period 1 become savings, which earn interest. As a result, forgoing a dollar of consumption today increases future consumption by more than a dollar.

Joan chooses among the points on this budget constraint according to her personal preferences. Consider, for example, point *D,* where Joan is consuming very little during her working life. Since she is spending very little in the present, any additional consumption now will have a high marginal value. She will be relatively eager to substitute present consumption for future consumption. At the other extreme, if she is consuming a great deal in the present, say at point *F,* additional consumption today will have a relatively low marginal value, while future consumption will have a high marginal value. Hence, she will be relatively eager to save more for the future. She chooses a point in between, *E,* where consumption in the two periods is not too different. She has *smoothed* her consumption. That is, consumption in each of the two different periods is about the same. This kind of saving, intended to smooth consumption over a worker's lifetime and to provide for retirement, is called **life-cycle saving.** In Figure 9.1, the difference between the first-period income, *w,* and what she consumes in the first period is her saving.

The Time Value of Money Because you can earn interest on your savings, the cost of a dollar of current consumption is more than simply $1.00 of future consumption. As we learned in Chapter 2, calculating costs correctly is one of the basic steps in making rational decisions. But what if we are comparing costs that occur at different times, such as the cost of current versus future consumption? Or to take a more specific example, suppose one store advertises a car stereo system for $400 and another advertises it for $425 with no payment for a full year. How can we compare these two? If you have the $400 to spend today, is it cheaper to pay $400 right now for the stereo or to pay $425 in one year?

To think about this comparison, consider what you could do with your $400 if you opted to buy from the store that lets you delay your payment. You might put the money in a bank. When you deposit money in a bank, you have lent it your money. In return, the bank pays you **interest.** If the interest rate is 5 percent per year, you will receive $420 in a year—the $20 is the interest payment, while the $400 is the repayment of the **principal,** the original amount you lent to the bank.

The interest rate is a price, and like other prices, it describes a trade-off. If the interest rate is 5 percent, by giving up $1.00 worth of consumption today, a saver can have $1.05 worth of consumption next year. Thus, the rate of interest tells us how much future consumption we can get by giving up $1.00 worth of current consumption. It tells us the relative price of purchases in the present and in the future.

Because interest rates are normally positive, $1.00 today becomes more than a dollar in the future. Thus a dollar today is worth more than a dollar in the future. Economists call this phenomenon the **time value of money.** The concept of **present discounted value** tells us precisely how to measure the time value of money. The present discounted value of $100 a year from now is what you would pay today for $100 in a year. Suppose the interest rate is 5 percent. If you put $95.24 in the bank today, then at the end of a year you will receive $4.76 in interest, which together with the original principal will total $100. Thus, $95.24 is the present discounted value of $100 one year from now, if the interest rate is 5 percent.

There is a simple formula for calculating the present discounted value of any amount to be received a year from now: just divide the amount by 1 plus the annual rate of interest (often denoted by *r*).

To check this formula, consider the present discounted value of $100. According to the formula, it is $100/(1 + r)$. In other words, take the present discounted value, $100/(1 + r)$, and put it in a bank. At the end of the year you will have

$$\frac{\$100}{1+r} \times (1+r) = \$100,$$

confirming our conclusion that $100/(1 + r)$ today is worth the same as $100 one year from now.

We can now evaluate the two options for purchasing the stereo. To compare $400 today with $425 in one year, we need to calculate the present discounted value of $425. If the interest rate is 5 percent, the present discount value of $425 is $404.76. Since this is greater than $400, you are better off paying for the stereo today.

Present discounted values depend on the rate of interest. If the interest rate increases, the present discounted value of future amounts will decrease. If the interest rate rises to 10 percent, the present discounted value of $425 falls to $386.96. Now it is cheaper to postpone payment for the stereo. You can take your $400, put it in the bank, and earn 10 percent interest. In one year, you will have $440. After paying $425 for the stereo, you are left with $15 more than if you had paid for it immediately.

The concept of present discounted value is important because so many decisions in economics are oriented to the future. Whether a person is buying a car or a house or saving for retirement, or a company is building a factory or making an investment, the decision maker must be able to value money that will be received one, two, five, or ten years in the future.

Wrap-Up

PRESENT DISCOUNTED VALUE

Present discounted value of $1.00 next year = $1.00/(1 + interest rate)$.

Inflation and the Real Rate of Interest The interest rate, we have seen, is a price. It tells us how many dollars we can get in the next period if we give up one dollar today. But dollars are of value only because of the goods that can be bought with them. If prices rise, then a dollar will buy less. Suppose a couple has been saving so that in a year they will have $40,000, which they plan to use to buy a BMW. If prices double between now and next year, their $40,000 will get them only a Honda Civic. Thus, to know how much we can actually purchase in the future if we save today, we need to take into account more than just the interest rate: we also need to consider how the general level of prices will change. The rate at which the general level of prices increases each year is the *rate of inflation*. If the inflation rate is 5 percent, then prices on average will be 5 percent higher in one year; if inflation is 10 percent, prices will go up 10 percent. Some prices will rise faster than the overall inflation rate; others will rise more slowly or even decline. For example, over the past twenty years computer prices have fallen while housing prices in many parts of the country have risen very rapidly. The inflation rate measures what is happening on average to prices in the economy.

Individuals want to know how much *consumption* they get tomorrow if they give up a dollar's worth of consumption today. The answer is given by the **real rate of interest.** This is distinguished from the **nominal rate of interest,** the rate posted at banks and printed in newspapers, which simply describes the number of dollars received next year in exchange for a dollar today. There is a simple relationship between the real interest rate and the nominal interest rate: the real interest rate equals the nominal interest rate minus the rate of inflation. If the nominal interest rate is 10 percent and the rate of inflation is 6 percent, then the real interest rate is 4 percent. By saving a dollar today, you can increase the amount of goods that you get in one year's time by 4 percent.

Consider an individual who decides to deposit $1,000 in a savings account. At the end of the year, at a 10 percent interest rate, she will have $1,100. But prices meanwhile have risen by 6 percent. A good that cost $1,000 in the beginning of the year now costs $1,060. In terms of "purchasing power," she has only $40 extra to spend ($1,100 − $1,060)—4 percent more than she had at the beginning of the year.

Wrap-Up

REAL INTEREST RATE

Real interest rate = nominal interest rate − rate of inflation.

Using the Model: Saving and the Interest Rate We can use the budget constraint to understand how Joan's saving decision will be affected if the interest rate changes. Keep in mind two points as we apply this model, however. First, just as we saw earlier that the relevant wage for labor supply decisions is the real wage, so the relevant interest rate for saving decisions is the real interest rate—that is, the interest rate adjusted for inflation. Also keep in mind that we have simplified the saving decision with our two-period model (current consumption on the one hand, future consumption on the other). In the real world, individuals usually earn interest on their savings year after year as they save for retirement. If you begin saving at the age of twenty-five, you might earn interest for forty years before retiring. Typically, the interest is compounded annually (or monthly), which means that each year you earn interest on the interest paid in previous years. Compounding makes a huge difference over long periods of time. If you set aside $100 at 5 percent interest for forty years, you might think that each year you would earn $5 in interest (5 percent of $100) and that at the end of the forty years you would have your $100 plus $200 in interest (40 × $5), or $300 in total. In fact, because you earn interest for thirty-nine years on the $5 of interest earned in year one, plus interest for thirty-eight years on the interest earned in year two, and so on, after forty years you end up with not $300 but $704!

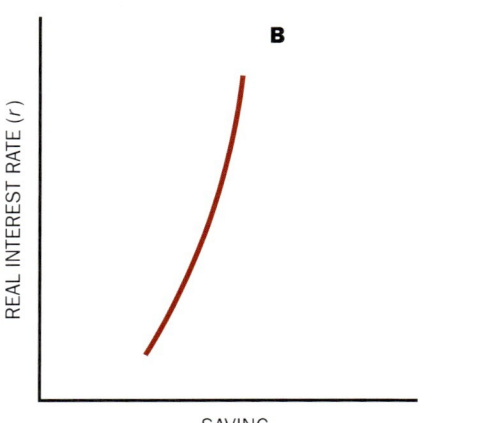

FIGURE 9.2

SAVING AND THE INTEREST RATE

An increase in interest rates rotates the budget constraint out from BC to B′C. Because the individual is better off, there is an income effect, leading to greater consumption in the present (and in the future). However, the higher interest rate makes future consumption cheaper; the substitution effect associated with the change in the slope of the budget constraint leads to greater current saving. In the typical case, the substitution effect is larger than the income effect; Joan's new choice will be on the new budget constraint to the left of E_1 and her saving increases. The saving function in panel B gives the level of saving at each real interest rate. The saving function in panel B illustrates this case, in which the saving function has a positive slope.

To focus on the key factors important for understanding saving decisions, we will continue to distinguish current from future consumption and apply interest only once. This simplification captures the essential characteristic of the saving decision, the choice between consumption now and in the future.

When the interest rate increases, Joan's budget constraint changes. Her new budget constraint is shown in Figure 9.2A as line $B'C$. If she does not save, the interest rate has no effect on her consumption. She simply consumes her income during her working years, with nothing left over for retirement. But for all other choices, the higher interest rate enables her to consume more during her retirement years.

The increased interest rate has both an income effect and a substitution effect. Because Joan is a saver, higher interest rates make her better off. Because she is better off, she consumes more today; that is, she reduces her saving. This is the income effect. But her return to savings—to postponing consumption—is increased. For each dollar of consumption she postpones, she gets more consumption when she retires. The opportunity cost of current consumption is now higher. This increase induces her to consume less—to save more. This is the substitution effect. Thus, the substitution and income effects work in opposite directions, and the *net* effect is ambiguous. Either may dominate. A higher interest rate may lead to more or to less saving.

What happens on *average* is a difficult empirical question. Most estimates indicate that the substitution effect outweighs the income effect, and thus an increase in real interest rates has a slightly positive effect on the rate of savings.

Panel B of Figure 9.2 shows the saving function, which gives the level of saving for each level of the real interest rate. It is derived by finding the choices between consumption today and in the future for different real interest rates, represented by rotating the budget constraint. The curve depicted has the typical shape. Increases in the real interest rate lead to slight increases in saving; the substitution effect slightly outweighs the income effect. But the saving curve could be vertical; the income effect and the substitution effect balance. Or it can even be backward bending; the income effect slightly outweighs the substitution effect.

Wrap-Up

THE SAVING DECISION

The saving decision is a decision of *when* to consume: today or tomorrow.

The slope of the budget constraint between consumption today and consumption tomorrow is determined by the real rate of interest.

A principal motive of saving is to smooth consumption to ensure that one's consumption while working and during retirement is about the same.

Other Factors Affecting Saving We have now seen how the techniques of consumer choice analysis presented in Chapter 5 can be applied to individuals' decisions about saving. The two basic determinants are income and interest rates. As incomes rise, individuals want to consume more in their retirement, and hence must save more. As interest rates change, the income and substitution effects work in different directions, so the net effect is ambiguous.

The saving decision in the United States also involves an even more important determinant: Social Security. How much individuals need to save for their retirement depends in part on how large a check they will get from the Social Security Administration when they stop working. A generous government system reduces the individual need to save for retirement, so one effect of Social Security is to reduce the overall level of saving in the United States. The Social Security checks mailed out each month to retired workers are paid for by taxes on individuals who currently work. As the members of the large baby boom generation born after World War II

Thinking Like an Economist
WEALTH DISTRIBUTION AND INTEREST RATES

Government policies aimed at increasing the interest rate individuals receive, such as exempting certain forms of savings from taxation, are based on the belief that an increase in the interest rate on savings will significantly increase total (aggregate) saving in the economy. Though the impact of these provisions on the aggregate saving rate is debatable, the distributional impact is not. Since wealthy people save more, a reduction in taxes on interest—which increases the effective interest rate the saver receives—obviously benefits them more and increases the degree of income inequality. According to the Survey of Consumer Finances (2001), almost 80 percent of households in the top 20 percent of the income distribution saved. These families had an average income in 2001 of just over $200,000 and an average net worth of $2 million. In contrast, only 30 percent of households in the bottom 20 percent of the income distribution saved. These families had an average income of $10,000 and an average net worth of just $52,000.

Low-income households save little and therefore enjoy little direct benefit from policies designed to increase the returns on saving.

Internet Connection

HOUSEHOLD SAVING

The Federal Reserve Board conducts a survey of households every three years, called the Survey of Consumer Finances. Each one provides a wealth of information on household saving. The most recently available survey was conducted in 2001, and you can find it and information about it at www.federalreserve.gov/pubs/oss/oss2/2001/scf2001home.html.

begin to retire, many are raising concerns about the future financial health of the entire system. The problems with the Social Security program and the reforms proposed by President George W. Bush and others are discussed in Chapter 17.

Even as Social Security payments have become more generous, private saving schemes have grown over the last fifty years. Three explanations are commonly put forward for this development. First, as individuals' life spans have increased well beyond normal retirement age, the need for more income late in life has increased faster than the generosity of Social Security. In fact, to reduce the financial burden on the system, the age at which a worker qualifies to receive Social Security benefits has gradually been increased. Individuals born in 1937, for example, could receive full benefits at age 65; those born in 1967 must wait until they are 67. Second, as we saw in Chapter 8, individuals who earn higher incomes may decide to enjoy more leisure, one form of which is earlier retirement—a choice that increases their need for retirement income. Finally, surveys indicate that many younger workers are concerned that the Social Security benefits received by their parents and grandparents will not be available to them. If the huge cost of the program forces cuts in the benefits of future retirees, younger workers will have to rely more on their own savings rather than on Social Security in their retirement.

Case in Point

WHY IS THE U.S. SAVING RATE SO LOW?

Between 1959 and 1992, the personal saving rate for U.S. households averaged 7.4 percent of disposable income (income after taxes). Since 1993, the saving rate has averaged only 3.6 percent (Figure 9.3). Why?

Economists have given several reasons for the low and falling saving rate among U.S. households. First, Social Security benefits are relatively generous, reducing the need for individuals to save for their retirement, and that generosity grew markedly in the 1970s. Second, it has become much easier to borrow for all kinds of purchases. In other words, the capital market in this country has improved its capacity to serve individual borrowers. Third, Americans prefer to consume now rather than later. Fourth, the value of household wealth from investments in housing and corporate stocks in the United States rose dramatically through the 1980s and 1990s. As people saw their wealth rise, they spent more and saved less. The figure suggests that the personal saving rate rose after the stock market crashed in 2001. Finally, there is the effect of the new economy. Many who observed increases in productivity as a result of new technologies concluded that the economy would grow faster, leading to higher incomes in the future. The income effect of higher expected future income works to increase current consumption, reducing saving today.

Aggregate Saving The sum of the saving of all individuals in society is **aggregate saving.** At any time, some individuals are saving and others are spending their savings (or, as economists say, *dissaving*). Aggregate saving is the two activities taken together. The *aggregate saving rate* is aggregate saving divided by aggregate income. *Demographic* factors—that is, factors relating to population—in particular the rate of growth of the population, are important determinants of the aggregate saving rate. Retirees typically dissave. That is, they withdraw money from savings accounts and cash in stocks and bonds if they have any (to supplement their main income sources, Social Security and interest on investments). There is considerable concern about the low aggregate saving rate in the United States (discussed further below), which is explained in part by our aging population. A slowly growing population, like that of the United States, has a larger proportion of elderly and, on that account, a lower aggregate saving rate than faster-growing populations with higher birthrates.

Forms of Savings To simplify our discussion, we have assumed that savings earns a single rate of interest, *r*. In fact, there are many different ways in which individuals can save, and these may offer different interest rates. For example, if you

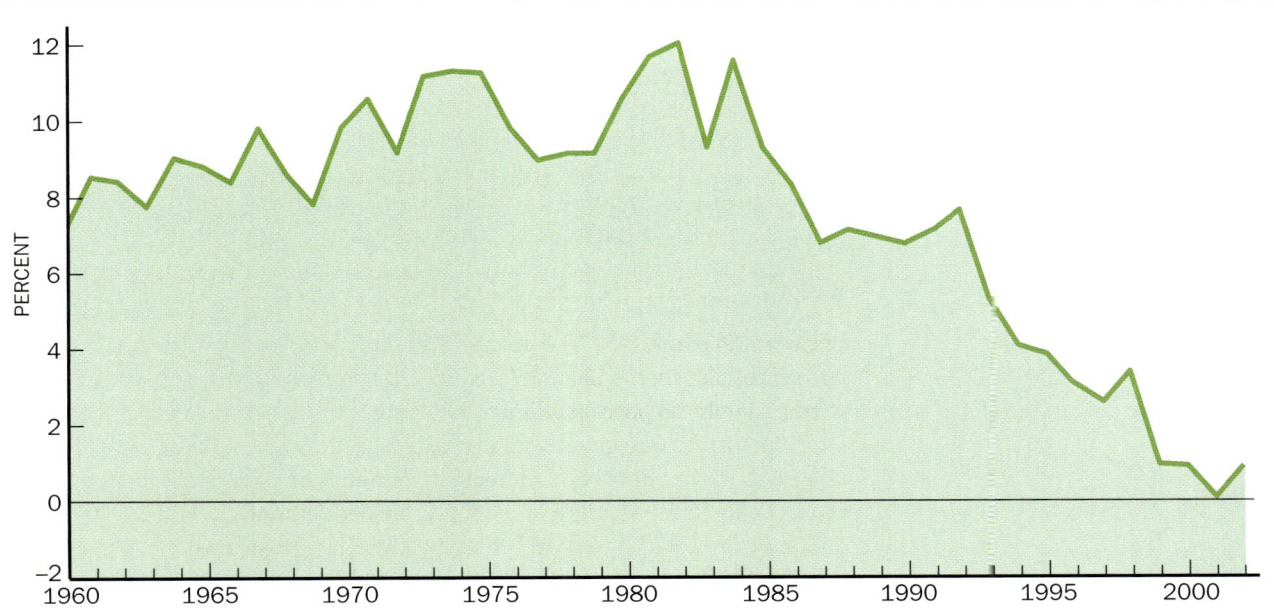

FIGURE 9.3
U.S. PERSONAL SAVING RATE, 1980–2002

U.S. households saved far less of their disposable income throughout the 1990s and into the first years of the twenty-first century than they had done in earlier decades.

SOURCE: *Economic Report of the President* (2005).

want to save, you can put money into a savings account at a bank. This earns interest and is very safe, because the federal government insures savings accounts with balances up to $100,000. The tremendous boom in the stock market in the 1990s encouraged many people to put some of their savings into stocks. Stocks earn a higher return on average than savings accounts, but they are much riskier. The stock market can go down as well as up. Real estate has also been an attractive place to put savings, but it too is risky. Rather than discussing the various savings options that are available to households, our focus in this chapter is on the broad outlines of the capital market and the role played by the interest rate in affecting saving decisions.

Demand in the Capital Market

Our goal here is to understand how the supply of savings by households and the demand for savings by firms result in a market equilibrium. In the preceding sections we worked through the supply side of the market. Now we turn to demand. The demand side of the capital market is driven by firms that borrow the savings of households to fund their purchases of **capital goods**—the machines, tools, buildings, and other equipment used in the production process. We therefore begin our analysis with firms' demand for capital goods.

Applying the same principle we used earlier to derive the demand for labor, we know that firms will demand capital (capital goods) up to the point at which the value of the marginal product of capital is equal to the price. The marginal product of capital is just the additional output obtained if one more unit is employed. It is the extra output obtained by adding another machine. But what is the price of capital?

A quick answer is that the price of a piece of equipment is simply what it costs to buy it. If a new computer server to handle Internet orders costs the firm $20,000, isn't that the price of this particular piece of capital? The answer is no—and to see why more is involved, let's think about the decision of a new start-up company as it evaluates whether to buy this computer. To keep things simple, suppose Andrea and Bryan, the company founders, plan to sell the server after one year for $12,000. They can borrow the $20,000 to buy the server from their bank, and the bank charges them interest on this loan. Let's suppose for our example that the interest rate the bank charges is 5 percent. What has it cost them to use the equipment?

Andrea and Bryan pay $20,000 for the server. At the end of the year, they sell the server for $12,000, but they also have to repay the bank. Since the bank charged them 5 percent interest, at the end of the year they owe the bank $21,000 (the $20,000 they borrowed plus $1,000 in interest). So the net cost of using the server is $21,000 − $12,000 = $9,000. A critical part of this cost is the interest Andrea and Bryan had to pay the bank. If the interest rate had been 10 percent, the cost of the computer would have been $10,000 ($20,000 + $2,000 − $12,000, since interest now totals $2,000). *The user cost of capital increases when the interest rate rises.*

The interest rate would have played exactly the same role if Andrea and Bryan had not needed to borrow from the bank. Suppose they had savings of their own that they could use to purchase the computer. When they use their own savings to buy the computer, there is an opportunity cost associated with the purchase. Andrea and Bryan could have left their $20,000 in the bank. If the interest rate is 5 percent, they would have earned $1,000 in interest over the year. This opportunity cost must be included in calculating the cost of capital. So when the interest rate is 5 percent, the total cost of the server is $9,000, regardless of whether they borrow from the bank or use their own funds. An increase in the interest rate raises the cost (including opportunity costs) of using the server.

This simple example illustrates an important point—the user cost of capital will increase with the interest rate. At a higher interest rate, firms will demand less capital and will need to borrow less. At lower interest rates, firms will demand more capital and need to borrow more.

Figure 9.4 shows the demand for loanable funds in the capital market as a downward-sloping relationship between the interest rate and the quantity of funds firms borrow. The figure also shows the supply of loanable funds as an upward-sloping line; it is shown as a steep line because the income and substitution effects of a change in the interest rate have opposing effects on saving. The net effect, though, is some increase in saving as the interest rate increases. In the loanable funds or capital market, the "price" is the interest rate, and the interest rate will adjust to bring supply and demand into balance. In the figure, the equilibrium interest rate is r^*.

We can now explain why the equilibrium interest rate is positive. If it were zero or negative, prospective borrowers would demand more funds than prospective savers would be willing to supply. Indeed, negative interest rates would enable borrowers to consume today and pay back less in the future, and force savers to receive less in the future than the amount they saved. Only at a positive interest rate can the demand for loans be made equal to the supply.

In our economy, borrowers and savers do not usually meet face-to-face. Instead, banks and other financial institutions serve as intermediaries, collecting savings from those who want to save and disbursing money to those who want to borrow. These intermediaries help make the market for loans work smoothly. For their services, the intermediaries charge fees, which can be measured as the difference between the interest rate they pay savers and the interest rate they charge borrowers.

New Technologies and the Demand for Capital Modern economies have undergone tremendous changes as new computer and information technologies have transformed the ways goods are produced and sold. The development of new technologies has led firms to undertake investments in new equipment. To analyze the impact this change might have on the interest rate, we can use our model of the loanable funds market.

Figure 9.5 shows demand and supply as a function of the rate of interest. The new technology increases the marginal product of capital and increases firms' demand for capital at each rate of interest. To purchase this additional capital, firms borrow more. At each rate of interest, the demand for funds shifts to the right. The equilibrium rate of interest rises.

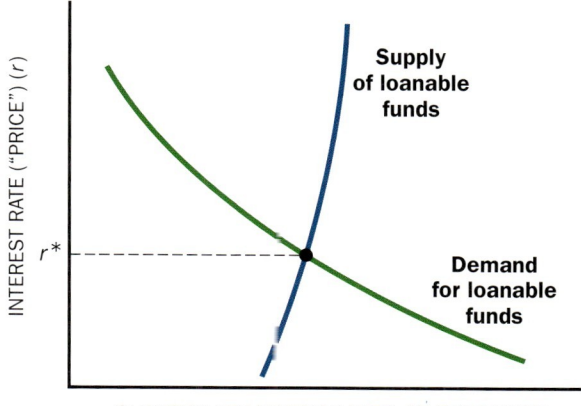

Figure 9.4

SUPPLY AND DEMAND FOR LOANABLE FUNDS

The amount of money loaned (or borrowed, from the other perspective) is the quantity, and the interest rate is the price. At the equilibrium interest rate r^*, the supply of loanable funds equals the demand.

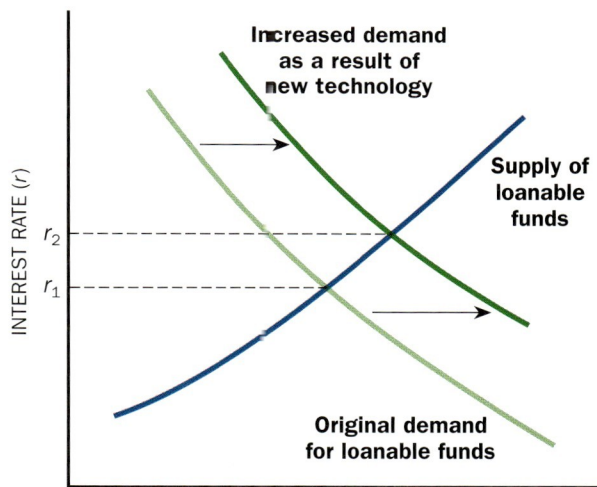

FIGURE 9.5

THE EFFECTS OF NEW TECHNOLOGIES THAT INCREASE THE DEMAND FOR CAPITAL

If new technologies increase the demand for capital by firms, the demand for funds will shift to the right as firms attempt to borrow more to purchase new equipment. If the supply of funds from saving does not shift, the equilibrium interest rate rises from r_1 to r_2.

A Behavioral Perspective on Saving

In Chapter 5, we introduced some of the new insights on how people behave that have come from research in psychology and behavioral economics. Many of these insights have proven particularly useful in understanding household saving decisions.

Earlier we discussed the importance of the desire to smooth consumption over a person's lifetime in influencing saving. A basic implication of the economist's standard model of saving is that people should save during their peak earning years so that when they retire, and their income drops, they will have accumulated enough to ensure that their consumption does not fall. Yet there is a great deal of evidence that when people retire, their income *and* their consumption drops. They have not saved enough for their retirement and so are forced to scale back the amount they consume. Behavioral economics offers some interesting perspectives that help explain why individuals undersave.

One reason may be that people simply lack the self-control necessary to postpone consumption. The standard model of choice that economists employ assumes people can rationally balance the benefits of consuming today versus the advantages of saving so that more consumption can be enjoyed in the future. But people often find it very difficult to make sacrifices in the present, even if they recognize the benefits to be gained in the future. Smoking provides a good example. There is a saying that the best time to quit smoking is tomorrow—the smoker is always tempted to have that cigarette today and promise (himself) that tomorrow will be different and he will quit. Of course, when tomorrow comes around, he falls into the same pattern. The result is that many people never are able to quit smoking. The self-control assumed by the standard model of rational choice appears to be in short supply.

Lack of self-control would make reducing current consumption quite difficult, for the benefits of such self-denial may not be seen for ten or twenty years. It may also explain why most saving done by American households takes the form of *forced savings,* occurring automatically without the need for an explicit decision every month. There are three common forms of forced saving. First, many workers participate in pension plans through their place of employment. Each month, the employer sets aside funds for the worker's pension, to which a certain amount deducted from the worker's paycheck may also be added. This is a form of saving for the worker. Second, Americans who own their own homes typically buy those homes by borrowing ("taking out a mortgage"), and they make a mortgage payment each month. Part of this payment represents the interest on the amount that was borrowed; the rest goes toward repaying the principal. This repayment builds the family's equity in their home, another common form of saving. A final example of forced saving is provided by the automatic withholding of income tax from paychecks for salaried jobs. Many people have too much withheld each pay period so that when they file their tax return in April of each year, they are owed a refund from the government. These refunds are often used to purchase a big-ticket item that the taxpayer might otherwise not have had the willpower to save up for.

Despite offering important insights into how people actually make choices, behavioral economics in some ways may explain too much. Lack of self-control makes intuitive sense as an explanation for low savings, but how do we then account for the many countries with high rates of saving? Many Asian countries, for example, have saving rates that average 30 to 40 percent of income. A traditional economic approach would focus on differences in the returns to saving (perhaps due to differences in the way taxes are structured in different countries), average family size, or the age distribution of the population to explain why saving rates differ so markedly across countries. A behavioral perspective suggests that cultural factors might also be important.

One area in which the insights of behavioral economics may be very useful is in designing public policies to increase the level of saving. For example, behavioral economists have identified the importance of the status quo effect (see Chapter 5), which predicts that people resist changes to their current circumstances. In particular they resist making choices that actively require a decision to be made. As a consequence, when presented with a number of options, many people will simply pick whatever option is the default—the one that is chosen automatically without further action on their part. The status quo effect can help explain why many people do not take advantage of some of the best ways to save for retirement, such as participating in what is called a 401(k) plan. In 1978, section 401(k) of the U.S. Internal Revenue Code created a new saving account that allowed workers to put aside some of their income for retirement. Its big advantage is tax deferral: the worker pays taxes not on the income put into the 401(k) or on any interest earned on the account but on the money when it is taken out of the account—after the worker is retired, when she usually has a lower tax rate. Many employers will match workers' contributions to 401(k) accounts, making them even more valuable. When workers are offered the option to participate in a 401(k) plan via an automatic paycheck deduction, the number that do so can depend on what the default option happens to be. If workers must explicitly choose to sign up for the account, fewer end up participating than when enrollment in the plan is automatic and deliberate action must be taken to opt out. This is an example of the status quo effect at work—peoples' choices are shaped not just by their rational evaluation of the pros and cons of different options but also by their reluctance to make changes. Policies designed to encourage saving need to increase the incentives to save, as suggested by the economist's basic model of consumer choice; but to be fully effective, they also must take into account the status quo effect.

Education and Human Capital

Why go to college? Many answers spring to mind, but to tackle this question from an economic perspective, and to understand why educational choices are similar to saving decisions, we will focus on the costs and benefits of education.

Education is one of the most important determinants of workers' productivity. Staying in school longer, which usually means delaying entry into the labor force, increases expected annual income. On average, high school graduates earn more than those without high school degrees; those with some college earn more than

This dental student improves his human capital by acquiring valuable skills and knowledge.

those who only have a high school degree; those with a college degree earn more than those who started college but never finished. A student has lower income while in school but can expect to earn high incomes in the future. In addition, working *harder* in school, and giving up leisure, may result in better grades and skills, which in turn will result in higher wages in the future. Thus, students face a trade-off between leisure and income today and income and consumption in the future.

Spending a year in college has its obvious costs—tuition, room, and board. But there are also opportunity costs, in particular the income that would have been received from a job. These are just as much part of the cost of going to school as any direct tuition payments. Economists say that the investment in education produces **human capital,** making an analogy to the *physical capital* investments that businesses make in plant and equipment. Human capital is developed by formal schooling, on-the-job training, and many other investments of time and money that parents make in their children, individuals make in themselves, and employers make in their employees.

The United States invests an enormous amount in human capital. In fact, the cumulative value of human capital is greater than that of physical capital. As much as two-thirds to three-fourths of all capital is human capital. This investment is financed both publicly and privately. Local, state, and federal governments spend about one-quarter of a trillion dollars a year on education. Government spending on primary and secondary education is the largest category of expenditure at the local and state levels, accounting for more than 20 percent of the total.

The enormous increase in education in the past fifty years is illustrated in Table 9.1. Among those 65 and older, more than 30 percent do not have a high school degree; of those 25 to 44, only one in eight has not received a high school degree. Similarly, the percentage with at least a bachelor's degree is more than one and a half times as high for those 25 to 44 as for those 65 and older.

e-Insight
FINANCING THE NEW ECONOMY

We have seen how the capital market links households who save with firms that invest, so that saving equals investment at the equilibrium interest rate. But how do firms actually get their hands on household saving? The answer is that financial intermediaries such as banks and investment companies perform the function of transferring funds between households and firms. Their job is to make sure that the households' money is well invested, so that the households can get it back with a return.

Banks are perhaps the most important financial intermediary. In the nineteenth century, banks mainly lent money to firms to help finance their inventories. The inventories were held as collateral—that is, if the borrower defaulted on the loan, the lender could seize the inventories. Gradually, banks expanded their lending activities—for instance, to finance houses and commercial real estate, in such cases holding the buildings as collateral. The past decade's revolution in information technology has presented special problems to these traditional forms of finance. Today firms invest heavily in software and new ideas. If the idea does not pan out, the firm may go bankrupt, but there is no collateral: there is little of value that the creditor can seize.

In the United States, financial markets have adapted, and there now is a new form of financial institution—venture capital firms. Typically, the funds are provided by either wealthy private investors or institutions, such as universities, seeking high returns. The venture capital firms have developed expertise in assessing new ideas in the new economy—the most successful of the venture capital firms have an impressive record of picking winners. But they offer more than capital; they typically also give managerial assistance and take an active role in oversight. After providing the initial capital that enables a firm to get established, the firm supported by the venture capital firms typically "goes public"—that is, it sells at least some of its shares on the market. It is at this point that venture capitalists reap their gains.

While the first venture capital firms concentrated on Silicon Valley (the area surrounding Stanford University where much of the early development of computers occurred), more recently they have expanded their focus to other areas of the country and other sectors.

Table 9.1
YEARS OF SCHOOLING BY AGE

Age group (in 2003)	% with less than a high school degree	% with a high school degree but no bachelor's degree	% with at least a bachelor's degree
25–34	13	57	30
35–44	12	59	29
45–54	11	59	30
55–64	15	58	27
65–74	25	56	19
75 and older	33	52	15

SOURCE: *Statistical Abstract of the United States, 2004* (www.census.gov/prod/2004pubs/04statab/educ.pdf).

EDUCATION AND ECONOMIC TRADE-OFFS

The production possibilities curve introduced in Chapter 2 can illustrate how decisions concerning investments in human capital are made. To accomplish this, we divide an individual's life into two periods: "youth" and "later working years." Figure 9.6 depicts the relationship between consumption in youth and in later life. As the individual gives up consumption in his youth, staying in school longer increases his expected future consumption because he can expect his income to go up. The curve has been drawn with a rounded shape. It shows diminishing returns: spending more on education today (reducing consumption) raises future income, but each additional investment in education provides a smaller and smaller return.

Point A represents the case in which Everett is a full-time student through four years of college, with little income until graduation (his youth) but with a high income in later life. Point B represents the consequences of dropping out of school after high school. When he does this, Everett has a higher income in his youth but a lower income in later life. Other possible points between A and B represent cases where Everett drops out of college after one or two years.

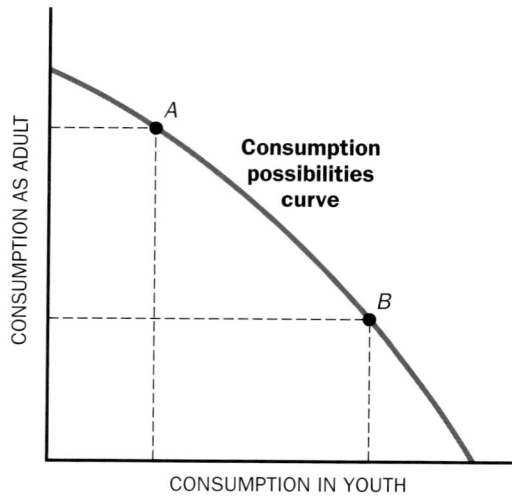

Figure 9.6

EDUCATION AND THE TRADE-OFF BETWEEN CURRENT AND FUTURE CONSUMPTION

Point A represents a choice of a reduced consumption and better education in the present, with a higher consumption in the future. Point B represents the choice of higher consumption and less education now, with a lower level of consumption in the future.

The Basic Competitive Model

We now have completed our description of the basic competitive model. Households make decisions about how much to consume and what goods to purchase. They decide how much labor to supply and how much to save. The firm in the competitive model takes the price it receives for the goods it sells as given. The firm also takes the prices of the inputs it uses, including the wages it pays workers and the cost of capital goods, as given. At these prices, the firm chooses its outputs and inputs to maximize profits. Prices adjust to ensure that demand and supply are equal. In the labor market, wages bring demand and supply into balance; in the capital market, the interest rate is the "price" that adjusts to balance supply and demand.

We have now seen where the supply and demand curves that were introduced in Chapters 3 and 4 come from, and why they have the shapes they do. Whether we examine the household's demand for goods, its supply of labor, or its savings decision, the effects of price changes on the household's choices can be analyzed in terms of income and substitution effects. We also demonstrated that firms balance marginal cost and price in deciding on production levels, and they set the value of the marginal product equal to the price of an input in deciding on their demand for factors of production such as labor and capital. An increase in the real wage reduces the firm's demand for labor. An increase in the interest rate reduces the demand for capital. In the next chapter, we will put all these results together to sketch a model of the complete economy.

Review and Practice

SUMMARY

1. The interest rate is determined in the capital market—also called the loanable funds market. The supply of loanable funds comes from savings, as some households and firms spend less than their income. The demand arises from those households and firms that spend more than their income.
2. In making a decision to save, people face a trade-off between current and future consumption. The amount of extra consumption an individual can obtain in the future by reducing present consumption is determined by the real rate of interest.
3. A dollar received in the future is worth less than a dollar received today. The present discounted value tells us how much a future dollar amount is worth today. The present discounted value of a future amount falls when the rate of interest rises.
4. The real interest rate adjusts to balance supply and demand in the capital market.
5. The interest rate is an important part of the cost of using capital. If the interest rate increases, the cost of using capital increases. Firms' demands for funds for investment decrease as they cut back on their purchases of capital goods.
6. Human capital adds to economic productivity just as physical capital does. It is developed by education, on-the-job training, and investments of time and money that parents make in their children.

KEY TERMS

capital market
loanable funds market
life-cycle saving
interest
principal
time value of money
present discounted value
real rate of interest
nominal rate of interest
aggregate saving
capital goods
human capital

REVIEW QUESTIONS

1. How does a choice to consume in the present determine the amount of consumption in the future?
2. What is the price of future consumption in terms of present consumption?
3. For savers, how will the income effect of a higher interest rate affect current saving? How will the substitution effect of a higher interest rate affect current savings?
4. What are some of the factors, besides incomes and interest rates, that affect saving?
5. Describe how students invest time and money to acquire human capital.

PROBLEMS

1. This chapter focused on how interest rates affect savers. If an individual is a net debtor (that is, she owes money), what is the income effect of an increase in interest rates? Will an increase in the interest rates that she has to pay induce her to borrow more or borrow less?
2. In the context of the life-cycle model of saving, explain whether you would expect each of the following situations to increase or decrease household saving.
   (a) More people retire before age 65.
   (b) There is an increase in life expectancy.
   (c) The government passes a law requiring private businesses to provide more lucrative pensions.
3. Explain how each of the following changes might affect people's saving.
   (a) Inheritance taxes are increased.
   (b) A government program allows college students to obtain student loans more easily.
   (c) The government promises to assist anyone injured by natural disasters such as hurricanes, tornadoes, and earthquakes.
   (d) More couples decide against having children.
   (e) The economy does far worse than anyone was expecting in a given year.
4. Economists are fairly certain that a rise in the price of most goods will cause people to consume less of those goods, but they are not sure whether a rise in interest rates will cause people to save more. Use the ideas of substitution and income effects to explain why economists are confident of the conclusion in the first case but not in the second.

5. Suppose a new technology makes capital more productive, leading firms to want to borrow more at each rate of interest in order to purchase more capital. Using supply and demand diagrams of the loanable funds market, show what the likely effect on the equilibrium rate of interest would be.
6. Suppose younger households decide that they cannot rely on Social Security and must save more on their own for their retirement years. What is the likely effect on the equilibrium rate of interest? Will the equilibrium amount of borrowing rise or will it fall?
7. We have all heard about winners of $10 million jackpot lotteries. The winner, however, does not get $10 million in cash on the spot, but rather typically gets a measly $500,000 for twenty years. Why is the present discounted value of the prize much less than $10 million? Calculate the present discounted value if $r = 5$ percent.
8. Consider an individual who is borrowing. Assume the nominal interest rate remains the same but the rate of inflation increases. What happens to the real interest rate? Why do you expect the individual to borrow more?

Appendix A: Indifference Curves and the Saving Decision[1]

This appendix investigates the saving decision using the indifference curve approach applied in the appendix to Chapter 5 to the consumption decision and in Chapter 8 to the labor supply discussion. Let's first look at the choice between leisure and consumption.

DECIDING HOW MUCH TO SAVE

Choosing how much to save is a decision about how much of lifetime income to consume now and how much to consume in the future. This trade-off is summarized in the two-period budget constraint introduced in the chapter, with present consumption measured along the horizontal axis and future consumption along the vertical axis. The slope of the budget constraint is $1 + r$, where r is the rate of interest, the extra consumption we get in the future from forgoing a unit of consumption today.

Figure 9.7 shows three indifference curves. The indifference curve through point A gives all the combinations of consumption today and consumption in the future about whose choice the individual is indifferent (she would be just as well off, no better and no worse, at any point along the curve as at A). Since people generally prefer more to less consumption, they would rather be on a higher than a lower indifference curve. The highest indifference curve a person can attain is one that is tangent to the budget constraint. The point of tangency we denote by E. The individual would clearly prefer the indifference curve through A, but no point on that curve is attainable because the whole indifference curve is above the budget constraint. She could consume at F, but the indifference curve through F lies below that through E.

As we learned in the appendix to Chapter 5, the slope of the indifference curve at a certain point is the marginal rate of substitution at that point. In this case, it tells us how much future consumption a person requires to leave him just as well off after his current consumption decreases by 1 unit. At the point of tangency, the slope of the indifference curve is equal to the slope of the budget constraint. The marginal rate of substitution at that point, E, equals $1 + r$. If the individual forgoes a unit of consumption, he gets $1 + r$ more units of consumption in the future, and this is exactly the amount he requires to compensate him for giving up current consumption. On the other hand, if the marginal rate of substitution is less than $1 + r$, it pays the individual to save more. To see why, assume $1 + r = 1.5$, while the person's marginal rate of substitution is 1.2. By reducing his consumption by a unit, he gets 1.5 more units in the future, but he would have been content getting only 1.2 units. He is better off saving more.

Figure 9.7

INDIFFERENCE CURVES AND SAVING BEHAVIOR

An individual will choose the combination of present and future consumption at E. Point A would be more desirable, but it is not feasible. Point F is feasible, but it lies on a lower indifference curve and is therefore less desirable.

---

[1] You will need to have read the appendix to Chapter 5 in order to follow this appendix.

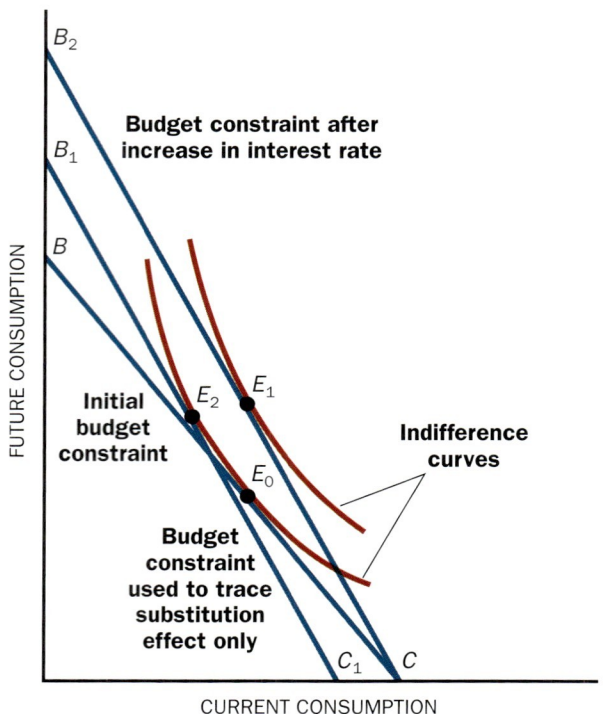

Figure 9.8

INCOME AND SUBSTITUTION EFFECTS OF A HIGHER INTEREST RATE

An increase in the interest rate rotates the budget constraint, moving it from BC to B_2C. The substitution effect describes what happens when relative prices are changed but Maggie remains on the same indifference curve; there is a shift in the budget line from BC to B_1C_1, and an increase in saving from E_0 to E_2. The income effect is the result of an outward shift of the budget line, keeping relative prices the same; the income effect is described by the shift from B_1C_1 to B_2C, and the increase in present consumption from E_2 to E_1.

CHANGING THE INTEREST RATE

Indifference curves and budget constraints enable us to see the effect of an increase in the interest rate. Figure 9.8 shows the case of an individual, Maggie, who works while she is young and saves for her retirement. The vertical axis gives consumption during retirement years, the horizontal axis consumption during working years. An increase in the rate of interest rotates the budget constraint, moving it from BC to B_2C. It is useful to break the change down into two steps. In the first, we ask what would have happened if the interest rate had changed but Maggie remained on the same indifference curve. This is represented by the movement of the budget constraint from BC to B_1C_1. As a result of the increased interest rate, Maggie consumes less today—she saves more. This is the substitution effect, and it is seen in the movement from E_0 to E_2 in the figure.

In the second step we note that since Maggie is a saver, the increased interest rate makes her better off. To leave Maggie on the same indifference curve after the increase in the interest rate, we needed to reduce her income. Her true budget constraint, after the interest rate increase, is B_2C, parallel to B_1C_1. The two budget constraints have the same slope because the after-tax interest rates are the same. The movement from B_1C_1 to B_2C is the second step. It induces Maggie to increase her consumption from E_2 to E_1. At higher incomes and the same relative prices (interest rates), people consume more every period, which implies that they save less. The movement from E_2 to E_1 is the income effect.

Thus, the substitution effect leads her to save more, the income effect to save less, and the net effect is ambiguous. In this case, there is no change in saving.

Appendix B: Calculating Present Discounted Value

In the text, we described how to calculate the present discounted value (PDV) of a dollar received a year from now. The present discounted value of a dollar received two years from now can be calculated similarly. But how much *today* is equivalent to, say, $100 two years from now? If I were given $PDV today and I put it in the bank, at the end of the year I would have PDV(1+r)$. If I left it in the bank for another year, in the second year I would earn interest on the total amount in the bank at the end of the first year, $r \times \text{PDV}(1+r)$. Therefore, at the end of the two-year period I would have:

$$\text{PDV}(1+r) + [r \times \text{PDV}(1+r)]$$
$$= \text{PDV}(1+r)(1+r)$$
$$= \text{PDV}(1+r)^2.$$

Thus, the $PDV of $100 in two years is $100/(1+r)^2$. If I put $100/(1+r)^2$ in the bank today, I would have $100/(1+r)^2 \times (1+r)^2 = \$100$ in two years. In performing these calculations, we have taken account of the interest on the interest. This is called **compound interest.** (By contrast, **simple interest** does not take into account the interest earned on interest that has been previously earned.)

TABLE 9.2

PRESENT DISCOUNTED VALUE OF $100

Year received	Present discounted value
Next year	$\frac{1}{1+r} \times 100 = \frac{100}{1+r}$
Two years from now	$\frac{1}{1+r} \times \frac{100}{1+r} = \frac{100}{(1+r)^2}$
Three years from now	$\frac{1}{1+r} \times \frac{100}{(1+r)^2} = \frac{100}{(1+r)^3}$

Table 9.3

CALCULATING PRESENT DISCOUNTED VALUE OF A THREE-YEAR PROJECT

Year	Return	Discount factor ($r = 0.10$)	Present discounted value ($r = 0.10$)
1	$10,000	$\frac{1}{1.10}$	$ 9,091
2	$15,000	$\frac{1}{(1.10)^2} = \frac{1}{1.21}$	$12,397
3	$50,000	$\frac{1}{(1.10)^3} = \frac{1}{1.331}$	$37,566
Total	$75,000	—	$59,054

If the rate of interest is 10 percent and is compounded annually, $100 today is worth $110 a year from now and $121 (*not* $120) in two years' time. Thus, the present discounted value today of $121 two years from now is $100. Table 9.2 shows how to calculate the present discounted value of $100 received next year, two years from now, and three years from now.

We can now see how to calculate the value of an investment project that will yield a return over several years. We look at what the returns will be each year, adjust them to their present discounted values, and then add these values up. Table 9.3 shows how this is done for a project that yields $10,000 next year and $15,000 the year after, and that will be sold in the third year for $50,000. The second column of the table shows the return in each year. The third column shows the discount factor—what we multiply the return by to obtain the present discounted value of that year's return. The calculations assume an interest rate of 10 percent. The fourth column multiplies the return by the discount factor to obtain the present discounted value of that year's return. In the bottom row of the table, the present discounted values of each year's return have been added up to obtain the total present discounted value of the project. Notice that it is much smaller than the number we obtain simply by adding up the returns, which is the "undiscounted" yield of the project.

Learning Goals

In this chapter, you will learn

1. How competitive markets maximize consumer and produce surplus
2. How competitive markets result in economic efficiency
3. How taxes create deadweight losses that reduce efficiency
4. How governments may intervene in markets to combine efficiency with acceptable distribution of wealth and income
5. How markets are interrelated, and how changes in one market will affect other markets in the economy

Chapter 10

THE EFFICIENCY OF COMPETITIVE MARKETS

In earlier chapters, we focused on the product market and saw that supply and demand come into balance at an equilibrium price and quantity. In equilibrium, the quantity of goods demanded by consumers equals the quantity supplied by firms. We have also seen that labor and capital markets achieve equilibrium similarly. In the labor market, labor supply and demand come into balance at an equilibrium wage; in equilibrium, the supply of labor by households equals the demand for labor by firms. In the capital market, equilibrium is achieved through adjustment in the interest rate; in equilibrium, the amount of savings supplied by households equals the amount of borrowing by firms. When all three markets are in equilibrium, the basic economic questions—What gets produced? By whom? How? For whom?—are resolved through the interactions of households and firms in the marketplace. When all of the economy's central markets have achieved equilibrium in this way, economists say that the economy is in **general equilibrium.**

Understanding how markets provide answers to these basic economic questions is important. But we also are interested in evaluating whether markets do a good job. When the assumptions of the basic competitive model hold, will the economy produce the right amounts of all the thousands and thousands of different goods and services? Will society's scarce resources be used *efficiently?* Once we evaluate how markets in our basic competitive model operate, we will be ready to extend the model in Part Three to deal with situations in which markets do not work perfectly (because competition is not perfect, for instance).

215

Competitive Markets and Economic Efficiency

The forces of demand and supply determine what is produced, how it is produced, and who receives the goods that are produced. To many people, relying on competitive markets seems like an undesirable way of addressing the fundamental economic questions. Such critics often complain that markets result in too much of some goods being produced, or too few of others; that allowing markets free rein leads to inequalities in income and wealth; or that society's scarce resources could be used more efficiently if only the government would do something.

Economists have long been concerned with these issues. Are there circumstances in which markets do a good job in allocating society's scarce resources? Are there circumstances in which they don't? By and large, economists have concluded that *competitive* markets, the markets in our basic competitive model, make efficient use of society's scarce resources. This faith in markets can be traced back to Adam Smith's 1776 masterpiece, *The Wealth of Nations*. Smith argued that workers and producers, interested only in helping themselves and their families, were the basis of the success of the economy. As Smith put it,

> Man has almost constant occasion for the help of his brethren, and it is in vain for him to expect it from their benevolence only. He will be more likely to prevail if he can interest their self-love in his favour, and shew them that it is for their own advantage to do for him what he requires of them. . . . It is not from the benevolence of the butcher, the brewer, or the baker, that we expect our dinner, but from their regard to their own interest. We . . . never talk to them of our own necessities but of their advantages.[1]

In short, Smith argued that individuals pursuing their own self-interest would best promote the public interest. His insight was that individuals work hardest—and best—to help the overall economic production of the society when their efforts help themselves. Smith used the metaphor of the "invisible hand" to describe how self-interest leads to social good: "He intends only his own gain, and he is in this, as in many other cases, led by an invisible hand to promote an end which was no part of his intention. . . . By pursuing his own interest he frequently promotes that of the society more effectually than when he really intends to promote it."[2]

This insight is one of the most fundamental in social science, and one that is not at all obvious. There is more to running an economy efficiently than individuals simply working hard. How do they know what to produce? How is it that the *uncoordinated* pursuit of self-interest then leads to efficiency? One of the most important achievements of modern economic theory has been to establish in what sense and under what conditions the market is efficient.

---

[1] *The Wealth of Nations* (1776), Book One, Chapter II.

[2] Ibid., Book Four, Chapter II.

CONSUMER AND PRODUCER SURPLUS

To understand why competitive markets are efficient, we need to measure the benefit that consumers gain from buying goods in such a market, as well as measure the benefits that firms gain from selling in it. We will then show that equilibrium in the competitive market leads to the greatest possible total gain for consumers and firms.

To evaluate the outcome in a competitive market, we can make use of Figure 10.1, which shows the market demand and supply curves for a market in equilibrium at a quantity Q_c and a price p_c. Can we measure the benefits that accrue to consumers and firms from participating in this market? From Chapter 5, we know that the gain to consumers is measured by consumer surplus. The consumers who purchase the good will do so only if their willingness to pay is greater than the market price. The magnitude of the *net* benefit that they receive from, say, the nth unit of the good they purchase is the difference between what they have to pay for that good—the market price—and what they were willing to pay for that good, as reflected in the demand curve. Accordingly, the area shaded in blue measures the total consumer surplus.

Firms also gain from participating in the market. As we learned in Chapter 7, the market supply curve reflects the marginal costs of producing the good. At the equilibrium quantity, Q_c, the marginal cost of producing the last unit of output is p_c, the equilibrium price. Just as the demand curve shows consumers' willingness to pay, so the supply curve shows firms' willingness to produce; if the market price were p_1, firms would be willing to produce only the quantity Q_1. The supply curve has a positive slope, reflecting the fact that marginal cost rises as output increases. At an output of Q_1, the marginal cost of production is equal to p_1, so the marginal cost of producing Q_1 is less than the competitive equilibrium price p_c. Since the firm is able to sell all it produces at the competitive market price p_c, it sells all but the last (marginal) unit for more than its marginal cost production. The magnitude of the profit, the net benefit, that firms receive from selling, say, the nth unit of the good is the difference between what they receive, the market price, and the price at which they would have been willing to produce the good, the marginal cost. The total gain to firms, called **producer surplus**, is the difference between the supply curve and the market price. The producer surplus is the green area in the figure.

We measure the total gain to both consumers and producers by adding together consumer surplus and producer surplus. We can now state an important result: *The equilibrium price and quantity in a competitive market lead to the highest possible level of total surplus.* At quantities such as Q_1, which are below the market equilibrium quantity Q_c, consumers are willing to pay p_2 while firms are willing to sell at p_1. The value to consumers exceeds the cost to firms of producing an extra unit. Total surplus could be increased if the quantity were increased. At output levels greater

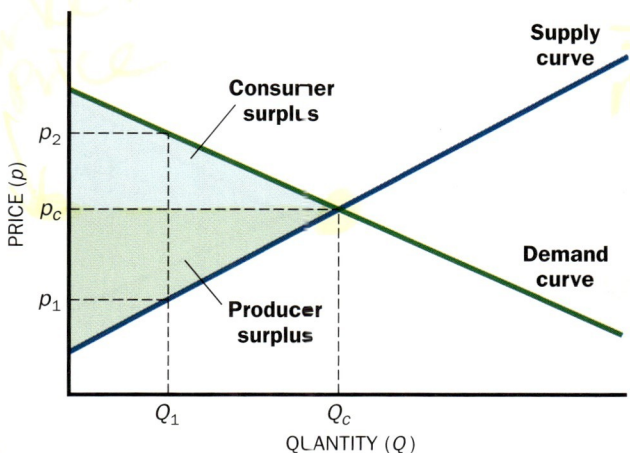

Figure 10.1

THE COMPETITIVE MARKET EQUILIBRIUM MAXIMIZES CONSUMER AND PRODUCER SURPLUS

When a competitive market is in equilibrium at the price p_c and quantity Q_c, at which demand and supply are equal, the sum of consumer surplus and producer surplus reaches its highest possible value. Consumer surplus is the blue area between the demand curve, showing willingness to pay, and the market price. Producer surplus is the green area between the supply curve (showing marginal cost) and the market price. If quantity is Q_1, firms are willing to supply an additional unit at a price p_1, while consumers are willing to pay p_2. The value to consumers exceeds the cost to producers, and total surplus can be increased if production expands. At quantities above Q_c, surplus can be increased by reducing output. At the market equilibrium, p_c and Q_c, the sum of consumer and producer surplus is maximized.

Figure 10.2

THE EFFECTS OF RENT CONTROL

Panel A of Figure 10.2 shows the supply and demand curves for rental apartments. The equilibrium rent at which supply equals demand is R^*. At this rent, the total surplus to renters and landlords is maximized. In panel A, the blue area is the consumer surplus—the value of apartments to renters in excess of the actual rent, R^*, they have to pay. The green area is the surplus that goes to landlords.

than Q_c, the marginal cost exceeds what consumers are willing to pay for the last unit, and so total surplus would be increased by reducing output. At Q_c and p_c, the sum of consumer and producer surplus reaches its highest level.

Fundamentals of Competitive Markets 1

HOUSEHOLDS AND FIRMS ARE PRICE TAKERS

In competitive markets, there are many firms and many consumers. Because each consumer and each firm is small relative to the size of the market, each takes prices as given. Firms, maximizing profits, produce at the level where price equals marginal cost. Households, making rational choices, purchase up to the point where the marginal willingness to pay equals the market price.

Example: Efficiency Losses from Rent Control In Chapter 4, we used the basics of supply and demand to illustrate why rent control interferes with the workings of a competitive market. We showed how rent control could create an artificial scarcity of housing, reducing the supply of low- and moderately priced apartments and making it more difficult for newcomers to find a place to live at a reasonable price. Now we can use the concepts of consumer and producer surplus to see how rent control reduces economic efficiency.

Panel A of Figure 10.2 shows the supply and demand curves for rental apartments. The equilibrium rent at which supply equals demand is R^*. At this rent, the total surplus to renters and landlords is maximized. In panel A, the blue area is the consumer surplus—the value of apartments to renters in excess of the actual rent, R^*, they have to pay. The green area is the surplus that goes to landlords.

Panel B illustrates what happens when the local government imposes a law that prevents rents from rising above R_1. A rental shortage results, as there will be an excess of demand over supply at R_1. We can use this simple supply and demand model of the market for apartments to see what happens to consumer surplus and producer surplus. The blue area of panel B equals consumer surplus at the rent R_1. The green area is the landlords' surplus. Comparing panels A and B, we can see that *total surplus is smaller as a result of rent control*. Total surplus has fallen by the area shown in yellow. The reduction in total surplus measures the inefficiency resulting from rent control.

Our analysis also highlights the distributional impact of policies such as rent control. Look again at panel B. Total surplus falls when the rent ceiling is R_1, and the available supply of apartments also falls, from Q^* to Q_1. Some consumers may be unable to find an apartment when rent control is imposed. Few apartments are available at or below the median rental in cities with rent control; in cities without rent control, it is much easier to find an apartment that is reasonably priced. Those consumers who do happen to get a rent-controlled apartment benefit from the policy. They would have been willing to pay more to get an apartment, but they only have to pay R_1. Renters who are fortunate enough to find a rent-controlled apartment gain, while landlords and those who cannot find housing lose.

In the long run, the supply of apartments is more elastic. Low rents discourage the construction of new apartments and cause some landlords to remove units from the rental market (converting them to condominiums and selling them, for example). Consumer surplus falls as rent control leads to a decline in the quantity of apartments available for rent. Thus, the cost of rent control in terms of the inefficient allocation of resources and its distributional impact can change in the long run. In general, the distributional impact is smaller in the long run, while the efficiency cost is greater. In the long run, landlords will put their money elsewhere—where they will get a normal return on their capital. The benefits to rent control will diminish, as the decreasing supply of rental apartments will result in more and more of those who would like to get rent-controlled apartments simply finding that none are available.

Fundamentals of Competitive Markets 2

THE EQUILIBRIUM PRICE MAXIMIZES CONSUMER PLUS PRODUCER SURPLUS

When the market clears, firms are able to sell the quantity that maximizes their profits at the market price, and households are able to purchase the quantity that maximizes their utility at the market price. At the equilibrium price, marginal cost equals consumers' willingness to pay. At a price above the equilibrium price, the marginal cost of producing one more unit is less than consumers' marginal willingness to pay. At a price below the equilibrium price, the marginal cost of producing one more unit is greater than consumers' marginal willingness to pay. At the equilibrium price in a competitive market, consumer plus producer surplus is maximized.

Internet Connection

DIGITAL ECONOMIST

The Digital Economist provides an online graphic demonstration of consumer surplus. You can test your understanding of how consumer surplus is calculated at www.digitaleconomist.com/cs_4010.html.

TAXES AND EFFICIENCY

Economists use the law of demand and supply to study the impact of taxes on consumers and producers. In Chapter 4 we learned that taxes imposed on producers can be passed on, or shifted, to consumers in the form of higher prices. There, two examples were contrasted. In the first, the law of supply and demand was used to study the impact of a tax on cigarette producers. When the demand for the taxed good is very inelastic, as is true of cigarettes, most of the burden of the tax is shifted to consumers. The second example involved a tax on one particular type of cheese, cheddar. In this case, the demand for the taxed good is very elastic, since close substitutes for cheddar cheese are available. When demand is elastic, most of the tax is borne by producers. Using the concepts of consumer surplus, producer surplus, and efficiency, we can gain additional insights into the effects of a tax.

Figure 10.3 shows the markets for cigarettes in panel A and the market for cheddar cheese in panel B. In each case, the equilibrium quantity without a tax is denoted by Q_0. The tax on the output of an industry paid by firms can be thought of as increasing the costs of production. This increase in cost shifts the supply curve up by the amount of the tax. Because the demand curve for cigarettes is relatively inelastic, the main impact of the tax is to raise the price to consumers. The price received by producers falls slightly, as does the quantity produced in the new equilibrium. In contrast, when the demand curve is relatively elastic, as shown in panel B for cheddar cheese, the effect is to cause a larger fall in the price producers receive and a smaller rise in the price paid by consumers.

The figure also shows what happens to consumer surplus when a good is taxed. In panel A, the entire blue area is equal to consumer surplus without the tax. After the tax, consumer surplus is equal only to the blue hatched area. Producer surplus is also reduced. It is equal to the entire orange region without the tax and the orange hatched area with the tax. Because the demand curve for cigarettes is inelastic, the reduction in consumer surplus is greater than the reduction in producer surplus, reflecting the fact that here the burden of the tax is shifted mainly to consumers.

While both consumer surplus and producer surplus fall, not all of this is lost to society—after all, the government collects revenue from the tax on cigarettes, and this revenue is then available to spend on government services. The tax revenue that is collected equals the tax per unit of output times the quantity of output produced. The difference between the price consumers pay and the price received by producers is equal to the tax on each unit of output. So the tax revenues collected will equal the area outlined in green. When we add up consumer surplus, producer surplus, and the revenue collected by the government, we can see that this total is less than the total surplus without the tax—the efficiency cost of the tax is measured by the area outlined in orange. This is called the **deadweight loss** caused by a tax. A tax thus has a cost beyond the revenue actually collected by the government.

Panel B illustrates the situation for a market in which the demand curve is relatively elastic. Here, the deadweight loss of the tax (the area outlined in orange) is larger. Because consumers are more sensitive to price when the demand curve is elastic, the tax causes them to substitute away from the taxed good. The tax "distorts" consumers' choices more in this case, and the resulting efficiency loss is larger.

Figure 10.3
TAXES AND EFFICIENCY

A tax on the output of an industry shifts the supply curve up by the amount of the tax. Panel A shows that if the demand curve is relatively inelastic, as is the case with cigarettes, most of the tax is passed on to consumers. Both consumer surplus and producer surplus fall, but most of the tax burden falls on consumers. The area outlined in green is equal to the revenue the government collects from the tax. Consumer and producer surplus fall by more than the revenue collected by the government. The deadweight loss due to the tax is shown as the area outlined in red. Panel B repeats the analysis for a good whose demand curve is relatively elastic. More of the burden of the tax falls on producers, and the deadweight loss is larger.

Efficiency

In the basic competitive model, with each consumer and each firm taking the market price as given, the equilibrium between demand and supply ensures the largest possible joint gain to consumers and firms. This is why most economists believe that the basic competitive model provides an important benchmark for evaluating how well resources are allocated. Taxes on specific goods create efficiency losses, as does interfering with the law of supply and demand through policies such as rent control. These policies may have desirable effects (a tax on cigarettes helps to reduce smoking, for instance), but those effects must be balanced against the inefficiencies they create. As we have seen before, trade-offs must be made.

If the conditions of the basic competitive model are satisfied, markets do a good job of allocating society's resources efficiently. But the benchmark provided by the basic competitive model is also useful because it helps us understand how markets can fail when the basic assumptions of the model do not hold. In Part Three, we consider a number of factors that cause markets to be inefficient. But first, we need to examine more closely what economists mean when they talk about the efficiency of markets.

PARETO EFFICIENCY

In everyday usage, we say something is efficient if it involves little waste. Economists relate the concept of efficiency to concern with the well-being of those in the economy. When no one can be made better off without making someone else worse off, the allocation of resources is called **Pareto efficient,** after the great Italian economist and sociologist Vilfredo Pareto (1848–1923). Typically, economists' use of the term refers to Pareto efficiency. Saying that a market is efficient is a compliment. In the same way that an efficient machine uses its inputs as productively as possible, an efficient market leaves no way of increasing output with the same level of inputs. The only way one person can be made better off is by taking resources away from another, thereby making the second person worse off.

It is easy to see how an allocation of resources might not be Pareto efficient. Assume that the government is given the job of distributing chocolate and vanilla ice cream and pays no attention to people's preferences. Assume, moreover, that some individuals love chocolate and hate vanilla, while others love vanilla and hate chocolate. Some chocolate lovers will get vanilla ice cream, and some vanilla lovers will get chocolate ice cream. Clearly, this arrangement is Pareto inefficient. Allowing people to trade resources—in this case, ice cream—makes both groups better off.

There is a popular and misguided view that *all* economic changes represent nothing more than redistributions. Gains to one only subtract from another. Rent control is one example. In this view, the only effect of rent control is redistribution—landlords receive less and are worse off by the same amount that their tenants' rents are reduced (and the tenants are better off). In some countries, unions have expressed similar views and see wage increases as having no further consequences than redistributing income to workers from those who own or who manage firms. This view is mistaken because it ignores consequences beyond the redistribution in each of these instances. Rent control that keeps rents below the level that clears the rental housing market does more than just take money out of the pocket of landlords and put it into the pocket of poor renters. It affects the amount of housing that landlords are willing to supply. It results in inefficiencies. For those concerned about renters who cannot afford the going rate, there are better approaches, such as vouchers to help those with low incomes pay for rent, that make the renters as well as the landlords better off than under rent control. Thus, with rent control, the economy is not Pareto efficient.

CONDITIONS FOR THE PARETO EFFICIENCY OF THE MARKET ECONOMY

For the economy to be Pareto efficient, it must meet the conditions of exchange efficiency, production efficiency, and product-mix efficiency. Considering each of these conditions separately shows us why the basic competitive model attains Pareto efficiency. (Recall the basic ingredients of that model: rational, perfectly informed households interacting with rational, profit-maximizing firms in competitive markets.)

Exchange Efficiency Exchange efficiency requires that whatever the economy produces must be distributed among individuals in an efficient way. If I like chocolate ice cream and you like vanilla ice cream, exchange efficiency requires that I get the chocolate and you get the vanilla. When there is exchange efficiency, there is no scope for further trade among individuals.

The price system ensures that exchange efficiency is attained. In deciding how much of a good to buy, people balance the marginal benefit they receive by buying an extra unit with the cost of that extra unit, its price. Hence, price can be thought of as a rough measure of the *marginal* benefit an individual receives from a good— that is, the benefit she receives from one more unit of the good. For those who like chocolate ice cream a great deal and vanilla ice cream very little, this will entail consuming many more chocolate ice cream cones than vanilla ones. And conversely for the vanilla lover. Notice that no single individual or agency needs to know who is a chocolate lover and who is a vanilla lover for the goods to get to the right person. Not even the ice cream stores have to know individual preferences. Each consumer, by his own action, ensures that exchange efficiency is attained.

Production Efficiency For an economy to be Pareto efficient, it must also be **production efficient.** That is, it must not be possible to produce more of some goods without producing less of other goods. In other words, Pareto efficiency requires that the economy operate along the production possibilities curve first introduced in Chapter 2.

Figure 10.4 shows the production possibilities curve for a simple economy that produces only two goods, SUVs and sedans. If the economy is at point I, inside the production possibilities curve, it cannot be Pareto efficient. At I society could produce more of both SUVs and sedans; and by distributing them to different individuals, it could make people better off. Prices signal to firms the scarcity of each of the inputs they use. When all firms face the same prices of labor, capital goods, and other inputs, they will take the appropriate actions to economize on each of these inputs, ensuring that the economy operates along its production possibilities curve.

Product-Mix Efficiency The third condition for Pareto efficiency is **product-mix efficiency.** That is, the mix of goods produced by the economy must reflect the preferences of those in the economy. The economy must produce along the production possibilities curve at a point that reflects what consumers want. The price system again ensures that this condition will be satisfied. Both firms and households look at the trade-offs. Firms look at how many extra sedans they can produce if they reduce their production of SUVs. The result is given by the slope of the production possibilities curve, and is called the **marginal rate of transformation.** Firms compare this trade-off with the relative benefits of producing the two goods— given by the relative prices. Similarly, households look at the relative costs of SUVs and sedans—again given by the relative prices—and ask, given those trade-offs, whether they would like to consume more SUVs and fewer sedans or vice versa.

Figure 10.4

THE PRODUCTION POSSIBILITIES CURVE

The production possibilities curve shows the maximum level of output of one good given the level of output of other goods. Production efficiency requires that the economy be on its production possibilities curve. Along the curve, the only way to increase production of one good (here, SUVs) is to decrease the production of other goods (sedans).

EFFICIENCY 223

Thinking Like an Economist
EXCHANGE AND DISTRIBUTION

The concepts of consumer surplus and producer surplus remind us that *exchange* in competitive markets can benefit both buyers and sellers. The demand curve for a good shows the total willingness to pay for each unit of the good. Though consumers are willing to pay more for the marginal unit at lower quantities, all units are purchased at the market price, which reflects the value of the last unit purchased. Thus, the total utility of the units purchased by consumers is greater than the total cost to consumers. Similarly, the supply curve reflects the marginal cost of producing each unit of a good. The market equilibrium price will equal the marginal cost of the last unit produced. Because marginal cost increases as the firm produces more, the price the firm receives is greater than the marginal cost of producing every unit except the last.

Consumer surplus and producer surplus also remind us that exchange has *distributional effects*. The gains from exchange need not be evenly distributed. If demand is relatively elastic while supply is inelastic, consumer surplus is small while producer surplus is large. If demand is relatively inelastic while supply is very elastic, consumer surplus is large while producer surplus is small.

Changes in preferences are reflected quickly—through the operation of demand and supply curves—in changes in prices. These changes are then translated by firms into changes in production. Assume that the economy is initially producing at point E along the production possibilities curve in Figure 10.4. Consumers decide that they like SUVs more and sedans less. The increased demand for SUVs will result in the price of SUVs increasing, and this price rise will lead to an increased output of SUVs; at the same time, the decrease in demand for sedans will result in the price of sedans falling, and this change in turn will lead to a decreased output of sedans. The economy will move from E to a point such as E_1, where there are more SUVs and fewer sedans produced; the mix of goods produced in the economy will have changed to reflect the changed preferences of consumers.

Wrap-Up

THREE CONDITIONS FOR PARETO EFFICIENCY

1. Exchange efficiency: Goods must be distributed among individuals in a way that leaves no scope for gains from further trade.
2. Production efficiency: The economy must be on its production possibilities curve.
3. Product-mix efficiency: The economy must produce a mix of goods reflecting the preferences of consumers.

COMPETITIVE MARKETS AND PARETO EFFICIENCY

We now know that when economists say that market economies are efficient, or that the price system results in economic efficiency, they mean that the economy is Pareto efficient: no one can be made better off without making someone else worse off. We have also shown why competitive markets ensure that all three of the basic conditions for Pareto efficiency—exchange efficiency, production efficiency, and product-mix efficiency—are attained.

The argument that competitive markets ensure Pareto efficiency can be put somewhat loosely in another way: a rearrangement of resources can benefit only people who voluntarily agree to it. But in competitive equilibrium, people have already agreed to all the exchanges they are willing to make; no one wishes to produce more or less or to demand more or less, at the prices given.

Pareto efficiency does *not* say that there are no ways to make one or many individuals better off. Obviously, resources could be taken from some and given to others, and the recipients would be better off. We have seen how, for instance, government interventions in the market, such as rent control, do benefit some individuals—those who are lucky enough to get the rent-controlled apartments. But in the process, others are made worse off.

Fundamentals of Competitive Markets 3

THE COMPETITIVE MARKET ECONOMY IS PARETO EFFICIENT

The equilibrium in the competitive market economy is Pareto efficient—no one can be made better off without making someone else worse off. In the competitive economy, the conditions for exchange efficiency, production efficiency, and product-mix efficiency are all satisfied.

COMPETITIVE MARKETS AND INCOME DISTRIBUTION

Efficiency is better than inefficiency, but it is not everything. In the competitive equilibrium, some individuals might be very rich, while others live in dire poverty. One person might have skills that are highly valued, while another does not. Competition may result in an efficient economy with a very unequal distribution of resources.

The law of supply and demand in a competitive economy determines how the available income will be divided up. It determines how much workers are paid for their labor and the return to owners of capital on their investments. By determining wages and the return to capital, the market thus determines the distribution of income.

EFFICIENCY

Knowing how the distribution of income is determined is important, because it tells us how the nation's economic pie is divided: it provides the answer to the question "For whom are goods produced?" While competitive markets produce economic *efficiency*—no one can be made better off without making someone else worse off—competitive markets may also produce distributions of income that seem, at least to some, morally repugnant. An economy in which some individuals live in mansions while others barely eke out a living may be efficient, but that hardly makes the situation desirable. Left to themselves, competitive markets may provide an answer to the question "For whom are goods produced?" that seems unacceptable.

This unacceptable response does not mean that the mechanism should be abandoned, at least not under the conditions assumed in our basic model—perfectly informed, rational consumers and firms interacting in competitive markets. Even if society as a whole wishes to redistribute income, it should not dispense with competitive markets. Instead, *all* that is needed is to redistribute in any way desired the wealth that people possess, and then leave the rest to the workings of a competitive market.

Of course, redistributing wealth is easier said than done; and as a practical matter, virtually all of the ways that the government engages in redistribution affect the workings of the market economy. Taxes on wages affect the labor market; taxes on capital, the capital market; taxes on luxuries, markets for specific goods.

Perhaps the most important impact of government on the distribution of "wealth" is in the sphere of education—in ensuring that everyone has a certain amount of human capital. By providing all individuals, regardless of the wealth of their parents, with a free basic education, government reduces the degree of inequality that otherwise would exist. Still, as we will see in Chapter 17, the magnitude of inequality in the United States remains high—larger than in most other developed countries.

Frequently government interferences with the market are justified on the grounds that they increase equality. These government policies are often based on the widely held but mistaken (as we have already seen) view that all redistributions are just that—some individuals get more and others get less with no further repercussions. We now know that changing relative prices to achieve redistribution—say, by imposing rent control—will have other effects as well. Such changes interfere with the economy's efficiency. One consequence of lower rents for apartments, for example, is that the return on capital invested in rental housing will fall. As a result, the economy will invest too little in rental housing and therefore too few apartments will be made available. Because of this underinvestment, the economy is not efficient.

Thus, interventions in the economy justified on the grounds that they increase equality need to be treated with caution. To attain an efficient allocation of resources with the desired distribution of income, *if* the assumptions of the competitive model are satisfied by the economy, the *sole* role of the government is to alter the initial distribution of wealth. Not only can it rely on the market mechanism thereafter, but its interference with the market may actually result in the economy not being Pareto efficient.

Both of the results just presented—that competitive markets are Pareto efficient and that every Pareto-efficient allocation, regardless of the desired distribution of income, can be obtained through the market mechanism—are *theorems*. That is, they are logical propositions that follow from basic definitions and assumptions, such as what is meant by a competitive economy and what is meant by Pareto efficiency. When these assumptions are not satisfied, market economies may not be Pareto efficient, and more extensive government interventions may be required to obtain Pareto-efficient allocations. Later chapters will explore these circumstance in greater detail.

Still, two important lessons that emerge are worth noting here: there are costs associated with redistributions that entail interventions in market mechanisms, and those costs have to be weighed against the benefits; and redistributions can make use of the price mechanism, rather than trying to override it. One cannot repeal the laws of supply and demand. Interventions like rent control can impose large costs. Some alternative forms of interventions, such as housing subsidies, may achieve comparable distributional objectives at less cost. If government cannot *costlessly* redistribute, it should look for efficient ways of redistributing—that is, ways that reduce the costs as much as possible. This is one of the main concerns of the branch of economics called the *economics of the public sector*.

General Equilibrium Analysis

When we applied the idea of market equilibrium in earlier chapters, we focused on one market at a time. The price of a good is determined when the demand for that good equals its supply. The wage rate is determined when the demand for labor equals its supply. The interest rate is determined when the demand for savings equals its supply. This kind of analysis is called **partial equilibrium analysis.** In studying what is going on in one market, we ignore what is going on in other markets—as we did earlier in this chapter when we analyzed the efficiency cost of rent control and the impact of a tax on cigarettes. In each case, we focused just on the demand and supply in the market for apartments and the market for cigarettes.

Interdependencies in the economy make partial equilibrium analysis overly simple, because demand and supply in one market depend on prices determined in other markets. For instance, the demand for skis depends on the price of ski tickets, ski boots, and possibly even airline tickets. Thus, the equilibrium price of skis will depend on the price of ski tickets, ski boots, and airline tickets. By the same token, the demand for ski tickets and ski boots will depend on the price of skis. **General equilibrium analysis** broadens our perspective, taking into account the interactions and interdependencies throughout the various parts of the economy.

THE BASIC COMPETITIVE EQUILIBRIUM MODEL

Economists view the entire economy as made up of numerous different markets, all interrelated. Individuals and firms interact in these different markets. In the labor market, for example, the supply of labor reflects the outcome of decisions by households as they determine the amount of labor they wish to supply. Households supply labor because they want to buy goods. Hence, their labor supply depends on both wages and *prices*. It also depends on other sources of income. If we assume, for the sake of simplicity, that households also have savings that yield a return, then we can see that the labor supply is connected to the product market and the capital market.

Equilibrium in the labor market requires that the demand for labor equal the supply. Normally, when we draw the demand curve for labor, we simply assume that

p, the price of the good(s) being produced, and the interest rate (here, r) are kept fixed. We focus our attention solely on the wage rate, the price of labor. Given p and r, we look for the wage at which the demand and supply for labor are equal. This is a *partial equilibrium analysis* of the labor market. But in fact all markets are interrelated; the demand for labor depends on the wage, on the interest rate, and on the price at which the firm sells its output.

The labor market is only one of the three markets, even in our highly simplified economy. There is also the market for capital to consider. In Chapter 9, we saw how

Thinking Like an Economist
INDIRECT TRADE-OFFS AND AIR SAFETY FOR CHILDREN

General equilibrium analysis calls attention to the fact that trade-offs often exist across markets. The benefits of an action taken in one market may be offset by related costs that arise in another market. This same reasoning applies to government policies, as policymakers work to balance the costs and benefits of expenditure programs and regulations. Sometimes the costs of a policy arise through its indirect repercussions. Such indirect trade-offs helped determine regulations related to air safety for children.

States require small children in cars to ride in specially designed safety seats. So why shouldn't small children traveling by plane be required to ride in safety seats as well? It seems clear that in at least a few cases, such seats would save a child's life in an airplane crash. Nevertheless, after considering the full potential consequences of requiring child safety seats in planes, the Federal Aviation Administration (FAA) argued against it.

On the benefit side, the FAA estimated that mandatory safety seats would save the life of one child in one airline crash every ten years. But parents would have to pay as much as $185 to buy the safety seats themselves, in addition to paying for a regular airplane seat for the child. Under current regulations, children under two years old are allowed to sit in their parents' laps, avoiding the expense of an airline ticket. With those extra costs, the FAA estimated that 20 percent of the families who now fly with small children would either stay home or drive. The additional driving would lead to 9 additional highway deaths, 59 serious injuries, and 2,300 minor injuries over the same ten-year period, according to FAA estimates.

Even those who feel that saving an additional child's life has a value that cannot be reduced to a price tag, however high, must look beyond the market being regulated. Looking beyond airlines makes it clear that reducing airline deaths by requiring child safety seats for infants and toddlers is almost certain to cause even greater total loss of life.

households determine their saving, which in turn determines the available supply of capital. The supply of capital is affected, in general, by the return it yields (the interest rate r) plus the income individuals have from other sources, in particular from wages. Since the amount individuals are willing to save may depend on how well-off they feel, and how well-off they feel depends on the wage rate relative to prices, we can think of the supply of capital, too, as depending on wages, interest rates, and prices. In Chapter 9 we learned how to derive firms' demand for capital. This depends not just on the interest they must pay but also on the price at which goods can be sold, and on the cost of other inputs such as labor.

Equilibrium in the capital market occurs at the point at which the demand and supply for capital are equal. Again, partial equilibrium analysis of the capital market focuses on the return to capital, r, at which the demand and supply of capital are equal, but both the demand and supply depend on the wage rate and the price of goods as well.

Finally, there is the market for goods. Chapter 5 showed how to derive households' demand for goods. We can think of the household at first deciding on how much to spend and then deciding how to allocate what it spends over different goods. Of course, with a single consumption good, the second choice does not exist. In our simplified model, then, we can think of the demand for goods at any price as being determined by household income, which in turn depends on the wage and the interest rate.

Similarly, in Chapter 7, we analyzed how firms determine how much to produce. They set price equal to marginal cost, where marginal cost depends on wages and the interest rate. Equilibrium in the goods market requires that the demand for goods equal the supply of goods. Again, while in the simple partial equilibrium analysis we focus on how the demand and supply of goods depend on price, p, we know that the demand and supply of goods also depend on both the wage rate and the return to capital.

The labor market is said to be in equilibrium when the demand for labor equals the supply. The product market is in equilibrium when the demand for goods equals the supply. The capital market is in equilibrium when the demand for capital equals the supply. The economy as a whole is in equilibrium only when all markets clear simultaneously (demand equals supply in all markets). The general equilibrium for our simple economy occurs at a wage rate, w; price, p; and interest rate, r, at which all three markets are in equilibrium.

In the basic equilibrium model, there is only a single good, but it is easy to extend the analysis to the more realistic case where there are many goods. The same web of interconnections exists between different goods and between different goods and different inputs. Recall from Chapter 3 that the demand curve depicts the quantity of a good—for instance, soda—demanded at each price; the supply curve shows the quantity of a good that firms supply at each price. But the demand curve for soda depends on the prices of other goods and the income levels of different consumers; similarly, the supply curve for soda depends on the prices of inputs, including the wage rate, the interest rate, and the price of sugar and other ingredients. Those prices, in turn, depend on supply and demand in their respective markets. The general equilibrium of the economy requires finding the prices for each good and for each input such that the demand for each good equals the supply, and the demand for each input equals the supply. *General equilibrium entails prices, wages, and returns to capital that ensure all markets for goods, labor, and capital (and other factors of production) clear.*

Wrap-Up

EQUILIBRIUM IN THE BASIC COMPETITIVE MODEL

The labor market clearing condition: The demand for labor must equal the supply.
The capital market clearing condition: The demand for capital must equal the supply.
The goods market clearing condition: The demand for goods must equal the supply.

Case in Point

THE LABOR MARKET AND THE WIDENING WAGE GAP

A general equilibrium perspective can help us understand how changes in one market affect other markets. Often those repercussions on other markets feed back to cause further changes in the market originally affected. As a case in point, a general equilibrium analysis is needed to analyze how wages for skilled and unskilled workers are affected by changes in technology.

Those who have a college education are paid more on average than those who fail to complete high school. The average wage of workers with at least four years of college is two-thirds higher than that of workers whose education ended with a high school diploma. Because unskilled workers generally cannot perform the same jobs as skilled workers, it is useful to think about the wages of these two groups as determined in separate labor markets, as illustrated in Figure 10.5. Panel A shows the demand and supply curves of unskilled workers, and panel B those for skilled workers. The equilibrium wage for skilled workers is higher than that for unskilled workers.

What happens if a change in technology shifts the demand curve for skilled labor to the right, to DS_1, and the demand curve for unskilled labor to the left, to DU_1? The wages of unskilled workers will decrease from wu_0 to wu_1, and those of skilled workers will increase from ws_0 to ws_1. In the long run, this increased wage gap induces more people to acquire skills, so the supply of unskilled workers shifts to the left, and that of skilled workers shifts to the right. As a result, the wage of unskilled workers rises from wu_1 to wu_2, and that of skilled workers falls from ws_1 to ws_2. These long-run supply responses thus dampen the short-run movements in wages.

Over the past two decades, the ratio of wages of college graduates to high school graduates, as well as the ratio of wages of high school graduates to nongraduates, has increased enormously. Indeed, the real wages (that is, wages adjusted for changes in the cost of living) of unskilled workers have fallen dramatically (by as much as 30 percent). Though there have been shifts in both demand and supply curves, the primary explanation of these shifts is a change in the relative demand for skilled labor, probably attributable largely to changes in technology.

While we can be fairly confident of the predicted shifts in long-run labor supply, how fast they will occur is less clear. At the same time that these supply shifts occur,

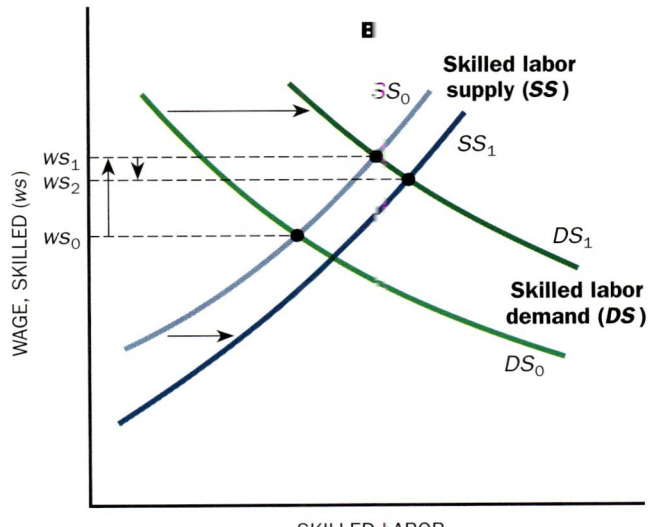

Figure 10.5

THE MARKET FOR SKILLED AND UNSKILLED LABOR

In panel A, new advanced technology shifts the demand curve for unskilled labor to the left, and reduces wages from wu_0 to wu_1. In panel B, the new technology shifts the demand curve for skilled labor out to the right, and thus raises wages from ws_0 to ws_1. Over time, this increased difference in wages may lead more individuals to obtain skills, shifting the supply curve for unskilled labor back to the left, raising wages for unskilled labor somewhat from wu_1 to wu_2, and shifting the supply curve for skilled labor to the right, reducing wages for skilled labor from ws_1 to ws_2.

there may be further shifts in the demand curves, exacerbating wage differences. The question is, How long will it take for the wage gap to be reduced to the levels that prevailed in the 1960s? In the meantime, many worry about the social consequences of steadily increasing wage (and income) inequality.

Case in Point

THE MINIMUM WAGE AND GENERAL EQUILIBRIUM

When the first minimum wage law was adopted by passage of the Fair Labor Standards Act of 1938, it had general equilibrium effects that altered the character of the country.

Initially the minimum wage law required that wages be no lower than 32.5 cents per hour. Because wages were much lower in the South than in the North, many more workers were affected there. For example, 44 percent of southern textile workers were paid below the minimum wage, but only 6 percent of northern textile workers were. The law had a particularly strong impact on African Americans in the South. Many lost their jobs and migrated North. The way to boost employment in

The effects of the first minimum wage were far reaching, and included the migration of many African Americans to the North.

the South was to raise the productivity of the workforce, so southern states were eager to attract new capital investment that would increase labor productivity and restore employment.

Gavin Wright, a professor of economics at Stanford University, described the situation this way: "The overall effect of this history on black Americans is complex, mixed, and ironic. Displacement and suffering were severe. Yet in abolishing the low-wage South, the federal government also destroyed the nation's most powerful bastion of racism and white supremacy. The civil rights movement of the 1960s was able to use the South's hunger for capital inflows as an effective weapon in forcing desegregation. Similarly, migration to the North allowed dramatic increases in incomes and educational opportunities for many blacks; yet the same migration channeled other blacks into the high-unemployment ghettos which if anything have worsened with the passage of time."[3]

A partial equilibrium analysis of the effects of enacting a minimum wage would look only at how the law affected labor markets. But for society as a whole, the effects of enacting such a law were far more momentous, touching on issues such as racial desegregation and the growth of urban ghettos.

GENERAL EQUILIBRIUM OVER TIME

A general equilibrium perspective focuses on the interrelationships among markets, including markets at different points in time. For example, the supply (and demand) for exhaustible natural resources like oil will depend on the price of oil

---

[3]Gavin Wright, "The Economic Revolution in the American South," *Journal of Economic Perspectives 1* (Summer 1987): 161–78.

today, but it will also depend on prices expected in the future. The role played by prices expected in the future is important for understanding how quickly the limited supply of a natural resource will be used.

Just as we did in Chapter 9 when we discussed household saving, we will simplify by considering only two periods, today and the future. Let's also assume that known reserves of oil are one billion barrels. The oil can be sold now or left in the ground and sold in the future. Oil producers will want to sell the oil today if they think prices in the future will be lower, and they will want to leave it in the ground today and sell it in the future if they expect prices then will be higher. Of course, we learned in Chapter 9 that we cannot compare prices today and in the future directly—a dollar in the future is not worth as much as a dollar today because today's dollar could always be invested, earning interest and thus yielding more than a dollar in the future. To compare prices in the future with prices today we need to look at the *present discounted value* of the future price (Chapter 9 explained how to calculate this figure). If the expected price of oil in one year is $55 per barrel and the interest rate is 10 percent, then the present discounted value of that $55 is $55/1.1 = $50.

We can now restate the comparison that oil producers will make. Oil producers will compare the current price with the present discounted value of the future price of oil. If the current price is above the present discounted value of the future price, they have an incentive to sell all one billion barrels today. But an attempt to sell all the oil reserves today will depress the current price of oil, pushing it down toward the present discounted value of the future price. In the opposite case, when the current price is less than the present discounted value of the future price, oil producers have an incentive to save the oil and sell it in the future. But because the oil is withheld from the market today, the current price will rise, until it equals the presented discounted value of the future price. Thus, market forces will tend to make the current price and the present discounted future price equal. By definition, in equilibrium an oil producer must be indifferent between the choices of selling an extra barrel today and saving it to sell in the future. This tells us that the current price and the presented discounted future price will be equal in equilibrium.

If the current price and the present discounted future price are equal, oil producers have no preference as to when they sell the oil. What then determines how much oil will actually be sold today? To answer this question we need to know something about the demand for oil, both today and in the future. In equilibrium, the quantity demanded today and in the future, when the current and present discounted future prices are equal, must add up to the total amount of oil—in our example, one billion barrels.

We can now understand how the price of oil is affected by such factors as the development of new technologies or more fuel-efficient cars. Suppose these developments lower the demand for oil in the future. The demand curve for oil in the future then shifts to the left, lowering the future price of oil. Whenever the present discounted future price of oil falls, oil producers will want to sell more of their oil today. As we have seen, an increase in the supply of oil today causes the current price of oil to fall. The current price must adjust until it again equals the present discounted future price, and total demand today and in the future equals one billion barrels. Because reduced demand in the future lowers the current price of oil, it leads to higher current consumption of oil and an increase in the quantity of oil produced today.

WHEN PARTIAL EQUILIBRIUM ANALYSIS WILL DO

In the examples of the widening wage gap and the price of oil, general equilibrium analysis is clearly important. But can we ever focus on what goes on in a single market, without worrying about the reverberations in the rest of the economy? Are there circumstances in which partial equilibrium analysis will provide a fairly accurate answer to the effect of, say, a change in a tax? When will the sort of analysis we used earlier in this chapter to analyze the impact of a tax on cigarettes and cheddar cheese be sufficiently accurate?

Partial equilibrium analysis is adequate, for example, when the reverberations from the initial imposition of a tax are so dispersed that they can be ignored without distorting the analysis. Such is the case when individuals shift their demand away from the taxed good toward many, many other goods. Each of the prices of those goods changes only a very little. And the total demand for the factors of production (such as capital and labor) changes only negligibly, so that the second-round changes in the prices of different goods and inputs have a very slight effect on the demand and supply curve of the industry analyzed. In these circumstances, partial equilibrium analysis will provide a good approximation of what will actually happen.

Our earlier analysis of a tax on cigarettes is an example of partial equilibrium analysis providing a good approximation. Since expenditures on cigarettes are a small proportion of anyone's income, an increase in their price will have a small effect on overall consumption patterns. While the reduced quantity demanded of cigarettes (and the indirect changed demand for other goods) will slightly change the total demand for labor, this effect is so small that it will have no noticeable impact on the wage rate. Similarly, the tax will have virtually no effect on the return to capital.

Under these circumstances, when more distant general equilibrium effects are likely to be so faint as to be indiscernible, a partial equilibrium analysis of a tax on cigarettes is appropriate.

Looking Beyond the Basic Model

This chapter has brought together the pieces of the basic competitive model. It has shown how the competitive equilibrium in an ideal economy is achieved. To the extent that conditions in the real world match the assumptions of the basic competitive model, there will be economic efficiency. Governments will have little role in the economy beyond establishing a legal framework within which to enforce market transactions.

What are the consequences when the underlying assumptions are not valid? Which of the assumptions are most suspect? What evidence do we have to assess either the validity of the model's underlying assumptions or its implications? The next part of this book is devoted to these questions, and to the role of government that emerges from the answers.

Review and Practice

SUMMARY

1. General equilibrium in the basic competitive model occurs when wages, interest rates, and prices are such that demand is equal to supply in all labor, capital, and product markets. All markets clear.
2. The competitive equilibrium maximizes the sum of consumer and producer surplus.
3. Under the conditions of the basic competitive model, the economy's resource allocation is Pareto efficient: that is, no one can be made better off without making someone worse off.
4. The distribution of income that emerges from competitive markets may be very unequal. However, under the conditions of the basic competitive model, a redistribution of wealth can move the economy to a more equal allocation that is also Pareto efficient.
5. Changes in one market will have effects on other markets. To analyze the effects of a tax, for example, general equilibrium analysis takes into account the effects in all markets. But when the secondary repercussions of a change are small, partial equilibrium analysis, focusing on only one or a few markets, is sufficient.

KEY TERMS

general equilibrium
producer surplus
deadweight loss
Pareto efficient
exchange efficiency
production efficiency
product-mix efficiency
marginal rate of transformation
partial equilibrium analysis
general equilibrium analysis

REVIEW QUESTIONS

1. How does the economy in general equilibrium answer the four basic economic questions: What is produced, and in what quantities? How are these goods produced? For whom are they produced? Who makes the economic decisions?
2. What is meant by Pareto efficiency? What is required for the economy to be Pareto efficient? If the conditions of the basic competitive model are satisfied, is the economy Pareto efficient?
3. What is the difference between partial and general equilibrium analysis? When is each one especially appropriate?
4. If the distribution of income in the economy is quite unequal, is it necessary to impose price controls or otherwise change prices in the competitive marketplace to make it more equal?

PROBLEMS

1. Decide whether partial equilibrium analysis would suffice in each of these cases, or whether it would be wise to undertake a general equilibrium analysis.
   (a) A tax on alcohol
   (b) An increase in the Social Security tax
   (c) A drought that affects farm production in the midwestern states
   (d) A rise in the price of crude oil
   (e) A major airline going out of business
   Explain your answers.
2. Explain how each of the following might interfere with exchange efficiency.
   (a) Airlines that limit the number of seats they sell at a discount price
   (b) Doctors who charge poor patients less than rich patients
   (c) Firms that give volume discounts
   In each case, what additional trades might be possible?
3. Assume that in the steel industry, given current production levels and technology, 1 machine costing $10,000 can replace 1 worker. Given current production levels and technology in the automobile industry, 1 machine costing $10,000 can replace 2 workers. Is this economy Pareto efficient; that is, is it on its production possibilities curve? If not, explain how total output of both

goods can be increased by shifting machines and labor between industries.

4. Consider three ways of helping poor people to buy food, clothing, and shelter. The first way is to pass laws setting price ceilings to keep these basic goods affordable. The second is to have the government distribute coupons that give poor people a discount when they buy these necessities. The third is for the government to distribute income to poor people. Which program is more likely to have a Pareto-efficient outcome? Describe why the other programs are not likely to be Pareto efficient.

5. Suppose the supply of rental apartments is completely inelastic in the short run. Show that imposing a ceiling on rents that is below the equilibrium rent does not cause any inefficiency by demonstrating that total consumer and producer surplus is not reduced by the rent ceiling. If the supply of rental apartments is more elastic in the long run, explain why a ceiling on rents would reduce the total surplus.

6. If you do not know whether you would be able to get a rent-controlled apartment, under what circumstances might you nonetheless vote for rent control? Why would your enthusiasm for rent control wane over time?

Part 3
IMPERFECT MARKETS

Learning Goals

In this chapter, you will learn

1. The key ways many markets fall short of the perfect competition envisioned in the basic competitive model

2. The different forms of imperfect competition and their consequences

3. How imperfect information can affect markets

4. What economists mean by externalities, and how they affect markets

5. What a public good is, and why markets undersupply public goods.

Chapter 11

INTRODUCTION TO IMPERFECT MARKETS

In the two centuries since Adam Smith enunciated the view that markets ensure economic efficiency, economists have investigated the basic competitive model with great care. Nothing they have discovered has shaken their belief that markets are, by and large, the most efficient way to coordinate an economy. However, economists have also found significant ways in which modern economies do not fit the basic competitive model. These differences can cause markets to operate inefficiently, and they may provide a rationale for government involvement in the economy.

Before we can understand the role of government in the economy, we need to understand how the differences between modern economies and the world envisioned in our basic competitive model affect the ways markets work. If competition is less than perfect, do markets still produce efficient outcomes? If they do not produce efficient outcomes, is too much produced or is too little produced? If people do not have enough information about, say, the quality of goods, will markets be efficient? And if the outcomes when information is imperfect are not efficient, what can government do about it? What sorts of policies will improve the situation?

In this part of the book, we address these questions. We begin by outlining four important ways in which some markets may differ from the basic competitive model. These differences can help account for the important role that government plays in our economy. We examine how these differences affect the ability of private markets to efficiently use society's scarce resources. Subsequent chapters explore each of these differences in greater depth. By considering when markets fail to produce efficient outcomes and why, we can greatly extend the range of insights that economics has to offer and better understand some of the dissatisfactions with markets and some of the roles of public policy. And going beyond the competitive model will help us make sense of many of the economic changes associated with new technologies and the information revolution.

As we explore the economics of imperfect markets, the five key concepts introduced in Chapter 1—trade-offs, incentives, exchange, information, and distribution—continue to serve as guides to thinking like an economist. Individuals, firms, and government still face trade-offs when markets are imperfect, though perhaps different ones from those in the world of the basic competitive model, and they must be weighed in any economic analysis. Trade-offs necessitate choices, which we can understand if we focus on incentives. Gaining an understanding of how market imperfections affect the outcome of market exchange will be especially critical. Throughout, we will highlight the effects of market imperfections on not only the level but also the distribution of economic welfare. The basic concepts of economics apply beyond the basic competitive model in which competition is perfect and everyone has all the information they need. In exploring the role of imperfect competition and imperfect information in market economies, economists have continued to find that these foundational concepts are crucial.

Extending the Basic Competitive Model

In Part Two, we made several simplifying assumptions to enable us to focus on key factors that explain how markets work. So that we could better understand how prices and quantities are determined and evaluate the nature of market outcomes, we concentrated on the essence of the market rather than on detailed descriptions of actual markets. In any field, theorizing often ordinarily takes place on a high level of generality.

The main assumptions in the basic competitive model include the following:

1. Firms and individuals take market prices as given—because each is small relative to the market because their decisions do not affect the market price.
2. Individuals and firms have perfect information about the quality and availability of goods, and about the prices of all goods.
3. Actions by an individual or firm do not directly affect other individuals or firms except through prices.
4. Goods can be enjoyed only by the buyer—if I buy and eat a slice of pizza, it is no longer available for you to eat; if you buy a bike, we cannot both use it at the same time.

Frequently, however, we would like to analyze what happens if a firm has the power to set prices, or consumers are uninformed about the quality of different goods, or actions by one individual directly affect others (a cigarette smoker creating secondhand smoke, for example), or there are goods we can all consume simultaneously (like national defense). We can extend our basic competitive model to deal with these cases, and we begin by considering each of our main assumptions in turn.

First, most markets are not as competitive as those envisioned by the basic model. In Part Two, we assumed markets have so many buyers and sellers that no individual household or firm believes its actions will affect the market equilibrium price. The basic competitive model focuses on products such as wheat or pig iron, which may be produced by different firms but are essentially identical and are perfect substitutes for one another. If a firm raises its price slightly above that of other firms, it loses all its customers. In that model, there is no room for brand loyalty, yet it is hard to think of a consumer product without attaching a brand name to it. If BMW raises the price of its cars, it may lose some customers to other makes, but it won't lose them all. A BMW enthusiast would probably pay more for a BMW than for an Audi. Likewise, if Nike charges slightly more than Adidas for running shoes, it will not lose every customer. Because it takes the market price as given, a firm in the competitive model does not need to consider how other firms will react when it considers changing the quantity it produces. However, when BMW and Nike make production and pricing decisions, they must worry about how their rivals will react. In the real world, many firms devote enormous resources to efforts designed to anticipate others' actions and reactions.

Second, buyers and sellers seldom have all the information that the basic competitive model assumes. In the basic competitive model, buyers know everything about what they are buying, whether it is stocks or bonds, a house, a used car, or a refrigerator. Firms know the productivity of each worker they hire; and when workers take employment at a firm, they know exactly what is expected of them in return for the promised pay. Yet in most markets, participants do not have complete information. A buyer of a used car may not know the true condition of the car, a high school student choosing among colleges doesn't have complete information about the quality of the teachers or the availability of courses she desires, and a firm hiring a new worker doesn't know precisely how productive he will be.

Third, firms and consumers bear all the consequences of their actions in the basic competitive model—but not in reality. Whenever an individual or firm can take an action that directly affects others but for which it neither pays nor is paid compensation, economists say that an **externality** is present. (The effect of the action is "external" to the individual or firm.) Externalities are pervasive. A hiker who litters, a driver whose car emits pollution, a child whose play leaves a mess behind, a person who smokes a cigarette in a crowded room, a student who talks during a lecture—each creates externalities. In each case, others—not just the agent—suffer the consequences of the action. Externalities can be thought of as instances when the price system works imperfectly. The hiker is not "charged" for the litter she creates. The car owner does not pay for the pollution his car makes.

While these examples are of negative externalities, externalities also can be positive. A homeowner tending a well-kept garden that provides a benefit to the neighbors creates a positive externality; so does a hiker who picks up litter along a trail.

Fourth, in the basic competitive model, when one person consumes a good, it is not available for others to consume. If John buys a gallon of gas for his car, Sarah cannot also use that gallon of gas. But some goods, called **public goods,** do remain available for others to consume. They represent extreme cases of externalities. (Normally, we think of these as positive externalities—for example, all *benefit* from the provision of national defense. However, some individuals—equally affected—may dislike the public good; for them, it acts like a negative externality.) The consumption (or enjoyment) of a public good by one individual does not subtract from that of other individuals (in this case, consumption is said to be *nonrivalrous*). Public goods also have the property of *nonexcludability*—that is, it costs a great deal to exclude any individual from enjoying the benefits of a public good. The standard example of a public good is national defense. Once the United States is protected from attack, it costs nothing extra to protect each new baby from foreign invasion. Furthermore, it would be virtually impossible to exclude a newborn from the benefits of this protection.

Imperfect competition, imperfect information, externalities, and public goods all represent cases in which the market does not produce economic efficiency. Economists refer to these problems as **market failures** and have studied them closely. The market "fails" not by ceasing to exist but by failing to produce efficient outcomes. Government *may* be able to correct such a market failure and improve economic efficiency. But before considering government policies to correct these failures, we first need to understand clearly how it is that market outcomes may be inefficient.

Though it describes an oversimplified world, the basic competitive model continues to provide important and powerful insights. For that reason, most economists use it as the starting point for building a richer, more complete model of the modern economy. This richer model is the focus of Part Three. In the next several chapters, we will examine how adding the complications of imperfect competition, imperfect information, externalities, and public goods to the basic model increases the ability of economics to explain our economy.

Fundamentals of Imperfect Markets 1

IMPERFECT MARKETS LEAD TO MARKET FAILURES

When the market is perfectly competitive, consumers and firms have perfect information, and there are no externalities (positive or negative) and no public goods, market outcomes will be efficient. When these conditions do not hold, markets are inefficient and there can be a role for government policies that lead to more efficient outcomes.

Imperfect Competition and Market Structure

When economists look at markets, they look first at the **market structure**—that is, how the market is organized. The market structure that formed the basis of the competitive model of Part Two is called **perfect competition.** For example, there are so many wheat farmers (producers) that no individual farmer can realistically hope to move the price of wheat from that produced by the law of supply and demand.

Frequently, however, competition is not "perfect" but limited. Economists group markets in which competition is limited into three broad categories. In the most extreme case, there is no competition: a single firm supplies the entire market. This is called **monopoly.** Your local electrical company may have a monopoly in supplying electricity in your area. In a court case in 1999, Microsoft was found to have a near monopoly in the market for personal computer operating systems. Because the profits of a monopolist would normally attract other businesses into the market, the firm must take advantage of some barrier to entry to maintain its monopoly position. In Chapter 12, we will discuss some of those barriers.

In the second structure, several firms supply the market, so there is *some* competition. This is called **oligopoly.** The automobile industry is an example, with a relatively small number of global producers. The defining characteristic of oligopoly is that the small number of firms forces each to be concerned with how its rivals will react to any action it takes. If General Motors offers low-interest-rate financing, for instance, other companies may feel compelled to match the offer, a predictable response that General Motors will have to take into account before acting. By contrast, a monopolist has no rivals and considers only whether special offers help or hurt itself. And a firm facing perfect competition never needs to resort to any special offer—it can always sell as much as it wants at the market price.

The third market structure contains more firms than an oligopoly but not enough for perfect competition. This is called **monopolistic competition.** An example is the market for laptop computers. IBM, HP, Toshiba, Sony, Gateway, Dell, and others produce their own brand of laptops. Each is slightly different from the others, similar enough that there is considerable competition—so much that profits may be driven down to zero—but different enough to make competition limited and prevent the companies from being price takers. The degree of competition under monopolistic competition is greater than that in oligopoly, because monopolistic competition involves a sufficiently large number of firms that each firm can ignore the reactions of any rival. If one company lowers its price, it may gain a large number of customers. But the number of customers it takes away from any single rival is so small that none of the rivals is motivated to retaliate.

Both oligopolies and monopolistic competition are in-between market structures, allowing some but not perfect competition. They thus are referred to as **imperfect competition.**

Wrap-Up

ALTERNATIVE MARKET STRUCTURES

Perfect competition: Many, many firms, each believing that nothing it does will have any effect on the market price.

Monopoly: One firm.

Imperfect competition: Several firms, each aware that its sales depend on the price it charges and possibly other actions it takes, such as advertising. There are two special cases:

Oligopoly: Sufficiently few firms that each must be concerned with how its rivals will respond to any action it undertakes.

> *Monopolistic competition:* Sufficiently many firms that each believes that its rivals will not change the price they charge should it lower its own price; competition strong enough that profits may be driven down to zero.

PRICE AND QUANTITY WITH IMPERFECT COMPETITION

In the basic model of perfect competition, each firm takes the market price as given. If one firm tries to raise its price, even slightly, it will lose all of its customers. When competition is imperfect, a firm will lose some but not all of its customers if it charges a slightly higher price. In conditions of imperfect competition, firms do not simply "take" the price as dictated to them by the market. They "make" the price. They are the *price makers*.

Whether a firm is a price taker or a price maker, it tries to maximize profits. In determining output, the firm will compare the extra or **marginal revenue** that it will receive from an extra unit of output with the extra or marginal cost of producing that extra unit. If marginal revenue exceeds marginal cost, it pays to expand output. Conversely, if marginal revenue is less than marginal cost, it pays to reduce output. Whether the firm operates in a market characterized by perfect or imperfect competition, it will produce at the output level at which marginal revenue equals marginal costs.

The essential difference between a firm facing perfect competition and one facing imperfect competition lies in the relationship between marginal revenue and price. For a competitive firm, marginal revenue equals the price. For instance, the marginal revenue received by a wheat farmer for one more bushel of wheat is just the price of a bushel of wheat. But under imperfect competition, a firm knows it cannot simply sell as much as it would like at the current price. The firm recognizes that its demand curve is downward sloping; if it wants to sell more, it has to be more proactive—for example, by lowering its price. Or it might try to shift its demand curve to the right by spending more on advertising. For the sake of simplicity, in this chapter and the next two we will focus on the case in which the firm lowers its price if it wants to increase sales. (Chapter 15 will investigate the role of advertising.) By changing its price, the firm will influence its sales. What needs to be emphasized here is that the firm cannot sell an extra unit of output at the present market price. Thus marginal revenue is not equal to the present market price when competition is imperfect.

In the case of a monopoly, for example, the firm controls the entire market; a doubling of its output therefore doubles industry output, which will have a significant effect on price. If Alcoa, in the days when it had a monopoly on aluminum, had increased its production by 1 percent, the total market supply of aluminum would have increased by 1 percent. If Alcoa leaves its price unchanged, that extra aluminum will not be sold; buyers were already purchasing the quantity they demanded. An increase in market supply will cause the equilibrium price to fall. Market price will continue to fall until the quantity demanded has increased by 1 percent.

How much the price must change as sales change will depend on whether the firm is a monopolist, a monopolistic competitive firm, or an oligopolist. If the firm is a monopolist, it controls the entire market, by definition, so the demand curve it faces is the market demand curve. By contrast, a firm such as PepsiCo will need to know how rivals like Coca-Cola will respond before it can determine how its sales will be affected if it changes its price. In either case, *marginal revenue will be less than price*. To sell more, the firm must lower its price, reducing the revenue it receives on all units that it produces.

To maximize profits, firms will set marginal cost equal to marginal revenue. When competition is imperfect, however, marginal revenue is less than price. Consequently, at the output level that maximizes profit, marginal cost is also less than price. In other words, the market price will be too high—it exceeds the cost of producing the last unit sold. Under conditions of perfect competition, producers would have an incentive to increase production when price exceeds marginal cost: an efficient outcome. Imperfect competition, in contrast, results in too little being produced at too high a price.

GOVERNMENT POLICIES

Because imperfect competition leads to an inefficient outcome, with too little produced at too high a price, government has taken an active role in promoting competition and in limiting the abuses of market power.

Antitrust laws are designed to break up monopolies, to prevent monopolies from forming, and to restrain firms from engaging in practices that restrict competition. For instance, before two large firms in an industry can merge, or before one can acquire another, they must seek government approval. The government will seek to determine whether the merger of the two firms will *significantly* reduce competition. The most recent highly publicized antitrust case involved the U.S. government and Microsoft, with the government arguing that Microsoft had a near monopoly in the market for operating systems and that it had abused that market power—not only setting prices above the competitive levels but also using its market power to deter and destroy rivals.

Internet Connection

THE FEDERAL TRADE COMMISSION

The Federal Trade Commission (FTC) enforces consumer protection and antitrust laws and plays an important role in eliminating unfair or deceptive practices while ensuring that American markets function competitively. The FTC provides articles at www.ftc.gov/bcp/menu-internet.htm on what to watch out for in e-commerce and when making purchases or seeking information over the Internet.

International Perspective
TRADE AND COMPETITION

As a result of the increasing globalization of the world economy, firms must compete with both foreign and domestic rivals. Even a firm that is the sole domestic producer of a product may be unable to take advantage of its monopoly position because of competition from foreign producers. Government actions to open a country to trade can therefore help promote competition. New Zealand provides a case in point.

New Zealand had a long history of restricting imports to protect domestic firms. Since the New Zealand economy was small, many industries had very few firms—sometimes only one. Besides the typical problems that accompany monopolies (too little produced at a price that is too high), domestic firms frequently offered only a narrow range of products. For example, suppose you wanted to buy some auto paint to touch up a scratch on your car. Because New Zealand had a domestic paint producer, imports of paint were restricted. But the small size of the New Zealand market limited the demand for any given type of paint. Consequently, the New Zealand paint industry offered few colors. If your car was an unusual hue, you were out of luck.

In 1984, a new Labour government was elected in New Zealand that implemented a new strategy to improve competition. The government realized that the regulatory structure that had developed to address the inefficiencies of monopoly could be eliminated; competition could be increased simply by removing the country's many trade barriers. There is no need to worry if only a single paint firm is located in New Zealand—that firm's market power will be limited if it must compete with foreign paint producers. Today, consumers can choose from a wide variety of products, and the prices of domestic firms are kept down by competition from foreign firms that can now sell their goods in New Zealand.

In some cases, the government may decide not to break up a firm even if it is a monopoly. It may believe, for instance, that it is more efficient for a single firm to provide the service. In this case, the firm is called a **natural monopoly.** Typically the government establishes a regulatory body to oversee such a monopoly. Industries that have been characterized in the past as *regulated monopolies* include local cable TV, electrical utility, and telephone. Firms in these industries normally must obtain the approval of the regulatory agency before they can raise the price they charge.

In Chapters 12 and 13 we will discuss some of the ways government attempts to limit the power of monopolies and promote competition. The policies that government uses depend on the source of imperfect competition and on the structure of the market.

Fundamentals of Imperfect Markets 2
IMPERFECT COMPETITION

Imperfectly competitive markets are characterized according to their market structure as monopolies, oligopolies, or monopolistic competition. In all cases, firms maximize profits by setting marginal cost equal to marginal revenue. Because marginal revenue is less than the market price, too little is produced at too high a price.

Imperfect Information

The model of perfect competition that was developed in Part Two assumed that market participants, whether consumers, firms, or the government, had *perfect information*. They had full information about the goods being bought and sold. Seldom do we actually approach this standard, and economists have gained new insights into how markets function by incorporating **imperfect information** into their models. Interestingly, economists' understanding of the importance of imperfect information deepened at almost the same time that new technologies improved the ability of firms and households to gather, process, and transmit information.

THE INFORMATION PROBLEM

The basic competitive model assumes that households and firms are well informed: they know their opportunity set, or what is available and at what price. More strikingly, they know every characteristic of every good, including how long it will last. For some purchases, we do have very good information, so the assumption of the basic model is a reasonable one. When I buy my favorite breakfast cereal at the grocery store, I know all I need to know.[1] Typically, though, we must make decisions about what to buy with much less than perfect information.

The model also assumes that consumers know their preferences; that is, they know what they like. They know not only how many oranges they can trade for an apple but also how many oranges they want to trade. In the case of apples and oranges, this assumption may make sense. But how do students know how much they are going to enjoy, or even benefit from, a college education? How does an individual know whether she would like to be a doctor, a lawyer, or a writer? She gets some idea about the different professions by observing those who practice them, but her information is at best incomplete.

According to the basic model, firms too are perfectly well informed. They know the best available technology. They know the productivity of each applicant for a job. They know precisely how hard every worker is working and how good a job each is doing. They know the prices at which inputs can be purchased from every possible supplier (and all the input's characteristics). And they know the prices at which they can sell the goods, not only today but in every possible circumstance in the future.

HOW BIG A PROBLEM?

That individuals and firms are not perfectly well informed is, by itself, not necessarily a telling criticism of the competitive model, just as the observation that markets are not perfectly competitive does not cause us to discard the model. The relevant issues are as follows: Can the competitive model mislead us in these situations? Are there important economic phenomena that can be explained only by taking into account

---

[1] Of course, to gain information about the cereal, I had to try it initially. So even in this example, the information was not automatically available. Often, gaining information about a good requires actually using it.

One benefit of this degree is that it conveys information about its recipient.

imperfect information? Are there important predictions of the model that are incorrect as a result of the assumption that consumers and firms are well informed?

Increasingly, over the past two decades, economists have come to believe that the answer to these questions is yes. For example, college graduates receive a higher income on average than high school graduates, perhaps not only because they have learned things in college that make them more productive but also because their college degree conveys valuable information to employers. Employers cannot easily learn in an interview which applicants for a job will be productive workers. They therefore use a college degree as a criterion to judge applicants. College graduates *are,* on average, more productive workers. But it is wrong to conclude from this that college has necessarily *increased* students' productivity. It may simply have aided firms in sorting those students who are more productive from the less productive.

HOW PRICES CONVEY INFORMATION

The price system provides brilliant solutions for some information problems. We have seen how prices play an important role in coordinating production and communicating information about economic scarcity. Firms do not have to know what John or Julia likes, or what their trade-offs are. The price tells the producer the marginal benefit of producing an extra unit of the good, and that is all the firm needs to know. Similarly, a firm does not need to know how much iron ore is left in Minnesota, the cost of refining iron ore, or a thousand other details. All it needs to know is the price of iron ore. This tells the company how scarce the resource is, and how much effort it should expend in conserving it. Prices and markets provide the basis of the economy's incentive system. But there are some information problems that markets do not handle, or do not handle well. And imperfect information sometimes inhibits the ability of markets to perform the tasks that they carry out so well when information is complete.

MARKETS FOR INFORMATION

Information has value; people are willing to pay for it. In this sense, we can consider information to be a good like any other. There is a market for information, at a price—just as there is a market for labor and a market for capital. Indeed, our economy is sometimes referred to as an *information economy*. And every year, investors spend millions of dollars on newsletters that give them information about stocks, bonds, and other investment opportunities. Magazines sell specialized information about hundreds of goods. One of the major impacts of the growth of the Internet has been to reduce the cost of all types of information.

Yet even with all the new information technologies, the markets for information are far from perfect, and for good reasons. Most obviously information is *not* just like any other good. When you buy a chair, the furniture dealer is happy to let you look at it, sit on it, and decide whether you like it. When you buy information, you cannot do the same. The seller can either say, "Trust me. I'll tell you what you need to know," or show you the information and say, "Here's what I know. If this is what you wanted to know, please pay me." You would rightfully be skeptical in the first scenario and might be unwilling to pay in the second. After you were given the information, what incentive would you have to pay?

e-Insight
INFORMATION, COMPETITION, AND THE INTERNET

The Internet is having a profound effect on consumer choices and on the nature of competition. One way it has done so is by providing consumers with easily accessible information at a low cost. For example, rather than pay a series of time-consuming visits to various car dealers when you want to shop for a car, you can now do your shopping from home over the Internet. Consumers can comparison shop using Web sites that provide car reviews and pricing information. They can even buy a car online and have it delivered to their doorstep. Many economists argue that by increasing the information consumers have, the new information technologies will enable actual markets to more closely approximate the basic competitive model, with its assumption that consumers are fully informed.

The Internet also increases competition. Local retail (bricks-and-mortar) stores must now compete against online sellers. Consumers can easily check prices at various online sellers, and there are even digital agents called "bots" that search Internet sites for the best available deals. Because consumers can comparison shop on the Web with little effort, Internet sellers are forced to offer low prices.

In business-to-business (B2B) commerce, the sheer number of firms linked through the Internet enables larger pools of buyers and sellers to be brought together, creating new marketplaces and lower costs for many businesses. For instance, the major U.S. auto manufacturers are moving their purchasing operations online, forming a marketplace for parts and other items that is estimated to handle almost $250 billion of purchases each year. As competition among parts suppliers increases, the auto manufacturers expect to gain significant cost savings. But some antitrust experts worry that to the extent that the U.S. auto manufacturers *cooperate* in purchasing, they may actually reduce competition among the buyers. Single buyers (called *monopsonists*) or limited competition among buyers is just as bad for economic efficiency as monopoly sellers or limited competition among sellers.

Some cases present a basic problem of credibility. You might think, If a stock tipster *really* knows that a stock's price is going to go up, why should he tell me, even if I pay him for the information? Why doesn't he go out and make his fortune with the information? Or is it that he really is not sure, and would just as soon have me risk my money rather than risk his?

Most important, even after the firm or consumer buys all the information thought to be worth paying for, the information is still far from perfect. Some information is simply too costly to obtain relative to the benefit of having it. So imperfect information is a fact of life, and in Chapter 15 we will examine the ways it can affect economic behavior and the structure of markets.

GOVERNMENT POLICIES

The market inefficiencies resulting from imperfect information can take a number of forms. Government concern about the pitfalls for ill-informed consumers has motivated a number of pieces of **consumer protection legislation.** For example, the Wheeler-Lea Act of 1938 made "deceptive" trade practices illegal and gave the Federal Trade Commission power to stop false and deceptive advertising. Truth-in-lending legislation requires lenders to disclose the true interest rate being charged. Truth-in-packaging legislation makes it less likely that consumers will be misled by what is printed on an item's package.

The Securities and Exchange Commission, which regulates the sale of stocks and bonds, requires the firms selling these securities to disclose a considerable amount of information. Of course, simply publishing the information is not enough—the public must be confident of its accuracy. For that reason, companies must hire accounting firms to audit their financial statements. Not surprisingly, many of the largest busi-

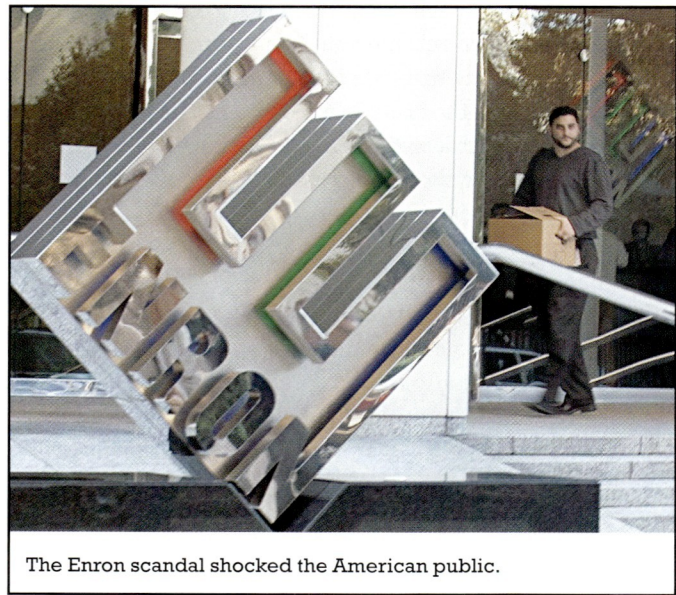

The Enron scandal shocked the American public.

ness scandals in recent years have involved misleading accounting practices. The best-known case is that of the energy-trading firm Enron. Between 1996 and 1999, Enron used accounting tricks to report profits of $2.3 billion to potential investors, while reporting to the U.S. tax authorities that it had lost $3 billion. In one of the many legal cases that resulted from Enron's collapse, the accounting firm Arthur Andersen, once one of the world's five largest, was found guilty of obstructing justice by destroying documents related to its role in auditing and approving Enron's financial statements (the Supreme Court later overturned the conviction on the grounds that the judge's instructions to the jury were too broad). And the Enron case is not unique. In January 2005, McKesson Corporation, the largest drug distributor in the United States, agreed to pay almost $1 billion to former investors who, in a single day in 1999, lost $8.6 billion—the value of McKesson stock had collapsed after it became known that the company had misreported its revenues.

Often, legislation mandating that more information be supplied is of only limited effectiveness. One problem occurs when consumers try to take in and process the information. A cereal manufacturer may disclose not only what is required but also vast amounts of other information, which may or may not be important. How are consumers to know what to pay attention to? They cannot absorb everything. Occasionally, as in the case of warnings about the dangers of smoking, government regulators for this reason have required the disclosures to be of a specific form and lettering size to make them stand out. But making this kind of intervention universal would be, at the very least, extremely costly.

Another problem with outlawing deceptive advertising is the difficulty of drawing a clear line between persuasion and deception. Advertisers are good at walking along the edge of any line—a suggestive hint may be legal but an explicit claim might be called deceptive. Congress or the courts cannot be expected to draw a line between informative and noninformative advertising for every product in the economy.

Most of the problems arising from imperfect information are not easily remedied. For example, firms will have imperfect information concerning potential employees, no matter what the government does. However, the government often must deal with the consequences. Imperfect information can lead to imperfect competition. In some markets, such as the health insurance market, the consequences are severe, and there has been considerable dissatisfaction with the way these markets work. Government has intervened in a variety of ways, but these efforts clearly have not remedied the problems—and some observers question whether they have even improved matters.

Fundamentals of Imperfect Markets 3

IMPERFECT INFORMATION

Consumers and firms must constantly make decisions based on less-than-perfect information. Markets for information exist, but information is not like normal goods—you cannot usually "try before you buy." Many government policies are designed to help improve the information on which consumers and investors base their decisions.

Externalities

Even when there is perfect competition and information, the market may supply too much of some goods and too little of others. One of the reasons for this is externalities. Externalities arise whenever an individual or firm can take an action that directly affects others without paying for a harmful outcome or being paid for a beneficial one. When externalities are present, firms and individuals do not bear all the consequences of their action.

A common example of a negative externality is the air pollution emitted by a factory. The factory benefits from not installing pollution-control devices, which would raise the cost of its product. When firms do not have to pay for the pollution they emit, society as a whole bears the negative consequences. If firms had to pay for their pollution, they would find ways to produce less of it—by adopting cleaner technologies, for instance. Government environmental regulations, which we will discuss in Chapter 18, are usually designed to ensure that firms bear the costs of the pollution they create.

When there are externalities, the market's allocation of goods will be inefficient, because the producer fails to take into account "social costs" in deciding how much to produce. To put it another way, the price of a good such as steel, determined in competitive markets by the law of supply and demand, reflects only *private costs,* the out-of-pocket costs to the firms. If firms do not have to pay *all* the costs (including the costs of pollution), equilibrium prices will be lower and output higher than they would be if firms took social costs into account. When the production of a good like steel entails a negative externality—such as smoke and its effects on the air—the market level of production is too high.

The inefficiency of market outcomes in the presence of externalities can be understood by considering an important characteristic of market outputs in the basic competitive model. There, the market price is equal both to the value consumers place on the last unit of output and to the cost to firms of producing that last unit. Thus, at the margin, the value of the last good produced is just sufficient to cover the costs of producing it. When an externality is present, this balance no longer holds. If the price consumers pay does not fully reflect the costs of producing the good (a negative externality), consumers will demand too much of the good and too much will be produced. If there are social benefits in addition to the private benefits to consumers (a positive externality), too little will be produced.

GOVERNMENT POLICIES TOWARD EXTERNALITIES

Because externalities lead to market inefficiencies, they can justify the government's intervention in markets. The government can prevent the overproduction of goods that accompanies negative externalities either by establishing regulations (for instance, environmental regulations that restrict the levels of pollution) or by providing incentives (for instance, imposing fees or fines on polluters).

Thinking Like an Economist
INCENTIVES AND THE ENVIRONMENT

When economists think about environmental issues, they focus on the incentives faced by individuals and firms. If too much air pollution is produced, economists try to understand why firms and individuals have an incentive to engage in activities that generate excessive pollution. If too many fish are taken, economists ask, Why don't fishermen have an incentive to preserve the fish stocks? In both of these examples, individuals and firms harm the environment because they do not have to bear the full cost of their actions. Take the case of fishermen. Each fisherman has to take into account the cost of operating his boat and the wages he needs to pay his crew. But he does not have to pay for the impact of his fishing on the total stock of fish. If he takes more fish, his action reduces the stock available to other fishermen, but no individual fisherman has to account for this cost imposed on others. No one fisherman has an incentive to limit his own take to preserve the remaining fish stock.

Here and in many other cases of externalities, the source of the problem can be traced to the lack of property rights over valuable resources such as clean air or the stock of commercially valuable fish. When a valuable resource is not privately owned, individuals and firms do not need to pay a price to use it. If the stock of fish were privately owned, the owner would charge each fisherman a fee to take fish. When the cost to society of the resource is not reflected in what the user has to pay, there is no incentive to economize on its use. Sometimes, assigning property rights is easy. In the case of a small lake, the government can auction off the exclusive right to fish to a single individual, who might extract the fish herself or might charge others for fishing. Either way, she would have an incentive to ensure that the resource is used efficiently. But more often, there is no reasonable or easy property rights solution: who should be given the right to the air? Indeed, the inability of political leaders to address this question is at the center of the failure of attempts to reduce the greenhouse gas emissions that are leading to global warming. As an alternative to property rights solutions, governments can provide appropriate incentives by designing taxes to make users pay the full social costs of their activities, ensuring that individuals and firms have incentives to economize on all of society's scarce resources.

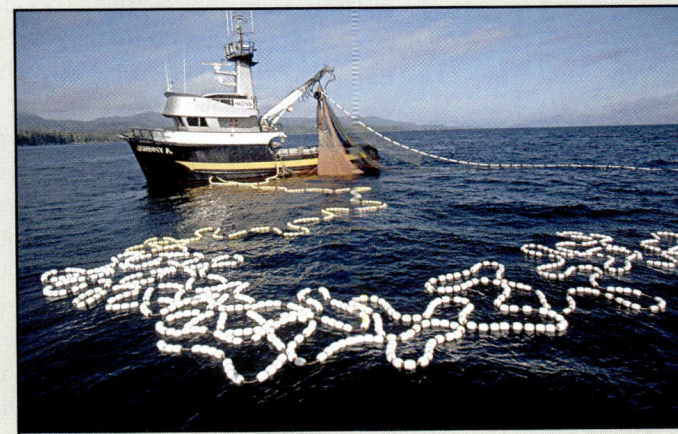

A fishing boat trawls the Clarence Strait in Alaska for salmon.

When the production of a good involves positive externalities, the market level of production is too low, and the government can try to enlarge the supply. The renovation of an apartment building in a decaying part of a city is an example of a positive externality; it will probably enhance the value of the buildings surrounding it. A government subsidy can lower the cost of rejuvenating old buildings. In equilibrium, the subsidy will increase the number of buildings that are renovated.

Fundamentals of Imperfect Markets 4

EXTERNALITIES

When individuals or firms do not have to pay for the actions they take that directly affect others, the market outcome will be inefficient. In the presence of externalities, the producer takes into account the private goods of production but fails to take into account all the social costs. When the direct effect of production on others is negative, as in the case of pollutants generated by a firm or second-hand smoke caused by a cigarette smoker, too much of the good is produced.

Public Goods

The final category of market failure arises when public goods are present. The marginal costs of providing a *pure public good* to an additional person are strictly zero, and it is impossible to exclude people from receiving the good. Many public goods that government provides are not *pure* in this sense. The cost of an additional person using an uncrowded interstate highway is very, very small, but it is not zero, and it is possible, though relatively expensive, to exclude people from (or charge people for) using the highway.

Figure 11.1 compares examples of publicly provided goods by setting them against the strict definition of a pure public good. It shows ease of exclusion along the horizontal axis and the (marginal) cost of an additional individual using the good along the vertical axis. The lower left corner represents a pure public good. Of the major public expenditures, only national defense is close to a pure public good. Completely uncongested highways, to the extent they exist, are another example. The upper right corner represents a pure private good (health services or education), where the cost of exclusion is low and the marginal cost of an additional individual using the good is high.

Many goods have one but not both of the main properties of pure public goods to some degree. Fire protection is like a private good in that exclusion is relatively easy—if the fire department were run as a private firm, individuals who refuse to contribute could simply not be helped in the event of a fire. But fire protection is like a public good in that the marginal cost of covering an additional person is low. Most of the time, firefighters are not engaged in fighting fires but are waiting for calls. Protecting an additional individual has little extra cost. Only in the rare event when two fires break out simultaneously will there be a significant cost to extending fire protection to an additional person.

Sometimes the marginal cost of using a good to which access is easy (a good that possesses the property of nonexcludability) will be high. When an uncongested highway turns congested, the costs of using it rise dramatically, in terms not of wear and tear but of the time lost by drivers using the road. It is costly to exclude individuals by charging for road use—as a

Figure 11.1

PUBLICLY PROVIDED GOODS

Pure public goods are characterized by nonrivalrous consumption (the marginal cost of an additional individual enjoying the good is zero) and nonexcludability (the cost of excluding an individual from enjoying the good is prohibitively high). Goods provided by the public sector differ in the extent to which they have these two properties.

practical matter, this can be done only on toll roads, and ironically, the tollbooths often contribute to the congestion.[2]

Many of the goods that are publicly provided, such as education and health services, have high costs associated with providing the service to additional individuals. For most of these goods, exclusion is also relatively easy. In fact, many of these goods and services are provided privately in some countries, or provided both publicly and privately. Though they are provided publicly in this country, they are not *pure* public goods, in the term's technical sense.

Private markets undersupply public goods. If a shipowner uses a port near which a lighthouse should be located, he could weigh the costs and benefits of constructing the lighthouse. But if there were one large shipowner and many smaller owners, it would not pay any one of the small owners to build the lighthouse; and the large shipowner, in deciding whether to construct the lighthouse, would take into account only the benefits she would receive, not the benefits to the small shipowners. If the costs of construction exceeded the benefits she alone would receive, she would not build the lighthouse. But if the benefits accruing to *all* the shipowners, large and small, were taken into account, those benefits might exceed the costs. It would then be desirable to build the lighthouse.

One can imagine a voluntary association of shipowners getting together to construct a lighthouse in these circumstances. But what happens if some small shipowner refuses to contribute, thinking that even if he does not contribute, the lighthouse will still be built anyway? This is the **free-rider problem** that accompanies public goods; because it is difficult to preclude anyone from using them, those who benefit from the goods have an incentive to avoid paying for them. Every shipowner has an incentive to free ride on the efforts of others. When too many decide to do this, the lighthouse will not be built.

Governments bring an important advantage to bear on the problem of public goods. They have the power to coerce citizens to pay for them. There might be *some* level of purchase of public goods—lighthouses, highways, parks, even police or fire services—in the absence of government intervention. But such societies would be better off if the level of production were increased, and if citizens were forced to pay for that increased level of public services through taxes.

Fundamentals of Imperfect Markets 5

PUBLIC GOODS

A pure public good can be provided to an additional person at a zero marginal cost and it is impossible to exclude people from receiving the good. Private markets undersupply public goods because of the free-rider problem.

---

[2]New technologies enable drivers to be charged for tolls without stopping at tollbooths. Scanners identify cars equipped with special tags as they pass, automatically billing the driver. Thus, new technologies can convert what was a public good into a private good.

Looking Ahead

We have now examined four situations in which markets may fail to develop an efficient allocation of society's scarce resources. In each of these cases—imperfect competition, imperfect information, externalities, and public goods—a role for government exists. Government can employ a variety of policies to promote competition, address the problems created by externalities and imperfect information, and supply public goods.

In the next several chapters, we will study market failures in more detail, beginning, in Chapter 12, with the analysis of imperfect competition—including the extreme case, that of a monopoly. Chapter 13 shows how public policy mitigates the results of imperfections of competition. Subsequent chapters will deal with strategic behavior when competition is imperfect (Chapter 14), with imperfect information in the product market (Chapter 15), and with the effects of imperfect competition and imperfect information on labor markets (Chapter 16).

Review and Practice

SUMMARY

1. By and large, private markets allocate resources efficiently. However, in a number of areas they do not, as in the cases of imperfect competition, imperfect information, externalities, and public goods.
2. Economists identify four broad categories of market structure: perfect competition, monopoly, oligopoly, and monopolistic competition.
3. When competition is imperfect, the market will produce too little of a good and the market price will be too high.
4. The basic competitive model assumes that participants in the market have perfect information about the goods being bought and sold and their prices. However, information is often imperfect.
5. Individuals and firms produce too much of a good with a negative externality, such as air or water pollution, since they do not bear all the costs. They produce too little of a good with positive externalities since they cannot receive all the benefits.
6. Public goods are goods that cost little or nothing for an additional individual to enjoy, but that cost a great deal to exclude an individual from enjoying them. National defense and lighthouses are two examples. Free markets underproduce public goods.

KEY TERMS

externality
public goods
market failures
market structure
perfect competition
monopoly
oligopoly
monopolistic competition
imperfect competition
marginal revenue
antitrust laws
natural monopoly
imperfect information
consumer protection legislation
free-rider problem

REVIEW QUESTIONS

1. What is the difference between perfect competition and imperfect competition?
2. What does it mean when an economist says that monopoly output is "too little" or a monopoly price is "too high"? By what standard? Compared with what?
3. What role does information play in the basic competitive model? How does the market for information differ from the market for a good such as wheat?
4. What is an example of a positive externality? of a negative externality? Why are goods with negative externalities often overproduced? Why are goods with positive externalities often underproduced? Give an example for each.
5. What sorts of policies can government use to address the problem of externalities?
6. What two characteristics define a public good? Give an example. Why will private markets not supply the efficient level of public goods?

PROBLEMS

1. Which do you think best describes each of the following markets—perfect competition, monopoly, oligopoly, or monopolistic competition?
   (a) The market for automobiles
   (b) The market for soy beans
   (c) The market for portable music players
   (d) The market for dining out in a large city
2. Briefly explain why marginal revenue is equal to the market price for a firm in a perfectly competitive market but is less than the current market price for a firm in an imperfectly competitive market.
3. Colleges and universities compete for students, and students shop for colleges. Is the market for college placements characterized by perfect competition? Does Harvard face a horizontal demand curve or a downward-sloping demand curve? Is the market for college placements characterized by perfect information? Describe how students' information about colleges might be imperfect. Describe how colleges' information about prospective students might be imperfect.

4. Each of the situations below involves an externality. Tell whether it is a positive or a negative externality, or both, and explain why a free market will overproduce or underproduce the good in question.
   (a) A business undertaking research and development projects
   (b) A business that discharges waste into a nearby river
   (c) A concert given in the middle of a large city park
   (d) An individual who smokes cigarettes in a meeting
5. When some activity causes a negative externality like pollution, would it be a good idea to ban the activity altogether? Why or why not? (Hint: Consider marginal costs and benefits.)
6. Do highways provide an example of a public good? Can you describe a situation in which the marginal costs of an additional driver on the highway might be high? How might society deal with this problem?
7. Many highways have designated car pool or high-occupancy lanes. Generally, only cars containing at least two people can use these lanes. Single drivers are fined heavily if they are caught using these lanes. With new technologies, it is possible to charge drivers using car pool lanes by recording identifying markings on the car and billing the owners. Would allowing single drivers to pay to use car pool lanes increase economic efficiency? Explain.
8. Group projects are often assigned in classes, with everyone in the group receiving the same grade for the project. Explain why a free-rider problem might arise in this situation.

Learning Goals

In this chapter, you will learn

1. Why monopolies produce too little at too high a price
2. The economic factors that lead to monopolies
3. How economists measure the degree of competition in a market
4. How monopolistic competition differs from perfect competition and pure monopoly
5. Why oligopolies need to think strategically
6. What factors lead to barriers to entry

Chapter 12

MONOPOLY, MONOPOLISTIC COMPETITION, AND OLIGOPOLY

As we discussed in Chapter 11, many markets in our economy are not well described by the perfectly competitive model. For years, AT&T was the only long-distance telephone carrier. Kodak controlled the market for film, and Alcoa the market for aluminum. Some firms so dominated a product that their brand name became synonymous with the product—for example, Kleenex, or Jell-O. These firms did not simply take the market price as given: they recognized that their actions could affect the market price. And the power to affect prices will influence a firm's decision about how much to produce.

In some industries, a handful of firms dominate the market, producing similar but not identical products: think of soft drinks (Coca-Cola, Pepsi, Canada Dry) or running shoes (Nike, Adidas, Reebok). Other industries may include a large number of firms, each producing a similar but slightly different product. When one firm raises its price a little—say, by 2 or 3 percent—it loses some customers, but it does not lose all customers, as would happen under perfect competition. If such a firm lowers its price by 2 or 3 percent, it gains additional customers but not the entire market.

Picking up where the discussion in Chapter 11 left off, this chapter explores markets in which there is either limited competition or no competition at all. It explains why output in these markets is typically lower than it would be under more competitive conditions, and it identifies the various factors that limit competition.

Monopoly Output

Economists' concerns about monopolies and other forms of restricted competition stem mainly from their observation that the output, or supply, of firms within these market structures is less than that of firms that face perfect competition, and prices are higher as well. To understand these concerns, we consider a monopolist that charges the same price to all its customers, and show how it decides on its level of output.

A monopolist, just like a competitive firm, will try to maximize profits. Both compare the marginal revenue and the marginal cost of producing more. For both, the basic principle for determining output is the same. Each produces at the output level at which marginal revenue equals marginal cost. The key difference lies in their marginal revenue. When a competitive firm decides on its output level, it takes the market price as given. Such a firm faces a horizontal demand curve—it can sell as much as it wants at the market price. In contrast, the monopolist is the sole supplier to the market, so its demand is the *market demand curve*. As we have already seen, market demand curves are downward sloping. The monopolist can increase its sales only by lowering its price.

Because the monopolist faces a downward-sloping demand curve, its marginal revenue is not equal to the market price. To understand why, we can break the marginal revenue a monopolist receives from producing one more unit into two separate components. First, the firm receives revenue from selling the additional output. This additional revenue is just the market price. But to sell more, the monopolist must reduce its price. Unless it does so, it cannot sell the extra output. Marginal revenue is the price it receives from the sale of the one additional unit *minus* the loss in revenue from the price reduction on all other units. Thus, for a monopolist, the marginal revenue for producing one extra unit is always less than that unit's price.

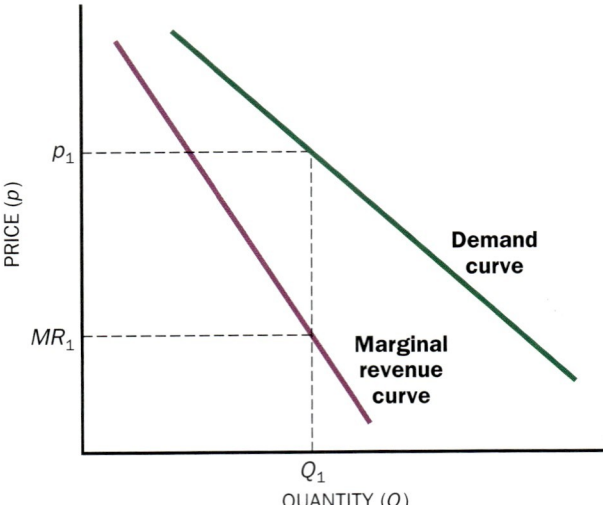

Figure 12.1

DEMAND CURVE AND MARGINAL REVENUE CURVE FOR A MONOPOLIST

Because the monopolist faces a downward-sloping demand curve, marginal revenue is less than price. To sell an extra unit of output, the monopolist must accept a lower price on every unit sold. At the quantity Q_1, the market price is p_1 and the marginal revenue is MR_1.

Figure 12.2

MARGINAL REVENUE EQUALS MARGINAL COST

A perfectly competitive firm gains or loses exactly the market price (p^*) when it changes the quantity produced by one unit. To maximize profits, the firm produces the quantity where marginal cost equals marginal revenue, which in the competitive case also equals price. Panel B shows the downward-sloping marginal revenue curve for a monopolist. A monopolist also chooses the level of quantity where marginal cost equals marginal revenue. For a monopolist, however, marginal revenue is lower than price.

In Chapter 7, we used a graph that showed the firm's marginal cost together with the market price to determine how much output the firm should produce to maximize profits (see Figure 7.3). We can use a similar graph to illustrate how much a monopoly will produce, once we recognize that for a monopolist, marginal revenue will be less than the market price.

Figure 12.1 shows the relationship between the demand curve and the marginal revenue of the monopolist. If the monopolist wants to sell the quantity Q_1, the market price must be p_1. Marginal revenue is less than price, so the marginal revenue curve lies below the demand curve. At the quantity Q_1, marginal revenue is MR_1, less than the price p_1.

Figure 12.2A shows the output decision of a competitive firm. Marginal revenue is just equal to the market price, p^*. The competitive firm produces at Q^*, where marginal cost is equal to the market price. Panel B shows the output decision of a monopolist. Marginal revenue is always less than price. The monopolist produces an output of Q_m, since at that output level, marginal cost is equal to marginal revenue. Both the monopolist and the competitive firm maximize profits by producing where marginal cost equals marginal revenue. The difference is that for the monopolist, marginal revenue is less than price.

Note that in the case of a monopolist, since marginal revenue is less than price and marginal revenue is equal to marginal cost, marginal cost is less than price. The price is what individuals are willing to pay for an extra unit of the product; it measures the marginal benefit to the consumer of an extra unit. Thus, the marginal benefit of an extra unit exceeds the marginal cost of producing that extra unit. This is the fundamental reason why monopolies reduce economic efficiency.

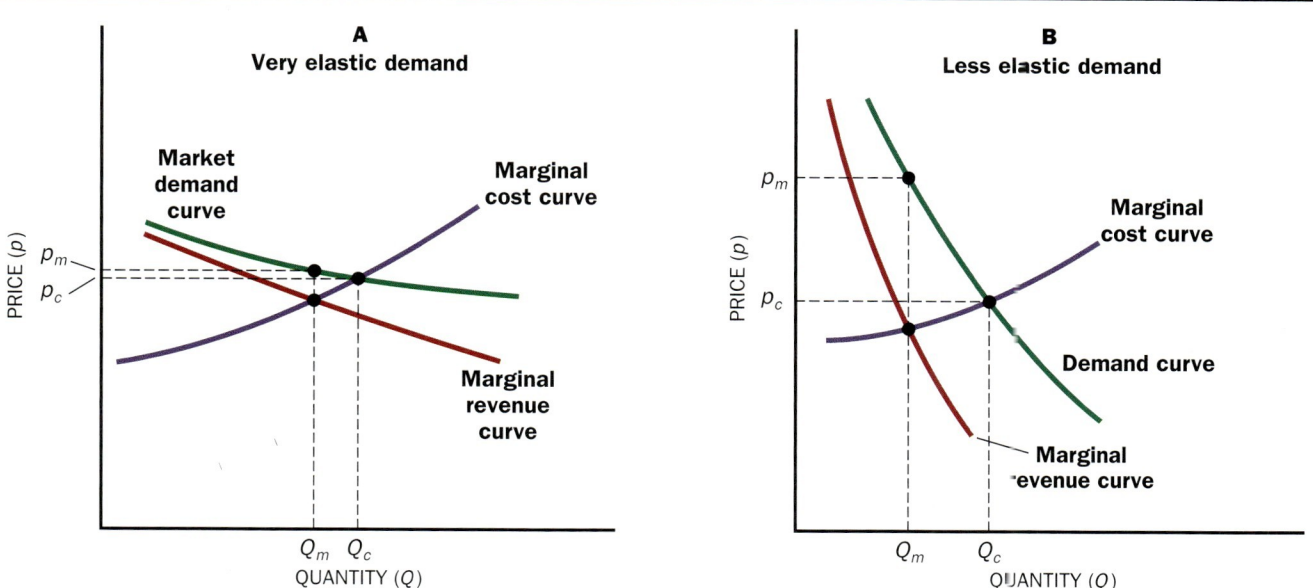

Figure 12.3
MONOPOLY AND THE ELASTICITY OF DEMAND

In panel A, a monopoly faces a very elastic market demand; prices therefore do not fall much as output increases, and monopoly price is not much more than the competitive price. In panel B, showing a monopoly that faces a less elastic market demand, price falls quite a lot as output increases, and the monopolist maximizes profit at a price substantially above the competitive price.

The extent to which output is curtailed depends on the magnitude of the difference between marginal revenue and price. This in turn depends on the shape of the demand curve. When demand curves are very elastic (relatively flat), prices do not fall much when output increases. As shown in Figure 12.3A, marginal revenue is not much less than price. The firm produces at Q_m, where marginal revenue equals marginal cost. Q_m is slightly less than the competitive output, Q_c, where price equals marginal cost. When demand curves are less elastic, as in panel B, prices may fall a considerable amount when output increases, and then the extra revenue the firm receives from producing an extra unit of output will be much less than the price received from selling that unit.

The larger the elasticity of demand, the smaller the discrepancy between marginal revenue and price.

Wrap-Up

THE FIRM'S SUPPLY DECISION

All firms maximize profits at the point where marginal revenue (the revenue from selling an extra unit of the product) equals marginal cost. For a competitive firm, marginal revenue equals price. For a monopoly, marginal revenue is less than price.

AN EXAMPLE: THE ABC-MENT COMPANY

Table 12.1 gives the demand curve facing the ABC-ment Company, which has a monopoly on the production of cement in its area. There is a particular price at which it can sell each level of output. As it lowers its price, it can sell more cement. Local builders will, for instance, use more cement and less wood and other materials in constructing a house.

For the sake of simplicity, we assume cement is sold in units of 1,000 cubic yards. At a price of $10,000 per unit (of 1,000 cubic yards), the firm sells 1 unit; at a price

TABLE 12.1

DEMAND CURVE FACING THE ABC-MENT COMPANY

Cubic yards (thousands)	Price	Total revenues	Marginal revenues	Total costs	Marginal costs
1	$10,000	$10,000	$8,000	$15,000	$2,000
2	$ 9,000	$18,000	$6,000	$17,000	$3,000
3	$ 8,000	$24,000	$4,000	$20,000	$4,000
4	$ 7,000	$28,000	$2,000	$24,000	$5,000
5	$ 6,000	$30,000	0	$29,000	$6,000
6	$ 5,000	$30,000		$35,000	

of $9,000, it sells 2 units; and at a price of $8,000, 3 units. The third column of the table shows the total revenues at each of these levels of production. The total revenues are just price multiplied by quantity. The marginal revenue from producing an extra unit (of 1,000 cubic yards) is just the difference between, say, the revenues received at 3 units and 2 units or 2 units and 1 unit. Note that in each case, the marginal revenue is less than the price.

Figure 12.4 shows the firm's demand and marginal revenue curves, using data from Table 12.1. At each level of output, the marginal revenue curve lies below the demand curve. As can be seen from the table, not only does price decrease as output increases, but so does marginal revenue.

The output at which marginal revenue equals marginal cost—the output chosen by the profit-maximizing monopolist—is denoted by Q_m. In our example, $Q_m = 4,000$ cubic yards. When the number of cubic yards increases from 3,000 to 4,000, the marginal revenue is $4,000, and so is the marginal cost. At this level of output, the price, p_m, is $7,000 (per 1,000 cubic yards), which is considerably in excess of marginal costs, $4,000. Total revenues, $28,000, are also in excess of total costs, $24,000.[1]

Figure 12.4

DEMAND AND MARGINAL REVENUE

At each level of output, the marginal revenue curve lies below the demand curve.

MONOPOLY PROFITS

Monopolists maximize their profits by setting marginal revenue equal to marginal cost. The total level of monopoly profits can be seen in two ways, as shown in Figure 12.5. Panel A shows total revenues and total costs (from Table 12.1) for each level of output of the ABC-ment Company. The difference between revenues and costs is profits—the distance between the two curves. This distance is maximized at the output $Q_m = 4,000$ cubic yards. We can see that at this level of output, profits are $4,000 ($28,000 − $24,000). Panel B calculates profits using the average cost diagram. Total profits are equal to the profit per unit multiplied by the number of units produced. The profit per unit is the difference between the unit price and the average cost, and total monopoly profits is the shaded area $ABCD$. Again, the sum is $4,000: ($7,000 − $6,000) × 4.

A monopolist enjoys an extra return because it has been able to reduce its output and increase its price from the level that would have prevailed under competition. This return is called a **pure profit**. Because these payments do not elicit greater effort or production on the part of the monopolist (in fact, they derive from the monopolist's *reducing* the output from what it would be under competition), they are also called **monopoly rents**.

---

[1] In this example, the firm is indifferent to the choice between producing 3,000 or 4,000 cubic yards. If the marginal cost of producing the extra output exceeds $4,000 by a little, then it will produce 3,000 cubic yards; if the marginal cost is a little less than $4,000, then it will produce 4,000 cubic yards.

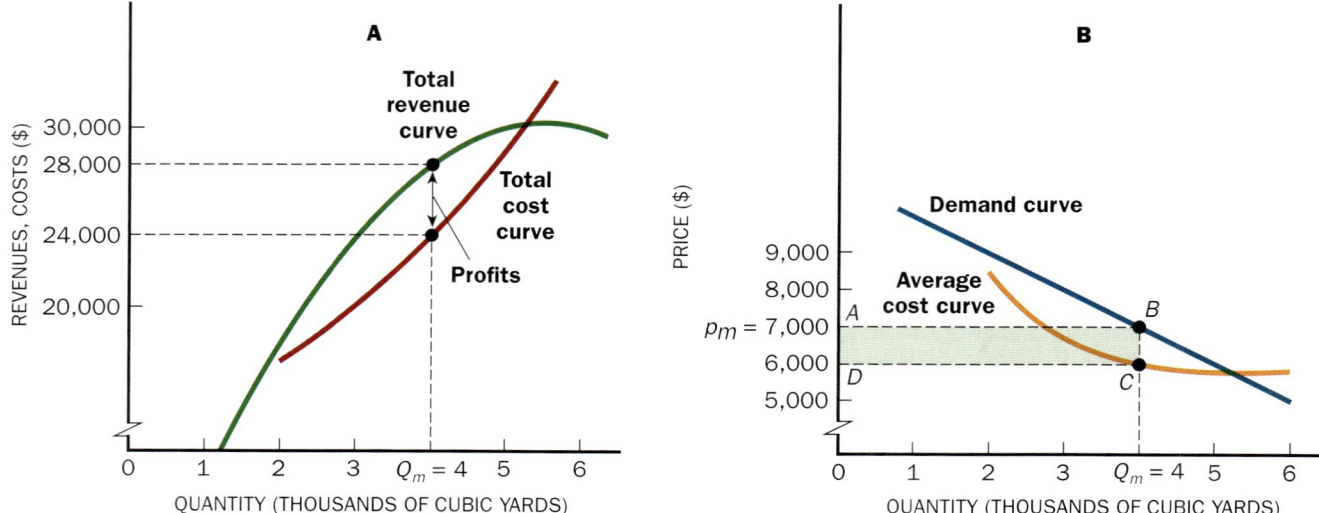

Figure 12.5

PRICE EXCEEDING AVERAGE COST LEADS TO PROFIT

Panel A shows profits to be the distance between the total revenue and total cost curves, maximized at the output Q_m = 4,000 cubic yards. Profits occur when the market price is above average cost, as in panel B, so that the company is (on average) making a profit on each unit it sells. Monopoly profits are the area $ABCD$, which is average profit per unit times the number of units sold.

PRICE DISCRIMINATION

The basic objective of monopolists is to maximize profits, and they accomplish this by setting marginal revenue equal to marginal cost, so price exceeds marginal cost. Monopolists can also engage in a variety of other practices to increase their profits. Among the most important is **price discrimination:** that is, charging different prices to different customers or in different markets.

Figure 12.6 shows a monopolist setting marginal revenue equal to marginal cost in the United States and in Japan. The demand curves in the two countries are different. Therefore, though marginal costs are the same, the firm will charge different prices for the same good in the two countries. (By contrast, in competitive markets, price equals marginal cost, so that regardless of the shape of the demand curve, price remains the same except for the different costs of delivering the good to each market.) Because prices in the two countries differ, middleman firms will enter the market, buying the product in the country with the low price and selling it in the other country. A company may attempt to thwart the middlemen—as many Japanese companies do—by, for instance, having distinct labels on the two products and refusing to provide service or honor any guarantees outside the country in which the good is originally delivered.

Within a country, a monopolist can also practice price discrimination *if* resale is difficult and *if* it can distinguish between buyers with high and low elasticities of demand. Because the retransmission of electricity is restricted, an electricity company can make its charge for each kilowatt hour depend on how much electricity the

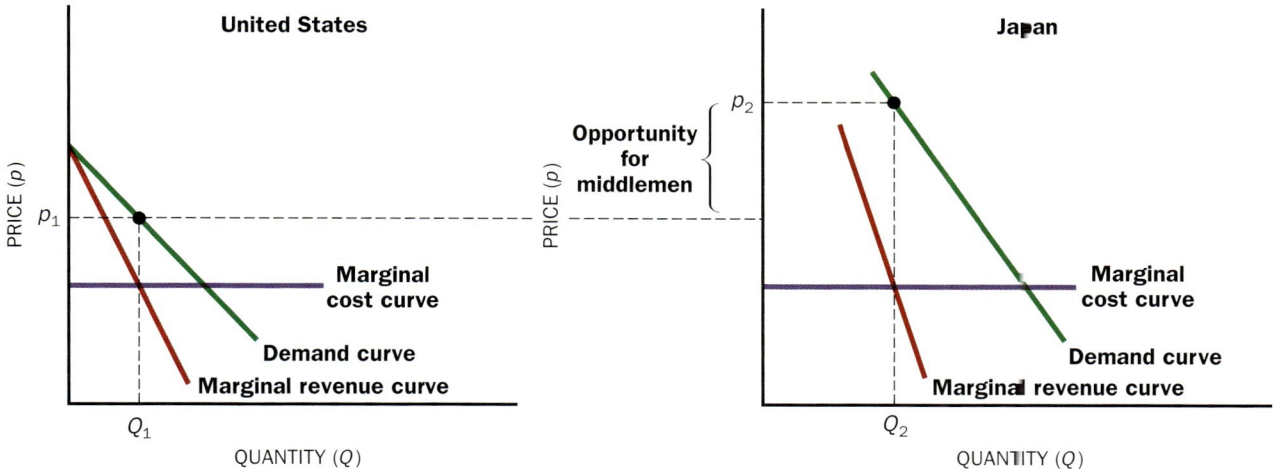

Figure 12.6
PRICE DISCRIMINATION

A monopolist that sells products in two different countries may find itself facing different demand curves. Though it sets marginal revenue equal to the same marginal cost in both countries, it will charge different prices.

customer uses. If the company worries that large customers charged the same high prices as its small customers might install their own electric generators, or switch to some other energy source, it may lower the price to them. An airline with a monopoly on a particular route may not know whether a customer is buying a ticket for business purposes or for a holiday trip, but by charging more for refundable tickets or tickets purchased at the last minute, it can effectively discriminate between business travelers and vacationers. Business customers are more likely to need the flexibility of a refundable ticket or to make their travel plans at the last minute, while vacationers have many alternatives. They can travel elsewhere, on another day, or by car or train. Such business practices enable the monopolist to enjoy greater profits than it could if it charged a single price in the market. Firms facing imperfect competition also engage in these practices, as we will see. Airlines again provide a telling example. Though the Robinson-Patman Act, which Congress passed in 1936, was designed to restrict price discrimination, it is only partially successful.

Economies of Scale and Natural Monopolies

The technology needed to produce a good can sometimes result in a market with only one or very few firms. For example, it would be inefficient to have two firms construct power lines on each street in a city, with one company delivering electricity to one house and another company to the house next door. Likewise, in most locales, there is only one gravel pit or concrete plant. These situations are called **natural monopolies.**

International Perspective
SOUTH AFRICA, AIDS, AND PRICE DISCRIMINATION

In perfectly competitive and well-functioning markets, goods cannot be sold at two different prices. Those who purchased the good at the low price could resell the good in the high-price market, making a pure profit. But in some markets, reselling the good is difficult; in others, governments prohibit or limit resale.

Research and testing account for the major cost of producing drugs. These are fixed costs that the drug manufacturers recoup by charging prices that are considerably in excess of the manufacturing costs. If they can practice price discrimination, the price they charge in each market will depend on the price elasticity *in that market*. But if they worry about resale, they may charge the same price in all markets.

Drug companies have developed some effective remedies against AIDS—not cures but treatments that can substantially prolong life. They charge $10,000 and more a year for treatment, a cost few in the developing countries can afford. The actual cost of manufacturing the drugs is much, much less. But the drug companies have been reluctant to sell the drugs at lower prices in these countries for two reasons. They worried that it would lower profits *in those countries;* and, probably more importantly, they worried about resale, which would lower profits in their own home markets (the United States, Europe). But charging high prices in, say, South Africa, the country with one of the highest incidence of HIV infection in the world, in effect condemned millions in that country to a premature death. Naturally, South Africa balked. It passed a law allowing the importation of drugs at lower prices, drugs possibly made by manufacturers that had ignored standard patent protections. The drug companies sued on the grounds that the law violated their basic economic rights. But protesters around the world argued that intellectual property rights must be designed to balance the rights of potential users and the rights of producers, that the benefits to the poor in Africa far outweighed the loss in profits. In April 2001 they successfully pressured the drug companies to drop their suit against South Africa.

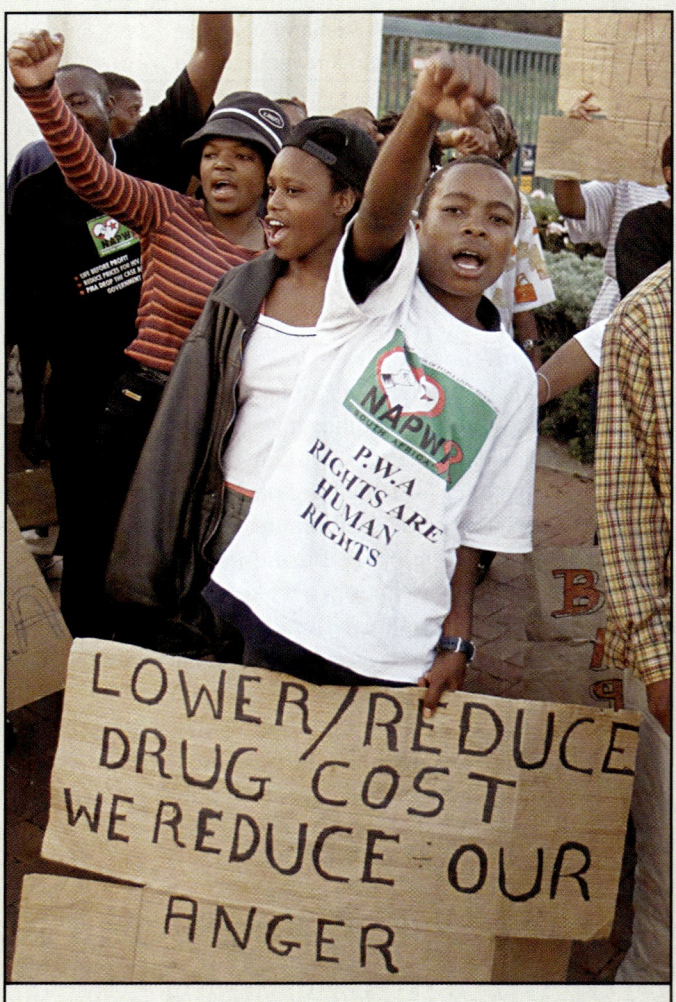

Protesters in South Africa objected to the high price of AIDS drugs.

A natural monopoly occurs whenever the average costs of production for a single firm decline as output increases up to levels beyond those likely to emerge in the market. When the average costs of production fall as the scale of production increases, we say there are economies of scale, a concept first introduced in Chapter 6. In Figure 12.7, the demand curve facing a monopoly intersects the average cost curve at an output level at which average costs are still declining. At large enough outputs, average costs might start to increase; but that level of output is irrelevant to the actual market equilibrium. For instance, firms in the cement industry have U-shaped average cost curves, and the level of output at which costs are minimized is quite high. Accordingly, in smaller, isolated communities, there is a natural monopoly in cement.

A natural monopolist is protected by the knowledge that it can undercut its potential rivals. Since entrants typically are smaller and average costs decline with size, the average costs of new firms are higher. Therefore, the monopolist feels relatively immune from the threat of entry. So long as it does not have that worry, it acts like any other monopolist, setting marginal revenue equal to marginal cost.

In some cases, even when a market is occupied by a natural monopolist, competition can still exist *for the market*. Competition to be that single supplier is so keen that price is bid down to average cost, at p_r. If the firm were to charge a slightly higher price, another firm would enter the market, steal the entire market with its lower price, and still make a profit. Markets for which there is such fierce competition are said to be *contestable*. Contestability requires that sunk costs be low or zero. If they are significant, a firm that entered the market could be undercut by the incumbent firm, which might lower price to its marginal cost (since so long as price exceeds marginal cost, it makes a profit on the last unit sold). The lower prices that result are sometimes referred to as a *price war,* and the result of a price war is that the entrant encounters a loss—when set equal to marginal cost, price is substantially below average cost. The entrant knows that even if it leaves at this juncture, it loses its sunk costs, which are, by definition, the expenditures that are not recovered when the firm shuts down. But anticipating this outcome, the potential rival does not enter the market. Thus, despite sustained current profits, other firms may choose not to enter the market. In fact, sunk costs appear to be sufficiently important that few markets are close to perfectly contestable. Even in the airline industry, where sunk costs are relatively low—airlines can fly new planes into markets that seem profitable or out of markets that seem unprofitable—they act as a sufficiently large barrier to entry that there are sustained profits in certain routes, especially those out of airline hubs (like American Airlines' hub in Dallas–Fort Worth). Just as most markets are not perfectly competitive, so most natural monopolies are not perfectly contestable, though the threat of competition (or potential competition) may limit the extent to which an incumbent monopolist exercises its monopoly power.

Whether a particular industry is a natural monopoly depends on the size of the output at which average costs are minimized relative to the size of the market.

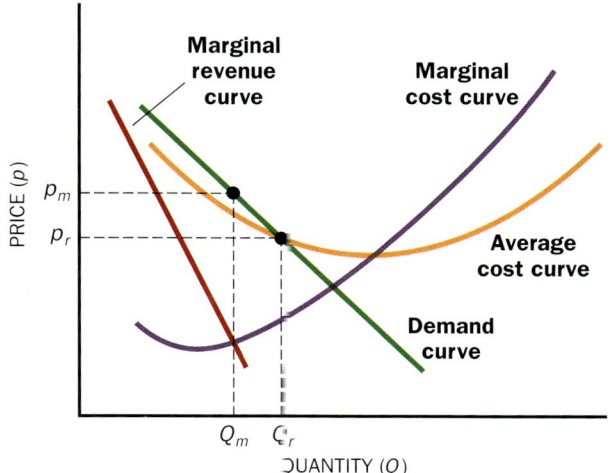

Figure 12.7

NATURAL MONOPOLY

In a natural monopoly, average cost curves are downward sloping in the relevant range of output. A firm can charge the monopoly price p_m. If the market is *contestable*, potential competition prevents the firm from charging a price higher than average costs. The equilibrium price is p_r.

The size of the market depends largely on transportation costs. If, somehow, the cost of transporting cement were lowered to close to zero, then there would be a national cement market. Many firms then would be competing against each other—the size of the national market is far larger than the output at which average costs are minimized.

The size of output at which costs are minimized depends in part on the magnitude of fixed costs. Since research is a fixed cost, its growing importance in many industries has increased the size of output at which average costs are minimized. At the same time, new technologies and business arrangements are enabling many firms to reduce their fixed costs. Today, firms need not have a personnel department for routine matters like paying checks; they can contract for such services as needed.

Because both technology and transportation costs can change over time, the status of an industry as a natural monopoly also can change. Telephone service used to be a natural monopoly. Telephone messages were transmitted over wires, and installing and using duplicate lines would have been inefficient. As the demand for telephone services increased, and as alternative technologies such as satellites and cell phones developed, telephone services ceased to be a natural monopoly. Today, consumers in most communities can choose from among several firms that provide telephone service.

Assessing the Degree of Competition

In the real world, few industries match the extreme cases of monopoly and perfect competition. Usually industries have some degree of competition. How then should that degree of competition in an industry be assessed?

One way to do this is to ask, What will happen if a firm in that industry raises its price? How much will sales of its product fall? In other words, what is the elasticity of demand for the firm's output? The lower the elasticity of demand—the less the quantity demanded falls when price is increased—the greater the firm's market power.

Two factors affect the elasticity of the firm's demand curve and, therefore, its market power. The first is the number of firms in the industry—more generally, how concentrated production is within a few firms. The second is how different the goods produced by the various firms in the industry are.

NUMBER OF FIRMS IN THE INDUSTRY

Competition is likely to be greater when there are many firms in an industry (textiles, shoes) than when a few companies dominate (home refrigerators and freezers, greeting cards, soft drinks). Table 12.2 gives the percentage of output that is

Table 12.2

DEGREE OF COMPETITION IN VARIOUS INDUSTRIES

	Market share of top 4 firms (percent)
Motor vehicle manufacturers	
Book publishers	41.8
Grocery stores	30.9
Electronic shopping and mail-order houses	19.0
Air transportaation	18.7
Furniture stores	8.1
Truck transportation	7.6
Florists	1.7

SOURCE: 2002 Economic Census (www.census.gov/epcd/www/concentration.html).

produced by the top four firms in a variety of industries ranging from books to furniture. This fraction is called the **four-firm concentration ratio,** one of several measures used to study industry concentration. When the four-firm percentage is high, as in the automobile or book publishing industry, companies have considerable market power. When it is low, as in the case of furniture or florists, market power is low; each firm faces a practically horizontal demand curve.[2]

PRODUCT DIFFERENTIATION

The amount of competition also depends on the extent of differences between the products of an industry. In some industries, the goods produced are essentially identical, as in the case of agricultural goods such as wheat and corn. More typically, the firms in an industry with imperfect competition produce goods that are **imperfect substitutes**—goods sufficiently similar that they can be used for many of the same purposes, but different in ways that reflect consumer preferences. Kellogg's Corn Flakes and the store brand may look alike, but more people purchase the Kellogg's version, even though it is more expensive. Many of the goods people buy belong to clusters of imperfect substitutes: beverages (Coke, Pepsi, and store-brand colas), cars (Toyota Camry, Honda Accord, Ford Taurus, and other four-door sedans), clothing (Land's End, L.L. Bean, and Eddie Bauer), computers, cameras, telephone service, building materials, and many more. Economists refer to this phenomenon as **product differentiation.**

Because product differentiation is a source of market power, firms devote considerable effort to producing goods that are slightly different from those of their

---

[2] In both theory and practice, a critical issue in evaluating the extent of competition is defining the relevant market.

e-Insight

NETWORK EXTERNALITIES, THE NEW ECONOMY, AND MONOPOLY POWER

Network externalities arise whenever an individual benefits from an increase in the number of individuals that are part of the network. A telephone is not much use if there is no one at the other end of the line. The value of a telephone is increased as more people have telephones.

Assume there are two different telephone systems that do not interconnect. A new subscriber having to decide between them is likely to sign up with the one with the larger number of subscribers. Thus, a firm that is initially in the lead will, over time, increase its dominance; an entrant will find it difficult to make headway. And this in turn will enable the dominant company to exercise monopoly power. It can charge a price considerably in excess of its costs of production without worrying about a new entrant coming in and stealing its customers.

Government can limit the ability of this firm to abuse its monopoly power by imposing restrictions—for example, by insisting that the dominant telephone network allow an entrant to interconnect, so that the subscribers in the new network can talk to the subscribers of the dominant network. Effective enforcement of these restrictions may be difficult, however; for example, the dominant firm might provide low-quality interconnectivity but blame the problems on the entrant.

The problem of network externalities is common in the new economy. If more people use the Windows operating system, then independent software developers will write more applications that work with Windows. If relatively few people use Apple's operating system (or Unix), then developers have little incentive to write software that works on that operating system. But if there are many applications that work on Windows, and few that work on Apple, customers will be induced to employ Windows. In fact, Windows has become the dominant operating system: more than 90 percent of all personal computers use it.

But such market dominance almost invites abuse, and Microsoft evidently found the invitation difficult to resist. Such abuse can take a number of forms. Many in the software industry realized that Microsoft's market power would be reduced if they could create a computer language that would enable programs to work on many alternative operating systems with equal, or almost equal, effectiveness. Sun Microsystems developed Java to do just that. Had this effort been successful, it would have broken the network externality. Microsoft sought to frustrate these efforts by developing a version of Java that was specifically adapted to Windows.

Another innovation that might have served as a platform for other applications and been applicable across operating systems was Netscape, an early entrant into Internet browsers. Microsoft sought to quash Netscape, not only by developing its own competing browser but also by delivering its browser free and insisting that computer manufacturers who purchased its operating system (to be installed on the computers they sell) *not* install Netscape as well. (This stipulation is called an *exclusionary practice*.) Microsoft's behavior led to legal suits being filed against it by the U.S. Justice Department, as well as by several individual states. As a result of these challenges, Microsoft agreed to stop some of its abusive practices; however, the company has faced additional legal problems in Europe, where the European Union Commission has found the company guilty of exploiting its monopoly power in the market for media players. Microsoft must now offer a version of its Windows XP operating system in Europe that does not include its media player software.

competitors. When goods are perfect substitutes, individuals will choose whichever is cheapest. In an imaginary world where all brands of cornflakes really are perfect substitutes for all consumers, they would all sell at the same price. By contrast, if most consumers view the different brands as imperfect substitutes, the demand curve facing each firm will be downward sloping, which means that each firm has some degree of market power.

Equilibrium with Monopolistic Competition

In most industries there is some but limited competition. The number of firms in the industry is perhaps the most important determinant of the nature of competition. If the fixed costs are large—not so large as to result in a single firm but sufficiently large that there are only two, three, or four firms—then the outcome is a natural oligopoly. We discuss oligopolies in the next section; we here consider the case in which fixed costs are relatively small—sufficiently small that the numerous firms drive profits to zero, but sufficiently large that only a single firm produces any single product. However, because these products are *close* but not perfect substitutes, each firm faces a downward-sloping demand curve. This is the case of monopolistic competition, first analyzed by Edward Chamberlin of Harvard University in 1933.

The market for women's dress shoes is one such industry. The producers include Steve Madden, Bass, Diverse, Naturalizer, Bruno Magli, Nine West, and many more. No two firms produce exactly the same shoes, but the shoes made by the different companies are close substitutes. Each producer faces a downward-sloping demand curve, but each firm has a small portion of the overall market. The market for fine pens provides another example. There are many manufacturers (Montblanc, Parker, Cross, Aurora, Pelikan, etc.). Each produces pens that differ from the pens of the others, each has a downward-sloping demand curve, and each is small relative to the total market for fine writing instruments.

Figure 12.8 illustrates a market in which there is monopolistic competition. Assume initially that all firms are charging the same price, say p_1. If one firm were to charge a slightly lower price, it would steal some customers away from other businesses. And if it should raise its price above that of its rivals, it would lose customers to them. Each firm assumes that the prices charged by other firms will remain unchanged as it changes its price or the quantity it produces. The demand curve facing each firm is thus the one shown in the figure.

In deciding how much to produce, the firm sets marginal revenue equal to marginal cost. The market equilibrium is (p_1, Q_1), with marginal revenue equaling marginal cost. In the equilibrium depicted in the figure, price exceeds average costs. One can think of this situation as a sort of minimonopoly, where each firm has a monopoly on its own brand name or its own store location.

But if existing firms are earning monopoly profits, there is an incentive for new competitors to enter the market until profits are driven to zero, as in the perfectly competitive model. *This is the vital distinction between monopolies and firms in monopolistic competition.* In both cases, firms face downward-sloping demand curves. In both cases, they set marginal revenue equal to marginal cost. But monopolistic competition raises no barriers to entry, which continues so long as profits are positive. As firms enter, each firm's share of the industry demand is reduced. The demand curve of each firm thus shifts to the left, as depicted in panel B. This process continues until the demand curve just touches the average cost curve, at point (p_e, Q_e), where profits are zero.

The figure also shows the firm's marginal revenue and marginal cost curves. As we have said, the firm sets its marginal revenue equal to its marginal cost. This equality

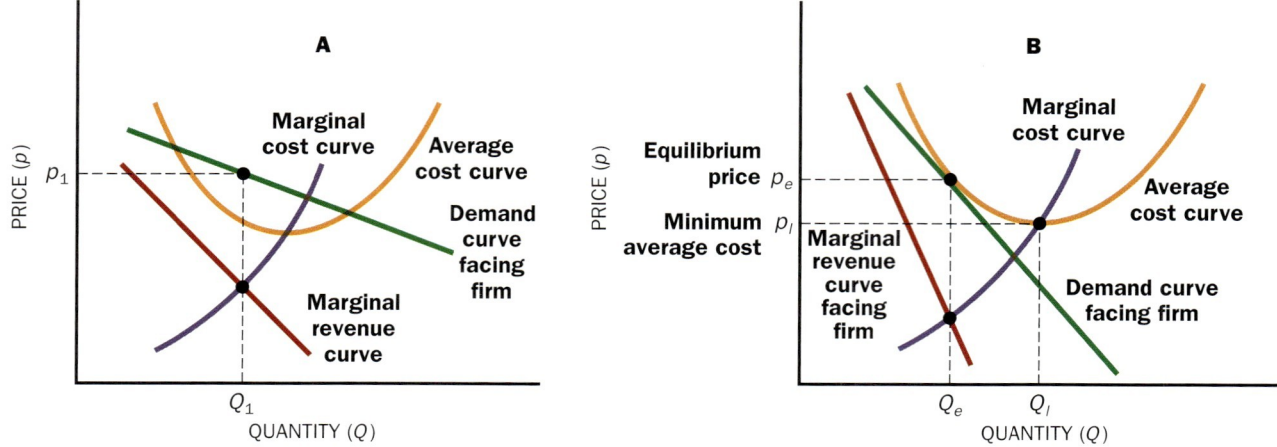

Figure 12.8

PROFIT MAXIMIZING FOR A MONOPOLISTIC COMPETITOR

A monopolistic competitor chooses the quantity it will produce by setting marginal revenue equal to marginal cost (Q_1), and then selling that quantity for the price given on its demand curve (p_1). In panel A, the price charged is above average cost, and the monopolistic competitor is making a profit, enticing other firms to enter the market. As firms enter, the share of the market demand of each firm is reduced, and the demand curve facing each firm shifts to the left. Entry continues until the demand curve just touches the average cost curve (panel B). When the firm produces the quantity Q_e, it just breaks even; there is no incentive for either entry or exit.

occurs at exactly the level of output at which the demand curve is tangent to the average cost curve. At any other point, average costs exceed price, so profits are negative. Only at this point are profits zero. Accordingly, this is the profit-maximizing output.

The monopolistic competition equilibrium has some interesting characteristics. Note that in equilibrium, price and average costs exceed the minimum average costs at which the goods could be produced. *Less is produced at a higher price.* But there is a trade-off here. Whereas in the perfectly competitive market every product was a perfect substitute for every other one, the world of monopolistic competition offers variety in the products available. People value variety and are willing to pay a higher price to obtain it. Thus, that goods are sold at a price above the minimum average cost does not necessarily indicate that the economy is inefficient.

Oligopolies

In oligopolies there are just a few firms, so each worries about how its rivals will react to anything it does. This is true of the airline, cigarette, aluminum, and automobile industries, as well as a host of others.

If an oligopolist lowers its price, it takes the chance that rivals will do the same and deprive it of any competitive advantage. Worse still, a competitor may react to a price cut by engaging in a price war and cutting the price still further. Different oligopolies behave quite differently. The oligopolist is always torn between its desire to outwit competitors and the knowledge that by cooperating with other oligopolists to reduce output, it will earn a portion of the higher industry profits.

A firm that is part of an oligopolistic market must think *strategically*. In deciding what to do, it faces four key questions: (1) Should it cooperate with other firms or compete? When firms cooperate rather than compete, economists say the firms are *colluding*. (2) If it cannot collude explicitly (because there are laws barring such behavior), how can it reduce the effectiveness of competition through *restrictive practices* or other means? (3) How can it deter entry? Like a monopolist, it knows that the entry of other firms will erode profits. (4) How will rivals react to whatever it does? Will they, for instance, match price decreases? In the next four subsections, we take up each of these questions in turn.

Note the contrast between both competitive and monopolistic competitive models on the one hand and pure monopoly on the other. In the latter, there is no competition, hence no need to take actions to restrict competition; in the former, by assumption, there are so many competing firms that attempts to restrict competition are fruitless.

COLLUSION

In some cases, oligopolists enter into **collusion** to maximize their profits. In effect, they act jointly as if they were a single monopoly, and split up the resulting profits. The prevalence of collusion was long ago noted by Adam Smith, the founder of modern economics: "People of the same trade seldom meet together, even for merriment and diversion, but the conversation ends in a conspiracy against the public, or in some contrivance to raise prices."[3] A group of companies that formally operate in collusion is called a **cartel.** The Organization of Petroleum Exporting Countries (OPEC), for instance, acts collusively to restrict the output of oil, thereby raising oil prices and hence the profits of member countries.

In the late nineteenth century, two or more railroads ran between many major cities. When they competed vigorously, profits were low. So it did not take them long to discover that if they acted collusively, they could raise profits by raising prices.

In the steel industry at the turn of the century, Judge Elbert H. Gary, who headed the U.S. Steel Company, the largest of the firms, regularly presided over Sunday dinners for prominent members of his industry at which steel prices were set. In the 1950s, a cartel that included General Electric and Westinghouse colluded in setting the prices of electrical generators. And in the 1990s, the government uncovered price-fixing by Archer Daniel Midland (ADM).

But the mere fact that collusion is illegal inhibits it. Because the members of the cartel cannot get together to discuss price-fixing or restricting output, they typically must rely on *tacit collusion*—each restricting output with an understanding that the others will too. They cannot sign a contract that can be enforced in a court of law, simply because collusion to fix prices is illegal; hence they must rely on self-enforcement, which can be difficult and costly. Moreover, their artificially high prices—well in excess of the marginal cost of production—tempt each firm to cheat, to expand production. The members of the cartel may try to discipline those that cheat. They may even incur losses in the short run to punish the cheater, in the belief

---

[3]*Wealth of Nations* (1776), Book One, Chapter X, Part II.

OPEC leaders met in Caracas, Venezuela, in September 2000.

that the long-run gains from "cooperation" (that is, collusion) are worth the temporary sacrifice. For instance, if a firm cuts its price or expands its output *and the cheating is detected,* the other firms in the cartel may match, or even more than match, the price cuts or capacity expansions. The cheater ends up not only with lower profits than anticipated but also with lower profits than it would have obtained had it cooperated.

A variety of *facilitating practices* can make collusion easier by making punishment for cheating easier. Some industries maintain cooperative arrangements—one firm, for instance, may draw on the inventories of another, in the case of an unanticipated shortfall—from which cheaters are excluded.

Sometimes, policies that *seem* to be highly competitive actually have exactly the opposite effect. Consider the "meeting-the-competition clauses" by which some members of the oligopoly commit themselves to charging no more than any competitor. This sounds highly competitive. But think about it from the perspective of rival firms. Assume one firm is selling for $100 an item that costs only $90 to produce, so it is making a $10 profit. Consider another firm that would like to steal some customers away. It would be willing to sell the item for $95, undercutting its rival. But then it reasons that if it cuts its price, it will not gain any customers, since its rival has already guaranteed to match the lower price. Further, the second firm knows that it will make less money on each sale to its current customers. Price-cutting simply does not pay. Thus, a practice that appears highly competitive in fact facilitates collusion.

Circumstances are always changing, necessitating adjustments in outputs and prices. The cartel must coordinate these changes. The illegality of collusion makes this coordination particularly difficult, all the more so since the interests of the members of the cartel may not coincide—some may find their costs lowered more than others and therefore seek a greater expansion of output than others. Were there to be perfect collusion, in which industry profits were maximized, some might have to contract production and others expand it, with profits of some firms actually decreasing and others increasing. The gainers could, in principle, make payoffs to the losers and still be better off. However, these side payments are also illegal, and thus must be subtle and hard to detect if they occur at all. While perfect coordination is seldom possible, some industries have found a partial solution by allowing one firm to play the role of the *price leader*. In the airline industry, American Airlines for a long time acted as a price leader. As it increased or decreased prices, others followed suit.

Using Game Theory to Model Collusion Economists apply a branch of mathematics called **game theory** to study collusion among oligopolists. Its basic aim is to shed light on strategic choices—that is, on how people or organizations behave when they expect their actions to influence the behavior of others. For instance, when executives at a major airline decide to change fares for flights on a certain route, they have to consider how their competitors might respond to the price change. And the competitors, when deciding how to respond, have to consider how the first airline might answer in turn. These are strategic decisions, just like those typical of players in various sorts of games, such as chess, football, or poker.

Using game theory, the economist views the participants in a given situation as players in a game, whose rules define certain moves. The outcomes of the game—what each participant receives—are referred to as its payoffs, and they depend on what each player does. Each participant in the game chooses a strategy; he decides what moves to make. In games in which each player has the chance to make more than one move (there is more than one round, or period), moves can depend on what has happened in previous periods. Game theory begins with the assumption that each player in the game is rational and knows that her rival is rational. Each is trying to maximize his own payoff. The theory then tries to predict what each player will do. The actions depend on the rules of the game and the payoffs.

One example of such a game is called the **prisoner's dilemma.** Two prisoners, A and B, alleged to be conspirators in a crime, are put into separate rooms. A police officer goes into each room and makes a little speech: "Now here's the situation. If your partner confesses and you remain silent, you'll get five years in prison. But if your partner confesses and you confess also, you'll only get three years. On the other hand, perhaps your partner remains silent. If you're quiet also, we can send you to prison for only one year. But if your partner remains silent and you confess, we'll let you out in three months. So if your partner confesses, you are better off confessing, and if your partner doesn't confess, you are better off confessing. Why not confess?" This deal is offered to both prisoners.

Figure 12.9 shows the results of this deal. The upper left box, for example, shows the result if both A and B confess. The upper right box shows the result if prisoner A confesses but prisoner B remains silent. And so on.

From the combined standpoint of the two prisoners, the best option is clearly that they both remain silent and each serves one year. But the self-interest of each individual prisoner says that confession is best, whether his partner confesses or not. However, if they both follow their self-interest and confess, they both end up

Figure 12.9

THE PRISONER'S DILEMMA

Both prisoners would be better off if both remained silent, but their individual incentives lead each one to confess. From the standpoint of prisoner A, confessing is the better strategy if prisoner B confesses, and confessing is the better strategy if prisoner B remains silent. The same holds for prisoner B.

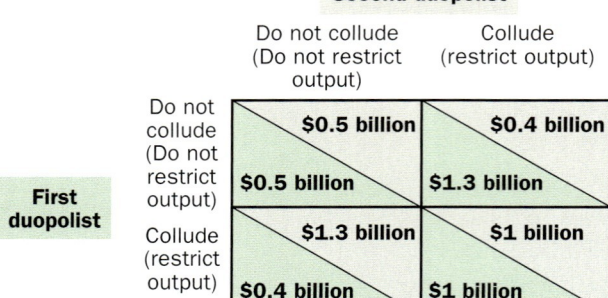

Figure 12.10

THE PROBLEM OF COLLUSION AS A PRISONER'S DILEMMA

The payoffs for the duopolists delineate a prisoner's dilemma. Both firms would be better off if both colluded (restricted output), but their individual incentives lead each to not collude (not restrict output).

worse off, each serving three years. The prisoner's dilemma is a simple game in which both parties are made worse off by independently following their own self-interest. Both would be better off if they could get together to agree on a story, and to threaten the other if he deviated from the story.

The prisoner's dilemma game can be used to illustrate the problem of collusion among oligopolists. Let us work with the example of a *duopoly*, which is a market with two firms. Figure 12.10 shows the level of profits of each if both collude and restrict output (both get $1 billion), if neither restricts output (both get $0.5 billion), or if one restricts output and the other does not (the one that does not gets $1.3 billion, the one that does gets $0.4 billion). As each firm thinks through the consequences of restricting output, it will quickly realize that if the other firm restricts output, its best strategy is to expand output; and if the other firm fails to restrict output, its best strategy is also to expand output. Thus the firm finds that regardless of what the other does, it pays to expand output rather than to restrict it. Since the other firm will reach the same conclusion, both will conclude that it does not pay to restrict output. Hence, both will expand output; they do not collude to restrict output.

The central point is that even though the firms see that they could both be better off colluding, the individual incentive to cheat dictates the strategy that each follows.

So far we have considered the prisoner's dilemma when each player makes only a single move to complete the game. But if firms interact over time, then they have additional ways to try to enforce their agreement. For example, suppose each oligopolist announces that it will refrain from cutting prices as long as its rival does. But if the rival cheats on the collusive agreement, then the first oligopolist will respond by increasing production and lowering prices. This strategy is called *tit for tat*. If this threat is credible—as it may well be, especially after it has been carried out a few times—the rival may decide that it is more profitable to cooperate and keep production low than to cheat. In the real world, such simple strategies may play an important role in ensuring that firms do not compete too vigorously in markets that have only three or four dominant firms.

The commonness and success of such strategies have puzzled economists. The logic of game theory suggests that these approaches would not be effective. Consider what happens if the two firms expect to compete in the same market over the next ten years, after which time a new product is expected to come along and shift the entire configuration of the industry. It will pay each firm to cheat in the tenth year, when there is no possibility of retaliation, because the industry will be completely altered in the next year. Now consider what happens in the ninth year. Both firms can figure out that it will not pay either one of them to cooperate in the tenth year. But if they are not going to cooperate in the tenth year anyway, then the *threat* of not cooperating in the future is completely ineffective. Hence in the ninth year, each firm will reason that it pays to cheat on the collusive agreement by producing more than the agreed-on amount. Collusion breaks down in the ninth year. As they reason backward through time, this logic will lead collusion to break down almost immediately. However, if there is no certain date at which the collusion will end, it is possible for collusion to carry on indefinitely. Whenever the firms contemplate cheating, on any agreement to collude, each will compare the initial increase in profits from cheating with the future reduction in profits when the other firm retaliates. The firms therefore may decide to continue colluding.

It is not just among traditional business firms that collusion occurs. A few years ago, the U.S. Justice Department investigated collusion by a group of colleges and universities, including several Ivy League schools. The claim was that these schools colluded to set financial aid awards. The schools had agreed to all offer the same scholarship package to students who had been accepted by more than one of the schools. Thus, the colleges were agreeing not to use larger financial awards to compete for these students. Their collusion helped the schools hold down their costs. In 1991, the eight Ivy League universities signed an agreement with the Justice Department in which they agreed to no longer cooperate in setting their financial aid offers.

RESTRICTIVE PRACTICES

If members of an oligopoly could easily get together and collude, they would. Their joint profits would increase. We have seen, however, that there are significant impediments to collusion. As a result, oligopolists typically resort to other ways of increasing profits. One approach is to restrict competition.

Firms engage in a number of **restrictive practices** to limit competition. Some were made illegal by the Federal Trade Commission Act of 1914. While these practices may not increase profits for the firms quite as successfully as the collusive arrangements discussed above, they do raise prices. In some cases, consumers may be even worse off than under outright collusion. Many restrictive practices are aimed at the wholesalers and retailers who sell a producer's goods. When one firm buys or sells the products of another, the two companies are said to have a "vertical" relationship. Such restrictive practices are called *vertical restrictions,* in distinction to the price-fixing arrangements among producers or among wholesalers selling in the same market, which are referred to as *horizontal restrictions*.

One example of a vertical restriction is the use of *exclusive territories:* a producer gives a wholesaler or retailer the exclusive right to sell a good within a certain region. Beer and soft drink producers, for instance, typically give their distributors exclusive territories. Coca-Cola manufactures its own syrup, which it then sells to bottlers who add the soda water. Coca-Cola gives these bottlers exclusive territories, so the supermarkets in a particular area can buy Coke from only one place. A store in Michigan cannot buy the soft drink from Coca-Cola bottlers in New Jersey, even if the price in New Jersey is lower. In 1979, Indiana passed a law prohibiting exclusive territories for beer within the state. As a result, beer prices there are substantially lower (adjusting for other differences) than in other states.

Another restrictive practice is *exclusive dealing:* a producer insists that any firm selling its products not sell those of its rivals. When you go into an Exxon gas station, for instance, you can be sure you are buying gas refined by the Exxon Corporation, not Texaco or Sunoco. Like most refiners, Exxon requires stations that want to sell only its brand of gasoline.

A third example of a restrictive practice is *tie-ins,* which force a customer who buys one product to buy another. Mortgage companies, for example, used to insist that those who obtained mortgages from them purchase fire insurance as well. Nintendo designs its console so that it can be used with only Nintendo games. In effect, it forces a tie-in sale between the console and the software. In the early days of computers, IBM designed its computers so that they could be used only with IBM "peripherals," such as printers.

A final example is *resale price maintenance*. Under this restrictive practice, a producer insists that any retailer selling his product must sell it at the "list" price. Like exclusive territories, it is designed to reduce competitive pressures at the retail level.

Consequences of Restrictive Practices Firms engaging in restrictive practices *claim* they are doing so not because they wish to restrict competition but because they want to enhance economic efficiency. Exclusive territories, they argue, provide companies with a better incentive to "cultivate" their territory. Exclusive dealing contracts, they say, provide incentives for firms to focus their attention on one producer's goods.

Despite these claims, restrictive practices often reduce economic efficiency. Exclusive territories for beer, for example, have limited the ability of very large firms, with stores in many different territories, to set up a central warehouse and distribute beer to their stores more efficiently. And regardless of whether they enhance or hurt efficiency, restrictive practices may lead to higher prices by limiting competitive pressures.

Some restrictive practices work by increasing the costs of, or otherwise impeding, one's rivals. In the 1980s, several major airlines developed computer reservation systems that they sold at very attractive prices to travel agents. If the primary goal of these systems had been to serve consumers, they would have been designed to display all the departures near the time the passenger desired. Instead, each airline's system provided a quick display for only its own flights—United's, for instance, focused on United flights—although with additional work, the travel agent could find out the flights of other airlines. Airlines benefited from these computer systems not because they best met the needs of the consumer, but because they put competitors at a disadvantage and thereby reduced the effectiveness of competition.

An exclusive dealing contract between a producer and a distributor also exemplifies how one firm may benefit from hurting its rivals. The contract might force a rival producer to set up its own distribution system, at great cost, when the already-existing distributor might have been able to undertake the distribution of the second product at relatively low incremental cost. The exclusive dealing contract increases total resources spent on distribution.

Courts have responded inconsistently to these and similar practices—in some circumstances ruling that they are illegal because they reduce competition, while in others allowing them, having been persuaded that they represent reasonable business practices.

> **Wrap-Up**
>
> ## FORMS OF RESTRICTIVE PRACTICES
>
> Exclusive territories
> Exclusive dealing
> Tie-ins
> Resale price maintenance

ENTRY DETERRENCE

Oligopolists use restrictive practices to reduce competition and thereby increase profits. Another way to reduce competition is to prevent other firms from entering the market. This is called **entry deterrence**.

Entry deterrence is intended to limit the number of firms—the fewer the firms, presumably the weaker the competitive pressure. Natural barriers to entry, such as the large fixed costs discussed earlier in the chapter, put some limits on competition, but they are not so impermeable as to block it entirely. Businesses already in the market often try to supplement the natural barriers by *strategic barriers*—that is, acting in ways that make the market unattractive for new firms.

The issue of entry barriers is at the center of the theory of monopoly and oligopoly, which must explain why new firms don't enter the market despite the pull of profits. What are the barriers to their entry? Thus, our discussion of entry deterrence applies to both monopolies and oligopolies.

Government Policies as Barriers to Entry Many early monopolies were established by governments. For example, in the seventeenth century, the British

---

Internet Connection
KEEPING TRACK OF OLIGOPOLIES

The Web site www.oligopolywatch.com provides numerous articles and news stories about oligopolies. Many of the stories report on the latest mergers and acquisitions by large corporations, describing how these often serve to reduce the number of sellers in a market to just a few different producers. For example, more than 80 percent of all the music titles produced in the United States are controlled by just five major record label conglomerates: Time Warner, EMI Group, Universal Music Group (UMG), Bertelsmann Music Group (BMG), and Sony. In 2000, Time Warner and EMI announced plans to merge, further consolidating the industry, but opposition from European Union regulators led the two companies to eventually call off the proposed merger.

These same corporations also own distribution companies that control more than 80 percent of the wholesale market.

government gave the East India Company a monopoly on trade with India. More recently, governments have often granted monopolies to providers of such services as electricity, telephones, and cable television. Today, however, the most important monopolies granted by governments are patents. A patent gives inventors the exclusive right to produce or license others to produce their discoveries for a limited period of time (generally twenty years). The argument for patents is that without property rights in their discoveries, inventors would have no economic incentive to innovate. The framers of the U.S. Constitution thought promoting "the Progress of Science and useful Arts" to be so important that they included the granting of patents among the powers of the newly created Congress.

Single Ownership of an Essential Input Another barrier to entry is a firm's exclusive ownership of some raw material. For example, an aluminum company might attempt to become a monopolist by buying all the sources of bauxite, the main ore of aluminum. A single South African company, De Beers, has come close to monopolizing the world's supply of diamonds.

Information as a Barrier to Entry Information can act as a barrier to entry when consumers do not know and cannot easily assess the quality of a new product. In the computer printer market, for example, firms such as HP, Epson, and Canon dominate; because these firms have already established reputations for producing high-quality printers, a new entrant unknown to consumers would need to sell at a price significantly below those of the other firms. Imperfect information about the production costs and responses of incumbent firms too can act as a barrier to entry. Potential entrants may know that they can undercut the incumbent firm's current price, but they do not know how much the incumbent will (or can afford to) lower its prices.

Market Strategies for Entry Deterrence Established firms often pursue strategies to convince potential entrants that even though they are currently making high levels of profits, these profits will disappear if the new firm enters the market. Two major forms of such **entry-deterring practices** are *predatory pricing* and *excess capacity*.

In predatory pricing, an incumbent firm deliberately lowers its price below the new entrant's cost of production in order to drive the new arrival out and discourage future entry. The incumbent may lose money in the process, but it hopes to recoup its losses when the entrant leaves and it is free to raise prices back to the monopoly level. Predatory pricing is an illegal trade practice, but changing technologies and shifting demand often make it difficult to ascertain whether a firm has actually engaged in predatory pricing or has simply lowered its price to meet the competition (see the following Thinking Like an Economist box).

Firms can also build more production facilities than are currently needed. By readying extra plants and equipment—excess capacity—even if they are rarely used, the incumbent sends a signal to potential entrants that it is willing and able to engage in fierce price competition.

These strategies are most likely to be effective if there are some sunk costs. Assume the incumbent firm has constant marginal costs and can respond to the entry of another firm by lowering its unit price to marginal cost. A potential entrant,

Thinking Like an Economist
TRADE-OFFS, AMERICAN AIRLINES, AND PREDATION

Firms with market power like to keep it that way, as they can earn high profits by being the only, or the dominant, firm in a market. One of the ways in which they do this is to be a *predator*. Like a predatory animal that eats up rivals, predatory firms lower their prices in an attempt to drive out competitors. A firm may find it can earn higher profits overall if it sacrifices some profit in the short run by cutting its prices to keep rivals out of its market.

This behavior is illegal. For instance, in 1999 the U.S. Justice Department accused American Airlines of predation. The Justice Department alleged that repeatedly, when a new, low-cost carrier entered a market, American Airlines would slash its prices and increase the number of its flights, in an attempt to drive the entrant out of the market. As soon as it was successful, it would cut back on its flights and raise prices. While consumers benefited in the short run from the price war, in the long run they suffered from higher prices caused by lack of competition. Courts have the difficult task of trying to determine whether the lowering of prices is just a normal response to competition, or a predatory action intended to kill a firm entering the market.

One part of the test that is commonly employed asks, Did the predatory firm give up profits today in anticipation of earning them back later from its monopoly position? One way of answering is to compare price and average variable cost. If price is below average variable cost, clearly the firm could not be maximizing its profits, because it would have been better off simply shutting down.

A more refined approach looks at price in comparison with marginal cost. If price is less than marginal cost, a firm should reduce production. Marginal cost is often hard to observe, however, and courts have had to rely on proxies. If the firm is operating at or near an efficient level of production, so that average total costs are minimized, then marginal cost equals average total costs (recall Figure 6.6).

The American Airlines case involved an expansion of output. In competitive markets, so long as the marginal cost curve is upward sloping, a lower price will be associated with lower output, since price must equal marginal cost. But predation occurs in markets that are not competitive. Still, it seemed peculiar that as a new entrant stole some of the demand facing American Airlines, it reacted by increasing supply. The Justice Department alleged that a closer look at American Airlines's behavior showed that it had given up profitable opportunities in order to drive out its rival. The additional revenue that it received from expanding its output was lower than the costs it incurred (including the opportunity cost associated with the profits the planes would have earned on alternative routes).

Predation cases present courts with difficult trade-offs because they assess the risk of finding an innocent party guilty versus that of finding a guilty party innocent. Consumers benefit from the lower prices in the first phase of predation. Courts worry that if firms that really were not engaged in predation are found guilty, competition will be stifled. But if predation really is occurring, then competition in the long run will be suppressed, and consumers will face higher prices and worse service. In most of the airline routes where the Justice Department alleged predation, after the entrant left, prices returned to high levels and service was cut back.

The courts ultimately ruled in favor of American Airlines and dismissed the suit brought by the Justice Department. The ruling was upheld on appeal on the grounds that the airlines did not set fares below average variable cost. Thus, the Justice Department failed to establish that American was pricing below an appropriate measure of cost.

American Airlines planes at Miami International Airport

with marginal costs equal to those of the incumbent, will realize that once it enters, it too must set price equal to marginal cost and therefore will be unable to recover even a small sunk cost. Hence, it chooses not to enter. And the incumbent firm, aware of this calculation, can charge a monopoly price unchallenged.

> **Wrap-Up**
>
> ## ENTRY DETERRENCE
>
> *Government policies:* These include grants of monopoly (patents) and restrictions on entry (licensing).
>
> *Single ownership of an essential input:* When a single firm owns the entire supply of a raw material, entry is by definition precluded.
>
> *Information:* Lack of technical information by potential competitors inhibits their entry; lack of information by consumers concerning the quality of a new entrant's product discourages consumers from switching to the new product, and thus inhibits entry.
>
> *Market strategies:* These include actions such as predatory pricing and excess capacity aimed at convincing potential entrants that entry would be met with resistance, and thus would be unprofitable.

The Importance of Imperfections in Competition

Many of the features of the modern economy—from frequent-flier mileage awards to offers to match prices of competitors, from brand names to the billions spent every year on advertising—not only cannot be explained by the basic competitive model but also are inconsistent with it. They reflect the imperfections of competition that affect so many parts of the economy. Most economists agree that the extreme cases of monopoly (no competition) and perfect competition (where each firm has *no* effect on the market prices) are rare, and that most markets are characterized by some, but imperfect, competition.

Review and Practice

SUMMARY

1. Both monopolists and firms in conditions of perfect competition maximize their profits by producing at the quantity at which marginal revenue is equal to marginal cost. However, marginal revenue for a perfect competitor is the same as the market price of an extra unit, while marginal revenue for a monopolist is less than the market price.
2. Since in a monopoly price exceeds marginal revenue, buyers pay more for the product than the marginal cost to produce it; there is less production in a monopoly than there would be if price were set equal to marginal cost.
3. Imperfect competition occurs when a relatively small number of firms dominate the market or when firms produce goods that are differentiated in ways that reflect consumer preferences.
4. An industry in which fixed costs are so large that only one firm can operate efficiently is called a natural monopoly. Even when there is only one firm (or a few firms), the threat of potential competition may be sufficiently strong that price is driven down to average costs; there are no monopoly profits. Such markets are said to be contestable. If, however, there are sunk costs or other barriers to entry, markets will not be contestable, and monopoly profits can persist.
5. With monopolistic competition, barriers to entry are sufficiently weak that entry occurs until profits are driven to zero; there are few enough firms that each faces a downward-sloping demand curve, but a sufficiently large number of firms that each ignores rivals' reaction to what it does.
6. Oligopolists must choose whether to seek higher profits by colluding with rival firms or by competing. They must decide what their rivals will do in response to any action they take.
7. A group of firms that have an explicit and open agreement to collude is known as a cartel. While the gains from collusion can be significant, important limits are posed by the incentives to cheat and the need to rely on self-enforcement, and by the difficulty of coordinating the responses necessitated by changing economic circumstances. Although cartels are illegal under U.S. law, firms have tried to find tacit ways of facilitating collusion—for example, by relying on price leaders and "meeting-the-competition" pricing policies.
8. Even when they do not collude, firms attempt to restrict competition with practices such as exclusive territories, exclusive dealing, tie-ins, and resale price maintenance. In some cases, a firm's profits may be increased by raising its rival's costs and making the rival a less effective competitor.

KEY TERMS

pure profit *or* monopoly rents
price discrimination
natural monopoly
four-firm concentration ratio
imperfect substitutes
product differentiation
collusion
cartel
game theory
prisoner's dilemma
restrictive practices
entry deterrence
entry-deterring practices

REVIEW QUESTIONS

1. Why is price equal to marginal revenue for a perfectly competitive firm but not for a monopolist?
2. How should a monopoly choose its quantity of production to maximize profits? Explain why producing either less or more than the level of output at which marginal revenue equals marginal cost will reduce profits. Since a monopolist need not fear competition, what prevents it from raising its price as high as it wishes to make higher profits?
3. What are the primary sources of product differentiation?
4. Under what circumstances will price be equal to average costs, so that even though there is a single firm in the market, it earns no monopoly rents?
5. What is a natural monopoly?

6. Describe market equilibrium under monopolistic competition. Why does the price charged by the typical firm exceed the minimum average cost, even though other firms may enter the market?
7. What are the gains from collusion? Why is there an incentive for each member of a cartel to cheat by producing more than the agreed-on amount? What is the "prisoner's dilemma" and how is it related to the problem of cheating? What are the other problems facing cartels?
8. Name some ways that firms might facilitate collusion, if explicit collusion is ruled out by law.
9. What are barriers to entry? How can firms try to deter entry?
10. Name and define three restrictive practices.

PROBLEMS

1. Explain how it is possible that at a high enough level of output, if a monopoly produced and sold more, its revenue would actually decline.
2. Assume there is a single firm producing cigarettes, and the marginal cost of producing cigarettes is a constant. Suppose the government imposes a 10-cent tax on each pack of cigarettes. If the demand curve for cigarettes is linear (that is, $Q = a - bp$, where Q = output, p = price, and a and b are constants), will the price rise by more or by less than the tax?
3. With what strategies might a furniture firm differentiate its products?
4. Suppose a gas station at a busy intersection is surrounded by many competitors, all of which sell identical gas. Draw the demand curve the gas station faces, and draw its marginal and average cost curves. Explain the rule for maximizing profit in this situation. Now imagine that the gas station offers a new gasoline additive called zoomine, and begins an advertising campaign that says: "Get zoomine in your gasoline." No other station offers zoomine. Draw the station's demand curve after this advertising campaign. Explain the rule for maximizing profit in this situation, and illustrate it with an appropriate diagram.
5. Explain how consumers may benefit from predatory pricing in the short run, but not in the long run.

6. Assume the demand curve faced by a monopolist is given by the following table:

Price	Demand	Total revenue	Marginal revenue
55	45		
60	40		
65	35		
70	30		
75	25		
80	20		
85	15		
90	10		
95	5		
100	0		

(a) Fill in the columns of the table for total revenue and marginal revenue.
(b) Draw the demand curve and the marginal revenue curve.
(c) If the firm's marginal cost is $75, what is the equilibrium monopoly price? How much does a monopolist produce?
(d) What would be the price and quantity produced if this were a competitive market (assume marginal costs to be $75)?

7. How might cooperative agreements between firms—to share research information, share the costs of cleaning up pollution, or address shortfalls of supplies—end up helping firms to collude in reducing quantity and raising price?
8. Explain why each of the following might serve to deter entry of a competitor.
    (a) Maintaining excess production capacity
    (b) Promising customers that you will undercut any rival
    (c) Selling your output at a price below that at which marginal revenue equals marginal cost (Hint: Assume entrants are unsure about what your marginal costs are. Why would they be deterred from entering if they believed you have low marginal costs? Why might a lower price lead them to think that you had low marginal costs?)
    (d) Offering a discount to customers who sign up for long-term contracts

9. Explain why frequent-flier programs (in which airlines give credits, convertible into travel awards for each mile traveled) might reduce competition among airlines. Put yourself in the role of consultant to one of the airlines in the days before any airline had such programs. Would you have recommended that the airline adopt the program? What would you have *assumed* about the responses of other airlines? Would this have been important to your assessment?
10. At various times, Nintendo has been accused of trying to stifle its competitors. Among the alleged practices have been (a) not allowing those who produce games for Nintendo to produce games for others; and (b) discouraging stores that sell Nintendo from selling competing games—for instance, by not fulfilling their orders as quickly, especially in periods of shortages. Explain why these practices might increase Nintendo's profits.
11. Consider two oligopolists, with each choosing between a "high" and a "low" level of production. Given their choices of how much to produce, their profits will be:

Firm A

	High production	Low production
High production	A gets $2 million profit B gets $2 million profit	A gets $1 million profit B gets $5 million profit

Firm B

	High production	Low production
Low production	A gets $5 million profit B gets $1 million profit	A gets $4 million profit B gets $4 million profit

Explain how firm B will reason that it makes sense to produce the high amount, regardless of what firm A chooses. Then explain how firm A will reason that it makes sense to produce the high amount, regardless of what firm B chooses. How might collusion assist the two firms in this case?

Learning Goals

In this chapter, you will learn

1. The sources of economic inefficiency that result from imperfect competition
2. The different policies that governments have adopted to deal with imperfect competition
3. The role of antitrust policies in limiting market domination and curbing practices that restrict competition

Chapter 13

GOVERNMENT POLICIES TOWARD COMPETITION

Motivated by both political and economic concerns, governments have taken an active role in promoting competition and in limiting the abuses of market power. In this chapter, we review the economic effects of limited competition and look at government policies to reduce its negative effects.

The Drawbacks of Monopolies and Limited Competition

Four major sources of economic inefficiency result from monopolies and other imperfectly competitive industries: restricted output, managerial slack, insufficient attention to research and development, and rent-seeking behavior. The problems stand out most plainly in the context of monopolies (the focus here), but they also arise in imperfectly competitive markets.

RESTRICTED OUTPUT

Monopolists, like competitive firms, are in business to make profits by producing the kinds of goods and services that customers want. But monopolists can make profits in ways not available to competitive firms. One way is to drive up the price of a good by restricting output, as discussed in Chapters 11 and 12. They can, to use the popular term, gouge their customers. Consumers, by *choosing* to buy the monopolist's good, are revealing that they are better off than they would be without the product. But they are paying more than they would if the industry were competitive.

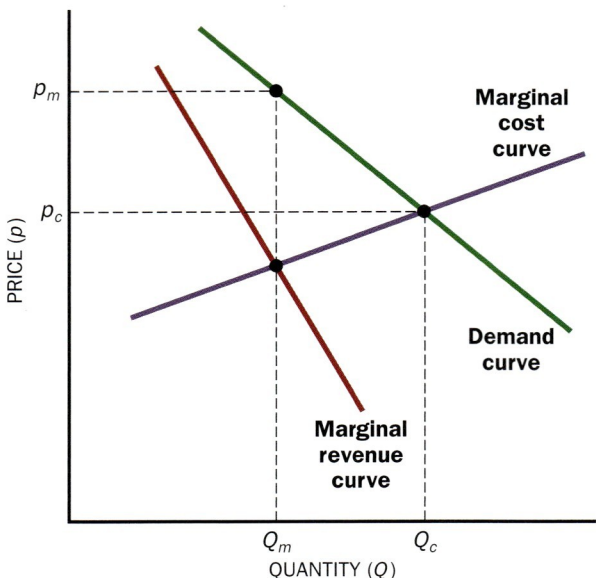

FIGURE 13.1

WHY MONOPOLY OUTPUT IS INEFFICIENT

With perfect competition, price is set equal to marginal cost: output is at quantity Q_c, and price at p_c. A monopolist will set marginal revenue equal to marginal cost, and will produce at quantity Q_m and price p_m, where the market price exceeds marginal cost.

A monopolist who sets marginal revenue equal to marginal cost produces at a lower level of output than a corresponding competitive industry—an industry with the same demand curve and costs but in which there are many producers rather than one—where price equals marginal cost. Figure 13.1 shows that the monopoly output, Q_m, is smaller than the competitive output, Q_c, where the price under competition, p_c, equals marginal cost. The price under monopoly, p_m, is higher than p_c.

The price of a good, by definition, measures how much an individual is willing to pay for an extra unit of it. It measures, in other words, the marginal benefit of the good to the purchaser. With perfect competition, price equals marginal cost, so that in equilibrium the marginal benefit of an extra unit of a good to the individual (the price) is just equal to the marginal cost to the firm of producing it. At the monopolist's lower level of output, the marginal benefit of producing an extra unit—the price individuals are willing to pay for an extra unit—exceeds marginal cost.

By comparing the monopolist's production decision with the collective decisions regarding output made by firms in a competitive market, we can estimate the value of the loss to society incurred by a monopoly. To simplify the analysis, in Figure 13.2 marginal cost is assumed to be constant, the horizontal line at the competitive price p_c. The monopolist produces an output of Q_m, at the point where marginal revenue equals marginal cost, and finds that it can charge p_m, the price on the demand curve corresponding to the output Q_m.

Two kinds of loss result, both related to the concept of consumer surplus introduced in Chapter 5. There we saw that the downward-sloping demand curve implies a bounty to most consumers. At points to the left of the intersection of the price line and demand curve, people are willing to pay more for the good than they have to. With competition, the consumer surplus in Figure 13.2 is the entire shaded area between the demand curve and the line at p_c.

The monopolist cuts into this surplus. First, it charges a higher price, p_m, than would be obtained in the competitive situation. This loss is measured by the rectangle *ABCD*, the extra price multiplied by the quantity actually produced and consumed. It is not a loss to society as a whole but a transfer of income, as the higher price winds up as revenues for the monopoly. But the monopolist also reduces the quantity produced. While production in a competitive market would be Q_c, a monopoly produces the lower amount, Q_m. This second kind of loss is a complete loss to society, and is called the *deadweight loss* of a monopoly. Consumers lose the surplus to the right of Q_m, denoted by triangle *ABG*, with no resulting gain to the monopolist.

Some economists, such as Arnold Harberger of UCLA, have argued that these costs of monopoly are relatively small, amounting to perhaps 3 percent of the monopolist's output value. Others believe the losses from restricting output are higher. Whichever argument is right, output restriction is only one source of the inefficiencies monopolies introduce into the economy.

MANAGERIAL SLACK

Chapter 6 argued that any company wants to minimize the cost of producing whatever level of output it chooses to produce. But in practice, companies already earning a great deal of money without much competition often lack the incentive to hold costs as low as possible. The lack of efficiency when firms are insulated from the pressures of competition is referred to as **managerial slack.**

In the absence of competition, it can be difficult to tell whether managers are being efficient. How much, for instance, should it cost for AT&T to put a call through from New York to Chicago? In the days when AT&T had a monopoly on long-distance telephone service, it might have claimed that its costs were as low as possible. However, not even trained engineers could really tell whether this was true. When competition developed for intercity telephone calls, shareholders in AT&T could compare its costs with those of Sprint, MCI, and other competitors; competition therefore provided each company with an incentive to be as efficient as possible.

REDUCED RESEARCH AND DEVELOPMENT

Competition motivates firms to develop new products and less expensive ways of producing goods. A monopoly, by contrast, may be willing to let the profits roll in, without aggressively encouraging technological progress.

Not all monopolists stand pat, of course. Bell Laboratories, the research division of AT&T, was a fountain of important innovations throughout the period during which AT&T was a virtual monopolist in telephone service. The laser and the transistor are but two of its innovations. But AT&T was also in a unique position. The prices it charged were determined by government regulators, and those prices were set to encourage the expenditure of money on research. From this perspective, AT&T's research contribution was largely a consequence of government regulatory policy.

In contrast to Bell Labs, the American automobile and steel industries are often blamed for falling behind foreign competition because of their technological complacence. By the end of World War II, these industries had attained a dominant position in the world. After enjoying high profits for many years, they lost a significant share of the market to foreign firms in the 1970s and 1980s. Foreign automobile and steel firms, for example, were able to undersell their U.S. counterparts during the 1980s, not only because they paid lower wages but also because their technological advances had made production processes more efficient.

More recently, analysts have expressed concern that firms with monopoly power not only engage in less innovation than they would under competition but also seek actively to quash innovations by rivals that could reduce their market power. And even if they do not

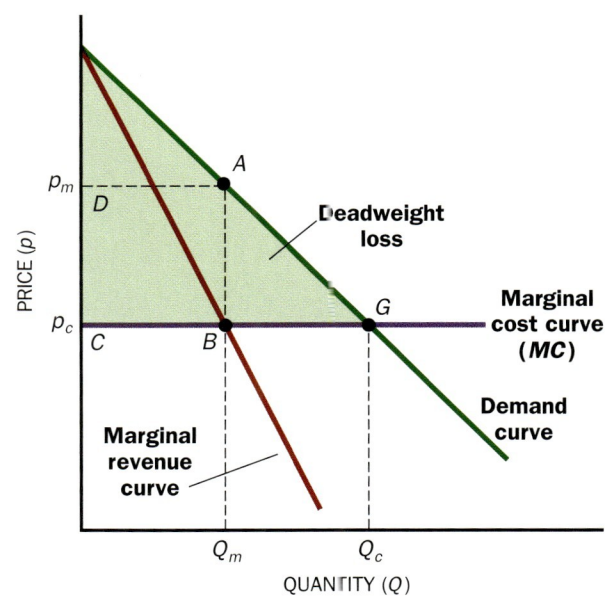

FIGURE 13.2

MEASURING THE SOCIAL COST OF MONOPOLY

The higher, monopoly price removes some of the consumer surplus. Part of this loss (the rectangle ABCD) is simply a transfer of income from consumers to the monopolist; the remainder (the triangle ABG) is known as the deadweight loss of monopoly.

deliberately try to inhibit innovative activities of potential rivals, they may stifle progress indirectly. Some of the most important inputs into the innovation process are prior innovations themselves, and by raising the "price" associated with these earlier discoveries (through their market power), monopolists reduce the incentives for follow-up inventions.

RENT SEEKING

The final source of economic inefficiency under monopoly is the temptation for monopolists to expend resources in economically unproductive ways. In particular, they may seek to deter the entry of other firms into their market. Because the profits a monopolist receives are called *monopoly rents,* the attempt to acquire or maintain already-existing rents by acquiring or maintaining a monopoly position in some industry is referred to as **rent seeking.**

Sometimes a firm's monopoly position is at least partly the result of government protection. Many less-developed countries grant a company within their country a monopoly to produce a good, and they bar imports of that good from abroad. In these circumstances, firms will give money to lobbyists and politicians to maintain regulations that restrict competition so that they can keep their profits high. Such activities are socially wasteful. Real resources (including labor time) are used to win favorable rules, not to produce goods and services. There is thus legitimate concern that the willingness of governments to restrict competition will encourage firms to spend money on rent-seeking activities rather than on making a better product.

To gain and hold a monopoly position, the firm would be willing to spend up to the amount it would receive as monopoly profits. The waste from this rent-seeking activity can be much larger than the loss from reduced output.

FURTHER DRAWBACKS OF LIMITED COMPETITION

We saw in Chapter 12 that markets in which a few firms dominated were more common than monopolies, and some of the inefficiencies discussed above are smaller under limited competition. Output is lower than under perfect competition but higher than under monopoly, for example. And competition to produce new products (research and development) is often intense, as we will see in Chapter 20. But other inefficiencies are worse in markets with limited competition than in monopoly markets. Firms under imperfect competition, for example, devote much attention to practices designed to deter entry, to reduce the force of competition, and to raise prices. Their expenditures may increase profits but they waste resources and make consumers worse off. Under imperfect competition firms may, for instance, maintain excess capacity to deter entry. A firm may gain a competitive advantage over its rival not by lowering its own costs but by raising the rival's—for instance, by denying it the use of existing distribution facilities. A firm may also spend money on uninformative (but persuasive) advertising.

e-Insight

USING THE INTERNET TO ENHANCE PRICE DISCRIMINATION

In 2000, the online retailer Amazon.com conducted a marketing test that generated an immediate outcry of foul play from consumer advocates. Amazon.com had offered different customers different prices on DVDs; and when the pricing strategy became public, it claimed that the prices were set randomly in an attempt to determine how consumers would respond to different prices. Analysts were skeptical, fearing that Amazon.com was using information collected from the previous purchases of individual consumers to fine-tune its prices. Customers from wealthier neighborhoods with a record of buying more expensive items might be receiving higher price quotes. Newspaper commentators accused Amazon.com of "unfair" pricing, and the marketing test was suspended.

Consumers have long accepted that airlines will offer different fares to travelers on the same flight, according to when tickets were purchased. Travelers who can plan in advance receive discount fares, while business travelers who need to get to a newly scheduled meeting pay much more. Because the business traveler's demand is highly inelastic, airlines can charge her a higher price. People who can plan ahead and easily adjust travel dates and times will be more price sensitive—their demand curve is more elastic. By offering only price-sensitive customers lower fares, airlines can sell more seats without having to offer the same low price to everyone.

In imperfectly competitive markets, as we saw in Chapter 12, firms can try to boost profits through price discrimination—charging different prices to different consumers. The Internet is opening up new opportunities for this sales strategy. Here's an example of how it might work. Knowing that a blizzard is predicted for the weekend, early in the week you log onto a hardware site to order extra lanterns, batteries, and candles. The Web site is programmed to check orders of emergency supplies from your zip code against a national weather database. Knowing that you are facing a blizzard, the hardware online retailer decides that your demand is inelastic, and raises the prices for the purchase and delivery of the items you need.

By providing firms with more detailed information about their customers, the Internet may open new possibilities for firms in imperfectly competitive markets to engage in price discrimination.

Policies Toward Natural Monopolies

If imperfect competition is as disadvantageous as the previous analysis has suggested, why not simply require that competition be perfect? To answer this question, we need to recall the reasons, discussed in Chapter 11, why competition is imperfect.

One reason is that the cost of production may be lower if there is a single firm in the industry, leading to a natural monopoly. In the case depicted in Figure 13.3, average costs are declining throughout the relevant levels of output, though marginal costs are constant; there are very large fixed costs. Natural monopolies present a difficult policy problem. Like any other firm, a natural monopolist will produce at the level where marginal revenue equals marginal cost—at Q_m, in Figure 13.3. At this level, it will charge a price of p_m, which is higher than the marginal cost at that point. Thus, it will produce less and charge more than it would if price were equal to

FIGURE 13.3

A PROBLEM WITH REGULATING A NATURAL MONOPOLY

A natural monopoly will set marginal revenue equal to marginal cost, and produce at quantity Q_m and price p_m. In perfect competition, price would be equal to marginal cost, at Q_c and p_c. However, the perfectly competitive outcome is not possible in this case, since it would force the natural monopoly to produce at below its average cost, and thus to be making losses.

marginal cost, as would be true under perfect competition (the output level Q_c and the price p_c in the figure).

However, a decreasing average cost curve necessarily precludes perfect competition. To understand why, recall that under perfect competition, price equals marginal cost. Now look again at Figure 13.3 and consider what would happen if price were driven down to marginal cost. In the figure, marginal cost is equal to p_c. At a price equal to p_c, the quantity demanded is equal to Q_c. But at that quantity, the firm's average costs are greater than p_c. When average costs are declining, marginal costs are less than average costs. Hence, a price equal to marginal cost would be less than average costs. But if the firm sells its output at a price that fails to cover its average costs, it will lose money. So when average costs are declining, profits will be negative when price equals marginal cost, as shown by the shaded area in the figure. No firm will be able to stay in business if it always loses money.

There is old joke about a firm that loses money on every sale but makes it up in volume. Of course, selling more when there is a loss on each sale just makes the firm even worse off. And that would be exactly the condition of a firm with declining average costs that set price equal to marginal cost.

If the government wanted a natural monopoly to produce at the point where marginal cost equaled price, it would have to subsidize the firm to offset its losses. But the taxes that would have to be raised to provide the subsidy impose other economic costs; thus the severity of the two distortions—caused either by a firm charging a price above marginal cost or by the taxes required to fund the subsidy to eliminate the first distortion—would have to be compared. Moreover, the government would likely have a difficult time ascertaining the magnitude of the subsidy needed. Managers and workers in the firm would have an incentive to exaggerate the wage and other costs necessary to produce the required output, because exaggeration would win them a bigger subsidy from the government.

Governments have found three different solutions to the problem of natural monopolies.

PUBLIC OWNERSHIP

In some countries, government simply owns natural monopolies, such as electric power, gas, and water. There are problems with public ownership, however. Governments often are not particularly efficient as producers.

Managers of such monopolies commonly lack adequate incentives to cut costs and modernize vigorously, particularly since government is frequently willing to subsidize the industry when it loses money. In addition, public ownership tends to politicize business decisions. Political influence may affect where public utilities, for example, locate their plants—politicians like to see jobs created in their home districts—and whether they prune their labor force to increase efficiency. Publicly run firms may also be under pressure to provide some services at prices below marginal cost and to make up the deficit with revenues from other services, a practice referred to as **cross subsidization.** Thus, business customers of utilities are sometimes charged more, relative to the actual costs of serving them, than are households. This practice in effect involves a hidden tax and a hidden subsidy; businesses are taxed to subsidize households. The same phenomenon can be seen in our most important public monopoly, the U.S. Postal Service. It charges the same price for delivering mail to small rural communities as it does to major cities, in spite of the large differences in costs. Small communities have their mail services subsidized by larger ones.

How much less efficient the government is as a producer than the private sector is difficult to determine. Efficiency comparisons between government-run telephone companies in Europe and America's private firms provided much of the motivation for the late-twentieth-century **privatization** movement—the movement to convert government enterprises into private firms. Britain sold its telephone services and some other utilities, Japan its telephones and railroads, France its banks and many other enterprises. Not all publicly run enterprises are less productive than their private counterparts, however. For example, Canada has two major rail lines, one operated by the government and one private, which differ little in the efficiency with which they are run—perhaps because of competition between the two. Many of the publicly owned enterprises in France seem to run as efficiently as private firms, perhaps because the high prestige afforded to those who work in the French civil service enables it to recruit from among the most talented people in the country. There may also be less difference between government enterprises and large corporations—particularly when both are subjected to some market pressure and competition—than popular conceptions of governmental waste would suggest.

REGULATION

Some countries leave the natural monopolies in the private sector but regulate them. This is generally the U.S. practice. Local utilities, for instance, remain private, but their rates are regulated by the states. Federal agencies regulate interstate telephone services and the prices that can be charged for interstate transport of natural gas.

The aim of regulation is to keep the price as low as possible, commensurate with the monopolist's need to obtain an adequate return on its investment. In other words, regulators try to keep price equal to average costs—where average costs include a "normal return" on what the firm's owners have invested in the firm. If they are successful, the natural monopoly will earn no monopoly profits. Such a regulated output and price are shown in Figure 13.4 as Q_r and p_r.

Two criticisms have been leveled against regulation as a solution to the natural monopoly problem. The first is that regulations often introduce inefficiencies in several ways. The intent is to set prices so that firms obtain a "fair" return on their capital. But to make the highest level of profit, firms respond by investing as much capital as

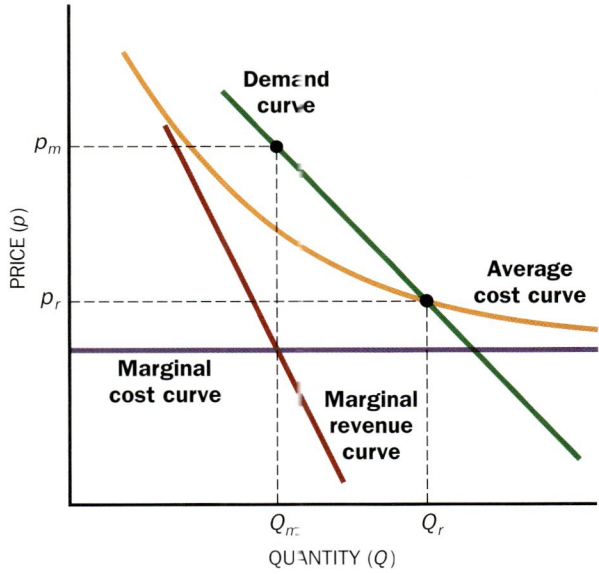

FIGURE 13.4

REGULATING A NATURAL MONOPOLY

Government regulators will often seek to choose the point on the market demand curve where the firm provides the greatest quantity at the lowest price consistent with the firm covering its costs. The point is the quantity Q_r and price p_r, where the demand curve intersects the average cost curve.

possible—sometimes too much. In addition, some groups, often businesses, may be required to pay extra-high prices so that other groups can be subsidized. Cross subsidies are no less a problem for natural monopolies if they are privately owned and regulated than if they are owned and operated by the government. Furthermore, companies have little incentive to innovate if their success in lowering costs is always followed by lower regulated prices rather than by higher profits. U.S. regulators have recognized that unless they reward innovation, it will not happen. They have agreed to allow the utilities to retain much of the increased profits they obtain from improved efficiency, at least for a few years.

The second criticism is that the regulators lose their focus on the public interest. The theory of **regulatory capture** argues that regulators are frequently pulled into the camps of those they regulate. Sometimes bribery and corruption are to blame, but far more common is that over time, employees of a regulated industry develop personal friendships with the regulators, who in turn come to rely on their expertise and judgment. Worse, regulatory agencies (of necessity) tend to hire from among those in the regulated industry. By the same token, regulators who demonstrate an "understanding" of the industry may be rewarded with good jobs in that industry after they leave government service.

ENCOURAGING COMPETITION

The final way government deals with the hard choices posed by natural monopolies is to encourage competition, even if it is imperfect. To understand this strategy,

International Perspective
THE DARKER SIDE OF PRIVATIZATION

In many countries around the world, where government used to own a large share of industry, privatization has had a marked impact on the economic landscape. Those favoring privatization argued that it would not only improve efficiency but also reduce corruption, by eliminating government enterprises as a source of income and patronage.

But privatization itself has turned out to be a major source of corruption; indeed, in many parts of the world it has come to be called *briberization*. When state assets are sold at below market prices, those who are lucky enough to get control of them win a huge bonanza. (In Russia, instant billionaires were created.) And to be sure, those who control the privatization process get ample kickbacks.

The problem is that the sale of a large corporation involves a host of technical details. To begin with, potential buyers have to be certified—will they really come up with the cash they promise? The rules for conducting the sales have routinely been written and implemented in ways that serve the interests of some at the expense of others. As a result, rather than being those most capable of managing the corporation, the winners are the most politically connected or are willing to bribe the most. This in turn has meant that the promised benefits of privatization—increased efficiency—often have not been realized. In many countries in the former Soviet Union and Eastern Europe, privatization has led more often to the stripping away of assets than to the creation of more efficient firms.

let us first review why competition may not be viable when average costs are declining over the relevant range of output.

If two firms divide the market between them, each faces higher average costs than if either one controlled the whole market. By undercutting its rival, a firm would be able to capture the entire market *and* reduce its average costs. By the same token, a natural monopolist knows that it can charge a price above its average cost without worrying about entry. Rivals that might enter the market, trying to capture some of the profits, know that the natural monopolist has lower costs because of its larger scale of production, and so can always undercut them.

Even under these conditions, some economists have argued that a monopolist would not in fact charge higher than average costs, because a rival could enter any time and grab the whole market. Analysts have argued that in the software industry, such a worry leads Microsoft to lower its prices. By keeping its prices lower than it would if no potential rival could enter the market, Microsoft promotes the wider use of its software. As people use programs such as Microsoft's Word and Excel, they become familiar with them and more reluctant to switch to something new, thereby creating a greater obstacle for a new entrant to overcome. Similarly, in small countries such as New Zealand, the threat that a large foreign firm could enter the market and take it over if the local monopoly charged above average costs restrains the monopoly's ability to raise its prices. On this argument, all that is required to keep prices low is potential competition.

Most economists are not so optimistic about the effectiveness of potential, as opposed to actual, competition. They note that potential competition has not been able to keep airline prices down in those markets in which actual competition is limited to one or two carriers.

In the late 1970s and 1980s, many governments became convinced that competition, however imperfect, might be better than regulation, and they began a process of deregulation. Deregulation focused on industries such as airlines, railroads, and trucking in which increasing returns to scale are limited. Recall that it is increasing returns to scale that lead to declining average costs. Thus, reformers believed that competition had a chance of succeeding in these industries. Government also sought to distinguish parts of an industry where competition might work from parts where competition was unlikely to be effective. In the telephone industry, for example, competition among several carriers was strong for long-distance telephone service, and there were few economies of scale in the production of telephone equipment. Accordingly, regulation in these areas was reduced or eliminated.

The virtues of competition have been realized, for the most part. Trucking—where the arguments for government regulation seemed most suspect—was perhaps the most unambiguous success story, as prices have fallen significantly. Railroads appear more financially sound than they did under regulation. But coal producers, who rely on railroads to ship their coal, complain that railroads have used their monopoly power to charge them much higher tariffs.

Airline deregulation has become more controversial. After its initial success—marked by new firms, lower fares, and more extensive routings—a rash of bankruptcies has reduced the number of airlines. Many airports, including those at St. Louis, Atlanta, and Denver, are dominated by one or two carriers, and travelers from these communities often must pay extremely high fares. A pattern of discriminatory pricing has developed, and businesspeople who cannot make reservations weeks in advance are charged four or more times the fare of a vacationer for the same seat.

Deregulation has not yet extended to natural monopolies like water. But the deregulation of electricity is well under way, implemented in more than half the U.S. states.

Case in Point

CALIFORNIA ELECTRICITY DEREGULATION

California was among the states in the forefront of electricity deregulation. Economists recognized that there were many potential suppliers of generating capacity and many potential retailers of electricity services. The only natural monopoly was in the transmission between the generators of electricity and the retailers. Breaking up the old electricity companies, which integrated all these functions, could lead to competition in all areas except transmission. Increased competition in the parts of the system where it was possible would lead to greater efficiency, and ultimately to lower prices and better service—or so it was hoped.

In 2000, deregulation appeared to be a disaster: electricity prices soared, shortages of generating capacity led to brownouts and interrupted service, electricity companies went bankrupt, and a massive government bailout was needed. Clearly, things had not gone as planned. Not surprisingly, there was plenty of finger-pointing. Critics blamed deregulation. Proponents said that even with

Shasta Dam is a hydroelectric facility in California.

deregulation, government had retained too large a role—it had put ceilings on the prices companies could charge consumers and prevented the use of long-term contracts. Well-intentioned or not, these restrictions exposed electricity companies like Pacific Gas and Electric to an impossible squeeze: high gas prices led to high wholesale prices for electricity that were greater than the controlled retail prices. And the way deregulation was done allowed energy traders like Enron to manipulate the market. Enron was doing more than just gouging California—it was also engaging in a variety of allegedly fraudulent accounting practices that were designed to boost its stock price. Eventually, the company collapsed, and the schemes that enabled Enron to create profits by exploiting the partially deregulated California energy market were revealed during the court cases that attended its bankruptcy.

Wrap-Up

APPROACHES TO THE PROBLEM OF NATURAL MONOPOLY

Public ownership
Regulation
Encouraging competition

Antitrust Policies

Only some of the failures of competition arise from natural monopolies. Other imperfections, as we have seen, are the result of sharp business practices intended to develop market power by deterring entry or promoting collusion. When encouraging competition does not work, government sometimes resorts to enforcing competition through *antitrust law*, the body of law designed to restrict anticompetitive practices.

As we will see, these policies have often been controversial. Consumer groups and injured businesses tend to support them, arguing that without them, firms would focus more on competition-reducing strategies than on efficiently producing products that customers like. But many businesses claim that such policies interfere with economic efficiency. For instance, even if the most efficient way to distribute its products is through exclusive territories for distributors, the firm might worry that such a contract might be ruled illegal.

Table 13.1 lists the major landmarks of U.S. antitrust policy. These take the form of legislation and relevant judicial decisions. They fall into two categories: (1) limiting market domination and (2) curbing restrictive practices.

Table 13.1
MAJOR ANTITRUST LEGISLATION AND LANDMARK CASES

Sherman Antitrust Act, 1890	Made acts in restraint of trade illegal.
Standard Oil and American Tobacco cases, 1911	Broke up both firms (each of which accounted for more than 90% of its industry) into smaller companies.
Clayton Act, 1914	Outlawed unfair trade practices. Restricted mergers that would substantially reduce competition.
Establishment of the Federal Trade Commission, 1914	Established to investigate unfair practices and issue orders to "cease and desist."
Robinson-Patman Act, 1936	Strengthened provisions of the Clayton Act, outlawing price discrimination.
Alcoa case, 1945	Alcoa, controlling 90% of the aluminum market, was found to be in violation of the Sherman Act.
Tobacco case, 1946	The tobacco industry, a concentrated oligopoly, was found guilty of violation of the Sherman Act on the basis of tacit collusion.
Celler-Kefauver Antimerger Act, 1950	Placed further restrictions on mergers that would reduce competition.
Du Pont Cellophane case, 1956	Broadened the definition of market. Ruled that a 20% market share was insufficient to establish market power.

LIMITING MARKET DOMINATION

In this section, we look at how government tries to limit economic power. In the decades following the Civil War, entrepreneurs in several industries attempted to form **trusts.** These were organizations that controlled a market. One individual had a controlling interest in a firm, which in turn had a controlling interest in all the other firms in the industry. Through the addition of more layers—firms that controlled firms that controlled firms, and so on—a relatively small ownership stake could be leveraged into enormous economic power.

Among the most famous of the nineteenth-century trusts was the oil industry trust; John D. Rockefeller and his partners eventually controlled 90 percent of all oil sold in America between 1870 and 1899. In the early 1900s, Andrew Carnegie and J. P. Morgan merged many smaller steel companies to form U.S. Steel, which in its heyday sold 65 percent of all American steel.

Concern about these so-called robber barons led to passage of the Sherman Antitrust Act of 1890, which outlaws "every contract, combination in the form of a trust or otherwise, or conspiracy in restraint of trade or commerce." Further, "every person who shall monopolize, or attempt to monopolize, or combine or conspire with any other person or persons, to monopolize any part of the trade or commerce among the several States, or with foreign nations, shall be deemed guilty of a misdemeanor." (A 1974 amendment made violations felonies.) Two important decisions based on the Sherman Act led to the breakups of Standard Oil and American Tobacco in 1911, each of which had dominated its respective industry.

The Sherman Act was supplemented by the Clayton Act in 1914, which forbade any firm to acquire shares of a competing firm when that purchase would substantially reduce competition. The act also outlawed interlocking directorates (in which the same individuals serve as directors of several firms) among firms that were supposedly in competition. These antimerger provisions were further strengthened in 1950 by the Celler-Kefauver Antimerger Act.

The government does not care about absolute size itself. In the 1960s, huge firms called *conglomerates* were formed that brought together such disparate enterprises as a steel company, an oil company, and a company making films. For example, United Airlines for a few years owned Hertz rental cars and Westin Hotels (both sold in the late 1980s). But while large, these conglomerates generally did not have a dominant position in any one market, and thus the antitrust laws were not concerned with them. The early antitrust laws were particularly concerned with **horizontal mergers,** and thus with competition within a market. These are distinguished from **vertical mergers,** in which a firm buys a supplier or a distributor, thereby amalgamating the various stages in the production process within a firm. Thus, Ford made its own steel, and General Motors bought out Fisher Body (the maker of GM's car bodies), as well as many of the specialized firms that produced batteries, spark plugs, and other components.

Under current court interpretations, market power per se is also not a primary concern. To be convicted of an antitrust violation, the firm must be shown to have acquired its market position by anticompetitive practices or to have used its market power to engage in anticompetitive practices.

DEFINING MARKETS

We have seen that the extent to which a firm's demand curve is downward sloping, enabling it to raise its price without losing all its customers—its market power—is related to the number of firms in the industry and the extent of product differentiation. Both factors are important for purposes of antitrust enforcement, since the government must first define "the market" before it can determine whether a firm dominates its market.

Internet Connection

U.S. DEPARTMENT OF JUSTICE AND ANTITRUST LAWS

At www.usdoj.gov/atr/overview.html, the Department of Justice explains the mission of its Antitrust Division and its role in preventing monopolies from depriving consumers of the benefits of competition.

Thinking Like an Economist

INCENTIVES AND THE REMEDY TO THE MICROSOFT MONOPOLY PROBLEM

In 1999, Judge Thomas Penfield Jackson found Microsoft guilty of violating U.S. antitrust laws. He then was faced with a difficult problem: what remedy to impose. Jackson was keenly aware of the *incentives* that Microsoft faced; its profitability depended on its ability to preserve its market power, and it therefore had strong incentives to stifle innovations that might reduce that market power. For instance, Sun Microsystems had developed a language, Java, that would enable programmers to develop applications to run not just on Microsoft's Windows operating system but on other operating systems as well. One of the reasons why Microsoft's operating system was so dominant was that rivals started with a marked disadvantage—a lack of applications to run on their operating systems. By changing all of that, Java would result in real competition in the market for operating systems. Microsoft similarly worried that Netscape might serve as a platform through which competition in the operating system might be enhanced, and it sought to quash this threat by bundling its own browser, Internet Explorer, free with the Windows operating system. Microsoft had done what comes naturally to monopolists—it simply sought to maximize its long-run profits by reducing the threat of competition. The judge worried that no matter how he scolded Microsoft, or what fines he imposed, Microsoft had every incentive to continue these anticompetitive practices. Moreover, he was aware of how difficult detecting and proving anticompetitive behavior can be, and Microsoft had already demonstrated its willingness to face risks of antitrust prosecution. Hence, the only way to alter behavior was to alter incentives, and doing so entailed changing the structure of the enterprise. The Department of Justice proposed splitting Microsoft into two, with one company focusing on applications and the other focusing on the operating system. The application company would have every incentive to ensure that its applications could be used on as many operating systems as possible. The hope was that Microsoft Word might then be written to work on more operating systems, like Linux, so that

Market Bounds and Globalization Over the past two hundred years, the geographical scope of markets has grown enormously. Technological improvements in transportation, from steam-powered ships to railroads to airplanes, have lowered the cost of transportation and expanded the boundaries of markets. As a market expands, it may become more competitive—as happened in the U.S. auto industry during the 1980s and 1990s, when the big three domestic firms (Ford, General Motors, and Chrysler) faced increasing competition from Japanese, European, and Korean manufacturers. Today, the degree of competition in a market must be judged by a global assessment rather than by a simple examination of how many firms produce a good in the United States. Because of the Internet, many markets have enlarged even more. Twenty years ago, a local bookstore might have been the only bookseller in a town; now that same business must face competition from online vendors such as Amazon.com and Borders.com.

Product Differentiation All firms that produce the same good and sell in the same location are clearly in the same market, but definitions become more ambigudemand for them would increase. And restraining the operating system company from writing applications would at least prevent a repeat of what had happened with Netscape and the browser market.

Some critics thought the judge, in approving the Justice Department's recommendations in 2000, went too far; others thought he did not go far enough. Those in the former camp worried that he overlooked important economies of scope—efficiencies that arose from the close interaction between those writing the operating system and those developing applications. These advantages, they contended, more than offset the disadvantages from the loss in competition. Moreover, they believed that Microsoft's monopoly power was temporary; within a few years, surely competition would erode its dominant position. Already, Linux was rapidly growing as an alternative operating system. They argued that Microsoft had achieved its dominant position by strong innovation, and it was wrong to punish this success now by breaking the company up.

But critics on the other side said that at least a significant part of Microsoft's success was due to its ruthless business practices, and such behavior should not go unpunished. And more was at stake: Microsoft represented a threat to innovation. Few would invest in innovation if they believed that any innovation threatening Microsoft's competitive position would be suppressed by Microsoft. Many Silicon Valley firms shared this fear.

These critics worried that the Microsoft application company still might not write programs for other operating systems, that there might be sweetheart deals between the two companies; they argued for other approaches to changes Microsoft's incentives. For instance, some suggested limiting intellectual property protection—and requiring the disclosure of the code—for operating systems of a firm with a dominant position (like Microsoft) to, say, three to five years. Doing so would automatically create a competitor to, say, Windows XP—the freely available Windows 2000. Only if Windows XP were markedly better than Windows 2000 would people pay anything for it. This approach would enhance Microsoft's incentives to innovate. Meanwhile, application programmers would have an incentive to write programs that worked better and better with the freely available 2000 operating system. The hope was that out of this competition, consumers would benefit not only from lower prices but also from innovations, possibly leading to programs that crash less often and are tailored better to the needs of particular groups of users, that run faster, and that perform new tasks.

ous when goods produced by different firms are imperfect substitutes. What, for example, is the market for beer? Those in the industry might claim that premium beers and discount beers really constitute two different markets, as relatively few customers cross over from one to the other. In the 1950s, DuPont had a virtual monopoly on the market for clear wrapping paper, but it fought off charges of monopoly by arguing that its product was one among several "wrapping materials." It claimed that brown paper was a good, though not perfect, substitute for clear wrapping paper, and that DuPont did not have a particularly large share of this larger market.

Legal Criteria Today, the courts look at two criteria in defining a market and market power. First, they consider the extent to which a change in price for one product affects the demand for another. If an increase in the price of aluminum has a large positive effect on the demand for steel, then steel and aluminum may be considered to be in the same market—the market for metals. Second, if a firm can raise its price, say by 5 percent, and lose only a relatively small fraction of its sales, then it is "large"—that is, it has market power.

Before one large company can acquire or merge with a competitor, it must convince the government that the acquisition would not seriously interfere with the overall competitiveness of the market.

CURBING RESTRICTIVE PRACTICES

In addition to promoting competition by limiting the degree of concentration within an industry, the government works to limit restrictive practices. The history here begins with the 1914 Federal Trade Commission Act. The first ten words of the act read: "Unfair methods of competition in commerce are hereby declared unlawful." President Woodrow Wilson defined the purpose of the new commission as being to "plead the voiceless consumer's case." Since then, a number of laws have been passed by Congress to specify what is "unfair."

Many of the restrictive practices targeted by the government involve the relations between a firm and its distributors and suppliers. Such practices include tie-ins, exclusive dealing, and price discrimination. We have already encountered all three in Chapter 12. Tie-ins require a consumer to purchase additional items when she buys a product. In exclusive dealing, a producer says to a firm that wants to sell its product, "If you sell my product, you cannot sell that of my rival." Price discrimination entails charging different customers different prices on grounds unrelated to the costs of serving those customers. The Robinson-Patman Act of 1936 strengthened the provisions outlawing price discrimination, making it easier to convict firms engaged in the practice. Other practices discussed in Chapter 12 designed to deter entry or promote collusion are illegal as well.

The precise definition of an illegal restrictive practice has changed over time with varying court interpretations of the antitrust laws. Some practices are illegal per se—firms conspiring to fix prices, for example. In 1961, General Electric, Westinghouse, and other producers of electrical equipment were found guilty of such conspiracy. More recently, several huge price-fixing cases were prosecuted successfully, most notably one against ADM (Archer Daniel Midland) involving lysine, citric acid, and high-fructose corn syrup. The corporations paid more than $100 million in fines, and some of their officials went to prison. Most practices, however, are not so clear-cut, and today a "rule of reason" prevails: they are acceptable if they can be shown to be reasonable business procedures, designed to promote economic efficiency. The efficiency gains are balanced against the higher prices resulting from the reduced competition.

Consider the example of Budweiser beer, which delivers its product through distributors. In any area, there is only one distributor, and the distributors are not allowed to compete against one another. The New York attorney general has argued that this system, by restricting competition, raises prices. Anheuser-Busch has replied that the system of exclusive territories enhances the efficiency with which beer is delivered and is necessary to ensure that customers receive fresh beer. They have maintained that their distribution system satisfies the rule of reason, and thus far their view has prevailed in the courts.

States have also been accused of adopting laws that restrict competition in ways designed to favor in-state firms. In December 2004, the U.S. Supreme Court heard arguments brought by a small Virginia winery against New York's laws restricting direct sales by out-of-state wineries to residents of New York. A challenge to a similar law in Michigan was also heard by the courts. The states argued that they were given regulatory power over the sale of alcoholic beverages by the Twenty-first Amendment to the Constitution, adopted to repeal Prohibition in 1933. However, because the New York and Michigan restrictions apply only to out-of-state producers while allowing in-state producers to ship directly to consumers, the laws have the effect of limiting competition. In May 2005, the Supreme Court ruled in favor of the Virginia winery and struck down the New York and Michigan laws that had restricted sales by out-of-state wineries.

ENFORCING THE ANTITRUST LAWS

Today antitrust laws are on the books at both state and federal levels, and they are enforced by both criminal and civil courts. The government takes action not only to break up existing monopolies but also to prevent firms from obtaining excessive market power.

The Federal Trade Commission (FTC) and the Antitrust Division of the Department of Justice are at the center of the government's efforts to promote competition. The FTC works like a law enforcement agency, investigating complaints it receives. It can provide advisory opinions on how an individual business should interpret the law, provide guidelines for entire industries, and even issue specific rules and regulations that businesses must follow. When necessary, the FTC enforces these decisions in court.

One interesting and controversial aspect of the antitrust laws is the use they make of *private* law enforcement. Any firm that believes it has been injured by the anticompetitive practices of another firm can sue; if successful, it can receive three times the dollar value of the damages and attorney fees incurred. The treble damages provision helps encourage private firms to call violations to the attention of the government. For example, in 1974 MCI sued AT&T, claiming that the latter had used unfair trade practices to hurt MCI in its attempt to enter the long-distance telephone business. In 1982, the jury estimated that MCI had, as a result of AT&T's activities, lost $600 million in profits, and ordered AT&T to pay triple that amount—$1.8 billion—in damages to MCI. The award was subsequently reduced on appeal to higher courts.

Two arguments favor private enforcement of antitrust laws. First, those who are injured by anticompetitive practices are in the best position to detect a violation of the law. Second, government may be lax in the enforcement of these laws because cartels and dominant firms may wield a great deal of political influence.

On the other side of the argument are concerns about the rising costs of antitrust litigation—the number of private suits doubled between the 1960s and the 1970s. And many worry that businesses use the threat of an antitrust suit as a way of raising a rival's costs. Thus, Chrysler charged General Motors with an antitrust violation when GM proposed a joint venture with a Japanese firm, only to drop the action when it found a Japanese partner for its own joint venture.

Wrap-Up

ANTITRUST POLICIES

Antitrust policies are designed to ensure competition in the marketplace by
- Limiting market dominance
- Curbing restrictive trade practices

The problems faced in designing and enforcing antitrust policies include
- The problem of defining the market
- Determining how to deal with firm practices that may *both* reduce competition *and* enhance efficiency

Enforcement of antitrust regulations can involve criminal or civil penalties.

Case in Point

COKE AND PEPSI PLAY MERGER

The Coca-Cola Company and PepsiCo, Inc., dominate the market for carbonated soft drinks. Early in 1986, each proposed to grow larger through acquisition. In January, PepsiCo proposed buying 7-Up, the fourth-largest soft drink manufacturer, for $380 million. In February, Coca-Cola proposed buying Dr. Pepper, the third-largest, for $470 million.

The mergers would have made the big even bigger. Coca-Cola and PepsiCo already held 39 percent and 28 percent of the market, respectively, while Dr. Pepper had 7 percent and 7-Up had 6 percent. The next largest firm in the market after 7-Up was R. J. Reynolds (known for Canada Dry and Sunkist), which held 5 percent of the soft drink market.

The Federal Trade Commission announced that it would oppose the mergers. To assess the impact on competition in such cases, the government often uses what is called the Herfindahl-Hirschman index (HHI). The HHI is calculated by summing the squares of the market shares. If the industry consists of a single firm, then the HHI is $(100)^2 = 10,000$. If the industry consists of 1,000 firms, each with 0.1 percent of the market, then the HHI is $(0.1)^2 \times 1,000 = 10$. Thus, higher values of the HHI indicate less competitive industries.

Merger guidelines used by the federal government divide markets into three categories, with different policy recommendations. The divisions and policy recommendations are given in Table 13.2.

Before the mergers, assuming that the 15 percent of the market not accounted for by the big five was divided equally among fifteen small producers, a somewhat simplified HHI for the soft drink industry was

$$\text{HHI} = 39^2 + 28^2 + 7^2 + 6^2 + 5^2 + 15\,(1)^2 = 2{,}430.$$

If we plug in the 34 percent share that PepsiCo would have after acquiring 7-Up, the PepsiCo–7-Up merger would raise the HHI to 2,766. The two proposed mergers together would raise the HHI to 3,312.

After the FTC announced its opposition, PepsiCo immediately gave up on purchasing 7-Up. Coca-Cola pushed ahead with its plan to buy Dr. Pepper until a federal judge ruled that it was a "stark, unvarnished" attempt to eliminate competition that "totally [lacked] any apparent redeeming feature."

The court case did bring a secret to the surface, however. The trial disclosed certain Coca-Cola company memos written after PepsiCo's offer for 7-Up had been made. In the memos, Coca-Cola executives expressed fear that the FTC might allow the PepsiCo merger, despite the agency's guidelines. By announcing plans to buy Dr. Pepper, Coca-Cola hoped that the FTC would step in and block *both* mergers, as it did, thereby preventing PepsiCo from using a merger to catch up in size to Coca-Cola.[1]

Table 13.2
HERFINDAHL-HIRSCHMAN INDEX

Level of HHI	Policy recommendation
Less than 1,000, unconcentrated	Mergers allowed without government challenge
Between 1,000 and 1,800, moderately concentrated	Mergers challenged if they raise the industry HHI by more than 100 points
Above 1,800, concentrated	Mergers challenged if they raise the industry HHI by more than 50 points

---

[1] See the following *Wall Street Journal* articles: Timothy K. Smith and Scott Kilman, "Coke to Acquire Dr. Pepper Co. for $470 Million," February 21, 1986, p. 2; Andy Pasztor and Timothy K. Smith, "FTC Opposes Purchase Plans by Coke, Pepsi," June 23, 1986, p. 2; Pasztor and Smith, "Coke Launched Dr. Pepper Bid to Scuttle Plans by PepsiCo, Documents Indicate," July 29, 1986, p. 3; Pasztor and Smith, "Coke's Plan to Buy Dr. Pepper Is Blocked by U.S. Judge, Pending Decision by FTC," August 1, 1986, p. 3.

Review and Practice

SUMMARY

1. Economists have identified four major problems resulting from monopolies and imperfect competition: restricted output, managerial slack, lack of incentives to make technological progress, and wasteful rent-seeking expenditures.
2. Since for a natural monopoly average costs are declining over the range of market demand, a large firm can undercut its rivals. And since marginal cost for a natural monopoly lies below average cost, an attempt by regulators to require it to set price equal to marginal cost (as in the case of perfect competition) will force the firm to make losses.
3. Taking ownership of a natural monopoly enables the government to set price and quantity directly. But it also subjects an industry to political pressures and the potential inefficiencies of government operation.
4. In the United States, natural monopolies are regulated. Government regulators seek to keep prices as low and quantity as high as is consistent with the natural monopolist being able to cover its costs. However, regulators are under political pressure to provide cross subsidies and are prone to being "captured" by the industry they are regulating.
5. In some cases, potential competition may be as effective as public ownership or government regulation at keeping prices low.
6. Antitrust policy is concerned with promoting competition, both by making it more difficult for any firm to dominate a market and by restricting practices that interfere with competition.
7. Under the "rule of reason," companies may seek to defend themselves from accusations of anticompetitive behavior by claiming that the practice in question also leads to greater efficiency. In such cases, courts must often decide whether the potential efficiency benefits of restrictive practices outweigh their potential anticompetitive effects.

KEY TERMS

managerial slack
rent seeking
cross subsidization
privatization
regulatory capture
trusts
horizontal mergers
vertical mergers

REVIEW QUESTIONS

1. What does it mean when an economist says that monopoly output is "too little" or a monopoly price is "too high"? By what standard? Compared with what?
2. Why might a monopoly lack incentives to hold costs as low as possible?
3. Why might a monopoly lack incentives to pursue research and development opportunities aggressively?
4. What might an economist regard as a socially wasteful way of spending monopoly profits?
5. Explain why the marginal cost curve of a natural monopoly lies below its average cost curve. What are the consequences of this?
6. If government regulators of a natural monopoly set price equal to marginal cost, what problem will inevitably arise? How might government ownership or regulation address this problem? What are the problems of each?
7. What is the regulatory capture hypothesis?
8. Explain the difference between a horizontal and a vertical merger.
9. Explain how the government uses antitrust policies to encourage competition, by making it more difficult for a firm to dominate a market and by curbing restrictive practices. What are some of the problems in implementing antitrust policy and some of the current controversies surrounding it?

PROBLEMS

1. Before deregulation of the telephone industry in 1984, AT&T provided both local and long-distance telephone service. A number of firms argued that they could provide

long-distance service between major cities more cheaply than AT&T, but AT&T argued against allowing firms to enter only the long-distance market. If those other firms (which had no technological advantage) could actually have offered long-distance service more cheaply, what does that imply about cross subsidies in AT&T's pricing of local and long-distance service? What would have happened if AT&T had been required to continue offering local service at the same price, but competition had been allowed in the long-distance market?

2. Explain the incentive problem involved if regulators ensure that a natural monopoly will be able to cover its average costs.

3. Explain how some competition, even if not perfect, may be an improvement for consumers over an unregulated natural monopoly. Explain why such competition will not be as good for consumers as an extremely sophisticated regulator, and why it may be better than many real-world regulators.

4. Smalltown, USA, has one bookstore, one newspaper, one movie theater, one nightclub, one grocery store, one hair salon, one college, and one department store. Does it follow that each of these is a monopolist? In each case, explain what sources of competition the firm might face that would limit its market power.

5. For each pair, explain whether you think they are part of the same or separate markets
   (a) Ice cream manufacturers and frozen yogurt manufacturers
   (b) Doctors and dentists
   (c) Doctors and chiropractors
   (d) Public universities and private universities
   (e) Trade schools and universities

6. Before the 1980s, many industries in New Zealand were dominated by a single firm. To limit the social cost of monopoly, these firms were heavily regulated by the government. After winning election in the 1980s, New Zealand's Labour Party shifted the government's focus from regulating domestic firms to eliminating restrictions on imports. Explain why reducing the barriers that had prevented New Zealanders from buying imported goods could reduce the market power of the domestic firm, even if there continues to be only one domestic firm in the industry.

Learning Goals

In this chapter, you will learn

1. How game theory can help us understand strategic behavior
2. What the Nash equilibrium is in the prisoner's dilemma game
3. Why backward induction is critical for thinking strategically
4. How reputation can play a role in repeated games
5. How game theory can help us understand why threats and promises may not always be credible

Chapter 14

STRATEGIC BEHAVIOR

During the 2000 television season, viewers were enthralled by the first season of the show *Survivor*. Sixteen contestants were marooned on Pulau Tiga, an uninhabited island off the coast of Borneo, and at the end of each episode, the survivors voted to kick out one of their members. The last surviving contestant collected $1 million. By episode 13, the original group had been reduced to just three final contestants: Kelly, Rudy, and Rich. In the course of a trial that involved answering questions about the thirteen previously evicted castaways, Kelly won immunity in the first round of voting that would reduce the group to the final pair. She still had to decide, though, how to cast her own vote. If, as seemed certain, Rudy votes against Rich and Rich votes against Rudy, Kelly's vote would decide who stays and who leaves. How should Kelly vote?

To know whom she should vote out in the first round, Kelly must think about how she was likely to fare in the final round. Kelly must think backward from the end of the contest. Rudy seemed popular with the audience and with the other thirteen contestants who would get to vote for the final winner. So Kelly would reason that if the final contest came down to her and Rudy, Rudy would probably win. On the other hand, Rich seemed to be very unpopular. So Kelly would reason that if it came down to a choice between her and Rich, she would probably win. Her best chance would be to face off against Rich, not Rudy, in the final voting. Even if Kelly really dislikes Rich, her best strategy is to oust Rudy. As it turned out, that is exactly what happened. Rich and Kelly voted against Rudy. Unfortunately for Kelly, the voters ended up picking Rich over her, but her strategy was still the right one.

The participants in *Survivor* had to think strategically. They needed to anticipate how their rivals would respond to the decisions they themselves made. They had to consider how their own position would depend on who else survived and who didn't, and they had to use that information in deciding how to vote.

Thinking strategically doesn't help just in a made-up environment such as a television show. We all face situations that call for strategic thinking. Economists try to understand the choices individuals and firms make, and researchers studying strategic behavior have extended the reach of economics into many new areas.

Economists examine the choices made by rational individuals and profit-maximizing firms. In the basic competitive model presented in the first two parts of this book, individuals and firms do not need to behave strategically. Consumers and firms can buy or sell as much as they want at the market price. A firm does not need to worry about how its rivals will react if it decides to produce more. Nor does a monopoly, but for a different reason: a monopoly has no rivals. In the basic competitive model and in a monopoly model, **strategic behavior**—decisions that take into account the possible reactions of others—plays no role.

Things were different in Chapter 12 when we studied oligopolies. With only a few firms in the industry, each firm needs to be concerned about how its rivals might react whenever it contemplates expanding production or cutting its price. Strategic behavior becomes important. When AMD considers cutting the prices of its various computer processor chips, it must try to assess how Intel will respond. If Intel reacts by also cutting prices, then AMD may not gain much market share and its revenues will decline as a result of the lower prices. But if Intel keeps its prices unchanged, AMD may gain market share and its revenues might rise as it sells more chips.

Because oligopolies engage in strategic behavior, Chapter 12 used game theory—and the simple prisoner's dilemma game—to demonstrate why it may be difficult for firms to collude. In this chapter, we return to the prisoner's dilemma and see how its basic insights can be applied to other areas of economics. The usefulness of game theory goes well beyond this simple model, however, for decisions and choices often must incorporate the potential reactions of others. You will learn more about game theory and how it helps us understand the choices made by individuals, firms, unions, and governments. Game theory provides a framework for studying strategic behavior. Using this framework, economists have found that many instances of strategic behavior can be understood by relying on the core concepts of incentives and information.[1]

Review of the Prisoner's Dilemma

Let's very briefly recall the prisoner's dilemma game introduced in Chapter 12. Two prisoners, A and B, are alleged by the police to be conspirators in a crime. After being taken into custody, the two are separated. A police officer tells each, "Now here's the situation. If your partner confesses and you remain silent, you'll get five years in prison. But if your partner confesses and you confess also, you'll both get three years. On the other hand, if both you and your partner remain silent, we'll be able to convict you only of a lesser charge and you'll get one year in prison. But if your partner remains silent and you confess, we'll let you out in three months." The same deal is offered to both prisoners.

---

[1]If you would like to learn even more about game theory, an accessible textbook is available: Avinash Dixit and Susan Skeath, *Games of Strategy*, Second Edition (New York: W. W. Norton, 2004).

Figure 14.1, which reproduces a diagram from Chapter 12, shows the results of the deal the police have offered the prisoners. This type of grid, showing the payoffs to each player, is called a **game table.** In Chapter 12, we saw that based on self-interest, each individual prisoner believes that confession is best, whether his partner confesses or not. But by following self-interest and confessing, each ends up worse off than if neither had confessed. The prisoner's dilemma is a simple game in which both parties suffer because they independently act in self-interest. Both would be better off if they could get together to agree on a story and if each could threaten to punish the other if he deviates from the story.

This simple game has been widely applied in economics and in other fields such as international relations and political science. In Chapter 12, we used it to explain why two oligopolists would find it difficult to sustain an agreement to collude. We will discuss some further examples of the prisoner's dilemma and then consider other types of game situations. First, though, we will need to clarify our method of analyzing strategic situations to make predictions about how individuals and firms will behave.

FIGURE 14.1

PRISONER'S DILEMMA GAME

Each prisoner's dominant strategy is to confess.

	Prisoner B Confesses	Prisoner B Remains silent
Prisoner A Confesses	B gets 3 years / A gets 3 years	B gets 5 years / A gets 3 months
Prisoner A Remains silent	B gets 3 months / A gets 5 years	B gets 1 year / A gets 1 year

DOMINANT STRATEGIES

Behaving strategically means that each player must try to determine what the other player is likely to do. Will your accomplice confess or keep quiet? Will your rival match price reductions if you cut your prices? The decision of one player depends on how she thinks the other player will respond.

In the basic prisoner's dilemma game, we assume that players reason along the following lines: "For each choice that I might make, what is the best choice for the other player to make?" In analyzing the prisoner's dilemma, we ask, "If prisoner A doesn't confess, what is the best strategy for prisoner B? If prisoner A confesses, what is the best strategy for prisoner B?" In both cases, we conclude that confessing is prisoner B's *best response*. If B's best response is to confess, no matter what prisoner A does, then A will conclude that B will confess, so A needs to decide what his best response is to prisoner B confessing. As we saw, prisoner A's best option is also to confess.

Such a strategy—one that works best no matter what the other player does—is called a **dominant strategy.** Recall that an objective of game theory is to predict what strategy each player will choose. When a player has a dominant strategy, that is the strategy we should predict a rational decision maker will choose.

NASH EQUILIBRIUM

It is easy to predict the outcome of a game—its equilibrium—if each player has a dominant strategy. Each will play his dominant strategy. Thus, in the prisoner's dilemma, the equilibrium is both players confessing. The situation is not quite so simple when only one player has a dominant strategy, or when neither player has one; we will learn about such games later. To predict the equilibrium outcomes in these more complex games, we need to look more closely at why confessing is the equilibrium in the prisoner's dilemma.

In the prisoner's dilemma, each prisoner confesses because doing so leads to the best, or *optimal* payoff—the least amount of time in prison—given what the other prisoner can be expected to do. The outcome is an equilibrium in the sense that neither prisoner would change her chosen strategy if offered the chance to do so at the end of the game. By confessing, both have played their best response. Such an equilibrium is called a **Nash equilibrium,** and it is the most fundamental idea for predicting the actions of players in a strategic game.

John Nash developed the notion that bears his name when he was just twenty-one years old and a graduate student in mathematics at Princeton University. Economists have found the concept of Nash equilibrium extremely useful for predicting the outcomes of games and understanding economic problems. In recognition of its importance, John Nash shared the 1994 Nobel Prize in Economics. Nash is not an economist; he is a mathematician and the only winner of the Nobel Prize in Economics whose life has been the subject of a best-selling biography and a popular movie. Published in 1998, *A Beautiful Mind* by Sylvia Nasar chronicles Nash's early mathematical brilliance, his struggle with mental illness, and his eventual recovery. On being informed he had won the Nobel Prize, Nash commented that he hoped it would improve his credit rating.

The prisoner's dilemma arises in many contexts, both in economics and in other social sciences. The following examples, briefly sketched, provide some illustrations.[2]

Example: Collusion In Chapter 12, we studied an application of the prisoner's dilemma to the problem faced by two rivals who can benefit by colluding to restrict output. Colluding results in a higher price and therefore greater profits for each. The higher price can be maintained only if both firms continue to restrict output. But at the higher price, each firm perceives that it would be even better off if it could expand its output a little and sell more at the high price. Of course, this means that each firm has an incentive to cheat on their agreement to restrict output, just as each prisoner had an incentive to confess. And if both firms fail to stick to their bargain, their expansion causes the price, and their profits, to fall, thereby making each worst off than if they had continued to collude. In this game, each firm has a dominant strategy—cheat on the agreement by expanding output. Here, the outcome in which each firm expands is the Nash equilibrium; each firm is choosing its best response, given the actions of its rival. When both players have a dominant strategy, as in the prisoner's dilemma, both will choose to play it; no other outcome would satisfy the definition of a Nash equilibrium. In this case, there is only one Nash equilibrium, a situation economists describe by saying there is a *unique Nash equilibrium.*

Example: Politicians and Negative Ads Why do politicians engage in negative advertising even though they all promise not to?

---

[2]You should test your understanding of each example by filling out a game table, identifying the dominant strategy for each player, and finding the Nash equilibrium.

Consider the case of politicians A and B. If neither runs a negative campaign, the public thinks highly of both of them, but neither gains any advantage over the other. If both run negative campaign ads, the public thinks poorly of both, but again neither gains an advantage. Each is tarred by the other's ads. If politician A runs a clean campaign, politician B can gain an advantage by running a negative ad that tarnishes A's reputation. Conversely, A gains by running a negative ad if politician B runs a clean campaign.

Each politician will reason as follows: "If my opponent runs a negative ad, I'm better off if I also run negative ads. And if my opponent doesn't run a negative ad, then I can gain an advantage if I run negative ads. Either way, I'm better off if I run negative ads." Each politician has a dominant strategy, and in this unique Nash equilibrium both run negative campaign ads, despite their promises not to.

Example: Military Spending Two countries, A and B, are locked in a military balance. Each must decide whether to build a new generation of missiles. If neither builds the missile system, the military balance is preserved and each country will remain secure. If one builds the system while the other does not, one will gain a military advantage. If they both build the system, they each spend billions of dollars, but neither gains an advantage: each country now has the new missile system, preserving the military balance.

Each country reasons that if the other country fails to build the system, it can gain an advantage by going ahead and building the system. Both also know that if one country builds the new missiles, the other will be worse off if it fails to build the missile system as well. Each country has a dominant strategy—build the missile system. Both countries spend billions, only to find themselves left in the same military balance as before.

Example: Sports Owners and Player Salaries Sports teams compete to hire the best players. Suppose there are just two teams, the Yankees and the Athletics. If both teams collude and keep salaries low, the owners' profits go up. If the Yankees' owner instead offers high salaries while the Athletics owner does not, the Yankees will attract all the good players and will generate higher profits for the owner. Meanwhile, the Athletics end up with weaker players and have a poor season. Low attendance causes the owner to lose money. Conversely, if the Athletics offer high salaries and the Yankees do not, the Athletics get all the good players and earn the higher profits, while the Yankees lose money. If both offer high salaries, neither team gets all the good players, but increased salary costs cut into the owners' profits.

In a Nash equilibrium, both team owners offer players high salaries, and the owners are worse off than if they been able to collude to keep salaries down. Of course, our simple example ignores all the other factors—TV revenues, cable deals, sales of team paraphernalia, and so on—that support total payrolls and thus affect salaries and profits. But the example does suggest one of the factors behind the desire of owners in most professional sports to institute caps on player salaries. Without such caps, each owner has an incentive to try to outbid the others for the best players. A salary cap enables the owners to collude more effectively.

> **Wrap-Up**
>
> ## THE PRISONER'S DILEMMA
>
> In the prisoner's dilemma, each player has a dominant strategy. In a unique Nash equilibrium, the players choose their dominant strategy. Yet the players are worse off in this Nash equilibrium than if they had chosen their alternative strategy. Applications of the prisoner's dilemma arise in many branches of economics, as well as in other social sciences and in everyday life.

Strategic Behavior in More General Games

In the prisoner's dilemma, both players have a dominant strategy. In most games, however, this is not the case. What each player finds it best to do depends on what the other player does, and determining the outcome of a game is therefore harder. But we can often make an accurate prediction by thinking through the consequences from each player's perspective, just as we did in the prisoner's dilemma.

GAMES WITH ONLY ONE DOMINANT STRATEGY

Consider the positions of two firms deciding on whether to cut prices. Discounters Delux and Quality Brands compete with each other. Discounters Delux promises its customers the lowest prices; it would suffer a large loss of customers if it failed to deliver on that promise. Quality Prices has higher costs; perhaps it provides better health care benefits to its workers or spends more on the displays in its stores. Because of these higher costs, it would prefer not to cut prices. However, it risks losing some of its business if it does not match Discounters Delux's price reductions. The profits each expects to earn are shown in Figure 14.2. The payoffs to Discounters Delux are below the diagonal lines, while those of Quality Brands are above the diagonals.

Discounters Delux has a dominant strategy—reduce prices. It makes more in profits under this strategy, regardless of what Quality Brands does. Quality Brands, in contrast, does not have a dominant strategy. If Discounters Delux reduces prices, Quality Brand's best response is to cut prices as well, since otherwise it would lose too many sales. However, if Discounters Delux does not reduce prices, then Quality Brands is better off not reducing its prices.

Even though Quality Brands does not have a dominant strategy, we can predict its move if we reason as follows. Quality Brands

FIGURE 14.2

PRICE-CUTTING GAME

Discounters Delux has a dominant strategy, which is to reduce prices. Thus, the best response for Quality Brands is also to cut prices.

International Perspective
BEGGAR-THY-NEIGHBOR TARIFF POLICIES

During the international depression of the 1930s, many countries debated whether to impose restrictions on international trade. Some argued that restricting imports from other countries would boost the demand for goods produced domestically. Increased demand, in turn, would enable domestic firms to expand employment and production. By reducing the demand for goods produced in other countries, such policies would lead to fewer sales by foreign firms, who would then have to cut production and employment. The gains at home would come at the expense of foreign producers and workers, so these were often called "beggar-thy-neighbor" policies. The trade wars of the 1930s can be understood as another example of the prisoner's dilemma.

In 1930, the United States passed the Smoot-Hawley Tariff Act. This act raised tariffs on imported goods, making them more expensive for American consumers and thereby providing an incentive for Americans to shift their demand to domestically produced goods. Other countries did not stand by idly while American tariffs reduced their market in the United States. They retaliated by raising their tariffs on goods produced in the United States. The result was that all countries suffered from the decline in world trade. By imposing tariffs that reduced trade, all countries lost the benefits of trade.

The outcome in the sort of trade war set off by the Smoot-Hawley Act can be illustrated in terms of a simple game. The diagram shows the payoffs to each of two countries that are deciding whether to impose trade restrictions. Payoffs to country A are shown below the diagonal line in each box; payoffs to country B, above the diagonal. The payoffs are defined as the gains (or losses) to a country's income relative to what that income would be if neither imposed trade restrictions. The numbers are hypothetical and can be thought of as, say, tens of billions of dollars. Each country gains the most if it is the only one to impose restrictions. Both are worse off if both impose restrictions and better off if neither imposes them.

Each country has a dominant strategy—impose trade sanctions. Country A, for example, would reason as follows: "If country B imposes trade restrictions, our country will be better off if we also impose restrictions. If country B does not impose restrictions, we are also better off if we impose restrictions. Therefore, we should impose trade restrictions regardless of what country B does." Country B would reason in exactly the same manner. Unfortunately, when they both impose restrictions, both are left worse off than if no restrictions had been imposed.

Another way to look at this situation is to recognize that both countries would be better off if they could cooperate and mutually agree not to impose trade restrictions. The problem is, our simple example provides no mechanism to ensure that they cooperate. Just as in the collusion example discussed in Chapter 12, each player has an incentive to violate any voluntary agreement not to impose trade restrictions. One of the roles of international organizations such as the World Trade Organization (WTO) is to lay down rules designed to promote international trade and cooperation, enabling nations to make credible commitments not to raise tariffs or other barriers to trade. The WTO can impose sanctions on the countries that violate these rules.

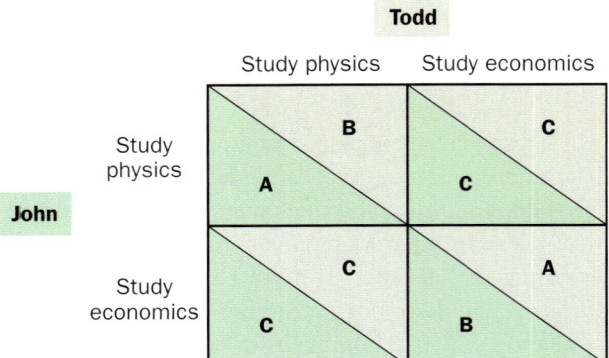

FIGURE 14.3

THE STUDY GAME

Neither player has a dominant strategy, but there are two Nash equilibria: both study physics or both study economics.

knows that Discounters Delux will reduce prices, since that is Discounters Delux's dominant strategy. So the fact that Quality Brands would find it best to keep prices high if Discounters Delux keeps its prices high is irrelevant. Quality Brands knows that Discounters Delux will cut prices, and therefore its best strategy is also to cut prices. The outcome, or equilibrium, in this game will have both firms reducing their prices.

GAMES WITHOUT DOMINANT STRATEGIES

Both the prisoner's dilemma game and the price-cutting game have unique Nash equilibria. Often, however, a game will have more than one Nash equilibrium, as the following example illustrates.

Two friends are enrolled in the same physics and economics classes. They both know that studying together is much more efficient than studying alone. By working through problems together, each will greatly improve his performance on upcoming tests in the two classes. However, John is really worried about his physics grade and would prefer that he and Todd focus on physics. Conversely, Todd is most worried about economics and would rather devote their study time to it. The game table for their circumstances is shown in Figure 14.3, with the payoffs expressed in the average grade for the two courses (the letter below the diagonal line in each box is the payoff to John).

Does either John or Todd have a dominant strategy? No. If John insists on studying physics, Todd is better off joining John in hitting the physics books than in going it alone and studying economics. On the other hand, if John is willing to study economics, then Todd's best response is obviously to study economics too. Similarly, John's best strategy is to study physics if that is what Todd also does, while John's best strategy is to study economics if Todd does that instead. Neither player has a dominant strategy, one that is best regardless of what the other does.

Even though there are no dominant strategies in this game, there are two Nash equilibria—either both friends study physics or both study economics. If Todd pulls out Stiglitz and Walsh's economics textbook and starts reviewing the material on trade-offs and incentives, John's best strategy is to join him. Studying economics is John's best choice, given that Todd is studying economics. After all, if he goes off and studies physics by himself, his average grade in the two classes will be a C; while if he instead studies economics with Todd, he will do worse in physics, but he will do so much better in economics that his average grade will be a B. The same is true for Todd—given that John is studying economics, Todd's best strategy is to join him. So the lower right box in the diagram is a Nash equilibrium. But it is not the only one. The upper left box, where both end up studying physics together, is also a Nash equilibrium. While it may not enable us to predict a *unique* equilibrium in a game, the concept of a Nash equilibrium can help eliminate some outcomes. Neither the upper right nor the lower left box in the diagram is a Nash equilibrium. If Todd studies physics, then studying economics alone is not John's best response.

Internet Connection
THE ZERO-SUM GAME SOLVER

Some games have a fixed total payoff: in *Survivor,* the winner receives $1 million and the next few survivors receive smaller amounts. Nothing the contestants do can affect the total prize money available. If one contestant receives more, another receives less. Games like this are called *zero-sum games.* When we think of games, we usually think of sports or chess, or perhaps gambling—all zero-sum games. In sports, one team wins and the other loses. In gambling, every dollar you win is someone else's loss. While many people think that economic exchange is a zero-sum game, you should understand by now that it is not—exchange can leave *both* parties better off. On the Web site of Professor David Levine at UCLA, you can find a program that will find the solution to any two-person zero-sum game. Invent a game yourself and find its solution at http://levine.sscnet.ucla.edu/Games/zerosum.htm.

Wrap-Up
THE BASIC TYPES OF GAMES

1. The prisoner's dilemma—both players have dominant strategies and the game has one Nash equilibrium. Application: understanding why collusion is difficult.
2. The price-cutting game—only one player has a dominant strategy and the game has one Nash equilibrium. Application: understanding competition between duopolists.
3. The study game—neither player has a dominant strategy and there are two Nash equilibria. Application: understanding banking panics (see p. 322).

Repeated Games

In the basic prisoner's dilemma game, each party makes only one decision. The game is played just a single time. The two players could do better if they could somehow cooperate and agree not to pick the dominant strategy. But when the game is actually played, each has an incentive to break any prior agreement and do what is in his own best interest. If the players or parties interact many times, then the strategies for each can become more complicated. There may be additional ways to try to enforce cooperation that would benefit both parties. Games that are played many times over by the same players are called **repeated games.**

To see how the nature of the game is changed when it is repeated, let us consider the actions of two politicians running for the Senate. At the start of an election campaign, suppose each candidate announces that she will refrain from running negative ads as long as her rival does. But if the rival cheats on this agreement and runs a negative ad, the other candidate responds by running her own negative attack ads. Can this threat of retaliation ensure that the two candidates run clean campaigns?

Imagine that there are several weeks remaining until the date of the election. Each candidate will figure that she should run negative ads in the last week of the campaign: this is her best strategy, because the threat of retaliation carries no force after the election. There is no longer any payoff in continuing to cooperate, since the campaign (and the game) ends on election day. The agreement breaks down the week before the election.

Now consider what happens two weeks before the election. Both candidates know that the other will start running negative ads the following week. But if they are not going to honor their agreement during the last week of the campaign anyway, then the threat of future retaliatory attacks is completely meaningless. Hence, each candidate will reason that it pays to cheat on the agreement by running a negative ad. The agreement breaks down two weeks before the election. Reasoning backward through time, we see that the agreement not to run negative ads will break down almost immediately, no matter when the election is held.

This example illustrates an important principle of strategic thinking: think first about the end of the game and work backward from there to identify the best current choice. Making decisions in this way is called **backward induction.** For each decision a player can make, she needs to work out her opponent's optimal response and what her own payoff will be. Then, in the first stage of the game, she can adopt the strategy that gives her the highest payoff.

Backward induction also applies in the various games considered earlier, from Kelly making her decision in *Survivor* to the players in a prisoner's dilemma game. For example, prisoner A reasoned, "Suppose my partner confesses; what is my best strategy? And if my partner does not confess, then what is my best strategy?" Each thought about the consequences of his opponent's choices and worked backward to determine what he should do.

Our analysis of collusion in a repeated game setting may seem too pessimistic about the ability of firms or individuals to cooperate. Certainly we see that individuals often do find ways to cooperate, trading a short-term gain to establish longer-term relationships that yield higher benefits. And firms behave similarly, offering services or providing higher-quality products that lower their immediate profits but contribute to higher profits in the future. In strategic games that do not have a finite end—that always offer the possibility of another round—a variety of strategies may enable players to cooperate to achieve better outcomes.

Wrap-Up

BACKWARD INDUCTION

When strategic interactions occur for a repeated but fixed number of times, the best approach is to start from the end of the game and work backward to determine the optimal strategy. Backward induction helps the player focus on the future consequences of his current decision.

REPUTATIONS

Developing good reputations can be useful when players are engaged in repeated interactions. A firm that relies on local customers for repeat business has more of an incentive to develop a reputation for good service than does one with little repeat business. A car mechanic might have an incentive to pad the bill or otherwise cheat a customer if he never expects to service that particular car again, but in the long run he might profit more by gaining a reputation for good service and relying on repeat business from his customers.

Gaining a reputation is costly in the short run—initially the car mechanic will be unable to charge any more than do garages unconcerned about their reputations. His lower profits in the short run are like an investment: they will pay off in the future when the reputation he has developed enables him to charge more than most mechanics.

TIT FOR TAT

Economists have set up laboratory experiments, much like those used in other sciences, to test how individuals actually behave in these different games. The advantage of this sort of **experimental economics** is that the researcher seeking the crucial determinants of behavior can change one aspect of the experiment at a time. One set of experiments has explored how individuals cooperate in situations like the prisoner's dilemma. These experiments tend to show that participants often evolve simple strategies that, although sometimes apparently irrational in the short run, can be effective in inducing cooperation (collusion) as the game is repeated a number of times. One common strategy is tit for tat. In the case of two oligopolists, one might threaten to increase output if the other does, even if doing so does not maximize its short-term profits. If the rival finds this threat credible—as it may well be, especially after it has been carried out a few times—the firm may decide that it is more profitable to cooperate and keep production low than to cheat. In the real world, such simple strategies may play an important role in ensuring that firms do not compete too vigorously in markets in which there are only three or four dominant firms.

Internet Connection
THE PRISONER'S DILEMMA

You can play a repeated game version of the prisoner's dilemma against a computer at www.princeton.edu/-mdaniels/PD/PD.html. Try a tit-for-tat strategy and see how the computer responds.

INSTITUTIONS

In many situations, institutions ensure that a cooperative outcome is reached. International organizations such as the World Trade Organization (WTO) serve to enforce agreements that promote international trade. Member countries agree to abide by certain rules that forbid the type of trade restrictions and beggar-thy-neighbor policies that proved so disastrous during the 1930s. Professional sports leagues impose salary caps, which limit the ability of teams to boost salaries. Deposit insurance eliminates the incentive for depositors to withdraw funds when there are rumors of financial trouble at their bank, because they know their money is protected even if their bank fails.

Case in Point

BANKING PANICS

Between 1930 and 1933, the United States suffered a massive financial panic that forced about nine thousand banks to fail. This disruption of the financial system contributed to the severity of the Great Depression, when unemployment reached levels as high as 25 percent of the labor force. As banks closed their doors, businesses that relied on bank credit to finance their inventories and investments were forced to cut back production and lay off workers. How can game theory help us understand why so many banks failed?

During the banking panics of the early 1930s, depositors rushed to withdraw their savings, leading to many bank failures.

If you have a deposit in a commercial bank today, the federal government insures it (up to $100,000): if your bank makes bad investments and goes bankrupt, the federal government will make sure that you receive all your money back. Before 1933, however, bank deposits were not insured. If your bank went bankrupt, you could lose everything—that is, unless you acted at the first hint of trouble and withdrew your deposits before the bank ran out of cash. Banks lend out most of the money they receive as deposits, holding only a small fraction as cash to meet daily unpredictable fluctuations in deposits and withdrawals. If all depositors were to suddenly demand their money back, a bank would quickly run out of cash and be forced to close. That's what almost happened to George Bailey's bank in the movie *It's a Wonderful Life,* and it is exactly what happened in real life in the 1930s as depositors raced to be the first to withdraw their deposits. When they all tried to withdraw their deposits at the same time, there simply was not enough money on hand to pay everyone. Thousands of banks had to shut their doors. Everyone would have been better off leaving their deposits alone, since in that case the banks could have remained open.

The concept of Nash equilibrium can help us understand bank runs and financial panics. Consider a simple example of a bank with just two depositors—call them A and B. Each depositor must decide whether to try to withdraw her deposits from the bank or to leave them there. Assume each has deposited $1,000 at the bank. The bank has used these funds to make loans and investments but keeps $200 on hand in its vault. If the bank's loans are repaid, the bank can pay an interest rate of 5 percent to its depositors.

If neither depositor tries to withdraw funds from the bank, let us assume they both will eventually receive the full value of their deposits plus the 5 percent interest (for a total of $1,050). If depositor A withdraws while depositor B does not, A can take out $200, all the cash the bank has on hand. The bank then must shut its doors, and depositor B receives nothing. The reverse happens if depositor B tries to withdraw its funds while A does not. If both try to withdraw their money, the most each can get is $100. The payoffs are shown in Figure 14.4.

Clearly both depositors are better off if neither attempts a withdrawal. In that case, they both would eventually receive $1,050. This is also a Nash equilibrium. If depositor A leaves her money in the bank, depositor B's best strategy is to do the same. Conversely, if depositor B leaves her money in the bank, depositor A's best strategy is to do the same. Each reasons as follows: "If the other leaves her deposits in the bank, my best strategy is also to leave my deposits in the bank." So there is an equilibrium in which neither depositor tries to withdraw funds, and the bank stays open.

Just as in the earlier example of the two friends deciding what to study, there are two Nash equilibria to the deposit withdrawal game. The second Nash equilibrium occurs when both depositors try to withdraw their money and the bank fails. In this case, each reasons as follows: "If the other depositor tries to withdraw, I'm better off if I also try to withdraw. That way, at least I get $100,

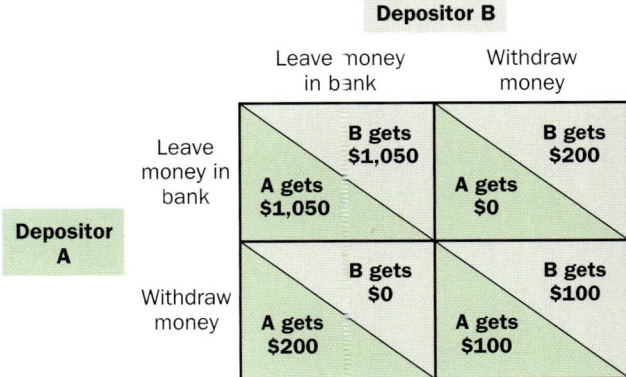

FIGURE 14.4

A BANK PANIC AS A STRATEGIC GAME

Like the study game, this game has two Nash equilibria: both withdraw money or both leave money in the bank. The equilibrium in which both leave their money in the bank leaves both better off than if they both withdraw their money.

which is better than nothing." So there is an equilibrium in which each rushes to the bank, and the bank is unable to fully meet its obligations to the two depositors. The bank fails.

In this example, there is a good equilibrium—the one in which the bank remains open and the depositors eventually receive all their money plus interest—and a bad equilibrium, when the bank is forced to close. In the prisoner's dilemma, in contrast, the only equilibrium was inferior to an alternative set of strategies (neither prisoner confesses). The example of John and Todd illustrated another possible outcome: one of the two equilibria was preferred by Todd and the other by John.

Financial panics can be thought of as shifts from the good to the bad equilibrium. Such a shift can occur if depositors start to worry about the financial soundness of the banking sector, even if such fears are unfounded. The simple argument illustrated by this game provides part of the rationale behind federal deposit insurance. Deposit insurance gives each depositor confidence that her money is safe, regardless of what other depositors do. No depositor has an incentive to try to outmaneuver others by getting her money out first.

Sequential Moves

In the prisoner's dilemma, each player must make a choice without knowing what the other has done. The players move simultaneously. In many situations, however, one player must move first, and the second player then responds directly to what the first has done. This is called a **sequential game,** since players take turns and each can observe what choices were made in earlier moves. In such a game, the player who moves first must consider how the second player will respond to each possible move he can make.

Sports offer many instances of strategic behavior. The baseball manager deciding whether to bring in a relief pitcher is a prime example of someone playing a sequential game. Conventional wisdom in baseball says that a left-handed batter has more success against a right-handed pitcher, and a right-handed batter does better against a left-handed pitcher. Does that mean that if a right-handed player is coming to bat, the manager should bring in a right-handed pitcher? Not necessarily. Once a right-handed pitcher is brought in, the manager of the other team can send a left-handed pinch hitter to the plate. So a manager considering a change of pitchers needs to think about how his counterpart will respond to each of the possible pitching choices he can make.

This example illustrates an important aspect of a sequential game. The player who moves first must anticipate how the second player will respond. Take the case of a firm facing the potential entry of a new rival into its market. Suppose a software firm, call it Redhat, is considering the launch of a new operating system that will compete with Microsoft Windows. Redhat must decide whether to enter the business or stay out. If it enters, Microsoft must decide whether to peacefully compete or to wage a price war. Suppose that Redhat enters and Microsoft competes peacefully. Assume Microsoft will earn profits of $50 billion and Redhat $10 billion on its operating system. If instead Microsoft engages in a price war, assume both firms will lose money, with Microsoft losing $1 billion and Redhat losing $500 million. If Redhat decides not to enter, it earns $0, while Microsoft earns profits of $80 billion. Will Redhat enter? And will Microsoft engage in a price war?

To simplify this complex scenario we can use a **game tree** diagram, which is the standard way to represent a sequential game. Different branches on a game tree indicate the various outcomes that could occur, given all the possible strategies the players could follow. For example, the entry game involving Microsoft and Redhat is represented by the game tree of Figure 14.5. At the end of each branch, the payoffs to Redhat and Microsoft are shown. The first number is Redhat's payoff; the second is Microsoft's.

Each node—the points at which new branches split—represents a decision point for one of the players. In this game, Redhat moves first (node 1). Microsoft moves second, after it has learned whether Redhat has entered or not. If Redhat decides to enter, we move along the upper branch of the game tree from node 1 to node 2. Microsoft must then choose whether to compete peacefully or wage a price war. From node 2, we move along the upper branch if Microsoft competes peacefully, and the payoffs are $10 billion to Redhat and $50 billion to Microsoft; or we move along the lower branch if Microsoft wages a price war, in which case the payoffs are –$500 million and –$1 billion, respectively. If Redhat decides not to enter, we move along the lower branch from node 1. Here, there is nothing further Microsoft must decide, so the game ends and the players receive the payoffs shown ($0 for Redhat and $80 billion for Microsoft).

In deciding whether to enter, Redhat's managers will reason as follows: "If we enter, Microsoft can either wage a price war or compete peacefully. In the former case, it loses $1 billion, and in the latter case it makes $50 billion. Clearly, once we enter, it will be in Microsoft's best interest to compete peacefully, so we should enter."

This example again illustrates backward induction. "Thinking strategically" requires that one think first about the end of the game, and work backward from there to determine the best current choice. Redhat asks itself what Microsoft will do if Redhat has entered. It works backward from there to determine if it should enter.

Using backward induction is easy when a game tree is employed . At each node that leads to an end to the game, determine the best strategy of the player who makes a decision at that node. Then work backward. At node 2, Microsoft's best strategy is to compete peacefully. It gets $50 billion that way, while it would lose $1 billion in a price war. Now work back to the previous node—node 1, where Redhat makes its decision. From its analysis of Microsoft's options at node 2, Redhat knows that if it enters the market, Microsoft will compete peacefully, leaving Redhat with a $10 billion profit. Redhat's other option at node 1 is not to enter, which would leave it with profits of $0. Clearly, Redhat's best strategy is to enter.

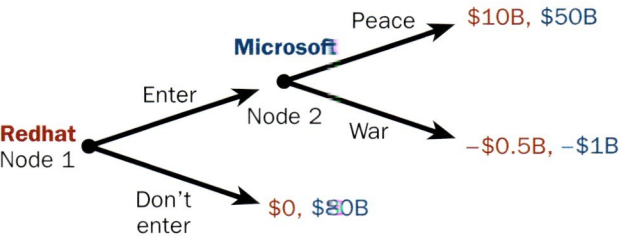

FIGURE 14.5

GAME TREE FOR A SEQUENTIAL GAME

Redhat makes the first move. If Redhat decides to enter the market, Microsoft may then choose between peaceful coexistence or a price war. By reasoning backward from these options, we can see that Redhat will enter the market and Microsoft will choose to compete peacefully.

Thinking Like an Economist
INFORMATION AND THINKING STRATEGICALLY

Information plays a critical role in strategic behavior, but sometimes in surprising ways. Take the prisoner's dilemma, for example. Each prisoner must make a decision about whether to confess without knowing what the other prisoner has done. It might seem that the outcome would change if one prisoner could know the other's choice in advance, but it turns out that providing this extra information makes no difference. It is still best to confess, because confessing is a dominant strategy: it is the best strategy for each prisoner, regardless of what the other did.

In the absence of a dominant strategy, changing the information that the player has *is* likely to alter the player's best strategy. Consider the case of an insurance company that offers health insurance. Suppose the insurance company can obtain information such as whether an individual smokes. Since smoking is associated with many health problems, the insurance company will offer different policies to smokers and nonsmokers; smokers will pay higher insurance premiums to reflect the likelihood they will incur higher medical bills. Now suppose a law is passed that forbids the insurance company from collecting such information. Governments frequently pass such laws on the grounds that collecting certain types of information is an invasion of privacy. If the company offers just a single policy to everyone, it faces an adverse selection problem of the type we will consider in Chapter 15—those with the poorest health are the ones most likely to buy the insurance. But if the firm thinks strategically, it might reason along the following lines: "If we offer only one type of policy, we run the risk that only those with health problems will buy it and we will lose money. Instead, let's offer two different policies. One will have a high deductible, so that patients themselves have to pay a large amount for doctor visits and other services before insurance kicks in. The other policy will have a low deductible, with insurance paying for most medical services. We will charge more for the policy with the low deductible. The low-deductible policy will be more attractive to individuals who think they will need lots of medical services. It will be attractive to smokers. The policy with the high deductible will be more attractive to individuals who think they are less likely to need lots of medical care. It will be attractive to nonsmokers. By offering these separate policies, we can get individuals to reveal information about their health risks."

By thinking strategically, the insurance company is able to overcome some of the information problems it faces. By offering different policies, it is able to separate individuals into high- and low-risk groups.

Time Inconsistency

Threats and promises are common components of strategic behavior. We have already discussed the case of a monopolist who threatens to wage a price war if another firm enters its market (our Redhat and Microsoft example). In that case, the firm that is considering entering the market understands that once it enters, the existing firm's best strategy is to compete peacefully. Because the potential entrant can use backward induction to make this determination, the initial threat is ineffective in deterring entry—it is not credible.

Now instead of looking at this problem from the perspective of the firm contemplating entrance, consider the situation of the monopolist trying to protect its market. It makes sense for the monopolist to try to scare off potential rivals by threatening a price war if any business attempts to enter the industry. But are these threats *time consistent;* that is, will it be in the monopolist's best interest to act in a manner consistent with its statements by actually carrying out the threat? The answer is no; as we have seen, the monopolist's best strategy if a rival enters the market is simply to compete peaceably. We can describe the threat as *time inconsistent;* it will not make sense to actually carry out the threat when it comes time to do so. The rival, knowing that the monopolist will not do as it threatened, knows that the threats can be ignored.

Time inconsistency arises in many contexts, usually in situations in which one player's promise or threat is designed to influence the other player's actions. Consider the case of Sarah, who has just graduated from high school. Her parents believe that holding down a summer job will help Sarah learn responsibility, so they offer to help pay her college tuition in the fall if she works during the summer. The implicit threat is that they will not help with her tuition if Sarah loafs around over the summer and does not work.[3] But Sarah can see that such a threat is time inconsistent. If she hangs out at the beach with her friends all summer, the only choice her parents face in the fall is whether to help her pay for college. Because Sarah knows her parents want her to receive a college education, regardless of how lazy she is, she knows they will help pay for college whatever she does. Since she would rather loaf than work, she does not get a job. Her parents' threat, designed to force her to find a job, was ineffective because it was time inconsistent. Sarah knew they would never actually carry out the threat, because it would not be their best strategy come the fall.

COMMITMENT

Consider again the situation faced by Sarah's parents at the end of the summer. At that point, it was too late to affect Sarah's summer activities, so the threat to not fund her college is no longer worth carrying out. Things would have been different if her parents could have somehow tied their hands in a way that would have prevented them from paying for Sarah's tuition unless she had actually worked during the summer. A demonstrated commitment to undertake a future action may be necessary for threats or promises to be credible.

Military strategists commonly face the problem of making threats credible. During the cold war, the United States stated that it would not rule out being the first to use nuclear weapons. This policy raised the possibility that if the Soviet Union invaded Western Europe, the United States would retaliate against the Soviet Union with nuclear weapons if necessary. Such retaliation would then lead the Soviet Union to launch a nuclear strike against the United States. A Soviet military planner using backward induction might reason that if the Soviet Union invaded Europe, the U.S. government would be faced with the choice of either launching a nuclear attack on the Soviet Union, and having millions of Americans killed in the ensuing nuclear war, or accepting a Soviet victory in Europe. Faced with that choice, the United States might decide to accept a Soviet victory. The U.S. threat to retaliate would not be credible. One argument for maintaining thousands of U.S. troops in Europe was that their loss in a Soviet invasion would force the U.S. military to launch a strike against the Soviet Union. By committing troops to Europe, the Americans made their threat more credible.

Imperfectly competitive markets provide a firm many opportunities to take concrete actions that deter rivals when threats alone would not be credible. A variant of the earlier example of Microsoft and Redhat can illustrate this point. Consider a coffee company, which we'll call Northwest Coffee, that opens a coffee store on every

---

[3]This example is from Herb Taylor, "Time Inconsistency: A Potential Problem for Policymakers," *Economic Review* (Federal Reserve Bank of Philadelphia), March/April 1985, pp. 3–12.

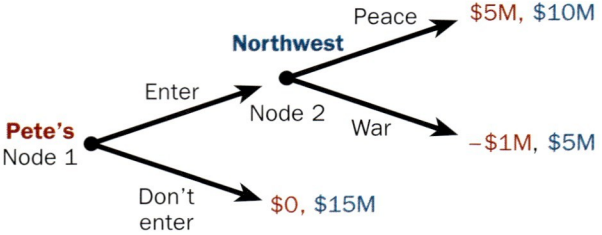

FIGURE 14.6

MARKET ENTRY GAME WITHOUT COMMITMENT

Northwest may threaten to wage a price war if Pete's Coffee enters the market, but such a threat lacks credibility.

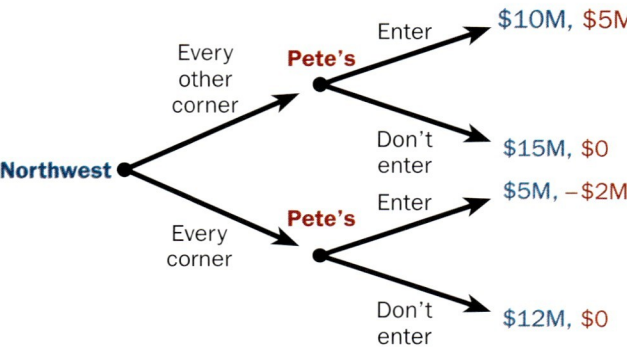

FIGURE 14.7

MARKET ENTRY GAME WITH COMMITMENT

Even though it costs more to operate stores on every street corner, Northwest will do so in order to prevent Pete's Coffee from entering the market. Opening stores on every street corner serves as a commitment mechanism.

other corner of a city's downtown. To deter a potential rival, Pete's Coffee, from opening stores on the empty corners, Northwest Coffee might threaten a price war if a rival opens up competing stores. The game tree and payoffs are shown in Figure 14.6.

Just as in our earlier example, Pete's Coffee can use backward induction to determine that if it enters, Northwest will find it more profitable to compete peacefully. Any threat by Northwest Coffee would not be credible.

Now let's change the game so that Northwest first decides whether to open on every *other* corner, or on *every* corner. The order of play now starts with Northwest's choice about how many stores to open. In the second stage of the game, Pete's Coffee must decide if it will enter. When it makes that decision, it knows whether Northwest has opened on every corner or only on every other corner. The new game tree appears in Figure 14.7.

First, note that if Northwest opens on every other corner and Pete's Coffee enters, the payoffs—$10 million for Northwest Coffee and $5 million for Pete's Coffee— reflect the previous finding that Northwest will not wage a price war. Second, the new branches of the tree show the possible outcomes if Northwest opens on every corner. Because of its added costs, Northwest's profit is smaller when it opens the additional stores and Pete's Coffee stays out of the market ($12 million) than if it opens only on every other corner and Pete's stays out ($15 million). If Northwest has a store on every corner and Pete's Coffee decides to enter the market, Northwest's profits fall to $5 million, while Pete's Coffee ends up losing $2 million.

We again use backward induction to determine the Nash equilibrium. Start from the Pete's Coffee decision node along the top branch (the branch followed if Northwest opens on every other corner). If it finds itself at this node, the best strategy is for Pete's Coffee to enter the market, earning $5 million. Now look at the Pete's Coffee decision node along the bottom branch (the branch followed if Northwest opens on every corner). Here, the best strategy is to not enter. That way, at least, it does not lose any money.

By applying backward induction, we can now analyze Northwest Coffee's decision at the start of the game. Northwest knows that if it puts a store on every other corner, Pete's will enter and Northwest will earn $10 million. If it opens on every corner, Pete's will not enter, and Northwest will earn $12 million. Northwest's best strategy therefore is to open a store on every corner. Even though the decision may appear to be counterintuitive, lowering Northwest's profits from $15 million to $12 million, the extra stores are worth opening because they deter a potential rival. Northwest's extra stores are a more credible threat to a potential rival than is a promise to engage in a price war. Stores that are open and in place serve as a commitment mechanism that deters potential rivals from entering. Northwest is worse off than if it opened fewer stores and Pete's stayed out of the market, but it is better off than if Pete's had entered.

Review and Practice

SUMMARY

1. In perfectly competitive markets, firms and consumers can decide how much to produce and how much to consume without taking into account how others might react. In imperfectly competitive markets, firms must take into account how their rivals will respond to the firms' production or pricing decisions. Firms must behave strategically in such situations. Individuals also face many situations in which they must behave strategically. Economists use game theory to predict how individuals and firms will behave.
2. In a Nash equilibrium, each player in a game is following a strategy that is best, given the strategies followed by the other players. A game may have a unique Nash equilibrium, or it may have several equilibria.
3. A dominant strategy is one that is best regardless of what the other player chooses to do. Looking for dominant strategies can help analysts predict behavior.
4. Backward induction is crucial for strategic behavior. Thinking strategically means looking into the future to predict how others will behave, and then using that information to make decisions.
5. Strategic choices are often designed to influence the choice of others. Once others have made their choices, however, carrying out the initial strategy may no longer be best. When this is the case, the original strategy was time inconsistent.

KEY TERMS

strategic behavior
game table
dominant strategy
Nash equilibrium
repeated game
backward induction
experimental economics
sequential game
game tree
time inconsistency

REVIEW QUESTIONS

1. Firms in perfectly competitive markets do not need to behave strategically. Why not? Why do oligopolists need to behave strategically? Does a monopolist need to behave strategically?
2. Professional sports leagues often have salary caps that limit the amount individual teams can pay players. Using the prisoner's dilemma game, explain why such a restriction might make the team owners better off.
3. What is a dominant strategy? Explain why each player in the prisoner's dilemma has a dominant strategy.
4. What is a Nash equilibrium? What is the unique Nash equilibrium in the prisoner's dilemma game? Can a game have more than one Nash equilibrium? Give an example to illustrate your answer.
5. In the prisoner's dilemma, each player has a dominant strategy and there is a unique Nash equilibrium in which the players choose their dominant strategy. Give an example of a game in which only one player has a dominant strategy. What is the Nash equilibrium?
6. This chapter opened with a discussion of the television show *Survivor*. What principle of strategic behavior did Kelly need to use?
7. What is a sequential game? Why does the player who moves first need to use backward induction?
8. An old saying, when a parent punishes a child, is "This hurts me more than it hurts you." Drawing on the idea of a repeated game, explain why a parent might still punish the child even if doing so really did hurt her more than the child.
9. Why might threats and promises not be credible?

PROBLEMS

1. Consider two oligopolists, each choosing between a "high" and a "low" level of production. Given their

choices of how much to produce, their profits will be as follows:

Explain how firm B will reason that it makes sense to produce the high amount, regardless of what firm A chooses. Then explain how firm A will reason that it makes sense to produce the high amount, regardless of what firm B chooses. How might collusion assist the two firms in this case?

2. Use the prisoner's dilemma analysis to describe what happens in the following two situations:
(a) Consider two rivals—say, producers of cigarettes. If Benson and Hedges alone advertises, it diverts customers from Marlboro. If Marlboro alone advertises, it diverts customers from Benson and Hedges. If they both advertise, each retains its customer base.

Are they genuinely unhappy with government regulations prohibiting advertising? In practice, cigarette firms have complained quite bitterly about such government restrictions, including those aimed at children. Why?
(b) Consider two rivals—say, producers of camera film, Fuji and Kodak. Consumers want a film that accurately reproduces colors and is not grainy. Assume that initially, the two firms had products that were comparable in quality. If one does research and improves its product, it will steal customers from its rivals. If they both do research and develop comparable products, then they will continue to share the market as before. Thus, the hypothetical payoff matrix (in millions of dollars) appears below (the profits in the case of research take into account the expenditures on research):

Explain why both will engage in research, even though doing so reduces their profits. Could this choice make society better off, even though their profits are lower?

3. Draw the game tree for the game discussed on pages 324–325 in which Microsoft moves first and decides whether to threaten a price war; Redhat then decides whether to enter; and finally, Microsoft decides whether to compete peacefully or wage the price war. Verify that Microsoft's decision at the first stage of the game has no effect on Redhat's strategy.

4. Suppose firm A is a monopolist. Firm A threatens a price war if any potential rival enters its market. Suppose firm B is contemplating such a move. The game tree is as follows (firm B's payoffs are shown first; firm A's are shown second):

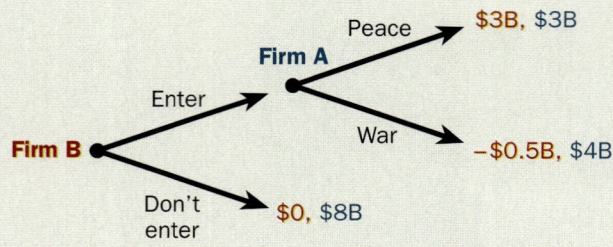

Should firm B enter? Is firm A's threat credible? Why? What makes this example different from the outcome in the Redhat-Microsoft example given in the text?

5. Draw the game tree for the sequential game between Sarah and her parents that was described on page 327. The first move is Sarah's; she decides whether to work during the summer or not work. At the end of the

summer her parents decide whether or not to pay for Sarah's tuition. Using backward induction, what is the equilibrium for this game? Now add a new first stage in which Sarah's parents announce that they will only pay for the tuition if Sarah works. Is this announcement credible? Use this example to explain what is meant by time inconsistency.

6. "Tying one's hands" can be a way to commit credibly to a certain course of action. In the 1960s film *Dr. Strangelove,* the Soviet Union deployed a doomsday device that could destroy the world and would be automatically triggered if the United States attacked. Explain how such a device could serve as a credible threat to deter a U.S. attack. In the movie, the Soviet Union did not inform the United States that the device had been deployed. Why was this a really bad strategy?

7. Suppose Quality Brands and Discounters Delux are involved in a repeated price-cutting game. Explain what a tit-for-tat strategy would be. Is a promise to "match any available price" a way for one firm to signal that it is playing tit for tat? Explain.

8. Restaurants often locate along major highways. Since most customers at such restaurants will not return, does the restaurant have an incentive to develop a reputation for good food? If reputations are important, which restaurant will have a greater incentive to offer good service—one that is part of a national chain (such as McDonald's or Burger King) or one that is locally owned?

9. How might a cultural or group norm or expectations about "correct" behavior, such as that summarized in the old saying "honor among thieves," help enforce cooperation in the prisoner's dilemma?

Learning Goals

In this chapter, you will learn

1. About the critical ways information affects markets
2. What the adverse selection problem is, and how it affects markets
3. What the incentive problem is, and how it affects markets
4. How search and advertising are explained by imperfect information

Chapter 15

IMPERFECT INFORMATION IN THE PRODUCT MARKET

It was never any secret to economists that the real world did not match the model of perfect competition. Theories of imperfect competition and monopoly such as those covered in Chapters 11 and 12 have been put forth from Adam Smith's time to the present.

Another limitation of the model of perfect competition has recently attracted attention: its assumption of perfect information—that market participants are fully informed about the goods being bought and sold. By incorporating *imperfect information* into their models, economists have come a long way in closing the gap between the real world and the world depicted in the perfect competition, perfect information model of Part Two.

This chapter provides an overview of the major information problems of the product market, the ways in which market economies deal with them, and how the basic model of Part Two has to be modified as a result. In Chapter 16, we will see how information problems affect labor markets. We start our analysis of information problems by examining a market you may be familiar with—the used-car market.

The Market for Lemons and Adverse Selection

Have you ever wondered why a three-month-old used car sells for so much less—often 20 percent less—than a new car? Surely cars do not deteriorate that fast. The pleasure of owning a new car may be worth something, but in three months, even the car you buy new will be "used." Several thousand dollars is a steep price to pay for this short-lived pleasure.

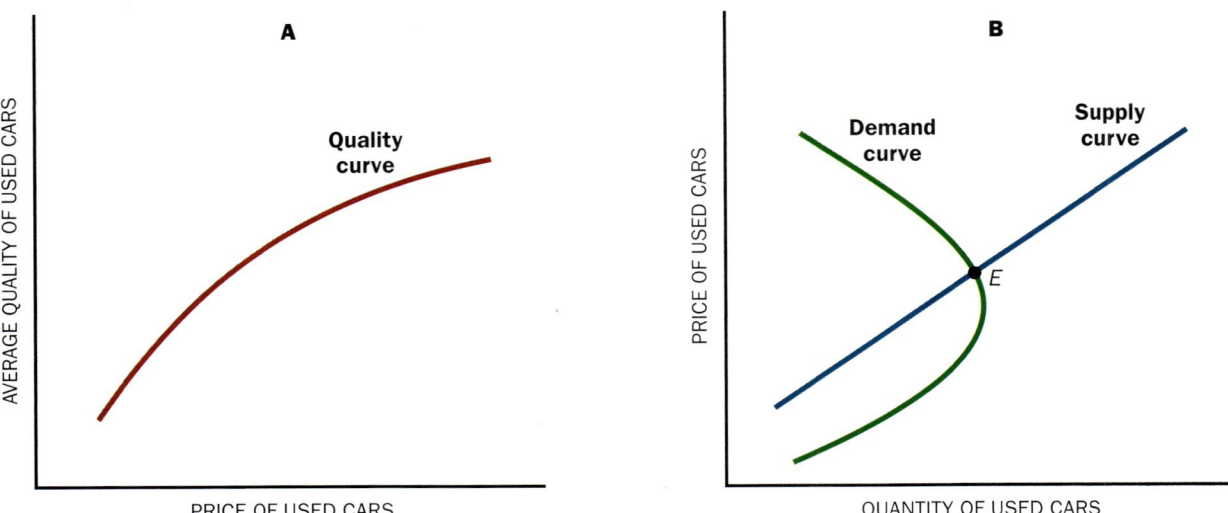

Figure 15.1

A MARKET WITH LEMONS

Panel A shows the average quality of a used car increasing as the price increases. Panel B shows a typical upward-sloping supply curve, but a backward-bending demand curve. Demand bends back because buyers know that quality is lower at lower prices, and they thus choose to buy less as the price falls. Panel B shows the market equilibrium is at point E.

George Akerlof of the University of California at Berkeley has provided a simple explanation, based on imperfect information. Some cars are worse than others. They have hidden defects that become apparent to the owners only after they have driven the cars for a while. Such defective cars are called *lemons*. One thing after another goes wrong with them. While warranties may reduce the financial cost of having a lemon, they do not eliminate the bother—the time it takes to bring the car into the shop, the anxiety of knowing there is a good chance of a breakdown. The owners, of course, know they have a lemon and would like to pass it along to someone else. Those with the worst lemons are going to be the most willing to sell their car. At a high used-car price, they will be joined by owners of better-quality cars, who perhaps just want to replace their cars with the latest model. As the price drops, more of the good used cars will be withdrawn from the market as the owners decide to keep them. And the average quality of the used cars for sale will *drop*. We say there is an **adverse selection** effect. The mix of those who elect to sell changes adversely as price falls.

Figure 15.1 shows the consequences of imperfect information for market equilibrium in the used-car market. Panel A depicts, for each price (measured along the horizontal axis), the average quality of used cars being sold in the market. As price increases, average quality increases. Panel B shows the supply curve of used cars. As price increases, the number of cars being sold in the market increases, for all the usual reasons. The demand curve is also shown. This curve has a peculiar shape—upward as well as downward sloping—because as price decreases, the average quality decreases. But demand depends not just on price but on quality—on the "value" being offered on the market. If, as price falls, quality deteriorates rapidly, then the quantity demanded will actually *fall* as price falls—consumers are getting less for their dollars. The equilibrium is depicted in panel B.

The situation just described is characterized by **asymmetric information** between sellers and buyers. That is, the seller of the used car has more information about the product than does the buyer. Many markets, and not just the market for used cars, are characterized by asymmetric information. The founders of a new high-tech start-up company may know more about the potential value of the company's stock than a typical investor does; an individual buying car insurance knows more about her driving abilities than the car insurance company does; the manufacturer of a kitchen refrigerator knows more about how reliable the product is than the customer who is contemplating its purchase does. One of the consequences of asymmetric information is that there may be relatively few buyers and sellers, far fewer than there would be with perfect information. Economists use the term **thin** to describe markets in which there are relatively few buyers and sellers. Sometimes particular markets may be so thin as to be essentially nonexistent. When there are important markets missing from an economy, it is said to have an **incomplete** set of markets. The used-car market, for example, is a thin one. Buyers may know that there are some legitimate sellers, people who for one reason or another prefer to always drive a new car. But mixed in with these are people who are trying to dump their lemons. The buyers cannot tell the lemons apart from the good cars. Rather than risk it, they may simply decide not to buy. (Of course, the low demand drives down the price, increasing the proportion of lemons. It is a vicious cycle.) The problems that arise when markets are thin and distorted by adverse selection, as used-car markets are, help explain why the price of a relatively new used car can be so much lower than the price of a brand-new vehicle.

SIGNALING

If you have a good car and you want to sell it, you would like to persuade potential buyers that it is good. You could tell them that it is not a lemon, but why should they believe you? There is a simple principle: *actions speak louder than words*. What actions can you take that will convince buyers of the quality of your car?

That Kia is willing to provide a ten-year, 100,000-mile warranty on its cars says something about the confidence Kia has in its product. The warranty is valuable to the buyer, not only because it reduces his risk of having to spend a mint to repair the car but also because he believes that Kia would not have provided the warranty unless the chances of defects were low. Actions such as this are said to **signal** higher quality. A signal is effective if it differentiates goods—here between high-quality cars and low-quality cars. The cost to the producer of a ten-year guarantee is much higher for a car that is likely to fall apart within ten years than for a car that is unlikely to break down. Customers know this, and thus can infer that a firm willing to provide this warranty is selling high-quality cars.

When you go to a car dealer, you want to know that it will still be around if you have trouble. Some firms signal that they are not fly-by-nights by spending a great deal of money on their showroom. Expensive furnishings lead visitors to infer that they would find it too costly to just pack up and leave.

Actions such as providing a better guarantee or a larger showroom are taken not just for the direct benefit that the consumer receives from them, but because they persuade consumers that the product is a better product or the firm is a better business to deal with. In a sense, the desire to convey information "distorts" decisions, insofar as they no longer conform to what they would have been in a world of perfect information. For example, if customers receive no direct benefit from a luxurious showroom, the cost of building and maintaining it is a waste of resources.

JUDGING QUALITY BY PRICE

There is still another clue that buyers use to judge the quality of what they are about to purchase: price. Consumers base inferences about the quality of goods on the price charged. For example, they know that on average, if the price of a used car is low, their chance of getting a lemon is higher. Many if not most sellers know that buyers know this.

In markets with imperfect information, firms *set* their prices. And in setting their prices, they take into account what customers will think about the quality of the good being sold. Concerns about the (correct or incorrect) inferences that consumers may make about quality impede the effectiveness of price competition. In the used-car example, we saw that as price rose, the average quality of cars on the market increased. But if firms think customers believe that cars being sold at a lower price are lower quality, then they will not lower the price—to do so would scare away customers who perceive that such "bargains" must be lemons. Under such circumstances, even if firms cannot sell all they would like at the going price, they still will not cut prices.

Information problems fascinate economists because they turn the basic competitive model upside down. Economists have long recognized that prices convey critical information about scarcity in a market economy. But only recently have the other informational roles of prices—and their consequences—become clear. When they can, sellers will manipulate prices to control the information conveyed. Buyers, for their part, usually see through these manipulations. And their suspicion that the seller is trying to pass off a lemon discourages trade. When these sorts of information problems are severe, markets are thin or even nonexistent. Moreover, price competition may be limited. Even when there is an excess supply of goods, firms may not cut their prices and the market may not clear.

Wrap-Up

SOLUTIONS TO ADVERSE SELECTION PROBLEMS IN MARKET ECONOMIES

Signaling
Judging quality by price

The Incentive Problem

Providing incentives that motivate individuals to make the best choices is one of the central economic problems. The central problem of incentives, in turn, is that individuals do not bear the full consequences of their actions. The multibillion-dollar collapse of many savings and loan associations in the 1980s—though fraud may have played a part—is attributable largely to incorrect incentives. Because S & L deposits were guaranteed by the government, depositors had no incentives to check on what the S & Ls were doing. For the same reason, the owners of many S & Ls had an incentive to take high risks. If they were successful, they kept the gains. If they failed, the government picked up the loss.

When there is a misalignment of incentives such as occurred in the S & Ls, we say there is a problem of **moral hazard.** The term originated in the insurance industry. Individuals who purchased insurance had an inadequate incentive to avoid the insured-against event—indeed, if they were insured for more than 100 percent of the loss, they would have an incentive to bring it about. Though the term was originally associated with insurance fraud, its use by economists today has no ethical overtones. For example, an individual who has fire insurance has less of an incentive to avoid a fire. The benefit to her, for instance, of putting in a sprinkler system may not be worth the cost—because she need not take into account the expected cost to the fire insurance company. Thus the fire insurance company is likely to require a sprinkler system; or it may change her calculations by offering a discount on the premiums of individuals with such systems, so that it would pay for her to have a sprinkler installed.

In the basic competitive model of Part Two, private property and prices provide incentives. Individuals are rewarded for performing particular tasks. Incentive problems arise when individuals are not rewarded for what they do, or when they do not have to pay the full costs for what they do. In our economy, such problems are pervasive.

In product markets, firms must be given the incentive to produce quality products, and here, too, information is an important part of the picture. If customers could always tell the quality of the product they were getting, firms that produced higher-quality products would always be able to charge a higher price, and no company could get away with producing shoddy goods.

MARKET SOLUTIONS

In simple transactions, incentive problems can be solved by stipulating penalties and rewards. For example, many companies need to have goods delivered. They contract with trucking firms, promising to pay a certain amount if the goods are delivered safely and on time to their destination. The contract might stipulate how much will be deducted from the total payment for each day the goods are late or for any damage that occurs while they are in the truck. The agreement thus has built-in incentives for the trucking firm to perform adequately.

But most transactions, even relatively simple ones, are more complex than this one. The more complicated the transaction, the more difficult it is to solve the incentive problem. Say you want your grass mowed, and your neighbor's twelve-year-old son wants to mow it. You want him to take good care of your power mower. When he sees a rock in the mower's path, he should pick it up. But what incentive does he have to take care of the mower? If you plan to charge him for repairs if the mower does hit a rock, how can you tell whether the rock was hidden by the grass? If he owned his own mower, he would have the appropriate incentives—an illustration of why private property combined with the price system provides such an effective solution to the incentive problem. But your neighbor's son probably does not have the money to buy his own power mower. Under these conditions, an incentive problem is inevitable. Either you let him use your lawn mower and bear the risk of his mistreating it. Or you lend him money to buy his own, in which case you bear the risk of his not paying you back.

Many private companies must hire people to run machinery worth hundreds or thousands of times more than a lawn mower. Every company would like its workers to exert effort and care, to communicate clearly with one another and take responsibility for their actions. Beyond a reliance on private property and prices, the market economy has other partial solutions to these incentive problems, loosely categorized as contract solutions and reputation solutions.

CONTRACT SOLUTIONS

When one party (firm) agrees to do something for another, it typically signs a contract, which specifies the conditions of the transaction. For example, a firm will agree to deliver a product of a particular quality at a certain time and place. There will normally be "escape" clauses. If there is a strike, if the weather is bad, and so on, the delivery may be postponed without penalty. These *contingency clauses* may also make the payment depend on the circumstances and manner in which the service is performed.

Contracts attempt to deal with incentive problems by specifying what each of the parties is to do in each situation. But no one can think of every contingency. And even if such foresight was possible, writing down all the possibilities would be prohibitively time-consuming.

There are times when complying with all the terms of the contract would be extremely expensive for the supplier. He could make the promised delivery on time, but only at a very great cost; a delay of just one day would save him a great deal. To provide suppliers with the incentive to violate the terms only when doing so is really economically worthwhile, most contracts allow delivery delays, but with a penalty. The penalty gives the supplier the incentive to provide timely, but not overly costly, deliveries.

Sometimes the supplier may think it simply is not worth complying with the contract. If she violates the agreement, she is said to be in *breach* of the contract. When a contract has been breached, the parties usually wind up in court, and the legal system stipulates what damages the party breaking the contract must pay to the other side. Contracts, by specifying what parties are supposed to do in a variety of circumstances, help resolve incentive problems. But no matter how complicated the contract, ambiguities and disputes will always remain. Contracts are incomplete and enforcement is costly, and thus they provide only a partial resolution of the incentive problem.

REPUTATION SOLUTIONS

Reputation plays an extremely important role in providing incentives in market economies. A reputation is a form of guarantee. Even though no particular individual or firm can collect anything from this guarantee—it is not a "money-back" guarantee—all know that the reputation of the person or company will suffer if it does not perform well. The desire to maintain a good reputation is what provides firms with an incentive to produce high-quality goods. It provides contractors with an incentive to complete a house on or near the promised date.

For reputation to be an effective incentive mechanism, firms must lose something if their reputation suffers. The "something" is, of course, profits. For reputations to provide incentives, there must be profits to lose.

Thus, we see another way in which markets with imperfect information differ from markets with perfect information. In competitive markets with perfect information, competition drives price down to marginal cost. In markets, competitive or not, in which quality is maintained as the result of a reputation mechanism, price must remain above marginal cost.

In markets where reputation is important, competition fails to lead to price-cutting, because prices that are "too low" give firms no incentive to maintain their reputation. Consumers, aware of this dynamic, come to expect low-quality goods. Here again, we see why cutting prices will not necessarily bring firms more customers. Even companies with (initially) good reputations are unlikely to find price-cutting a successful long-term strategy.

Reputation as a Barrier to Entry Competition is frequently very imperfect in markets where reputation is important. The necessity of establishing a reputation acts as an important barrier to entry and limits the degree of competition in these industries. Given a choice between purchasing the product of an established firm with a good reputation and the product of a newcomer with no reputation at the same price, consumers will normally choose the established firm's good. In selecting a new TV, at a given price you will probably choose a Sony over a new brand with no track record for quality and reliability. To win customers, the newcomer must offer a sufficiently low price, often accompanied with strong guarantees. Entering a market thus becomes extremely expensive.

Wrap-Up

SOLUTIONS TO INCENTIVE PROBLEMS IN MARKET ECONOMIES

Private property and prices
Contracts
Reputations

THE MARKET FOR HEALTH INSURANCE

The market for health insurance provides an illustration of the impact imperfect information can have. It is estimated that about 45 million Americans are without health insurance, and even those with insurance often feel dissatisfied with their coverage. Understanding the problems with health care and the policy debates that these problems have generated requires an understanding of the market for health insurance, a market in which information, or rather the lack of information, plays a major role.

The United States spends a larger fraction of its national income on health care than most other developed countries, but its figures for life expectancy are lower and for infant mortality are higher. Information problems and associated market failures are a large part of the reason. Moral hazard—the reduced incentive to economize on health care expenditures when a large fraction of the tab is picked up by insurance firms—is one source of market failure. Adverse selection—the attempt of each insurance firm to take the lowest-risk applicants, leaving those with high medical costs to others—is another. In some countries, the first of these problems is addressed by rationing the availability of health care and the second is overcome by having a universal health care system that covers everyone, not just those at low risk.

In the standard model, consumers are assumed to be well-informed. But consumers go to the doctor for information, to find out what is wrong with them. Moreover, they typically must rely on the doctor's advice. Economists worry that under a fee-for-service system, in which doctors are paid for each of the services they perform, there is an incentive to provide excessive care. *Excessive* here means the marginal cost exceeds the marginal benefit to the patient. Making sure that health care dollars are used efficiently requires that the marginal benefits of a particular treatment, prescription, or procedure are balanced against the marginal costs. Consumers can be expected to balance marginal benefits and costs when they purchase most goods, but health care differs because consumers may lack the information needed to assess the potential benefits of care and because those with insurance typically bear only a small fraction of the marginal costs.

Today, more and more doctors work in "managed care" organizations, or HMOs, where they are paid a flat fee up front. They then provide whatever care is needed and receive no extra income from doing extra procedures. On average, doctors working in managed care charge less and perform fewer surgeries, with no noticeable effect on patient health. Critics worry that under managed care, doctors have an incentive to underprovide services, since they receive no compensation at all for providing care at the margin. Newspaper accounts of managed care programs denying patients treatment have galvanized legislators to enact a patients' bill of rights. But while admitting that there may be occasional abuses, advocates argue that any managed care organization guilty of repeated abuses would lose its patients. Reputations can provide effective discipline. When employers provide a level playing field between fee-for-service and managed care plans—contributing an equal amount for each and making employees pay for the extra costs if they choose the more expensive fee-for-service plans—more than half their employees, on average, choose the managed care plan. Evidently, the employees do not feel that the benefits of the extra services provided under fee-for-service are worth the extra cost.

Case in Point

BUYING HEALTH INSURANCE

Have you ever seen an advertisement for health insurance which stresses that no physical exam is required? What can economics, and the notion of adverse selection, tell us about who is likely to buy such insurance and whether it is a "good" deal?

Health insurance is designed to let individuals share the risks that are associated with health needs. To see how such insurance might work, let's suppose there is a medical condition that affects 1 person in 100. This condition can be treated through surgery, but the cost of the surgery is $50,000. Let's assume that the chances of needing the surgery are the same for everyone. Without insurance, 99 of the 100 will not have to pay anything, but one unlucky person will have to pay $50,000. Under an insurance plan, 100 people could each contribute $500. Whoever ends up needing the operation has its cost paid by the insurance. The other 99 are "out" $500, but they have been insured against the much larger cost they would have had to pay had they required the surgery. If all 100 were equally likely to need the operation, and the cost of the surgery is $50,000, then charging everyone $500 is the fair price

Health insurance is designed to let individuals share the risk of needing expensive health care, such as surgery.

for the insurance. A private company could offer this insurance since it will collect enough from selling the insurance to cover the amount it expects to have pay out.[1] Most people would probably find the option of paying $500 to avoid the much larger cost of the operation a good deal.

But suppose some people know that they are more likely than others to need the operation. Perhaps, like heart disease, the likelihood of needing surgery is higher if there is a family history of the disease. Suppose other individuals know they are extremely unlikely to develop the condition. Now, if an insurance company offers insurance for $500, all the individuals at high risk will see this as a good deal—they will purchase the insurance. But the individuals at low risk will not; for them, it is not worth $500. So the insurance company finds that only the bad risks buy the insurance—an example of adverse selection.

To continue our example, suppose 50 of our 100 individuals are in the high-risk group and buy the insurance. The insurance company collects $500 from each, for a total of $25,000: only half of what is needed to pay for an operation. The insurance company therefore has to charge $1,000 in order to break even. Given the overall likelihood of someone in the general population needing the operation (1 in 100), the insurance company appears to be overcharging; the ratio suggests that $500 is the fair price. And at the premium of $1,000, the low-risk people find the insurance even less attractive. They see themselves as providing a large subsidy to the high-risk individuals. But if the insurance company cannot distinguish between high-risk and low-risk individuals, the adverse selection effect will force it to charge more. So if you think you are at low risk for health problems, an insurance plan that does not require a medical exam is likely to be a bad deal. The adverse selection problem also explains why health and life insurance companies typically require medical exams—their incentive is to insure only healthy individuals, or at least to make certain that the premiums charged reflect the risks.

The Search Problem

A basic information problem is that consumers must find out what goods are available on the market, at what price, and where. Households must learn about job opportunities as well as opportunities for investing their savings. Firms, by the same token, have to figure out the demand curve they face, and where and at what price they can obtain inputs. Both sides of the market need, in other words, to find out about their opportunity sets.

In the basic competitive model of Part Two, a particular good sells for the same price everywhere. If we see what look like identical shoes selling for two different prices at two neighboring stores—$25 at one and $35 at the other—it must mean (in that model) that the stores are really selling different products. If the shoes are in fact identical, then what the customer must be getting is a combination package:

---

[1] For the sake of simplicity, this ignores any administrative cost the firm would have to include in the price charged to those who buy its insurance.

Thinking Like an Economist

INCENTIVE AND INFORMATION PROBLEMS IN THE HOUSING MARKET

For most Americans, buying or selling a house is likely to be the largest financial transaction they ever engage in. For people selling houses, setting the right price is critical. Set the price too high, and the house may remain unsold for months; set it too low, and the house sells quickly but the seller ends up with less money. Most people rely on a real estate agent to help them sell their homes, and the agent's job is to recommend a price at which to list the home, advertise it to attract potential buyers, and help the owner negotiate a final sale.

Because real estate agents know more about the local housing market than the typical client does, they can use their informational advantage to help sell the home. In their book *Freakonomics,* the University of Chicago economist Steven Levitt and his co-author Stephen Dubner highlight some of the ways real estate agents signal information about a house to other agents and to potential buyers. Words in ads such as "fantastic," "spacious," "charming," or "great neighborhood" actually are associated with lower sales prices, while "granite," "state-of-the-art," "Corian," "maple," and "gourmet" are associated with higher sales prices. Levitt and Dubner argue that the second set of descriptive terms tell potential buyers about particular attributes of the house. If all you can say about a house is that it is "spacious," potential buyers may take that as a signal that the place isn't all that great—otherwise, the ad would list its specific attractive features.

Interestingly, when real estate agents sell their *own* homes, they are much more likely to employ specific terms like "granite" or "maple," knowing that doing so is likely to yield a higher sales price.

Why then would they use adjectives like "fantastic" when they are hired to sell the homes of others? The answer lies in the incentives agents face. Suppose an agent lists her own home for $400,000. If she receives an offer of $380,000, she may decide to reject it and wait longer for the higher asking price. After all, she gives up $20,000 if she accepts the offer. But when it is *your* home she is selling, the situation is quite different. The agent typically receives a commission that is equal to a percentage of the sales price. After the costs of advertising and the share that goes to the agent's company are subtracted, only 1.5 percent of the sales price ends up in the agent's pocket. So if you reject the $380,000 offer in hopes of getting an offer of $400,000, the agent stands to gain only about an extra $300 (1.5 percent of $20,000), a far cry from the $20,000 she would gain if it were her home. In selling her own home, the agent has a big incentive to reject the lower offer; but when it comes to your home, the agent's incentive is to encourage you to accept. Giving up the chance of an extra $300 is too small a gain to make the agent want to pass up a sale that guarantees her a commission of $5,750 (1.5 percent of $380,000).

SOURCE: Steven D. Levitt and Stephen J. Dubner, *Freakonomics* (New York: William Morrow, 2005).

the shoes plus the service of having the shoes fitted. And the more expensive store is providing a higher-quality service.

Yet as we know from experience, essentially the same good may be sold at different stores for different prices, and it is not always possible to account for the observed differences in prices by differences in other attributes, such as the location of the store or the quality of the service provided. In these cases, we say there is **price dispersion**. If the act of finding out all prices were itself costless (or information were perfect, as in the standard competitive model), consumers would search until they found the cheapest price. And no store charging more than the lowest price on the market would ever have any customers. But in a world of costly information, a high-price store may still be able to keep some customers—and its higher profit per sale offsets its lower level of sales. Thus, price dispersion can persist.

Given price dispersion, combined with variations in quality, households and firms must spend considerable energy searching. Workers search for a good job. Firms look for good workers. Consumers search for the lowest prices and best values. The process by which this kind of information is gathered is called **search.**

Search is an important, and costly, economic activity. Because it is costly, a search stops before you have *all* the relevant information. A Google search may turn up thousands of references, but you are unlikely to scroll through more than the first few pages of the results. Because links that appear near the top of the list are more likely to be clicked on, the order of search results is extremely important. A site on the second or third page might be an even better source for the information you are seeking, but navigating through all the links until the perfect one is located is just too time-consuming. Similarly, after buying a new shirt for a special occasion, you may worry that you might have found an even better one if only you had visited one more store. But in truth, there should be no regrets. Going to more stores is costly in terms of your time, and there is always a chance you would not have found anything

e-Insight
INFORMATION TECHNOLOGY AND MIDDLEMEN

Perhaps the defining characteristic of the new economy is the role of information technologies. These new technologies make possible the collection, analysis, and transmission of vast amounts of information—more efficiently than anyone could have conceived even ten years ago. The new technologies no doubt will improve the flow of information in all markets, including product markets. Some have suggested that it will completely eliminate the need for middlemen such as retailers and wholesalers. Instead, consumers will be able to deal directly with producers. Those claims are greatly exaggerated.

To be sure, in some markets information technologies will diminish the role of middlemen. Already, many consumers are buying computers, insurance, books, and airline tickets over the Internet. The Internet will make an enormous difference in the dissemination of prices about homogeneous products—a particular form of wheat, or steel, or a new Buick with a deluxe sound system, leather seats, and so forth. But the hardest choices often involve differences in quality and characteristics. In fact, most retailers see their job as searching among producers and making judgments about the quality of the goods that different manufacturers produce. Retailers who establish a good reputation do so on the basis of the quality they offer at a particular price range. Because much of the relevant information concerning quality and characteristics cannot be conveyed easily over the Internet, consumers still need direct access to the product. For instance, without actually sitting in a driver's seat, how can an auto shopper detect whether the controls of a car feel right? The same point can be made for various other products. Thus, information technology is unlikely to make middlemen obsolete. We may visit a local bookseller less frequently, but instead we browse an online retailer such as Amazon.com or Borders.com for the latest books. Searching for books by visiting each individual publisher's Web site would be too time-consuming (and thus costly). Most travelers find it more convenient to search travel sites that show flights and fares for several airlines than to check the online home of each carrier. The Internet has changed the nature of middlemen, and may have made them more competitive and efficient, but they still have an important role to play in the modern economy.

Internet Connection

JOB SEARCH

The Internet's ability to disseminate information makes it a natural way for workers seeking new jobs and firms seeking new employees to exchange information. Several private companies have established sites for matching workers and jobs. One of the best known is Monster.com (www.monster.com). The Monster.com network consists of sites in more than a dozen countries. The U.S. government has also taken advantage of the Internet; all current job openings in the federal government are listed at www.usajobs.opm.gov.

better. There is even a chance that by the time you returned to buy the shirt you had originally thought acceptable, it would have been sold to someone else. Continuing a search has benefits, but there are also costs. When deciding whether to search further, you need to compare the marginal benefits to the marginal costs.

The expected marginal benefit of searching declines with the amount of search. In general, people search the best prospects first. As they search more and more, they look at less and less likely prospects. On the other hand, the marginal cost of additional search rises with increased search. The more time people spend in search, the less time they have to do other things; thus the opportunity cost of spending an extra hour searching increases. The amount of search chosen will be at the point where the expected marginal benefit just equals the marginal cost.

An increase in price (or quality) dispersion will normally increase the marginal benefit of searching—there is a chance of picking up a really good bargain, and the difference between a good buy and a bad buy is larger. Thus, the amount of search will increase.

SEARCH AND IMPERFECT COMPETITION

Firms know and take advantage of the costliness of search. They know they will not lose all their customers if they raise their prices. And if a store lowers its price slightly, it will not immediately attract *all* the customers from the other stores. Customers have to learn about the competitive price advantage, a process that takes time. Moreover, even when people do hear of the lower price, they may worry about the quality of the goods being sold, the nature of the service, whether the goods will be in stock, and so on.

The fact that search is costly means that the demand curve facing a firm will be downward sloping. Competition is necessarily imperfect.

Consider, for instance, the demand for a portable MP3 player. When you walk into a store, you have some idea what it should sell for. The store asks $195 for it. You may know that somewhere you might be able to purchase it for $5 less. But is it worth the additional time, trouble, and gasoline to drive to the other stores that might have it, looking for a bargain? Some individuals are willing to pay the extra

$5 simply to stop having to search. As the store raises its price to, say, $200, $205, or $210, some people who would have bought the MP3 player at $195 decide that it is worth it to continue shopping around. The store, as it raises its price, loses some but not all of its customers. Thus, it faces a downward-sloping demand curve. If search were costless, everyone would go to the store selling the MP3 player at the lowest price, and any store charging more than that would have no sales. Markets in which search is costly are, accordingly, better described by the models of imperfect competition introduced in Chapters 11 and 12.

Costly search is also responsible for some of the strategic behavior by firms that was studied in Chapter 14. For example, some stores, in order not to lose customers, guarantee to match the lowest price available, if the customer can prove that another store has a better price. This common sales tactic ensures that the customer benefits from searching for a lower price; at the same time the firm, by matching the price, ensures that it does not lose a customer. In fact, while an offer to match any price sounds like a good offer, most economists believe it is simply a way for firms to keep prices high by letting any competitors know that they will not gain many sales by cutting prices.

SEARCH AND THE LABOR MARKET

The economics of search—a comparison of the costs and benefits of search—has important applications in the labor market. While older workers typically stay with an employer for years, younger workers often leave after a period of a few weeks or months. How can we explain these differences?

To begin, consider the positions of a sixty-year-old and a thirty-year-old contemplating a job search. Even should the sixty-year-old find a better job, he is likely to enjoy the job for at most a few years. For the thirty-year-old, the marginal benefit of additional search is much greater: there is at least the *possibility* that she will stay with the new employer for two decades or more. Each worker evaluates the marginal benefit and the marginal cost of additional search, but their evaluations yield different answers.

Two other factors reinforce these outcomes. First, the younger worker is likely to be less informed about her own preferences (what she likes and does not like) and about the job market. Moving from job to job provides additional information about both. Second, employers recognize such a learning process as normal, so there is little stigma associated with a younger worker moving about. By contrast, employers worry that an older worker who is looking for a new job may know that he is about to be dismissed or demoted because of inadequate job performance. Excessive job mobility for an older worker is often interpreted as a "bad" sign.

SEARCH AND INFORMATION INTERMEDIARIES

Some firms play an important role by gathering information and serving as intermediaries between producers and customers. One of the functions of stores such as Wal-Mart and Macy's, for example, is to economize on customers' search costs. The stores' buyers seek out literally hundreds of producers, looking for the best buys and the kinds of goods that their customers will like. Stores can earn a reputation for the quality of the selection they offer their buyers. Customers still have a search problem—they may have to visit several stores—but doing so is far less costly than if they had to search directly among producers. In addition, magazines like *Consumer Reports* provide readers with detailed information on product quality and price, saving consumers considerable search cost. Today, numerous Internet sites enable consumers to compare prices offered by different online sellers, again helping to reduce search costs.

Advertising

Customers have an incentive to find out where the best buys are. Firms have a corresponding incentive to tell customers about the great deals they are providing. Companies may spend large sums to bring information about their products, prices, and locations to potential customers. In the United States, many firms spend 2 percent, 3 percent, or more of their total revenue on advertising. This figure varies greatly across industries, however. Motion picture producers spend more than 12 percent of their sales revenue on advertising, but motion picture theaters spend only about 1 percent. Department stores spend more than 3 percent, while drug stores spend less than 1 percent.

Advertising can serve the important economic function of providing information about what choices are available. When a new airline enters a market, it must announce its presence to potential customers. When a new product is developed, that fact has to be publicized. When a business is having a sale, it must let people know. A firm that wants to be successful cannot just lower its prices and wait for customers. Companies need to actively recruit new customers and convey information. Thus, advertising plays an important role in improving the efficiency of markets when information is imperfect. It also supports the entire network television industry—rather than paying a direct price to watch network programs, as cable subscribers do, we pay an indirect price: we sit through the commercials that are scattered through our favorite shows, and the networks receive revenue by selling time to firms who wish to advertise.

But not all advertising is designed to convey factual information about product prices or characteristics. Take the typical beer or car advertisement. It provides almost no information about the product; instead, it seeks to create an image, one with which potential buyers will identify. That these advertisements succeed in persuading individuals either to try a product or to stick with that product rather than trying another is a reminder that consumer behavior is much more complicated than the simple theories of competitive markets suggest. Few people decide to go out and buy a car or new shoes solely because they saw a TV ad. But decisions about what kinds of clothes to wear, what beer to drink, and what car to drive are affected by a variety of considerations, including how peers view the consumers or how they see themselves. These views, in turn, can be affected by advertising.

To emphasize the different roles played by advertising, economists distinguish between *informative advertising* and *persuasive advertising*. The intent of the former is to provide consumers with information about the price of a good, where it may be acquired, or what its characteristics are. The intent of persuasive advertising is to make consumers feel good about the product. To that end, advertisers may even provide "disinformation," seeking to confuse consumers into perceiving differences among goods that are essentially the same.

ADVERTISING AND COMPETITION

Advertising is both a cause and a consequence of imperfect competition. In a perfectly competitive industry, in which many producers make identical goods, it would not pay any single producer to advertise the merits of its product. We do not see advertisements for wheat or corn. If such advertising were successful, it would simply shift the demand curve for the product out. This increase in the total demand for wheat would have a negligible effect on the wheat grower who paid for the advertisement. The industry as a whole might benefit, however, if all the wheat farmers could get together and advertise as a group. In recent years, associations representing producers of milk, oranges, almonds, raisins, and beef have done just that.

But if advertising can create in consumers' minds the perception that products are different, then firms will face downward-sloping demand curves. There will be imperfect competition. And once imperfect competition exists, advertising can be used to increase the demand for a firm's products.

Figure 15.2

HOW ADVERTISING CAN SHIFT THE DEMAND CURVE

Successful advertising shifts the demand curve facing a firm. When the imperfect competitor equates its new marginal revenue with its old marginal cost, it will be able to raise both its price and its output.

ADVERTISING AND PROFITS

The objective of advertising is not only to change the slope of the demand curve—by creating the perception of product differentiation—but also to shift the demand curve out, as in Figure 15.2. The increase in advertising by one firm may divert customers away from rivals, or it may divert customers away from other products. Advertising a particular brand of cigarettes may succeed in inducing some smokers to switch brands and inducing some nonsmokers to smoke.

The increase in profits from shifting the demand curve consists of two parts. First, the firm can sell the same quantity it sold before but at a higher price—p_3, rather than p_1. Profits then increase by the original quantity (Q_1) times the change in price ($p_3 - p_1$), the rectangle *ABCD* in the figure. Second, because the advertising has shifted the firm's marginal revenue curve up, it can adjust the quantity it sells. As usual, the imperfectly competitive firm sets marginal revenue equal to marginal cost, so it increases output from Q_1 to Q_2. The additional profits thus generated are measured by the area between the marginal revenue and marginal cost curves between Q_1 and Q_2. Marginal cost remains the same, so the second source of extra profits is the shaded area *EFG*. The net increase in profits is the area *ABCD* plus the area *EFG* minus the cost of advertising.

So far, in studying the effect of an increase in advertising on one firm's profits, we have assumed that other firms keep their level of advertising constant. Determining the effect of advertising on both industry and firm profits is more problematic once the reactions of other firms in the industry are taken into account. To the extent that advertising diverts sales from one firm in an industry to another, it may, in equilibrium, have little effect on demand. For example, assume that Nike shoe ads divert customers from Reebok to Nike and vice versa for Reebok ads. Figure 15.3 shows the demand curve facing Reebok (1) before advertising, (2) when only Reebok advertises, and (3) when both companies advertise. The third demand curve is the same as the first. Price and output are the same; profits are lower by the amount spent on advertising. We have here another example of a prisoner's dilemma. If the firms could cooperate and agree not to advertise, they would both be better off. But without such cooperation, it pays each to advertise, regardless of what the rival does. The government-mandated ban on cigarette advertising on radio and TV may have partially solved this prisoner's dilemma for the tobacco industry—in the name of health policy.

In practice, when all cigarette firms advertise, the ads do more than just cancel each other out. Some people who might not otherwise have smoked are persuaded to do so, and some smokers are persuaded to smoke more than they otherwise would have. But the shift in a particular firm's demand curve when all companies advertise is still much smaller than it is when only that firm advertises.

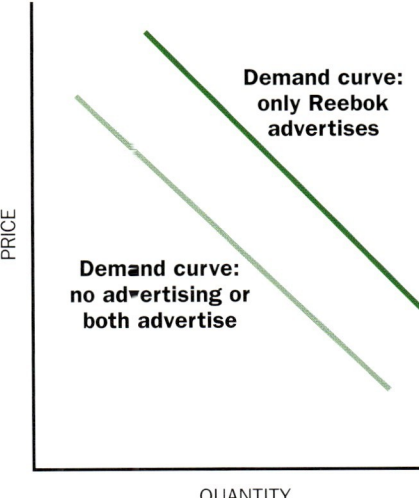

Figure 15.3

HOW ADVERTISING CAN CANCEL OUT OTHER ADVERTISING

If only one company advertises, the demand curve for its product may shift out. But if both companies advertise, the resulting demand curve may be the same as it would be if neither advertised.

Wrap-Up

CONSEQUENCES OF IMPERFECT INFORMATION

In the presence of adverse selection problems, quality may be affected by price.
    Adverse selection can lead to thin markets or the failure of markets to even exist.
    Signaling plays an important role in adverse selection problems.
In the presence of weak or misdirected incentives, moral hazard problems arise.
    Contingent contracts and reputation are important solutions for incentive problems.
In the presence of price dispersion, consumers must engage in search.
    Because searching is costly, firms face downward-sloping demand curves and competition is imperfect.
In the presence of imperfect information, firms engage in advertising.
    Advertising can be used to change perceptions of product differences, altering the slope of the demand curve.
    Advertising can be used to shift the demand curve.

The Importance of Imperfect Information

The modern economy has sometimes been called "the information economy." The name is justified in part because the major advances in computer technology have greatly enhanced the capacity to process information, and in part because such a large fraction of total economic activity now revolves around collecting, processing, and disseminating information. Personnel officers focus on finding out about potential employees; lending officers attempt to assess the likelihood that potential borrowers will default; market researchers try to determine the potential market for some new product; large retailers send buyers out to scour the world for new suppliers of the clothes they sell. But no matter how much information we have, we seldom have as much as we would like.

Not only is information imperfect, but different people have different information. Information is asymmetric. The seller of a car knows more about her car's problems than the buyer. The worker may know more about his strengths and weaknesses than does the firm where he is interviewing for a job. The borrower may know more about some of the contingencies that may affect his ability to repay the loan than the lender. Because the parties to a transaction do not always have an incentive to be perfectly truthful, it may be difficult for the more informed party to convey convincingly what she knows to others.

That individuals and firms typically make decisions based on imperfect information fundamentally affects the behavior of markets in various ways. For their part, firms and individuals attempt to compensate for the scarcity of information. In many markets in which problems of adverse selection and moral hazard arise, firms adjust prices to convey information about quality. Moreover, individuals and firms may attempt to signal information about their characteristics and work to establish a reputation.

Review and Practice

SUMMARY

1. The basic competitive model assumes that participants in the market have perfect information about the goods being bought and sold and their prices. In the real world, information is often imperfect. Economists have modified the basic model so that it includes a number of limitations on information.
2. A problem of adverse selection may arise when consumers cannot judge the true quality of a product. As the price of the good falls, the quality mix changes adversely, and the quantity demanded at a lower price may actually be lower than at a higher price.
3. Producers of high-quality products may attempt to signal that their product is better than those of competitors; for instance, they may provide better warranties.
4. When consumers judge quality by price, they may agree on some price that offers the best value. Firms will have no incentive to cut prices below this "best value" price, even when, at this price, the amount they would be willing to supply exceeds demand. As a result, the market can settle on an equilibrium with an excess supply of goods.
5. When there is perfect information, private property and prices supply the correct incentives to all market participants. When information is imperfect and incentives are not correct, two methods of adjusting them are to employ contracts with contingency clauses and to rely on reputation. For firms to have an incentive to maintain a good reputation, they must earn profits by doing so. Thus equilibrium price exceeds marginal cost. (Reputation may also serve as a barrier to entry.)
6. Costly search may lead to price dispersion and imperfections of competition as each firm faces a downward-sloping demand curve.
7. Advertising attempts to change consumers' buying behavior, either by providing relevant information about prices or characteristics, by using persuasion, or both.

KEY TERMS

adverse selection
asymmetric information
thin or incomplete markets
signal
moral hazard
reputation
price dispersion
search

REVIEW QUESTIONS

1. Why would "lemons" not be a problem for consumers in a world of perfect information? Why do they lead to a backward-bending demand curve in a world of imperfect information?
2. Why is signaling unnecessary in a world of perfect information? What does it accomplish in a world of imperfect information?
3. Explain why, if consumers think that quality increases with price, there will be cases in which firms will have no incentive to cut prices in an attempt to attract more business.
4. How do contingency clauses in contracts help provide appropriate incentives? What are some of the problems in writing contracts that provide for all the relevant contingencies?
5. What role does reputation have in maintaining incentives? What is required if firms are to have an incentive to maintain their reputations? How might the good reputation of existing firms serve as a barrier to the entry of new firms?
6. What are the benefits of searching for market information? What are the costs? How does the existence of price dispersion affect the benefits? Could price dispersion exist in a world of perfect information? How do the costs of search affect the nature of competition in a market?
7. Describe how advertising might affect the demand curve facing a firm. How do these changes affect prices? profits?
8. What is moral hazard? What is adverse selection? Give an example of each.

PROBLEMS

1. How does imperfect information help explain why used cars cost more when sold by car dealers than by private individuals?
2. For each situation, state whether it reflects a problem of adverse selection or of moral hazard.
   (a) A person drives faster because his new car has air bags.
   (b) A high school football team visits an "all you can eat" restaurant.
   (c) A real estate agent who advertises that she will buy your house from you if she fails to sell it in six weeks sets a low selling price for your house.
   (d) An insurance company that offers health insurance without requiring a medical exam finds that only people with health problems buy its insurance.
3. Explain how the incentives of someone to look after a car she is renting may not suit the company that is renting the car. How might a contingent contract help solve this problem? Is it likely to solve the problem completely?
4. L. L. Bean, a mail-order company, has a long-standing policy that it will take back anything it has sold, at any time, for any reason. Why might it be worthwhile for a profit-maximizing firm to enact such a policy?
5. Would you expect to see greater price dispersion within a metropolitan area, or between several small towns that are fifty miles apart? Why?
6. How do costs of search help explain the success of department stores?
7. Suppose a professor assigns a group project to a class. Each student in a group will receive the same grade, based on the project submitted by the group. Will this lead to a moral hazard problem? Explain.

Learning Goals

In this chapter, you will learn

1. About the economic effects of labor unions on wages and employment
2. About the factors that limit union power
3. About the factors that explain wage differentials
4. About the incentive problems that face firms seeking to motivate workers

Chapter 16

IMPERFECTIONS IN THE LABOR MARKET

Part Two emphasized the similarity between the labor market and markets for goods. Households demand goods and firms supply them, with the price system as intermediary. Likewise, firms demand labor and workers supply it, with the wage as intermediary. Firms hire labor up to the point at which the value of the marginal product of labor is equal to the wage, just as they would buy coal up to the point at which the value of the marginal product of coal is equal to the price of coal.

This chapter takes another look at the labor market. Just as we saw in the preceding five chapters some of the ways in which product markets differ from their depiction in the basic competitive model, here we will see important ways in which labor markets differ from their depiction in the basic competitive model. We will find that labor markets, like product markets, are characterized by imperfect competition. Unions are the most obvious manifestation, and we will take a look at their history as well as their impact on wages and employment—the prices and quantities of the labor market.

Information problems affect the labor market even more significantly than product markets, in part because workers are not like computer chips. They have to be motivated to work hard, and they are concerned with working conditions and how their current pay compares with that offered by other firms. Firms are aware of the importance of these considerations in attracting and keeping employees, and they design employment and compensation policies accordingly.

Labor Unions

Labor unions are organizations of workers, formed to obtain better working conditions and higher wages for their members. The main weapon they have is the threat of a collective withdrawal of labor, known as a *strike*.

A BRIEF HISTORY

Labor unions are less important institutions in our economy than they used to be, and they have always played a smaller role in the United States than in many European countries. Unionization in the United States began in the late nineteenth and early twentieth centuries. A variety of craft unions were established, consisting of skilled workers such as carpenters, plumbers, and printers. In 1886, the American Federation of Labor (AFL) was formed. Led by Samuel Gompers, the AFL gathered together a number of these craft unions to enhance their bargaining power.

The Rise of Unions In the 1930s, two events strengthened union power: the confederation of major industrial unions into the Congress of Industrial Organizations (CIO) and the passage of the Wagner Act, which provided legal status to unions. The CIO represented a major change in two respects. First, it embraced all workers, unskilled as well as skilled; and second, it represented all the workers in a company. These industrial unions, by uniting all workers across job categories, enhanced workers' bargaining strength. Their leaders, such as Walter Reuther of the United Automobile Workers (UAW), attained national prominence, and the unions were able to obtain for their workers substantial wage increases and improvements in working conditions. The 1935 Wagner Act set up the National Labor Relations Board, which established procedures for certifying labor unions and preventing certain practices on the part of firms trying to block workers from unionizing.

The Decline of Unions Prompted by concerns that the balance had swung too far in favor of unions, Congress in 1947 passed the Labor-Management Relations Act, better known as the Taft-Hartley Act. This law addressed two issues. First,

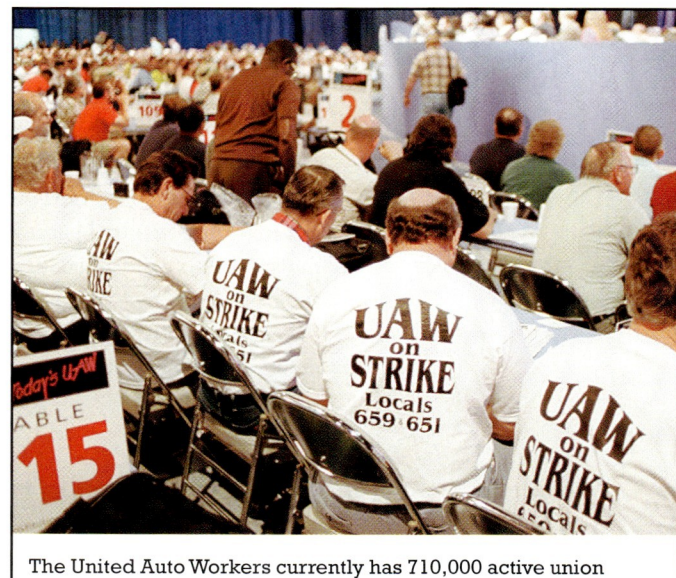

The United Auto Workers currently has 710,000 active union members.

unions had claimed that when they negotiated a better contract or better working conditions, they were providing benefits to all workers at an establishment. Thus, they demanded that all laborers at unionized companies join the union, a requirement that established **union shops.** Critics of union shops thought that the right to work should not be limited to members of unions. The Taft-Hartley Act left it to the individual states to decide whether to outlaw union shops, and many states subsequently passed **right-to-work laws.** These laws gave workers the right to hold a job without belonging to a union—or, to put it the way unions do, the right to receive union pay without paying union dues.

The second concern addressed by the Taft-Hartley Act was the devastating effect on the country of strikes by national unions. A shutdown of the railroads or the steel or coal industry could have ramifications far beyond the firms directly involved. The new law gave the president the power to declare, when national welfare was at stake, an eighty-day cooling-off period, during which workers had to return to work.

Since the mid-1950s, union power has declined steadily in the United States. Figure 16.1 traces the sharp increases of union membership in the 1930s, and again during World War II, when the government encouraged unionization in all military plants. But since then, unions have had only limited success in recruiting new members, and the union share of nonagricultural employment has thus been falling. It fell below 20 percent in 1984, where it remains today. In fact, not only the union share but also the actual number of unionized workers has been declining. Today there are about 16 million union members, 2 million fewer than there were in 1960.

Figure 16.1
UNIONIZATION OF THE U.S. LABOR FORCE

The percentage of the U.S. labor force belonging to unions increased sharply in the 1930s and early 1940s but has been largely declining since 1950.

SOURCE: U.S. Census Bureau, *Historical Statistics of the United States, Colonial Times to 1970, Employment and Earnings* (various issues).

Internet Connection
UNIONS ON THE INTERNET

The American Federation of Labor–Congress of Industrial Organization (AFL-CIO) is the largest union organization in the United States. Its home page is at www.aflcio.org. Traditional unions such as the United Automobile Workers (UAW) (www.uaw.org) organize workers in manufacturing industries. Today, many workers are employed in public-sector jobs, and AFSCME, the American Federation of State, County and Municipal Employees, is a major organizer of public-sector and health industry workers (www.afscme.org).

Though total union membership has fallen, today's union member is much more likely to work in the public sector than was true in the past. In 1960, the percentage of union members working in the public sector was only 6 percent. Today it is closer to 40 percent, while only about one in ten nongovernmental workers belongs to a union. Why the recent and continuing decline in union membership among workers in the private sector?

One explanation is that working conditions for workers—whether as a result of union pressure or technological progress—have improved enormously. Workers therefore see less need for unions.

A second reason is related to the changing nature of the American economy. Unions have declined as the traditionally unionized sectors (such as automobiles and steel) have weakened, and the service sector, in which unions have been and continue to be weak, has grown.

Third, unions may be less effective in competitive markets. When competition is limited, there are monopoly (or imperfect competition) profits or rents. Unions may be successful in winning a share in those rents for their workers. But when markets are competitive, firms cannot charge more than the market price for their goods; and if they are to survive, they simply cannot pay their workers more than the competitive wage.

In the late nineteenth and early twentieth centuries, for example, high wages in shoe and textile mills in New England drove plants to the nonunionized South. High wages also drive American firms to manufacture abroad. Unless unions manage to ensure that their workers are more productive than average, it is only when these sources of competition are restricted that unions can succeed in keeping their wages above average for long. In this view, the increased competition to which American industry is subjected, both from abroad and from the deregulation of trucking, oil, airlines, banking, telephone service, and so on, has led to a decline in the ability of unions in the private sector to garner higher wages for their workers.

A final explanation of the growth and decline of unions is the changing legal atmosphere. When laws support or encourage unions, unions prosper. When they do not, unions wither. Thus, the Wagner Act set the stage for the growth of unions in the 1930s. The Taft-Hartley Act paved the way for their decline in the post–World War II era.

ECONOMIC EFFECTS

The source of union power is collective action. When workers join together in a union, they no longer negotiate as isolated individuals. The threat of a strike (or a work slowdown) poses many more difficulties for an employer than does the threat of any single employee quitting.

In the perfectly competitive model of labor markets, workers are price takers; the market wage is given. But when there is a downward-sloping demand curve for labor, as in Figure 16.2,[1] unions have some power to be price setters. As a result of this power, a worker at a particular level of skill who works in a unionized establishment will be paid more than a comparable worker in a competitive industry. The firm would like to hire that lower-priced, nonunion worker, and the nonunionized worker could easily be induced to move, but the firm has a union contract that prevents it from hiring anyone at a lower wage. But as the union raises the price of labor (the wage), firms will employ fewer workers. Higher wages are obtained at the expense of lower levels of employment. In the figure, when wages rise from the competitive level w_c to w_m, employment is reduced from L_c to L_m.

Figure 16.2

THE UNION AS A MONOPOLY SELLER OF LABOR

Unions can be viewed as sellers of labor, with market power. When they increase their wage demands, they reduce the demand for their members' labor services.

Short-Run Gains at the Expense of Long-Run Losses

Sometimes unions can increase both employment and wages, at least for a time. They present the employer with, in effect, two alternatives: either pay a high wage *and* maintain an employment level above the labor demand curve for that wage, or go out of business. If the employer already has sunk costs in machines and buildings, he may accede to the union demands. In effect, the union takes away some of the employer's monopoly profits or return to capital. In competitive markets, where there are no monopoly profits, the higher wages can only come out of employers' return to capital. But these employers will lose interest in investing in more capital. As capital wears out, an employer has less and less to lose from the union threat. As she refuses to invest more, jobs decrease. Even if the union makes short-run gains, they come at the expense of a long-run loss in jobs.

Effects on Nonunion Workers

The gains of today's union members not only may cost future jobs but also may come at the expense of those in other sectors of the economy, for two reasons. First, the higher wages may well be passed on to consumers in the form of higher prices, particularly if product markets are not perfectly competitive. Second, the increased wages (and reduced employment) in the union sector drive down wages in the nonunionized sector, as the supply of nonunion labor increases. Some argue the opposite—that high union wages "pull up" wages in

---

[1]Chapter 8 showed how the demand curve for labor is derived in competitive markets. Firms hire labor up to the point at which the wage equals the value of the marginal product of labor. The derivation of the demand curve for labor in monopolies and imperfectly competitive markets follows along similar lines. Firms hire labor up to the point at which the marginal revenue—that is, the extra revenue they obtain from selling the extra output they produce from hiring an extra unit of labor—is equal to the wage.

nonunion firms. The nonunion firms may, for instance, pay higher wages to reduce the likelihood of unionization. In particular sectors this effect is important, but most economists believe that the overall impact of union gains on nonunion workers is negative.

Job Security and Innovation The economy as a whole benefits from innovation, but particular groups within it are likely to suffer. In an innovative economy, those workers who are dislocated by new inventions are expected to learn new skills and seek out new jobs. Without the shifts of labor in response to changes in demand (resulting from either new technologies or changes in tastes), the economy will be inefficient.

Technological changes may threaten the job security that unions seek for their members. As a result, unions have attempted to retard innovations that might decrease the demand for their members' services. An efficient economy requires job transitions, but they are costly and the costs are borne largely by the workers. Before the advent of unions and laws providing unemployment compensation, the human toll was considerable. Individuals could not buy insurance against these employment risks, but they could form unions—and union attempts to enhance job security were a response to this important problem. Today many countries are looking for ways of insulating workers against the risks of job transition without impeding the labor mobility that is so important for economic efficiency.

Unions and Politics We have seen that the fortunes of unions depend, to a large extent, on the legal environment in which they operate. Unions have also learned that what they cannot get at the bargaining table they may be able to obtain through the political process. For example, they have actively campaigned for higher minimum wages.

At the same time, unions have shown in their political stances that they recognize the economic forces that determine both the strength of their bargaining positions and, more generally, the level of wages. Thus, they have been active supporters of policies of high employment. They have sought to restrict imports from abroad (believing that such restrictions will increase the demand for American products and therefore the demand for labor). And historically they have been proponents of limits on immigration (recognizing that increases in the supply of labor lead to reductions in wages).

Finally, unions have been strong advocates, through the political process, of safer working conditions. Today, the Occupational Safety and Health Administration (OSHA) attempts to ensure that workers are not exposed to unnecessary hazards. OSHA seeks to make much less likely the kinds of episodes that occurred in the asbestos industry, which knowingly exposed workers to life-threatening risks.

LIMITS ON UNION POWER

In the United States, no union has a monopoly on *all* workers. At most, a union has a monopoly on the workers currently working for a particular firm. Thus, the power of unions is partly attributable to the firm's inability to easily replace its employees.

When a union goes on strike, the firm may be able to hire some workers, but it is costly to bring in and train a whole new labor force. Indeed, most of the knowledge needed to train the new laborers is in the hands of the union members. While one bushel of wheat may be very much like another, one worker is not very much like another. Workers outside the firm are not perfect substitutes for other workers, particularly skilled ones, inside.

The Threat of Replacement In industries in which skills are easily transferable across firms or in which a union has not succeeded in enlisting the support of most of the skilled workers, a firm can replace striking workers, and union power will be limited. Caterpillar, a manufacturer of tractors and road-making equipment, weathered a seventeen-month strike by the UAW that began in 1993. Eventually, management announced that if workers did not return to their jobs, they would be replaced. The union caved in shortly after the firm made good its threat.

In today's global economy, the threat to move jobs overseas provides another limit to union power. Even if the union has a monopoly on all workers in an industry, its reach does not extend to foreign workers. The ability of firms to relocate to other countries reduces a union's ability to gain higher wages.

In many cases, however, workers' skills are specific to the firm. Just as, from the employer's perspective, workers outside the firm are not perfect substitutes for workers within the firm, so from the workers' perspective one job is not a perfect substitute for another. Thus, there is often value to both workers and to firms in preserving ongoing employment relationships.

The Threat of Unemployment Unions understand that in the long run, higher wages—other things being equal—mean lower levels of employment. When job opportunities in general are weak, concern about the effects of union contracts on employment increases. Maintaining jobs rather than raising wages may become the union's chief priority if the industry is shrinking, perhaps owing to increased competition from imports or owing to technological changes that have increased the industry's competition from new products. A rise in overall unemployment in the economy is also likely to limit a union's ability to seek wage hikes.

> **Wrap-Up**
>
> ## UNIONS AND IMPERFECT COMPETITION IN THE LABOR MARKET
>
> Economic effects of unions:
> - Higher wages for union members, with fewer union jobs and lower wages for nonunion members
> - Improved job security, sometimes at the expense of innovation and economic efficiency
> - Minimum wages, restrictions on imports, improved working conditions, and other gains achieved through the political process

Determinants of union power:
　Political and legal environment
　Economic environment: salience of the threat of replacement and unemployment

Wage Differentials

The basic competitive model suggests that if the goods being sold are the same, prices will also be the same. Wages are the price in the labor market; but even in the absence of unions, similar types of workers performing similar types of jobs are sometimes paid quite different wages. For example, some secretaries are paid twice as much as others. How can economists explain differences like these?

An understanding of wage differentials begins with the observation that although different jobs may have the same title, they can be quite different. Some are less pleasant, require more overtime, and are in a less convenient location. These are **nonpecuniary attributes** of a job. Other nonpecuniary attributes include the degree of autonomy provided the worker (that is, the closeness with which her actions are supervised) and the risk she must bear, whether from physical hazard or from variability in income. Economists expect wages to adjust to reflect the attractiveness or unattractiveness of these nonpecuniary characteristics. **Compensating wage differentials** arise because firms have to compensate their workers for the negative aspects of a job.

Other differences are accounted for by differences in the productivity of workers. These are *productivity wage differentials.* Some workers are much more productive than others, even those with the same experience and education.

Compensating and productivity wage differentials fall within the realm of the basic competitive model analysis. But other wage differentials are due to imperfect information. It takes time to search out different job opportunities. Just as one store may sell the same object for a higher price than another store, one firm may hire labor for a lower wage than another firm. The worker who accepts a lower-paying job simply because he did not know about the higher-paying one down the street illustrates an *information-based differential.*

Limited information has important implications for firms. First, in the standard competitive model, firms face a horizontal supply curve for labor. If they raise wages slightly above the "market" wage, they can obtain as much labor as they want. In practice, mobility is more limited. Even if workers at other firms knew about the higher wage offer, they might be reluctant to switch. They may worry that they are not well matched for the job, or that the employer is offering high wages because the work is unattractive.

Second, firms worry about the quality of their workforce. If an employer offers a higher wage to someone working for another firm and the worker accepts, the employer might worry about the signal the acceptance sends about the worker's quality. Did his current employer—who presumably knows a lot about the worker's productivity—fail to match the job offer because his productivity does not warrant the higher wage? Does the worker's willingness to leave demonstrate a "lack of loyalty," or an "unsettled nature"—in which case, he may not stick with the new firm long enough to make his training worthwhile? These concerns again impede labor mobility, leading employers to prefer to keep their existing labor force even when there are lower-paid workers with similar credentials whom they might recruit at a lower wage.

Different groups of individuals may differ in their mobility. For instance, older workers may be much more reluctant to move than younger workers. Sometimes, firms take advantage of these differences to cut their own costs. Knowing that older workers will not leave even if their wages fail to keep pace with inflation, employers may hold back raises from them. Their lack of mobility provides a rationale for employers to engage in age discrimination.

DISCRIMINATION

Discrimination is said to occur if two workers of seemingly similar *work-related* characteristics are treated differently. Paying higher wages to better-educated workers is not discrimination, as long as the higher level of education is related to higher productivity. If older workers are less productive, then paying them lower wages is not discrimination. But if they are just as productive as younger workers, then taking advantage of their lower mobility to pay them less *is* discrimination.

Forty years ago, there was open and outright discrimination in the labor market. Some employers simply refused to hire African Americans. Today much of the discrimination that occurs is more subtle. Firms seek to hire the best workers they can for each job at the lowest cost possible, operating with imperfect information. In making predictions about future performance, employers use whatever information they have available. Employers may have found that those receiving a degree from a well-established school are more productive, on average, than those receiving a degree from a less-established college. Of the African Americans and Hispanics who are college graduates, more may have gone to less-prestigious schools. Screening the applicant pool to pick those with degrees from well-established colleges effectively excludes many African Americans and Hispanics. This more subtle form of discrimination is called **statistical discrimination.**

Some discrimination reflects neither old-fashioned prejudice nor statistics. Employers may just feel more comfortable dealing with people with whom they have dealt in the past. Highly uncertain about who is a good worker, and knowing that a bad worker can do enormous damage, top management may rely on certain trusted employees for recommendations. And such judgments are inevitably affected by friendships and other ties. Many claim that if discrimination is to be eliminated, this associative form, based on "old boy networks," has to be broken.

When firms pay lower wages to, say, women or minorities, they are practicing **wage discrimination.** Today, wage discrimination is perhaps less common than **job discrimination,** the denial to disadvantaged groups of equal access to better-paying jobs. Women are often said to face a "glass ceiling": they can climb up to middle management jobs but can't get beyond that level to reach top management.

Some market forces tend to limit the extent of discrimination. If a woman earns less than a man of comparable productivity, it pays a firm to hire her. Not to do so costs the firm profits. To put it another way, the firm pays a price for discriminating.

If there are enough firms that put profits above prejudice, then the wages of women will be bid up toward the level of men of comparable productivity.

Beginning in the 1960s, the government has taken an active stance in combating discrimination. In 1964, Congress passed the Civil Rights Act, which banned employment discrimination and set up the Equal Employment Opportunity Commission to prosecute cases of discrimination. The reach of these laws was extended in 1975 when the government prohibited age discrimination; in 1990, job discrimination against qualified individuals with disabilities was barred.

Beyond this, the federal government has required its contractors to undertake **affirmative action.** They must actively seek out minorities and women for jobs, and actively seek to promote them to better-paying positions. Affirmative action has occasionally taken the form of quotas that specify that a certain number or fraction of positions be reserved for minorities or women. Critics claim that quotas are discriminatory—they imply that a minority individual would be chosen over a more qualified white male. One of the objectives of antidiscrimination laws was to discourage thinking in racial or gender terms. Courts have reaffirmed this aim, allowing quotas only in special circumstances such as redressing the effects of specific instances of past discrimination.

> ### Wrap-Up
>
> ### EXPLANATIONS OF WAGE DIFFERENTIALS
>
> Unions: Unions may succeed in obtaining higher wages for their workers.
>
> Compensating differentials: Wage differences may correspond to differences in the nature of the job.
>
> Productivity differentials: Wage differences may correspond to differences in the productivity between workers.
>
> Information-based differentials: Wage differences may be a reflection of workers' not having perfect information about the opportunities available in the market, and employers' not viewing all workers as perfect substitutes for one another.
>
> Imperfect labor mobility: Differentials are preserved because of the reluctance of individuals to move between jobs.
>
> Discrimination: Wage differentials and hiring and promotion decisions can sometimes be traced to nothing more than differences of race or sex.

Motivating Workers

The discussion to this point has treated workers as if they were machines. Workers have a price—the wage—analogous to the price of machines. But even to the most profit-hungry and coldhearted employer, people are different from machines. They bring adaptability and a multitude of skills and experiences to a job. Most machines can do only one task, and even robots can only follow their programs. However, machines have one advantage over humans: except when they break down, they do what they are told. Workers, in contrast, have to be motivated if they are to work hard and to exercise good judgment.

This requirement can be viewed as an information problem. In the basic competitive model of Part Two, workers were paid to perform particular tasks. The employer knew perfectly whether the worker performed the agreed-on task in the agreed-on manner. If the worker failed to do so, he did not get paid. The pay was the only form of motivation required. But in reality, workers frequently have considerable discretion. And because employers have limited information about what a worker is doing at each moment, they have to motivate members of their workforce to exercise their abilities to the fullest.

To motivate workers, employers use both the carrot and the stick. They may reward workers for performing well by making pay and promotion depend on performance, and they may punish workers for shirking by firing them. Sometimes a worker is given substantial autonomy; sometimes she is monitored closely. The mix of carrots and sticks, autonomy and direct supervision, varies from job to job and industry to industry. Among other factors, it depends on how easy it is to supervise workers directly and how easy it is to compensate workers on the basis of performance.

PIECE RATES AND INCENTIVES

When the pay of workers increases for higher productivity and falls for lower productivity, they will have appropriate incentives to work hard. The system of payment in which a worker is paid for each item produced or each task performed is called a **piece-rate system.** But relatively few Americans are paid largely, let alone exclusively, in this way. Typically, even workers within a piece-rate system get a base pay *plus* additional pay, which goes up as they produce more.

Why don't more employers enact a piece-rate system, if it would improve incentives? One major reason is that piece rates leave workers bearing considerable risk. A worker may have a bad week because of bad luck. For example, salespeople, who are often paid commissions on the basis of sales—a form of piece rate—may simply find little demand for their products, no matter how hard they have worked.

A firm, by providing a certain amount of guaranteed pay, gives the worker a steady income and reduces the risk she must bear. But compensation that is less dependent on a piece rate gives the worker less incentive to work hard. There is thus a trade-off between risk and incentives. Compensation schemes must find some balance between offering security and offering incentives linked to worker performance. In many jobs, employers or managers achieve this balance by providing both a guaranteed minimum compensation (including fringe benefits) and bonuses that depend on performance.

A second reason that more employers do not use piece-rate systems is their concern for quality, which can be difficult to measure even when the quantity—say, the output of workers on an assembly line—is obvious. If pay depends just on the number of items produced, the worker has an incentive to emphasize quantity over quality. The result may be less profitable for the firm than a lower level of higher-quality output.

In any case, most workers are engaged in a variety of tasks, only some of which can easily be defined and rewarded by means of a piece-rate system. For example, although employers would like experienced workers to train new workers, employees who are paid on a piece-rate system have little incentive to do this, or to help their co-workers in other ways. Similarly, when salespeople are paid on the basis of commissions, they have little incentive to provide information and service to any potential customers except those perceived as likely to buy immediately. Even if providing information enhances the likelihood that a customer will return to the store to purchase the good, there is a fair chance that someone else will get the commission. To observe this effect at work, visit a car dealer's showroom, make it clear that you are not going to buy a car that day, and see what service you get.

EFFICIENCY WAGES

When output is easily measured, then the carrot—basing pay at least partially on performance—makes sense. And when effort is easily monitored, then the stick—firing workers for not exerting adequate effort—makes sense. But monitoring effort continuously is often expensive. An alternative is to monitor less frequently, and impose a big penalty if the worker is caught shirking. One way of imposing such a penalty is to pay above-market wages and benefits. Then, if a worker is fired, he suffers a large income loss. The higher the wage, the greater the penalty from being fired. Similarly, rewarding workers with higher pay who are observed to be working hard whenever they are monitored provides incentives for workers to continue to apply themselves.

In these cases, higher wages help motivate workers and lead to increased productivity. Additional factors may persuade a firm to pay wages higher than are absolutely necessary to recruit the desired number of workers. High wages reduce labor turnover, lead to more loyalty and higher-quality work by employees, and enable the firm to attract more productive workers. The theory that higher wages increase workers' net productivity, for any or all of these reasons, is called the **efficiency wage theory.** While conventional theory emphasizes that increased productivity leads to higher wages, efficiency wage theory emphasizes that higher wages lead to increased productivity.

UPS exemplifies a firm that has adopted a conscious strategy of developing a reputation as an excellent employer. It treats its employees well, offering good benefits and salaries. It also encourages workers to gain promotions. The availability of these benefits and opportunities makes the loss of a job especially costly for UPS workers. But because employees feel they are well treated by UPS, they are likely to show more loyalty to the firm, working harder and ensuring a high level of labor productivity. In the long run, UPS benefits from this approach, even though in the short run it might be able to raise its profits by scaling back employee benefits or promotion opportunities.

Efficiency wage theory provides an explanation for some wage differentials. In jobs in which the costs of monitoring workers on a day-to-day basis are very high or the damage a worker can do is very great (for instance, by punching one wrong button the worker can destroy a machine), employers are more likely to rely on high wages to ensure that workers perform well.

These "wages of trust" may explain why pay in more capital-intensive industries (which require massive investments) is higher for workers with otherwise comparable skills than it is in industries using less capital. They may also explain why workers entrusted with the care of much cash (that they could steal) earn higher wages than other workers of comparable skills. It is not so much that they are paid more because they are trustworthy, but that they become more trustworthy because they are paid more—and the threat of losing those high wages encourages honest behavior.

Case in Point

MINIMUM WAGES

Legislating a minimum wage below which it is illegal to hire workers has been sharply criticized by economists as hurting exactly the people it is designed to help—those at the bottom of the wage scale.

Critics base their reasoning on the traditional demand and supply model of Part Two. There, an increase in wages above the market equilibrium results in lower employment. Those who manage to get jobs are better off; those who are forced into unemployment are worse off. If the objective is to reduce poverty, the minimum wage, from this perspective, seems counterproductive.

But as this chapter has pointed out, markets for labor are different from markets for many other commodities. Workers have to be motivated to work hard. High wages lead to increased productivity, less absenteeism, and lower labor turnover. Presumably, rational firms would take these consequences into account in setting wages. Even so, if the government forces firms to pay higher wages through minimum wage legislation, the increased productivity may largely offset the increased wages, making the employment effect very small.

In labor markets in which there is imperfect competition, minimum wages could actually lead to increased employment. Because of imperfect mobility, firms face an upward-sloping supply curve. Since all workers in a similar job have to be treated the same, the cost of hiring an additional worker may be much higher than the new

Does minimum wage legislation help or hurt low-income workers?

employee's salary. Not only must the firm raise the wage offered to the *new* worker, it must also raise the wage paid to all existing workers. This cost discourages the firm from hiring additional employees. The imposition of a minimum wage limits the expense of hiring an additional worker to just that employee's wage. And because their marginal cost of adding to their workforce is lower, firms that are required to pay a minimum wage in fact will hire more workers.

These perspectives are consistent with several recent empirical studies that have shown there to be negligible, or even positive, employment effects from a minimum wage.

Some economists have also pointed to broader positive consequences of minimum wages: they induce firms to invest more in their workers in order to increase their workers' productivity. Gavin Wright, a distinguished economic historian at Stanford University, has argued that minimum wages played a vital role in the transformation of the South. It was a region that had been vastly poorer than the North from the end of the Civil War to the Great Depression, and its economy had been largely based on very low wages. The minimum wage catalyzed dramatic changes, shifting the South away from low-wage industries to dynamic industries paying higher wages.

A further alleged advantage of raising the minimum wage is that it increases the incentive to work by increasing the income gap between someone on welfare and someone with a job.

OTHER INCENTIVES

Other important incentives to increase job performance are enhanced possibilities of promotion, and thus higher salaries, for those who perform well. But, as already noted, assessing achievement is often difficult. One way to figure out who is performing well is to set up a contest among workers and promise the winner some valuable prize, like a cash bonus. Consider a firm trying to figure out how much to pay its sales force when it is promoting a new product. If a salesperson is successful, does that success demonstrate good salesmanship, or is the new product able to "sell itself"? All sales representatives are in roughly the same position. The representative who sells the most gets a bonus—and wins the contest.

At the upper end of the corporate hierarchy, the top executives of America's largest firms are paid much more, on average, than their counterparts in many other industrial economies; their salaries often run into the millions of dollars. Economists continue to debate why this is. Some interpret these salaries as the payoffs of contests, others as reflecting the large contributions of these managers or as wages of trust. But some suspect that top managers have enough control over the firm to divert a considerable amount (though still a small fraction) of its resources to their own betterment in the form of higher compensation.

COMPENSATING WORKERS

We saw earlier that the wage a firm has to pay adjusts to take into account nonpecuniary attributes. Some of these nonpecuniary attributes reflect decisions made by the firm: the company can try to make the workplace more attractive; it can try to make it safer; it can even try to lower the stress level of its employees. Such changes may affect the workers' level of performance. In choosing how to organize the workplace, firms consider the impact of their decisions both on productivity and on how much they will have to pay to recruit workers.

Today, much of the compensation a worker receives takes the form not of direct cash but of **fringe benefits;** these include health insurance, retirement pay, and life insurance. In recent years, fringe benefits have constituted an increasing share of total compensation.

Employers' reliance on fringe benefits rather than simply paying a straight salary to workers is largely explained by the tax code. If employees are paid income and then purchase health insurance on their own, they must pay income tax on the money. But if the company buys the insurance for them, the fringe benefit is not counted as income. From the firm's perspective, it costs less to provide workers with health insurance than to raise their wages enough to enable employees to buy the insurance themselves. In addition, many employers use fringe benefits as an incentive for employees to stay with the company. For example, firms often require that the employee remain with the company for a period of several years before becoming eligible for the company pension plan. Such benefits show that employers are not eager to lose their long-term employees, and would rather offer some added benefits than go through the cost and trouble of hiring and training new workers. But why—other than for tax reasons—they should rely so heavily on rewarding their workers through better fringe benefits rather than through cash bonuses remains unclear.

e-Insight
LABOR MARKETS AND THE INTERNET

One of the main *imperfections* in the labor market is that searching for a new job is costly. Information is imperfect and is expensive to acquire. Help-wanted ads play an important role in making the labor market work, but individuals in one city often cannot easily obtain current newspapers from other cities that might have job opportunities.

Employment agencies and government employment services have helped make the labor market work better. But the Internet promises a revolution in labor markets—or at least a vast improvement. Almost without cost, individuals can see the help-wanted ads in newspapers in other cities. Employers can post free help-wanted ads and can provide far more complete descriptions both of the job and of the characteristics of the employees that they seek. Eighty percent of the world's largest 500 firms use Web sites for job recruitment, as do more than 90 percent of American firms. Existing employment agencies (including government-provided services) have used the Internet to extend their scope, and new firms have been created. Much of the information relevant both to the employer and to the employee will still be obtained by face-to-face contact, during an interview, and this process will remain costly. Still, by lowering search costs, the Internet holds out the promise of enormously increasing the efficiency of labor markets.

> **Wrap-Up**
>
> ## WAYS OF MOTIVATING WORKERS
>
> Piece rates, or pay based on measured output.
>
> Threats: firing workers whose efforts or performance are deemed inadequate.
>
> Efficiency wages: introducing an extra cost to those dismissed for unsatisfactory performance.
>
> Relative performance: promotions, contests.
>
> Fringe benefits, such as health insurance and retirement pay.

Review and Practice

SUMMARY

1. The proportion of U.S. workers in unions has declined since the 1950s. Possible reasons include laws that have improved working conditions in general; the decline of manufacturing industries, where unions have traditionally been stronger than in service industries; increased competition in the product market, providing firms with less latitude to pay more than market wages; and a legal atmosphere that has shifted away from encouraging unions.
2. Union gains in wages are typically made at the cost of lower employment, at least in the long run, and lower wages in the nonunion sector. Unions also have played an important role in enhancing job security, though sometimes at the expense of innovation. They have accomplished some of their gains for workers through the political process; for instance, unions have pushed legislation promoting occupational safety and health as well as the minimum wage.
3. Union power is limited by the ability of companies to bring in new, nonunion workers and to threaten union workers with unemployment.
4. Explanations of why two workers doing the same job may receive different wages include compensating differentials (differences in the nature of jobs), productivity differentials (differences in productivity between workers), imperfect information (workers do not know all the job opportunities that are available), and discrimination.
5. Employers try to motivate workers and induce high levels of effort through a combination of direct supervision, incentives for doing well, and penalties for doing badly. They pay wages higher than workers could get elsewhere (efficiency wages), give promotions and bonuses, and base pay on relative performance (contests).

KEY TERMS

union shops
right-to-work laws
nonpecuniary attributes
compensating wage differentials
statistical discrimination
wage discrimination
job discrimination
affirmative action
piece-rate system
efficiency wage theory
fringe benefits

REVIEW QUESTIONS

1. Has the power of unions in the U.S. economy been shrinking or growing in the last few decades? Why? In what sector has union growth been largest? Why might this be so?
2. What effect will successful unions have on the level of wages paid by unionized companies? on the capital investment for those companies? What effect will they have on wages paid by nonunionized companies?
3. How might greater job security for union workers possibly lead them to become less efficient?
4. Does it make sense for a union to resist the introduction of an innovation in the short run? in the long run?
5. What are alternative explanations for wage differentials?
6. How do piece rates provide incentives to work hard? Why is there not a greater reliance on piece-rate systems?
7. What is efficiency wage theory?

PROBLEMS

1. In what ways are labor markets similar to product markets? In what ways are they different?
2. Explain how both these points can be true simultaneously:
   (a) Unions manage to raise the wage paid to their members.
   (b) Unions do not affect the average level of wages paid in the economy.

3. How might each of the following factors affect the power of unions?
   (a) A state passes a right-to-work law.
   (b) Foreign imports increase.
   (c) The national unemployment rate falls.
   (d) Corporate profits increase.
4. Suppose a worker holding a job that pays $15 per hour applies for a job with another company that pays $18 per hour. Why might the second company be suspicious about whether the worker is really worth $18 per hour? How might the worker attempt to overcome those fears?
5. Imagine that a company knows that if it cuts wages 10 percent, then 10 percent of its employees will leave. How might adverse selection cause the amount of work done by the company to fall by more than 10 percent?
6. Advances in computer technology have enabled some firms to monitor their typists by a system that counts the number of keystrokes they make in a given workday. Telephone operators are sometimes monitored according to how many calls they take, and how long they spend on an average call. Would you expect such information to increase productivity? Why or why not?
7. When someone is promoted from middle-management to top executive, her salary often doubles or more. Why does this seem puzzling, from the perspective of the theory of competitive markets? Why might a profit-maximizing firm offer such a large raise?

Part 4
ISSUES IN PUBLIC POLICY

Learning Goals

In this chapter, you will learn

1. The three basic reasons why governments intervene in the economy
2. The characteristics of a good tax system and how the U.S. system measures up
3. About the major transfer programs of the government
4. About current controversies in the economics of the public sector

Chapter 17

THE PUBLIC SECTOR

Throughout American history, the issue of the role of government in the economy has been at the center of political discussions. Today's debates focus on the sizable imbalance between the federal government's spending and its tax revenues and on the future financial health of government programs that provide retirement income (Social Security) and health insurance (Medicare) to the elderly.

The impact of the government on the economy is huge, much larger than raw statistics on the size of the government might suggest (e.g., federal tax receipts and expenditures have averaged around 20 percent of GDP over the past fifty years, while state and local government taxes and expenditures now total around 14 percent of GDP). The government influences the economy not only through taxes and expenditures but also through myriad regulations that affect every aspect of economic life. This chapter describes what the government does, why it does what it does, the trade-offs it faces in choosing what to do, and how those choices are made.

The United States has a federal structure in which responsibilities are divided between the federal government and state and local governments. Federal expenditures represent about two-thirds of total government spending. State and local governments are responsible for education (their single largest category of expenditures), local roads, law enforcement, and fire protection.

One way of understanding what the federal government does is to look at what it spends its money on. Figure 17.1 shows how its spending has changed over the past half century. In the 1950s, defense expenditures represented more than half of all expenditures; by 2000 defense had fallen to just 16 percent of the total. Though this figure has risen to close to 20 percent as a result of the wars in Afghanistan and Iraq, it is still a significantly smaller share of government expenditures than in earlier years. A half century ago, Social Security and welfare expenditures were about an eighth of the total; today they are three-eighths. In recent years the federal

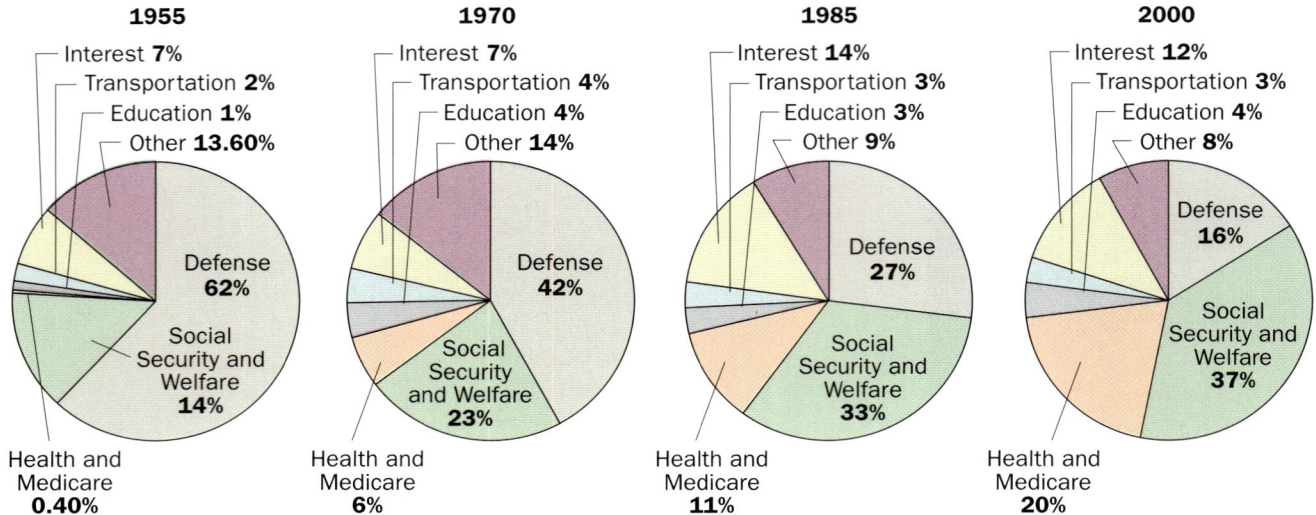

Figure 17.1

THE CHANGING PATTERN OF FEDERAL EXPENDITURES

Since 1955 there has been a steady increase in the share of federal funds allocated to Social Security, welfare, health, and Medicare. During the same period, the share allocated to defense has dropped dramatically.

SOURCE: U.S. Census Bureau, *Statistical Abstract of the United States* (1997), Table 518, and (2000), Table 533.

government has become more involved in school reform, but most spending on education in the United States is undertaken by state and local governments; it accounts for about 4 percent of federal spending.

But as already noted, the impact of the federal government cannot be gauged just by taxes and expenditures. First, it provides the legal system that enables the private sector to function. For example, the government creates and enforces contract laws, which structure agreements between two parties. The government also makes and enforces bankruptcy laws, which determine whose bills must be paid when an individual or corporation cannot meet debt obligations and files for bankruptcy.

Second, the government is responsible for maintaining the macroeconomic stability of the economy—preventing or at least minimizing recessions and depressions on the one hand, and runaway inflation on the other. Third, the government creates and enforces regulations designed to promote competition, preserve the environment, and protect consumers and workers. While there is considerable debate about the costs of these regulations, and about whether the benefits exceed those costs, few doubt that the regulations have succeeded in creating cleaner air, less-polluted waterways, and even safer cars and workplaces.

Although everyone values these benefits of government, many have worried that the taxes levied to finance government activities are a drag on the economy and interfere with its efficiency.

Why Does the Government Intervene in the Economy?

There are three basic reasons why the government intervenes in the economy: (1) to improve economic efficiency by correcting market failures; (2) to pursue social values of fairness, or equity, by altering market outcomes; and (3) to pursue other social values by mandating the consumption of some goods, called merit goods, and prohibiting the consumption of other goods, called merit bads. The next three sections address each of these reasons for government participation in the economy.

International Perspective

THE SIZE OF GOVERNMENT IN DIFFERENT COUNTRIES

The increase in central (federal) government expenditures during the twentieth century was dramatic, but expenditures in the United States are still among the smallest of any of the major industrialized economies in proportion to the size of the economy. In Denmark, Sweden, and the United Kingdom, government expenditures are more than one-third of GDP; in the United States, they are less than one-fifth. Of the major industrialized countries, only Japan and Australia spend less than one-third of GDP on the public sector. As a significant portion of U.S. federal expenditures goes to defense (about 3 percent of GDP), the relative size of its nondefense expenditures is particularly low viewed from this international perspective.

In the United States, federal spending on nondefense public-sector programs amounts to about 17 percent of GDP. In Sweden and the United Kingdom, this figure is 39 and 34 percent, respectively. The key difference lies in social insurance and welfare programs, which are proportionally much larger in those countries than in the United States.

These foreign comparisons prove different things to different people. Advocates of more government spending argue that the United States is out of step with global norms. Opponents of more government spending argue that other industrialized nations would do better to reduce public expenditures.

One factor to keep in mind is the smaller role played by local governments in those countries. In the United States, state and local government spending is about 14 percent of GDP, bringing total government expenditures close to 31 percent—a figure more in line with other countries.

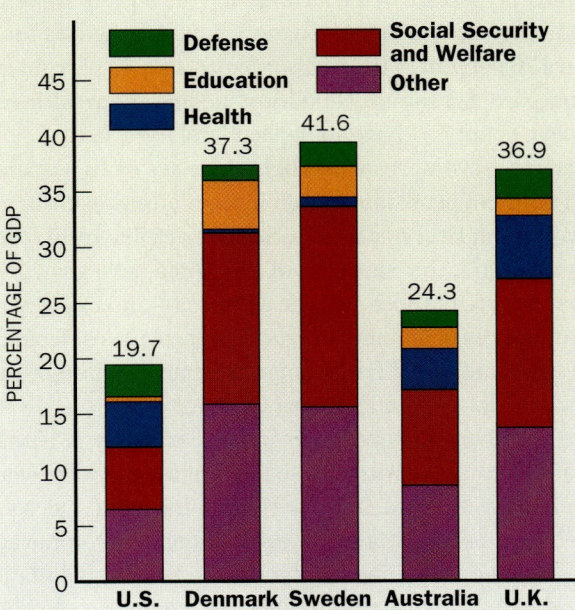

SOURCE: *Government Finance Statistics Yearbook* (2000) and *Economic Report of the President* (2001).

Correcting Market Failures Chapter 11 described four sources of market failure in the economy: imperfect competition, imperfect information, externalities, and public goods. Government programs are aimed at redressing market failures in each of these major categories. For instance, under imperfect competition, firms use their market power to raise prices and reduce output. Antitrust policies set by government attempt to maintain a competitive marketplace and restrain firms from abusing their market power. Imperfect information may impede the efficient functioning of product and labor markets. Governments establish regulations to require firms to produce information on their products and on their financial condition. Moreover, governments often play a large role in providing *social insurance* that helps protect against the risks of unemployment or illness, in part to provide relief for problems caused by imperfect information. In the presence of externalities, firms produce too little of goods (like research) accompanied by positive externalities and too much of goods (such as those that generate pollution) accompanied by negative externalities. Governments subsidize the former and tax or otherwise regulate the latter.

Equity and the Redistribution of Income But even if markets were efficient, they would result in some individuals receiving too low of an income to survive at a standard of living that is viewed as socially acceptable. In the market, individuals' incomes are related to their ownership of assets and their productivity. Those with little education receive low wages. And even in the United States, most individuals have few assets: the bottom 75 percent of households by wealth own less than 15 percent of total wealth, and the average wealth of the bottom 25 percent of all households was less than $1,100 in 2001. Income in the United States is highly unequal: the top 10 percent of households receive 30 percent of the income, and the bottom 20 percent receive just 2 percent of total income. Wealth is even more concentrated, as the top 10 percent of households have 70 percent of the wealth; the bottom 50 percent, only 3 percent. Some countries have even greater inequality of income and wealth, while others, such as many European countries, have somewhat less.

Inequality raises concerns for several reasons. High levels are often associated with a variety of social and political problems, which in turn often result in a climate that does not favor investment. East Asia and Latin America illustrate the two extremes. Over the past thirty years, the countries of East Asia have grown very rapidly—at more than twice the rate of those in Latin America—and many economists believe that the greater degree of equality in East Asia provides at least part of the explanation. Many of the countries of Latin America, characterized by great inequality, are plagued by urban violence and political unrest.

In most societies, there is a concern about *social justice* or *fairness*. It seems morally wrong for so many of society's goods to go to so few. But fairness, like beauty, is often in the eye of the beholder. Many of those with high incomes and wealth believe that they *deserve* their fortunes. Attitudes toward inequality differ markedly across countries and have changed over time. In the United States, inequalities explained by individual effort are far more acceptable than inequalities linked to inheritance. Wealth that results from a brilliant innovation is more acceptable than wealth gained by the exercise of monopoly power or political influence (as wielded by the nineteenth-century "robber barons").

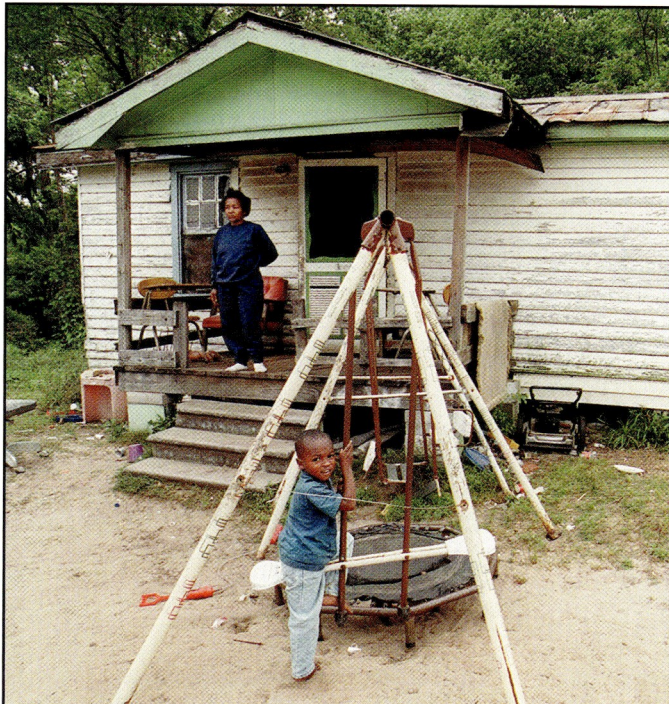
The lifetime prospects for children born into poor families are much bleaker than those of children born into rich families.

Concern is particularly acute about two groups—the very poor and children. The public finds it especially disturbing that even in the United States, supposedly the land of opportunity, the lifetime prospects of a child born into a poor family and a child born into a rich family are markedly different—and much bleaker for the poor child. This troubling disparity helps explain the widespread support for high-quality public education; for Pell Grants, which help make a college education affordable to students with low family incomes; and for Project Head Start, which provides preschool education for poor children.

The government provides a variety of programs aimed at the very poor. These programs attempt to provide a basic *safety net,* to ensure that all have a minimal level of income (through welfare programs), housing, food (through food stamps), and health (through Medicaid). Programs that take income from some people and *redistribute* it to others are called **transfer programs.** Many government programs, including education, have a redistributive component, which is especially important in social insurance programs. Low-wage individuals, for instance, get back more than they contribute to Social Security.

Merit Goods and Bads Some government activities, however, neither correct market failures nor redistribute income. Rather, they attempt to impose social values on individuals, to force or encourage them to do more of some things and less of others. Governments try to discourage drug taking and encourage education. These are called **merit goods.** Such merit goods (and bads) need to be distinguished from externalities: no one else may be harmed by someone smoking marijuana, yet many governments make it illegal. Moderate drinking or cigarette smoking may have an adverse effect only on the drinker or smoker, yet government still tries to discourage the consumption of alcohol and tobacco through high taxes. In these instances, the government interferes with the general principle of **consumer sovereignty,** which holds that individuals are the best judges of what is in their own interests and promote their own well-being. The government acts *paternalistically.* Many economists believe that government should limit such behavior to its oversight of minors—few object to compulsory education requirements for children but many question whether government should dictate what adults should or should not do, so long as their actions do not cause harm to others.

WRAP-UP

REASONS FOR GOVERNMENT INTERVENTION IN THE ECONOMY

To correct market failures: Market failures such as externalities provide a rationale for government intervention, which aims at improving economic efficiency.

To pursue equity: Market outcomes, even when they are efficient, might fail to satisfy social standards of equity. Government may intervene to redistribute income.

To promote and discourage merit goods and bads: Sometimes government imposes social values, by mandating the consumption of merit goods (education) and prohibiting the consumption of merit bads (illicit drugs).

EQUITY-EFFICIENCY TRADE-OFFS

We have seen that government programs have multiple objectives. If the only task of the government were to address market failures, it would face difficult technical issues—for instance, how best to reduce pollution. But the hardest problems are those that involve *trade-offs,* especially between improving the efficiency of the market and promoting equity. Equity—a sense of fairness—might suggest that the rich and wealthy should contribute not only more to support the government but proportionately more (i.e., a larger fraction of their income). The United States has a **progressive** income tax system that is designed to do exactly that; tax rates for higher-income individuals are set above those for lower-income individuals. (Conversely, tax systems in which the poor pay a higher proportion of their income to the government are **regressive**.) The inefficiencies associated with such taxation arise from the **marginal tax rate,** the extra tax that an individual pays on the last dollar earned. If the marginal tax rate is high, incentives to work harder are

e-Insight
THE NEW ECONOMY AND INEQUALITY

Income inequality in the United States has increased significantly over the past twenty years. One reason for this change has been the increasing premium earned by skilled workers. In 1980, college graduates received a wage 43 percent higher, on average, than that received by those with only a high school education; by 1990, that premium had increased to just over 70 percent. Over the 1990s, it continued to increase, rising to 75 percent by the end of the decade.

The job skills demanded by the new, information-based economy are often cited as a major cause of the growth in the wage premium for skilled workers. In fact, two opposing forces have been at play. On the supply side, there has been a marked increase in the skills of the U.S. labor force. In 1980, only 20 percent of the workforce had a college degree; by 2000, this fraction had risen to almost 30 percent. But at the same time that the supply of college-educated workers was increasing, the new economy was generating an increasing demand for skilled labor. The rise in the college wage premium since 1980 suggests that increases in demand have outpaced increases in supply (at any given wage).

Economists debate how much of the premium's rise has been caused by the introduction of new computer-related technologies. According to a survey of human resource managers, new information technologies have led many organizations to decentralize decision making, a shift that has increased the demand for highly educated workers able to use computers. Some economists believe that the wage premium associated with computer skills will erode over time as these skills become widely disseminated.

reduced. Thus, if high-income individuals have a high income because their wages are high, and their wages are high because they are more productive, then the effect of a progressive income tax on those who are the most productive is to discourage them from working.

Though governments often must make hard trade-offs, sometimes equity and efficiency go together. Providing educational opportunities for the poor may be equitable and efficient, as encouraging the use of these human resources may also improve the efficiency of the economy. And in many poor countries, large numbers of landless peasants work under sharecropping contracts in which the landlord gets one out of two dollars they earn. It is as if the sharecroppers face a 50 percent tax rate. Redistributing land to the poor may increase both efficiency and equity.

The U.S. Tax System in Practice

One out of every three dollars of the U.S. economy's total output goes to the government. Not surprisingly, the question of how the government raises its revenue attracts a great deal of attention. Nobody likes taxes, but they are necessary if the government is to provide public goods and services and if it is to reduce income inequality by redistribution.

CHARACTERISTICS OF A GOOD TAX SYSTEM

While the design of the tax system is a perennial subject of controversy—views of how to balance the equity-efficiency trade-off differ markedly, as is wholly predictable—there is broad consensus on five *principles* of a good tax system.

Fairness The first criterion is fairness. But fairness is not always easy to define. Economists focus on two points: **horizontal equity,** the notion that individuals who are in identical or similar situations should pay identical or similar taxes, and **vertical equity,** the notion that people who are better off should pay more taxes.

Efficiency The second criterion for a good tax system is efficiency. The tax system should interfere as little as possible with the economy's allocation of resources, and it should raise revenue with the least cost to taxpayers. Very high taxes may discourage work and saving, and thereby interfere with the efficiency of the economy. Taxes that narrowly target particular goods—such as excise taxes on perfume, boats, and airline tickets—discourage individuals from purchasing those goods, and thereby also interfere with efficiency.

Sometimes, taxes can be used to improve economic efficiency or to advance broader social purposes: taxes on pollution can improve the environment; taxes on cigarettes discourage smoking, leading to improvements in public health. Such taxes are said to yield a "double dividend," increasing overall efficiency or promoting social purposes at the same time that they generate revenue.

Administrative Simplicity The third criterion is administrative simplicity. Taxation is an expensive process, both to those who must pay taxes and to the government that must collect them. In addition to the costs of running the IRS, billions of hours are spent each year in filling out tax forms, hours that might be spent producing goods and services or enjoyed as additional leisure time. Billions of dollars are spent by taxpayers and by the IRS on tax software, accountants and lawyers in the annual ritual of preparing and processing tax forms. Finally, having a simple tax system reduces the likelihood that a would-be tax evader will succeed.

Flexibility The fourth criterion is flexibility. As economic circumstances change, it may be desirable to change tax rates. A good tax system should permit such adjustments with relative ease.

Transparency The fifth criterion is transparency. A good tax system is one in which it can be ascertained what each person is paying in taxes. The principle of transparency is analogous to the principle of "truth in advertising." Taxpayers are consumers of public services. They should know what they (and others) are paying for the services they are getting.

Wrap-Up

CRITERIA FOR EVALUATING A TAX SYSTEM

Fairness
Efficiency
Administrative simplicity
Flexibility
Transparency

THE SCOPE OF THE U.S. TAX SYSTEM

The U.S. government raises tax revenues from a variety of sources. The earnings of individuals and corporations yield **individual income taxes** and **corporation income taxes.** Real estate—buildings and land—is subject to taxation by most states; these payments are known as **property taxes.** Large bequests and gifts are taxed, through **gift** and **estate taxes.** Special provisions apply to the taxation of capital gains (the increase in value of an asset between the time an individual purchases it and the time she sells it). Furthermore, wage income is subject not only to the income tax but also to the **payroll tax** (the tax levied on a company's payroll, half of which is deducted from employees' paychecks). Revenues from the payroll tax finance two programs: Social Security (retirement and disability income) and Medicare (medical care for the aged).

There are also taxes on the purchase of specific goods and services, known as **excise taxes.** The two heaviest excise taxes are on alcohol and tobacco, also known as **sin taxes.** The excise taxes on air travel and gasoline are sometimes called **benefit taxes** because the proceeds are spent on benefits (e.g., airports and roads) for those who purchase the good. Excise taxes on perfume, large cars, yachts, and expensive fur coats, aimed at the rich, are referred to as **luxury taxes.** Other excise taxes, such as the one on telephone services, have no particular justification other than to raise revenue. Most states impose a general tax on purchases of goods and services, known as a **sales tax,** though often some items (such as food) are exempted.

As this list indicates, few transactions in our economy escape taxation. Figure 17.2 shows the relative importance of various taxes at the federal and at the state and local levels. At the federal level (panel A), the single most important source of revenue is the tax on individuals' income (contributing almost half of total revenue), followed by the payroll tax. At the state and local levels (panel B), the sales tax is the most important revenue source.

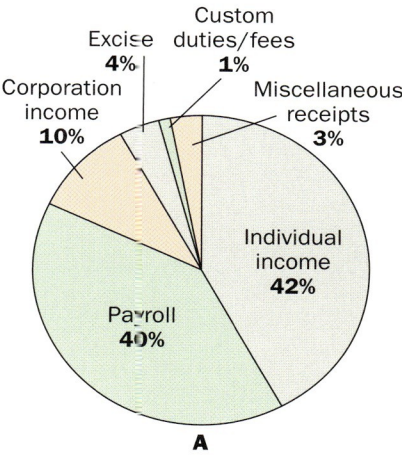

A
Sources of Federal Tax Revenues 2003

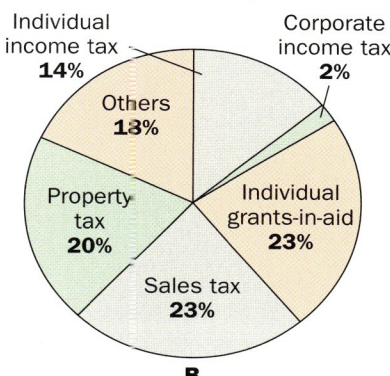

B
Sources of State and Local Tax Revenues 2003

Figure 17.2

THE IMPORTANCE OF VARIOUS TAXES

At the federal level, the largest share of taxes comes from the individual income tax, followed by the payroll tax and the corporate income tax, as shown in panel A. Sources of revenue at the state and local level are more fragmented, as seen in panel B; they include sales and property taxes, as well as revenue received from other levels of government.

SOURCE: Bureau of Economic Analysis, *National Income and Product Accounts* (2004), Tables 3.2 and 3.3 (www.doc.gov)

GRADING THE U.S. TAX SYSTEM

How well does the U.S. tax system measure up against the five principles of a good tax system? Equally important, have the major changes in the tax laws over the past decade resulted in improvements? During the past quarter century, the U.S. income tax system has undergone five major reforms, in 1981, 1986, 1993, 1997, and 2001. The announced intent of each was to make the system more efficient, more fair, and administratively more simple. But trade-offs always had to be made, and the reforms approached them differently; indeed, each tended to undo what was widely viewed as the excesses of its predecessor. Meanwhile, worries about soaring government expenditures limited the extent to which various social goals could be pursued through new programs. Hence, government instead used tax expenditures—such as tuition tax credits and deductions—to pursue these objectives in the tax bills of 1993, 1997, and 2001, inevitably complicating the tax system greatly.

Fairness As noted, the U.S. federal income tax system is, overall, progressive. Low-income individuals are exempt from paying any income tax whatsoever. Beyond a certain level of income (depending on family size—for a family of four, the critical level in 2004 was $22,100), the tax rate is then 10 percent. Thus, for each $100 an individual earns, he must pay an extra $10 of taxes; this is his *marginal tax rate*. At higher levels of income, the marginal tax rate increases further, eventually reaching 39.1 percent on incomes above $315,900 (for a family of four).

The **average tax rate** gives the ratio of taxes to taxable income. While the marginal tax rate shows big jumps, the average tax rate increases smoothly. Figure 17.3 shows the 2000 marginal and average income tax rates for a typical family of four that did not itemize its deductions.

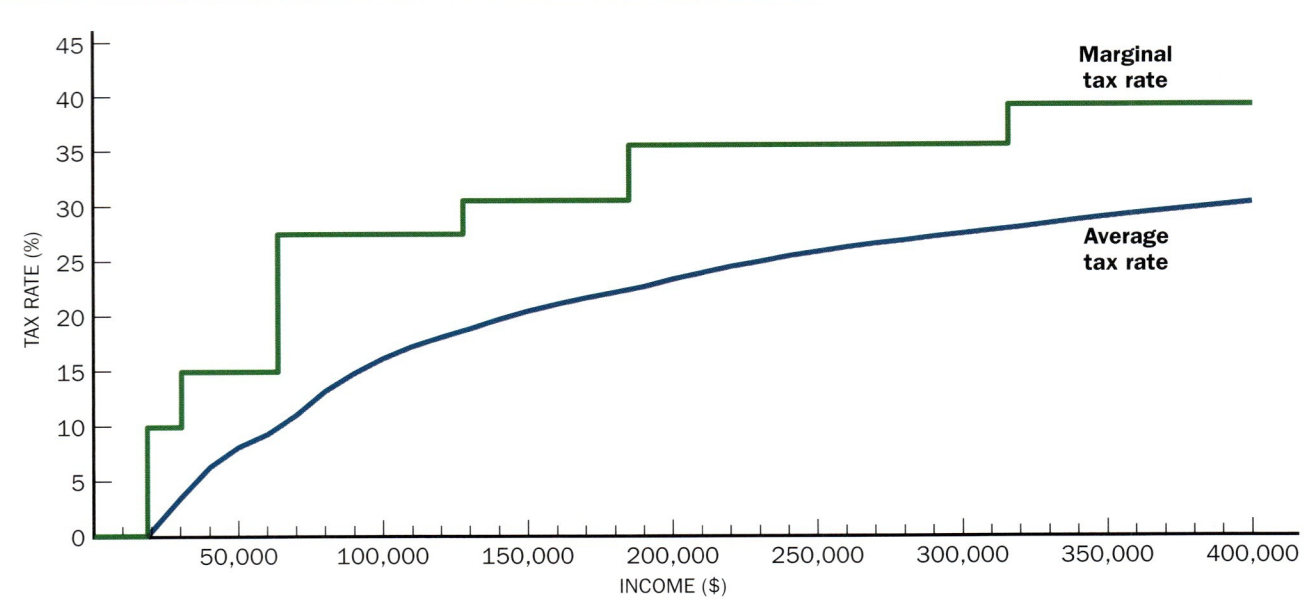

Figure 17.3

MARGINAL AND AVERAGE FEDERAL INCOME TAX RATE

Marginal tax rates change by jumps, as shown in the table, but average tax rates increase gradually.

SOURCE: Tax Relief Act of 2001.

The income tax is only one of several income-related taxes that U.S. citizens pay. The payroll (Social Security) tax is another that increases with income up to a fixed level. An **earned-income tax credit** is designed to supplement the income of low-income workers with families; as a person's income increases beyond a given level, the payments she *receives* under this program decrease.

To assess the overall progressivity of the U.S. tax system, we have to look not only at federal taxes but at all taxes—including the corporate income tax and state and local taxes.

Many state and local taxes are regressive, because lower- and middle-income individuals spend a larger fraction of their income on items that are subject to state sales taxes than do the rich. Our current *total* tax system—combining the slightly progressive federal tax system with the slightly regressive state and local tax system—is, in the judgment of most economists, only modestly progressive.

Tax changes in recent years have alternately decreased and increased the degree of progressivity. In 1981 and 1986, marginal tax rates on upper-income individuals, for instance, were brought down markedly; in 1993, they were increased again, though to levels that were still lower than they had been in 1981. The tax cut passed by Congress in 2001 phases in lower marginal tax rates over a number of years. Prior to 1986, capital gains—the increases in the value of assets over time—were taxed at lower rates (varying from 40 to 50 percent of the "normal" rate) than were other forms of income. Reform abolished this special treatment, but in 1997 it was restored. Earlier, we noted that wealth is heavily concentrated; not surprisingly, the rich benefited enormously from this provision. At the same time, other changes in the tax law helped those with lower incomes, especially those with children, and the 2001 tax changes reduced the marginal tax rate from 15 percent to 10 percent on the first $6,000 of taxable income ($12,000 for married couples).

Efficiency The U.S. tax system today, while considerably more efficient than it was fifteen years ago, still has much room for improvement. Its inefficiencies are related to two factors: the progressivity of the tax system and the extent to which different kinds of income and different expenditures are treated differently. The *marginal* tax rates distort labor supply, for instance, and the variations in marginal tax rates discussed earlier affect this distortion.

Similarly, the distortions associated with differential taxation have increased, decreased, and again increased over time. As we noted, the 1981 tax law encouraged certain kinds of investment, while the 1986 law created a more level playing field than had existed for decades. Changes in the tax law since then have introduced new distortions—some, such as provisions favoring the oil and gas industries, largely reflect the influence of special interests while others, such as those promoting education, demonstrate the use of the tax system to pursue social objectives.

The U.S. income tax system has many provisions intended to encourage some types of economic activity and discourage others. For instance, the U.S. income tax allows certain child care payments to be taken as a credit against tax payments owed. The government thus subsidizes child care. Similarly, when firms spend money on R & D, their expenditures may reduce the amount they have to pay in taxes. Such arrangements are called **tax subsidies.** These subsidies cost the government money, just as if the government paid directly for child care or research. Accordingly, the revenue lost from a tax subsidy is called a **tax expenditure.**

Administrative Simplicity Americans live in a complex society, and their tax laws reflect and contribute to this complexity. As legislators have sought to ensure that the tax laws are fair and apply uniformly to all people in similar situations, the laws have become increasingly complex. High tax rates make it worthwhile for individuals and businesses to think hard about legal means of minimizing taxes. It may pay a businessperson to devote almost as much energy to tax avoidance as to designing and producing a better product. The tax law has evolved out of this constant battle between the government and taxpayers; as each new way of reducing tax payments is discovered, the law is modified to close the loophole. Inevitably another hole is discovered, and another repair job is attempted. Today the federal tax law fills tens of thousands of pages.

The objective of administrative simplicity seems to remain elusive. Many economists are convinced that the United States could have a tax system that is truly simple to administer, but only if other objectives are given up. Some of its complexity derives from the effort to have a progressive income tax and to tax the income from capital.

Flexibility One of the weakest aspects of the U.S. tax system is its lack of flexibility. Any time a tax change is proposed, all of the issues discussed here are raised. Its effects on different groups and on efficiency are debated. Basic issues of values—how progressive should the tax system be?—are aired once again, while special-interest groups try to take advantage of the chance to have favorable treatment written into the code. Changing the tax law is thus extremely difficult—and very time-consuming.

Transparency Though the merits of transparency are widely preached, governments often prefer citizens to be ignorant of their total tax bill. The worry is that knowledge might lead to "sticker shock" and that opposition to taxes might grow. The overall impact of some taxes is more obvious than others. For instance, individuals pay sales taxes in dribs and drabs; they never get a clear view of their total payments. That may be one reason why politicians seem to love the sales tax so much. Of all the parts of the tax system, the ultimate burden imposed by corporate income tax is perhaps the least transparent. Although corporations write the check to the IRS, most economists agree that much of the onus of paying taxes is shifted to individuals and households, through reduced wages, higher product prices, or both.

Transfers

Earlier we noted the role of government in redistributing income: very poor individuals receive more from the government than they contribute in taxes. There are five major public benefit programs for low-income Americans: welfare, Medicaid, food stamps, supplemental security income (SSI), and housing assistance. Until

1997, the program commonly known as "welfare" was AFDC (Aid to Families with Dependent Children), which provided cash assistance to poor families, mostly households with only one parent present. It was replaced by a new program called TANF (Temporary Assistance to Needy Families). Medicaid provides health care to the poor. The food stamp program offers vouchers for the purchase of food. SSI provides cash assistance to the low-income elderly and disabled, to supplement their Social Security benefits. Housing assistance programs include public housing and rental vouchers. In addition, states and localities provide different amounts of general assistance to those who fall between the cracks. Food stamps and SSI are federal programs (states can supplement SSI benefits). The other programs vary from state to state, with the federal government typically providing only broad program guidelines but footing much of the bill.

Our discussion here focuses on the most controversial program areas: welfare, housing, and social insurance.

WELFARE

From 1935 until 1997, AFDC was the primary cash program in the U.S. welfare system. The states not only administered AFDC but also set benefit levels and had some discretion over rules. The federal government provided a fraction of the funds, which varied from approximately one-half to three-fourths, depending on the state's per capita income. Programs in which federal outlays depend on state expenditures are called **matching programs.** The federal matching subsidy presumably resulted in raising the benefit levels above what they would have been if the states had been required to pay the full (marginal) costs themselves. States were given considerable discretion in determining the level of expenditures. Not surprisingly, there were considerable discrepancies in the level of benefits provided by the states; the highest benefits, in Alaska, were more than seven times the lowest benefits, in Mississippi.

Starting in 1997, TANF replaced AFDC. TANF represented a marked departure from the earlier system in two ways. First, it replaced the old system of matching grants with **block grants,** a fixed amount of money, with states given great flexibility in spending that money (including discretion in determining the eligibility of needy families and the benefits and services those families receive). Second, TANF focused on moving individuals from welfare to work. The states were given broad leeway in the design and operation of their welfare-to-work programs, but the use of TANF funds had to be consistent with the federal priorities: strong work requirements, time limits to receiving assistance, a reduction in welfare dependency, and the encouragement of two-parent families.

Under TANF, most recipients of aid must find work or participate in "work activities" such as job-training programs to keep their benefits. Among those exempt from this requirement are single parents with a child under six; they cannot be penalized for not working if they are unable to find adequate child care. In a major break with past welfare programs, TANF puts explicit time limits on participation. A family with an adult who has received federally funded assistance for a total of five years is not eligible for cash aid under the TANF program. After the introduction of TANF, employment among low-income single mothers with children under six rose significantly. The incidence of poverty among children, which had already been falling, continued to decline, although it rose slightly during the economic recession in 2001.

When the original TANF legislation was passed by Congress in 1996, the program was designed to expire in 2002. However, on nine occasions since 2002, Congress has temporarily extended it. The most recent extension, passed in March 2005, reauthorized TANF until September 30, 2005.

HOUSING

Public housing projects have been described, with some justification, as warehouses of the poor. By failing to integrate the poor thoroughly into the communities in which they live, public housing projects can help perpetuate the cycle of poverty. Moreover, many housing programs are inequitable. They provide generous benefits to those lucky enough to receive them, but many with the same income and family size get nothing. Worse still, providing a subsidy that is tied to a particular dwelling impedes labor mobility. Finally, though the costs of public housing are high, its quality is often much lower than housing of similar cost in the private sector.

All these drawbacks have led the government to reduce its role in directly supplying low-income housing and to turn increasingly to more market-based solutions. The most common is to subsidize the cost of housing for the poor by supplying rental vouchers. As recipients use the vouchers, thereby increasing demand for low-income housing, more builders are induced to provide housing for them. Vouchers have several other advantages. They allow individuals to shop for their housing over broader areas, not just in the designated projects, and they can be made "portable," so that individuals can relocate to pursue job opportunities without losing their housing subsidy. Unfortunately, vouchers are no panacea. Long waiting lists, time limits on using the voucher once it is received, and the disinclination of builders and landlords to provide low-income housing when the demand for housing generally is so strong limit their effectiveness.

Wrap-Up

GOVERNMENT TRANSFER PROGRAMS IN THE UNITED STATES

Welfare: TANF (Temporary Assistance for Needy Families)

Medicaid: health care for the poor

Food stamps: vouchers for the purchase of food

Supplemental security income: cash assistance to the low-income elderly and disabled

Housing assistance: public housing and rental vouchers

SOCIAL INSURANCE

The United States has a variety of what are referred to as middle-class **entitlement programs,** so named because individuals do not have to demonstrate poverty to receive benefits. The most important of these are the social insurance programs. Social insurance programs are like private insurance, in that people nominally pay for their own protection through a tax on wage income, the payroll tax. But in other important ways, they are *not* like private insurance, as we will see in the paragraphs that follow.

The Burden of Social Insurance Programs Social Security is supported by a tax on wages, 50 percent paid by the employer and 50 percent by the employee. This division of the tax is entirely superficial; the consequences of the tax are essentially the same as they would be if the worker paid the entire amount.

Figure 17.4 uses demand and supply curves for labor to demonstrate this point. Consider a payroll tax imposed on the employer based on what she pays her workers. The vertical axis measures the wage *received* by the employee. Since the cost of a worker is the wage received by the employee *plus* the tax, the tax shifts the demand curve down. In the new equilibrium, workers' wages have fallen. The wage received by a worker is precisely the same as it would have been had the same tax been imposed on the worker directly. While normally the wage falls by less than the amount of the tax, the extent to which it falls depends on the elasticity of the demand and supply curves. The figure shows the "normal" case where the supply of labor is relatively inelastic, in which case wages fall by almost the full amount of the tax. According to another view, Social Security has relatively little impact on labor supply, by and large, because benefits increase with contributions (though the increase in benefits may not be *fully* commensurate with the increase in contributions); the program is largely a forced savings program. Indeed, most individuals are not forced to save more, or at least much more, than they otherwise would. As we note in the next paragraph, the program has a redistributive aspect. Some individuals therefore receive back less than they contribute, and for them there is a disincentive effect not unlike the disincentive effects that would arise if a similar amount of redistribution occurred through the income tax system.

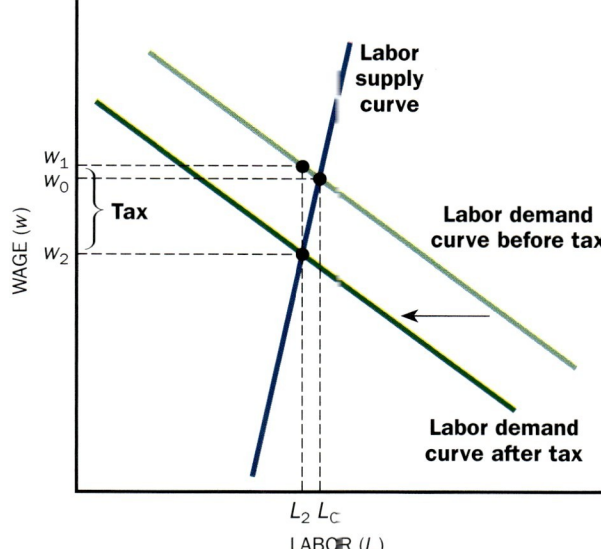

Figure 17.4

THE INCIDENCE OF PAYROLL TAXES

The payroll tax introduces a wedge between the cost to an employer of an individual working an hour more (wage plus tax) and what the worker receives. The magnitude of the wedge does not depend on whether the tax is levied on the employer or employee. The tax leads to fewer workers being hired at the equilibrium wage, reduced from w_0 to w_2.

How Social Insurance Is More Than an Insurance Program In any insurance program, some individuals receive back more than they contribute, others receive less. That is, in a sense, the whole purpose of insurance. David may pay for fire insurance year after year, but if his home never burns down, he doesn't receive anything back from the insurance company. Clara may have the misfortunate to have her house burn down, and may receive back from the insurance company a payment that greatly exceeds what she had paid in. Those lucky enough not to have their houses go up in flames in effect help pay for those who do suffer a loss. Similarly, no one knows whether the upcoming year will bring serious illness. So people buy health insurance that covers hospitalization. Those who remain healthy essentially pay for the hospitalization of those who need it. But the premiums of an individual's private insurance policy will, on average, cover the costs of what the policyholder can expect to receive (plus the costs of administration, which are often substantial). Social insurance programs, in contrast, often lack a close connection between the amount contributed and the amount contributors expect to receive. In the case of Social Security, for example, the retirement payments of single high-wage earners are less per dollar contributed than those of low-wage families with a single earner. Thus, the Social Security program performs a redistributive as well as an insurance function.

In the United States, Social Security faces a serious financial shortfall over the next several decades as the large post–World War II generation of baby boomers retires; social insurance programs in many other countries anticipate similar difficulties. Many argue that these financing problems could be solved by undertaking modest reforms, such as increasing the minimum age at which retirees can start collecting benefits. More radical proposals call for establishing individual retirement accounts for younger workers. These accounts would tie the benefits an individual receives more closely to the taxes the individual has paid, thereby diminishing the redistributive role of social insurance.

Designing Government Programs

Even when there is agreement about *what* the government should do, analysts often disagree on *how* it should do it. Take, for instance, the problem of pollution. The government can tax those who pollute, it can regulate pollution, or it can subsidize actions that abate pollution. Or consider education. At the elementary and secondary level, the government provides free public education to all; it is a *producer*. But at the university level, education is not free to all. Instead, state governments subsidize those who choose to go to state universities or colleges, and the federal government gives grants to low-income individuals to use for any university or college, public or private. A variety of considerations go into making these choices. When the government is an inefficient producer, as often happens, it makes more sense for it to provide the money to individuals, who can make purchases from the more efficient private producers. In the case of higher education, the U.S. government improves the access of those from poor or disadvantaged backgrounds by offering educational *grants* to individuals rather than by providing the education itself. Such grants to individual students are more controversial when it comes to elementary or secondary education. In school *voucher* programs, grants go directly to the parents of school-age children, to be spent at either public or private elementary and secondary schools. Many critics of school vouchers, while supporting the same basic concept in higher education, believe that such programs would weaken public schools by draining away their pupils and funds. Supporters of vouchers argue that giving parents a choice in where to send their children would force public schools to improve.

Government Failures

Decisions about whether the government should intervene and *how* it should intervene thus depend on one's views of the efficiency and efficacy of government. One of the main rationales for government action that we noted above is to correct market failures. But proponents of a limited role for government argue that government often not only fails to correct the problems of the market but makes matters even worse. Noting that many of the difficulties facing the private sector—such as imperfect information—also plague the public sector, they then point to several more that are especially acute in the public sector, such as problems relating to incentives and commitments and to budgetary constraints and processes.

In fact, the evidence on government inefficiency is mixed. Government has long played an important role in the economy, and the list of its commonly accepted successes is correspondingly long. The amazing increase in agricultural productivity over the past seventy-five years is generally attributed to the government's support of research and its outreach to train farmers in the new technologies. Key advances in computer technology and jet engines were the result of government support. The development of the vital telecommunications sector has relied on government support—from Samuel Morse's first telegraph line between Baltimore and Washington in 1842 to the birth and growth of the Internet in the 1970s and 1980s. Today we can more safely breathe the air in our cities and drink and swim in the water from our lakes and rivers, largely because of actions undertaken by government.

Critics of government draw on a number of widely cited studies comparing the efficiency of the government and the private sector in similar activities—such as collecting garbage—to suggest that the public sector is systematically less efficient. But two important caveats must be added. First, much of the government activity is in areas where output is hard to measure or the quality of an individual's contribution is hard to assess, and accordingly where the private sector too has a hard time designing effective incentive systems. Second, public enterprises are every bit as efficient as private enterprises. For instance, in the United States, the administrative and transaction costs are a much smaller percentage of contributions for Social Security than they are for privately provided annuities (insurance policies that pay a fixed amount every year of an individual's retirement). The government-run Canadian National Railroad appears to be as efficient as the privately run Canadian Pacific Railroad. And even the much-maligned U.S. Postal Service has managed to score productivity improvements in the past fifteen years that exceed the average for the U.S. economy. One reason cited for these successes is competition: the post office has to compete with private-sector competitors such as FedEx and UPS, and Canadian National Railroad had to compete with Canadian Pacific.

Still, failures of government are well-recognized, from public housing projects that rival the worst provided by any slumlord to cost overruns on defense projects. And some of the government successes have had questionable side effects: for example, the interstate highway system, while greatly reducing transportation time, contributed to the urban sprawl that blights many of our cities. Given the frequency with which government failures occur, it is natural to ask if there are *systemic* reasons for them? Four major factors underlie systemic government failure: incentive problems, budgeting problems, information problems, and the nature of political decision making. While the first three can afflict any large organization, including private-sector businesses, they often have particularly severe effects in government programs.

INCENTIVES AND CONSTRAINTS

Unlike private organizations, government has the power of coercion. It can force people to pay taxes, it can prohibit firms from paying less than the minimum wage if they engage in interstate commerce, and so on. But since this power carries with it enormous potential for abuse, certain procedures have been developed to protect the public against arbitrary use of government power. These procedures are collectively called *due process*.

Such procedures have the potential to create incentive problems, as can be seen from the set of rules governing civil service employment. These rules are designed to ensure that there is no discrimination against or other arbitrary treatment of government workers. But the rules are often inflexible and make it difficult to pay comparable salaries to public officials who do their jobs as well as similarly qualified and dedicated persons in the private sector—or to offer them the same opportunities for rapid promotion. It is even more difficult for government to demote or fire incompetent and lazy workers. Thus, the public sector's ability to recruit and manage staff with maximum efficiency typically is limited.

In addition to the constraints of due process, the government has trouble making long-term commitments that are perceived to be binding. Any Congress can reverse decisions made by previous Congresses, though it may try to design both legislation and legislative rules in ways that discourage later about-faces. Such limitations on the government's ability to make binding commitments can have major economic consequences. Take, for example, a government promise that it will pursue a policy of maintaining low inflation. The current government may convince investors of its commitment to keeping inflation low. But it has no control at all over what happens after the next election—as investors know. They therefore make their own assessments of inflation risk, which may interfere with the effectiveness of what the government is trying to do today. The current government can make it more costly for future governments to increase the rate of inflation; for instance, it can issue short-term bonds, so that the interest cost to the government would rise quickly if inflation started to pick up.

Also undermining government efficiency, and sometimes leading to perverse decisions against the broad interests of society, are the political pressures inherent in the democratic process. A prime example here is legislators' concerns about the next election. These can lead to so-called pork barrel projects that create jobs in a pivotal legislator's home district but make no economic sense from a national perspective. Moreover, the enormous cost of running for office provides incentives for elected officials to pay particular attention to the views and needs of those who contribute to their campaign funds. Thus lobbyists, among others, can wield influence far out of proportion to the importance of the interests they represent.

BUDGETING AND SPENDING PROCEDURES

The budgeting and spending constraints on government decision makers differ from those of the private sector in three major ways. The first is in their severity. Unlike a private firm, which faces the prospect of bankruptcy if enough of its ventures yield losses, a public enterprise can more easily turn to the government for budgetary help. This is the problem of *soft budget constraints*. Amtrak, for example, continues to lose money in its overall railroad operations, in spite of government promises that it will turn a profit. A major reason for the continuing loss is a set of labor rules *imposed by the government* requiring that workers be compensated if they are laid off or forced to relocate even a short distance. Soft budget constraints such as these weaken the incentives for public management to be efficient. There is nothing quite like the threat of bankruptcy to focus managerial attention.

The second budgetary difference between the private and public sectors—a factor that works in the opposite way from the soft budget constraints—is the annual appropriations process. This can force short-term spending constraints on the public sector that are not cost-effective in the long run. Limited investment flexibility is a particularly unfortunate consequence of the annual appropriations system.

The third budgetary constraint on government is the anti-efficiency effects of some of the procedures implemented to ensure strict cost control. Government has instituted detailed accounting, competitive bidding, and other procurement procedures to avoid waste and corruption. Yet these procedures can cost more than they save—and not just because of the extra bureaucracy involved. When purchasing T-shirts, for example, the government in its efforts to ensure that the specifications were accurate and precise—so that bidders were competing to supply *exactly* the same product—created thirty pages of documentation in small print that prospective bidders had to follow carefully. These forms of bureaucratic red tape reduce the supply of bidders willing to sell to the government and increase the cost to the government of goods and services.

IMPERFECTIONS OF INFORMATION

Information problems plague government just as they plague the private sector. As a result, there are often adverse *unintended* (and often unforeseen) *consequences* of even well-intentioned programs. We already noted one example: the expansion of the superhighway system in the 1950s may have led to urban sprawl, weakened the inner cities, and increased air pollution (from increased driving); none of these effects was even widely discussed, let alone anticipated. Urban renewal programs, designed to increase the quality of housing, often resulted in a decreased supply of affordable housing for the poor, thus aggravating the housing problems they faced and even contributing to homelessness.

Table 17.1
VOTING PREFERENCES

	Jessica's preferences	Ralph's preferences	Brutus's preferences
First choice:	Young and Romantic	Third and Goal to Go	Automatic Avengers
Second choice:	Third and Goal to Go	Automatic Avengers	Young and Romantic
Third choice:	Automatic Avengers	Young and Romantic	Third and Goal to Go

COLLECTIVE DECISION MAKING

A fourth important reason for public failures relates to how government decisions get made. Governments are not always consistent in their actions. This inconsistency may not be surprising, given that government choices do not reflect the preferences of a single individual. More fundamentally, majority voting may not yield a determinate outcome even when only three people choose among only three alternatives, as was noted more than two hundred years ago by the Frenchman Marquis de Condorcet—a phenomenon referred to as the **voting paradox.** Consider the simple example of three people who want to go to a movie together. They have narrowed their choices down to three possibilities, which they rank as shown in Table 17.1.

When they compare each of the films, they find that *Young and Romantic* is preferred over *Third and Goal to Go* by a two-to-one margin and *Third and Goal to Go* is preferred to *Automatic Avengers,* also by a two-to-one margin. Taking this information alone, they might reason that—since *Young and Romantic* is preferred over *Third and Goal to Go* and *Third and Goal to Go* is preferred over *Automatic Avengers—Young and Romantic* is also preferred to *Automatic Avengers.* But when they put it to a vote, they find that *Automatic Avengers* is preferred to *Young and Romantic* by a two-to-one margin. There is no majority winner. Majority voting can compare any two of these choices but is incapable of ranking all three of them.

The Nobel laureate Kenneth Arrow proved an even more remarkable result. All voting systems (two-thirds majority, weighted majority, or any other), under some circumstances, yield the same kind of indecision. Inconsistencies are simply inherent in the decision-making process of any democratic government. The only way around this problem is to entrust a single individual with all decisions. Such a system yields consistent choices but is hardly democratic!

Economists have looked carefully at how political processes are affected by *incentives*—for example, the incentives of politicians, of political parties, of government bureaucrats, and of special interests to curry favor with these political actors to influence legislation. *Public choice* theory is a branch of economics that analyzes the outcomes of political processes, assuming that each of the participants acts rationally. James Buchanan of George Mason University received a Nobel Prize for his contributions in developing public choice theory. As an understanding of how campaign contributions affect the behavior of politicians, and thus the outcomes of political processes, has become widespread, growing numbers of legislators and activists have argued for the need to reform campaign contribution laws.

Wrap-Up

SOURCES OF PUBLIC FAILURES

Incentives and constraints
    Due process
    Constrained ability to make long-term commitments
    Political pressures
    Pork barrel projects
    Power of lobbyists who make campaign contributions
Budgeting and spending constraints
    Soft budget constraints
    Annual appropriations process
    Rigid procurement rules
Imperfect information
    Unforeseen changes in behavior resulting from government action
Problems in collective decision making

Current and Recent Controversies in the Economics of the Public Sector

A good number of the controversies in public policy revolve around the role of the government in the economy. In the following paragraphs, we describe three of the *major* issues.

DEALING WITH THE DEFICIT

The past twenty-five years have seen large swings in the federal government's budget balance. In 1981, President Ronald Reagan engineered a large tax cut. As a result, the U.S. government's expenditures outpaced its revenues and the government ran huge deficits that continued throughout the 1980s. At its worst, the deficit reached almost $300 billion in the early 1990s. When the government runs a deficit, spending more than it collects in taxes, it must borrow to make up the difference. The federal debt is the total amount that the government owes as a result of this borrowing, and it rose from $3,500 for every man, woman, and child in the United States in 1981 to just over $14,000 in 1996.

When President Bill Clinton took office in 1993, he managed to slow the growth of expenditures, mainly by cutting defense spending (a task made far easier by the end of the cold war), and to increase taxes, mainly on individuals in the upper 2 percent of the income distribution. At the same time, the rate of growth of the U.S. economy picked up, increasing the growth in tax revenues.

By 1998, the budget situation had improved so much that the government actually ran a surplus, its first since 1969. Because the government was collecting more revenue than it was spending, it could use the excess (the surplus) to repay some of its debt. There was even talk that the government would eventually be able to repay all of its base borrowing and reduce the debt to zero. The debate over how to cut the deficit was apparently over; now the political issue was how to spend the surplus. Three views dominated the discussions. Some wanted to continue to use the surplus to reduce the debt; others wanted large tax cuts; still others wanted to use the funds to increase spending on a variety of social programs—from financing Social Security and health care for the elderly to improving education for the poor.

Tax cuts won out in the first months of President George W. Bush's presidency. In June 2001, President Bush signed into law a new tax reform that provided extensive tax cuts over a ten-year period. At the same time, the economy was entering a slowdown that caused tax revenues to decline; and the September 11, 2001, terrorist attack on the United States and the wars in Afghanistan and Iraq led to large hikes in defense spending. Rather than enjoying the expected surpluses, the U.S. government was confronted with massive deficits. By 2004, the deficit reached an all-time high of more than $400 billion, nearly $17,000 for every person in the country.

Dealing with the deficit is complicated by the other two major areas of controversy: Social Security and health care.

SOCIAL SECURITY

As President Bush began his second term in January 2005, the future of Social Security was being actively debated. The main component of Social Security, and the focus of our discussion, is the provision of retirement income to the elderly; it also supports survivors and those with disabilities. Currently, Social Security is a **pay-as-you-go program:** the taxes paid by today's workers go to pay the benefits of today's retirees. The tax rate now is 12.4 percent on all income up to $90,000 (half the tax is taken out of the worker's paychecks, and the other half is paid directly by the employer). Under a pay-as-you-go program, each generation of workers contributes to the retirement payments for previous generations. Under a **fully funded program,** in contrast, each worker has an individual account. Contributions are invested until the worker retires, when the proceeds finance that worker's retirement.

The Social Security program has been running a surplus since 1984. This will end as members of the large baby boom generation, born between the late 1940s and early 1960s, begin to retire and the program's balance between its expenditures and taxes collected starts to shift. By 2018, the program will begin paying out more in benefits than the smaller number still working are paying in; the difference will be covered from the surplus, which will be exhausted around 2040. At that point, additional sources of revenue will be needed if the current law's promises of benefits are to be honored.

While all agree that some changes to Social Security will be needed, what form those changes should take and how large they have to be are intensely debated. Calling the situation a crisis, President Bush has sought major changes to the very nature of the program. He has proposed that younger workers be allowed to divert some of the Social Security taxes they pay into individual retirement accounts, which then could be invested as each individual chooses. At retirement, benefits would be paid both from the traditional Social Security program and from the balance in the individual account. Proponents of retirement accounts argue that they will enable individuals to earn, on average, higher rates of return on their contributions than they do under the current Social Security program.

Opponents of retirement accounts make three points. First, they argue that the advocates have made unrealistic assumptions about the average returns on worker's contributions. Second, they stress that a system of individual accounts involves more risk for each individual; for example, the stock market might decline significantly just as a worker was about to retire, wiping out a large part of her account if it were invested heavily in stocks. Third, opponents point out that if younger workers divert some of their Social Security taxes into separate accounts, the funds available to provide benefits to the current retirees will go down. To come up with the money to keep paying for these promised benefits, therefore, the government will need to do one of three things: raise other taxes; borrow more now, thereby worsening the already huge budget deficit; or cut back on other government programs.

Most critics of the president's proposals recognize that if nothing is done, Social Security in time will face financial problems. However, they argue that these can be fixed with relatively minor adjustments in the program. One suggestion is to index the level of a retiree's initial benefit payment to the level of prices rather than to the general level of wages (as is currently done). Since wages on average rise faster than prices, tying payments to the latter would reduce the growth in future payments. At the same time, the indexing would ensure that the purchasing power of the benefits did not decline.

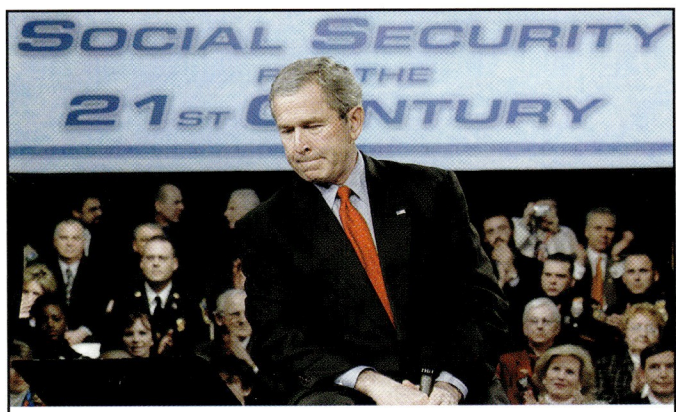

President Bush has been urging Americans to consider a major reform of the Social Security system.

A second adjustment often mentioned is to raise the age at which one can start collecting retirement benefits. Currently, that age is being gradually increased. For example, anyone born before 1937 could start receiving full benefits at age sixty-five. Someone born in 1947, however, has to wait until she is sixty-six years old, an individual born in 1957 must wait until they are sixty-six and a half, and anyone born in 1967 must be sixty-seven. The argument in favor of increasing the retirement age is that because people live much longer now than they did when the Social Security program was first established, they might reasonably expect to retire somewhat later.

A third proposal is to raise Social Security taxes, in one (or both) of two ways. First, the basic tax rate, currently 12.4 percent, could go up. It is estimated that an increase of 1 to 2 percent would cover the projected shortfall. There seems to be little political support for this approach, but somewhat less hostility toward the second: raising the income cap. Now the tax is paid only on the first $90,000 of income; taxing incomes instead up to $125,000 or $150,000 would bring in more revenue.

A fourth possibility is to accept a reduction in the level of benefits that future retirees will receive. Analysts estimate that if no adjustments are made, the system will be able to pay about 70 percent of what is now promised. This option, like an increase in the basic tax rate, lacks political support.

The Social Security program is often called the "third rail" of American politics, threatening a fatal shock to any politician who dares to propose any changes. Until some reforms are made, however, its fiscal stability will remain in doubt.

HEALTH CARE

There has long been dissatisfaction with certain aspects of the U.S. health care system, and yet it has proven hard to reform. The United States spends a larger fraction of its GDP on medical care than any country in the world, but its health indicators (such as child mortality and life span) are lower than those in many other countries of comparable income. (This outcome is explained in part by the relatively high level of inequality in the United States. Poverty and poor health are closely associated, as low income leads to poor health and poor health leads to low income. Most other countries also do a better job than the United States in making sure that all citizens have access to health care.) Health care costs have been rising faster than the cost of living in general. The federal government has two major programs: Medicaid, which provides health care for the poor, and Medicare, which provides health care for the aged. Both have become increasingly expensive.

Not only do Americans spend more, with seemingly poorer results, than do residents of other countries, but they also have a greater sense of *insecurity*. In most advanced industrialized countries, everyone is guaranteed the right to a reasonably high level of health care; that is, there is effectively some form of comprehensive insurance. While most Americans receive health care coverage from their employers, many lack any insurance. For them a major illness can be a financial disaster. Most Americans do manage to receive health care in one way or another, but it is a major source of anxiety, especially for middle-income Americans who are too well-off to receive Medicaid.

Health care is different from most other commodities in several respects. Most health care is paid for by the government or insurance companies, not by individuals. Hence, individuals do not have an incentive to economize on these expenditures. Individuals also are often not in a position to judge well the necessity or quality of the services being provided. They must rely on the judgment of a physician. But under the standard fee-for-service system, the physician has an incentive to provide services, some of which may be of marginal value. To make matters worse, since individuals do not bear much of the cost, they have little incentive to monitor value; so long as the expected benefits exceed the costs they bear, they will wish the services to be performed. Moreover, doctors fear that a medical malpractice suit may be brought if they fail to provide a service that may be of benefit. Thus for many, "defensive medicine" has become a way of life.

Early attempts to correct these problems relied on a massive increase in the use of an alternative system called the health maintenance organization (HMO), or managed care. After paying a fixed annual amount, individuals are charged nominal fees for each doctor's visit. To gain access to a specialist, a patient must sometimes be referred by a primary care physician. But while the fee-for-service system may have an incentive for excessive provision of services, HMOs have an incentive, equally worrisome, not to supply services that are needed. In principle, an HMO that is excessively restrictive would lose customers to its competitors, but in practice, competition is limited. Thus, in the early 1990s, HMOs were widely lauded as the solution to the country's soaring health care costs; but by the late 1990s, HMOs were viewed as part of the problem. They were criticized, for instance, for "drive-by deliveries"—requirements that new mothers could stay in the hospital for only a day or two after a normal birth.

Today, the high cost of pharmaceuticals is causing much concern. Drug companies are constantly introducing new prescription medications, and more and more Americans are taking them. For the elderly—up to a third of whom are thought to lack insurance that covers their drugs—the financial burden of paying for them can be crushing. The growing awareness that the identical drugs cost less in other countries has led many to argue for new laws that would allow Americans to legally purchase drugs from pharmacies outside the United States, particularly in Canada. Drug manufacturers and the Bush administration have argued that the importation of drugs from other countries poses too great a safety risk.

In 2003, Congress added a major drug benefit to the Medicare program; it comes into effect fully only in 2006. Almost immediately after the bill's passage, concerns were raised about the new benefit's long-term cost, estimated to exceed $700 billion over the next decade. As the prices of prescription drugs have soared, many have called for the government to be given the power to negotiate discounts from the drug companies, something that the 2003 legislation specifically prohibits. They also have demanded more loudly that Americans be allowed to import drugs from Canada, where the federal government imposes price ceilings on drugs under patent and where health insurers negotiate with drug companies to obtain lower prices for the specific drugs that they cover. States such as Minnesota have saved money by purchasing drugs from Canada. However, the Canadian market is smaller than that in the United States, and if more Americans purchase drugs from Canadian sources,

Internet Connection
POLICY ANALYSIS

Washington, D.C., is home to many research groups that focus on government programs and policies. Among the better known are the Brookings Institution (www.brookings.org), the American Enterprise Institute (www.aei.org), and the Urban Institute (www.urban.org). These institutions post on their Web sites research and policy pieces dealing with major public-sector issues and debates. Some, like the American Enterprise Institute, are associated with conservative views. Others, such as the Brookings Institution, tend to be associated with more liberal views. In any case, the best of these institutions provide thoughtful and careful analyses of major economic policy issues.

shortages in Canada are likely to occur. Such shortages are particularly likely if U.S. manufacturers carry out their threat to stop shipping to Canadian pharmacies that sell to the United States.

Reformers cite four major tasks that remain on the health care agenda:

1. Reducing the number of uninsured Americans, particularly through programs targeted at the unemployed and at children.
2. Containing the soaring costs of health care in ways that are socially acceptable. In many countries, health care benefits are rationed to contain costs; that is, government programs provide assistance only to *some* of those who need it. For example, those over eighty-five years old may not be eligible for a hip replacement or must wait until all those who are younger and need the surgery get it.
3. Developing programs for nursing home care; today, many of the elderly must rely on Medicaid, the government program for low-income elderly, for long-term care.
4. Promoting healthy habits (e.g., better diet and more exercise), while discouraging activities such as smoking that are known to cause disease. Medical care is only one factor affecting health, and perhaps not the most important. Expenditures in broader areas of living and the environment may more effectively improve health status in general than increased spending targeted at medical care.

Review and Practice

SUMMARY

1. Government plays a pervasive role in the economy, influencing the economy through taxes, expenditures, and myriad regulations that affect every aspect of economic life.
2. In the United States, federal government spending over the past fifty years has shifted away from defense and toward Social Security, health care, and welfare. These areas accounted for 57 percent of expenditures in 2000.
3. There are three basic reasons why the government intervenes in the economy: (1) to improve economic efficiency by correcting market failures, (2) to pursue social values of fairness by altering market outcomes, and (3) to pursue other social values by mandating the consumption of merit goods (such as education) and outlawing the consumption of merit bads (such as illicit drugs).
4. Sometimes government faces a trade-off between improving the efficiency of the economy and promoting equity. The U.S. income tax illustrates this trade-off. In the interest of equity, the system requires the wealthy to pay a greater share of the tax than the poor. On the other hand, the progressive income tax discourages from work those who are the most productive.
5. A tax system can be judged by five criteria: fairness, efficiency, administrative simplicity, flexibility, and transparency.
6. Government transfer programs alter the income distribution by transferring resources from those who are relatively wealthy to those who are relatively poor. In the United States, there are five major transfer programs: welfare, Medicaid, food stamps, supplemental security income, and housing assistance.
7. Just as markets may fail, attempts by the government to intervene in the economy may also fail. Four major factors underlie systematic government failure: incentive problems, budgeting problems, information problems, and the nature of political decision making.
8. Some of the most important areas of public policy debate regarding the economic role of government relate to the federal budget deficit, reform of the Social Security system, and reform of the U.S. health care system.

KEY TERMS

transfer programs
merit goods
consumer sovereignty
progressive tax system
regressive tax system
marginal tax rate
horizontal equity
vertical equity
individual income taxes
corporation income taxes
property taxes
gift and estate taxes
payroll tax
excise taxes
sin taxes
benefit taxes
luxury taxes
sales tax
average tax rate
earned-income tax credit
tax subsidies
tax expenditure
matching programs
block grants
entitlement programs
voting paradox
pay-as-you-go program
fully funded program

REVIEW QUESTIONS

1. Name some of the ways that government touches the lives of all citizens, both in and out of the economic sphere.
2. Explain the rationale for government intervention in the economy in connection with economic efficiency, equity, and the role of merit goods.
3. What are the five characteristics of a good tax system? How well does the U.S. tax system fare in terms of these criteria? What is the difference between horizontal equity and vertical equity? What is the difference between a progressive and a regressive tax?

4. How do tax and redistribution programs affect incentives? How do social insurance programs affect incentives? Describe some of the trade-offs involved.
5. How can redistribution take place through an entitlement program like Social Security, to which all workers contribute and from which all retirees receive benefits?
6. What are some of the major controversies in the realm of policy and public-sector economics?

PROBLEMS

1. In each of the following areas, specify how the government is involved, either as a direct producer, a regulator, a purchaser of final goods and services distributed directly to individuals or used within government, or in some other role.
   (a) Education
   (b) Mail delivery
   (c) Housing
   (d) Air travel
   (e) National defense
   In each of these cases, think of ways that part of the public role could be provided by the private sector.
2. Assume that a country has a simple tax structure, in which all income over $10,000 is taxed at 20 percent. Evaluate a proposal to increase the progressivity of the tax structure by requiring all those with incomes over $100,000 to pay a tax of 80 percent on income in excess of $100,000. Draw a high-wage earner's budget constraint. How does the surtax affect her budget constraint? What happens to her incentives to work? Is it possible that imposing the tax actually will reduce the tax revenues the government receives from the rich?
3. Imagine that Congress decided to fund an increase in Social Security benefits by increasing the payroll tax on employers. Would this prevent employees from being affected by the higher tax? Draw a diagram to illustrate your answer.
4. Consider an individual contemplating whether to quit her job and go on welfare. How might the fact that welfare is time limited affect her decision? Is it possible that time-limited welfare may not only lead people to leave welfare but also reduce the number who go on welfare?
5. The president is trying to decide which of three goals he should put at the top of his agenda—Social Security reform (s), a middle-class tax cut (m), and preserving the safety net for the poor (p). He puts the matter before his advisers in three separate meetings. Assume he has three advisers, and he takes a vote in each meeting. His political adviser's ranking is {m-s-p}, his economic adviser's ranking is {s-p-m}, and his health care adviser's ranking is {p-m-s}. What is the outcome?
6. What is the difference between a pay-as-you-go retirement system and a fully funded system? Explain why the former may run into problems if a large generation is followed by a generation with many fewer members.
7. Assume that initially prescription drug prices are lower in Canada than in the United States, and suppose all barriers to drug trade between the two countries are removed. In the absence of any price controls, what would you predict will happen to drug prices in the United States? in Canada? How does the difference in the size of the two countries' populations affect your answer? If Canada has a system of price controls on prescription drugs, what would you predict will happen in the Canadian drug market if barriers to trade are eliminated?

Learning Goals

In this chapter, you will learn

1. Why many environmental problems are the result of externalities that cause market failures

2. The four types of policy responses to environmental problems and their implications for economic efficiency

3. Whether natural resources are depleted too rapidly in a market economy

Chapter 18

ENVIRONMENTAL ECONOMICS

Among the most contentious issues today is the impact of the economy on the environment. Usually, the discussion portrays economic activity and environmental concerns as diametrically opposed. Producing more goods and services generates more pollution, uses up more and more land, and contributes to global warming. It may seem that the fundamental perspective of economics—that of scarcity—hardly applies to things like pollution. After all, most people think we have too much pollution, not a scarcity of it. Yet the tools of economics can provide critical insights into the causes of environmental pollution, and these insights help shape the ways that government has tried to design policies to protect the environment.

The basic competitive model yielded the conclusion that markets would produce efficient outcomes. But we have seen, in Chapter 11 and again in Chapter 17, that in some situations, markets fail to produce efficient outcomes. In those circumstances, government may have an economic role to play. This justification for government involvement in the market is known as the *market failure approach* to the role of government.

Many environmental problems are the result of a market failure that arises because of the presence of externalities—costs and benefits of a transaction that are not fully reflected in the market price. In this chapter, we focus on negative externalities and the issues of environmental protection.

Negative Externalities and Oversupply

The basic competitive model assumes that the costs of producing a good and the benefits of selling it all accrue to the seller, and that the benefits of receiving the good and the costs of buying it all accrue to the buyer. This is often not the case. As was explained in Chapter 11, the extra costs and benefits not captured by the market transaction are called *externalities*.

Externalities can be either positive or negative, depending on whether individuals enjoy extra benefits they did not pay for or suffer extra costs they did not incur themselves. Goods for which there are positive externalities—such as research and development—will be undersupplied in the market (see Chapter 20). In deciding how much of the good to purchase, each individual or firm thinks only about the benefits it receives, not the benefits conferred on others. By the same token, goods for which there are negative externalities, such as air and water pollution, will be over-supplied in the market. The inability of the market to fully capture the costs and benefits of a trade provides a classic example of a market failure and a possible role for the public sector.

Figure 18.1A shows the demand and supply curves for a good—say, steel. Market equilibrium is the intersection of the curves, the point labeled E, with output Q_p and price p_p. Chapter 10 explained why, in the absence of externalities, the equilibrium E is efficient. The price reflects the marginal benefit that individuals receive from an extra unit of steel (it measures their marginal willingness to pay for an extra unit). The price also reflects the marginal cost to the firm of producing an extra unit. At E, marginal benefits equal marginal costs.

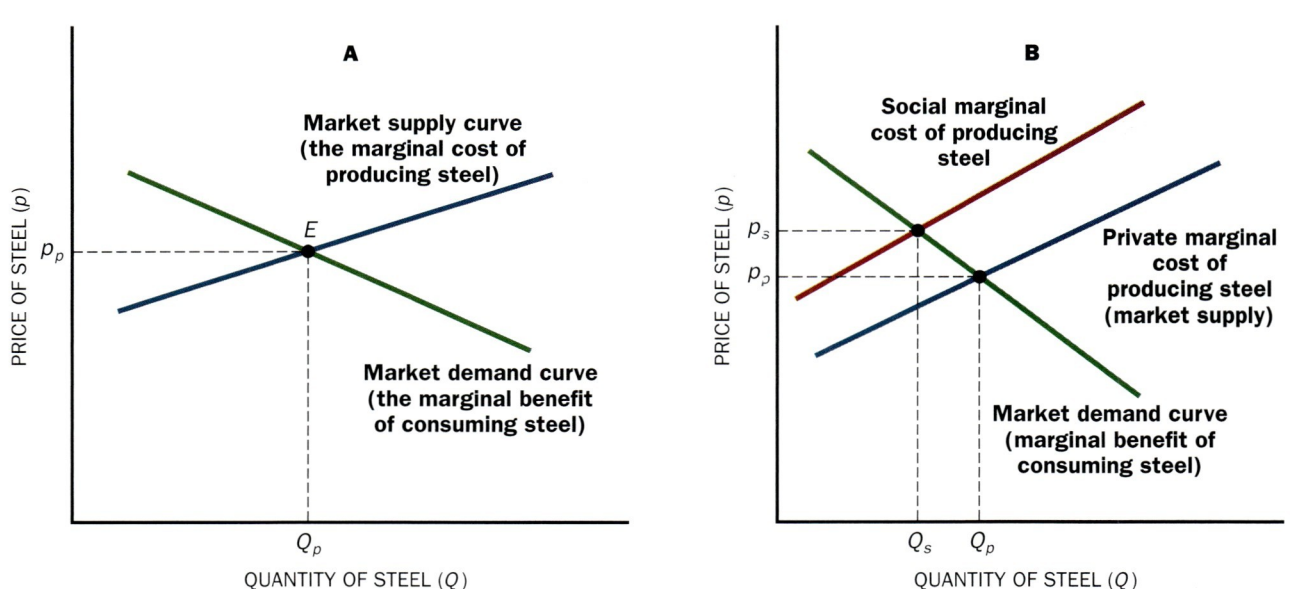

Figure 18.1

HOW NEGATIVE EXTERNALITIES CAUSE OVERSUPPLY

In a perfectly competitive market, the market supply curve is the (horizontal) sum of the marginal cost curves of all firms, while market demand reflects how much the marginal unit is worth to any consumer. In panel A, the equilibrium, at quantity Q_p and price p_p, will be where private marginal cost is equal to the marginal benefit.

If society as a whole faces broader costs, like pollution, then the social marginal costs will exceed the private costs. If the supplier is not required to take these additional costs into account (as in panel B), production will be at Q_p, and the quantity produced will exceed the amount Q_s where marginal cost is equal to marginal benefit for society as a whole.

Consider what happens if, in the production of steel, there is an externality—producers are polluting the air and water without penalty. The **social marginal cost**—the marginal cost borne by all individuals in the economy—will now exceed the **private marginal cost**—the marginal cost borne by the producer alone. Note that in a competitive industry, the supply curve corresponds to the horizontal sum of all producers' *private* marginal cost curves. Panel B contrasts the two situations. It shows the social marginal cost curve for producing steel lying above the private marginal cost curve. Thus, with social marginal costs equated to social marginal benefits, the economically efficient level of production of steel will be lower, at Q_s, than it would be, at Q_p, if private costs were the only ones.

The level of production of steel, which generates negative externalities, will therefore be too high in a free market. We can also ask, What about the level of expenditure on pollution abatement? Such expenditures confer a positive externality—the benefits of the equipment, the cleaner air, accrue mainly to others. Figure 18.2 shows a firm's demand curve for pollution-abatement equipment in the absence of government regulation. It is quite low, reflecting the fact that the firm itself derives little benefit. That is, the firm's marginal private benefit from expenditures on pollution-abatement equipment is small. The firm sets its marginal private benefit equal to the marginal cost of pollution abatement, which results in a level of expenditure on pollution abatement at E. The figure also depicts the marginal social benefit of pollution abatement, which is far greater than the marginal private benefit. Efficiency requires that the marginal social benefit equal the marginal cost, point E'. Thus, economic efficiency requires greater expenditures on pollution abatement than there would be in the free market.

One of government's major economic roles is to correct the inefficiencies resulting from externalities. Among the many types of negative externalities, perhaps the most conspicuous are those that harm the environment.

Figure 18.2

HOW POSITIVE EXTERNALITIES CAUSE UNDERSUPPLY

The private marginal benefit includes just the benefits received by the firm; but since pollution-abatement equipment provides a positive externality, it will have a social marginal benefit that is higher. If the firm takes only its private benefit into account, it will operate at point E, using less equipment than at the point where marginal benefits are equal to marginal costs for society as a whole (E').

Policy Responses to Problems in the Environment

As the negative externalities associated with pollution and other environmental issues are increasingly recognized, the various approaches of governments seeking to curtail their bad effects have received considerable attention from economists and others. This section evaluates several of the major options.

PROPERTY RIGHTS RESPONSES

Large-scale environmental degradation is a conspicuous form of negative externalities. Having identified these market failures, what can the government do to improve

International Perspective
GLOBAL WARMING

Many environmental problems are local in nature. The pollution of a stream or a toxic waste site mainly affects people in the neighborhood. But some environmental hazards have an impact on the entire planet and therefore require international cooperation. For instance, the Montreal Convention signed in 1990 limited the emissions of chemicals that had led to the depletion of ozone in the atmosphere. Ozone depletion was linked to a higher incidence of certain types of cancer caused by radiation normally blocked by the ozone layer. The agreement was remarkably successful: with little cost to the economy, the use of these chemicals was phased out, even ahead of schedule.

Today, the most serious global environmental problem is probably global warming, the increased temperature of the earth caused by the buildup of the so-called greenhouse gases, such as carbon dioxide, that trap the sun's energy just as a greenhouse does. The evidence of the buildup of these gases is strong, and there is mounting data about the consequences. A series of international panels of experts have concluded that the impacts are likely to be large: they include the melting of the polar ice cap and a rise in the sea level, resulting in the inundation of low-lying regions of the world. In 1992 at Rio de Janeiro, an international convention was signed committing the world's governments to controlling the emission of greenhouse gases. In 1997, a further agreement, making the reductions binding, was signed in Kyoto. However, then-president Bill Clinton never submitted the Kyoto Protocol on global climate change to the Senate for ratification because opposition to it was very strong. In 2001, President George W. Bush announced formally that the United States would not ratify the treaty. The outrage from the rest of the world at this declaration was particularly strong because the United States is the largest producer of greenhouse gases, emitting 36 percent of the world's total. Opponents of the Kyoto Protocol argue that it does not do enough to limit emissions from rapidly developing economies such as China's: while mandatory limits are set for developed economies, developing countries are subject only to voluntary limits. In 1997, the U.S. Senate had voted 95–0 to oppose any agreement that did not incorporate mandatory limits on developing countries as well. In addition, many argue that the economic costs of limiting emissions are too great.

Supporters of the treaty note that on a per capita basis, emissions from the developing economies are much lower than they are from the United States. Further, it seems unfair to ask countries struggling to boost economic growth and reduce poverty to bear the costs of limiting greenhouse gas emissions, when it is the past pollution of the rich, developed countries that has created the problem. Drawing on arguments of equity, the developing economies such as China and India called for mandatory limits on the rich countries first, combined with initially voluntary targets for the developing countries.

To come into effect, the Kyoto Protocol needed to be ratified by a set of countries that accounted for 55 percent of total greenhouse gas emissions in 1990. By 2004, industrialized countries accounting for 44 percent of 1990 emissions had ratified the treaty. It was finally pushed over the 55 percent hurdle in late 2004, when President Vladimir Putin announced that Russia, which accounted for 17 percent of 1990 emissions, would ratify the treaty. Russia had a large economic incentive to vote for the Kyoto Protocol, since it allows countries that reduce their emissions below the level of their quota to sell the unused portion to countries that fail to meet their target. Because of its economic contraction following the collapse of the former Soviet Union, Russia's emissions are 25 percent lower than the 1990 level, while the treaty required of the nation only a 5 percent reduction. Thus, Russia can potentially earn billions by selling its unused quotas.

matters? Some economists, led by the Nobel laureate Ronald Coase of the University of Chicago Law School, argue that government should simply rearrange property rights. **Coase's theorem** says that with appropriately designed property rights, markets could take care of externalities without direct government intervention. Consider, for example, the case of a small lake in which anyone can fish without charge. Each fisherman ignores the fact that the more fish he takes out of the lake, the fewer there are for others to take out. No fisherman has an incentive to worry about whether there will be fish in the lake in the future, either. Why should he? After all, if he leaves fish in the lake today, someone else might take them out tomorrow. If all fishermen think this way, the lake will quickly be overfished, likely to the point of wiping out the fish stock. If the government were to rearrange property rights and grant the right to fish to a single individual, then she would have every incentive to fish efficiently. There would no longer be any externality. She would have an incentive to take into account both the long-term and the short-term effects of her decisions. She would realize that if she fished too much today, the lake would contain fewer fish tomorrow. If it were a large lake, she might let others do the fishing and charge them for each fish caught or regulate the amount of fish they could catch. But the prices she charged and the regulations she imposed would be designed to ensure that the lake was not overfished.

The point of this example is that the problem of overfishing is solved with only limited government intervention. All the government has to do is assign the property rights correctly.

Coase envisioned that once property rights were assigned, market solutions or bargaining among potential users would ensure efficient outcomes. Consider the conflict between smokers and nonsmokers over whether to allow smoking in a room. Smokers confer a negative externality on nonsmokers. Coase suggests a simple solution. Give the rights to the air to one individual, say, a smoker. He has the right to decide whether to allow smoking or not. For the sake of simplicity, assume that there are only two individuals in the room, one a smoker and the other a nonsmoker. If the value of fresh air to the nonsmoker exceeds the value of smoking to the smoker, the nonsmoker would offer the smoker enough money to compensate him not to smoke. Conversely, if the property rights were given to the nonsmoker, and if the value of smoking to the smoker exceeded the value of fresh air to the nonsmoker, then the smoker could compensate the nonsmoker.

Coase argued not only that assigning property rights ensures an efficient outcome but also that how the property rights are assigned affects only the distribution of income, not economic efficiency. Whether smoking would be allowed would depend merely on whether the value of smoking to smokers exceeded or was less than the value of fresh air to nonsmokers.

The appeal of Coase's theorem is that it assigns a minimal role to government. Government simply makes the property rights clear, and leaves the efficient outcome to private markets. Opportunities to apply the theorem are limited, however, because the costs of reaching an agreement may be high, particularly when large numbers of individuals are involved. Imagine the difficulties of assigning property rights to the atmosphere, and arranging that all the individuals adversely affected by air pollution negotiate with all those contributing to it!

Thinking Like an Economist
ENVIRONMENTAL AND ECONOMIC TRADE-OFFS

In economics, what matters are *incentives,* not *intentions*—and well-intentioned acts often have unintended consequences. In 1973, Congress passed an important piece of legislation, the Endangered Species Act, intended to protect species that are threatened with extinction. If, for instance, a rare species, like the spotted owl, was discovered to be nesting in a tree on your property, you would not be allowed to cut down the tree. The act brought to the fore the point that we often think of private property too simplistically: If I own something, I should be able to do with it what I like, *so long as I don't harm anyone else.* But there's the rub. What you do with your property does affect others. If you build a tall building on your property, blocking out the light that your neighbors receive, you are affecting them. If you build a dirty, noisy factory in a quiet residential neighborhood, you are affecting your neighbors. Such interdependence explains why most cities have *zoning laws* restricting the use of land; there are residential zones and business zones and manufacturing zones. But society as a whole benefits from the preservation of endangered species; in that sense, destroying the habitat of an endangered species has repercussions that touch others beyond the owners of the land.

In 1993, a heated dispute arose over the spotted owl in the Pacific Northwest. Environmentalists, concerned about the destruction of the spotted owl's habitat, had acted on a provision of the Endangered Species Act to halt logging, thereby threatening the livelihood of hundreds of people in the area. In the region as a whole, there were new bases for economic growth—for instance, software and other high-tech industries were moving in, attracted in part by the natural beauty of the environment. But the loggers lacked the requisite skills to join

Today there is general agreement that while assigning property rights clearly may take care of some problems, most externalities, particularly those concerning the environment, require more active government intervention.

REGULATION

Government's first response to the need for intervention to address environmental externalities was to regulate. Electric utilities that burned high-sulfur coal would not be allowed to emit sulfur dioxide into the atmosphere. They would be required to install scrubbers, devices that removed the sulfur from the fumes. And cars would be required to have catalytic converters. This approach is sometimes called the **command and control approach.**

It quickly ran into problems. The same environmental benefits often could be achieved at much lower costs in ways that were not allowed by the regulations. This weakness arose in part because the regulations did not (and could not) allow for the myriad variations in the circumstances of different firms, and in part because the regulatory process is always slow (at best) in incorporating newly developing technologies. Worse still, the command and control approach failed to provide incentives for the development of new technologies to reduce environmental in such developments. The end of logging would have presented them with bleak prospects. There seemed to be a clear *trade-off*: which was more important, the livelihood of the loggers or the survival of the spotted owl? There was one way out of this box: if the value of preserving the spotted owl exceeded the economic damage to the loggers, those benefiting from preservation could pay off the loggers. Alternatively, the federal government might have used general tax revenues to compensate the loggers. But at the time, the government's budget was severely constrained. A compromise was sought, whereby enough area was kept closed to protect the spotted owl's habitat while enough was kept open for logging to protect many of the jobs.

Critics of the Endangered Species Act pointed out the perverse incentives created by the law. For example, if you had a tree of the type that a spotted owl might nest in, you would have an incentive to cut it down before the owl nested in it. That way, your later desire to develop your land would not be encumbered by a court injunction issued because the land contained a habitat for an endangered species. Some worried that these *unintended consequences* were so large that they reversed the act's intended effects.

Which is more important, the livelihood of loggers or the survival of the spotted owl?

damage, since it often would not allow those technologies to be used, even if they did a better job.[1]

Moreover, politics inevitably intrudes into the setting of regulations, resulting in higher than necessary costs. High-sulfur coal producers worried that the cost of scrubbers would put them at a competitive disadvantage relative to low-sulfur coal producers. (This is the correct market outcome from the viewpoint of economic efficiency, because the social cost of high-sulfur coal—including its negative environmental impacts—was greater than that of the low-sulfur coal.) So they succeeded in getting Congress to mandate that users of low-sulfur coal also had to have scrubbers, though for them such devices were unnecessary. In another example, ethanol producers (dominated by a single firm, Archer Daniels Midland) persuaded regulators to require a corn-based gasoline additive to reduce pollution rather than an oil-based one—even though the latter is cheaper and may be better environmentally.

Another reason economists are wary of regulations is that the costs they impose are often hidden. As the costs of environmental regulation rise, it becomes clear that better analysis when designing regulations is needed. Such analysis should look

---

[1] On the other side, advocates argue that in some cases the tight regulations have "forced" the development of new technologies to meet environmental standards that could not be met with existing technologies.

at cost and benefit, encouraging government to undertake regulations only when benefits exceed costs, and to focus on those areas where environmental risks are greatest. These principles, supported by most economists, would seem to be unexceptionable, and are in fact reflected in presidential Executive Orders issued to guide the implementation of regulations. But some environmentalists take a "purist" stand. They argue that a child's health should not be submitted to the cold calculus of costs and benefits. And they worry about "paralysis by analysis"—that the process of doing the cost-benefit analyses will effectively bring environmental regulation to a halt.

TAXES AND SUBSIDIES

Most economists believe that taxes and subsidies provide a better way than regulation to encourage the behavior desired by society. Taxes are the stick, while subsidies are the carrot. Both share the aim of adjusting private costs to account for social costs.

Panel A of Figure 18.3 shows the supply and demand curves for steel. If the production of steel generates a negative externality in the form of pollution, then the social marginal cost of producing steel is higher than the private marginal cost. The market equilibrium leads to a production level of Q_p, which exceeds the socially optimal quantity Q_s. Panel B illustrates how a tax on the production of steel can lead to

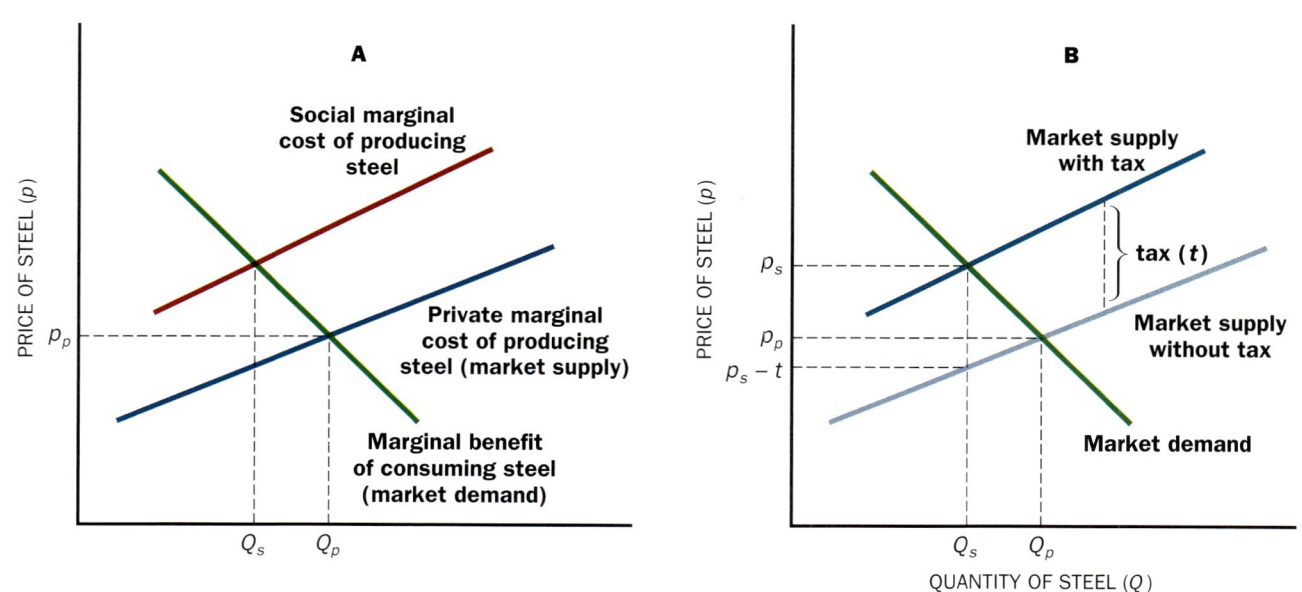

Figure 18.3

USING A TAX IN THE PRESENCE OF A NEGATIVE EXTERNALITY

When production leads to a negative externality, such as pollution in the case of steel production, the firm's costs do not reflect the total social cost of production. The market equilibrium, before a tax is imposed, is at a price p_p and quantity Q_p (see panel A). The efficient level is at quantity Q_s. Panel B depicts the effects of imposing a tax on steel producers. The tax increases their costs, and the market supply curve shifts up. The new equilibrium price is p_s and the equilibrium quantity is Q_s.

the socially optimal level of production. The tax, t, increases the firm's costs of producing steel, shifting up the market supply curve. The new market equilibrium is now at the socially optimal quantity Q_s. The equilibrium price is p_s; purchasers of steel pay a price that correctly reflects the social cost of producing steel. Doing so ensures that the marginal benefits are set equal to the marginal costs. Steel-producing firms receive the market price less the tax, $p_s - t$, an amount that equals their private marginal cost of producing steel.

Taxes on pollution are similar to fines for violating regulations in one respect—both increase the cost of and thereby discourage pollution. But taxes differ from regulation in a fundamental way. Regulations are a clumsy tool. They penalize firms for polluting over a specific level, but polluters who stay just below that level get off scot-free. Pollution taxes can be set so that they reduce aggregate pollution by the same amount as a regulator would under a command and control system. But the economic effects are very different. Taxes add the cost of pollution to the costs that a company has to cover to remain in business. As a result, companies have an incentive to reduce their pollution as far as possible and to find new, low-cost ways of reducing pollution or to devise new production methods that are less polluting, rather than keeping pollution just below the legal standard. This is "efficient pollution abatement," as the producers who pollute less gain their reward in lower costs.

Subsidies such as tax credits for pollution-abatement devices are an alternative way of providing incentives to reduce pollution. Subsidies are economically inefficient. Take the case of steel firms. When they receive subsidies, firms are not paying the full costs. Part of the costs are being picked up by the government. Producers therefore can sell (and users can buy) steel for less than its full cost of production, and steel and pollution production thus remain above the socially efficient level. Clearly, firms prefer subsidies to taxes.

THE MARKETABLE PERMIT RESPONSE

Still another approach to curbing pollution is **marketable permits.** Companies purchase (or are granted) a permit from the government that allows them to emit a certain amount of pollution. Again, the government can set the amount so that the company produces the same level of pollution as it would under the command and control approach. However, companies are allowed to sell their permits. Thus, if a company cuts its pollution in half, it can sell some of its allowance to another company that wants to expand production (and hence its emission of pollutants).

The incentive effects of marketable permits are very much like those of taxes. A market for pollution permits encourages development of the best possible anti-pollution devices, rather than keeping the pollution just under some government-set limit. If the government wishes to reduce pollution over time, the permits can be designed to reduce the amount of pollution they allow by a prescribed amount each year. In the United States, this sort of shrinking marketable permit was used to reduce the amount of lead in gasoline during the early 1980s. Variants of this idea have recently been adopted to help control other forms of air pollution, such as sulfur dioxide.

The effects of acid rain are easy to see in forests throughout the northeastern United States and Canada.

Case in Point

REDUCING ACID RAIN

Forests throughout the northeastern United States and Canada have been damaged by acid rain—that is, rain polluted by sulfuric and nitric acids. These acids result from the reaction of sulfur dioxide (SO_2) and nitrogen oxides in the atmosphere. In the United States, coal-fired power plants in the Northeast and Midwest are the primary sources of the SO_2 that contributes to acid rain. The Clean Air Act Amendments of 1990 established programs to reduce the emissions of SO_2.

As part of this program, owners of pollution-producing plants are given permits, called *allowances,* that give them rights to emit a certain amount of SO_2. The critical aspect of the program is that these permits are tradable. A plant that has a larger allowance than it needs can sell the unused portion to another plant that wishes to emit more than its allotted amount. A plant that finds the marginal cost of reducing SO_2 emissions to be greater than the price of a permit will choose to purchase a permit; a firm that finds the marginal cost of reducing emissions to be less than the price of a permit will want to sell a permit. As a consequence, the market price for permits will measure the marginal cost of reducing emissions.

A simple example illustrates how a system of tradable permits can reduce the total cost of lowering emissions. Consider the case of two plants with different marginal costs of cutting back on their emissions of SO_2. For the sake of illustration, suppose the relevant cost data are those given below:

Reduction in Emissions	Plant A Total Cost	Plant A Marginal Cost	Plant B Total Cost	Plant B Marginal Cost
0	$0	$0	$0	$0
1	$1	$1	$0.5	$0.5
2	$3	$2	$1.5	$1
3	$6	$3	$3	$1.5
4	$10	$4	$5	$2
5	$15	$5	$7.5	$2.5
6	$21	$6	$10.5	$3

In this example, plant B is able to reduce emissions at a lower cost than plant A.

Now suppose the goal is to reduce emissions by 6 units. One approach might be to require each plant to cut emissions by 3 units. In this case, the cost of reducing emissions would be $6 at plant A and $3 at plant B for a total cost of $9. However, the marginal cost of achieving the last reduction in emissions at plant A was $3, while plant B would be able to gain a further reduction (to 4) in its emissions at a marginal cost of only $2.

Instead of requiring each plant to reduce its emissions by the same amount, suppose the same overall reduction of 6 units is achieved by having plant A cut emissions by 2 units and plant B by 4 units. The total cost is now only $3 + $5 or $8. We have achieved the same overall reduction in pollution more efficiently by having the plant that can cut emissions at a lower marginal cost (plant B) cut back the most.

If the two plants can participate in a market for permits, plant A would find it advantageous to purchase a permit from plant B. By cutting back by only 2 units instead of 3, plant A can reduce its costs by $3. Plant B, having sold a permit to plant A, must cut its emissions back further, from a reduction of 3 to a reduction of 4. This raises its costs by $2. As long as the price of a permit is between $2 and $3, both firms gain. Society gains by achieving the desired reduction in emissions at the least cost.

While the SO_2 tradable permit system has been in place only since the mid-1990s, the evidence indicates that it has achieved emission goals in a cost-effective manner.[2]

WEIGHING THE ALTERNATIVE APPROACHES

Incentive programs, such as taxes or marketable permits, have an important advantage over direct controls, like regulations. The issue of pollution is not whether it should be allowed—after all, it is virtually impossible to eliminate all pollution in an industrial economy. Nor would such elimination be efficient; its costs would far exceed its benefits. The real issue is how sharply pollution should be limited. The *marginal* benefits have to be weighed against the marginal costs. This calculation is not performed under regulation. If instead government ascertains the marginal social cost of pollution and sets charges or marketable permits accordingly, private firms will engage in pollution control up to the point at which the marginal cost of pollution control equals the marginal social return of pollution abatement (which is just the marginal cost of pollution). Each firm will have the correct marginal incentives.

Governments often prefer direct regulations because they believe that they can control the outcomes better. But such control can be illusory. If an unreachable standard is set, it is likely to be repealed. For example, as automobile companies have found the costs of various regulations to be prohibitive, they have repeatedly appealed for a delay in the enforcement of those regulations, often with considerable success.

It must also be kept in mind that choosing the socially efficient method of pollution abatement is the easy part of the policy problem. Figuring out the "right" level of pollution to aim for is much harder. Uncertainty about the consequences of pollution abounds, and how to value certain options is hotly debated. To what extent can environmental degradation be reversed? How much value should be placed on the extinction of a species like the spotted owl, or the preservation of the Arctic wilderness? No matter what approach is chosen to externalities and the environment, such questions will remain controversial.

---

[2]See Richard Schmalensee et al., "An Interim Evaluation of Sulfur Dioxide Emissions," and Robert N. Stavins, "What Can We Learn from the Grand Policy Experiment? Lessons from SO_2 Allowance Trading," in *Journal of Economic Perspectives* 12, no. 3 (Summer 1998): 53–68, 69–88.

> **Wrap-Up**
>
> ## SOLVING THE PROBLEM OF EXTERNALITIES
>
> Externalities, which occur when the extra costs and benefits of a transaction are not fully reflected in the market price, give rise to market failure. Four main solutions have been proposed and used:
> 1. The reassignment of property rights
> 2. Regulations that outlaw the negative externality
> 3. Tax and subsidy measures to encourage the behavior society wants
> 4. Marketable permits

Natural Resources

A recurrent theme among environmentalists is that our society is squandering its natural resources. We are using up oil and energy resources at an alarming rate, hardwood timber forests that took hundreds of years to grow are being cut down, and supplies of vital resources like phosphorus are dwindling. There are repeated calls for government intervention to enhance the conservation of our scarce natural resources. Those who believe in the infallibility of markets reply, Nonsense! Prices give the same guidance to the use of natural resources that they give to any other resource. Prices measure scarcity, and send consumers and firms the right signals about how much effort to expend to conserve resources, so long as consumers and firms are well informed, and so long as there is not some other source of market failure.

There is, in fact, some truth in both positions. Prices, in general, do provide signals concerning the scarcity of resources; and *in the absence of market failures,* those signals lead to economic efficiency. We have seen some cases in which a private market economy without government intervention will not be efficient—when there are negative externalities (pollution) or when a resource (like fish in the ocean) is not priced.

But what about a privately owned resource, such as bauxite (from which aluminum is made) or copper? The owner of a bauxite mine has a clearly defined property right. Let's assume that he pays a tax appropriate to any pollution his mining

Internet Connection

THE NATIONAL CENTER FOR ENVIRONMENTAL ECONOMICS

The National Center for Environmental Economics (NCEE) conducts and supervises economic research on environmental issues. Its Web site is www.epa.gov/economics/.

operation causes. Thus, the price he charges will reflect both social and private costs. The question of resource depletion now boils down to the question of whether his bauxite is worth more to him in the market today or left in the ground for future extraction. The answer depends on how much the owner of the bauxite thinks it will be worth in the future, say thirty years from now. If the owner expects it to be sufficiently more valuable thirty years from now to compensate him both for waiting and for all the uncertainties associated with trying to predict what the bauxite will be worth that far in the future, he will keep the bauxite in the ground.

In Chapter 9, we learned how to calculate the future value of something in terms of its present discounted value. For example, if the price of the bauxite next year is expected to be $25 per ton and the interest rate is 10 percent, the present discounted value of that $25 is found by dividing $25 by 1 plus the interest rate, or 1.1. At an interest rate of 10 percent, next year's expected price of bauxite is equivalent to a price today of $25/1.1 = $22.73. If the interest rate is 10 percent, then a dollar a year from now is worth 10 percent less than a dollar today (a dollar today could be invested and would yield $1.10 in one year). If the current price of bauxite is above $22.73, it will pay to mine the bauxite today and sell it. If the current price is less than $22.75, the owner of the bauxite mine will find it more profitable to leave the bauxite in the ground and mine it next year.

Now looking ahead to what the bauxite might be worth thirty years from now. Suppose the owner's best guess is that in thirty years bauxite will be selling for $75 per ton and that the interest rate will remain 10 percent for the next thirty years; then the present discounted value of bauxite today will be $75/(1.1)^{30} = 4.30. If the current price is greater than $4.30, it will pay to mine the bauxite now—the price expected in the future is not high enough to compensate the owner for waiting. If the interest rate falls to 5 percent, however, the present discounted value rises to $75/1.05^{30} = 17.35. Now, if the current price is less than $17.35, it will pay to leave the bauxite in the ground. At a lower interest rate, the owner of the bauxite has a greater incentive to leave the bauxite in the ground until some future time. Higher interest rates increase the incentive for firms to extract the bauxite earlier.

If this miner and all other bauxite producers choose to bring the bauxite to market today, depleting the world's supply of bauxite, there are two possible reasons for their decision. Perhaps this is the socially efficient outcome—society values bauxite more highly today than it will tomorrow. Or perhaps the miners have miscalculated the value of bauxite thirty years from now and underestimated future prices, though they have every incentive to forecast as accurately as they can. If they have indeed miscalculated, we might view the result as a market failure; but there would be no reason to expect a government bureaucracy to do any better than the firms at guessing future prices.

However, there are two plausible reasons why private owners may habitually tend to undervalue future benefits of a natural resource. First, in countries where property rights are not secure, owners of a resource may feel that if they do not sell it soon, there is a reasonable chance that it will be taken away from them. There may be a revolution, for example, in which the government will take over the resource with no or only partial compensation to the owners. Even in countries like the United States, where owners are not worried about government confiscating their property, they might fear that more stringent regulations will make it more expensive to extract the resource in the future, or that higher taxes will make it less attractive to sell the resource in the

e-Insight

INFORMATION AND THE ENVIRONMENT

In addition to employing regulation and taxation, some governments have sought to control pollution by requiring firms to disclose the type and level of toxic substances they are emitting into the air or water. Such information disclosure has proved to be extremely effective. Pressure brought by local communities, and worries on the part of firms about acquiring a bad reputation, have induced polluting firms to reduce their levels of emissions. In this effort, the Internet has proved to be an important tool. For instance, Environmental Defense, a not-for-profit environmental advocacy group, maintains an Internet site called Scorecard (www.scorecard.org) that provides a wide range of information on pollutants.

---

future. Second, individuals and firms often face limited borrowing opportunities and very high interest rates. In these circumstances, capital markets discount future returns at a high rate, far higher than society or the government would discount them.

Sometimes government has aggravated the waste of natural resources. For example, much of the timber in the United States lies on government lands. The government, in making the land available, has paid less attention to concerns about economic efficiency than it has to the pleading of timber interest groups. Government policies aimed at restricting the import of foreign oil have also encouraged the use of domestic resources, a seemingly perverse policy of "drain America first." Government policies intended to keep the price of water low for farmers has led to many negative outcomes: excessive use of water has drained water from underground basins filled over centuries, lowered the water table, and in some cases leached out the soil. In each of these instances, private property rights and market outcomes would have supplied solutions that almost everyone in society would regard as better than what happened.

Merit Goods and the Environment

In this chapter, we have explained how externalities provide a rationale for government intervention in the economy. To some people, how we treat the environment and the earth's natural resources is not just a matter of economic efficiency: it is a moral issue. They argue that the question of, say, allowing whaling should not be approached narrowly from the perspective of economic costs and benefits. This view reflects the principle of merit goods discussed in Chapter 17. The government sometimes becomes involved not just because markets have failed to produce efficient outcomes but out of a belief that there are values that supersede those reflected in individual preferences, and government has the right and duty to impose those values on its citizens. Such a view rejects the basic premise of *consumer sovereignty,* which holds that individuals are the best judges of their own welfare, and argues that in certain selected areas, there is a role for *paternalism*—government can make better choices in some matters than individuals.

Review and Practice

SUMMARY

1. Government may have a role in the economy when markets fail to produce an efficient outcome. When positive or negative externalities exist, markets will not provide an efficient outcome.
2. One way to deal with externalities is to assign clear-cut property rights.
3. Governments may deal with environmental externalities by imposing regulatory measures (the command and control approach), levying taxes and granting subsidies, or issuing marketable permits.
4. In a perfect market, natural resources are used up at an efficient rate. However, privately owned resources may be sold too soon, for two reasons. First, owners may fear that if they do not sell the resources soon, new government rules may prevent them from selling at all or, in any case, may lower the return from selling in the future. Second, interest rates facing owners may be high, so they may value future income less than society does in general. High interest rates lead to a faster exploitation of natural resources.

KEY TERMS

social marginal cost
private marginal cost
Coase's theorem
command and control approach
marketable permits

REVIEW QUESTIONS

1. Name several market failures. Why do economists see the existence of these market failures as a justification for government action?
2. Why will a free market produce too much of goods that have negative externalities, like pollution? Why will a free market produce too little of goods that have positive externalities, like pollution controls?
3. What are the advantages and limitations of dealing with externalities by assigning property rights?
4. What are the advantages of marketable permits over command and control regulation? What are the advantages of using taxes on polluting rather than subsidies for pollution-abatement equipment?
5. How do markets work to allocate natural resources efficiently? In what cases will markets fail to give the correct signals for how quickly a resource like oil should be depleted?

PROBLEMS

1. Marple and Wolfe are two neighboring dormitories. Wolfe is considering giving a party with a very loud band, which will have a negative externality in the form of a sort of sound pollution for Marple. Imagine that the school administration decides that any dormitory has the right to prevent another dorm from hiring a band. If the band creates a negative externality, how might the residents of Wolfe apply the lessons of Coase's theorem to hire the band they want?

    Now imagine that the school administration decides that no dormitory can prevent another dorm from hiring a band, no matter how loud. If the band provides a negative externality, how might the residents of Marple apply the lessons of Coase's theorem to reduce the amount of time they have to listen to the band? How would your answer change if the band provided a positive externality?

2. The manufacture of trucks produces pollution of various kinds; for the purposes of this example, let's call it all "glop." Producing a truck creates one unit of glop, and glop has a cost to society of $3,000. Imagine that the supply of trucks is competitive and market supply and demand are given by the following data:

Price (thousand $)	19	20	21	22	23	24	25
Quantity supplied	480	540	600	660	720	780	840
Quantity demanded	660	630	600	570	540	510	480

Graph the supply curve for the industry and the demand curve. What are equilibrium price and output? Now graph the social marginal cost curve. If the social cost of glop were taken into account, what would be the new equilibrium price and output?

If the government is concerned about the pollution emitted by truck plants, explain how it might deal with the externality through fines or taxes and through subsidies. Illustrate the effects of taxes and subsidies by drawing the appropriate supply and demand graphs. (Don't bother worrying about the exact units.) Why are economists likely to prefer fines to subsidies?

3. Consider a small lake with a certain number of fish. The more fish that one fisherman takes out, the fewer fish are available for others to take out. Use graphs depicting private and social costs and benefits to fishing to describe the equilibrium and the socially efficient level of fishing. Explain how a tax on fishing could achieve the efficient outcome. Explain how giving a single individual the property right to the fish in the lake might also be used to obtain an efficient outcome.

   The more fish taken out this year, the fewer fish will be available next year. Explain why if there is a single owner for the lake, the fish will be efficiently extracted from it. Assume that anyone who wants to fish can do so. Would you expect that too many fish would be taken out this year?

4. Consider a crowded room with an equal number of smokers and nonsmokers. Each smoker would be willing to pay $1.00 to have the right to smoke. Each nonsmoker would be willing to pay $0.50 to have the room free from smoke. Assume there is a rule that says no smoking is allowed. Could everyone be made better off if smoking is allowed? How? If property rights to clean air are assigned to the nonsmokers, how might the efficient outcome be obtained? What difference does it make to the outcome whether there is initially a rule that smoking is allowed or that smoking is not allowed? What problems might you envision occurring if no smoking is allowed unless all the nonsmokers agree to allow it?

5. The following table gives the demand for water for two households, the Joneses and the Lopezes. Suppose these two households are the only ones in the market. Draw the individual demand curves for each household and the market demand curve. If the total quantity of water available is 80 units, what price would equate demand and supply?

   Assume the local water authority has set the price at 3. Now suppose there is a water shortage, and the total quantity of water available falls to 60 units. Suppose the local water authority keeps the price unchanged and rations the available water supply, with each household receiving 30 units. What is the marginal benefit of an extra unit of water to the Joneses? to the Lopezes? Is the allocation of water between the two households efficient? Suppose the water authority let the price of water rise until market demand equated supply (60 units). How much would the Joneses consume? How much would the Lopezes consume? Is the allocation efficient?

Price	Demand by the Jones family	Demand by the Lopez family
2	50	40
3	45	35
4	40	30
5	35	25
6	30	20
7	25	15
8	20	10

Learning Goals

In this chapter, you will learn

1. How international trade can benefit all countries
2. The role comparative advantage plays in determining what countries produce and trade
3. Why countries erect barriers to trade and who the winners and losers are when international trade is restricted
4. Why international trade agreements are often controversial

Chapter 19

INTERNATIONAL TRADE AND TRADE POLICY

Exchange was one of the core concepts in economics discussed in Chapter 1. Economists often use the words *trade* and *exchange* interchangeably. When Chip goes to work, he exchanges, or trades, his labor services for income. When Juanita purchases a new cell phone, she exchanges, or trades, income for the product she chooses. The subject of international trade—the exchange of goods and services across national borders—is an extension of the basic principle of exchange. Individuals in our economy are involved in countless voluntary trades. They "trade" their labor services (time and skills) to their employer for dollars. They then trade dollars with a multitude of merchants for goods (such as gasoline and groceries) and services (such as plumbing and hairstyling). A firm trades the goods it produces for dollars, and then trades those dollars for labor services

Why is it that people engage in all these complex sets of economic exchanges with one another? The answer is that people are better off as a result of trading. Just as individuals *within* a country find it advantageous to trade with one another, so too do countries find trade advantageous. And just as it is impossible for any individual to be self-sufficient, it is impossible for a country to be self-reliant without sacrificing its standard of living.

Trade Between Countries

The United States has long been part of an international economic community. Its participation has grown in recent decades—a process often referred to as *globalization*—increasing the interdependence among the United States and its trading partners. How has this development affected the three major markets in the U.S. economy?

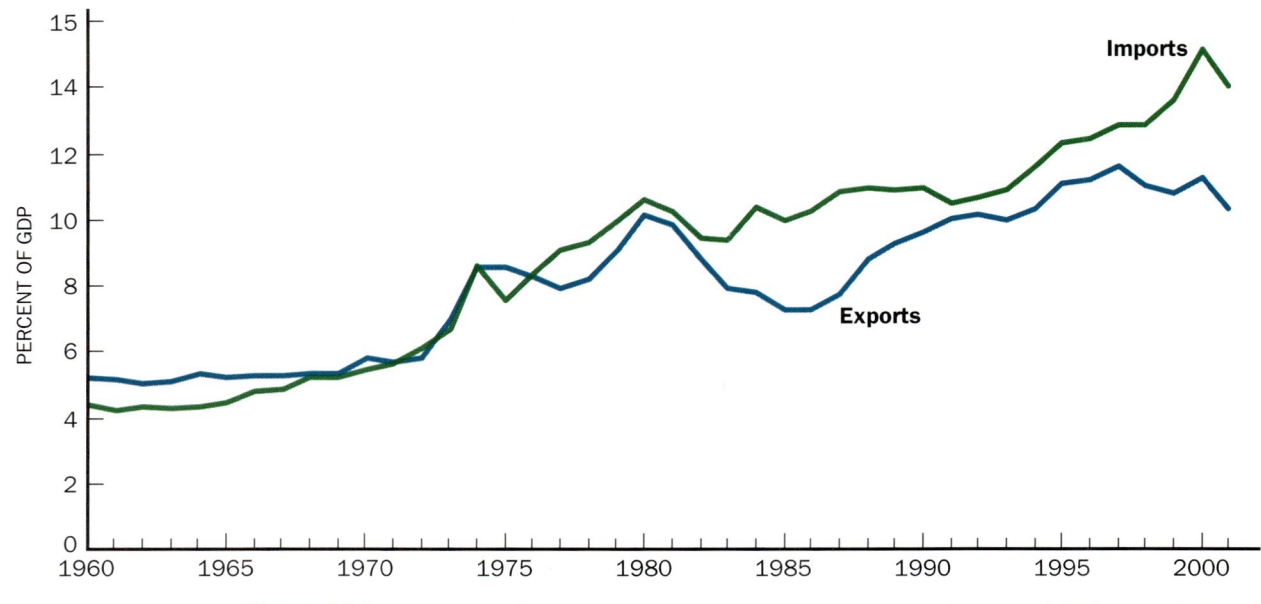

Figure 19.1
INTERNATIONAL TRADE

Here, U.S. imports and exports are expressed as a fraction of GDP. Note that trade has increased over time, and that imports have exceeded exports since the mid-1970s.

SOURCE: *Economic Report of the President* (2004).

INTERDEPENDENCE IN THE PRODUCT MARKET

Foreign-produced goods are commonplace in U.S. markets. In the 1990s, for instance, more than one-fourth of the cars sold in the United States were imported (**imports** are goods produced abroad but bought domestically), along with a third of apparel items, a third of the oil, and virtually all the diamonds. Many of the materials essential for the U.S. economy must also be imported from abroad. At the same time, American farmers export almost two-fifths of the agricultural goods they produce (**exports** are goods produced domestically but sold abroad), including almost three-fourths of the wheat and one-third of the cotton.

Imports have grown in recent decades, not only in dollar terms but also as a percentage of overall production. Exports have grown almost as much. Figure 19.1 shows how exports and imports have increased relative to the nation's total output. As a percentage of GDP, both have more than doubled over the past twenty-five years. Countries with smaller economies are even more dependent on international trade than the United States is. Britain and Canada import one-fourth of their goods, France one-fifth.

INTERDEPENDENCE IN THE LABOR MARKET

International interdependence extends beyond simply the shipping of goods between countries. More than 99 percent of U.S. citizens either came here from another country or are descended from people who did. Though the flow of immigrants, relative to the size of the population, has slowed since its peak a century ago, millions still arrive each year.

The nations of Europe have increasingly recognized the benefits that result from this international movement of workers. One of the most important provisions of the treaty establishing the European Union, an agreement initially among most of the countries in western Europe but now extended to include many in eastern Europe, allows for the free flow of workers within the member countries.

INTERDEPENDENCE IN THE CAPITAL MARKET

The United States has become a major borrower from abroad, but the country also invests heavily overseas. In 2002, for example, U.S. private investors owned approximately $180 billion worth of assets (factories, businesses, buildings, loans, etc.) in foreign countries, while foreign investors owned $707 billion worth of assets in the United States. American companies have sought out profitable opportunities abroad, where they can use their special skills and knowledge to earn high returns. They have established branches and built factories in Europe, Japan, Latin America, and elsewhere in the world. Foreign companies have likewise invested in the United States. Major automobile producers such as Toyota and BMW have built factories in the United States to manufacture cars.

MULTILATERAL TRADE

Often, we think of trade as a two-way exchange—the United States sells airplanes to Japan and buys Japanese-produced consumer electronics. Such transactions between two individuals or countries are called **bilateral trade.** But exchange between two parties is often less advantageous than that among several parties, called **multilateral trade.** Such trades are often observed among sports teams. One highly publicized trade in 2004 involved the Boston Red Sox, the Chicago Cubs, the Montreal Expos, and the Minnesota Twins. At its heart were three shortstops—Nomar Garciaparra, a five-time all-star, who went from the Red Sox to the Cubs; Alex Gonzalez, who went from the Cubs to Montreal; and Orlando Cabrera, who went from Montreal to Boston—but other players and a fourth team (the Twins) were also involved. No two of the teams were willing to make a bilateral trade, but all thought they could benefit from the multilateral deal.

Countries function similarly. China imports oil from the Arabian countries. The Arabian countries want wheat and food for their oil, not just the textiles that China can provide. So the Arabian countries use revenue obtained by selling oil to China to buy wheat and food from the United States, and the United States buys textiles from China. This three-way trade, shown in Figure 19.2, offers gains that two-way trade cannot. The scores of nations that are active in the world economy create patterns far more complex than these simple examples.

When trade is multilateral, the trade between any two countries may not balance. In Figure 19.2, the Arab nations send oil to China but get no goods (only yuan) in return. No one would fault this trade policy. Yet some members of Congress,

Figure 19.2

MULTILATERAL EXCHANGE

The figure illustrates exchange in international trade. Note that no two of the countries have the ingredients for a mutually beneficial exchange.

newspaper columnists, union leaders, and business executives complain that because the United States imports more from a particular country (often China or Japan) than it exports to that country, the trade balance is "unfair." According to a misguided popular cliché, "Trade is a two-way street." But trade in the world market is a complex network involving hundreds of possible streets. While the overall U.S. trade deficit raises legitimate concerns, there is no reason why U.S. exports and imports with any particular country should be balanced.

Comparative Advantage

We have so far focused on exchanges of existing goods. But clearly, most of what is exchanged must first be produced. Trade enables individuals and countries to concentrate on what they produce best.

Some countries—because they have more highly educated workers, more capital (plant and equipment), or more abundant natural resources—may be more efficient at producing almost all the different goods that their citizens wish to consume. The possession of superior production skills is called having an **absolute advantage.** Why would a country with an absolute advantage wish to trade with countries that are less efficient? And how can such disadvantaged countries successfully engage in trade? The answer to these questions lies in the principle of **comparative advantage,** which states that individuals and countries specialize in those goods in whose production they are *relatively,* not absolutely, most efficient.

To see what comparative advantage means, let's say that both the United States and Japan produce two goods, computers and wheat. The amount of labor needed to produce these goods is shown in Table 19.1. (These numbers are all hypothetical.) The United States is more efficient (spends fewer worker hours) at making both products. America can rightfully claim to have the most efficient computer industry in the world, and yet it imports computers from Japan. Why? The *relative* cost of making a computer (in terms of labor used) in Japan, relative to the cost of producing a ton of wheat, is low, compared with that in the United States. That is, in

Table 19.1

LABOR COST OF PRODUCING COMPUTERS AND WHEAT (WORKER HOURS)

	United States	Japan
Labor required to make a computer	100	120
Labor required to make a ton of wheat	5	8

Internet Connection

DAVID RICARDO

The economist David Ricardo developed the theory of comparative advantage. Born in 1772, Ricardo was the third of seventeen children. He was a successful stockbroker before retiring at age forty-two to write about economics. The Library in the Virtual Economy at Biz/ed—a Web site devoted to business and economics education—provides a brief biography of this famous economist and discusses his contributions to the theory of comparative advantage at www.bized.ac.uk/virtual/economy/library/economists/ricardo.htm.

Japan, it takes 15 times as many hours (120/8) to produce a computer as a ton of wheat; in the United States, it takes 20 times as many hours (100/5) to produce a computer as a ton of wheat. While Japan has an absolute *dis*advantage in producing computers, it has a *comparative* advantage.

The principle of comparative advantage applies to individuals as well as countries. The president of a company might type faster than her secretary, but it still pays to have the secretary type her letters, because the president may have a comparative advantage at bringing in new clients, while the secretary has a comparative (though not absolute) advantage at typing.

PRODUCTION POSSIBILITIES CURVES AND COMPARATIVE ADVANTAGE

The easiest way to understand the comparative advantage of different countries is to use the production possibilities curve first introduced in Chapter 2. Figure 19.3 depicts parts of hypothetical production possibilities curves for two countries, China and the United States, producing two commodities, textiles (garments) and airplanes. In both, point *E* represents the current level of production. Let us look at what happens if each country changes its production by 100 airplanes.

China has a comparative advantage in producing textiles. If it reduces its airplane production by 100, its textile production can be increased by 10,000 garments. This trade-off between airplanes and garments is called the *marginal rate of transformation*. By contrast, if the United States reduces its airplane production by 100 airplanes, its textile production can be increased by only 1,000 garments. Conversely, if it increases its airplane production by 100, it will have to reduce its garment production by only 1,000 garments. We can now see why the world is better off if each country exploits its comparative advantage. If China moves from *E* to *E'* (decreasing airplane production by 100),

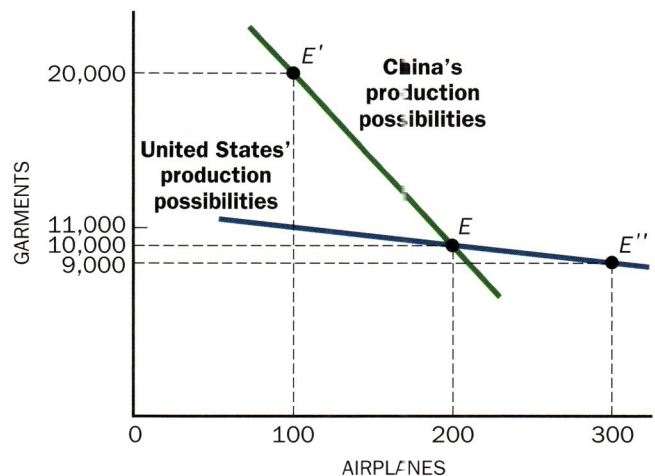

Figure 19.3

EXPLOITING COMPARATIVE ADVANTAGE

The production possibilities schedules for China and the United States, each manufacturing two commodities, textiles and airplanes, illustrate the trade-offs at different levels of production. Point *E* shows the current level of production for each country; *E'* and *E"* illustrate production decisions that better exploit each country's comparative advantage.

10,000 more garments can be produced. If the United States at the same time increases its airplane production by 100 from E to E''', it will produce only 1,000 fewer garments. In the new situation, the world production of airplanes is unchanged (100 + 300 = 200 + 200), but world production of garments has increased by 9,000 (the difference between 20,000 + 9,000 and 10,000 + 10,000). So long as the production trade-offs differ—that is, so long as the marginal rates of transformation differ—it pays for China to specialize increasingly in textiles, and the United States to specialize increasingly in airplanes. Notice that the analysis depends on knowledge only about the production trade-offs. We do not need to know how much labor or capital is required in either country to produce either airplanes or garments.

Though it pays countries to increase the production and export of goods in which they have a comparative advantage and to import goods in which they have a comparative disadvantage, doing so may not lead to complete specialization. Thus the United States continues to be a major producer of textiles, in spite of heavy imports from the Far East. Its engagement in this industry does not violate the principle of comparative advantage: not all textiles require the same skill and expertise in manufacturing. While China may have a comparative advantage in inexpensive textiles, the United States may have a comparative advantage in higher-quality textiles. At the same time, the comparative advantage of other countries is so extreme in producing some goods—TVs and VCRs, for example—that it does not pay for the United States to produce them at all.

COMPARATIVE ADVANTAGE AND SPECIALIZATION

To see the benefits of specialization, consider the pencil. A tree of the right kind of wood must be felled; it must be transported to a sawmill, and there cut into pieces that can be further processed into pencil casings. Then the graphite that runs through the pencil's center, the eraser at its tip, and the metal that holds the two together must each be produced by specially trained people. The pencil is a simple tool. But to produce it by oneself would cost a fortune.

Why Specialization Increases Productivity Specialization increases productivity, thereby enhancing the benefits of trade, for three reasons. First, specializing eliminates the time it takes a worker to switch from one production task to another. Second, by repeating the same task, the worker becomes more skilled at it. And third, specialization creates a fertile environment for invention.

Dividing jobs so that each worker can practice and perfect a particular skill (called the *division of labor*) may increase productivity hundreds or thousands of times. Almost anyone who practices activities—cooking, writing, adding a column of numbers, and so on—will be quite a lot better at them than someone who has not practiced. Similarly, a country that specializes in producing sports cars may develop a comparative advantage in their manufacture. With its relatively large scale of production, it can divide tasks into separate assignments for different people; as each becomes better at his own tasks, productivity is increased.

e-Insight

THE UNITED STATES' COMPARATIVE ADVANTAGE IN THE INTERNET AGE

The United States holds a comparative advantage in information technology and Internet-based commerce. Large U.S. firms such as Microsoft, Intel, and Sun Microsystems have led the surge in information technology over the past two decades, and Internet-based businesses such as Amazon, Google, and eBay have come to define the so-called new economy. How has the United States established itself as a leader in this field? Let's consider this question from the standpoint of the sources of comparative advantage described in this chapter.

The key to the United States' success in the information revolution has been its ability to innovate. U.S. firms have developed new types of computers and software, as well as new applications of these resources across various industries. This prowess in innovation derives from acquired endowments, superior knowledge, and specialization.

The human skills needed for innovation represent acquired endowments that have led to superior knowledge, some of which was gained as a by-product of America's massive expenditures on defense-related research. Another aspect of acquired endowments that has played a major role is the distinctive set of *institutions* in the United States that are particularly well suited for promoting research. These institutions include a special set of financial institutions (venture capital firms) that are better able to supply capital to new and small enterprises, which have played a pivotal role in the new economy, and strong research universities, which often have close ties to firms that can translate basic research into market applications. More broadly, both American labor and capital seem more able and willing to bear the high risks associated with new innovative enterprises, many of which may fold after a relatively brief existence. Americans' willingness to bear these risks may be connected to the generally high levels of employment that have characterized the U.S. economy for the past two decades.

Partly as a result of these acquired advantages and of superior knowledge, the United States has developed a relative specialization in high-tech industries; it has become, to a large extent, the world's research center.

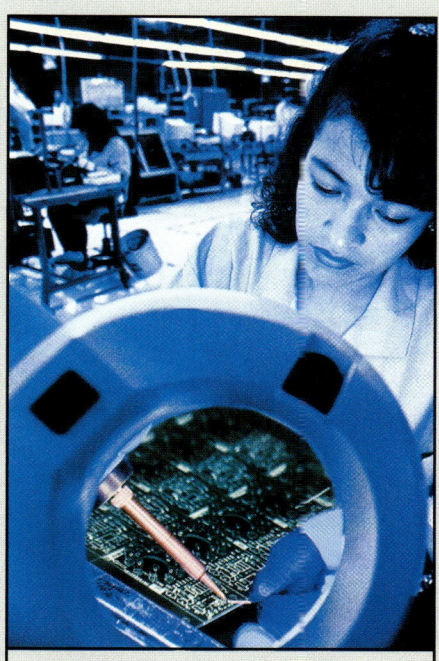

Intel's strength in computer chip production exemplifies the U.S. comparative advantage in information technology.

At the same time, the division of labor often leads to invention. As someone learns a particular job extremely well, she might figure out ways of doing it better—including devising a machine to do it. Specialization and invention reinforce each other. A slight initial advantage in the production of some good leads to greater production of that good, thence to more invention, and thence to even greater production and further specialization.

Limits of Specialization The extent of the division of labor, or specialization, is limited by the size of the market. Specialization has greater scope in mass-produced manufactured goods like picture frames than in custom-made items like the artwork that gets framed. That is one reason why the costs of production of mass-produced goods have declined so much. Similarly, there is greater scope for specialization in a big city than a small town. That is why small stores specializing in a particular food or type of clothing thrive in cities but are rare in smaller towns.

The very nature of specialization limits its benefits. Repetitive jobs can lead to bored and unproductive workers. And single-track specialization inhibits the new insights and ideas that engagement in a variety of work activities can spark.

WHAT DETERMINES COMPARATIVE ADVANTAGE?

Earlier we learned that comparative advantage determines the pattern of trade. But what determines comparative advantage? In the modern world, this turns out to be a complex matter.

Natural Endowments In first laying down the principle of comparative advantage in the early 1800s, the great British economist David Ricardo used the example of Portugal's trade with Britain. In Ricardo's example, Portugal had an absolute advantage in producing both wool and wine. But it had a comparative advantage in producing wine, and Britain had a comparative advantage in producing wool. In this and other early examples, economists tended to assume that a nation's comparative advantage was determined largely by its *natural endowments*. Countries with soil and climate that are *relatively* better for grapes than for pasture will produce wine; countries with soil and climate that are relatively better for pasture than for grapes will produce sheep (and hence wool).

In the modern economy, natural endowments still count: countries such as China that have an abundance of low-skilled labor relative to other resources have a comparative advantage in producing goods like textiles, which require a lot of handwork. But in today's technological age nations can also act to *acquire* a comparative advantage.

Acquired Endowments Japan has little in the way of natural resources, yet it is a major player in international trade, in part because it has *acquired endowments*. Japan's case underscores the principle that by saving and accumulating capital and building large factories, a nation can acquire a comparative advantage in goods like steel that need large amounts of capital for their production. And by devoting resources to education, a nation can develop a comparative advantage in those goods that require a skilled labor force. Thus, the resources—human and physical—that a country has managed to acquire for itself can also give rise to comparative advantage.

Superior Knowledge In the modern economy, comparative advantage may come simply from expertise in using resources productively. Switzerland has a comparative advantage in watches because, over the years, the people of the country have accumulated superior knowledge and expertise in watchmaking. Belgium has a comparative advantage in fine lace; its workers have developed the requisite skills. A quirk of fate might have led Belgium to acquire a comparative advantage in watches and Switzerland in lace.

Specialization Earlier we saw how comparative advantage leads to specialization. Specialization may also lead to comparative advantage. The Swiss make fine watches, and have a comparative advantage in that market because of years of unique experience. Such superior knowledge, however, does not explain why Britain, Germany, and the United States, which are at roughly the same level of technological expertise in building cars, all trade cars with one another. How can each country have a comparative advantage in making cars? The answer lies in specialization.

Both Britain and Germany may be better off if Britain specializes in producing sports cars and Germany in producing luxury cars, or the converse, because specialization increases productivity. Countries enhance, or simply develop, a comparative advantage by specializing just as individuals do. As a result, similar countries enjoy the advantages of specialization even when they specialize in different variations of products that are fundamentally similar.

Interactions The different sources of comparative advantage can serve to reinforce each other. Pittsburgh provides a good example of some of these interactions. Its rivers and deposits of bituminous coal (natural endowments) gave it an early comparative advantage as a location for industries such as steel production. George Westinghouse, founder of the corporation that bears his name, came to Pittsburgh because he needed steel for a tool he had designed to get derailed train cars back onto their tracks, and he could take advantage of Pittsburgh's established steel industry. Carnegie Technical Schools, the ancestor of today's Carnegie Mellon University, was created to help supply the area's industries with the engineers they needed. The availability of engineers (acquired endowments) made Pittsburgh an attractive place for other industries to locate.

> **Wrap-Up**
>
> ## THE FIVE BASES OF COMPARATIVE ADVANTAGE
>
> *Natural endowments,* which consist of geographical determinants such as land, natural resources, and climate
>
> *Acquired endowments,* which are the physical capital and human skills a nation has developed
>
> *Superior knowledge,* including technological advantages, which may be acquired either as an accident of history or through deliberate policies
>
> *Specialization,* which may create comparative advantages between countries that are similar in all other respects
>
> *Interactions,* which reinforce the other sources of comparative advantage

The Perceived Costs of International Interdependence

If the argument that voluntary trade must be mutually beneficial is so compelling, why has there been, from time to time, such strong antitrade sentiment in the United States and many other countries? This antitrade feeling is often labeled **protectionism,** because it calls for "protecting" the economy from the effects of trade. Those who favor protectionism raise a number of concerns. Some of the objections to international trade parallel the objections to trade among individuals noted earlier. Was the trade a fair deal? Was the seller in a stronger bargaining position? Such concerns, for individuals and countries, revolve around how the *surplus* associated with the gains from trade is divided. Weak countries may feel that they are being taken advantage of by stronger countries. Their weaker bargaining position may lead to the stronger countries getting *more* of the gains from trade. But this outcome does not contradict the basic premise: both parties gain from voluntary exchange. All countries—weak as well as strong—are better off as a result of voluntary exchange.

Thinking Like an Economist
EXCHANGE AND THE GLOBALIZATION CONTROVERSY

In recent decades, transportation and communication costs have come down markedly. So too have artificial barriers to the movements of goods and services—trade barriers such as tariffs and quotas. The result is that the economies of the world are now more closely integrated than ever before.

From an economic perspective, this trend toward globalization would seem to offer a great benefit to the world. As we know, one of the core ideas of economics is that *voluntary exchange* is mutually beneficial to the parties involved. Yet globalization has been a subject of great controversy. For instance, some critics see globalization as a one-sided process mainly benefiting rich countries and large multinational firms. Others on the opposite side of the debate see it as the best opportunity to increase the standards of living in poor countries. How do we make sense of this controversy from an economic perspective? A close look at the globalization controversy shows that some of the criticisms are misplaced, while others have merit.

Globalization no doubt has made us more aware of the huge inequalities around the world. Some workers in China, Africa, and India, for instance, earn less than a dollar a day working under conditions that appear inhumane by American standards. But, for the most part, globalization has not caused their misery; it has only brought their plight to global attention. Many of these workers have moved to jobs in seemingly awful factories—some run by multinational firms, others selling their goods to multinational firms—because their previous jobs were even worse or because they had no previous jobs. It may seem cruel for corporations to exploit these workers, especially when working conditions could be improved at moderate expense. But even so, in many cases the workers have benefited from globalization.

Another economic aspect of globalization is that the *distribution* of its benefits may be highly uneven. For example, the owners of factories that make goods for multinational firms typically benefit more than the workers they employ. As a result, even if everyone is better off, inequality increases. Critics attacking the issue from a normative stance—emphasizing social values about fairness—may see increased inequality as the primary concern. In their view, the poor, who in some cases may benefit the least from globalization, are the very people who deserve to benefit more. But even if we agree with this con-

But trade among individuals and trade among countries differ in one important way. Some individuals within a country benefit from trade and some lose. Since the trade as a whole is beneficial to the country, the gains to the winners exceed the losses to the losers. Thus, in principle, those who benefit within the country could more than compensate those who don't. In practice, however, those who lose remain losers and obviously oppose trade, arguing that it results in lost jobs and reduced wages. Such worries have become particularly acute as unskilled workers face competition with low-wage unskilled workers in Asia and Latin America: how can they compete without lowering their income?

These concerns figured prominently in the debate in 1993 over ratification of the North American Free Trade Agreement (NAFTA), which allows Mexican goods into the United States with no duties at all. Advocates of NAFTA pointed out that (1) more jobs would be created by the new export opportunities than would be lost through competition from Mexican firms and (2) the jobs that were created paid higher wages, reflecting the benefits from specialization in areas where the United States had a comparative advantage.

tention, we have to recognize that it does not refute the basic economic principle about the benefits of voluntary exchange.

A further criticism of globalization maintains that some individuals are actually made worse off. Can this be? The answer is yes, and an example helps illustrate the point. The theory of comparative advantage says that countries should produce the goods that they are relatively good at producing. But when they are protected from foreign competition, firms may produce goods that are not part of the country's comparative advantage. The United States may produce cheap clothes, simply because of the limits put on importing inexpensive foreign-made clothes. Removing the protection may make the production of the inexpensive clothes unprofitable. The factory may have to shut down, and workers will be left unemployed. But in theory, these conditions should not last for long. If markets work well, some new enterprises will be created to take advantage of the country's comparative advantage. Resources are redeployed from where they are less productive to where they are more productive, a shift that increases the country's income. But this process does not happen automatically, or always quickly; in the meanwhile, those who are pushed into unemployment often object to the removal of the protection.

Such problems are especially severe in developing countries, where there is a shortage both of entrepreneurs and of capital to start new enterprises. Workers who lose their jobs can be at particular risk, since they have no unemployment insurance or welfare system to fall back on. In many cases it may be true that the gains of those who benefit from freer trade more than offset the losses of those who suffer. Therefore, in principle, the gainers could compensate the losers so that everyone could be made better off. But in practice, the compensation is seldom paid. Thus, although a country may benefit from globalization, some of its citizens may suffer until the process of redeployment works itself out.

Are the jobs of these Chinese workers a cost or a benefit of globalization?

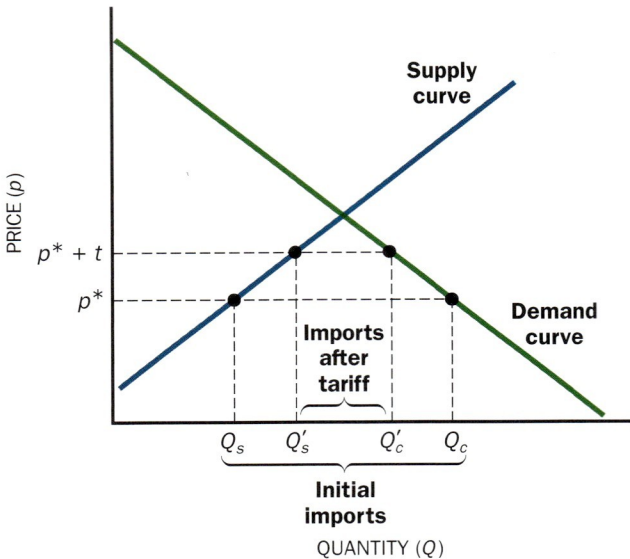

Figure 19.4

EFFECT OF TARIFFS

A small country faces a horizontal supply curve for a good at the international price, p^*. In the absence of tariffs, the price in the country will be p^*. The country will produce Q_s (the quantity along the supply curve corresponding to p^*), consume Q_c (the quantity along the demand curve corresponding to p^*), and import $Q_c - Q_s$. A tariff at the rate t increases the price in the country to $p^* + t$, lowers aggregate consumption to Q'_c (the quantity along the demand curve corresponding to $p^* + t$), and increases domestic production to Q'_s (the quantity along the supply curve corresponding to $p^* + t$). Domestic producers are better off, but consumers are worse off.

Opponents of free trade are not swayed by these arguments, but instead stress the costs to workers and communities as particular industries shrink in response to foreign imports. The textile worker in North Carolina who loses his job as a result of imports of inexpensive clothing from China cannot instantly convert himself into a computer programmer in California or an aircraft engineer working for Boeing. But the fact is that jobs are being destroyed and created all the time, irrespective of trade. Over the long run, the increased demand for computer programmers and aircraft engineers leads to higher salaries for those workers, thereby strengthening the incentives for young workers to gain the skills needed for these jobs and for others to relocate to areas where new jobs are being created. The declining demand for textile workers lowers salaries for textile workers, reducing the incentives for workers to remain in that industry. The United States is characterized by a high degree of labor mobility, and as jobs are created in one part of the country and disappear in other parts, individuals and families often move to seek new employment opportunities.

On balance, the country benefits from these changes, but the benefits are not distributed evenly. The unemployed textile worker sees only the economic hardship she faces and the cost of free trade. For this reason, many economists argue that policies must be implemented to help retrain and relocate workers displaced by trade so that they too can share in the benefits that accrue from international interdependence. To the extent that such assistance increases the number of winners, it should reduce opposition to trade.

While the perceived costs of economic interdependence cannot be ignored—especially when they become the subject of heated political debate—the consensus among the vast majority of economists is that the country as a whole benefits from freer trade. We can summarize this central tenet as follows: *There are gains from voluntary exchanges. Whether it occurs between individuals or across national borders, voluntary exchange can benefit all. Trade enables parties to specialize in activities in which they have a comparative advantage.*

Trade Policies

In spite of the gains from trade, countries have imposed a variety of barriers to it. In the remainder of this chapter, we explore some of the common trade barriers and the major initiatives to remove them.

COMMERCIAL POLICY

Countries that have *no* barriers to trade are said to practice **free trade**, but most countries engage in some form of protectionism—that is, in one way or another they restrict the importation of goods. Policies directed at affecting either imports or exports are referred to as **commercial policies.** This and the next section examine the forms that trade barriers take, their economic costs, and their economic and political rationale. The final section explores international attempts to reduce them.

There are five major categories of trade barriers—tariffs, quotas, voluntary export restraints, other *nontariff barriers,* and a set of so-called fair trade laws that, by and large, actually serve to impede trade.

TARIFFS

Tariffs are simply a tax on imports. Since a tariff is a tax that is imposed only on foreign goods, it puts the foreign goods at a disadvantage and discourages imports.

Figure 19.4 shows the effect of a tariff: a downward-sloping demand curve for the product, and an upward-sloping domestic supply curve. For the sake of simplicity, we consider the case of a country sufficiently small that the price it pays for a good on the international market does not depend on the quality purchased. In the absence of a tariff, the domestic price is equal to this international price, p^*. The country produces Q_s, consumes Q_c, and imports the difference, $Q_c - Q_s$. When a tariff is imposed, the price that consumers have to pay is increased from p^* to $p^* + t$, where t is the tariff. Domestic production is increased (to Q'_s)—producers are better off as a result. But consumers are worse off, as the price they pay is increased. Their consumption is reduced to Q'_c. Since production is increased and consumption reduced, imports are reduced; the domestic industry has been protected against foreign imports.

Quantifying the Losses to Society from Tariffs We can quantify the net loss to society caused by tariffs. The difference between the amount consumers are willing to pay and what they have to pay is called *consumer surplus.* For the last unit consumed, the marginal benefit exactly equals the price paid, and so there is no consumer surplus. But for the first units consumed, individuals typically would be willing to pay far more—reflected in the fact that the demand curve is downward sloping in Figure 19.5. Initially, the consumer surplus is given by triangle *ABC,* the area between the demand curve and the price line, p^*. After the price increase, it is given by the triangle *ADE.* The net loss is the trapezoid *BCED.*

But of this loss, the rectangle *BDHF* represents increased payments to producers (the increased price, *BD,* times the quantity that they produce), and *HFGE* is the tariff revenue of the government (imports, *HE,* times the tariff). A portion of the increased payments to domestic producers covers the cost of expanding production. The rest represents a difference between price and the marginal cost of production—increased profits. This is the area *BIHD.* Thus, the societal loss is represented by two triangles, *EGC* and *HFI.* The triangle *EGC* is similar to the loss to consumers arising from a monopolist's raising his price. The triangle *HFI* is a waste

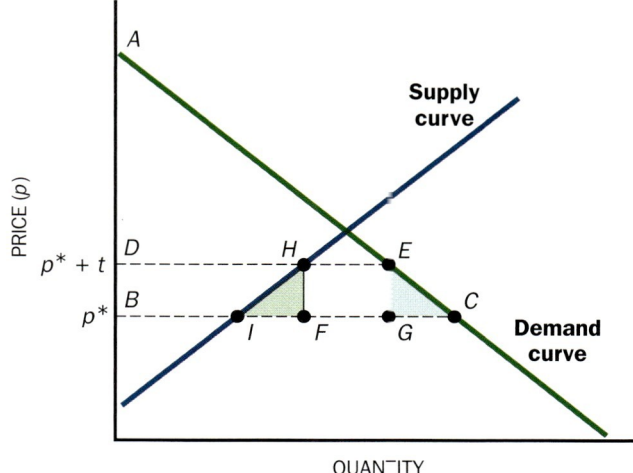

Figure 19.5

QUANTIFYING THE NET LOSS TO SOCIETY FROM IMPOSING TARIFFS

The societal loss from imposing tariffs is represented by the two triangles, *EGC* and *HFI.*

of resources resulting from the cost of domestic production exceeding the costs of purchasing the good abroad, as the economy expands production because of the tariff.

QUOTAS

Rather than setting tariffs, many countries impose **quotas**—limits on the amount of foreign goods that can be imported. For instance, in the 1950s, the United States imposed a quota on the amount of oil that could be imported, and until 2005 strict quotas controlled imports of textiles.

Producers often prefer quotas. Because the quantity imported is limited, the domestic price increases above the international price. Quotas enable domestic producers to know precisely the magnitude of the foreign supply. If foreign producers become more efficient or if exchange rates change in their favor, they still cannot sell any more. In that sense, quotas provide domestic producers with greater certainty than do tariffs, insulating them from the worst threats of competition.

Quotas and tariffs both succeed in raising the domestic price above the price at which the good could be obtained abroad. Both thus protect domestic producers. There is, however, one important difference: quotas enable those possessing permits to import to earn a profit by buying goods at the international price abroad and selling at the higher domestic price. The government is, in effect, giving away its tariff revenues. These profits are referred to as **quota rents.**

VOLUNTARY EXPORT RESTRAINTS

In recent years, international agreements have reduced the level of tariffs and restricted the use of quotas. Accordingly, countries have sought to protect themselves from the onslaught of foreign competition by other means. One approach that became popular in the 1980s was the use of *voluntary export restraints* (VERs). Rather than limiting imports of automobiles, for example, the United States persuaded Japan to limit its exports.

There are two interpretations of why Japan might have been willing to go along with this VER. One is that it worried the United States might take a stronger action, such as imposing quotas. From Japan's perspective, VERs are clearly preferable to quotas, because VERs allow the quota rents to accrue to Japanese firms. A second interpretation is that VERs enable Japanese car producers to act collectively in their self-interest to reduce production and raise prices, engaging in a kind of collusion otherwise illegal under American antitrust laws. The VER "imposed" output reductions on the Japanese car producers that they would have chosen themselves if they had been permitted to under law. No wonder, then, that they agreed to go along! The cost to the American consumer of the Japanese VER was enormous. American consumers paid more than $100,000 in higher prices for every American job created.

OTHER NONTARIFF BARRIERS

VERs and quotas are the clearest nontariff barriers, but today they are probably not the most important. A host of regulations have the same effect of imposing barriers to trade. For instance, health-related regulations have been abused in ways that restrict trade. When, in 1996, Russia threatened to halt U.S. exports of chickens on the grounds that its health regulations were not satisfied, U.S. chicken exporters were faced with a nontariff barrier. Various types of regulations have been used to establish nontariff barriers.

During the 1980s, as tariff barriers were being reduced, nontariff barriers increased. A study by the International Monetary Fund concluded that whereas about one-eighth of all U.S. imports were affected by protectionism in 1980, by the middle of the 1990s the figure had risen to one-fourth. It is estimated that trade barriers (including nontariff barriers) may prevent consumers and business from buying as much as $110 billion in imports they would otherwise have purchased. Japan was particularly harmed by these actions. By the early 1990s, about 40 percent of Japan's exports to the United States were limited by some form of U.S. protectionism.

Wrap-Up

COMPARISON OF QUOTAS AND TARIFFS

Both can be used to restrict imports by the same amount, with the same effect on consumers and domestic producers.

In the case of quotas, the difference between domestic price and international price accrues to the importer, who enjoys a quota rent.

In the case of tariffs, the difference accrues to government as tariff revenues.

VERs (voluntary export restraints) are equivalent to quotas, except that the quota rents are given to foreign producers.

"FAIR TRADE" LAWS

Most people believe competition should be fair. When someone can undersell them, they suspect foul play. The government has imposed a variety of laws to ensure that there is genuine and fair competition domestically. Laws have also been enacted by most countries to ensure "fair competition" in international trade. But most economists believe that in practice these are protectionist measures, reducing competition and restricting imports. To ensure fair competition, economists argue that the same laws that apply domestically should be extended internationally—that is, there should not be two standards of fairness, one applying domestically, the other internationally. The two most important "fair trade" laws that represent nontariff barriers are antidumping laws and countervailing duties.

International Perspective
SURROGATE COUNTRIES AND CANADIAN GOLF CARTS

Question: How, if Canada did not produce golf carts, could the cost of Canadian golf carts be used to accuse Poland of dumping? Answer: The United States sometimes achieves wonders when its markets are at stake.

The standard criterion for judging whether a country is dumping is whether it is selling commodities on the U.S. market at prices below those for which it sells them at home or elsewhere, or at prices below the costs of production. For nonmarket economies, the Department of Commerce formulated a special criterion: Is the price below what it would have cost to produce the good in a "comparable" (or "surrogate") country?

The Department of Commerce, which is responsible for implementing the law, knows no shame. In a famous case involving Polish golf carts, it decided that the country most like Poland was Canada—at a time when Poland's per capita income was a fraction of Canada's, and when Canada did not make comparable golf carts. Thus, the Commerce Department faced the question: What would it have cost for Canada to produce these golf carts, had it chosen to do so? Not surprisingly, the resulting cost estimate was higher than the price the real golf carts were being sold for in the United States, and Poland was found guilty of dumping.

Similar charges have been made on similar grounds against Russian sales of natural resources. For years, Western countries had preached to the Soviet Union and the other socialist countries the virtues of the market. Beginning in 1989, with the demise of communism, former iron-curtain countries sought to transform their economies into market economies. Under the old regime, these countries had traded mainly with themselves, and generally engaged in barter. In the new era, they sought to enter international markets, like any other market economy.

Though the design and production quality of many of its manufactured goods made them unsuitable for Western markets, Russia had a wealth of natural resources—including uranium and aluminum—that it could produce on a competitive basis. Moreover, with the reduction of defense expenditures—good news from virtually every perspective—Russia's demand for many of these raw materials was greatly reduced.

American producers attempted to discourage Russian exports by filing, or threatening to file, dumping charges. Though Russia was probably not selling these commodities at prices below those prevailing at home or elsewhere, or at prices below the cost of production, the "surrogate" country criterion made the dumping charges a very real threat. Russia agreed to a cutback in aluminum production in 1994, to be matched by cutbacks in other countries.

To the Commerce and State Departments, this may have seemed a reasonable way to avoid trade conflict. But consumers paid dearly, in higher prices for aluminum and products using aluminum.

Antidumping Laws Dumping refers to the sale of products overseas at prices that are not only lower than those in the home country but below cost. Normally, consumers greet discounted sales with enthusiasm. If Russia is willing to sell aluminum to the United States at low prices, why should we complain? One possible concern is that by selling below cost, the foreign companies hope to drive American firms out of business. Once they have established a monopoly position, they can raise prices. In such a case, American consumers gain only in the short run. In competitive markets, however, this scenario simply cannot occur, for firms will have no power to raise prices. In almost all of the cases in which dumping has been found, markets are sufficiently competitive that foreign firms have no hope of establishing monopoly positions.

As administered, the antidumping laws are more frequently used as a protectionist tool. If dumping is discovered, a duty (tariff) is levied equal to the difference between the (calculated) cost of production and the price. Critics of the dumping laws worry that other countries will imitate American practices. If so, just as the international community has eliminated tariff barriers, a whole new set of trade barriers will have been erected.

Countervailing Duties A second trade practice widely viewed as unfair is for governments to subsidize domestic firms' production or exports. For example, the government may give certain domestic industries tax breaks or pay a portion of the firms' costs. These subsidies give the companies receiving them an unfair advantage. Trade is determined on the basis not of comparative advantage but of relative subsidy levels.

The usual logic of economics seems to be reversed. If some foreign government wants to subsidize American consumers, who benefit from the lower prices, why should they complain? Presumably, they would have a grievance only if the subsidies are part of a policy intended to drive American firms out of business and establish a monopoly position, after which prices will be raised. Most foreign subsidies do not fall into this category.

Opposition to these subsidies arises from the companies who see their businesses hurt. While the gains to consumers outweigh the losses to businesses, the gain to each consumer is small, and consumers are not well organized. Producers, being far better organized, are able and willing to bring their case to Washington. In response, Congress has passed laws allowing the U.S. government to impose **countervailing duties,** that is, taxes that offset any advantage provided by these subsidies.

But even governments that preach against other countries providing subsidies engage in the practice themselves, most commonly in agriculture. At various times, the U.S. government has subsidized the export and production of wheat, pork, peaches, and a host of other commodities.

Political and Economic Rationale for Protection

Free trade, by enabling each country to concentrate production where it has a comparative advantage, can make all countries better off. Why is protection nevertheless so popular? The basic reason is simple: protection raises prices. While the losses to consumers from higher prices exceed the gains to producers in higher profits, producers are well organized and consumers are not;

hence producers' voices are heard more clearly in the political process than are consumers'.

There is an important check on firms' ability to use the political process to advance their special interests: the interests of exporters, who realize that if the United States closes off its markets to imports, other countries will reciprocate. Thus, exporting firms like Boeing have forcefully advocated an international regime of freer and fairer trade through the kind of international agreements that will be described in the next section.

But before turning to a review of these international agreements, we need to take a closer look at some of the other economic aspects of protection. While free trade may make the country as a whole better off, certain groups may actually become worse off. Those especially affected include displaced firms and workers, low-wage workers, and those in industries that enjoyed limited competition without free trade.

DISPLACED FIRMS AND WORKERS

China has a comparative advantage in inexpensive textiles while the United States has a comparative advantage in manufacturing complex goods, like advanced telephone exchanges. If the United States starts to import textiles from China, U.S. textile manufacturers may be driven out of business, and their workers will have to find work elsewhere. More than offsetting these losses are the gains to the export industries. In principle, the gainers in those industries could more than compensate the losers, but such compensation is seldom made: hence, the losers oppose moves to open trade.

Typically, economists shed few tears for the lost profits of the businesses that are hurt when trade becomes open. After all, such a loss is just one of the risks that businesses face, and for which they are typically well compensated. New innovations destroy old businesses. But barring the door to new technologies or to cheaper products from abroad is bad economics—and bad economic policy.

Often, however, more sympathy is felt for workers affected by trade—though there is no reason why concern should be greater over displacements caused by open trade than by new innovations. When the economy is running at close to full employment, workers who lose their jobs typically do find new positions. But they often go through a transition period of unemployment, and when they eventually do find a new job, chances are good that their wages will be lower (in the United States, in recent years, a worker who succeeds in finding full-time employment experiences on average a 10 percent wage decline). While these particular laborers are worse off, workers as a whole benefit, because those who get newly created jobs in the export industries are paid far more (on average 13 to 15 percent more) than the average for the economy. Concern about the transitional costs borne by displaced workers has motivated Congress to pass laws to provide special assistance for these workers in finding new jobs and obtaining the requisite training.

BEGGAR-THY-NEIGHBOR POLICIES

Concerns about unemployment have provided the strongest motivation for protectionist policies. The argument is simple: if Americans do not buy foreign goods, they will spend the money at home, thereby creating more jobs for Americans. Deliberate attempts to increase national output and employment by reducing imports are called **beggar-thy-neighbor policies,** because the jobs gained in one country are at the expense of jobs lost in another. Such efforts ignore an important fact: if we do not buy goods from abroad, foreign purchasers will not buy our goods. As a result, U.S. exports to other countries will fall in tandem with our imports from other countries, causing jobs in our export industries to disappear. The benefits of specialization are denied to everyone, and national incomes fall.

The worst instances of these beggar-thy-neighbor policies occurred at the onset of the Great Depression. In 1930, the United States passed the Hawley-Smoot Tariff Act, raising tariffs on many products to a level that effectively prohibited many imports. Other countries retaliated. As U.S. imports declined, incomes in Europe and elsewhere in the world fell. As incomes declined and as these countries imposed retaliatory tariffs, they bought fewer goods from the United States. U.S. exports plummeted, contributing further to the economic downturn in the United States. The downturn in international trade that was set off by the Hawley-Smoot Tariff Act, charted in Figure 19.6, is often pointed to as a major factor contributing to the depth and severity of the Great Depression.

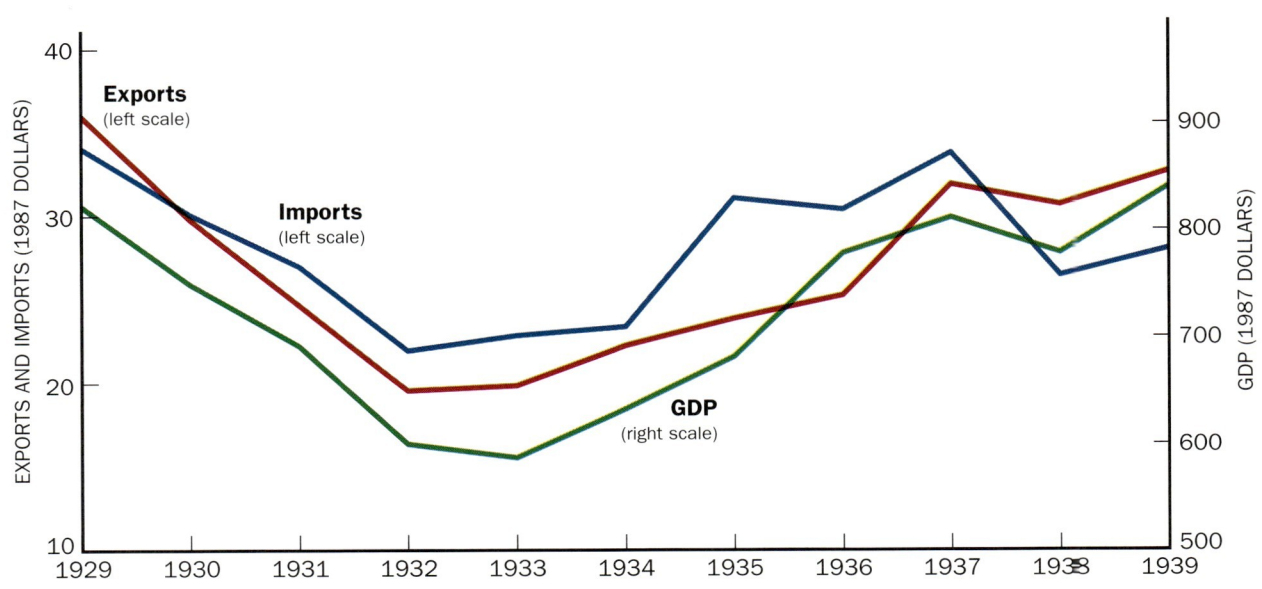

Figure 19.6

THE DECLINE IN INTERNATIONAL TRADE AND THE GREAT DEPRESSION

U.S. exports and imports fell dramatically during the Great Depression. One contributing factor in the decline in trade was the Hawley-Smoot Tariff Act, passed in 1930.

SOURCE: Bureau of Economic Analysis (www.bea.gov).

> **Wrap-Up**
>
> ## INTERNATIONAL TRADE AND JOBS
>
> Restricting imports as a way of creating jobs tends to be counterproductive.
>
> It is the responsibility of macroeconomic policy, not trade policy, to maintain the economy at full employment.

WAGES IN AFFECTED SECTORS

Beyond these short-run problems of transition and unemployment, long-run problems may face workers in affected sectors. The United States has a comparative advantage in producing goods such as airplanes and high-tech products that require highly skilled workers. As the United States exports more of these goods, its demand for these workers increases, driving up their wages. Similarly, the United States has a comparative disadvantage in producing goods that require much unskilled labor, such as lower-quality textiles. As imports compete against these U.S. industries and their production decreases, the demand for unskilled labor decreases. As a result, the wages of the unskilled workers are driven down.

This loss in income for unskilled workers is often blamed on imports from third world countries like China, where wages are but a fraction of those in the United States. The consensus among economists who have looked closely at the matter is that international trade explains a relatively small part of the decline in wages—perhaps 20 percent. Nonetheless, those who see their livelihood being threatened are among the most ardent advocates of trade restrictions. Again, economists argue that the appropriate response is not to restrict trade but to increase skills. The workers gaining the skills are better off, as their wages rise commensurately with the increase in their productivity. In addition, as more workers become skilled, the supply of workers still unskilled is reduced; and the smaller supply of unskilled workers leads to a rise in their real wages, offsetting the adverse effects of trade.

> **Wrap-Up**
>
> ## EFFECTS OF TRADE ON WAGES
>
> International trade may lower wages of unskilled U.S. labor and those working in industries where competition is limited.
>
> International trade raises wages of skilled U.S. workers.

INCREASED COMPETITION

International trade also has other adverse effects in industries in which competition is limited. Limited competition enables firms to enjoy monopoly or oligopoly profits.

Thinking Like an Economist
DISTRIBUTION AND TRADE LIBERALIZATION

Trade liberalization may make a country as a whole better off, but it does not make everyone in the country better off. The gains to the winners are large enough that, in principle, any losers could be compensated, to everyone's benefit. But in practice, compensation is seldom made. Thus, trade liberalization often entails trade-offs to balance the gains of one group in the economy against the losses of another group. The problem is that often the losers are among the poorest in the country. For example, trade liberalization threatens to force low-paid textile workers in United States into unemployment. It is little comfort for the textile workers in South Carolina to know that new jobs are being created for aircraft engineers in Seattle or that all American consumers of textile products are now better off. In the United States, however, labor markets work reasonably well, and the laid-off textile worker can eventually get a new job, though often at markedly reduced wages.

While low-wage textile workers in the United States are hurt by trade liberalization, low-wage textile workers in developing economies gain. Trade liberalization increases the demand for the textiles they produce, and thus increases the demand for their labor. Unfortunately, matters can be far bleaker for those in developing countries to whom trade liberalization brings increased competition. In many developing countries, unemployment is 15 percent or more, so the loss of a job is likely to have severe consequences.

In Mexico, since the North American Free Trade Agreement was enacted wages have soared for those who produce goods for American car companies or other firms near the border of Texas. But in the south of Mexico, the poor have become even poorer. Highly subsidized American corn has depressed the already low incomes of Mexican farmers. To be sure, urban workers benefit, since they can buy corn for a lower price than would otherwise have been possible.

When diverse groups are affected so differently, it is not clear whether trade liberalization is a good thing *in the absence of policies to address its distributional effects*. But such assessments are not made by economists; in democracies, they are left to the political processes. Society as a whole does benefit from trade liberalization, and the role of the economist is to point out this potential for gain. Economists also have a role to play in explaining who will be affected, and to what degree.

Workers often receive some of these extra profits: particularly when the industries are unionized, they may earn wages far higher than workers of comparable skill employed elsewhere in the economy. After international trade introduces more competition, monopoly and oligopoly profits get competed away. Firms are forced to pay competitive wages—that is, the lowest wage that they can for workers with a given skill.

From the perspective of the overall economy, this competition that erodes market power and induces greater efficiency and responsiveness to consumers is one of the major virtues of free trade. From the perspective of those who see their higher wages and profits vanishing, it is one of free trade's major vices.

THE INFANT INDUSTRY ARGUMENT

While job loss and decreased wages and profits from international competition provide much of the political motivation behind protection, economists have asked if there are any *legitimate* arguments for protection. That is, are there circumstances where protection may be in the *national* interest, and not just in the interests of those being protected? Two arguments have been put forward.

The first is the **infant industry argument.** Costs in new industries are often high, dropping as experience is gained. The infant industry argument is that firms, particularly in less-developed countries, will never be able to get the experience required to produce efficiently unless they are protected from foreign competition.

Economists have traditionally responded to this argument skeptically. If it pays to enter the industry, eventually entrants will earn profits. Thus, the firm should be willing to initially charge a price below cost to gain the necessary experience, because today's losses will be more than offset by future profits. But more recently, the infant industry argument has found more favor. Firms can operate at a loss only if they can borrow funds. If capital markets do not work well, firms may not be able to borrow even if their eventual prospects are reasonable. Such market failures are a particular danger in less-developed countries.

This may be a legitimate argument. But it points to a need not for protection but for assistance, which can take the form of loans or direct subsidies. Economists argue for direct assistance rather than protection because the assistance is trans-

e-Insights

TRADE LIBERALIZATION IN INFORMATION TECHNOLOGY AND FINANCIAL SERVICES

In recent years, there have been important trade agreements in information technology (IT) and financial services. This is a distinct change from the past, when trade agreements focused on traded goods, such as cars, steel, and textiles. But the two areas draw markedly different reactions in many developing countries: while IT liberalization has been welcome, there is extensive opposition to liberalizations in financial services. Why the difference?

Economic theory says that unilateral liberalization—opening up one's market to the cheaper goods of foreigners—is a good thing. Even if domestic producers are worse off, their losses are more than offset by the gains of consumers. Unfortunately, producers often have a greater voice in the political process, and consumers cannot unite to compensate the producers for their losses. Countries therefore often resist trade liberalization. But IT is different. Most developing countries do not have a large IT sector that would be hurt by liberalization. Instead, both producers and consumers in developing countries are purchasers of IT products, and both gain by having access to IT at lower prices.

Financial service liberalization is quite a different matter. The existing domestic banks in developing countries fear greater competition from foreign banks. The greater efficiency of foreign banks is not their only worry; depositors may feel safer putting their money in a large American or European bank than in a small domestic bank. In addition, many firms in developing countries believe that the foreign banks are more likely to lend to Coca-Cola and IBM than to small domestic firms, and there are some grounds for these concerns. The government, too, may worry that the foreign banks will be less subject to pressure from the government. Sometimes such pressure is part of corruption—members of the government lean on the bank to lend to their friends. But it can also be part of economic policy—the government leans on the bank to increase lending in an economic downturn and to contract lending when the economy is overheated. In developing countries, this "guidance" from the government may be an important tool for macroeconomic stability.

Today, as many countries liberalize their financial markets, they are asking, "How can we gain the advantages of the new competition without suffering the disadvantages?" Until they find effective ways of ensuring a flow of capital to small domestic businesses, banks in developing countries will find powerful allies in resisting financial market liberalization.

parent: everyone can see that it is a subsidy to producers. Economists criticize protection because it is a hidden tax on consumers, with the proceeds transferred to producers. The lack of transparency encourages industries to spend resources on persuading government to impose these hidden taxes that benefit themselves.

STRATEGIC TRADE THEORY

Another argument for protection is that it can give a country a strategic trade advantage over rivals by helping to reduce domestic costs. There may be economies of scale: the larger the level of production, the lower the marginal costs. Protection ensures a large domestic sales base, and therefore a low marginal cost. The instances in which **strategic trade theory** might provide a rationale for protection appear relatively rare, however. Even then, it tends to be effective only when foreign governments do not retaliate by taking similar actions.

International Cooperation

Recognizing both the temptation of shortsighted trade policies and the potential gains from trade, nations large and small have engaged since World War II in a variety of efforts to reduce trade barriers.

GATT AND THE WTO

The **General Agreement on Tariffs and Trade (GATT),** an organization established after World War II, was replaced in 1995 by the **World Trade Organization (WTO).** GATT was founded on three guiding principles: *reciprocity*—if one country lowered its tariffs, it could expect other countries in GATT to lower theirs; *nondiscrimination*—no member of GATT could offer a special trade deal that favored only one or a few other countries; and *transparency*—import quotas and other nontariff barriers to trade should be converted into tariffs to allow their effective impact to be ascertained.

The lowering of trade barriers has proceeded in a number of stages, called *rounds* (the Kennedy Round, completed in 1967; the Tokyo Round, completed in 1979; the Uruguay Round, completed in 1994, and the Doha [Qatar] Round, currently slated to be completed by the end of 2005). Collectively, the rounds have reduced tariffs on industrial goods markedly, from an average of 40 percent in 1947 to less than 5 percent today.

The Uruguay Round produced agreements to reduce agricultural subsidies and to ensure that intellectual property rights—patents and copyrights—were respected. It also created the WTO to help enforce the trade agreements. Previously, a country that believed it was suffering from an unfair trade practice could bring a case to a GATT panel that would examine the evidence. However, there was little in the way of effective enforcement of subsequent decisions. Under the WTO, a country injured by an unfair trade practice will be authorized to engage in retaliatory actions. For example,

Brazil won a major WTO case in 2004 against U.S. cotton subsidies. That decision is under appeal; if the United States loses the appeal and then fails to remove its subsidies to cotton farmers, Brazil will be able to retaliate against U.S. exports to Brazil.

The Doha Round began in 2001 and almost collapsed in 2003 when delegates from developing nations walked out in protest over the subsidies that developed nations such as the United States and members of the European Union provide to their farmers. The European Union has agreed in principle to eliminate exports subsidies on farm products; the United States has not yet made a similar commitment.

THE GROWING PROTEST AGAINST THE WTO

In December 1999, the WTO held a meeting in Seattle to launch a new round of trade negotiations. But thousands of protesters—some violent—dominated the stage. What brought on such a vehement reaction? Old-fashioned protectionist sentiment played a role, but there were other important factors.

Some WTO critics believed that the agenda in previous rounds of trade negotiations had been set by the more advanced industrial countries—to further their interests—and that the outcomes reflected their economic power. Not only had they gained the lion's share of the benefits, but they had done so at the expense of some poorer countries. The World Bank estimated that after the round of trade negotiations concluded in 1994, the poorest region in the world, sub-Saharan Africa, was actually worse off. While poorer countries were forced to cut their tariffs against goods produced in the more advanced industrial countries, the more advanced industrial countries continued to protect their agricultural sectors. While financial services had been opened up, industries that relied more heavily on unskilled workers, such as the construction and maritime industries, remained closed.

Thousands of protesters converged in Seattle to protest the WTO conference held there in December 1999.

Environmental and human rights issues were two other prominent areas of intense debate. Environmentalists and human rights advocates wanted to use trade policy to help achieve their objectives. They worried that countries with inadequate protections of the environment or of labor rights would be able to undercut American firms, whose losses would increase pressure within the United States to erode those standards here. The insistence by some on including clauses in trade agreements concerning labor and the environment was met with an equally adamant resistance by others, threatening to stall all efforts at trade liberalization. There was consensus on a few issues—for example, countries should not be allowed to export goods produced by child or prison labor. But beyond that, the debate raged on and it is likely to continue in the foreseeable future.

Case in Point

THE BANANA WAR

How could a dispute over bananas lead to unemployment among Scottish cashmere workers? The explanation lies in the spillover effect of the banana war between the United States and the European Union (EU). This dispute revolved around the claim by the United States that the EU was following discriminatory trade practices.

Beginning in 1993, the EU imposed a banana import tariff that favored producers in former European colonies in the Caribbean, Africa, and the Pacific over those in Latin America. The United States and five Latin American countries complained to the WTO. The United States claimed that EU banana import tariffs were harming the country. Since the United States does not produce bananas, one might reasonably ask how it could be harmed by the EU's policy on banana imports. While not a producer itself, the United States is home to two food distributors, Chiquita Brands and Dole, that do grow bananas in Central America.

The WTO ruled that the EU regime was in violation of GATT and ordered the EU to change its policies. The EU did, instituting a new banana import regime on January 1, 1999. However, the United States and Latin America banana producers argued that the new policy still effectively discriminated against them, and the dispute was sent to the WTO Dispute Settlement Body. The United States claimed victory in the banana war when, in April 1999, the Dispute Settlement Body accepted the results of the WTO arbitrators, agreeing that the new EU policies harmed the United States. This decision paved the way for the United States to impose sanctions against EU products. The WTO ruled that the United States could impose $191 million in sanctions against the EU, an amount determined by estimating the economic damages to the United States resulting from the EU policies.

To retaliate against Europe, the United States imposed 100 percent tariffs on a range of European products, effectively doubling their prices in the United States. The list of goods hit by the punitive tariffs included Scottish cashmere, Italian cheese, and German coffee makers. The targeted products were chosen to bring maximum political pressures on the EU. The WTO ruling allowed the United States to impose these high tariffs until the EU revised its banana policy to eliminate discrimination against Latin American producers. The EU conceded defeat, and the banana war ended.

REGIONAL TRADING BLOCS

GATT and WTO have made some progress in reducing trade barriers among all countries. But the difficulties of reaching agreements involving so many parties have made progress slow. In the meantime, many countries have formed *regional trade blocs,* agreeing with their more immediate neighbors not only to eliminate trade barriers but also to facilitate the flow of capital and labor. Perhaps the most important of these is the **European Union,** the successor to the *Common Market,* which now embraces most of Europe. The **North American Free Trade Agreement, NAFTA,** creates a free trade zone within North America—that is, an area within which goods and services trade freely, without tariffs or other import restrictions. There are also many smaller free trade zones, such as those between New Zealand and Australia, and among groups of countries in Latin America and in Central America.

While the gains from internationally coordinated reductions in trade barriers are clear, the gains from regional trading blocs are more controversial. Reducing trade barriers within a region encourages trade by members of the trading bloc. Lowering barriers among the countries involved results in **trade creation.** But it also leads to **trade diversion.** Trade is diverted away from countries that are not members of the bloc but might, in fact, have a comparative advantage in a particular commodity. Under these conditions, the global net benefits will be positive if the trade creation exceeds the trade diversion. Typically, when trade blocs are formed, tariffs against outsiders are harmonized. If the external trade barriers are harmonized at the lowest common level (rather than at the average or highest levels) at the same time that internal trade barriers are lowered, the effects of trade creation are more likely to exceed those of trade diversion.

Expanding regional trading blocs to cover investment flows raises particular anxieties, especially when the bloc includes countries with very different standards of living. During the debates over NAFTA, some argued that Mexico would suck up huge amounts of investment that would otherwise have gone to businesses in the United States. According to this view, American firms would move to Mexico to take advantage of the low-wage labor and the capital that flowed to Mexico would not be available for investment in the United States.

Such arguments failed to take into account that capital markets were already global. Capital flows to good investment opportunities wherever they are. Good opportunities to invest in the United States will attract capital, regardless of how much Americans invest in Mexico. Investment barriers impede this flow of capital to its most productive use, thereby lowering world economic efficiency.

Often trade debates are based on a "zero-sum" view of the world, the belief that when one country (Mexico) gains, another (the United States) must lose. For example, many people argue that when a country imports, it loses jobs: the gains to foreign workers from their exports are at the expense of domestic firms to which those jobs somehow belonged. The debate over "outsourcing"—the move by U.S. firms to import goods and services that these same firms formerly produced in the United States—is of this sort. Earlier in this chapter we learned what was wrong with this argument. The theory of comparative advantage says that when countries specialize in what they produce best, *both* countries are better off. Workers enjoy higher

Internet Connection
THE WORLD TRADE ORGANIZATION

The World Trade Organization (WTO) is the global organization that deals with the rules of trade between nations. The WTO's Web site, www.wto.org, contains material for a range of users, from the general public to students, academics, and trade specialists. It includes introductions to WTO activities and a large database of official documents. In recent years, the WTO has become a focus of protest by those opposed to globalization and free trade. One group that has actively campaigned against the WTO is Global Trade Watch, whose Web site (www.citizen.org/trade/) provides information on the views of those fighting what they identify as the WTO's model of globalization.

wages when they move into sectors where their productivity is highest, and consumers benefit from the lower prices. So too with investment. When investment flows to where its return is highest, world output (income) is increased.

But just as not everyone necessarily gains from trade according to comparative advantage, so too not everyone will necessarily gain from the free flow of capital. There will be some investment diversion from other countries to Mexico, as Mexico becomes more attractive to investors throughout the world because of its improved access to the huge American market. Most economists believe that the net effect on investment in the United States will be negligible, and could even be positive. Industries within the United States that see their opportunities expand by selling more to Mexico will increase their investment, more than offsetting the reduced investment from firms that decline in the face of competition from Mexican imports.

In fact, investment flows augment the gains from trade that would occur in their absence because there are important trade-investment links. American companies producing abroad tend to use more parts from America, just as French companies producing abroad tend to use more French parts. Thus, flows of investment often serve as a precursor to exports.

Wrap-Up
AREAS OF INTERNATIONAL COOPERATION

Multilateral trade agreements—WTO
    Based on principles of reciprocity, nondiscrimination, and transparency

Regional trade agreements—NAFTA, European Union
    Risk of trade diversion rather than trade creation
    May be better able to address complicated issues, such as those involving investment

Review and Practice

SUMMARY

1. The benefits of economic interdependence apply to individuals and firms within a country as well as to countries within the world. No individual and no country is self-sufficient.
2. The principle of comparative advantage asserts that countries should export the goods in which their production costs are relatively low.
3. Specialization tends to increase productivity for three reasons: specializing eliminates the time it takes a worker to switch from one production task to another, workers who repeat a task become more skilled at it, and specialization creates a fertile environment for invention.
4. A country's comparative advantage can arise from natural endowments, acquired endowments, superior knowledge, specialization, or interactions of these factors.
5. There is a basic difference between trade among individuals and trade among countries: trade among countries may actually leave some individuals within the country worse off. Though free trade enhances national income, fears about job loss and wage reductions among low-skilled workers have led to demands for protection.
6. Countries protect themselves in a variety of ways besides imposing tariffs. The most important nontariff barriers are quotas, voluntary export restraints, and regulatory barriers. Quotas and voluntary export restraints are now banned by international agreement.
7. While all countries benefit from free trade, some groups within a country may be harmed. In the United States, unskilled workers and those in industries where, without trade, there is limited competition may see their wages fall. Some workers may lose their jobs and may require assistance to find new ones.
8. Laws nominally intended to ensure fair trade—such as antidumping laws and countervailing duties—often are used as protectionist measures.
9. Beggar-thy-neighbor policies, which attempt to protect jobs by limiting imports, tend to be counterproductive.
10. The WTO, which replaced GATT, provides a framework within which trade barriers can be reduced. It is based on reciprocity, nondiscrimination, and transparency.

KEY TERMS

imports
exports
bilateral trade
multilateral trade
absolute advantage
comparative advantage
protectionism
free trade
commercial policies
tariffs
quotas
quota rents
dumping
countervailing duties
beggar-thy-neighbor policies
infant industry argument
strategic trade theory
General Agreement on Tariffs and Trade (GATT)
World Trade Organization (WTO)
European Union
North American Free Trade Agreement (NAFTA)
trade creation
trade diversion

REVIEW QUESTIONS

1. Why are all voluntary trades mutually beneficial?
2. Does a country with an absolute advantage in a product necessarily have a comparative advantage in that product? Can a country with an absolute disadvantage in a product have a comparative advantage in that product? Explain.
3. Why does specialization tend to increase productivity?
4. "A country's comparative advantage is dictated by its natural endowments." Discuss.
5. What are the various ways in which countries seek to protect their industries against foreign imports?
6. How do tariffs and quotas differ?
7. Why are consumers worse off as a result of the imposition of a tariff?
8. What are nontariff barriers to international trade?

9. How is it possible that while there are gains to free trade, some groups are harmed? Which are the groups in the United States that are most adversely affected?
10. What are beggar-thy-neighbor policies? What are their consequences?
11. What is meant by trade diversion versus trade creation?

PROBLEMS

1. David Ricardo illustrated the principle of comparative advantage in terms of the trade between England and Portugal in wine (port) and wool. Suppose in England it takes 120 laborers to produce a certainty quantity of wine, while in Portugal it takes only 80 laborers to produce the same quantity. Similarly, in England it takes 100 laborers to produce a certain quantity of wool, while in Portugal it takes only 90. Draw the opportunity set for each country, assuming each has 72,000 laborers. Assume each country commits half its labor to each product in the absence of trade, and designate that point in your graph. Now describe a new production plan, with trade, that can benefit both countries.
2. If you continue with the example of Problem 1, which country has an absolute advantage in wine? in wool? Which country has a comparative advantage in wine? in wool?
3. For many years, an international agreement called the Multifiber Agreement limited the amount of textiles that the developed economies of North America and Europe could buy from poor countries in Latin America and Asia. Textiles can be produced by relatively unskilled labor with a reasonably small amount of capital. Who benefited from the protectionism of the Multifiber Agreement? Who suffered? The Multifiber Agreement expired on January 1, 2005. Who should benefit from its end? Who will suffer?
4. Both the European Union and the United States produce cars and television shows. Assume the labor costs (in worker hours) required for the production of cars and programs is as follows:

LABOR COSTS OF PRODUCING CARS AND TV SHOWS (WORKER HOURS):

	European Union	United States
Labor required to make a car	100	80
Labor required to to produce a TV show	600	400

Assume each region has 240,000 worker hours to divide between producing cars and television shows. Initially, assume workers are divided equally between producing cars and television shows.

(a) What are the initial levels of production of cars and TV shows in each region? What is total production in the two regions?
(b) Draw the production possibilities curves for the two regions.
(c) Which region has an absolute advantage in producing cars? Which region has an absolute advantage in producing television shows?
(d) Which region has a comparative advantage in producing cars? Which region has a comparative advantage in producing television shows?
(e) Starting with the initial levels of production, demonstrate how comparative advantage can be exploited to raise joint production of cars by 10 while leaving television show output unchanged.

5. In 2002, President George W. Bush imposed tariffs on foreign-produced steel. Who gained from this policy? Who lost? (In 2003, the WTO ruled that the tariffs were illegal.)
6. Many Americans have objected to the importation of textiles and garments from poor countries because the conditions of production in those countries is much worse than it is for most American workers. If these imports from poor countries are reduced, who benefits? Who loses?
7. If Mexican workers receive a third of the wages that U.S. workers do, why don't all American firms move down to Mexico?
8. If Mexico becomes a more attractive place to invest, is the United States helped or hurt?

Learning Goals

In this chapter, you will learn

1. How technological change and imperfect competition are linked
2. About the role of patents in promoting innovation
3. Why basic research is a public good
4. How governments promote technological progress

Chapter 20

TECHNOLOGICAL CHANGE

For much of the twentieth century, the United States has led the world in discovering and applying new technologies. Alexander Graham Bell and the telephone, the Wright brothers and the airplane, Thomas Edison and a host of electrical devices, for example, are all familiar early success stories. This tradition of innovation and invention continued as Americans came up with products such as the transistor and the laser. U.S. companies such as IBM, Eastman Kodak, and Xerox grew to become household names. More recently, Intel, Microsoft, Google, and Genentech have experienced rapid growth and financial success based on their innovations.

The great strength of the market economy has been its ability to increase productivity, raise living standards, and innovate. Yet the basic competitive model on which we focused in Part Two simply *assumed* the state of technology as given. In fact, the huge changes in living standards that modern economies have experienced over the past two hundred years and the truly amazing differences between the economy in 1900 and the economy in 2000 are in large part due to technological change. We are not manufacturing more of the same goods as the economy in 1900. We are making goods that the people of 1900 never dreamed of. Instead of producing more horse-drawn carriages, we produce cars and airplanes. Instead of producing more horseshoes, we produce tires and jogging shoes. Key to the whole process of economic growth, then, is technological progress—thinking up new ways to do not just old things but also entirely new things. And for this reason, *ideas* are central to explaining economic growth. Indeed, economists estimate that as much as two-thirds of all increases in productivity prior to 1973 were attributable to technological progress.

We have become so accustomed to the current level of technological change that it is hard to believe how different the expectations of reputable economists were in the early 1800s. Real wages of workers were little higher than they had been more than four hundred years earlier, when they had increased after the deaths of a large part of the population of Europe in the bubonic plague created a scarcity of labor. After half a millennium of slow progress at best, Thomas Malthus, one of the greatest economists of that time, saw population expanding more rapidly than the capacity of the economy to support it. His prediction of declining living standards earned economics the nickname of "the dismal science." Today, many continue to predict that the world economy will be unable to grow faster than the population and that living standards must inevitably decline. Such forecasts have been proved wrong over and over again by technological advances.

If we are to understand what determines the pace of innovation, we must go beyond the basic competitive model by recognizing two important factors. First, industries in which technological change is important are almost always imperfectly competitive. Second, the basic competitive model of Part Two assumed that individuals and firms receive all the benefits and pay all the costs of their actions, yet the basic research that leads to technological change can produce important *positive externalities.*

Alexander Graham Bell, Henry Ford, the Wright brothers, and others were all rewarded for their inventions, some richly so. But these inventors reaped but a fraction of what society gained. Similarly, Tim Berners-Lee, Robert Cailliau, and their colleagues at the European particle physics center (CERN) in Geneva, Switzerland, invented the World Wide Web and hypertext markup language, or HTML, in 1990, and since then programmers from around the world have been able to use and benefit from their ideas.[1] The creation of these new products conferred benefits well beyond what consumers had to pay for them.

Links Between Technological Change and Imperfect Competition

In modern industrialized economies, competition often takes the form of trying to develop both new products and new ways of making existing products. In industries in which technological change is important, such as the computer and drug industries, firms devote considerable resources to R & D—research (discovering new ideas, products, and processes) and development (perfecting, for instance, a new product to the point at which it can be brought to the market).

Technological change and imperfect competition are inevitably linked for four major reasons. First, to make R & D expenditures pay, and therefore stimulate innovation, inventions are protected from competition by patents (which are specifically designed for that purpose). Second, industries in which technological change is important typically have high fixed costs—costs that do not change as output increases—and thus their average costs decrease over a wide range of output, another characteristic that limits competition. Third, industries characterized by rapid technological change are also industries in which the benefits of increasing experience in a new production technique can lead to rapidly decreasing costs. Finally, because

---

[1] For an interesting history of the Internet, see Janet Abbate's *Inventing the Internet* (Cambridge: MIT Press, 1999).

e-Insight

THE NEW ECONOMY AND INNOVATION

The new economy sometimes has been characterized as an innovation in the process of innovation. Just as the Industrial Revolution represented a marked change in the way that goods are produced, the new economy has strikingly changed how ideas are produced and disseminated.

A century ago, inventors like Edison, Westinghouse, and the Wright brothers, working alone or with a few assistants, created innovations that transformed the economy, but in the past hundred years the innovation process has been centered around large corporations, such as DuPont and AT&T, with vast laboratories and research budgets in the hundreds of millions of dollars. In the new economy, small firms once again seem to be playing a central role. Evidently, important innovations can occur on a far smaller scale—and then when they are successful, production can be quickly ramped up.

One of the reasons for this speed—and one of the reasons why the Internet has increased productivity—is that these innovations help markets work better. New firms can obtain from others much of what they previously had to provide for themselves, including a sizable portion of their accounting and personnel services. And, at least in some cases, the Internet has significantly lowered the costs of marketing.

Because of the new technologies, and especially the Internet, new ideas can be disseminated far more quickly today. It used to take years, sometimes decades, for discoveries to spread from one part of the economy to another.

The Internet has both increased productivity and enabled new ideas to spread more quickly.

banks are generally unwilling to lend funds to finance R & D, raising capital is difficult for new and small firms. All these factors make entry difficult, and reduce competition of the sort assumed by the basic competitive model.

PATENTS AND THE PRODUCTION OF IDEAS

Ideas appear to be important for technological change, but how are ideas produced? Can we use some of the basic concepts of economics to understand the process?

Most advances result from the deliberate allocation of resources to R & D. The typical large corporation may spend as much as 3 percent of its revenue on research. Though many discoveries have occurred almost by accident (such as Alexander Fleming's discovery of penicillin), in the modern economy these are more the exception than the rule. In order for firms and individuals to have an incentive to allocate their valuable time and resources to research, they must reap a return. They can profit from their work in one of two ways—either by using it themselves to make or sell a product or by licensing the right to use it to others. In either case, however, the inventor has to prevent others from freely using the idea. Otherwise, the inventing firm would have a hard time getting a return, because competition would drive the price down to the marginal cost of producing the product. And the expense of discovery is itself a fixed cost; once it is made and developed, it typically lowers the marginal cost of production. In short, for the inventor to obtain a return, she must be able to exclude users who do not pay for her invention. But some ideas are not very excludable. After Henry Ford had devised the modern assembly line, he might have kept it secret for a while by barring visitors to his factory, but certainly anyone who saw one could set up the same process in another factory. Most software companies keep their source code secret in order to exclude users who have not paid a licensing fee. To increase the incentive to invent, inventors must be given property rights to their work. If property rights are insecure—if a firm planning on undertaking research is

Thinking Like an Economist
INTELLECTUAL PROPERTY RIGHTS AND DISTRIBUTION

As the importance of innovation in the economy has grown, so too has the importance of intellectual property rights. Hence, it was no surprise that the United States pushed for stronger intellectual property protection in the so-called Uruguay Round of the World Trade Organization's trade negotiations, completed in 1994. Many developing countries objected to this initiative.

The key to understanding this dispute lies in the nature of intellectual property rights. How these rights are defined—for instance, the length of the patent—has significant distributional effects. Most inventions are produced in the developed world; stronger intellectual property rights increase the incomes of the patent holders but force consumers in the developing world to pay higher prices. In the past, businesses outside the more advanced countries often freely pirated books, copied CDs, and produced goods such as drugs that were covered by patents. Not surprisingly, many in these developing countries objected to stronger intellectual property rights protections. Two issues in particular grabbed popular attention.

The first concerned the patenting of drugs derived from plants and animals in the developing world. While the drug companies insisted that they should be rewarded for creating useful medicines, those in the developing countries maintained that the medicinal properties of the matter used were already well known and that the companies merely verified them. Moreover, they argued that local people deserved greater returns for preserving the biodiversity on which such drugs depend.

The second issue also concerned drugs. Previously, companies in countries like South Africa had manufactured knockoff drugs, selling them for a fraction of the prices charged by the drug companies from the advanced industrial countries. Under the Uruguay Round agreement, people in developing countries would have to pay whatever the drug companies in the developed countries decided. In the case of life-preserving AIDS drugs, this policy would condemn thousands to a premature death, as few could afford the prices the drug companies insisted on charging. At first, the U.S. government backed the American firms, threatening trade retaliation if South Africa refused to comply. But in the end, the international outrage was so great that the American government and the drug companies caved in and agreed to provide the drugs at cost.

uncertain about whether it will be allowed to capture the benefits of any new process, machine, or article of manufacture that it produces—then fewer resources will be invested in research and the production of these innovations.

Society has another consideration, however. Producing a new idea may be very costly, but it needs to be produced only once. Your laptop embodies thousands of new ideas, but these ideas do not have to be reproduced each time a new laptop is manufactured. The screen, memory chips, and case did have to be produced for each laptop; they are examples of **rivalrous goods**—the memory chips in your laptop cannot be in your roommate's laptop. But the same is not true of the machine's design. Goods whose consumption or use by one person does not exclude consumption by another are **nonrivalrous goods**—a concept we introduced in Chapter 11. If both you and your roommate are taking economics, both of you can use an idea like the law of supply and demand. If your roommate does her homework first, the idea is still available to you when you get around to studying. The marginal cost of *using* such a nonrivalrous good is zero: it costs nothing to use the idea one more time. So from society's perspective, the idea should be freely available to anyone who wants to use it.

Recall that in Chapter 11, a *pure public good* was defined as always available to others and as having a marginal cost of zero when provided to an additional person (it is nonrivalrous). Most types of knowledge come close to satisfying this definition, though it is rarely entirely *impossible* to exclude consumption by others. Thus, we can think of knowledge or an idea as a public good. And like other public goods, it is accompanied by a tension between providing incentives for its production, on the one hand, and ensuring it is widely used, on the other.

Societies address this tension through **patents.** The U.S. Constitution empowers Congress to grant "for limited Times to Authors and Inventors the exclusive Right to their respective Writings and Discoveries." Economists refer to this creative output as **intellectual property.** The limited time for most inventions is currently twenty years. During this period, other producers are precluded from making or using the invention in a product of their own, without the permission of the patent holder. A patent holder may allow others to use its patent (typically for a fee, called a **royalty**) or to sell its product.

THE TRADE-OFF BETWEEN SHORT-TERM EFFICIENCY AND INNOVATION

The patent system grants the inventor a temporary monopoly, enabling her to appropriate some part of the returns on her inventive activity. In Chapter 12, we saw that compared to a firm in a competitive market, a monopoly produces a lower level of output that sells at a higher price. In Chapter 10, we saw that competitive markets, in which price is equal to marginal cost, ensure economic efficiency. In our early analysis, we assumed the state of technology as given. We refer to this kind of economic efficiency as **static efficiency.**

But the overall efficiency of the economy requires harmonizing these short-term concerns with the long-term objectives of stimulating research and innovation. Firms will innovate only if they can reap a return on their investment, and that in

Figure 20.1
ECONOMIC EFFECT OF PATENTS

Here, an innovation has reduced the marginal cost of production from c_0 to c_1. Before the innovation, the equilibrium price is p_0, which equals c_0. However, an innovator with a patent will drop the price to p_1, just below p_0, and sell the quantity Q_1. Total profits are the shaded area $ABCD$. When the patent expires, competitors reenter the market; price falls to p_2, which equals c_1; and profits drop to zero.

turn requires that they possess some degree of monopoly power. An economy in which short- and long-term concerns are appropriately balanced is said to have the property of **dynamic efficiency.**

A key provision of the patent law that affects how static efficiency is weighed against the incentives for innovation necessary for dynamic efficiency is the *life of the patent*. If the life of a patent is short, then firms can appropriate the returns from their innovation only briefly. They thus have less incentive to innovate than if the patent protection (and monopoly) lasted longer. If the life of a patent is long, then they enjoy large incentives to innovate but the benefits of the innovation are reduced. Consumers, in particular, must wait a long time before prices fall. The twenty-year patent period is intended to strike a balance between benefits to consumers and return to investments in R & D.

An Example: The Sweet Melon Company Figure 20.1 illustrates the effect of a patent owned by the Sweet Melon Company on a new, cheaper process for producing frozen watermelon juice. To keep things simple, the marginal cost of production is constant in this example. Before the innovation, all producers face the same marginal cost of c_0. Sweet Melon's innovation reduces the marginal costs of production to c_1. Imagine that this industry is perfectly competitive before the innovation, so that price equals marginal cost, c_0. But now Sweet Melon is able to undercut its rivals. With patent protection, the firm sells the good for slightly less than p_0. Its rivals drop out of the market because at the new, lower price, they cannot break even. Sweet Melon now has the whole market. The company sells the quantity Q_1 at the price p_1, making a profit of AB on each sale. Total profits are shaded area $ABCD$ in the figure. The innovation pays off if the profits received exceed the cost of the research. (These profits may be thought of as "rents" associated with the firm's superior technology.)

When the patent expires, other firms using the less-expensive technology enter the industry. Competition forces the price down to the now lower marginal costs, c_1, and output expands to Q_2. The new equilibrium is at E. Consumers are clearly better off. Static economic efficiency is enhanced, because price is now equal to marginal cost. But Sweet Melon reaps no further return from its expenditures on R & D.

If no patent were available, competitors would immediately copy the new juice-making process, and the price would drop to c_1 as soon as the innovation became available. Sweet Melon would receive absolutely no returns. (In practice, of course, imitation takes time, during which the company would be able to obtain *some* returns from the innovation.) If the patent were made permanent, consumers would enjoy only a small benefit from the innovation, since other companies could not compete. Output would remain at Q_1, slightly greater than the original output, and the price would remain high.

Breadth of Patent Protection How broad a patent's coverage should be is as important as its duration. If an inventor comes up with a product quite similar to, but in some way distinct from, one that has already been patented, can this inventor also be granted a patent? Or does the original patent cover "minor" variants? This issue became critical in the early days of the American automobile industry.

Soon after Henry Ford's Model T had burst into the American marketplace—its sales rocketed from 58,000 in 1909 to 730,000 in 1916—Ford was taken to court for infringing upon the patent of George Baldwin Selden, who argued that his patent covered all self-propelled, gasoline-powered vehicles. Selden tried to force Ford and other pioneers of the automobile industry to pay royalties to him, but Ford successfully challenged the patent claim. Recently controversies have concerned patents in genetic engineering and superconductivity. Does a firm that decodes a fraction of a gene and establishes a use for that information, for example, get a patent? If so, does the patent cover the fraction in question or the whole gene?

The original innovators have every incentive to claim broad patent coverage, encompassing their own product and those that are in any way related. Later entrants argue for narrow coverage, so that they will be allowed to produce variants and applications without paying royalties. As usual in economics, there is a trade-off. Broad coverage ensures that the first inventor reaps more of the returns on her innovation. But excessively broad coverage inhibits follow-on innovation, as others see their returns to further developing the idea squeezed by the royalties they must pay to the original inventor.

Trade Secrets If patents protect the profits of innovation, why do many firms not bother to seek patent protection for their new products and processes? A major factor in this decision is the patent process itself, which requires applicants to disclose the details of the new product or process—information that may be extremely helpful to a firm's rivals in furthering their own R & D programs.

To prevent such disclosure, companies sometimes prefer to keep their own innovations a **trade secret.** A trade secret is simply an innovation or production process that a firm does not disclose to others. The secret formula for Coca-Cola, for example, is not protected by a patent. Trade secrets play an important role in metallurgy; new alloys usually are not patented. But trade secrets have one major disadvantage compared with patents. If a rival firm *independently* discovers the same new process—for making an alloy, say—it can use the process without paying royalties, even though it was second on the scene.

Some of the returns to an invention come simply from being first in the market. Typically, the firm that first introduces a new product has a decided advantage over rivals, as it builds up customer loyalty and a reputation. Latecomers often have a hard time breaking in, even if there is no *patent* or trade secret protection.

Limitations to Patents There are other limitations to the use of patents. Many of the most important ideas are not *patentable*—for instance, the basic mathematics behind the inner workings of computers, discovered by Alan Turing. Turing received no return on his innovation, which was of immense value. The *ideas* that led to the transistor or to the laser—the understandings of the underlying physics—similarly were not patentable.

What is considered patentable has changed over time. A recent new category of patents involves business applications. Thus, the *idea* of a mutual fund with certain distinctive characteristics, or a special type of auction provided by an Internet firm, might today be patentable. Some people believe that these new patents have provided much of the spur for the new economy. But many of these patents are being challenged on the grounds that they are not sufficiently *novel* and nonobvious to deserve protection.

Case in Point

ELI WHITNEY AND THE COTTON GIN

Obtaining a patent does not necessarily guarantee the inventor a return on the discovery. Others may "infringe" on the patent—that is, use the idea without paying for it—forcing the inventor to go to court for redress. The story of Eli Whitney and the cotton gin provides a famous example.

Late in the eighteenth century, the textile mills of England and the northern American states were up and humming, but they seemed always to be short of cotton. The kind of cotton grown in the southern United States could have filled the need, but separating the seeds from the cotton was labor-intensive and hence costly. Eli Whitney invented the cotton gin to perform that task inexpensively, then did what an inventor is supposed to do. He applied for a patent and received one in 1794. After finding a partner to put up the money, he started a business to make machines that would clean the seeds out of cotton. The cotton gin turned out to be a wonder, bringing prosperity to the American South. But Whitney received little of the benefit.

The problem was that Whitney's machine was both very effective and very simple. Cotton planters found it easy to copy the cotton gin, and they were careful to make a few minor changes in their versions. When Whitney sued for patent infringement, courts in cotton-growing states tended to find that his patent had not been infringed. Eventually, the states of South Carolina, North Carolina, Tennessee, and Georgia agreed to pay a lump sum to Whitney to purchase the rights to his invention, though the amount paid was barely enough to enable Whitney and his partner to recoup their expenses.

Whitney continued his lifelong career as an inventor, but he never bothered to patent an invention again. As he once wrote: "An invention can be so valuable as to be worthless to the inventor." Whitney's experience was extreme. Today patent laws provide essential protection for scientific firms engaged in producing new and better products. They may choose to share their new technology by selling others the use of their patents in return for royalties, which represent a substantial fraction of the revenues of some firms.

Whitney's cotton gin

R & D AS A FIXED COST

Patents and trade secrets are not the only reasons why industries in which technological change is important are generally not perfectly competitive. A second explanation is that R & D expenditures are fixed costs. That is, the cost of inventing something does not change with the frequency of its use in production.[2] The size of fixed costs helps determine how competitive an industry is. The larger the fixed costs relative to the size of the market, the greater the likelihood it will have few firms and limited competition.

---

[2] R & D expenditures can themselves be varied. Differences in the expenditure level will affect when new products will be brought to market and whether a firm will beat its rivals in the competition for new products.

Because expenditures on R & D are fixed costs, industries with large R & D expenditures face declining average cost curves up to relatively high levels of output. We saw in Chapter 6 that firms typically have U-shaped average cost curves. The presence of fixed costs means that average costs initially decline as firms produce more; but for all the reasons discussed in Chapter 6, there is some level of output beyond which average costs increase. When there are large fixed costs, large firms will have lower average costs than small firms and enjoy a competitive advantage (Figure 20.2). Industries with large fixed costs thus tend to have relatively few firms and limited competition. It is not surprising, therefore, that the chemical industry—in which R & D is tremendously important—is highly concentrated.

Increased size also provides firms with greater incentives to undertake research. Suppose a small firm produces 1 million pens a year. If it discovers a better production technology that reduces its costs by $1 per pen, it saves $1 million a year. A large firm that makes the same discovery and produces 10 million pens a year will save $10 million a year. Thus, large firms have more incentive to engage in R & D, and as they do, they grow more than their smaller rivals.

But while a large firm's R & D department may help the firm win a competitive advantage, it may also create managerial problems. Bright innovators can feel stifled in the bureaucratic environment of a large corporation, and they may also feel that they are inadequately compensated for their research efforts. In the computer industry, for example, many capable people have left the larger firms to start up new companies of their own.

Thus, size has both advantages and disadvantages when it comes to innovation. Important inventions and innovations—including nylon, transistors, and the laser—have been produced by major corporations; on the other hand, small enterprises and individual inventors have produced Apple computers, Polaroid cameras, and Kodak film, all of which sparked the growth of major corporations. One objective of antitrust policies is to maintain an economic environment in which small, innovative firms can compete effectively against established giants.

Figure 20.2

COSTS OF RESEARCH AND DEVELOPMENT

R & D costs are fixed costs—they do not vary with the scale of production. In industries that are R & D intensive, average costs will be declining over a wide range of outputs. Firms with low levels of output (Q_1) have higher average costs than those with higher output (Q_2).

LEARNING BY DOING

Some increases in productivity occur not as a result of explicit expenditures on R & D but as a by-product of actual production. As firms gain experience in manufacture, their costs fall. This kind of technological change is called **learning by doing.** The systematic relationship between cumulative production experience and costs—often called the **learning curve**—was first noticed in the aircraft industry; as more planes of a given type were produced, companies found that their costs of production fell dramatically. Such a learning curve is said to be *steep*.

This is the third reason why technological change and imperfect competition go together: the marginal cost falls as the scale of production (and the experience accumulated) increases. The first firm to enter an industry therefore has an advantage over other firms. Even if some of what the first company has learned spills over into other firms, not all of it does. Because of the knowledge the first firm has gained, its costs will be below those of potential rivals, and thus it can always undercut them. Since potential entrants know of this advantage, they are reluctant to enter industries in which learning by doing has a significant impact on costs. By the same token, companies realize that if they can find a product that provides significant benefits from learning by doing, the profits they earn will be relatively secure. Hence, just as firms race to be the first to obtain a patent, so too they race to be the first to enter a product market in which there is a steep learning curve. This behavior is commonly displayed in the computer chip industry.

When learning by doing is important, firms will produce beyond the point at which marginal revenue equals *current* marginal costs, because producing more today has an extra benefit. It reduces future costs of production. How much extra a firm produces depends on the rapidity with which experience pays off.

ACCESS TO CAPITAL MARKETS

Banks are generally unwilling to lend funds to finance R & D expenditures, because the ventures are often very risky and their risks cannot be insured. When a bank makes a loan for a building, the bank winds up with the building if the borrower defaults. If the bank lends for R & D and the research project fails, or a rival beats the firm to the patent office, the bank may wind up with nothing. Banks also often have a hard time judging the prospects of an R & D endeavor—inventors are always optimistic about their ideas. In addition, the inventor is often reluctant to disclose all the information about his idea, either to banks or to potential investors, fearful that someone will steal his idea and beat him either to the market or to the patent office.

Established firms in industries with limited competition and growing demand have little difficulty financing their research expenditures—they can pay for R & D out of their profits. For this reason, most R & D occurs in such firms. In contrast, raising capital *is* a problem for new and small firms, and also for firms in industries in which intense competition limits the profits that any one company can earn. Thus, a firm's dominant position in an industry may be self-perpetuating. Its greater output gives it more to gain from innovations that reduce the cost of production. And its greater profits give it more resources to expend on R & D.

Today much of the R & D in new and small companies is financed by venture capital firms. These firms raise capital, mainly from pension funds, insurance companies, and wealthy individuals, and then invest it in the most promising R & D ventures. Venture capital firms often demand, as compensation for their risk taking, a significant share of the new enterprise, and they usually keep close tabs on how their money is spent.

SCHUMPETERIAN COMPETITION

Although competition in markets in which innovation is important may not live up to the ideal of perfect competition discussed in Chapter 2, it still can be intense. Competition focuses on producing new products as much as on selling old products at lower prices. This kind of competition is often referred to as *Schumpeterian competition,* after a great economist of the early twentieth century, Joseph Schumpeter. Schumpeter began his career in Austria (serving from spring to October 1919 as minister of finance to the emperor of the Austro-Hungarian Empire), and ended it as a distinguished professor of economics at Harvard. His vision of the economy was markedly different from that of the competitive equilibrium model. That model focuses on equilibrium, a changeless condition. He questioned the very concept of equilibrium: to him the economy was always in flux, and the economist's role was to understand the forces driving its changes.

Schumpeter argued that the economy was characterized by a process of creative destruction. An innovator could, through a new product or lower costs of production, establish a dominant position in a market. But eventually, that dominant position would be destroyed, as another new product or process was invented.

He worried that the giant corporations he saw being formed during his lifetime would stifle innovation and end this process of creative destruction. His fears, so far, have been unfounded; indeed, many of the largest firms, like IBM, have not been able to manage the innovative process in a way that keeps up with upstart rivals.

Modern-day Schumpeterians often turn to biology to help them understand the process of change, describing changes as *evolutionary.* They see a slow process of change, with many random elements; firms that are the fittest—that, by luck or skill, manage to discover new products or new ways of doing business that are better, in a particular environment, than their rivals—survive, and their practices spread to other firms.

As respect for and understanding of the importance of innovation have grown, so too have the number of economists who think of themselves as Schumpeterians.

Wrap-Up

COMPETITION AND TECHNOLOGICAL CHANGE

HOW COMPETITION AFFECTS TECHNOLOGICAL CHANGE

Competition spurs R & D:	Competition impedes R & D:
A new innovation enables firms to enjoy profits (profits are driven to zero in standard markets).	Competitors may imitate, thus eroding returns from innovation.
Unless firms innovate, they will not survive.	Competition erodes the profits required to finance R & D.

HOW TECHNOLOGICAL CHANGE AFFECTS COMPETITION

R & D spurs competition:	R & D impedes competition:
R & D provides an alternative to prices as a way for firms to compete; it is one of the most important arenas for competition in modern economies.	Patents give a single firm a protected position for a number of years.
	The fixed costs of R & D give large firms an advantage; thus industries in which R & D is important may have few firms.
	Learning by doing gives a decided advantage to the first entrant into a market.
	Limited access to capital markets for financing R & D is a disadvantage to new and small firms.

Basic Research as a Public Good

R & D expenditures on inventions or innovations almost always give rise to externalities. Externalities arise, as we first noted in Chapter 11, whenever one individual's or firm's action produces costs or benefits to others. The total benefits produced by an R & D expenditure are referred to as its *social benefit*. Even when they have patents, inventors appropriate only a fraction of the social benefit of an invention. A firm that discovers a cheaper way of producing is likely to lower its price during the life of the patent to steal customers away from its rivals, a move that benefits consumers. After the patent expires, consumers benefit even more as rivals beat the price down further. And the benefits of an invention developed by researchers in one industry spill over to others. The transistor, which revolutionized electronics, was invented at AT&T's Bell Laboratories. AT&T reaped the benefits from its direct application to telephone equipment. But the benefits in better radios, television sets, and other products accrued to other firms and many more consumers.

From society's viewpoint, a particularly valuable kind of R & D is **basic research**—the kind of fundamental inquiry that produces a wide range of applications. Basic research in physics, for example, led to the ideas behind so many of the things we take for granted today—the laser, the transistor, atomic energy. The private returns to firms from any basic research they might undertake—which would dictate the amount of R & D spent on basic research in the absence of government intervention—are negligible in comparison with its social benefits. Indeed, the externalities flowing from basic research are so extreme that it can be considered a public good.

Recall the two defining properties of public goods. First, it is difficult to exclude anyone from their benefits. Basic research involves the discovery of underlying scientific principles or facts of nature. Such facts—for example, superconductivity, or even the existence of certain materials that exhibit superconductivity at temperatures considerably above absolute zero—cannot be patented.

Second, the marginal cost of an additional individual enjoying a public good is zero (i.e., consumption is nonrivalrous). Informing an additional person of a basic discovery does not detract from the knowledge that the original discoverer has, though doing so may reduce the potential profits she might earn from it. Indeed, sharing the fruits of basic research as soon as they are available can yield enormous benefits—as other researchers use this knowledge to seek further innovations.

As is true of all public goods, private markets yield an undersupply of basic research. Accordingly, the government supports basic research through the National Science Foundation, the National Institutes of Health, and other organizations. Some of the expenditures of the Department of Defense on R & D also go into basic research. Still, economists are voicing increasing concern that expenditures on basic research are inadequate. Support by the federal government for R & D, outside of defense, has fallen, as a percentage of the nation's output, over the past thirty years, and more than half of government R & D expenditures remain defense related. This emphasis explains why, while the United States devotes about the same proportion of its economy to R & D as do Japan and Germany (as shown in Figure 20.3), less of the total is spent in developing new products and processes to make American industry more competitive. And more is spent in developing better and more effective weapons.

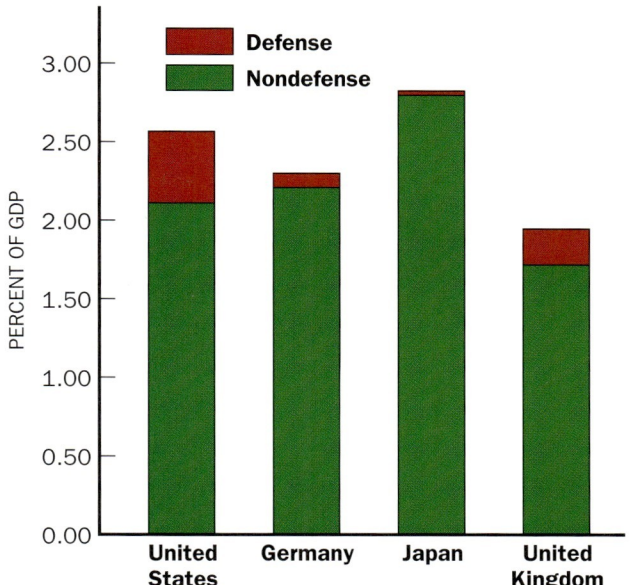

Figure 20.3

COMPARISON OF R & D EXPENDITURES ACROSS COUNTRIES

Total U.S. expenditures, as a percentage of the nation's output, are similar to those of other major industrialized countries. The difference lies in how these expenditures are allocated: U.S. expenditures are concentrated more heavily in defense than those of Germany or Japan.

SOURCE: National Science Foundation, *Science and Engineering Indicators* (2000).

Government Promotion of Technological Progress

Government's efforts to stimulate innovative activity enjoys widespread support, as long as that encouragement takes the form of protecting intellectual property rights and supporting basic R & D. But its other methods of promoting R & D have generated more criticism.

SUBSIDIES

One way in which government has sought to encourage new technologies is through subsidies. Critics of this approach argue that governments have a poor track record in choosing what to subsidize. As evidence, they note that the Concorde, the supersonic airplane developed with the support of the French and British governments that flew commercially from 1976 to 2003, was never able to pay for itself. Closer to home, the U.S. government has spent billions of dollars in an unsuccessful attempt to develop synthetic fuels. Broad-based subsidies, such as R & D tax credits, do not depend on government selection of particular projects, but their relatively high cost to the government makes them controversial. Critics claim that little additional research is generated per dollar of tax revenue lost.

In response, supporters of more active involvement of government in R & D claim that applied research has large positive externalities, implying that the private sector underinvests in it. Policies that support particular sectors of the economy are called **industrial policies** (a term applied to all sectors, including agriculture). They admit that government has not always picked winners. But advocates note that R & D is by its very nature risky. Moreover, they claim that government's successes have in fact been impressive. They point, for example, to the more than 1,000 percent increase in the productivity of agriculture over the past century. This improvement has resulted not only from research undertaken at state agricultural colleges (which the federal government has helped for more than a century) but also from government-supported diffusion of knowledge through agricultural extension services.

International Complications Subsidies have, however, raised the specter of unfair competition in the international arena. Countries facing competition from foreign firms that receive government subsidies often impose countervailing duties—that is, taxes on imports that are intended to offset the benefits of those subsidies. This outcome creates problems; if, for instance, Europe and the United States become engaged in a contest to support some industry, the industry will benefit, but at the expense of the taxpayers in both countries. Thus, international agreements have tried to reduce the extent of subsidization. Broad-based R & D subsidies (such as those provided through the tax system) are still permitted, but more narrowly focused subsidies are either prohibited or viewed as questionable practices.

PROTECTION

Firms in less-developed countries often argue that they need to be insulated from competition from abroad in order to develop the knowledge base required to compete effectively in world markets. This is the **infant industry argument** for protection. Most economists are skeptical. They see this argument mainly as an excuse by rent-seeking firms eager to insulate themselves from competition so they can raise prices and increase profits. The best way to learn to compete is to compete, not to withdraw from competition. If some help is needed to enable firms to catch up, it should be provided in the form of subsidies, whose costs—unlike the hidden costs of higher prices that result from protection—are explicit and obvious.

RELAXING ANTITRUST POLICIES

The antitrust policies explored in Chapter 13 were founded on the belief that government should push markets toward the model of perfect competition. But an increasing awareness of the importance of R & D in modern industrial economies has led some to reconsider this stance.

A major argument for change is that cooperation aimed at sharing knowledge and coordinating research among firms in an industry has the effect of internalizing the externalities of R & D, thereby providing firms with an incentive to invest. But antitrust authorities have long worried that cooperation in R & D could easily grow into cooperation in other areas, such as price setting, which would not serve the public interest. Public policy has tried to find an effective balance. In 1984, the National Cooperative Research Act was passed to allow some cooperative ventures. Enterprises registered under the act are shielded from the risk of paying triple damages in a private antitrust suit but are not shielded from all antitrust risk. By the end of the 1980s, more than a hundred such ventures had been registered. Among the best-known are the Electric Power Research Institute, formed by electric power companies; Bell Communications Research, formed by local telephone companies; and Sematech, a consortium of computer chip manufacturers.

Wrap-Up

TECHNOLOGICAL CHANGE AND THE BASIC COMPETITIVE MODEL

Basic competitive model	Industries in which technological change is important
Assumes fixed technology	The central question is what determines the pace of technological change. Related issues include what determines expenditure on R & D and how learning by doing affects the level of production.
Assumes perfect competition, with many firms in each industry	Competition is not perfect; industries where technological change is important tend to have relatively few firms.
Perfect capital markets	Firms find it difficult to borrow to finance R & D expenditures.
No externalities	R & D confers benefits to others besides the inventor; even with the protection afforded by patents, the inventor appropriates only a fraction of the social benefits of an invention.
No public goods	Basic research is a public good: the marginal cost of an additional person making use of a new idea is zero (nonrivalrous consumption), and it is often difficult to exclude others from enjoying the benefits of basic research.

Internet Connection
COMPETITIVENESS

The Council on Competitiveness is a nonprofit organization that focuses on the role of innovation and technological change in enhancing the international competitiveness of American firms. Its Web site (www.compete.org) offers forums on issues related to technological innovation and national economic performance.

Technological Change and Economic Growth

Living standards in the United States are far higher today than they were one hundred years ago. The reason is that productivity—the amount produced by the average worker per hour—has increased enormously. Underlying these increases is technological change. In the 1970s and 1980s the pace of growth in productivity in the United States slowed down markedly, from almost 3 percent to around 1 percent. In the latter half of the 1990s, it picked up again, by some measures surpassing even pre-1970 rates. Some of the change has to do with changes in levels of investment in capital, but much of it has to do with the pace of innovation, which has resulted largely from the deliberate allocation of resources to R & D. No wonder then that governments focus so much attention on the issue of how to create an economic environment that is conducive to innovation. While the *incentives* provided by intellectual property protection and government expenditures on basic research are important, several other features of the economy have played a vital role in helping the United States maintain a dominant position. These factors include financial markets (especially venture capital firms) that are willing to finance new ventures, a labor force that is willing to take the risks associated with working for an upstart firm likely to fail, a university system that has attracted the best scientists from around the world, and close ties between research universities and corporations.

Review and Practice

SUMMARY

1. Ideas are different from the goods envisioned in the basic competitive model—they are nonrivalrous.
2. Industries in which technological change is important are almost necessarily imperfectly competitive. Patents are one way the government makes it difficult and costly for firms to copy the technological innovations of others. A firm with a patent will have a government-enforced monopoly. The expenditures on R & D are fixed costs; when they are large, there are likely to be few firms in the industry, and price competition is more likely to be limited.
3. Long-lasting and broad patents reduce competition (at least in the short run), but provide greater incentives to innovate. Excessively broad patent coverage may discourage follow-on innovation.
4. Learning by doing, which provides companies (or countries) that begin making a product first an advantage over all later entrants in lowering costs of production, may be a source of technological advantage.
5. Research and development generally provides positive externalities to consumers and other firms. But since the innovating firm cannot capture all the social benefits from its invention, it will tend to invest less than a socially optimal amount.
6. Basic research has both of the main properties of a public good: it is difficult to exclude others from the benefits of the research, and the marginal cost of an additional person making use of the new idea is zero.
7. A number of governmental policies encourage technological advance: patents, direct spending on research, tax incentives to encourage corporate R & D, temporary protection from technologically advanced foreign competitors, and the relaxation of antitrust laws to allow potential competitors to work together on research projects.

KEY TERMS

rivalrous goods
nonrivalrous goods
patents
intellectual property
royalty
static efficiency
dynamic efficiency
trade secret
learning by doing
learning curve
basic research
industrial policies
infant industry argument

REVIEW QUESTIONS

1. In what ways do industries in which technological change is important not satisfy the assumptions of the basic competitive model?
2. Why do governments grant patents, thereby conferring temporary monopoly rights? Explain the trade-off society faces in choosing whether to offer patents for long or short terms, and whether to offer broad or narrow patents.
3. How do the effects of learning by doing provide an advantage to incumbent firms over prospective entrants?
4. Why might it be harder to raise capital for R & D than for other projects? How can established firms deal with this problem? What about start-up firms?
5. How do positive externalities arise from R & D? Why do externalities imply that there may be too little expenditure on research by private firms?
6. Explain how basic research can be thought of as a public good. Why is society likely to underinvest in basic research?
7. What are the arguments for and against industrial policies?
8. What possible trade-off does society face when it considers loosening its antitrust laws to encourage joint R & D ventures?

PROBLEMS

1. Imagine that Congress is considering a bill to reduce the current twenty-year life of most patents to eight years.

What negative effects might this change have on the rate of innovation? What positive effect might it have for the economy?

2. Suppose that many years ago, one inventor received a patent for orange juice, and then another came forward and requested a patent for lemonade. The first inventor maintained that the orange juice patent should be interpreted to cover all fruit juices, while the second inventor argued that the original patent included only one particular method of making one kind of juice. What are the trade-offs for society as it sets rules for deciding cases such as these?

3. Although a patent ensures a monopoly on that particular invention for some time, it also requires that the inventor disclose the details of the invention. Under what conditions might a company (like Coca-Cola) prefer to use trade secrets rather than patents to protect its formulas?

4. Why might a company invest in R & D even if it does not believe it will be able to patent its discovery?

5. Learning by doing seems to be important in the semiconductor industry, in which the United States and Japan are the main producers. Explain why U.S. and Japanese firms may race to try to bring out new generations of semiconductors. If learning by doing is important in the semiconductor industry, why might other nations try to use an infant industry strategy to develop their own semiconductor industry?

Part 5
INTRODUCTION TO MACROECONOMICS

Learning Goals

In this chapter, you will learn

1. How important historical events such as the Great Depression have shaped the field of macroeconomics

2. The three important goals of macroeconomic performance

3. What the key concepts that define core ideas in economics are

4. What markets are, and which are the principal markets that make up the economy

5. Why economics is called a science, and why economists often disagree

Chapter 21

MACROECONOMICS AND THE ECONOMIC PERSPECTIVE

Macroeconomics is the study of the overall economy—not the study of employment levels and prices in a particular industry but the study of total employment and unemployment and the general level of prices throughout the economy. It is also concerned with the effects on the overall economy of government policies. Macroeconomics deals with the *aggregate* economy. To begin to get a sense of the field of macroeconomics, it is useful to start with a brief history of the macroeconomy. The episodes described in this brief history have been important in shaping the field of macroeconomics, and we will use them throughout the following chapters to illustrate macroeconomic topics.

Imagine the world in 1929, three-quarters of a century ago. The stock market was booming, and no end to the good times was in sight. True, some commentators were saying the market was overvalued, that a crash was sure to come, but most investors were optimistic about the future. Unemployment was low, and the general level of prices was stable.

Only one year later, the world had changed forever. The October 1929 stock market crash wiped out almost a quarter of the value of the New York stock market; similar crashes occurred in other countries. The Dow industrial average (the precursor of today's Dow Jones industrial average, a measure of stock market prices), which had hit a high of 381 in September 1929, fell to 41 in July 1932. Unemployment rose to previously unseen levels throughout the world economy. By 1933, one of every four workers in the United States was unemployed. The United States and other industrialized economies still had the same buildings, plants, and equipment as before, the same labor force was available and apparently willing to work, yet many of these resources lay idle. This period, the 1930s—now indelibly linked with hardship and depressed economic conditions—is commonly called the **Great Depression.**

Out of this catastrophe, macroeconomics was born. While the science of economics can be dated to the publication in 1776 of Adam Smith's *The Wealth of Nations,* the birth of macroeconomics as a separate branch within economics can be dated to the publication in 1936 of John Maynard Keynes's *The General Theory of Employment, Interest, and Prices.* Prior to Keynes's time, economists had studied the behavior of the entire economy and placed special emphasis on understanding the role of money and the general level of prices. But the modern field of macroeconomics, with its stress on understanding why economies experience episodes like the Great Depression and why employment and production grow and fluctuate over time, begins with Keynes. Our understanding of the forces influencing aggregate economies has evolved dramatically since Keynes wrote, but his work helped define the field and has had lasting impacts (both good and bad) on economic policy.

Not just macroeconomics, but many of the government policies and programs we take for granted today, such as Social Security and federal insurance for bank deposits, grew out of the experience of the 1930s. Perhaps its most important legacy is the general acceptance of the notion that governments are responsible for ensuring that periods like the Great Depression never reoccur. In the United States, the Employment Act of 1946 requires the federal government to cultivate "conditions under which there will be afforded useful employment opportunities . . . for those able, willing, and seeking to work, and to promote maximum employment, production, and purchasing power."

The impact that the Great Depression has had on the subsequent history of the United States and other major economies can teach us a great deal about macroeconomics and important government policies.

The Commitment to Full Employment and Growth

Before the Great Depression, the United States and other industrialized economies had gone through frequent periods of rapid economic growth followed by declines in production. These declines were often accompanied by financial panics in which banks were forced to close their doors, refusing to let depositors withdraw their funds.[1] The Roaring Twenties was one period associated in the popular mind with a booming economy. This pattern of periods of rapid growth alternating with periods of decline has continued to today, although the fluctuations in economic activity since World War II have generally been milder than those experienced before the war (see Figure 21.1). Looking back over the most recent fifteen years, we see that the 1990s was a period of rapid growth, high employment, and rising incomes in the United States. In early 2001, the boom times of the 1990s came to an end. The stock market collapsed as the dot-com bubble burst. Unemployment began to rise. By most measures, the downturn was short and mild, with the economy growing again by the end of 2001. Yet unemployment remained stubbornly high and many

---

[1] Each Christmas season, the movie *It's a Wonderful Life* is shown on television. A central event in the movie is the threatened failure of the bank owned by the character played by Jimmy Stewart.

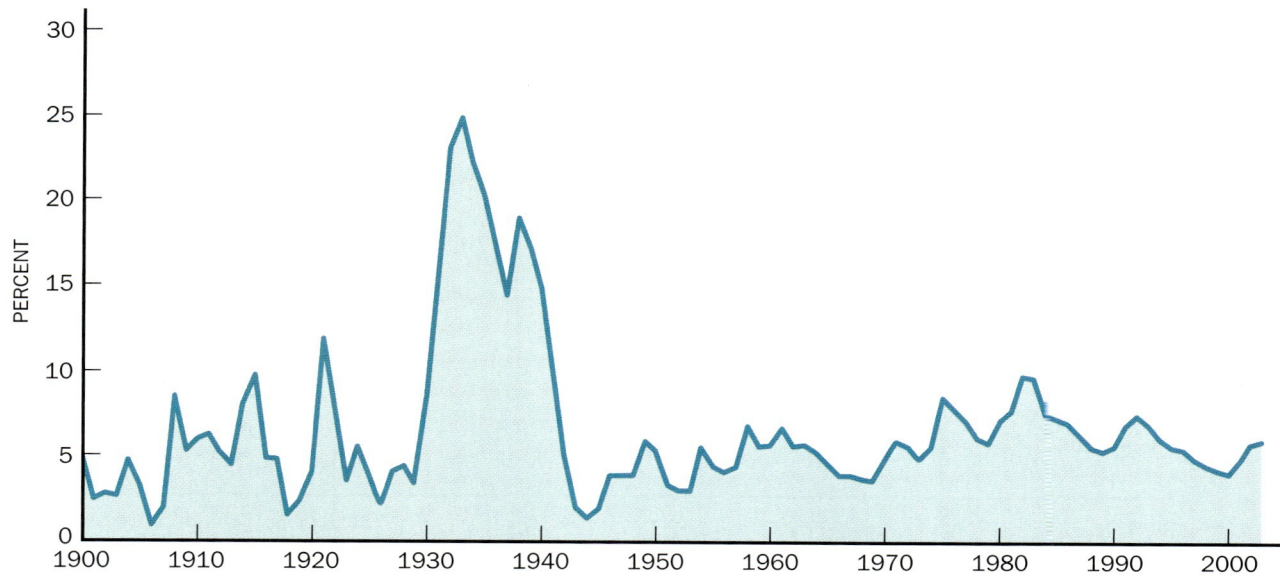

Figure 21.1

UNEMPLOYMENT, 1900–2003

The proportion of the labor force unemployed and seeking jobs rose to 25 percent during the Great Depression. Since 1960, unemployment has fluctuated around an average of about 6 percent, but it has risen to almost 10 percent (in 1983) and fallen to as low as 3.5 percent (in 1969). After reaching 7.5 percent in 1992, the unemployment rate fell steadily over the rest of the 1990s and was at 4.0 percent in 2000. It then rose to 6.0 percent in 2003.

SOURCE: *Economic Report of the President* (2004), Table B-42.

talked of a "jobless recovery." It was not until 2004 that employment growth fully recovered.

When the Great Depression hit, it was not confined to the United States. Figure 21.2 shows that production declined in all the major industrial economies, with the United States and Germany being hit the hardest. We often think of the "global economy" and the close international linkages we have today as uniquely characteristic of the modern world, but the economies of Europe and North America were also linked in the 1920s, and economic crises took on a global dimension, just as they can today.

The world economy recovered slowly from the dramatic depths of the Great Depression. The United States produced less in 1936 than it had in 1929. And in 1937 another decline occurred, helping to solidify our view of the 1930s as an entire decade of hardship. Only with the increased production associated with the advent of World War II did incomes in the United States significantly surpass earlier levels and unemployment return to more normal levels. The massive increase in orders to factories for war materials stimulated firms to expand production and hire workers. By 1944, the unemployment rate had fallen to 1.2 percent of those willing to work.

The end of World War II brought new worries that the economy would lapse back into recession and the hard times of the 1930s. The fear was that when the strong demand for production arising from the wartime needs of the government ended, firms would again be idle and the era of massive unemployment would return. Fortunately, while production declined from its wartime peaks, the economy did not

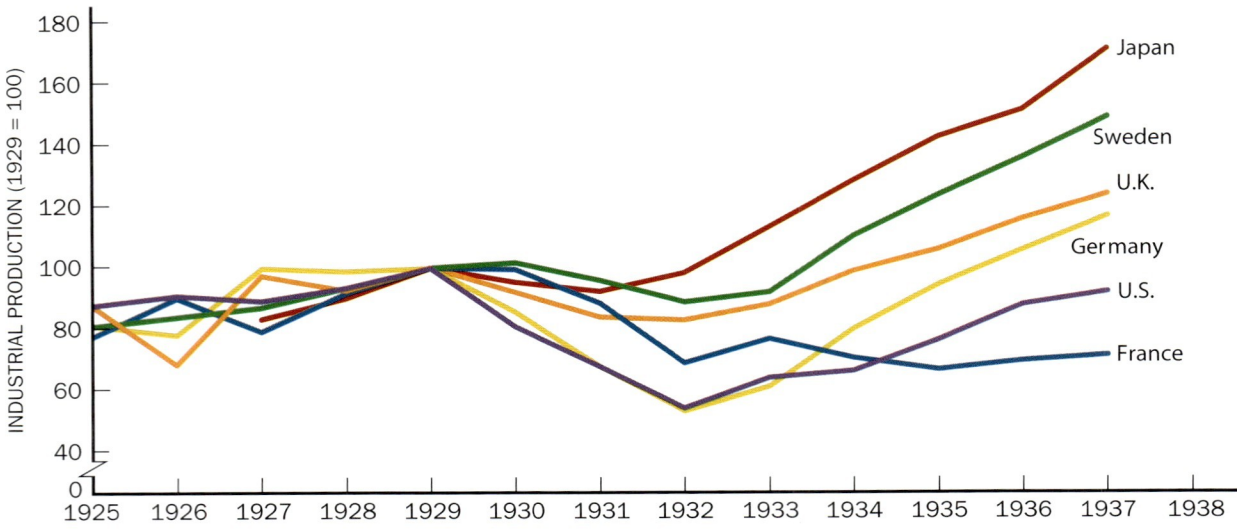

Figure 21.2
INDUSTRIAL PRODUCTION

The Great Depression was not limited to the United States. All industrial economies suffered declines in economic activity and production in the 1930s. The index of industrial production for each country is scaled so that all the indexes equal 100 for the year 1929.

SOURCES: League of Nations, *World Production and Prices* (Geneva: League of Nations, 1936), Appendix II, p. 142; and *World Production and Prices* (Geneva: League of Nations, 1938), Table 1, p. 44.

revert to the conditions of the Great Depression. The late 1940s saw strong growth in economic activity, in part fueled by household spending as Americans moved to the suburbs, built homes, and had children. During the war years, few consumer goods had been available, purchases of some goods had been rationed, and households had been urged to save by buying war bonds to help finance the war effort. Americans wanted to enjoy the return of peace and prosperity by using the incomes they had earned during the war to buy new cars, homes, and appliances.

The shift from wartime production and the demands for military goods to peacetime production and the demands for civilian goods represented a tremendous change in what the economy produced. Assembly lines that had been making tanks for the government shifted to making automobiles for consumers. Construction boomed as it met the demand for new homes. Resources—workers and capital—had to be shifted from what they had been producing to meet the new needs and desires of Americans. Jobs had to be created for the millions of soldiers returning from the war.

The end of the war also saw the government accepting responsibility for preventing a recurrence of the Great Depression, an acceptance formalized when the U.S. Congress passed the Employment Act in 1946. Among its provisions was the establishment of the president's Council of Economic Advisors, a three-member committee of economists who advise the president.[2] While economists have debated how much power the government actually has to influence macroeconomic developments, the voting public often shows that it expects the president to ensure continued economic growth, low inflation, and low unemployment.

[2]Professor Stiglitz was chair of President Clinton's Council of Economic Advisors from 1995 to 1996.

Today, a slight rise in the unemployment rate brings demands for the government to do something to "get the economy moving again." And for good reason: In today's economy, when an extra 1 percent of the labor force becomes unemployed, incomes in the economy fall by about $160 billion. A commitment to maintaining full employment was absent in the 1930s, or at least there was much less agreement over whether the government could (as well as whether it should) stimulate the economy.

GETTING THE COUNTRY MOVING AGAIN

The attempts by government to pursue the goals established by the Employment Act have helped economists learn about how the economy operates.

The 1960s saw the first active use of government policy to try to reduce overall unemployment. During the 1960 presidential election, John F. Kennedy narrowly defeated Richard Nixon in what had been the closest presidential race in U.S. history until the contest between George W. Bush and Al Gore in 2000. In part, Nixon's defeat was due to the slowdown in economic activity and rise in unemployment that the country experienced in 1959. During the six years from 1958 through 1963, the unemployment rate averaged almost 6 percent; ten years before it had been 2.8 percent. Kennedy's Council of Economic Advisors proposed a policy based on the ideas of John Maynard Keynes that was designed to stimulate the economy and bring the unemployment rate down to 4 percent, a level that at the time was believed to be consistent with "full employment." The policy called for a major tax cut. Those who opposed the cut argued that it would be fiscally irresponsible and lead to a deficit, with the government spending more than it received in taxes. They contended that inflation would rise and the cost of lower unemployment would be higher inflation. The government would need to decide how much inflation it was willing to tolerate to get unemployment down.

In what is perhaps the most famous macroeconomic policy experiment, the federal government did cut taxes in 1964. At the same time, federal government expenditures rose because of the Vietnam War and President Lyndon Johnson's War on Poverty programs. The unemployment rate did subsequently fall; in fact, it fell below 4 percent, reaching as low as 3.5 percent by 1969. Unfortunately, this fall in unemployment was accompanied by rising inflation; the general level of prices in the United States rose by only 1 percent in 1963, but by 1969 prices were rising at an annual rate of 6.2 percent. To some extent, policymakers at the time thought that higher inflation was simply the price they had to pay to maintain lower unemployment. They saw this as a trade-off: lower unemployment required accepting higher inflation, but inflation could always be reduced again, they believed, by letting average unemployment return to the levels of the late 1950s and early 1960s.

STAGFLATION

During the 1970s, policymakers discovered that the trade-off between unemployment and inflation they thought they were facing had somehow disappeared. Instead, the 1970s saw unemployment and inflation both rise. During the first half of the 1970s, unemployment averaged 5.4 percent, essentially the same level as before the Kennedy tax cut; yet as unemployment rose from the low levels of the late 1960s, inflation remained high. Chapter 31 will explain why the unemployment–inflation trade-off seemed to disappear in the 1970s. Policymakers found themselves confronting very different economic situations from those in the previous decade.

One new situation was caused by a disruption of oil supplies and a rise in oil prices. In the 1970s, the members of the Organization of Petroleum Exporting Countries (OPEC) were able to raise the world price of oil significantly. This action both contributed to the general increase in prices in oil-importing countries and changed the behavior of households and firms. Higher gas prices created incentives for consumers to economize on gas, and households started buying smaller, more fuel-efficient automobiles. In the United States, many of these cars were produced in other countries, particularly Japan, because U.S. automakers were slow to alter the products they made to respond to changes in consumer demand. Firms also needed to adjust their production techniques to conserve energy and adopt more energy-efficient equipment, as well as to produce the more energy-efficient goods that consumers now desired.

During the 1970s, unemployment averaged more than 6 percent, while inflation averaged more than 7 percent per year. This experience with high inflation *and* high unemployment was called **stagflation.** Numerous attempts to control inflation were made without success. In 1971, President Nixon imposed price and wage controls. These temporarily reduced inflation but failed to address the underlying causes, described in Chapter 31. As soon as the controls were lifted, inflation reappeared.

THE CONQUEST OF INFLATION

At the end of the 1970s, most industrial economies continued to suffer unacceptably high rates of inflation. The last big oil price increase of the decade occurred in 1979 and helped push inflation rates to new highs in many countries.

The turning point in the battle against inflation actually occurred in October 1979, when Paul Volker, President Jimmy Carter's newly appointed chairman of the Federal Reserve System, shifted economic policy. Under Volker, the Federal Reserve adopted policies designed to reduce inflation. Chapter 32 will describe how the Federal Reserve is able to affect the economy. As part of its policy changes, the Federal Reserve began to focus more on controlling the money supply. Interest rates rose to record highs, but Volker's policies succeeded in getting inflation down. Reducing inflation wasn't costless, however. By 1982, unemployment reached 10 percent, the highest level in the post–World War II era. President Ronald Reagan's ratings in the polls sank to low levels. Many Democrats thought Reagan was sure to be defeated when new elections were held in 1984.

But during 1984 the economy expanded. Chapter 24 will explain why increases in unemployment tend to be temporary, with the economy eventually returning to full employment. By the time of the presidential election, the unemployment rate had fallen to 7.2 percent, yet inflation remained relatively low. With the macroeconomy improving, Reagan coasted to a landslide reelection victory.

GOVERNMENT DEFICITS AND TRADE DEFICITS

The economy continued to expand during the rest of the 1980s, and inflation remained under control. New macroeconomic issues emerged, however, and the last half of the 1980s and much of the 1990s were dominated by concern over two deficits. One was the federal government's budget deficit. Tax cuts and increases in defense spending under President Reagan helped push the budget into deficit, as federal spending exceeded tax revenues. Little success was achieved in the 1980s in reducing this deficit, and the gap between what the federal government spent and what it collected in taxes reached a peak of $290 billion in 1992. When the government spends more than it receives in taxes, it must borrow, just as you would if you spent more than your income. The total amount the government owed rose from about $700 billion in 1980 to $3.7 trillion in 1997—that is, $3,700,000,000,000, or about $13,500 for every man, woman, and child in the United States. Ours was not the only country showing an imbalance between government spending and tax revenues. Other countries faced the difficult task of balancing spending desires with available tax revenues. Germany, France, Italy, Japan, and the United Kingdom all had deficits in the second half of the 1990s that were larger, relative to the size of their economies, than the deficit of the U.S. federal government. Each government had to make trade-offs, deciding which programs to scale back or which taxes to increase.

The second focus of attention in the 1980s and 1990s was the trade deficit, the difference between what the United States purchases from other countries (our imports) and what we sell to other countries (our exports). Some argued that the trade deficit was costing American workers their jobs and that we should "buy American." Others pointed out that trade provided access to new markets for American producers and more product choices for American consumers. They also argued that international capital markets allowed firms and the government to borrow from foreign lenders, increasing the availability of credit needed to build the new plants and equipment that contribute to future economic growth.

GETTING THE ECONOMY MOVING (AGAIN)

In the presidential election of 1992, Bill Clinton's campaign slogan, "It's the economy, stupid!" struck a responsive chord among voters. After almost eight years of economic growth, the U.S. economy had stalled during the summer of 1990. The overall level of production in the economy declined throughout the rest of 1990 and into 1991. With firms producing less, they needed fewer workers; the unemployment rate rose. This was enough to sink President George H. W. Bush's reelection bid. Strong economic growth in the second half of the 1990s, with low unemployment and low inflation, contributed significantly to President Clinton's reelection in 1996.

As the century ended, the United States was enjoying its strongest economic performance in decades. Unemployment had fallen to the lowest level since the 1970s, and inflation remained low. American workers were becoming more productive, perhaps owing to the computer and technological revolution that was changing the way the economy operates, and their productivity was improving prospects for long-term growth in living standards.

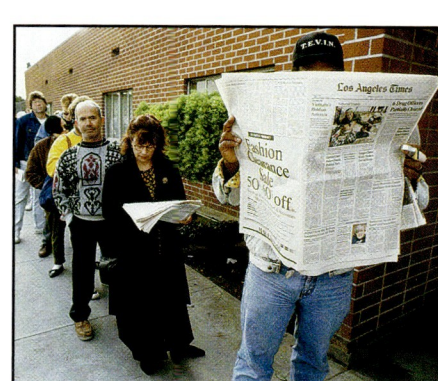

Rising unemployment played a role in Bill Clinton's defeat of George H. W. Bush in the 1992 presidential election.

The information technology revolution was also having an impact on the distribution of income. New technologies increased the demand for better-educated workers, which helped increase the incomes of college-educated workers. At the same time, many manufacturing jobs—jobs that had provided decent wages for workers with less education—moved overseas as competition forced firms to shift production to lower-cost locations. The 1990s saw a widening of the income gap between college-educated workers and those with only a high school diploma.

The last half of the 1990s also saw a tremendous swing in the government's budget outlook. In 1998, the federal government ran its first surplus since 1969, and by 2000, the federal government surplus had grown to more than $200 billion. At the time, the outlook was for years of future surpluses. The turnaround in the budget was due to a combination of factors. Congress had agreed to some tax increases and to restraints on the growth of spending. The booming economy of the 1990s led to higher incomes, which in turn led wage earners to pay more in taxes. Likewise, the stock market boom boosted tax revenues from capital gains.

Meanwhile, many other major economies were experiencing quite different macroeconomic conditions. Asia had been wracked by financial crises, rising unemployment, and stagnating growth, while many European countries found that their unemployment rates remained stubbornly high through most of the 1990s.

As the year 2000 ended, the boom times of the 1990s in the United States also came to a close. High-tech firms were scaling back operations or even going out of business. When President George W. Bush took office in 2001, the macroeconomy was already slowing and unemployment, which was only 4.2 percent at the end of 2000, rose throughout 2001, reaching 5.8 percent by December. A recession officially began in March 2001. Bush had promised tax cuts as he campaigned during 2000, and once in office he pushed them through Congress. At the time, he argued that lower taxes would encourage households to spend more, helping to boost the economy.

NEW CHALLENGES

The first years of the twenty-first century saw heated debates over unemployment, the fiscal deficit, and the risks of deflation. The economic slump that began in early 2001 was over by late 2001, yet the subsequent economic recovery seemed unable to produce lasting employment gains. The unemployment rate remained stubbornly high, beginning to fall only at the end of 2003. The growth in overall economic output while employment remained weak raised concerns about a "jobless recovery" in which firms take advantage of new production techniques and of longer hours put in by employees to gain increases in production without adding new workers.

The tax cuts introduced by President Bush, the rise in expenditures associated with the war on terrorism, and the fall in tax revenues caused by the sluggish economy all served to push the federal budget back into deficit. The federal deficit for 2004 was $412 billion. Many state and local governments also found their budget situation worsening, forcing major reductions in expenditures. Just as in the early 1990s, large budget deficits now loom for the foreseeable future.

A new concern surfaced during 2003 as **deflation**—a situation in which overall prices actually fall—seemed possible. The United States had not experienced significant periods of deflation since the Great Depression of the 1930s, and many were concerned that falling prices would again be associated with depressed economic conditions. Many pointed to the experience of Japan, where deflation had accompanied a decade-long recession during the 1990s. The Federal Reserve under Alan Greenspan had shifted policy in early 2001 to help stimulate economic growth by lowering interest rates, but by 2003, interest rates were almost down to zero, and some feared that the Federal Reserve would be unable to provide further stimulus.

Concerns lessened during 2004 as the economy continued to grow, unemployment edged downward, and fears of deflation disappeared. With the economy expanding, Federal Reserve policymakers gradually began to raise interest rates as they focused on preventing an upswing in inflation.

As this book goes to press in 2005, two major macroeconomic issues are dominating the news. President Bush has made Social Security reform a major part of his domestic agenda. Both Democrats and Republicans agree that some changes must be made to the Social Security program to ensure its future financial health, but the two parties differ significantly in the ways they want to change the program. Some of the issues at the heart of this debate will be discussed in Chapter 38. The second major issue is the federal government's budget deficit. Tax cuts and spending increases since 2000 have led to massive deficits. The impact of government deficits on the economy will be studied in Chapter 25.

"Deflation" was a concern that occupied policymakers in the first years of the twenty-first century. The U.S. economy had not experienced severe deflation since the Great Depression of the 1930s.

THE THREE KEY GOALS OF MACROECONOMIC PERFORMANCE

For more than half a century, the American government has been formally committed to achieving a number of important macroeconomic goals. As the Employment Act of 1946 states, the "Congress hereby declares that it is the continuing policy and responsibility of the Federal Government . . . to promote maximum employment, production, and purchasing power." These goals were further defined in the Full Employment and Balanced Growth Act of 1978, better known as the Humphrey-Hawkins Act, after the bill's chief authors, Senator Hubert Humphrey (D-Minn.) and Representative Augustus Hawkins (D-Calif.). The Humphrey-Hawkins Act formally makes it the policy of the federal government to "promote full employment and production, increased real income, balanced growth, a balanced Federal budget, adequate productivity growth, proper attention to national priorities, achievement of an improved trade balance through increased exports and improvement in the international competitiveness of agriculture, business, and industry, and reasonable price stability."

Three of these aims have come to represent the key goals of macroeconomic policies—full employment, economic growth, and price stability. Full employment ensures that all those willing and able to work can find jobs; economic growth ensures that material standards of living will rise; and a low and stable rate of inflation aids individuals in planning for the future. Macroeconomists are constantly studying the causes of slow growth, unemployment, and inflation. Understanding the causes of these problems is the first step toward designing policies to improve macroeconomic performance.

Wrap-Up

THREE GOALS OF MACROECONOMIC POLICY

Rapid growth
Full employment
Low inflation

A Look Ahead

Our task, taken up in the next three chapters, is to understand how economists measure the aggregate economy's performance. How do we measure the aggregate output of the entire economy? How do we measure unemployment? How do we measure the general level of prices and inflation?

In Parts Six to Nine, we will learn about the factors that account for growth, inflation, and economic fluctuations. We also will learn how government policies affect the economy, and how these policies can be used to achieve macroeconomic goals. What happens to the aggregate economy depends not only on government policies but also on the individual decisions made by thousands of firms and millions of households. Microeconomics helps economists understand how firms and households make choices—what trade-offs they face, how they respond to incentives, the effects of information on their choices, and the role markets and exchange play in determining what is produced and how income is distributed. Macroeconomics helps economists understand how the choices of firms and households, together with government policies, affect the aggregate economy.

Review and Practice

SUMMARY

1. The three major goals of macroeconomic policy are high and sustainable economic growth, full employment, and low inflation.

KEY TERMS

Great Depression
stagflation
deflation

REVIEW QUESTIONS

1. What trade-off between inflation and unemployment did President Kennedy's Council of Economic Advisors believe they faced? What happened to inflation and unemployment after the 1964 tax cut?
2. What is stagflation? When has the United States experienced stagflation?
3. When has the United States experienced the combination of low inflation *and* low unemployment?
4. What are the key goals of macroeconomic policy?

PROBLEMS

1. Look at the front pages of a newspaper this week. What macroeconomic issues are in the news?
2. What is the current unemployment rate in the United States? What is the current rate of inflation? (Go to the Web site of the Bureau of Labor Statistics at www.bls.gov to find this information.)
3. Which two deficits were of concern in the 1980s and 1990s? What happened to these two deficits in the 1990s? What has happened to them during the past five years?

Learning Goals

In this chapter, you will learn

1. What gross domestic product (GDP) is
2. The three ways we can measure GDP
3. The difference between nominal and real GDP
4. How the unemployment rate is measured
5. The four types of unemployment
6. What the natural rate of unemployment is
7. What Okun's Law tells us

Chapter 22

MEASURING OUTPUT AND UNEMPLOYMENT

Every month, when the United States Bureau of Labor Statistics releases its latest figures on the unemployment rate, newspapers and the radio and TV news give them significant coverage. The same is true when new data on economic growth become available. Measures of unemployment and of growth in the economy are yardsticks that are used to gauge economic performance. Such yardsticks help analysts judge how successful economies have been in achieving such policy goals as low unemployment and strong growth. In addition to being frequent topics in the news, many of the most common economic yardsticks—the gross domestic product, the unemployment rate, and the consumer price index—figure prominently in political debates and presidential election campaigns.

In this chapter, we discuss what economists mean by the gross domestic product, what it measures, and how the government goes about actually measuring it. Then, we turn to the unemployment rate and examine how it is measured. Without an understanding of these common yardsticks, we cannot assess their strengths and weaknesses as measures of economic performance. It is especially important to understand the weaknesses of our measures so that we do not make errors in assessing economic conditions. The issues that arise in measuring inflation, another key indicator of economic performance, are discussed in the following chapter.

Measuring Output and Growth

To gauge the economy's success in raising living standards, we need to start by understanding how we measure the total output of the economy. We will learn later in this chapter that the aggregate income of the economy is equal to the aggregate output of goods and services that the economy has produced. Measuring output is our starting point for assessing the economy's performance.

485

GROSS DOMESTIC PRODUCT

The output of the economy consists of millions of different goods and services. We could report how much of each good or service the economy produced. This would yield a list that might include 1,362,478 hammers, 473,562,382 potatoes, 256,346 heart operations, and so forth. Such a list might be useful for some purposes, but it would not provide us with the information we want. If the following year the number of hammers produced goes up by 5 percent, the potato crop yield goes down by 2 percent, and the number of heart operations performed rises by 7 percent, has the economy's total output gone up or down? And by how much?

We need a single number that summarizes the output of the economy. But how do we add up hammers, potatoes, heart operations, and the millions of other products produced in the economy? We do this by totaling the *money value* of all the *final* goods and services produced. By money value, we mean the dollar value of output. By final goods and services, we mean those goods and services sold for final usage and not those used to make other products. Since the money value of hammer production and the money value of heart operations are in the same units (dollars), we can add them together. The money value of final output is called the **gross domestic product,** or **GDP.** It is the standard measure of the value of the output in an economy. It sums up the total money value of the final goods and services produced within a nation's borders during a given time period, usually a year. It makes no difference whether the production takes place in the private or public sector, or whether the goods and services are purchased by households, the government, or the foreign sector.[1]

Wrap-Up

GROSS DOMESTIC PRODUCT

The total money value of all final goods and services produced for the marketplace within a nation's borders during a given period of time (usually a year).

Table 22.1 illustrates the calculation of GDP for a simple economy that produces just two goods, personal computers (PCs) and compact discs (CDs). The table shows the number of PCs and CDs produced in two different years, and the average prices at which they were sold. GDP in year 1 is found by multiplying the quantities of each good sold in year 1 by its price in year 1. This gives the money value of PC and CD production. Adding the resulting money values together gives us GDP for this economy. Using the data in the table, we calculate GDP to be $2,550 million in year 1 and $2,985 million in year 2. GDP grew by 17 percent—100($2,985−$2,550)/$2,550—from year 1 to year 2.

---

[1]We use prices not only because they are a convenient way of making comparisons but also because they reflect how consumers value different goods. If the price of an orange is twice that of an apple, it means an orange is worth twice as much (at the margin) as an apple.

Table 22.1
CALCULATING GDP

	Prices and Quantities			
Year	Price of PCs	Quantity of PCs	Price of CDs	Quantity of CDs
1	$1,800.00	1.0 million	$15.00	50.0 million
2	$1,850.00	1.2 million	$17.00	45.0 million
GDP in year 1	= value of PCs + value of CDs = $1,800 × 1.0 million + $15 × 50.0 million = $2,550 million.			
GDP in year 2	= value of PCs + value of CDs = $1,850 × 1.2 million + $17 × 45.0 million = $2,985 million.			

Nominal vs. Real GDP There is one problem with using money as a measure of the economy's output. The value of a dollar changes over time. Candy bars, books, movie tickets, hammers, and heart operations all cost more today than they did ten years ago. We do not want to be misled into believing the economy is producing more when, in fact, prices may simply have risen. In our example from Table 22.1, for instance, one of the reasons why GDP was higher in year 2 than in year 1 was that the prices of the two goods were higher. Even if output had remained unchanged in year 2 at 1.0 million PCs and 50.0 million CDs, GDP would have risen to $2,700 million simply because prices rose.

To keep the comparisons of different years straight, economists adjust GDP for changes in the average level of prices. Unadjusted GDP is known as **nominal GDP;** that is what we calculated in Table 22.1. The term **real GDP** is used for the GDP numbers that have been adjusted for changes in the general level of prices. Real GDP gives a truer year-to-year measure of how much the economy actually produces. One way to think of real GDP is to ask, What would GDP be if all prices had remained unchanged? That is, from the example in Table 22.1, we could ask what GDP would have been in year 2 if prices had remained unchanged from year 1. Table 22.2 gives us the answer. Real GDP in year 2 using year 1 prices is $2,835 million. Since we are using the same prices to make this comparison, the measure of real GDP changes only if the quantities of the goods produced change. In this example, real GDP ($2,835 million) is less than nominal GDP ($2,985 million from Table 22.1), and this tells us that part of the increase in nominal GDP that we found in Table 22.1 reflected price increases. When we use year 1 prices to calculate real GDP in subsequent years, year 1 is called the *base year*.

When economists talk about adjusting nominal GDP for price changes to obtain a measure of real GDP, they say they "deflate" nominal GDP using a measure of the average level of prices called a *price index*. The price index for GDP is called the **GDP**

Table 22.2

NOMINAL AND REAL GDP

Real GDP (using year 1 as the base year):
    real GDP in year 1   = $2,550 million
    real GDP in year 2   = $1,800 × 1.2 million + $15 × 45.0 million
                                = $2,835 million.	

Price index (GDP deflator) using year 1 as base year:
    GDP deflator, year 1   = 100
    GDP deflator, year 2   = 100 × (year 2 nominal GDP)/(year 2 real GDP)
                               = 100 × (2,985/2,835)
                               = 105.3.	

Deflating nominal GDP:
                  real GDP in year 2   = nominal GDP/price index
                                            = $2,985/1.053 = $2,835 billion.	

deflator. As we have already seen, nominal GDP reflects changes in prices and quantities, while real GDP is a measure of how much quantities have changed. Real GDP can be defined by the equation

$$\text{real GDP} = \frac{\text{nominal GDP}}{\text{price index}}.$$

If nominal GDP has risen by 3 percent in the past year but prices have also risen by 3 percent, then real GDP would be unchanged. Since we have calculated nominal GDP and real GDP for the economy of Tables 22.1 and 22.2, we can determine that the price index must equal 1.053 (see Table 22.2). This is normally reported as 105.3 (so in the base year the price index is equal to 100), indicating that for this example, prices rose by 5.3 percent from year 1 to year 2.

This approach encounters a problem when *relative* prices change dramatically. If the price of computers falls rapidly as the output of computers increases—as has happened over the past two decades—then real output, using an earlier base year such as 1987, may be distorted. The large increases in computer production are valued at the high prices that existed earlier. Doing so places a high value on computer output, and GDP will look as if it is increasing very rapidly. When the base year used to calculate real GDP is changed—as it is periodically—the growth of the economy will appear to diminish suddenly; in the *new* base year, computer prices are lower, so each computer "counts" for less in GDP. Of course, the growth of the economy did not really diminish; it was only that our previous yardstick distorted the picture.

To address this problem, the Bureau of Economic Analysis (BEA), the agency in the Department of Commerce responsible for the GDP numbers, changed its approach in January 1996. It now provides a measure called the chain-weighted real GDP, which is designed to avoid some of the problems that arise when the prices of certain goods, such as computers, change greatly from the base year.

MEASURING GDP: THE VALUE OF OUTPUT

The general accounting system we use to measure GDP is called the National Income and Product Accounts (NIPA) and is produced by the Bureau of Economic Analysis. In the national income accounts, there are three approaches to measuring GDP (whether real or nominal), each of which yields the same result. Two concentrate on output data. The third—relying on the fact that the value of output becomes income to someone—uses income figures to obtain a measure of output.

The Final Goods Approach On the face of it, measuring GDP is a straightforward task; we gather together the dollar value of all goods and services sold in a country and then add them up. Unfortunately, matters are not this simple, because it is first necessary to distinguish between final goods and intermediate goods. Final goods—such as automobiles, books, bread, and shoes—are sold for final use by consumers, firms, the government, or foreigners. Intermediate goods are used to produce outputs—like coal used to make steel or silica used to make silicon computer chips. A good such as a blank CD can be either a final good or an intermediate good, depending on how it is used. The **final goods approach** used to measure GDP adds up the total dollar value of goods and services produced, categorized by their ultimate users.

The reason why it is so important to distinguish between final and intermediate goods is that the value of the final goods *includes* the value of the intermediate goods that went into making the final goods. When Ford sells a truck for $25,000, that figure may include $250 worth of Uniroyal tires. It would be double counting to list both the value of the truck and the value of the tires on the truck in GDP. Likewise for steel, plastic, and other components that go into making the truck. In fact, cases in which some intermediate goods are used to produce other intermediate goods could lead to even triple or quadruple counting.

One way of calculating the value of the final goods produced in the economy is to consider where those goods go. There are four possibilities. Some of the final goods are consumed by individuals—we call this aggregate *consumption* (and we include all consumption goods, regardless of where they are produced—we will see later how we correct for goods produced in other countries). Some are used by firms to build buildings and make machines—this is called aggregate *investment* (again, we include all investment goods that firms purchase, regardless of where they are

Internet Connection

THE BUREAU OF ECONOMIC ANALYSIS

The home page of the Bureau of Economic Analysis can be found at www.bea.gov. You can find the latest GDP data at this site.

produced). Some are *government purchases*. And some of the goods, called *exports*, go to other countries. If we did not import any goods (that is, buy goods produced in other countries), then GDP would simply consist of goods that went for private consumption, private investment, government purchases, or exports. But not all such goods are produced in this country. For instance, many consumer electronics and automobiles that individuals purchase are produced in other countries. To calculate GDP using the final goods approach, we therefore need a final step of subtracting the amount imported. Thus,

$$GDP = C + I + G + X - M,$$

where C is consumption, I is investment, G is government purchases, X is exports, and M is imports. The difference between exports and imports is referred to as *net exports*. This equation is an *identity*; that is, it is always true (by definition) that the GDP equals consumption plus investment plus government purchases plus net exports.

But what, you might ask, about goods produced during a given year that are still unsold at its end? The value of these goods should be counted in GDP—after all, they were produced during the year—but how can they be counted in final sales if the firms that produced them have not sold them by December 31? An example will help illustrate how this problem is solved in the National Income and Product Accounts. Suppose Dell Computer produces a new laptop on December 1, 2004, but the laptop has not been sold by the end of the year. Instead, it remains in the firm's inventory. This is treated by NIPA as a final sale to the firm itself—it is as if Dell purchased the laptop for its own use. The increase in firms' inventories is counted as part of final sales to firms and included in investment. If Dell sells the laptop to a consumer in January 2005, the sale adds to consumption but it *reduces* inventory holdings. Thus, when we add together consumption purchases and inventory investment, the two transactions cancel each other out—the laptop is correctly counted in 2004 GDP and not in 2005 GDP.

The final goods approach to calculating GDP in the United States can be illustrated using the figures for 2003. According to the Bureau of Economic Analysis,[2] the values for the components of GDP were as follows:

Category	Billions of $
Consumption	7,609.8
+ Investment	1,596.6
+ Government purchases	2,041.4
+ Exports	1,019.8
− Imports	1,523.0
= GDP	10,744.6

By adding these components together, we find that the value of all final goods and services produced within the borders of the United States during 2003 was $10,744.6 billion.

---

[2] www.bea.gov.

Wrap-Up

GDP equals consumption plus investment plus government purchases plus exports minus imports.

Case in Point

IS SOFTWARE A FINAL GOOD OR AN INTERMEDIATE GOOD?

Measuring output might seem straightforward when the economy produces cars and wheat and houses, but what happens when it produces ideas? The new technologies and the new economy they have created have forced the economists and statisticians at the Bureau of Economic Analysis to revise the National Income and Product Accounts. Such updates and revisions are nothing new; the bureau is always trying to improve its estimates of economic activity. However, the new economy has created some unique problems. One of the major changes in the *1999 Comprehensive Revision of the National Income and Product Accounts* dealt with how software is treated in GDP. Thinking about the correct way to measure the price and quantity of software highlights the differences between final and intermediate goods.

Prior to the new revisions, business and government expenditures on software were treated inconsistently. Software that was bundled in a product—a suite of office software programs such as a word processor and spreadsheet that was installed on a computer, for instance—was treated as a final good and included as an investment. After all, the computer is an investment good, and the value of the software installed on it represents part of its value. If a business purchased the software separately to install on a computer, however, it was treated as an intermediate good. The same was true of software a business produced itself. The costs a business incurred in producing software for its own use was treated as a business expense similar to that for any other intermediate good.

Under the new rules, all software expenditures are treated as investment spending. This is appropriate because software, like other investment goods, produces a flow of services that lasts more than one year. In fact, the Bureau of Economic Activity estimates that the average life of software is between three and five years. The effects of these new rules will be to raise GDP by the amount of software businesses and government agencies purchase and by the amount of software they produce for their own use. These expenditures were not counted as part of GDP when they were viewed as intermediate goods. By treating them as a final good, GDP is increased by the amount spent on them.

How much difference does this make? The revisions boosted GDP during the late 1990s by more than $100 billion per year. This is a large number, but it represents a change in GDP of only around 1 percent.

The Value-Added Approach A second way to calculate the value of GDP is to study the intermediate goods directly. The production of most items occurs in several stages. Consider the automobile. At one stage in its production, iron ore, coal, and limestone are mined. At a second stage, these raw materials are shipped to a steel mill. A third stage involves a steel company combining these ingredients to make steel. Finally, the steel and other inputs such as rubber and plastics are combined by the auto firm to make a car. The difference in value between what the automaker pays for intermediate goods and what it receives for the finished cars is called the firm's **value added.**

$$\text{value added} = \text{firm's revenue} - \text{costs of intermediate goods.}$$

GDP can be measured by calculating the value added at each stage of production.

$$\text{GDP} = \text{sum of value added of all firms.}$$

The Income Approach The third method used to calculate GDP involves measuring the income generated by selling products, rather than the value of the products themselves. This is known as the **income approach.** Firms have four claims on their revenue. They must pay for labor they have hired, pay interest on any funds they have borrowed, pay for any intermediate goods they have purchased, and pay indirect taxes such as sales taxes to the government. Anything left over represents the firm's income. Some income must be set aside to replace equipment worn out during the production process (called *depreciation,* which we will discuss later), and the rest is the firm's profit.

$$\text{revenue} = \text{wages} + \text{interest payments} + \text{cost of intermediate} \\ \text{inputs} + \text{indirect taxes} + \text{depreciation} + \text{profits.}$$

But we already know that the firm's value added is its revenue minus the cost of intermediate goods. Therefore,

$$\text{value added} = \text{wages} + \text{interest payments} + \\ \text{indirect taxes} + \text{depreciation} + \text{profits.}$$

And since GDP is equal to the sum of the value added of all firms, it must also equal the sum of the value of all wage payments, interest payments, indirect taxes, depreciation, and profits for all firms:[3]

$$\text{GDP} = \text{wages} + \text{interest payments} + \\ \text{indirect taxes} + \text{depreciation} + \text{profits.}$$

People receive income from wages, from capital, and from profits of the firms they own (or own shares in). And when firms spend to replace old equipment, that

---

[3]This ignores a few small adjustments such as net income payments from the rest of the world and net subsidies to government enterprises.

spending represents income for those who produce the new equipment. Thus, the right side of this identity is the total income of all individuals and the government revenue from indirect taxes. This is an extremely important result, one economists use frequently, so it is worth highlighting: *aggregate output equals aggregate income*.

Differences Between Individual Incomes and National Income

The notion of income used to calculate GDP differs slightly from the way individuals commonly think about income, and it is important to be aware of the distinction.

First, people are likely to include in their view of income any capital gains they earn on assets. *Capital gains* are increases in the value of assets and accordingly do not represent current production (output) in any way. The national income accounts used to calculate GDP do not include capital gains.

Second, profits that are retained by a firm are included in national income, but individuals may not perceive these retained profits as part of their own income. Again, this is because the GDP accounts measure the value of production, and profits are part of the value of production, whether these profits are actually distributed to the owners of the firm (its shareholders) or are retained by the firm.

Comparison of the Final Goods and Income Approach As Table 22.3 shows, the value of GDP is the same whether it is calculated in terms of final goods output or in terms of income. It is no accident that the two approaches to measuring GDP lead to identical results; it is a consequence of the circular flow of the economy. Every dollar of revenue each firm receives after paying for its intermediate inputs is paid out in the form of wages, profits, interest, rents, or indirect taxes. Income flows back to firms when households purchase consumption goods or when household saving is borrowed by firms to purchase investment goods, such as plant and equipment, or by the government to spend in excess of its tax revenues.

Table 22.3

TWO APPROACHES TO U.S. GDP, 2003

Final Goods	Billions of $	Income	Billions of $
Consumption	7,609.8	Employee compensation	6,179.1
Investment	1,596.6	Profits, rents, interest, etc.	2,448.0
Government expenditures	2,041.4	Indirect taxes	783.5
Net exports	−503.2	Depreciation	1,334.0
Total	10,744.6	Total	10,744.6

SOURCE: www.bea.doc.gov/bea/dn1.htm.

POTENTIAL GDP

Real GDP is a measure of how much the economy actually produces. But sometimes workers may not be fully employed, and some plants and equipment may be operating at less than normal capacity. At other times, the economy may produce more than would normally be sustainable. Firms may put on extra shifts, increase overtime, and delay maintenance in order to temporarily increase output. Another important macroeconomic measure of real output, **potential GDP,** indicates what the economy would produce if labor were fully employed at normal levels of overtime and if plants and machines were used at their normal rates. Real GDP will fall below potential GDP when the economy has above-normal levels of unemployed resources.

In some circumstances, real GDP can exceed potential GDP by a considerable amount. Even when the economy is operating at its normal potential, some unused capacity remains. By fully utilizing this capacity, the economy's real GDP can temporarily exceed its potential. Individuals may be willing to temporarily put in extra overtime; other workers may take a second job when the labor market is particularly strong. Such steps enable real GDP to be greater than would occur at more normal levels of utilization and work hours. One common example of actual production greatly exceeding the economy's normal potential is when a country mobilizes for war. Figure 22.1 shows how real GDP and potential GDP have increased over the past forty years. Output does not grow smoothly; the jagged progression in the figure shows the effects of short-term fluctuations around an upward trend. Sometimes these fluctuations

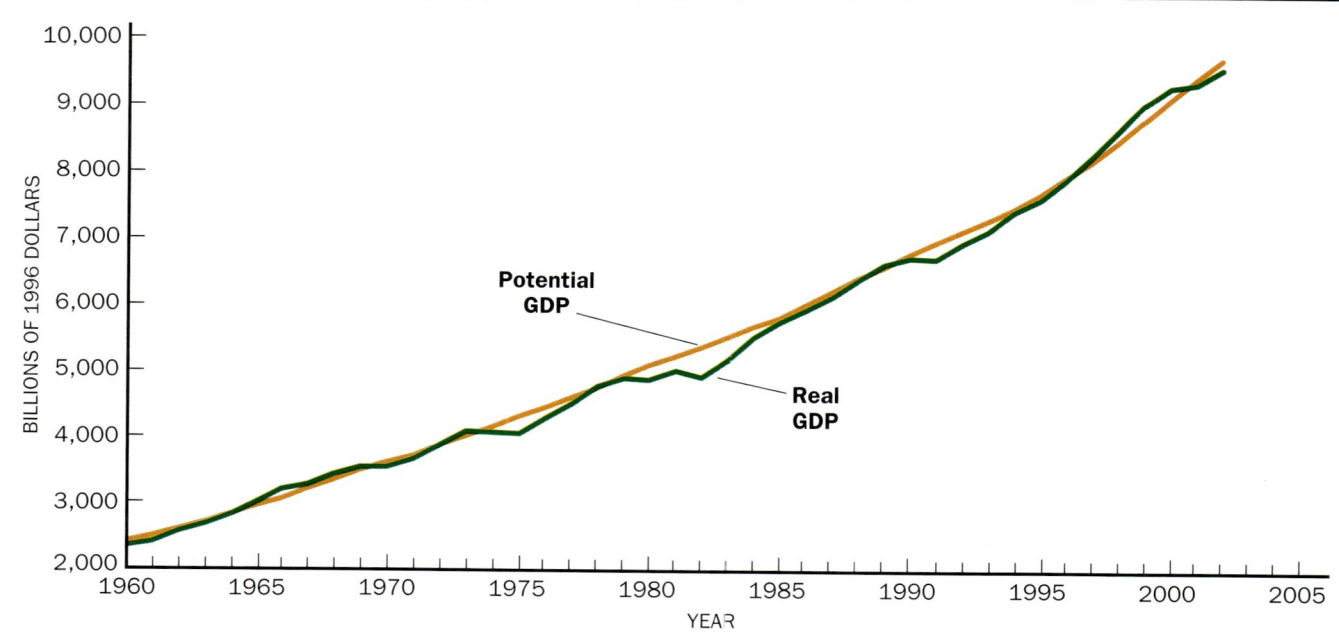

Figure 22.1
POTENTIAL AND REAL GDP

Potential GDP measures how much the economy would produce if it used all its resources at normal levels of overtime and capacity utilization. Real GDP shows what the economy actually produces. Notice that both have been growing over time.

SOURCES: Bureau of Economic Analysis and Congressional Budget Office.

International Perspective
WHAT GETS MEASURED IN THE GDP?

In the United States, illegal activity is not counted as part of GDP. If we are trying to get a measure of market economic activity, excluding occupations like the drug trade means that GDP misses one type of output. For the United States, this omission is unlikely to have a major impact on the usefulness of GDP statistics. But if illegal activity is a major source of income in a given country, then failing to count that income as part of GDP may give a misleading picture of its economy.

Colombia provides a case in point. Colombia is a major exporter of illegal drugs. Drugs are grown, processed, and transported. Each of these steps represents economic activity, yet the incomes generated directly by the trade in illegal drugs have been excluded from its GDP.

The Colombian government has begun to add income earned from illegal drug crops to GDP. It is estimated that treating drug crops like legal crops in this calculation may add as much as 1 percent to Colombia's GDP. The drug trade involves much more than just growing the crops—processing and transporting them are also huge businesses. But as of now, those aspects are omitted from Colombia's GDP. Including them would increase the drug trade's impact on the figures.

While adding even part of the value of drug-related income will raise Colombia's reported GDP, the new figure does not mean the country's income is any higher—it simply means that more of it is being counted in the official statistics. The change does highlight an important point, however. Often the exact definition of a statistic changes over time, or the methods used to collect the data change. Variables that have the same name in two different countries may not measure quite the same thing. We must keep these possible variations in mind when making international comparisons of GDP, especially when comparing economies that are quite different. If a particular type of economic activity—say, bread making—is done through markets in one economy and at home in another, bread consumption as measured in GDP will be higher in the former.

Robert Summers and Alan Heston carried out one of the best attempts to construct consistent international data on GDP. Their data, known as the Penn World Table, are available on the Web at http://pwt.econ.upenn.edu/.

For sound economic reasons, Colombia includes the illegal coca leaf crop in its calculation of GDP.

represent only a slowdown in real growth; sometimes output actually falls. The dips in real GDP from 1971 to 1973, from 1980 to 1981, from 1990 to 1991, and in 2001 represent periods when U.S. economic output actually declined. A strong upward fluctuation is called a **boom**, and a downward one is called a **recession**. A severe recession is called a **depression**. The last depression, called the Great Depression because of its length and depth, began in 1929. The economy did not fully recover until World War II. While there is no technical definition of a boom, a recession is generally said to have occurred when real GDP falls for at least two consecutive quarters. (For statistical purposes, a year is divided into quarters, each three months long.)

Low utilization of capacity, like the unemployment of workers, represents a waste of scarce economic resources. In recessions the economy operates well below its potential. Unemployment is high and a large fraction of machines remain idle or underutilized.

Because the difference between the actual level of GDP the economy produces and its potential level of GDP is an important measure of fluctuations, economists have a special name for it. The percentage difference between GDP and potential GDP is called the **output gap.** When the economy is in a recession, actual GDP is less than potential and the output gap is negative. If actual GDP is greater than potential, the output gap is positive. The output gap will play an prominent role in Part Seven when we examine economic fluctuations in more detail.

Wrap-Up

ALTERNATIVE APPROACHES TO MEASURING GDP

Measuring the value of output:
  consumption + investment + government purchases + net exports
  sum of value added in each stage of production
Measuring income:
  employee compensation + profits, interest, rents + indirect taxes + depreciation
Output = income

PROBLEMS IN MEASURING OUTPUT

The U.S. economy is constantly changing—new industries emerge, old industries decline, new technologies lead to new products and different methods of production. Does the way our economy is being fundamentally altered by new technologies mean that economists will need to rethink how we measure the economy's output? Three problems cause particular difficulties for measuring output.

Measuring Quality Changes With many products, such as computers, improvements in quality occur every year. GDP statisticians try to make adjustments for these changes in quality. But in some sectors, such as the financial and health sectors and the computer industry, the adjustments may be inadequate. Because these sectors are expanding rapidly, the magnitude of the real growth of GDP may be understated.

Measuring Service Output Defining and measuring output in the service sector of the economy are increasingly complex and difficult tasks. Because the service sector is a growing share of the economy, the conventional GDP measure may understate the real growth of the economy.

Measuring Nonmarket Goods Nonmarket goods and services, such as housework done by family members, also present problems. The statistics underestimate the true level of production in the economy, because they ignore such activity. While GDP is designed primarily to measure only market economic activity, there are two important exceptions to this restriction. GDP does include a measure of the value of owner-occupied housing, and it includes the value of homegrown food consumed by farm families. In general, though, nonmarket activity is not included, because without prices a value cannot be assigned to the output.

Conclusions GDP provides our best estimate of the level of production for markets. But changes in the nature of production, from growth in the underground economy to new technological innovations, can affect the ability of GDP to provide an accurate picture of the economy's performance.

MEASURING THE STANDARD OF LIVING

GDP tells us something about the overall level of economic activity in a nation, the goods and services produced for the market. But it is only a partial measure of a society's overall well-being. Literacy rates (the percentage of the population that can read or write), infant mortality rates (the fraction of infants that die), and life expectancy are other social indicators that are often employed in attempts to gauge a nation's standard of living. Real GDP does not take into account these other important components. But at the same time, there is a strong connection between high levels of real GDP per capita and high levels of literacy, high levels of health, and high environmental quality. People in countries that are rich as measured by real GDP per capita are able to enjoy better health, longer life expectancy, higher levels of education, cleaner water, and cleaner air than can people in poor countries.

A GREEN GDP

The national income accounts do not take note of the depletion of the stock of natural resources or the deterioration in the quality of the environment that producing GDP may cause. Harvesting a hardwood forest may increase a country's GDP, but it decreases the country's assets. The output is not sustainable—a fact that a "green GDP" would recognize by subtracting the decrease in the natural resource base from conventional GDP. Such a measure would better indicate whether an economic activity is adding to the nation's wealth or subtracting from it by using up natural resources. A measure of living standards, unlike a measure of goods and service produced for the marketplace, should include changes in the quality of the environment, as well as changes in such factors as levels of health and of crime.

Constructing a means of calculating a green GDP is difficult. Compare the problem of measuring the value of auto production with the problem of measuring the value of the decline in the California sea otter population. In the former case, we can collect statistics on the number of cars produced, and we can use the prices we observe in the marketplace to assign a value to that production. In contrast, while

Green GDP takes account of exhausted natural resources, such as this clear-cut section of forest near Willamette National Forest in Oregon.

we may be able to measure the drop in the otter population, how do we value this decline? There is no market price that we can use. And unless we can value the change in the otter population, the change in old-growth forests, the change in air quality, and the production of cars in a common measure (say dollars), we cannot add them up to obtain an overall measure of a green GDP. So developing an environmental measure of the economy's production is inherently problematic.

Unemployment

Discussions of unemployment frequently take center stage during presidential elections. In the 1992 campaign, two slogans that struck a responsive cord were "Jobs, Jobs, Jobs" and "It's the economy, stupid!" During the 2000 campaign, Vice President Al Gore emphasized the economy's strong performance over the previous eight years. In the 2004 election, candidates focused on the "jobless recovery." The unemployment rate is the most common measure of the economy's performance in creating jobs.

Though the central economic goal over the long run is to increase living standards, unemployment becomes a source of immediate concern when the economy goes into a downturn. Unemployment represents an underutilization of resources. People who are willing and able to work at current market wages are not being productively employed. To the unemployed individuals and their families, unemployment represents economic hardship. People unemployed for a long time will be unable to meet current expenses—utilities, rent, and so on—and will have to move to less-expensive housing and otherwise reduce their standard of living.

Unemployment not only costs individuals their paychecks, it can deal a powerful blow to their self-respect, and their families may be forced to choose between poverty and the bitter taste of government or private charity. Many families break up under the strain.

Unemployment presents each age group of workers with different problems. For the young, having a job is necessary to develop job skills. Persistent unemployment for them not only wastes valuable human resources today but also reduces the future productivity of the labor force. Young people who remain unemployed for an extended period are especially prone to becoming alienated from society and turning to antisocial activities such as crime and drug abuse.

For the middle-aged or elderly worker, losing a job poses different problems. Despite federal and state prohibitions against age discrimination, employers are often hesitant to hire older applicants. If older workers are unemployed for long periods of time, they may lose some of their skills. And the job that the unemployed older worker does succeed in getting often entails lower wages and less status than previous jobs and may make less than full use of his or her skills. Such changes burden the dislocated workers and their families with much stress.

Unemployment is very costly to communities as well. If people in a town are thrown out of work—say, because a big employer closes down or decides to move—their neighbors are also likely to suffer, since there is less income circulating to buy everything from cars and houses to gasoline and groceries. As higher unemployment results in fewer people paying local taxes, the quality of schools, libraries, parks, and police can be threatened.

Unemployment also may reinforce racial divisions in a society. The rate of unemployment for African Americans is generally more than twice that for whites. By 2000, with overall unemployment at its lowest level in thirty years, all groups were benefiting from the strong labor market—unemployment for African Americans was lower than at any time since 1969. As the economy entered a recession in 2001, unemployment rates for all groups rose. By the end of 2002, the unemployment rate for African Americans peaked at 11.4 percent, while white unemployment was only 5.2 percent. The economy was starting to recover by 2002, but unemployment had declined only modestly by the end of 2003. By December 2004, though, the unemployment rate for whites had fallen to 4.6 percent, while the rate for African Americans was still over 10 percent.

UNEMPLOYMENT STATISTICS

In the United States, unemployment data are collected by the Department of Labor, which surveys a representative mix of households every month. The survey takers ask each household whether a member of the household is currently employed, and if not, whether that member is currently seeking employment. The *labor force* is the total number of people employed or actively seeking employment. The **unemployment rate** is the ratio of the number seeking employment to the total

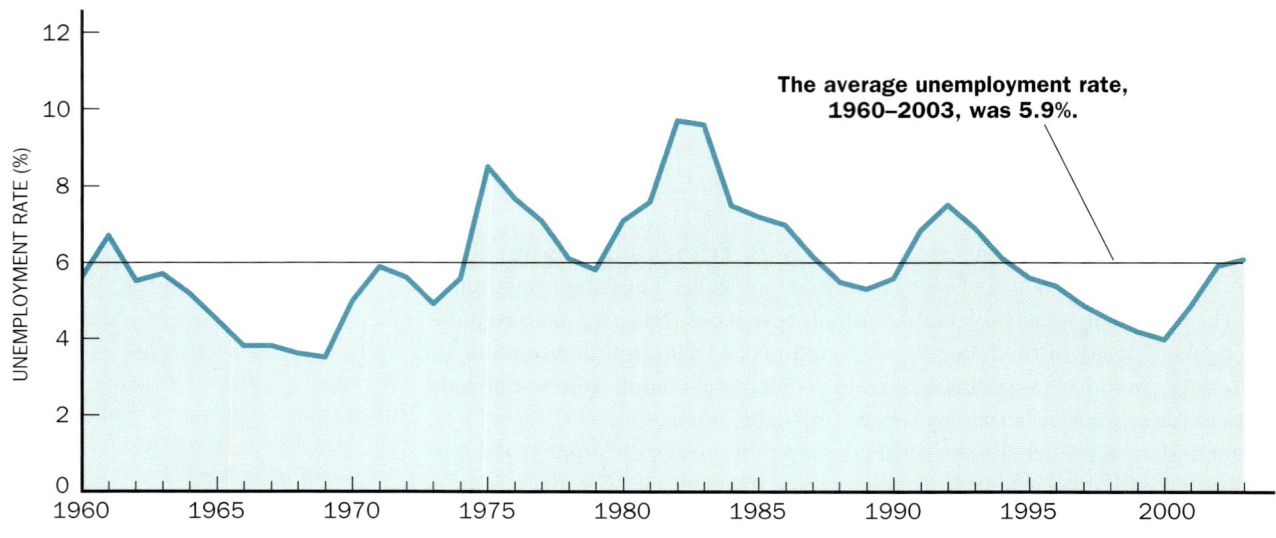

Figure 22.2

OVERALL U.S. UNEMPLOYMENT RATE

Unemployment in the United States rises during recessions and falls during booms. Between 1960 and 2003, it averaged 5.9 percent. It reached a low of 3.5 percent during 1969 and a high of 9.7 percent in 1982.

SOURCE: *Economic Report of the President* (2004).

labor force. If there are 127 million workers employed and 6 million say they are looking for a job but cannot find one, then the total labor force is 133 million, and the

$$\text{unemployment rate} = \frac{\text{number unemployed}}{\text{labor force}}$$

$$= \frac{\text{number unemployed}}{\text{number employed} + \text{number unemployed}}$$

$$= \frac{6 \text{ million}}{127 \text{ million} + 6 \text{ million}} = 4.5 \text{ percent}.$$

The unemployment rate does not include individuals who are not working but who also are not actively seeking a job. Such individuals are not counted as part of the labor force.

Figure 22.2 plots the unemployment rate for the United States since 1960. The figure illustrates two facts. First, unemployment is persistent; it has averaged just under 6 percent since 1960, and the lowest it has been during this period was 3.5 percent (in 1969). Second, the level of unemployment can fluctuate dramatically. By the end of the 1990s, unemployment in the United States had fallen to levels not seen in thirty years, but as recently as 1983, the unemployment rate was nearly 10 percent. Fluctuations in unemployment were even more pronounced in earlier periods. In the worst days of the Great Depression of the 1930s, more than one-fourth of

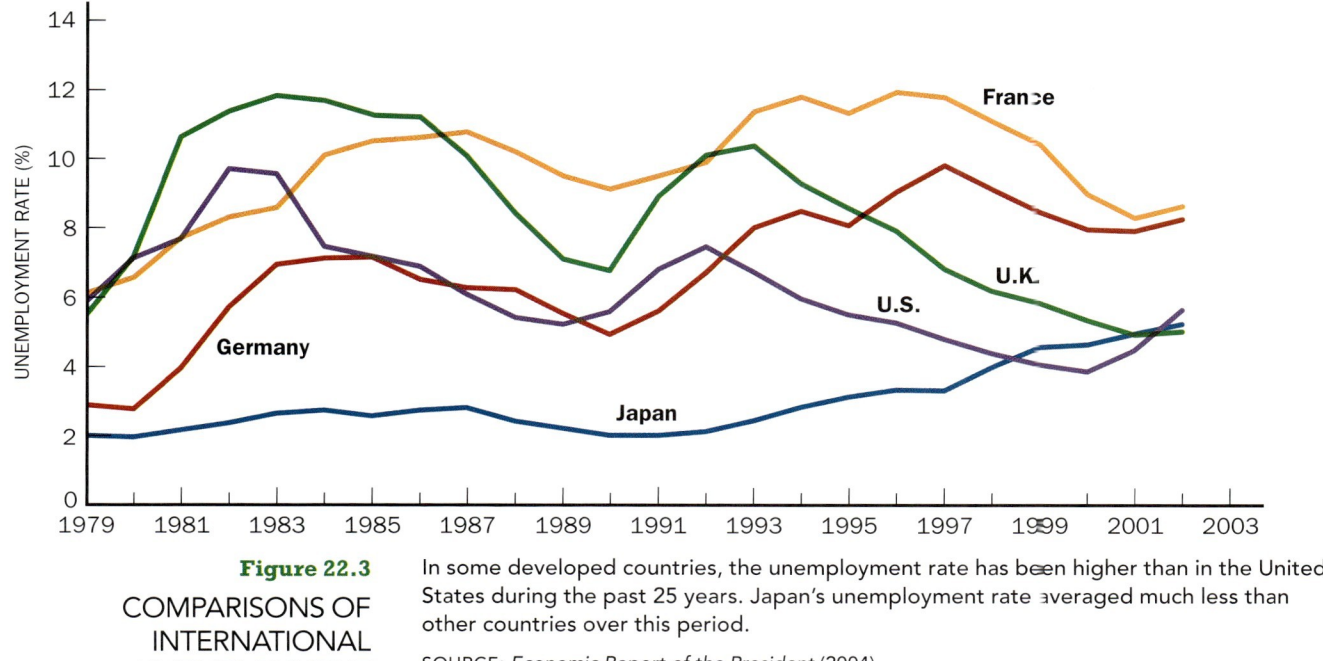

Figure 22.3

COMPARISONS OF INTERNATIONAL UNEMPLOYMENT

In some developed countries, the unemployment rate has been higher than in the United States during the past 25 years. Japan's unemployment rate averaged much less than other countries over this period.

SOURCE: *Economic Report of the President* (2004).

the U.S. labor force was unemployed. The unemployment rate among those who worked in manufacturing was even higher—at one point, one out of three workers in manufacturing had lost their jobs.

In recent years, unemployment in other countries often was worse than in the United States (Figure 22.3). In the 1960s, U.S. unemployment rates exceeded those in other major industrialized economies; but European unemployment rates rose dramatically during the 1980s and generally now exceed the rate in the United States. Japan historically has had very low levels of unemployment, but in 1999 the unemployment rate in Japan surpassed that of the United States for the first time. Unemployment in many developing countries is more than 20 percent.

One problem with the unemployment measure is that many individuals are *discouraged* from even looking for a job, especially in a prolonged downturn. Because they are not actively seeking employment, the statistics will not count them as unemployed and thus underestimate the number who would choose to work if a job were available. The fraction of the working-age population that is employed or seeking employment is called the **labor force participation rate.** Because of the effect of discouraged workers, the labor force participation rate tends to decline in recessions and rise in booms.

FORMS OF UNEMPLOYMENT

Even when output is equal to potential, unemployment is not zero. To understand why, we must distinguish between different kinds of unemployment. Economists define four: seasonal, frictional, structural, and cyclical.

Right before Christmas, there is a huge demand for retail salespeople to work in department stores and shopping malls across the nation. In many parts of the country, construction slows down in the winter because the weather makes outdoor work impossible. Conversely, tourism often increases in the summer, as does the number of jobs that cater to tourists. The supply of labor also increases in the summer, as high school and college students enter the labor force on a temporary basis. Unemployment that varies predictably with the seasons is called **seasonal unemployment.** Since these movements in employment and unemployment reflect normal seasonal patterns, the unemployment rate reported on the news is adjusted according to the average amount of seasonal unemployment. These adjustments are called *seasonal adjustments*. If on average the unadjusted unemployment rate is 0.4 percent higher in the summer than at other times during the year, the seasonal-adjusted unemployment rate for July will be the measured unemployment rate minus 0.4 percent.

While workers in construction, agriculture, and tourism regularly face seasonal unemployment, other workers become unemployed as a part of a normal transition from one job to another. For example, new college graduates may spend a month or more looking for a job before finding one. During that month, they are counted as unemployed. This kind of unemployment is referred to as **frictional unemployment.** If people could move from one job to another instantaneously, there would be no frictional unemployment. In a dynamic economy such as in the United States, with some industries growing and others declining, there will always be movements from one job to another, and hence there will always be some frictional unemployment. Not all frictional unemployment represents wasted resources—searching for a new job can be a valuable use of time.

Most individual bouts of unemployment are short-lived; the average person who loses a job is out of work for only about three months. However, about 10 percent of the jobless are unemployed for more than six months. This kind of long-term unemployment often results from structural factors in the economy and is called **structural unemployment.** Substantial structural unemployment is quite often found in the same market as firms with job openings, because the unemployed lack the skills required for the newly created jobs. For example, there may be vacancies for computer programmers while construction workers are unemployed. Similarly, there may be job shortages in parts of the economy that are expanding rapidly (as in the Sunbelt and Silicon Valley during the 1990s) and unemployment in areas that are suffering decline (as in Michigan when the demand for U.S. cars fell).

Seasonal, frictional, and structural unemployment occur even when the economy is operating at its potential level of output. The sum of seasonal, frictional, and structural unemployment is called the **natural rate of unemployment**.

There is a fourth type of unemployment, however, that is associated with economic fluctuations. Unemployment that increases when the economy slows down and decreases when the economy goes into a boom is called **cyclical unemployment** and is one of the fundamental concerns of macroeconomics. Government policymakers are particularly interested in reducing both the frequency and the magnitude of this kind of unemployment, by reducing the frequency and magnitudes of recessions that give rise to it. Government also seeks to reduce its impact by providing unemployment compensation to those temporarily thrown out of work.

Wrap-Up

FORMS OF UNEMPLOYMENT

Seasonal
Frictional
Structural
Cyclical

OUTPUT GAPS AND THE NATURAL RATE OF UNEMPLOYMENT

Earlier, we defined the output gap as the percentage gap between GDP and potential GDP. When the output gap is zero, real GDP is equal to potential GDP and the economy is at full employment. *Full employment* means not that the total unemployment rate will be zero—there will still be seasonal, frictional, and structural unemployment—but that there is no cyclical unemployment. The unemployment rate that occurs when the output gap is equal to zero is the natural rate of unemployment. When the output gap is equal to zero, the actual unemployment rate equals the natural rate of unemployment. When the output gap is positive, the actual unemployment rate will be below the natural rate of unemployment; when the output gap is negative, it exceeds the natural rate of unemployment.

The natural rate of unemployment can change over time because of such factors as changes in the age composition of the labor force. For example, young workers typically experience higher unemployment rates than do older workers; thus, when the baby boom generation first began entering the labor force in the 1960s, the unemployment rate associated with a zero output gap rose. In the 1970s and 1980s, most economists thought the natural rate of unemployment was around 6 percent. Because workers in their forties and fifties tend to experience lower unemployment rates, the natural rate of unemployment fell as the baby boomers aged. Today, many economists put the natural rate at around 5 to 5.5 percent.

The connection between fluctuations in the unemployment rate and fluctuations in the economy's production is illustrated in Figure 22.4. The horizontal axis plots the output gap. On the vertical axis is the unemployment rate. The downward-sloping relationship between the output gap and the unemployment rate stands out clearly. Arthur Okun, who served as chairman of the Council of Economic Advisors under President Lyndon Johnson, showed that as the economy pulls out of a recession, output increases by a greater percentage than the rise in employment. And as the economy goes into a recession, output decreases by a greater percentage than the reduction in employment. This result is called **Okun's Law.** Current estimates of the relationship between the output gap and employment predict that a 1 percent increase in the unemployment rate will correspond to about a 2 percentage point reduction in the output gap.

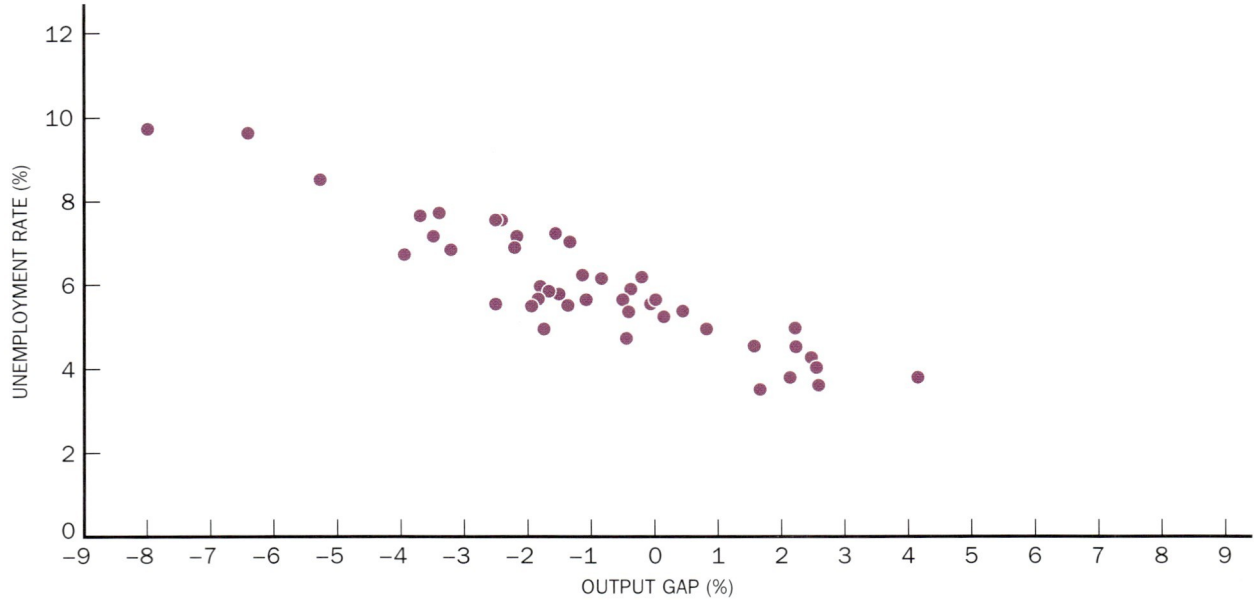

Figure 22.4
OKUN'S LAW, 1959–2002

Okun's Law relates fluctuations in output relative to potential (the output gap) and fluctuations in the unemployment rate. For every 1 percentage point change in the unemployment rate, the output gap changes approximately 2 percentage points.

Figure 22.4 shows that when the output gap is zero, so that real GDP equals potential GDP, the unemployment rate in the United States is usually around 5.5 percent. If real GDP falls below potential GDP and the output gap becomes negative, then unemployment rises above 5.5 percent. This makes sense—when the output gap is zero, the unemployment rate should be equal to the natural rate of unemployment, which, as we have already noted, is usually estimated to be about 5.5 percent.

Okun's Law provides an easy way to link fluctuations in unemployment with fluctuations in the output gap. It can also help us estimate the cost of a recession. In the boom year of 1999, the number of unemployed Americans fell below 6 million. By 2002, just over 8 million American workers were seeking work but unable to find it. From the standpoint of the economy, the loss from an increase in unemployment during a recession is the output that could have been produced if those workers had remained employed. This lost output represents the *opportunity cost* of the higher unemployment, and we can use Okun's Law to roughly calculate it. Unemployment reached 5.8 percent in 2002. Using an estimate of 5.5 percent for the natural rate, we find that cyclical unemployment was 5.8 minus 5.5 percent, or 0.3 percent. According to Okun's Law, that would be associated with a 2 × 0.3 = 0.6 percent negative output gap. With real GDP in 2002 equal to roughly $10 trillion, a 0.6 percent output gap means the economy was producing 0.6 percent of $10 trillion, or $60 billion ($60,000,000,000), less per year than its potential. This is the opportunity cost of the rise in unemployment during the recession, an amount equal to just under $200 per person in the United States.

Flows and Stocks

GDP is a measure of output *per year*. Rate measurements such as these are called **flows.** When a financial reporter says, "The quarterly GDP statistic, just released, shows that GDP was $10 trillion per year," she does not mean that $10 trillion of goods and services were produced during the quarter. Rather, the production during the quarter was $2.5 trillion; and if that rate were sustained for a whole year, the total value of goods and services produced would be four times as much: $10 trillion.

Flow statistics need to be contrasted with **stock** statistics, which measure an item at a single point in time. The unemployment rate is a stock—the number of workers unemployed in a particular month as a fraction of the total labor force in that month. Another important figure is the capital stock—the total value of all the buildings and machines that underlie the economy's productive potential. The amount in your bank account is a third example of a stock statistic.

The relationship between stocks and flows is simple. The stock of capital at the end of 2000, for example, consists of the stock of capital at the end of 1999 plus or minus the flows into or out of the stock during 2000. Investment is the flow into the stock of capital. Depreciation is the flow out of the capital stock.

Review and Practice

SUMMARY

1. Gross domestic product (GDP) is the typical way of measuring the value of national output. Real GDP adjusts GDP for changes in the price level.
2. GDP can be calculated in three ways: the final goods approach, which adds the value of all final goods produced in the economy in a given year; the value-added approach, which adds the difference between firms' revenues and costs of intermediate goods; and the income approach, which adds together all income received by those in the economy. All three methods give the same answer.
3. Aggregate output in the economy is equal to aggregate income.
4. Economists distinguish between flows—such as output per year—and stocks—such as the total value of buildings and machines in an economy at a given time (the capital stock).
5. Unemployment imposes costs both on individuals and on society as a whole, which loses what the unemployed workers could have contributed and must supply what is needed to support them in other ways.
6. Seasonal unemployment occurs regularly in sectors such as tourism, construction, and agriculture. Frictional unemployment results when people are in transition between one job and another or when they first enter the labor market to search for work. Structural unemployment occurs when the economy changes, as the new jobs being created have requirements different from the old jobs being lost. Cyclical unemployment increases or decreases as the level of actual real output fluctuates around potential GDP.
7. Seasonal, frictional, and structural unemployment account for the positive unemployment rate even when the economy operates at potential GDP.
8. The natural rate of unemployment is the sum of seasonal, structural, and frictional unemployment.
9. Okun's Law is a relationship between the cyclical unemployment rate and real GDP relative to potential GDP (the output gap).

KEY TERMS

gross domestic product (GDP)
nominal GDP
real GDP
GDP deflator
final goods approach
value added
income approach
potential GDP
boom
recession
depression
output gap
unemployment rate
labor force participation rate
seasonal unemployment
frictional unemployment
structural unemployment
natural rate of unemployment
cyclical unemployment
Okun's Law
flow
stock

REVIEW QUESTIONS

1. What is the difference between nominal GDP, real GDP, and potential GDP?
2. What are the differences among the final goods approach to measuring GDP, the value-added approach, and the income approach?
3. What is the GDP deflator?
4. What are some problems that arise in measuring output?
5. What are the differences between seasonal, frictional, structural, and cyclical unemployment?
6. When there is a reduction in the number of hours worked in the economy, is this normally shared equally by all workers? Are workers in some groups more affected by increased unemployment than those in other groups?
7. What is the natural rate of unemployment?
8. What is Okun's Law?

PROBLEMS

Use the following data for Questions 1–3, and round your answers to the nearest tenth. Assume the economy of Slugian produces two products, lectures and coffee. Output and prices of these two goods for 2002 and 2003 are given in the table:

	Quantities	Prices
2002: Lectures	1,400 lectures	$75 per lecture
2002: Coffee	35,000 cups	$1.55 per cup
2003: Lectures	1,450 lectures	$76 per lecture
2003: Coffee	40,000 cups	$1.45 per cup

1. What was nominal GDP in 2002 for this economy? What was it in 2003? What was the percentage rate of change in nominal GDP between 2002 and 2003?
2. Using 2002 prices as your base year, what was real GDP in 2002? What was real GDP in 2003? What was the percentage rate of change in real GDP between 2002 and 2003?
3. What was the percentage rate of increase in prices in this economy between 2002 and 2003 as measured by the GDP price deflator?
4. Given the following information about the U.S. economy, how much did real GDP grow between 1980 and 1990? Between 1990 and 2000?

	1980	1985	1990	1995	2000
Nominal GDP (trillions)	$2.80	$4.21	$5.80	$7.40	$9.96
GDP deflator (1996=100)	57	73.7	86.5	98.1	106.9

5. Go to the Web site of the National Income Accounts at the Bureau of Economic Analysis (www.bea.doc.gov/bea/dn1.htm). What is the latest figure on the economy's nominal GDP? On real GDP? What was the growth rate of real GDP during the most recently available quarter?
6. Go to the Web site of the Bureau of Labor Statistics (www.bls.gov/) and find the latest data on the unemployment rate. What was the unemployment rate for the most recently available month? How has the unemployment rate changed over the past year?
7. For each of the cases listed, state whether the person is in the labor force or not. If the person is in the labor force, is he or she employed or unemployed? Give your reasons in each case.
   (a) John recently retired from IBM and is looking for a part-time job to supplement his retirement income.
   (b) Christina works 10 hours each week at Starbucks; she would like to find a full-time job.
   (c) Ben recently quit his job at the campus bookstore to have more time to surf.
   (d) Michelle just graduated from college; she has been sending out her resumé but has yet to land a job.
8. Are you currently in the labor force? If so, are you employed or are you unemployed? Explain.
9. If the output gap is a negative 2 percent, what does Okun's Law tell us will be the level of cyclical unemployment?
10. Firms typically do not fire workers quickly as the economy goes into a recession—at least not as quickly as their output is reduced. How might you expect output per worker and output per hour to move over the business cycle?
11. Suppose the Farsighted Forecasting Group, an organization of private economists, predicts that the output gap will fall by 4 percent over the next year. According to Okun's Law, by how much is the unemployment rate likely to rise?

Learning Goals

In this chapter, you will learn

1. The costs of inflation
2. How the consumer price index is measured
3. The recent history of inflation in the United States

Chapter 23

THE COST OF LIVING AND INFLATION

In the 1920s, the years of silent pictures, a movie ticket cost a nickel. By the late 1940s, in the heyday of the Hollywood studios, the price was up to $0.50. In the 1960s, the price of a movie was $2.00, and now it is more than $8.00. This steady rise is no anomaly. Most other goods have undergone similar price increases over time. This increase in the general level of prices is called *inflation*. While unemployment tends to be concentrated in certain groups within the population, everyone is affected by inflation. Thus, it is not surprising that when inflation becomes high, it almost always rises to the top of the political agenda.

Ensuring that inflation remains low and stable is one of the key goals of macroeconomic policy. In this chapter, you will learn about the costs of inflation and why it is desirable to make sure that inflation remains low. You will also learn about the price index that is used to measure the cost of living. Finally, the chapter ends with a review of American's experience with inflation.

The Costs of Inflation

It is not inflation if the price of only one good goes up. It *is* inflation if the prices of *most* goods go up. The **inflation rate** is the rate at which the *general level* of prices increases. When inflation is positive—that is, the average price level is rising—a dollar buys less and less over time. Or, to put it another way, it takes more and more dollars to purchase the same bundle of goods and services. While the costs of unemployment are apparent—it causes not only a loss in output but also the misery of those who cannot secure gainful work—the costs of inflation are more subtle.

People sense there is something wrong with the economy when there is high inflation. Workers worry that paychecks will not keep pace with price hikes, a failure that will erode their standard of living. Investors worry that the dollars they receive in the future will be worth less than the dollars they invested, leaving them with less than enough to live comfortably in their old age.

When inflation is anticipated, many of its economic costs disappear. Workers who know that prices will be rising by 5 percent this year, for example, may negotiate wages that rise fast enough to offset inflation. Firms may be willing to agree to these larger wage increases since they anticipate being able to raise the prices of the goods they produce. Lenders know that the dollars they will be repaid will be worth less than the dollars they lent, so they take this loss in value into account when setting the interest rate they charge or when deciding whether to make a loan.

But even when inflation is not fully anticipated, workers and investors can immunize themselves against its effects by having wages and returns *indexed* to inflation. For instance, when wages are perfectly indexed, a 1 percent increase in the price level results in a 1 percent increase in wages, preserving the workers' purchasing power. In recent years, both Social Security payments and tax rates have been indexed. Many countries, including the United Kingdom, Canada, and New Zealand, sell indexed government bonds so that savers can put aside money knowing that the returns will not be affected by inflation.

WHO SUFFERS FROM INFLATION?

Although indexing softens the effects of inflation, its protection is far from complete. So who suffers from inflation today? Many people may suffer a little because indexing does not fully protect them, but some are more vulnerable than others. Among the groups most imperfectly protected are lenders, taxpayers, and holders of currency.

Lenders Since most loans are not fully indexed, increases in inflation mean that the dollars that lenders receive back from borrowers are worth less than those they lent out. Many people put a large part of their retirement savings into bonds or other fixed-income securities. These people will suffer if an inflationary bout reduces the purchasing power of their savings. The extent to which they will suffer depends in large measure on whether the price changes were anticipated, as interest rates can adjust to completely compensate lenders for any inflation that was anticipated.

Taxpayers Our tax system is only partially indexed, and inflation frequently hurts investors badly through the tax system. All returns to investment are taxed, including those that do nothing more than offset inflation. Consequently, real after-tax returns are often negative when inflation is high. Consider a rate of inflation of 10 percent and an asset that yields 12 percent before tax. If the individual has to pay a 33 percent tax on the return, the after-tax yield to the investor is only 9 percent—not even enough to compensate for inflation. The after-tax real return in this example is –1 percent.

Holders of Currency Inflation also makes it expensive for people to hold currency because as prices rise, the currency loses its value. Since currency facilitates a variety of transactions, inflation interferes with the efficiency of the economy by discouraging its holding. By taking away the real value of money, inflation acts as a tax on those who hold money. Economists refer to this distortionary effect as an *inflation tax.*

This distortion is not as important in modern economies, where individuals frequently put their money into interest-paying checking accounts instead of keeping their cash. As the rate of inflation increases, the interest rate paid on checking accounts normally increases as well. Even in Argentina in the 1970s, when prices were rising at 800 percent *a month,* bank accounts yielded more than this. Still, poorer individuals who do not have checking accounts—and therefore must hold much of what little wealth they have in the form of currency—are adversely affected. According to the Federal Reserve's 2001 Survey of Consumer Finances, almost 10 percent of American families do not have a checking, savings, or money market account. These families tend to have low incomes and little wealth.

THE ECONOMY

There are two costs of inflation to the economy as a whole. The first has to do with relative prices. Because price increases are never perfectly coordinated, increases in the rate of inflation lead to greater variability in relative prices. If the shoe industry makes price adjustments only every three months, then in the third month, right before its price increase, shoes may be relatively cheap; conversely, right after the price increase, shoes may be relatively expensive. On the other hand, the prices of groceries might change continually throughout the three-month period. Therefore, the ratio of the price of groceries to the price of shoes will change continually. An average inflation rate of only 2 or 3 percent per year does not cause much of a problem. But when the average rate is 10 percent per month, inflation causes real distortions in how society allocates its resources. When inflation gets very high, individuals and firms tend to allocate considerable time and resources to avoiding its costs and to taking advantage of the discrepancies in prices charged by different sellers. Rather than carrying money, which quickly erodes in value, people rush to deposit their money in interest-bearing bank accounts.

The second economy-wide cost of inflation arises from the risk and uncertainty that it generates. If indexing were perfect, the uncertainty about the rate of inflation would be unimportant. But as indexing is not perfect, the resulting uncertainty makes it difficult to plan. People saving for their retirement cannot know how much to put aside if they do not know what a dollar will be worth in the future when they retire. Business firms borrowing money are uncertain about the price they will receive for the goods they produce. Firms are also hurt when they build wage increases into multiyear contracts to reflect *anticipated* inflation. If for any reason a firm finds that the prices it can charge have increased less rapidly than anticipated in the contract, the employer suffers.

Because of these economy-wide costs, countries that experience periods of very high inflation also tend to experience slower real economic growth.

The Costs of Deflation

Our focus has been on the costs of inflation—rising prices—since that has been the experience of the United States and most other countries over the past fifty years. But inflation in many countries declined significantly during the 1980s, and falling prices—**deflation**—has in some places become the concern. Japan, for instance, recently experienced several years of falling prices.

Many of the costs associated with inflation also make deflation costly. Variability in relative prices and increased uncertainty can arise when average prices are falling, just as they can when average prices are rising. And while inflation can hurt lenders, deflation can hurt borrowers. When prices are falling, the dollars a borrower must pay back are worth more than the dollars that were borrowed. In the United States, the 1870s and the 1930s were periods of declining prices. Borrowers, particularly farm families, were hard hit as the wages they earned or the prices they received for their crops fell. Many were forced to leave their farms. These periods have had a lasting impact on America's cultural history. L. Frank Baum's *The Wizard of Oz*, for example, has been interpreted as an allegory on the dangers of the gold standard and in favor of raising the money supply by coining silver. (In Chapter 28, we will learn why a rise in the money supply—as occurred with the discoveries of gold in South Africa in the 1880s—can lead to rising prices.) John Steinbeck's *The Grapes of Wrath* chronicles the hardships faced by Oklahoma farmers who were displaced during the 1930s.

Periods of deflation also have been associated with financial and banking crises. If firms that have taken loans are unable to repay them because of falling prices, they may be forced into bankruptcy. But their failure will prevent them from repaying the banks that have lent money, which therefore may become bankrupt in turn.

The hyperinflation in Germany in the early 1920s was so severe that paper deutsche marks were more valuable as stove fuel than as actual money.

Wrap-Up

REAL COSTS OF INFLATION

Variability in relative prices

Resources devoted to mitigating the costs of inflation and taking advantage of price discrepancies

Increased uncertainty

Case in Point

HYPERINFLATION IN GERMANY IN THE 1920s

Following World War I, the victorious Allied nations required Germany to make substantial "reparations." But the sheer size of the reparations, combined with the wartime devastation of German industry, made payment nearly impossible. In *The*

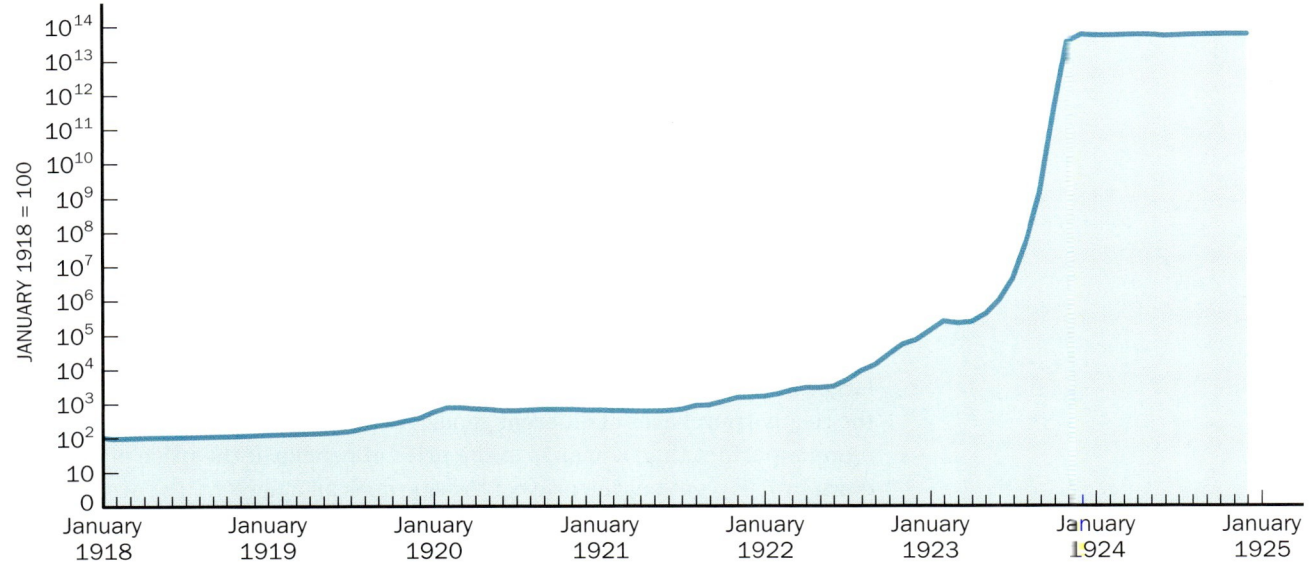

Figure 23.1
HYPERINFLATION: GERMANY'S PRICE LEVEL (LOG SCALE)

Inflation in Germany during the 1920s reached levels that may seem unbelievably high. At the end of 1923, prices were 36 billion times higher than they had been two years earlier.

SOURCE: Thomas Sargent, "The Ends of Four Big Inflations," in R. Hall, ed., *Inflation, Causes and Effects* (Chicago: University of Chicago Press, 1982).

Economic Consequences of the Peace, John Maynard Keynes, then an economic adviser to the British government, warned that the reparations were too large. To pay for some of Germany's financial obligations, the German government started printing money.

The resulting increase in both the amount of circulating currency and the price level can be seen in Figure 23.1. From December 1921 to December 1923, the average price level increased by a factor of 36 billion.[1] People made desperate attempts to spend their currency as soon as they received it, since the value of currency was declining so rapidly. One story Keynes often told was that Germans would buy two beers at once, even though one was likely to get warm, for fear that otherwise, when it came time to buy the second beer, its price would have risen.

At an annual inflation rate of 100 percent, money loses half its value every year. If you save $100 today, in five years it will have a buying power equal to only $3. It is possible for nominal interest rates to adjust even to very high inflation rates; but when those high inflation rates fluctuate in unanticipated ways, the effects can be disastrous.

Periods of hyperinflation create a massive redistribution of wealth. If an individual is smart or lucky enough to hold assets in a form such as foreign funds or land, then the hyperinflation will do little to reduce that person's real wealth. Those who cannot avail themselves of these "inflation-proof" assets will see their wealth fall.

---

[1]Thomas Sargent, "The Ends of Four Big Inflations," in R. Hall, ed., *Inflation, Causes and Effects* (Chicago: University of Chicago Press, 1982), pp. 74–75.

Measuring Inflation

If the prices of all goods and services rose by the same proportion, say, 5 percent, over a year, then measuring inflation would be easy: the rate of inflation that year would be 5 percent. Difficulties arise because the prices of different goods rise at different rates, and the prices of some goods even decline. For example, since the years 1982–1984, which the United States uses as a base reference period, the price of apparel rose by 24 percent, the price of medical care by 186 percent, and the price of housing by 80 percent, yet the price of personal computers fell by 77 percent between 1998 and 2003. To determine the change in the overall price level, economists calculate the *average* percentage increase in prices. But since some goods loom much larger in the typical consumer's budget than others, this calculation must reflect the relative purchases of different goods. A change in the price of housing is much more important than a change in the price of pencils. If the price of pencils goes down by 5 percent but the price of housing goes up 5 percent, the overall measure of the price level should go up.

Economists have a straightforward way of reflecting the differing importance of different goods. They ask, What would it cost consumers to purchase the same bundle of goods this year that they bought last year? If, for example, it cost $22,000 in the year 2005 to buy what it cost consumers $20,000 to purchase in 2004, we say that prices, *on average,* rose by 10 percent. Such results are frequently expressed in the form of a *price index,* which, for ease of comparison, measures the price level in any given year relative to a common base year.

The price index for the base year is, by definition, set equal to 100. The price index for any other year is calculated by taking the ratio of the price level in that year to the price level in the base year and multiplying it by 100. For example, if 2004 is our base year and we want to know the price index for 2005, we first calculate the ratio of the cost of a certain bundle of goods in 2005 ($22,000) to the cost of the same bundle of goods in 2004 ($20,000), which is 1.1. The price index in 2005 is therefore $1.1 \times 100 = 110$. The index 110, using 2004 as a base, indicates that prices are 10 percent higher, on average, in 2005 than in 2004.

There are several different price indexes, each using a different bundle of goods. To track the movement of prices that are important to American households, the government collects price data on the bundle of goods that represent how the average household spends its income. This index is called the **consumer price index, or CPI.** To determine the bundle, the government, through the Bureau of Labor Statistics (BLS) of the Department of Commerce, conducts a Consumer Expenditure Survey. The information from the survey is then used to determine the importance of more than 2,000 different expenditure categories. Weights are assigned to the expenditure categories to reflect the importance of each in household spending. For example, new cars receive a weight of 4.6 out of 100, while men's footwear receives a weight of 0.241. Currently, the CPI is based on an expenditure survey conducted over the period 1993–1995. This survey involved more than 30,000 households who provided information on their buying habits. In the past, a new expenditure survey was conducted once a decade or so. However, the BLS now plans to update the bundle every two years. The BLS provides answers to many questions about the CPI at www.bls.gov/cpi/cpifaq.htm.

To see how a price index like the CPI is constructed, we can calculate one for Bob, who spends all his income on rent, Big Macs, and CDs. Let's suppose his total expenditures during 2003 were $1,500 each month, of which $1,000 went for rent, $200 for 100 Big Macs (which cost $2 each), and $300 for 15 CDs (which cost $20 each). In 2004, his rent increases to $1,200 and Big Macs go up in price to $2.25, while the price of a CD falls to $18. What has happened to Bob's price index? We want to know how much it costs, in year 2004, to buy the same basket of goods Bob purchased in 2003. In 2003, these goods cost $1,500. In 2004, they cost $1,695: $1,200 for rent, $225 for 100 Big Macs, and $270 for 15 CDs. Bob's cost of living has increased. Setting the value of the index equal to 100 in the base year of 2003, Bob's price index in 2004 will equal $100 \times 1,695/1,500 = 113$.

The inflation rate is the percentage change in the price index. So if we look at Bob's price index, it rose from 100 to 113 between 2003 and 2004, an increase of 13 percent. Inflation as measured by his price index was 13 percent in 2004. Now let's look at the actual CPI for the United States. The CPI in 2003 was 184.0; that is, the general level of consumer prices was 84.0 percent higher than it had been in the base years of 1982–1984. In 2004, the index rose to 187.6. The inflation rate in 2004 was the percentage change in the CPI from 2003 to 2004, or $100 \times (187.6 - 184.0)/184.0 = 1.96$ percent.

Summarizing the movements of masses of prices into a single index provides an easy way to look at price trends over time. The advantages of an index are that once an index number is calculated for a given year, we can compare it with any other year. For example, the CPI for 1973 was 44.4, and for 2002 it was 179.9. Between those years, the index rose by 135.5, so the increase was

$$100 \times 135.5/44.4 = 305 \text{ percent.}$$

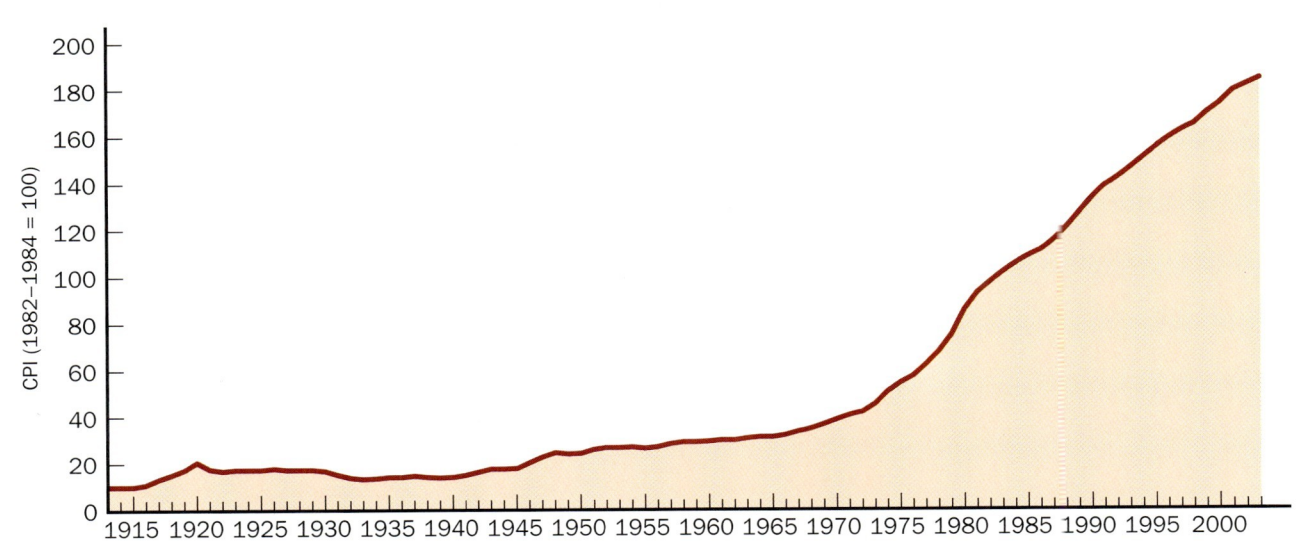

Figure 23.2
THE CONSUMER PRICE INDEX FOR 1913 TO 2003

Consumer prices have risen significantly since the early years of the twentieth century, with most of the increases occurring since 1970.

SOURCE: Bureau of Labor Statistics.

Internet Connection

IMPROVING OUR MEASURE OF THE CPI

The Bureau of Labor Statistics undertook a major revision of the consumer price index in 1998. Details of the changes can be found at www.bls.gov/opub/mlr/1996/12/art1abs.htm.

On average, prices rose 305 percent from 1973 to 2002. Figure 23.2 shows the CPI since 1913.

Case in Point

THE PRICE INDEX MAKES A DIFFERENCE

Price indexes increasingly have come to play an important role in recent economic debates. The Social Security benefits of the elderly rise with the cost of living index (the CPI),[2] and tax brackets and tax exemptions also change with the index. If the index overstates the increases in the cost of living, the real benefits (purchasing power) of the elderly increase, and real inflation-adjusted tax revenues fall. Both distortions increase the budget deficits of the government—the first by increasing its outlays, the second by reducing its receipts.

By early 1994, it had become apparent that the price index the federal government used for adjusting both benefits and tax brackets was seriously flawed—overstating the rate of inflation by between 0.5 and 1.5 percent a year. The government made several changes to partly correct the errors in the index.

The upward bias stems from three problems. The first is the "fixed basket problem." The CPI is calculated by comparing how much it costs to purchase a particular market basket of goods that represents an average consumer's expenditure pattern. But expenditure patterns change steadily over time, while the market basket is revised only infrequently. For instance, in February 1998, the market basket was revised; it is now based on spending patterns in 1993–1995; previously it was based on 1982–1984 expenditure patterns. As people buy more of the goods that have become relatively less expensive (such as computers) and less of the goods that have become relatively more expensive, the index increasingly overweights goods whose prices have risen the most.

---

[2]When a worker retires, his or her initial Social Security benefits are determined by a formula that is indexed to the general level of wages. However, once a worker begins to receive benefits, future benefit levels are indexed to the CPI.

The second major problem is "quality adjustment." New products, which both offer new functions and better perform the existing functions of older products, constantly enter the market. To compare the prices of the new products with the old, some quality adjustment must be made. If the price goes up by 10 percent but the new product lasts longer and works better, then in a real sense the price increase is less than 10 percent and may even represent a price reduction. Sometimes, the quality adjustments are easy; one machine can do what two machines did before. But usually the comparisons are difficult. If we measure the quality of computers by calculations per second, memory, and disk storage, the rate of decrease in computer prices is phenomenal. But even this does not fully reflect their improvements in quality. We can do things with the computer now that were unimaginable twenty-five years ago at any price. And how do we determine the relative value of a new drug that cures a previously incurable disease? The Bureau of Labor Statistics tries to make adjustments for quality. But the consensus is that these adjustments are imperfect and result in an overestimate in the inflation rate of anywhere between a few tenths of a percentage point to more than 1 percent.

The third problem is technical, having to do with the way the data are collected and the details of the calculations.

Many economists believe that the recent revisions will not fully eliminate the CPI bias. They argue that as a result, Social Security and taxes should be indexed to the CPI rate of inflation minus 1 or 0.5 percent.

ALTERNATIVE MEASURES OF INFLATION

The CPI provides one measure of inflation, based on what the average consumer buys. Other price indexes can be calculated using different market baskets. One different measure of prices is the **producer price index,** which measures the average level of prices of goods sold by producers. This index is useful because it gives us an idea of what will happen to consumer prices in the near future. Usually, if producers are receiving higher prices from their sales to wholesalers, eventually retailers will have to charge higher prices. These will be reflected in a higher CPI.

Internet Connection

THE INFLATION CALCULATOR

The Bureau of Labor Statistics has a handy inflation calculator that allows you to find out how much it costs today to purchase goods that cost $100 in some earlier year. For example, it takes $731 today to purchase goods you could have bought for $100 in 1949. Try it out at www.bls.gov/cpi/home.htm.

e-Insight
MEASURING THE PRICE AND QUANTITY OF SOFTWARE

Measuring prices might seem easy—just go out to stores (or log on to e-commerce sites) and record the prices. Unfortunately, it is not that simple. A price index needs to measure how the price of an individual good or service changes over time, and this process is complicated because the quality of the good or service also can change over time. A car with air bags may cost more than a car without air bags, but in part that is because the two cars are not identical. In such a case, the auto firm's cost of adding air bags can be used to estimate how much of the price change is due to quality improvements (the addition of the air bags) and how much represents a change in the price of a car. Adjusting for quality changes is a particularly significant problem with many of the goods and services associated with the new economy, information technologies, and e-commerce.

Software provides an interesting case in point. Anyone who has used software for a number of years knows that today's programs have been improved in countless ways over the programs of the past. Word-processing software purchased for $100 today has many more features than a word-processing program purchased for $350 in 1985. A price index for software has to correct for these changes in quality.

The Bureau of Economic Analysis at the Department of Commerce tries to adjust for quality changes when it calculates its price index for software, but it does so only for prepackaged software, the type you might buy at the campus bookstore. Other types of software are treated differently. Many businesses develop specialized software for their own uses (called *business own-account software*), and the bureau bases the price index for this class of software on the cost of producing it. So if it costs the same to write a program today as it did ten years ago, the bureau assumes that the programs are of equal quality. But this is unlikely—a programmer today can write in one hour a program that does what was impossible ten years ago. Finally, the price of a third class of software—called *custom software*—is based on an average of the prices for business own-account software and prepackaged software. The price of prepackaged software gets a weight of 25 percent, with business own-account software prices receiving a weight of 75 percent. Like the treatment of business own-account software, this method is likely to underestimate the quality improvements in custom software, and therefore to overestimate the price index for constant-quality software. The Bureau of Economic Analysis takes this approach because, unfortunately, the detailed information needed to develop better measures of software prices and changes in the quality of software is not available.

SOURCE: Dale W. Jorgenson and Kevin J. Stiroh, "Raising the Speed Limit: U.S. Economic Growth in the Information Age," *Brookings Papers on Economic Activity* 2000, 1 (2000): 61–211.

In Chapter 22 we observed that real GDP is nominal GDP adjusted for the price level. The price index we used for calculating real GDP is called the *GDP deflator*. It represents a comparison between what it would cost to buy the total mix of goods and services produced within the country today and what it cost in a base year. In other words, the GDP deflator is a weighted average of the prices of different goods and services, where the weights represent the importance of the goods and services in GDP.

The goods and services whose prices go into the GDP deflator are different from those that go into the CPI. For example, households do not purchase Boeing 747s, so their price is not included in calculating the CPI, but the United States produces these planes, so their price is included when we calculate the GDP deflator. Households purchase foreign goods, so their prices are factored into the CPI, but they are not included in the GDP deflator since GDP measures only production within the country's borders. Because of these differences we will obtain slightly different measures of inflation, depending on which price index we use.

The American Experience with Inflation

As we have learned, the inflation rate is the percentage increase in the price level from one year to the next. Figure 23.3 shows the inflation rate for the United States during the past century. Three interesting features stand out.

First, prices were relatively stable for much of the century, with the inflation rate under 5 percent except in three periods: around World War I, around World War II, and during the period 1973–1981. Indeed, from the start of the twentieth century until the early 1960s, the average inflation rate was only about 1 percent per year.

Second, prices can actually fall as well as rise. During the recession that followed World War I, prices fell by more than 15 percent, and during the Great Depression of the 1930s they fell by more than 30 percent. In fact, at the end of the

Figure 23.3
THE INFLATION RATE

The inflation rate is the percentage increase in the price level in a given year. Notice that inflation was low through most of the early part of the last century, although it was high during both world wars. Inflation rose sharply in the 1970s, and then fell during the 1980s. It has remained relatively low since the early 1990s.

SOURCE: Bureau of Labor Statistics.

nineteenth century, the concern was deflation, which is a steady *decline* in the price level. Borrowers at that time who were in debt and had not anticipated the fall in prices found that the dollars they had to pay back were worth far more than the dollars they had borrowed. They were as upset about this as investors (lenders) are when inflation makes the value of the dollars they get back from an investment or loan worth less than the value of the dollars they originally put in.

During the past fifty years, however, inflation has been a major concern in the United States. The 1970s are often referred to as the era of the Great Inflation, and by 1980s, inflation had risen to more than 13 percent. Inflation fell during the 1980s, and remained low and relatively stable throughout the rest of the twentieth century. The possibility that the United States would experience deflation emerged as a concern early in the twenty-first century, but this worry soon faded, and the United States has continued to have low rates of inflation.

Review and Practice

SUMMARY

1. The inflation rate is the percentage increase of the price level from one year to the next.
2. The economy-wide costs of inflation are related to the distortions that inflation creates in relative prices and in the increased risk and uncertainty it generates.
3. The consumer price index (CPI) is a measure of the cost of living for the typical household. The rate of change of the CPI is one of the most common measures of inflation.
4. U.S. inflation was low through most of the early part of the twentieth century, rose sharply in the 1970s and early 1980s, fell to lower levels in the rest of the 1980s, and remained low throughout the 1990s. In different countries at different times, inflation has sometimes been very high, with prices increasing by factors of tens or hundreds in a given year.

KEY TERMS

inflation rate
deflation
consumer price index (CPI)
producer price index

REVIEW QUESTIONS

1. When the prices of different goods change at different rates, how do we measure inflation?
2. Are all groups of people affected equally by inflation? Why or why not?
3. What are the major costs of inflation?
4. Which decade, the 1970s, 1980s, or 1990s, saw the highest average rate of inflation in the United States? Which of these decades saw the lowest average inflation rate?

PROBLEMS

1. Geoffrey spends his allowance on three items: candy, magazines, and movie video rentals. He is currently receiving an allowance of $34 per month, which he is using to rent 4 movies at $3 apiece, buy 10 candy bars at $1 apiece, and purchase 4 magazines at $3 apiece. In each of the following cases, calculate Geoffrey's price index (CPI) for this basket of goods, with the current price level equal to 100:
   (a) The price of movies rises to $4.
   (b) The price of movies increases by $1 and the price of candy bars falls by $0.20.
   (c) The prices of movies and magazines both increase by $1 and the price of candy bars falls by $0.20.
2. An increase in the consumer price index will often affect different groups in different ways. Think about how different groups will purchase items such as housing, travel, or education in the CPI basket, and explain why they will be affected differently by increases in components of the CPI. How would you calculate an "urban CPI" or a "rural CPI"?
3. Using the following information on the consumer price index, calculate the rate of inflation in each year from 2000 to 2003.

Year	1999	2000	2001	2002	2003
CPI	166.6	172.2	177.1	179.9	184

4. Wartimes are usually associated with inflation. According to the Inflation Calculator at www.bls.gov/cpi/home.htm, what would $100 in 1860 be worth in 1865? By how much did prices rise during the Civil War?
5. According to the Bureau of Labor Statistics's Inflation Calculator (see Question 4), by how much did prices rise between 1973 and 1983? 1983 and 1993? Between 1993 and 2003? During which of these ten-year periods was inflation the highest? By how much did prices rise between 1983 and 2003? Between 1973 and 2003?

Part 6
FULL-EMPLOYMENT MACROECONOMICS

Learning Goals

In this chapter, you will learn

1. How full employment is achieved in market economies
2. The factors that determine real wages, output, and the real interest rate at full employment
3. The role that the capital market plays in maintaining full employment

Chapter 24

THE FULL-EMPLOYMENT MODEL

Every year, about 1.7 million Americans enter the labor force. Creating jobs for these workers is critically important for the health of the economy and for the general welfare of society. With so many new workers each year, it may seem amazing that market economies like that of the United States are able to create employment opportunities for almost all who seek them. Between 1955 and 2000, for example, the American labor force grew by 117 percent, almost 76 million workers—and incredibly, the number of jobs also grew by 117 percent. This remarkable ability of the economy to generate millions of new jobs is the result of competitive markets. No government official can calculate where to place the millions of new workers who are expected to enter the labor force over the next decade. But past experience makes us confident that somehow, somewhere, the economy will create jobs for them. The economic theories we explore in this and the next four chapters help explain the ability of market economies to create jobs.

Though the economy does generate jobs, the process does not always occur smoothly—in some years, job growth slows and unemployment rises; in other years, when the economy is expanding, the opposite happens. But over the long run, jobs are created to employ those who want to work.

To understand how this happens, we focus on the *aggregate* behavior of the economy—on movements in such macroeconomic variables as total output, interest rates, and average wages—when resources are fully used. We will also focus on a period of time that is long enough so that all wages and prices have had time to adjust to shifts in supply and demand. Many wages and prices do not respond rapidly to such changes, a factor that will play an important role when we turn to economic fluctuations in Part Seven. Eventually, however, wages and prices do adjust to bring supply and demand into balance. By using a time horizon that is long enough for these adjustments to occur, we will gain insights into many important macroeconomic phenomena. For example, the framework we develop in this chapter will be used in Chapter 25 to understand the implications of the large budget deficits that the U.S. government is currently running. Chapter 26 will explore the role of international financial markets, the economy's trade balance, and exchange rates, while Chapter 27 will focus on the factors that account for long-run economic growth. But to organize our discussion of these important economic topics, we will need a model that explains how the adjustment of real wages and the real interest rate help ensure that the economy is able, on average, to achieve and maintain full employment. There is another reason for beginning with a study of the long run: often, policies are proposed that may seem sensible at first sight but that over time have undesirable consequences. To fully evaluate macroeconomic policies, we must not neglect their long-run impact on employment, interest rates, and economic growth.

Macroeconomic Equilibrium

The model we employ here is the basic competitive model described in Chapters 2 and 9. In it, large numbers of households and firms interact in the labor, product, and capital markets. Households supply labor to firms that use it to produce goods and services. Firms compensate workers by paying wages. Households use their income to purchase the goods and services that firms produce. Households also save, and their savings finance firms' investments in the plant and equipment needed to undertake production. For the use of their funds, households earn interest and dividends from firms.

Two key lessons emerge from a study of macroeconomics. First, all markets are interrelated. What happens in one market will have an impact on other markets. The demand for labor, for instance, depends on the level of output in the product market. Second, wages, interest rates, and prices adjust to ensure that demand equals supply in each market. One of our major assumptions in this part of the book will be that wages, interest rates, and prices adjust so that the labor, product, and capital markets are in equilibrium. That is, they all clear, with the quantity demanded equal to the quantity supplied.[1]

While assuming that markets clear would be inappropriate if we were studying the year-to-year behavior of the economy, it is a useful simplification for helping us understand how the aggregate economy behaves over decades. The assumption that prices, wages, and interest rates adjust to balance supply and demand throughout the economy gives us powerful insights into some of the basic issues of macroeconomics.

---

[1] What happens when markets do not clear is the topic of Part Seven and will be important for understanding short-run fluctuations in the economy. In this and the next few chapters, however, our assumption is that there has been enough time for wages, interest rates, and prices to adjust to clear all markets. Some markets, such as financial markets, adjust very quickly to clear every day; others, such as the labor market, may take many months to clear if there are shifts in demand or supply.

In macroeconomics, we stress aggregates—the economy's total output, rather than the output of individual industries or types of goods and services. We examine total employment, and average wages. In looking at these aggregates, we ignore the richness of the microeconomic detail that captures the thousands of different products that the economy produces and the many characteristics that differentiate one worker from another. The basic premise of macroeconomics is that we can learn a great deal about the aggregates, as well as gain insights into many important policy issues, without inquiring into such details.

To bring our macroeconomic perspective into focus, we discuss each of the three major markets—labor, product, and financial capital—in turn. We then describe how real wages and the real interest rate play critical roles in balancing supply and demand in these markets so that the economy can maintain full employment.

The Labor Market

Full employment in the labor market occurs when the demand for labor equals the supply of labor. No qualified worker who wishes to get a job at the going market wage will fail to get one. No firm that wants to hire a worker at the going wage will fail to find a qualified employee. Adjustments in wages ensure that this will occur. Of course, when economists say that there is full employment of the labor force—that the demand for labor is equal to the supply of labor—there are still always some workers who will be unemployed. As we learned in Chapter 22, this unemployment occurs as workers transition between jobs and new entrants to the labor force search for positions, as mismatches occur between the location or skill requirements of new jobs and those of the unemployed, and as unemployment in some sectors fluctuates to reflect normal seasonal patterns. These sources of unemployment are called *frictional, structural,* and *seasonal unemployment.* Thus, even at full employment, the unemployment rate will not be zero.

In understanding how the economy reaches full employment, the relationship between nominal wages (w) and the price level (P) is very important. Workers earn wages, and they use those wages to buy goods and services. What matters to workers is how much their wages will buy. If a worker's wage goes from $6 per hour to $12 per hour but at the same time the prices of all the things she buys also double, the real value of her wage has not changed. What workers care about is their *real* wage, the nominal wage corrected for changes in the price level. Firms also will be concerned with the real wage, since what will matter to them is the cost of labor (the nominal wage) relative to the price firms receive for their output (the price level).

The real wage is obtained by dividing the nominal wage by the price level, or w/P. The real wage provides a measure of the purchasing power of wages. Average nominal wages, the price level, and average real wages since 1965 are shown in Figure 24.1. As the figure illustrates, nominal wages have risen significantly over this period. But the prices of the goods and services that workers buy have also risen. When we correct for the increases in the price level, the real wage actually declined during the first half of the 1990s and by 2002 was little changed from its value in 1980.

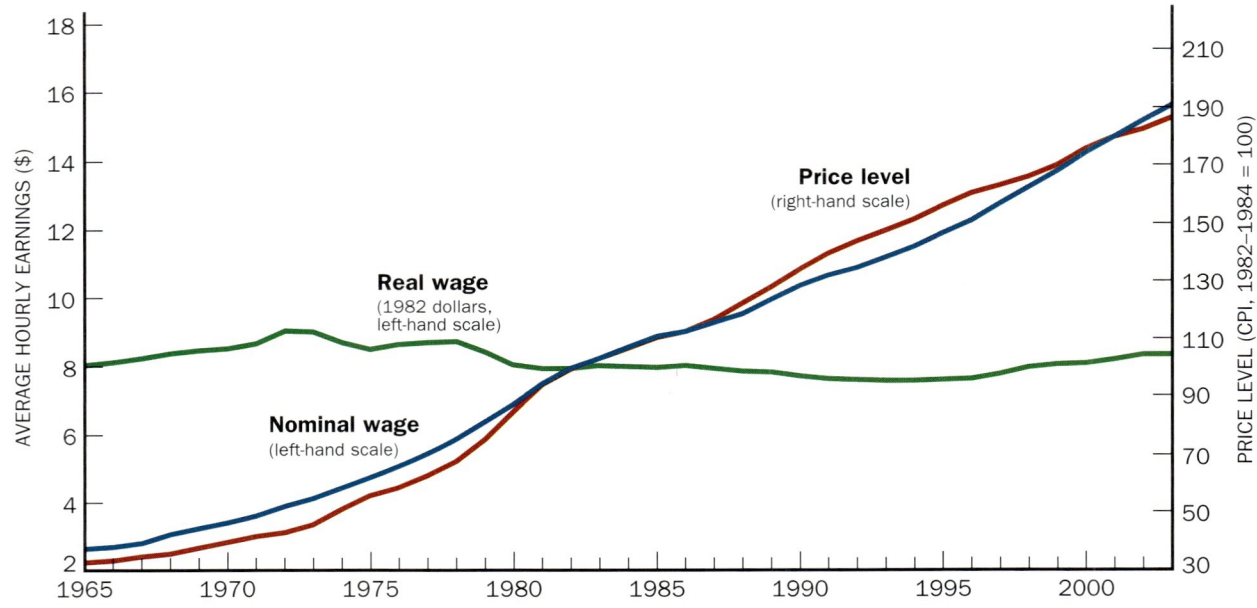

Figure 24.1

NOMINAL WAGES, THE PRICE LEVEL, AND REAL WAGES

The solid blue line shows that average nominal wages in the United States have risen significantly since 1965. The red line shows that the price level also has risen over this period. With average nominal wages and the price level rising at roughly the same rate, average real wages (shown by the green line) in 2003 were only slightly higher than they had been in 1965.

SOURCE: *Economic Report of the President* (2004), Table B-47.

Wrap-Up

REAL WAGES

The real wage is the nominal or dollar wage adjusted for prices.

Workers care about the real wage that they receive because it measures the purchasing power of their wages.

Firms care about the real wage because it measures the cost of labor.

Figure 24.2 shows the aggregate labor market, with the real wage (w/P) on the vertical axis, the quantity of labor (L) on the horizontal axis, and the aggregate demand and supply curves for labor. With a given set of equipment and technology, the aggregate demand for labor depends on the wages firms must pay, the prices firms receive for the goods and services they produce, and the prices they have to pay for nonlabor inputs such as raw materials and equipment. With the prices of goods and inputs held constant, the aggregate labor demand curve traces out the quantity of labor demanded by firms at different wages. At lower wages, the quantity of labor demand is greater. There are two reasons for this. First, as wages fall, labor becomes relatively less expensive compared with the price of the goods that firms produce. Because profits are greater, firms have an incentive to expand production and hire more workers. Second, as wages fall relative to the cost of machines, it pays firms to substitute workers for machines. Thus, the demand curve for labor slopes down, as shown in the figure.

The two reasons for the negative slope of the aggregate labor demand curve stress the importance of wages relative to the costs of other inputs and the price of the output being produced. If wages fall *and all other prices in the economy also fall in proportion*, the demand for labor will not change. That is why we show the demand for labor as a function of the real wage, w/P.

The figure also shows an aggregate labor supply curve. To simplify matters, the labor supply curve is drawn as a vertical line—we assume that the labor supply is perfectly inelastic. That is, either individuals are in the labor force, working a full (forty-hour) workweek, or they are not. In principle, workers might enter and exit the labor force as real wages go up or down, or they might reduce or increase the hours they work in response to such changes. When real wages rise, two factors are at work. First, higher wages mean the returns for working are greater. Thus workers should want to work more hours—the opportunity cost of leisure is now higher, and the substitution effect works to induce individuals to work more as real wages rise. But higher wages mean that workers have higher incomes, which lead them to want to increase their consumption—including their consumption of leisure. So there is an income effect acting to reduce labor supply as real wages rise. The income and substitution effects act in opposite directions.[2] In Figure 24.2, we assume they offset one another, so that as real wages change, labor supply remains constant.

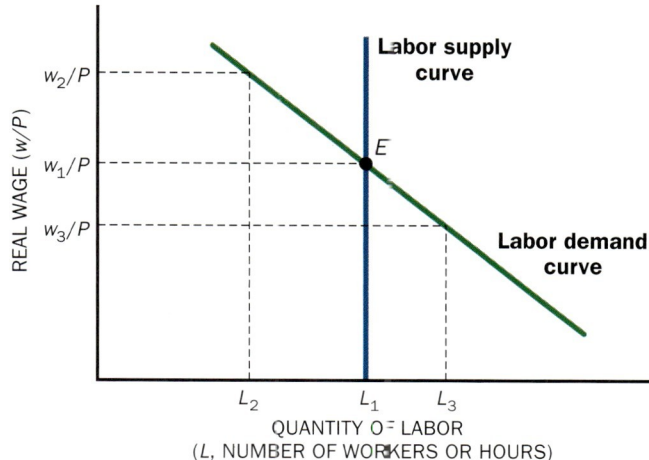

Figure 24.2
EQUILIBRIUM IN THE LABOR MARKET

Equilibrium in the labor market is at the intersection of the labor demand and labor supply curves. If the real wage is above w_1/P, where demand equals supply, there will be unemployment, putting pressure on wages to fall as workers compete to offer their services. Below w_1/P there will be excess demand for labor, which will put pressure on wages to rise.

Basic supply and demand analysis implies that market equilibrium should occur at the intersection of the demand and supply curves, point E. The reason for this is straightforward. If the real wage happens to be above the equilibrium real wage w_1/P—say, at w_2/P—the demand for labor will be L_2, much less than the supply, L_1. There will be an excess supply of workers. Those in the labor force without jobs will offer to work for less than the going wage, bidding down the average wages of those already working. The process of competition will lead to lower wages, until eventually demand again equals supply at point E. Likewise, if the real wage is lower than w_1/P—say, at w_3/P—firms in the economy will demand more labor than is supplied. Competing with one another for scarce labor services, they will bid the wage up to w_1/P.

SHIFTS IN THE DEMAND AND SUPPLY OF LABOR

The full-employment model makes clear predictions about the consequences of shifts in the demand and supply of labor. First, let's consider shifts in the supply curve of labor. These can occur because young people reaching working age

---

[2]To review the definitions of income and substitution effects, see Chapter 5.

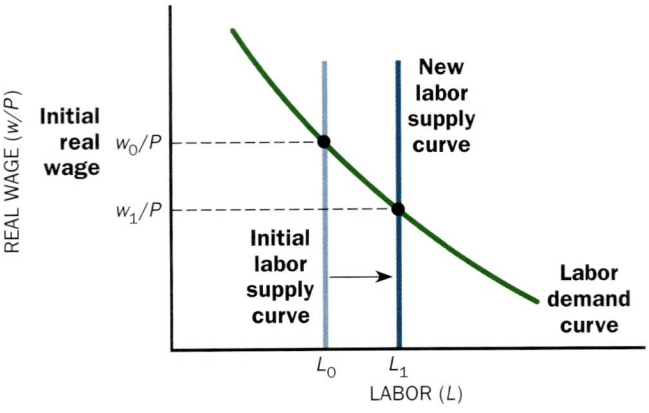

Figure 24.3

EFFECTS OF A SHIFT IN THE SUPPLY OF LABOR

A shift of the supply curve to the right leads to a fall in real wages.

outnumber old people retiring, because of new immigrants, or because of social changes such as the entry of more women into the labor force. For example, the U.S. labor force expanded rapidly in the 1970s as the baby boomers entered the labor force and more and more women worked outside the home. The consequences of such a large shift in the labor supply curve are depicted in Figure 24.3. The supply curve of labor (shown here as vertical) shifts to the right. At each real wage, there are more individuals in the labor force. The equilibrium real wage falls. This fall in the price of labor indicates to firms that labor is less scarce than it was before and they therefore should economize less in its use. Firms respond to the lower real wage by creating more jobs, and employment rises to absorb the increase in labor supply.

Now let's look at the effects of a shift in the demand curve for labor. First, consider the case of a decrease in investment, which leads to a reduction in the quantity of machines and equipment available for use by workers. This in turn reduces the productivity of workers, thereby shifting the demand curve for labor to the left, as depicted in panel A of Figure 24.4. For a given real wage, firms want to hire fewer workers than before. The equilibrium real wage falls.

Panel B depicts the effects of technological progress on the demand for labor. As technological change increases the productivity of workers, each hour of labor input produces more output. From the perspective of the firm, higher labor productivity lowers its effective cost of labor, as it now is able to produce more output per hour of labor hired. At each wage, the demand for labor will rise, shifting the demand for labor curve to the right. The equilibrium real wage rises.

These examples suggest that increases in investment and improvements in technology lead to an increase in the demand for labor (a rightward shift in the labor demand curve). Although this is generally true, the demand for some types of labor, especially unskilled labor, may actually decline with investment in new equipment and technology. At the same time, the demand for skilled workers may increase. In this case, the labor market is really made up of two markets, one containing skilled and the other unskilled workers. An increase in investment or technology may increase the demand for skilled workers, as in panel B, but decrease the demand for unskilled workers, as in panel A. Here, a focus only on the aggregate labor market is not sufficient to understand an interesting macroeconomic phenomenon—the increase in wage inequality based on skill levels that has occurred in the United States in recent years.

Wrap-Up

LABOR MARKET EQUILIBRIUM

Real wages adjust to equate labor demand with labor supply.

An increase in labor supply at each real wage (a rightward shift in the labor supply curve) lowers the equilibrium real wage, enabling firms to create additional jobs.

Figure 24.4
EFFECTS OF CHANGES IN INVESTMENT AND TECHNOLOGY

New investment or technological change shifts the demand curve for labor. Panel A shows the effects of a reduction in investment. Workers have fewer machines and equipment to work with, and the demand curve for labor shifts to the left, lowering real wages. Panel B shows an improvement in technology. The demand curve shifts to the right, as workers' marginal productivity increases, leading to higher real wages.

Technological change or new investment increases the demand for labor (shifts the labor demand curve to the right) at each real wage and increases the equilibrium real wage. Increases in labor productivity increase aggregate labor demand and cause the equilibrium real wage to rise.

Case in Point

MASS MIGRATION IN THE NINETEENTH CENTURY

The nineteenth century provides a case study in how labor markets adjust to changes in labor supply. Between 1820 and 1920, 60 million emigrants left Europe for the New World (Argentina, Brazil, Canada, and the United States) and Australia, and about 36 million entered the United States. This mass movement of people had a major impact on wages in both North America and Europe, just as our theory predicts.

Land was scarce and labor was abundant in Europe in 1850. As a consequence, wages were low. In North America, by contrast, land was abundant and labor was scarce. Consequently, wages were high.[3] In 1850, the average real wage in Europe was about half what it was in the New World. Real wages in Ireland, for instance, were 42 percent of the American level. This wage differential provided a powerful

---

[3]To help follow the discussion, you might find it useful to draw two supply and demand diagrams, one to represent the European labor market in 1850 and one to represent the North American labor market. Since our focus here is on labor supply and migration, draw the labor demand curves to be the same in both markets. For Europe, the labor supply curve is to the right of where it is for North America. The equilibrium real wage for this time period is therefore higher in North America.

e-Insight
LABOR MARKETS AND THE INTERNET

One of the main *imperfections* in the labor market is that it is expensive, in terms of time and money, to search for a new job. Information is imperfect and is costly to acquire. Help-wanted ads play an important role in making the labor market work, but individuals in one city often cannot easily and regularly obtain up-to-date newspapers from other cities to search out their job opportunities.

Employment agencies and government employment services have helped make the labor market work better. But the Internet promises a revolution—or at least a vast improvement—in labor markets. Almost without cost, individuals can see the help-wanted ads in newspapers in other cities. Employers can costlessly post help-wanted ads and provide far more complete descriptions of the job and of the characteristics of the employees that they seek. Eighty percent of the world's largest 500 firms use Web sites for job recruitment and more than 90 percent of American firms do. Existing employment agencies (including government-provided services) have used the Internet to extend their scope, and new firms have been created. Much of the information that is most relevant—from the perspective of both the employer and the employee—still will be obtained only by a face-to-face interview, and this process will remain costly. Still, by lowering search costs, the Internet holds out the promise of vastly increasing the efficiency of labor markets.

---

inducement for workers to migrate from Europe to areas offering higher living standards.

The mass migrations of the late nineteenth century shifted the North American labor supply curve to the right and the European labor supply curve to the left. Our theory predicts that wages adjust to balance the quantity of labor demanded and the quantity of labor supplied. Real wages needed to fall in the United States and rise in Europe in response to these shifts in labor supply.

Did this adjustment of wages occur? Irish real wages doubled between 1855 and 1913, with most of the increase occurring between 1860 and 1895. Average American wages also were rising during this period as a result of rapid accumulation of capital and growth in the wages of skilled workers. But average wages in Ireland rose faster, closing the gap between what workers earned in Ireland and what workers earned in the United States. Just as the theory predicted, real wages adjusted in response to shifts in labor supply to bring the quantity demanded and the quantity supplied into balance in the labor market.[4]

The Product Market

Just as the real wage adjusts to ensure that the demand for labor equals the supply, so too—in our full-employment model—adjustments will occur in the product and

---

[4]For a discussion of the impact of mass migration during the late nineteenth century and of other aspects of the globalization that occurred during this period, see K. H. O'Rourke and J. G. Williamson, *Globalization and History* (Cambridge, Mass.: MIT Press, 1999).

capital markets to ensure that the demand for goods equals the economy's output when it is at full employment.

POTENTIAL GDP

At any point in time, the economy has a given capital stock (a set of machines, equipment, and buildings) that, together with labor and materials, produces output. If more workers are hired, output increases. The relationship between employment and output with a fixed amount of capital is called the **short-run aggregate production function,** depicted in panel A of Figure 24.5. The figure illustrates that as more workers are hired, output goes up, but at a diminishing rate. There are *diminishing returns to labor*. With a fixed amount of capital, the amount of equipment and machinery available for each worker falls as the number of workers employed goes up. For example, the first workers hired may each have their own desktop computers, but as new workers are hired and the amount of capital remains fixed, workers must share computers. As a consequence, output increases as the additional workers are hired, but it does so at a diminishing rate. Diminishing returns to labor also occur because the most productive workers are likely to be hired first; as employment rises, workers with less training and fewer skills will be hired.

In the long run, when the labor market is in equilibrium, we achieve a condition called full employment. Panel B of Figure 24.5 shows the labor market, with the equilibrium real wage at the level that makes the demand for labor equal to the fixed supply. With this fixed supply of labor at full employment, the level of output can be found using the short-run aggregate production function in panel A. The equilibrium level of output when the economy is at full employment is referred to as its **potential GDP** or the **full-employment level of output.** If the supply of labor is not fixed but instead depends on the real wage, so that the supply curve of labor has a positive slope, full employment occurs when labor demand and labor supply are equal. Given the equilibrium level of employment at full employment, potential GDP is found from the short-run aggregate production function.

Potential GDP will be affected if the economy's stock of plant and equipment changes, if technology changes, or if there are changes in the equilibrium that defines full employment. Increases in the stock of plant and equipment would increase the amount of output that can be produced at each level of employment. As a consequence, the short-run aggregate production function would shift upward, increasing potential GDP. Similarly, new technological innovations would shift the short-run aggregate production function upward and increase potential GDP. Increases in labor supply would raise the equilibrium level at full employment and, for a given level of plant and equipment and technology, raise potential GDP.

Figure 24.5

EQUILIBRIUM IN THE LABOR MARKET AND THE DETERMINATION OF POTENTIAL GDP

Panel A shows the short-run aggregate production function; in the short run, with given technology and a given set of plant and equipment output increases as more labor is employed, but with diminishing returns. Panel B shows the labor market with a fixed supply of labor L^f. The equilibrium real wage is w/P^*. At full employment, potential GDP is Y^f.

DEMAND AND EQUILIBRIUM OUTPUT

For the product market to be in equilibrium, the supply of goods and services produced by firms in the economy must balance with the demand for the economy's goods and services. Firms will not continue to produce at the full-employment level if their products go unsold. If the economy is to maintain full employment, the total level of demand in the economy must adjust to balance output at full employment. The economy's financial sector—what we called the *capital market* in Chapter 1—plays a critical role in achieving this balance. By examining that role, we can see more clearly how the interrelation of markets helps ensure macroeconomic equilibrium.

A useful starting point in understanding how demand adjusts to equal full-employment output is the circular flow of income. Figure 24.6 shows the circular flow of income for a closed economy. Notice that we have ignored the government sector for the moment.

The circular flow diagram illustrates the flow of goods and income that links households, business, and financial sectors. In the diagram, the purple lines indicate flows of real resources and goods and services; the green lines represent the payments for those commodities. Households supply resources (labor, capital, land)

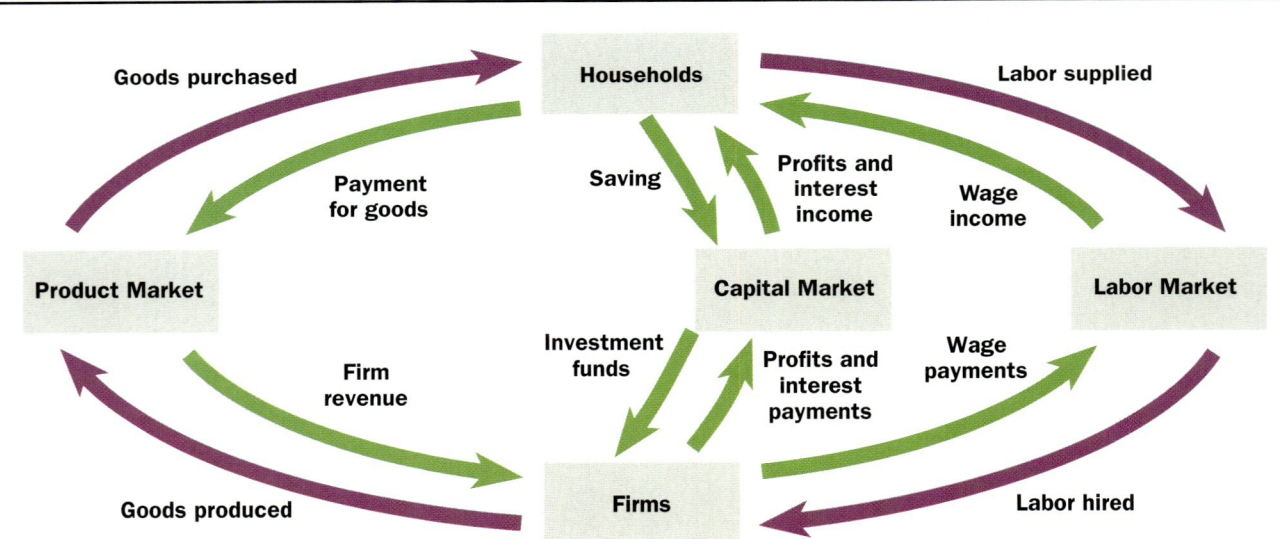

Figure 24.6
THE CIRCULAR FLOW OF INCOME

The circular flow of income provides a summary picture of how the flows of commodities and payments link the household and firm sectors of the economy. Households provide resources, such as labor, to firms and receive income payments in return. They use this income to purchase goods and services in the product market. The revenue that firms obtain from selling in the product market enables them to make the income payments to households for the labor and other resources that they have used. Saving from the household sector flows into the capital market, where it is available to firms that wish to borrow for investment projects.

to firms and in return receive payments for those resources. We have already learned in Chapter 22 that these income payments will equal the value of total production. This means that the household sector receives enough income to purchase all the goods and services that firms have produced.

Of course, households do not choose to spend all their income on goods and services; they save part of it. In our circular flow diagram, this action is shown by the flow of saving to the financial capital market. Thus, household saving is a *leakage* out of the spending stream.

While households in the aggregate do not spend all their income, other sectors of the economy spend more than the incomes they receive. Firms, for example, may wish to invest in buildings, new plant, and equipment. To do so, they need to borrow funds in the capital market. Investment spending is an *injection* into the spending stream.

The total level of spending will balance with the level of output at full employment if the leakages out of the spending stream in the form of saving are balanced by injections into the spending stream in the form of investments. We portray this algebraically by noting that in a closed economy with no government sector, the total demand for what is produced is equal to consumption spending (C) by households plus investment spending (I) by firms. In equilibrium at full employment, consumption and investment spending must add up to full-employment output (Y^f), or $C + I = Y^f$. Subtracting C from both sides of this equation tells us that demand will balance output at full employment if $I = Y^f - C$. But $Y^f - C$ is saving at full employment. So demand will balance output at full employment if investment equals full-employment saving.

But what ensures that this condition is satisfied? To answer this question, we must look at the role of the capital market.

Wrap-Up

PRODUCT MARKET EQUILIBRIUM

When the economy is at full employment, output is equal to potential GDP. This is the output that can be produced by the available labor force with the given set of plant and equipment at normal levels of work hours and capacity utilization.

Increases in the labor supply (rightward shifts in the labor supply curve), increases in the stock of plant and equipment as a result of new investment, and technological change all increase potential GDP.

Total spending will equal potential GDP if leakages at full employment equal injections. In a closed economy with no government sector, leakages are equal to saving and injections are equal to investment.

The Capital Market

When households save, they make funds available to borrowers. Whenever firms undertake investment, they need to borrow.[5] The financial capital market is the market in which the supply of funds is allocated to those who wish to borrow. For this reason, it is also called the **loanable funds market.** In a closed economy with no government sector, equilibrium in the capital market requires that savings (the supply of funds) equal investment (the demand for funds). Our analysis of each builds on the basic competitive model of Part One.

HOUSEHOLD SAVING

The most important determinants of household saving are income and interest rates. Each year, families have to decide how much of their income to spend on current consumption and how much to save for future consumption, for retirement, for emergencies, to pay for their children's college education, or to buy a new car or new home. On average, families with higher incomes spend more *and* save more. Of course, before families can decide how much to consume and how much to save, they must pay any taxes that they owe. What is relevant for consumption and saving decisions is how much income a household has after paying taxes; this is called its **disposable income.** When the government increases taxes, disposable income is reduced. Households will typically reduce both their consumption spending and their saving when disposable income falls.

Because we are ignoring the government sector in this chapter (we add the government in Chapter 25), we also ignore taxes; disposable income therefore will equal total income. In this chapter, we also assume that the stock of plant and equipment, as well as the labor supply, is given. With wages and prices adjusting to ensure that the labor market always clears, aggregate output is fixed at potential GDP, the full-employment level of output. Recalling from Chapter 22 that aggregate income is equal to aggregate output, we can also say that total income is equal to potential GDP.

With income fixed at its full-employment level, the level of saving will depend on the return that households can earn on their savings. When households save, they set aside current income so that they will have more to spend in the future. What matters as they decide how much to save is the interest rate their savings can earn, *corrected for changes in the prices of what they buy.* The interest rate corrected for changes in prices is called the **real rate of interest.** The formula for the real rate of interest is simple: the real interest rate is equal to the market interest rate *minus* the rate of inflation. If the market interest rate is 5 percent and inflation is 2 percent, the real return on your savings is 3 percent.

The real interest rate is the correct measure of the return on savings because it takes into account changes in prices. The evidence, at least for the United States, suggests that household saving is relatively insensitive to change in the real inter-

---

[5]For the sake of simplicity, we have so far assumed that households are the only source of saving. Firms may also save so that they can finance their investment spending from their own cash reserves. This does not change our analysis, since we can think of the firm as borrowing the funds from itself.

est rate (perhaps rising slightly with it). For the sake of simplicity, then, we will often assume saving is completely inelastic—that is, it does not change at all as the real interest rate varies. In this case, changes in the real rate of interest do not lead to any change in saving. This results in a vertical saving function, as shown in Figure 24.7.

The assumption that saving does not respond to changes in the real interest rate might seem to be inconsistent with one of our key economic concepts—that incentives matter. Because a rise in the real rate of interest provides a greater incentive to save, it should lead to an increase in household saving. However, an offsetting income effect works in the opposite direction. If the adults in a household are saving for the college expenses of their children or for their own retirement, a higher real rate of interest means that they need to save less each year to reach their goal in the future. For example, suppose you want to have $15,000 saved up in ten years. If the real rate of interest is 2 percent, you must save $1,370 annually; if the real rate of interest rises to 10 percent, the amount needed each year drops to $941.25. You can reduce your current level of saving and still achieve your goal of $15,000. The income effect of a rise in the real rate of interest works to reduce saving, while the substitution effect of a rise in the real interest rate, the direct incentive effect of the higher return, acts to increase saving. The two effects pull in opposite directions, and the evidence suggests that the result is essentially a draw. That is why household saving is not very sensitive to the real interest rate and why we will often assume it is completely inelastic.

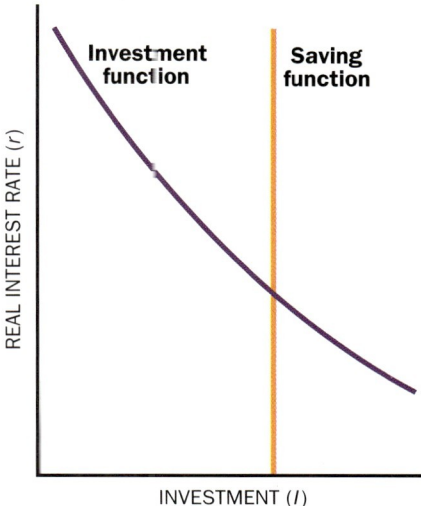

Figure 24.7

THE SAVING FUNCTION AND THE INVESTMENT FUNCTION

If saving is unresponsive to the real interest rates, then the saving function will be vertical. The investment function slopes downward to the right, tracing out the levels of real investment at different real interest rates. As the interest rate falls, investment increases.

INVESTMENT

Economists use the word *investment* in two different ways. Households think of the stocks and bonds they buy as investments—**financial investments.** These financial investments provide the funds for firms to buy capital goods—machines and buildings. The purchases of new machines and buildings represent firms' investment, referred to as **capital goods investment** or simply as *investment. In macroeconomics, when we refer to* investment, *it is to physical investment in capital goods, not financial investment.*

Firms invest to increase their capacity to produce goods and services. They expect returns from the sales of this additional production to cover the costs of the additional workers and raw materials required, as well as the cost of the funds that financed the investment, leaving the firm with a profit.

There are two key determinants of investment: firms' expectations concerning future sales and profits, which for now we will assume to be fixed, and the real rate of interest. Many firms borrow to finance their investment. The cost of these funds—what they have to pay back to the financial sector for using the borrowed funds—is the interest rate. Since the firm pays back a debt with dollars whose purchasing power depends on inflation, the relevant cost is the real rate of interest.

The higher the real rate of interest, the fewer the investment projects that will be profitable—that is, the fewer the projects that will yield a return sufficient to compensate the firm for the risks undertaken after interest on the borrowed funds is paid back. Even if the firm is flush with cash, the interest rate matters. The real interest rate then becomes the opportunity cost of the firm's money—that is, what the firm could have obtained if, instead of making an investment, it had simply decided to lend the funds to some other firm.

The **investment function** gives the level of (real) investment at each value of the real rate of interest. The investment function slopes downward to the right; investment increases as the real interest rate decreases. This is depicted in Figure 24.7, which shows the real interest rate on the vertical axis and the level of real investment on the horizontal axis.

Wrap-Up

SAVING VERSUS INVESTMENT

What we often call investing (putting money into a mutual fund, purchasing shares in the stock market) is actually *saving*—setting aside part of our income rather than spending it. These funds are then made available through the financial system to individuals and firms who wish to purchase capital goods such as plant and equipment or build new office buildings, shopping malls, or homes.

Investment refers to such additions to the physical stock of capital in the economy. As the real interest rate rises, the cost of borrowing funds for these investment projects rises. As a result, fewer projects will look profitable, fewer households will buy a new car, and fewer homes will be constructed.

Saving may rise as households reduce consumption to take advantage of higher rates of return on their savings. However, the evidence suggests this effect is small, so we will often assume that saving is inelastic.

EQUILIBRIUM IN THE CAPITAL MARKET

The equilibrium real interest rate is the rate at which saving and investment balance, as depicted in Figure 24.8. Panel A shows saving increasing as the real interest rate rises, while panels B and C illustrate the case of an inelastic saving curve. The impact of an increased demand for investment at each real interest rate is shown in panels A and B. In panel A, both the equilibrium real rate of interest and the equilibrium levels of saving and investment increase. Because the rise in the interest rate induces households to save more, in the new equilibrium the quantity of investment is able to rise. In panel B, only the equilibrium real interest rate changes as a result of the shift in investment demand. Because saving is inelastic in panel B, the change in the interest rate leaves saving unaffected. As a consequence, the quantity of investment must also be unchanged (since saving and investment are equal in equilibrium). Despite the rightward shift in the investment function, the real interest rate increases enough to keep investment unchanged.

Panel C illustrates the effects of a shift in the saving curve. A rightward shift in the saving curve, perhaps caused by households wishing to set aside more for retirement, results in a fall in the equilibrium real rate of interest and a rise in equilibrium investment.

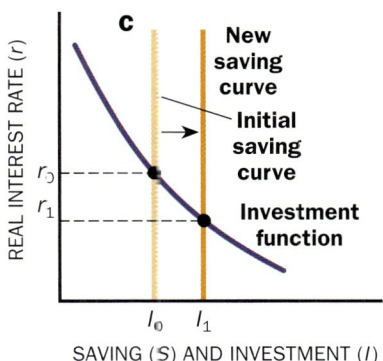

Figure 24.8

EQUILIBRIUM IN THE CAPITAL MARKET AT FULL EMPLOYMENT

Equilibrium requires that the demand for funds (investment) equal the supply (saving). The level of desired investment decreases as the real interest rate increases.

In panel A, saving increases slightly with increases in the real interest rate. In panels B and C, saving is not interest sensitive, so the saving curve is a vertical line. The equilibrium level of investment is simply equal to the full-employment level of saving.

A shift in the investment function is depicted in panels A and B. In panel A, equilibrium investment is increased from I_0 to I_1, while in panel B, with inelastic saving, the only effect is to increase the equilibrium real interest rate from r_0 to r_1, leaving investment (and saving) unchanged.

Panel C shows a rightward shift in the saving curve. The level of saving increases at each real interest rate. In the new equilibrium in the capital market, the real interest rate has fallen from r_0 to r_1 and investment has increased from I_0 to I_1.

When the real interest rate adjusts to balance demand and supply in the capital market, saving will equal investment. We can express this same result by saying that when the capital market is in equilibrium, leakages from the spending stream equal injections. This was the condition needed to ensure that the product market was in equilibrium. Therefore, the capital market plays a critical role in ensuring product market equilibrium.

Wrap-Up

CAPITAL MARKET EQUILIBRIUM

In long-run equilibrium, full employment saving equals investment.

Increases in investment at each real interest rate (shifts to the right in the investment function) lead to a higher equilibrium real interest rate. Equilibrium investment will be unchanged if the saving curve is vertical; equilibrium investment will rise if the saving curve has a positive slope.

Increases in saving at each real interest rate (shifts to the right of the saving curve) lead to a lower equilibrium real interest rate and higher levels of investment.

Capital market equilibrium ensures that leakages equal injections at full-employment output (potential GDP). When saving is equal to investment at full-employment output, aggregate demand equals the economy's full-employment level of output.

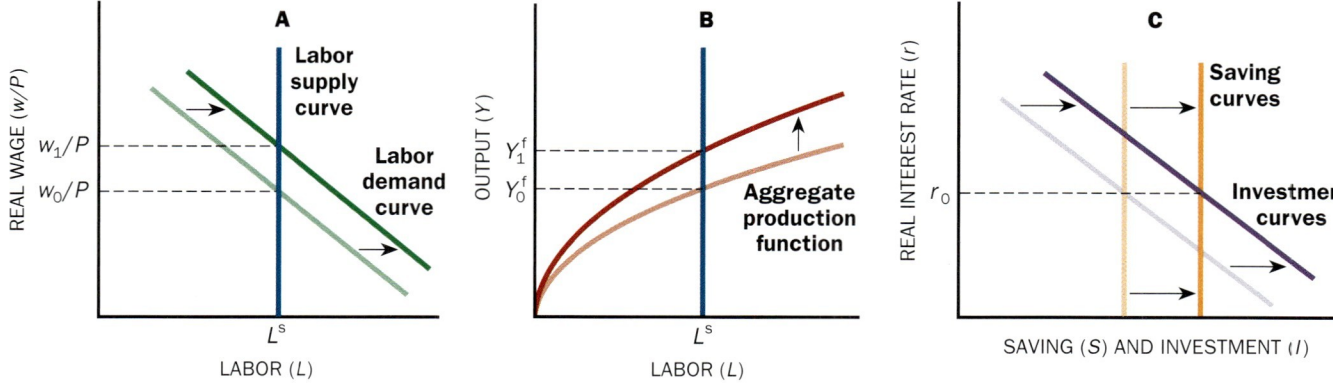

Figure 24.9

EFFECTS OF INTRODUCING PERSONAL COMPUTERS INTO THE ECONOMY

Panel A depicts the labor market. The labor supply curve is drawn as a vertical line at L^s. Personal computers increase the marginal product of workers, resulting in a rightward shift of the labor demand curve and an increase in the equilibrium real wage from w_0/P to w_1/P. Panel B depicts the aggregate production function; it shifts up because of the introduction of computers and the increased productivity of workers. Potential GDP increases from Y_0^f to Y_1^f. Panel C depicts the capital market. Investment increases as firms purchase personal computers, and saving increases as a result of increased income. Both the investment and saving curves shift to the right. There may be no net effect on the real interest rate (r_0) as shown here. The actual effect on the interest rate depends on the relative shifts of the saving and investment curves.

The General Equilibrium Model

We can now describe the general, long-run equilibrium of the economy. General equilibrium is a situation in which all the economy's markets are in balance—the labor, product, and capital markets all clear. General equilibrium in the full-employment model occurs when employment and the real wage have adjusted to ensure that the labor market is in equilibrium at full employment, output is equal to potential GDP, and the real interest rate is at the level ensuring that full-employment saving is equal to investment.

Start with the labor market. The real wage adjusts to ensure that the demand for labor equals the supply of labor. This adjustment determines both the equilibrium real wage and the level of employment that constitutes full employment. In the product market, the short-run aggregate production function then determines the level of output produced by firms when the economy is at full employment. This output level is potential GDP—the output that the labor supply, working with the available stock of plant and equipment, can produce when the economy is at full employment. Finally, the capital market balances leakages and injections in the circular flow of income. The real interest rate adjusts to ensure that at the full-employment level of income, saving is equal to investment. This equality also ensures that aggregate demand will equal aggregate supply at the full-employment level of output. The product market clears.

USING THE GENERAL EQUILIBRIUM MODEL

The general equilibrium model is useful because it enables us to understand the effects of various changes in the economy—from the market in which these changes originate to all the other markets in the economy.

Consider the effects on the economy of the introduction of personal computers. By making workers more productive, personal computers increase the marginal product of workers. This change increases the quantity of labor demanded at each real wage, causing a shift in the labor demand curve to the right. The equilibrium real wage rises, as shown in Figure 24.9, panel A.

The change in technology yields greater worker productivity. This change is represented by an upward shift of the short-run production function as shown in panel B. The improvement in productivity yields an increase in full-employment output. Product market equilibrium can be maintained only if aggregate demand also rises so that firms are able to sell the new higher level of output they are producing. As we have seen, this change in demand will occur if the real interest rate adjusts to maintain saving equal to investment in the capital market. Investment at each level of the real interest rate may rise as firms take advantage of the profit opportunities opened up by the new computer technology. At the same time, the increase in full-employment income leads to increases in both consumption and saving at each interest rate. The increases in investment and saving at each interest rate are represented by a rightward shift in both the investment and the saving curves (panel C). In equilibrium, the real interest rate may either rise, fall, or stay the same (as illustrated in panel C), depending on the relative magnitudes of the shifts. Whatever the impact on the real interest rate, we can conclude that equilibrium investment will rise.

We have focused here on the current effects of these changes, but there are important future effects as well. A higher level of investment today will lead to more plant and equipment tomorrow. The economy's future capacity will increase, and this expansion will contribute to future economic growth, a topic we will examine in Chapter 27. Thus, links exist not only between all markets today but also between today's and future markets.

The basic full-employment model also can be used to examine the impact on the labor, product, and capital markets of the rise in labor force participation rates among women. The *labor force participation rate* is the fraction of a group that is in the labor force (either employed or seeking work). In 1970, the female labor force participation rate was 43 percent, compared to 80 percent for men. By 1999, the female rate had risen to 60 percent. The change has pumped almost 20 million additional workers into the U.S. economy.

The effects of this change are shown in Figure 24.10. The increased supply of workers shifts the labor supply curve to the right. As panel A shows, the equilibrium real wage falls, while equilibrium employment rises. Because the level of employment now associated with equilibrium in the labor market has increased, potential GDP rises; this is shown in panel B. With higher incomes, households will increase both their consumption spending and their saving at each level of the real rate of interest. This impact on the capital market is shown in panel C as a rightward shift in the saving curve. While equilibrium saving and investment rise, the equilibrium real interest rate falls.

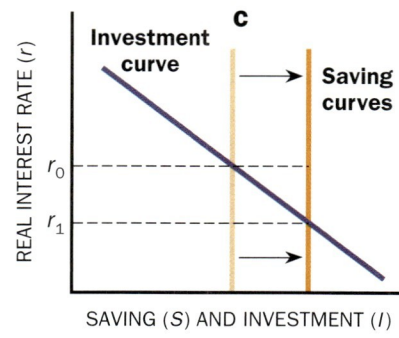

Figure 24.10

EFFECTS OF AN INCREASE IN THE SUPPLY OF LABOR

Panel A depicts the labor market. As more women enter the labor force, the labor supply curve shifts to the right, from L_0 to L_1. This results in a decrease in the equilibrium real wage from w_0/P to w_1/P and an increase in employment. Panel B depicts the aggregate production function; with employment higher, potential GDP rises from Y_0^f to Y_1^f. Panel C depicts the capital market. Saving increases as a result of increased income; the saving curve shifts to the right. The real interest rate falls, and in the new equilibrium, both saving and investment have increased.

We have used the full-employment model to analyze the impacts of two important changes in the economy: those associated with the introduction of a new technology (personal computers) and those associated with a change in the labor force. To focus on the effects each would have, we studied each change in isolation, assuming that nothing else was changing. In fact, both effects have been at work for more than thirty years. Both have combined to expand employment and raise potential GDP. Since the introduction of new technologies tends to raise real wages, while the expansion in the labor supply tends to lower real wages, their combined effect on real wages could be to increase them, decrease them, or leave them unchanged.

Computer technology has increased the productivity of a wide range of workers.

542 **CHAPTER 24** THE FULL-EMPLOYMENT MODEL

Review and Practice

SUMMARY

1. Macroeconomic equilibrium focuses on equilibrium levels of aggregates: employment, output, saving, and investment.
2. The real wage equates the demand for labor with the supply of labor. Increases in labor supply at each real wage are reflected in lower real wages, which induce firms to create additional jobs to match the increases in supply.
3. The full-employment level of output is that level of output which the economy can produce with its given stock of plant and equipment, when labor is fully employed. It will increase with increases in the labor supply or as a result of new technologies.
4. The real interest rate (which takes into account inflation) equates investment and saving. The desired level of investment decreases with increases in the real rate of interest. Household saving depends on income and the real interest rate. When the economy is at full employment, the interest rate is the main variable of concern in determining saving. Saving increases slightly with increases in the real interest rate.
5. A decrease in saving leads to a higher real interest rate and lower investment. A decrease in investment at each real interest rate leads to an unchanged or lower level of investment, depending on the elasticity of saving.
6. An increase in saving leads to a lower real increase rate and to increased investment. An increase in investment at each real interest rate leads to unchanged or higher investment, depending on the elasticity of saving.
7. When saving and investment are equal, the demand for goods and services will equal the level of output at full employment. The capital market balances leakages and injections in the circular flow of income.
8. All the markets in the economy are interlinked. Changes in one market have effects in all other markets.

KEY TERMS

full employment
short-run aggregate production function
potential GDP
full-employment level of output
loanable funds market
disposable income
real rate of interest
financial investments
capital goods investment
investment function

REVIEW QUESTIONS

1. How do competitive markets with flexible wages and prices ensure that labor is always fully employed? What induces firms to create just the right number of additional jobs to match an increase in the number of workers?
2. Describe the effects of changes in labor supply on equilibrium real wages and potential GDP (full-employment level of output).
3. What determines the economy's productive capacity or aggregate supply or potential GDP? How does aggregate supply increase when labor supply increases?
4. What is investment? Why does investment decrease when the real interest rate increases? What role do expectations play in investment?
5. What determines the level of saving? Explain why, if taxes are fixed, disposable income in a full-employment economy is fixed. Explain why saving may not be very sensitive to the real interest rate.
6. How are leakages and injections balanced? Why will demand and supply in the product market be equal if leakages and injections are equal?

PROBLEMS

1. In the text, we assumed that the labor supply did not depend on the real wage. Assume that at higher real wages, more individuals wish to work. Trace through how each of the steps in the analysis has to be changed. Show the equilibrium in the labor market. What happens to real wages, employment, GDP, and saving if the labor supply function shifts to the right?

2. An increase in capital resulting from an increase in investment allows a given number of workers to produce more. Show the effect on the short-run production function and the full-employment level of output.
3. Trace through how the effects of a change in one market—such as an increase in the supply of labor—have effects on other markets. How was it possible for the labor supply to increase markedly, as occurred during the 1970s and the 1980s, with relatively little change in real wages?
4. The following table gives average hourly nominal wages in nonagricultural industries and the price level in the United States from 1995 to 2002.

Year	Nominal Wage	Price Level	Real Wage
1995	11.43	152.4	7.50
1996	11.82	156.9	7.53
1997	12.28	160.5	7.65
1998	12.78	163.0	7.84
1999	13.24	166.6	7.95
2000	13.76	172.2	7.99
2001	14.31	177.1	8.08
2002	14.77	179.9	8.21

(a) In what year did the nominal wage rise the most?
(b) In what year did the real wage rise the most?
(c) Did you get the same years for both (c) and (b)? If you didn't, what accounts for the difference?

5. Figure 24.9 showed the impact of personal computers on full-employment output, the real wage, and the real interest rate when the labor supply curve is vertical. Suppose instead that the labor supply curve is upward sloping. How does this change affect your conclusions about the impact of personal computers?
6. Using the full-employment model, discuss the effect on employment, output, the real rate of interest, investment, and saving if households become more optimistic about the future and as a result reduce their current saving.
7. Suppose the introduction of a new technology for production causes an increase in investment at each real interest rate. What will be the impact of this change on the equilibrium real rate of interest and the level of saving and investment if the interest rate elasticity of household saving is zero? How do your answers change if the interest rate elasticity of household saving is positive?

Learning Goals

In this chapter, you will learn

1. The composition of government expenditures and revenues in the United States

2. How government deficits and surpluses affect the capital market

3. How the government affects the economy's full-employment equilibrium

4. The consequences of fiscal deficits and surpluses for output, investment, and future generations

5. The recent experiences with deficits and surpluses in the United States

Chapter 25

GOVERNMENT FINANCE AT FULL EMPLOYMENT

News stories are filled with debates over government spending and tax policies. In the United States, the federal government spends more than $2 trillion each year on everything from national defense to Social Security to national parks to health and education. State and local governments spend another $1.5 trillion on schools and a variety of services, including police, fire, and health. To pay for these expenditures, governments levy taxes and, when taxes are not sufficient to cover expenditures, they borrow.

During the 1980s and through most of the 1990s, the U.S. government consistently spent more than it raised in tax revenues. To cover this deficit, the government had to borrow in the capital market, just as a firm or household would. The ballooning budget deficit emerged as a major national issue; by the 1992 presidential election, public opinion polls were persistently ranking the huge deficits among the central problems facing the country. By 1998, deficits had apparently been vanquished and the U.S. federal government was collecting more in taxes than it was spending. Debates during the 2000 presidential campaign focused on what to do with these excess tax revenues. Should they be used to finance additional government spending? Or should taxes be cut? In early 2001, Congress took up the debate and eventually approved a large tax cut. Quickly, however, the situation again changed: the war on terrorism led to unanticipated increases in spending while the tax cut and an economic slowdown reduced the government's revenues. By 2002, the federal government was once again spending more than it raised in tax revenues, and a major issue during the 2004 presidential campaign was how to deal with these deficits.

In this chapter, we begin by briefly discussing the major components of the federal government's expenditures and revenues. Then we extend the full-employment model developed in Chapter 24 to include the government sector. By adding the

A
Outlays 2002

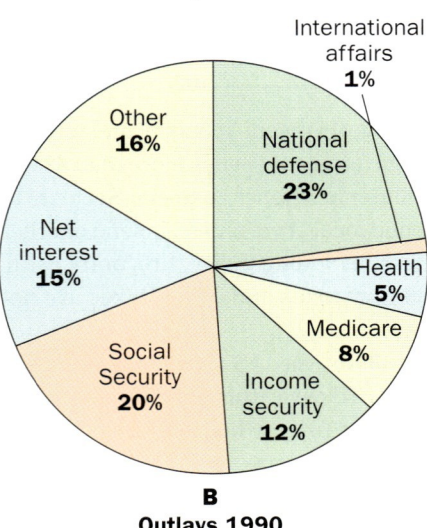

B
Outlays 1990

Figure 25.1

THE COMPOSITION OF FEDERAL GOVERNMENT SPENDING

The composition of the federal budget changed between 1990 and 2002: Medicare, income security, and social security programs grew, while net interest and defense spending fell as a percent of the total budget.

SOURCE: *Economic Report of the President* (2004).

government to our full-employment model, we will learn how government decisions about taxes and spending affect the full-employment economy. The chapter concludes with a discussion of some of the major budgetary issues facing the U.S. federal government.

The Composition of Spending and Taxes

The federal government spends more than $2 trillion per year. This total can be divided into two basic categories: **discretionary spending** and **nondiscretionary spending**. Discretionary expenditures—which include spending on the military, government operations, and most education and training programs—are decided on an annual basis. Each year, Congress and the president have the *discretion* to change their levels. Nondiscretionary spending has two components. First, the government must make interest payments on the national debt. Second, the government in various programs has established **entitlements**—certain benefits, such as Social Security, Medicare, and food stamps, to which individuals who meet criteria specified by law are *entitled*.

Panel A of Figure 25.1 shows the composition of federal spending in 2002, by major categories. Health, Medicare, Social Security, income security, and net interest are largely nondiscretionary expenditures, and in 2002 they constituted almost 70 percent of all spending. Panel B shows the same categories in 1990. By comparing the two panels, we see how the composition of government spending changed during this period. Defense spending shrank as a proportion of total spending, while the proportion of spending represented by health, Medicare, Social Security, and income security rose. Increases in health costs were particularly dramatic, doubling from 5 percent of the budget in 1990 to 10 percent in 2002. Net interest payments fell as a proportion of total spending, reflecting the low level of interest rates in 2002 and the decline in the debt caused by the surpluses between 1998 to 2001.

The sources of the government's revenue during this period changed only slightly. As shown in Figure 25.2, individual income tax payments represented just under half of the federal government's receipts in 1990 and 2002.

Extending the Basic Full-Employment Model

Although the basic full-employment model ignored the role of the government, in reality, the government plays a central role in all economies. Major macroeconomic policy issues often center around the impact of government spending and taxation decisions. To address these important policy issues, we need to extend the basic full-employment model.

Adding the Government

Introducing government into the analysis affects both the product market and the capital market. In the product market, the government has an impact on the economy in two ways. First, the government's purchases of goods and services produced by firms affect demand in the product market. Second, taxes subtract from demand in the product market because they reduce disposable income, lowering consumption spending.[1] In the capital market, governments affect the economy if they need to borrow to cover deficits when spending exceeds tax revenues or if they repay government debt when tax revenues exceed spending.

Figure 25.3 shows the circular flow of income when the government sector is added to our model. Households pay taxes to the government sector. These payments, just like household saving, represent a leakage from the spending stream. The government sector's purchases of goods and services represent an injection into the spending stream similar to investment spending. If tax revenues fall short of government expenditures, the government has a **fiscal deficit,** and it will need to borrow in the capital market to cover the difference. If the government runs a **fiscal surplus,** so that its tax revenues exceed its expenditures, then the government, like the household sector, will be a net saver and will represent a source of saving for the economy.

The government *deficit* represents the additional borrowing in a given year, while the accumulated amount the government owes—its *debt*—reflects all the borrowing it has done in the past. When the government runs a surplus, as it did from 1998 to 2001, it takes in more in revenue than it is spending. That surplus is used to repay the government's debt.

THE GOVERNMENT AND THE CAPITAL MARKET

Focusing on the capital market makes clear the effects of the government on the economy's full employment. In Chapter 24, we examined a simplified economy, one with no government and no trade with other countries (i.e., a *closed* economy). There, we saw that at the equilibrium real interest rate, saving was equal to investment. Now let's see how equilibrium in the capital market and the real interest rate are affected when we bring government into the picture. If government expenditures (G) exceed tax revenues (T), then the government must borrow to obtain the funds necessary to finance its expenditures. This means the government will compete with private borrowers for the saving of the private sector. Less saving is available for private investment.

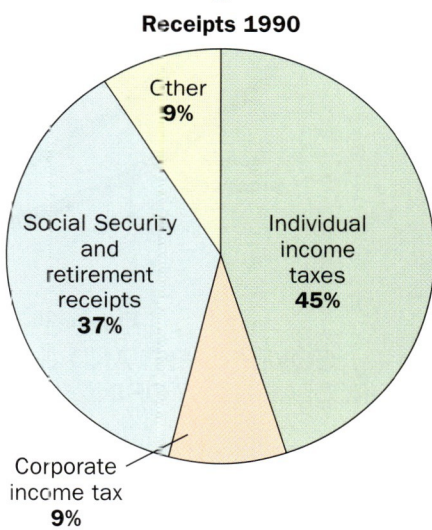

Figure 25.2

THE COMPOSITION OF FEDERAL GOVERNMENT REVENUE

The importance of different sources of federal revenue remained relatively constant between 1990 and 2002.

SOURCE: *Economic Report of the President* (2004).

---

[1] Governments also can affect the economy as producers of goods. In the U.S. economy, the government is not a major producer of goods and services and so we will neglect that aspect of the government in our analysis. However, government production is very important in some areas of the economy, education being a prime example.

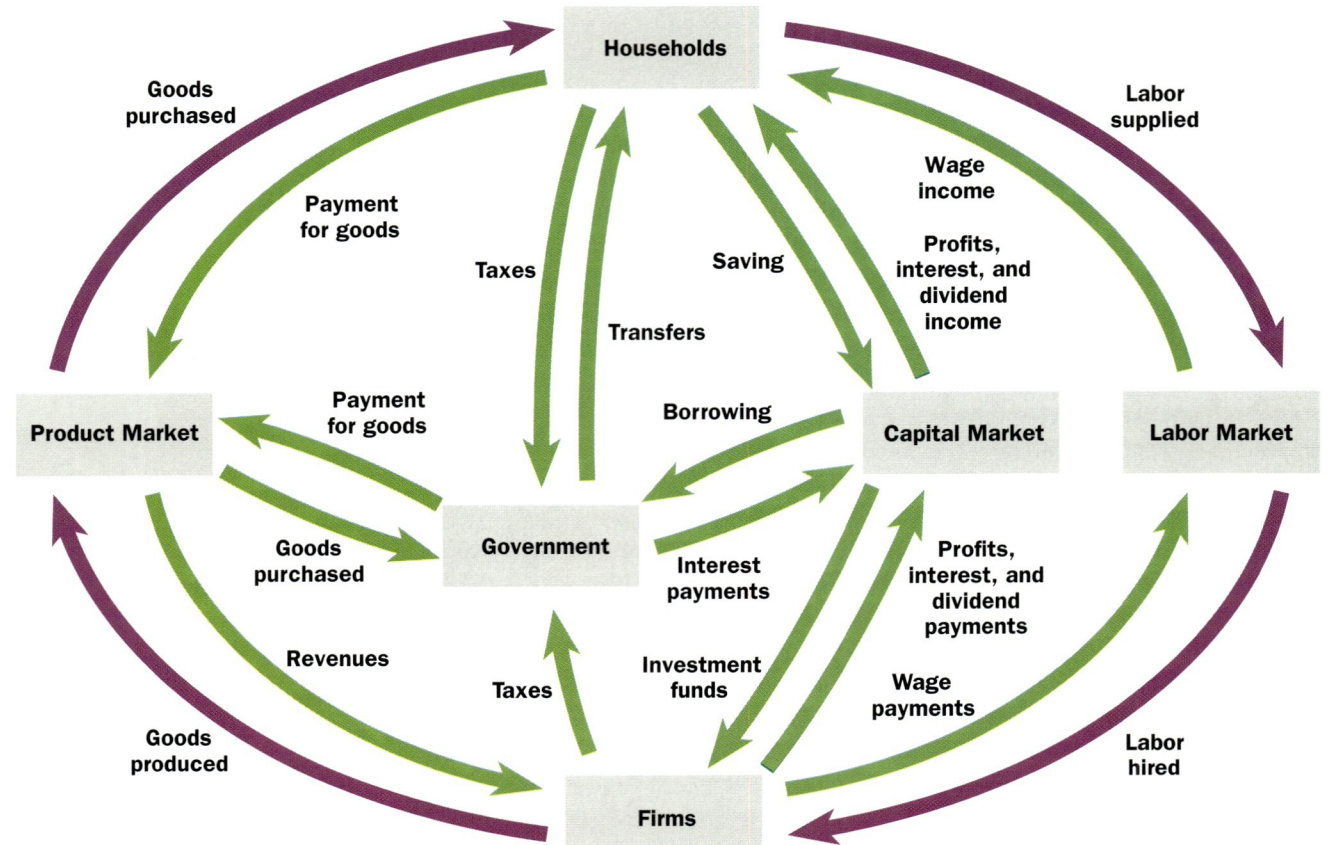

Figure 25.3

GOVERNMENT AND THE CIRCULAR FLOW OF INCOME

The government purchases goods and services in the product market and receives tax revenues from households and firms. It also makes transfer payments, such as Social Security benefits, to households. Government purchases represent an injection into the spending flow, while taxes (the amount after transfers) represent a leakage. If government expenditures exceed revenues, the government will need to borrow in the capital market. If government revenues exceed expenditures, the government surplus adds to the supply of funds in the capital market. When the capital market is in equilibrium, leakages will again balance injections, and demand and supply in the product market will be equal.

When the government runs a deficit, private saving (S_p) takes on two purposes—to finance private investment (I) and to finance the government's deficit ($G - T$). Equilibrium in the capital market occurs when private saving is equal to investment plus the deficit, or

$$S_p = I + (G - T).$$

Alternatively, we can think of the deficit as *negative public government saving* (S_g):

$$G - T = -S_g.$$

From this perspective, the first equation can be rewritten as

$$S_p = I - S_g,$$

or

$$S_p + S_g = I.$$

The left side is called **national saving,** the combined saving of the private (households and businesses) and public (government) sectors. When the capital market in a closed economy is in equilibrium, *national saving equals investment.*

The effect in the capital market of a government deficit is illustrated in Figure 25.4. The investment schedule is downward sloping. Saving is assumed to be unresponsive to the interest rate. The initial level of national saving is S_0. The capital market is in equilibrium when the real rate of interest is r_0. Now suppose the government increases expenditures without increasing taxes so that it needs to borrow an amount equal to its deficit, $G - T$, the excess of spending over revenue. The increase in the government deficit reduces national saving, so the saving schedule is now shifted to the left, to S_1. It is shifted to the left by the amount the government has borrowed. Equilibrium in the capital market now occurs at a higher real interest rate (r_1). The higher real interest rate reduces private investment spending. As a consequence, government borrowing is **crowding out** an equal amount of private investment. That is, a rise in government spending is simply displacing private investment spending.

Figure 25.4

EFFECTS OF INCREASED GOVERNMENT DEFICIT ON THE CAPITAL MARKET

An increased government deficit (reduced public saving) reduces national saving. With a leftward shift in the saving curve, the equilibrium level of real interest rates is higher and the equilibrium level of investment is lower.

When the government has a budget surplus, the opposite effects occur. With a surplus, public saving is positive. A cut in government expenditures without a corresponding reduction in taxes increases the surplus and shifts the national saving schedule to the right. As a result, the equilibrium real interest rate falls and private investment rises.

Our analysis tells us that *when all else is held constant,* an increase in the government deficit will raise the equilibrium real rate of interest at full employment. Other factors—shifts in the investment function or in private saving—can also affect the equilibrium real rate of interest (as we learned in Chapter 24). Thus, as we assess the impact of the government on real interest rates, the full-employment model predicts that an increase in the deficit will increase the equilibrium real rate of interest *relative to what it would have been without the deficit increase.* To understand the actual evolution of the economy's real interest rate, we need to take these other factors into account. For example, in the late 1990s, an investment boom associated with new information technologies created such a strong demand for capital that it offset the effects on the real interest rate of the federal budget deficit reduction that occurred at the same time. In the first years of the current century, investment collapsed after the bubble in technology stocks burst in 2000 and the recession of 2001 began. This decrease in the demand for capital worked to offset the impact of the big increase in the budget deficit.

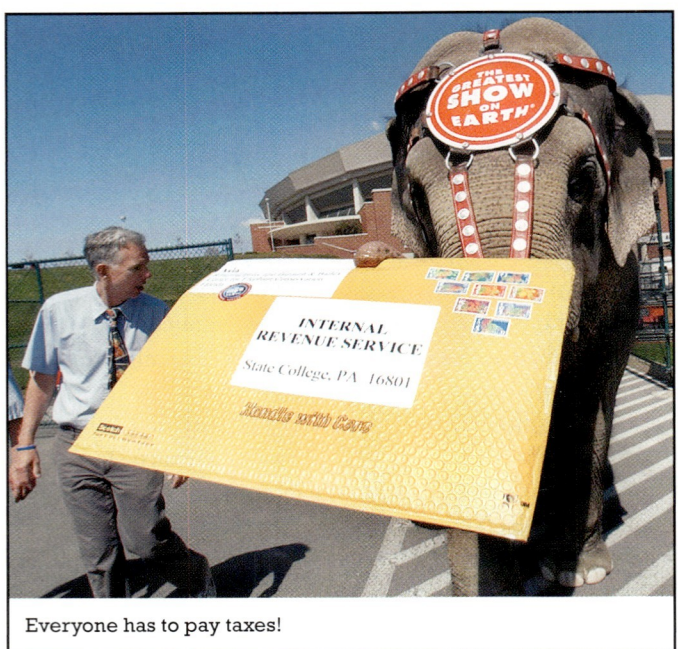
Everyone has to pay taxes!

The Effects of Changes in Taxes While we have focused on changes in expenditures, the same analysis enables us to understand how the economy would be affected by a tax cut not balanced by a cut in government expenditures. A tax cut increases households' disposable income. To make the example concrete, suppose taxes are reduced by $100 billion. As a result, disposable income rises by the full $100 billion that households no longer need to pay to the government as taxes. They will use this additional disposable income to increase their current consumption spending and to increase their saving.[2] For example, aggregate consumption might rise by $90 billion and saving by $10 billion. If this is the case, private saving will rise by $10 billion, but national saving will fall because the government's deficit rises by $100 billion. Therefore, national saving falls by $90 billion. The leftward shift in the savings curve leads to a higher equilibrium real interest rate and a lower level of investment.

Balanced Budget Changes in Expenditures and Taxes The previous examples considered cases in which expenditures or taxes were changed, leading to changes in public saving. But what happens if the government changes *both* expenditures and taxes by the same amount so that public saving remains unchanged? Suppose initially that the government has a balanced budget: that is,

---

[2]This does not mean every household will use some of the tax cut to increase their saving. Many households might decide to spend the entire amount. Others might decide to save it all. But when we add up all the households in the economy, both aggregate consumption and aggregate saving will have increased.

revenues match expenditures. In 1998, for example, both U.S. federal government receipts and expenditures were roughly $1.7 trillion. Now suppose that the government increases its expenditures, say, by $100 billion. To pay for these expenditures, suppose the government increases taxes by an equal amount. We would describe this as a *balanced budget change in taxes and expenditures*. Since both expenditures and revenues increase by the same amount, the government's overall budget remains in balance. What will be the effect on the macroeconomy of such a balanced budget increase in spending?

Since taxes have risen by $100 billion, the private sector's disposable income—income after paying taxes—has been reduced by $100 billion. When disposable income falls, households typically adjust by reducing both their consumption and their saving. For example, to pay the additional $100 billion in taxes, total consumption might fall by $90 billion and saving by $10 billion. The reduction in consumption and saving totals $100 billion, the amount that households needed to pay the higher taxes.

The reduction in disposable income from the tax increase reduces private saving. Since public saving is unchanged (remember, expenditures and taxes were increased by the same amount), national saving falls. In the capital market, the national saving curve shifts to the left. With an unchanged investment schedule, the equilibrium real interest rate rises and the equilibrium investment level falls. This is an important conclusion. Equal changes in government revenues and expenditures—balanced budget changes in taxes and expenditures—affect investment and the real interest rate. A balanced budget *increase* in taxes and expenditures will *reduce* consumption and investment and *raise* the real interest rate. A balanced budget *decrease* in taxes and expenditures will *increase* consumption and investment and *lower* the real interest rate.

A balanced budget change in expenditures and taxes shifts how output is allocated to private uses (consumption and investment) and public uses (government purchases). Think of total output as a pie to be divided among various uses. A balanced budget change does not alter the total size of the pie; under our assumption that the economy remains at full employment, output remains at its full-employment level. Its effect is simply to change how the pie is divided. If government expenditures and taxes increase, private-sector spending on consumption and investment shrinks—it is crowded out—to make room for increased public-sector spending. Crowding out occurs even if the government increases taxes enough to fully pay for the increased expenditures, as individuals adjust to higher taxes in part by reducing private saving.

In this example, the total pie—full-employment output—was treated as fixed. It is important to understand why this is the case. In Chapter 24 we learned that full-employment output depends on the economy's capital stock, its technology, and the level of employment that occurs when demand and supply balance in the labor market. None of these factors is likely to be affected directly by changes in general government expenditures or taxes. Thus full-employment output, potential GDP, will remain unchanged. However, government expenditures can have an impact on *future* income levels and growth. For example, increased government purchases that lower private-sector investment will reduce the amount of capital that the economy has in the future, thereby lowering full-employment income in the future. When we discuss economic growth and productivity in Chapter 27, we will consider some types of government expenditures and taxes that might affect the discovery of new technologies, the productivity of capital, and the demand for labor by firms. When we deal with these policies, we will need to investigate their impact on potential GDP.

LEAKAGES AND INJECTIONS

We have focused our discussion of government deficits on the capital market. Recall, however, that when the capital market is in equilibrium, balancing national saving and investment, the leakages and injections in the circular flow of income will also be balanced. This result holds just as it did in Chapter 24 when we ignored the government sector. Leakages from the spending flow now consist of household saving and taxes, while injections into the spending flow consist of investment and government expenditures. As they adjust to ensure that national saving equals investment, real interest rates also ensure that leakages equal injections at full-employment output. The total demand for the goods and services produced by firms will balance the total output that is produced at full employment.

Adding Government   Incorporating the government into our model gives us three sources of aggregate demand—consumption, investment, and government purchases:

$$\text{demand} = C + I + G.$$

For the economy to be at equilibrium at full employment, demand must equal full-employment income. When the capital market is in equilibrium, desired investment equals national saving (the sum of private saving and government saving). Private saving at full employment is equal to full-employment income Y^f minus consumption and taxes. Government saving is equal to taxes minus expenditures. We can express capital market equilibrium as

$$I = S_N = S_p + S_g = (Y^f - C - T) + (T - G).$$

Rearranging this expression implies that

$$C + I + G = Y^f,$$

which is to say that demand from consumption spending, investment, and government spending equals full-employment income. Thus, aggregate demand equals full-employment output and the product market is in equilibrium at full employment when the capital market is in equilibrium.

International Perspective
DEFICITS IN OTHER COUNTRIES

When the United States ran a huge budget deficit during the 1980s, it was not alone. Most other major economies also witnessed the same problems of deficits and growing government debt. The figure shows estimates from the International Monetary Fund (IMF) of the "structural" budget deficit as a percentage of potential GDP for the United States, Japan, and other major industrialized economies (Canada, France, Germany, Italy, and the United Kingdom). The structural deficit is that part of the government's deficit that is left after it is corrected for the type of business cycle factors we will be studying in Part Seven. It corresponds to an estimate of the budget *if the economy were at full employment.* As the figure shows, only Japan among the major industrialized economies experienced a budget surplus during the 1980s.

During the 1990s, the budget situation improved in the United States and the other industrialized economies, again with the exception of Japan. The 1990s, when most industrialized economies enjoyed strong economic growth, are sometimes described as "the lost decade" in Japan, as growth stagnated after the rapid economic expansion of the previous thirty years.

According to the IMF's estimates, the United States had achieved a balanced budget by 1998 and ran surpluses in 1999 and 2000. However, that budget situation changed dramatically after 2001 as a result of tax cuts that reduced government revenue and spending increases that were necessitated by the war on terrorism. But unlike in the 1980s, the other industrialized economies did not show a similar budget picture. In fact, for 2004, the deficit as a percent of potential GDP in the industrialized economies fell to under 2 percent, even as it rose to exceed 4 percent in the United States.

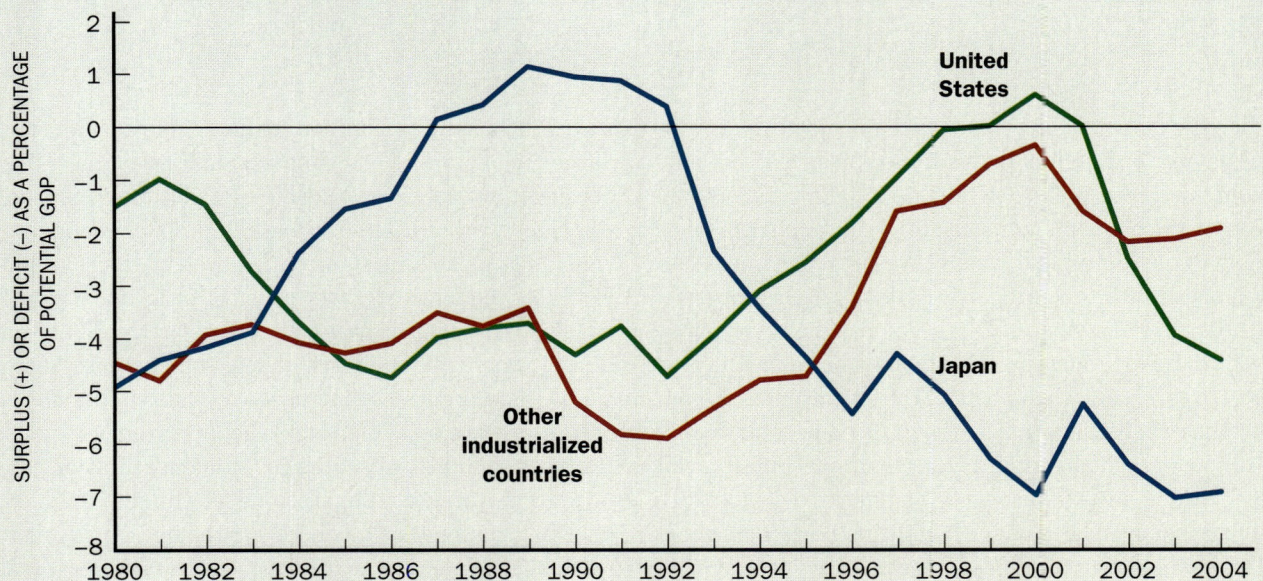

STRUCTURED SURPLUS AS A PERCENTAGE OF POTENTIAL GDP

SOURCE: IMF, *World Economic Outlook* (2004).

Wrap-Up

GOVERNMENT DEFICITS AND SURPLUSES

Government expenditures and taxes affect the capital market.

Increases in taxes reduce disposable income, and thereby decrease private saving. The equilibrium real interest rate is higher and private investment is lower.

When the government spends more than it receives in revenue, it must borrow to finance its deficit. A deficit reduces public saving, leading to higher real interest rates and lower private investment.

The lower the level of private investment, the smaller the increase in the capital stock. With a smaller capital stock, potential GDP in the future is lower.

A surplus has the opposite effect. When the government spends less than it receives in revenue, public saving and thus national saving rise. This increase leads to lower real interest rates and higher private investment. Higher private

Thinking Like an Economist
DISTRIBUTION, DEFICITS, AND INTERGENERATIONAL TRANSFERS

If you borrow money to buy a car, you can enjoy the car now without paying for it in full. Instead, you can spread the payments out over a relatively long time period. The same is true of governments that borrow. Instead of raising enough in taxes right now to pay for all its expenditures, a government can borrow and use future taxes to repay its debt. But this approach raises the issue of distribution. Let's suppose the government borrows $20 billion today, uses the money to reduce the current level of taxes, and then plans to raise taxes in fifty years to repay the money that it has borrowed. In fifty years, most of the taxpayers who benefited from the tax reduction will have died, and many of those whose higher taxes will repay the debt are not even alive now, when the money is being borrowed. Does this mean that government borrowing results in a transfer of wealth between generations, from future taxpayers to today's?

Some economists argue that the answer is no. They point out that those future taxpayers are the children of today's taxpayers. Rather than spend the tax cut, today's taxpayers can save it, and simply pass it on to their children in the form of a larger inheritance. The children would then have the extra wealth they need to pay the higher taxes they will face. They therefore will not have to reduce their own consumption spending to pay for the tax cut enjoyed by their parents.

Most economists, however, do not believe that private savings increases in this way when taxes are cut. They observe that when people find their disposable incomes higher as a result of a tax cut, they increase their consumption spending. They may save some of the tax cut, but private saving does not increase enough to offset the government's dissaving (deficit). As a consequence, national saving falls. In the capital market, the fall in national saving increases the full-employment equilibrium real interest rate. Investment falls. Lower investment means less capital (plant and equipment) is built, and future generations inherit a smaller stock of capital. The distribution of wealth between generations is affected: current taxpayers have been able to consume more, while future generations will have less capital and therefore lower incomes.

investment increases the capital stock, thereby increasing potential GDP in the future.

Evaluating Government Deficits and Surpluses

We have seen that government deficits and surpluses have significant impacts. Deficits reduce national saving, increase the real interest rate, and reduce investment, and surpluses have the opposite effect. But while our analysis tells us what the consequences of deficits and surpluses are, it does not tell us whether governments should or should not run deficits.

Economists have traditionally argued that government borrowing, just like individual borrowing, may or may not make sense, depending on the purpose for which the funds have been borrowed. It makes sense to borrow to buy a house that you will live in for many years or a car that you will drive for several years. Borrowing is a way to spread the payments for the house or the car over time, so that you can pay for the purchase as you use it. It also makes sense to borrow for an educational degree that will lead to a higher-paying job in the future. But paying this year for a vacation from two years ago makes no economic sense.

Countries are in a similar position. Borrowing to finance a road or a school that will be used for many years may be quite appropriate; borrowing to pay for this year's government salaries or current operating costs poses real problems. Governments in many countries—sometimes the dictators or corrupt regimes of the past—have taken on more debt than they can comfortably pay off, forcing them to raise taxes sharply and reduce citizens' living standards. Others have simply failed to repay what they owe, thereby jeopardizing their ability to borrow in the future.

Financing government expenditures by borrowing rather than by raising taxes— deficit financing—results in higher levels of private consumption in the short run, since individuals' taxes are lower. Thus, borrowing to finance government expenditures can serve to shift the burden onto future generations. For example, the U.S. government financed some of its World War II expenditures by borrowing rather than raising taxes by the full amount necessary to cover the war effort. This debt was discharged, in part, by taxes paid by workers long after the war ended. Thus, some of the cost of the war was borne by the generation who entered the labor force *after* the war. Since these later generations benefited from the Allied victory in World War II, an argument can be made in this case that sharing the burden across generations made sense. If governments borrow for spending that benefits only the current generation, however, forcing future generations to share the cost is less defensible.

There is another way that government borrowing shifts the burden of expenditures onto future generations. When the economy is at full employment, more consumption implies less saving. To maintain the economy at full employment, the real interest rate must rise to balance saving and investment—and a higher equilibrium interest rate reduces investment. As we will see in Chapter 27, lower investment in the present can reduce economic growth in the future, leading to lower incomes and consumption.

Reducing the deficit or actually running a surplus has the opposite effect. It allows the real interest rate to fall, stimulating private investment and thereby promoting economic growth and better living standards in the future.

Wrap-Up

CONSEQUENCES OF GOVERNMENT DEFICITS

If the government runs deficits,
> Some of the burden of current expenditures is shifted to future generations directly.
> Government deficits also reduce national saving, raise the real interest rate, and lower the level of private investment, thereby making future generations worse off.

If the government runs surpluses,
> Some of the burden of future expenditures is shifted to the current generation.
> Also, repaying government debt increases national saving, lowers the real interest rate, and increases private investment, thereby making future generations better off.

Government Deficits and Surpluses: Our Recent Experiences

In 1981, federal taxes were cut in the United States, but expenditures on defense and social programs (medical, income security, and Social Security) increased. Figure 25.5 shows the resulting increase in the federal deficit. In twelve years, from 1981 to 1992, the deficit more than quadrupled from $60 billion per year to $280 billion per year. The economy grew over the period shown in the figure, as did the price level, so a better measure of the size of the deficit is obtained by expressing the nominal deficit as a percentage of nominal GDP. Even after making this adjustment, we see that the increase in the deficit was dramatic, as panel B shows. The United States experienced the first major peacetime deficits in its history.

During President Bill Clinton's first term, a number of measures were adopted to raise taxes and limit the growth in federal spending. These succeeded in reducing the deficit. Beginning in 1998, the federal government actually started to run a surplus, with tax revenues exceeding government expenditures. The surpluses were short-lived, however. The federal budget swung back into deficit in 2002 as a result of three factors: the economy entered a recession in 2001, and thus the taxes

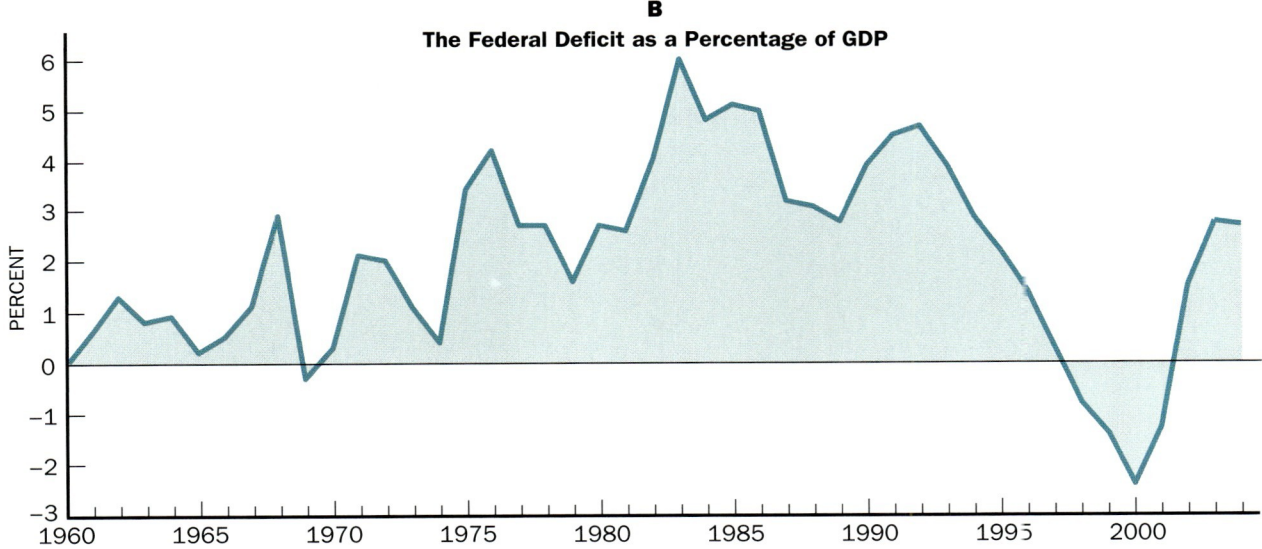

Figure 25.5

THE FEDERAL DEFICIT

Federal borrowing increased dramatically between 1975 and the early 1990s, fell sharply in the late 1990s, and rose steeply again after 2000. Panel A shows the nominal deficit; panel B shows the deficit as a percentage of nominal GDP.

SOURCE: *Economic Report of the President* (2004).

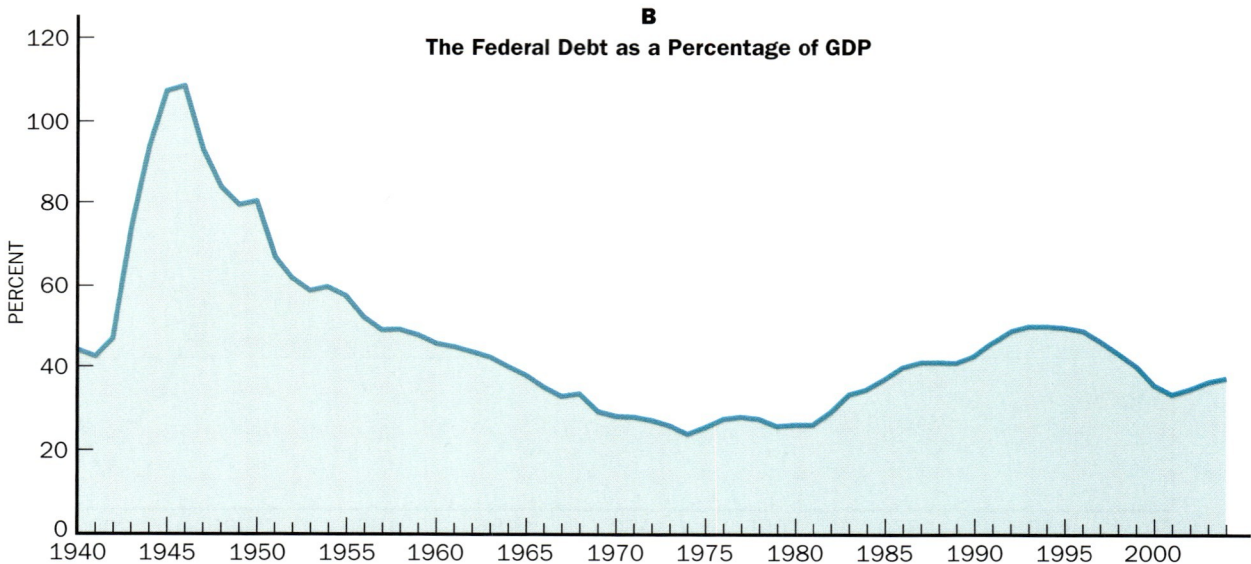

Figure 25.6

THE FEDERAL DEBT

The federal debt fell after World War II and rose rapidly after 1982 (panel A). Expressing the debt relative to GDP, panel B shows that the debt reached a peak relative to the size of the economy immediately after World War II, rose between 1982 and 1996, and declined from 1996 until 2000.

SOURCE: *Economic Report of the President* (2004).

collected fell; Congress passed a large tax cut in 2001 (followed by another in 2003); and the war on terrorism led to a rise in federal government spending.

Panel A of Figure 25.6 shows the U.S. federal debt, the accumulated effect of past deficits. The deficits of the 1980s and 1990s pushed the federal debt to record peacetime levels. Debt was reduced during 1998 to 2001 as the government enjoyed budget surpluses. Panel B shows the debt as a percentage of GDP to adjust for the inflation and real economic growth that has occurred over the sixty-odd years shown. As the graph reveals, the debt today is smaller relative to the size of the economy than it was immediately following World War II.

Factors Affecting the Federal Budget

Figure 25.7 shows federal outlays and receipts as a percentage of GDP since 1960, together with projections for 2004 through 2010. Projecting what will happen to the deficit even a few years into the future is often difficult. In 1996, for example, the Congressional Budget Office (CBO) was predicting that the federal government would run a deficit of $259 billion in 2001. In fact, the government enjoyed a surplus in 2001 of $127 billion. In January 2001, the CBO projected a surplus of $397 billion

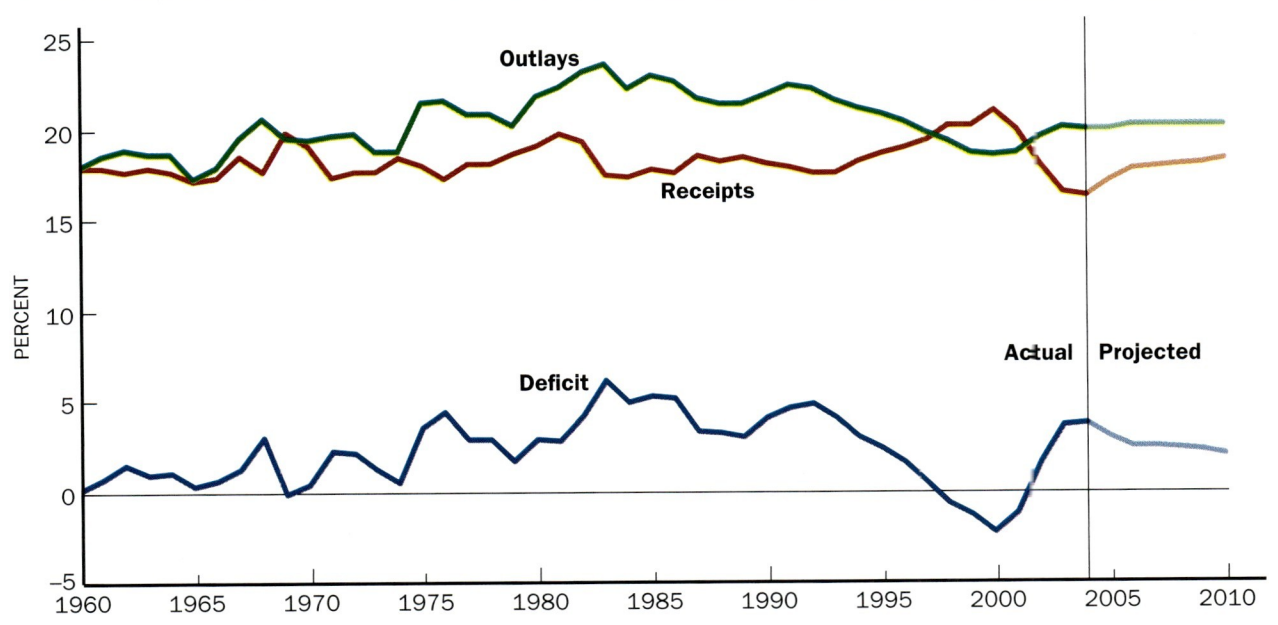

Figure 25.7

FEDERAL OUTLAYS AND REVENUE AS A PERCENTAGE OF GDP

The gap between federal outlays and revenues as a percentage of GDP reached a peak of 6 percent in 1983. In 2000, the surplus of revenues over outlays was 2.4 percent of GDP.

SOURCE: Congressional Budget Office.

for 2004. As of 2005, it was clear that the government, instead of running a surplus in 2004, saw the deficit soar above $400 billion.

One reason budget projections often turn out wrong is that in making its calculations the CBO, by law, must assume there will be no changes in tax or expenditure programs. Yet these programs do change, partly in response to the CBO's figures. In the 1990s, the large projected deficits led Congress to change taxes and curb growth in expenditures; in 2000, with the CBO projecting future surpluses, Congress cut taxes to reduce future revenues. Another reason for the projections' inaccuracy is that unforeseen events can alter the government's fiscal position. For example, the recession that started in 2001, further tax cuts, the terrorist attacks of September 11, 2001, and the rise in spending for homeland security all contributed to turning the projected surpluses into actual deficits.

RISK FACTORS FOR THE FEDERAL BUDGET

Three broad factors are likely to play important roles in determining the future budget outlook for the federal government.

Defense Spending From 1983 to 1988, defense spending averaged 6 percent of GDP. The end of the cold war was followed by reductions in defense spending. By 2002, this category had fallen to slightly over 3 percent of GDP. The war on terrorism has led to a rise in defense spending, and it is uncertain how these expenditures will trend in the future.

Higher Social Spending on the Elderly As the elderly population in the United States has grown, not only in absolute number, but also as a proportion of the population, federal expenditures on programs such as Social Security and Medicare (providing health care to the aged) have increased dramatically. These programs are projected to continue to grow, with significant implications for the federal budget. A central question is how much of the government's revenues needs to be set aside to help pay for future Social Security and Medicare benefits.

Increasing Health Expenditures Through Medicare and Medicaid, its program that provides health care to the poor, the government has assumed an increasing share of total health care expenditures, which have soared in recent years. The addition of a prescription drug benefit to Medicare and the rapid increase in drug prices will significantly affect the government's need for revenue in the future. New but expensive medical technologies and the aging of the population are also contributing to the swift escalation of medical costs.

Review and Practice

SUMMARY

1. When the government runs a deficit or a surplus, the capital market is affected. If there is a deficit, the government must borrow in the capital market to finance the deficit.
2. In the full-employment model, an increase in government expenditures matched by an increase in taxes reduces disposable income. This drop, in turn, reduces both consumption and saving at full-employment output. Saving decreases, the equilibrium real interest rate rises, and the equilibrium level of investment falls.
3. Changes in government revenues and expenditures do not affect full-employment output or employment, but they do alter how output is divided between consumption, investment, and government purchases.
4. During the past twenty-five years, the budget of the U.S. federal government has swung from large deficits in the 1980s and early 1990s to surpluses from 1998 to 2001, and then back to large deficits.
5. Government borrowing can be an economic burden for future generations in several ways. First, future generations may bear the responsibility of paying off the debt; there is a transfer of wealth from one generation to another. Second, government borrowing can raise real interest rates and crowd out private investment, thereby reducing future output and wages.
6. Future expenditures by the government on homeland security, Social Security, and Medicare are likely to increase in the future.

KEY TERMS

discretionary spending
nondiscretionary spending
entitlements
fiscal deficit
fiscal surplus
national saving
crowding out

REVIEW QUESTIONS

1. What is the relationship between deficit spending and the government's debt?
2. What are the consequences of an increased deficit for private investment and the real rate of interest?
3. How do government deficits and surpluses affect different generations?
4. Name three factors that contributed to the elimination of deficits at the end of the 1990s.
5. Name three factors that contributed to the return of deficits after 2001.

PROBLEMS

1. Suppose households save 5 percent of their disposable income. If the government increases expenditures and taxes by $100 billion, by how much will saving decline? By how much will consumption decline? What happens to investment? (Assume a closed economy.)
2. Redo Question 1 but assume that households save 10 percent of their disposable income. What happens to consumption and investment? Why does investment decline more with a higher saving rate?
3. The primary deficit is defined as the difference between tax revenues and government expenditures, *excluding interest payments;* it represents what the deficit would have been, had the government not inherited any debt. Discuss why the concept of a primary deficit may or may not be useful or relevant.
4. "The resources that were spent fighting World War II were spent during the period 1940–1945. Hence, the generations that were alive and paying taxes during that period are the generations that bore the burden of the cost of the war, regardless of how it was financed." Discuss.
5. Why does the way the government uses a surplus make a difference for investment spending? Consider the following scenarios:

(a) Assume the government reduces income taxes. What is the total impact on national saving, taking into account the reduction in the surplus and the change in private saving? What is the impact on investment? (Hint: How does your answer depend on the sensitivity of saving to the interest rate?)

(b) Assume the government increases expenditures. What is the total impact on national saving, taking into account the reduction in the surplus and the change in private saving? What is the impact on investment? (Hint: How does your answer depend on the type of expenditures the government increases?)

Learning Goals

In this chapter, you will learn

1. The role of the capital market in an open economy
2. How the net exports and international capital flows are related
3. What exchange rates are, how they are determined, and how they affect the trade balance

Chapter 26

THE OPEN ECONOMY AT FULL EMPLOYMENT

Modern economies are open economies—actively engaged in international trade and linked to international financial markets. The increasing globalization of the world's economies, and what it means for individual countries and their citizens, has occasioned often strident political debate. Because it is part of the global economy, the United States is affected by, and in turn affects, international economic developments. A financial crisis abroad can have an impact on the value of the dollar and on U.S. exports and imports. U.S. budget deficits influence interest rates and net exports.

The United States and other countries are linked by exchanges both of goods and services and of financial assets. In 2003, the United States sold more than $1 trillion worth of goods and services to the rest of the world. Exports as a percentage of total GDP equaled almost 10 percent; in 1970, they totaled only 5 percent. Americans purchased more than $1.4 trillion in products from other countries in 2003. But these exchanges of goods and services aren't the only international trades that take place. Trade also occurs in financial capital—a British firm borrows money in the U.S. capital market, and interest is paid to Japanese investors who own U.S. government bonds, as well as to U.S. investors who hold Korean government debt. Financial linkages have also grown tremendously over recent decades. It is estimated that foreign-owned assets in the United States grew from $142 billion in 1990 to more than $500 billion in 1999. These flows of financial funds from one country to another play a major role in unifying the global economy. The international exchange of goods and capital has important implications for the macroeconomy.

In this chapter, we extend the full-employment model developed in Chapter 24 to include the foreign sector. By extending the model, we will be able to explore how the international flows of savings affect the domestic capital market and the relationship between national saving and investment. We will also examine how the international financial linkages between countries are related to the balance between exports and imports. Finally, we will discuss how the value of the dollar relative to other currencies is determined in foreign exchange markets, and how the dollar's value affects U.S. exports and imports.

The Open Economy

Globalization and the increasing integration of the world economy are topics encountered in the news all the time. Whether at our local auto dealer, computer store, or grocery store, we find goods produced in many other countries. Financial markets, too, are global in nature. News reports of financial crises in other countries can affect the U.S. stock market. To understand the macroeconomic implications of being part of a world economy, we need to extend our full-employment model to incorporate international trade and finance. In doing so, we turn from the analysis of a closed economy and focus on an open economy. An **open economy** is one whose households and firms trade with other countries and borrow from and lend to other countries. The basic lessons learned from the study of the closed economy continue to guide our analysis of the open economy.

International trade affects the product market because net exports represent a demand for what the economy produces. More importantly, an open economy has access to international sources of funds for financing domestic investment or for financing government deficits. National saving is the domestic source of funds. If the demand for funds for investment exceeds domestic national saving, firms and governments in an open economy can borrow abroad. To understand the role that international trade and international flows of financial capital play, we again start our analysis with the capital market.

THE CAPITAL MARKET IN THE OPEN ECONOMY

Because households and firms in an open economy can borrow or lend abroad, foreign borrowing and lending must be accounted for when we look at equilibrium in the capital market. The moneys coming into the United States—to be deposited in U.S. banks, to buy U.S. government bonds, or to be lent directly to Americans for any reason—are called **capital inflows**. U.S. dollars going to other countries for similar purposes are called **capital outflows**. In the closed economy, as we saw in Chapter 24, equilibrium occurs when national saving and investment are equal. In the open economy, investment can be financed *either* from domestic sources of saving *or* by borrowing abroad, essentially making use of foreign sources of saving, thus:

national saving (S_N) + borrowing from abroad (NCF) = investment (I).

We have denoted net borrowing from abroad by NCF, which stands for **net capital inflows** (the inflows minus the outflows). If net capital inflows are positive, then the domestic economy is borrowing more from foreigners than it is lending to foreigners. In 2002, for example, national saving in the United States totaled $1.54 trillion (of which private saving was $1.57 trillion and government saving was –$30 billion), while private investment was $1.93 trillion. The difference between investment and national saving was $390 billion, which was financed by a net capital inflow. Because this investment was financed by borrowing from abroad, it represents the amount that foreigners have invested in the United States, and so it is also called *net foreign investment.*

When the capital market in an open economy is in equilibrium, *national saving plus net capital inflows equals private investment.* National saving plus capital flows from abroad can be thought of as the "sources" of funds, and investment can be thought of as the "use" of these funds.

The reaction in the capital market is different if the country is a **small open economy** rather than a **large open economy.** A small open economy is one that is too small to affect the rest of the world with shifts in its domestic saving or investment; it can borrow or lend internationally at the world rate of interest. A large open economy can also borrow and lend in the international capital market. However, domestic shifts in saving or investment in such an economy are substantial enough to affect that market's equilibrium world rate of interest.

The Capital Market in the Small Open Economy Capital market equilibrium requires that national saving plus net capital inflows equal private investment. The implications this has for the economy will depend on the relationship of the supply of funds from both domestic and foreign sources to the real interest rate. A small open economy like Switzerland faces a perfectly elastic supply curve of funds at the world real interest rate. If borrowers in Switzerland were to pay a slightly higher interest rate than that paid in other countries, those with financial capital to lend would divert their funds to Switzerland. If Switzerland were to pay slightly less than the interest rate available in other countries (adjusted for risk), it would not obtain financial capital. Those who have financial investments in Switzerland can take their funds and invest them abroad to earn higher interest rates. These flows of international financial capital play an important role in the global economy. For a small country, the interest rate is determined by the international capital market. Effectively, such a country takes the interest rate as fixed. This is shown in Figure 26.1, where the interest rate is fixed at r^*. A fixed interest rate, in turn, means that the level of investment is fixed, at I^* in Figure 26.1. Any shortfall between the level of domestic national saving and the level of domestic investment is funded by borrowing from abroad. In Figure 26.1, if the level of national saving is given by S_0, the amount of funds borrowed from abroad is B_0. A reduction in the amount of domestic saving increases the amount of foreign borrowing (B_1) but leaves investment unaffected.

This result contrasts with our earlier result for a closed economy, one in which there is no foreign borrowing or lending. There, we noted that lower national saving (a shift to the left in the saving curve) results in less investment. The effect of an increase in government expenditures

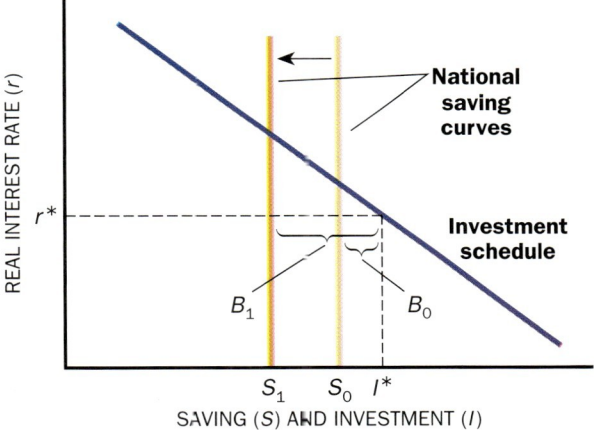

Figure 26.1

SUPPLY OF SAVING IN A SMALL OPEN ECONOMY

In a small open economy, the real interest rate, r^*, is determined by the international capital market. That in turn determines the level of investment, I^*. In the figure, saving is assumed to be fixed, unaffected by the interest rate. If domestic national saving equals S_0, the shortfall, B_0, is made up by borrowing from abroad. A reduction in national saving to S_1, caused, for example, by an increase in the government's deficit, leads to increased international borrowing, B_1, but leaves investment unchanged.

matched by an equal increase in taxes likewise differs in the two economies. In a closed economy, increased taxes reduce national saving, and hence reduce investment (see Figure 7.4 on p. 159). In a small open economy, investment is unchanged. The fall in domestic national saving is fully offset by increased borrowing from abroad (resulting in a net capital *inflow*).

We showed in Chapter 25 that in a closed economy, an increase in government expenditures not matched by an increase in taxes reduces investment and raises the real interest rate. Again, the situation is different in a small open economy. An increase in the government's deficit in a small open economy reduces national saving, but this reduction just leads to an increase in net capital inflows. Domestic investment is left unchanged.

Though investment is unaffected, the increased borrowing from abroad has consequences for the future. Foreigners who have lent funds must be repaid. Income used to repay foreign borrowing is not available for raising domestic standards of living. Access to foreign funds alleviates the need for investment to fall when national saving falls, but the effects of borrowing from abroad on future standards of living are much the same as the effects of a lower level of investment. These effects will be discussed more fully in Chapter 34.

Wrap-Up

THE CAPITAL MARKET IN A SMALL OPEN ECONOMY

In a *closed economy,* changes in the level of national saving affect the real interest rate and investment. An increase in the government's deficit reduces national saving, thereby resulting in a higher real interest rate and lower investment.

In a *small open economy,* the real interest rate is determined by international capital markets. Changes in the level of national saving do not affect the real interest rate or investment. An increase in the government's deficit does not raise the real interest rate; instead, it increases net capital inflows (borrowing from abroad).

The Capital Market in a Large Open Economy: The U.S. Case The United States is a large open economy. Trade is important; in 2002, exports totaled about 10 percent of GDP. Capital flows are also important—the United States has been a net borrower from abroad every year since 1981. But the United States is such a large part of the world economy that changes in its saving function—unlike those in a small country such as Switzerland—affect the international interest rate, with global ramifications. The U.S. economy represents about one-quarter of world output and one-fifth of world saving. A decrease in the level of U.S. saving (implying less national saving at each real interest rate) raises world real interest rates and leads to less investment in the United States. When the world real interest rate rises, investment falls in other open economies as well. Because the full impact is spread throughout the world, the effect on U.S. investment is far less than it would be if the United States were a closed economy.

The discussion so far has also assumed that the world's capital markets are fully integrated. However, this is far from the truth. Individuals know more about what is going on in their own country than about what is going on abroad. American investors require slightly higher returns on foreign investments to compensate for this increased risk. In recent years, as the flow of information has increased, the magnitude of this risk premium—the extra return they must earn for taking the risk of investing abroad—has decreased. But because financial capital still does not flow perfectly freely, interest rates are not equal in all countries, and a decrease in U.S. saving is not fully made up by an increased flow of capital from abroad.

While capital from abroad does not fully offset changes in U.S. saving, foreign saving has been an important source of funds for the United States. In 2002, for example, foreign capital flows were equal to 20 percent of U.S. private investment spending. An increase in U.S. interest rates relative to rates in other countries makes it more attractive for foreigners to lend to American firms and the U.S. government. Conversely, a decrease in U.S. interest rates relative to rates in other countries makes such lending less attractive for foreigners. Thus, the total supply of saving available to finance U.S. investment—the sum of national saving plus net capital inflows—increases as the U.S. interest rate rises. Even if national saving is unresponsive to changes in interest rates (as we have often assumed in drawing a vertical national saving curve), the total supply of funds will increase with the U.S. interest rate. This means that we should draw the saving curve as having a positive slope when we take into account both domestic and foreign sources of saving.

What are the implications of a positively sloped saving curve? Suppose the U.S. investment function shifts to the right. Many economists have argued that this type of shift occurred in the 1990s as firms increased investment at each interest rate to take advantage of new technologies. In a closed economy, such a shift would raise the real interest rate, and investment would be constrained by the availability of domestic saving. But in today's integrated world economy, an investment boom in the United States can be financed by capital inflows. An increase in U.S. investment at each real interest rate raises world interest rates, but the resulting capital inflow increases the supply of saving and results in more investment than would occur when investment must be financed solely from domestic sources.

Wrap-Up

A LARGE OPEN ECONOMY: THE UNITED STATES

The United States is a large open economy. Reductions in the U.S. national saving rate are reflected in increases in the real interest rate internationally (and therefore in the United States also), and reduced levels of investment. But the effects on investment in the United States are smaller than would be the case if the economy were closed, because an increase in U.S. interest rates will attract foreign saving (a capital inflow).

The Basic Trade Identity

The capital market balances saving and investment. In doing so it balances leakages and injections from the spending stream, ensuring that aggregate spending equals potential GDP at full employment. In Chapter 25, we showed that this equation remains valid when the government is added to the basic full-employment model. The same continues to hold true for an open economy. Reexamining the connection between capital market equilibrium and aggregate spending in an open economy, we find an important relationship between net capital flows and the balance between exports and imports.

When the capital market is in equilibrium, investment equals private saving (S_p) plus government saving (S_g) plus net capital inflows:

$$S_p + S_g + NCF = I.$$

Private saving is income minus consumption and taxes: $S_p = Y - C - T$. Government saving is $T - G$, where G represents government purchases. Thus capital market equilibrium implies

$$(Y - C - T) + (T - G) + NCF = Y - C - G + NCF = I.$$

When an economy engages in international trade, there are four sources of aggregate demand: consumption, investment, government purchases, and net exports (NX). Net exports are equal to exports minus imports. In an economy in equilibrium, these four sources of demand must add up to the total output being produced:

$$Y = C + I + G + NX.$$

If we substitute this into the previous equation to eliminate Y, we find that

$$I + NX + NCF = I.$$

Subtracting investment (I) from both sides gives us our key result:

$$NX + NCF = 0.$$

That is, net exports (NX) plus net capital inflows (NCF) equal zero. If net capital flows are positive, net exports must be negative (imports exceed exports). When net exports are negative, we say the country has a **trade deficit.** If net capital flows are negative, net exports must be positive and the country has a **trade surplus.**

The United States has a large net capital inflow and net exports are negative. The large net capital inflow into the United States and the large U.S. trade deficit are not separate phenomena. A country like Japan that lends more aboard than it borrows has a negative net capital inflow and its net exports are positive.

To understand better the relationship between foreign borrowing and the trade deficit, let's trace what happens when an American buys a German car. It appears to be a simple matter: the buyer pays American dollars to a car dealer. The car dealer buys the car—in dollars—from an importer. The importer buys the car from the German manufacturer, who wants to be paid in euros. For the importer, this is no problem. He goes to a bank, perhaps in Germany, and exchanges his dollars for euros. But the bank will not hold on to those dollars. It will sell them, either to someone wanting dollars to purchase U.S. goods or to someone wanting to invest in a dollar-denominated asset.

Every dollar an American spends to buy a foreign import eventually comes back, either to buy American exports or to buy an investment in the United States. We can express this relationship by a simple equation:

$$\text{imports } (IM) \text{ into the United States} = \text{exports } (E) + NCF.$$

Subtracting exports from both sides, we obtain the **basic trade identity:**

$$\text{trade deficit} = IM - E = -NX = NCF.$$

This is just what we obtained earlier by considering the equilibrium in the capital market. The sum of net exports and net capital flows is equal to zero.

Thus, a trade deficit and a net inflow of foreign capital are two ways of describing the same thing. This can be reframed yet again: the only way American consumers and businesses can import more from abroad than they export is if foreigners are willing to make up the difference by lending to or investing in the United States.

In a world of multilateral trade, the accounts between any particular country and the United States do not have to balance. Assume that Japan and Europe are in trade balance and the United States and Europe are in trade balance. Assume also that Japanese investors like to put their money into Europe and Europeans like to invest in the United States. Europe will have a zero net capital inflow, with its positive capital inflow from Japan offset by its negative outflow to the United States. Under these circumstances, the U.S. trade deficit with Japan is offset by a capital inflow from Europe. But what must be true for any country is that *total* imports minus *total* exports (the trade balance) equals *total* net capital inflows.

The basic trade identity can describe a capital outflow as well as a capital inflow. In the 1950s, the United States had a substantial trade surplus, as the

Internet Connection
U.S. TRADE DATA

You can find the latest data on U.S. foreign trade, from information on the overall trade balance to the specifics of our trade with individual countries, at www.ita.doc.gov/td/tic/.

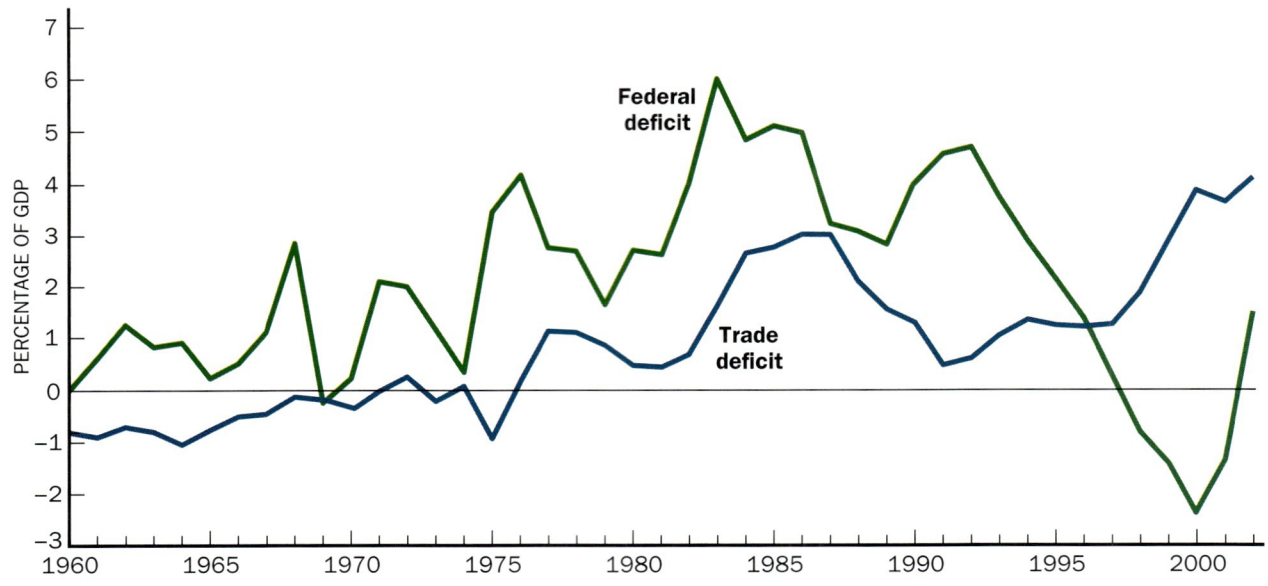

Figure 26.2

THE U.S. FISCAL DEFICIT AND TRADE DEFICIT

Increases in government deficits in the 1980s were accompanied by increases in foreign borrowing. During the late 1990s, the fiscal deficit fell but investment boomed. Beginning in 2001, the government's deficit again increased—and with it, the trade deficit.

SOURCE: *Economic Report of the President* (2004).

country exported more than it imported. Europe and Japan did not receive enough dollars from selling exports to the United States to buy the imports they desired, and they borrowed the difference from American households and firms. There was a net capital outflow from the United States that gradually accumulated. Japan now exports more than it imports, with the difference equal to its capital outflow.

The basic trade identity implies that if U.S. public saving and investment are unchanged and private saving falls, then the U.S. interest rate will rise to attract additional capital inflows, and foreigners will end up holding more American assets. But the identity does not specify which assets they will hold. They may buy government bonds or they may buy stocks or bonds of U.S. companies. In 2003, for instance, foreign investors purchased almost 60 percent of the new debt issued by the U.S. Treasury.

Case in Point

THE TRADE DEFICIT

At the same time that the fiscal budget deficit in the United States was exploding in the 1980s, so too was the trade deficit. From about $20 million a year from 1977 to

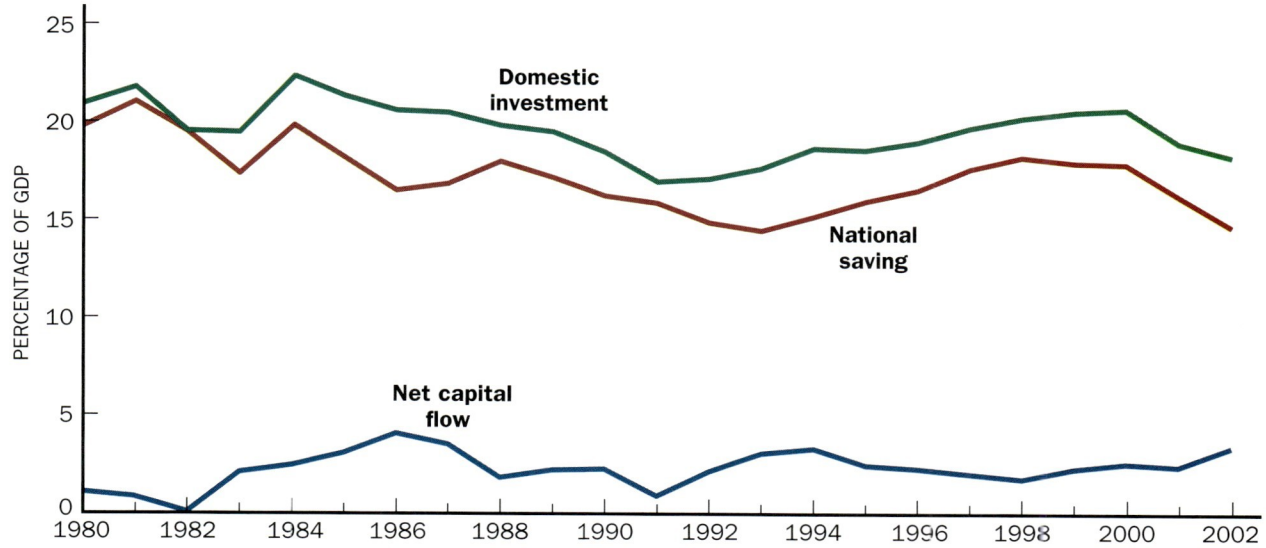

Figure 26.3

NATIONAL SAVING, DOMESTIC INVESTMENT, AND NET CAPITAL FLOWS

During the 1980s, the large federal budget deficits reduced national saving. To finance the high level of private investment, the United States had a large capital inflow. In the late 1990s, the budget deficit was eliminated, and government became a net saver. However, private saving declined and investment rose; investment continued to exceed national saving. At the end of the period shown, the federal government was again running a large deficit, reducing national saving. Since capital inflow is equal to the trade deficit, the United States continues to run a trade deficit.

SOURCE: *Economic Report of the President* (2004).

1982, it soared (in nominal terms) to $142 billion in 1987. It then fell to $20 billion in 1991 before ballooning again, reaching $609 billion (5 percent of GDP) in 2004.

Figure 26.2 shows the trade and federal budget deficits. The two have often moved together. This is no accident; we have already noted that for an open economy, an increase in the government's deficit results in increased foreign borrowing if domestic saving remains constant. But it is important to note that while the trade and fiscal deficits often move together, they are by no means in lockstep. During the late 1990s, for example, the U.S. fiscal deficit fell dramatically while the trade deficit widened significantly. The reason is straightforward—net capital flows reflect the difference between national saving and investment. Looking at Figure 26.2, we can see that the fiscal deficit was reduced in the 1990s. Yet the trade deficit has continued to grow. The reason is that the other two factors at work—private saving and investment—moved to offset the reduction in the fiscal deficit. Figure 26.3 shows domestic investment, national saving, and net foreign borrowing (capital flow) as a percentage of the GDP. By the late 1990s, the U.S. economy was experiencing a record-setting economic boom, increasing the attractiveness of this country as a place to invest. And even though the U.S. private saving rate fell to record lows in the late 1990s, the rise in government saving increased total national saving. Still, the increase in national saving was less than the increase in investment. The net effect was a rise in foreign borrowing (and a larger trade deficit).

e-Insight
HIGH-TECH EXPORTS AND IMPORTS

The United States has emerged as the international leader in many aspects of the new information and computer technologies. Silicon Valley in northern California, home to such firms as Intel, Apple, Sun Microsystems, and Google, has become synonymous with the information-based economy. We thus might naturally expect the United States to be a major exporter of computer-related products. The figure shows the amount, in millions of dollars, of computer-related products exported from and imported to the United States in 2003. It is not surprising that the U.S. is a net importer (i.e., imports exceed exports) of audio and video equipment. Asian companies such as Sony have long dominated this market. But the United States also imports more computer equipment than it exports.

The figure illustrates two important aspects of trade. First, for many categories of products, the United States is both an exporter *and* an importer. For example, the United States produces cars for export, and it imports cars from Asia and Europe. The United States produces semiconductors for export as well as importing semiconductors.

Second, trade reflects both microeconomic and macroeconomic factors. That the United States leads the world in computing technologies does not necessarily imply that it will be a net exporter of computers. We learned in this chapter that the overall balance between exports and imports reflects the balance between a country's national saving and investment. If national saving is less than investment, borrowing from foreigners must finance the difference. The basic trade identity tells us that when the United States is a net borrower from foreigners, it also must have a trade deficit: imports will exceed exports. The overall U.S. trade deficit grew from $163.1 billion in 1998 to $496.3 billion in 2003. Mirroring this deterioration of the overall trade balance, U.S. imports of computers rose from $7.3 billion in 1998 to $19.7 billion in 2003, as net exports of computers went from a surplus of $1.8 billion in 1998 to a deficit of $11.7 billion in 2003.

Many foreign-made computers are powered by American-made computer chips, such as those being manufactured here.

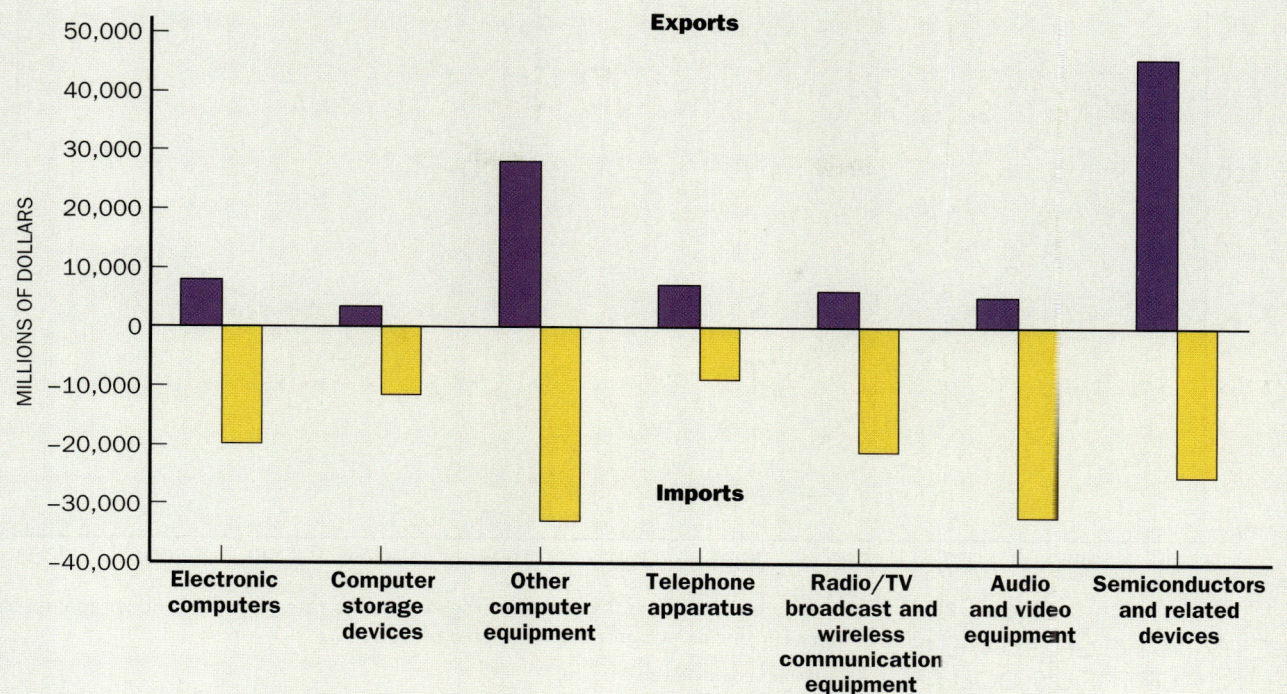

SOURCE: U.S. Census Bureau.

EXCHANGE RATES

If a country borrows more (or less) from abroad, what ensures that net exports adjust? The answer is the **exchange rate.** The exchange rate tells how much of one currency can be bought with a given amount of another currency. For instance, in 2004, one dollar could be exchanged for approximately 108 Japanese yen. Exchange rates may change rapidly. In August 1998, a dollar could buy 144 yen. But in January 1999, it could buy only 113 yen. This represents a 21 percent fall in the value of the dollar relative to the yen in just five months. When the dollar becomes less valuable relative to another currency, we say the dollar has **depreciated.** When the dollar becomes more valuable relative to other currencies, we say the dollar has **appreciated.** When the dollar-yen exchange rate fell from 144 to 113 in 1998, the dollar depreciated relative to the yen and the yen appreciated relative to the dollar. Since the United States trades with many countries, it is often useful to measure the value of the dollar relative to an average of other currencies. A standard measure of the value of the dollar is the *trade-weighted exchange rate:* an average of the exchange rates between the dollar and the currencies of our trading partners that reflects the amount of trade the United States does with the other

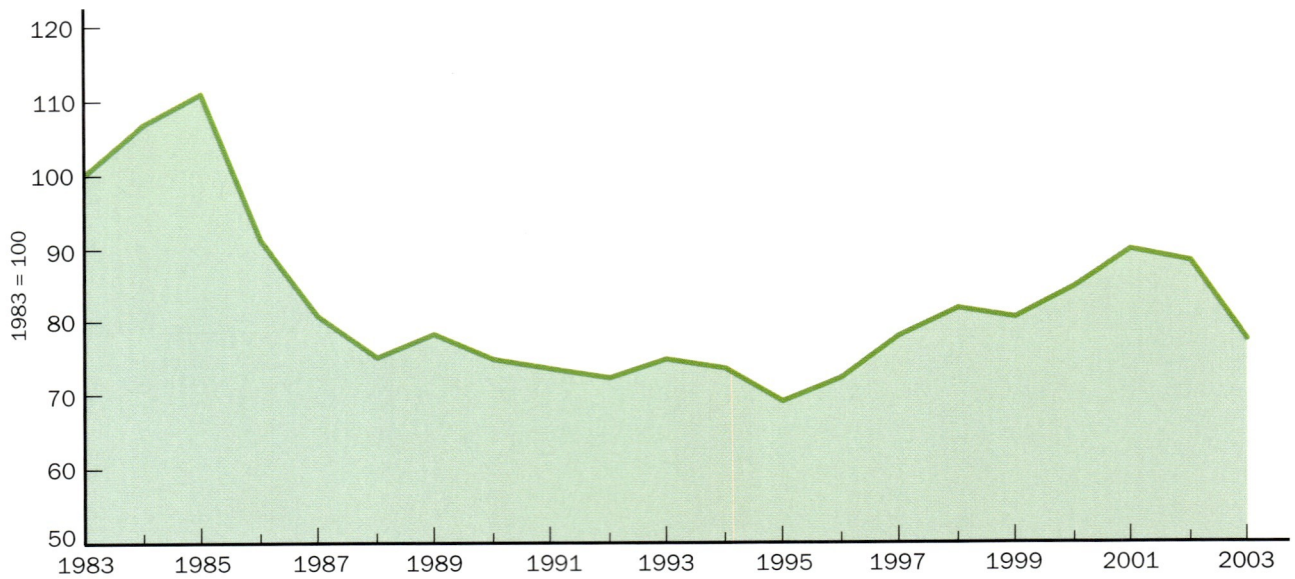

Figure 26.4

THE TRADE-WEIGHTED VALUE OF THE U.S. DOLLAR

The figure shows an index of the average exchange rate of the U.S. dollar against other major currencies, weighted by the value of trade.

SOURCE: Federal Reserve Board.

countries. So, for example, the U.S. dollar–Canadian dollar exchange rate is given more weight in the measure than is the U.S. dollar–New Zealand dollar exchange rate because the United States engages in much more trade with Canada. Figure 26.4 shows the trade-weighted value of the U.S. dollar.

Thus, the exchange rate is a price—the relative price of two currencies. Like any price, the exchange rate is determined by the laws of supply and demand. For the sake of simplicity, let's continue to focus on the exchange rate between the dollar and the yen (ignoring the fact that in the world trading system, all exchange rates are interlinked). Figure 26.5 depicts the market for dollars in terms of the exchange rate with the yen. The exchange rate in yen per dollar is on the vertical axis, and the quantity of U.S. dollars is on the horizontal axis. The supply curve for dollars represents the quantity of dollars supplied by U.S. residents to purchase Japanese goods and to make investments in Japan. At higher exchange rates—when the dollar buys more yen—Americans will supply larger quantities of dollars. A Japanese good that costs 1,000 yen costs $10 when the exchange rate is 100 but only $6.67 when the exchange rate rises to 150. Americans will therefore wish to buy more Japanese goods as the exchange rate rises, and the supply curve of dollars thus slopes upward to the right. The demand

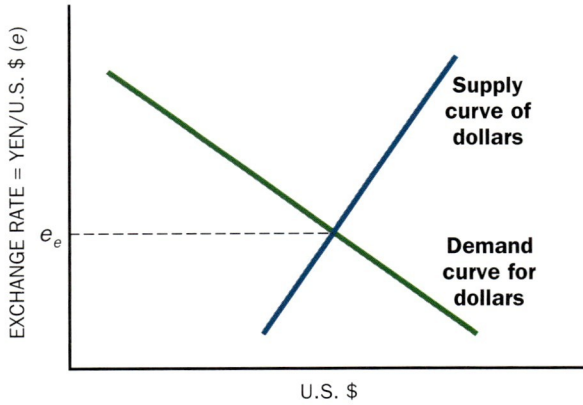

Figure 26.5

EQUILIBRIUM IN THE MARKET FOR DOLLARS

The exchange rate is the relative price of two currencies. The equilibrium exchange rate, e_e, occurs at the intersection of the supply and demand curves for dollars.

curve for dollars represents the dollars demanded by the Japanese to purchase American products and to make investments in the United States. At higher exchange rates—when it takes more yen to buy one dollar—the Japanese demand lower quantities of dollars, resulting in a demand curve that slopes downward to the right. The equilibrium exchange rate, e_e, lies at the intersection of the supply and demand curves for dollars.

Now we can see how the exchange rate connects the flow of capital and goods between countries. We continue with the case of the United States and Japan. Suppose the United States wants to borrow more from Japan. Higher U.S. interest rates will attract more Japanese investment to the United States. Japanese demand for dollars increases at each exchange rate, shifting the demand curve for dollars

Thinking Like an Economist
NET EXPORTS AND THE EXCHANGE RATE

Incentives matter, and that is why the balance between exports and imports is affected by the exchange rate. Consumers have choices—for most goods, they can buy a brand produced in the United States, or they can buy a brand produced abroad. Similarly, firms may purchase the inputs they need for production from domestic suppliers or from foreign suppliers. In making choices, consumers and firms alike will respond to the incentives provided by prices. If domestically produced goods rise in price relative to foreign-produced goods, the demand for the domestic goods will fall and the demand for the foreign-produced goods will rise. The exchange rate affects these decisions by affecting the relative prices of domestic and foreign-produced goods.

If the dollar depreciates, it takes more dollars to buy each unit of foreign currency. For example, in 2001, it cost 90 cents to buy one euro. Thus, any good or service with a price of 100 euros would cost $90 to buy. By 2003, the dollar had fallen in value relative to the euro, so that it cost $1.13 to buy a euro. The same 100 euro good now cost an American buyer $113, not $90. Because the dollar's depreciation makes the European-produced good more expensive, our imports from Europe will tend to fall. From the perspective of a European, however, American goods have become less expensive. A U.S. good that sells for $100 cost 111 euros in 2001 (1 euro could buy $0.90, so it took 111 euros to buy the $100 U.S. good), but by 2003, that same $100 good cost only 88.5 euros.

What is important in determining the relative price of foreign and domestic goods is the *real* exchange rate: the exchange rate adjusted for changes in the general level of prices in different countries. Suppose in our previous example that the general price level in the United States had risen by 25 percent between 2001 and 2003 so that instead of still costing $100, the U.S. good had risen in price to $125 in 2003. Then, to Europeans, the fall in the value of the dollar by 25 percent (from $0.90 to $1.13 per euro) would just offset the rise in the dollar price from $100 to $125: the good would still cost 111 euros. Similarly, from the perspective of the American consumer, the good that cost 100 euros in 2001 costs $113 in 2003, a 25 percent rise. Thus, its price has not changed relative to the general level of U.S. prices—the real exchange rate would be unchanged.

In fact, however, prices in the United States rose by only 4 percent between 2001 and 2003. Thus, the 25 percent depreciation of the dollar more than offset that rise and represented a large real depreciation in value. This will create incentives for American consumers and firms to purchase fewer foreign goods and services. Conversely, it will boost U.S. exports by creating incentives for foreign consumers and firms to purchase American products.

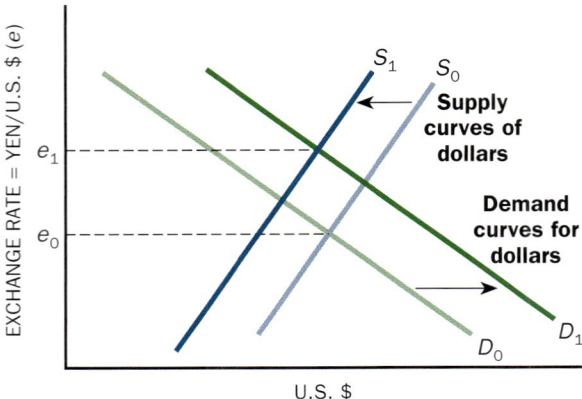

Figure 26.6

EXCHANGE RATE EFFECTS OF INCREASED FOREIGN BORROWING

The equilibrium exchange rate is e_0 before the increase in U.S. borrowing from Japan. Higher interest rates in the United States attract Japanese investment, shifting the demand curve for U.S. dollars to the right. At the same time, more Americans decide to invest in their own country rather than abroad, shifting the dollar supply curve to the left. The equilibrium exchange rate rises from e_0 to e_1. At the higher exchange rate, the dollar buys more yen, so U.S. imports of Japanese products increase. Conversely, U.S. goods are now more expensive for the Japanese, so U.S. exports decrease.

to the right, as depicted in Figure 26.6. The higher U.S. interest rates also will make Japanese investments relatively less attractive to American investors, who will therefore increase their investments at home. Americans will be willing to supply fewer dollars at each exchange rate, shifting the supply curve for dollars to the left. These shifts in the supply and demand curves for dollars cause the exchange rate to rise from e_0 to e_1—the dollar appreciates and the yen depreciates.[1] Since the dollar can now buy more Japanese products, U.S. imports increase (i.e., Japanese exports increase). Since the yen can now buy fewer U.S. products, U.S. exports fall. Changes in the exchange rate thus ensure that the trade deficit moves in tandem with foreign borrowing.

Is the Trade Deficit a Problem?

So far, our discussion has shown the relationship between the trade deficit and the international capital flows that reflect differences between national saving and investment. But we have not said anything about whether a trade deficit is good or bad. Certainly much of the popular discussion about the United States' huge trade deficit suggests that it is a major problem.

---

[1] Later, in Chapter 34, we will see that matters are somewhat more complicated. Investors have to take into account expectations concerning future changes in the exchange rates as well.

Trade deficits mean the country is borrowing from abroad. As is true of borrowing from any other source, such borrowing can be sensible or not depending on its reason.

In its first century, this country borrowed heavily from abroad. By contrast, for most of the twentieth century, the United States lent more money to foreign countries and investors than it borrowed. This pattern is typical. In the early stages of economic development, countries borrow to build up their economies, and they repay the loans with a portion of their economic gains. More mature economies typically lend capital.

The enormous U.S. trade deficits in the 1980s reversed this pattern. When the government borrows year after year, the cumulative budget deficits lead to a high level of government debt. Similarly, when the country borrows from abroad year after year, the cumulative trade deficits (cumulative capital inflows) lead to a high level of debt to foreigners.

The effects of the trade deficits of the 1980s were to convert the United States from the world's largest creditor nation at the beginning of the decade to the world's largest debtor nation by its end. Figure 26.7 shows the net international position of the United States—the value of all American-owned assets abroad plus what others owe Americans minus the value of all assets within the United States owned by foreigners and what Americans owe foreigners. In the mid-1980s, the United States became a net debtor nation. As a result, the U.S. economy will have to pay interest, dividends, and profits to foreign investors each year, spending more dollars abroad for these payments than it is receiving.

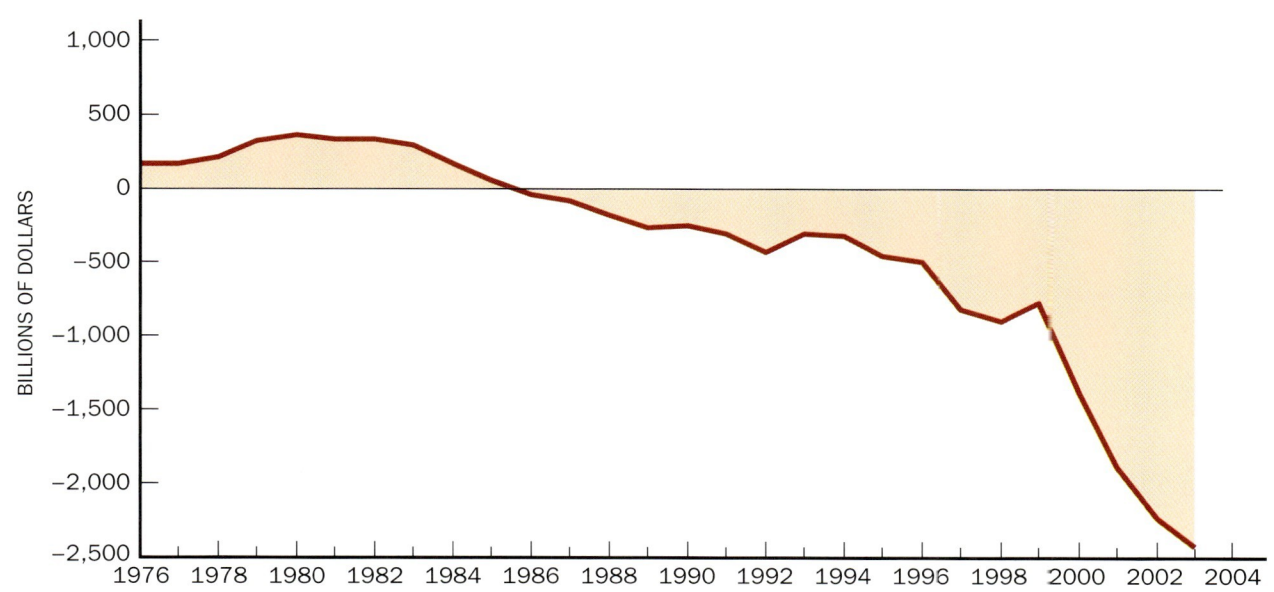

Figure 26.7
THE UNITED STATES BECOMES A DEBTOR NATION

The United States was a large creditor nation in the beginning of the 1980s; that is, American-held foreign assets exceeded foreign-held U.S. assets. By 1992, it had become a large debtor nation: foreign-held U.S. assets exceeded American-held foreign assets.

SOURCE: *Survey of Current Business* (BEA, Department of Commerce).

But is this good or bad? Suppose you borrow a large sum from a bank. In the future, unless you used the borrowed funds to make an investment that yielded a return at least equal to the interest you had to pay the bank, you would be unable to consume as much as you would otherwise, for the simple reason that you must pay the bank interest as well as principal. The same applies to foreign borrowing. During the 1980s, the large trade deficits were caused by the large fiscal budget deficits that reduced national saving. Because the foreign borrowing was not being used to finance investment spending that would boost future income, the concern was that the large trade deficits represented a future burden on the economy. In contrast, the trade deficit in the late 1990s was a reflection of strong investment spending. But at the beginning of the twenty-first century, with the U.S. government again running a huge budget deficit, the concern again arose that the large trade deficit resulting from these budget deficits represents a future burden.

Review and Practice

SUMMARY

1. In an open economy, investment can be financed from domestic national saving or borrowing from abroad.
2. In a small open economy, changes in national saving will not affect the international real interest rate or the level of domestic investment. Changes in national saving will affect the level of net capital inflows.
3. In a large open economy such as the United States', a fall in national saving will raise the real interest rate. This rise attracts net capital inflows and moderates the decline in domestic investment.
4. The basic trade identity states that net exports plus net capital inflows equal zero. A trade deficit must equal net capital inflows; a trade surplus must equal capital outflows.
5. Changes in the exchange rate ensure that net exports move in tandem with net capital flows.

KEY TERMS

open economy
capital inflows
capital outflows
net capital inflows
small open economy
large open economy
trade deficit
trade surplus
basic trade identity
exchange rate
depreciation
appreciation

REVIEW QUESTIONS

1. What are the consequences of an increased government deficit for private investment in an open economy and in a closed economy?
2. What is the relationship between the trade deficit and an inflow of foreign capital?
3. What is the relationship between the trade deficit and the fiscal deficit?
4. What is the saving-investment identity for an open economy?
5. What is the exchange rate? How is it determined? What role do adjustments in the exchange rate play in ensuring that capital inflows equal the trade deficit?

PROBLEMS

1. Suppose a certain country has private saving of 6 percent of GDP, capital inflow of 1 percent of GDP, and a balanced budget. What is its level of investment? If the budget deficit is 1.5 percent of GDP, how does your answer change?
2. Why does it make a difference if a country borrows abroad to finance the expansion of its railroads or to finance increased Social Security benefits for the elderly?
3. U.S. foreign indebtedness is greater than that of Mexico, Brazil, and Argentina combined. Does this necessarily mean that the United States has a larger debt problem than those countries? Why or why not? Can you think of a situation in which an individual with debts of larger value may actually have less of a debt problem than someone with less debt?
4. If Congress were to pass a law prohibiting foreign investors from buying U.S. Treasury bills, would this prevent government borrowing from leading to capital inflows? Discuss.
5. Japan had large trade surpluses during the 1980s. Would this cause Japan to be a borrower or to be a lender in international capital markets?
6. If a nation borrowed $50 billion from abroad one year and its imports were worth $800 billion, what would be the value of its exports? How does the answer change if, instead of borrowing, the nation lent $100 billion abroad?
7. If U.S. investments increase and world interest rates rise, what is the effect on private investment in other countries? What is the effect on U.S. national saving?

Learning Goals

In this chapter, you will learn

1. The role of labor productivity in raising living standards
2. The factors that lead to productivity growth
3. The sources of economic growth
4. The role of technological change and new ideas

Chapter 27

GROWTH AND PRODUCTIVITY

The changes that took place in the U.S. standard of living during the twentieth century are hard to comprehend. In 1900, the average American's level of consumption was little higher than the average citizen's in Mexico or the Philippines today. Life expectancy was low, in part because diseases such as smallpox, diphtheria, typhoid fever, and whooping cough were still common. People were fifteen times more likely to catch measles in 1900 than they are today. The abundance of land meant that relatively few Americans were starving, but luxuries were scarce. People worked as long as they could, and when they could no longer work, they became the responsibility of their children; there was no easy retirement. Most of the goods that people consume today—from DVDs to cellular phones to frozen pizzas—could not even be conceived of in 1900.

During the nineteenth century, the living standards in England and a few other European countries were perhaps slightly higher than that of the United States. In Asia, Africa, and Latin America, where the vast majority of people lived then as they do now, standards of living were much lower. Famines, which parts of Africa still suffer from today, were common in even Europe's poorer areas, such as Ireland. More than a tenth of the Irish population died during the potato famine of 1845–1848, and more than another tenth migrated to the United States.

The tremendous improvements in our standards of living are the fruits of economic growth—our ability to produce more of the things that provide for our material well-being. To analyze the factors that account for economic growth, we can use the insights provided by the full-employment model that we have used in the previous three chapters. The full-employment model provides what we can think of as a snapshot of the economy. We assumed the economy's capital stock—its plant and equipment—was fixed, and we assumed the labor force was fixed. Now we will look at the economy through a sequence of snapshots in order to obtain a movie that captures the changes occurring over time. At each point, the full-employment model shows how real wages and the real interest rate adjust to ensure that the economy produces at potential GDP. Over time, new investment leads to more machines and buildings, population growth and immigration lead to increases in the labor force, and innovation and research and development generate technological changes that alter what the economy produces and how it is produced.

Rising Standards of Living

Table 27.1 compares the United States in 1900 and 2000. Such a comparison reveals an enormous boost in living standards, demonstrated not just in higher incomes and life expectancy but also in higher levels of education, improved medical services, and a cleaner environment. If we are interested in the economy's ability to provide material goods and services to its residents, then we should focus on **income per capita** and how it has grown. Income per capita is total income divided by the population. Over the twentieth century, the population of the United States grew from 76 million to 281 million, but real GDP grew even more, raising incomes per capita by more than 400 percent—from $6,701 to $34,935, in real terms.

Figure 27.1 shows that during the 1960s, real income per capita grew rapidly. That growth slowed during the 1970s and 1980s, but beginning in the last half of the 1990s, its pace increased. The growth rate of income per capita (Y/N) is equal to the growth rate of output (Y) minus the growth rate of the population (N).

We can write income per capita as the product of output per hour and hours per person:

$$Y/N = (Y/H) \times (H/N).$$

Table 27.1

THE UNITED STATES IN 1900 AND 2000

	1900	2000
Population	76 million	281 million
Life expectancy	47 years	77 years
GDP (in 2000 dollars)	$510 billion	$9,817 billion
GDP per capita (in 2000 dollars)	$6,701	$34,935
Average hours worked each week in manufacturing	59	42
Average hourly wage in manufacturing (2000 dollars)	$5.33	$14.37
Number of telephones	1.3 million	>200 million
% of those age 5–19 enrolled in school	51 percent	92 percent

SOURCES: *Economic Report of the President* (2004); *Statistical Abstract of the United States* (2003).

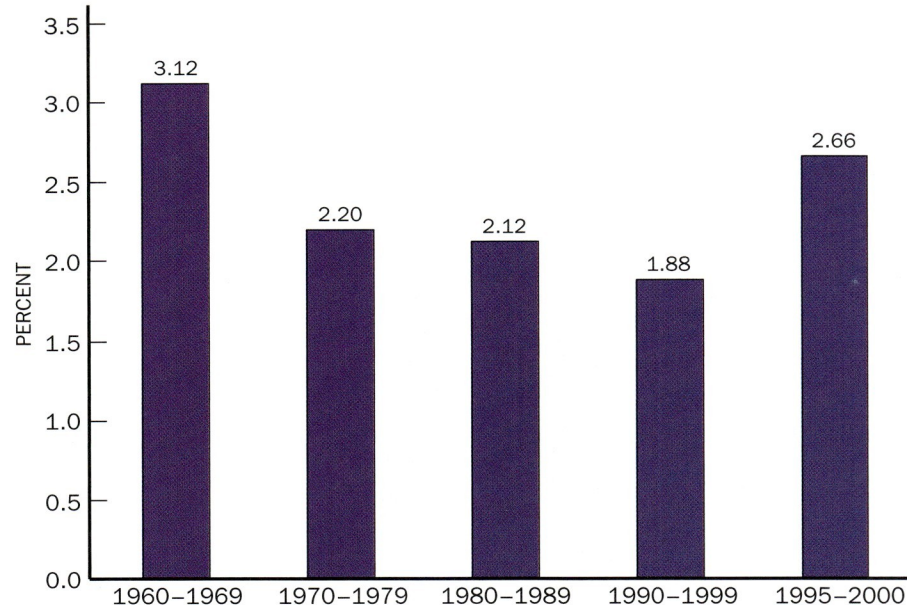

Figure 27.1

PER CAPITA OUTPUT GROWTH

The growth rate of total output per capita declined over the 1970s, 1980s, and the early 1990s. It rose again in the late 1990s.

SOURCE: *Economic Report of the President* (2004).

Output per hour (Y/H) is what we identified in Chapter 22 as *labor productivity*. Hours per person (H/N) reflects both the average number of hours people work and the **labor force participation rate.** The labor force participation rate is the fraction of the population that is actually in the labor force. For income per capita to rise, either labor productivity must rise or the number of hours worked must grow faster than the population.

In many countries, rapid growth in income per capita follows increases in labor force participation. For example, a customary restriction on women's engaging in work outside the home may be loosened. Thus the United States did experience growth in labor force participation, particularly during the 1970s and 1980s, as women entered the labor force in ever greater numbers. The only other way to increase hours per person is to raise the average hours worked—that is, individuals must work longer and sacrifice leisure. For developed economies such as the United States', the key to improving living standards lies in the other element in the equation: growth in labor productivity.

The roles of labor productivity and of hours worked in accounting for economic growth in the United States are shown in Figure 27.2, which expresses the growth rate of total output as the sum of the two factors:

$$\text{growth rate of output} = \text{growth rate of output per hour} + \text{growth rate of hours worked}.$$

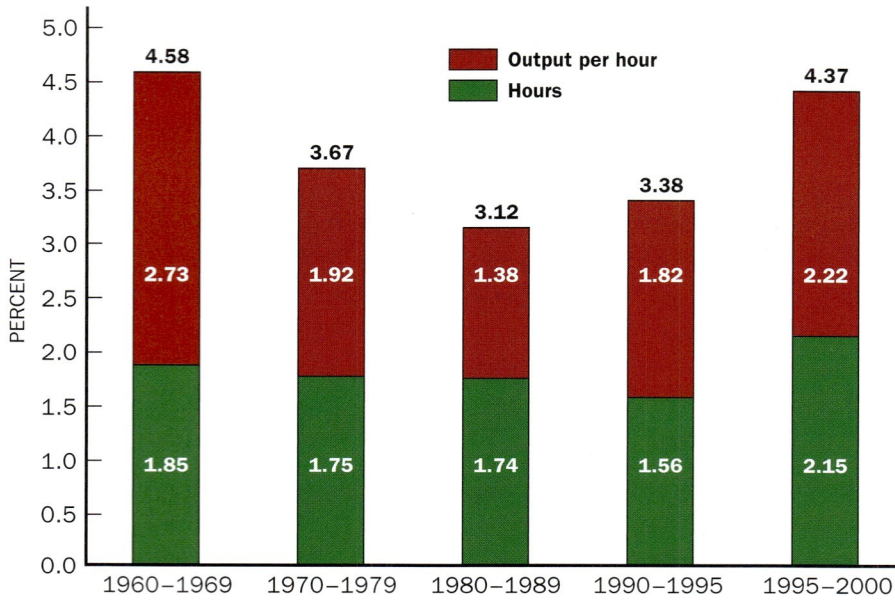

Figure 27.2

OUTPUT GROWTH—HOURS AND PRODUCTIVITY

The growth rate of total output is equal to the growth rate in the number of hours worked plus the growth rate of labor productivity. Total growth slowed during the 1970s through the first half of the 1990s, a decline accounted for by the decline in the growth rate of productivity. Productivity growth increased during the second half of the 1990s.

SOURCE: *Economic Report of the President* (2004).

Two important points stand out from Figure 27.2. First, overall growth declined after the 1960s but then picked up again in the late 1990s. Second, the decline during the 1970s and 1980s was attributable to a decline in productivity growth. This fall—the "productivity slowdown," as it was called—began in 1973, and was not just an American phenomenon: all the industrial economies grew more slowly after 1973.

Wrap-Up

GROWTH IN PER CAPITA INCOME

The growth rate of per capita income is the sum of the growth rate of labor productivity and the growth rate of hours worked per person.

The number of hours worked per person depends on the labor force participation rate and the average number of hours that each worker works.

Labor productivity is the amount of output produced on average per hour worked.

The growth rate of output is the sum of the growth rate of labor productivity and the growth rate of total hours worked.

Growth in labor productivity is the key to rising standards of living.

Explaining Productivity

For almost a century, the United States has been at the center of the technological advances that have changed the world. The telegraph, telephone, laser, transistor, airplane, assembly line, jet engine, atomic reactor, memory chips . . . the list of U.S. technological achievements goes on and on. Beyond these pathbreaking developments are countless smaller improvements: better as well as new products, and less-expensive ways of making old products. The country has reaped a huge reward from these productivity-enhancing changes—it is through these productivity increases that rising standards of living are possible.

Though a rise in the average rate of productivity growth from about 2 percent to 3 percent may seem inconsequential, it in fact matters enormously because the differences compound over time. Consider this simple calculation. Two countries start out equally wealthy, but one grows at 2 percent a year while the other grows at 3 percent. The difference in productivity would be barely perceptible for a few years. But after thirty years, the slower-growing country would be only three-fourths as wealthy as the faster-growing one.

One way to grasp the importance of even small differences in growth rates is to compare how long it takes for income to double. To do this, we can make use of the *rule of seventy*—dividing the growth rate into 70 will tell us the approximate number of years needed for income to double. For example, if an economy grows at 5 percent per year, income will double in 14 years (70/5 = 14).

Average annual growth rate	Number of years for income to double
1 percent	70
2 percent	35
3 percent	23
4 percent	18
5 percent	14
6 percent	12
7 percent	10
8 percent	9

The difference between growing at 3 percent per year instead of 2 percent may sound small, but as the table shows, over time it is substantial.

Lower growth in productivity means that, on average, people will have less of everything—smaller houses, poorer health care, less travel, and fewer government services than otherwise. When output growth is sustained through increases in the number of hours worked rather than through productivity gains—when families

Internet Connection

HOW FAST IS MODERN ECONOMIC GROWTH?

Measuring the rise in per capita income is one way to assess economic growth and rising living standards, but another way is to ask how many hours a typical worker must work in order to purchase some specific good. For example, in 1895, the average worker needed to work 44 hours to earn the income necessary to purchase a set of dishes—today, it takes only about 3.6 hours. Brad DeLong, a professor at the University of California, Berkeley, provides further examples of how one can compare today's living standards to those of the past at www.j-bradford-delong.net/Comments/FRBSF_June11.html as he addresses the question, How fast is modern economic growth?

raise their income only by having both spouses working, for instance—reduction in leisure also leads to increased strain. In this case, to focus on the income increases alone would exaggerate the rise in living standards.

The critical role played by productivity growth in improving living standards accounts for the attention that has been given to the speedup in productivity growth since the mid-1990s. Many commentators argue that the tremendous advances in computer and information technologies in recent years will contribute to higher productivity growth and rising standards of living.

To understand these fluctuations in productivity, we need to understand what causes increases in output per hour in the first place. There are four key factors: saving and investment, education and the quality of the labor force, the reallocation of resources from low- to high-productivity sectors of the economy, and technological change. The following sections discuss each factor in turn.

THE CAPITAL STOCK AND THE ROLE OF SAVING AND INVESTMENT

Workers today are much more productive than they were one hundred or even twenty years ago. One important reason is that they have more and better machines to work with. An American textile worker can produce far more than a textile worker in India, partly because of the differences in their equipment: in India, handlooms similar to those used in America two hundred years ago are often still employed.

The amount of capital per worker increases when investment exceeds the amount of capital that depreciates. **Depreciation** is the amount of capital that wears out or becomes obsolete. Higher levels of investment relative to GDP increase the capital stock and result in more capital per worker, a process that economists call **capital deepening.** As capital per worker increases, the amount of output that each worker can produce increases. In Chapter 24, we introduced the concept of the aggregate production function: the relationship between employment and output, when the amount of capital is fixed. When we focus on economic growth, we need to take into account the increases in the capital stock that come about through investment. The effect of having more capital per worker is shown in Figure 27.3. As each worker has more capital to work with, output per worker (labor productivity) rises. But because of diminishing returns, the effects on labor productivity become smaller as the economy accumulates more and more capital.

Capital deepening can increase labor productivity and standards of living, as economies get more capital by investing in plant and equipment. In Chapters 24 to 26, we discussed the relationship between investment and saving. In a closed economy, national saving equals investment, as illustrated in Figure 27.4. In the figure, we assume saving does not depend on the real interest rate. A rise in saving (a shift in the saving curve to the right) leads to lower real interest rates, and lower real interest rates lead to higher investment. In a closed economy, the way to increase investment and obtain a faster-growing stock of capital is to increase national saving. One reason many people are concerned about the low rate of private saving in the United States and the large federal government deficits is that America's low national saving rate may in the future decrease the capital available per worker.

In an open economy, matters are more complicated. Domestic national saving need not equal investment, because a country can finance investment by borrowing from abroad. But even though the U.S. economy is open, U.S. saving and investment tend to move together. A reduction in national saving does lead to greater foreign borrowing—but not enough more to prevent some reduction in investment.

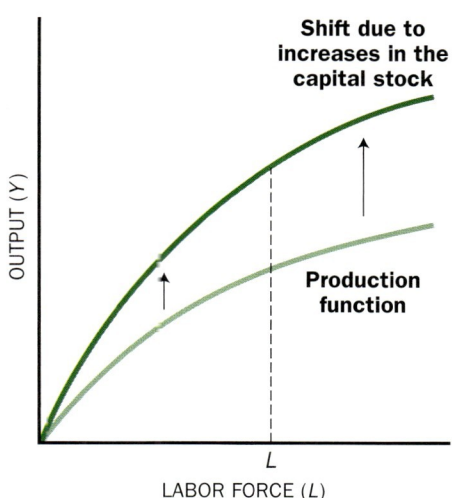

Figure 27.3
INCREASES IN CAPITAL AND THE PRODUCTION FUNCTION

The short-run aggregate production function relates employment to output for a given stock of capital and for a given level of technology. With more capital, workers will be more productive; thus at each level of employment, output will be higher. The effect of an increase in the economy's capital stock is shown by the shift in the production function.

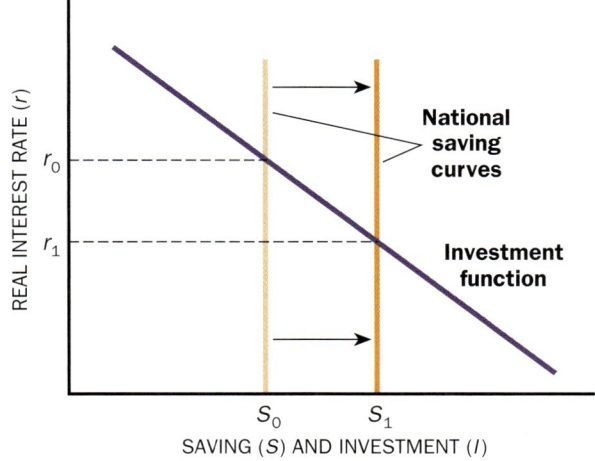

Figure 27.4
SAVING AND INVESTMENT

Higher saving rates lead to lower real interest rates and higher investment.

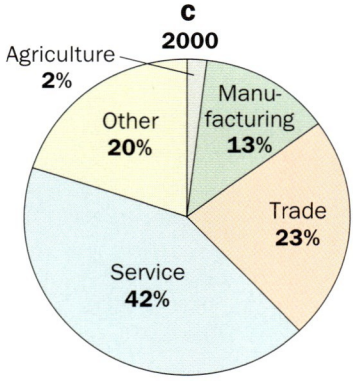

Figure 27.5

SECTORAL SHIFTS

Employment in the U.S. economy shifted from agriculture to manufacturing in the first half of the twentieth century, and from manufacturing to services in the second half.

SOURCES: *Historical Statistics of the United States* (1975), *Economic Report of the President* (2004).

THE QUALITY OF THE LABOR FORCE

As important as saving and investment rates are in explaining the growth rate of labor productivity, capital deepening is not the whole story. Even more important today is a second major source of productivity growth: a higher-quality labor force. Running a modern industrial economy requires a well-educated workforce. In addition, an economy on the cutting edge of technological change needs trained scientists and engineers to discover and shape innovations.

Spending money on education and training improves workers' skills and productivity. These expenditures are investments—just like investments in machines and buildings. And just as expenditures on plant and equipment result in physical capital, we say that expenditures on education and training result in **human capital**. Human capital is the stock of accumulated skills and experience that makes workers productive. Increases in human capital increase the amount of output that workers can produce and thus shift the aggregate production function up, just as increases in physical capital do.

The United States has a highly educated workforce. Even as the number of educated workers has increased, the returns to investing in education have grown. In 2000, the median full-time worker with at least a bachelor's degree earned about 90 percent more per week than one with only a high school diploma—up from 36 percent in 1979. Though some of this difference may be attributed to the likelihood that those who graduated from college are more able (and hence would have earned high incomes whether or not they had attended college), the returns to education appear significant even after factors such as family background and high school performance are taken into account. Just a year of college has been estimated to increase earnings by a minimum of 5 to 10 percent.

THE REALLOCATION OF RESOURCES FROM LOW- TO HIGH-PRODUCTIVITY SECTORS

During the past century, the United States has evolved from an agricultural economy to an industrial economy to a service economy. Figure 27.5 shows this dramatic structural change. The service sector, broadly defined, includes not only traditional services such as those provided by barbers and waiters but also the more sophisticated services provided by doctors and lawyers, educators, and computer programmers, among others. The medical sector alone has grown to the point that it accounted for about 15 percent of GDP in 2000.

The movement out of agriculture and into industry explains some of the productivity increase in the early part of the twentieth century. Though the level of productivity in agriculture was increasing rapidly, it remained lower than that in industry. Thus, as workers shifted out of low-productivity jobs in agriculture into high-productivity jobs in manufacturing, average productivity in the economy increased. With almost all labor now out of agriculture—and with agricultural productivity increased to the point that incomes in that sector are comparable to those in the rest of the economy—this kind of shift can no longer be a source of overall productivity growth. But other opportunities remain. Productivity in the telecommunications industry, other high-tech sectors, and export sectors is substantially higher than that in other parts of the economy. Telecommunications deregulation in the 1990s facilitated the movement of resources into that sector. Rapid innovation in computer technology is affecting all sectors of the economy. Increasing globalization will open up new opportunities for export growth. These changes are contributing to the overall increase in productivity that the United States has experienced since the mid-1990s.

TECHNOLOGICAL CHANGE AND THE ROLE OF IDEAS

While capital—both physical and human—is important for explaining the huge changes in living standards over the past two hundred years, just having more machines or better-educated workers cannot account for the truly amazing differences between the economy in 1900 and the economy today. We are not producing more of the same goods the economy produced in 1900; we are producing goods that the people of 1900 never dreamed of. Instead of using more machines to produce more horse-drawn carriages, we produce cars and airplanes. Instead of producing more horseshoes, we produce tires and jogging shoes. Key to the whole growth process, then, is technological progress—thinking up new ways to do old things and new ways to do entirely new things. This means that *ideas* are central to explaining economic growth. Indeed, economists estimate that as much as two-thirds of all increases in productivity prior to 1973 were due to technological progress.

Investment increases the economy's stock of physical capital, and education leads to increases in human capital, but what leads to technological progress? To understand the economics of technological progress, we need to start by considering how ideas are different from such goods as a laptop computer or a piece of chocolate cake. These goods are *rivalrous;* if I eat that piece of chocolate cake, you can't. But ideas are different. If both you and your roommate are taking economics, both of you can use an idea like the law of supply and demand. If your roommate does her homework first, the idea is still available to you when you get around to studying. When Tim Berners-Lee, Robert Cailliau, and their colleagues at the European particle physics center (CERN) in Geneva, Switzerland, invented the World Wide Web and hypertext markup language, or HTML, in 1990, programmers from around the world could use their ideas. If you use HTML to construct a Web page, the idea is still also available to others—it is a *nonrivalrous* good. This is a key property of ideas; they cannot be used up.

One of the major differences between the economy today and in 1900 is the routine nature of the change brought about by new ideas. This technological progress is accomplished through the activities of thousands of entrepreneurs and innovators, particularly in the computer industry, and thousands of scientists and engineers engaged in large-scale research projects in the business, government, and university sectors. Much of modern research is centered in huge laboratories, employing large numbers of people. While the government runs some of these—such as the Brookhaven, Argonne, and Lawrence laboratories that carry out research in basic physics—many are private, as was Bell Laboratories, where the transistor and

Modern textile manufacturing bears little resemblance to the traditional hand loom, which is still used in underdeveloped areas such as Darjeeling, India.

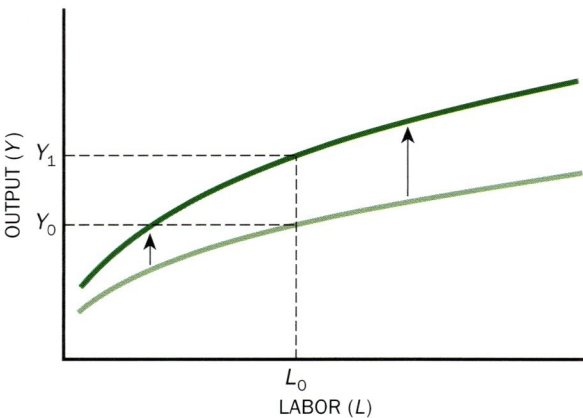

Figure 27.6

TECHNOLOGICAL CHANGE

Improvements in knowledge and technology shift up the production function; at each level of physical and human capital per worker, higher levels of output per worker can be achieved.

the laser were developed. Indeed, most major firms spend about 3 percent of their gross revenues on research and development (R & D).

We have become so accustomed to the current level of technological progress that it is hard to believe how different the view of reputable economists was in the early 1800s. Real wages of workers were little higher than they had been more than four centuries earlier, when the bubonic plague killed a large part of the population of Europe and thereby created a scarcity of labor that raised real wages. After half a millennium of slow progress at best, Thomas Malthus, one of the greatest economists of that time, saw population expanding more rapidly than the capacity of the economy to support it. His prediction of an inevitable decline in living standards earned economics the nickname of "the dismal science." Today, many continue to predict that the world economy will be unable to grow faster than the population and that living standards must necessarily decline. Such calculations have been proved wrong over and over again, as technological advances have rendered their premises false. The role of technological change in the economy's aggregate production is depicted in Figure 27.6. Improved technology enables the economy to achieve more output per worker at each level of physical and human capital per worker.

The Production of Ideas Knowing that ideas are important for economic growth tells us little about how they are produced. Can we use some of the basic ideas of economics to understand the production of ideas?

To start, think about the incentives that face a potential inventor. Those incentives will be greatest if the inventor can charge a fee to anyone who uses her new idea. She must be able to prevent its employment by those unwilling to pay. But some ideas are hard to maintain control over. Once Henry Ford came up with the idea of the modern assembly line, he might have kept it secret for a while by barring visitors to his factory, but certainly anyone who saw his new method of manufacture could take the idea and set up a new factory. Most software companies keep their source code secret in order to exclude its use by those who have not paid a licensing fee. The incentive to produce new ideas will be increased if inventors are able to profit from such licenses. To that end, inventors must be granted **property rights** to their ideas, as those ideas are given form in a specific process, machine, article of manufacture, composition of matter, or design. Property rights give their holder legal authority to determine how a resource is used, including the right to charge others for its use. If property rights are insecure, if a firm planning on engaging in research is uncertain about whether it will be allowed to capture the benefits of any new ideas it produces, then fewer resources will be invested into research and the production of new ideas.

Society has another consideration, however. Producing a new idea may be very costly, but it need be produced only once. Your laptop embodies thousands of new ideas, but these ideas did not have to be reproduced each time a new laptop was made. The screen, memory chips, and case did have to be produced for each laptop; they are examples of rivalrous goods—the memory chips in your laptop cannot be in your roommate's laptop. But the design of the laptop is a nonrivalrous good, and its marginal cost is therefore zero. So from society's perspective, the idea should be freely available to everyone. After all, it costs nothing to let others use it.

There is a tension, then, between providing incentives for the production of new ideas and ensuring that they can be widely used. Inventors need secure property rights that enable them to benefit from their ideas; they need to be able to exclude users who do not pay. Yet once an idea is invented, its zero marginal cost of production suggests that it should be freely available.

The digitization of music has brought the issue of intellectual property rights into sharp focus. Many music lovers think nothing of downloading and sharing music files at no cost, and companies such as Napster developed software to make this sharing possible. But the music actually "belongs" to the copyright holder, who has a right to demand payment for its use. Representatives of the music industry have repeatedly brought companies and individuals to court over the downloading and sharing of music files. Record labels cite declining sales of CDs as evidence that music piracy will reduce their financial incentives to find and market new artists. Now, major companies such as Apple and Sony run online music stores that allow individuals to download songs for a fee.

Society addresses the tension between making intellectual property widely available and protecting the property rights of inventors through copyright and patent laws. Once issued, a patent gives an inventor the exclusive rights to his invention. Because others can use it only with his permission, the inventor can impose a licensing fee to capture some of the benefits of his idea. But in the United States, patents are valid only for a fixed period (usually twenty years), and after they expire their ideas are freely available. Copyrights on written work generally now last for the life of the author plus seventy years. In this way, society both increases the incentive to produce new ideas and ensures that they eventually become available to everyone.

Expenditures on R & D Innovations and technological process do not simply happen. They require deliberate investment in research and development. Pharmaceutical manufacturers devote millions of dollars and thousands of scientists to the search for new drugs; companies such as Intel and AMD fund projects to develop the next generation of computer chips; and the thousands of firms that produce consumer goods ranging from household cleaners to garden hoses are constantly seeking improvements in their products as a way to increase their profits.

Industry accounts for about 65 percent of U.S. R & D expenditures, with the remainder provided by the government, universities, and nonprofit organizations. In 2002, just under 30 percent of R & D spending was by the government. Historically, roughly half of the federal spending on R & D has been for defense, which now accounts for about 15 percent of total U.S. R & D expenditures. This percentage has fallen steadily; it was more than 30 percent in 1970.

Some analysts put the private returns on R & D expenditures at more than 25 percent; and since many of the returns accrue to firms other than those undertaking the research, social returns are estimated to be even higher. Such rewards may make the relatively low level of investment in research somewhat surprising. High risk and limitations on the ability to borrow to finance R & D provide part of the explanation for this seeming underinvestment.

> **Wrap-Up**
>
> ## FACTORS CONTRIBUTING TO PRODUCTIVITY GROWTH
>
> Saving and investment (capital accumulation)
> Improved quality of the labor force
> Reallocation of labor from low-productivity to high-productivity sectors
> Technological progress

Total Factor Productivity: Measuring the Sources of Growth

In an advanced economy like that of the United States, reallocation of resources from low- to high-productivity sectors is not viewed as a major source of further growth. Investment in physical and human capital and technological change are therefore the three sources of growth in productivity. But how important is each? To assess the relative contribution of each, economists use **total factor productivity analysis,** a methodology that helps them determine the change in total output that can be "attributed" to increases in the stock of capital (both human and physical) and increases in the supply of labor. Any output growth that cannot be attributed to capital or labor is attributed to technological change.

Similarly, that part of economic growth that cannot be explained by increases in capital or labor is called the increase in **total factor productivity (TFP).** The increase in TFP reflects the increasing efficiency with which an economy's resources are used. Efficiency can increase because new production methods make it possible to produce more goods and services with the same inputs of labor and capital as before, or because innovations result in new, higher-valued goods and services being produced. The introduction of the assembly line by Henry Ford is an example of a change that enabled more cars to be produced with the same inputs. The past few decades—which have witnessed the development of personal computers, VCRs, DVDs, cell phones, new pharmaceuticals, and more—are replete with examples of innovations that change the nature of the goods and services the economy produces.

Figure 27.7 shows the sources of increases in productivity for three different periods—1959–1973, 1973–1995, and 1995–2000. We can draw several conclusions from the chart. First, the overall rate of growth was much higher before 1973 than it was during the period from 1973 to 1995. Second, between 1973 and 1995, almost all of the growth in output can be explained by increases in the inputs of capital and labor, while before 1973 and after 1995, there was a large

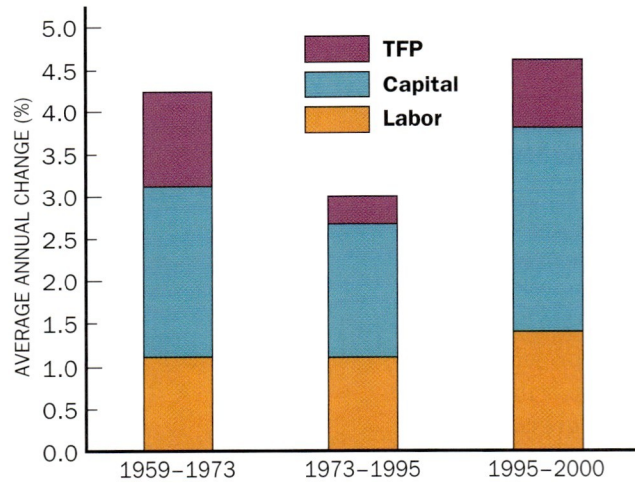

Figure 27.7

GROWTH ACCOUNTING

More than half the decline in growth between 1973 and 1990 is left unexplained after changes in the growth rates of capital and labor are accounted for. The second half of the 1990s saw an increase in TFP growth, returning it to levels similar to those seen in the 1959–1973 period. Increases in capital also account for the faster growth experiences during the second half of the 1990s.

SOURCE: D. W. Jorgensen, M. S. Ho, and K. J. Stiroh, "Projecting Productivity Growth: Lessons from the U.S. Growth Resurgence," *Federal Reserve Bank of Atlanta Economic Review* 87, no. 3 (2002): 1–13.

residual (i.e., TFP). The decrease in TFP appears responsible for most of the growth slowdown in the 1970s and 1980s. Third, the decline in productivity after 1973 was caused, in part, by a decline in the contribution of capital; but since 1995, increases in capital have, together with increases in TFP, accounted for the increase in the growth rate of output. The rapid growth at the end of the 1990s represented a return to the high growth rates of the 1950s and 1960s after two intervening decades of slow productivity growth.

These results pose major problems for those involved in long-term forecasting. Was the rapid growth in the 1959–1973 period an aberration? Or were the 1970s and 1980s atypical, with the late 1990s representing a return to the higher growth rates of earlier decades as fundamentally new technologies, such as computers, came into wider use? Throughout most of human history, technological change and economic growth have been rare. From this longer perspective, the aberration has been the past 250 years of economic growth.

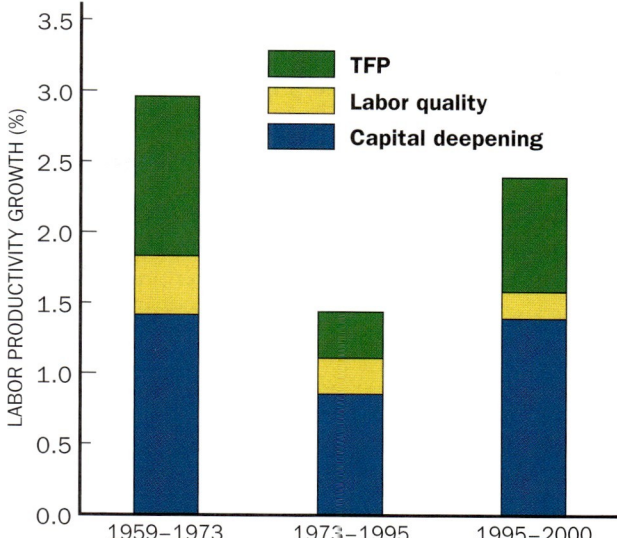

Figure 27.8

SOURCES OF LABOR PRODUCTIVITY GROWTH

Growth in labor productivity is due to capital deepening, increases in labor quality, and increases in total factor productivity. During the late 1990s, labor productivity growth increased because of the contributions of capital deepening and TFP.

SOURCE: D. W. Jorgensen, M. S. Ho, and K. J. Stiroh, "Projecting Productivity Growth: Lessons from the U.S. Growth Resurgence," *Federal Reserve Bank of Atlanta Economic Review* 87, no. 3 (2002): 1–13.

Case in Point

CALCULATING TOTAL FACTOR PRODUCTIVITY IN THE 1990s

Between 1995 and 2000, private domestic output in the United States grew by 20 percent, or 4.6 percent per year. Dale Jorgensen, Mun Ho, and Kevin Stiroh[1] in 2002 estimated that average labor productivity grew by 2.36 percent per year over this period—each hour of labor input produces more output than previously. The accounting used earlier to explain the contribution of various factors to economic growth also can be used to explain the sources of this growth in labor productivity.

One of the reasons why labor might become more productive is capital deepening. According to Jorgensen, Ho, and Stiroh, capital deepening accounted for 1.4 percentage points, or about 60 percent, of the 2.36 percent growth rate of labor productivity. Figure 27.8 shows that labor productivity growth increased during the second half of the 1990s, and part of this increased growth can be explained by capital deepening. But this source of labor productivity growth is still less today than it was in the 1959–1973 period.

A second source of labor productivity growth is increases in the *quality* of labor. Labor quality can increase through education or through shifts in the composition of the labor force. For instance, in the early 1970s, the baby boom generation entered the workforce and changed its composition—now more workers were younger and relatively inexperienced. Such a shift acts to reduce labor productivity. In the 1990s, as these baby boomers gained more work experience and training, the overall quality of the labor force increased, a change that contributed to rising labor

---

[1] D. W. Jorgensen, M. S. Ho, and K. J. Stiroh, "Projecting Productivity Growth: Lessons from the U.S. Growth Resurgence," *Federal Reserve Bank of Atlanta Economic Review* 87, no. 3 (2002): 1–13.

e-Insight
COMPUTERS AND INCREASED PRODUCTIVITY GROWTH

If the recent increases in productivity growth are due to new information and computer technologies, then we might expect that all the major industrialized economies would be benefiting from them. Panel A shows average labor productivity growth for the seven advanced economies known since 1976 as the "Group of Seven," or the G-7 (the G-7 became the G-8 with the addition of the Russian Federation in 1998). As the chart shows, only the United States has seen labor productivity increase in recent years. For all the other members of the group, productivity growth was higher from 1980 to 1995 than it has been since. Yet the new information and computer technologies are available to all these countries; so why hasn't growth increased in all of them? Should we conclude that the new technologies are not the source of America's increased productivity growth?

Perhaps the acceleration in U.S. productivity growth has not been matched in these other industrialized economies

PCs AND PRODUCTIVITY GROWTH

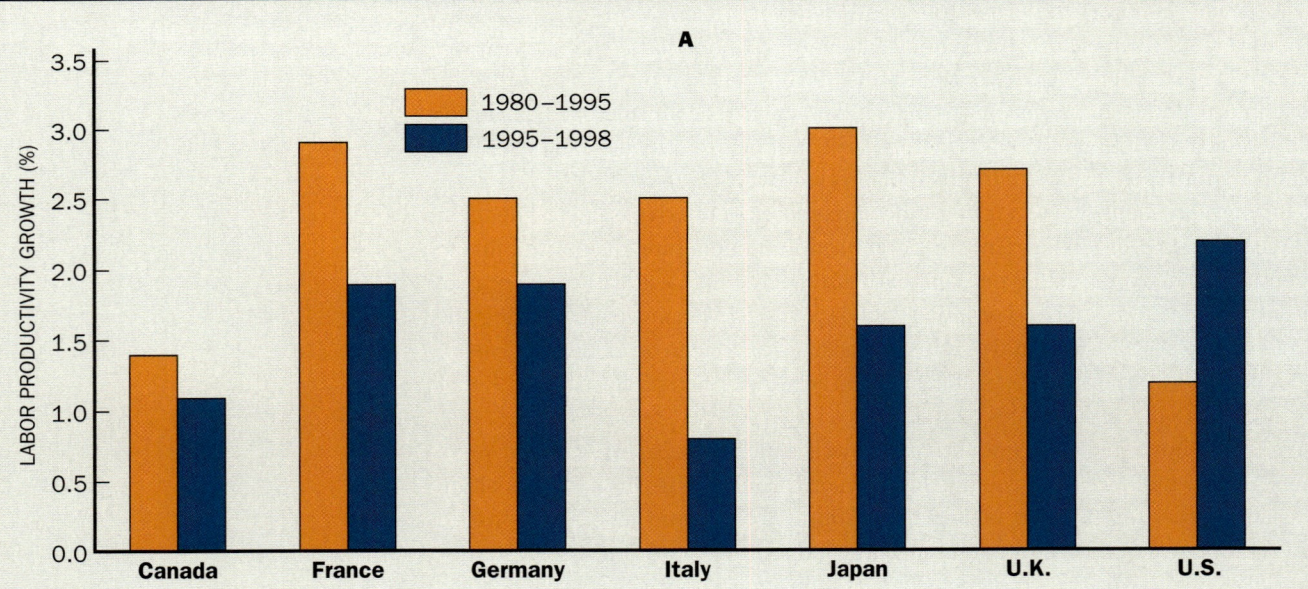

PRODUCTIVITY GROWTH IN THE G–7 COUNTRIES

Physicians can now make virtual house calls using time-saving technology such as videoconferencing.

because the United States has been more successful in adopting new technologies throughout the economy and has done so more quickly. For example, the Organization for Economic Cooperation and Development (OECD) estimated that in 1995 the number of personal computers (PCs) per capita was almost twice as high in the United States as in Canada and 75 percent higher than in the United Kingdom. As shown in Panel B, the change in productivity growth between the 1980–1995 and 1995–1998 periods does appear to be associated with the adoption of computers. The United States, with the most PCs per capita in 1995, experienced the biggest increase in growth, while Italy, with the fewest PCs per capita in 1995, had the largest growth slowdown. While this association between PCs and productivity growth cannot prove whether the adoption of computers has helped *cause* America's growth speedup, it is suggestive.

SOURCE: Casey Cornwell and Bharat Trehan, "Information Technology and Productivity," *Economic Letter*, No. 2000-34, Federal Reserve Bank of San Francisco, November 10, 2000.

productivity. In the second half of the 1990s, however, increases in labor quality accounted for less than 10 percent of the total growth in labor productivity.

The final source of labor productivity growth is increases in TFP. As the figure shows, TFP has increased significantly over the levels experienced between 1973 and 1995.

Fundamentals of Growth

GROWTH IN THE ECONOMY'S LABOR FORCE

The economy's potential output will increase with growth in the labor force. However, rising standards of living depend on increaasing the growth rate of *per capita* output. Growth in the *quality* of the labor force through investments in human capital that increase the skills of the work force will lead to higher incomes per capita.

GROWTH IN THE ECONOMY'S CAPITAL STOCK

Economic growth occurs when workers have more capital goods to work with. The success of many of the newly industrialized economies of Asia is due in large part to thier high rates of saving, which allowed them to invest and accumulate capital goods rapidly.

TECHNOLOGICAL CHANGE

Perhaps the most important sources of economic growth and rising standards of living are the productivity increases that arise from innovation and technological change.

Are There Limits to Economic Growth?

In the early 1800s, the famous British economist Thomas Malthus envisioned a future in which the ever-increasing labor force would push wages down to the subsistence level, or even lower. Any technological progress that occurred would, in his view, raise wages only temporarily. As the labor supply increased, wages would eventually fall back to the subsistence level.

Over the past century, there has been a decrease in the rate of population growth in developed countries, a phenomenon perhaps as remarkable as the increase in the rate of technological progress. We might have expected improved medicine and health conditions to cause a population explosion, but the spread of birth control and family planning has had the opposite effect, at least in the more-developed countries. Today family size has decreased to the point that in many countries population growth (apart from migration) has almost halted. Those who worry about the limits to growth today believe that *exhaustible* natural resources—such as oil, natural gas, phosphorus, or potassium—may pose a limit to economic growth as they are used up in the ordinary course of production.

Most economists do not share this fear, believing that markets do provide incentives for wise use of most resources—that as any good becomes more scarce and its price rises, the search for substitutes will be stimulated. Thus, the rise in the price of oil led to smaller, more efficient cars, cooler but better-insulated houses, and a search for alternative sources of energy such as geothermal resources and synthetic fuels, all of which resulted in a decline in the consumption of oil.

Still, there is one area in which the price system does not work well—the area of externalities. Without government intervention, for example, producers have no incentive to worry about air and water pollution. And in our globally connected world, what one country does results in externalities for others. Cutting down the rain forest in Brazil, for instance, may have worldwide climatic consequences. The less-developed countries feel that they can ill afford the costs of pollution control, when they can barely pay the price of any industrialization. Most economists do not believe that we face an either/or choice. We do not have to abandon growth to preserve our

Thinking Like an Economist
TRADE-OFFS AND THE COSTS OF ECONOMIC GROWTH

Faith in the virtues of economic progress is widespread. Few openly embrace the alternative of economic stagnation and lower standards of living. Yet not everyone benefits from changes in technology, and there may be environmental and other costs associated with growth.

In the early 1800s, English workmen destroyed labor-saving machinery rather than see it take over their jobs. They were referred to as *Luddites,* after their leader, Neil Ludd (whose role may have been largely mythical). Concerns about workers thrown out of their jobs as a result of some innovations are no less real today.

What needs to be kept in mind, and has already been stressed earlier in this book, is that technological progress *creates* jobs as it destroys them. Of course, it can be hard to retrain workers in declining industries to gain the skills necessary for new jobs, so middle-aged or older workers who lose jobs may have real difficulty in getting another one that is as good.

Not surprisingly, technical progress frequently meets with resistance. Although there is growing acceptance that such resistance is futile—change will eventually come—and that the benefits of economic progress exceed the costs, many also recognize the role of government in assisting individuals who are displaced by technological change in their transition to alternative employment. Such assistance can be thought of as a form of insurance. Most workers face the possibility that their jobs will be made technologically obsolete. Knowing that if they are thrown out of work for this reason they will be at least partially protected helps create a sense of security, something most workers value highly.

An important cost of economic growth can be its toll on the environment. As we noted in Chapter 22, a green GDP measure might give a different picture of growth as it would include the economic costs to the environment of producing more goods and services. Accounting for all the costs, as well as the benefits, of growth would provide a clearer picture of the trade-offs that growth can involve.

environment. Nevertheless, a sensitivity to the quality of our environment may affect how we go about growing. This sensitivity is building a new consensus in favor of **sustainable development**—that is, growth not based on the exploitation of natural resources and the environment in a way that cannot be sustained. In many cases, policies can be devised to improve economic efficiency, and thus promote economic growth, at the same time that they decrease adverse environmental effects. These include elimination of energy subsidies and certain agricultural subsidies that encourage farmers to use excessive amounts of fertilizers and pesticides.

Review and Practice

SUMMARY

1. The United States experienced a marked slowdown in the rate of productivity growth in the early 1970s, compared with the preceding two decades. Since the late 1990s there has been a remarkable increase in productivity growth. Even seemingly small changes in the rate of increase in productivity will have powerful effects on the standard of living over a generation or two.
2. There are four major sources of productivity growth: increases in the accumulation of capital goods (investment); qualitative improvements in the labor force; greater efficiency in allocating resources; and technological change. Since 1973 almost all of the increase in productivity can be attributed to increases in capital, improvements in human capital, and expenditures on research and development. In recent years, the relative role of human capital has increased and the role of physical capital has decreased.
3. Increases in human capital—improved education—are a major source of productivity increases. There are large returns to investments in education.
4. The twentieth century was marked by shifts in the U.S. economy from an agricultural base to an industrial base and then to a service base.
5. Improvements in technology, partly as a result of expenditures on research and development (R & D), are a major source of increases in productivity. Government supports R & D through both direct spending and tax incentives, though direct support for R & D that is not defense-related has actually declined during the past quarter century.
6. There has long been concern that certain natural resources (like oil) will run out someday, causing economic growth to halt. However, most economists would argue that the price of resources will increase as they become more scarce, and this rise will encourage both greater conservation and a search for substitutes.
7. Sustainable development requires growth strategies that use resources and the environment in ways that do not jeopardize future potential growth.

KEY TERMS

income per capita
labor force participation rate
depreciation
capital deepening
human capital
property rights
total factor productivity analysis
total factor productivity (TFP)
sustainable development

REVIEW QUESTIONS

1. True or false: "Since growth-oriented policies might have an effect of only a percent or two per year, they are not worth worrying much about." Explain.
2. What are the four possible sources of productivity growth?
3. What is the link between changes in the capital stock (investment) and the rate of growth of productivity in the short run? What is the link between changes in the capital stock and the *level* of productivity (output per worker) in the long run? What is meant by capital deepening?
4. What policies might the government use to increase investment in R & D?
5. What is total factor productivity and how is it measured?
6. Are there limits to economic growth? What was Malthus's view? Is growth limited by exhaustible resources?

PROBLEMS

1. Explain how the following factors would increase or decrease the average productivity of labor:
   (a) Successful reforms of the educational system
   (b) The entry of new workers into the economy
   (c) Earlier retirement
   (d) Increased investment

2. Explain why a rapid influx of workers might result in a lower output per worker (a reduction in productivity). Would the effect on productivity depend on the skill level of the new workers?
3. Explain, using supply and demand diagrams, how a technological change such as computerization could lead to lower wages for unskilled workers and higher wages for skilled workers.
4. Using the model of Chapter 26, discuss the effect on the level of investment for an open economy of (a) an increased government deficit; (b) an increase in government expenditure, financed by taxes on households that reduce their disposable income; (c) an investment tax credit. How will such policies affect future living standards of those living in the country?
5. Calculate the growth rate in the number of hours worked per capita, total output, and output per capita from the following information:

   Growth rate in number of hours worked = 1.5 percent
   Growth rate of the population = 1.2 percent
   Growth rate of productivity = 2.3 percent

   What happens to the growth rates of total output and per capita output if the growth rate of productivity rises to 3.3 percent? What happens to the growth rates of total output and per capita output if the growth rate of the population rises to 2.0 percent?
6. The table below gives growth rates for the United States for various time periods. Using these data, calculate the growth rate of average hours worked per capita for each period.

	1970–1979	1980–1989	1990–1999	2000–2002
Output	3.57%	3.12%	3.38%	2.27%
Output per capita	1.12%	1.31%	2.05%	2.26%
Productivity	1.92%	1.38%	1.82%	3.43%
Total hours	1.75%	1.74%	1.56%	−1.17%

7. Assume investments in human capital yield a return of 15 percent, private investments yield a total return of 10 percent, and public investments in research yield a return of 25 percent. Assume the deficit is $100 billion per year, and the government wishes to eliminate it. What will be the impact on economic growth of a deficit reduction package that consists of reducing Medicare expenditures by $50 billion, education expenditures by $40 billion, and research expenditures by $10 billion?

Learning Goals

In this chapter, you will learn

1. How the general level of prices is related to the money supply
2. The factors that determine the money supply in a modern economy
3. The role of the Federal Reserve, and the tools it can use to affect the supply of money

Chapter 28

MONEY, THE PRICE LEVEL, AND THE FEDERAL RESERVE

Our discussion of the full-employment model in Chapter 24 left out some crucial dimensions of the macroeconomy: most importantly, the role of money and the determination of the average level of prices and inflation. Most people find the topic of money fascinating, especially when they learn how banks "create" money. In modern economies, banks are active participants in the capital market *and* are key to understanding how the supply of money is determined. In this chapter, we concentrate on the role of banks and the government in the economy's financial market and on their role in affecting the price level and inflation.

While you might care about how much money you have because it provides a measure of how much you may be able to spend, macroeconomists focus on the supply of money in the economy because of its connection with the price level and inflation. Over the past fifty years, the general level of prices has risen significantly, as Figure 28.1 shows. The index of consumer prices has risen by more than 1500 percent since 1913. In other words, something that cost $1 in 1913 would cost more than $16 today. A rising price level—inflation—is associated with growth in the supply of money. As Figure 28.2 shows, the inflation rate has varied greatly since the early twentieth century. Unpredictable swings in inflation can be costly to the economy. The variability of relative prices associated with volatile inflation, the increased uncertainty about future prices that makes planning more difficult, and the capricious shifts in wealth between borrowers and lenders are some of the costs of inflation that were discussed in Chapter 23.

Our first task in this chapter is to explain how the general level of prices is determined in the full-employment model. Answering this question will lead us to a discussion of the role of money, how the money supply is determined, and how government policy can affect the money supply.

No discussion of prices and money is complete without an understanding of the role played by the Federal Reserve. In the United States, monetary policy is

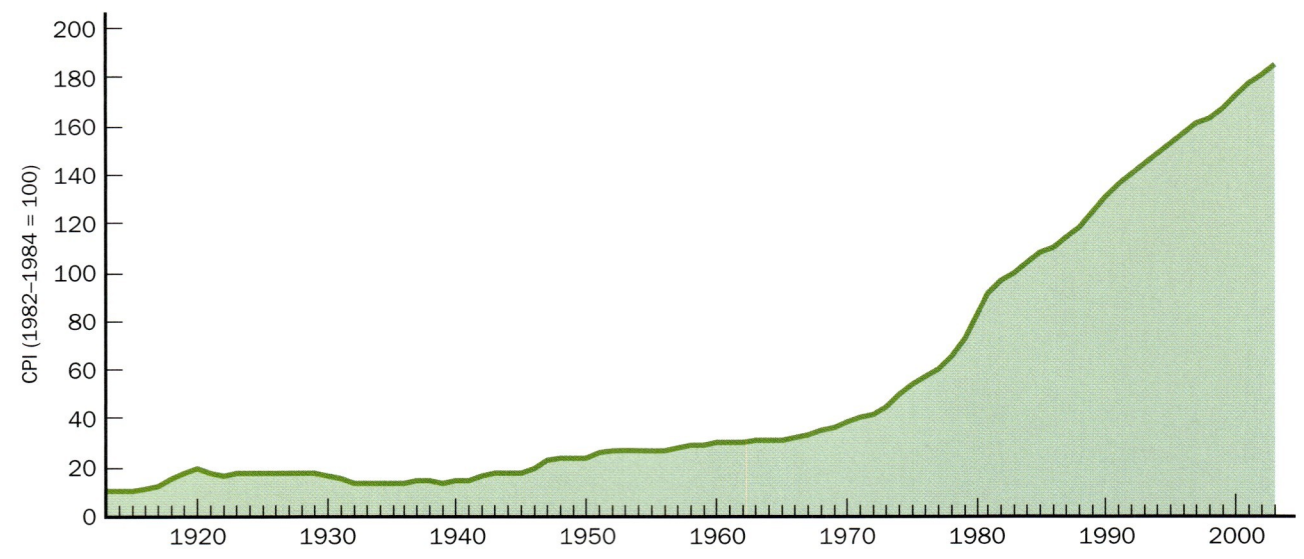

Figure 28.1

THE CONSUMER PRICE INDEX

During the past ninety years, the consumer price index has increased enormously. Most of the rise has occurred since 1973.

SOURCE: Bureau of Labor Statistics.

conducted by the Federal Reserve System. In this chapter, you will learn about the Federal Reserve and the policy tools it can use to affect the money supply.

Prices and Inflation

The discussion of the long-run, full employment model in Chapter 24 was conducted entirely in *real* terms; real output, real employment, real saving and investment, real wages, and the real rate of interest. *We were able to explain the factors that determine the economy's full-employment output level (potential GDP) without any mention of the aggregate price level.* We could do so because the economy's real equilibrium at full employment is independent of the level of prices. That is, regardless of whether the average level of prices is high or low, potential GDP is the same. This implication is represented in Figure 28.3, which has real output on the horizontal axis and the price level on the vertical axis. Potential GDP is denoted by Y^f. Since Y^f is determined by labor demand and labor supply (both of which depend on *real* wages) and the economy's aggregate production function (which depends on the state of technology and the capital stock), it will be the same at all price levels. Because full-employment output is independent of the price level, we have drawn a vertical line in Figure 28.3 at Y^f.

The price level simply tells us how many dollars (or euros in France or Germany, yen in Japan, pesos in Mexico) it takes to buy a basket of goods and services. We measure the price level by using price indexes (see Chapter 23), most commonly either the GDP deflator or the consumer price index (CPI). The GDP deflator reflects

Figure 28.2
THE RATE OF INFLATION

Inflation has fluctuated considerably over the past ninety years. It reached significant levels during World War I, World War II, and the Korean War, and was negative (i.e., prices fell) during most of the period between the two world wars. The period from the late 1960s until the early 1980s is sometimes described as the Great Inflation, because it represented an extended period of high inflation not associated with wartime.

SOURCE: Bureau of Labor Statistics.

the prices of all the goods and services that the economy produces as part of GDP. The CPI measures the prices of things purchased by households. In 2004, the CPI was equal to 189. This means that in 2004 it took $1.89 to purchase what could have been bought for $1.00 in the index base year (an average of prices in 1982–1984).

Because the price level tells us how much it costs to purchase goods and services, it is a measure of the value of money. If the price level rises, each dollar will buy fewer goods and services: the value of money falls. If the price level falls, each dollar will buy more goods and services: the value of money rises.

The value of money, like the value of other commodities, is determined by the interaction of demand and supply. To understand what determines the price level, we will need to examine the factors that affect the demand for and supply of money.

MONEY DEMAND

Money is a financial asset, just like stocks and bonds. But money differs from those other assets because we use it to carry out our day-to-day transactions. If you want to buy a cup of coffee, you cannot present the sales clerk with a share of Microsoft Corporation and expect change. In the United States, you have to present cash. Or you can pay with a credit card—but to pay for those credit purchases, you need to write a check at the end of the month. Cash and balances in checking accounts are the primary forms of money that we use. The more transactions we engage in, or the higher the average value of these transactions, the more of those forms of money

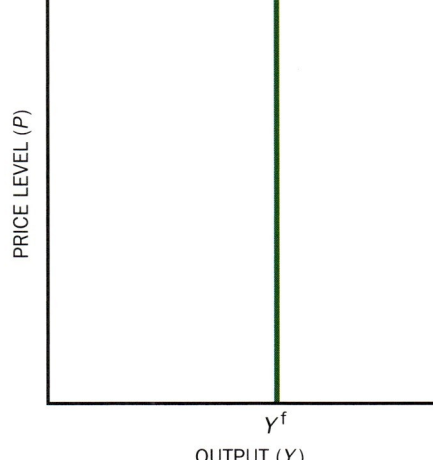

Figure 28.3

POTENTIAL GDP AND THE AGGREGATE PRICE LEVEL

The economy's potential GDP does not depend on the price level; this is represented by drawing a vertical line at potential GDP.

we need to hold. Money we do not need for transactions is better used to purchase financial assets that earn interest. Increases in the dollar value of transactions increase the demand for money; decreases in the dollar value of transactions decrease the demand for money.

A useful simplifying assumption is that the amount of money individuals hold is proportional to the dollar value, or nominal value, of their income. The same will be true when we aggregate the economy; the overall demand for money will be proportional to aggregate nominal income, which we measure by GDP. As we learned in Chapter 22, we can express GDP as PY, the price level (P) times the real GDP (Y). If nominal income in the economy rises, people hold, on average, more money. Nominal income can rise because of an increase either in real incomes or in the price level. If their real incomes rise, people will typically hold more money on average, since they are likely to increase consumption and thus engage in more transactions. Money demand also rises if the general level of prices rise, even if real income remains constant, because each transaction will involve more dollars. When every cup of coffee costs, say, $3 rather than $2.50, it takes $30 rather than $25 to fill up a tank of gasoline, and the bill for a trip to the grocery store is $60 rather than $50, individuals, on average, will need to hold more money to carry out their transactions.

Velocity The relationship between the aggregate demand for money and aggregate nominal income can be represented by the **quantity equation of exchange,** which defines the amount of money that individuals wish to hold as proportional to nominal GDP. We can write this equation as

$$MV = PY,$$

where M is the quantity of money demanded and PY is the nominal GDP. The final term in the equation is the factor of proportionality or **velocity,** V. Suppose, for example, that each individual in the economy held enough money to pay for one month's worth of spending. In this case, velocity for each individual would equal 12—annual expenditures would be twelve times the average level of money held. If an individual's annual income was $60,000, on average he would want to hold $5,000. If velocity were 26, so that on average individuals held an amount of money equal to only two weeks' worth of expenditures, someone with an annual income of $60,000 would hold $2,308. When we add up all the individuals in the economy, velocity enables us to predict the aggregate demand for money when the aggregate income is known. For example, suppose GDP is $11.2 trillion per year and velocity is 26. Then the demand for money will be $11.2 trillion divided by 26, or $43 billion. Velocity, therefore, is a measure of how many times a given dollar gets spent over the course of a year. The higher the value of velocity, the more times a dollar is spent—the faster it speeds from one transaction to another.

Velocity will depend on the methods available in the economy for carrying out transactions. If many purchases are made with money, V is larger than if money is rarely used in making transactions. If innovations in the financial industry reduce the average amount of money that individuals need to hold, velocity rises.

Since we are interested in the demand for money, we can rearrange the quantity equation to express it as

$$\text{money demand} = PY/V.$$

Money demand changes in proportion to changes in nominal income. An increase in velocity reduces the demand for money at each level of nominal income.[1]

MONEY SUPPLY

The supply of money is affected by government policies. In particular, governments influence the amount of money in circulation through *monetary policy*. In the United States, monetary policy is conducted by the Federal Reserve, commonly called "the Fed." How the Fed conducts policy and how monetary policy affects the economy will be discussed later in this volume (in Chapters 31, 32, and 33). For now, we will simply assume the government determines the supply of money. Our focus will be on understanding the consequences for the economy if the government changes that supply.

THE PRICE LEVEL

We now have the information we need to explain how the price level is determined when the economy is at full employment. The supply of money is set by the government. The demand for money depends on the dollar value of transactions in the economy. The supply of money and the demand for money must be equal when the economy is in equilibrium. If the supply of money increases, so that at the initial value of GDP the supply of money is greater than the demand for money, GDP must rise to restore the balance between money demand and money supply.

GDP can adjust through changes in either the price level or real GDP (or both). In a full-employment equilibrium, however, real GDP is determined by the level of employment consistent with equilibrium in the labor market and with the aggregate production function that determines how much the economy produces when employment is at that level. At full employment, GDP is equal to PY^f, where Y^f is full-employment real GDP. We can then write the requirement that the demand for money equal the supply of money as

$$\text{money demand} = PY^f/V = M = \text{money supply}.$$

For a given level of velocity, it is the price level P that adjusts to ensure that the demand for money is equal to the supply of money.

---

[1] The inverse of velocity, $1/V$, also has its own name—the Cambridge constant—after the formulation of money demand used by economists (including John Maynard Keynes) at Cambridge University in the early twentieth century, and it is usually denoted by k. We can then write the demand for money as kPY. The Cambridge constant is equal to the fraction of nominal income held as money.

What happens if the supply of money increases? At the initial price level P, individuals are now holding more money than they want to. The easiest way to reduce the amount of money you are holding is to spend it. From the perspective of firms, increased spending by consumers provides a signal to increase prices. Faced with higher prices, workers demand high nominal wages. As prices rise, individuals must hold more money to carry out the same transactions. Equilibrium between demand and supply for money is restored when prices have risen enough that the increase in the quantity of money demanded equals the increase in the money supply. Nominal wages will have risen by the same proportionate amount to maintain the real wage at the level that clears the labor market and maintains full employment. *An increase in the money supply leads to an increase in the general level of prices and nominal wages.*

In the labor market, as noted, the increase in the price level will be matched by an increase in the nominal wage, so that the *real* wage remains at its original level. At this real wage, the demand for labor continues to equal the supply of labor. Thus the effect on the labor market of an increase in the price level is simply a proportionate increase in the nominal wage. There are no real effects—the equilibrium real wage and the equilibrium level of employment are unaffected.

In the capital market, real saving and investment both depend on the real interest rate, which is not affected by the increase in the price level. Accordingly, the equilibrium real interest rate remains unchanged. Only the *nominal* levels of saving and investment change in proportion to the change in the price level.

We can say something more about how much the price level will increase if the money supply rises. We have assumed the demand for money is proportional to GDP. If the money supply rises by 10 percent, GDP must rise by 10 percent to ensure that the money demand increases by the same amount as the money supply. With full-employment output unaffected, this means that the price level must also rise by 10 percent. The aggregate price level will move in proportion to changes in the money supply.

Most economists agree that in a full-employment economy, a onetime change in the money supply affects the price level but little else in the long run. In particular, it does not affect the quantity of goods and services produced or the number of workers employed. An imaginary example may help us understand the point. Suppose that instantaneously, the entire supply of money in the economy was increased by a multiple of ten. In effect, we have tacked a zero onto the money supply. Stores,

Internet Connection

HOW MUCH CASH DO WE HOLD?

The Web site at the Federal Reserve Bank of Atlanta provides some facts and figures on America's money. For instance, did you know that in 1920, we had just over $50 in cash per person, while by 2000 this figure rose to over $2,000? Check out the site at www.frbatlanta.org/publica/brochure/fundfac/html/home.html.

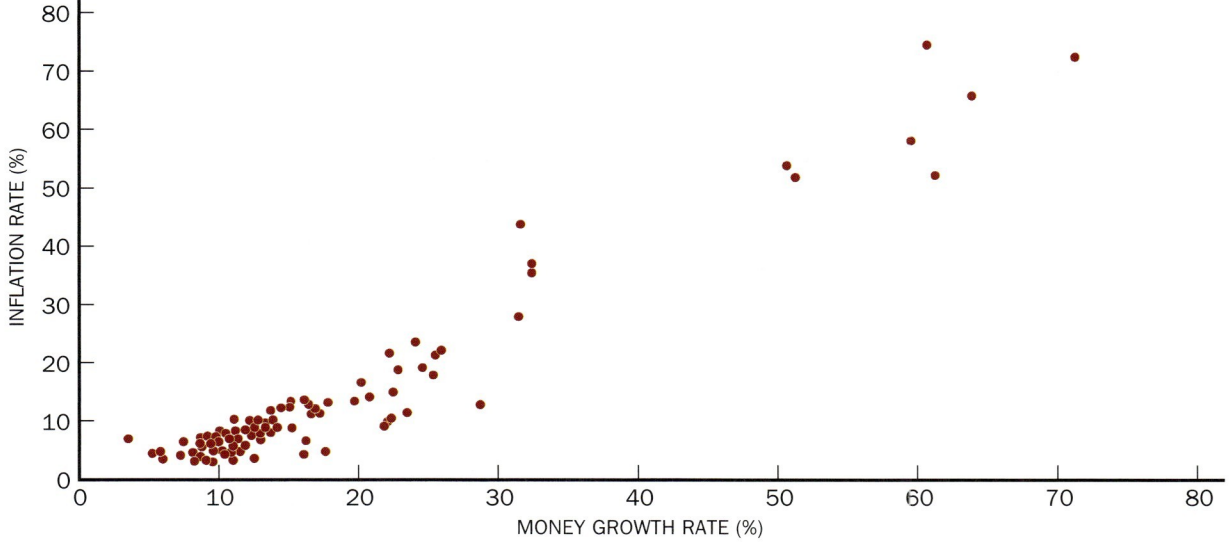

Figure 28.4

MONEY GROWTH AND INFLATION

Money growth and inflation are closely related, as this figure shows. Each dot represents the 1960–1990 average annual inflation rate and rate of money growth for a single country. In all, 110 countries are shown.

SOURCE: George T. McCandless Jr. and Warren E. Weber, "Some Monetary Facts," *Federal Reserve Bank of Minneapolis Quarterly Review* 19, no. 3 (Summer 1995): 2–11.

acting perfectly efficiently, and knowing that the money supply has multiplied by ten, would increase their prices tenfold. Thus, the actual amount of goods and services produced and consumed would be the same. There would be no real effects: the only difference would be the numbers on the bills, bank statements, and price tags.

The lesson is more general. A change in the supply of money accompanied by a proportionate change in the price level has no real effects on the economy. When changing the money supply has no real effect, we say that money is *neutral*. If the economy is at full employment and wages and prices are perfectly flexible, prices will change proportionally to any change in the money supply. Thus, the **neutrality of money** is a basic implication of the full-employment model.

Suppose that instead of thinking about onetime changes in the level of the money supply, we think about what would happen if the money supply grows at 10 percent per year. Then, the price level and nominal wages also would rise at 10 percent per year; the rate of inflation would be 10 percent per year, equal to the rate of growth of the money supply. Rapid money growth would be accompanied by high rates of inflation; low money growth would be accompanied by low rates of inflation. Figure 28.4 provides some evidence on this implication of the full-employment model. It shows average annual money supply growth rates and inflation rates for 110 countries for the period 1960–1990. Just as the full-employment model predicts, there is close to a one-for-one relationship between the growth rate of the money supply and the rate of inflation. Rapid money growth and high inflation go together; slow money growth and low inflation go together.

While the neutrality of money is a basic property of our full-employment model with flexible wages and prices, it is important to keep in mind the limitations of the model. If price increases themselves really had no real consequences, then inflation would not be a matter of much concern. But as we learned in Chapter 23, it *is* a concern. Later chapters will explore the more complicated effects of changes in the money supply and prices when the economy is not at full employment and wages and prices are not perfectly flexible.

> **Wrap-Up**
>
> ## MONEY AND THE PRICE LEVEL
>
> In the full-employment model, employment, the real wage, real output, and the real rate of interest are independent of the price level.
>
> Changes in the nominal supply of money produce proportional changes in the price level, nominal wages, and the nominal value of output.
>
> Money is neutral when changing the money supply has no real effect.

The Financial System in Modern Economies

We have now learned that the level of prices is related to the supply of money. But we have not discussed the role of banks, the financial sector, and government policy in determining the supply of money. We will begin by explaining the role that financial institutions play and how banks create money. We focus on banks because they are key players in financial markets generally and help provide an important link between government policy and the money supply.

The capital market is the market where the supply of funds is allocated to those who wish to borrow. In everyday language, we often refer to this as the country's financial market or financial system. Broadly speaking, a country's *financial system* includes all institutions involved in moving savings from households and firms whose income exceeds their expenditures and transferring it to other households and firms that would like to spend more than their current income allows.

The financial system in the United States not only makes it possible for consumers to buy cars, televisions, and homes even when they do not have the cash to do so, but it also enables firms to invest in factories and new machines. Sometimes money goes directly from, say, a household engaged in saving to a firm that needs some additional cash. For example, when Ben buys a bond from General Motors that promises to pay a fixed amount in 90 or 180 days (or in five or fifteen years), he is lending money directly to the company.

But most funds flow through *financial intermediaries*—firms that stand between the savers, who have extra funds, and the borrowers, who need them. The most important of these are banks, but there are many other financial intermediaries, including life insurance companies, credit unions, and savings and loan associations. All are engaged in looking over potential borrowers, ascertaining who among them are good risks, and monitoring their investments and loans. The intermediaries take "deposits" from consumers and put the funds into many different investments, thereby reducing risk. One investment might turn sour, but it is unlikely that many will. Diversifying provides the intermediary with a kind of safety it could not obtain if it put all its eggs in one basket. Financial institutions differ in who the depositors are, where the funds are invested, and who owns the institution. Table 28.1 provides a glossary of the major types of financial intermediaries.

Financial intermediaries have a key function in our financial system. After all, few firms have the resources to undertake investments in new buildings, factories, or equipment without borrowing. And in recent years, venture capitalists have played a critical role in providing the funding that enables high-tech firms to get started. In

Table 28.1
A GLOSSARY OF FINANCIAL INTERMEDIARIES

A variety of financial intermediaries take funds from the public and lend them to borrowers or otherwise invest them. Of the many legal differences between these institutions, the principal ones relate to the kinds of loans or investments made. The following list is ranked roughly by the asset size of each intermediary.

Commercial banks	Banks chartered by either the federal government (national banks) or a state (state banks) to receive deposits and make loans.	**Mutual funds**	Financial intermediaries that take funds from a group of investors and invest them. Major examples include stock mutual funds, which invest the funds in stocks; bond mutual funds, which invest in bonds; and money market mutual funds, which invest in liquid assets such as Treasury bills and certificates of deposit. Many mutual funds allow account holders to write checks against the fund.
Life insurance companies	Companies that collect premiums from policyholders out of which insurance payments are made.		
Savings and loan associations (S&Ls, or "thrifts")	Institutions originally chartered to receive deposits for the purpose of making loans to finance home mortgages; in the early 1980s, they were given more latitude in the kinds of loans they could make.		
		Institutional money market mutual funds	Money market mutual fund accounts held by institutions.
Credit unions	Cooperative (not-for-profit) institutions, usually organized at a place of work or by a union, that take deposits from members and make loans to members.	**CMA accounts (cash management accounts)**	Accounts at a brokerage firm (the name was trademarked by Merrill Lynch, the first to establish such accounts) that enable people to place stocks, bonds, and other assets into a single account, against which they can write checks.

return, venture capitalists often receive a share in the ownership of the new firm. For the sake of simplicity, our discussion in the rest of this chapter will focus on one very important group of financial intermediaries: commercial banks.

Traditionally, banks have been the primary avenue for businesses to raise capital. When the banking system collapses, as it did in the Great Depression in the United States, firms cannot obtain funds to make their investments, consumers lose their deposits, and the entire economy suffers. For this reason, governments have developed banking regulations intended to ensure greater financial stability. During the 1930s, hundreds of U.S. banks closed, leaving thousands destitute. Today, banks are more tightly regulated, and deposits are insured by the federal government so that individuals' losses will be limited even if their bank goes bankrupt. Problems can still occur, however. In the early 1980s, changes in government regulations allowed savings and loan associations (S&Ls), which traditionally had invested in home mortgages, to branch into much riskier areas, particularly commercial real estate. Almost immediately thereafter the commercial real estate market collapsed, bankrupting many S&Ls. Depositors were protected by federal deposit insurance, but the cost to the U.S. government reached around $150 billion.

In addition, the actions of commercial banks affect the supply of money, which in turn influences the overall level of prices in the economy. Because of their central role, banks are critical to how monetary policies affect the economy.

While our focus will be on banks, it is important to recognize that to varying degrees, other financial intermediaries perform the same functions. For instance, in accepting deposits and making loans, savings and loan associations today are almost indistinguishable from banks.

Case in Point

WHEN ATLANTA PRINTED MONEY

In the nineteenth and early twentieth centuries, in the rural South and West, cash for everyday transactions was often in short supply. Workers could not shop for food or clothing, bills were not paid, and the local economy lurched sideways or backward.

It was common in such cases for towns, private companies, and sometimes states to print their own currency, known politely as "scrip" and less politely as "soap wrappers," "shinplasters," "doololly," and many less-printable names. The idea was that issuing scrip could keep the local economy going until official currency became available again, at which point people could cash in their scrip.

The last major issue of scrip in the United States came during the Great Depression. In the early 1930s, banks were crashing right and left, and bank runs were a daily occurrence. Remember, these were the days before deposits were insured. When President Franklin Roosevelt took office in March 1933, one of his first major actions was to declare a "bank holiday." He closed all the banks for the week of March 6–12 to give everyone time to relax and get their bearings.

But these were also the days before checking accounts had become widespread; workers were paid weekly, in cash. If firms could not get to the bank, they could not pay their workers. How could the local economy react to these sorts of financial disturbances?

Each area adapted in its own way. Let's consider Atlanta.[2] The city printed about $2.5 million in scrip, in eight different issues, during the first half of the 1930s. One of the first payments was to schoolteachers, and the city made sure that Rich's, a prominent local department store, would take the scrip at full face value. Many other stores, however, would count the scrip only at 75 percent or less of face value. Note that by taking scrip, which it would later turn in to the city for cash, stores were effectively lending money to Atlanta, which had issued the scrip.

Such stories of scrip may sound antiquated today (though in its 1992 financial crisis, California paid its workers with something akin to scrip). But they emphasize the fact that without something to serve as a medium of exchange and a measure and (short-term) store of value, an economy simply cannot function. Today the Federal Reserve acts to ensure that currency is available. But in the 1930s, issuing scrip was one step a city could take on its own to cushion the ravages of the Great Depression.

Creating Money in Modern Economies

Banks have long played a key role in the financial sector. Indeed, today's money supply is created not by a mint or a printing press but largely by the banking sector. The money supply consists not only of the cash we carry but also the deposits in our checking accounts. The total level of deposits in the banking system is an important part of what we mean by the money supply. Whenever you make a deposit to or a withdrawal from your checking account, you are potentially affecting the overall quantity of money.

When you put $100 into the bank, the bank does not simply put it in a slot marked with your name and keep it there until you are ready to take it out. Banks know that not all their thousands of depositors will withdraw their money on any given day. Some people will withdraw their money in a week, some in two weeks, some not for a year or more. In the meantime, the bank can lend out the money deposited and charge interest on the loans it makes. The more money the bank can persuade people to deposit, the more it can lend out and the more money it will earn. To attract depositors, the bank pays interest on some of its deposits, effectively passing on (after taking its cut) the interest earned on its loans.

MONEY IS WHAT MONEY DOES

What do bank deposits and loans have to do with the total amount of money in the economy? When we talk about money, we often mean much more than just currency. In speaking of how much money someone makes, we are really referring to

---

[2] See William Roberds, "Lenders of the Next-to-Last Resort: Scrip Issue in Georgia During the Great Depression," *Economic Review of the Federal Reserve Bank of Atlanta,* September–October 1990, pp. 16–30.

her income. Or we say someone has a lot of money, but what we really mean is that he is wealthy, not that he has piles of currency stashed away.

Economists define *money* by the functions it serves, and three functions are critical.

Money as a Unit of Account Money serves as a means of measuring the relative values of different goods and services. This is its **unit of account** function. If a laptop computer costs $1,800 and a desktop computer costs $900, then a laptop is worth twice as much as a desktop. People wishing to trade laptops for desktops will trade at the rate of one laptop for two desktops. Money provides a simple and convenient measure of relative market values.

Imagine how difficult it would be for firms to track their profitability without money. Their accounting ledgers would record how many items were sold or purchased, but firms would not know whether these transactions had left them better or worse off. Firms need to know the relative value of what they sell and what they purchase, and money provides that unit of account.

Money as a Medium of Exchange Money's primary function is to facilitate trade—the exchange of goods and services. This is called its **medium of exchange** function. Trade that involves the direct exchange of goods without the use of money is called *barter*. For example, barter occurs when a mechanic fixes a plumber's bad speedometer cable in exchange for the repair of a leaky sink. Nations sometimes sign treaties phrased in barter terms; a certain amount of oil might be traded for a certain amount of machinery or weapons.

Barter works best in simple economies, and it also requires a *double coincidence of wants*. That is, one individual must have what the other wants, and vice versa. If Helen has compact discs (CDs) and wants DVDs, and Joshua has DVDs and wants CDs, bartering will make them both better off. However, if Joshua doesn't want CDs, then Helen's bartering for his DVDs will require that one or both of them search for people with other goods in hopes of putting together a multilateral exchange. Money provides a way to make multilateral exchanges much simpler. Helen sells her CDs for money, which she can use to buy Joshua's DVDs. Money is essential for the billions of exchanges that take place in a modern economy.

Money can be thought of as a social convention. People accept money in payment for what they sell because they know that others will accept it for what they themselves want to buy. Any easily transportable and storable good can, in principle, be used as a medium of exchange, and different cultures have chosen widely different goods to use as money. South Sea Islanders once used cowry shells. In World War II prisoner of war camps and in many prisons today, cigarettes are a medium of exchange.

All developed countries today use paper and metal coins produced by the government as currency. However, most business transactions require not currency but checks drawn on banks, credit cards whose balances are paid with checks, or funds wired from one bank to another. Since the promise of a transfer from a checking account is accepted as payment at most places, economists view checking account balances as money. Most people keep much more money in their checking accounts than they do in their wallets, so economists' measure of the money supply is much larger than the amount of currency in circulation.

Money as a Store of Value People will exchange what they have for money only if they believe that they can later exchange money for things they need. For money to serve as a medium of exchange, it must hold its value. Economists call this third function of money the **store of value** function. Governments once feared that paper money by itself would not hold its value unless it was backed by a commodity such as gold. People had confidence in paper money because they knew they could exchange it at banks for a precious metal.

Today, however, all major economies have *fiat money*—money that has value only because the government says it has value and because people are willing to accept it in exchange for goods. Dollar bills carry the message "This note is legal tender for all debts, public and private." The term *legal tender* means that if you owe $100, you have fully discharged that debt if you pay with a hundred dollar bill (or a hundred one-dollar bills).

We are now ready for the economic definition of **money.** Money is anything that is generally accepted as a unit of account, a medium of exchange, and a store of value. Money is, in other words, what it does.

MEASURING THE MONEY SUPPLY

What should be included in the money supply? A variety of things fulfill some of the functions of money. For example, in a casino, gambling chips are a medium of exchange, and they may even be accepted by nearby stores and restaurants. But no establishment except the casino is obligated to take chips; they are neither a generally accepted medium of exchange nor a unit of account.

Economists' measure of money begins with the currency people carry around. Economists then expand the measure to include other items that serve money's three functions. Checking accounts, or **demand deposits** (so called because you can get your money back on demand), are part of the money supply, as are some other forms of bank accounts. But what are the limits? It is helpful to imagine items on a continuum: at one pole are those that everyone would agree should be called money, at the other are those that should never be considered part of the money supply, and in between are what works as money in many circumstances.

Economists have developed several measures of the money supply to take account of this variety. The narrowest, called **M1,** is the total of currency, traveler's checks, and checking accounts. More simply, M1 is currency plus items that can be treated like currency throughout the banking system. In late 2003, M1 totaled $1.3 trillion.

A broader measure, **M2,** includes everything that is in M1, plus some items that are *almost* perfect substitutes for M1. Savings deposits of $100,000 or less (i.e., up to the limit covered by federal insurance) are included. So are certificates of deposit (deposits put in the bank for fixed periods of time, between six months and five years), money market funds held by individuals, and eurodollars, or U.S. dollars deposited in European banks. In late 2003, M2 totaled $6 trillion.

The common characteristic of assets in M2 is that they can be converted easily into M1. Economists describe as *liquid* an asset that is easily converted into M1 without losing value. You cannot just tell a store that the money needed to purchase a shirt is in your savings account. But if you have funds in a savings account, it is not

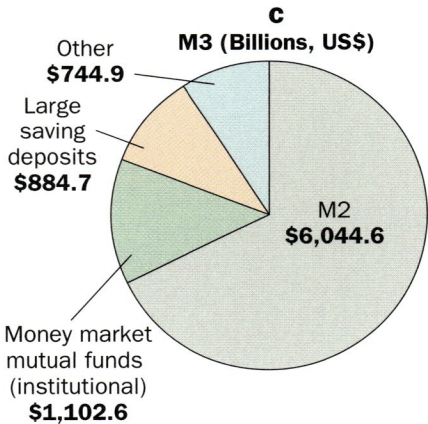

Figure 28.5

THE MEASURES OF MONEY IN 2003

The money supply can be measured in many ways, including M1, M2, and M3.

SOURCE: *Economic Report of the President* (2003), Tables B-69, B-70.

hard to change these funds into either currency or a checking account, so that you can pay for the shirt with cash or a check. A car is a much less liquid asset; if you want to convert your car into cash quickly, you may have to sell it for much less than you might get if you had more time.

A third measure of the money supply, **M3,** includes everything that is in M2 (and thus in M1) plus large-denomination savings accounts (more than $100,000) and institutional money market mutual funds. M3 is nearly as liquid as M2. In late 2003, M3 totaled $8.7 trillion.

Table 28.2 provides a glossary of the financial assets used in the various definitions of money, and Figure 28.5 shows the relative magnitude of M1, M2, and M3.

MONEY AND CREDIT

One of the key properties of money, as noted, is that it is the medium of exchange. However, many transactions today are completed without any of the elements of the money supply presented in M1, M2, or M3. They involve credit, not money. In selling a suit of clothes or a piece of furniture or a car, stores often do not receive money. Rather, they receive a promise from you to pay money in the future. Credit is clearly tied to money; what you owe the store is measured in dollars. You want something today, and you will have the money for it tomorrow. The store wants you to buy today and is willing to wait until tomorrow or next week for the money. There is a mutually advantageous trade. But because the exchange is not *simultaneous,* the store must rely on your promise.

Promises, the saying goes, are made to be broken. But if they are broken too often, stores will not be able to trust buyers, and credit exchanges will not occur. There is therefore an incentive for the development of institutions, such as banks, that can ascertain who is most likely to keep economic promises and can help ensure that such promises are kept once they have been made.

When banks are involved, the store does not need to believe the word of the shopper. Rather, the shopper must convince the bank that he will in fact pay. Consider a car purchase. Suppose the bank agrees to give Todd a loan, and he then buys the car. If he later breaks his promise and does not pay back the loan, the car dealer is protected. It is the bank that tries to force Todd to keep his commitment. Ultimately, the bank may repossess the car and sell it to recover the money it lent to Todd.

Modern economies have relied increasingly on credit as a basis of transactions. Banks have a long tradition of extending *lines of credit* to firms—that is, agreeing to lend money to a business automatically (up to some limit) as it is needed. As Visa and MasterCard and the variety of other national credit cards came into widespread use in the 1970s and 1980s, lines of credit also were extended to millions of consumers, who now can purchase goods even when they lack the currency or checking account balances to cover the price. Today, many can also get credit based on the equity in their homes (the difference between the value of the house and what they owe on their mortgage, which is the loan taken out to buy the house). This type of credit is called a *home equity loan.* When house prices increased rapidly in the 1980s and again in the 1990s, millions of home owners gained access to a ready source of credit.

Table 28.2

GLOSSARY OF FINANCIAL TERMS

One of the problems in defining money is the wide variety of assets that are not directly used as a medium of exchange but can be readily converted into something that *could* be so used. Should they be included in the money supply? There is no right or wrong answer. Below are definitions of eight terms, some of which have been introduced already. Each of these assets serves, in progressively less satisfactory ways, the function of money.

Currency	One, five, ten, twenty, and hundred dollar bills; pennies, nickels dimes, quarters, and half dollars.	**Certificates of deposit**	Money deposited in the bank for a fixed period of time (usually six months to five years), with a penalty for early withdrawal.
Traveler's checks	Checks issued by a bank or a firm such as American Express that you can convert into currency upon demand and are widely accepted.	**Money market accounts**	Another category of interest-bearing bank checking accounts, often paying higher interest rates but with restrictions on the number of checks that can be written.
Demand deposits, or checking accounts	Deposits that you can withdraw upon demand (that is, convert into currency upon demand), by writing a check.	**Money market mutual funds**	Mutual funds that invest in Treasury bills, certificates of deposit, and similar safe securities. You can usually write checks against such accounts.
Savings deposits	Deposits that technically you can withdraw only upon notice; in practice, banks allow withdrawal upon a demand (without notice).	**Eurodollars**	U.S. dollar bank accounts in banks outside the United States (mainly in Europe).

These innovations make it easier for people to obtain credit. But they also have changed how economists think about the role of money in the economy—blurring definitions that once seemed quite clear.

Case in Point

"BOGGS BILLS" AND THE MEANING OF MONEY

J. S. G. Boggs is an artist who explores the social meaning of money. He starts by drawing one side of a banknote, completely accurate except for some crucial details. The bill might say "In God We Rust" instead of "In God We Trust."

With the Boggs bill in hand, the artist sees if someone will accept it at face value in payment for actual goods or services. For example, he might offer a restaurant a $20 Boggs bill in exchange for a meal. If the restaurant accepts the bill and provides any change, Boggs notes the details of the transaction on the bill before turning it over. Boggs then sells the receipt and the change. An art dealer might purchase the receipt and change and then track down the restaurant and try to buy the Boggs bill. The dealer then resells the bill, the receipt, and the change. One such "transaction" sold for $420,000! The British Museum, the Museum of Modern Art, and the Smithsonian are among the museums holding Boggs transaction pieces in their permanent collections.

Boggs bills illustrate the social nature of fiat money—anything can serve as money if others are willing to accept it as money. As Boggs puts it, "Nobody knows what a dollar is, what the word means, what holds the thing up, what it stands in for. And that's also what my work is about. Look at these things, I try to say. They're beautiful. But what the hell are they? What do they do? How do they do it?"

The Secret Service has taken a dim view of Boggs's efforts and has taken him to court. In its 1998 ruling against the artist, the U.S. Court of Appeals for the District of Columbia stated, "Art is supposed to imitate life, but when the subject matter is money, if it imitates life too closely it becomes counterfeiting."

THE MONEY SUPPLY AND THE BANK'S BALANCE SHEET

The banking system's role in the economy is critical because demand deposits are an important component of the money stock, representing almost 50 percent of M1. An understanding of what determines the money stock in a modern economy begins

Thinking Like an Economist
EXCHANGE, MONEY, AND THE INTERNET

Imagine how difficult it would be to organize exchange without money. As individuals, we probably think about the value of money in terms of the wealth it represents. The cash we carry in our pockets has no intrinsic value—we cannot eat it, for instance—but it does represent value, because it can be exchanged for things that are of direct utility to us: food, clothing, housing, and the thousands of goods and services we consume.

An economist naturally thinks of the benefits that are gained from voluntary exchange, and so thinks of the social benefits that money provides by reducing the costs of exchanging goods and services. The music store employee does not have to accept compact discs (CDs) for wages and then find a landlord who is willing to rent an apartment for CDs. Instead, wages are paid in money, and the landlord is happy to take money for rent, knowing that she can use the money to purchase the goods and services she wants. Thus, the role of money in helping to carry out transactions cheaply and efficiently is the most important service it provides.

The classic problem faced by barter systems—the need to find someone who has what you want and wants what you have—may be reduced by the ability of the Internet to match sellers and buyers. A number of companies have set up Web sites that arrange barter transactions. Yet even with the information-processing capabilities of the Internet, these barter Web sites still rely on a form of money. Barter Systems, Inc. (www.bartersys.com) is typical. A seller receives "trade dollars," which then can be used to make purchases from other sellers. U.S. dollars are not used, but trade dollars serve just like a local currency to avoid the requirement of double coincidence of wants that makes barter inefficient.

Table 28.3

AMERICABANK BALANCE SHEET

Assets		Liabilities	
Loans outstanding	$28 million	Deposits	$30 million
Government bonds	$ 2 million		
Reserves	$ 3 million	Net worth	$ 3 million
Total	$33 million	Total	$33 million

with a look at the assets and liabilities of a typical bank. One convenient way to look at the assets and liabilities of a bank (or a firm or individual, for that matter) is to organize them in what is known as a *balance sheet*. A balance sheet simply lists all the assets of the bank in one column and the liabilities in a second column.

The assets of the bank are what the bank owns, including what is owed to it by others. Since the loans that the bank has made represent funds that the borrowers owe the bank, loans are listed as assets on the bank's balance sheet. Liabilities are what the bank owes to others. We can think of the bank's depositors as having lent money to the bank. That is why deposits are treated by the bank as liabilities.

Table 28.3 shows the balance sheet of a typical bank that we will call AmericaBank. Its assets are divided into three categories: loans outstanding, government bonds, and reserves. Reserves are the deposits the bank has not used to make loans or buy government bonds. The cash a bank keeps in its vault to meet daily business needs is one part of its reserves. Another part is kept in an account elsewhere. In the United States, the Federal Reserve acts as a bank for banks, and private banks that are members of the Federal Reserve System can have accounts with the Fed. The bank's riskiest assets are its loans outstanding. These consist of loans to business firms, real estate loans (mortgages), car loans, house-remodeling loans, and so on. Government bonds are more secure than loans to households or firms, and banks typically concentrate their holdings in Treasury bills (or T-bills)—short-term bonds maturing in thirty, sixty, or ninety days after their date of issue.[3] Most secure are the reserves that are held on deposit at the local Federal Reserve bank and the cash in the vault.

The amount of money that people need to set aside for emergencies depends (in part) on how easily they can borrow. The same is true for banks. If they can borrow easily from other banks to meet any shortfall, they need to keep very little in their reserves. In the United States, the Federal Reserve banks act as the banker's bank, lending money to other banks. (Banks do not, however, have an automatic right to borrow; the Fed must concur with the request. Many central banks use this discretionary power to steer private banks' behavior.) But unlike individuals, banks are

---

[3]Long-term bonds are volatile in price, because their price changes with changes in interest rates. By instead holding short-term government bonds, the banks avoid risk, since price changes are much less likely over relatively short periods of time.

Table 28.4

REQUIRED RESERVES

Bank deposits and type	Minimum reserve required (percentage of deposits)
Checking accounts at banks with more than $46.5 million in deposits	10
Checking accounts at banks with less than $46.5 million in deposits	3
All other deposits	0

SOURCE: *Federal Reserve Bulletin* (1999).

required to hold reserves, at levels imposed by the Fed. Today, the amount of reserves they hold is dictated more by regulations than by the banks' own perceptions of what is prudent. After all, holding T-bills is just as safe as holding reserves with the Fed—and yields higher returns. And the level of reserves required by the Fed is designed primarily with an eye not to maximizing their profit but to controlling the money supply and thereby the level of economic activity. Table 28.4 shows the current reserve requirements. This system of banking, in which banks hold a fraction of the amount on deposit in reserves, is called a **fractional reserve system.**

The liability side of AmericaBank's balance sheet consists of two items: deposits and net worth. Deposits include checking accounts, which are technically known as *demand deposits,* and a variety of forms of savings accounts, which are technically known as *time deposits.* The bank's net worth is simply the difference between the value of its assets and the value of its liabilities. In other words, if the bank's assets were sold and its depositors paid off, what remained would equal the net worth of the bank. By including net worth in the column for liabilities, we ensure that the numbers on both sides of the balance sheet always balance when we add up each column.

HOW BANKS CREATE MONEY

As we have seen, the currency manufactured by the Treasury is a relatively small part of the money supply. The rest of the money is created by banks. To understand this process, let us consider all 9,500 U.S. banks as one huge superbank. Now suppose that a multibillionaire deposits $1 billion in currency into her account with this superbank.

The bank knows it must keep enough funds to satisfy the reserve requirement set by the Fed. Currently, the Fed requires that reserves be 10 percent of demand deposits, so its reserve-to-deposit ratio must be 1 to 10. The bank also has a long line of loan applicants. When the bank makes a loan, it does not actually give the borrower currency. It credits him with funds in his checking account. It does this by

e-Insight
ELECTRONIC CASH

A TV ad shows a thirsty older gentleman who finds himself short of change for a soda trying to steal coins out of a fountain, while a young girl points her cellular phone at the same machine and retrieves a drink. The message? Cash is for old folks.

Cold, hard cash is becoming a rarity in the United States. Americans increasingly rely on credit cards and ATM cards for all but the smallest transactions. Credit card purchases are often an easy, if expensive, method of taking out a consumer loan. But even consumers who pay off their balances every month enjoy the convenience of using cards instead of cash. They get complete records of their purchases every month, they do not have to write checks for recurring bills, and they can collect such benefits as air miles for their purchases. Such consumers choose automatic credit card payment for their phone bills, magazine subscriptions, and even their medical and dental bills. Cash is reserved for occasional purchases of small items at convenience stores. Soon even these "microtransactions" that still require cash may be taken over by electronic payment options.

Electronic cash cards are plastic "smart cards" that resemble the phone cards now widely used for long-distance calls. They contain microchips that enable users to transfer money from bank accounts to the cards at special ATMs or phones. The cards can then be used to make purchases at participating merchants. The purchases take place almost instantly, because, unlike credit card and ATM transactions, they do not require authorization over a phone line or verification of a password. Merchants are eager for this technology, as authorization charges and password verification are expensive (an expense that explains the minimum purchase requirements for credit card or ATM card transactions in some stores). In a world of e-cash, consumers will never need to worry about minimum purchase requirements or about having the right change for a bus or a vending machine. The microchip in their e-cash card will communicate with the microchip at a store or vending machine, and once the chips determine that there are no security issues, the transaction is complete.

For further discussion of the future of cash, see Kevin P. Sheehan, "Electronic Cash," *FDIC Banking Review* 11, no. 2 (1998): 1–8.

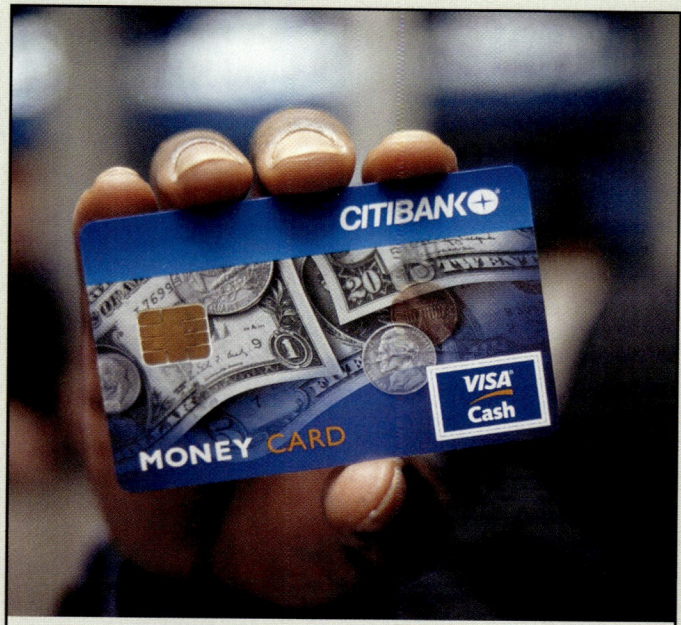

Money cards are now used to buy a wide variety of goods at all sorts of retail stores.

placing an entry into its books on both the left- and right-hand side of the balance sheet; there is a loan on the asset side and a deposit on the liabilities side. With the initial deposit of currency of $1 billion by the billionaire, the bank can make $9 billion worth of loans. If it lends $9 billion, its liabilities will have gone up by $10 billion (the $1 billion in currency originally deposited by the billionaire plus the $9 billion in new deposits that result from the new loans). On the asset side, the bank takes the $1 billion in currency to the Fed and is credited with the amount, so it now has $1 billion in reserves. Because its reserves have increased by $1 billion and its deposits by $10 billion, it has satisfied the 10 percent reserve requirement. The bank also has $9 billion in loans, so its assets have gone up by $10 billion, the $1 billion in reserves and the $9 billion in loans.

This relationship between the change in reserves and the final change in deposits is called the **money multiplier.** We can reach the same conclusion by a slower route, as shown in Table 28.5.

Money Multipliers with Many Banks The money multiplier works just as well when more than one bank is involved. Assume our billionaire deposits $1 billion in currency with BankNational, which then, after setting aside 10 percent to meet its reserve requirement, lends $900 million to Desktop Publishing. Desktop Publishing then orders equipment from ComputerAmerica, which banks with BankUSA. When Desktop Publishing writes a check for $900 million to ComputerAmerica, $900 million is transferred from BankNational to BankUSA. Once that $900 million has been transferred, BankUSA will find that it can lend more than it could previously. Out of the $900 million increase in deposits, it must set aside 10 percent, or $90 million, to satisfy the reserve requirement, but it can then lend out the rest, or $0.9 \times \$900 = \$810$ million. Suppose it lends the $810 million to the NewTelephone Company, which uses the money to buy a machine from Equipment Manufacturing. If Equipment Manufacturing promptly deposits its payment into its bank account at BankIllinois, then BankIllinois will find that its deposits have increased by $810 million; it therefore can lend $0.9 \times \$810 = \$729$ million after meeting the 10 percent reserve requirement. In this example, total deposits have increased by $1 billion plus $900 million $810 million plus $729 million, or $3.439 billion. But this is not the end of the process. As each bank receives a deposit, it will increase its lending. The process will continue until the new equilibrium is identical to the one described earlier in the superbank example, with a $10 billion increase in deposits. The banking system as a whole will have expanded the money supply by a multiple of the initial deposit, equal to 1/(reserve requirement).

In this example, there were no "leakages" outside the banking system. That is, no one decided to hold currency rather than put the money back into a bank, and sellers put all that they received into their bank after being paid. With leakages, the increase in deposits and thus the increase in the money supply will be smaller. In the real world these leakages are large. After all, currency held by the public amounts to almost 50 percent of M1. The ratio of M1 to currency plus reserves held by the banking system is under 3, and even for M2 the ratio is less than 10. Nevertheless, the increase in bank reserves will lead to an increase in the money supply by some multiple.

When there are many banks, individual banks may not even be aware of the role they play in this process of expanding the money supply. All they see is that their deposits have increased and therefore they are able to make more loans.

The creation of multiple deposits may seem somewhat like a magician's trick of pulling rabbits out of a hat; it appears to make something out of nothing. But it is, in

Table 28.5

SUPERBANK BALANCE SHEET

Before-deposit equilibrium

Assets		Liabilities	
Loans outstanding	$ 91 billion	Deposits	$100 billion
Government bonds	2 billion		
Reserves	10 billion	Net worth	3 billion
Total	103 billion	Total	103 billion

First round
(Add $1 billion deposits, $0.9 billion loans)

Assets		Liabilities	
Loans outstanding	$91.9 billion	Deposits	$101 billion
Government bonds	2 billion		
Reserves	10.1 billion	Net worth	3 billion
Total	104 billion	Total	104 billion

Second round
(Add $0.9 billion deposits, $0.81 billion loans to previous round[a])

Assets		Liabilities	
Loans outstanding	$92.71 billion	Deposits	$101.9 billion
Government bonds	2 billion		
Reserves	10.19 billion	Net worth	3 billion
Total	104.9 billion	Total	104.9 billion

Third round
(Add $0.81 billion deposits, $0.73 billion loans to previous round[a])

Assets		Liabilities	
Loans outstanding	$ 93.44 billion	Deposits	$102.71 billion
Government bonds	2 billion		
Reserves	10.27 billion	Net worth	3 billion
Total	105.71 billion	Total	105.71 billion

After-deposit equilibrium
(Add $10 billion new deposits, $9 billion new loans to original equilibrium)

Assets		Liabilities	
Loans outstanding	$100 billion	Deposits	$110 billion
Government bonds	2 billion		
Reserves	11 billion	Net worth	3 billion
Total	113 billion	Total	113 billion

[a]In each subsequent round, new deposits equal new loans of the previous round; new loans equal 0.9 × new deposits.

fact, a process with a physical trail. Deposits are created by making entries in records; today, electronic impulses create these records in computer files. The rules of deposit creation, which specify when certain entries can be made in these files—in particular, the fractional reserve requirements—also give rise to the system's ability to expand deposits by a multiple of the original deposit increase.

The money multiplier provides the link between the quantity of reserves in the banking system and the quantity of money. However, we have not yet explained where reserves come from. What determines the quantity of reserves, and therefore the money supply? To answer this question, we need to look more closely at the behavior of banks and the behavior of the Federal Reserve.

Wrap-Up

MONEY MULTIPLIER

An increase in reserves leads to an increase in total deposits by a multiple of the original increase.

If the reserve requirement is r percent, the maximum increase in deposits will be $1/r$ times any increase in reserves.

The Federal Reserve

We have already learned that the Federal Reserve serves as a bank for banks and that it sets the reserve requirement that determines the money multiplier. But the Fed's role in the economy extends much further. Federal Reserve decisions affect the level of reserves in the banking system, the money supply, and the rate of inflation. Learning about the tools the Fed can use and how they affect the supply of money is important for understanding the behavior of money and prices.

Our focus remains on the economy at full employment. As we will see in Part Seven, when the economy experiences fluctuations that lead to cyclical unemployment, the Federal Reserve plays an important stabilizing role. Like most central banks in the major industrial economies, the Fed has, in recent years, used its policy tools to influence the level of market interest rates rather than attempting to control the supply of money. Chapter 32 discusses how that influence is wielded.

The Federal Reserve is the **central bank** of the United States. A *central bank* is the government bank that oversees and monitors the rest of the banking system, serves as a bank for banks, and is responsible for the conduct of monetary policy. In Canada, the Bank of Canada is the central bank; in the United Kingdom it is the Bank of England; in the twelve-member European Economic and Monetary Union, it is the European Central Bank; and in Mexico, it is Banco de Mexico. A nation's central bank often functions largely to regulate commercial banks. The Fed's most important role, in contrast, arises from its responsibility for the conduct of monetary policy and the influence it has on the level of nominal interest rates and the supply of money.

The Federal Reserve was created by an act of Congress in 1913. In other countries, the central bank is a purely governmental institution, similar to the U.S. Treasury or the Environmental Protection Agency. When Congress set up the United States' central bank, however, it established a unique hybrid with both public and private aspects. The Federal Reserve is overseen by a seven-member Board of Governors in Washington, D.C. Governors are appointed to fourteen-year terms (although the average length of service is about seven years) by the president, subject to confirmation by the Senate. The president appoints one of the governors to serve as chair (also subject to Senate confirmation); the chair serves for four years and can be reappointed. From 1987 to 2005, the chair was Alan Greenspan, who was originally appointed by President Ronald Reagan and was reappointed by Presidents George H. W. Bush, Bill Clinton, and George W. Bush. Because the Fed chair plays a critical role in setting U.S. monetary policy, the chair is often described as the second most powerful person in the United States.

In addition to the Federal Reserve Board, the 1913 Federal Reserve Act established twelve regional Federal Reserve banks; their location is shown in Figure 28.6. These banks are officially "owned" by the private commercial banks that are members of the Federal Reserve System (about 3,700 member banks in total). The directors of each regional Federal Reserve bank are appointed by the member banks and by the governors of the Federal Reserve Board. These directors, in turn, choose the presidents of the regional Federal Reserve banks.

The Federal Reserve Board of Governors in Washington, D.C., and the regional Federal Reserve banks collectively form the *Federal Reserve System*. The structure

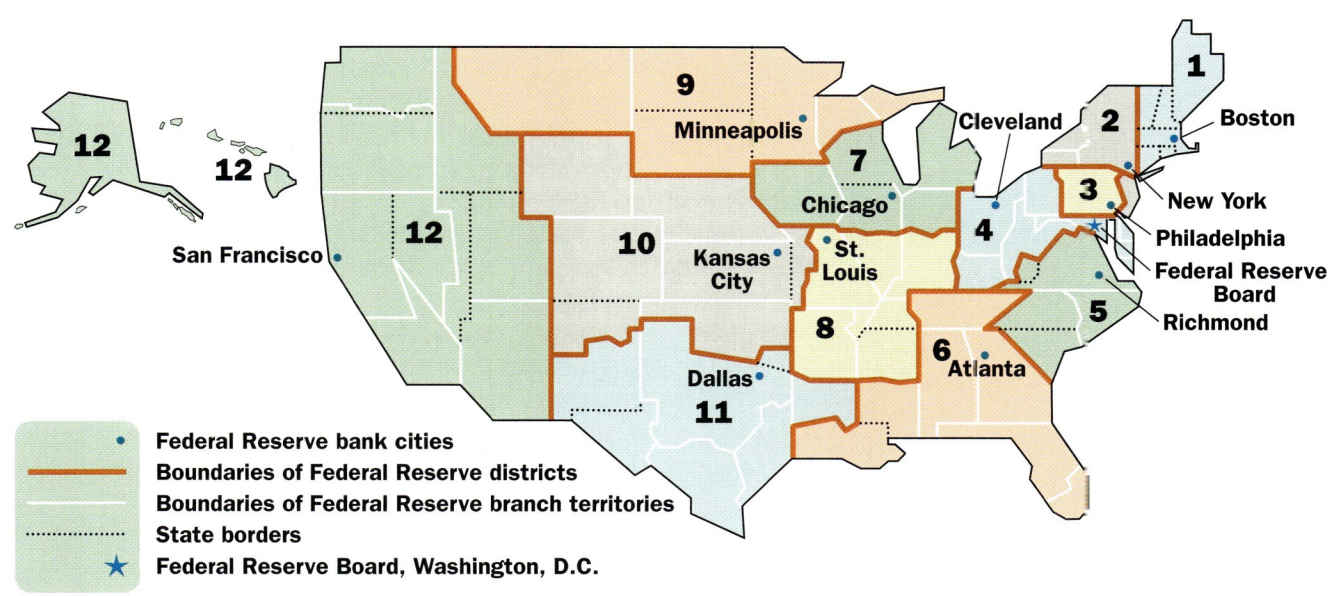

Figure 28.6 The nation is divided into twelve Federal Reserve districts.

FEDERAL RESERVE DISTRICTS

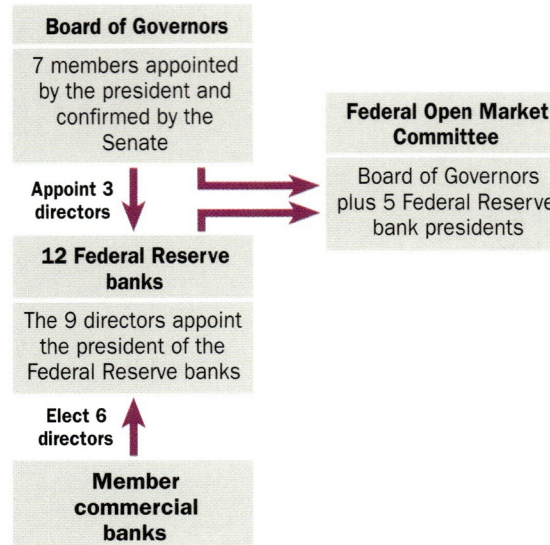

Figure 28.7

THE STRUCTURE OF THE FEDERAL RESERVE

The Federal Reserve operates at both a national level and a district level. The president appoints the Board of Governors; the district level includes some directors appointed nationally and some from within the district; and the Federal Open Market Committee includes the governors, appointed by the president, and representatives from the district banks.

of the Federal Reserve System is depicted in Figure 28.7. The **Federal Open Market Committee,** or **FOMC,** is responsible for making monetary policy. The name of the FOMC comes from the way the committee operates. The Fed engages in **open market operations**—so called because (as discussed in more detail below) they involve the Fed's entering the capital market directly, much as a private individual or firm would, to buy or sell government bonds. Once the FOMC has set its policy targets, its operations are carried out by the Federal Reserve Bank of New York because that bank is closest to the huge capital markets in New York City.

The FOMC has twelve voting members. These include the governors appointed by the president and some of the regional bank presidents, who are appointed, in part, by private member banks. The seven governors of the Federal Reserve are all voting members of the FOMC, as is the president of the Federal Reserve Bank of New York. The remaining four votes rotate among the other eleven presidents of the regional Federal Reserve banks.

HOW THE FED AFFECTS THE MONEY SUPPLY

Earlier, we said that the money supply depends on the level of bank reserves in the economy. Thus, by controlling the level of reserves, the Fed can affect the money supply. It uses three different policy tools: open market operations, the discount rate, and reserve requirements. Because open market operations are by far the most important of these tools, we will begin by describing what they are and how they affect the level of bank reserves.

Open Market Operations The Fed alters the stock of bank reserves through the use of open market operations during which it buys or sells financial assets, normally government securities. Imagine that the Fed buys $1 million of government bonds from a government bond dealer. The dealer deposits the Fed's $1 million check in its bank, AmericaBank, which credits the dealer's account for $1 million. (These transactions are in fact all electronic.) AmericaBank presents the check to the Fed, which credits the bank's reserve account with $1 million. AmericaBank now has the bond dealer's $1 million of new deposits on its books, matched by $1 million in new reserves; accordingly, it can lend out an additional $900,000, holding the remaining $100,000 to meet its 10 percent reserve requirement. As we saw earlier, the money multiplier then goes to work, and the total expansion of the money supply will be equal to a multiple of the initial $1 million in deposits. And credit—the amount of outstanding loans—will also increase by a multiple of the initial increase in deposits.

The purchase of the same bonds by a private citizen, Jane White, has quite a different effect. In this case, the dealer's deposit account goes up by $1 million but Jane's account goes down by $1 million. As a consequence, the dealer's bank gains $1 million in funds but Jane's bank loses $1 million in funds. The total funds available in the banking system as a whole remain unchanged. The money multiplier goes to work only when "outside" funds, in particular those from the Federal Reserve, are used for the bonds.

The process works in reverse when the Federal Reserve sells some of the government securities it holds. If the Fed sells $1 million to a bond dealer, the dealer pays with a check drawn against its account at its bank, NationalBank. The Fed presents the check for payment to NationalBank and deducts $1 million from NationalBank's reserve account. The total amount of reserves in the banking system has been reduced by $1 million. This change in reserves then has a multiplied impact in reducing the money supply and bank credit.

The **Open Market Desk** at the New York Federal Reserve Bank conducts the Fed's open market operations. But you might be wondering where the Fed gets the money to purchase government securities in the first place, especially since purchases (or sales) on a given day might amount to more than $1 billion rather than the $1 million of our example. When the Fed credited AmericaBank's reserve account for $1 million to settle the check it had used to purchase bonds, the Fed simply made an electronic entry in its bookkeeping system. In effect, it created the $1 million in reserves out of thin air! And when it sold government bonds and deducted $1 million from NationalBank's account, the reserves were simply gone.

Discount Rate Changes The Federal Reserve has another tool it can use to affect the level of reserves. Banks can obtain reserves by borrowing them from the Federal Reserve, which lends at an interest rate called the **discount rate.** By altering it, the Fed can influence how much banks borrow. When the Fed increases the discount rate, banks find borrowing reserves more expensive; they therefore borrow less and the total level of reserves in the banking system falls. If the Fed lowers the discount rate, banks will borrow more and the total level of reserves will rise. The discount rate is the only interest rate directly set by the Fed; all others are set in the market, by the forces of supply and demand.

Internet Connection

THE FEDERAL RESERVE BANKS AND INTERNATIONAL CENTRAL BANKS

Each of the regional Federal Reserve banks maintains a Web site that contains a variety of useful information related to monetary policy and general economic conditions. The Web site of the Board of Governors of the Federal Reserve System provides links to all the regional banks at www.federalreserve.gov.

The Bank for International Settlements in Basel, Switzerland, lists links to ninety-six central banks in countries around the world, from Albania to Zimbabwe. These can be found at www.bis.org/cbanks.htm.

Reserve Requirements Finally, the Fed establishes how much banks must hold as reserves. The reserve requirements are its third tool. If the Fed increases reserve requirements, banks must set aside a larger fraction of their deposits as reserves and thus can lend out less. A rise in the reserve requirement reduces the money multiplier and reduces the impact that a change in the level of reserves has on the money supply. A reduction in the reserve requirement increases the money multiplier and increases the effects of a dollar change in reserves on the money supply.

Wrap-Up

INSTRUMENTS OF MONETARY POLICY

1. Reserve requirements—the required ratio of reserves to deposits. The Fed can change the amount banks must hold as reserves. Increasing the reserve ratio forces banks to hold a larger fraction of deposits as reserves.
2. Discount rate—the rate that the Fed charges member banks on borrowed reserves. An increase in the discount rate raises the opportunity cost of borrowing from the Fed. As a result, banks reduce their borrowing and total reserve supply falls.
3. Open market operations—purchases and sales of Treasury bills by the Fed. When the Fed buys government bonds from the public, the stock of reserves is increased. When the Fed sells government bonds to the public, the stock of reserves falls.

Selecting the Appropriate Tool Of its three tools, the Federal Reserve uses open market operations most frequently. The effects of changes in the discount rate and in reserve requirements are inexact compared with the fine-tuning that open market operations make possible. Thus, the former are used infrequently, primarily to announce major shifts in monetary policy. Such changes can be quite effective in signaling the advent of tighter conditions (that is, higher interest rates and reduced credit availability) or looser conditions (that is, the reverse). Banks foreseeing a tightening of credit may cut back on their lending and firms may postpone their planned investment.

The Stability of the U.S. Banking System

The fractional reserve system explains how banks create money. It also explains how, without the Fed, banks can get into trouble. Well-managed banks, even before the establishment of the Fed and its reserve requirements, kept reserves equal to some average expectation of day-to-day needs. A bank could soon face disaster if one day's needs exceeded its reserves.

If (for good reasons or bad) many depositors lose confidence in a bank at the same time, they will attempt to withdraw their funds all at once. The bank simply will not have the money available, since most of it will have gone out in loans that cannot be called in instantaneously. This situation is called a *bank run*. Bank runs were as common in nineteenth-century America as they were in the old western movies, which often depicted customers in a small town lining up at the bank while it paid out what reserves it had on a first-come, first-served basis until nothing was left. Such a run could quickly drive even a healthy bank out of business. If a rumor spread that a bank was in trouble and a few savers ran to the bank to clean out their accounts, then other investors would feel they were foolish not to rush to the bank themselves and withdraw their deposits. One vicious rumor could result in a healthy bank shutting down, and the panic could set off a run on other banks, thus destabilizing the banking system and the whole economy.

REDUCING THE THREAT OF BANK RUNS

Bank runs and panics have periodically afflicted the American banking system. In fact, one reason the Fed was set up in 1913 was to make them less likely. The last major panic occurred in the midst of the Great Depression in 1933. Since then, the modern banking system has evolved a variety of safeguards that have ended the threat of bank runs for most banks. There are four levels of protection.

First, the Fed acts as a "lender of last resort." If a bank faces a run, it can turn to the Fed to borrow funds to tide it over. The certainty that the bank can meet its obligations means, of course, that there is no need for anyone to run to the bank. The Fed lends money when a bank faces a liquidity problem: that is, it has a temporary shortage of funds, but its assets still exceed its liabilities. It is, in other words, solvent. The objective of the next two measures is to reduce the likelihood that banks face problems of illiquidity or insolvency.

Second, the Fed sets reserve requirements. Even bank executives who might like to live recklessly, getting along on minimal reserves, are unable to do so.

The third level of protection is provided by the owners of the bank. Most banks are started by investors who put up a certain amount of money in exchange for a share of ownership. The net worth of the firm—the difference between the bank's assets and its liabilities—is this initial investment, augmented or decreased over time by the bank's profits or losses. If the bank makes bad investment decisions, then these shareholders can be forced to bear the cost. This cushion provided by shareholders not only protects depositors but also encourages the bank to be more prudent in its loans. If the bank makes bad loans, the owners risk their entire investment. But if the owners' net worth in the bank is too small, the owners may see themselves in a "Heads I win, tails you lose" situation. If risky investments turn out well, the extra profits accrue to the bank; if they turn out badly and the bank goes bankrupt, the owners lose little because they have little at stake. To protect against this danger, the government requires banks to maintain certain ratios of net worth to deposits. These are called *capital requirements*. Capital requirements protect against insolvency; they ensure that if the bank invests badly and many of its loans default, the bank will still be able to pay back depositors. (By contrast, reserves and the ability to borrow from the Fed protect against illiquidity; they ensure that if depositors want cash, they can get it.) On occasion a bank will make so many bad loans that its net worth shrinks to the point at which it can no longer satisfy the capital requirements.

As a fourth and final backstop, the government introduced the Federal Deposit Insurance Corporation (FDIC) in 1933. Since then, federal banks and savings and loans have had to purchase insurance, which guarantees that depositors can get all their money back, up to $100,000 per account. Because deposits are secured by the federal government, depositors fearing the collapse of a bank have no need to rush to withdraw their money. The deposit insurance thus not only protects depositors but also enormously increases the stability of the banking system. Simply because it exists, the threat against which it insures is much less likely to occur. It is as if life insurance somehow prolonged life.

Deposit insurance has an offsetting disadvantage, however: depositors no longer have any incentive to monitor banks, to make sure that banks are investing their funds safely. Regardless of what the bank does, their funds are protected. Thus—to the extent that capital requirements fail to provide banks with appropriate incentives to make good loans—bank regulators must assume the full responsibility of ensuring the safety and soundness of banks.

Review and Practice

SUMMARY

1. In the long run, the full-employment model implies that money is neutral. Changes in the quantity of money affect the price level and the level of nominal wages but leave real output, real wages, and employment unaffected.
2. Money is anything that is generally accepted in a given society as a unit of account, a medium of exchange, and a store of value.
3. The Federal Reserve is the central bank of the United States. Its policy actions affect the level of reserves and the money supply.
4. There are many ways of measuring the money supply. The most common measures in the United States are M1, M2, and M3. All include currency and demand deposits (checking accounts); M2 and M3 also include assets that are close substitutes for currency and checking accounts.
5. Financial intermediaries, which include banks, savings and loan institutions, mutual funds, insurance companies, and others, all form the link between savers who have extra funds and borrowers who desire extra funds.
6. Government is involved with the banking industry for two reasons. First, by regulating the activities banks can undertake and by providing deposit insurance, government tries to protect depositors and ensure the stability of the financial system. Second, by influencing the willingness of banks to make loans, government attempts to influence the level of investment and overall economic activity.
7. By making loans, banks can create an increase in the supply of money that is a multiple of any initial increase in the bank's deposits. If every bank lends all the money it can and every dollar lent is spent to buy goods purchased from other firms that deposit the checks in their accounts, the money multiplier is 1 divided by the reserve requirement imposed by the Fed. In practice, the multiplier is considerably smaller.
8. The Federal Reserve can affect the level of reserves by changing the reserve requirement, by changing the discount rate, or by conducting open market operations.
9. The chief tool of the Fed is open market operations, which affect the supply of reserves.
10. The reserve requirement, capital requirements, the Fed's status as lender of last resort, and deposit insurance have made bank runs rare.

KEY TERMS

quantity equation of exchange
velocity
neutrality of money
unit of account
medium of exchange
store of value
money
demand deposits
M1
M2
M3
fractional reserve system
money multiplier
central bank
Federal Open Market Committee (FOMC)
open market operations
Open Market Desk
discount rate

REVIEW QUESTIONS

1. What is meant by "the neutrality of money"?
2. What is the name of the committee that sets monetary policy for the United States? Who are the members of this committee?
3. What are the three characteristics that define "money"?
4. What are the differences between M1, M2, and M3?
5. What are the three instruments of the Federal Reserve?
6. Why do reserves fall if the Fed engages in an open market sale? Why do they rise if the Fed engages in an open market purchase?
7. Why do borrowed reserves fall if the Fed raises the discount rate?

PROBLEMS

1. Identify which of money's three traits each of the following assets shares, and which trait each does not share:
   (a) A house
   (b) A day pass for an amusement park
   (c) Russian rubles held by a resident of Dallas, Texas
   (d) A painting
   (e) Gold
2. Why will only the price level and money wages be affected by a change in the money supply in the full-employment economy? How is the rate of inflation related to the rate of growth of the money supply?
3. Down Home Savings has the following assets and liabilities: $6 million in government bonds and reserves; $40 million in deposits; $36 million in outstanding loans. Draw up a balance sheet for the bank. What is its net worth?
4. While gardening in his backyard, Bob finds a mason jar containing $100,000 in currency. After he deposits the money in his bank, where the reserve requirement is 5 percent, by how much will the money supply eventually increase? Suppose Bob decides to keep $5,000 of his find as cash and deposits only $95,000 in his bank. By how much will the money supply increase?
5. Why is it that the money supply changes when the Fed sells government bonds to a bank but the money supply does not change if a large corporation sells government bonds to a bank?
6. In 1999, there was broad concern about the Y2K computer problem. Banks and the Fed predicted that many people would want to hold additional cash in case there were financial problems on January 1, 2000. Use the money multiplier analysis to predict what would happen to deposits and the money supply if people increased their holding of cash and the Fed kept total reserves fixed.

Part 7
MACROECONOMIC FLUCTUATIONS

Learning Goals

In this chapter, you will learn

1. The terms economists use to describe economic fluctuations
2. Why economies experience fluctuations in production and employment
3. The four key concepts that help economists analyze short-run fluctuations in output and employment

Chapter 29

INTRODUCTION TO MACROECONOMIC FLUCTUATIONS

Modern economies are dynamic economies—new products are constantly being introduced, old ones disappear, consumer demand shifts from one good to another, technological innovations lead to job losses in some sectors and the creation of new jobs in others. Most of the time, these developments have effects that are primarily microeconomic in nature (felt in individual industries, for example). But sometimes, major disruptions affect the entire economy. Thus, large swings in oil prices, increases or decreases in government spending or taxes, shifts in consumers' attitudes that cause households to alter overall spending and saving levels, or modifications in Federal Reserve policy can lead to macroeconomic changes reflected in overall levels of production, employment, and inflation. By understanding the impact these factors have on the economy, we will better understand why unemployment in the United States reached nearly 11 percent in November and December of 1982 and why it fell to 3.9 percent in April 2000, why real GDP actually declined in 2001, and why inflation was over 10 percent in 1979 and only 3 percent in 2004.

To make sense of these sorts of fluctuations in the economy, we need to shift our focus from the long-run perspective adopted in Part Six, which allowed all wages and prices time enough to adjust and ensure that markets cleared, to a short-run perspective, in which adjustments in wages and prices may be incomplete. While the theory of long-run macroeconomics offers important insights into the effects of fiscal deficits on interest rates and exchange rates, the impact of changes in the supply of labor on the economy, the sources of economic growth, and the use of monetary policy to control inflation, it does not explain the fluctuations in real economic activity and employment that also characterize market economies.

Over the long run, the economy has managed to create jobs to keep pace with the increasing number of workers. But we also learned in Chapter 22 that in a dynamic market economy, the unemployment rate is never zero. Some firms and industries are shrinking—jobs are being lost—at the same time that new jobs are being created. Workers voluntarily quit jobs to relocate or look for better positions. In the United States, analysts estimate that 8 to 10 percent of workers—more than 10 million people—change jobs each year. Unemployment also varies seasonally. We call these normal patterns in unemployment structural, frictional, and seasonal unemployment. But at times the unemployment rate becomes much higher than usual, as the economy experiences periods of slow job growth and rising unemployment. Labor markets seem not to clear—the demand for labor is less than the supply. At other times, unemployment drops to unusually low levels, plant and equipment operate at high rates of utilization, and the economy booms. We call the fluctuations of the unemployment rate around its normal level *cyclical unemployment.* These fluctuations in the economy are the primary focus of Part Seven.

The key to understanding cyclical unemployment is the recognition of two important "facts" about modern economies. First, prices and wages do not always adjust quickly. As a result, the demand for labor and the supply of labor will not always balance—the economy can depart from full employment. Second, wages and prices eventually do adjust in response to demand and supply, bringing markets—including the labor market—back into balance. Given enough time, wages will normally adjust to restore full employment, returning the economy to the long-run equilibrium we studied in Part Six.

In this and the next four chapters, we will examine how the economy behaves when prices and wages have not adjusted to balance demand and supply in the labor market. This study will enable us to understand what causes cyclical unemployment, why the economy experiences fluctuations, and how monetary and fiscal policy affect inflation and cyclical unemployment.

Economic Fluctuations

All industrialized market economies experience fluctuations in the general level of economic activity. Panel A of Figure 29.1 shows the fluctuations in U.S. GDP over the past forty years. A smooth trend line has been drawn through the data, tracing out a hypothetical path the economy would have taken had it grown uniformly throughout this forty-year period. This trend line provides an estimate of the path of potential output—what the economy would produce if full employment were always maintained. The economy is sometimes above the trend line and sometimes below. The shaded bars in the figure mark out economic **recessions,** or periods during which output declines significantly. Over the time period shown, there were seven recessions; the most recent was in 2001. Panel B shows the percentage by which the economy has been above or below the trend line. As discussed in Chapter 22, the percentage deviation between actual and potential GDP is called the **output gap;** when the output gap is negative, the economy experiences higher than normal unemployment as firms scale back production and workers lose jobs. When output rises above potential and the output gap is positive, unemployment drops to low levels as employment rises and the economy's capital stock is utilized intensively. The close (negative) relationship between the unemployment rate and the output gap is illustrated in the figure.

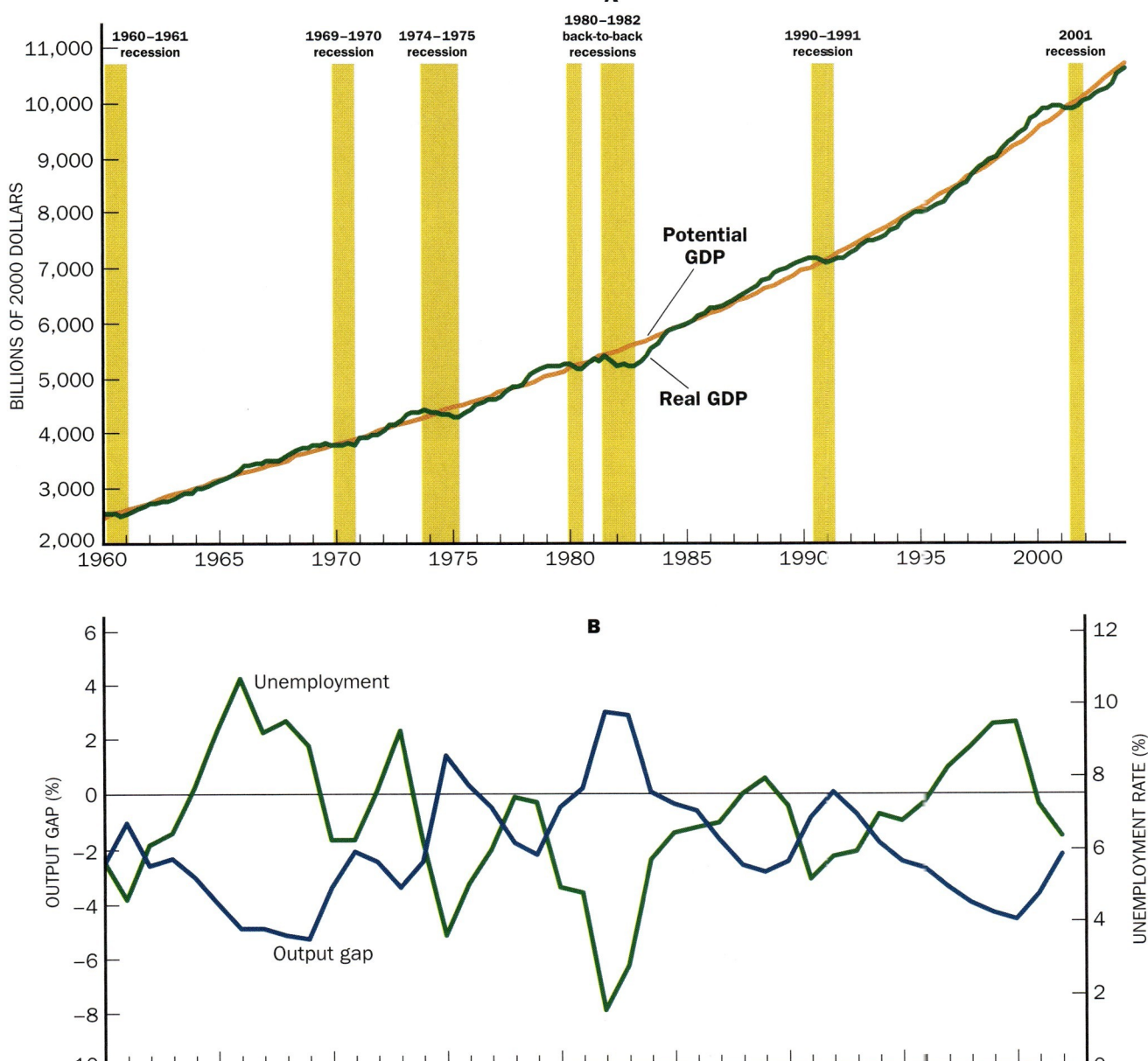

Figure 29.1

ECONOMIC FLUCTUATIONS: OUTPUT AND EMPLOYMENT

Panel A shows how real GDP from 1960 to 2003 has moved above and below potential GDP. Panel B compares the percentage deviations of GDP from potential (the output gap) with the unemployment rate. When the output gap is positive, unemployment tends to be low, and when the output gap is negative, unemployment tends to be high. The relation between the output gap and unemployment, as we learned in Chapter 22, is called Okun's Law.

SOURCES: *Economic Report of the President* (2004) and Congressional Budget Office, *The Budget and Economic Outlook* (January 2004).

ECONOMIC FLUCTUATIONS

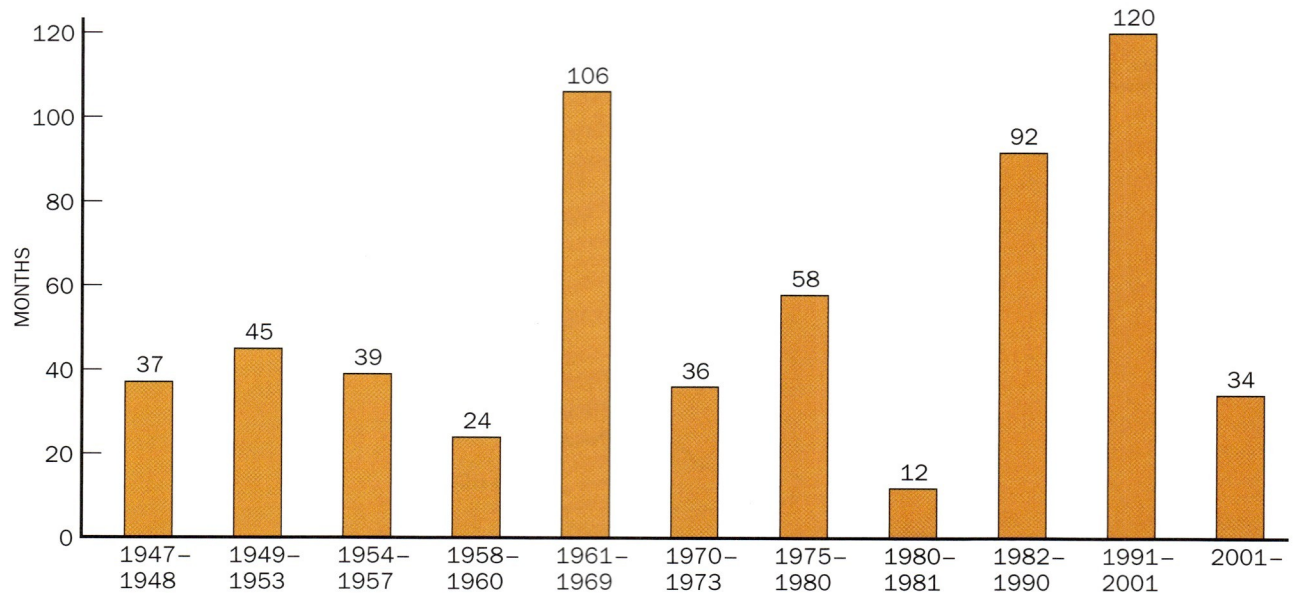

Figure 29.2

THE DURATION OF ECONOMIC EXPANSIONS

Over the past fifty-seven years, the duration of economic expansions has varied greatly. The average complete expansion has lasted 57 months; the shortest was 12 months, and the longest completed expansion was 120 months.

SOURCE: NBER Business Cycle Reference Dates (www.nber.org/cycles.html).

Since 1960, the unemployment rate has averaged just a little below 6 percent of the civilian labor force. But during recessions, it rises much higher. In 1982 and 1983, for example, the unemployment rate exceeded 9 percent for more than eighteen months. Perhaps the difference between 6 percent unemployment and 9 percent sounds small, but with a U.S. labor force numbering above 110 million at the time of the 1982 recession, those 3 percentage points translated into more than 3 million additional workers unemployed.

Economic **expansions** are periods in which output grows. Economists apply the terms **peaks** and **troughs,** respectively, to the points when the economy moves from an expansion to a recession and from a recession to a new period of economic expansion. A high point in output is a peak; a low point, a trough. These fluctuations in economic activity are called **business cycles,** which themselves differ in both length and severity. Since World War II, the length of time between recessions has varied significantly, as Figure 29.2 shows. The average duration of expansions since World War II has been 57 months; the shortest was 12 months, and the longest was 120 months (1991–2001).

Figure 29.3 provides a close-up of changes in real GDP since 1980. The four recessions that occurred during this twenty-five-year period can be seen clearly. The troughs were in 1980, 1982, 1991, and 2001, and the peaks were in 1981, 1990, and 2001. The expansion that peaked in 1981 was unusually short and weak, making the whole period from 1980 to 1982—a time associated with Federal Reserve Chairman Paul Volcker's actions to reduce inflation—one of weak economy growth. Since 1982, however, the United States has experienced more than 275 months of expansion, broken only by two brief recessions lasting only 8 months each: one in 1990–91 and the other in 2001.

Cyclical unemployment reflects unused labor resources. Periods of high unemployment also lead to idle factories and underutilized plant and equipment. There is a cost to the economy if its labor and capital resources are not fully employed. The output that could have been produced with these resources is the opportunity cost of cyclical unemployment.

Because of the potentially high costs, and the individual hardships, caused by high levels of cyclical unemployment, most governments attempt to manage macroeconomic policies to reduce its occurrence. In the United States, the Full Employment Act of 1946 and the Full Employment and Balanced Growth Act of 1978 (often called the Humphrey-Hawkins Act) reflect the commitment of the federal government to bear the responsibility for maintaining full employment. As noted in Chapter 21, the Humphrey-Hawkins Act mandates that the federal government "promote full employment and production, increased real income, balanced growth, a balanced Federal budget, adequate productivity growth, proper attention to national priorities, achievement of an improved trade balance, . . . and reasonable price stability." How governments try to achieve these goals and how successful their efforts have been are among the topics we will discuss in the next few chapters.

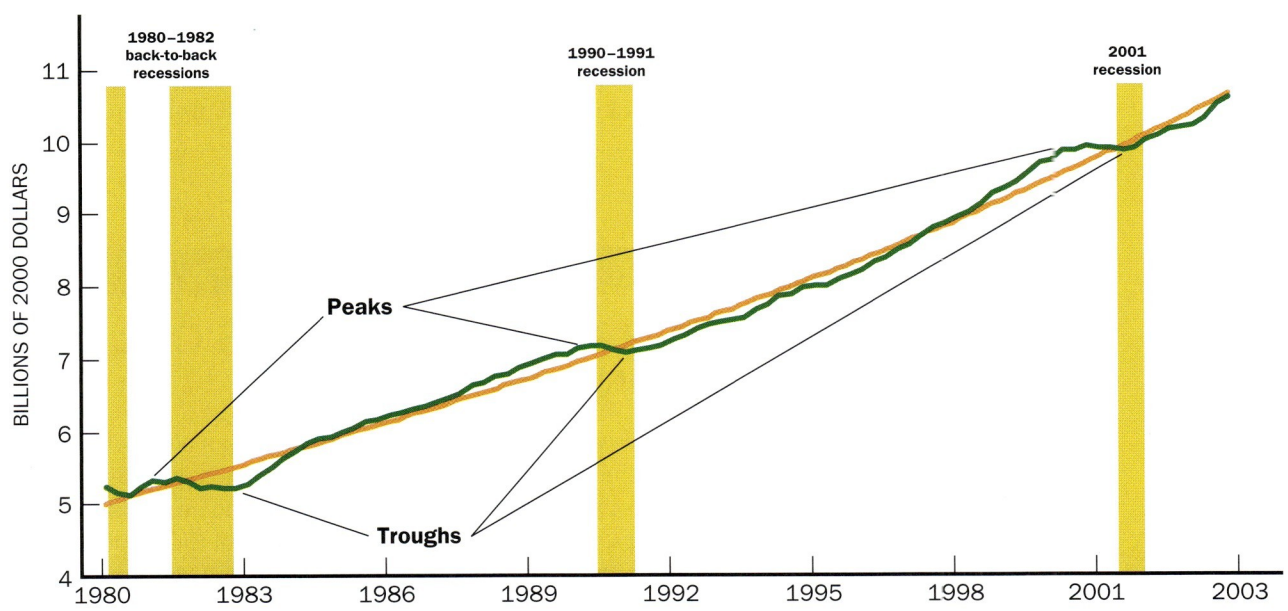

Figure 29.3

PEAKS AND TROUGHS SINCE 1980

There have been four economic recessions since 1980. After reaching a peak in January 1980, the economy entered a recession that lasted until July 1980, when the trough was reached. The next peak was in July 1981, making this the shortest expansion in U.S. history. The trough of the 1981–1982 recession came in November 1982. The economy then entered a long expansion, whose peak occurred in July 1990. The longest expansion on record lasted from the trough in July 1990 to the peak in March 2001. The recession of 2001 ended in November 2001.

SOURCE: NBER Business Cycle Reference Dates (www.nber.org/cycles.html).

Internet Connection

DATING BUSINESS CYCLE PEAKS AND TROUGHS

Almost all the data that economists use to study the economy are produced by the government. In the United States, the Department of Commerce and the Bureau of Labor Statistics within the Department of Labor collect much of the data economists use, such as the statistics on unemployment and GDP. The widely accepted dates for the peaks and troughs of business cycles, however, are determined by the members of the Business Cycle Dating Committee of the National Bureau of Economic Research (NBER), a private, nonprofit research organization. The NBER publishes business cycle dates going back to 1854; the entire list is available at the NBER's Web site (www.nber.org/cycles.html). The NBER defines a recession as "a recurring period of decline in total output, income, employment, and trade, usually lasting from six months to a year, and marked by widespread contractions in many sectors of the economy." In popular usage, the economy is usually considered to be in a recession if real GDP declines for two consecutive quarters.

Wrap-Up

ECONOMIC FLUCTUATIONS

Recessions: periods of significant decline in real GDP.

Expansions: periods of growth in real GDP.

Output gap: the deviation (a percentage) of observed real GDP from potential real GDP.

Case in Point

ESTIMATING THE OUTPUT COSTS OF A RECESSION

Recessions are periods when workers suffer from higher than normal levels of unemployment. By using the output gap and Okun's Law, economists have developed a way to estimate the opportunity cost of idle workers who are willing and able to work at the going wage. For example, Figure 29.1 shows that the output gap reached −8 percent during the 1982 recession. Since potential GDP in 1982 was approximately $5.2 trillion (in 2000 dollars), the cost of the recession in 1982 was about $420 billion (8 percent of $5.2 trillion) in lost income. The gap fell to only −3.2 percent in the recession of 1991; by then potential GDP had risen to $7.1 trillion, so a 3.2 percent shortfall represented a loss of $218 billion in 1991. These figures agree with most observers' view that the recession of 1982 was much more severe. Yet even a relatively mild recession is serious; to provide some perspective, in 1991 the total real value of expenditures by the federal government for all nondefense programs was only $183 billion.

Thinking Like an Economist
EMPLOYMENT FLUCTUATIONS AND TRADE-OFFS

We measure the cost of cyclical unemployment by the output that could have been produced if full employment had been maintained. This represents the *opportunity cost* to society of *cyclical* unemployment. Not all unemployment represents an opportunity cost, either to the individual worker or to society. A worker who voluntarily quits a job to look for another is classified as unemployed, but she must believe that the value of seeking a new job, one that either pays better or has other advantages over her old job, exceeds the temporary loss in wages. Time spent in job search can thus represent a productive use of time.

To measure the cost of employment fluctuations, we need to take into account the trade-offs that individuals face. For some, the value of time spent in leisure and other nonmarket activities (taking care of children, for example) is greater than the real wage that could be earned from working.

In Chapter 22 we learned that according to Okun's Law, the unemployment rate rises above the natural rate of unemployment level (the unemployment rate at full employment) by 1 percentage point for every 2 percentage points that the output gap shrinks. Using Okun's Law, we can translate an 8 percent output gap such as the United States experienced in the 1982 recession into an added 4 percentage points of unemployment. Since most estimates at the time placed the natural rate of unemployment at around 6 percent, the figure provided via Okun's Law (about 10 percent unemployment) is consistent with the actual 9.7 percent unemployment rate in 1982.

As a lingering result of the recession in 2001, the unemployment rate averaged 6.0 percent in 2002. Most estimates of the natural rate of unemployment for 2002 put it in the range of 5 to 5.5 percent. We can use this information, together with Okun's Law, to estimate the output cost of 2002's cyclical unemployment. For the purposes of this example, we will set the natural rate of unemployment at 5 percent.

Step 1: Cyclical unemployment is the difference between the actual unemployment rate (6 percent) and the rate estimated to correspond to full employment (5 percent), or 1 percent.

Step 2: Okun's Law tells us that the percentage gap between actual output and full-employment output is about twice the level of cyclical unemployment. So the lost output was roughly $2 \times 1 = 2$ percent of real GDP.

Step 3: In 2002, real GDP was $10 trillion. Thus $200 billion (2 percent of $10 trillion) is the value of the output lost as a result of cyclical unemployment that year.

Why Economies Experience Fluctuations

It is difficult to reconcile the economic fluctuations we observe, and the associated changes in unemployment, with the full-employment model. According to the full-employment model, the real wage—the nominal rate adjusted for the price level—always adjusts to ensure that the labor market clears: that is, labor demand and labor supply are equal. If, for whatever reason, the demand for labor were to fall, the real wage should simply decline to maintain full employment. In the real world, this rarely seems to happen. In the Great Depression of the 1930s, for example, when unemployment rose dramatically, real wages in the manufacturing sector for those who remained employed actually rose.[1] More recently, from 2000 to 2002, unemployment rose from 4 percent to 5.8 percent, yet real hourly earnings rose by 2.6 percent. Figure 29.4 shows little connection over the past forty years between the large fluctuations in the unemployment rate that the United States has experienced and movements in the real wage.

When the real wage fails to adjust in the face of a decline in the demand for labor, the labor market no longer clears: labor demand is less than labor supply. People are willing to work at the going wage, but the work is not there. Because firms demand fewer workers, they stop hiring and even lay off existing employees. As a result, unemployment rises.

Figure 29.5 illustrates what happens if there is a shift in the demand curve for labor with no corresponding fall in the real wage. The labor market is stuck in disequilibrium: demand does not equal supply. At the real wage w_0/P, the amount of labor that workers would like to supply remains L_0. But as the demand for labor shifts, the number of workers hired at w_0/P falls from L_0 to L_1. The difference,

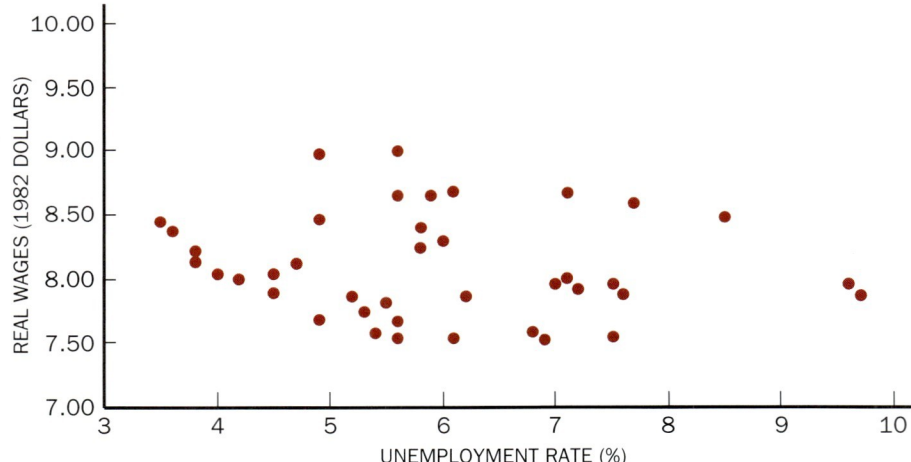

Figure 29.4

REAL WAGES AND UNEMPLOYMENT, 1964–2003

When real wages and unemployment are plotted on a graph, no pattern emerges. Apparently large changes in unemployment may be accompanied by relatively small changes in real wages.

SOURCE: *Economic Report of the President* (2004), Tables B-42, B-47.

---

[1]Nominal wages did fall during the Great Depression, but prices fell even more; consequently, the real wage rose.

$L_1 - L_0$, is the level of cyclical unemployment. People are willing to work *at the going real wage,* but the work is not there. The same argument holds even if there is a slight adjustment of the real wage that is too small to align demand and supply. *It is the failure of the real wage to adjust when the labor demand curve shifts to the left that leads to increases in unemployment.* But why don't real wages adjust quickly? By definition, the real wage is the nominal wage relative to the prices of goods and services; the failure of the real wage to adjust can therefore be traced to a lack of change in both nominal wages and many prices.

NOMINAL VERSUS REAL WAGES

When we discuss the labor market, it is important to keep in mind the distinction between the real wage and the money, or *nominal,* wage. The nominal wage is the wage expressed in dollars. The real wage is a measure of purchasing power, and what happens to the real wage as the nominal wage changes depends on how prices are changing. In 2003, the average hourly nominal wage in the private sector was $15.38. In 1982, it was $7.86. To compare these two wages, though, we need to take into account the marked overall rise in prices between 1982 and 2003. When expressed in terms of 1982 prices, the real wage in 2003 was equal to $8.29. Thus, while nominal wages almost doubled between 1982 and 2003, real wages increased by only 5 percent. Economists focus on real wages because individuals care about the purchasing power of their income, and firms care about the real costs of labor.

THE SLOW ADJUSTMENT OF NOMINAL WAGES

There are several reasons why nominal wages adjust slowly; we will briefly mention three.

Wage Contracts Some wages may be set by union contracts that typically last for a fixed period—three years is common. If the contract is signed just before an economic downturn, more than two years may pass before any wage adjustment can occur. Average union wages adjust slowly to changes in unemployment, since different contracts expire in different months and different years. Similar rigidities may persist even in the absence of any formal labor contract, because the relations between employers and employees are governed by a host of understandings developed over time. These implicit understandings are referred to as an **implicit labor**

Figure 29.5

CHANGES IN THE DEMAND FOR LABOR AND REAL WAGES

Panel A shows the labor market in equilibrium at full employment. The real wage is equal to w_0/P and employment is equal to L_0. In panel B, the labor demand curve has shifted to the left. Traditional theory predicts that when such a shift occurs, the real wage will fall to w_1/P. Full employment is maintained, although the level of employment in equilibrium declines to L_1. If the labor supply curve had been completely inelastic (vertical), the real wage would have fallen with no change in employment.

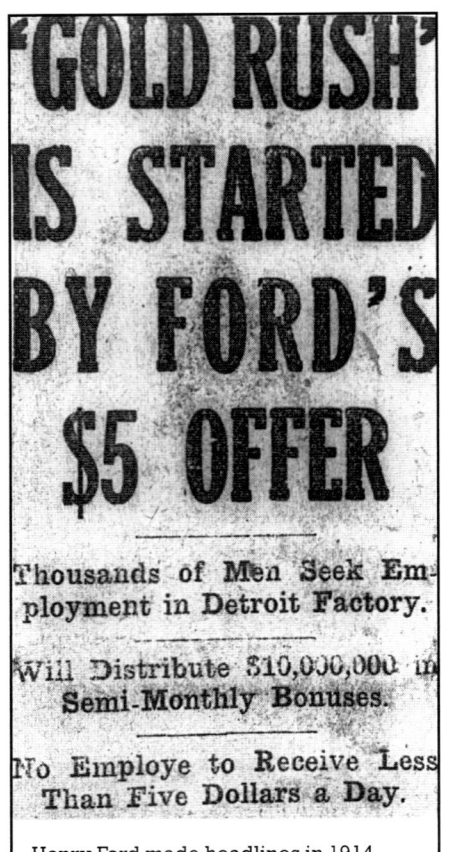

Henry Ford made headlines in 1914 when he doubled the standard wage for auto workers in an effort to promote productivity.

contract. Although most workers are not covered by formal contracts, wages or salaries are commonly adjusted only once a year, again contributing to the sluggish movement of nominal wages.

Efficiency Wages Firms want to pay the **efficiency wage:** that is, the wage that minimizes their total labor costs. *If paying higher wages leads to greater worker productivity, firms may find that their profits increase when they pay a real wage higher than the one at which the labor market would clear.* When Henry Ford opened his automobile plant in 1914, he paid his workers $5 per day—a rate more than double the going wage. The high wage ensured that Ford's employees worked hard, for they knew they would have trouble finding another job that paid as well if they were fired. Henry Ford knew that his new technique of production—the assembly line—when combined with motivated workers, would increase his profits. The high wage also reduced turnover of the workforce, because few workers wanted to quit a high-paying Ford job; and lower turnover saved Ford the cost of training a fresh, inexperienced worker each time someone with experience left. By boosting productivity and lowering turnover costs, the high wage paid off for Ford.

Productivity can depend on the wage for several reasons. One has already been mentioned: above-average wages create an incentive for workers to work hard and remain with the firm. Moreover, a firm that cuts its wages when demand falls may so sharply reduce worker morale and labor productivity that its costs of production actually increase. In addition, when a firm cuts wages, workers are more likely to quit to look for another job—and as the firm's **labor turnover rate** rises, it incurs increased costs of hiring and training new workers. Compounding the damage, those most likely to leave in response to a wage cut are a firm's best, most experienced workers, whose departure will significantly hurt overall productivity.

Risk and Uncertainty Cutting wages may be a risky strategy for a firm that wants to reduce its labor force. Whether the wage cut succeeds in encouraging workers to quit will depend on what other firms do—are they also cutting wages? The firm may reduce its uncertainty by simply laying off the workers it doesn't need.

To summarize, when sluggish nominal wages prevent the real wage from adjusting to maintain labor market equilibrium, shifts in labor demand will result in fluctuations in cyclical unemployment, as we illustrated in Figure 29.5. Such shifts in labor demand can occur fairly rapidly, mainly because of changes in output. Wages fail to fall enough to restore equilibrium (the balance between labor demand and labor supply) when labor demand shifts downward, resulting in a rise in cyclical unemployment.

THE SLOW ADJUSTMENT OF PRICES

In the short run, variation in the demand for goods and services has the most effect on changes in output and, therefore, on the demand for labor. If a firm experiences a decrease in demand, it can respond by either lowering its price or reducing the quantity it produces. If a firm experiences an increase in demand, it can respond by either raising its price or boosting production, since even in economic booms,

Thinking Like an Economist
INFORMATION AND MEASURING THE BUSINESS CYCLE

Designing macroeconomic policy requires accurate information about the economy. Economists' conclusions about the severity of business cycles and whether the economy has become more stable are affected by the quality of their information.

Though some recessions are more severe than others, most economists have accepted the view that recessions since World War II have been, on average, milder than the recessions experienced by the United States earlier in the century. Christina Romer of the University of California, Berkeley, disagrees. She notes that the macroeconomic data now available to economists are vastly better than the data used in the early decades of the twentieth century to gauge macroeconomic performance. She has argued that in large part the apparent decline in the severity of business cycles simply reflects improvements in our ability to measure fluctuations in the economy. However, most economists believe that better data do not explain the whole story. Economists do assess the economy more accurately today than was possible before World War II, but changes in the economy and improvements in economic policymaking also have helped make business cycles less severe.

Even though the quality of economic data has improved, accurately judging the behavior of the economy remains difficult. Policy must be based on some measures, such as potential GDP, that must be estimated rather than observed directly. During the 1970s, the growth of potential GDP slowed, but this slowdown was not apparent to analysts at the time. By overestimating potential GDP, the Federal Reserve, along with most other analysts, made errors in evaluating the level of the output gap and cyclical unemployment. These errors led to policy decisions that, in hindsight and with better data, now look to have been misguided.

---

firms normally have some spare capacity. *In the short run, firms typically adjust production rather than prices in response to changes in demand.* Economists have identified two key reasons for this tendency.[2]

The Role of Costs The first explanation emphasizes the implications of sluggish wage adjustment. Labor costs are, for most businesses, the major component of their costs of production. In competitive markets, prices move in tandem with marginal costs and changes in wages translate into changes in the marginal costs of production. Some firms, at least in the short run, use a simple rule of thumb in pricing their goods—they set price as a given markup over costs (e.g., 120 percent of costs). In this case, prices adjust slowly to changes in demand because wages (and therefore costs) adjust slowly.

Risk and Uncertainty Risk and imperfect information can significantly slow price adjustments just as they did wage adjustments. In perfectly competitive markets, firms simply take prices as given; with imperfect competition, firms have some

---

[2]In some cases, these explanations seem to explain too much—they suggest that in some situations, prices and wages will not adjust at all to, say, small changes in demand or costs. But the economy consists of many firms in different circumstances. Some may not be able to respond at all, while others may respond fully. The *average* for the economy demonstrates a slow response.

control over the price of the goods they produce. But firms face a great deal of uncertainty about the consequences of price changes. The effect of a lower price on a firm's sales depends on how other firms in the industry as well as its customers respond. If rivals lower their prices, the firm may fail to gain market share, and the price decline may simply put its profits into a nosedive. If rivals have no reaction, the firm may gain a competitive advantage. The behavior of customers is also unpredictable. If they think this is just the first of several price cuts, they may decide to wait until prices get still lower before they buy. Thus, a decrease in prices might even result in lower sales.

Often much greater uncertainty is associated with changing prices than with changing output and employment. When a firm cuts back on production, provided that the cuts are not too drastic, it risks only depleting its inventories below normal levels should sales be stronger than expected. If that happens, it can simply increase production. Thus its added risk is small, as long as production costs do not change much over time.

Since firms like to avoid risks, they try to avoid making large changes in prices (and wages, as discussed earlier). They would rather accept somewhat larger changes in the amount produced and in employment. As a result, prices are sticky.

Wrap-Up

CYCLICAL UNEMPLOYMENT

Cyclical unemployment is typically generated by shifts in the aggregate demand curve for labor when real wages fail to adjust. These shifts often arise from changes in aggregate output.

Real wages can fail to adjust because nominal wages and many prices are sticky.

Understanding Macroeconomic Fluctuations: Key Concepts

We have argued that the full-employment model of Part Six cannot explain cyclical unemployment. To understand economic fluctuations and how government policies can affect the economy, economists have developed a basic model that differs from the long-run, full-employment model in several critical respects. Fortunately for ease of understanding, the two models also share many features.

Four key ideas are fundamental to helping us understand economic fluctuations. A brief discussion of each will give an overview of the model of fluctuations, before each is developed in more detail in the remainder of this chapter and in the chapters that follow.

The first two fundamental ideas reflect behavior we observe around us—the slow adjustment of wages and prices. When wages (and prices) have had enough time to adjust, supply and demand will balance in all markets, including the labor market. Once this has happened, the level of employment, potential output, the real rate of interest, and the price level are determined as the full-employment model of Part Six explained. Because it takes time for wages and prices to adjust fully, we often refer to the full-employment model as describing the economy in the **long run**—a length of time sufficient to allow wages and prices to adjust to equilibrate supply and demand.

When wages or prices adjust sluggishly, the basic price mechanism that leads to equilibrium can't function effectively. The **short run** is that period during which wages or prices have failed to keep demand and supply in balance. In the short run, the level of employment can diverge from the full-employment level, and wages and prices will not respond quickly enough to move the economy back to full employment. But as noted above, once wages and prices have had enough time to adjust, the economy does return to full employment and the model of Part Six holds sway.

The third and fourth of our fundamental ideas entail simplifying assumptions about how individuals, firms, and economic policymakers behave. They will play an important role in clarifying the implications of the slow adjustment of wages and prices for short-run economic fluctuations.

STICKY WAGES

Our first key concept is one we have already discussed: the fundamental explanation for cyclical unemployment is that wages do not adjust quickly enough when either the demand or the supply for labor shifts. *At least for a while, and sometimes for extended periods of time,* the demand for labor at market wages can differ from the supply of labor. Because this is such a crucial assumption in macroeconomics, some of the reasons for the slow adjustment of wages have already been discussed in this chapter.

Fundamentals of Fluctuations 1

STICKY WAGES

In the short run, shifts in labor supply or demand often result in labor surpluses (high unemployment) or shortages (very low unemployment) because nominal wages tend to adjust slowly.

STICKY PRICES

Like nominal wages, many prices are also sticky. And just as shifts in labor demand lead to fluctuations in unemployment when wages fail to adjust, so shifts in product demand will lead to fluctuations in production. When demand for a firm's product falls, the firm might respond by lowering its price or by reducing production. Our analysis of economic fluctuations is based on a fundamental insight:

e-Insight
CYCLICAL AND STRUCTURAL PRODUCTIVITY

Productivity growth is the key to economic growth and rising standards of living, and the information technologies we associate with the "new economy" have contributed significantly to the rapid growth in productivity that the United States has enjoyed since the mid-1990s. When productivity increased sharply in 1996, few commentators thought the numbers heralded a new period of sustained rapid growth. By 2000, most were convinced that the economy's average, or *structural*, rate of productivity growth had risen.

One reason it can take several years to discover shifts in structural productivity growth is that the business cycle itself influences productivity. When the economy goes through recessions and booms, GDP and employment fluctuate. Measures of productivity such as output per hour—real GDP divided by the total number of hours worked—will be affected as GDP and employment change over the business cycle. It therefore can be difficult to determine whether productivity is changing because of a new structural growth rate or simply because of short-run business cycle fluctuations.

The best way to understand how the business cycle affects productivity is to visualize what happens in a small firm as the economy enters a recession. Let's call this firm YourPlace.com, a business offering specialized Internet consulting and troubleshooting services to other businesses. YourPlace.com employs 20 people: the owner, an accountant, a sales manager, 16 computer service technicians who actually visit the clients' sites and provide the consulting services, and a person who manages and coordinates their schedules. Suppose that initially YourPlace.com has 96 clients, with each service technician responsible for 6 clients. When the economy starts to go into a recession, YourPlace.com finds that the demand for its business services falls. Some of its clients may go bankrupt, while others may seek to lower their costs by scaling back their contracts with firms like YourPlace.com. Suppose YourPlace.com loses 12 clients; in response, it lays off 2 technicians. Even though business has fallen, it still needs the scheduler to handle its remaining 14 technicians, and it still needs its sales manager and its accountant. While YourPlace.com's business has dropped by 12.5 percent (from 96 to 84 clients), so that it is producing 12.5 percent less, its workforce fell by only 10 percent (from 20 to 18 employees). In other words, labor productivity goes down. (For the sake of simplicity, we are

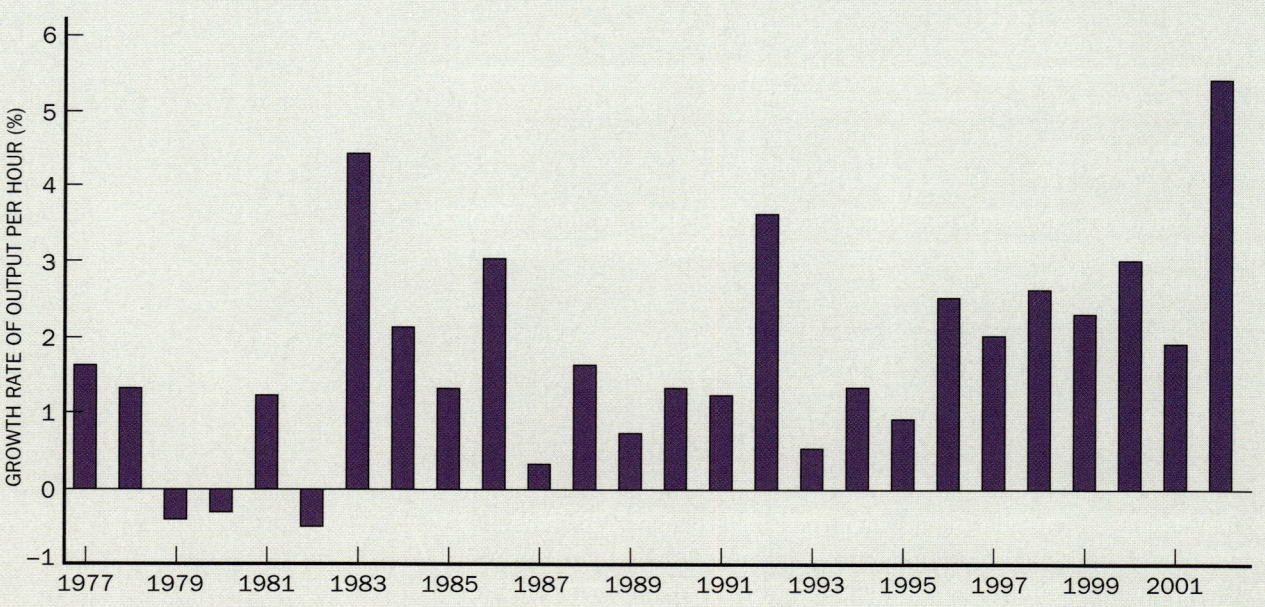

SOURCE: *Economic Report of the President* (2004).

assuming that the firm's output is proportional to the number of clients it has.)

When the economy comes out of the recession, the firm can hire new technical staff as it adds new clients. It doesn't need to add a new accountant or sales manager or scheduler. As a result, its output will increase more (in percentage terms) than its employment, and its labor productivity rises.

Labor productivity falls as the economy goes into a recession; it rises when the economy comes out of a recession. The bar graph, which shows jumps in labor productivity in 1983 and 1992 following the ends of recessions, illustrates this pattern very clearly. Such cyclical fluctuations in productivity can easily mask changes in structural productivity for a time—as happened in the United States in the 1990s. When productivity first increased, the economy was recovering from the 1990–1991 recession. In 1992, productivity grew by 3.7 percent, well above estimates for structural productivity growth. This rise was the normal cyclical effect of an economy coming out of recession.

Usually, once a recovery is well under way, productivity growth tends to settle in at the economy's structural rate. And that is what seemed to be occurring after the initial spurt in productivity growth in 1992; as the chart shows, productivity growth slowed significantly in 1993. But the increase in productivity growth that began in 1996 did not fit the expected pattern. By 1999, it was clear that the sustained rise in productivity growth represented a change in structural productivity growth rather than a temporary rise caused by cyclical factors. While debate still rages over the precise source of this increase, most economists attribute it to new information technologies.

At the beginning of 2001, the U.S. economy again entered a recession. Though productivity growth slowed, it remained much higher than in previous recessions. The recession ended in late 2001, and 2002 saw the expected postrecession jump in labor productivity. Because of the higher structural productivity growth rate *and* the cyclical contribution to productivity growth, labor productivity in 2002 grew at its fastest rate in at least fifty years.

in the short run, firms adjust production and employment in response to changes in demand. They initially adjust production, not prices. This is the second key concept in understanding fluctuations.

When demand at retail stores rises in December because it is the holiday season, stores could respond by raising prices and keeping sales relatively constant. Instead, they generally keep prices constant and satisfy the greater demand with increased sales. In some markets, prices do respond quickly to shifts in demand; competitive markets such as those for agricultural products or for commodities like oil are usually characterized by rapid price adjustments. In many markets, both price and production adjust. If an automobile company sees demand fall, it may offer rebates or other price reductions to spur demand, but it will also scale back production, perhaps closing an assembly line and laying off workers. Most markets, particularly those characterized by imperfect competition, undergo adjustments in production as demand shifts.

Fundamentals of Fluctuations 2

STICKY PRICES

In the short run, shifts in demand lead firms to adjust production and employment. This occurs because the prices of many goods and services tend to adjust slowly.

INFLATION ADJUSTMENT

The first two fundamental ideas for understanding economic fluctuations—that wages and prices do not adjust rapidly—set the stage for the model that is developed over the next two chapters. They imply that changes in demand will cause fluctuations in employment and production. But in macroeconomics, we are also interested in the factors that determine inflation, and our other two fundamental ideas will serve to link fluctuations in unemployment and inflation.

The adjustment of inflation turns out to be one of the keys to understanding how economies return eventually to full employment. While many prices are slow to adjust, they do not remain constant; the rate of inflation is the rate at which the aggregate price level is changing.

To understand the behavior of inflation, it is important to avoid two common confusions. The first potential problem involves a failure to distinguish between the *price level* and the *rate of inflation*. The price level is an index number that measures overall prices relative to a base year (the construction of price indexes is discussed in Chapter 23). In 2004, the consumer price index (CPI) was equal to 188.9. The base year for the CPI is an average of 1982–1984 prices. Because the CPI is by definition equal to 100 in the base period, the index shows that by 2004 the prices of the goods and services in its basket had risen 88.9 percent since that period. The *price level* in 2004 is higher than it was in 1982–1984.

The inflation rate tells us how fast the price level is rising. In 2004, the CPI inflation rate was 2.7 percent. In other words, the price level in 2004 was 2.7 percent higher than it had been in 2003. The higher the inflation rate, the faster the rise in the price level. A negative inflation rate (deflation) would indicate that prices were falling.

A higher price level does not mean that inflation is higher. For example, the price level was much higher in 2004 than it was in 1982, but the inflation rate was lower. Inflation in 1982 was 6.2 percent; in 2004, it was only 2.7 percent, and thus prices were rising more slowly.

The second potential confusion arises if *sticky* is not distinguished from *constant*. In calling wages and prices "sticky," economists mean that they fail to adjust rapidly in the face of shifts in supply and demand, not that they are constant—that is, that they never change. Both wages and prices do adjust over time. The rate at which the general level of prices changes, the inflation rate, will be one of the key macroeconomic variables in our model of short-run fluctuations.

What Causes Inflation to Adjust? The law of supply and demand tells us that whenever supply and demand are out of balance in a market, pressures will be brought to bear on the price in that market to adjust. The same applies for the aggregate economy. The balance between labor demand and supply, as reflected in cyclical unemployment, is an important factor influencing how wages change. As unemployment falls—that is, as labor markets become *tight*—firms must boost the wages they pay to attract new workers and retain their existing workforce. In unionized sectors, a tight labor market increases the bargaining power of unions, enabling them to negotiate larger wage increases. Wages therefore rise more rapidly in tight labor markets. Conversely, wages will rise more slowly when cyclical unemployment rises. For most firms, labor costs are their primary costs of production. If wage hikes outpace increases in workers' productivity, firms' labor costs rise. As labor costs go up, firms will raise their prices; when labor costs fall—as occurs, for instance, if labor productivity increases faster than wages rise—firms will cut their prices. This means that for a given rate of increase in labor productivity, prices will rise more rapidly—that is, inflation will be higher—when wages rise more rapidly; when wages rise slowly, so will prices, and inflation will be lower. Thus, cyclical unemployment affects wages, which in turn affect inflation.

This connection between cyclical unemployment and inflation points to a trade-off in the economy. When the economy experiences a business cycle expansion and enjoys lower unemployment, inflation is likely to start to rise. To lower inflation typically requires a period of high cyclical unemployment. Thus, if inflation is too high, the cost of lowering it will be temporarily high unemployment. Of course, cyclical unemployment isn't the only factor affecting inflation, but it is among the most important. The short-run trade-off between cyclical unemployment and inflation can present policymakers with hard choices.

Fundamentals of Fluctuations 3

SHORT-RUN INFLATION–UNEMPLOYMENT TRADE-OFF

In the short run, policymakers face a trade-off between unemployment and inflation. This trade-off occurs because attempts to reduce unemployment cause nominal wages to increase faster than labor productivity, raising firms' labor costs. Higher costs, in turn, lead to more rapidly rising prices (i.e., inflation increases). Attempts to reduce inflation require periods of high cyclical unemployment to reduce the rate of wage increases.

INFLATION, MONETARY POLICY, AND SPENDING

We have just set out three of the key concepts we will use as we explore how the economy behaves in the short run. These will help us begin to understand economic fluctuations, but they also open up new questions. For example, if firms respond to shifts in demand by adjusting production and employment, what explains the level of demand and its shifts? And is spending, like cyclical unemployment, also related to that other important macro variable, inflation?

The answer to this last question is yes. As inflation starts to rise, governments are likely to undertake policies designed to bring it back down. Maintaining stable, low rates of inflation is a primary goal of most countries, and central banks—the

Federal Reserve in the United States, for example, or the European Central Bank for the members of the Economic and Monetary Union—are the government institutions responsible for achieving this goal through their use of monetary policy. To keep inflation under control, central banks in developed and many developing economies seek to reduce aggregate spending when inflation rises and to boost spending when inflation falls. They follow such policies as a consequence of our third fundamental idea, that reducing inflation in the short run requires a rise in cyclical unemployment. Thus, when inflation rises, central banks act to reduce aggregate spending in accord with our second key concept, that firms react to a fall in demand by reducing production. When production falls, cyclical unemployment rises, and consequently the initial rise in inflation is moderated. Since central banks wish to keep inflation stable, they will also act to counter a decline in inflation by increasing aggregate spending and production. As the boost to production reduces cyclical unemployment, inflation begins to rise.

This relationship between inflation and aggregate spending depends critically on how monetary policy is conducted. The behavior of the economy, as it experiences disturbances, will depend on what policies the government institutes in response, just as it does on how firms and households respond to changing economic conditions. If we want to understand how the economy operates—how it adjusts, say, when world oil prices jump or there is a financial crisis in Asia—we will need to take into account the government's actions.

To understand short-run fluctuations in the economy, we particularly need to grasp the role of the Federal Reserve and its decisions regarding monetary policy. In Chapter 25, the basic tools of the Fed were explained. We also learned, however (see Chapter 24), that the real interest rate—that is, the nominal interest rate adjusted for inflation—has the most influence on households' saving decisions and firms' investment decisions. *In the long run,* at full employment, the real interest rate balances national saving and investment. *In the short run,* when the economy can fluctuate around full employment, the Fed is able to affect the real interest rate by influencing the nominal interest rate.

Like many other central banks, the Fed reacts to changes in inflation. If inflation increases, the Fed uses its policy tools to reduce aggregate spending. If inflation declines, the Fed uses its policy tools to increase aggregate spending. These responses help keep inflation low and stable. The Fed's concern with inflation has been most apparent during the past twenty-five years; during earlier periods, particularly the 1960s and 1970s, it was criticized for not taking strong enough action when inflation rose. In Chapter 31, we will see how an economy's short-run fluctuations in inflation and output depend on how central banks behave.

The type of monetary policy reaction to changes in inflation that we will incorporate into our model of economic fluctuations occurs most explicitly in countries whose central banks follow a policy of trying to keep inflation equal to a target value—so-called inflation-targeting policy regimes. But in fact a wide range of monetary policy behavior, and not just inflation targeting, is consistent with a link between inflation and spending. This link between inflation, monetary policy, and aggregate spending is our fourth key concept. It will be the focus of Chapter 31.

Fundamentals of Fluctuations 4

INFLATION, MONETARY POLICY, AND SPENDING

In the short run, central banks act to reduce aggregate spending when inflation increases and to increase aggregate spending when inflation falls. This relationship depends critically on the way in which the central bank reacts to inflation and how much importance it places on controlling inflation. Because this relationship depends on monetary policy, it can differ in different countries and at different times.

Case in Point

INFLATION TARGETING

During the 1990s, many central banks adopted policies that economists call *inflation targeting*. Under inflation targeting, the central bank strives to achieve a low and stable rate of inflation. In some countries, such as the United Kingdom, New Zealand, Canada, and Sweden, the government or the central bank formally announces a target for the inflation rate. In the United Kingdom, for example, the Bank of England's inflation target is 2 percent. We will learn more about inflation targeting in later chapters, but it is useful to discuss inflation-targeting policies here because they illustrate our four key concepts.

The basics of an inflation-targeting policy are simple. The central bank wants to keep the inflation rate equal to a targeted value. If inflation rises above the target, the central bank implements policies to reduce aggregate spending (key concept 4). Because wages and prices are sticky, this spending reduction causes firms to cut back production, leading to a rise in unemployment (key concepts 1 and 2). Higher cyclical unemployment moderates inflation (key concept 3) and helps bring the inflation rate back to the target. The process works in reverse when inflation falls below the central bank's target.

Wrap-Up

FUNDAMENTALS OF SHORT-RUN FLUCTUATIONS IN OUTPUT, EMPLOYMENT, AND INFLATION

1. *Sticky wages:* Wages do not adjust rapidly to shifts in labor supply and labor demand. As a result, the labor market may not always be in equilibrium.

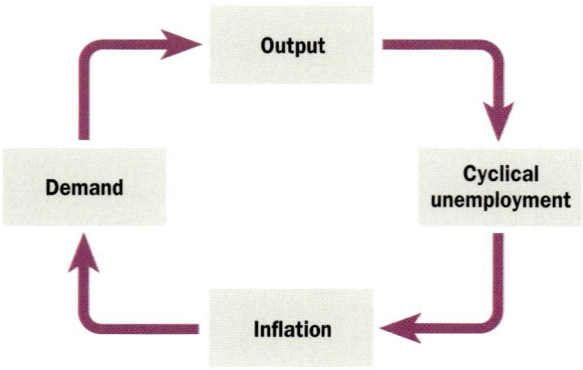

Figure 29.6

AGGREGATE DEMAND AND INFLATION

The four fundamental keys to understanding short-run fluctuations serve to link together demand, output, cyclical unemployment, and inflation. The next three chapters examine these links.

2. *Sticky prices:* When the labor market does not clear, shifts in the demand for goods and services in the product market lead firms to adjust production rather than simply change prices (see Chapter 30).
3. *Short-run inflation–unemployment trade-off:* A fall in cyclical unemployment leads to an increase in inflation—increases in cyclical unemployment reduce inflation. This relationship implies that policymakers face a trade-off in the short run between lower unemployment and higher inflation (see Chapters 31 and 33).
4. *Inflation, monetary policy, and spending:* As inflation rises, monetary policy works to reduce aggregate spending. When inflation falls, monetary policy acts to boost aggregate spending. This relationship between monetary policy, inflation, and aggregate spending can vary over time as the central bank's policy goals change (see Chapters 31 and 32).

LINKING THE FOUR KEY CONCEPTS

The four key concepts work together to explain how output and inflation are determined when the economy is not at full employment. Figure 29.6 shows how. We can start at any one of the boxes and use the key concepts to travel around the circle. For example, let's suppose something causes demand to drop. It might be a financial crisis in Asia or Latin America that reduces sales of U.S. goods in those countries. The drop in demand causes U.S. firms to scale back production—output falls. With production now at lower levels, firms do not need as many workers, so layoffs occur and cyclical unemployment rises. Wages fail to adjust quickly enough to keep the economy at full employment. High cyclical unemployment leads to slower wage growth, and inflation declines. In the face of a decline in inflation, the Fed acts to boost some types of spending, helping to offset some of the initial drop in demand that started the process.

Over the next few chapters, we will examine each of these links in detail, learning about how they operate and how they help us understand the causes of economic fluctuations.

Review and Practice

SUMMARY

1. Economies experience recessions and booms in which output fluctuates around its full-employment level. Recessions are periods in which real GDP declines; in booms, real GDP increases. The fluctuations in output are called business cycles.
2. If wages and prices do not adjust quickly enough to ensure that markets are always in equilibrium, so that demand and supply are balanced, the economy may experience fluctuations in cyclical unemployment.
3. To explain cyclical unemployment, we need to explain why the aggregate labor market does not clear. If real wages do not adjust when the demand curve for labor shifts to the left, then the quantity of labor supplied will exceed the quantity demanded at the prevailing wage and there will be cyclical unemployment.
4. Wages may be slow to adjust because of union contracts and implicit contracts that lead to infrequent wage changes. Firms minimize total labor costs by paying the efficiency wage. Cutting wages may raise costs by lowering productivity, as the best workers are most likely to leave, or by leading to higher labor turnover costs.
5. In the short run, firms adjust production in response to fluctuations in demand. Thus, aggregate demand plays a critical role in determining the short-run equilibrium level of output.
6. Our model of fluctuations will be built around four key components: (1) wages are sticky, (2) prices are sticky, (3) there is a trade-off between inflation and cyclical unemployment in the short run, and (4) inflation and aggregate spending are linked by monetary policy.

KEY TERMS

recessions
output gap
expansions
peaks
troughs
business cycles
implicit labor contract
efficiency wage
labor turnover rate
long run
short run

REVIEW QUESTIONS

1. If the labor market always clears, is there any unemployment? Any cyclical unemployment? What does it mean for the labor market "not to clear"? What gives rise to cyclical unemployment?
2. If the labor market always clears, what factors can cause fluctuations in the level of employment?
3. What inferences can you draw from the following two facts, assuming that both hold simultaneously?
   (a) The labor supply curve is relatively inelastic.
   (b) Large variations in employment coexist with relatively small variations in real wages.
4. What might shift the aggregate demand curve for labor?
5. What are the four key concepts that help explain economic fluctuations?
6. If cyclical unemployment increases, what would you expect to happen to inflation? If cyclical unemployment falls, what would be the effect on inflation?
7. If inflation falls, why will aggregate expenditures rise? If inflation rises, why will aggregate expenditures fall?
8. What are some explanations for sticky wages?
9. Give three reasons why productivity may depend on the level of wages paid.
10. How does an efficiency wage differ from a wage that clears the labor market?

PROBLEMS

1. In the 1970s, a large number of new workers entered the U.S. economy from two main sources. The baby boom generation grew to adulthood and the proportion of women working outside the home increased substantially. If wages adjust, what effect will these factors have on the equilibrium level of wages and quantity of labor? If wages do not adjust, how does your answer change? In which case will unemployment exist? Draw a diagram to explain your answer. What is the effect of the increased

labor supply on the product market? Illustrate your answer diagrammatically.

2. Soon after Iraq invaded Kuwait in August 1990, many firms feared that a recession would occur. Anticipating a lack of demand for their goods, they began cutting back on production. If wages adjust, what will happen to the equilibrium level of wages and employment? If wages do not adjust, how does your answer change? In which case will unemployment exist?

3. For the most part, macroeconomics focuses on aggregate employment, ignoring distinctions among different categories of workers, but it sometimes considers broad categories, such as skilled and unskilled workers. Assume, for the sake of simplicity, that there are just these two categories, and that in general they cannot be substituted for each other.
    (a) Draw demand and supply curves for skilled and unskilled workers, marking the initial equilibrium in each market.
    (b) Assume now there is a technological change that increases the demand for skilled labor at each wage, while it shifts the demand curve for unskilled labor to the left. If wages do not adjust, can there be job vacancies of one type of labor at the same time there is unemployment of another type?

4. Would you be more likely or less likely to observe implicit contracts in industries in which most workers hold their jobs for only a short time? What about industries in which most workers hold jobs a long time? Explain.

5. Go to the National Bureau of Economic Research's Web site (www.nber.org/cycles.html) and find the Business Cycle Reference Data for all peaks and troughs since 1854. What has been the average length of recessions since 1854? Since 1945? What has been the average length of expansions since 1854? Since 1945?

6. In the Case in Point on page 642, the cost of cyclical unemployment was estimated for 2002 by assuming that the unemployment rate associated with full employment was 5 percent. Suppose changes in the age structure of the workforce meant that full employment in 2002 was actually associated with an unemployment rate of 4.5 percent rather than the 5 percent figure used earlier. Recalculate the output costs of the recession. Explain why they are higher.

Learning Goals

In this chapter, you will learn

1. How equilibrium GDP is determined in the short run
2. What happens to GDP when the level of aggregate expenditures changes
3. The components of aggregate expenditures
4. How the real interest rate affects aggregate expenditures

Chapter 30

AGGREGATE EXPENDITURES AND INCOME

In Chapter 29, we learned that recessions and booms can result from shifts in the demand for the goods and services that the economy produces. When demand falls, firms scale back production and need fewer workers—current employees are laid off and few new ones are hired. Wages and prices fail to adjust quickly enough to ensure that the economy remains at full employment, and the unemployment rate rises. When demand increases, firms expand production and the economy expands—employment increases and the unemployment rate falls.

The task of this chapter is explaining the relationship between equilibrium output and **aggregate expenditures,** the name economists give to the overall demand for what the economy produces. Aggregate expenditures are the total spending by households, firms, government, and the foreign sector on the goods and services produced. There is a feedback relationship between spending and income—changes in spending affect the equilibrium level of production and income, and changes in income influence spending. Understanding the connection between aggregate expenditures and income is important. Shifts in aggregate expenditures, increased pessimism among households that results in a drop in consumption spending, and the introduction of new technologies that lead to increased investment spending by firms are important causes of economic fluctuations. We will also discuss the major factors that affect the three components of private expenditures: consumption, investment, and net exports.

Income–Expenditure Analysis

Aggregate expenditure has four components: consumption, investment, government purchases, and net exports.[1] We can think of aggregate expenditures as the

---

[1] Since our objective is to explain *real* GDP and employment, our focus continues to be on *real* consumption, *real* investment, *real* government purchases, and *real* net exports.

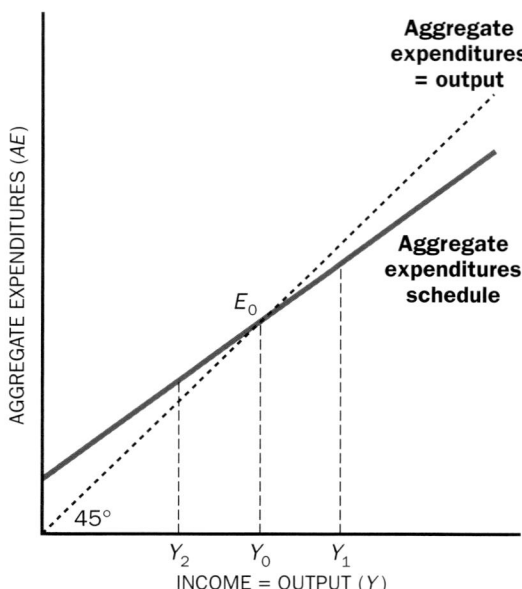

Figure 30.1

THE AGGREGATE EXPENDITURES SCHEDULE AND INCOME–EXPENDITURE ANALYSIS

The aggregate expenditures schedule gives the sum of consumption, investment, government purchases, and net exports at each level of national income. Aggregate expenditures increase with income. Equilibrium occurs at the intersection of the aggregate expenditures schedule and the 45-degree line, where aggregate expenditures equal income (at point E_0). At outputs greater than Y_0, such as Y_1, aggregate expenditures are less than output (remember, income equals output). Some goods that are being produced are not being sold; there are unintended accumulations of inventory. The reverse is true for outputs less than Y_0, such as Y_2.

total expenditures in the four parts of the economy: households spending on consumption, firms on investment goods, the government on public goods, and foreigner buyers on net exports. We have already seen in Chapter 22 that total income (output) is equal to the sum of consumption, investment, government purchases, and net exports. Income depends on spending, but spending also depends on income. When their income rises, for example, households will increase their consumption spending. This spending then becomes income for the producers of the goods and services purchased. Understanding the implications of this feedback loop is critical to understanding why the economy experiences fluctuations in production and employment.

The key to solving for the equilibrium level of output and the equilibrium level of aggregate demand is the **aggregate expenditures schedule.** The aggregate expenditures schedule traces out the relationship between aggregate expenditures and national income—the aggregate income of everyone in the economy. It is depicted in Figure 30.1, where the vertical axis measures aggregate expenditures and the horizontal axis measures national income.

The aggregate expenditures schedule has three critical properties. First, it is upward sloping—as national income goes up, so do aggregate expenditures. Changes in other variables (such as interest rates, tax rates, and exchange rates) cause the aggregate expenditures schedule to shift up or down, and they may even alter its slope. Later in this chapter, we will examine why expenditures increase with income and how the aggregate expenditures schedule is shifted by changes in other variables.

Second, as income increases by $1 billion, aggregate expenditures increase by less than $1 billion—consumers save some of their additional income. If a household's income increases by $1,000, its consumption might rise by $900 and its saving by $100. The same logic applies to other components of aggregate expenditures; they will rise less than the increase in income. Figure 30.1 also shows a line through the origin at a 45-degree angle. The slope of this line is one. All along this line, a change in the horizontal axis (income) is matched by an equal change in the vertical axis (aggregate expenditures). By contrast, the aggregate expenditures schedule is flatter than the 45-degree line, since aggregate expenditures increase less than dollar-for-dollar with increased income.

Third, at very low levels of national income, aggregate expenditures will exceed income. Households, for example, will use up their savings to maintain consumption if aggregate income falls to dramatically lower levels.

The facts that (1) the aggregate expenditures schedule slopes up, (2) the aggregate expenditures schedule is flatter than the 45-degree line through the origin, and (3) aggregate expenditures are greater than income at very low income levels imply that the aggregate expenditures schedule intersects the 45-degree line, as seen in Figure 30.1.

This brings us to our central questions: What determines the (short-run) equilibrium level of aggregate expenditures? Where on the schedule in Figure 30.1 will the economy find itself? To answer these questions, we need to add two more concepts to our analysis.

THE NATIONAL INCOME–OUTPUT IDENTITY

National income is equal to national output (as explained in Chapter 22). Their equality reflects the fact that when a good or service is purchased, the money that is paid must eventually wind up as someone's income—as wages, in the pockets of the workers in the firm that produced the good (or of the workers who produced the intermediate goods that were used in the production of the final good); as interest payments, in the pockets of those who lent the firm money; or as profits, in the pockets of the owners of the firm.[2] If Y is used to represent national income, this identity can be written as

$$\text{GDP} = \text{national income} = Y.$$

The equation allows us to interpret the horizontal axis in Figure 30.1 in two different ways. We can say that the aggregate expenditures schedule gives the level of expenditures at each level of national income. We also can say that it gives the level of expenditures at each level of national output.

EQUILIBRIUM OUTPUT

Normally, firms will produce only what they believe they can sell. As a result, the total output produced by all firms will equal the total demand for output. In equilibrium, aggregate expenditures, which we will denote by AE, must equal aggregate output (GDP). Since aggregate output also equals national income (Y), we have the simple equation

$$AE = \text{GDP} = Y.$$

In Figure 30.1, the 45-degree line through the origin is labeled "Aggregate expenditures = output." All points on the 45-degree line have the property that aggregate expenditures, measured on the vertical axis, equal aggregate output, measured on the horizontal axis. Only points on this 45-degree line satisfy the equilibrium requirement that aggregate expenditures equal output.

Equilibrium lies at the point on the aggregate expenditures schedule that also satisfies the "Aggregate expenditures = output" condition. That point is at E_0 in the figure, where the aggregate expenditures schedule intersects the 45-degree line. The corresponding equilibrium value of aggregate output, for given inflation and interest rates, is denoted Y_0.

The analysis that determines equilibrium output by relating income (output) to aggregate expenditures is called **income–expenditure analysis.** We can take two approaches to demonstrating that Y_0 is the equilibrium. The first way is to note that it is the only point that satisfies the two conditions for equilibrium. In equilibrium, everything produced must be purchased. Thus, aggregate expenditures must be equal to output, as represented by the 45-degree line. In equilibrium, the level of

---

[2]For the sake of simplicity, we will assume that the residents of the country neither receive money (net) from abroad nor make payments (net) abroad.

aggregate expenditures also must be what households, firms, government, and the foreign sector want to spend in total at that level of national income (output), as represented by the aggregate expenditures schedule. Only point E_0 is consistent with both conditions.

The second way is to consider what happens at a level of income, Y_1, in excess of Y_0. At that point, the aggregate expenditures schedule lies below the 45-degree line. What households, firms, government, and the foreign sector would like to spend at that level of national income, as reflected in the aggregate expenditures schedule, is less than national income (output). More goods are being produced than individuals want to buy. Some of the goods, like strawberries, cannot be stored. They simply spoil. The goods that can be stored go into inventories. Since firms find they cannot sell all the goods they produced, the income level Y_1 is not the equilibrium level of output. Firms will respond by cutting back production until national income falls to Y_0. At Y_2, in contrast, the aggregate expenditures schedule lies above the 45-degree line. Households, firms, government, and the foreign sector are spending more than national income. They are purchasing more than what is being produced. This is possible (temporarily) because firms can sell out of inventories. When firms find they are selling more than they are currently producing, they respond by increasing production. Aggregate output rises until equilibrium is restored at Y_0.

SHIFTS IN THE AGGREGATE EXPENDITURES SCHEDULE

The aggregate expenditures schedule can shift through a variety of changes in the economy that lead households, firms, the government, and the foreign sector to decide, at each level of income, to spend more or less. Panel A of Figure 30.2 shows what happens if the level of aggregate expenditures increases at each level of national income by the amount S. The new aggregate expenditures schedule is denoted AE_1. Equilibrium output increases from Y_0 to Y_1. The increase in equilibrium output *is greater than the amount S;* the size of the increase depends on the slope of the aggregate expenditures schedule.

To understand why, think about an economy that is initially in equilibrium at the output level Y_0 in panel A. At this level of income, the amount that households, firms, the government, and the foreign sector wish to purchase (given by the AE_0 schedule) is exactly equal to Y_0, the amount of output that firms are producing. Now, planned spending increases at each level of income, represented by the shift of the aggregate expenditures schedule to AE_1. If firms continued to produce at Y_0, demand would exceed output; inventories would decline and this would signal to firms that they should increase production.

As output rises, households find that their incomes have risen. This boost leads them to increase their spending. Consequently, aggregate expenditures end up increasing by more than the initial amount S that the aggregate expenditures schedule shifted up. If the aggregate expenditures schedule is steep, a rise in income increases spending significantly, and the final increase in equilibrium output will be large. If the schedule is flatter, rising income has a smaller impact on spending, and the final increase in equilibrium output will be smaller. In panel B of Figure 30.2, the aggregate expenditures schedule shifts up by the same amount as it did in panel A, but the aggregate expenditures schedule is flatter and, as a result, equilibrium output rises by less.

MATHEMATICAL FORMULATION

We can describe the equilibrium by using simple algebra. The aggregate expenditures equation can be written

$$AE = A + bY,$$

where A is the vertical intercept of the aggregate expenditures schedule (the value of AE when $Y = 0$), and b is the slope of the aggregate expenditures schedule (an increase in Y of \$1 increases AE by \$$b$). The fact that the slope is positive but less than 45 degrees implies that b is between 0 and 1. Equilibrium requires that aggregate expenditures equal income, which, under our simplifying assumptions, equals Y:

$$AE = Y.$$

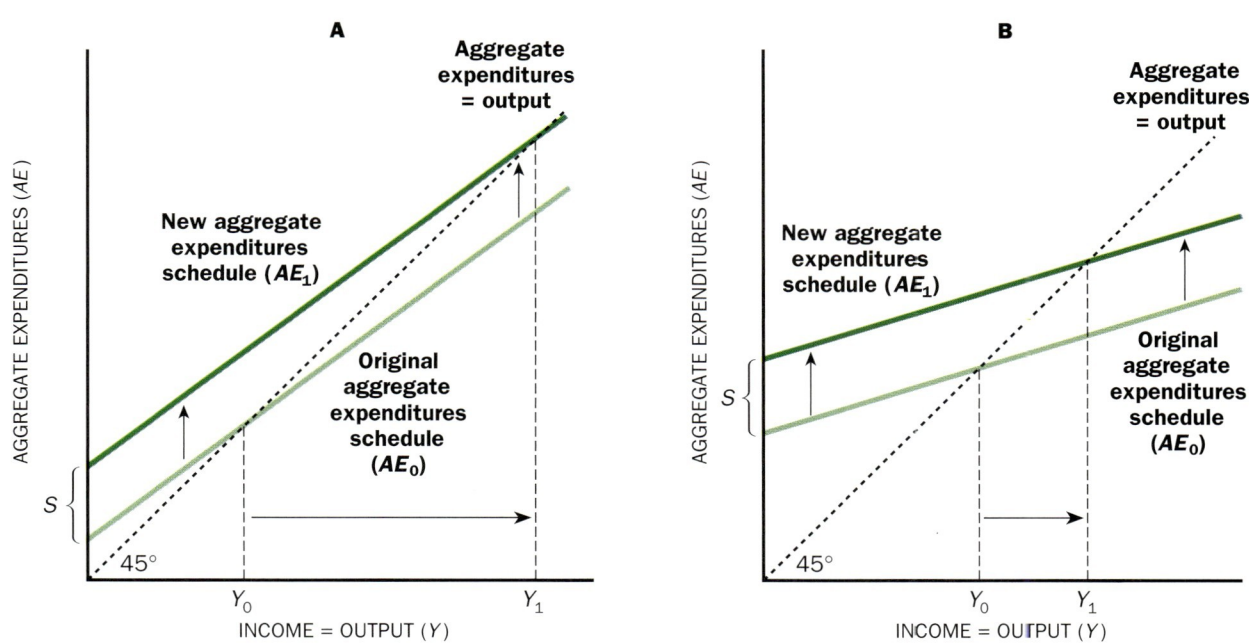

Figure 30.2

EFFECT OF A SHIFT IN THE AGGREGATE EXPENDITURES SCHEDULE

An upward shift in the aggregate expenditures schedule results in an increase in the equilibrium level of output. The magnitude of this increase in equilibrium output is greater than the magnitude of the upward shift; that is, $Y_1 - Y_0$ exceeds S, the magnitude of the shift.

The flatter the aggregate expenditures schedule, the smaller the magnitude of the increase in output resulting from a given upward shift in the schedule.

Substituting the second equation into the first equation yields

$$Y = A + bY,$$

which can be solved for Y:

$$Y = A/(1 - b).$$

This equation tells us that if A changes by $1, Y will change by $1/(1 - b)$. For example, if $b = .9$, a $1 increase in A increases Y by $10. The factor $1/(1 - b)$ is called the **multiplier**. It tells us how much total aggregate expenditures and output increase when the aggregate expenditures schedule shifts by $1.

Wrap-Up

INCOME–EXPENDITURE ANALYSIS

1. Equilibrium output is the point where the aggregate expenditures schedule equals output (income).
2. Increases in the aggregate expenditures schedule result in increases in equilibrium output. Decreases in the aggregate expenditures schedule result in decreases in equilibrium output.
3. The changes in equilibrium output are larger than the initial shift in the aggregate expenditures schedule. How much larger they are depends on the slope of the aggregate expenditures schedule. The steeper the slope, the greater the change.

As you will learn in the next few chapters, changes in aggregate expenditures will also influence interest rates, net exports, and inflation in ways that will act to reduce the ultimate effect of shifts in the aggregate expenditures schedule on equilibrium output. When we have incorporated these additional adjustments into our analysis, the change in equilibrium output per dollar change in the AE schedule is closer to 1.5 to 2 in the short run; it is close to 0 in the longer run as wages and prices have time to completely adjust.

A Look Forward

We have just learned two of the central principles of macroeconomics: (1) shifts in the aggregate expenditures schedule determine changes in the equilibrium output of the economy, and (2) the magnitude of these changes is greater than the magnitude of the shift up or down in the aggregate expenditures schedule. We also have learned that the magnitude of the change in output increases with the slope of the aggregate expenditures schedule. The remainder of this chapter explores two critical questions. First, why does the aggregate expenditures schedule have a positive slope and what determines that slope? And second, what factors lead to shifts in the aggregate expenditures schedule?

To address these questions, we will take a brief look at each of the four components of aggregate spending: (1) consumption: purchases by households of goods and services, such as food, television sets, and clothes; (2) investment: purchases of capital goods, machinery, and buildings by firms to help them produce goods and services; (3) government purchases, both of goods and services bought for current use (government consumption) and of goods and services such as buildings and roads bought for the future benefits they produce (public investment); and (4) net exports. We say *net exports,* because to determine the total purchases of goods and services produced domestically (and therefore included in GDP), we must subtract from the value of goods sold abroad (exports) the value of the goods and services purchased by U.S. households, businesses, and the government that were produced abroad (imports).

Consumption

Consumption is by far the largest component of aggregate expenditures. In the United States, consumer expenditures represent about two-thirds of total expenditures. Three factors are of primary importance in determining consumption. These are disposable income, expectations about future income, and wealth.

DISPOSABLE INCOME

Figure 30.3 shows real consumption and real GDP in the United States since 1960. The figure, in addition to illustrating that consumption is a large fraction of GDP, also reveals that the two tend to move together. That should not be surprising. Though GDP represents the economy's total output, national output is also equal to national income—and income is the most important determinant of consumption. On average, families with higher incomes spend more.

The measure of income most pertinent to household consumption is **disposable income,** the income of households after taxes are paid. Figure 30.4 plots aggregate real consumption against aggregate real disposable income for the United States from 1960 to 2002; the close relationship is quite obvious. As disposable income goes up, consumption rises; as disposable income falls, consumption falls.

The Marginal Propensity to Consume The amount by which consumption changes as income changes is called the **marginal propensity to consume,** or **MPC.** For example, if a household's disposable income rises by $2,000 per year and its consumption spending rises by $1,600 per year, the marginal propensity to consume is found by taking the change in consumption and dividing it by the change in income, or 1,600/2,000 = .8. Another household might increase its spending by $1,900 if its income rose by $2,000; the MPC of this second household would be .95. Since

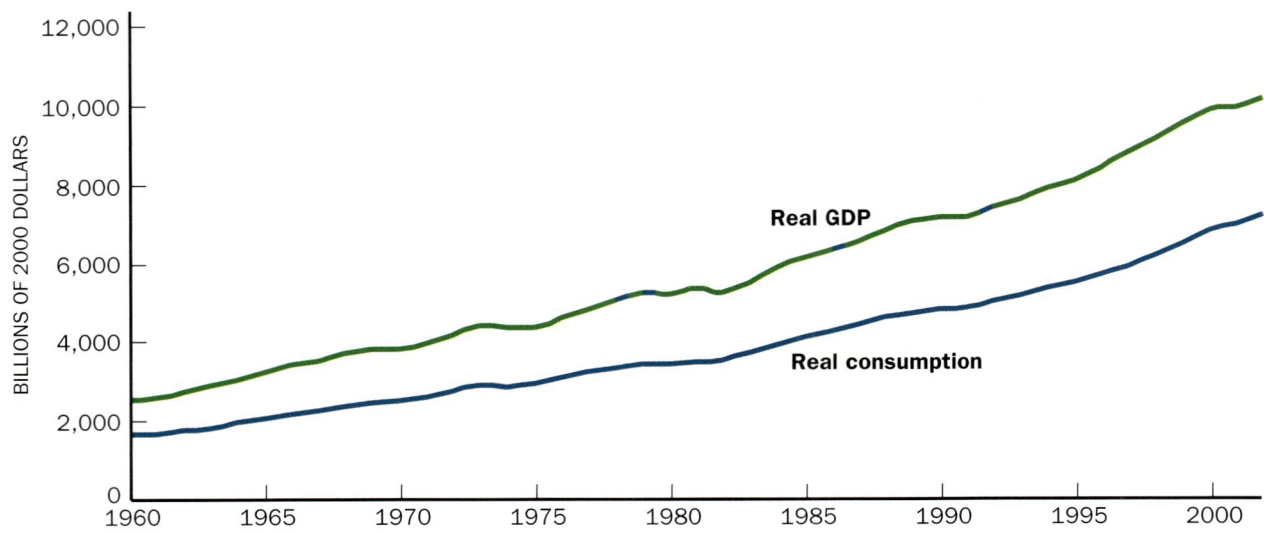

Figure 30.3

CONSUMPTION AND GDP

Real consumption spending is the largest component of aggregate expenditures. It moves closely with total real income in the economy.

SOURCE: *Economic Report of the President* (2004).

our concern is with the aggregate behavior of the economy, we are most interested in the change in aggregate consumption as aggregate income changes. The *aggregate MPC* can be thought of as an average, over the millions of households in the economy, of all the individual marginal propensities to consume. The aggregate MPC is equal to the slope of the aggregate consumption function.

The aggregate MPC conveys important information. Since consumption is a large fraction of total aggregate expenditures, the upward slope of the aggregate expenditures schedule shown in Figure 30.1 is closely related to the MPC. As aggregate income rises, disposable income rises, and households increase their consumption spending. If the MPC is high, indicating that changes in disposable income cause large changes in consumption, then the aggregate expenditures schedule will be steep. If households save a large fraction of any increase in income, then the MPC will be small and the aggregate expenditures schedule will be flatter.

The Marginal Propensity to Save Individuals must either spend or save each dollar of disposable income. The definition "disposable income = consumption plus saving" tells us that if consumption rises by 90 cents when disposable income rises by a dollar, saving must rise by 10 cents. The higher level of saving stemming from an extra dollar of income is called the **marginal propensity to save (MPS)**. Since the extra dollar is either spent or saved, the marginal propensity to consume and the marginal propensity to save must always sum to one:

marginal propensity to consume + marginal propensity to save = 1.

This relationship holds both for the individual households in the economy and for the aggregate economy. Thus if the MPS is large, the MPC must be small.

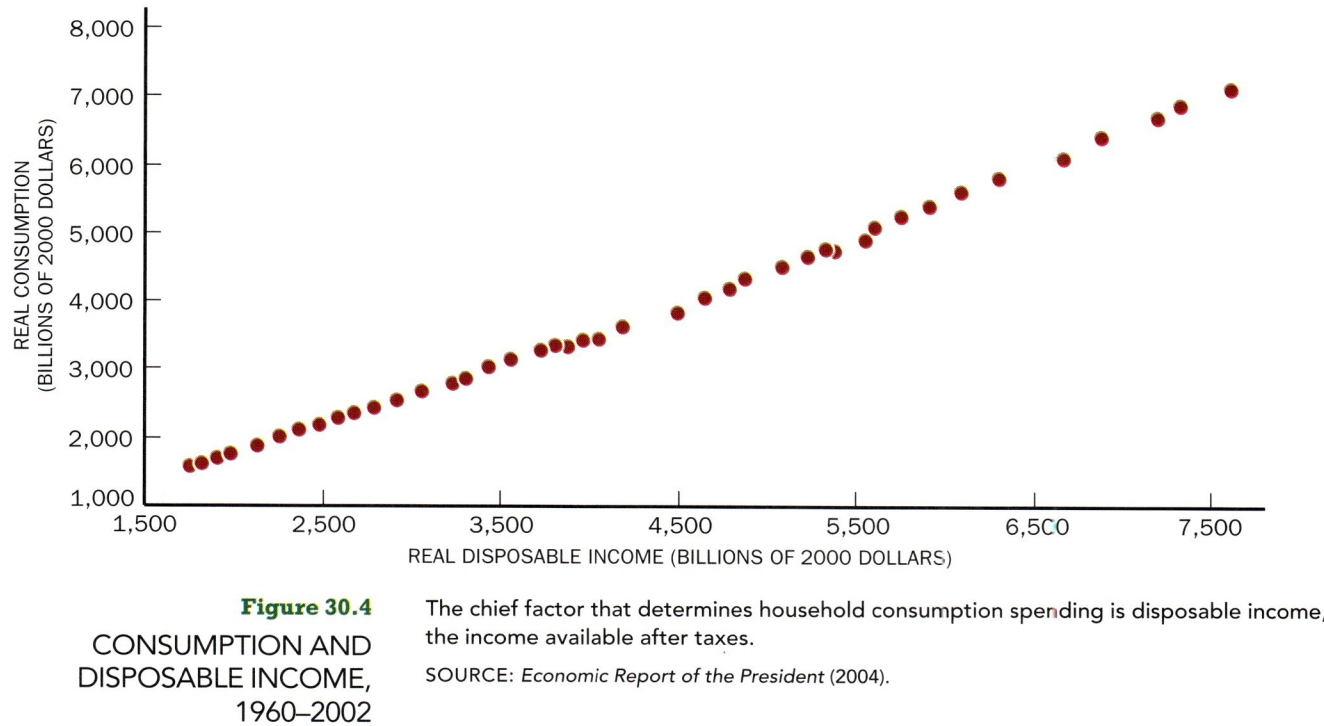

Figure 30.4
CONSUMPTION AND DISPOSABLE INCOME, 1960–2002

The chief factor that determines household consumption spending is disposable income, the income available after taxes.

SOURCE: *Economic Report of the President* (2004).

In that case, the aggregate expenditures schedule will be flatter than if the MPS is small.

Taxes and the Aggregate Expenditures Schedule Consumption spending by households depends on their disposable income. For a given level of total income, an increase in taxes reduces disposable income and leads to a fall in consumption. Tax increases therefore shift the aggregate expenditures schedule down. Tax decreases shift it up.

Taxes have a second effect on the aggregate expenditures schedule. The government's tax revenues typically go up when income rises and fall when income declines. Personal income taxes, for instance, are related to income. Individuals with higher incomes generally pay more in taxes. As total national income rises, tax revenues rise. This statement implies that disposable income will increase by less than the increase in total income. The same process works in reverse if income falls. As total income declines, so do taxes. Since people pay less in taxes, disposable income declines less than total income. For example, if the average tax rate on the last dollar of income earned (the marginal tax rate) is 30 percent, then a $1 fall in income reduces taxes by $0.30; disposable income falls by only $0.70.

What does this imply for the slope of the aggregate expenditures schedule? Because changes in total income lead to smaller changes in disposable income when taxes vary with income, the changes in consumption spending also will be smaller. Assume the marginal propensity to consume out of disposable income is .9 and the marginal tax rate is 30 percent. Of a $1 increase in total income, $0.30 must be paid in taxes, so disposable income rises by only $0.70. With a marginal propensity to consume of .9, consumption rises by .9 times the $0.70 increase in disposable income, or by $0.63. A rise in total income leads to a smaller rise in spending. The aggregate expenditures schedule is therefore flatter if marginal tax rates are high. As we have already learned, a flatter schedule means the multiplier will be smaller.

Taxes that increase with income are an example of an **automatic stabilizer.** Automatic stabilizers are factors that, like taxes, act to reduce the fall in aggregate expenditures as income declines or reduce the rise in aggregate expenditures as income rises. By reducing the multiplier, automatic stabilizers make the economy more stable. A shift down in the aggregate expenditures schedule results in a smaller drop in total output. A shift up results in a smaller rise in output. These effects occur automatically because tax revenues change automatically as income changes. Automatic stabilizers will be discussed more fully in Chapter 33.

The Marginal Propensity to Consume, Taxes, and the Multiplier

As Figure 30.4 suggests, consumption is closely related to disposable income. Suppose the relationship between the two is

$$C = a + MPC \times Y_d,$$

where MPC is the marginal propensity to consume, a is an intercept term (equal to the value of consumption if disposable income were zero), and Y_d is disposable income. If the other components of aggregate expenditures (in a closed economy, investment and government purchases) are equal to a fixed amount denoted by E, then total aggregate expenditures will be

$$AE = C + I + G = a + MPC \times Y_d + E.$$

Disposable income is equal to total income minus taxes. While taxes are of various types (for example, income taxes, payroll taxes such as Social Security and Medicare taxes, sales taxes, and property taxes), many are related to income. Just as the taxes that an individual pays usually increase as her income rises, so total taxes paid by households increase as total incomes in the economy rise. For the sake of simplicity, we will assume that taxes are equal to a constant fraction, t, of income. In this case,

$$Y_d = (1-t)Y.$$

Hence, in equilibrium, with aggregate expenditures equaling income,

$$Y = AE = a + MPC(1-t)Y + E.$$

If we now solve this equation for Y, we obtain

$$Y = (a + E)/[1 - (1-t)MPC].$$

As a numerical example, let $a = \$2$ trillion, $E = \$3$ trillion, $MPC = .8$, and $t = .25$. Substituting these into the expression for equilibrium output yields $Y = \$12.5$ trillion. If any of the components of E changes by $1, equilibrium output changes by $1/(1-(1-t)MPC)$. For example, suppose E increases to $4 trillion. Equilibrium output rises to $15 trillion. The multiplier is equal to the change in output ($15 trillion − $12.5 trillion = $2.5 trillion) per dollar change in E ($1 trillion), or 2.5. This can also be found directly as $1/(1-(1-t)MPC) = 1/[1-(1-.25) \times .8] = 2.5$. By contrast, the multiplier without taxes would be $1/(1-MPC) = 5$, or twice as large. The reason that the multiplier is larger without taxes is simple. Without taxes, every dollar of extra income translates into 80 cents of extra spending. With taxes, when income goes up by a dollar, disposable income rises by 75 cents and consumption increases by only $.8 \times .75$ cents = 60 cents.

EXPECTATIONS OF FUTURE INCOME

Current disposable income is a key determinant of consumption, but households' decisions about how much to consume are also influenced by their expectations about future income. If households expect that their income will fall in the future, they are likely to reduce their current consumption so that they can save more. By saving more today, they will be better able to preserve their standard of living when their income declines later. Thus, a projected or expected tax increase that will reduce future disposable income may reduce consumption spending even before it goes into effect. Conversely, if households expect that their future income will rise, they are likely to increase their consumption spending immediately. A projected or expected tax decrease can lead to a rise in consumption before households actually see their disposable income go up.

The dependence of current spending on expectations about future income has another very important implication. Households are likely to increase spending more when their current income rises if they expect the income increase to be permanent—that is, if they expect both their current and future income to be higher. Similarly, a tax cut viewed as temporary is likely to lead to a smaller increase in consumption than a tax cut that is viewed as permanent. Another way to express this implication is to say that the marginal propensity to consume out of permanent changes in income will be larger than the marginal propensity to consume out of temporary or transitory changes in income.

If consumption changes when expected future income changes, even when current income is still the same, then shifts in expectations will cause the aggregate expenditure schedule to shift. When households become more optimistic about their future income, aggregate consumption will increase at each level of current disposable income. The result is an increase in aggregate expenditures at each level of national income, shifting the aggregate expenditure schedule upward.

WEALTH

A third factor that is important for determining consumption is household wealth. Wealthier households will consume more (at each level of current income). Just as changes in individuals' wealth will affect their consumption choices, so changes in aggregate wealth will affect aggregate consumption.

For example, the stock market boom of the late 1990s caused many people to feel wealthier. As a result, they increased their consumption spending at each level of current income. These increases had the effect of shifting the aggregate expenditures schedule upward. When the stock market crashed in 2000, the same individuals experienced a drop in their wealth and reduced consumption spending; the aggregate expenditures schedule therefore shifted downward.

Wrap-Up

CONSUMPTION AND THE AGGREGATE EXPENDITURES SCHEDULE

Three key determinants of consumption are
1. Disposable income: the marginal propensity to consume and the tax rate, by affecting how much consumption changes when total income changes, affect the slope of the aggregate expenditures schedule and the multiplier.
2. Expectations about future disposable income: changes in expectations about future income shift the aggregate expenditures schedule.
3. Wealth: changes in household wealth shift the aggregate expenditures schedule.

Investment

Variation in investment spending is probably the principal cause of shifts in the aggregate expenditures schedule. The volatility of investment is shown in Figure 30.5. Since 1960, investment has averaged about 13 percent of GDP, but it has ranged from a low of 10 percent to a high of 17 percent.

Investment spending comprises three broad categories. The first is firms' purchases of new capital goods (everything from new factories and buildings to machinery to the cash registers, computers, and desks used by firms). These make up the **plant and equipment** component of total investment. Firms also invest in **inventories,** storing their output in anticipation of sales or storing the raw materials they will need to produce more goods. The third investment category consists of households' purchases of new homes, or **residential investment.**

The purchases of previously owned capital goods or houses do not count in investment spending because they are not purchases of current production. Recall from Chapter 22 that GDP is defined as total final goods and services *produced* in the current year. We exclude from investment any purchases of capital goods or houses that were built in earlier years. If one person buys a home built ten years ago, he might view it as an investment. But for the seller it is a "disinvestment," so the transaction represents no new investment in the economy but simply a change in who owns an existing asset.

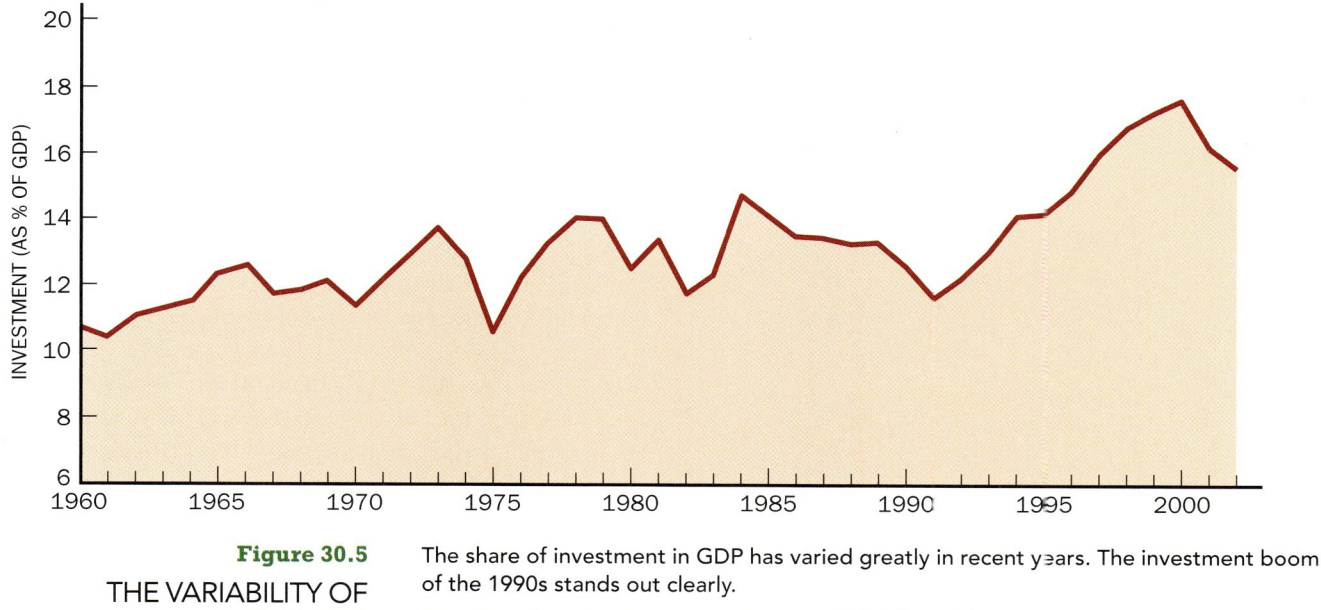

Figure 30.5
THE VARIABILITY OF INVESTMENT

The share of investment in GDP has varied greatly in recent years. The investment boom of the 1990s stands out clearly.

SOURCES: *Economic Report of the President* (2004), Table B-2.

INVESTMENT AND THE REAL INTEREST RATE

To undertake investment in new plants or equipment, firms must believe that the expected future returns will be large enough to compensate them for the risks of the investment. Moreover, firms are aware that a dollar in the future is worth less than a dollar today; if they had the dollar today, they could put it in a bank and get back the dollar *with interest* a year later. *As the interest rate rises, future dollars are worth less relative to today's dollars.* As a result, there will be fewer investment projects with future returns large enough to offset the forgone interest. To put the relationship between investment and interest another way, think of a firm as having to borrow money for the investment project. As higher interest rates increase the cost of undertaking the project, fewer projects will have an expected return high enough to yield a profit after those higher interest costs are paid. Thus, higher interest rates lead to lower levels of investment.

The relationship between interest rates and investment is the investment function introduced in Chapter 6. It is depicted as the downward-sloping curve in Figure 30.6. Of course, what matters for investment spending is the *real interest rate,* or the cost of funds after taking into account the effect of inflation. If the *nominal* interest rate increases but expected inflation increases by the same amount, firms' investment will be unaffected. (The real interest rate is the nominal interest rate minus the expected rate of inflation.) When there is inflation, the dollars that the firm uses in the future to pay back the funds borrowed today for investment will be worth less than those borrowed dollars. If inflation is 5 percent, then each year, the value of goods and services that a dollar can purchase drops by 5 percent. If the interest rate is 8 percent, the real cost of the loan is only 3 percent (the 8 percent nominal interest rate minus the 5 percent rate of inflation).

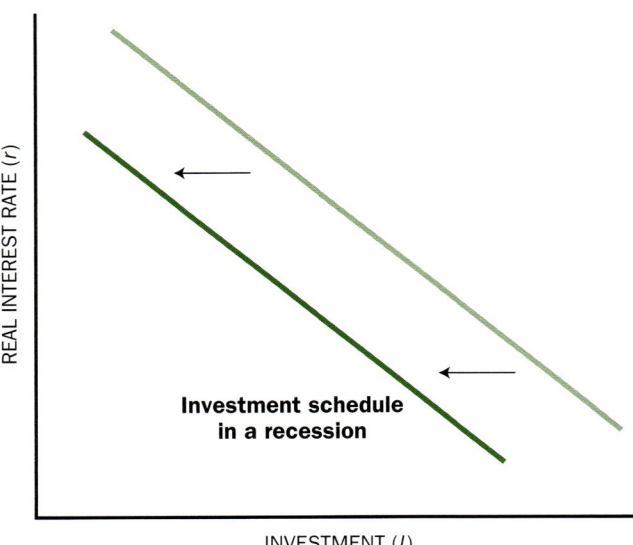

Figure 30.6

THE INVESTMENT SCHEDULE

At higher real interest rates, firms are willing to invest less. As the economy enters a recession, expectations of profits decrease, the ability to share risks decreases, and the availability of financing decreases. These changes lead to a shift in the investment schedule to the left.

While we have focused our discussion on investment spending by firms, the same principles are at work when individuals decide to make investment purchases—for example, buying a new car. If someone plans to take out a car loan, the interest rate on the loan is an important factor that will influence whether or not she buys a car and, if she does, what type of car she buys and how much she ends up spending on it. An increase in the interest rate on car loans will increase the cost of buying a car, and in response to the greater cost, some consumers will purchase less-expensive cars, while others may decide not to buy a new car at all. Even if a car buyer plans to pay cash, the interest rate is still relevant. Money earmarked for a car could instead be saved at the going rate of interest. An increase in the level of interest rates increases the opportunity cost (the forgone interest income) of spending the money on a car.

Investment Variability Investment decisions must be based on expectations about future returns. Predicting the future is always difficult. There may be *technological risks*—the firm may introduce a new technology that could prove unreliable. In most cases, there are *market risks*. Will there be a market for a new product? At what price will it sell? What will labor costs be in the future? What about the prices of energy and other inputs? Firms must base investment decisions on educated guesses, recognizing that much often remains uncertain.

The risks associated with investment spending are the primary reason that investment is so volatile. Expectations about the future may oscillate sharply. When sales are up today, firms may expect future sales to be high and perhaps even to continue to increase. In response, they will want to add more plant and equipment for the future—that is, they will want to invest more. If sales dip, firms may decide to scale back or even cancel their plans for new capital goods, and thus investment will fall. Changes in current output therefore will shift the investment schedule. For instance, when the economy goes into a recession, the investment schedule typically shifts to the left, as depicted in Figure 30.6. Expectations of future profits decrease, risks appear larger, and the ability and willingness to bear risks are reduced.

INVENTORY INVESTMENT

One of the most volatile components of investment is inventories—the materials that are held in storage awaiting either use in production or sale to customers. Inventories are typically very large. Usually, about $1.50 worth of goods and services is held in inventory for every $1 of goods sold each month.

Inventory investment is equal to the *change* in the stock of goods in inventory. Firms hold inventories of intermediate goods used as inputs in production; doing so facilitates production by ensuring that parts are available when they are needed. Similarly, stores hold inventories so that customers can obtain the goods they want without waiting; otherwise, they may seek those goods elsewhere. Finally, because gearing up a production facility and then closing it down as sales fluctuate can be costly, firms find it profitable to produce at a relatively constant rate, adding to inventories when sales weaken and selling out of inventories when sales strengthen.

Inventory investment is the most volatile component of aggregate expenditures. One reason for this variability may again be the impact of the availability of credit on naturally risk-averse firms. When the economy enters a recession, firms often find that their net worth is decreased. This can make it harder for them to obtain credit to finance their inventory investment. They may also become less willing to make any kind of investment, in inventories or otherwise. Indeed, when possible, they would like to disinvest, or convert their assets back into cash. By far, the easiest method of disinvestment is to sell off inventories.

As the economy goes into a recession or simply slows down, inventories often build up involuntarily. Retail stores, for instance, base their orders on expected sales; if the sales fail to materialize, the store holds the unsold merchandise as "inventories." This unintended accumulation of inventory can rapidly affect production, as stores respond by reducing their factory orders. Lower orders, in turn, lead quickly to cutbacks in production. The cutbacks in production as firms try to restore their inventories to a normal size relative to sales are referred to as *inventory corrections*. Cyclical variability induced by inventories is called *inventory cycles*.

> **Wrap-Up**

DETERMINANTS OF INVESTMENT

1. Investment spending will depend negatively on the real interest rate.
2. Shifts in the investment schedule can be caused by changing assessments of risk or changes in expectations about future returns.
3. Fluctuations in current economic conditions can affect current investment by altering firms' expectations about future sales.

MACROECONOMIC IMPLICATIONS OF INVESTMENT

Three important macroeconomic implications can be drawn from this discussion of investment spending. First, we have identified another reason for the positive slope of the aggregate expenditures schedule: as current output rises, firms will increase investment spending, while if current output falls, they will scale back their investment plans. Because both consumption and investment expenditures will rise as income increases, the slope of the AE schedule is positive.

Second, investment depends on the real interest rate: at each level of income, a rise in the real interest rate will lower investment. A higher real interest rate lowers total aggregate expenditures, shifting the AE schedule down. Conversely, a reduction in the real interest rate will shift the AE schedule up.

Figure 30.7

THE EFFECT OF AN INCREASE IN GOVERNMENT PURCHASES

Government purchases (G) are one of the components of aggregate expenditures. An increase in government purchases shifts the aggregate expenditures schedule up by the amount of the increase. Because of the multiplier effect, the increase in equilibrium output, $Y_1 - Y_0$, is greater than the increase in government purchases, ΔG.

Third, changing perceptions of risk or of future economic conditions affect investment expenditures. Their influence helps account for the volatility of investment, and they can be added to our list of factors that shift the aggregate expenditures schedule.

Government Purchases

The third component of aggregate expenditures is government purchases. In later chapters, when we discuss fiscal policy in the United States, we will usually focus on the expenditure and tax policies of the federal government. However, this category consists of the purchases of goods and services by *all* levels of government—federal, state, and local. In fact, of the total government purchases of roughly $2 trillion (about 18 percent of GDP), only about one-third—under $700 billion—are made by the federal government. Its total *expenditures* of about $3 trillion exceed those by state and local governments, but a large fraction of federal expenditures are for programs such as Social Security that do not directly purchase goods and services. The largest component of federal government purchases is defense, equal to roughly two-thirds of the total.

At this point in our analysis, it is useful to assume that total government purchases do not vary with income but instead are simply fixed—say, at $2 trillion. Earlier, we learned that taxes vary with income, so government revenue will rise and fall as income fluctuates. But because the government can borrow (run a deficit) when tax revenues are less than expenditures, and repay its debt when tax revenues exceed expenditures, government spending does not need to move in lockstep with tax revenues. In later chapters we will study in greater detail the role of fiscal policy, government expenditures, and tax policies. For now, though, we will assume that government purchases are fixed (in real terms).

Government purchases (*G*) are one component of aggregate expenditures. An increase in *G* will raise aggregate expenditures at each level of total income. This rise shifts the *AE* schedule up by the amount of the increase in *G*, as Figure 30.7 shows. Equilibrium again occurs at the intersection of the aggregate expenditures schedule and the 45-degree line. The total increase in equilibrium output depends on the size of the change in *G* and on the multiplier.

Net Exports

The analysis so far has ignored the important role of international trade. Such an omission is appropriate for a closed economy, an economy that neither imports nor exports, but not for an open economy, one actively engaged in international trade. Today, the United States and other industrialized economies are very much open economies.

The effect of exports and imports on aggregate expenditures is straightforward. Recall that what we are concerned with here is total purchases of *domestically* produced output. Consequently, exports of U.S.-produced goods to other countries represent another component of aggregate expenditures, just like consumption, investment, and government expenditures. However, some of what households, firms, and the government purchase are goods made abroad. To calculate the total demand for domestically produced goods, we must subtract the value of imports from the total. The net effect of international trade on aggregate expenditures is measured then by exports minus imports, or *net exports*. Exports minus imports are also sometimes referred to as the **balance of trade.**

Figure 30.8 shows net exports as a percentage of GDP for the United States. Since the mid-1970s, U.S. imports have exceeded U.S. exports, making net exports negative. Chapter 26, from the long-run perspective of the full-employment model, discussed how net exports were affected by the U.S. investment boom in the late 1990s and the large increases in the federal budget deficit in recent years. Our focus in the current chapter is on the short run, so just as we did when discussing the other components of aggregate expenditures, we need to ask whether net exports depend on income (and if so, how), and we need to ask what factors might shift net exports at each level of income.

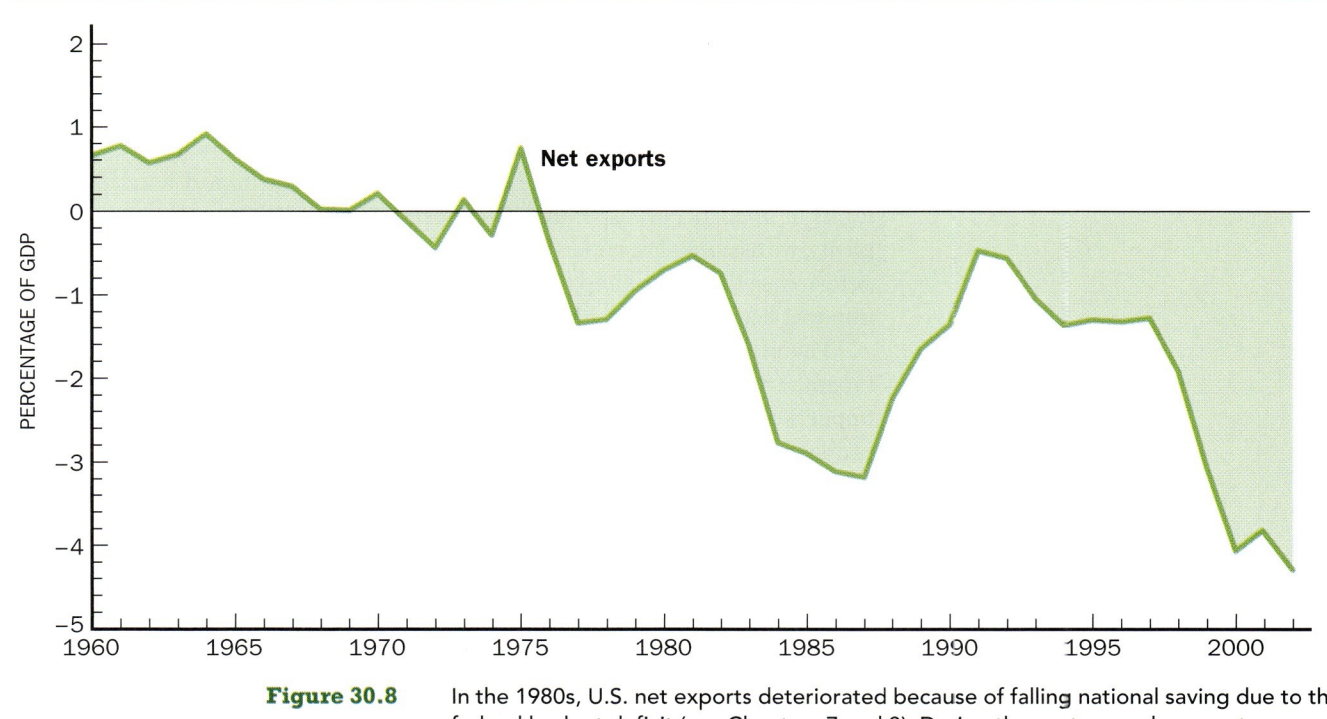

Figure 30.8

NET EXPORTS AS A PERCENTAGE OF GDP

In the 1980s, U.S. net exports deteriorated because of falling national saving due to the federal budget deficit (see Chapters 7 and 8). During the past several years, strong growth in U.S. incomes, recessions in many countries we trade with, and a burgeoning federal budget deficit have caused net exports to fall dramatically.

SOURCE: *Economic Report of the President* (2004).

EXPORTS

What foreign consumers buy from the United States depends on their income, not income in the United States. Exports may also depend on other factors, such as the marketing efforts of American firms and the prices of American goods relative to foreign goods. To simplify, we will assume that income in other countries does not depend on what happens in the United States. Exports, like government purchases, will not vary with U.S. income.

Exports do depend on the relative cost of goods produced in different countries. If the price of a Toyota 4Runner built in Japan rises relative to the cost of an American-manufactured Ford Explorer, consumers in other countries will buy more Ford Explorers and fewer Toyota 4Runners, so U.S. exports will rise.

The relative price of goods produced abroad and goods produced domestically is affected by the exchange rate, as explained in Chapter 26. If the dollar falls in value, U.S. goods become less expensive. As a result, consumers and firms in the rest of the world will tend to increase their purchases of U.S.-produced goods and U.S. exports will rise. Changes in the exchange rate affect exports at each level of income. A rise in the value of the dollar makes U.S.-produced goods more expensive on world markets and reduces U.S. exports; a fall in the value of the dollar has the opposite effect and increases U.S. exports.

IMPORTS

When their incomes rise, households buy not only more American-made consumer goods but also more goods from abroad. We can draw an **import function** in much the same way as the consumption function that we used to illustrate the relationship between disposable income and consumption. The import function shows the levels of imports corresponding to different levels of income. For the sake of simplicity, we assume that imports are bought by consumers and that disposable income determines the level of imports. The import function, depicted in Figure 30.9, shows imports rising as disposable income rises.

The **marginal propensity to import** gives the amount of each extra dollar of income that is spent on imports. If the marginal propensity to import is .1, then imports rise by $100 if income rises by $1,000 ($100 is .1 × $1,000). The marginal propensity to import is given by the slope of the import function.

As incomes increase, imports rise while exports remain unchanged. Thus net exports fall as income rises. This fact helps explain the decline in U.S. net exports in the latter half of the 1990s (see Figure 30.8). At a time when the U.S. economy was booming and many other countries were in recession, our imports rose significantly, reducing net exports.

Imports also depend on the relative cost of goods produced abroad and domestically, which in turn is affected by the exchange rate. If the dollar rises in value, foreign goods become less expensive. Households tend to increase their purchases of goods produced abroad, and imports rise. One reason for the big drop in U.S. net exports in the mid-1980s was a significant rise in the dollar's value. As foreign goods became less expensive, imports rose. Changes in the exchange rate affect imports at each level of income. A rise in the value of the dollar shifts the import function up; a fall in the value of the dollar shifts the import function down.

Changes in the exchange rate affect imports for the same reason that they affect exports. If the dollar rises in value, U.S. goods become relatively more expensive. Foreigners buy fewer American goods and our exports will fall. Since this exchange rate alteration makes foreign goods relatively cheaper, our imports rise, so net exports fall. Conversely, a fall in the value of the dollar will stimulate exports and reduce imports, leading to an increase in net exports.

MACROECONOMIC IMPLICATIONS

Net exports affect the aggregate expenditures schedule in two ways. First, net exports alter its slope. As incomes rise, imports also rise, thereby reducing the net increase in expenditures on domestically produced goods and services. Aggregate expenditures rise with income because consumption and investment increase, but the slope of the AE schedule will be flatter in an open economy. If the marginal propensity to import is small, then the slope of the AE schedule is reduced only slightly; if the marginal propensity to import is large, as it might be in a very open economy, then the slope will be reduced significantly.

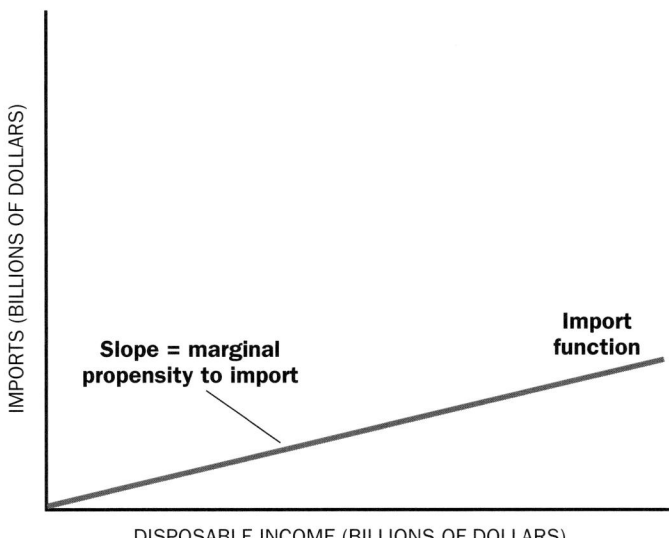

Figure 30.9

THE IMPORT FUNCTION

Imports (M) increase steadily as disposable income (Y_d) rises. The slope of the import function is equal to the marginal propensity to import.

Second, factors such as exchange rates and income developments in other countries can affect net exports and lead to shifts in the *AE* schedule. A recession in Europe will reduce U.S. exports and shift the aggregate expenditures schedule for the United States down. In the absence of any other change, equilibrium output in the United States will fall. In the late 1990s, the financial crises and subsequent recessions in many Asian economies raised the concern that the resulting fall in U.S. exports would lead to a recession here. The drop in exports shifted the *AE* schedule for the United States down. Fortunately, not everything else remained unchanged, and the United States continued to enjoy an economic boom. This bit of recent history illustrates an important point. We often use our theoretical models to illustrate what would happen if one factor changed, when all other things were held constant, because doing so enables us to understand clearly the distinct effects of changes in each factor. In the real world, however, many of the things we assumed to be constant are also changing, and we need to use our models to analyze simultaneous changes in many factors.

PUTTING INTERNATIONAL TRADE INTO THE EQUATION

When we add exports (X) and imports (M), aggregate expenditures are given by

$$AE = C + I + G + X - M.$$

Imports are related to disposable income by the import function,

$$M = MPI \times Y_d,$$

where MPI is the marginal propensity to import. Exports are assumed to be fixed. Hence, aggregate expenditures are

$$AE = a + MPC \times (1-t) \times Y + I + G + X - MPI \times (1-t) \times Y.$$

Since aggregate expenditures equal income, in equilibrium,

$$Y = (a + I + G + X)/[1 - (1-t)(MPC - MPI)],$$

so the multiplier is

$$1/[1 - (1-t)(MPC - MPI)].$$

If $t = .25$, $MPC = .8$, and $MPI = .1$, the multiplier is

$$1/[1 - .75(.8 - .1)] = 2.1,$$

smaller than it was in the absence of trade (2.5).

Calculating Equilibrium Output

At this point, it may be helpful to work through two simple examples, one illustrating the calculation of equilibrium GDP in a closed economy and the other showing the same calculation for an open economy. Suppose we have the following information on a closed economy. Each row in Table 30.1 gives the level of income (Y) in the first column and the levels of taxes (T), consumption (C), investment (I), and government purchases (G) at that level of income. I and G are assumed to be constant, regardless of the level of income, but both taxes and consumption rise with income. The final column calculates aggregate expenditures; it is simply equal to $C + I + G$ for our closed economy.

Equilibrium output occurs at the point where Y is equal to $C + I + G$. Using the information in Table 30.1, we can add up C, I, and G. If we do this, we find that equilibrium output is 7,000. At this output level, consumption is 4,600, investment is 1,200, and government purchases are 1,200; therefore, $AE = C + I + G = 4,600 + 1,200 + 1,200 = 7,000 = Y$.

Suppose G increases to 1,600. Recalculating aggregate expenditures ($C + I + G$) at each income level, we can find that the new equilibrium level of output will be 8,000. The increase of G by 400 increases Y by 1,000, so the multiplier is 2.5.

We also know that when taxes depend on income, the multiplier is equal to $1/[1 - (1 - t)MPC]$), where t is the marginal tax rate. Using the information in the table, we can see that as income rises by 1,000, say from 7,000 to 8,000, taxes increase by 250, one-fourth as much. So $t = .25$. As total income increases by 1,000, disposable income increases by 750. Consumption then rises by 600. In the same example, as

Table 30.1

EQUILIBRIUM OUTPUT IN A CLOSED ECONOMY

Y	T	C	I	G	AE
1,000	200	1,000	1,200	1,200	3,400
2,000	450	1,600	1,200	1,200	4,000
3,000	700	2,200	1,200	1,200	4,600
4,000	950	2,800	1,200	1,200	5,200
5,000	1,200	3,400	1,200	1,200	5,800
6,000	1,450	4,000	1,200	1,200	6,400
7,000	**1,700**	**4,600**	**1,200**	**1,200**	**7,000**
8,000	1,950	5,200	1,200	1,200	7,600
9,000	2,200	5,800	1,200	1,200	8,200
10,000	2,450	6,400	1,200	1,200	8,800
11,000	2,700	7,000	1,200	1,200	9,400
12,000	2,950	7,600	1,200	1,200	10,000
13,000	3,200	8,200	1,200	1,200	10,600

Y goes from 7,000 to 8,000, disposable income goes from 5,300 (7,000 − 1,700) to 6,050 (8,000 − 1,950). Consumption rises from 4,600 to 5,200, an increase of 600. The *MPC* is the increase in *C* per dollar increase in disposable income, or 600/750 = .8. Using these values, we can calculate the multiplier to be $1/(1 − (1 − .25) \times .8) = 1/(1 − .75 \times 8) = 1/(1 − .6) = 1/.4 = 2.5$, the same value we found directly by finding the new equilibrium after an increase in *G*.

How would things change if we were dealing with an open economy? In an open economy, aggregate expenditures consist of $C + I + G + X − M$, where X denotes exports and M denotes imports. Suppose we have the information in Table 30.2. Exports do not depend on the level of GDP; in our example, they are equal to 500. Imports rise with income, and the example assumes a marginal propensity to import of .1. Just as in the closed economy, equilibrium occurs when $Y = AE$. In this example, as in the previous one, the equilibrium level of GDP is 7,000. For this economy, net exports are positive at the equilibrium level of GDP. A comparison between the *AE* column in the two tables reveals that as income rises, aggregate expenditures increase faster in the closed economy than in the open economy. In the latter, a positive marginal propensity to import means that imports rise as income rises, reducing net exports.

Given a marginal propensity to import of .1, a marginal propensity to consume of .8, and a marginal tax rate of .25, the formula for the multiplier tells us that a $1 increase in *G* will increase equilibrium income by $1/[1 − .75(.8 − .1)] = 2.1$. If *G* increases by 400, then equilibrium income will increase by 840, from 7,000 to 7,840. Recall that in the closed economy described in Table 30.1, the multiplier was 2.5. Again, the marginal propensity to import explains why it is smaller in the open economy.

Table 30.2

EQUILIBRIUM OUTPUT IN AN OPEN ECONOMY

Y	T	C	I	G	X	M	AE
1,000	200	1,000	1,200	1,100	900	200	4,000
2,000	450	1,600	1,200	1,100	900	300	4,500
3,000	700	2,200	1,200	1,100	900	400	5,000
4,000	950	2,800	1,200	1,100	900	500	5,500
5,000	1,200	3,400	1,200	1,100	900	600	6,000
6,000	1,450	4,000	1,200	1,100	900	700	6,500
7,000	**1,700**	**4,600**	**1,200**	**1,100**	**900**	**800**	**7,000**
8,000	1,950	5,200	1,200	1,100	900	900	7,500
9,000	2,200	5,800	1,200	1,100	900	1,000	8,000
10,000	2,450	6,400	1,200	1,100	900	1,100	8,500
11,000	2,700	7,000	1,200	1,100	900	1,200	9,000
12,000	2,950	7,600	1,200	1,100	900	1,300	9,500
13,000	3,200	8,200	1,200	1,100	900	1,400	10,000

> **Wrap-Up**
>
> ## AGGREGATE EXPENDITURES AND OUTPUT
>
> Aggregate expenditures and output are equal where the aggregate expenditures schedule crosses the 45-degree line.
>
> Shifts in the aggregate expenditure schedule have a multiplied impact on the level of equilibrium output. This multiplier depends on the marginal propensity to consume, the marginal tax rate, and the marginal propensity to import.
>
> Factors that can shift the aggregate expenditures schedule up and increase equilibrium output include
> - increases in wealth or expectations of higher future disposable income
> - a reduction in the perceived risks of investment
> - a fall in the value of the dollar
> - a fall in the real rate of interest.

Aggregate Expenditures and the Real Interest Rate

Our discussion has highlighted a number of factors in addition to national income that can alter aggregate expenditures at each level of national income: expectations about future income, wealth, the exchange rate, and one of the most important, the real rate of interest. The impact of the interest rate on aggregate expenditures provides monetary policy a key means of affecting economic activity. Changes in the real interest rate influence investment spending and household purchases of new homes and durables like autos. Chapters 17 and 18 will discuss how interest rates also affect the exchange rate and therefore net exports. This connection offers another channel through which monetary policy can attempt to control aggregate expenditures.

Each of the aggregate expenditures schedules used in this chapter was drawn for a given real rate of interest. A change in the real rate of interest shifts the *AE* schedule. A decrease in the real rate, for instance, raises investment spending as credit becomes more readily available and firms find it less costly to borrow to undertake new projects. Such a decrease would therefore shift the *AE* schedule up, increasing the equilibrium level of GDP. An increase in the real interest rate has the opposite effect, shifting the *AE* schedule down and reducing equilibrium GDP.

For an open economy, interest rate changes can also affect net exports by causing the exchange rate to change. This link between interest rates and aggregate

Thinking Like an Economist

INCENTIVES AND THE REAL AFTER-TAX RATE OF INTEREST

In other chapters we have emphasized that real values determine incentives. Thus, decisions to save and invest respond to real interest rates. So far, deriving the real interest rate from the nominal interest rate has been straightforward: subtract the rate of inflation from the nominal interest rate. But for the sake of simplicity we have ignored another important factor, the effect of taxation. In the absence of taxes on interest income, a nominal interest rate of 2 percent and 0 percent inflation yields the same real return as a nominal interest rate of 6 percent and 4 percent inflation. If nominal interest income is taxed, then the relationship between the nominal interest rate, inflation, and the real interest rate becomes more complicated.

Suppose nominal interest income is taxed at a 25 percent rate. If inflation is 0 percent and the nominal interest rate is 2 percent, the *after-tax* nominal return would be the 2 percent return minus the taxes (.25 × 2 percent = 0.5 percent), leaving an after-tax nominal return of 1.5 percent. With 0 percent inflation, this is also the real return.

Now consider the situation when inflation rises to 4 percent. If the nominal interest rate were to rise to 6 percent, the after-tax return would be 6 percent minus taxes (.25 × 6 percent = 1.5 percent), leaving a nominal after-tax return of 4.5 percent. Since inflation was 4 percent, the *real after-tax* return is only 0.5 percent! Even though the nominal interest rate rose by the same amount as inflation, the real after-tax return fell.

To maintain the same 1.5 percent real after-tax return that was obtained with 0 percent inflation, the nominal interest rate would need to rise to 7.33 percent when inflation increases to 4 percent. With a nominal return of 7.33 percent, the nominal after-tax return would be 5.5 percent, and the real after-tax return would be 1.5 percent. The nominal interest rate must more than match increases in inflation in order to maintain the same real return. In this example, if inflation increases 4 percent, the nominal interest rate must rise 5.33 percent.

The relationship would be different if countries designed their tax systems to tax real returns rather than nominal returns. In the case of 4 percent inflation, a nominal interest rate of 6 percent would yield a real before-tax return of 2 percent and an after-tax return of 1.5 percent, the same after-tax return as was earned with 0 percent inflation and a 2 percent nominal interest rate.

expenditures will be explained in Chapter 34; here we can note that it serves to reinforce the negative effect on aggregate expenditures of a rise in the real rate. Thus the basic effects of interest rates on the *AE* schedule in a closed economy will also be observed when we are studying the determination of GDP in an open economy.

Wrap-Up

THE REAL INTEREST RATE AND EQUILIBRIUM OUTPUT

A fall in the real rate of interest increases investment spending and household purchases of durables and new homes. These increases shift the aggregate expenditures schedule up, raising equilibrium output.

Review and Practice

SUMMARY

1. Income-expenditure analysis shows how the equilibrium level of output in the economy is determined when firms produce to meet demand.
2. Equilibrium output is determined by the intersection of the 45-degree line and the aggregate expenditures schedule. The aggregate expenditures schedule shows the level of expenditures at each level of national income, while the 45-degree line represents the points where aggregate expenditures equal output.
3. Shifts in the aggregate expenditures schedule give rise to changes in equilibrium output. The magnitude of the increase in output resulting from an upward shift in the schedule depends on the slope of the schedule. Much of macroeconomic analysis focuses on what determines the slope of the schedule, what causes shifts in the schedule, and how government policies affect the schedule.
4. Aggregate expenditures are the sum of consumption, investment, government purchases, and net exports.
5. Consumption increases as disposable income increases. The amount by which consumption increases when disposable income increases by a dollar is called the marginal propensity to consume.
6. The multiplier tells us how much total aggregate expenditures and output increase when the aggregate expenditures schedule shifts up by $1. The multiplier is larger if the marginal propensity to consume is large.
7. If tax revenues rise with income, the aggregate expenditures schedule is flattened and the multiplier is reduced. Taxes act as an automatic stabilizer. Increases in government purchases shift the schedule up.
8. Imports increase with income. The relationship between imports and income is called the import function; its slope is the marginal propensity to import. Exports are determined by factors in other countries. Trade reduces the multiplier, because as income increases, some of it goes to purchase foreign rather than domestic goods.
9. Both imports and exports depend on the exchange rate. A fall in the value of the dollar increases exports and reduces imports; this increase in net exports shifts the aggregate expenditures schedule up.
10. Changes in the real interest rate affect investment, the exchange rate, and net exports. A rise in the real interest rate reduces investment and net exports, leading to a downward shift in the aggregate expenditures schedule. Consequently, the level of output consistent with equilibrium falls as the real interest rate rises.

KEY TERMS

aggregate expenditures
aggregate expenditures schedule
income–expenditure analysis
multiplier
disposable income
marginal propensity to consume (MPC)
marginal propensity to save (MPS)
automatic stabilizer
plant and equipment investment
inventory investment
residential investment
balance of trade
import function
marginal propensity to import

REVIEW QUESTIONS

1. What is the aggregate expenditures schedule? What are the components of aggregate expenditures?
2. If output is determined by aggregate expenditures, explain how the equilibrium level of output is determined. Why are points on the aggregate expenditures schedule above the 45-degree line not sustainable? Why are points on the aggregate expenditures schedule below the 45-degree line not sustainable?
3. What factors might cause shifts in the aggregate expenditures schedule? List at least four.
4. How is the multiplier affected by the marginal propensity to consume? By the marginal tax rate? By the marginal propensity to import?
5. Why does an increase in the real rate of interest lower equilibrium output?

PROBLEMS

1. In the economy of Consumerland, national income and consumption are related in this way:

National income	$1,500	$1,600	$1,700	$1,800	$1,900
Consumption	$1,325	$1,420	$1,515	$1,610	$1,705

   Calculate national saving at each level of national income. What is the marginal propensity to consume in Consumerland? What is the marginal propensity to save? If national income rose to $2,000, what do you predict consumption and saving would be?

2. To the economy of Consumerland, add the fact that investment will be $180 at every level of output. Graph the consumption function and the aggregate expenditures schedule for this simple economy (no government or net exports). What determines the slope of the aggregate expenditures schedule? What is the equilibrium output?

3. Calculate the effect of a one-dollar increase in investment on output for each of the following economies:
   (a) A simple consumption and investment economy where the *MPC* is .9
   (b) An economy with government but no foreign trade, where the *MPC* is .9 and the tax rate is .3
   (c) An economy with an *MPĆ* of .9, a tax rate of .3, and a marginal propensity to import of .1

4. If, at each level of disposable income, saving increases, what does this imply about what has happened to the consumption function? What will be the consequences for the equilibrium level of output?

5. If the government made it easier for people to borrow money, perhaps by enacting programs to help them get loans, would you expect consumption spending to become more sensitive or less sensitive to current income? Why? How is the marginal propensity to consume affected? How is the multiplier affected?

6. Suppose the consumption function is given by $C = a + bY_d$ where a and b are constants (b is the marginal propensity to consume), and Y_d is disposable income, equal to $Y - T$. Taxes vary with income and are equal to $t_0 + tY$ where t_0 and t are constants (t is the marginal tax rate).
   (a) What is the effect on consumption of a $1 change in total income?
   (b) What is the effect on saving of a $1 change in total income?

Learning Goals

In this chapter, you will learn

1. What a monetary policy rule is, and how it depends on inflation

2. What the aggregate demand–inflation (ADI) curve is, what determines its slope, and what causes it to shift

3. How the ADI curve can be used to understand important macroeconomic events

4. How output and inflation respond to aggregate demand shocks and aggregate supply shocks

Chapter 31

AGGREGATE DEMAND AND INFLATION

Every six weeks, the members of the Federal Open Market Committee (FOMC), the policymaking committee of the Federal Reserve, gather in Washington, D.C. They come from across the nation to discuss the state of the economy and to make decisions that can determine the outlook for U.S. inflation and unemployment over the next several years. Stock markets can rise or fall in anticipation of FOMC decisions. On April 14, 2000, when the government released the latest figures suggesting a rise in inflation, the Dow Jones Industrial Average fell 616 points, its largest one-day point loss ever, in response to investors' fears that the FOMC would raise interest rates. Nine months later, on January 3, 2001, the Dow jumped 300 points and the NASDAQ went up 325 points when the FOMC cut interest rates. Investors know that if the economy booms and inflation rises, the Fed will increase interest rates; if the economy slows and inflation falls, the Fed will lower interest rates. These decisions by the FOMC affect the cost of credit for major corporations as well as for small family businesses. They affect the cost of car loans, student loans, and home mortgages. The importance of the FOMC for everyone in the economy has spawned a distinct industry of "Fed watchers" who try to predict what the FOMC will do. Since 1986, the chair of the Federal Reserve has been Alan Greenspan, and Fed watchers closely follow every speech and statement made by Chairman Greenspan for clues about future policy actions.

The Fed's actions have an important influence on GDP and inflation. In Chapter 30, we learned that the economy's level of output (GDP) is determined in the short run by the level of aggregate demand. One factor that affects aggregate demand is the real rate of interest. We now need to bring inflation back into the picture so that we can understand the linkages among inflation, the real interest rate, and aggregate demand. Monetary policy plays a critical role in this story. This should not be surprising, for Chapter 28 has already noted that when the economy is at full employment, the average inflation rate is determined by monetary policy. In the

689

United States, monetary policy is the responsibility of the Federal Reserve, our central bank.

Keeping inflation low and stable is a primary responsibility of any central bank, and, particularly during the past twenty-five years, many countries have undertaken central bank reforms that specify low inflation as the major or even sole objective of monetary policy. To maintain control over inflation, the Fed needs to keep its eye on the level of aggregate demand relative to the economy's full-employment output. If aggregate demand rises relative to the economy's full-employment output, inflation will rise: firms can boost prices and low unemployment will lead to wage increases in excess of productivity gains that push up firms' costs. If demand falls relative to potential output, inflation will eventually moderate. To keep inflation stable, the Fed acts to reduce demand when it starts to rise and to increase demand when it falls.

In the previous two chapters, we focused on the first two of the four key concepts for understanding short-run economic fluctuations—wages and prices do not adjust fast enough to keep the economy always at full employment. As a result, unemployment and output fluctuate around the full-employment level, and equilibrium occurs when output equals aggregate expenditures. In this chapter, we bring into our analysis the third and fourth key concepts—there is a short-run trade-off between inflation and unemployment, and increases in inflation reduce aggregate spending. By the end of the chapter, you will have a simple framework for understanding many important macroeconomic debates.

The Real Interest Rate and the Capital Market

Any news report on the Fed and monetary policy is sure to involve a discussion of interest rates. The reason is simple: central bank policies influence the level of aggregate demand by affecting the cost and availability of credit. In Chapter 30, we examined the four components of aggregate expenditures—consumption, investment, government purchases, and net exports—and their determinants, and we learned that the real interest rate is one of the main factors influencing aggregate expenditures. To simplify the analysis in this and the next two chapters, we will concentrate on the case of a closed economy. This focus enables us to ignore net exports. Despite the growing importance of international trade, the vast bulk of goods and services purchased in the United States are produced in the United States, so even an initially circumscribed analysis can provide important insights into macroeconomics. In Chapter 35 we will discuss how the lessons learned from a study of a closed economy need to be modified when we deal with an open economy.

In a closed economy, a higher real interest rate lowers aggregate expenditures by two primary mechanisms: (1) it reduces the profitability of investment, leading businesses to scale back investment projects, and (2) it affects consumer loans and mortgages, causing households to cut back on purchases of new homes and of consumer durables such as autos.

When we discuss interest rates and monetary policy, it is natural to start with the capital market. We have already seen, in Chapter 24, how the real rate of interest balances saving and investment when the economy is at full employment. When the economy is not at full employment, saving and investment must still balance to ensure that the capital market is in equilibrium. Figure 31.1 shows capital market equilibria for two different levels of output. When the economy is producing at full employment, as we assumed in Part Six, the saving and investment schedules are given by S^f and I^f. (For the sake of simplicity, we have assumed saving does not vary with the real interest rate—that is why it is drawn as a vertical line.) The equilibrium real rate of interest is r_0. If the economy's output is at less than its full-employment level, household income will be lower, and households will save less at each value of the real interest rate. This outcome is shown by the saving schedule S_1, to the left of S^f. The saving schedule shifts left because the marginal propensity to consume is less than one—a one-dollar decline in income reduces consumption by less than a dollar, which means that saving is also reduced. If there is no change in the investment schedule, the capital market will again be in equilibrium at an income level below full employment when the real interest rate rises to r_1.

However, investment will not remain the same if GDP drops. When output falls and the economy enters a recession, the investment schedule will also be affected. Declines in production lead to higher unemployment of labor *and* lower utilization of plant and equipment. The drop reduces the need for new investment, and firms are less likely to invest when the business outlook is bleak. The leftward shift in the investment schedule is depicted by the investment schedule I_1 in Figure 31.1. In this case, the equilibrium real interest rate is r_2. Depending on the relative shifts of the saving and investment schedules, the new equilibrium real interest rate may be greater or less than r_0.

When the economy is at full employment, equilibrium in the capital market determines the full-employment real interest rate. But what determines output and the real interest rate at less than full employment? To answer this question, we turn now to the connection among inflation, spending, and monetary policy.

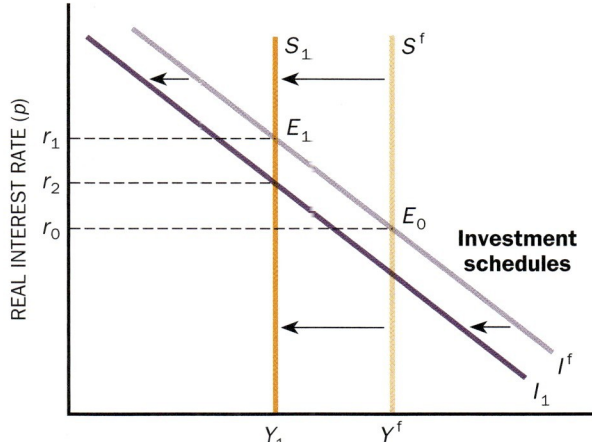

Figure 31.1

CAPITAL MARKET EQUILIBRIUM AT DIFFERENT INCOME AND INTEREST RATES

A fall in income from Y^f to Y_1 will shift the savings line to the left, from S^f to S_1. If the investment schedule remains unchanged, capital market equilibrium will occur at a higher real interest rate, r_1, and lower level of real income. A decline in output, however, is likely to shift the investment schedule to the left as firms reduce planned investment spending at each value of the real rate of interest. If the new investment schedule is I_1, the equilibrium real rate of interest is r_2. Depending on the magnitudes of the shifts, the final equilibrium real interest rate could be higher or lower than r_0.

The Aggregate Demand–Inflation Curve

In Chapter 29, we listed the effect of inflation on aggregate expenditures as the fourth of the key concepts for understanding short-run fluctuations of the economy. Now this relationship must be explored in more detail. Because monetary policy plays an important role in determining how changes in inflation affect aggregate expenditures, we need to focus on Fed policy.

THE FED'S POLICY RULE

The Fed is concerned about inflation, and it knows that as unemployment falls, inflation tends to rise (our third key concept). As inflation rises, the Fed acts to reduce aggregate demand in order to slow the economy down and lessen any upward pressure on inflation. The Fed can affect aggregate demand by influencing the real interest rate. An increase in the real interest rate will reduce investment spending, for example. As inflation falls, the Fed acts to lower the real interest rate to boost aggregate expenditures. These changes in aggregate demand move the economy's equilibrium level of output.

The Fed's systematic reaction to the economy is called a **monetary policy rule**. It describes how the Fed moves the interest rate in response to economic conditions. Initially, we will assume a very simple policy rule: the Fed raises interest rates when inflation increases and lowers interest rates when inflation falls. In 2004, for example, the Fed was concerned that inflation was rising, so it raised interest rates. In actuality, the Fed doesn't react only to inflation—a financial crisis might cause the Fed to lower interest rates even though inflation is unchanged, the Fed might be concerned that economic growth is slowing, and so on. For instance, on January 3, 2001, when the FOMC cut its interest rate target, it explained that "these actions were taken in light of further weakening of sales and production, and in the context of lower consumer confidence, tight conditions in some segments of financial markets, and high energy prices sapping household and business purchasing power. Moreover, inflation pressures remain contained."

When the Fed responds to factors other than inflation, the policy rule linking the interest rate to inflation changes. *A given policy rule reflects the adjustment of interest rates to inflation; a change in the policy rule occurs when, at a given level of inflation, the Fed sets a different interest rate than before.* Because the monetary policy rule describes how a central bank behaves, it can change over time. In the United States, as noted in Chapter 29, the Fed has taken much stronger action against inflation during the past twenty years than it did in the 1960s and 1970s.

There is one more point to keep in mind. Aggregate expenditures depend on the real interest rate (i.e., the nominal interest rate adjusted for inflation). To influence it, the Fed must move the nominal interest rate in the same direction as inflation, but by more. Thus, if inflation rises by 1 percentage point—say, from 3 to 4 percent—the Fed must raise the nominal interest by *more* than 1 percentage point to increase the real interest rate. Only then can it affect the real rate of interest and aggregate spending. To simplify our analysis here, we will postpone discussing the details of how the Fed affects the nominal interest rate until Chapter 32.

Inflation and Aggregate Expenditures Our discussion of the Fed's policy rule leads to the following conclusion: there is a negative relationship between inflation and aggregate expenditures.

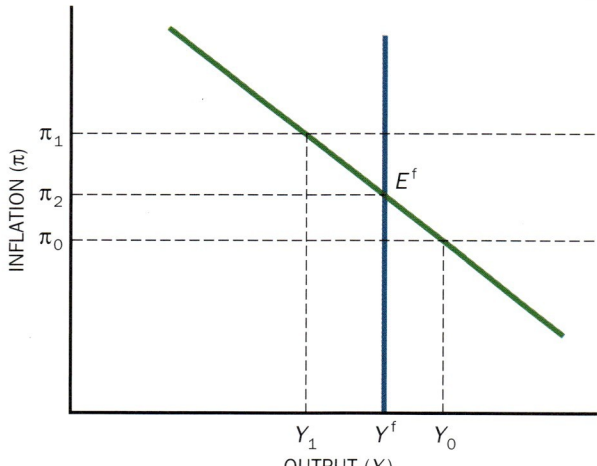

Figure 31.2

EQUILIBRIUM OUTPUT AND THE ADI CURVE

For each rate of inflation, the ADI curve shows the economy's equilibrium level of output. If inflation is π_0, the equilibrium output level is Y_0; at Y_0, aggregate expenditures equal output. At a higher inflation rate such as π_1, the real interest rate is higher, aggregate expenditures are lower, and the equilibrium level of output is only Y_1. The vertical line at Y^f denotes full-employment output.

Because equilibrium GDP is determined by aggregate expenditures in the short run, we can also say that there is a negative relationship between inflation and the short-run equilibrium level of GDP, given the central bank's policy rule. This relationship between inflation and GDP is called the **aggregate demand–inflation (ADI) curve** and is shown in Figure 31.2. Output (GDP) is on the horizontal axis, and inflation is on the vertical axis. The ADI curve in Figure 31.2 shows equilibrium output at each rate of inflation. If the inflation rate is π_0, equilibrium output will equal Y_0. At a higher inflation rate such as π_1, equilibrium output will be lower, equal to Y_1.

What Determines the Slope of the ADI Curve? When we use a demand and supply framework to analyze how price and quantity are determined, both the positions and the slopes of the demand and supply curves are important. Similarly, the adjustment of inflation and output to economic disturbances will depend on whether the ADI curve is relatively flat or relatively steep. Changes in inflation lead to changes in equilibrium output that are large when the ADI curve is relatively flat but small when the ADI curve is relatively steep. Understanding the factors that determine the slope of the ADI curve will be important for understanding the behavior of the economy in the short run.

The slope of the ADI curve in the closed economy has two main determinants. The first important factor is how the central bank adjusts interest rates as inflation changes—that is, the monetary policy rule. When the central bank responds more aggressively, a change in inflation will result in a larger change in the real rate of interest. A given change in inflation then leads to a larger fall in aggregate expenditures, making the ADI curve relatively flat. In contrast, a weaker reaction by the central bank will lead to a smaller rise in the real interest rate and a smaller decline in aggregate expenditures. As a result, the ADI curve will be relatively steep.

The second factor that affects the slope of the ADI curve is the impact of the real interest rate on the decisions by households and firms about how much to spend on consumption and investment. For example, if investment spending is very sensitive to the real interest rate, then the ADI curve will be quite flat—that is, a given change in the real interest rate caused by inflation will lead to a large change in aggregate expenditures. If investment and household spending do not respond much to changes in the real interest rate, then the ADI curve will be steep.

Figure 31.3 illustrates two different ADI curves. In an economy where the central bank responds aggressively to changes in inflation, or investment spending is very sensitive to changes in the real interest rate, or both, the ADI curve would be relatively flat, such as the curve labeled ADI_0. In an economy where the central bank responds weakly to changes in inflation, or investment spending is not very sensitive to changes in the real interest rate, or both, the ADI curve would be relatively steep, such as the curve labeled ADI_1.

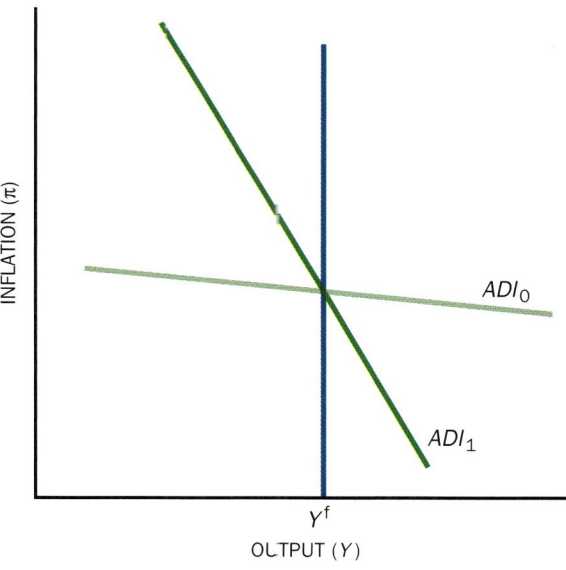

Figure 31.3

THE ADI SLOPE

If monetary policy responds aggressively to changes in inflation, or investment is sensitive to real interest rates, or both, the ADI curve will be flat, as illustrated by the curve ADI_0. If monetary policy does not respond strongly to changes in inflation, or investment is insensitive to real interest rates, or both, the ADI curve will be steep, as illustrated by the curve ADI_1. The vertical line at Y^f denotes full-employment output. Both ADI curves are drawn to be consistent with achieving full-employment output at the same rate of inflation.

Finally, although we have emphasized the role of the central bank's policy rule in producing the negative slope of the ADI curve, other factors are also at work. When the rise in prices outpaces the growth in money, the real value of money held by households and businesses is reduced. This reduction in real wealth may cause consumption and investment spending to decline. When prices rise more rapidly than nominal wages, real wages fall and this may cause consumption and spending to decline. In an open economy, more rapidly rising prices will, for a given exchange rate, increase the prices of domestically produced goods relative to foreign-produced goods. As a result, demand will shift away from domestic goods and toward foreign goods, reducing the overall demand for domestic output. These factors, like the monetary policy response we have emphasized, contribute to the negative relationship between inflation and GDP that is captured by the ADI curve.

To summarize, the negative relationship between inflation and short-run equilibrium GDP represented by the ADI curve is based on the following set of linkages:

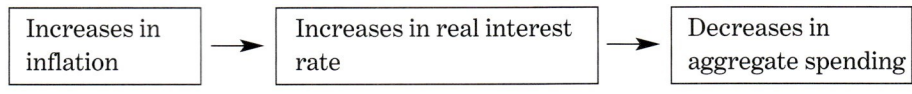

Wrap-Up

THE AGGREGATE DEMAND–INFLATION (ADI) CURVE

The ADI curve shows, for each value of inflation, the economy's short-run equilibrium level of output. Higher rates of inflation are associated with higher real interest rates, lower aggregate expenditures, and lower equilibrium output.

The central bank's monetary policy rule—the way monetary policy reacts to inflation—and the sensitivity of aggregate spending to the real interest are important in determining the negative slope of the ADI curve.

WHAT CAN SHIFT THE ADI CURVE?

Just as it is important to understand why the ADI curve has a negative slope, so too we need to understand the factors that can cause the curve to shift. For a given monetary policy rule, an ADI curve shows the equilibrium level of GDP for each rate of inflation. Movements in aggregate demand and GDP caused by changes in inflation translate into movements along a given ADI curve. Changes in any other factor that, for a given inflation rate, affect aggregate demand will *shift* the curve. Two of the most important examples of factors that can cause such a shift are fiscal policy and changes in the central bank's policy rule.

Fiscal Policy A change in government purchases or taxes alters the level of aggregate expenditures, and therefore output, for a given rate of inflation. An increase in government purchases, for example, raises aggregate expenditures at each level of the inflation rate; for every value of inflation, total expenditures (and therefore equilibrium GDP) are higher. This effect of a rise in government purchases is shown in Figure 31.4. The increase causes a rightward shift in the ADI curve. If the initial level of inflation was π_0, the initial level of output was Y_0. After the increase in government purchases, equilibrium output increases from Y_0 to Y_1. At the inflation rate π_0, output is now Y_1.[1]

Changes in taxes also shift the ADI curve. An increase in taxes reduces disposable income and leads to a fall in consumption. At each rate of inflation, aggregate spending will be lower. The ADI curve will shift to the left.

Changes in the Monetary Policy Rule The position of the ADI curve also depends on monetary policy. We have already learned how the slope of the ADI curve is affected by the policy rule that describes how the central bank adjusts the real interest rate in response to changes in inflation and how aggregate spending reacts to changes in the real interest rate. The slope has this automatic reaction to changes in inflation built into it. But we can also investigate what would happen if, at each rate of inflation, the central bank changed interest rates—that is, if the policy rule were to shift. For example, suppose the Fed decides to cut interest rates for a given rate of inflation. The Fed did just this in 1998 when it was concerned that the financial crisis in Asia would harm the United States. How will such an interest rate cut affect the ADI curve?

To answer this question, we need to work out the effects of the policy change on the real interest rate and then determine the impact on aggregate expenditures. That will tell us whether equilibrium GDP has increased or decreased. Since we are holding the rate of inflation constant, an increase in GDP will cause the ADI curve to shift to the right; a decrease in GDP will cause a shift to the left.

The Fed's decision to cut interest rates at a given rate of inflation first lowers the real rate of interest. We know that this reduction, in turn, will boost aggregate expenditures by lowering the cost of credit to households and firms. The rise in aggregate expenditures leads to an increase in equilibrium GDP. Hence, we can conclude that the ADI curve shifts to the right when, at each rate of inflation, the Fed cuts nominal interest rates.

We could run through the same steps to determine that the reverse happens to the ADI curve when the Fed raises interest rates at each rate of inflation. Since monetary policy ensures that each rate of inflation now leads to a higher real interest rate, aggregate expenditures will be lower. The fall in aggregate expenditures at each value of inflation lowers equilibrium GDP, shifting the ADI curve to the left.

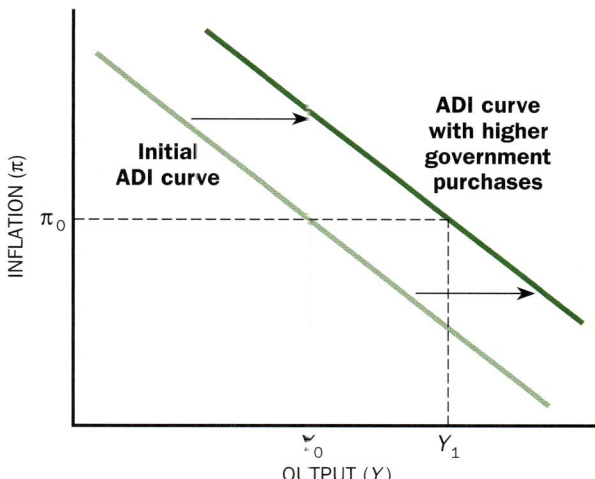

Figure 31.4

THE EFFECT OF GOVERNMENT PURCHASES ON AGGREGATE EXPENDITURES AND THE ADI CURVE

An increase in government purchases raises aggregate expenditures at each value of the rate. This increase in aggregate expenditures increases equilibrium output. At the initial inflation rate π_0, this change represents an increase in output from Y_0 to Y_1. The rise in government purchases causes the ADI curve to shift to the right, as shown.

---

[1] The size of the increase in output is determined by the magnitude of the initial increase in spending and the multiplier, as explained in Chapter 30.

International Perspective

HOW DO OTHER CENTRAL BANKS REACT TO INFLATION?

The reaction of the central bank to inflation is a critical factor in determining the slope of the ADI curve. One implication of the bank's role is that ADI curves in different countries may have different slopes, because central banks do not all react to inflation in the same way. Countries whose central bank responds aggressively to inflation, pushing up interest rates at its slightest hint and cutting interest rates whenever it falls below target, will have flatter ADI curves than will countries with central banks that fail to react to changes in inflation.

Three economists—Rich Clarida of Columbia and Jordi Galí and Mark Gertler of New York University—have estimated how various central banks respond to inflation. For the Federal Reserve, the German Bundesbank (prior to the formation of the European Economic and Monetary Union), and the Bank of Japan, they find strong evidence consistent with the type of policy rule we have used to represent monetary policy. When inflation increases, these central banks raise nominal interest rates by more than that increase. If inflation rises by 1 percentage point, the nominal interest rate must rise by more than 1 percentage point to ensure that the real interest rate rises. When inflation falls, these central banks reduce the nominal interest rates by more so that the real interest rate falls.

Yet despite their similar responses to inflation, Clarida, Galí, and Gertler also found some differences among these central banks. Of the three, the Bank of Japan was judged to respond the most strongly to changes in inflation, while the Bundesbank showed the weakest reaction. From what we have learned about the factors that affect the slope of the ADI curve, these differences in policy rules among Germany, Japan, and the United States mean that the slopes of each country's ADI curve will differ. Japan's response to inflation, because it is stronger, should produce a flatter ADI curve than Germany's. However, we also learned that the policy rule is not the only factor that affects the ADI slope, so we would also need to know how sensitive spending in each country is to changes in the real interest rate before we could make a final prediction about how their ADI slopes might differ.

Monetary policy rules can change over time. In the 1960s and 1970s, most central banks did not react as aggressively to inflation as they do today. Because inflation reached undesirable levels in the 1970s, central banks today focus on ensuring that inflation remains low and stable.

SOURCE: R. Clarida, J. Galí, and M. Gertler, "Monetary Policy Rules in Practice: Some International Evidence," *European Economic Review* 42, no. 6 (1998): 1033–1068.

OTHER FACTORS THAT CAN SHIFT THE ADI CURVE

While fiscal policy and monetary policy are key factors that can shift the ADI curve, similar effects occur if investment or consumption behavior changes at each value of the inflation rate. For example, the stock market boom of the 1990s boosted consumption spending for given levels of income and inflation. This type of wealth effect on consumption spending increases total aggregate expenditures and the equilibrium level of output. Greater optimism about the future can encourage consumption and investment spending, also increasing aggregate expenditures. For a given level of the inflation rate, equilibrium output would be higher, an outcome represented by a rightward shift of the ADI curve.

If households and firms become more pessimistic about the future and scale back their spending, or if wealth falls because of a stock market collapse, for example, aggregate expenditures would fall at each level of the inflation rate. The result is a leftward shift in the ADI curve.

> **Wrap-Up**
>
> ## FACTORS THAT SHIFT THE AGGREGATE DEMAND–INFLATION (ADI) CURVE
>
> Factors that increase aggregate expenditures at each rate of inflation (and shift the ADI curve to the right) include
> - increases in government purchases,
> - decreases in taxes,
> - an increase in wealth,
> - an increase in business or household optimism, and
> - a cut in interest rates at each rate of inflation.
>
> Factors that decrease aggregate expenditures at each rate of inflation (and shift the ADI curve to the left) include
> - decreases in government purchases,
> - increases in taxes,
> - a decrease in wealth,
> - an increase in business or household pessimism, and
> - an increase in interest rates at each rate of inflation.

Factors That Have Shifted the ADI Curve Over the past forty years, the ADI curve in the United States has been shifted by fiscal and monetary policy actions, as well as by changes in spending behavior by households and firms. Among the major factors affecting the ADI curve were

- The increase in government purchases associated with the Vietnam War in the 1960s
- The increase in interest rates that resulted from the major shift in Fed policy in 1979, which was designed to bring inflation down from the high levels reached in the 1970s
- The drop in consumption as households became more pessimistic at the time Iraq invaded Kuwait in 1990
- The increase in consumer spending due to the wealth effects of the stock market boom of the late 1990s
- The increase in investment spending associated with the introduction of new information technologies in the 1990s

For each of these examples, be sure that you can explain whether the ADI curve shifted to the left or to the right and why it did so.

Using the ADI Curve

We have now learned about one of the key components of the theory of economic fluctuations, the ADI curve. In the short run, firms adjust production in response to changes in demand at each level of inflation. That means that *the economy's short-run equilibrium GDP will be determined by the level of aggregate demand.* In Figure 31.2, the economy's equilibrium level of GDP will be Y_0 if the inflation rate is equal to π_0. If inflation is higher, say, at π_1, equilibrium output will be lower, at Y_1.

Figure 31.2 includes a vertical line at the economy's full-employment level of output, denoted as Y^f. As we know from Chapter 24, full-employment output, or potential GDP, is determined by the level of employment that occurs when labor demand and labor supply are balanced and by the economy's stock of capital and its current level of technology. Because full-employment output (and thus potential GDP) does not depend on the rate of inflation, we have drawn a vertical line at Y^f. If the inflation rate were equal to π_2, the economy's equilibrium would be at point E^f in the figure, and the economy would be at full employment.

In the short run, as already observed, wages and prices do not respond quickly enough to keep the labor market always in equilibrium at full employment. Employment and output fluctuate around their full-employment levels. In some markets—the stock market, or the market for gold and other commodities such as wheat or oil—prices move rapidly to adjust to shifts in demand and supply curves. But for most goods and services, whether sold by producers, wholesalers, or retailers, wages and prices change with considerable sluggishness. For now, we will assume that the inflation rate adjusts slowly in our short-run analysis of the product market and equilibrium output. This assumption is consistent with most empirical evidence, which suggests that output adjusts more rapidly than inflation when economic disturbances occur.

OUTPUT EFFECTS OF A SHIFT IN THE ADI CURVE

Consider what happens in the short run if the aggregate demand–inflation curve shifts to the left, as depicted in Figure 31.5 by the move from ADI_0 to ADI_1. A leftward shift in the ADI curve like that shown in the figure occurred in 1990 when American households became more pessimistic about the future and scaled back their consumption spending. Similarly, when Japan's financial sector collapsed in the early 1990s, households and firms reduced their spending, shifting the ADI curve for Japan to the left.

Suppose the economy starts out with an inflation rate equal to π_0. We have drawn a horizontal line at this initial inflation rate and labeled it IA_0 (for *inflation adjustment* line). The **inflation adjustment line** shows the current rate of inflation. We will use it to keep track of how the inflation rate adjusts when the economy fluctuates around full-employment output.

When the ADI curve shifts to ADI_1, the new equilibrium is at point E_1, where ADI_1 crosses the IA_0 line. At the inflation rate π_0, output falls from Y^f to Y_1, as firms will produce only the quantity they can sell. One result of the reduced output will be a decrease in the demand for labor. Because wages do not adjust quickly, this decrease leads to a fall in employment and a rise in cyclical unemployment. The economy enters a recession.

But the story does not end there. At point E_1, output is below potential, and there is cyclical unemployment. Because of the decline in production and the increase in unemployment, workers will likely have to settle for smaller wage increases, and firms will be less able to pass along cost increases by increasing their prices. As a result, inflation declines. This impact of cyclical unemployment on inflation was set out in Chapter 29 as the third of our four key concepts: increases in cyclical unemployment lead to declines in inflation, while decreases in cyclical unemployment lead to increases in inflation. Its implication for our analysis is that the economy will not remain at point E_1; instead, over time, inflation will start to come down.

Imagine that we return to Figure 31.5 after a few months. Inflation will have fallen from π_0 to some lower level. As long as output remains below the full-employment level, inflation will continue to decline. If the aggregate demand–inflation curve remains in its new position (ADI_1), the economy will move down along the aggregate demand curve as inflation falls. Along the ADI curve, aggregate spending rises as inflation falls, increasing the equilibrium level of output and moving the economy back toward full employment. The process of adjustment continues until eventually the inflation adjustment line has shifted down to IA_1, with GDP equal again to output at the full-employment level. Once the gap between GDP and potential GDP

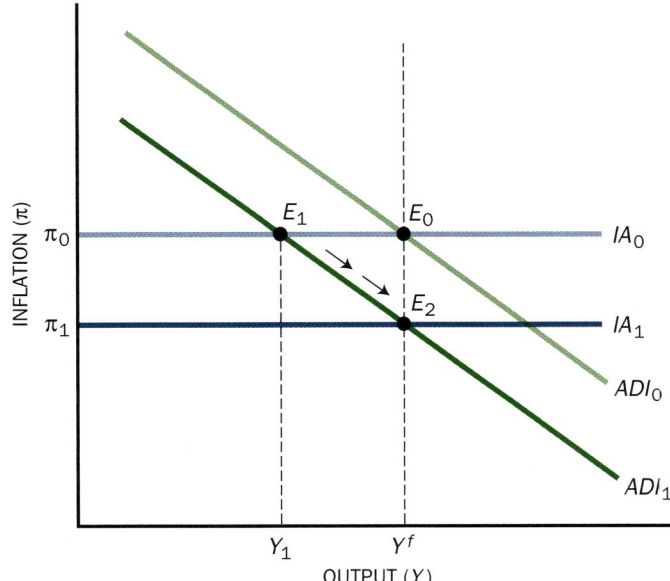

Figure 31.5

A RECESSION CAUSED BY A SHIFT IN AGGREGATE DEMAND

The full-employment level of output is given by the vertical line at Y^f. The initial inflation rate is π_0 and the aggregate demand inflation curve is ADI_0. The equilibrium is at E_0, with output equal to Y^f. If the ADI curve shifts to the left (to ADI_1), equilibrium GDP will fall below the full-employment level of output; the new short-run equilibrium level of GDP is Y_1. Eventually, if output remains below Y^f, inflation will decline and the economy will move down the ADI curve until full employment is restored at E_2 at an inflation rate of π_1.

is eliminated and the economy is back at full employment, there is no further downward pressure on inflation. Eventually the economy reaches a new long-run equilibrium at full employment at the point E_2, with an inflation rate of π_1.

Case in Point

THE VOLCKER DISINFLATION

In 1979 and 1980, there was widespread agreement that something should be done to halt inflation. At the time, inflation was at a postwar high and appeared to be moving even higher. The economy was at a point such as E_0 in Figure 31.5—it was at full employment (the unemployment rate was 5.8 percent in 1979, about equal to estimates of full employment at the time), but the inflation rate was very high (over 8 percent in 1979 as measured by the GDP price deflator).

Paul Volcker, then the chair of the Federal Reserve Board, pushed through a sharp increase in interest rates in order to choke off inflation. This action represented a major shift in the monetary policy rule. As a result of the higher real interest rates, firms cut back their investments, and households cut back their purchases of items such as new cars and homes. Interestingly, at the same time that the Fed was taking actions to restrict aggregate spending, fiscal policy was stimulating the economy. President Reagan cut taxes without cutting government expenditures by an

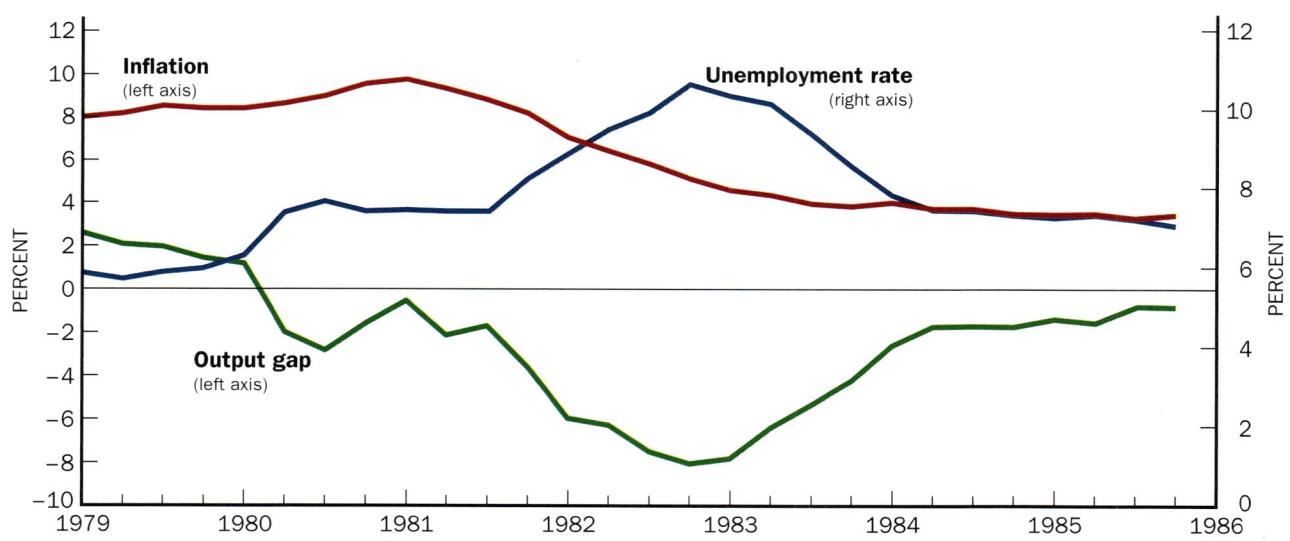

Figure 31.6

THE OUTPUT GAP, UNEMPLOYMENT RATE, AND INFLATION RATE IN THE 1980s

In the late 1970s and early 1980s, the Federal Reserve Board, worried about runaway inflation, acted to restrict credit and thus consumption and investment. The decrease in aggregate demand raised unemployment and lowered output below potential. The effects more than offset the expansionary effects of the 1981 tax cut. Inflation gradually declined, and by 1985, the economy was back at full employment, with a lower rate of inflation.

SOURCES: Unemployment, *Economic Report of the President* (2001), Table B-35; inflation, *Economic Report of the President* (2001), Table B-64; output gap, Federal Reserve Board.

offsetting amount. But the contractionary impact of monetary policy more than offset the expansionary effect of lower taxes, and the ADI curve shifted to the left, as shown in Figure 31.5.

Figure 31.6 shows the results of this shift in monetary policy. Output declined below potential GDP and the unemployment rate briefly hit a post–World War II high of 11 percent. However, the recession did succeed in curbing inflation, which dropped from around 9 percent in 1980 to just 3.2 percent in 1983.[2] As the economy moved to its new equilibrium at point E_2 in Figure 31.5, unemployment fell; by 1985, the economy was essentially back at full employment.

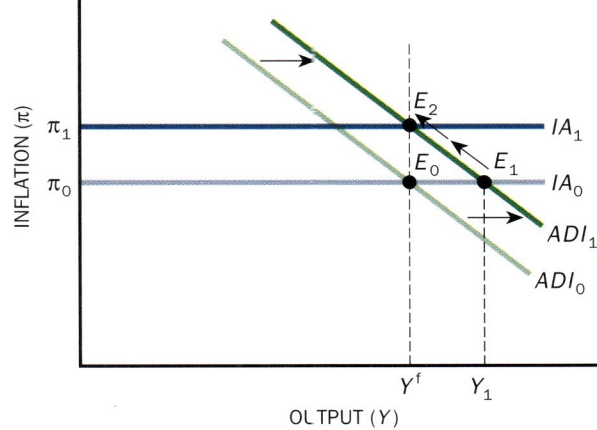

Figure 31.7

A BOOM CAUSED BY A SHIFT IN AGGREGATE DEMAND

If the aggregate demand curve shifts to the right (from ADI_0 to ADI_1), firms will increase production. Output and employment rise, and the new short-run equilibrium level of output is Y_1. Eventually, wages and prices will start rising more rapidly and the economy will move up the aggregate demand–inflation curve toward the full-employment equilibrium at point E_2, where output has returned to Y^f but inflation is now higher at π_1.

An Expansionary Shift in the ADI Curve

Figure 31.7 illustrates a different scenario, one in which the ADI curve has shifted to the right. This type of shift is caused by a positive shock to spending; perhaps firms have become more optimistic about the future and have increased investment spending on plant and equipment. Or perhaps the government has increased its purchases or cut taxes. In response to the growth in demand, firms expand production. They hire more workers, average weekly hours rise as workers work more, and unemployment falls. Firms utilize their plant and equipment more intensively, perhaps adding extra shifts or delaying maintenance in order to keep production lines running at top speed. These adjustments enable output to rise above levels associated with normal conditions. Output rises above Y^f, moving the economy to E_1; the new equilibrium level of output is now Y_1.

Just like a recession caused by a drop in spending, the boom caused by increased spending does not last forever. To attract and retain workers, firms are willing to increase wages more rapidly, and they can push up prices with less fear of losing markets. As inflation rises, the Fed boosts interest rates. As it does so, the economy's equilibrium level of output will tend to fall back toward the full-employment level. The economy moves up the ADI curve from point E_1 toward point E_2 in Figure 31.7. Eventually, output will return to Y^f at point E_2 with a higher rate of inflation.

Case in Point

THE KENNEDY TAX CUT

In 1963, the unemployment rate in the United States seemed to be stuck at an unacceptably high level, 5.5 percent. Ten years earlier it had been 2.8 percent. President

---

[2] The peak rate of inflation was even higher if measured by the consumer price index (CPI), reaching 13 percent in 1980.

John F. Kennedy's economic advisers believed that a cut in the individual income tax would cause households to consume more. This increased consumption would lead to a rightward shift in the ADI curve. An increase in aggregate expenditures, Kennedy's advisers believed, would result in increased output and a lower unemployment rate, not higher inflation. They argued that inflation would not rise, because the economy had excess capacity—productive workers and machines were lying idle. As a result, the shift in the ADI curve would be translated into increases in output, as shown in Figure 31.7.

Increases in output, as we have learned, imply increases in employment. The predictions of the economic advisers turned out to be correct. After taxes were cut in 1964, unemployment fell to 4.4 percent in 1965 and stayed under 4 percent for the rest of the 1960s. In addition, real GDP grew at the remarkable rate of 5.5 percent from 1964 to 1966, while inflation initially remained at low levels. Figure 31.8 shows these developments. Output was below potential in 1962 and 1963, but the output gap was shrinking and the unemployment rate was falling. The tax cut boosted the economy and pushed output above potential by 1965.

According to our model, wages and prices start to rise more rapidly when the economy is operating above potential. This is just what happened. Throughout the late 1960s, inflation rose. Eventually, the economy fell back toward potential GDP, just as the analysis illustrated in Figure 31.7 predicts. By the end of 1970, unemployment was back above 5.5 percent. Inflation, which had averaged 1.3 percent in 1963, averaged 5.7 percent in 1970.

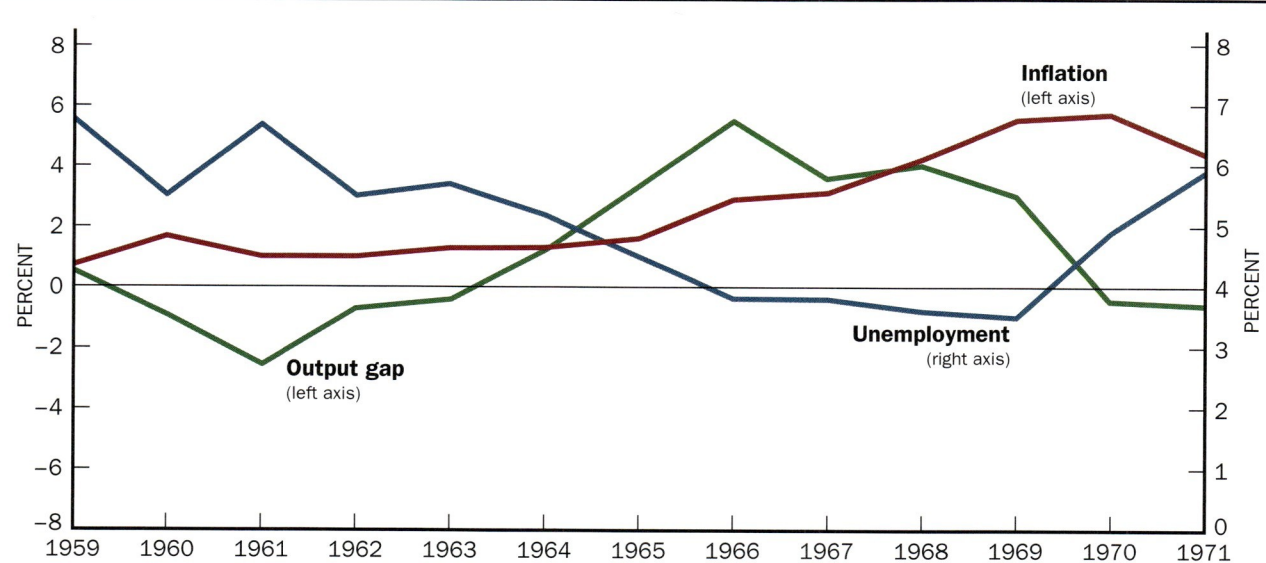

Figure 31.8

THE OUTPUT GAP, UNEMPLOYMENT RATE, AND INFLATION RATE IN THE 1960s

The increase in aggregate demand during the 1960s lowered unemployment. As the economy continued to expand above full-employment GDP, the rate of inflation increased. By the end of the decade, the economy was back at full employment but with a higher rate of inflation.

SOURCES: *Economic Report of the President* (2004) and Congressional Budget Office.

Thinking Like an Economist
TOUGH TRADE-OFFS

The Volcker policy to control inflation in late 1979 provides a graphic illustration of the trade-offs policymakers are often forced to make. Inflation had risen to unacceptable levels in the United States, but the only way the Federal Reserve could bring it down was to create a recession. It had to make a trade-off. The Federal Reserve could continue to let inflation remain at high levels, accepting the concomitant distortions. Or it could act to lower inflation, knowing that the cost would be an increase in cyclical unemployment, with all the attendant hardships for the unemployed.

In weighing the costs of higher cyclical unemployment against the benefits of lower inflation, we must remember an important implication of our model of fluctuations. The rise in cyclical unemployment would be temporary. Eventually, the economy would return to full employment. That may not be much comfort to the workers who lost their jobs during the recessions in 1980 and 1982, but it was an important fact for policymakers to keep in mind. In assessing trade-offs, we need to know whether the consequences of an action are likely to be permanent or only temporary. If the Federal Reserve policymakers had believed that its disinflation policies would lead to permanently higher unemployment, they might have made a different choice.

In April 1980, the federal funds rate peaked above 17.5 percent (for comparison, during the first half of 2004, the federal funds rate stood at 1 percent). Just two years earlier, in 1978, it had been only 6.89 percent. Of course, what matters for spending decisions is the real interest rate, so we need to adjust the federal funds rate for inflation. During 1978, inflation averaged almost 9 percent, while in 1980 it was more than 12 percent. Between 1978 and 1980, the real federal funds rate swung from a negative 2.11 percent (6.89 percent minus 9 percent inflation) to a positive 5.5 percent (17.5 percent minus 12 percent inflation). This rise in the real interest rate reduced aggregate expenditures, as we learned it would in Chapter 30.

The Federal Reserve's policy actions in 1979 and 1980 eventually did succeed in bringing inflation down. But cyclical unemployment rose significantly during the period of disinflation. From an average of 6 percent of the labor force in 1978–1979, the unemployment rate averaged 8.5 percent over 1980–1983.

In Chapters 33 and 37, we will learn more about the short-run trade-off between inflation and unemployment.

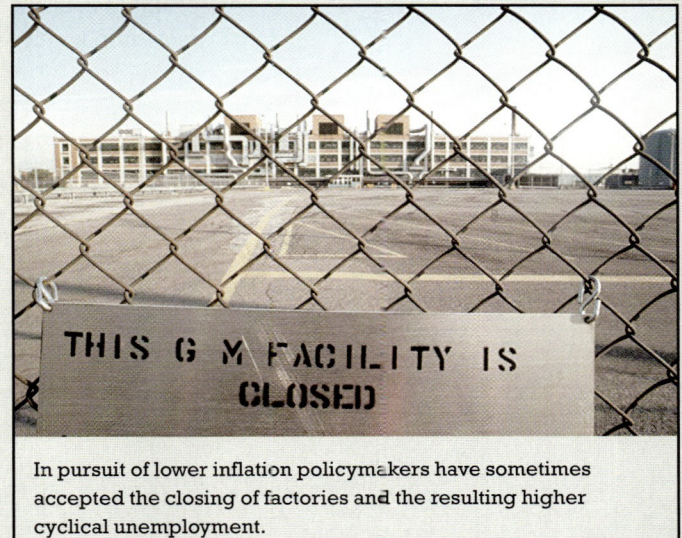

In pursuit of lower inflation policymakers have sometimes accepted the closing of factories and the resulting higher cyclical unemployment.

MACROECONOMIC POLICY AND SHIFTS IN THE ADI CURVE

Our examples have illustrated the effects on aggregate demand and output in the short run. For each example, we assumed the economy started out at full employment. Tracing through the effects of a single disturbance on output and employment in the short run can be useful. More commonly, however, we want to use our macroeconomic model not to focus on such effects but to analyze how policy might help maintain the economy at full employment. In Figure 31.5, the initial leftward shift in the ADI curve pushed the economy into a recession, with output at E_1, below the economy's full-employment output at point E_0. If the aggregate demand curve remains at ADI_1, inflation will eventually fall and the economy will reach full employment at point E_2 with an inflation rate of π_2. If inflation adjusts slowly, it may take a long time for full employment to be restored. An expansionary fiscal or monetary policy that shifts the aggregate demand curve to the right would push the short-run equilibrium output level closer to full employment. If the ADI curve is shifted all the way to ADI_0, full employment is restored at the original rate of inflation, π_0.

Shifts in the Inflation Adjustment Curve

So far, we have concentrated on the impact of shifts in the ADI curve on the economy. Such a focus is natural in that aggregate expenditures determine output (and employment) in the short run, and inflation typically adjusts relatively slowly. But economies also experience disturbances that directly affect inflation. Two of the most important are changes in energy prices and shifts in potential GDP.

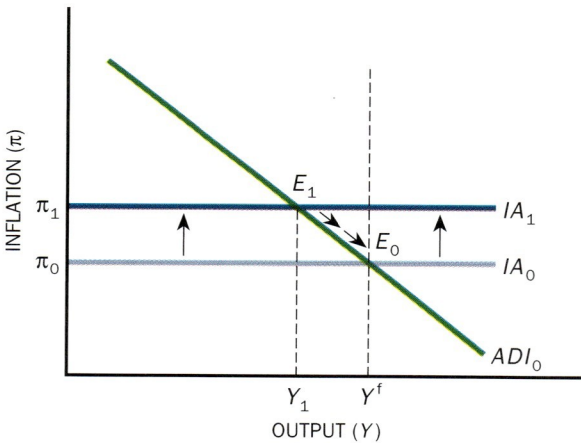

Figure 31.9

THE IMPACT OF AN INFLATION SHOCK

An increase in the cost of production at each level of output increases the inflation rate, shifting the inflation adjustment curve up, from IA_0 to IA_1. The short-run equilibrium is at the point of intersection between the inflation adjustment and ADI curves. The upward shift in the inflation adjustment curve moves the economy to E_1, where output has fallen to Y_1. If there are no further inflation shocks, inflation declines because output is below its full-employment level. Eventually, full employment and an inflation rate of π_0 are restored.

CHANGES IN ENERGY PRICES

For a given level of cyclical unemployment, inflation can be affected by shocks that alter firms' costs of production. For example, during the 1970s, oil prices increased dramatically. Oil prices also rose substantially in 2004, because of both greater demand for oil as the economies of China and the United States grew and fears of disruptions in supply as the fighting in Iraq continued. By raising the price of energy, an increase in oil prices pushes up the costs of production. In response, firms will raise prices, leading in turn to a jump in the inflation rate.

We can analyze the consequences of an inflation shock such as an oil price increase using the ADI curve and inflation adjustment line. To do so, suppose the economy is initially at full employment with an inflation rate equal to π_0. This condition is shown as point E_0 in Figure 31.9. The inflation shock causes inflation to increase to π_1, as shown by the upward shift in the inflation adjustment curve to IA_1. The new equilibrium is at E_1. Economic disturbances that shift the inflation adjustment curve—inflation shocks—are often also called **supply shocks.**

The economy will not remain at point E_1, however. Over time, inflation will decline because the economy is operating below potential GDP. As inflation falls, the IA curve shifts back down. Eventually, the equilibrium returns to point E_0, with the inflation rate and output back at their initial values.

Supply shocks present policymakers with difficult choices. To prevent output from declining and unemployment from rising, the central bank could cut interest rates at each rate of inflation (changing its policy rule). Such cuts would shift the ADI curve to the right. The central bank's effort to keep output equal to potential GDP will prevent unemployment from rising, but at the cost of leaving inflation at the higher level, π_1. Alternatively, if the central bank wants to prevent any rise in inflation, it must pursue a tighter policy and higher interest rates (changing its policy rule, this time toward a higher interest rate at each rate of inflation). When the ADI curve is shifted to the left, inflation can be maintained at π_0, but at the cost of a deeper recession and a larger increase in cyclical unemployment.

Case in Point

OIL PRICE SHOCKS OF THE 1970s

The Arab-Israeli War in 1973 led the Organization of Petroleum Exporting Countries (OPEC) to restrict oil exports to Western industrialized economies and to raise the price of oil sharply. The fuel and utilities component of the consumer price index jumped more than 16 percent in 1973. Overall inflation as measured by the GDP deflator rose from 4.14 percent in 1972 to 5.23 percent in 1973 to 8.58 percent in 1974 as the impact of higher oil prices raised the prices of goods and services throughout the economy.

The hike in inflation resulting from the oil price increases shifted the inflation adjustment curve up, as illustrated in Figure 31.9. Our model of fluctuations predicts a decline in output after such an inflation shock, and that is just what happened. Unemployment, which had averaged 4.9 percent in 1973, rose to 8.5 percent by 1975 as the economy entered a recession. Figure 31.10 shows the path of the output gap, unemployment rate, and inflation rate from 1972 until 1977. The high level of cyclical unemployment during the recession put downward pressure on inflation. As inflation declined during 1976 falling to 5.7 percent from 9.0 percent in 1975, output recovered and unemployment began to decline; it eventually reached 5.8 percent in 1979, a level close to most estimates of full employment.

A SHIFT IN POTENTIAL GDP

Changes in the economy's potential GDP can shift the inflation adjustment curve. Potential GDP might shift because of productivity changes or because of labor market changes that increase the level of employment associated with full employment, leading to higher output at full employment. Many of the recent discussions about the new economy and the impact of information technologies in boosting productivity can be thought of as arguing that potential GDP has risen.

Consider what happens if there is a productivity increase that boosts full-employment GDP. In Figure 31.11, the initial equilibrium is at E_0. Potential GDP shifts from the old level of potential output (Y_0^f) to the new, higher value (Y_1^f). If there is

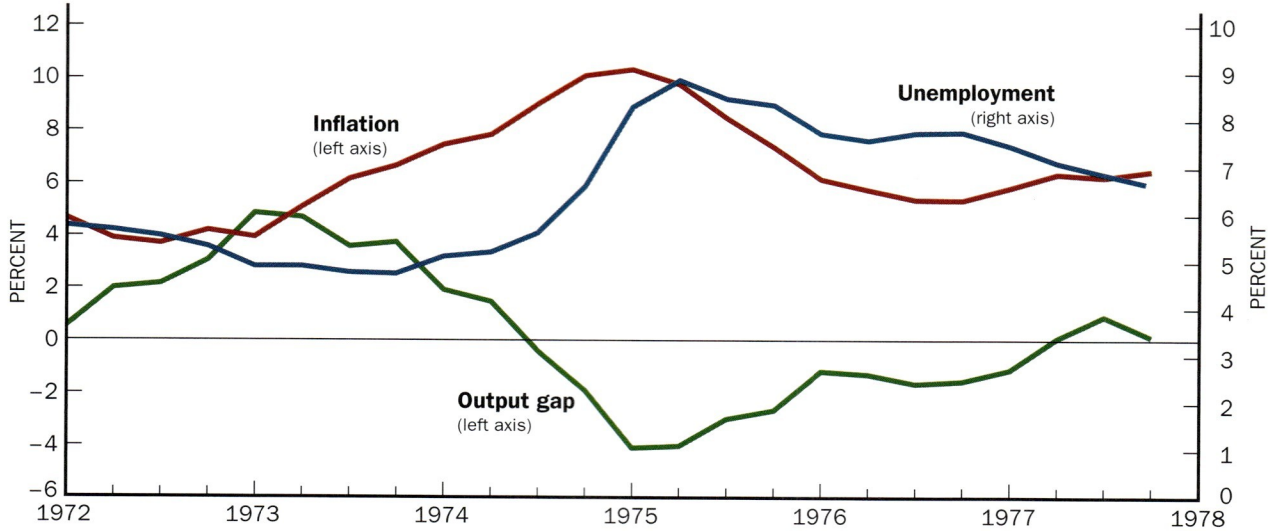

Figure 31.10

THE 1973 OIL PRICE SHOCK

In 1972, the U.S. economy was expanding, with output rising above potential (the output gap was positive) and unemployment declining. In 1973, OPEC sharply raised the price of oil. This inflation shock pushed up U.S. inflation and sent the economy into a recession. The output gap fell and unemployment rose. After peaking in 1975, inflation started to decline. As Figure 31.9 would suggest, falling inflation was associated with a rise in output and fall in unemployment as output returned to potential. A second oil price shock hit the economy in 1979.

SOURCES: *Economic Report of the President* (2003) and Congressional Budget Office, *The Budget and Economic Outlook*, January 2004.

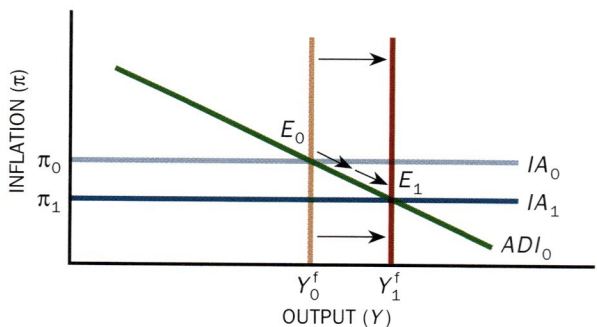

Figure 31.11

THE IMPACT OF AN INCREASE IN POTENTIAL GDP

If potential GDP increases from Y_0^f to Y_1^f, initially equilibrium remains at the point where the inflation adjustment line at the current inflation rate π_0 intersects with the ADI curve (E_0). Eventually, the economy achieves its new, higher level of potential GDP at the inflation rate π_1.

no change in the ADI curve, equilibrium output remains at point E_0 at the initial inflation rate π_0.

The economy will not remain at E_0, however. At an output equal to the old level of potential GDP, Y_0^f, firms now have excess capacity—the increase in productivity means they could produce more than before with the same resources. The change places downward pressure on inflation. As inflation declines, the real interest rate also falls, leading to an increase in aggregate expenditures and equilibrium output (i.e., to a movement along the ADI curve). Eventually the economy will reach point E_1, with output now at the new, higher level of potential GDP and inflation lower than initially.

In Figure 31.11, the ADI curve was held fixed. But if potential output rises, there may be a direct impact on the ADI curve as well. Higher potential output means that total incomes in the economy are higher. Households' desire to increase their consumption spending when they expect their real incomes to rise can lead to a rightward shift in the ADI curve. As a consequence, the economy may move to a higher level of output with very little change in inflation.

Case in Point

THE 1990s

Now that we have a complete model for understanding how the economy adjusts, we can use it to analyze the U.S. economy at the end of the 1990s. Figure 31.12 shows the unemployment rate, the output gap, and the inflation rate since 1990. The recession of 1990–1991 shows up clearly in the path of the unemployment rate, which rose from 5.6 percent of the labor force in 1990 to 7.5 percent in 1992. This recession was caused by demand factors that shifted the ADI curve to the left. Both consumption and investment spending dropped, as people became more pessimistic about the future at the time of the Gulf War.

Our model predicts that a drop in aggregate expenditures will lead to an increase in unemployment and a decline in inflation. Output will eventually return to potential (see Figure 31.5), so unemployment should return to its full-employment level, but inflation will remain lower. In the late 1980s and early 1990s, estimates of the unemployment rate at full employment were in the 5.5 to 6 percent range. As Figure 31.12 shows, by 1996 the unemployment rate had returned to its prerecession level, and inflation remained at a level lower than its prerecession value.

From 1996 to the end of the 1990s, the economy continued to expand, and both unemployment *and* inflation continued to fall. Economic output displayed strong

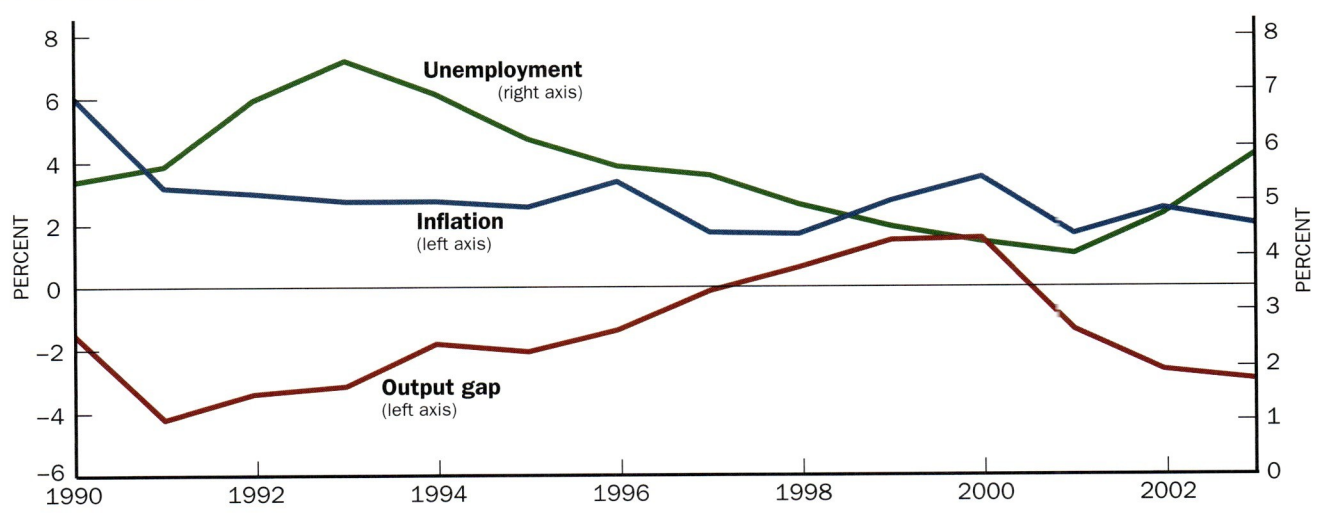

Figure 31.12

THE BOOM OF THE 1990s

The U.S. economy began the 1990s recovering from the recession of 1990–1991. Steady growth throughout the decade brought the output gap back to zero and led to a significant reduction in unemployment. Inflation remained stable. In 2001, the economy experienced a recession—GDP fell and unemployment rose.

SOURCES: *Economic Report of the President* (2003) and Congressional Budget Office, *The Budget and Economic Outlook*, 2004.

e-Insight
PRODUCTIVITY GROWTH AND THE PUNCH BOWL

To prevent inflation from rising, the Fed must not let the economy overheat—if output rises above potential, the tight labor market will lead wages to rise in excess of productivity growth. As firms face increasing labor costs, they will boost their prices, and inflation will rise. Sometimes it seems that just when the good times of low unemployment arrive, the Fed starts raising interest rates to slow things down. An old adage about monetary policy is that the job of the Fed is to take the punch bowl away just when the party really gets going. Increases in productivity growth brought on by new technologies will enable the Fed to leave the punch bowl out a bit longer during booms.

The Fed's actions have to do with the relationship between wage increases, productivity, and inflation. As long as wages do not increase faster than productivity, firms' costs of production will not rise. The reason is simple—firms may have to pay more to their workers, but their workers are producing more. The labor costs of producing each unit of output—unit labor costs—do not increase when wages rise at the same rate as productivity. The faster productivity grows, the faster wages can rise without fueling price increases.

Sometimes the Fed is criticized for raising interest rates whenever wages start to rise. It is not wage increases themselves that concern the Fed, however, but inflation. As long as wage increases are in line with increases in productivity, they do not increase firms' costs or contribute to inflation. So the Fed looks at unit labor costs to determine if wage increases are inflationary or not. As the chart illustrates, during the early 1980s, wage increases far outstripped increases in productivity, causing unit labor costs to rise rapidly. The opposite occurred during the 1990s. While wages started rising faster in the late 1990s, so did productivity.

The years 1999 and 2000 illustrate some of the difficulties facing the Fed as it makes its policy decisions. Wage growth had increased. If the observed increases in productivity growth heralded the arrival of a "new economy" in which such growth would remain strong, then wages could rise much faster than previously without arousing concerns that they would ignite a new bout of inflation. If the increased productivity growth turned out to be only temporary, then the faster wage growth would start to push up unit labor costs and prices. Information and computer technologies are transforming the economy, and if these changes lead

growth and the growth rate of productivity increased. These developments were consistent with a supply shock that lowered the unemployment rate at full employment and shifted the inflation adjustment curve down, as illustrated in Figure 31.11. As our model predicts, this resulted in lower unemployment and lower inflation. The prime candidate for such a favorable supply shock is the new computer and information technologies that have transformed so many parts of the American economy.

As the 1990s ended, the Fed was concerned that the booming economy would eventually lead to higher inflation. To guard against this, the Fed raised interest rates several times in 1999 and 2000. These interest rate hikes were designed to slow the economy by reducing demand, and signs that the economy's strong growth was weakening appeared by the end of 2000. The year 2000 also saw the collapse to sustained increases in productivity growth, workers' real wages will rise faster than was usual during the previous quarter century. But when wages outpace productivity, even workers in the new economy will discover that the Fed will have to put away the punch bowl to keep inflation under control.

LABOR COMPENSATION, PRODUCTIVITY, AND COST

SOURCE: *Economic Report of the President* (2004).

of the stock market and a drop in business investment. By December 2000, economic conditions were weakening much more quickly than had previously been expected. As a consequence, the Fed's concerns shifted; it now needed to focus on preventing the economy from entering a recession. In a dramatic action on January 3, 2001, the FOMC cut its interest rate target by a full half percentage point, from 6.5 percent to 6 percent. The move caught most commentators by surprise, since the decision was made between regularly scheduled committee meetings. The U.S. economy officially entered a recession in March 2001. The Fed cut its interest rate target several times more during 2001, bringing the rate down below 2 percent by the end of the year. Though the recession ended in November 2001, the economy did not recover rapidly. Amid continuing weak growth, the Fed continued to reduce interest rates; at the end of 2003, they were 1 percent. By that time, real output was growing strongly again, but cyclical unemployment had failed to decline significantly.

Internet Connection

THE FOMC

After each meeting of the FOMC, the committee releases a press statement that explains any policy action it has taken and highlights the economic conditions that most concern the FOMC members. These statements can be found at www.federalreserve.gov/fomc/.

In the middle of 2004, as economic growth recovered, the Fed's concerns again turned to preventing inflation from increasing. In June, the FOMC raised the interest rate modestly, and continued to raise the interest rate throughout the next year.

Wrap-Up

FACTORS THAT SHIFT THE INFLATION ADJUSTMENT LINE

Costs of production: an increase in firms' costs of production, such as an increase in energy prices, boosts inflation at each level of output. This rise shifts the inflation adjustment line up.

Potential GDP: an increase in potential GDP lowers inflation at each level of output. This reduction shifts the inflation adjustment line down.

Review and Practice

SUMMARY

1. Aggregate demand depends negatively on inflation. As inflation increases, the Fed or other central bank raises interest rates, thereby reducing aggregate expenditures. This negative relationship is called the aggregate demand–inflation or ADI curve.
2. At a given rate of inflation, the economy's equilibrium level of output is given by the ADI curve.
3. The slope of the ADI curve depends on the central bank's behavior. If it increases interest rates sharply when inflation rises, the impact on aggregate demand will be large and the ADI curve will be relatively flat. If the bank responds less strongly to inflation changes, the ADI curve will be steeper.
4. Changes in fiscal policy, private investment, consumption spending, or monetary policy at a given rate of inflation shift the ADI curve.
5. The slope of the ADI curve also depends on the responsiveness of investment to interest rate changes. If increases in the real interest rate have a large impact on investment and spending, the ADI curve will be relatively flat.
6. If GDP is below the full-employment level, inflation will fall, shifting the inflation adjustment line down and increasing equilibrium output. This process continues until full employment is restored.
7. If GDP is above the full-employment level, inflation will rise, shifting the inflation adjustment curve up and decreasing equilibrium output. Eventually full employment is restored.
8. Once inflation has adjusted, the economy will be at full employment. Shifts in the ADI curve affect GDP in the short run, but in the long run such shifts only affect the inflation rate.

KEY TERMS

monetary policy rule
aggregate demand–inflation (ADI) curve
inflation adjustment line
supply shocks

REVIEW QUESTIONS

1. How can the capital market be in equilibrium at different levels of aggregate output? If income is below the full-employment level, can we say whether the interest rate that balances saving and investment will be higher or lower than the equilibrium rate at full employment?
2. If the inflation rate is slow to adjust and is initially above a level at which aggregate expenditures equal potential GDP, what will be the level of output? What will happen if the aggregate demand–inflation (ADI) curve shifts to the left? To the right? If long-run potential GDP decreases? Increases?
3. How does the slope of the ADI curve depend on monetary policy?
4. If investment is not very sensitive to changes in real interest rates, will the ADI curve be relatively flat or relatively steep? Explain why.
5. If current output is below potential GDP, what will happen to the inflation rate? How does inflation adjustment move the economy back to full employment?
6. Use the ADI curve to describe some of the major episodes of the post–World War II period.

PROBLEMS

1. Use the ADI curve to describe how the economy would respond to a productivity shock that increases full-employment output. If there is no impact on the ADI curve, what will happen to output in the short run?
2. Suppose that as a result of the Fed's policy, the relationship between the real rate of interest and the inflation rate is given by the following table (all numbers are annual percentages):

Inflation	0	2	4	6	8	10
Real interest rate	3	4	5	6	7	8

The relationship between aggregate expenditures and the real interest rate is given by the following table (expenditures are in trillions of 2000 dollars):

Real interest rate	3	4	5	6	7	8
Aggregate expenditures	8.3	8	7.7	7.4	7.1	6.8

Plot the ADI curve. If inflation is 4 percent, what is the level of aggregate expenditures? Suppose investment now becomes more sensitive to interest rate changes. How would this affect the ADI curve?

3. Draw an ADI curve. As we move up and to the left on a given ADI curve, the real rate of interest increases. Explain why.
4. Suppose output is initially equal to potential GDP. Now assume the government cuts taxes (and assume government expenditures remain unchanged). How does this affect the ADI curve? What happens in the short run to equilibrium output? To unemployment? Over time, will inflation tend to rise or to fall? Explain how the adjustment of inflation works to return the output gap to zero. What happens to the real interest rate?
5. Suppose output is initially equal to potential GDP. Now assume the Fed shifts its policy rule by raising interest rates at each rate of inflation. How does this affect the ADI curve? What happens in the short run to equilibrium output? To unemployment? Over time, will inflation tend to rise or to fall? Explain how the adjustment of inflation works to return the output gap to zero. What happens to the real interest rate?
6. Suppose output is initially equal to potential GDP and inflation is equal to 2 percent. Suppose a new chair of the Federal Reserve is appointed. This new chair believes that average inflation should be reduced to 1 percent. To achieve this new lower rate of inflation, should the Fed shift its policy rule by raising interest rates at each rate of inflation or by lowering interest rates at each rate of inflation? What are the consequences for the output gap in the short run of the policy shift that results? What are the consequences for the output gap in the long run?
7. Go to the Federal Reserve's Web site (www.federalreserve.gov), follow the links to Monetary Policy and the FOMC, and find the press releases ("statements") from the last two FOMC meetings. Has the FOMC raised or lowered interest rates at these meetings? What reasons do the press releases give for these actions? Would you describe these actions as movements along a given policy rule (i.e., interest rate changes arising from a concern about inflation) or as shifts in the policy rule (i.e., policy actions in response to factors other than inflation)? If you feel the policy rule has shifted, what factors was the FOMC reacting to?

Learning Goals

In this chapter, you will learn

1. About the federal funds market and the federal funds interest rate
2. How the Federal Reserve uses its policy tools to influence the federal funds rate
3. The reasons that central banks today focus on interest rates rather than on the money supply

Chapter 32

THE FEDERAL RESERVE AND INTEREST RATES

In the previous chapter, we assigned a key role to the Federal Reserve's response to inflation in the model of short-run fluctuations. The downward slope of the aggregate demand–inflation curve reflected the Fed's policy reaction as inflation varied. What we did not discuss, though, was exactly how the Federal Reserve is able to move interest rates. Chapter 28 did examine the three basic tools of the Federal Reserve—open market operations, the discount rate, and reserve requirements—but there the focus was on how these are used to influence bank reserves and the money supply. The objective in this chapter is to explain how the Fed uses its tools to implement monetary policy by influencing market interest rates.

The Federal Funds Market

At meetings of its policymaking committee, the Federal Open Market Committee (FOMC), the Fed establishes a target interest rate. The FOMC focuses on the **federal funds rate;** and to understand what this key interest rate is and how the Fed is able to affect the economy, we need to understand the workings of a very important financial market, the **federal funds market.**

We usually think of banks lending to consumers wishing to buy cars or homes, or to firms seeking to build factories or stores or to finance their inventories. But banks also lend to each other. Often, a bank's need is very short-term; AmericaBank might borrow from NationalBank and repay the loan just one day later. Banks borrow and lend funds overnight in the federal funds market, and the interest rate on these loans is the federal funds rate. Before examining this market in detail, we will first look at the details of what the Fed does every business day to influence the level of reserves and the federal funds rate.

A DAY AT THE TRADING DESK

The Fed is able to affect the federal funds rate by controlling the supply of bank reserves in the federal funds market, and it does so by using **open market operations.** As we saw in Chapter 28, by entering the market directly to buy or sell government securities, the Fed is able to increase or decrease the supply of bank reserves. More specifically, these open market operations are conducted by the Trading Desk located at the Federal Reserve Bank of New York. In a typical workday, Trading Desk personnel gather information about reserve market conditions, evaluate this information to assess the level of reserves required to keep the funds rate at the target value set by the FOMC, and engage in actual open market operations to affect the supply of reserves.

Around 7 A.M. every morning, the staff at the Trading Desk begins the process of collecting information about financial developments. Information about factors that may affect reserves arrives from other Federal Reserve banks and is used to develop projections of reserve levels.

As the financial markets open in the United States, staff members talk with the primary dealers on government security markets and with the managers of reserve positions for the largest banks. These conversations provide the Trading Desk with information about the likely demand and supply conditions in the federal funds market. If the demand for reserves, at the current funds rate, exceeds the current supply, the funds rate will rise unless the Trading Desk increases the supply. If the supply of reserves at the current funds rate exceeds demand, the funds rate will fall unless the Trading Desk acts to reduce supply.

Reserve conditions can also be affected by the net cash flow of the U.S. Treasury, which has cash accounts with the Federal Reserve. If tax payments exceed government expenditures on a particular day, there will be a net flow of funds into the Treasury accounts at the Fed and a corresponding fall in funds held by the banking sector. This decline in total reserves in the banking sector pushes up the funds rate unless offsetting open market operations are undertaken. Treasury balances with the Fed are fairly stable from year to year, but they can fluctuate greatly from day to day. Once all this information is collected, the Trading Desk decides on its program for open market operations. A conference call then takes place between the Trading Desk, Federal Reserve Board staff in Washington, D.C., and one of the four presidents of a regional Federal Reserve bank (other than New York) currently serving as a voting member of the FOMC. This call, which lasts about fifteen minutes, reviews the plans formulated by the Trading Desk and the information about financial conditions on which it is based. Afterward, a member of the Federal Reserve Board staff prepares a brief summary report that is distributed to all the governors and reserve bank presidents.

The next step in the process is the actual execution of open market operations, which takes place at between 9:20 A.M. and 9:40 A.M. (EST) each day; a die is used to randomly choose the exact minute. The Trading Desk informs dealers of the details of the operation. Is it buying or selling? How much? Does the sale or purchase involve a repurchase (or resale) at a later date? (If the Trading Desk forecasts a change in reserve conditions that is expected to be temporary, it uses what are known as **repurchases** or **RPs,** transactions that involve, for example, a combined

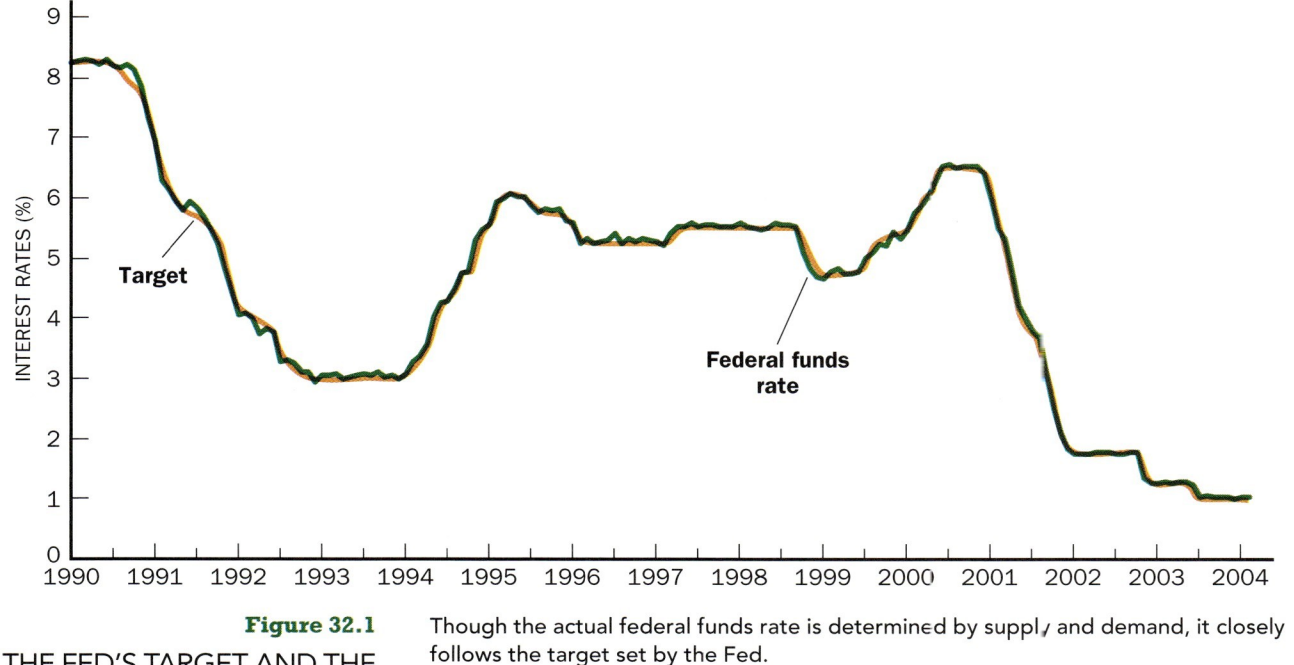

Figure 32.1

THE FED'S TARGET AND THE FUNDS RATE

Though the actual federal funds rate is determined by supply and demand, it closely follows the target set by the Fed.

SOURCE: Federal Reserve Board.

sale of a government security and an agreement to repurchase it at a future date—perhaps the next day.)

The last major activity of the day is a 3:15 P.M. telephone meeting with representatives of the government security market dealer firms. The interchange of information helps keep the Trading Desk informed of the dealers' perceptions of developments in the financial markets.[1]

The Fed's Target for the Funds Rate The activities of the Trading Desk are designed to affect the level of the federal funds rate, which plays a critical role in the economy precisely because it is the rate that the Federal Reserve can most directly control. At each FOMC meeting, the members of the committee must decide whether the federal funds rate should remain unchanged, be raised, or be lowered. Though the FOMC decides on its *target* for the funds rate, the rate itself is determined by the interplay of demand and supply in the market for federal funds. Thus the federal funds rate can diverge from the Fed's target—but by influencing supply in the federal funds market every day through its open market operations, the Fed can keep these divergences very small, as Figure 32.1 shows.

To grasp what the Fed does and how it affects the economy, we must examine the factors that determine demand and supply in the federal funds market. We can

---

[1] For an excellent and detailed discussion of how monetary policy is conducted in the United States, see Ann-Marie Meulendyke, *U.S. Monetary Policy and Financial Markets* (New York: Federal Reserve Bank of New York, 1998).

then understand how the Fed is able to influence the market to make sure the equilibrium level of the federal funds rate is kept close to the target established by the FOMC.

THE DEMAND FOR RESERVES

Banks hold reserves for two reasons. First, they must satisfy the legal reserve requirement imposed by the Fed. Second, even if reserve requirements were zero (as they are in some countries), banks need to hold some reserves to meet their daily transaction needs. Deposits and withdrawals cannot be predicted perfectly each day, so a bank must make sure it has enough cash on hand in case withdrawals happen to exceed deposits. Similarly, when Desktop Publishing writes a check to ComputerAmerica on its account at BankNational and ComputerAmerica deposits that check into its account with BankUSA, BankNational must have enough reserves to transfer to BankUSA to cover the check. Of course, BankNational will receive funds as it collects on checks it has received in deposits that are from accounts in other banks, but the daily balance of payments and receipts is unpredictable. BankNational needs to ensure that it has access to reserves to make certain it can always settle its account. The reserves a bank holds over and above its required reserves are called **excess reserves.** Because reserves do not earn interest, banks try to keep excess reserves to a minimum. In 2000, for example, required reserves totaled $40 billion, while excess reserves were only just over $1 billion.

What happens if a bank discovers that it does not have enough reserves to meet its needs? It has two options. It can try to borrow reserves from the Fed. If the Fed agrees to lend reserves to the bank, the interest rate on the loan is called the **discount rate.** Unlike interest rates on other types of loans, the discount rate is not determined by conditions of demand and supply; the Fed simply sets it. In some countries, the discount rate is linked directly to market-determined rates of interest. If the discount rate is increased, banks find it more expensive to borrow from the Fed.

The second option a bank has is to borrow reserves from another bank. Just as some banks find themselves short of reserves, other banks may find they have larger reserve holdings than they need. Since the Fed does not pay interest to banks on reserve account balances, and vault cash similarly earns the bank no interest, a bank with more reserves than it needs will want to lend them out in the federal funds market. In this way, it can earn the federal funds interest rate on its extra reserves. The federal funds rate adjusts to balance supply and demand in the federal funds market.

The quantity of federal funds demanded will fall if the federal funds rate increases. A higher federal funds rate makes it more costly to borrow reserves from other banks. Each bank has an incentive to take extra care to ensure that it does not run short of reserves. Figure 32.2 shows the demand for federal funds as a downward-sloping function of the funds rate.

Figure 32.2

THE DEMAND FOR RESERVES IN THE FEDERAL FUNDS MARKET

When the federal funds rate increases, it becomes more expensive to borrow reserves from other banks. Banks will turn to other sources (such as the Fed) or adjust their balance sheets to reduce the likelihood that they will need to borrow in the funds market.

The position of the demand curve for reserves will depend on banks' lending opportunities and on the general volume of transactions. Suppose, for example, that a new technological innovation causes firms to want to invest more money in new equipment. To finance this investment, firms try to borrow more from banks. As the quantity of bank loans demanded increases, interest rates on bank loans will rise. Any bank that was holding excess reserves will have a greater incentive to make additional loans because the interest that can be earned has risen (recall that reserves earn no interest). Other banks may not have an excess of reserves, but to take advantage of the higher returns on loans, they will try to borrow additional reserves in the federal funds market. Consequently, the demand curve for reserves shifts to the right.

Changes in the volume of transactions through the banking system also can shift the reserve demand curve. For example, as real incomes rise, the dollar volume of transactions in the economy will rise. Banks hold reserves because they cannot predict perfectly their daily flow of deposits and withdrawals. As these flows become larger, banks will need to hold additional reserves.

THE SUPPLY OF RESERVES

The supply of reserves arises from two sources. First, some banks have borrowed reserves from the Fed. These reserves are called **borrowed reserves.** As the federal funds rate increases, it becomes more expensive to obtain funds from other banks in the federal funds market, and banks instead borrow more from the Fed. If the discount rate is increased, borrowing from the Fed becomes more expensive and borrowed reserves fall. Such borrowing is not the main source of reserves, however. In 2000, borrowed reserves accounted for only $400 million out of a total stock of reserves equal to about $40 billion. The difference between **total reserves** and borrowed reserves is called **nonborrowed reserves.** The supply of nonborrowed reserves is under the Fed's immediate control, and it is by adjusting the supply of nonborrowed reserves that the Fed affects the funds rate.

OPEN MARKET OPERATIONS

In Chapter 28, we saw that open market operations are the Fed's most important tool for influencing the economy. Whenever the Fed buys government securities from the private sector in an open market purchase, it pays for them by simply creating nonborrowed reserves; whenever it sells government securities to the private sector, the level of nonborrowed reserves held by the banking sector is reduced. If the Fed wishes to increase nonborrowed reserves, it undertakes an open market purchase. If it wants to reduce nonborrowed reserves, it undertakes an open market sale.

Through these open market operations, the Fed can control the *total* supply of reserves. For example, suppose banks increase their borrowing from the Fed so that the level of borrowed reserves rises. The Fed can sell government securities to reduce the supply of nonborrowed reserves if it wants to keep total reserves from

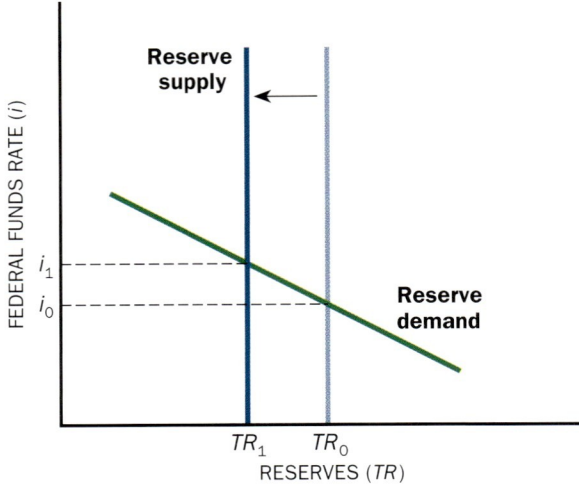

Figure 32.3

THE SUPPLY OF RESERVES AND EQUILIBRIUM IN THE FEDERAL FUNDS MARKET

The total supply of reserves consists of borrowed and nonborrowed reserves. The total reserves supply schedule is drawn as a vertical line. An open market sale decreases the total supply of reserves, shifting the reserve supply curve from TR_0 to TR_1.

The equilibrium federal funds rate is determined at the intersection of reserve demand and reserve supply. If the initial equilibrium funds rate is i_0 and the Fed wishes to increase the funds rate to i_1, it reduces the stock of nonborrowed reserves, shifting the supply schedule to the left until the equilibrium funds rate is i_1.

changing. Because the Fed, if it chooses, can always offset any change in borrowed reserves by adjusting nonborrowed reserves, we can simplify the situation by treating the supply of *total reserves,* the sum of borrowed and nonborrowed reserves, as controlled directly by the Fed. In Figure 32.3, the stock of total reserves set by the Fed is shown as a vertical line, labeled TR_0. An open market sale decreases total reserves, shifting the supply to TR_1.

EQUILIBRIUM IN THE FEDERAL FUNDS MARKET

We can now see how the Fed is able to affect the value of the funds rate through its control of the stock of total reserves. Figure 32.3 depicts the quantity of reserves demanded as depending negatively on the funds rate. Suppose the Fed's target for the federal funds rate is i_0. To achieve this target, the Fed must ensure that the funds market clears at the interest rate i_0, the point where the quantity of reserves supplied and the quantity demanded are equal. For this to occur, the level of total reserves the Fed will need to supply is TR_0. At this level, the supply curve for total reserves intersects the demand curve at the desired interest rate i_0.

Now, assume the Fed decides to increase its target for the funds rate (as it did in mid-2004). If the new target is i_1, the Fed must reduce reserve supply to TR_1. By engaging in open market sales, the Fed can reduce the supply of total reserves from TR_0 to TR_1. The new equilibrium funds rate is i_1, the desired target value. The funds rate is determined by supply and demand in the funds market, but by adjusting the supply of reserves, the Fed is able to keep the funds rate equal to its target.

As conditions change in the economy, the quantity of reserves demanded at each funds rate may shift. If its target for the funds rate is unchanged, the Fed has to adjust total reserves in response to any shifts in the demand curve for reserves. For instance, a change in bank deposits will shift the demand curve for reserves. The consequences of an increase in deposits that increases banks' demand for reserves are depicted in Figure 32.4. Initially, the funds market is in equilibrium with the funds rate at i_0. If the Fed does nothing, a rightward shift in the demand for reserves will push the funds rate up to i_1. To prevent this from happening, and to keep the funds rate at its target value i_0, the Fed must increase the supply of nonborrowed reserves through an open market purchase, thereby shifting the total reserve supply curve to the right. In this way, the Fed can respond to shifts in reserve demand and keep the funds rate equal to its target.

The demand for reserves at each funds rate will also shift if the Fed changes the required reserve ratio. Suppose the Fed increases the reserve ratio. At each level of deposits, banks must now hold a higher level of reserves. The reserve demand curve therefore shifts to the right. If the Fed keeps total reserves constant, the equilibrium funds rate rises. If the Fed wishes to prevent the funds rate from changing, it needs to engage in an open market purchase to increase the total reserve supply.

These shifts in the reserve demand curve illustrate another important consequence of a monetary policy that targets the funds rate. The rightward shift of the reserve demand curve shown in Figure 32.4 led to an equal shift in reserve supply to keep the funds rate from changing. While the funds rate remained constant, the *quantity of reserves* rose, from TR_0 to TR_1. Through the money multiplier process discussed in Chapter 28, this rise in reserves will increase the supply of money.

When monetary policy is implemented through control of the federal funds rate, shifts in the quantity of reserves demand are accommodated automatically. If banks' demand for reserves at each federal funds rate were to increase, the Fed would automatically allow the supply of reserves to rise so that the funds rate would not be affected.

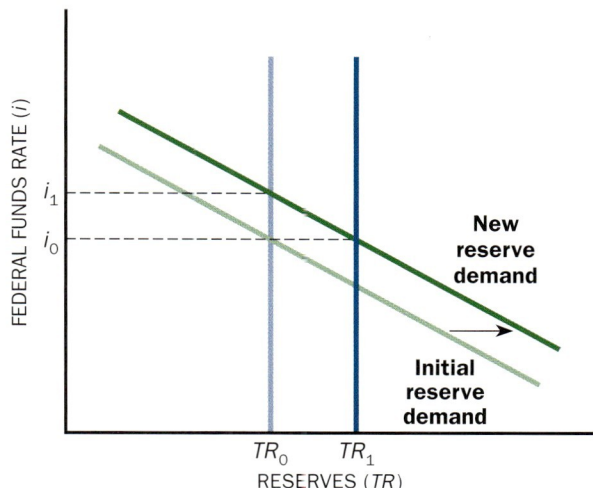

Figure 32.4

THE EFFECT OF AN INCREASE IN THE QUANTITY OF RESERVES DEMANDED

Suppose the demand curve for reserves shifts rightward. If the Fed leaves the stock of nonborrowed reserves unchanged, the funds rate rises to i_1, where reserve demand and reserve supply are again equal. If the Fed wishes to keep the funds rate at i_0, it increases nonborrowed reserves in order to shift the supply schedule to the right by an amount equal to the shift in demand. Total reserves rise from TR_0 to TR_1.

> **Wrap-Up**
>
> ## THE FEDERAL FUNDS MARKET
>
> 1. The federal funds rate is determined by supply and demand in the federal funds market.
> 2. The Fed is able to keep the funds rate equal to the target set by the FOMC by using open market operations to control the supply of total reserves.

Monetary Policy Operating Procedures

The actual manner in which a central bank implements monetary policy is often called the monetary authority's **operating procedures.** In the case of the Fed, the federal funds rate is the key interest rate used to implement monetary policy. Its policy goals and assessment of the economy led the FOMC to set a target for the funds rate. The Trading Desk at the Federal Reserve Bank of New York conducts the actual open market operations required to keep the funds rate equal to the target established by the FOMC. Implementing monetary policy in this fashion is often called an *interest rate operating procedure.*

An interest rate procedure is not the only way monetary policy can be implemented, and over the course of the past twenty-five years, the Fed has changed its operating procedures several times. The main alternative to an interest rate procedure is a *money supply operating procedure* that focuses on controlling a quantity—either a reserve quantity such as total reserves or a monetary aggregate such as

M1 (the total of currency, traveler's checks, and checking accounts). Rather than letting reserve supply adjust automatically to achieve an interest rate target, the Fed could decide on a target for the money supply or the quantity of reserves, letting the funds rate adjust automatically to clear the federal funds market.

Under a money supply procedure, just as under an interest rate procedure, monetary policy discussions start with an assessment of the state of the economy and a determination of what changes in policy are needed, if any, to achieve the agreed-on goals. Once the path for the money supply consistent with those goals of policy is determined, open market operations are conducted to supply a level of reserves that leads to the desired level of the money stock.

During the 1970s, many economists argued that the Fed should focus on controlling the money supply. They had two reasons. First, inflation was then the primary policy problem. Our full-employment model shows that the average rate of inflation and the average rate of money growth are related; if the monetary authority controls money growth, it can control inflation. Second, economists at the time saw a tight link between a measure of the money supply such as M1 and total dollar GDP. By controlling M1, the argument went, the Fed could control total aggregate income. In the 1980s, however, the tight link between M1 and nominal GDP appeared to break down, making a money supply operating procedure less useful for implementing monetary policy.

INFLATION, MONEY SUPPLY, AND THE NOMINAL RATE OF INTEREST

Because the link between money and nominal GDP became unstable in many countries, most central banks now implement monetary policy by setting a target interest rate. But such policies can lead to problems when inflation rises, as it did in the late 1960s. The full-employment model tells us that increases in the money supply provide the fuel for inflation. Under an interest rate policy, an initial increase in inflation can lead to automatic increases in the money supply that allow the inflation to continue.

Suppose prices have been stable in the economy—an inflation rate of zero. Then, suppose inflation rises to 5 percent. As prices rise, the dollar value of transactions in the economy increases. A sandwich that costs $5.00 one year will cost 5 percent more annually, or $5.25 after one year, $5.51 after two years, and $8.14 after ten years. People will want to hold, on average, about 5 percent more money each year, both as cash for everyday transactions and in their checking accounts. Thus the demand for money grows.

Because the volume of transactions through the banking system has increased, banks will need to hold more reserves to balance their payment flows. This increase in the demand for reserves at each value of the funds rate shifts the reserve demand curve to the right. If its target for the funds rate is kept unchanged, the Fed will need to increase the supply of reserves over time, allowing the money supply to rise with the increased demand for money. From our money multiplier analysis, we know that by allowing the supply of reserves to increase, the Fed also ensures that the quantity of money increases. *When the monetary authority tries to keep the nominal interest rate constant, the quantity of money automatically increases as prices rise. Inflation causes the money supply to automatically increase, further fueling and sustaining the inflation.*

In the full-employment model, we assumed that government controlled the supply of money directly. Because full-employment output is determined by such factors as labor supply, the capital stock, and the economy's technology, changes in the money supply led to proportional changes in the price level (see Chapter 28). When the central bank adjusts the reserve supply to achieve an interest rate target, the supply of money adjusts in line with prices. To halt the rise in inflation, the central bank must raise its target interest rate to prevent the ongoing expansion of the money supply. When inflation rose to high levels in the 1970s, central banks therefore shifted from interest rate operating procedures to procedures that focused more directly on controlling the money supply.

Review and Practice

SUMMARY

1. The federal funds market is the market in which banks can borrow or lend reserves.
2. The federal funds rate, which is the interest rate on overnight interbank loans, adjusts to balance the supply and demand for reserves.
3. The Federal Reserve can affect the market for reserves by changing the reserve requirement, by changing the discount rate, or by open market operations.
4. Open market operations are the chief tool used by the Fed to affect the market for reserves. By controlling the supply of reserves, they enable the Fed to achieve the target for the federal funds rate set by the FOMC.
5. Under a money supply operating procedure, open market operations can be used to achieve a target for the money supply. Because the speed with which money circulates in the economy (and therefore the optimal money supply) has become less predictable in recent years, most central banks implement policy by setting the nominal interest rate, an interest rate operating procedure.

KEY TERMS

federal funds rate
federal funds market
open market operations
repurchases (RPs)
excess reserves
discount rate
borrowed reserves
total reserves
nonborrowed reserves
operating procedures

REVIEW QUESTIONS

1. Why do nonborrowed reserves fall if the Fed engages in an open market sale? Why do they rise if the Fed engages in an open market purchase?
2. Why do borrowed reserves fall if the Fed raises the discount rate? Why do they rise if the federal funds rate increases?
3. If the FOMC raises its target for the federal funds rate, will the Fed need to increase or to decrease the supply of reserves? Will it need to engage in an open market purchase or a sale to accomplish this?
4. Why does the Fed increase the supply of reserves when prices rise if it is targeting the federal funds rate? What would happen to the funds rate if prices rose and the Fed held the supply of reserves fixed?

PROBLEMS

1. Why does an open market purchase increase the supply of reserves in the banking sector?
2. Using a supply and demand diagram of the federal funds market, show how an increase in reserve requirements would affect the equilibrium federal funds rate.
3. Suppose the economy's income falls, reducing the demand for money. If the Fed keeps its target for the funds rate constant, what happens to reserve demand and the supply of reserves? If instead the Fed keeps the supply of reserves constant, what happens to the funds rate?
4. In 1999, there was broad concern about the Y2K computer problem. Banks, and the Fed, predicted that many people would want to hold additional cash in case software glitches blocked access to their bank accounts on January 1, 2000. Use a money multiplier analysis (see Chapter 28) to predict what happens to deposits and the money supply if people increase their holdings of cash and the Fed attempts to keep the federal funds rate constant. What are the consequences for the money supply of the increased demand for cash?
5. Does money growth cause inflation, or does inflation cause money growth? Discuss. How does your answer depend on the behavior of the Fed?

Learning Goals

In this chapter, you will learn

1. Modern views of the macroeconomic trade-offs that policymakers face
2. The roles of automatic stabilizers and discretionary policy
3. The monetary policy rule and what it depends on
4. How monetary and fiscal policies differ in their impacts on the economy

Chapter 33

THE ROLE OF MACROECONOMIC POLICY

Economic policy debates have always been at the core of macroeconomics. After all, macroeconomics began as an attempt to understand the causes of the Great Depression of the 1930s and to formulate government policies that might end it. Discussions in the United States in recent years have been dominated by the debate over job creation after the 2001 recession, the huge federal government deficits and their possible impact on economic growth, and the implications of the trade deficit.

Economies are constantly buffeted by shocks and disturbances—the stock market collapse in 2000; the financial crises in Asia, Europe, and Latin America in the late 1990s; large swings in the federal budget deficit; new technological innovations transforming many sectors of the economy—that have the potential to create recessions or ignite inflation. In the face of these disturbances, policymakers must try to ensure that the economy continues to operate at potential GDP while inflation remains low and stable.

In this chapter, we will examine the role of both monetary and fiscal policy in affecting the economy in the short run. Chapters 29 to 31 have provided a framework for understanding the impact of government on the economy. In those chapters, the analysis treated policy in isolation—explaining how a change in fiscal or monetary policy affected the economy. But macroeconomic policy decisions are not taken in isolation—governments use monetary and fiscal policy to try to stabilize the economy, and this role of macroeconomic policy is the topic of the present chapter.

Inflation–Unemployment Trade-Offs

Economists focus on trade-offs: if we want more of one thing, what do we have to give up? Can we have lower average unemployment if we are willing to accept higher average inflation? Does keeping inflation low and stable mean that output and unemployment will fluctuate more? Chapter 31 provided the analytical basis for addressing these questions. Clearly, we would like to have both low (and stable) inflation and low (and stable) unemployment. Economists' understanding of the trade-offs that policymakers must face has evolved over time.

THE OLD INFLATION–UNEMPLOYMENT TRADE-OFF

Fifty years ago, most economists thought that there was a trade-off between the *average* level of unemployment and the *average* rate of inflation. Economists who believed that the costs of inflation were high argued for lower inflation and a higher unemployment rate, while those who held that the benefits of low inflation were far outweighed by the costs of high unemployment argued for lower unemployment rates and higher inflation. Thus, disagreements about policy largely hinged on disagreements about the relative *costs* of inflation and unemployment.

Attempts in the 1960s to exploit this trade-off by reducing unemployment to levels much lower than previously experienced led, as our analysis in Chapter 31 predicted, to higher inflation. And rather than remaining stable at its new higher level, the inflation rate continued to increase as long as unemployment remained below the economy's natural rate of unemployment. The economy ended up back at potential GDP, with the same average levels of unemployment as before but with higher inflation rates. During the 1970s, a consensus developed that the economy could not enjoy a sustained level of unemployment below the natural rate.

The experience of the 1960s and 1970s convinced most policymakers that no trade-off exists between average rates of inflation and average rates of unemployment. As we learned in Part Six, the average level of the unemployment rate and the rate of real economic growth are determined by such fundamentals as technological change, population growth, labor market institutions, and the skills of the workforce. Because these factors are unrelated to the economy's average rate of inflation, allowing average inflation to rise brings no *long-run* benefit in the form of faster growth or lower average unemployment. The choice facing policymakers appeared to be a simple one—the economy could operate at full employment with low inflation, or it could operate at full employment with high inflation. Obviously, low inflation was preferable.

THE NEW TRADE-OFF: OUTPUT STABILITY–INFLATION STABILITY

In recent years, economists such as John Taylor of Stanford University have argued that attempts to stabilize fluctuations in output and employment will cause inflation to fluctuate more. And attempts to stabilize fluctuations in inflation will cause output and employment to fluctuate more.[1] Thus policymakers face a different trade-off: one between fluctuations in the real economy (output and unemployment) and fluctuations in inflation. One important aspect of this shift in focus is that it encourages the use of macro policies to *stabilize* the economy rather than attempting to achieve unsustainable outcomes (such as an average unemployment rate below the natural rate). Later in this chapter we will see how the trade-off between stability in output and in inflation is affected by the policy rule followed by the central bank.

So far, our discussion has concentrated on the trade-offs that policymakers face. But even when they agree about the objectives, they may disagree about how best to achieve those objectives. Should fiscal policy be the main tool for stabilizing the economy? Or should monetary policy take the lead?

Fiscal Policy

Fiscal policy is defined as changes in government expenditures and taxes that are designed to achieve macroeconomic policy goals. In earlier chapters, we learned about the consequences of changes in fiscal policy. The full-employment model is useful for assessing the impact of budget deficits and surpluses on the real interest rate, investment, and growth. The model of short-run fluctuations in Chapter 31 provides a framework for analyzing how unemployment and inflation would be affected by swings in fiscal policy that shifted the aggregate demand–inflation (ADI) curve. These models offer insights into the effects of fiscal policy, but we now need to use those insights to focus on how fiscal policy can contribute to the macroeconomic goals of full employment, low and stable inflation, and economic growth. We will start by distinguishing between two types of policies—**automatic stabilizers** and **discretionary actions.**

AUTOMATIC STABILIZERS

One way that fiscal policy contributes to macroeconomic goals is by instituting automatic stabilizers. Automatic stabilizers are expenditures that automatically increase, or taxes that automatically decrease, when economic conditions worsen. We have

---

[1] John B. Taylor, "How Should Monetary Policy Respond to Shocks While Maintaining Long-Run Price Stability?—Conceptual Issues," in *Achieving Price Stability: A Symposium* (Kansas City, Mo.: Federal Reserve Bank of Kansas City, 1996), pp. 181–95.

already seen in Chapter 30 how income-related taxes serve as automatic stabilizers by reducing the multiplier. As incomes rise, individuals and business will have to pay more in taxes to local and state governments and to the federal government, an increase that automatically acts to limit spending increases and to keep overall aggregate spending more stable. For example, suppose the marginal tax rate is 30 percent—that is, for each additional dollar you earn, you have to pay 30 cents in taxes. When your income goes up by $1,000, your disposable income—what is left after taxes are paid—increases by only $700. The rest of your increased income—$300—must cover the taxes. If the marginal propensity to consume is .8, you increase your spending by .8 × $700, or $560. Without the increased tax bite, you would have increased your spending by significantly more: .8 × $1,000, or $800. Because taxes rise and fall with income, they help reduce swings in spending and, as a result, make the economy more stable.

Taxes aren't the only form of fiscal automatic stabilizers. Many transfer payments, such as unemployment benefits, adjust automatically as economic conditions change. When unemployment rises, unemployment benefits automatically increase, thereby helping to provide income support to those who receive them. As a result, the unemployed are not forced to reduce their consumption spending as sharply as they otherwise would. By limiting the decline in spending, automatic stabilizers make the economy more stable.

Automatic stabilizers influence the slope of the ADI curve. For example, the impact of an increase in inflation on aggregate spending will depend on the tax system. As the real interest rate rises when inflation increases and spending and income fall in reaction to the increased cost of credit, tax payments also fall. This decrease in tax payments cushions the decline in disposable income and household consumption spending. It acts to limit the extent to which spending, and therefore aggregate income, declines when inflation increases. As a consequence, an economy that makes much use of automatic fiscal stabilizers will have a steeper ADI curve than one without fiscal stabilizers.

The impact of automatic stabilizers on the ADI curve and the effect of spending shocks on short-run equilibrium are illustrated in Figure 33.1. The two sets of ADI curves show two economies, one with much stronger fiscal automatic stabilizers than the other. The economy with the stronger stabilizers has the steeper ADI curve (the light green line in the figure). To understand why, consider what happens if inflation rises. When inflation rises and the central bank boosts the real interest rate, spending falls and equilibrium income declines; but when automatic stabilizers kick in—taxes decline and government spending, particularly transfer spending, increase automatically—they act to cushion the decline in spending and output. The economy lacking these stabilizers will suffer a bigger decline in aggregate spending and output—and thus it has a flatter ADI curve, such as the blue line in the figure.

Automatic stabilizers also reduce the effect on the economy of shocks to GDP. A fall in government purchases shifts the ADI curve to the left, but the size of this shift is reduced by automatic stabilizers. Researchers have estimated that the federal tax system offsets about 8 percent of the impact of shocks to GDP.[2] As shown in the

---

[2] Alan J. Auerbach and Daniel Feenberg, "The Significance of Federal Taxes as Automatic Stabilizers," NBER Working Paper No. 7662, April 2000.

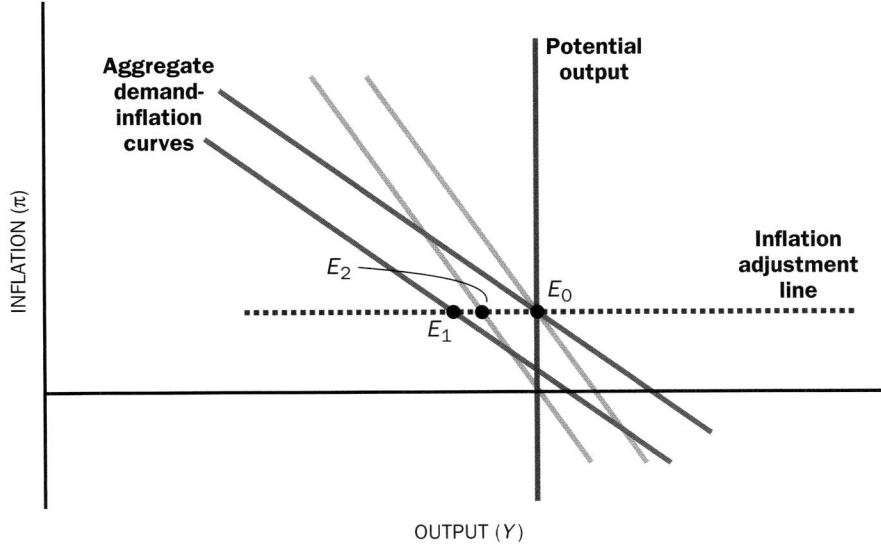

Figure 33.1
AUTOMATIC STABILIZERS

Automatic stabilizers affect the slope of the ADI curve and how it shifts in response to disturbances in spending. The light green ADI curve depicts an economy with stronger automatic stabilizers; the dark green ADI curve, one with weaker. When a spending shock shifts both to the left from the same starting point E_0, the light green ADI curve moves less as the automatic stabilizers dampen the impact of the shock. As a result, output and inflation fluctuate less (compare the short-run equilibria at E_1 and E_2). In the face of an inflation shock, stronger automatic stabilizers lessen the fluctuation of output.

figure, the smaller shift in the light green ADI curve reduces the fall in equilibrium output, increasing the economy's stability. In the face of inflation shocks, automatic stabilizers lead to smaller fluctuations in real output.

DISCRETIONARY POLICY ACTIONS

Fiscal policy has also been used to affect the economy deliberately rather than automatically. *Discretionary* policy actions represent conscious choices by the government. When we analyzed the impact of an increase in government purchases in the full-employment model of Part Six or discussed how a tax cut would shift the ADI curve, we were analyzing discretionary policy changes.

Fiscal policy has been used actively to help promote macroeconomic goals several times in recent history. Perhaps the most famous case was the 1964 Kennedy tax cut, which was designed to boost economic growth and reduce unemployment. The analysis in Chapter 30 explained why this policy succeeded in the short run but led to higher inflation in the long run. The late 1960s also saw an increase in government purchases associated with the Vietnam War, which contributed to an expanding economy and rising inflation (just what a rightward shift of the ADI curve would be expected to produce). To counteract these forces, President Lyndon Johnson imposed a 10 percent income tax surcharge in 1968; the hope was that this tax increase would cause households to scale back their consumption spending, thereby helping to offset the expansion in demand caused by the increased government spending. Unfortunately, the policy did not have the full effect that its designers had sought—because the tax surcharge was temporary, lasting only one year, most households had little reason to significantly change their behavior.

In the United States, discretionary fiscal policy is usually viewed as very slow to respond. As is discussed in greater detail at the end of this chapter, there are inevitably delays both in recognizing a problem and—more significantly—in drafting and passing legislation to address it. Congress rarely works swiftly. As a result of these lags in implementation, at least for the United States, fiscal policy operates mainly through automatic stabilizers in helping to stabilize the economy. When the economy enters a recession, tax revenues decline automatically as incomes fall. And as incomes and employment levels fall, some government expenditure programs, such as unemployment insurance, automatically increase. These responses help stabilize the disposable income and consumption spending of households.

Using Discretionary Fiscal Policy to Combat a Recession When the economy goes into a recession, the role of fiscal policy is usually hotly debated; despite their practical difficulties as tools to fine-tune the economy, discretionary policy actions are frequently proposed. During 1990 and 1991, the U.S. economy was caught in recession, and "It's the economy, stupid" was one of the most memorable lines from Bill Clinton's successful 1992 campaign against the incumbent president, George H. W. Bush. Clinton argued for a more active fiscal response to help end the recession, although by the time he took office, the economy was already expanding and the recession was clearly over.

In 2001, soon after President George W. Bush took office, the U.S. economy entered a recession, and the president used the emerging signs of an economic slowdown to push a tax cut through Congress. He argued that an expansionary fiscal policy was needed because of the recession. We can use the ADI framework to analyze the impact of a fiscal expansion during a recession.

Internet Connection

THE ECONOMIC REPORT OF THE PRESIDENT

Every February, the president's Council of Economic Advisors issues the *Economic Report of the President*. This report discusses the state of the economy and developments in fiscal policy. As well as providing a wealth of data on the economy, each chapter of the report deals with a current policy debate. The latest report can be found at www.gpoaccess.gov/eop/index.html.

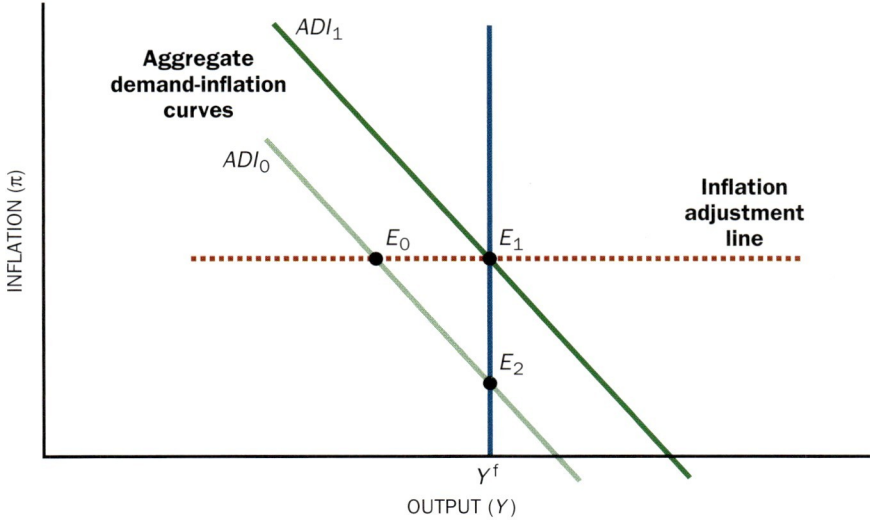

Figure 33.2
USING FISCAL POLICY TO END A RECESSION

The initial short-run equilibrium is at E_0, with the economy in recession. An expansionary fiscal policy—an increase in government purchases or a tax cut—would shift the ADI curve to the right and increase equilibrium output. If the fiscal stimulus can be designed to move the ADI curve to ADI_1, full employment would be restored at E_1. In the absence of any policy actions, full employment would eventually be restored as inflation declined, and the economy would be at E_2. If the adjustment of inflation is slow, the economy would experience a long period of high unemployment as it moves to E_2.

Figure 33.2 shows the economy in a recession at point E_0. Output is below the full-employment level Y^f. The decline in output, with the associated rise in cyclical unemployment, has resulted from a leftward shift in the ADI curve.

An expansionary fiscal policy can end a recession and eliminate the cyclical unemployment. Increasing government purchases or cutting taxes raises aggregate expenditures at each inflation rate, shifting the ADI curve to the right. If the size of the fiscal policy is judged correctly, the ADI curve can be shifted to ADI_1, moving the economy's short-run equilibrium back to full employment.

If no policy action were taken, the economy would eventually return to full employment at E_2. With high cyclical unemployment, inflation will tend to fall, shifting the inflation adjustment line down (not shown in the figure). As inflation declines, the Fed lowers the interest rate to stimulate aggregate expenditures, causing output to begin to increase. This process continues until full employment is restored at a lower rate of inflation at point E_2 in the figure.

THE FULL-EMPLOYMENT DEFICIT

Because tax revenues rise and fall with income, the government's surplus or deficit also varies with income. As the economy expands and tax revenues increase, the

International Perspective
FISCAL TRANSFERS

The role of fiscal policy and automatic stabilizers has been a topic of debate within the twelve European countries that all use the euro as their currency. There, the concern is the lack of automatic fiscal stabilizers that can help mitigate economic fluctuations within the euro zone when the economies of some members are in recession while those of others are booming.

The members of the European Economic and Monetary Union (EMU) that use the euro share a single monetary policy, conducted by the European Central Bank (ECB) in Frankfurt. The ECB bases that policy on overall economic conditions in the union, but what is right for the union might not be the best policy for individual countries within the union. For example, suppose Germany, France, and Italy, the three biggest economies in the union, are experiencing an economic boom, while Portugal is in a recession. The ECB might raise interest rates to dampen the boom in Germany, France, and Italy, but this action would make the Portuguese recession even worse. Because the ECB affects interest rates for the whole union, its policy cannot be tailored to meet the individual needs of each member country.

But how is this different from the situation in the United States, with fifty individual states? The Fed bases its policy on conditions in the entire country. Some states might be in recession and therefore would like the Fed's policy to be more expansionary, while for others, in a booming economy, a tighter policy would be better.

What the United States has, and Europe lacks, is a federal fiscal system that automatically helps stabilize the overall economy. If one state is in a recession, federal tax payments from that state fall and federal transfer payments to the state increase. Such transfers promote demand in that state. The federal system serves to shift income from expanding states to contracting states, helping to dampen demand in the booming states while helping to offset the recession in the contracting states.

No such fiscal transfers exist among the member countries of the EMU. Though the twelve members have a common monetary policy, their fiscal policies are not unified. If the economy of Germany is booming and Portugal's economy is in a slump, the increased tax payments generated by rising Germany incomes are not used to provide increased fiscal transfers to Portugal.

The headquarters for the European Central Bank

surplus will expand (or the deficit will shrink). When the economy goes into a recession, tax revenues fall, decreasing the surplus (or increasing the deficit). These automatic changes in the surplus or deficit show the effects of taxes' role as an automatic stabilizer. But how can we determine what part of, say, a larger deficit has resulted from a discretionary increase in government purchases rather than from a decline in overall economic activity?

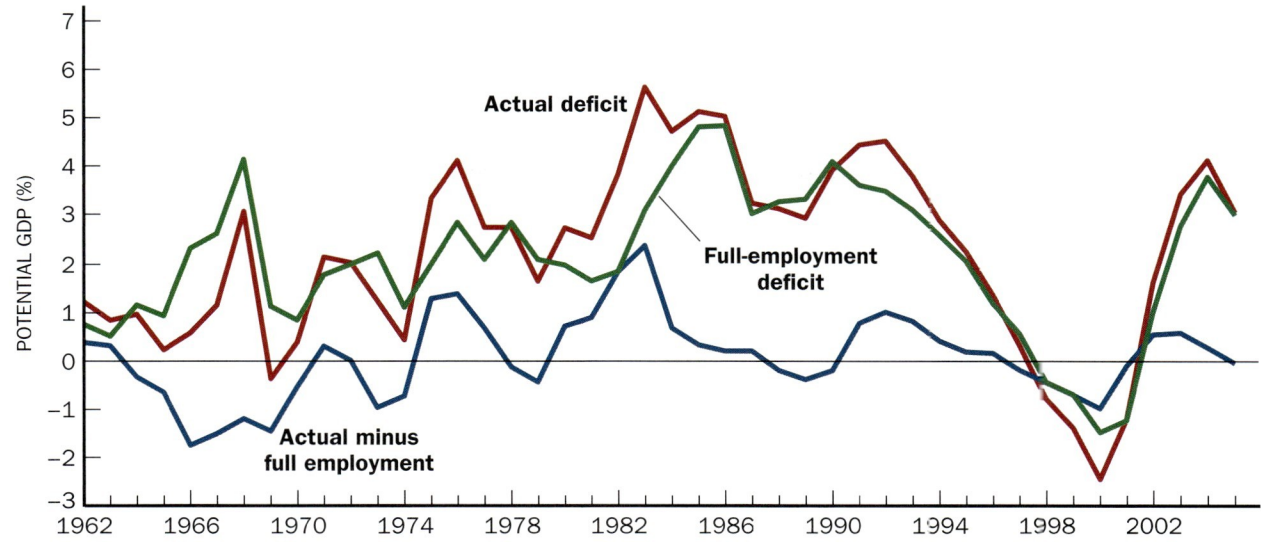

Figure 33.3
ACTUAL AND FULL-EMPLOYMENT DEFICITS

The government's deficit fluctuates with movements in GDP. The full-employment deficit provides an estimate of what the deficit would be if the economy were at full employment—that is, with the cyclical component of the deficit removed. The figure shows the difference between the actual and full-employment deficits (blue line). When cyclical unemployment is positive, the actual deficit exceeds the full-employment deficit.

SOURCE: Congressional Budget Office.

One way to separate out the effects of automatic stabilizers from these active changes in policy is to focus on the **full-employment deficit**—what the deficit would have been had the economy been operating at full employment. The full-employment deficit adjusts for the stage of the business cycle; it adjusts for the changes in taxes and spending that vary over the business cycles. For instance, in a recession when incomes fall, the actual deficit increases because tax revenues decline with the drop in income. The full-employment deficit corrects for this cyclical effect on taxes by calculating what the deficit would be if the economy had not gone into a recession. It changes, therefore, only when there are discretionary changes in taxes or spending and gives a better measure of the impact of discretionary fiscal policy actions.

If the economy booms and tax revenues swell, the full-employment deficit will be greater than the actual deficit; if the economy goes into a recession and tax revenues fall, the full-employment deficit will be less than the actual deficit. Most economists view the government as fiscally responsible so long as there is no deficit when the economy is at full employment—that is, the full-employment deficit should be zero. Balancing the budget at full employment would allow automatic stabilizers to work during business cycle fluctuations. Figure 33.3 shows the actual U.S. federal deficit and an estimate of the full-employment deficit. In 2003 (the last year shown), cyclical unemployment was almost zero, so the full-employment deficit and the actual deficit were equal.

> **Wrap-Up**
>
> ## FISCAL POLICY
>
> Automatic stabilizers increase expenditures and reduce taxes automatically as the economy goes into a recession. They act to reduce the impact of economic shocks on GDP by stabilizing aggregate expenditures.
>
> The full-employment deficit adjusts for the stage of the business cycle and gives a measure of what the deficit (or surplus) would be if the economy were at full employment. It provides a clearer picture of the effects of discretionary fiscal policy actions.

Monetary Policy

Monetary policy affects the level of nominal interest rates, the money supply, and average inflation in the economy. Decisions by the Federal Reserve about interest rates are a major focus of participants in the financial market and of news reports. Speeches by the chair of the Federal Reserve Board—from 1987 until January 2006, Alan Greenspan—are closely examined for hints about possible interest rate changes, and speculation can reach a fever pitch when the Federal Open Market Committee (FOMC) meets to decide on policy.

Some aspects of monetary policy are similar to automatic stabilizers as they work to keep the economy more stable. But like fiscal policy, monetary policy has also been used actively to achieve macroeconomic goals.

We have already mentioned one common behavior of the Fed in our discussion of the aggregate demand–inflation curve. As inflation increases, the Fed, like other central banks in major industrialized economies, raises the nominal interest rate. And the nominal rate is raised enough so that the real interest rate rises. This normal reaction works exactly as does an automatic stabilizer when the economy expands above potential and inflation starts to rise. Raising the interest rate curtails aggregate spending and helps stabilize the economy at its potential. A critical issue in the design of good monetary policy is determining how large such an increase should be. The strength of this response to an increase in inflation significantly affects the slope of the ADI curve.

BEHIND THE ADI CURVE—THE ROLE OF MONETARY POLICY

When the ADI curve was introduced in Chapter 31, we saw that as inflation increases in the short run, the Fed seeks to raise the real rate of interest. This increase lowers aggregate expenditures and equilibrium output. Now it is time to take a closer look at the role of monetary policy in affecting the shape and position of the ADI curve.

Conducting Monetary Policy The FOMC meets approximately every six weeks to decide on monetary policy. The central banks in most industrial economies conduct monetary policy by setting a target for a nominal interest rate; in the case of the United States, the target is the federal funds rate, the rate on overnight bank-to-bank loans. Chapter 32 explained how the Fed uses its control of bank reserves to achieve that target. At the close of each FOMC meeting, a vote is taken on whether to raise, lower, or leave unchanged the interest rate target, and any change is immediately announced in a press release. Occasionally, the FOMC will change its target between meetings, as it did on January 3, 2001, in response to mounting evidence that the economy was slowing down and an interest rate cut was necessary.

Figure 33.4 shows the Fed's target for the funds rate, the actual funds rate, and the prime interest rate—that is, the interest rate charged on loans to banks' best customers. Two facts stand out. First, the Fed is extremely successful in achieving its target, which in the figure is almost indistinguishable from the actual funds rate. Our focus here is not on how this is done—open market operations and their implications for the supply of reserves and of money were discussed in Chapter 32—but on the consequences of changes in interest rates for the economy and on the factors that influence the Fed in setting its target.

The second point illustrated by the figure is that the prime interest rate moves in tandem with the funds rate. The prime rate is always higher, reflecting the greater risk of business loans. But whenever the funds rate is raised or lowered, the prime rate also rises or falls. If an increase in the funds rate increases the real interest

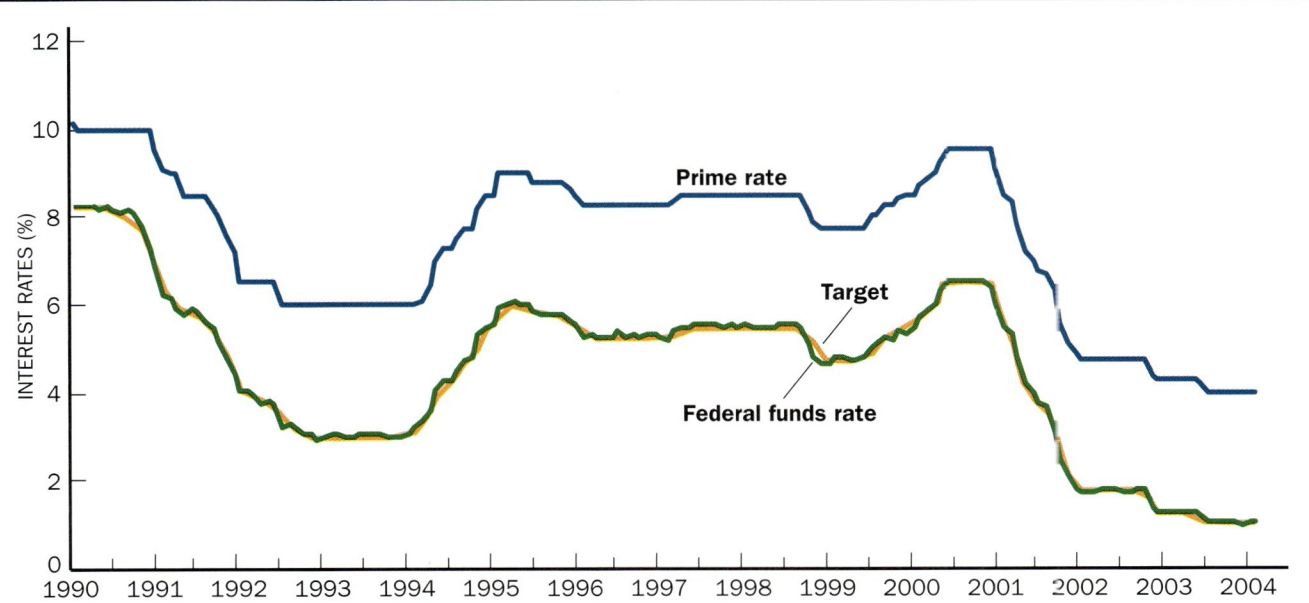

Figure 33.4

THE FED'S TARGET, THE FUNDS RATE, AND THE PRIME RATE

Though the actual funds rate is determined by supply and demand, it closely follows the target set by the Fed. The prime interest rate is the rate that banks charge on loans to their best business customers. It also moves closely with changes in the Fed's target for the funds rate.

SOURCE: Federal Reserve Board.

Internet Connection
THE BEIGE BOOK

The summary of economic conditions prepared for each meeting of the FOMC is published in what is known as the *Beige Book*. You can see the latest Beige Book at the Fed's Web site by going to www.federalreserve.gov/fomc/beigebook/2005/ (changing the year in the URL as appropriate).

rate, borrowing will become more costly: the real cost of auto loans, mortgage interest rates, and commercial loans to firms will increase. As credit becomes more costly, households and firms will scale back their spending plans.

Because changes in the funds rate affect the entire range of market interest rates, we simplified the discussion in previous chapters by assuming that the Fed sets the level of nominal interest rates. In Chapter 32, we learned that other approaches to implementing monetary policy are also used. For example, between 1979 and 1985, the Fed often focused more closely on various measures of the money supply than on the funds rate. Since 1985, however, setting a target for the funds rate has been the Fed's main tool of monetary policy. Chapter 32 explained *how* the Fed influences interest rates; what we need to examine now is *why* the Fed decides to raise or lower market interest rates. And to do that, we must examine the goals of monetary policy.

Case in Point
ANNOUNCING THE FED'S DECISIONS

After each FOMC meeting, any policy decisions are conveyed to the Federal Reserve Bank of New York for implementation. In recent years, these directives have specified the average value for the federal funds rate that the FOMC believes is consistent with its policy objectives. The FOMC also issues a press release that summarizes any policy actions taken during the meeting and offers an assessment of economic conditions. For example, the press release of August 10, 2004, begins

> The Federal Open Market Committee decided today to raise its target for the federal funds rate by 25 basis points [i.e., 1/4 of a percentage point] to 1-1/2 percent.
>
> The Committee believes that, even after this action, the stance of monetary policy remains accommodative and, coupled with robust underlying growth in productivity, is providing ongoing support to economic activity. In recent months, output growth has moderated and the pace of improvement in labor market conditions has slowed. This softness likely owes importantly to the substantial rise in energy prices. The economy nevertheless appears poised to resume a stronger pace of expansion going forward. Inflation has been somewhat elevated this year, though a portion of the rise in prices seems to reflect transitory factors.

The Committee perceives the upside and downside risks to the attainment of both sustainable growth and price stability for the next few quarters are roughly equal. With underlying inflation still expected to be relatively low, the Committee believes that policy accommodation can be removed at a pace that is likely to be measured. Nonetheless, the Committee will respond to changes in economic prospects as needed to fulfill its obligation to maintain price stability.

REAL INTEREST RATES AND NOMINAL INTEREST RATES

To understand the links between the Fed's decisions and real output and inflation, we must start by recalling an important distinction between *real interest rates* and *nominal interest rates*. The nominal, or market, interest rate gives the percentage rate of return on a deposit, loan, or financial asset *without taking into account the effects of inflation*. When prices are rising, the value of a dollar is falling since each dollar will buy fewer and fewer goods and services over time. The dollars a borrower repays are worth less than the dollars that were borrowed. When prices are falling, the value of a dollar is rising since each dollar will buy more and more goods and services over time. The dollars a borrower repays are then worth more than the dollars that were borrowed. The nominal interest rate as a measure of the cost of a loan or the rate of return on a financial asset fails to correct for these changes in the value of money.

The real rate of interest is the percentage return on a deposit, loan, or other financial asset *after the effects of inflation are taken into account*. It represents the change in the real purchasing power that the lender receives. If the market rate of interest is 6 percent and inflation is 2 percent, the real interest rate is 4 percent; 2 percentage points of the 6 percent nominal interest rate represent compensation for the falling value of the dollar. The relationship between the real rate of interest, the nominal rate of interest, and inflation[3] is given by

$$\text{nominal rate of interest} = \text{real rate of interest} + \text{inflation}.$$

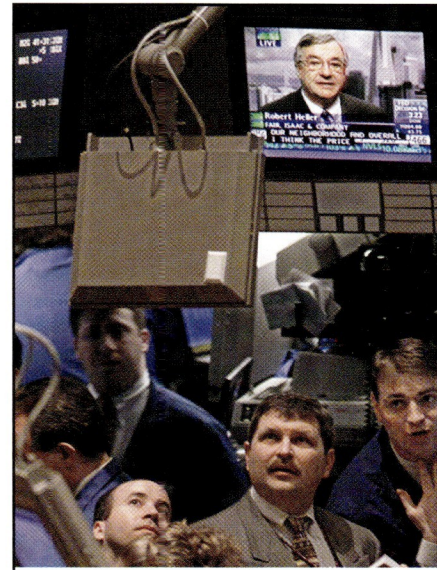

New York Stock Exchange traders listen to the results of a recent FOMC meeting.

Figure 33.5 shows the nominal federal funds rate, the inflation rate, and the nominal funds rate minus the inflation rate as a measure of the real interest rate. Two points are worth noting. First, the level of nominal and real interest rates can differ significantly. In the 1970s, for instance, the nominal funds rate was high, yet the real rate was negative for most of the decade. In the 1990s, the nominal funds rate was lower than it had been in the 1970s, yet the real rate was higher. Second, the average level of the funds rate moves closely with inflation. Periods of high inflation typically are associated with a high nominal interest rate; periods of low inflation typically are associated with a low nominal rate.

Given the definition of the nominal interest rate, it is easy to understand why nominal interest rates are high when inflation is high. Both borrowers and lenders

---

[3]We are ignoring taxes on interest income here.

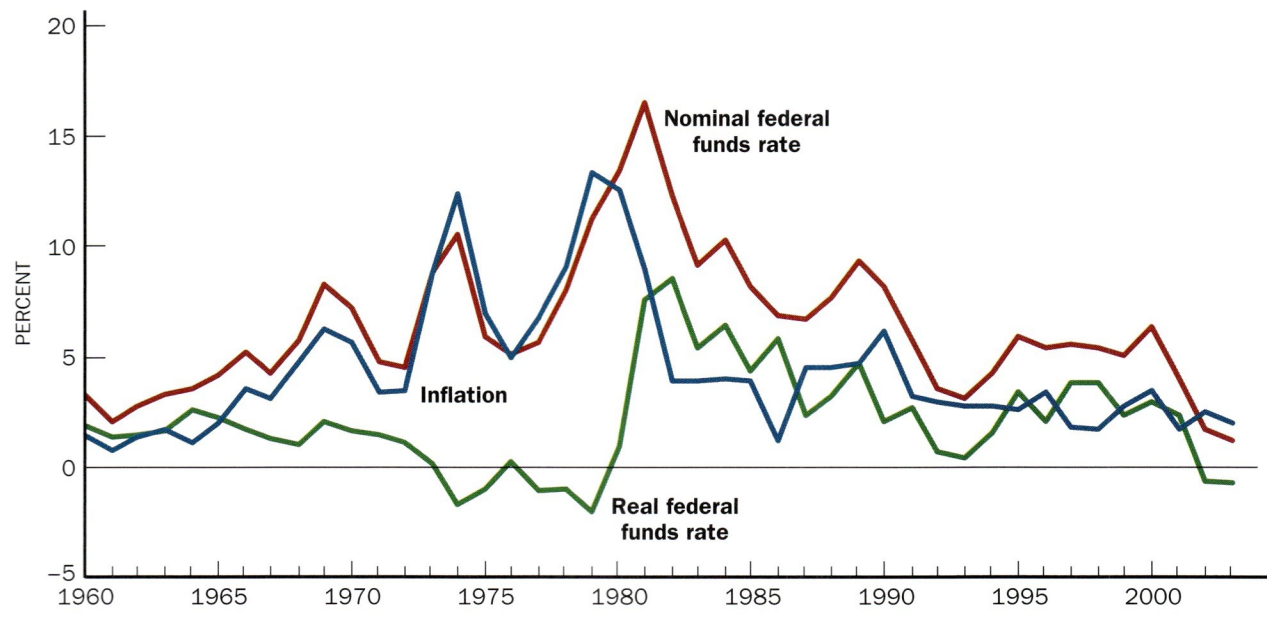

Figure 33.5
NOMINAL AND REAL FEDERAL FUNDS RATES

The nominal federal funds rate is the market interest rate most directly influenced by Federal Reserve policy. The major channel through which policy has its effects is the real federal funds interest rate (the market rate adjusted for inflation). During the 1970s, the funds rate was high, but so was inflation. Consequently, the real interest rate was low, and at times even negative.

SOURCE: *Economic Report of the President* (2004).

care about the real interest rate, which determines the purchasing power they must give up to borrow or the purchasing power they receive by making the loan. If inflation rises, lenders demand and borrowers are willing to pay a higher market interest rate. And a market interest rate of 10 percent with inflation equal to 6 percent represents the same real interest rate as a market rate of 5 percent with inflation of 1 percent. The interest rates we hear or read about are nominal; they are not adjusted to take into account changes in the value of money. Economic decisions—decisions about how much to consume or save, whether to invest in a new plant, or whether to buy a new home—are based on real interest rates.

THE CENTRAL BANK POLICY RULE

In setting its nominal interest rate target, the Fed attempts to influence the level of aggregate expenditures. When inflation rises, or when it expects inflation to rise, the Fed raises the nominal interest rate. But because the spending plans of households and firms depend on the real interest rate, the Fed must raise the nominal interest rate enough to ensure that the real interest rate rises. When it does so, aggregate expenditures fall, lowering equilibrium output and reducing the upward pressure on prices. Similarly, if the economy is entering a recession and inflation is falling, the Fed will reduce the nominal interest rate to lower the real interest rate, stimulate aggregate expenditures, expand output, and moderate the recession.

We illustrate the connection between inflation and the nominal interest rate the central bank sets in panel A of Figure 33.6. The real interest rate is the nominal rate minus inflation, so the nominal interest rate must rise proportionally more than increases in inflation to ensure that the real interest rate increases.[4] This means that the slope of the line in the figure is greater than 1. If the inflation rate increases from π_0 to π_1, the nominal interest rate is raised from i_0 to i_1. The change in the nominal interest rate, i_1 to i_0, is greater than the change in the rate of inflation, π_1 to π_0.

The relationship between inflation and the interest rate set by the central bank is an example of the type of **monetary policy rule** we introduced in Chapter 31. A policy rule is just a description of how the central bank behaves. We have assumed that the policy rule takes a very simple form: the central bank changes the nominal interest rate in response to changes in inflation. We will discuss later in this chapter how the central bank may respond to other macroeconomic variables. Even our simple rule, though, captures important aspects of actual Fed behavior over the past twenty years. It implies that the real rate of interest increases as inflation rises, as shown in panel B of Figure 33.6. Conversely, a fall in inflation leads to a decline in the real interest rate.

Because the Fed sets a target for the nominal federal funds interest rate, we have discussed monetary policy in terms of its effects on interest rates. The relationships shown in panel B would also arise if the central bank instead targeted the money supply. Such was the case from 1979 until 1984, while Paul Volcker was chair of the Federal Reserve; policy focused on target growth rates for measures of bank reserves and the money supply. As an increase in the inflation rate drives prices up faster, individuals will need more money on hand to carry out transactions. The demand for money, including bank deposits, rises. Banks will need to hold more reserves—at each level of the federal funds rate, the demand for reserves shifts up. If the Fed holds the supply of reserves constant, the funds rate will rise. So the policy rule represented in Figure 33.6 would also hold under a policy focused on controlling money supply.

The policy rule illustrates how the Fed responds to inflation. If the Fed reacts to other factors, the line representing the policy rule will shift. For example, suppose at a given rate of inflation the Fed decides to lower interest rates, as it did in January 2001 to offset rising unemployment. This action would shift the entire policy rule downward; at each rate of inflation, the nominal (and real) interest rate would therefore be lower.

Figure 33.6

INTEREST RATES AND INFLATION: THE FED'S POLICY RULE

To ensure that the real interest rate increases when inflation rises, the Fed must raise the nominal interest rate more than proportionally with an increase in inflation. In panel A, at an inflation rate of π_0, the central bank sets the nominal rate equal to i_0; the real rate of interest is $r_0 = i_0 - \pi_0$. If inflation increases to π_1, the nominal interest rate increases to i_1. This increase is greater than the increase in inflation, so the real rate, shown in panel B, increases as inflation rises.

---

[4] If nominal interest income is taxed, the nominal rate will need to rise proportionally more than inflation to ensure that the real, after-tax interest rate rises.

Do Central Banks Respond Only to Inflation? We have assumed that the central bank adjusts policy when inflation changes. This convenient simplification captures an important aspect of how many major central banks conduct policy today. It helps explain why the Fed did not initially raise interest rates as the unemployment rate fell to very low levels in the late 1990s—as long as inflation seemed stable, the Fed did not alter its policy.

But few central banks (if any!) react *only* to inflation. The goals of monetary policy are low, stable inflation *and* overall economic stability and growth. If the economy enters a recession, central banks normally lower interest rates to help stimulate aggregate expenditures and moderate the rise in unemployment. That the Fed cannot simply look at inflation is illustrated by two recent cases in point.

Thinking Like an Economist
REAL VALUES MATTER FOR INCENTIVES

Economists believe that to understand how individuals and firms behave, we should assume they make rational decisions. In making decisions, individuals and firms respond to incentives. But to affect decisions, a change in incentives has to be a *real* change—it has to reflect an actual alteration in the trade-offs the decision maker faces. A worker will thus be concerned with how much her wages can purchase—the real value of wages, not simply their amount in terms of dollars. If a worker's nominal wage rises by 10 percent but prices also rise by 10 percent, her incentive to supply labor is unaffected. Supplying an extra hour of labor increases her nominal income by more than before, but it yields the same real income as it did before prices and wages rose. The incentive to work is unchanged.

Similarly, households and firms will base decisions about borrowing and investing on the *real* costs of borrowing and the *real* returns to investing, and the riskiness associated with each. In deciding whether to borrow to finance a car, an individual must weigh the consumption of other goods and services that must be given up in order to make that purchase. If the interest rate on the car loan is 12 percent, but he expects prices and his nominal income to be rising at 3 percent each year because of inflation, then the dollars he uses each year to pay the interest on the loan will be worth 3 percent less than the year before. The effective real interest rate on the loan is 9 percent. Now suppose that when he took out the car loan, inflation had been zero rather than 3 percent per year. His incentive to borrow would be unaffected if the interest rate on the loan fell to 9 percent: though he would pay fewer dollars each year, those dollars would be worth more since there is no inflation. The real cost is the same; so if nothing else has changed, the incentives to borrow are also unchanged.

The riskiness of an investment also depends on inflation. Suppose you invest in a bond that will pay you 8 percent interest for the next six years. It may seem to be riskless—after all, you know you will receive 8 percent on your investment. But if inflation turns out to average 2 percent, your real return will only be 6 percent; and if inflation averages 8 percent, your real return will be zero! Because there is always some uncertainty about future inflation, real returns will be uncertain even when the nominal rate of return is fixed.

Economic decisions are based on the real interest rate, not the nominal interest rate. Changes in the real interest rate alter individuals' incentives to act.

Case in Point

THE INTEREST RATE CUT OF JANUARY 3, 2001

The effects of the interest rate hikes engineered by the Fed during 1999 and the first part of 2000 started to make themselves felt by the end of 2000. And when signs of a slowdown in economic activity began to appear, they seemed to indicate that the economy might be headed toward a recession. On January 3, 2001, new figures showed that auto sales by U.S. domestic manufacturers were down almost 8 percent from the level of a year earlier. Chrysler announced that it would be shutting down five of its twelve North American factories for two weeks, putting as many as 30,000 workers on temporary furloughs. The day before, the National Association of Purchasing Management released its index of activity in the manufacturing sector during December—which had fallen to its lowest level since the previous recession, in 1991. Declines in the stock market during the last few months of 2000 had also created concerns that households would become more pessimistic about the economy and scale back their spending.

At the same time, inflation appeared to be relatively stable, averaging just under 3 percent during the last six months of 2000. It actually edged upward in early 2001; during the first six months of 2001, the inflation rate averaged above 4.5 percent. If the Fed were concerned only with inflation, it might have responded by raising interest rates. But faced with growing evidence that the chances of a recession were rising, the FOMC cut its federal funds rate target from 6.5 percent to 6 percent on January 3, 2001. By cutting interest rates, the FOMC hoped to stimulate investment and consumption spending. A central bank that cared only about the rate of inflation would not have taken this action; in fact, as the January 3 case shows, the Federal Reserve is concerned not just with inflation but also with maintaining overall economic stability.

SEPTEMBER 11, 2001

On September 11, 2001, the terrorist attack on the World Trade Center in New York City caused not only a grievous loss of life but a tremendous shock to the U.S. economy's financial sector. The attack led to a one-week closure of the New York Stock Exchange and disrupted the payments system through which transactions between banks are cleared. For example, one side effect of the suspension of air flights within the United States was to slow the process of clearing checks. In periods of great uncertainty, banks and other financial institutions often contract their lending activity, and the demand for safe assets such as money generally increases. The Fed needed to make sure that any rise in money demand was satisfied. Shortly before September 11, deposits at Federal Reserve Banks had averaged under $20 billion. They rose to more than $100 billion on September 12, as the Fed provided additional reserves to the banking system to meet the demand for money.[5] This reaction illustrates how central banks must respond to ensure macroeconomic stability whenever the economy is threatened with disruption, even if inflation remains low and stable.

---

[5] See Christopher J. Neely, "The Federal Reserve Responds to Crises: September 11 Was Not the First," *Review* (Federal Reserve Bank of St. Louis), 86, no. 2 (2004): 27–42.

e-Insight

THE DOT-COM BUBBLE AND MACROECONOMIC STABILITY

Just think if in June 1996 you had invested $20,000 in a little-known and fledgling new company called Yahoo. It would have been a risky decision; Yahoo was offering a free service to users of the Internet—something that most Americans still knew little about. A share of stock in Yahoo was selling for $2.09.

It would have been a great investment decision. As the year 2000 dawned, each share of Yahoo's stock was worth $176.50 and your $20,000 investment would have been worth $1,688,995! This represented a 255 percent annual return. A year later, in January 2001, things would have looked a bit different. You would no longer be a millionaire, since your Yahoo stock had plunged until it was worth only $262,010, a fall of 84 percent. Each of your shares would have been selling for just $27.38.

The experiences of Yahoo were mirrored by hundreds of other dot-com firms that had begun in the 1980s and 1990s as small start-ups and then saw their share prices break all records for growth as investors clamored for their shares when these companies "went public." Thousands of dot-com millionaires, and quite a few billionaires, were created, and millions of Americans who had never before thought of investing in stocks started speculating in the market. Fluctuations in the New York Stock Exchange or the Nasdaq exchange became part of daily conversations. But just as quickly, it seemed, the high-flying days ended during 2000. Dot-com start-ups started going bankrupt, and the technology-heavy Nasdaq index, after reaching a peak at just over 5,000 in March 2000, had fallen to 2,291.46 by New Year's Day in 2001. By March 2001, it was below 2,000.

The stock market affects macroeconomic conditions and in turn is influenced by economic conditions. Several times during the 1990s, the stock market was feared to be a source of instability in the economy. For example, consumption spending was fueled by soaring stock prices in the mid-1990s, a situation that concerned the Federal Reserve for two reasons. First, increased consumption spending in an economy already experiencing a strong expansion threatened to overheat the

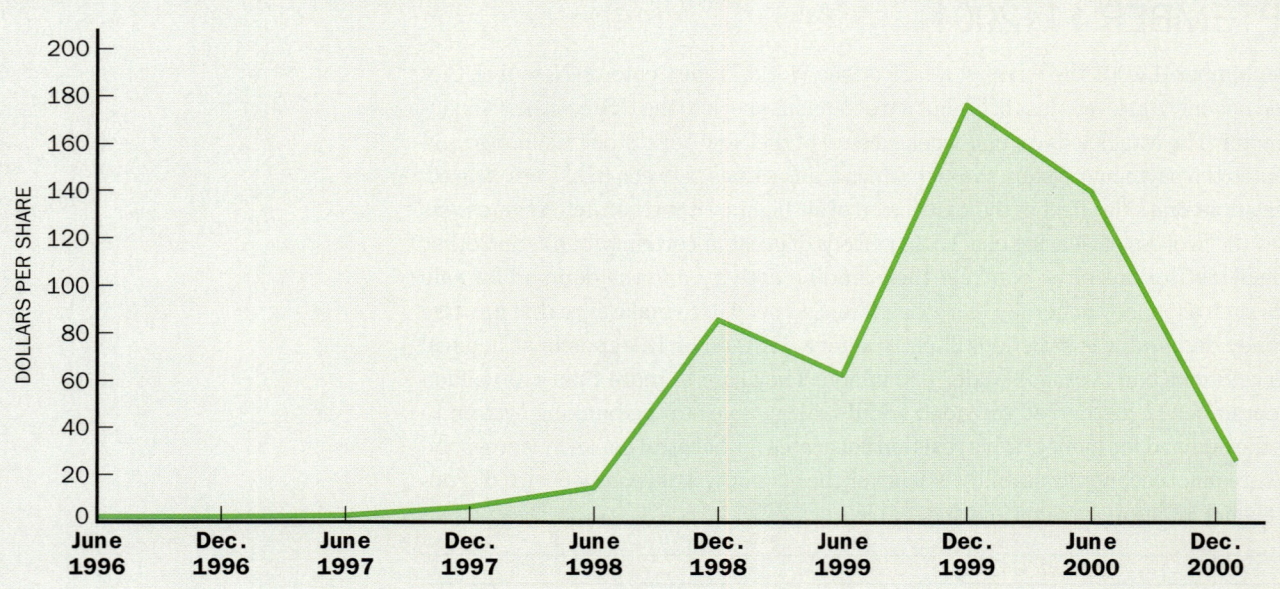

THE PRICE OF YAHOO'S STOCK

economy and lead to a resurgence of inflation. Second, many feared that the stock market boom was based on unrealistic expectations about the value of the new dot-com businesses. Although many of these firms had yet to actually earn profits, investors were bidding their stock prices higher and higher in expectation of future profitability. If expectations were to become less optimistic, the stock market might collapse suddenly, leading to spending cutbacks by households as they saw their wealth fall.

The stock market boom generated by dot-com businesses represented a major source of uncertainty for the Federal Reserve. Was the boom based on realistic expectations of the value of new economy firms? Or was it simply so much "irrational exuberance," as Federal Reserve Chair Greenspan labeled it in a widely quoted speech of December 1996? Did it reflect the fundamental soundness of the new economy, or was it setting the economy up for an inevitable market crash, much as had occurred in 1929? When the market slumped in the fall of 1998, the Fed cut interest rates, and this action helped restore optimism to the market. During the summer of 2000, the market drifted downward as the Fed boosted interest rates to slow the economy and head off a possible increase in inflation. Many economists have argued that the Fed should act to tighten monetary policy whenever a stock market boom seems to be based simply on expectations of continued unrealistic increases in stock prices—a so-called speculative bubble. Yet as so many changes are affecting the economy, and as new firms producing totally new products are constantly emerging, judging whether the stock market was reflecting the fundamental reality of the new economy or simply irrational exuberance is a difficult task.

THE POSITION OF THE POLICY RULE

We can further explore the position of the monetary policy rule by asking what nominal interest rate a central bank would want to target if the economy were at full employment. Two factors will be important: the equilibrium real rate of interest at full employment and the target inflation rate that the central bank would like to achieve.

The Equilibrium Real Interest Rate Recall from Chapter 24 that the full-employment model made an important prediction about the real interest rate: when the economy is at full employment, the real interest rate does not depend on the inflation rate or on monetary policy. Consequently, monetary policy cannot influence what real interest rate will balance savings and investment at full employment.

This implication of the full-employment model has significant consequences for monetary policy and the relationship between the nominal interest rate and inflation. Suppose, for instance, that the equilibrium real interest rate when the economy is at full employment is 3 percent. A central bank that could control the real interest rate directly would want to set it at 3 percent to keep the economy at full employment. But because central banks work indirectly, we must ask, What nominal interest rate will the central bank wish to set when the economy is at full employment?

The answer to this question depends on the average rate of inflation the central bank would like to achieve. Many central banks, such as the Bank of England, aim to keep inflation equal on average to 2 percent.[6] The nominal interest rate, in

---

[6]Central banks set a target for inflation slightly above zero because they want to avoid the possibility of deflation (i.e., falling prices or negative inflation). Moreover, because most common measures of inflation are thought to contain a slight upward bias, price stability would still lead to a small but positive measured rate of inflation.

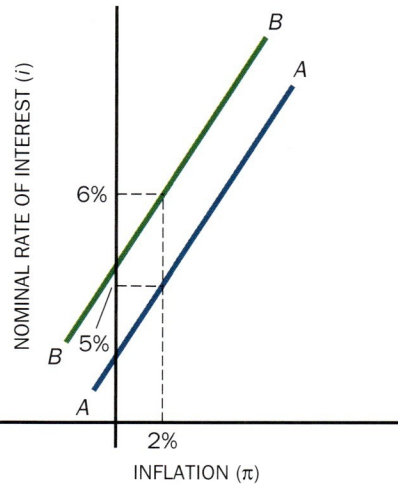

Figure 33.7

THE MONETARY POLICY RULE AND THE EQUILIBRIUM REAL INTEREST RATE AT FULL EMPLOYMENT

The central bank's policy rule needs to be consistent with the economy's equilibrium real interest rate at full employment and the central bank's target inflation rate. If the equilibrium real interest rate at full employment is 3 percent and the central bank's inflation target is 2 percent, then the nominal interest rate must be 5 percent when inflation is equal to its target, as shown by the policy rule line AA.

If the equilibrium real interest rate at full employment rises to 4 percent, the central bank must set the nominal rate equal to 6 percent when inflation is on target. The entire policy line shifts up to BB.

our hypothetical full-employment economy, must then be 5 percent—the full-employment equilibrium real interest rate (3 percent) plus the desired inflation rate (2 percent). Figure 33.7 shows the policy rule for this example (the line labeled *AA*); when inflation is equal to 2 percent, the policy rule shows that the central bank sets the nominal interest rate equal to 5 percent.

If the equilibrium real rate of interest at full employment changes, the central bank will need to shift its policy rule. For example, in Chapter 24, we learned that an increase in the fiscal deficit would increase the equilibrium real interest rate at full employment. Suppose the full-employment real interest rate rises from 3 percent to 4 percent. Now, when inflation is on target (equal to 2 percent), the central bank must ensure that the nominal interest rate at full employment is 6 percent—the 4 percent real rate plus 2 percent for inflation. The monetary policy rule must shift up, as illustrated by the line labeled *BB* in Figure 33.7. When the full-employment real interest rate falls—owing to a reduction in the fiscal deficit or a rise in household saving, for example—the central bank must shift its policy line down. Thus, the position of the policy rule will depend on the economy's full-employment equilibrium real interest rate.

These shifts in the policy rule as the full-employment equilibrium real interest rate changes are not automatic; the Fed must make an explicit decision to alter its policy rule. Failure to do so can harm the economy, and some of the policy errors of the past forty years can be attributed to the Fed's not adjusting its policy rule when the full-employment equilibrium real interest rate changed.

The 1960s provide a case in point. As already noted in this chapter, the 1964 tax cut and the expansion in government spending associated with the Vietnam War and the War on Poverty pushed the U.S. economy above potential output by the end of the decade, causing, inflation to start to rise. Figure 33.8 illustrates this situation. The initial equilibrium, at full employment, is labeled as E_0. The fiscal expansion shifted the ADI curve to the right, leading to the economy's new, short-run equilibrium at E_1. As we learned in Chapter 31, the inflation adjustment curve shifts up when the output gap is positive. Eventually, full employment is restored at E_2, with a higher rate of inflation.

The fiscal expansion raised the full-employment equilibrium real interest rate. In response, to prevent inflation from rising, the Fed should have shifted its policy rule. At each inflation rate, it should have set a higher interest rate. Doing so would have counteracted the rightward shift in the ADI curve; as a result, full employment would have been restored at E_0, with both output *and* inflation returning to their original levels.

This simple statement of what the Fed should have done ignores an important complication: the equilibrium real rate of interest cannot be directly observed by economists. The Fed must try to estimate the equilibrium real rate, a task that can be difficult. Thus even if the Fed recognizes the need to adjust its policy rule, it may not know by how much. For example, tax cuts and expenditure increases that took place between 2001 and 2004 are projected to lead to huge fiscal deficits over the next several years. These deficits will increase the equilibrium real interest rate. But the effects of the deficits will depend on how the president and Congress eventually adjust taxes and expenditures to deal with the deficit and on when those adjustments are made.

The Inflation Target The position of the monetary policy rule also depends on the central bank's target inflation rate. As we just learned, at full employment the central bank will set the nominal interest rate equal to the equilibrium real interest rate plus the target for the rate of inflation. Suppose the central bank decides to lower its inflation target from 2 percent to 1 percent. And let's assume the full-employment equilibrium real interest rate is 3 percent. Figure 33.9 depicts the initial policy rule, the one for a target inflation rate of 2 percent, as AA. When inflation is equal to the target, the nominal interest rate is 5 percent (the 3 percent real interest rate plus 2 percent inflation). When the inflation target is reduced to 1 percent, the nominal interest rate at full employment falls from 5 percent to 4 percent (the 3 percent real interest rate plus the new target inflation rate of 1 percent). The policy rule shifts up to BB, as illustrated in the figure. At each rate of inflation, the nominal rate is now set at a higher value.

Figure 33.8

A FISCAL EXPANSION WHEN THE FED'S POLICY RULE DOES NOT ADJUST AND WHEN IT DOES

The figure illustrates the consequences if the Fed fails to adjust its policy rule when the equilibrium real interest rate at full employment changes. A fiscal expansion shifts the aggregate demand–inflation curve from ADI_0 to ADI_1. In the short run, equilibrium output rises and the new equilibrium is at E_1. If the Fed does not adjust its policy rule, the economy eventually returns to full employment at E_2 with higher inflation. The green arrows show the path the economy takes. To prevent the fiscal expansion from leaving inflation higher, the Fed must raise interest rates at a given rate of inflation. This shift in the Fed's policy rule is necessary because a fiscal expansion raises the real interest rate that balances the capital market at full employment. If the Fed's policy rule shifts, then the ADI curve is shifted back to ADI_0, the economy returns to full employment, and inflation returns to its initial level at E_0 along the black arrow.

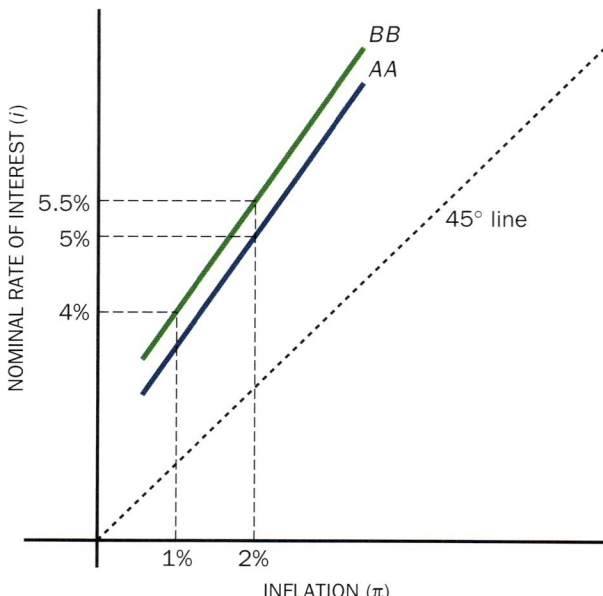

Figure 33.9

THE EFFECT OF A SHIFT IN THE INFLATION TARGET ON THE CENTRAL BANK'S POLICY RULE

The position of the monetary policy rule depends on the central bank's target for inflation. Policy rule AA is based on an inflation target of 2 percent and an equilibrium real interest rate of 2 percent at full employment. If the central bank reduces its inflation target to 1 percent, the policy rule shifts up. At a given inflation rate, the central bank will set nominal interest rates higher.

This shift in the policy rule does succeed in lowering inflation. If the economy initially has 2 percent inflation, the central bank increases the nominal interest rate in line with the new policy rule BB. As shown in the figure, the nominal rate rises to 5.5 percent. Since inflation is still equal to 2 percent, this represents a rise in the real interest rate from 3 percent to 3.5 percent, which dampens aggregate spending and causes output to decline in the short run. The decline puts downward pressure on inflation. The economy suffers an increase in cyclical unemployment in the short run, but eventually full employment is restored at a lower rate of inflation.

THE SLOPE OF THE POLICY RULE

The slope of the monetary policy rule tells us how much the central bank adjusts interest rates when inflation changes. Suppose the central bank reacts aggressively to inflation, hiking interest rates whenever inflation rises and cutting them sharply whenever it falls. Such behavior would be represented by a policy rule that has a steep slope, indicating that changes in inflation lead to large changes in interest rates. In contrast, the policy rule for a central bank that reacts more moderately to changes in inflation would be relatively flat. Many central banks react more strongly to inflation today than they did in the 1970s. Therefore, we would draw a steeper policy rule to reflect current practices of central banks than we would if we wanted to represent their behavior in the 1970s.

The slope of the policy rule is important because, as we learned in Chapter 31, it helps determine the slope of the ADI curve. If the central bank reacts aggressively to changes in inflation, aggregate expenditures will vary more as inflation changes; the ADI curve will be relatively flat. If the central bank has little response as inflation changes, then aggregate expenditures will be less affected by inflation and the ADI curve will be steeper.

The slope of the ADI curve significantly affects how the economy responds to inflation shocks. As we learned in Chapter 31, a positive inflation shock causes inflation to increase and output to decline in the short run by an amount that depends on how much aggregate expenditures fall. If the ADI curve is steep—either because changes in inflation lead to little change in interest rates or because changes in interest rates induce little change in aggregate spending—the impact of an inflation shock on output will be small. Because the rise in cyclical unemployment is small in this case, the moderating effects of a recession on wage growth and inflation are small, and it may take longer for inflation to return to its initial level. If the ADI curve is flat—either because changes in inflation lead to large changes in interest rates or because changes in interest rates induce large changes in aggregate spending—the impact of an inflation shock on output will be larger. But because cyclical unemployment increases more in the latter case, the downward pressures on wage growth and inflation are larger, and the initial rise in inflation is likely to be reversed more quickly.

This discussion returns us to the trade-offs that were examined earlier in this chapter. By responding strongly to changes in inflation, the central bank can keep inflation more stable but at the cost of larger fluctuations in real output and unemployment. By responding less aggressively to changes in inflation, real output and unemployment can be kept more stable but at the cost of greater instability in inflation.

Wrap-Up

THE MONETARY POLICY RULE

A monetary policy rule describes how the central bank adjusts its policy in response to economic conditions. Inflation is one of the major factors that central banks respond to.

The position of the policy rule will depend on the central bank's target rate of inflation and the equilibrium real rate of interest at full employment.

The slope of the policy rule affects the slope of the ADI curve. If the central bank reacts aggressively to inflation, the ADI curve will be relatively flat. Inflation shocks will lead to larger movements in output but inflation will be more stable. Weaker policy responses to inflation lead to more stable output but less stability in inflation.

Interactions Between Monetary and Fiscal Policies

So far, we have treated monetary and fiscal policies as if they were entirely distinct. In the United States, fiscal policy is the responsibility of Congress and the president, while monetary policy is the responsibility of the Federal Reserve. This division of labor makes it convenient to discuss them separately. In fact, what is important for the economy is the net impact of both types of policies and the important interactions between them. Consider the earlier discussion of a fiscal stimulus. If the Fed raises interest rates as the stimulus occurs, monetary policy may partially or totally offset the expansionary effect of fiscal policy, pulling in the opposite direction. This happened in the early 1980s, when restrictive monetary policy more than offset expansionary fiscal policy and the economy went into a major recession.

We also have seen how a change in fiscal policy may require the Fed to alter its policy rule. If one of the goals of monetary policy is to maintain a low and stable inflation rate at full employment, then the central bank will need to offset the effects that fiscal policy might otherwise have on inflation.

Both fiscal policy and monetary policy can be used to expand aggregate demand and increase output in the short run. Both types of policies can be used to dampen aggregate demand when inflation threatens to increase. But they do more than just affect aggregate demand. Because these two policies have different implications for investment, they can have different longer-run effects on the economy. A monetary expansion lowers real interest rates, stimulating investment. In contrast, a fiscal expansion reduces national saving and results in a higher real interest rate and lower investment. Using fiscal policy to stimulate the economy, by reducing private investment, may have harmful effects on future potential output.

Fiscal and monetary policies differ as well in their impact on exports and imports. A monetary expansion that lowers interest rates will also tend to cause the currency to depreciate as foreign investors seek higher returns elsewhere.[7] A depreciation decreases imports (by making foreign goods more expensive) and increases exports. In contrast, a fiscal expansion that causes interest rates to rise also causes the currency to appreciate; net exports fall as foreign goods become less expensive.

In recent decades, monetary policy has been the chief tool for macroeconomic stabilization policies, and discretionary fiscal policy has played little role in the United States. The chief reason, as already noted, is the lags inherent in the fiscal policy process—particularly the **inside lag,** or time needed to implement the necessary expenditure or tax changes. First, it takes time to recognize the need to stimulate or restrain aggregate spending. Data are subject to revision, and conflicting developments often can frustrate attempts to determine the true condition of the economy. For example, after the 2001 recession, one survey of households tended to indicate strong employment growth even as a survey of firms showed continued job losses. Then, after some change in the economy is recognized, there is the delay due to the time it takes to design a package of new tax or spending initiatives (whether increases or cuts) and get it approved by Congress. While the delay in recognizing changed economic conditions is the same whatever the approach, the inside lag is much longer for fiscal than for monetary policy. Postwar recessions have lasted less than a year on average. By the time—often longer than a year—a tax bill is approved by Congress, the economy is entering a different phase of the business cycle. A policy that makes sense when it is introduced may easily turn out to be inappropriate when it comes into effect. This unwieldiness limits the effectiveness of discretionary fiscal policy. In contrast, the FOMC meets every six weeks, and, if conditions warrant, committee members can hold telephone conferences more frequently. Hence, monetary policy can act swiftly to deal with new economic developments.

Monetary and fiscal policies also differ in the speed with which a policy action affects the economy. Monetary policy stimulates the economy by lowering interest rates, thereby increasing investment in equipment and housing and increasing net exports. Even after firms see a decrease in the real interest rate, it may take some time before they commit to new investment, and before the capital goods industry starts producing the newly ordered goods. Similarly, though in the long run a lower real interest rate leads to increased demand for housing, it takes a while before plans are drawn up, permits are obtained, and construction starts. Typically, six months or longer must pass before monetary policy's effects on output are realized. By contrast, increased government purchases have a direct and immediate effect on total spending. The time required for the change in policy to affect the economy is called the **outside lag,** and it is normally shorter for fiscal policy.

---

[7]The reason that interest rate changes affect the exchange rate is discussed in Chapter 35.

> **Wrap-Up**

DIFFERENCES BETWEEN MONETARY AND FISCAL POLICY

Effects on Aggregate Demand

Fiscal policy and monetary policy have different effects on the economy. Expansionary fiscal policy raises the real interest rate and crowds out private investment spending. Expansionary monetary policy lowers the real interest rate and stimulates private investment spending.

Policy Lags

Inside lag: The time required to recognize a need for a change in policy and to implement the policy change. The inside lag is much shorter for monetary policy.
Outside lag: The time required for the change in policy to affect the economy. The outside lag is normally shorter for fiscal policy.

Review and Practice

SUMMARY

1. The actual fiscal deficit increases in a recession as tax revenues decline. This process provides an important automatic stabilizer. To measure discretionary shifts in fiscal policy, economists look at the full-employment budget deficit.
2. The aggregate demand–inflation (ADI) curve depends on the monetary policy rule used by the central bank. The slope of the policy rule affects the slope of the ADI curve, while shifts in the policy rule are reflected in shifts in the ADI curve.
3. If the central bank wants to keep inflation stable, it must adjust its policy rule whenever the equilibrium full-employment real interest rate changes. The policy rule must be shifted up if the full-employment real interest rate increases, leading to a higher nominal interest rate at each inflation rate.
4. The monetary policy rule shifts if the central bank alters its target for inflation. If it reduces its inflation target, the policy rule shifts up, leading to a higher nominal interest rate at each rate of inflation.
5. Both fiscal and monetary policies can affect aggregate demand and output in the short run. They have different effects on the interest rate. A fiscal expansion raises the real interest rate; a monetary expansion lowers the real interest rate. Consequently, investment will be higher in the short run if monetary policy is used to stimulate the economy.
6. The inside lag is shorter for monetary policy than for fiscal policy. The outside lag is shorter for fiscal policy.

KEY TERMS

automatic stabilizer
discretionary action
full-employment deficit
monetary policy rule
inside lag
outside lag

REVIEW QUESTIONS

1. What are automatic stabilizers and how do they affect the economy?
2. What happens to the government surplus when the economy goes into a recession? What happens to the full-employment surplus when the economy goes into a recession?
3. How does the slope of the ADI curve depend on the monetary policy rule?
4. If the central bank wants to keep inflation equal to its target, how must the monetary policy rule shift if the equilibrium full-employment real interest rate falls?
5. How does the monetary policy rule shift if the central bank's target for inflation is reduced? How does this reduction affect the ADI curve?
6. In addition to the effects of monetary policy on aggregate demand that operate through the real interest rate, what other channels are there through which monetary policy may affect aggregate expenditures?
7. Compare the effects of monetary and fiscal policies on the level of investment and the composition of output.

PROBLEMS

1. Why would the economy be more stable or less stable if there were no automatic stabilizers?
2. In recent years, many central banks have placed increased emphasis on controlling inflation. Suppose the central bank of the nation of Economica decides that it will move interest rates sharply whenever inflation differs from its desired target of 1 percent. Previously, policymakers in Economica had adjusted interest rates only slightly in response to inflation.
   (a) How will this switch in policy affect the central bank's monetary policy rule?
   (b) How will it affect the slope of the ADI curve?
   (c) Suppose Economica suffers an inflation shock that increases inflation. Use a graph to illustrate how output and inflation respond under both the old and the new policy rules.

3. Assume that the economy is currently at full employment with an inflation rate of 2 percent. The government embarks on a major new expenditure program that increases aggregate expenditures (assume that full-employment output is unaffected).
   (a) If the central bank's policy rule remains unchanged, what will be the short-run and long-run effects on output and inflation of this change in fiscal policy? What will be the long-run effects on the real interest rate at full employment?
   (b) Suppose the central bank's policy rule adjusts to reflect the change in the full-employment real interest rate. Will this alter the short-run or long-run effects of the fiscal expansion?
4. In late 2000, there were signs the U.S. economy might be heading into a recession. Some argued that the rise in energy prices during 2000 was the cause of the economic slowdown. Others pointed to the decline in the stock market and argued that this decline in wealth would reduce consumption spending. Assume the economy is initially at full employment.
   (a) Using the ADI-IA (inflation adjustment) framework, explain how a rise in energy prices would affect output and inflation in the short run.
   (b) Using the ADI-IA framework, explain how a fall in stock prices would affect output and inflation in the short run.
   (c) Suppose you are chair of the Federal Reserve Board. If your *only* concern is keeping inflation stable, would you raise interest rates or would you lower them if you believe energy prices are the cause of the slowdown? Would you raise interest rates or would you lower them if you believe the stock market decline is the cause of the slowdown?
   (d) Suppose you are chair of the Federal Reserve Board. If your *only* concern is keeping unemployment stable, would you raise interest rates or would you lower them if you believe energy prices are the cause of the slowdown? Would you raise interest rates or would you lower them if you believe the stock market decline is the cause of the slowdown?
5. Suppose a fall in net exports due to a recession among our major trading partners causes a recession in the United States.
   (a) If fiscal policy is used to stimulate the economy and return it to full employment, what happens to the real interest rate, investment, and future output?
   (b) If monetary policy is used to stimulate the economy and return it to full employment, what happens to the real interest rate, investment, and future output?
6. In parliamentary governments, such as the United Kingdom, the prime minister can announce a change in taxation or expenditure and implement that change almost immediately. How might this fact affect the balance between the use of monetary and fiscal policy for short-run stabilization?

Part 8
THE GLOBAL ECONOMY

Learning Goals

In this chapter, you will learn

1. What factors determine international exchange rates
2. How fixed exchange rate systems differ from flexible exchange rate systems
3. How a fixed exchange rate system restricts the use of monetary policy

Chapter 34

THE INTERNATIONAL FINANCIAL SYSTEM

After working all year, you have saved enough to buy that new, fuel-efficient Toyota Prius. You have located one at a local car dealer, and the price is $20,000. You give the dealer $20,000 and drive away. But is that the end of the transaction? No. The car was built in Japan, so Toyota needs yen, the Japanese currency, and not U.S. dollars to pay the workers in Japan who manufactured it. The dealer who imported the Prius to the United States therefore will need to convert those dollars into yen to pay Toyota; the dealer needs to sell dollars and buy yen. Similarly, when Boeing sells an airplane to Garuda Indonesia, it needs to convert the Indonesian rupiah into U.S. dollars to pay its workers, suppliers, and owners. The market in which different currencies can be bought and sold is called the *foreign exchange market:* it enables the car dealer to sell dollars and buy yen and Boeing to sell rupiah and buy U.S. dollars.

Every day, U.S. exporters like Boeing receive payments from their sales in foreign countries that they need to convert to dollars, while U.S. importers need foreign currencies to pay their foreign suppliers. Foreign investors wishing to purchase American assets need to buy dollars, while others may be selling American assets in order to switch their investments into a different country. If Toyota decides to expand its production facilities in the United States, it will need to purchase dollars to carry out its investment plans. All these transactions involve one or more currencies and give rise to a huge volume of foreign currency trading—about $1.5 trillion every day.

The international financial system that has developed to carry out these trades, and that enables Americans to invest in Brazilian stocks and Ford to buy Volvo, Japanese investors to buy U.S. Treasury bonds and Toyota to build assembly plants in Tennessee, links together the members of the global economy. Because of these financial links, international factors can play a critical role in the macroeconomy.

Opening a country's financial markets to foreign investors can have many benefits. The most important is that domestic investment is no longer constrained by domestic saving. There are also potential costs, however, a point driven home in 1996 and 1997 when a financial crisis that began in Thailand spread to other countries in Asia and Latin America, and again in 1998 when Russia faced a financial crisis that led to the largest one-day fall in prices on the London stock exchange in a decade. In this chapter, we will focus on the factors that affect foreign currency trading and how international capital flows in foreign exchange markets influence the value of the dollar.

Determining the Exchange Rate

The starting point for understanding the international financial system is the foreign exchange market, in which currencies of different countries are bought or sold. This market has no single location; instead, it involves thousands of currency traders at computer terminals around the globe, buying and selling different currencies. Most trading is heavily concentrated, though, in three major centers: London, New York, and Tokyo. London is the largest, with a daily trading volume of more than $600 billion.

The *exchange rate* is the rate at which one currency can be traded for another. If the dollar–yen exchange rate is 110, then $1 will buy 110 yen. Systems in which exchange rates are determined by the law of supply and demand, without government interference, are called **flexible exchange rate systems.** The United States, Japan, and the European Economic and Monetary Union (EMU) all have flexible exchange rate systems. We have already looked briefly, in Chapter 26, at how exchange rates are determined by supply and demand in the foreign exchange market. Governments often intervene in foreign exchange markets, and later in this chapter we will examine the different forms that this intervention takes. But first we need to understand what determines the exchange rate in a flexible exchange rate system.

Consider a world consisting of only two currencies, the U.S. dollar and the euro used by members of the EMU. Americans and Europeans exchange dollars for euros. There are three reasons why Europeans might want dollars and therefore be willing to supply euros in trade for dollars in the foreign exchange markets: to buy American goods (American exports, or imports into Europe), to make investments in the United States (that is, to buy U.S. stocks, other financial assets, or real assets such as land or factories), or to speculate—that is, if Europeans think that the dollar is going to gain value relative to the euro, speculators might want to buy dollars now and sell them later when they are more valuable. Similarly, there are three reasons why Americans might want euros, and accordingly supply dollars to the foreign exchange market to trade for euros: to buy European goods, to make investments in Europe, or to speculate if they think that the euro is going to become more valuable relative to the dollar. The question is, How many euros will an American get in exchange for a dollar, or, conversely, how many dollars will a European get in exchange for a euro? The exchange rate can be thought of as the *relative price* of dollars and euros. It will tell us how many dollars it takes to purchase one euro and how many euros it will take to purchase one dollar.

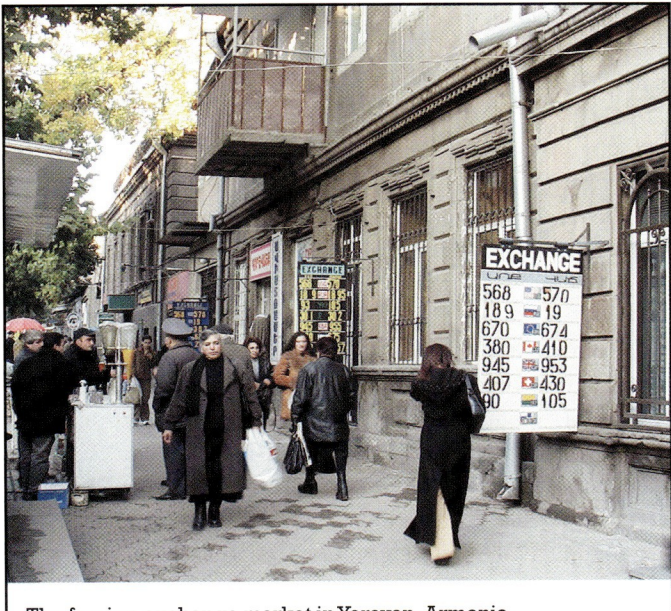
The foreign exchange market in Yerevan, Armenia

SUPPLY AND DEMAND IN THE FOREIGN EXCHANGE MARKET

In competitive markets, prices are determined by demand and supply. Similarly, exchange rates are determined by demand and supply in foreign exchange markets. In our example of just two currencies—dollars and euros—it makes no difference whether we look at things from the perspective of the demand for and supply of dollars or from the perspective of the demand for and supply of euros. The European supply of euros on the foreign exchange market is equivalent to the European's demand for dollars. The U.S. supply of dollars is equivalent to Americans' demand for euros.

Panel A of Figure 34.1 shows supply and demand curves in the foreign exchange market. The horizontal axis measures the volume of dollars; the vertical axis measures the exchange rate, the value of the dollars in terms of euros. We express the value of the dollar as the number of euros it takes to buy 1 dollar in the foreign exchange market. Thus, if the exchange rate is 2 euros to the dollar, the dollar is expensive in terms of euros—it takes 2 euros to buy 1 dollar. If the exchange rate is one half a euro to the dollar, the dollar is cheap—it only takes a half a euro to buy 1 dollar (or, equivalently, 1 euro will buy 2 dollars). The higher the exchange rate, the more expensive the dollar is in terms of euros.

The demand for dollars has been drawn as a downward sloping curve. As the exchange rate falls, dollars become cheaper. Just as demand for a good goes up when its price falls, so, as dollars become cheaper, Europeans will want to purchase more of them.

The supply curve of dollars has been drawn in the figure with a positive slope. As the exchange rate rises, Americans will be able to get more euros for every dollar they sell in the foreign exchange market. As they do so, the supply of dollars will increase. The equilibrium exchange rate is the value of dollars in terms of euros that balances the demand for dollars and the supply of dollars. In the figure, e_0 is the equilibrium exchange rate. At a lower exchange rate such as e_1, the demand for dollars exceeds the supply of dollars. Just as in the market for wheat, if demand exceeds supply, the price will rise. In this case, the value of the dollar will rise. At an exchange rate such as e_2, supply exceeds demand and the dollar will fall in value.

Panels B and C illustrate the effects on the exchange rate of a shift in the supply of dollars and the demand for dollars, respectively. In panel B, the supply curve has shifted to the right, increasing the supply of dollars at each exchange rate. Perhaps a change in European tax law has made investing in Europe more attractive to American firms (other factors that might shift the supply curve will be discussed below). At the initial exchange rate e_0, there is now an excess supply of dollars. The dollar will fall in value until the new equilibrium is reached at the exchange rate e_1.

Panel C illustrates another change in the foreign exchange market—this time a shift to the left in the demand curve for dollars, reflecting a smaller demand for dollars at each exchange rate. Such a shift might be caused by a change in U.S. tax law that makes it less attractive for European firms to invest in the United States. At the initial exchange rate e_0, there is now an excess supply of dollars. The value of the dollar falls until the new equilibrium is reached at the exchange rate e_1. At this lower value, the demand for dollars and the supply of dollars are again equal.

Earlier, we noted three reasons why Europeans might wish to sell euros to buy dollars and, conversely, Americans might wish to sell dollars to buy euros. We can now discuss how each of these factors affects demand and supply in the foreign exchange market.

Exports and Imports Consider what happens if a U.S. firm sells a product in Europe. Suppose, for example, Levi Strauss sells jeans in Europe. The company can do three things with the euros it receives for the goods it has sold. First, it could try to convert them into dollars. Second, it could sell the euros to an American firm

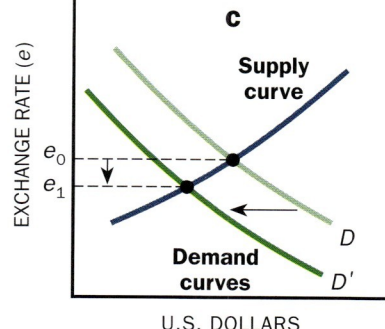

Figure 34.1

THE EXCHANGE RATE

In equilibrium, the exchange rate is determined where the demand for dollars equals the supply, as in panel A. A rightward shift in the supply curve of dollars (panel B) or a leftward shift in the demand curve for dollars (panel C) results in a lower exchange rate; that is, the dollar depreciates.

that wants to use the euros to buy European goods and import those goods back into the United States. Third, it could lend the euros to a European borrower. To simplify the discussion, we will imagine that no one in Europe would lend to anyone in America, and no one in America would lend to anyone in Europe. Foreign borrowing and lending will be considered separately.

A European firm that sells goods in the United States will find itself in a similar position. The firm will receive U.S. dollars, and it could try to convert them into euros or sell them to a European importer who needs them to buy American goods for import back into Europe. In a situation in which some parties (U.S. exporters and European importers) want to trade euros for dollars, while others (U.S. importers and European exporters) wish to trade dollars for euros, mutually beneficial exchanges are clearly possible.

Figure 34.2 illustrates the market for foreign exchange (dollars and euros in our two-currency example). The supply curve for dollars is determined by U.S. importers who want to sell dollars to buy the euros they need and by European exporters who want to sell the dollars they have earned. At a low value of the dollar, such as e_1, U.S. imports (European exports) will be low because dollars buy few euros. From the perspective of Americans, European goods are expensive—it takes many dollars to purchase European goods. At a high value of the dollar, such as e_2, U.S. imports (European exports) will be high because, from the perspective of Americans, European goods are cheap. Thus, the supply curve of dollars in the foreign exchange market slopes up.

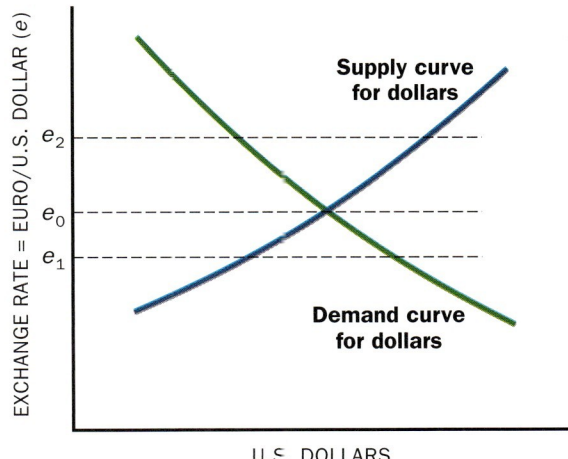

Figure 34.2

THE EQUILIBRIUM EXCHANGE RATE

At the exchange rate e_2, supply exceeds demand. At e_1, demand exceeds supply. At e_0 equilibrium is achieved.

The demand curve for dollars is determined by U.S. exporters who want to sell the euros they have earned and buy dollars and by European importers who want to buy dollars to purchase American goods. At a low value of the dollar, such as e_1, U.S. exports (European imports) will be high because a euro buys many dollars. From the perspective of Europeans, American goods are cheap. At a high value of the dollar, such as e_2, U.S. exports (European imports) will be low because, from the perspective of Europeans, American goods are expensive. Thus, the demand curve of dollars in the foreign exchange market slopes down. The value of the dollar at which the demand for dollars equals the supply of dollars is the equilibrium exchange rate—in the figure, this point is e_0—where exports and imports are equal. As we will see, exports and imports need not be equal once we take foreign borrowing and lending into account.

We can use the demand and supply model of the foreign exchange market to analyze how the equilibrium exchange rate is affected when other factors change and shift the demand or supply curves. For example, suppose Americans adopt a "buy American" campaign that reduces the demand for European imports at each value of the exchange rate. We can represent the impact of this campaign by a leftward shift in the supply curve of dollars as U.S. imports (European exports) fall, as illustrated in Figure 34.3. The equilibrium exchange rate rises. When the dollar rises in value relative to other currencies, we say that the dollar **appreciates.** Because the higher value of the dollar makes U.S. goods more expensive for foreigners, U.S. exports fall. In the new equilibrium, both U.S. imports *and* exports have fallen by the same amount, since exports equal imports in equilibrium. A "buy American"

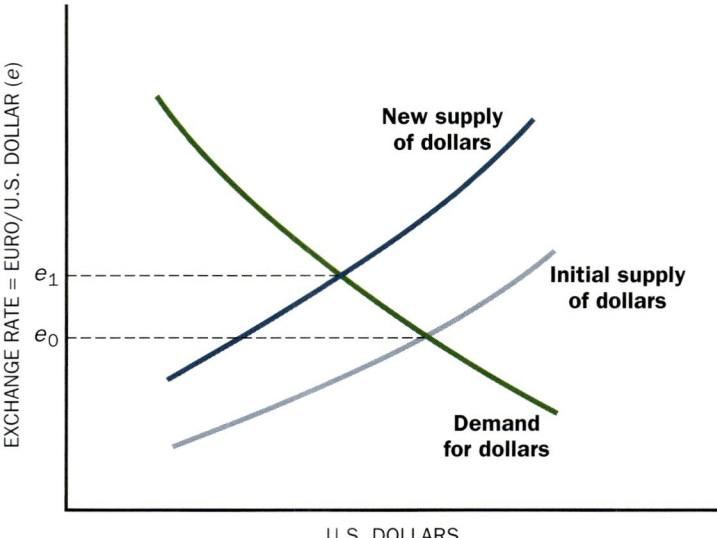

Figure 34.3

THE IMPACT OF A "BUY AMERICAN" CAMPAIGN ON THE EQUILIBRIUM EXCHANGE RATE WITH NO BORROWING OR LENDING

The supply of dollars is determined by the U.S. demand for imported goods and the demand for dollars is determined by the foreign demand for U.S. goods. The figure shows that a "buy American" campaign that causes Americans to import less at any exchange rate shifts the supply of dollars curve to the left and results in a higher exchange rate (a higher value of the dollar). At the higher exchange rate, U.S. exports fall below their initial level.

campaign increases output and employment in industries that produce substitutes for the goods that had been imported, but output and employment decline in U.S. export industries. In contrast, a change that increased the demand by Americans for European goods—perhaps a shift in tastes—would cause the dollar to fall in value; when the dollar falls in value, we say the dollar **depreciates.** Such a shift in tastes would increase American imports from Europe *and* American exports.

Foreign Borrowing and Lending The massive amount of international borrowing and lending now commonplace is the second factor that affects supply and demand in the foreign exchange market and determines the exchange rate. Financial capital markets, the markets in which funds are borrowed and lent, are global. Investors in Japan, Europe, and the United States, constantly seeking to maximize their returns, will shift their funds from Japan or Europe to the United States if returns there are highest. If returns drop in the United States, funds will move to other countries where returns are higher. When investors respond quickly and shift their funds in response to slight differences in expected returns, economists say that capital is **perfectly mobile.**

In today's world, capital is highly but not perfectly mobile. American investors may still feel slightly more comfortable keeping their money invested in the United

States than moving it to Europe or Japan. And this preference becomes even stronger when they contemplate investing in countries threatened by political or economic instability. Many countries have defaulted on their debts; recent examples include Russia, which in 1998 defaulted on some of the debt it owed and called a moratorium on interest payments to foreign creditors, and Argentina, which in 2002 defaulted on payments it owed. The more stable the political and economic environment of the world, the more mobile capital becomes across countries.

When foreign borrowing and lending occurs, it affects the equilibrium exchange rate, which thus is no longer just a matter of balancing imports and exports. The international flows of financial capital will influence demand and supply in the foreign exchange market, as illustrated in Figure 34.4. Consider the case of foreign investors who want to take advantage of the rates of return available in the United States on U.S. stocks, bonds, real estate, or other American assets. To buy U.S. assets, they need dollars, and therefore the demand for dollars increases. On the other hand, Americans who wish to invest in European assets such as shares of a German company or bonds issued by the Japanese government will need to sell dollars to buy foreign currencies, thereby increasing the supply of dollars in the foreign exchange market. How these new motives for supply and demand affect the equilibrium exchange rate depends on the relative amounts that foreigners want to invest in the United States and Americans want to invest abroad.

Because of international borrowing and lending, interest rates in different countries significantly influence exchange rates. If interest rates in Japan rise relative to interest rates available in the United States, investors will want to put their money into Japanese investments. To do so, the investor will first need to buy yen; thus an increase in Japanese interest rates will increase the demand for yen and boost the currency's value. Similarly, if interest rates in the U.S. rise relative to rates in other countries, the demand for dollars will rise and the equilibrium exchange rate will rise to reflect a higher value of the dollar. If U.S. interest rates fall relative to those available in other countries, the demand for dollars will also fall and the dollar will depreciate. An important implication of this discussion is that changes in interest rates in different countries will affect equilibrium exchange rates and the foreign exchange market.

Speculation The third important factor in determining the exchange rate is speculation. The demand for any asset depends on beliefs about what that asset could be sold for in the future; that is, it depends on expectations. If Americans believe that the Japanese yen is going to increase in value relative to the dollar, they may want to buy yen. For instance, consider what happens if the current exchange rate is 200 yen to the dollar and investors believe that the yen is going to appreciate to a value of 100 to the dollar by the end of the month. They believe, in other words, that if they took $1,000 and bought 200,000 yen (each dollar exchanged for 200 yen), at the end of the month they could exchange the yen back into dollars and receive $2,000 (100 yen buying each dollar). By holding yen for a month, they would earn a phenomenal 100 percent return. American investors

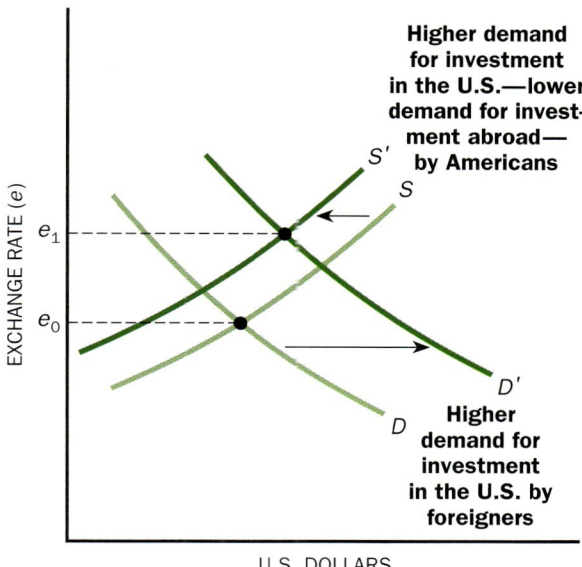

Figure 34.4

INCREASED ATTRACTIVENESS OF INVESTING IN THE UNITED STATES

As some Americans decide not to invest abroad, the supply curve of dollars shifts to the left. As more foreigners wish to invest in the United States, the demand curve shifts to the right. Both shifts serve to increase the equilibrium exchange rate.

with such a belief will want to hold more yen today, and the resulting increase in the demand for yen will cause the equilibrium value of the yen to rise. In this way, expectations about future changes in exchange rates are translated *immediately* into changes in exchange rates *today*.

Seeking currency to benefit from the possible gains from its appreciation is called *foreign exchange speculation*. Once it is added to the picture, exchange rates depend not only on the demand for and supply of exports, imports, and investment today but also on expectations about future changes in those factors.

Thinking Like an Economist
INCENTIVES AND THE REAL EXCHANGE RATE

Whether their concern is real GDP, real consumption, real interest rates, or real exchange rates, economists focus on *real* variables. In the case of real GDP, they look at a measure of production and correct for changes in the general level of prices. In the case of the real interest rate, they find that saving and investment decisions are based on interest rates corrected for changes in price levels. Similarly, when dealing with exchange rates, economists distinguish between the *nominal* exchange rate—how many euros or pesos one dollar can buy—and the **real exchange rate**—the nominal exchange rate adjusted for changes in the relative price levels in different countries. It is this relative price of domestic and foreign goods that affects our incentives to choose between oods produced in different countries and thus affects net exports.

To understand why we need to adjust for relative prices in different countries, consider an Italian bike that sells for 1,430 euros in Italy. An American consumer trying to decide between the Italian bike and an American-made bike that sells for $1,200 needs to know the exchange rate between euros and dollars. Let's suppose it is 1.1 euros to the dollar. Thus $1,300 is required to obtain the 1,430 euros needed to buy the bike. So the consumer needs to compare the features of the U.S.-built bike for $1,200 with the Italian bike for $1,300 to decide which is the better buy. The U.S. bike costs 8 percent less than the Italian bike. To make this price comparison, we needed to know three things—the dollar price of the U.S. bike, the euro price of the Italian bike, and the nominal exchange rate.

Now suppose prices are rising an average of 2 percent per year in the United States and 5 percent in Italy. If nothing else changes, the price of the U.S. bike would rise to $1,224 and the Italian bike to 1,502 euros after a year. If the nominal exchange rate is still 1.1 euros to the dollar, the dollar price of the Italian bike would be $1,365. The U.S. bike now costs about 10 percent less than the Italian bike. Even though the *nominal* exchange rate has not changed, the relative price of the two bikes has changed. The U.S. bike is now relatively cheaper, so consumers are likely to buy more U.S. bikes and fewer Italian bikes. If the euro falls to 1.13 euros to the dollar, then the relative price of the two bikes would remain unchanged.

This example illustrates why we need to adjust for changes in the price levels to determine whether a change in the nominal exchange rate will affect net exports. If the change simply reflects differences in the price levels in different countries, the relative price of domestic and foreign goods will not change, and net exports will not be affected. Such was the case in our example when the nominal exchange rate rose from 1.1 to 1.13 euros to the dollar. In practice, when the nominal exchange rate rises or falls, the real exchange rate usually moves similarly. But when two countries have very different inflation rates, distinguishing between the nominal exchange rate and the real exchange rate can be very important.

Expectations about changes in the exchange rate in fact play a role in all overseas investment. Suppose you have saved up some money for a new car, but you don't plan to buy it until the summer you graduate from college, eighteen months away. A savings account, U.S. government bonds, and the stocks of an American company are among the many options you have for investing the funds until you need them. You also could choose to invest in European assets. If you do, you will first need to sell your dollars for euros. But in eighteen months, you will need dollars for your new car; you will have to sell the European assets you purchased and then convert the euros you receive back into dollars. Thus, in deciding whether to make investments in Europe while you wait to buy your new car, you must form expectations about how much the dollar will be worth in eighteen months when you want to sell euros for dollars. If you think the euro will rise in value (i.e., the dollar will fall in value) over the next year and half, investing in Europe will look more attractive, since you anticipate that each euro will get you more dollars when it is sold. But if you think the euro will fall in value (the dollar will rise in value) over the next eighteen months, then investing in Europe will look less attractive because each euro will get you fewer dollars when you need them.

As this simple example illustrates, expectations that the dollar will fall in value in the future make investing abroad look more attractive. Conversely, expectations that the dollar's value will rise make investing abroad look less attractive. The same is true from the perspective of a foreign investor: investing in the United States looks less attractive if the dollar is expected to fall and more attractive if the dollar is expected to rise in value.

The role played by expectations helps us understand how speculation in foreign exchange markets can introduce a source of instability. Suppose investors suddenly decide the Mexican peso is going to fall in value, perhaps because new reports of corruption have caused worries about Mexico's political stability. Each investor will want to sell pesos before they fall in value; but as all investors attempt to sell, the collapsing demand for pesos pushes its value down immediately. Thus expectations that the peso would depreciate become self-fulfilling. This process is key in international currency crises, a topic we will return to later.

Wrap-Up

WHAT DETERMINES THE EXCHANGE RATE?

The U.S. exchange rate is determined by the supply of and demand for dollars. Foreigners' demand for U.S. dollars and Americans' supply of dollars are determined by

1. Underlying trade factors: the overseas demand for U.S. goods (U.S. exports) and Americans' demand for foreign goods (U.S. imports)
2. Underlying investment factors: the returns to investments in the United States and abroad
3. Speculation based on expectations about future changes in the exchange rate.

Exchange Rate Management

Fluctuations in exchange rate can have important effects on an economy. As a country's currency appreciates, its exports become more expensive for foreign buyers, causing declines in production and employment in export-producing industries. Many developing countries have foreign debts that must be repaid in dollars. Depreciation in their currency will make buying the dollars to repay their debt more expensive, increasing its burden. Because of the link between interest rates and exchange rates, central banks in many countries have attempted to use their influence over interest rates to "manage" the exchange rate. In some cases, they have simply tried to smooth out day-to-day fluctuations in the foreign exchange market. In others, they have tried to permanently move the exchange rate higher or lower. There are two extremes of this continuum. At one pole, countries have flexible exchange rates that move in response to fluctuations in demand and supply; they do not intervene directly in the foreign exchange market. At the other pole, countries fix their exchange rates, announcing a value and then intervening in the foreign exchange market to keep the exchange rate at that level.

Fixed Exchange Rate Systems The United States has had a flexible exchange rate for more than three decades. Before 1971, the world had a **fixed exchange rate system:** that is, exchange rates were pegged at a particular level. Thus the U.S. dollar was pegged to gold, valued at $32 per ounce, while other currencies were fixed in terms of the dollar. Exchange rates changed only as the result of explicit government decisions. Before the euro was introduced as the common currency of the European Economic and Monetary Union, the member countries of the union permanently fixed the exchange rates between their currencies. Often smaller countries will decide to fix their exchange rate relative to an important trading partner. Estonia's exchange rate, for example, is fixed in terms of the euro. From this brief description, three questions follow: How does a country "fix" its exchange rate? What are the consequences of fixed exchange rates for monetary policy? And what are the pros and cons of a fixed exchange rate system?

Fixing the Exchange Rate Let's suppose the government of Mexico has decided to fix the exchange rate between the peso and the dollar at 9 pesos to the dollar; this was approximately the peso-dollar exchange rate in 1998. Figure 34.5 depicts the foreign exchange market for pesos. It is important to note that we have drawn the figure to represent the market for pesos, so the quantity on the horizontal axis is expressed in terms of pesos and the exchange rate is dollars per peso. (Our earlier figures focused instead on the dollar exchange rate; the quantity along the horizontal axis was dollars, and the vertical axis was

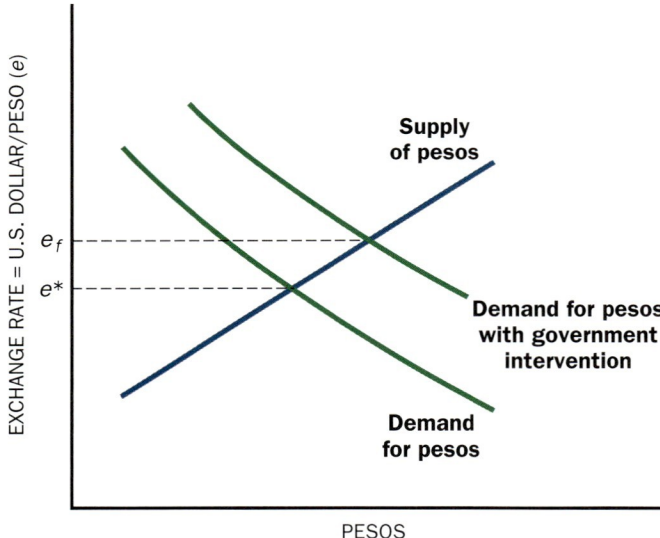

Figure 34.5

GOVERNMENT INTERVENTION IN A FIXED EXCHANGE RATE SYSTEM

If the "fixed" value for the dollar-peso exchange rate under the fixed exchange rate system, e_f, differs from the market equilibrium rate, e^*, then sustaining the fixed exchange rate requires government intervention. When e_f is above e^*, the government enters the foreign exchange market demanding pesos (supplying dollars or other foreign currencies) until the equilibrium exchange rate is equal to the pegged rate e_f.

expressed in terms of the value of the dollar.) As drawn in Figure 34.5, the market equilibrium exchange rate (e^*) is below the pegged rate (e_f). Without some sort of government intervention, the peso will depreciate until the exchange rate reaches e^*. At the pegged rate e_f, the supply of pesos exceeds the demand for pesos. To keep the value of the pesos from falling, the Mexican government would need to shift the demand curve for pesos to the right, as shown in the figure. The government can do this by buying pesos with the dollars, other foreign currencies, or gold that it holds. Thus, to keep the exchange rate equal to the level e_f, the government will need to intervene in the foreign exchange market to offset shifts in the demand or supply of the currency.

Much as speculation can be destabilizing, as discussed earlier, it can also be stabilizing. If the exchange rate should fall to e^*, foreign investors convinced that the government is planning to intervene to bring it back to e_f will seek to buy pesos now, when they are cheap. Later, after the government intervenes, their value will rise and the speculators expect to earn large profits by then selling the pesos and buying dollars. But their actions shift the demand curve for pesos to the right, helping to drive the equilibrium exchange rate back to e_f.

Problems can arise when investors believe that the equilibrium exchange rate and the pegged rate are far apart. Recall that the way the Mexican government attempted to sustain the exchange rate was by selling its holdings of dollars, other currencies, or gold for pesos. But if the government has insufficient resources and investors believe that the government will be unable to, or unwilling to, sustain the exchange rate at e_f, a disaster may follow. Once investors are convinced that the peg will be abandoned and the exchange rate will fall, they expect a capital loss on their peso holdings. Their best bet is to try to unload pesos before the peg is abandoned. The supply curve shifts to the right, widening the gap between the peg and the equilibrium exchange rate. To sustain the peg, the government now has to use up even more of its non-peso holdings. The gap between supply and demand at the original rate e_f becomes enormous. Eventually, the government may be forced to abandon the pegged rate, letting the exchange rate fall and proving the speculators who dumped pesos to have been correct.

When the government announces a new, lower exchange rate under a fixed exchange rate system, it is said to **devalue** the currency.

Monetary Policy Under a Fixed Exchange Rate System One cost of a fixed exchange rate system is the loss of a key tool of macroeconomics policy—monetary policy. To understand why this loss occurs, recall first that monetary policy affects the interest rate and credit conditions, influencing aggregate expenditures and therefore output and inflation. With this in mind, suppose Canada decides to fix the Canadian dollar–U.S. dollar exchange rate. Given a high degree of capital mobility between Canada and the United States, consider what would happen if interest rates in Canada were above those in the United States. Investors would shift funds from the United States into Canada to take advantage of the higher returns. This increased demand for the Canadian dollar would cause it to appreciate. If Canadian interest rates were below those in the United States, the reverse would occur, causing the Canadian dollar to depreciate. Only if Canadian interest rates are equal to interest rates in the United States will the exchange rate between Canadian dollars and U.S. dollars remain constant. Thus, to maintain a fixed exchange rate, the Bank of Canada (Canada's central bank) must ensure that it keeps the Canadian interest rate equal to the U.S. interest rate. If the Bank of Canada tries to reduce interest rates slightly, perhaps in an attempt to stimulate Canadian investment spending if Canada is in a recession, foreign investors will sell Canadian dollars as they take their capital out of the country to earn higher yields in the United States. To prevent the exchange rate from changing, the Bank of Canada would have to push interest rates back up. Similarly, any attempt to raise interest rates would attract a capital inflow that would push the value of the currency up. To keep the exchange rate at its pegged rate, the central bank would have to lower interest rates back down. By the same argument, if the Federal Reserve increases the U.S. interest rate, the Bank of Canada will have to follow suit and raise the Canadian interest rate if it wishes to maintain its fixed exchange rate. *In a small open economy under a fixed exchange rate system with perfect capital mobility, the central bank must keep the interest rate equal to the foreign interest rate. The country cannot run an independent monetary policy.*

This result can help us understand three important recent episodes. First, it helps explain why the European economies decided to adopt a common currency once they integrated their economies and fixed their exchange rates. No individual country in the monetary union can run an independent monetary policy, so the members of the union have given up their own national currencies and delegated monetary policy for the entire union to the European Central Bank.

Second, it helps us understand why in 1992 the United Kingdom dropped out of the European Monetary System, a system of fixed exchange rates that preceded the Economic and Monetary Union. The United Kingdom was in a recession, and many economists argued for interest rate cuts to help expand aggregate expenditures. As long as the United Kingdom wanted to maintain its fixed exchange rate, it could not cut interest rates. Because speculators thought the country might drop out of the European Monetary System and cut interest rates, they expected the pound to depreciate. This expectation shifted the demand curve for pounds to the left; and to offset this downward pressure on the pound exchange rate, the Bank of England had to keep its interest rates higher than those in Germany just when domestic factors called for interest rate cuts. Finally, the system collapsed; the United Kingdom dropped out of the European Monetary System, cut its interest rates, and let the pound depreciate against the other European currencies.

Third, the loss of monetary control under a fixed exchange rate system explains why countries that have experienced high inflation rates often decide to fix their exchange rate as part of a disinflation policy. In fact, while the loss of an independent monetary policy is one of the chief arguments against a fixed exchange rate system, paradoxically it is also one of the chief arguments in favor of this system for countries that have a history of high inflation and bad monetary policy.

Pegging the nominal exchange rate forces a high-inflation country to bring its own inflation rate down. If it does not, its exports will become more and more expensive as its price level rises faster than that of other countries (a real appreciation). As its net exports decline, the demand for its currency, at the fixed exchange rate, falls. To maintain the fixed exchange rate, the central bank must raise interest rates. Doing so reduces aggregate expenditures, reducing output and ultimately inflation.

One of the attractions of the European Monetary System of fixed exchange rates for countries like Italy was that it linked their monetary policy with that of Germany, a low-inflation country. Before the creation of the EMU, Italy's inflation rate was higher than Germany's. Maintaining a fixed nominal exchange rate with Germany forced Italy to bring down inflation by reducing its net exports, thereby reducing aggregate expenditures, output, and eventually inflation.

Reducing Exchange Rate Volatility A major argument for a fixed exchange rate system is that it reduces risks from exchange rate volatility. Many economists have been concerned about the high degree of volatility in exchange rate markets. Exchange rates have fluctuated greatly, both on a day-to-day and on a longer-term basis. The Japanese yen went from 94 yen to the dollar in 1995 to 131 yen in 1998, back to 107 yen in 2000, and then to 110 in 2004. The euro went from 87 cents in early 2002 to $1.25 two years later. The dollar has had single-day declines of more than 1 percent against the German mark (February 18, 1985), and more than 1 percent against the Japanese yen (October 14, 1987). This may not seem like a lot, but a 1 percent decline every business day for a year would result in the exchange rate declining by more than 240 percent within that year. Many of these gyrations, particularly the ones that happen from day to day, cannot be explained by any correspondingly large changes in the economy. They seem explainable only in terms of large shifts in expectations.

As was noted above, dollars or yen are assets. That is why the value of the exchange rate today depends on what investors expect the exchange rate will be next year. Thus, the stability of the exchange rate depends on the stability of the expectations of investors. For instance, when the dollar is lower, foreign investors might expect it to rise again. In that case, as the value of the dollar declines, the expected return to holding dollars increases: investors believe that the dollar is likely to appreciate and that they will benefit from a capital gain when it does. Here expectations help stabilize the market, since foreign investors may help limit any decline in the dollar by buying it as it falls.

But if as the dollar depreciates foreign investors expect further depreciation, then their willingness to invest in America may actually decrease as the dollar falls in value. In that case, an initial decline in the value of the dollar in effect shifts the demand curve for dollars down, leading to further decreases in value.

Whatever their cause and whatever the nature of expectations concerning future movements, huge swings in exchange rates add to the risk of doing business in the world market and thus discourage businesses and countries from pursuing their comparative advantages. If the exchange rate appreciates greatly, exporters suddenly find that the market for their goods has dried up, unless they drastically cut prices; either way, their profits are dramatically reduced. Even American firms that produce only for the American market face great risks as a result of exchange rate fluctuations. Shoe manufacturers may find the American market flooded with cheap Brazilian shoes if the dollar appreciates relative to the Brazilian real; again, they either lose sales or must cut their prices, and in either case, profits fall.

Exporting and importing firms can take steps to mitigate the effects of foreign exchange risks in the short run—say, the next three to six months. Consider an American firm that exports abroad. It has a contract to deliver so many ball bearings to France at so many euros per ball bearing. But it pays its workers in dollars, not euros. If the euro depreciates, when the firm takes the euros it receives

International Perspective
GLOBAL FINANCIAL CRISES

The decade of the 1990s witnessed three global financial crises. The first occurred in 1992, forcing the United Kingdom, Italy, and Sweden to abandon pegged exchange rates and leading several other members of the European Monetary System (EMS) to devalue their currencies. The second occurred in 1994 with the collapse of the Mexican peso. The collapse raised concerns among speculators about the financial health of other Latin American countries, and their currencies also came under pressure. This process by which concerns about one country spread to others is called *contagion*. Because the 1994–1995 crisis was centered in Latin America, the fallout from the Mexican crisis has been called the *tequila effect*.

The third crisis of the 1990s was set off in mid-1997 when speculators began selling the Thai currency, the baht. In June, the Thai government stopped fixing the value of the baht and it immediately devalued. As investors continued to shift into safer currencies, such as the dollar, the Thai economy continued to suffer. Between June 1997 and December 1998, the Thai stock market lost almost half its value—as if the Dow Jones average in the United States had fallen from 11,000 to 5,500. As stock prices and other asset prices fell, banks that had lent money using the inflated asset values as collateral were threatened.

Initially, no one expected what seemed to be an isolated event in Thailand to lead to a global financial crisis. It did, because investors' assessments of the risks of investing in emerging market economies like Thailand's changed. Investors started pulling funds out of Indonesia, Malaysia, and the Philippines. As these countries were forced to let their currencies depreciate, Singapore and Taiwan stopped fixing the value of their currencies out of concern that their exports would otherwise be at a competitive disadvantage. As investments in emerging markets looked increasingly risky, investors wanted out. They started selling holdings in other Southeast Asian economies. The Hong Kong stock market fell 23 percent in just four days in October 1997. Even the U.S. market was hit by fears of a crisis. The Dow Jones industrial average dropped 554 points on October 27, 1997, at that time the largest one-day point loss ever. In Asia, selling pressure spread from Thailand to Indonesia, South Korea, Taiwan, and Malaysia before jumping around the globe to hit Russia and Brazil.

WORLD INDUSTRIAL PRODUCTION

SOURCE: IMF, *World Economic Outlook* (1999).

As speculators withdrew capital, the governments of the affected countries faced difficult choices. One option was to simply let their currencies depreciate. Unfortunately, in many of these countries, domestic banks and firms had borrowed heavily from foreign sources; a devaluation would make it more difficult to repay these loans because it would raise the domestic currency value that must be repaid. Devaluation would therefore threaten the solvency of the banking sector of these countries. The second option was to prevent a devaluation by raising interest rates high enough to halt the capital outflow. But doing so would severely constrict investment, cut aggregate expenditures, and lead to output declines and increases in unemployment.

The devastating economic consequences of financial crises are clear from the declines in production in Latin America during 1995 and 1996 and the declines in Asia in 1998 and 1999. The chart illustrates the very high rates of economic growth experienced in Asia throughout most of the 1990s. These growth rates started falling in Asia in mid-1997, turning negative in 1998.

and converts them into dollars, its revenues will fall short of the dollars it has already paid to workers. It can insure itself by making a contract (with either a bank or a dealer in the foreign exchange market) for the future delivery or sale of those euros at a price agreed on today. It can thus avoid the risk of a change in the foreign exchange rate. However, firms cannot easily buy or sell foreign exchange for delivery two or three years into the future. Since many investment projects have a planning horizon of years or even decades, investors are exposed to foreign exchange risks against which they cannot insure themselves. But, as noted above, even firms that do not buy or sell in foreign markets are exposed to risks from foreign exchange rate fluctuations: American firms cannot buy insurance against the longer-term risk that the American market will be flooded with cheap imports as a result of an appreciation of the U.S. dollar. These risks are reduced if the exchange rate is fixed.

FLEXIBLE EXCHANGE RATE SYSTEMS

Today, while most governments do not peg the exchange rate at a particular value, they do frequently intervene in the foreign exchange markets, buying and selling in an attempt to reduce day-to-day variability in exchange rates. Rather than let the exchange rate freely *float* as demand and supply vary, as would occur under a flexible exchange rate system, governments take action. Economists sometimes refer to this as a *"dirty float" system*.

Stabilizing the Exchange Rate Given the costs of exchange rate instability, some have demanded that the government should actively try to stabilize the exchange rate. Producers are particularly concerned that the real exchange rate be stabilized, so that if inflation in the United States is higher than in foreign countries, American exporters can still sell their goods abroad. As Figure 34.6 shows, there have been large movements in real exchange rates, just as there have been in nominal exchange rates.

Any government program to stabilize the (real) exchange rate must meet three requirements. First, the government must choose what the exchange rate should be. Second, it must have a mechanism for keeping the real exchange rate at that value.

European Monetary Union, Frankfurt, Germany

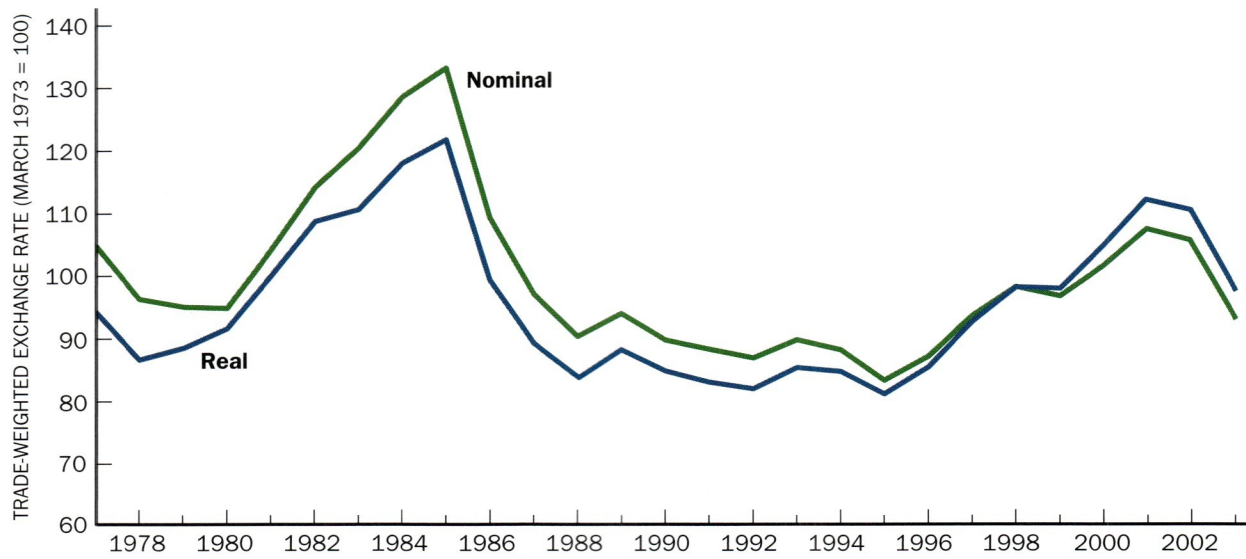

Figure 34.6
VOLATILITY OF NOMINAL AND REAL EXCHANGE RATES

Both the nominal and real exchange rates for the United States fluctuated considerably over the 1980s. The figure shows the trade-weighted value of the dollar relative to other currencies, unadjusted (nominal) and adjusted (real) for price-level changes in the United States and abroad.

SOURCE: *Economic Report of the President* (2004).

For example, if the dollar seems to be climbing too high against the yen, a plan might propose that the Fed sell dollars and buy yen, thereby pushing up the demand for yen and increasing the supply of dollars. Producers in the United States may be delighted by this move; demand for exports will increase, as will demand for goods that compete closely with imports. But producers in Japan will have just the opposite reaction. If the Japanese government, responding to these pressures, were to intervene simultaneously and start selling yen and buying dollars, the two efforts would offset each other. In effect, it would be as if the U.S. government sold dollars in exchange for yen directly to the Japanese government, with private markets unaffected.

This brings up a third requirement of exchange rate stabilization proposals: there must be some degree of cooperation among countries. This is particularly true in the modern world economy, where no single country is dominant. There are several big players—Japan, the Economic and Monetary Union, and the United States—and setting exchange rates requires these governments to work together.

Case in Point

CURRENCY BOARDS AND DOLLARIZATION

Currency crises in Latin America and Asia have increased interest in new forms of monetary reform that could avoid future crises. Two suggestions that have figured prominently in discussions are a **currency board** and **dollarization**.

Under a currency board, the exchange rate between the local currency and, say, the dollar is fixed by law. The central bank holds enough foreign currency to back all the domestic currency and reserves it has issued. This precaution makes a run on the currency unlikely—the central bank always has enough dollars to pay off anyone who shows up wanting to exchange the domestic currency for dollars. Since there is never any fear the country will run out of reserves, investors will have no reason to panic and try to get their funds out before the pegged rate is abandoned.

Argentina operated with a currency board between 1991 and 2001. Because Argentina had a history of high inflation, a currency board was viewed as a means of establishing a credible, low-inflation environment by tying the Argentinean currency to the U.S. dollar. The disadvantages of a currency board are two. First, exchange rate adjustments can help ensure macroeconomic stability when two countries face different economic disturbances. For example, a recession in Argentina might be lessened by an exchange rate depreciation that spurs exports. A currency board, like other fixed exchange rate systems, leaves countries unable to conduct an independent monetary policy. If a country has a history of bad monetary policy, however, such a limitation may be desirable. Second, under a currency board the central bank cannot create reserves in the event of a domestic banking crisis—it can no longer serve as the lender of last resort.

A more extreme solution to exchange rate volatility and currency crises is to simply abandon the domestic currency and use the U.S. dollar, a policy called *dollarization*. Ecuador *dollarized* in 2000; the Ecuadorian currency, the sucre, is no longer used for transactions and all prices are quoted in U.S. dollars. By eliminating the possiblity of exchange rate changes and tying itself to Federal Reserve policy, it is argued, countries can benefit from the effects of reduced risk and lower uncertainty. Like other fixed exchange rate systems, dollarization removes mone-

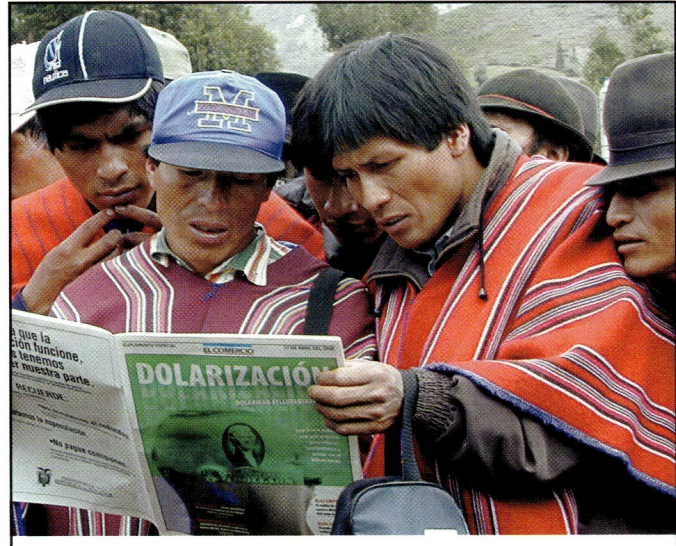
Ecuadorians read about their country's switch to the U.S. dollar as the official currency in 2000.

tary policy from a country's control—in this case, giving it to the Fed. The potential drawback is that the Fed bases its policy decisions on U.S. economic conditions and would be unlikely to alter monetary policy in response to a domestic economic or financial crisis in a country that had switched to dollars.

At the time it dollarized, Ecuador faced the threat of hyperinflation. By adopting the dollar as its currency, Ecuador has enjoyed low inflation instead. Thanks to high oil prices, real output has grown.

Can Governments Stabilize Exchange Rates? Some economists are skeptical about the ability of government to stabilize the exchange rate even in the short run. If the current exchange rate between the peso and the dollar is 10 pesos to the dollar, and if the market knows that the exchange rate must change in the near future to 12 pesos to the dollar, it will be futile for the Mexican government to try to maintain the current exchange rate in the short run. Mexican investors, believing that there will be a devaluation of the peso, know that the gains from holding assets in dollars will be enormous. By converting their pesos to dollars and holding them for the short period until the peso is devalued, they obtain a large return.

The result will be what is referred to as a *run* on the peso, as those holding assets denominated in pesos seek to sell them now. This run will be too large for the Mexican government to stop by buying pesos and selling dollars, as more private individuals are willing to sell pesos and buy dollars than the Mexican government has resources to cope with. The government may be successful in postponing the fall of the peso for a few days, but in doing so it may pay a huge price. It would have obtained the capital gain on the dollars it held if it had not sold dollars for pesos. Instead, the capital gain is earned by private individuals. If the government spends $1 billion trying to support the peso and the peso goes down 20 percent (as in our example), the cost of the short-run support is more than $200 million.

Critics of government stabilization programs make several points. First, they stress the difficulties in determining the equilibrium exchange rate that is supposed to be stabilized. Is there any reason, they ask, to believe that government bureaucrats are in a better position to make judgments about the equilibrium exchange rate than the thousands of investors who buy and sell foreign exchange every day? If the government makes mistakes, as it is almost bound to do, it can actually contribute to destabilizing the exchange rate rather than to stabilizing it.

Exchange rates often need to change. For example, if one economy grows faster than another or has higher inflation than another, the exchange rate will have to adjust to compensate. How will a scheme for stabilizing exchange rates let them adjust naturally while controlling them at the same time?

Second, critics of government stabilization programs question whether international economic cooperation is achievable. Running domestic economic policy is difficult enough. For example, will a country take steps to raise its exchange rate and thus hurt its exporters to keep a political agreement with foreign countries?

Thus, there are serious questions about whether stabilizing the currency is possible either economically or politically.

Review and Practice

SUMMARY

1. In a flexible exchange rate system, exchange rates are determined in the foreign exchange market by the forces of supply and demand.
2. The demand for and supply of dollars are determined by exports and imports, by foreigners' desire to invest in the United States and Americans' desire to invest abroad, and by speculators who base their demands for various currencies on expectations about changes in future exchange rates.
3. In the absence of foreign borrowing and lending, exports and imports would always need to balance.
4. A rise in interest rates will attract a capital inflow and cause the exchange rate to rise; a fall in interest rates will cause the exchange rate to fall.
5. Under a fixed exchange rate system, the government must intervene in the foreign exchange market to ensure that demand and supply balance at the pegged exchange rate.
6. In a small open economy with perfect capital mobility, under a fixed exchange rate system the domestic interest rate must equal the foreign interest rate. Monetary policy therefore must be used to peg the exchange rate and cannot be used to address other macroeconomic goals.
7. It may not be possible for the government to stabilize exchange rates effectively. It is difficult to determine the equilibrium exchange rate that is supposed to be stabilized, and international coordination may not be achievable.

KEY TERMS

flexible exchange rate systems
appreciation
depreciation
perfectly mobile capital
real exchange rate
fixed exchange rate system
devaluation
currency board
dollarization

REVIEW QUESTIONS

1. Name three factors that cause exchange rates to shift.
2. If the European Central Bank raises interest rates in Europe while the Fed leaves U.S. interest rates unchanged, would you expect the dollar to appreciate or to depreciate?
3. Why are expectations concerning changes in the exchange rate important? How do relative rates of inflation affect those expectations?
4. What are the costs of exchange rate instability? How might the government attempt to reduce instability in exchange rates?
5. What problems result from government attempts to stabilize the exchange rate at a level that is not the equilibrium level?
6. Can a country run an independent monetary policy to achieve domestic economic policy goals if it is committed to maintaining a fixed exchange rate?
7. Under a fixed exchange rate system, when will speculation by foreign investors be stabilizing? When will it be destabilizing?

PROBLEMS

1. Tell whether each of the economic actors in the following list would be suppliers or demanders in the foreign exchange market for U.S. dollars:
   (a) An American tourist in Europe
   (b) A Japanese firm exporting to the United States
   (c) A British investor who wants to buy U.S. stocks
   (d) A Brazilian tourist in the United States
   (e) A German firm importing from the United States
   (f) A U.S. investor who wants to buy real estate in Australia
2. Explain whether each of the following changes would tend to appreciate or to depreciate the U.S. dollar, using supply and demand curves for the foreign exchange market to illustrate your answers:
   (a) Higher interest rates in Japan
   (b) A boycott of American goods by Europeans
   (c) A tight U.S. monetary policy
   (d) An expansionary U.S. fiscal policy

3. Suppose that at the start of 2001, a U.S. investor put $10,000 into a one-year euro investment. If the exchange rate was 1.5 euros per dollar, how much would $10,000 be in euros? Over the course of the year, the euro investment paid 10 percent interest. But when the investor switched back to dollars at the end of the year, the exchange rate was 2 euros per dollar. Did the change in the exchange rate earn the investor more money or less money? How much? How does your analysis change if the exchange rate had fallen to 1 euro per dollar?
4. If the government wanted to reduce the trade deficit by altering the exchange rate, what sort of monetary policy should it employ? Explain.
5. If the government succeeds in raising the exchange rate, who benefits and who is injured?
6. Suppose Americans go on a "buy American" campaign that reduces imports. Use a supply and demand model of the foreign exchange market to show how this campaign would affect the value of the dollar. Does the change in the exchange rate act to increase the reduction in imports or does it partially offset the initial reduction in imports? Explain.

Learning Goals

In this chapter, you will learn

1. How open economy factors affect the ADI curve
2. How foreign events can affect the U.S. economy
3. How monetary and fiscal policies affect the exchange rate and net exports
4. How open economy factors influence the effectiveness of monetary and fiscal policies

Chapter 35

POLICY IN THE OPEN ECONOMY

The previous chapter focused on the foreign exchange market, and on some of the differences between flexible and fixed exchange rate systems. The world's three major economic blocs—the United States, the European Union, and Japan—all have adopted flexible exchange rate systems. The forces of supply and demand that were discussed in Chapter 34 operate to determine the relative values of the dollar, the euro, and the yen. The purpose of this chapter is to incorporate exports, imports, and international financial capital flows into the model of short-run fluctuations that was developed in Part Seven.

When short-run fluctuations associated with business cycles were first discussed, for the sake of simplicity we focused on a closed economy, ignoring the role of international trade and financial linkages. Now it is time to add the international dimension to the model to see if any of the basic conclusions we reached in the earlier chapters need to be altered. Fortunately, the fundamental connections between inflation, interest rates, and output operate in much the same manner as before. But by adding in the linkages that tie together the global economy, we can better understand how U.S. fiscal policy and Federal Reserve decisions affect the value of the dollar and the U.S. trade balance. In addition, these new linkages with monetary policy can affect the economy, and international factors can be a source of economic fluctuations.

The aggregate demand–inflation (ADI) curve and the inflation adjustment (IA) line form the core framework for understanding economic fluctuations. Our main objective in this chapter will be to see how international trade in goods and financial assets affects these two key relationships. We will focus on economies like that of the United States that have a flexible exchange rate determined by the interplay of supply and demand in the foreign exchange market.

The ADI Curve and the Open Economy

In the closed economy, the components of aggregate spending are consumption, investment, and government purchases. In the open economy, net exports must be added to this list. An increase in net exports, just like an increase in government purchases, leads firms to expand production and employment. If foreigners purchase more U.S.–produced goods and services, U.S. exports rise. The firms producing these goods increase production and employment. If U.S. residents switch from buying goods produced in the United States to buying more foreign goods—purchasing Olympus rather than Kodak cameras or Heineken beer rather than Bud—U.S. firms see demand drop, and they respond by cutting back production and employment. The impact of exports and imports on domestic aggregate demand is measured by *net exports*—exports minus imports.

The ADI curve developed in Chapter 31 summarized the relationship between aggregate demand and inflation in a closed economy. Increases in inflation lead to increases in the real interest rate, and these reduce household and business spending on consumption and investment. This connection between inflation and demand continues to hold in an open economy like the U.S. economy—changes in inflation continue to result in interest rate changes through the actions of monetary policy. But these interest rate changes now affect the exchange rate—the value of the dollar relative to other currencies such as the euro, the yen, or the peso—and net exports. To understand how they do so is our next task.

INFLATION, THE INTEREST RATE, AND THE EXCHANGE RATE

How does an increase in inflation affect the exchange rate? When inflation increases, monetary policy responds to cause the real interest rate to increase. The impact of inflation on the real interest rate depends on the central bank's monetary policy rule, as we learned in Chapter 33. International investors constantly seek out the most attractive financial investments around the globe; thus, when interest rates rise in the United States, they sell financial assets in other countries in order to invest here. As they do so, exchange rates are affected.

If interest rates in the United States rise relative to the rates of return available in other countries, international investors, rather than lending funds in the capital markets of Japan or Europe, will lend their funds in U.S. capital markets to take advantage of those higher rates. But borrowers in the U.S. capital market want to borrow dollars, not yen or euros. International investors therefore need to buy dollars in the foreign exchange market if they want to lend those dollars to U.S. borrowers.[1] This increase in the demand for dollars causes the price of dollars to rise, just as a rightward shift in the demand curve for any other good would cause its price to rise.

---

[1] See Chapter 34 for a discussion of the foreign exchange market.

While this discussion has focused on the demand for dollars by foreign investors, the supply of dollars in the foreign exchange market will also be affected. With U.S. interest rates higher, U.S. investors will be less likely to buy foreign securities, thereby reducing the supply of dollars in the foreign exchange market. Again, the result is to raise the value of the dollar as demand increases and supply decreases.

Our discussion took as its starting point a rise in U.S. interest rates. Though the increase leads to an appreciation of the dollar, from the perspective of other countries it causes their currencies to depreciate. For example, if U.S. interest rates rise relative to interest rates in Canada, the Canadian dollar will depreciate, falling in value relative to the U.S. dollar. To take another example: in June 2000, the European Central Bank boosted interest rates. Because higher returns could now be earned on European financial assets, investors sold off some holdings of dollar assets in order to invest in euro assets. But to make those investments, they needed to use their dollars to buy euros. The greater demand for euros pushed up the price of euros in terms of dollars—that is, the exchange rate changed and euros appreciated relative to dollars.

Two points are worth noting. First, the value of the dollar is affected by changes in interest rates in other countries. This point illustrates just one of the ways in which international economic developments can affect the U.S. economy. Second, in our examples of how interest rates affect exchange rates, interest rates in one country change relative to interest rates in other countries—and that change is what causes investors to shift funds in pursuit of higher returns. If the Fed raises the interest rate in the United States and other countries respond by increasing their interest rates, the dollar will not appreciate.

THE EXCHANGE RATE AND AGGREGATE EXPENDITURES

Changes in the value of the dollar affect net exports. As the dollar appreciates, U.S. exports fall and imports rise. As dollars become more expensive, foreign buyers find that U.S. goods cost more in terms of their own currencies. Faced with this increase in cost, they will buy fewer goods produced in the United States. And conversely, foreign goods are now cheaper for Americans to purchase since dollars buy more in terms of other currencies. U.S. imports rise as Americans buy more goods produced abroad.

The fall in exports and rise in imports mean that U.S. *net* exports fall. Thus the total demand for U.S. goods and services (consumption plus private investment plus government purchases plus net exports) falls. As firms producing for the export market see their sales decline, and as consumers shift their spending toward imported goods, total production and employment in the U.S. decline.

As a result, the ADI curve continues to have a negative slope when we take into account that modern economies are open economies. Just as in our earlier analysis, a rise in inflation leads the central bank to boost the real interest rate, and this increase reduces private spending, particularly investment spending. In addition, as the interest rate rises, the dollar appreciates; net exports are therefore reduced. So equilibrium output falls when inflation rises, because investment spending *and* net exports fall. A movement along a given ADI curve now involves changes in both the interest rate and the exchange rate.

Net Exports and Shifts in the ADI Curve Net exports depend on the real exchange rate, but they also can be affected by other factors. For instance, U.S. exports will be affected by the level of income in other countries. If incomes in Mexico rise, Mexicans will buy more goods and services, including more U.S.-produced goods. So U.S. exports to Mexico will rise when incomes in Mexico rise. And similarly, if Mexico suffers a recession, U.S. exports to Mexico will fall.

Shifts in net exports at a given real exchange rate cause the ADI curve to shift, just as shifts in government purchases do. A case in point occurred in the late 1990s. Financial crises in several Asian and Latin American economies led to severe recessions in many of these countries. As incomes fell, households and firms cut back spending. As a consequence, the demand for U.S.-produced goods fell, lowering U.S. exports. At the same time, the financial crises reduced the value of many Asian currencies relative to the dollar. This rise in the value of the dollar also acted to reduce U.S. net exports. At a given rate of inflation, total demand for U.S. goods fell, shifting the ADI curve to the left.

If this shift in net exports had been the only factor affecting the U.S. economy at the time, the impact would have been to push the United States into a recession. But in fact, the 1990s was one of the strongest periods of U.S. growth in the twentieth century. So what happened? Is our model wrong? Two things prevented the Asian financial crisis from creating a recession in the United States. First, domestic consumption and investment spending remained very strong in the United States. The growth in these components of demand served to offset the drop in net exports. The second factor was the Fed's response. As problems in Asia developed during 1995, the Fed cut the federal funds rate. The Fed's target for the funds rate fell from 6 percent in 1995 to 5.25 percent in February 1996. This action is a good example of the type of stabilization policy discussed in Chapter 33. To offset a potential leftward shift in the ADI curve due to a drop in net exports, the Fed cut the interest rate to boost investment spending.

Foreign Interest Rates and Shifts in the ADI Curve Policy actions by foreign governments also have the potential to affect interest rates and exchange rates. If the European Central Bank, for example, decides to raise interest rates in Europe, euro assets become more attractive and the euro appreciates in value relative to the dollar. This appreciation makes European goods more expensive for Americans to buy, and it makes American goods cheaper for Europeans to buy. The appreciating euro increases U.S. net exports as our exports rise and our imports fall. For a given inflation rate in the United States, this increase in demand for U.S. output means the ADI curve has shifted to the right. In the short run, U.S. output rises. The effect of a rise in European interest rates on U.S. output is illustrated in Figure 35.1.

This discussion can be summarized in two points. First, the ADI curve is downward sloping in the open economy, just as it was for the closed economy. There is a new channel from inflation to spending, however, and this affects the slope of the ADI curve—as inflation rises, and the real interest rate rises, the value of the domestic currency

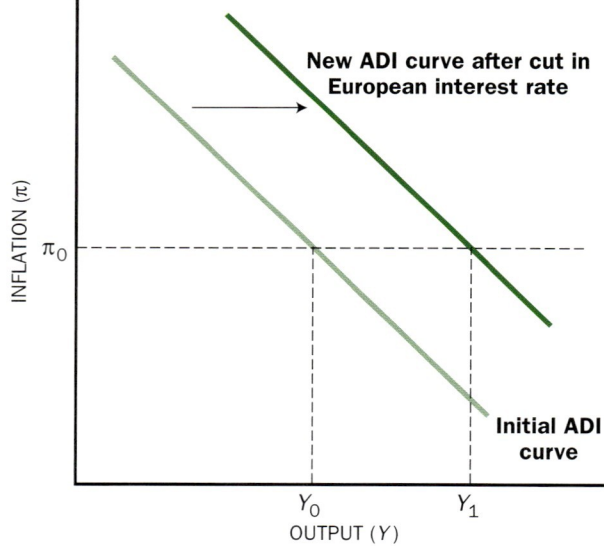

Figure 35.1

THE EFFECTS OF A RISE IN EUROPEAN INTEREST RATES ON U.S. OUTPUT

If European interest rates rise, the dollar will depreciate. This depreciation increases U.S. exports, and the increased demand leads to a rise in U.S. output.

rises and its appreciation reduces net exports. Second, international developments—booms or recessions abroad or changes in foreign interest rates—can have a direct impact on the U.S. economy by shifting the ADI curve.

> **Wrap-Up**
>
> ## INTERNATIONAL FACTORS THAT AFFECT THE SLOPE OF THE ADI CURVE
>
> When monetary policy increases interest rates in response to a rise in inflation, the dollar appreciates. An appreciation reduces net exports, one of the components of aggregate spending. A rise in inflation leads to a fall in investment and net exports.
>
> When monetary policy decreases interest rates in response to a fall in inflation, the dollar depreciates. A depreciation increases net exports, one of the components of aggregate spending. A fall in inflation leads to an increase in investment and net exports.
>
> ## INTERNATIONAL FACTORS THAT SHIFT THE ADI CURVE
>
> Factors that increase aggregate expenditures at each rate of inflation (and shift the ADI curve to the right) include
>
> economic booms abroad
>
> a rise in interest rates abroad.
>
> Factors that decrease aggregate expenditures at each rate of inflation (and shift the ADI curve to the left) include
>
> economic recessions abroad
>
> a fall in interest rates abroad.

The Exchange Rate and Inflation

Because net exports are one of the components of aggregate spending, fluctuations in net exports can affect the equilibrium level of output. Fluctuations in output around potential output in turn will affect inflation. The impact of output on inflation was summarized in Chapters 29 and 31. But changes in the exchange rate can also influence inflation more directly.

IMPORTED INPUTS

The prices in dollars that American firms must pay for imported goods depend both on the prices charged by the foreign producers of these goods *and* on the value of the dollar. If the dollar falls in value (depreciates), foreign goods cost more, just as

Thinking Like an Economist
INTEREST PARITY AND INCENTIVES

Wherever expected returns on different assets are unequal (after adjusting for any differences in risk), an economist sees a profit opportunity. By selling the lower-yielding assets and buying the higher-yielding one, an investor can increase her total return. Investors have an *incentive* to adjust their portfolios to take advantage of the opportunity offered by the higher-yielding assets. This idea—that investors seek out the highest returns—lies at the heart of what is known as the **interest parity condition,** which states that expected returns will be equal in different countries. Whenever expected returns differ across countries, the attempts by investors to take advantage of these differences by shifting funds from one country to another will cause exchange rates to adjust. In equilibrium, with perfect capital markets, expected returns would have to be equal in different countries.

When expected returns differ in, say, Canada and the United States, investors have an incentive to sell their holdings in the country with the lower return and invest in the country with the higher return. For example, suppose the interest rate is 8 percent in Canada and 5 percent in the United States. Furthermore, suppose investors do not expect any change in the Canadian-U.S. exchange rate. Such conditions create a strong incentive to sell financial assets in the United States and invest in the high-yielding Canadian assets. As investors try to take advantage of the high Canadian interest rates by buying Canadian assets, they first need to buy Canadian dollars. This increased demand for Canadian dollars causes the currency's value to rise—the Canadian dollar appreciates. Its rise may lead investors to worry that it is overvalued and likely heading for a fall, perhaps back to its earlier value. Now, the 8 percent interest rate in Canadian starts to look less attractive. If the Canadian dollar is expected to fall, say by 2 percent, then investing in Canadian financial assets will yield a return of only 6 percent (an 8 percent interest rate minus the 2 percent depreciation). This is still better than the 5 percent return in the United States, but the incentive to shift funds to Canadian is smaller than it was initially. As investors continue to respond to the incentive offered by the higher expected returns in Canada, the Canadian dollar will continue to appreciate. In this example, once investors expect a future 3 percent depreciation of the Canadian dollar, they no longer have any incentive to shift funds out of the United States and into Canada.

When capital markets are perfect, any difference in expected returns is quickly eliminated as investors respond to the incentives offered by these differences, a process economists call *arbitrage*. If you look at the major industrial economies—countries whose financial markets are closely linked—and see interest rates higher in one country than in another, you can therefore conclude that investors must believe that the currency of the country with the higher interest rate is going to depreciate.

---

if the foreign producers had raised their prices. Firms face increased costs for inputs when the value of the dollar falls; and if firms set prices as a markup over costs, prices will rise. As a consequence, inflation rises temporarily. For a given output gap and inflation expectations, changes in the exchange rate can shift the IA line.

CONSUMER PRICE INFLATION AND THE EXCHANGE RATE

The most relevant price index for measuring changes in the cost of living is the consumer price index (CPI), which is an index of the prices of goods and services that households purchase—including those that are foreign-produced. The price of French cheese does not figure in the U.S. GDP price index, since the U.S. does not produce French cheese. But U.S. households buy French cheese, so their price is

> **Internet Connection**
>
> ## FOREIGN EXCHANGE RATES
>
> The Universal Currency Converter at www.xe.com/ucc/ enables you to find out how much $1 is worth in any of more than seventy other currencies, from the Algerian dinar to the Zambian kwacha. Historical series on U.S. dollar exchange rates with many countries are provided by the Federal Reserve at www.federalreserve.gov/releases/F10/hist/.

included in the CPI. Because the CPI includes both domestically produced and foreign-produced goods, it is affected by changes in the exchange rate.

If the dollar appreciates, the dollar prices of foreign goods will fall. Because the CPI includes foreign consumer goods while the GDP price index does not, the CPI will fall relative to the GDP index. When the dollar depreciates, the opposite will occur: the CPI index will rise relative to the GDP index. Fluctuations in the exchange rate are one reason for the differences in reported inflation rates, differences that depend on which price index is used to measure inflation.

Comparing Monetary and Fiscal Policies in the Open Economy

In today's open economy, policymakers designing macroeconomic policies must take into account the effects of the exchange rate. In a closed economy, expansionary monetary policy has a short-run effect on aggregate expenditures through lower interest rates and an increase in available credit, while expansionary fiscal policy eventually crowds out private investment. In the open economy, we have already seen how the effects of changes in exchange rates, and their impact on net exports, come into play when we analyze macroeconomic policy. In an open economy, the relative utility of monetary and fiscal policies changes—monetary policy becomes more effective in the short run while fiscal policy becomes less so.

MONETARY POLICY WITH FLEXIBLE EXCHANGE RATES

When discretionary monetary policy actions are undertaken, their impact on the economy is reinforced by the exchange rate. Suppose the Fed decides to raise interest rates in the United States. And suppose Japan, members of the European Economic and Monetary Union, and other countries do not match the interest rate increase. The higher yields on U.S. bonds make them more attractive to both foreign and U.S. investors. The resulting demand for U.S. dollars leads the dollar to appreciate.

The dollar's appreciation discourages exports and encourages imports. Thus, monetary policy succeeds in dampening aggregate demand both through the interest rate effect on private investment spending—the channel that operates in a closed economy—and through the effect the exchange rate has on net exports. This impact on net exports reinforces the effect on investment, strengthening monetary policy's influence on aggregate expenditures and output.

When monetary policy expands the economy by lowering interest rates, the exchange rate depreciates; this depreciation encourages exports and discourages imports. The improvement in net exports is part of the overall impact of monetary policy in expanding aggregate expenditures. For small economies in which net

e-Insight

NEW TECHNOLOGY AND THE INTEGRATION OF WORLD FINANCIAL MARKETS

New information technologies are leading to tremendous reductions in the costs of carrying out transactions—particularly in financial markets. Today, you can search the Web for low-cost brokers and trade in financial stocks and bonds in markets in New York, London, Frankfurt, or Tokyo, right from your home computer.

The increased integration of world financial markets alters the impact that fiscal policy has on the economy. To see how it does so, imagine a world in which shifting investment funds from one country to another is prohibitively expensive. Economists describe such a world as one in which transaction costs are very high. High transaction costs will limit opportunities to take advantage of high returns in other countries. If you consider investing in the United Kingdom, you first need to sell your dollars to buy pounds, the local currency. Buying pounds will involve a transaction fee. Next, you need to buy a U.K. financial asset such as a bond with your pounds, and the purchase will also involve a transaction fee. Finally, when your investment pays interest to you in pounds, you have to convert those pounds back into dollars. Again, you have to pay a transaction fee. As an investor, you need to evaluate the return you can earn from investing in a foreign country by taking into account the interest rate available, any change in the exchange rate you expect, *and* your unavoidable transaction costs.

Even though U.K. interest rates might be higher than interest rates in the United States, the difference may not be enough to compensate for the transaction fees you will have to pay if you try to shift your investments to the United Kingdom. If you do not shift your investments, you do not need to buy pounds. When fees are high, the rise in U.K. interest rates does not increase the demand for pounds, and the value of the pound does not rise.

In this imaginary world, an expansionary fiscal policy in the United Kingdom leads to a rise in U.K. interest rates, but this rise in interest rates does not lead to an appreciation of the pound.

Now consider what happens in today's world with its lower transaction costs. Again, assume there is an expansionary fiscal policy in the United Kingdom. As interest rates start to rise in the United Kingdom, the higher returns attract international investors. These investors buy pounds so that they can shift their investments into U.K. assets. As a result, the value of the pound rises, increasing the price of U.K. exports on world markets and lowering the price of imported goods to U.K. consumers. The United Kingdom's net exports decline. Because net exports are one of the components of aggregate expenditures, the fall in net exports offsets the initial expansionary fiscal policy. As transaction costs fall, world financial markets become more closely integrated, making exchange rates more sensitive to interest rate movements and reducing the impact that fiscal policy can have on the economy.

exports are a large fraction of total spending, these exchange rate effects are the main channel of monetary policy.

Although monetary policy may be more effective in the short run in an open economy, one of our key earlier conclusions continues to hold: as wages and prices eventually adjust, the economy returns to full employment. So even in an open economy, the long-run effect of monetary policy is on inflation, not on output or unemployment.

FISCAL POLICY WITH FLEXIBLE EXCHANGE RATES

Though changes in the exchange rate tend to reinforce the impact of monetary policy, they act to reduce the impact of fiscal policy. The reason again can be traced to the way interest rates move. We have already learned that a fiscal expansion that shifts the ADI curve to the right increases output and eventually inflation. As inflation starts to rise, the central bank will act to raise interest rates. Since central banks react to anticipate future increases in inflation, interest rates are likely to rise even if initially the actual increase in inflation is small. Also, a fiscal expansion raises the equilibrium full-employment real interest rate. As we learned in Chapter 33, a central bank that desires to maintain a stable inflation rate will shift its monetary policy rule when the equilibrium full-employment real interest rate changes. In the case of a fiscal expansion, this shift will lead to higher interest rates.

As interest rates increase, the exchange rate will appreciate, thereby dampening net exports. Any decline in net exports works to offset the original fiscal stimulus to aggregate expenditures. As a consequence, the exchange rate adjustment limits the impact of fiscal policy on expenditures. In the long run, as the economy returns to full employment, an increase in the government's deficit crowds out private investment and net exports, as the full-employment model of Chapter 26 explains.

Exchange rates, unlike wages and prices, adjust very rapidly, but exports and imports often do not adjust as quickly. A change in government expenditures may have an immediate impact on aggregate expenditures, while the offsetting movements in net exports may occur much later.

Wrap-Up

POLICY IN AN OPEN ECONOMY

In an open economy, the force of monetary policy is strengthened because it may affect the real exchange rate and, through the exchange rate, the level of aggregate expenditures. This effect reinforces the impact of monetary policy on aggregate expenditures through interest rates and credit availability.

In an open economy, the force of fiscal policy is dampened because it may affect the real exchange rate and, through the exchange rate, the level of net exports. The change in exchange rates caused by a fiscal expansion reduces net exports, offsetting some of the expansion's impact.

International Perspective

IS A STRONG DOLLAR GOOD FOR THE UNITED STATES?

Politicians and news commentators frequently associate the "strength" of a nation's currency with the underlying health of its economy. And concerns are often expressed when the value of a currency falls. The experience with the euro provides a case in point. The euro came into existence on January 1, 1999, when eleven European countries joined together to form a monetary union. The exchange rate between the euro, its new currency, and the dollar was initially $1.16. That is, it took $1.16 to purchase one euro. Over the next seventeen months, the euro declined in value. By May 2000, an American could buy a euro for only 91 cents. The fall in the euro caused some to worry greatly as they suggested that the weakness of the euro was a sign of the monetary union's failure.

But is a weak currency really bad for an economy? Should the European Central Bank have taken action to prevent the euro from weakening? Since early 2002, the euro has strengthened against the dollar. Should the Fed have acted to prevent this fall in the dollar's value? To answer these questions, we can focus on the role that exchange rates play in helping to stabilize the macroeconomy and on how different sectors of the economy are affected.

Movements in the exchange rate serve to offset fluctuations in aggregate expenditures. In this way, they help stabilize the economy. For instance, at the end of the 1990s, European economies were in recession. As the euro fell in value, European goods became cheaper on world markets. As a result, Europe's exports increased. The fall in the euro made imported goods more expensive for Europeans to buy, thereby decreasing Europe's imports. The falling euro boosted Europe's net exports, helping to end the recession. If the European

THE EURO–DOLLAR EXCHANGE RATE

SOURCE: Federal Reserve Board, Release G.5, 2004.

Central Bank had increased the interest rate to try to prevent the weakening of the euro, it would have made Europe's recovery from recession more difficult.

A weak currency will boost exports and reduce imports; a strong currency has the opposite effect. The United States has a huge trade deficit. The fall in the value of the dollar over the past few years will help reduce this deficit by making foreign goods more expensive for Americans and making American goods cheaper for foreigners. Thus, if you buy lots of imported goods, you benefit from a strong dollar. But if you are a business that sells abroad, your sales suffer from a strong dollar. If you work for a company that competes against foreign imports, your company is hurt by a strong dollar. Farmers therefore may see world demand for American wheat fall when the dollar appreciates, while consumers enjoy lower prices for imported electronics goods. Exchange rate movements create both winners and losers; so, apart from buttressing macroeconomic stability, a strong dollar has no grounds to be always preferred.

One additional argument is often made in favor of maintaining a strong dollar. Foreign investors have lent the United States huge amounts over the past twenty years. If they think the dollar will fall in value, they may sell their holdings of U.S. financial assets. Because the United States has been able to maintain a high level of investment, despite its low national savings rate, by borrowing from abroad, these foreign sources of funds might dry up if the dollar were to weaken. However, what matters most in attracting foreign investors is not the level of the exchange rate but the rate of return that these investors expect to earn; and those returns depend on U.S. interest rates and the expected rate of dollar depreciation. If foreign investors expect the dollar to fall, then interest rates will have to rise to continue to attract foreign investment to the United States.

Policy Coordination

Net exports provide one of the channels through which economic conditions in one country affect others. Interest rates provide another linkage. Because of these connections, the major industrialized economies of North America, Europe, and Asia meet regularly to discuss global economic conditions and often try to coordinate macroeconomic policies. The summits of the Group of Eight, or G-8, consisting of the United States, Canada, Japan, Germany, France, Italy, the United Kingdom, and Russia provide a forum for discussions of international economic developments. In recent years, these discussions have included such topics as the ongoing Japanese recession and policies to end it, the emerging market economies and the Russian economy, the role of international organizations such as the International Monetary Fund and the World Bank, and the debt burden of developing nations.

The argument that countries may gain from coordinating their macroeconomic policies is best illustrated with an example. Suppose two countries are in recession. Each contemplates using expansionary fiscal policy to try to speed its return to full employment. Each realizes, however, that if it expands fiscal policy while the other country does not, its currency will appreciate. Such appreciation would have a detrimental impact on the net exports of the country undertaking the fiscal expansion and negate some of the effect desired from the policy action. But suppose both countries could agree to undertake fiscal expansions. As their economies expand, interest rates in *both* countries will rise, and thus the exchange rate can remain at its initial level—the fiscal expansions are not offset by a movement in exchange rate.

Review and Practice

SUMMARY

1. In the open economy, net exports are a component of aggregate spending. Both imports and exports depend on the real exchange rate. A lower real exchange rate increases exports and reduces imports.
2. Changes in the real interest rate affect investment, the exchange rate, and net exports. A rise in the real interest rate reduces domestic investment and net exports, leading to a downward shift in aggregate expenditures.
3. The aggregate demand–inflation (ADI) curve in an open economy has a negative slope—the level of output consistent with equilibrium falls as inflation rises. The ADI curve can shift if incomes abroad fluctuate or if foreign interest rates rise or fall relative to the U.S. interest rate.
4. Exchange rate movements can have a temporary but direct effect on U.S. inflation. If the dollar depreciates, the prices of imported inputs rise, and firms may pass this increase through in the form of higher prices.
5. Exchange rate movements can directly affect the consumer price index (CPI) measure of inflation, because the CPI includes the prices of imported goods purchased by households.
6. Monetary policy is more effective in an open economy—changes in interest rates affect private investment, but they also cause reinforcing changes in net exports through the exchange rate channel.
7. Fiscal policy is less effective in an open economy—the change in exchange rate causes net exports to offset the initial fiscal action.

KEY TERM

interest parity condition

REVIEW QUESTIONS

1. What is the relationship between the interest rate and the exchange rate? What is the relationship between the exchange rate and net exports?
2. As we move up and to the left on a given ADI curve, what happens to the value of the domestic currency and net exports?
3. If firms import a lot of raw materials, what impact would a depreciation in the dollar have on the inflation adjustment (IA) curve?
4. How does a fiscal expansion affect the real exchange rate and net exports?
5. How does a monetary policy expansion affect the real exchange rate and net exports?
6. If the United States raises its interest rate and Canada does not, will the Canadian dollar appreciate or will it depreciate? If Canada follows the United States and also raises its interest rate, what will happen to the value of the Canadian dollar?

PROBLEMS

1. Explain how U.S. net exports would be affected by each of the following:
   (a) An economic expansion in western Europe
   (b) Financial crises in Asia and Latin America that cause the U.S. dollar to appreciate
   (c) An interest rate increase by the European Central Bank
2. Using the information in the table below, calculate the real exchange rate between the nations of Nordamer and Sudamer (the nominal exchange rate is the number of Nordamer dollars that can be purchased with one Sudamer dollar):

	Price level in Nordamer	Price level in Sudamer	Nominal exchange rate
Year 1	100	100	1
Year 2	110	100	1.1
Year 3	121	100	1.21
Year 4	133	100	1.33

   (a) Has the Sudamer dollar appreciated or depreciated in nominal terms?
   (b) Has the real exchange rate appreciated or depreciated?
   (c) Have Nordamer goods become less expensive for Sudamers to buy? Explain.

3. Suppose a fall in net exports due to a recession among our major trading partners causes a recession in the United States.
   (a) If fiscal policy is used to stimulate the economy and return it to full employment, what happens to the real interest rate, investment, and future output?
   (b) If monetary policy is used to stimulate the economy and return it to full employment, what happens to the real interest rate, investment, and future output?
4. The United States is a major export market for Canadian goods. Use the ADI and IA framework to illustrate how Canadian output and inflation will be affected if the Fed increases interest rates.
5. Suppose the U.S. economy is in a recession. The government is considering using expansionary fiscal or monetary policy to help get the economy back to full employment. Which type of policy will result in a higher level of net exports?
6. True or false: "A contractionary monetary policy hurts export industries; a fiscal contraction helps export industries." Explain why fiscal and monetary policies might have different effects on industries that produce a lot of goods for export.

Learning Goals

In this chapter, you will learn

1. How developing economies differ from developed economies such as the United States, Japan, and western Europe

2. What the impediments to growth in developing economies are, and what policies these countries can pursue to improve their standards of living

3. What *globalization* is and why some people are skeptical of it

4. How resources were allocated under the old communist system, and how the transition economies have fared since the collapse of communism

Chapter 36

DEVELOPMENT AND TRANSITION

Every year, thousands of Mexicans risk their lives to cross into the United States. The reason is simple: they seek a way out of their poverty. In the United States, a family of four is said to be in poverty—to have insufficient income for a minimal standard of living—if its income is less than $18,811. This income is about equal to that of the *average* family of four in Mexico! The average income per capita in Mexico is one-sixth of that in the United States. The minimum wage in the United States is now more than $5 an hour. In many developing countries, workers receive a mere $1 a day. Figure 36.1 shows the huge differences in income per capita between developed countries such as the United States and Italy and *less-developed countries* such as Ethiopia and Nigeria. These less-developed countries sometimes are referred to as the *third world* and sometimes as *developing countries*. Unfortunately, many of these low-income countries have not been developing—some have even been declining, with income per capita falling. Today, three-fourths of the world's population live in these developing countries.

Another group of countries also differs markedly from the advanced industrial countries. These are the so-called *economies in transition*—in transition from communism to a market economy. Figure 36.2 shows how these countries, the most important of which is Russia, have fared since the ending of communism. In many cases the transitions to market economies have yet to bear fruit, and in some cases the results have been disastrous.

There have been exceptions to this picture: countries such as Hungary and Poland have recently joined the European Union, signaling closer economic integration with western Europe, and China, the most populous country in the world and a half century ago one of the poorest, has grown rapidly. In the past two decades, incomes in China have soared, and the poverty rate has fallen from 80 percent to 5 percent.

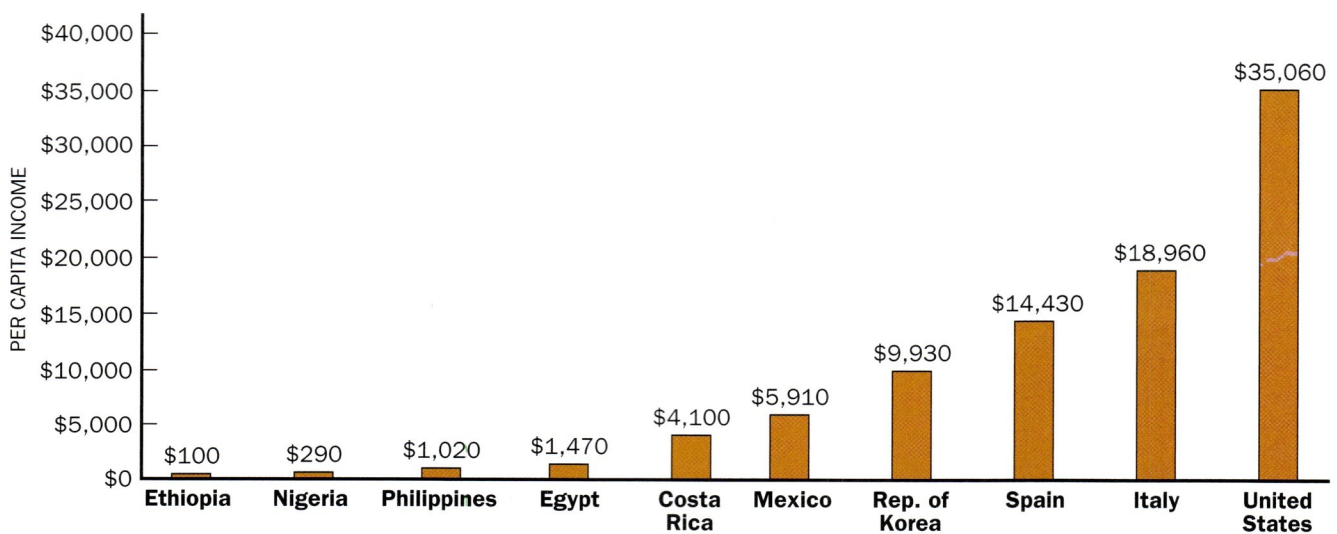

Figure 36.1

DIFFERENCES IN PER CAPITA INCOME

Some middle-income countries such as Costa Rica have per capita incomes that are up to ten times those of the world's poorest nations, and yet only one-tenth of those of the world's wealthiest nations.

SOURCE: *World Development Indicators 2004,* www.worldbank.org/data/.

This chapter explores the issues of economic development and transition. We will see that many of the challenges faced by developing and transitional economies relate to the process by which the world has become increasingly integrated economically. This process, called *globalization,* has created opportunities for some countries, but it has also been a source of contention and even conflict.

Development

Three-fourths of the world's population live in **less-developed countries,** or **LDCs.** Statistics cannot convey the full measure of what it means to live in an LDC, but they can provide a start. In the United States, life expectancy at birth is about 78 years. In Peru, it is 70 years; in India, 63 years; and in Ethiopia, 42 years. In the United States, 7 infants die for every one thousand live births; in Brazil, 31 die; in Pakistan, 84; and in Ethiopia, 116. The average American completes twelve years of schooling, while the average African gets only five years. India, with a population three and a half times that of the United States, has a GDP roughly one-twentieth that of the United States. This means that per capita income in India is about 1 percent of that in the United States.

The statistics connect with one another in a vicious cycle. Little or no education, malnutrition, and poor health care reduce productivity and thus incomes. With low incomes, people in the LDCs cannot afford better education, more food, or better health care. In many African countries, whose standards of living were already low, population has been growing faster than national income, and thus per capita income

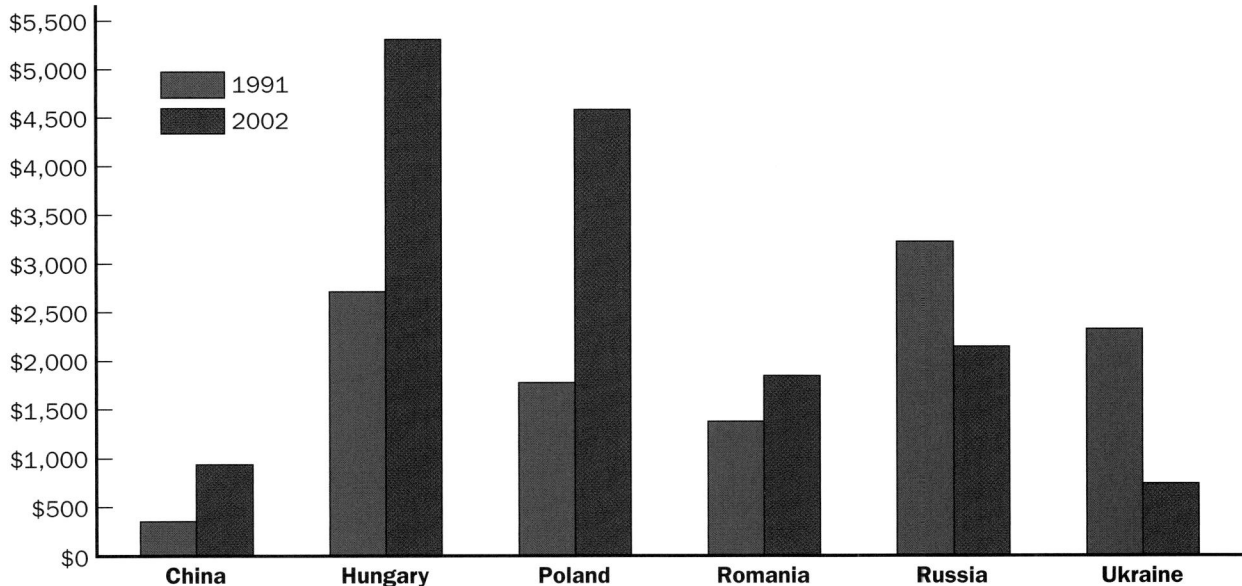

Figure 36.2

INCOME PER CAPITA IN THE TRANSITION ECONOMIES

The figure shows how some economies that are in transition from communism to a market economy have fared over the past decade. While some countries, such as China, Hungary, and Poland, have made progress, the nations of the former Soviet Union such as Russia and Ukraine have not.

SOURCE: World Bank (http://devdata.worldbank.org/data-query/).

has been falling. Life is getting worse, not better. The AIDS epidemic has ravaged Africa and threatens much of the rest of the developing world, making a bad situation even worse. Some countries, like Zambia, have seen life expectancy fall by ten years in less than a decade. More than one-fourth of the population in southern Africa is infected with HIV.

The United Nations and the World Bank (a bank established by the major industrialized countries after World War II that provides loans to LDCs) group countries into three categories: low-income countries, with GDP per capita of $735 or less in 2002; high-income countries, with GDP per capita above $9,076; and middle-income countries, with GDP per capita in between. The low-income countries are the LDCs. The high-income countries are referred to as **developed countries.** Because their higher level of income is based on their higher level of industrialization, they also are referred to as the **industrialized countries.** In the Western Hemisphere, hardly 200 miles lie between one of the richest countries, the United States, with a per capita income of $35,060 in 2002, and one of the poorest, Haiti, with a per capita income of $440.

The income gap between high-income countries, including the countries of western Europe, the United States, Canada, Japan, Australia, and New Zealand, has narrowed considerably over the past hundred years, but the gap between the high-income countries and the low-income countries has not. However, there are signs that change is possible. Some countries have made notable progress in recent years.

Internet Connection
THE WORLD BANK'S DEVELOPMENT GOALS

The World Bank has established goals for reducing poverty, improving education, reducing child mortality, and achieving other indicators of economic development and improved standards of living. They are listed at www.developmentgoals.org.

First, several countries have moved from the circle of LDCs to the ranks of middle-income countries. These are referred to collectively as **newly industrialized countries,** or **NICs** for short. Those with success stories include the "gang of four": South Korea, Taiwan, Singapore, and Hong Kong. In the thirty years after the devastating Korean War, for instance, South Korea moved from being a backward country to a major producer—not just of simple products such as textiles but of automobiles (the Hyundai) and computers, whose production requires a reasonably high level of technological expertise. Even more impressive, Japan has moved from the category of middle-income country to become one of the most prosperous nations in the world. But the success stories are not limited to East Asia: Botswana, while today suffering greatly from AIDS, has managed to have sustained growth of more than 8 percent annually for thirty years, among the most impressive records anywhere in the world. India, which for decades after independence hardly seemed to grow, has experienced sustained growth of more than 5 percent for a decade.

Second, there have been pockets of remarkable progress *within* the LDCs. In the early 1960s, agricultural research centers around the world (funded largely by the Rockefeller Foundation) developed new kinds of seeds, which under proper conditions enormously increase yields per acre. The introduction and dissemination of these new seeds—accompanied by far-reaching improvements in agricultural practices, known as the **green revolution**—led to huge increases in output. India, for example, finally managed to produce enough food to feed its burgeoning population and now sometimes exports wheat to other countries.

Third, even the grim statistics for life expectancy—62 years in Bangladesh and 46 years in sub-Saharan Africa (compared to 78 years in the United States, as noted above)—represent improvements for many countries. But these improvements have a darker side in some countries: a population explosion reminiscent of the Malthusian nightmare. Thomas Malthus envisioned a world in which population growth outpaced increases in the food supply. In Kenya during the early 1980s, for instance, improved health conditions enabled the population to grow at 4.1 percent a year, a remarkable rate at which the population would double every seventeen years, while output increased at only 1.9 percent a year. Increases in output do nothing to improve per capita income when the population grows even faster.

LIFE IN A LESS-DEVELOPED COUNTRY

Just as there are large differences between the LDCs and the industrialized countries, so there are large differences among the LDCs. The largest LDC of all, China, has a communist government. The second-largest, India, functions as the world's largest democracy. Literacy standards in Costa Rica rank with those of the industrialized countries, whereas more than half of the adult population in sub-Saharan Africa is illiterate. One must be careful in generalizing about LDCs. Still, certain observations are true for *most* of them.

Table 36.1 summarizes some of the most important dimensions of living standards, contrasting the United States, a high-income country; Mexico (its nearest neighbor to the south), a middle-income country; and India, a low-income country.

Incomes and life expectancies in most LDCs are low. A large fraction of the population lives in the rural sector and is engaged in agriculture. Lacking modern equipment like tractors, the farmers work on small plots (an acre or two, compared to an average of more than a hundred acres in the United States). In many cases, they lack the resources to buy productivity-increasing inputs such as fertilizer and pesticides; on average they use less than half the fertilizer per acre that farmers in more-developed countries use. In many countries, most farmers are landless, tilling the landlord's land under **sharecropping** arrangements that give the landlord half the output. In several countries with policies of **land reform,** land has been

Table 36.1

STANDARD OF LIVING MEASUREMENTS IN THE UNITED STATES, MEXICO, AND INDIA

Category	United States	Mexico	India
GNP per capita ($)	35,060	5,910	480
Life expectancy (years)	78	72	63
Agriculture as percentage of GDP	2	5	28
Energy consumption per capita (kilograms of oil equivalent)	8,076	1,501	479
Annual average growth of population (%)	1	1.8	1.8
Infant mortality rate (per 1,000 live births)	7	30	70
Maternal mortality rate (per 100,000 live births)	8	48	410
Urban population (% of total)	77	74	28
Television sets (number per 1,000 people)	847	261	69
Personal computers (number per 1,000 people)	458.6	47	2.7

SOURCE: *World Development Report 2004*. Data are for the most recent year available, 2002 in most cases.

redistributed to the peasants. Such land reforms were a precursor to the remarkable growth in Taiwan and Japan. In other countries, such as the Philippines and Peru, the land reforms have been only partially successful.

Over the past fifty years, most LDCs have experienced gradual urbanization. Those who live in the cities have a much higher standard of living, including access to better education and health facilities. The marked differences between the cities and rural areas have led some to refer to these economies as **dual economies.** While there are large income disparities between rural and urban sectors, disparities within the urban sectors are equally large: government workers and those few lucky enough to get jobs in manufacturing earn many times the average wage. These high wages attract migrants from the rural sector, often resulting in high urban unemployment (exceeding 20 percent) in some cities.

One reason for the poverty in LDCs is a lack of resources. These countries have less physical capital per capita and less human capital, with high illiteracy rates and a low average number of years of schooling. The lower levels of physical capital per capita are not the result of low saving rates—in fact, the saving rates of most LDCs are considerably higher than the rate in the United States. Because of their high population growth rates, they have to save a lot just to stand still.

High population growth rates have another effect. They have increased enormously the proportion of the young, who depend on others for their income. And they have made the task of improving educational levels even harder, creating a vicious circle. Typically, less-educated women have larger families, in part because they are less likely to be informed about family planning but also because the opportunity cost of having children is lower—they forgo less income. If educational levels can be improved, this vicious cycle can be turned into a virtuous cycle: more-educated women have smaller families, lowering population growth rates. Between 1980 and 2000, the average population growth rate for countries with 1980 per capita incomes below $1,000 was 3.3 percent per year. For those with 1980 per capita incomes between $1,000 and $3,000, it was 2.6 percent per year; with 1980 incomes over $3,000, only 1.3 percent. These lower rates reduce the proportion of the young and make the task of further improving educational levels easier.

Low educational levels and lack of capital prevent these economies from availing themselves of much of the most advanced technologies. With important exceptions, they specialize in low-skill *labor-intensive* industries (those whose products require much labor relative to the amount of equipment they employ), like textiles.

These problems are compounded by *institutional* failures. The lack of good financial institutions means that what capital is available may not be invested well; the lack of financial markets means that businesses cannot obtain some of the inputs they need; and the lack of good legal systems means that creditors find it difficult to force a recalcitrant borrower to repay, and consequently are willing to lend only at high interest rates that can compensate them for their risk. All these failures inhibit the entry of new firms and the expansion of old firms.

Many LDCs also are marked by high levels of inequality. Their limited incomes are shared even more unequally than are the incomes in the more advanced countries, leading to high levels of poverty. Throughout the developing countries as a whole, the number in poverty, living on less than $2 a day, was 2.8 billion at the end of the twentieth century, and the number in absolute poverty, living on less than $1 a day, was 1.2 billion.

Some of this inequality is simply due to the law of supply and demand. Because unskilled labor is abundant and skilled labor and entrepreneurs are scarce, unskilled wages are low and those who have skills prosper. Indeed, earlier theories suggested that inequality contributed to economic growth. Sir Arthur Lewis, who received the Nobel Prize for his work on development economics, argued that what he called the **surplus of labor** kept wages low and profits high. Workers earning subsistence wages could not save, but capitalists could; thus higher profits contributed to a higher saving rate. In this view, there is a trade-off between growth and equality. Current views are different. Today, many economists believe that growth and equality are in fact complementary, as evidenced by the East Asian miracle.

Wrap-Up

SOURCES OF PROBLEMS IN LESS-DEVELOPED COUNTRIES

A lack of resources, both human and physical, and high population growth, which makes raising educational levels difficult

The lack of financial markets and inadequate legal systems

A high level of income inequality

THE SUCCESS OF EAST ASIA

The most successful efforts at development, anywhere at any time, have been in East Asia in the decades after World War II. Sustained growth over three to four decades has led to eightfold or greater increases in per capita income. There are several ingredients to this success:

- Macroeconomic stability—avoiding for the most part high inflation or high levels of unemployment. As part of this strategy, governments maintained a high level of fiscal responsibility, eschewing the huge budget deficits that characterize many LDCs.
- High saving rates. With saving rates of 25 percent or more, the countries could invest heavily.
- Smart investment of savings. As important as the high level of saving is the fact that the savings were invested well; in other countries with high saving rates (either forced, as in the communist countries, or the result of a natural resource bonanza, as in Venezuela), they were not.
- Heavy investment in education, including the education of women. This investment resulted in a highly skilled labor force that was able to absorb new technologies.
- Heavy investment in technology. What separates developed from less-developed countries is not only a shortage of capital but also a "gap" in knowledge. East Asian countries developed technology policies aimed at

closing this gap, with remarkable success. Some countries, like Singapore, encouraged foreign firms to invest directly, bringing with them access to foreign markets as well as new technology. Other countries, like Korea, focused on licensing new technologies from the more advanced countries.
- Political and social stability, which provides an environment conducive to investment.

So impressive have the outcomes in East Asia been that many refer to them as the *East Asian miracle*. Some economists, however, find nothing miraculous in them—the growth can be explained largely by standard economics of the kind that we have studied in this text (see Chapter 27). High saving rates, high investment in both capital and education, and knowledge are part of the standard recipe. Still, one point argues for a miracle: no other set of countries has been able to achieve similar outcomes.

Underlying these successes were both good policies (such as those that led to macroeconomic stability) and strong institutions (such as newly created financial institutions that allocated the capital well). Three features of East Asia's development strategy deserve special attention: the roles of government, exports, and egalitarian policies.

The Role of Government Perhaps the most distinctive feature of the East Asia model was the balance the countries achieved between the role of the state and the role of the market. Their governments pursued market-oriented policies that encouraged development of the private sector. They sought to augment and "govern" the market, not to replace it.

They also fostered high saving rates—often in excess of 25 percent. In Japan, more than a third of these savings went into accounts at the postal savings banks established by the government. In Singapore, the government established a provident fund, to which all workers were required to contribute 40 percent of their income.

These governments also influenced the allocation of capital in myriad ways. Banks were discouraged from making real estate loans and loans for durable consumer goods. This action helped to increase private saving rates and to discourage real estate speculation, which often serves to destabilize the economy. As a result, more funds were available for investment in growth-oriented activities like purchasing new equipment. In addition, governments established development banks to promote long-term investment in sectors such as shipbuilding, steel mills, and the chemical industry. These interventions have been more controversial, and their success has been mixed. On the positive side, the steel firms in Taiwan and Korea are among the most efficient in the world. With more mixed results, the Japanese and Korean governments took a variety of initiatives to promote certain industries, including the computer chip industry. By the early 1980s, Japan seemed poised to completely dominate that market. During the late 1980s and early 1990s, a series of agreements reached between Japan and the United States lowered tariffs on semiconductors and allowed U.S. manufactures access to the Japanese market. These changes served to level the playing field, enabling American producers such as Intel to draw on America's comparative advantage in chip production and reassert leadership in the industry. The dangers of government intervention are often symbolized by the Japanese government's failed attempt to discourage Honda (originally a manufacturer of motorcycles) from entering the auto market, arguing that there were already too many producers.

Export-Led Growth A second factor that distinguished the countries of East Asia from less successful LDCs was their emphasis on exports. A growth strategy focusing on exports is called **export-led growth.** Firms were given a variety of encouragements to export, including increased access to credit, often at subsidized rates.

Export-led growth enables firms to produce according to their long-term comparative advantage. This is not current comparative advantage, based on current resources and knowledge. It is dynamic comparative advantage, which relies on acquired skills and technology, and on recognition of the importance of learning by doing—that skills and productivity improve with production experience. When an LDC emphasizes exports, demand for the goods it produces is not limited by the low income of its citizens. The world is its market.

Advocates of export-led growth also believe that the competition provided by the export market is an important stimulus to efficiency and modernization. The only way for a firm to succeed in the face of keen international competition is to produce what consumers want, at the quality they want, and at the lowest possible cost. This keen competition forces specialization in areas where low-wage LDCs have a comparative advantage, such as in the production of labor-intensive products.

Finally, export-led growth has facilitated the transfer of advanced technology. Producers exporting to developed countries not only come into contact with efficient producers within those countries but also learn to adopt their standards and production techniques.

Fostering Equality Another distinctive aspect of East Asia's development strategy was its emphasis on equality. Examples of these egalitarian policies include Singapore's home ownership program; the almost universal provision of elementary and secondary education, extended to girls as well as boys; and the land redistribution programs that were the precursor of growth in several of the countries, including Taiwan and Japan. In many of these countries, the governments also tried to curb excessive wage inequality and to discourage conspicuous consumption by the rich. Their experience has shown that high saving rates are possible without either the oppressiveness of Soviet-style governments or vast inequalities. The equality measures have actually promoted economic growth. The land reforms have resulted in increased agricultural production, and the high educational levels have directly increased productivity and facilitated the transfer and adoption of more advanced technology. More education for women is associated with smaller families, and thus with declining rates of population growth.

Wrap-Up

EAST ASIA'S SUCCESS

Key ingredients to East Asia's success include macroeconomic stability, high saving rates to finance investment, investment in education and in technology, and political and social stability.

Governments pursued market-oriented policies that encouraged saving and investment.

Growth strategies emphasized *export-led growth*.

Income equality was fostered.

ALTERNATIVE DEVELOPMENT STRATEGIES

The development strategies pursued by East Asia stood in marked contrast to those followed in much of the rest of the world, and many economists attribute, at least in part, the differences in performance to differences in strategies. As the developing countries first experienced independence, many came under the sway of socialism and government took a central role in planning development. Having been dominated by foreign governments, they worried that opening themselves up to foreign investment would lead to a new form of domination—domination by large multinational firms. Some countries, trying to reduce their reliance on imports, focused on *import substitution* policies, and a few, like Brazil, had a short period of success following that strategy. But by and large, the countries following these strategies stagnated or grew very slowly.

Even before the end of the cold war seemed to provide convincing proof that the socialist or planning model was badly flawed, its weaknesses as implemented in the developing countries seemed apparent. Governments did not do a good job of planning, often managing and allocating resources inefficiently. "White elephants" such as huge and inefficient steel mills dotted the landscape. Protectionist barriers were erected, nominally to help support domestic industries but all too often to allow friends of the government to enjoy high profits insulated from outside competition. In some cases, the inefficiencies were so extreme that the value of the inputs imported for use in production was greater than the value of the output, had it been sold at international prices. Protection had been granted using the *infant industry argument*—the argument that new industries had to be protected until they could establish themselves sufficiently to meet the competition. But in many of the developing countries, the infants seemed never to grow up: protection became permanent.

In the early 1980s a new development strategy emerged. Recognizing the limits of a state-dominated economy, many countries swung to the other extreme, arguing for a minimal role for government. Governments were urged to privatize and liberalize, to sell off state companies and eliminate government intervention. These policies, together with macroeconomic stability, were often referred to as the *Washington consensus,* since they were advocated by the U.S. Treasury and two international institutions located in Washington, the International Monetary Fund (IMF) and the World Bank. In many cases, these policies proved little better than their predecessors in promoting growth over an extended period of time. Reducing tariff barriers led to losses of jobs, and the developing economies were not able to generate new enterprises. Advocates believed that liberalization would lead resources to move from low-productivity uses to high-productivity uses, as the theory of comparative advantage suggested; in practice, workers frequently moved from low-productivity jobs into unemployment. All too often the policies that were designed for macroeconomic stability included very high interest rates—so high that new investment to create new jobs simply was not forthcoming.

By the mid-1990s, it became increasingly clear that neither of the extremes—the Washington consensus or state-dominated planning—provided much help. The success of the East Asian countries, even after taking into account the setback of the financial crisis of 1997–1998, stood in marked contrast to the experiences of those that had tried one or the other of these recipes for success. The East Asian countries had been more successful not only in producing growth but also in reducing poverty. Markets were seen to be at the center of development, but government had a vital role in catalyzing change and in helping to make the markets work better, to transform the economy and society through education and technology, and to regulate the economy so that it could function better. Greater attention was focused on how to make not only markets but also governments work better.

GLOBALIZATION AND DEVELOPMENT

The six decades since World War II have seen major efforts at reducing trade barriers. However, from the developing countries' perspective, the trade liberalization agenda has been driven primarily by the interests of the advanced industrialized countries, which continue to subsidize agriculture and protect textiles, making it difficult for the less-industrialized countries to sell some of the main goods that represent their comparative advantage.

These concerns are but one part of a broader dissatisfaction with globalization and the international economic institutions that help manage it. **Globalization** is the name given to the closer integration of the countries of the world—especially the increased level of trade and easier movements of capital—brought on by lower costs of transportation and communication. There are three important international economic institutions: the World Trade Organization (WTO), which provides a venue for international trade agreements and resolving trade disputes; the IMF, which was created to help support global financial stability, providing funds to countries in times of crisis, but which has expanded its activities to include giving assistance to developing and transition economies; and the World Bank, which promotes development and the alleviation of poverty in poor and middle-income countries.

Case in Point

A HISTORICAL PERSPECTIVE ON GLOBALIZATION

There has been much discussion of globalization, the closer integration of the economies around the world. The most dramatic aspect of globalization is the growth of trade, of exports and imports. But there are other aspects. Workers migrate from one country to another, multinational firms do business across borders, billions of dollars of capital flow from one country to another, and ideas and knowledge are ceaselessly communicated via the Internet.

It is sometimes forgotten, however, that the world went through a process of globalization once before. In the decades before World War I, trade grew enormously, eventually reaching a percentage comparable to that attained more recently. World War I and the Great Depression led to retrenchment. As the economies of the world plunged into a downturn at the end of the 1920s, they erected trade barriers.

Today, many analysts worry about a possible backlash against globalization—as evidenced by protest marches in Seattle, Washington, Prague, and Genoa. While many of the marchers saw globalization as threatening their own jobs, others took a broader moral stance: they viewed the way globalization had been proceeding as fundamentally unfair, as rich countries ordered the poor to open their markets to them while keeping their own markets protected. After the round of trade negotiations completed in 1994 (called the Uruguay Round, after the place where it was initiated), the poorest region in the world, sub-Saharan Africa, was actually worse off, while the United States and Europe boasted enormous gains.

Economists argue that free trade enables each country to benefit by taking advantage of its comparative advantage. Even the unilateral opening up of a market makes the country as a whole better off. But some individuals may be worse off, and typically they are not compensated. Finding ways to ensure that *all* can benefit from lower trade barriers can convert a conflict into a win-win situation, but few countries have successfully done so.

In poor developing countries, the problems are even more complicated. In these countries, unemployment rates are high, entrepreneurship is limited, and capital is scarce. Bringing down trade barriers can destroy jobs and enterprises quickly, but the country may not be able to make the investments required for it to take advantage of its comparative advantage. Jobs are destroyed faster than they are created, throwing into question the argument that the country as a whole benefits. While moving workers from low-productivity employment to employment of higher productivity as measured by comparative advantage would increase national income, moving workers from low-productivity employment to unemployment would lower national income. To increase incomes, the opening up of trade must be accompanied by other measures to help these poor countries take advantage of their comparative advantage.

Trade Giving less-developed economies access to the U.S. markets is a win-win policy. American consumers win by having a greater variety of goods at lower prices. The LDCs benefit by having a huge market for their goods. The United States has a system of preferential treatment for poor countries called the *general system of preferences,* or GSP. Of course, as always with trade, some U.S. producers and their workers complain about the loss of jobs to these low-cost competitors. As argued in Chapter 19, the total benefits to trade generally outweigh the losses to certain groups. In many cases, however, these potential losers have more influence. Many developing countries find that even as they open up their markets to U.S. products, the United States does not fully reciprocate, especially in areas such as agriculture and textiles—sectors that are of particular importance to developing countries. Though the European Union has not done much better, its members have agreed on a striking initiative, offering to eliminate all trade barriers to the lowest-income countries on all commodities except guns.

While the world as a whole, and the LDCs in particular, has much to gain from globalization—after all, we saw how growth in East Asia was spurred by its exports—unless those in developing countries can be persuaded that the playing field has been made more level, hostility toward globalization may grow.

Outsourcing One source of opposition to globalization in the United States has been the perception that jobs in America are being moved overseas in what has come to be called **outsourcing,** the process by which firms buy goods and services from others rather than producing the goods and services themselves. Outsourcing is not a new phenomenon. For example, car manufacturers have long outsourced the production of many car parts to independent firms. The practice has become controversial because many believe that Americans ranging from phone operators staffing customer help lines to software engineers are losing their jobs as firms move production to other countries or purchase the services from foreign firms. For example, new information technologies have made feasible the electronic transmission of tax returns to India for overnight processing, reducing the demand for American tax preparers.

Although outsourcing generated a great deal of news and debate during the presidential campaign in 2004, two facts are frequently ignored. First, very few U.S. jobs have moved overseas. The U.S. Labor Department reported that in the first quarter of 2004, there were 239,361 mass layoffs (layoffs that involved 50 or more workers); of these workers, only 9,985 lost jobs that were moved to a different location, and in only about half those cases (affecting 4,633 workers) did the job move to a foreign country. Overall, less than 2 percent of the mass layoffs could be described as the result of outsourcing to a foreign country. This practice is not responsible for the major changes in American patterns of employment.

Second, the United States benefits from what could be called *insourcing*—the employment of American workers by foreign firms. Toyota, for example, has established manufacturing facilities in the United States and is a major employer of American workers. Infosys Technologies of Bangalore, India, a company that helps U.S. firms shift jobs to India, opened a major consulting operation in California in

e-Insight

INDIAN ENGINEERS IN SILICON VALLEY AND SILICON VALLEY'S CAPITAL IN INDIA

Globalization and the increasing integration of the world economy can allow both investment capital *and* workers to move across borders, seeking more profitable opportunities. Nothing better illustrates this interchange than the investment by venture capitalists and U.S.-based firms in India's Silicon Valley and the immigration of high-tech workers from India to California's Silicon Valley. U.S. firms are investing in software design and research facilities in India to take advantage of that country's well-trained computer workforce and lower wages. At the same time, many engineers from India are moving to the United States to find higher-paying employment.

During the 1990s, the rapid expansion of high-tech jobs in places such as California's Silicon Valley led to an increased demand for engineers and others with the skills the computer industry needed. To meet it, Congress expanded the H-1B visa program that allows individuals with certain skills to immigrate to the United States. While potential immigrants can qualify for an H-1B visa in a wide range of occupations, most often they have sought computer-related jobs. According to the U.S. Immigration and Naturalization Service (now the Bureau of Citizenship and Immigration Services), just under half of the H-1B visas granted between October 1999 and February 2000 were for occupations classified as in systems analysis and programming. The next most common occupation was in electrical and electronics engineering, accounting for 5.4 percent of the visas. (Occupations in economics ranked seventh on the list, making up 2.3 percent of the H-1B visas.) Nearly 43 percent of all H-1B visas were granted to individuals from India. Among other countries of origin, China, representing fewer than 10 percent of H-1B visas, was a distant second.

In 2000, Congress raised the number of H-1B visas that could be issued each year from 115,000 to 195,000. The bill's passage by a vote in the Senate of ninety-six to one demonstrated the broad political support that this program to bring skilled workers to the United States enjoyed. This support

Fueled by an influx of American capital investment, successful high-tech firms like Infosys are making Bangalore the Silicon Valley of India.

eroded significantly in 2001 as a result of two factors. First, the United States experienced an economic recession in 2001, and many high-tech firms began laying off workers. Second, the terrorist attacks on the World Trade Center in New York City and on the Pentagon on September 11, 2001, led to a new concern with homeland security and a desire to tighten controls on the number of foreigners entering the United States. While Congress did not move immediately to reduce the availability of H-1B visas that could be issued, the number was eventually reduced in 2004 from 195,000 to 65,000.

The movement of workers from India to the United States represents just one example of how globalization promotes the flow of resources—in this case human capital—across borders in search of higher returns. The same process is at work in the flow of investment capital from the United States to India. In recent years, such giants as Microsoft, Oracle, Intel, Cisco, and AOL have invested heavily in India. Operating research and development facilities in India has several advantages for these firms, chief among them the presence of a well-educated workforce and significantly lower wages. As long as there are limits on how many workers can be brought to the United States, it can make sense for a technology firm to move to where the workers are.

Opening facilities in India also enables firms to engage in around-the-clock software and product development. Project work does not have to come to a halt when night falls in Silicon Valley—with a twelve-hour time difference, the workday is just beginning in India, where workers can take up the uncompleted tasks. The Internet has helped make this transfer of work possible, as a software firm can electronically move new code under development between its California and India locations.

The inflow of capital investment has helped fuel the development of local high-tech firms in India as well, and the area around Bangalore is now known as the Silicon Valley of India. Increased capital investment in India provides both new jobs for Indian engineers and the funds that have enabled local high-tech firms in India to expand.

2004 with plans to hire 500 workers. While some American jobs may move to other countries, new jobs are being created by foreign firms that locate in the United States.

The movement of jobs is part of the process of globalization. Like free trade, this process can benefit all countries. But also like free trade, its overall benefits do not necessarily translate into gains for each and every individual. Those workers whose jobs are lost do suffer, just as they would if their jobs moved to another state or disappeared because of changes in technology. In the long run, economies gain by implementing policies that help these workers find new jobs rather than by trying to preserve existing jobs.

THE PROGNOSIS FOR DEVELOPMENT

Overall, the divide between the haves and have-nots has not decreased over the past century. There have been successes, where the gap has narrowed, and failures, where it has widened. The choice of policies appears to make a difference. Some countries have adopted policies that promoted increased growth and reduced poverty. Others have pursued policies that led to some growth but had little impact on poverty (or even increased it). Still other countries seem to have stagnated or declined. Unfortunately, the prognosis is for these patterns to continue. China and India are poised to take advantage of the new economy represented by the Internet and information technologies and thereby further narrow the gap between them and the more advanced industrialized countries. But the possibility that Africa can do the same remains remote. Its current standard of living, already low, is threatened by the AIDS epidemic and continuing civil strife, conditions that make it difficult to attract foreign capital and that are not conducive even to domestic investment. As a result, the gap between Africa and the rest of the world is likely to widen.

> **Wrap-Up**
>
> ## DEVELOPMENT
>
> In LDCs, per capita income is a fraction of that enjoyed in the developed countries.
>
> The newly industrialized countries (NICs) of East Asia have achieved rapid economic growth and have closed the income gap with developed countries. China and India also appear poised to narrow the income gap. Others, particularly countries in Africa, may see the income gap widen even further.
>
> Successful development has been based on macroeconomic stability, high saving and investment (in physical and human capital), and government policies promoting financial markets, strong legal systems, and income equality.

Economies in Transition

There were two great economic experiments in the past century. The first was the move from markets to communism that began in Russia in 1917, which proved an unmitigated disaster. The second was the move from communism to a market economy, which began in Eastern Europe about 1990 and in China in the late 1990s. This second great experiment also led to disappointing outcomes in some of the countries involved. Before we can understand the reason for these failures, we have to understand the system that prevailed before the transition.

THE COMMUNIST ECONOMIC SYSTEM

Communism represented an alternative method of allocating resources to the market. Although there was variation in how the system worked from country to country, the basic system was developed in the Soviet Union, and we describe that system here. Under communism, the state owned the means of production—the factories, the land, virtually everything except each individual's personal possessions. The government established a vast bureaucracy to determine what was to be produced and how it was to be produced. It decided how many cars would be produced, how many would have two doors, how many would have four doors, and so on. Knowing how much steel would be required to produce cars, tractors, and the myriad other products using steel, the state calculated the total amount of steel required. It could then work out how much iron ore would be needed. Intricate calculations of this kind allowed it to determine how much of every good should be produced. It then worked backward, figuring out how much each plant in the country should produce. Factory managers were given production quotas—they should produce so many tons of steel, or so many nails. Factory managers also were allocated inputs with which to produce the output. This system was called **central planning.**

The Failures of Communism The central planners decided on wage levels and prices as well. Consumers did get to choose what to buy, but many commodities were *rationed.* For example, each individual was allowed to buy only so many pounds of sugar a month. Unfortunately, everything did not go according to plan. Often there were shortages, especially for consumer goods. People had to wait in line for hours to get the food they wanted every day, and they endured month-long waits for consumer durables or a car. Factories also faced shortages: they often could not get the inputs they needed. Deliveries did not occur on time, and when the materials arrived they often were of poor quality. Factories that had been told to produce nails produced nails, but they paid little attention to whether the nails were too brittle or too soft to be used. They had incentives to meet the numerical quotas set by the central planners, but no incentives to produce what others wanted. They figured out ways of getting around the system; if they had to obtain more steel to meet their quotas, they would find some firm that had been delivered more steel than it needed and make a trade. Managers traded favors with each other—various forms of barter occurred. Thus, an underground market developed.

The shortage of consumer goods was partly caused by an emphasis on *development.* In 1917, at the time of the Soviet revolution, Russia was a relatively backward country. In the 1930s, Stalin wanted to push the country forward quickly. He saw the road to success as heavy industrialization and pushed the building of steel mills and the like. The hostility throughout the world toward the Soviet Union's communist system led the country to adopt an inward-looking economic policy; the communist countries largely traded with each other. They wanted to be self-reliant.

For a while these strategies worked. The Soviet Union grew so rapidly that after World War II it became one of the world's two superpowers. It developed missiles and nuclear weapons and even sent the first man into space. By 1956, Nikita Khrushchev, then the Soviet Union's leader, could boast that his country, with communism, would bury the West, with its capitalism. Western textbooks described a trade-off between growth and freedom; they granted that the Soviet Union might be able to grow faster, but they asked whether the price, the sacrifice in freedom, was worth it.

But the Soviet Union's achievements masked growing problems in its economy: in particular, an agricultural sector that was stagnating and an industrial sector that, outside the military, could not keep up with the rapid pace of innovation in the West. The gap between living standards grew. Mikhail Gorbachev, who became the Soviet Union's leader in 1985, began a process of political and economic reforms, called *perestroika,* but events escaped his control. In 1991, popular protests stopped an attempted military coup, followed soon after by the breakup of the Soviet Union; each of the so-called republics that had constituted it became an independent state.

Wrap-Up

THE COMMUNIST SYSTEM IN THE SOVIET UNION

The government owned the means of production and determined what should be produced and how it should be produced under a system of central planning.

Because wages and prices were set by the government, they could not function to balance supply and demand. Shortages were common and many goods were rationed.

By the 1980s, the failures of Soviet agriculture and Soviet industry's inability to keep up with rapid innovation in the West led first to attempts at economic and political reform and then to the collapse of the Soviet Union.

THE MOVE TOWARD A MARKET ECONOMY

Russia and many of the other new republics quickly moved toward a market economy. They believed that replacing the inefficient central planners with markets and the price system would solve their economic woes. Private property would provide incentives. Free trade would provide competition; a supply of inputs to Russia's factories; a supply of consumer goods to Russia's consumers, who had been deprived of so much for so long; and a ready market for what Russia produced. The cornerstones of its strategy were thus *privatization* and *liberalization*—eliminating the myriad constraints that marked the Soviet system. Replacing the inefficient Soviet system thus was bound to raise living standards. The optimists thought it would happen overnight; the pessimists, that it might take six months or perhaps a year.

What happened in the next decade came as a surprise. For most of the countries, growth in the decade after the beginning of the transition was slower than growth during the decade before the transition. The economy of the former superpower has shrunk to the point where it is comparable with that of the Netherlands or Denmark. Social statistics reflect the deteriorating economic conditions: life spans are shorter, and divorce rates are higher. While 2 percent of the population was in poverty at the beginning of the transition, a decade later the number was estimated to be approaching 40 percent.

There are some exceptions to this bleak picture: Poland has a GDP today that is 50 percent higher than it was a decade ago, and China, another country making the transition from central planning to a market economy, has seen its income quadruple over the past twenty years.

What accounts for these transition successes *and* failures? To be sure, because each country began the transition in different circumstances, some had an advantage over others. Poland and several of the other Eastern European countries had a higher standard of living before becoming communist than did Russia; China had a much lower level of income. The countries of Eastern Europe had easier access to Western markets, and the lure of entry into the European Union helped speed up the reforms required for admission. Some countries, like Uzbekistan, are landlocked, a limitation that poses distinct problems. A few countries have been plagued with ethnic strife or conflicts with their neighbors (such as between Armenia and Azerbaijan). Some countries produced commodities, such as cotton and gold, that had ready markets in the West; others, accustomed to producing such goods as parts for Russian tractors or cars, found themselves with limited markets.

Gradualism Versus Shock Therapy In the beginning of the transition, many countries faced a problem of extremely high inflation. Under communism, prices were controlled at levels that were too low, and goods were thus rationed. When the restrictions were abolished, prices soared. The initial challenge for these countries was to bring this inflation under control. Many adopted a policy that was referred to as *shock therapy*—dramatic reductions in government expenditures and very tight monetary policy. This policy induced deep recessions but did manage to get inflation under control. At that point, two schools of thought developed.

The first argued for a continuation of rapid change. As they said, "You cannot cross a chasm in two jumps." They pushed for quick privatization and liberalization. After privatization, the owners of the assets would have an incentive to manage their assets well. Trade liberalization would ensure that there were competing products available from abroad, encouraging efficiency and ensuring that even if the number of firms in the domestic market was low, their ability to exercise market power would be limited.

The second argued for more gradual change. In the battle of metaphors, they pointed out that "It takes nine months even to have a baby." According to the gradualists, time was needed to establish the *institutional infrastructure* underlying a market economy, institutions without which market economies simply cannot function but that those in the West simply take for granted. Earlier, in the context of development, we noted the importance of legal and financial institutions, and a tax system must also be in place. Russia is a country rich in natural resources. Selling those resources for a pittance, or giving them away, would leave future governments coping with a shortage of revenues unless they could impose taxes on the newly privatized companies. Gradualists also argued that changes were needed not only in the economy but also in the society; change could not be imposed from above, especially in a democracy. For democratic reforms to be durable (sustainable), time was needed to change the mind-set of the people, and there would have to be demonstrated successes. The problems confronting Russia and the other countries were particularly severe because the people had been indoctrinated throughout their lives in the evils of capitalism, and because there was little "rule of law"—or at least the kinds of laws required for a market economy—on which to build.

Well-functioning markets require both competition and private property. But if both could not be obtained simultaneously, which should be stressed more? Some advocates of rapid change, like Andrei Shleifer of Harvard University, took the position that the underlying legal structure mattered little; once private property was introduced, owners would create political pressure to build the necessary institutional infrastructure. They argued that the specific recipients of the state's assets mattered little, since even if the first-round owners were not particularly efficient managers, they would have an incentive either to resell the assets to someone who was an efficient manager or to hire efficient managers.

In the end, the shock therapy approach won out in policy circles, especially in the West. The U.S. Treasury and the IMF pushed for rapid privatization and liberalization. They argued not only for eliminating trade barriers but also for opening up capital markets. Doing so, they asserted, would demonstrate to outside investors that Russia was a business-friendly place in which to invest. To be sure, they said that the institutional infrastructure was important, but they believed that this infrastructure would develop in time.

Not all the countries followed their advice. Poland and Slovenia, once their hyperinflation was contained, took a more gradualist strategy. China charted its own innovative course of development and transition, but it too was based on gradualism. The decade-long decline of Russia and most of the other countries that followed the shock therapy approach laid bare the weaknesses in this strategy, as compared to that followed by China and Poland.

A Comparison of Transition Strategies Consider some of the key differences between transition strategies in Russia and China:

- China placed more emphasis on creating jobs and enterprises than on restructuring enterprises. In China, *local* townships and villages took their savings and created millions of new enterprises. These new businesses represented a new institutional form: they were not really private, but neither were they like the old government-run, state-owned enterprises.
- China put more emphasis on competition than on privatization. In a sense, the new township and village enterprises were publicly owned, but each had to compete against the other; thus the reforms promoted efficiency. Local control and competition helped solve the *governance problem.* The old state enterprises had suffered from a lack of effective oversight. Government bureaucrats in Moscow or Beijing simply could not keep tabs on what was going on in remote provinces. By contrast, those living in the townships and villages could see clearly whether jobs were being created and their incomes were rising, and how they were faring relative to neighbors. This transparency put enormous pressure on managers.
- The gradualist approach built on existing institutions, the communes (townships and village authorities) that previously had been responsible for agriculture. But early on in the reforms, China introduced what it called the *individual responsibility system,* in which land was effectively turned over to the farmers and they reaped the benefit of their own hard work—a standard application of the conventional theory of incentives. The communes then turned their attention from agriculture to industrialization. Because the new enterprises were put in the villages and townships, there was much less social disruption than would have occurred had the industrialization been centered in urban areas. The contrast with Russia could not have been greater. There, the erosion of *social capital*—a sense of "community" and of law and order—had enormous consequences. The entire process of reform was conducted in ways that seemed unfair to the average Russian. While a few oligarchs became billionaires, the government did not pay workers and retirees what was their due. Inflation had wiped out

the value of existing savings. Mafia-like activity made it increasingly difficult for ordinary individuals to conduct business. Overall, according to a World Bank study, corruption in the region was second only to that in Africa.
- Privatization of Russia's major revenue sources at bargain-basement prices not only lent a sense of unfairness to the whole process but also, since an effective tax collection system had not been put into place, left the government continually facing a revenue shortage.

The Future of Transition The debate about the transition continues to rage. Those who led the reform in Russia and its Asian republics claim that things would have been even worse had there not been shock therapy. They are hopeful that success is "just around the corner." The critics of shock therapy say that China, Slovenia, Poland, and Hungary show that alternative approaches were possible, and that Russia would have fared better if *their* advice had been heeded. They worry about a backlash resulting from the failures—a return not to communism but to authoritarianism or nationalism—and periodic attacks on parts of the media have been unsettling. They contend that Russia's huge inequality, together with the devastation of the middle class, does not bode well for Russia's future. Only time will tell.

In many respects, China has been the most successful transition economy. It has an increasing and thriving private sector, which includes high levels of innovation in the new economy, but it faces many challenges. It has moved gradually, in part to preserve the authoritarian political control exercised by the Communist Party, and the process of democratization is just beginning. The process of restructuring the large state-owned enterprises lies largely ahead. While all parts of China have seen growth, the disparity between the richest parts, largely along the coast, and the poorer parts, in the western regions, is increasing.

Meanwhile, many of the countries of eastern Europe that were part of the Soviet Union have become part of the European Union. They are adapting their legal systems and beginning to integrate their economies with Europe's. While their transition may not be easy, for them there is a bright light at the end of the tunnel.

Wrap-Up

TRANSITION STRATEGIES

The two basic strategies the former communist countries have followed are called *gradualism* and *shock therapy*.

The more gradual reform strategy stresses the creation of competition and the development of the institutional infrastructure necessary for markets to function adequately. Countries following this strategy have fared better over the past decade than those adopting shock therapy.

Review and Practice

SUMMARY

1. In less-developed countries, or LDCs, life expectancies are usually shorter, infant mortality is higher, and people are less educated than in developed countries. Also, a larger fraction of the population lives in rural areas, and population growth rates are higher.
2. In recent years, newly industrialized countries (NICs) such as South Korea, Singapore, Hong Kong, and Taiwan have managed to improve their economic status dramatically. Other LDCs, like India, have expanded food production considerably. But the standard of living in some of the poorest LDCs, such as many African nations, has actually been declining, as population growth has outstripped economic growth.
3. Among the factors contributing to underdevelopment are lack of physical capital, lack of education, lack of technology, and lack of developed capital markets. The factors interact: low education levels impede the transfer of advanced technology; low incomes make it difficult to invest heavily in education.
4. The success of the countries of East Asia is based partially on activist government policies. These include helping to develop and use markets rather than replacing them; maintaining macroeconomic stability; promoting high levels of investment (including in public infrastructure) and saving; providing strong support for education, including the education of women; improving capital markets, which facilitate an efficient allocation of scarce capital; promoting exports; fostering equality; and promoting technology. The policies of these countries helped to create a positive investment climate (including for foreign investors) and to reduce population growth.
5. Under communism, the state was responsible for all production: central planners decided what to produce, how it was to be produced, and for whom it was to be produced. While there were some successes, especially in the system's early decades, eventually the lack of incentives, the central planners' lack of information, and the distortions that were rife in the system took their toll.
6. The transition to a market economy has not been easy. In most countries, output fell markedly and poverty increased markedly. A few countries fared well.
7. After more than ten years of transition, it now appears that the countries that rapidly brought inflation down to moderate levels, then took a more gradual approach to broader reforms—with greater emphasis on creating an institutional infrastructure, creating jobs and new enterprises, and creating competition—have done better than those that adopted a more wholesale, shock therapy approach.

KEY TERMS

less-developed countries (LDCs)
developed countries
industrialized countries
newly industrialized countries (NICs)
green revolution
sharecropping
land reform
dual economies
surplus of labor
export-led growth
globalization
outsourcing
central planning

REVIEW QUESTIONS

1. List some important ways in which LDCs differ from more-developed countries. How have different developing countries fared over recent decades?
2. What are the most important factors inhibiting growth in the LDCs? Why is capital shortage *alone* not the most important factor? How do some of the factors interact with each other?
3. How does rapid population growth make it more difficult for a country's standard of living to increase?
4. What are some of the factors that contributed to the East Asian miracle?
5. Why might fostering equality promote economic growth?

6. What are some of the roles that government can play in promoting economic development and growth?
7. How were resources allocated under the former Soviet (communist) system?
8. What were some of the problems with the communist system, and why was the switch to a market economy expected to lead to increased incomes?
9. What were two of the different strategies for moving from communism to a market economy?
10. How have different countries fared in the transition? How do you explain the different performances?

PROBLEMS

1. In the United States, the economy grew by 2.6 percent per year (in real terms) during the 1980s. In India, the economy grew by 5.3 percent during the 1980s. However, population growth in the United States was 0.8 percent annually, while population growth in India was 2.1 percent annually. Which country increased its standard of living faster for the average citizen? By how much?
2. Nominal GNP in Kenya was 9 billion shillings in 1967 and 135 billion shillings in 1987. The price level in Kenya (using 1980 as a base year) rose from 40 in 1967 to 200 in 1987, and the population of Kenya increased from 10 million to 22 million in those twenty years. What was the total percentage change in real GNP per capita in Kenya from 1967 to 1987?
3. True or false: "LDCs do not have much capital because their rates of saving are low. If they saved more or received more foreign aid, they could rapidly expand their economic growth." Discuss.
4. How might each of the following hinder entrepreneurs in LDCs?
   (a) Lack of functioning capital markets
   (b) Pervasive government control of the economy
   (c) Lack of companies that offer business services
   (d) A tradition of substantial foreign control of large enterprises
5. What is the economist's case for having the government be responsible for providing infrastructure?
6. If many LDCs simultaneously attempted to pursue export-led growth, what would be the effect in world markets on the quantities and prices of products sold mainly by LDCs, such as minerals, agricultural goods, and textiles? What effect might these quantities and prices have on the success of such export-led growth policies?
7. Explain how the idea of import substitution conflicts in the short run with the idea of comparative advantage. Need the two ideas conflict in the long run? Why or why not?
8. Why might a family in an LDC face a lower opportunity cost of having more children than a family in a developed country?

Part 9
FURTHER TOPICS IN MACROECONOMICS

Learning Goals

In this chapter, you will learn

1. What the short-run Phillips curve is and why it shifts
2. The three factors that affect inflation
3. The short-run inflation–unemployment trade-off and the role of expectations

Chapter 37

INFLATION AND UNEMPLOYMENT

During the 1970s, the most pressing macroeconomic policy issue facing industrialized economies was inflation. Despite repeated attempts to reduce it, inflation remained stubbornly high throughout the decade. Figure 37.1 shows the inflation rates for the United States, Japan, and western Europe. All display roughly similar patterns. Inflation had remained relatively low during the 1960s, but it jumped to much higher levels in the following decade.

To understand how governments might control inflation, we need to understand what causes inflation. How do we explain why some countries have higher rates of inflation than others? What are the costs of reducing inflation? Why do the United States and most other industrialized economies have lower inflation rates today than they did twenty-five years ago? And why do some countries continue to suffer from high rates of inflation?

We have already learned about the costs of inflation in Chapter 23. Many of these costs are associated with *variability* in inflation rates. Countries that experience high average inflation also experience greater inflation variability than do countries with low average inflation. It is this unpredictability that can impose large costs on the economy. When inflation turns out to be higher than anticipated, lenders lose as the dollars they receive are worth less than the dollars they lent; borrowers gain since the dollars they repay are worth less than the dollars they borrowed. Conversely, if inflation turns out to be lower than anticipated, borrowers lose and lenders gain. The possibility of these unanticipated gains and losses increases uncertainty and the general level of risk in the economy. We also learned in Chapter 23 that inflation imposes further costs on the economy as individuals devote resources to trying to avoid its costs.

If inflation disrupts the economy, why don't governments simply get rid of it? The answer is that normally, inflation can be reduced only at a cost—only if the unemployment rate is allowed to increase temporarily. This chapter looks at that short-run trade-off. Most economists believe that in the long run, there is no trade-off—the full-employment model shows that once real wages have adjusted, the economy will be at full employment, no matter what the rate of inflation might be.

In Chapter 31 we assumed that inflation rises and falls as the economy moves above or below potential GDP. The adjustment of inflation played a critical role in eventually moving the economy to full employment. In this chapter, we will examine the foundations of inflation adjustment in more detail. Three factors are important for explaining how inflation varies over time. First, while wages do not adjust quickly to keep demand equal to supply, they do respond over time whenever demand does not equal supply. Increases in cyclical unemployment lead to lower inflation; decreases in cyclical unemployment lead to higher inflation. Second, wages and prices depend on workers' and firms' expectations about inflation. For example, if workers expect prices to rise faster, they will demand higher wage increases. An increase in *expected* inflation leads to an increase in *actual* inflation. Third, economies occasionally experience inflation shocks—increases in costs such as the dramatic rise in oil prices of the 1970s. We will see that increases in inflation expectations or inflation shocks that boost actual inflation force policymakers to make difficult trade-offs.

Short-Run Inflation Adjustment

The framework for thinking about how demand and supply pressures influence the rate of change of wages is summarized in a famous relationship called the **Phillips**

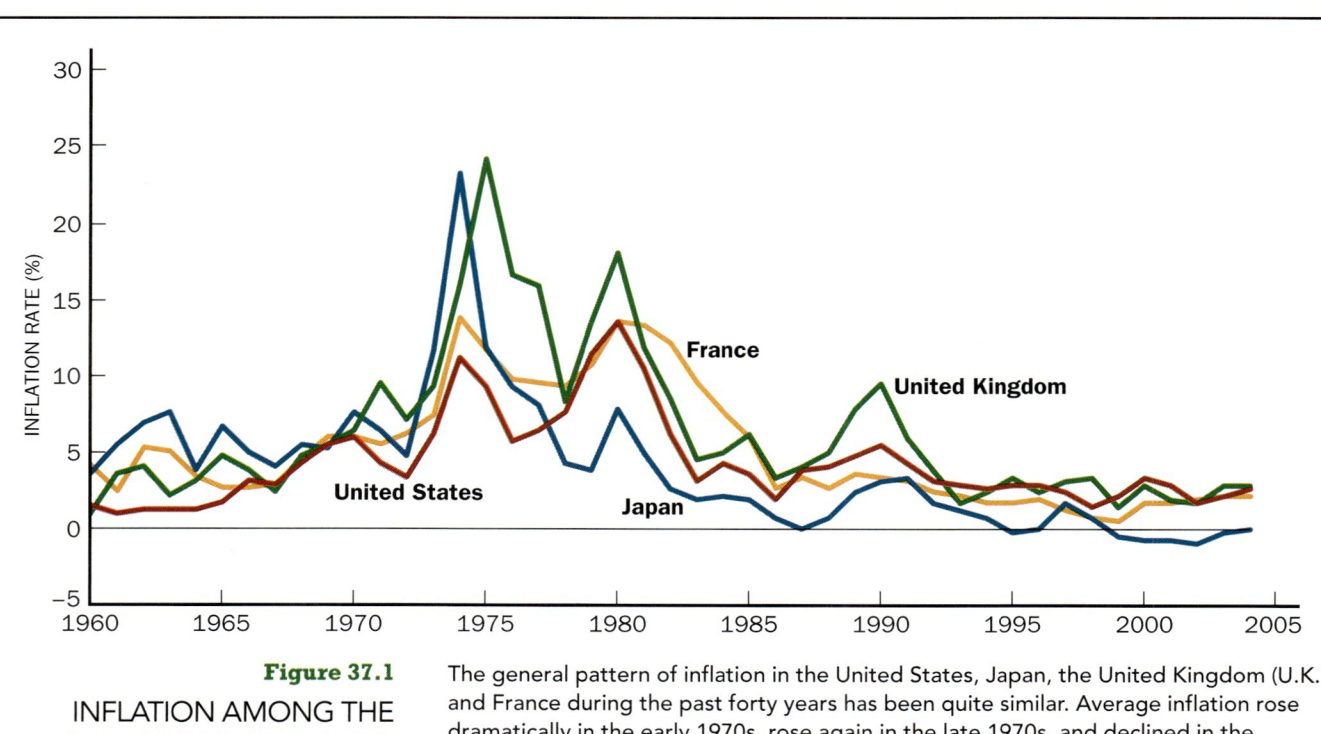

Figure 37.1

INFLATION AMONG THE MAJOR INDUSTRIALIZED ECONOMIES

The general pattern of inflation in the United States, Japan, the United Kingdom (U.K.), and France during the past forty years has been quite similar. Average inflation rose dramatically in the early 1970s, rose again in the late 1970s, and declined in the early 1980s.

SOURCE: International Financial Statistics (2005).

curve. A. W. Phillips was a New Zealander who taught economics in England during the 1950s. He examined data from England on unemployment and the rate of increases in nominal or money wages. He found a negative relationship between the two, and this relationship is known as the *Phillips curve*. At higher unemployment rates, money wages rose more slowly. At lower unemployment rates, money wages rose more quickly. The relationship he found is shown in Figure 37.2.

The logic behind the Phillips curve is straightforward. If unemployment is low, firms have greater difficulty hiring workers. The result is upward pressure on wages, as firms attempt to attract workers by paying more. If unions and firms negotiate over wages, the union will be in a stronger bargaining position, better able to get larger wage increases, if labor markets are "tight." At low unemployment rates, workers are more likely to decide that the time is right to look for another job. Firms that do not keep pace with wage increases elsewhere may discover that their best workers are leaving. If workers believe that finding another job will be easy, they may worry less about being fired. As a consequence, they may not work as hard. To maintain worker productivity, firms will need to raise wages more rapidly. In contrast, if unemployment is high, there will be little upward pressure on real wages. Money wages will increase more slowly or even decrease for some workers.

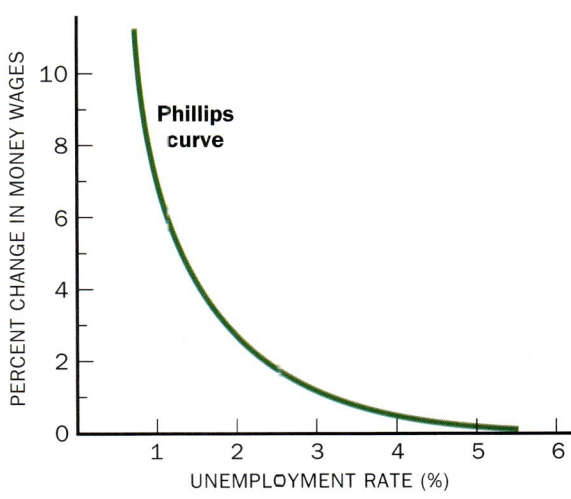

Figure 37.2

THE ORIGINAL PHILLIPS CURVE

The Phillips curve shows that the rate of wage growth rises as the unemployment rate falls. The curve shown here is the one Phillips plotted in 1958 for the British economy.

From Wages to Prices The Phillips curve relates unemployment to the rate at which wages are changing. The bigger the imbalance between labor demand and labor supply, the faster money wages will change.

The link between the rate at which wages are changing and the rate at which prices are changing—the rate of inflation—is direct. Labor costs are, for most businesses, the major component of their costs of production. In competitive markets, prices will move in tandem with marginal costs, and an increase in wages will translate directly into an increase in the marginal costs of production. Some firms, at least in the short run, use a simple rule of thumb in setting prices—they set price as a given markup over costs (e.g., 120 percent of costs). Under that system, changes in the rate at which wages are changing will translate directly into changes in the rate of inflation. Figure 37.3 shows the close historical relationship between the two.

Because they move together, we can replace the rate of nominal wage increase on the vertical axis of the Phillips curve with the rate of inflation. Even though Phillips himself originally studied the behavior of unemployment and wages, it is more common today to see Phillips curves that have the inflation rate on the vertical axis. We will adopt this practice from now on when we use the Phillips curve.

The Phillips Curve and Cyclical Unemployment The relation between inflation and unemployment that Phillips found for the United Kingdom also has been found for other countries. Figure 37.4, which shows inflation and unemployment for the United States during different periods, reveals an important fact. The Phillips curve seems to shift. During periods of relative low inflation, such as 1960 to 1969 and 1984 to 2003, the inflation-unemployment relation is closer to the origin

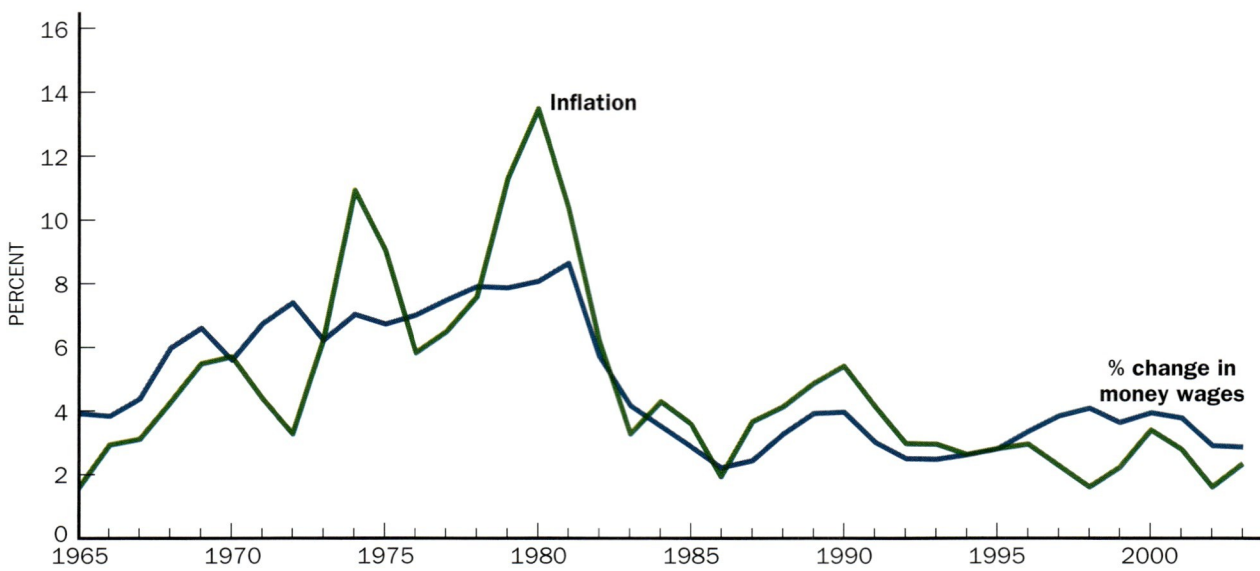

Figure 37.3

THE RATE OF WAGE INCREASE AND INFLATION MOVE TOGETHER

The original Phillips curve related the rate of wage increase to the rate of unemployment. Because the rate of increase in money wages moves closely with the overall rate of inflation, we also use the Phillips curve to relate inflation to the rate of cyclical unemployment.

SOURCE: *Economic Report of the President* (2004), Tables B-47, B-64.

than it was during the high inflation period from 1974 to 1983. In other words, the relationship between inflation and unemployment is not stable. Understanding why the Phillips curve shifts is a primary objective of this chapter. To explain these shifts, economists draw on the concept of the natural rate of unemployment and the role of expectations.

The Natural Rate of Unemployment There are reasons why unemployment is always positive. Not every worker is qualified to do every job. When there is unemployment of autoworkers and excess demand for computer programmers, unemployment in Detroit and vacancies in Seattle occur at the same time. In Chapter 22, we referred to this type of unemployment as *structural*. By the same token, there will always be some workers moving between jobs. This latter type of unemployment is referred to as *frictional* unemployment. Structural and frictional unemployment account for positive unemployment even at full employment. The unemployment rate that occurs at full employment, when the economy is producing at potential output, is usually called the **natural rate of unemployment.**

The pressures on wages that lead to increases or decreases in inflation are produced by *cyclical* unemployment—that is, fluctuations in total unemployment around the natural rate. When output is below potential so that cyclical unemployment is positive, total unemployment exceeds the natural rate of unemployment. Labor markets are slack, and wages rise more slowly. When output rises above potential output, then total unemployment falls below the natural rate, labor markets are

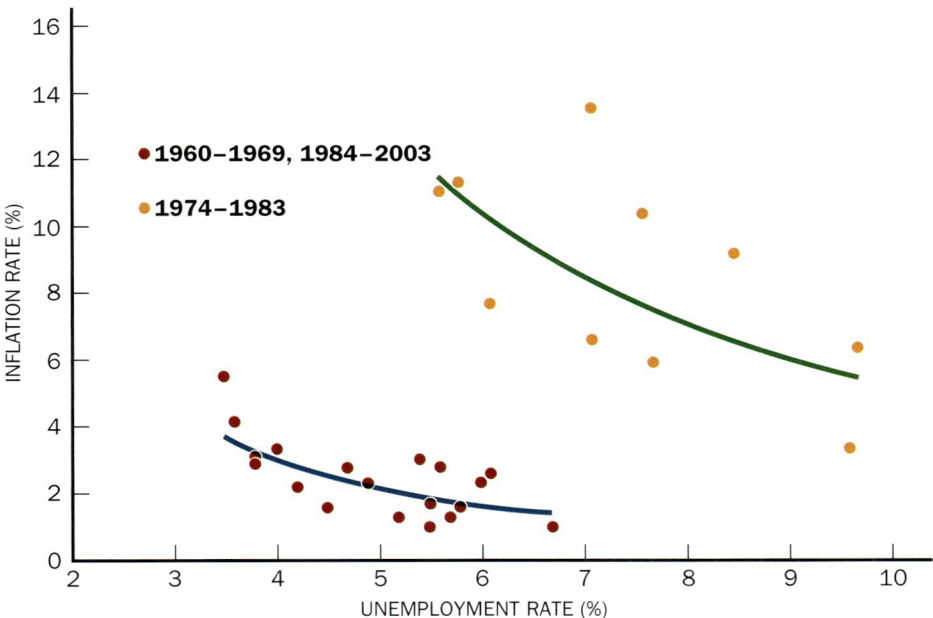

Figure 37.4

THE PHILLIPS CURVE FOR THE UNITED STATES

The figure depicts the Phillips curve relationship for the United States during different periods. Notice that the Phillips curve has shifted over time.

SOURCE: *Economic Report of the President* (2004).

tight, and wages rise more rapidly. It is the rate of cyclical unemployment, not the total level of unemployment, that best measures the inflationary pressures in the economy.

In Chapter 31, we combined the aggregate demand–inflation (ADI) curve with an inflation adjustment (IA) line. We drew the IA line as a horizontal line at the economy's current rate of inflation. If equilibrium output rose above or fell below full-employment output, we shifted the IA line to reflect the changes in inflation over time. The horizontal IA line provided a starting point for understanding how fluctuations in the economy can cause inflation to rise or fall. Now we can use our knowledge of the Phillips curve to elaborate on the relationship between output and inflation. As output expands and unemployment falls below the natural rate, inflation will rise. The resulting relationship between output and inflation is called the **short-run inflation adjustment (SRIA) curve**. It is shown as the green line in Figure 37.5. In the figure, Y^f is the economy's potential level of output. If actual output rises above potential, say to Y_1, unemployment falls below the natural rate and wages rise more rapidly. Higher wages increase the costs of production for firms, and prices rise more rapidly. Because the inflation rate increases to π_1, the short-run inflation adjustment curve in Figure 37.5 is drawn with a positive slope, rather than as a horizontal line.

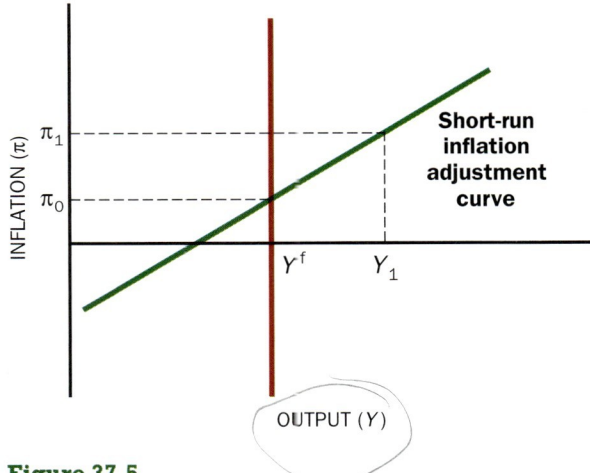

Figure 37.5

THE INFLATION ADJUSTMENT CURVE

Increases in output above potential lead to higher inflation. Y^f is potential output. If the economy expands from Y^f to Y_1, inflation rises from π_0 to π_1. The expansion in output causes unemployment to fall below the natural rate. The result is that wages increase faster, and inflation rises.

> ### Wrap-Up
>
> ## INFLATION AND CYCLICAL UNEMPLOYMENT
>
> The *natural rate of unemployment* is the unemployment rate when the economy is at potential GDP and cyclical unemployment is zero.
>
> The *short-run inflation adjustment (SRIA) curve* shows the rate of inflation at each level of output relative to potential GDP, for a given expected rate of inflation.
>
> The SRIA curve has a positive slope. If output increases above potential, inflation increases. If output falls below potential, inflation falls.

THE ROLE OF EXPECTATIONS: SHIFTS IN THE SHORT-RUN INFLATION ADJUSTMENT CURVE

Figure 37.4 illustrated a second characteristic of the relationship between unemployment and inflation—the relationship does not seem to be stable. It has shifted over time. Though the relationship between cyclical unemployment and inflation was stable in the 1960s, that stability disappeared in the 1970s. The U.S. economy experienced high unemployment *and* high inflation. *Stagflation* was the term coined to describe this undesirable situation. High inflation occurred while output was below potential. At other times, output was above potential, yet inflation was low. The SRIA curve is not stable.

There is a simple explanation for this instability: the level of cyclical unemployment is not the only factor that affects wages. For one thing, expectations of inflation also matter. Take the case of a union contract. If workers and firms expect that inflation will be 3 percent per year over the life of the contract, then the nominal wage called for in the contract will rise 3 percent per year even if the negotiated real wage remains constant. Employers are willing to let the nominal wage increase, because they believe they will be able to sell what they produce at higher prices.

If unemployment is low and people are expecting inflation, wages may rise even faster than is necessary simply to offset expected inflation. When unemployment is low and output above potential, workers enjoy better job prospects and are more likely to quit to take better jobs, while firms will find it harder to hire replacements. Wages will rise faster as firms try both to prevent their existing workers from leaving and to attract new workers. If an inflation rate of 3 percent is expected, nominal wages might rise at 5 percent per year (3 percent to compensate for increases in the cost of living and 2 percent because labor markets are tight). If workers and firms expect a much higher rate of inflation, say, 10 percent, then low unemployment may lead money wages to rise at 12 percent per year (10 percent to compensate for the rising cost of living, plus 2 percent because labor markets are tight).

Because expectations of inflation affect actual inflation, the SRIA curve shows the relationship between output (relative to potential) and inflation, *for a given expected rate of inflation*. This is represented diagrammatically in Figure 37.6. A vertical line is drawn at the level of full-employment output Y^f to indicate that Y^f does not depend on the rate of inflation. The position of the SRIA curve depends on the level of expected inflation. Because it includes inflationary expectations, we refer to it as the *expectations-augmented SRIA curve.*

To better understand the role of the natural rate of unemployment, consider how expectations about inflation are affected both by recent experience and by anticipated changes in policy and economic conditions. Take the simple case of **adaptive expectations**[1]—that is, expectations that respond or adapt to recent experience. Assume an economy in which prices have been stable for an extended period of time. Given this historical experience, workers and firms expect zero inflation. The SRIA curve is represented in Figure 37.6 by the curve labeled "Expected inflation = 0." Suppose the government reduces unemployment below the natural rate by expanding output above potential (where actual inflation equals expected inflation). In the short run, the actual inflation rate rises to π_1. With actual inflation now positive, workers and firms will not continue to expect zero inflation. They will come to expect positive inflation. If they now expect inflation to be π_1, the expectations-augmented SRIA curve shifts up, so there will be a higher rate of inflation at each level of output. The new SRIA curve is labeled "Expected inflation = π_1" in Figure 37.6. If the government continues to maintain output above Y^f, inflation will rise to π_2. Now workers and firms will start to expect inflation at the rate π_2, and this higher expected inflation will be incorporated into wage- and price-setting behavior. The expectations-augmented SRIA curve shifts up again as shown in Figure 37.6 by the curve labeled "Expected inflation = π_2." Inflation rises further.

We can now understand why the data on unemployment and inflation for the United States shown in Figure 37.4 seem to shift over time. The 1960–1969 period was one of low average inflation. The data from this period show the negatively sloped relationship between inflation and unemployment that is implied by the SRIA curve. Both inflation and expected inflation were much higher from 1974 to 1983. The SRIA curve in that period shifted up, as can be seen in Figure 37.4. Finally, the period since 1984 has seen much lower inflation and reductions in inflationary expectations. Declines in expected inflation have shifted the SRIA curve again—this time in, toward the origin, as our analysis predicts.

The recognition that the SRIA curve shifts as inflationary expectations change brings us to an important conclusion: *When output remains above potential (the unemployment rate remains below the natural rate of unemployment), the rate of inflation increases; when it remains below potential (the unemployment rate remains above the natural rate), inflation decreases. An economy cannot keep its unemployment rate below the natural rate without facing ever-increasing rates of inflation.* An economy cannot "buy" higher output and lower unemployment by accepting a slightly higher (but stable) inflation rate.

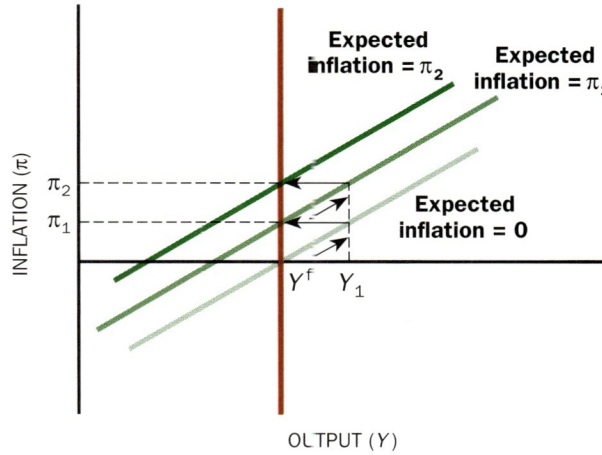

Figure 37.6

SHORT-RUN INFLATION ADJUSTMENT CURVES AND INFLATION EXPECTATIONS

Increases in output above potential lead to higher inflation for a given expected rate of inflation. Suppose expected inflation is initially equal to zero and the economy is at potential output Y^f. The SRIA curve is labeled "Expected inflation = 0." If output increases to Y_1, inflation rises to π_1. If workers and firms now expect an inflation rate of π_1, the SRIA curve shifts up, increasing the inflation rate associated with any given output. If output were to remain at Y_1, inflation would rise to π_2. The SRIA curve therefore shifts up again as expectations adjust to the new, higher rate of inflation. Inflation will be stable only when output is equal to potential.

---

[1]Expectations are called *adaptive* if they respond to recent experience. Adaptive expectations are also called *backward-looking,* since they respond to actual past experience. *Forward-looking expectations* respond to anticipated future developments.

Thinking Like an Economist
DISTRIBUTIONAL EFFECTS OF INFLATION AND UNEMPLOYMENT

Inflation and cyclical unemployment impose macroeconomic costs on the economy. Each does so by affecting the lives of millions of individuals. However, not everyone is affected equally. Even when cyclical unemployment reaches very high levels, as it did during the 1982 recession, only a small fraction of the total labor force bears the direct hardship of losing a job, and the burden does not fall evenly on different groups in the population. For example, unemployment rates differ significantly by race and age in the United States. Even during the long expansion of the 1990s, unemployment rates for blacks remained about double the overall rate and more than double the rate for whites (see figure). Young workers experience much higher rates of unemployment than do older workers. For young black workers, the unemployment rate exceeded 30 percent in 2003. The overall labor force has not experienced that level of unemployment since the Great Depression of the 1930s.

The figure shows three recessionary periods—1982–1984, 1990–1991, and 2001. All unemployment rates rise during recessions and fall during expansions. And as Christina and David Romer of the University of California, Berkeley, have recently documented, increases in unemployment are positively related to increases in the fraction of the population living in poverty.

The other macroeconomic problem—inflation—also influences the distribution of well-being in the economy, although its effects on the poorest households seem to be small. As we learned in Chapter 23, inflation, particularly if it is unexpected, redistributes wealth from creditors to debtors. Those who have borrowed funds are able to repay in dollars whose value has fallen as a result of inflation. Romer and Romer found, however, that inflation has little actual effect on the financial conditions of the poorest households. The reason for this is straightforward: the poor have few financial assets or liabilities.

SOURCE: Christina Romer and David Romer, "Monetary Policy and the Well-Being of the Poor," *Economic Review* (Federal Reserve Bank of Kansas City), 84 (1999): 21–49.

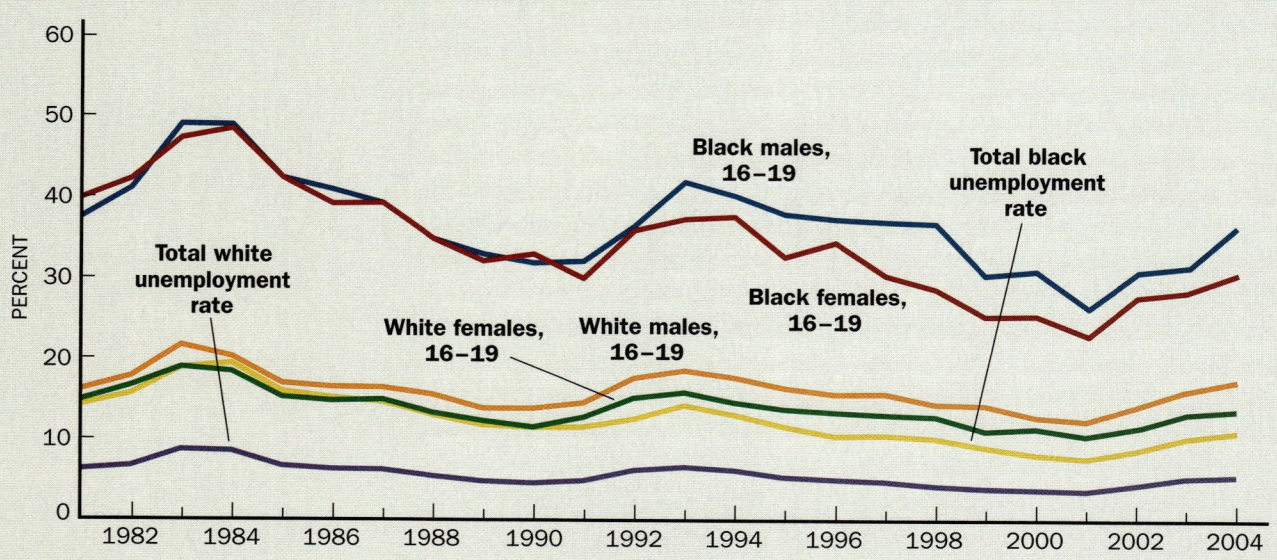

UNEMPLOYMENT RATES

SOURCE: *Economic Report of the President* (2004).

An important implication of this conclusion is a consensus belief about macroeconomic policy: governments should not try to use macroeconomic policies to maintain the unemployment rate below the natural rate or output above potential. Expansionary policies will temporarily lower unemployment and boost income, but eventually unemployment returns to the natural rate. Thus, the policy question is whether the *temporary* fall in unemployment is worth the potential cost of higher inflation.

A key issue for policymakers is identifying the natural rate of unemployment and potential GDP in a dynamic economy. At one time, economists thought the natural rate was around 6 percent. Unemployment rates below that level were expected to lead to increases in the inflation rate. When the unemployment rate fell below 6 percent in 1995 and below 5 percent in 1997 without causing inflation to rise, economists needed to reassess their estimates. We will discuss shifts in the natural rate later in this chapter.

Wrap-Up

BASICS OF INFLATION ADJUSTMENT

Short-run inflation adjustment (SRIA) curve: shows the relationship between inflation and output *for given inflation expectations;* the higher that output is, relative to potential, the higher the inflation rate.

Expectations-augmented SRIA curve: the SRIA curve with expectations of inflation explicitly incorporated. The level of inflation associated with any level of output depends on expectations concerning inflation; the higher the inflationary expectations, the higher the level of inflation associated with any level of output. As inflationary expectations increase, the SRIA curve shifts up.

Case in Point

NOBEL VIEWS ON INFLATION AND UNEMPLOYMENT

Our understanding of the shifting relationship between unemployment and inflation owes much to the contributions of Milton Friedman and Robert Lucas, the 1976 and 1995 winners of the Nobel Prize in Economics. Friedman and Lucas are two of the giants of monetary economics. Friedman is most widely known for his emphasis on the role of monetary policy as a force in shaping the course of inflation and business cycles. He is best known to the lay public for his advocacy of free markets. Lucas is probably unfamiliar to most noneconomists, but like Friedman, he has made fundamental contributions to the study of money, inflation, and business cycles.

Milton Friedman, Nobel Laureate, 1976

During the 1960s, most economists believed that a stable Phillips curve allowed lower average unemployment rates to be achieved if one were willing to accept a permanently higher (but stable) rate of inflation. Friedman argued that such a trade-off could not persist. Expanding the economy to lower unemployment would lead to increases in nominal wages as firms attempted to attract additional workers. Firms would be willing to pay higher nominal wages if they expected prices for their output to be higher in the future owing to the economic expansion. Workers would recognize that inflation had increased, and would therefore demand more rapid wage increases. Inflation would not stabilize at a higher level but would continue to increase. Inflation would remain stable only when the economy returned to its natural rate of unemployment.

Most economists have followed Friedman in accepting that there is no long-run trade-off that would permanently allow lower unemployment to be traded for higher inflation. This acceptance can be attributed in part to the contributions of Lucas, who demonstrated the striking implications of assuming individuals formed their expectations rationally. He stressed the forward-looking nature of expectations. Expectations of a future economic expansion could immediately raise expectations of inflation, shifting up the Phillips curve. Inflation would rise without even a temporary decline in unemployment.

This chapter has shown how experiences with inflation lead individuals to revise their expectations concerning inflation, a change that shifts the short-run Phillips curve. But Lucas emphasized that workers in their wage bargains and firms in their price-setting behavior can also be forward-looking—they can anticipate inflation and thereby shift the short-run Phillips curve even before the inflation is actually experienced. For instance, if the government were to announce its intention to change its target for inflation, many individuals might adjust their inflation expectations.

These expectations-driven shifts can be both good news and bad news for the economy. On the one hand, inflation can pick up quite quickly—even when the economy has an unemployment rate above the natural rate, expectations that future inflation will be higher can push up inflation immediately. The good news is that inflation can be brought down quite quickly as well by this mechanism, without a period of painful unemployment.

Friedman argued that the growing evidence for the instability of the vintage Phillips curve for the 1960s was instrumental in forcing the profession to adjust its thinking. As Friedman put it, "The drastic change that has occurred in accepted professional views was produced primarily by the scientific response to experience that contradicted a tentatively accepted hypothesis—precisely the classical process for the revision of a scientific hypothesis."[2]

The insights of Friedman and Lucas continue to guide developments in macroeconomics. Their work on the links between inflation and unemployment has influenced the course of economic theory *and* the most practical of policy discussions. For example, Lucas's theory of rational expectations stresses the role of credibility in the conduct of monetary policy. This emphasis continues to have a major impact on policy discussions.

Robert Lucas, Nobel Laureate, 1995

[2] Milton Friedman, "Nobel Lecture: Inflation and Unemployment," *Journal of Political Economy* 185 (1977): 451–472.

Internet Connection

WINNERS OF THE NOBEL PRIZE IN ECONOMICS

You can learn more about the research contributions of Milton Friedman, Robert Lucas, and other winners of the Nobel Prize in Economic Sciences at www.almaz.com/nobel/economics/economics.html.

SHIFTS IN THE NATURAL RATE

Though the *concept* of the natural rate of unemployment is well accepted, economists do differ in their judgments of the critical level of unemployment below which inflation increases. Because the natural rate itself may vary over time, our estimates of it are quite imprecise. In the late 1980s, most economists thought it was around 6 percent or slightly higher. As the unemployment rate fell to 5.6 percent in 1995, then to 5.4 percent in 1996, and eventually to 3.9 percent in 2000 without evidence that inflation was increasing, more and more economists believed the natural rate had decreased. Today, few economists believe the evidence is strong enough to yield a precise value; the best that can be done is to identify a range of plausible values. Most current estimates of the natural rate fall in the range of 5 to 5.5 percent.

Some of the changes in the natural rate are predictable. There is always some frictional unemployment, as people move from job to job. Such movements are more common among new entrants into the labor force; in the 1970s, these were numerous as the baby boomers reached working age and as more women began working outside the home. As a result, the natural rate increased. In the 1990s, these trends reversed themselves, partially accounting for the decline in the natural rate of unemployment. Government policies to help workers move quickly from one job to another may lower the natural rate. Similarly, because competitive pressures have increased and unionization has decreased, wages more frequently fall and are slower to rise. This change too has helped lower the natural rate.

Case in Point

THE BABY BOOMERS AND THE NATURAL RATE

The natural rate of unemployment is not a constant. One reason it changes is that the demographics of the labor force change over time. The prime example of the role of demographics is provided by the effect of the baby boomers.

We have focused on the overall unemployment rate, the fraction of the total civilian labor force that is unemployed. However, not all groups in the labor force experience the same unemployment rate. Teenagers, for example, have much higher unemployment rates than older workers. At the end of 2000, while the overall unemployment rate averaged only 4 percent, the rate for females sixteen to nineteen years old was 11 percent; for teenage males, over 13 percent. In contrast, the unemployment rates for older workers were much lower.

These differences in the unemployment experiences of different age groups have important implications for the total unemployment rate when the age distribution of the population is changing. The total unemployment rate is equal to a weighted average of the unemployment rates of different age groups. The weight placed on the unemployment rate of teenagers, say, will equal the number of teenagers in the labor force as a fraction of the total labor force. So if teenage workers represent 6 percent of the total labor force, as they did in 2000, the teenage unemployment rate will receive a weight of .06 (6 percent) in calculating the overall unemployment rate.

Because teenagers experience higher rates of unemployment, a change in the age distribution can alter the overall unemployment rate. This is exactly what happened in the 1960s, when the post–World War II baby boom generation started entering the labor force. Their entry boosted the natural rate; the same labor market conditions resulted in a higher measured overall unemployment rate because there were more young workers than previously. One recent estimate concluded that the baby boomers added 1.8 percent to the unemployment rate between 1959 and 1980. As boomers aged, they entered periods of life typically associated with low unemployment rates. This effect has cut almost 1.5 percent off the overall unemployment rate since 1980.

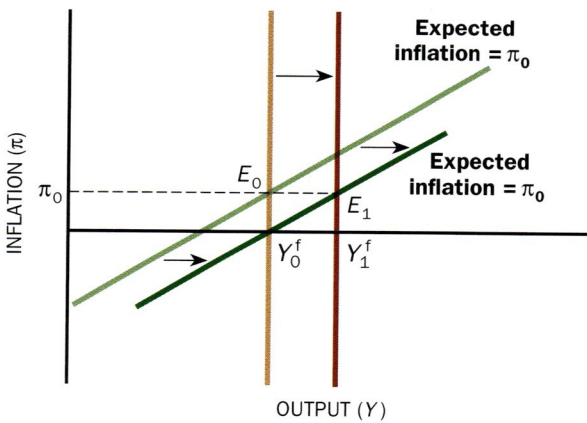

Figure 37.7

THE POSITION OF THE SRIA CURVE WILL SHIFT IF POTENTIAL GDP SHIFTS

An increase in the economy's potential GDP will shift the SRIA curve. In the figure, the economy is initially at point E_0 at full employment (output equals potential) and at an inflation rate of π_0 that is fully incorporated into expectations. If potential output rises from Y_0^f to Y_1^f, the SRIA curve then goes through the point E_1, where expected inflation and actual inflation are equal and output is at the new level of potential GDP.

SHIFTS IN POTENTIAL GDP

The inflation adjustment curve relates inflation to the state of the economy, measured by a comparison of actual output with potential output: the output gap. Positive output gaps—output levels above potential—accompany unemployment rates below the natural rate. Negative output gaps—output levels below potential—accompany unemployment rates above the natural rate. Just as measuring cyclical unemployment is difficult because the natural rate can shift, measuring the output gap is difficult because the economy's potential output level can shift.

Figure 37.7 shows the impact of an increase in potential output on the inflation adjustment curve. Initially, the economy's potential GDP is Y_0^f. Vertical lines are drawn at Y_0^f and Y_1^f to remind us that full-employment output does not depend on the inflation rate. If inflationary expectations are equal to π_0, the SRIA curve is positively sloped and goes through the point E_0. If potential increases to Y_1^f, the SRIA curve shifts to the right, going through the point E_1, since actual inflation and expected inflation are equal when the economy is at potential.

INFLATION SHOCKS

During 1973 and again in 1979, there were major increases in the price of oil. In 1973, supplies of oil to the United States were disrupted by the oil embargo imposed by the Organization of Petroleum Exporting Countries (OPEC) as a result of the 1973 Arab-Israeli War. The sharp increases in inflation caused by these oil price increases are clearly visible in Figure 37.1. As this experience suggests, other factors besides cyclical unemployment and expectations influence inflation.

The basic relationship between output and inflation that we summarized in the inflation adjustment curve started with the Phillips curve relationship between cyclical unemployment and wage increases. We then argued that wages and prices move in tandem, and thus the SRIA curve links cyclical unemployment and inflation. While Figure 37.3 shows that wages and prices generally move together, it also shows that inflation exceeded wage increases at the time of the oil price shocks. The oil price changes altered the relationship between wages and prices.

The reason is straightforward. Wages are a large part of the costs that firms face. But firms have other important costs as well, and the cost of the energy involved in producing is one of them. For a given increase in wages, prices will rise more as these other costs rise. The oil price hikes of the 1970s increased inflation relative to wages, as shown in Figure 37.3. Such events are called **inflation shocks,** and they produce temporary shifts in the SRIA curve. For given inflation expectations and output, a positive inflation shock increases the actual rate of inflation.

Some economists have argued that the late 1990s were a repeat of the 1970s but in reverse. That is, the United States was again hit by an inflation shock—but this time, a negative shock that temporarily shifted the SRIA curve down. Inflation was lower at each level of output. Put another way, we can say that inflation was lower at each level of cyclical unemployment. Two pieces of evidence are consistent with this interpretation. First, if we again look back to Figure 37.3, we see that just as inflation was pushed above the rate of wage increases by the positive inflation shocks of the 1970s, so during the 1990s inflation fell below wage increases. Second, at the end of the 1990s, unemployment plummeted. In April 2000, for example, the overall jobless rate fell to 3.9 percent, the lowest level since 1970. Despite this evidence of tight labor markets, inflation had not increased, as the SRIA curve would imply should happen. This stability, too, might indicate that the economy was experiencing a negative inflation shock.

Fundamentals of Inflation

CYCLICAL UNEMPLOYMENT

Movements in cyclical unemployment cause fluctuations in the rate of wage growth relative to productivity growth. In tight labor markets, wages will rise more rapidly; in periods of high unemployment, wage growth will slow and wages may decline. These fluctuations in firms' wage costs are passed through into prices and lead to fluctuations in the rate of inflation. As a consequence, fluctuations in the output gap will be positively associated with fluctuations in the rate of inflation.

EXPECTATIONS

Wage and price decisions will be influenced by the expectations about inflation that are held by individuals and firms. If higher inflation is expected, wage growth will rise, leading to an increase in actual inflation. This happens because workers and firms are concerned with real wages, and nominal wages must increase faster to maintain real wages when inflation is higher.

INFLATION SHOCKS

Factors such as oil price changes that affect the cost of production will lead to fluctuations in the rate of inflation. When oil prices increase, firms pass the higher cost on to consumers by raising prices.

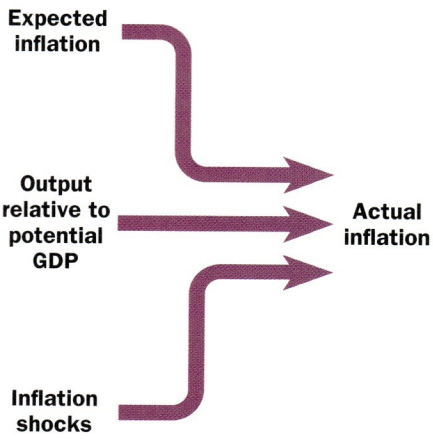

Combining the Aggregate Demand–Inflation and Inflation Adjustment Curves

The SRIA curve summarizes the impact of cyclical unemployment and the output gap—the difference between output and potential GDP—on inflation for given inflation expectations. The aggregate demand–inflation curve developed in Chapter 31 summarizes the short-run impact of inflation on real interest rates, aggregate expenditures, and equilibrium output. Putting the two together enables us to understand the factors that determine both output *and* inflation in the short run.

Equilibrium in the short run occurs where the ADI and SRIA curves intersect. Figure 37.8 adds the ADI curve to Figure 37.7. The initial SRIA curve is drawn for an expected inflation rate equal to π_0. In the situation depicted, the short-run equilibrium occurs at point E_1 with output equal to Y_1 and inflation equal to π_1. Two aspects of this short-run equilibrium are important to note. First, the economy is producing at an output level above potential (Y^f). Second, the inflation rate π_1 is greater than people had expected.

The economy will not remain at point E_1, however, because inflation is now higher than people had expected. Inflation expectations will rise. As we learned in this chapter, a rise in inflation expectations causes the SRIA curve to shift up. As the SRIA curve shifts up, the economy's equilibrium moves along the ADI curve (shown by the arrow). Inflation continues to rise and output falls. This movement along the ADI curve involves rising interest rates. As inflation expectations rise, so does actual inflation. In response to rising inflation, the Fed raises interest rates and aggregate expenditures fall. Equilibrium output declines toward the full-employment level. Eventually, full-employment output is reached at an inflation rate of π_2. At this point, equilibrium output is equal to Y^f (so the economy is on its ADI curve) and both actual inflation and expected inflation are equal to π_2.

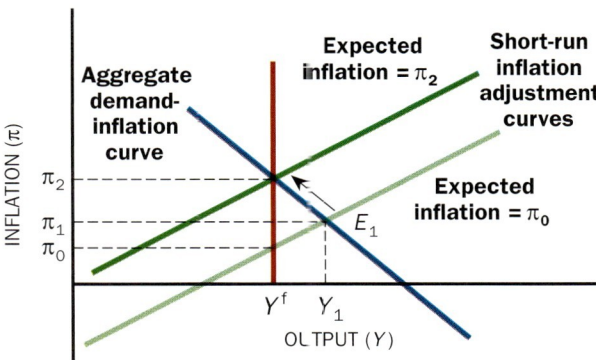

Figure 37.8

COMBINING THE ADI AND SRIA CURVES

The economy's short-run equilibrium is at the point where the ADI and SRIA curves intersect: E_1, in this figure. At E_1 output is above potential and inflation exceeds expected inflation. As people revise upward their expectations of inflation, the SRIA curve shifts up. Eventually, output returns to Y^f at an inflation rate equal to π_2. At that point, output is equal to potential and inflation is equal to expected inflation.

Review and Practice

SUMMARY

1. *Other things being equal,* in the short run, higher unemployment is associated with lower inflation. This relationship is called the Phillips curve.
2. *Other things being equal,* lower output is associated with lower inflation. This relationship is called the short-run inflation adjustment (SRIA) curve.
3. The level of inflation associated with any particular level of cyclical unemployment or output gap will increase as expectations of inflation increase. As a result, if the government attempts to maintain unemployment at too low a rate, the inflation rate will continually increase, as each increase in inflation is built into individuals' expectations. The expectations-augmented inflation adjustment curve reflects the effects of inflationary expectations.
4. The unemployment rate at which inflation is stable—at which actual inflation is equal to expected inflation—is called the natural rate of unemployment. Saying that inflation is stable when the output gap is zero expresses the same idea.
5. The natural rate of unemployment can change because of changes in the structure of the labor force or increasing competition in labor and product markets.
6. Inflation shocks such as oil price fluctuations will affect inflation, for given levels of output and inflationary expectations. A sharp rise in oil prices, for example, shifts the SRIA curve up.

KEY TERMS

Phillips curve
natural rate of unemployment
short-run inflation adjustment (SRIA) curve
adaptive expectations
inflation shocks

REVIEW QUESTIONS

1. Why is there a trade-off between cyclical unemployment and inflation in the short run?
2. What role do changes in expectations play in shifting the SRIA curve? What difference does it make whether expectations are adaptive or rational?
3. Why, if unemployment is kept below its natural rate, will the rate of inflation rise? What is the long-run trade-off between unemployment and inflation?
4. What factors affect the natural rate of unemployment?
5. What is an example of an inflation shock? How does a positive inflation shock affect the inflation adjustment curve?

PROBLEMS

1. Jennifer earns $40,000 per year, but her wages are not indexed to inflation. If over a period of three years inflation is at 5 percent and Jennifer receives raises of 2 percent every year, how much has the actual buying power of her income changed over that time?
2. What would be the effect on the short-run inflation adjustment curve of an announcement that OPEC—the cartel of oil-producing countries—had fallen apart, and thus the price of oil was expected to fall dramatically?
3. While playing around with old economic data in your spare time, you find that in 1963 the unemployment rate was 5.7 percent and the inflation rate was 1.6 percent; in 1972, the unemployment rate was 5.6 percent and the inflation rate was 3.4 percent; in 1979, unemployment was 5.8 percent and inflation was 13.3 percent; in 1988, unemployment was 5.5 percent and inflation was 4.4 percent; in 1996, unemployment was 5.4 percent and inflation was 3.3 percent. Does this evidence necessarily imply anything about the shape of the SRIA curve? How might you interpret these data?
4. A simple form of adaptive expectations has expectations equal to inflation in the previous year. If inflation in year t is written as π_t, then expected inflation in year t would be π_{t-1}. Suppose we write the Phillips curve relationship between unemployment and inflation as

$$\pi_t = \pi_{t-1} - .5 \times (U_t - U^*),$$

where U_t is the unemployment rate for year t and U^* is the natural rate. Assume $U^* = 5$ percent. Suppose initially in year 1 the inflation rate is 4 percent per year and the unemployment rate is 5 percent (i.e., $U_1 = U^* = 5$ percent). Now suppose in year 2 the unemployment rate falls to 4 percent and remains there. Complete the next four rows of the table. What is the inflation rate in year 7?

Year	Unemployment	Expected Inflation	Inflation
1	5 percent	4 percent	4 percent
2	4 percent	4 percent	4.5 percent
3	4 percent	4.5 percent	5 percent
4			
5			
6			
7			

5. Return to the situation of year 1 in the previous problem. By how much would unemployment need to rise to lower inflation in year 2 to 3 percent? Suppose unemployment is kept at this higher level. What happens to inflation in year 3? In year 4? How many years does it take to get inflation down to zero? Make a table like the one in the previous problem to show your results.

6. Suppose the Phillips curve in Problem 5 is replaced by

$$\pi_t = \pi_{t-1} - (U_t - U^*).$$

Redo Problem 5 with this new Phillips curve. What can you conclude about the role that the slope of the Phillips curve plays in determining the effects of a decline in unemployment?

7. The relationship between the output gap and unemployment summarized in Okun's law takes the form

$$U_t - U^* = -.5 \times (Y_t - Y^f)/Y^f,$$

where $(Y_t - Y^f)/Y^f$ is the percentage gap between output at time t and full-employment output. Use this expression for Okun's law and the Phillips curve from Problem 6 to derive the inflation adjustment curve linking inflation and the output gap.

8. The United States at the end of the 1990s witnessed rapid growth in real income and historically low rates of unemployment. Suppose two hypotheses for this decline are offered. The first is that productivity has increased owing to new technologies and that the natural rate of unemployment has fallen. The second is that the economy has been in a cyclical boom and unemployment has fallen well below the natural rate. How might you distinguish between these two hypotheses? Do they have different implications for inflation?

9. Suppose people expect higher inflation in the future. What are the short-run effects of this change in expectations on unemployment and actual inflation? How can monetary policy maintain the economy at full employment? If policy succeeds in maintaining full employment, what happens to inflation?

10. Using the ADI-SRIA framework, show how the economy adjusts to a negative aggregate demand shock in the short run and in the long run.

11. If individuals based their expectations of inflation on inflation in the recent past, we can write the SRIA schedule as

$$\pi_t = \pi_{t-1} + a \times (Y_t - Y^f),$$

where a is a constant, π_t is inflation at time t, Y_t is output at time t, and Y^f is potential output. Suppose the ADI curve is given by

$$Y_t = A - b \times \pi_t.$$

Assume that initially output is equal to potential and inflation is 8 percent. If $A = 116$, $Y^f = 100$, $a = .25$, and $b = 2$, fill in the rest of the following table to show how the economy would respond if A falls by 5.

Period	Inflation	Expected Inflation	Output
0	8 percent	8 percent	100
1	7.17 percent	8 percent	96.67
2			
3			
4			
5			

Use an ADI-SRIA graph to explain why output and inflation behave in the way you calculated.

12. Using a spreadsheet program repeat Problem 11 but calculate inflation, expected inflation, and output for twenty periods. Does output return to Y^f? What is the new long-run equilibrium rate of inflation? Plot output and inflation on the vertical axis, with the time period on the horizontal axis, to show how they move over time.

Learning Goals

In this chapter, you will learn

1. Why economists disagree about the impact of government deficits
2. Why economists disagree about the usefulness of macroeconomic stabilization policies
3. What the main debates over the goals of monetary policy are

Chapter 38

CONTROVERSIES IN MACROECONOMIC POLICY

Parts Six and Seven provide the tools you can use to analyze many important macroeconomic policy debates. You have learned how monetary and fiscal policy affect the economy, and how economic disturbances can lead to fluctuations in output, employment, and inflation. Much of the analysis represented positive economics—we asked what the impact of a policy action would be without asking whether the policy was good or bad. Now we need to apply the tools we have gained to questions of normative economics: What are good policies? How should policies be designed and implemented? What sorts of policymaking institutions seem to produce good policies? And we will use what we have learned to understand some of the most important current controversies in macroeconomics.

Three controversies will constitute the focus of this chapter. The huge increase in the U.S. federal budget deficit over the past few years has worried most economists, but some argue that these deficits are not cause for concern. So the first controversy we will discuss can be summarized in a simple question: Do fiscal deficits matter? A second controversy centers on the role of macroeconomic stabilization policies. Some economists have argued that any discussion of macroeconomic policies to help stabilize the economy is misguided. They either view the costs of business cycles as too small to worry about or believe that attempts to use monetary and fiscal policy to stabilize business cycles will actually make the economy more unstable. The question here is, Should governments attempt to stabilize the economy? Finally, the appropriate goals of monetary policy are a matter of debate. In many countries, governments have passed legislation to make price stability or low inflation the sole goal of monetary policy. In the United States, in contrast, the Federal Reserve has a mandate to keep inflation low *and* promote full employment; moreover, neither of these objectives is quantified. Many economists have called on the Federal Reserve to formally establish a numerical target for the rate of inflation. Alan Greenspan has opposed such a move, while other members of the Federal Open

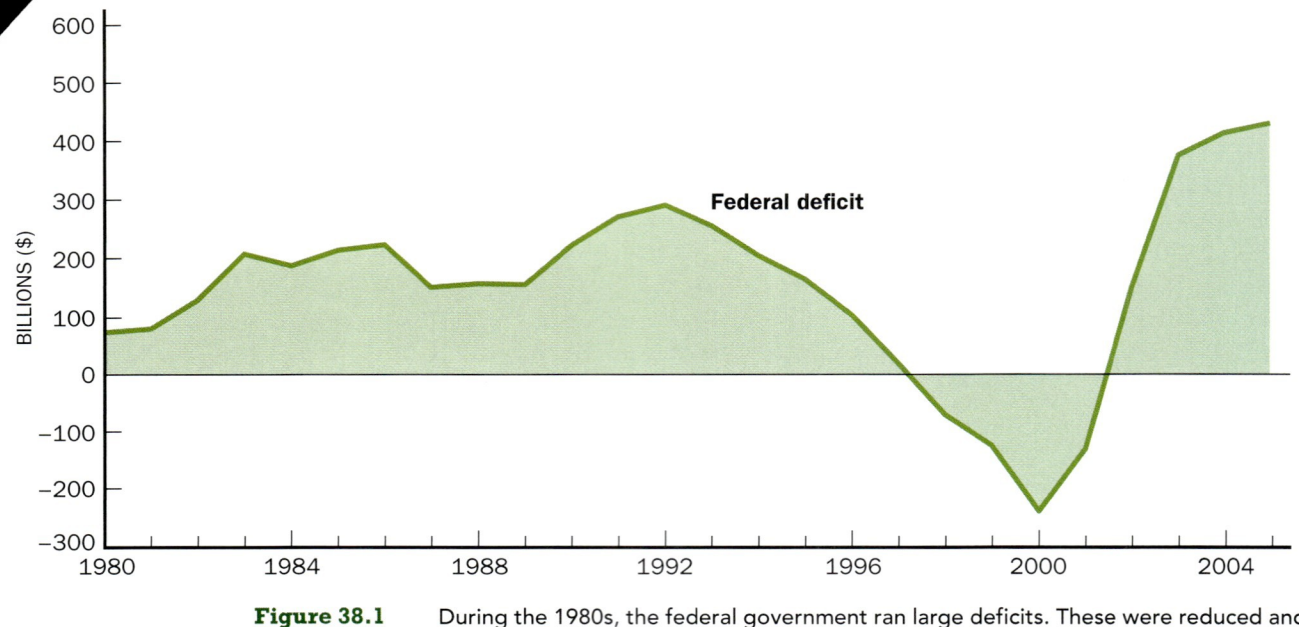

Figure 38.1

THE U.S. FEDERAL BUDGET DEFICIT

During the 1980s, the federal government ran large deficits. These were reduced and eventually eliminated by the end of the 1990s. The budget stance shifted back to deficits after 2001.

SOURCE: *Economic Report of the President* (2005).

Market Committee (FOMC) have supported it. This issue gives us a third question: Should the Fed target inflation?

Do Deficits Matter?

The budget of the U.S. federal government deteriorated rapidly between 2000 and 2004. In 2000, the federal budget had a $236 billion surplus; by 2004, the deficit was $520 billion, equal to about 4.5 percent of GDP. Figure 38.1 shows the big swings in the federal budget picture over the past twenty-five years. By the end of the 1990s, the United States appeared to have solved its budget problems after the large deficits that began in the 1980s. Through a blend of tax increases and restrictions on spending growth, the deficit had been eliminated and replaced by a surplus. And looking into the future, the Congressional Budget Office produced budget projections showing huge surpluses for the first decade of the twenty-first century.

Beginning in 2001, several events combined to push the budget back into deficit. First, the economic recession that began in 2001 reduced incomes and thereby reduced the government's tax receipts, since most tax revenues are linked to income and spending. This cyclical factor was only temporary, however. By 2002, the economy was growing again; by 2004, the lingering effects of the recession on tax revenues were gone. But other factors continue to have an impact. Fulfilling campaign promises made before the 2000 election, President George W. Bush succeeded in shepherding a large tax cut through Congress in 2001. The September 11, 2001, terrorist attacks on the United States led to substantial increases in military expenditures. And the expiration in 2002 of the "pay-as-you-go" rule introduced in the 1990s removed a significant restraint on government spending.

But if we focus just on the current deficit, we will miss the big picture as far as the federal budget is concerned. Because of the aging of the American population, health care (Medicare and Medicaid) and Social Security payments are expected to grow significantly as a fraction of GDP. If huge deficits are to be avoided, either the generous benefits of current programs will have to be reduced or large tax increases will be necessary.

But should we care about these deficit forecasts? Does it matter whether the government pays for its expenditures by raising enough tax revenue or instead simply borrows? Despite the big increase in the deficit, some commentators have claimed that deficits are unimportant to the overall health of the economy. To understand their arguments, it will be helpful to briefly review the traditional view on the impact of deficits.

DEFICITS AND THE TRADITIONAL VIEW

In Chapter 25, the full-employment model was expanded to include government spending and taxing. We learned that a government deficit reduces national saving. When the government runs a deficit, spending more than it receives in revenue, it must borrow in the capital market, thereby reducing the amount of saving available for private investment. Figure 38.2A depicts the effect of a fiscal deficit on the capital market in a closed economy. The deficit increases the equilibrium real interest rate, and reduces the equilibrium level of private investment spending by crowding out private investment spending. Over time, lower levels of investment reduce incomes as the economy accumulates less capital. Thus, the analysis of Chapter 25 concluded that deficits do matter.

Reducing the deficit or actually running a surplus has the opposite effect (see Figure 38.2B). It enables the real interest rate to fall, stimulating private investment and thus promoting economic growth and better future living standards.

But is this always the case? Do deficits always reduce future income? We saw in Chapter 26 that in one case—the small open economy—deficits do not affect the interest rate or investment. For such an economy, the supply curve of saving is horizontal, at the interest rate set by the global world capital market. A fiscal deficit results in borrowing from abroad—a capital inflow—without changing the interest rate. Private investment is not crowded out, as would be the case in a closed economy. Instead,

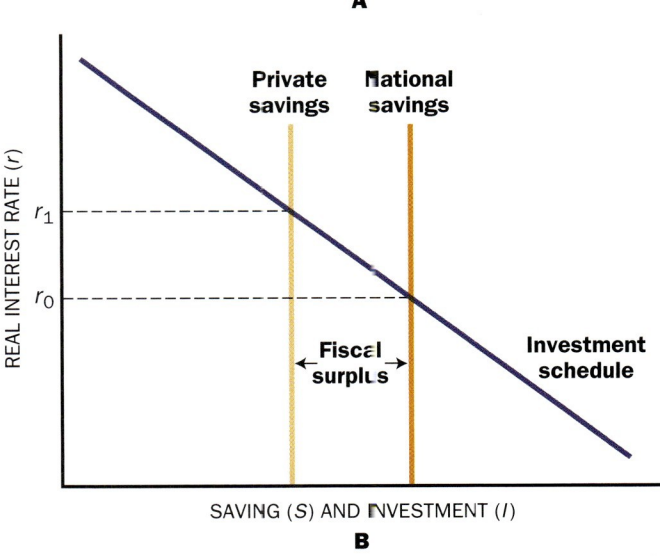

Figure 38.2

THE GOVERNMENT BUDGET AND THE CAPITAL MARKET IN A CLOSED ECONOMY

A budget deficit reduces national savings, leading to a higher equilibrium real interest rate and lower investment, as depicted in panel A. A surplus has the opposite effect, as illustrated in panel B.

the country must pay some of its national income each year to foreign investors as interest on its borrowing. A surplus in a small open economy would have the opposite effect, leading to a capital outflow.

That an increase in the fiscal deficit leaves private investment in the small open economy unaffected might suggest that it has no long-term consequences for economic growth. After all, since investment has not changed, the economy's future stock of capital is not reduced (as would happen in a closed economy with a deficit). Remember, though, that borrowing from abroad is what keeps the level of investment from being crowded out in the small open economy—it has a capital inflow. This borrowing will need to be repaid in the future to the foreign investors, and that repayment will render some of the income produced by the economy's capital stock unavailable to domestic residents.

ECONOMIC CONSEQUENCES OF DEFICITS AND SURPLUSES

Those holding the traditional view conclude that deficits reduce future income, either because lower private investment spending leads to a smaller stock of capital or because foreign borrowing must be repaid. This analysis is incomplete, however, focusing only on the costs of government borrowing. A complete evaluation of the government's budget must also consider the purposes to which the borrowed funds are put.

As we noted in Chapter 25, economists have traditionally assessed the wisdom of government and individual borrowing by the same criterion: the purpose for which the money is used. Just as it makes sense for individuals to borrow for purchases that will be put to long-term use (a house, a car) or will lead to future gains (e.g., a higher-paying job made possible by an advanced degree), so too countries appropriately borrow to finance projects that will be used for many years (a road, a school, industrial development). Similarly, taking on more debt than can be comfortably paid off or borrowing to cover this year's expenses creates real problems for both individuals and countries.

In the United States, concern is growing that most government borrowing today (as was true in the 1980s) is not being used for investment projects that will raise future incomes. The expenditures now projected to boost future deficits are mainly in the areas of Social Security and health care. Some health care spending can be viewed as an investment, making individuals (and thus the economy) more productive by improving their health. However, most goes to the elderly, who are no longer in the labor force; these payments, like those from Social Security, are used to finance consumption spending.

HOW FUTURE GENERATIONS ARE AFFECTED BY GOVERNMENT DEBT

As a result of past borrowing, the U.S. government currently owes over $5 trillion, or roughly $17,000 for every man, woman, and child in the nation. By borrowing rather than raising taxes to finance its expenditures, it has shifted the burden of reduced consumption to future taxpayers. During World War II, the U.S. government borrowed money rather than raise taxes by the full amount necessary to finance the war effort. Suppose that the bonds it issued were purchased by forty-year-old workers. Then, thirty years later, after those forty-year-olds retire, the government decides to pay off the bonds by raising taxes on those currently in the labor force. In effect, the government is transferring funds from these younger workers to those (now retired) who were working during the war. Thus, part of the cost of the war is borne by the generation who entered the labor force *after* the war. The lifetime consumption of those who purchased the bonds is little affected. The war (to the extent it is financed by debt, or government bonds) affected the form of their savings, which might otherwise have been put into stocks or bonds issued by firms, but not the total amount they have available to spend over the course of their lives.

Because deficits will force the government eventually to raise tax revenues or cut expenditures to repay its borrowing, they serve to shift resources from one generation to another. By reducing taxes today and running a deficit, the government enables current taxpayers to benefit at the expense of future taxpayers who will have to repay the debt.

ALTERNATIVE VIEWS

The discussion so far represents the current dominant views—which, according to some economists, overstate the burden of the debt on future generations. They give two different reasons for their belief.

The "Debt does not matter because we owe it to ourselves" Argument It used to be argued that the United States' fiscal deficit does not matter because we simply owe the money to ourselves. The budget deficit was compared to the effect on a family's wealth of one member borrowing from another. The borrower may be better off and the lender worse off, but the indebtedness really makes little difference to the family as whole. Financing government expenditures by debt, it was argued, could lead to a transfer of resources between generations, but this transfer would still keep all the buying power in the hands of U.S. citizens.

This argument is wrong on three counts. First, even if we owe the money to ourselves, the debt affects investment and thus future wages and productivity, as discussed in Chapter 25. Second, today we do not owe all the money to ourselves. The United States financed part of its deficits by borrowing abroad and becoming indebted to foreign investors. The consequences of spending beyond one's means are the same for a country and a family. Eventually the price of the consumption binge has to be paid—by future generations, in the case of a national spending spree. And third, simply to pay interest on the debt requires high levels of taxes; and taxes introduce distortions into the economy, discouraging work and saving (though economists disagree over the *quantitative* significance of this effect).

Ricardian Equivalence Some economists, most notably Robert Barro of Harvard University, argue that deficits will not raise real interest rates or lower investment. Barro bases his argument on an analysis originally developed by David Ricardo, an eighteenth-century English economist. Ricardo noted that when the government cuts taxes and runs a deficit, it must borrow to finance its expenditures. The government will need to raise taxes in the future to pay back what it has borrowed. If households correctly perceive that a tax cut today means higher taxes tomorrow, they will save any current windfall in order to ensure that they have the resources needed to pay the higher taxes in the future. According to Barro, even if they expect higher taxes to take effect after they are no longer alive, current taxpayers care enough about their children that they will pass on what they gain from any tax cut; this bequest will give their children the wealth that is needed to pay the higher taxes. On this account, private saving rises by the full amount of the tax cut. When private saving increases by the same amount that public saving has fallen, national saving is unchanged. The equilibrium real interest rate is unaffected, as is investment.

This argument does highlight an important fact. Governments must pay for their expenditures; if they cannot cover them with today's revenues, they will have to increase tax revenues in the future. Borrowing is equivalent to taxing, in this view—hence, the name *Ricardian equivalence*. But Ricardo himself ultimately rejected the view that deficits do not matter; and most economists today point out that the evidence does not support Barro's theoretical claim. During the 1980s and early 1990s, when the fiscal deficits were huge, private saving actually declined rather than increased. Today, private saving has not increased, although enormous deficits are projected for the future. Proponents of Ricardian equivalence do not find this evidence conclusive, arguing that a deficit may not lead individuals to save more if they believe that in the future the government will cut expenditures rather than raise taxes.

Wrap-Up

CONSEQUENCES OF GOVERNMENT DEFICITS

1. Issuing bonds reduces national saving, raises the real interest rate, and makes future generations worse off.
2. Foreign indebtedness may increase, reducing future standards of living.

The Goals of Macroeconomic Policy

The goals of macroeconomic policy in the United States are spelled out in the Full Employment and Balanced Growth Act of 1978, more commonly known as the Humphrey-Hawkins Act. It mandated the federal government to "promote full employment and production, increased real income, balanced growth, a balanced Federal budget, adequate productivity growth, proper attention to national priorities, achievement of an improved trade balance[,] . . . and reasonable price stability." The Humphrey-Hawkins Act set specific "interim" goals for unemployment (4 percent) and inflation (3 percent). These were ambitious targets: in 1978, actual unemployment was 6.1 percent and inflation was 9 percent. Over the next five years, unemployment averaged just under 8 percent, twice the interim goal of 4 percent, and inflation averaged 8.5 percent. Neither of the basic objectives of macroeconomic policy—low unemployment and low inflation—was achieved. At other times, the economy has managed to enjoy low unemployment and high growth with low inflation. In 2000, for instance, unemployment averaged 4 percent while inflation was 3.3 percent.

Our basic model, developed in Part Six, predicts that the economy tends to return to full employment; but at full employment, the rate of inflation can be either high or low. Policymakers should aim both to stabilize the economy around full employment (i.e., stabilize output around potential GDP) and to maintain an average inflation rate that is low and stable.

Yet even when average inflation is low, policymakers must continually make trade-offs. Consider the situation faced by the Federal Reserve in 2000. Unemployment, which in 1998 and 1999 had fallen to its lowest levels in almost thirty years, continued to remain well below previous estimates of its natural rate—the unemployment rate associated with full employment. Was it only a matter of time before inflation increased? Or had the natural rate of unemployment fallen, allowing lower rates of unemployment to be sustained without fear of inflation? If the Fed raised interest rates too soon, it might hasten the end of the boom unnecessarily; if it waited too long, inflation might increase. The Fed did raise interest rates in 2000; and by the end of the year, there were signs the economy was slowing. In January 2001, the Fed reversed course and cut interest rates as it moved to forestall a recession. The Fed faced the opposite situation in the spring and summer of 2004. Employment growth was finally beginning to pick up, but so was inflation. Should the Fed keep interest rates low to promote job growth? Or should it raise rates to head off an upsurge in inflation?

Economists differ in how they evaluate the trade-offs that policymakers face. A key to understanding their various positions is recognizing that unemployment and inflation affect different groups. Low-wage workers and other disadvantaged groups are the most likely to benefit from policies that stress low unemployment, and to bear the costs of high unemployment if inflation increases and must then be reduced. Since these workers have little savings, they bear little of the direct costs of inflation. The costs of *unanticipated* increases in inflation typically fall most heavily on those who hold long-term bonds—and who see the value of those bonds decrease as nominal interest rates rise, as happens when inflation increases. Unanticipated increases in inflation may also affect workers if their pension funds are invested in long-term bonds.

Because the costs of unemployment and inflation are not borne equally by all, it is not surprising that different groups take different positions in policy debates. To make economic policy—an exercise in normative economics—one must have both an understanding of how the economy operates (the role of positive economics) and a set of values to guide choices when they arise. Very often, economists reach different policy conclusions even when they share the same model of the economy. This outcome is to be expected, since each economist will evaluate the relative costs and benefits of policies differently. But a perhaps more fundamental question splits many economists—should governments even attempt to intervene to stabilize the macroeconomy? Or do such attempts simply worsen economic performance?

THE NONINTERVENTIONIST PERSPECTIVE

Those who share the view that government should not intervene to stabilize the economy differ in their reasons. Some believe that the economy is efficient, leaving little for the government to add. Others believe that government actions are ineffective, while still others argue that they do have significant effects but often simply make matters worse. We now take a closer look at each of these perspectives.

Real Business Cycle Theory: Intervention Is Unnecessary Intervention is clearly unnecessary if the economy always operates efficiently at full employment. Real business cycle theorists, led by Ed Prescott of the Arizona State University, attribute the economy's fluctuations to external shocks, such as the 1973 and 1979 oil price increases, or to shifts in the economy's underlying productivity, as may have occurred in the late 1990s. More importantly, these theorists believe that markets adjust quickly—prices and wages are sufficiently flexible that full employment will be rapidly restored—and certainly in less time than it would take for government to recognize a problem, act, and have an effect. According to real business cycle theorists, the fluctuations we observe are not signs that output is deviating from potential; instead, they argue that potential GDP fluctuates, with wages and prices adjusting to ensure that all markets clear.

Since the economy is at full employment, government need worry only about keeping inflation low and stable. The central bank just needs to set a low target for inflation and ensure that it is achieved.

New Classical Macroeconomics: Intervention Is Ineffective Some noninterventionists, while not claiming that all fluctuations are efficient, still argue that the government cannot affect output even in the short run. If the government attempts to expand the economy, shifting the aggregate demand–inflation (ADI) curve to the right, all market participants recognize that higher inflation will result. So price- and wage-setting behavior and expectations adjust immediately in anticipation of the higher inflation, and the short-run inflation adjustment (SRIA) curve shifts up, leaving the economy with higher inflation and no expansion in real output.

The new classical view also argues that inflation can be reduced without leading to higher unemployment. By reducing its inflation target, the monetary authority shifts the ADI curve to the right. If market participants are convinced that the inflation target has been reduced, they will immediately adjust their wage and price behavior, and lower inflation is achieved at no cost.

The new classical economists, led by Robert Lucas of the University of Chicago, strongly advance the view that predictable and systematic macroeconomic policies are largely ineffective in influencing real output and employment.

Intervention Is Counterproductive Some noninterventionists accept that government policies can affect the economy, and they may see shortcomings

Thinking Like an Economist
TRADE-OFFS AND CHOICES

When economists analyze the decisions of individual households making consumption purchases, they focus on two aspects. First, what are the choices available to a given household? These are defined by the household's income and the prices of the different goods it could purchase. With limited income, buying more of one thing means buying less of something else—the household faces trade-offs. Second, what are the preferences of the household? Faced with the same possibilities, different individuals will make different choices because they vary in what they like to do or consume.

Economists use this same perspective to analyze actions by economic policymakers. First, they focus on the trade-offs.

In the case of cyclical unemployment and inflation, they ask what the short-run trade-offs are—if unemployment is reduced slightly, how much will inflation rise over, say, the next year? And they need to understand the long-run trade-offs. Will the reduction in unemployment be only temporary? Once the policymakers understand the trade-offs, they can assess the costs and benefits of the different options and decide on the actual policies they want to implement. A policymaker who believes inflation is very costly will make different choices than one who sees its costs as less significant. Even if they agree about the way the economy behaves, differences in preferences will lead to differences in policy recommendations.

---

in markets, but they have little confidence in the ability of governments to improve macroeconomic performance. Indeed, some believe that intervention is counterproductive, for two reasons.

First, they recognize that there are important *lags* that make policymaking difficult. It takes time for the government to recognize a problem—and the lags in getting data, revisions in preliminary data, and the often conflicting information available can leave policymakers in great uncertainty as they try to assess the state of the economy. And after a problem is recognized, more time is needed before action can be taken. The Federal Open Meeting Committee of the Federal Reserve meets frequently, but fiscal policy actions may require congressional approval, which can easily take many months to secure. Finally, there are time lags between when a policy action is taken and when it has an impact on the economy. Interest rate changes by the Fed, for example, take six months or more to significantly affect output and even longer to influence inflation. Lags by themselves would not be a problem if the government could accurately forecast. But everyone, including government economists, sees the future with a cloudy crystal ball.

Because of these lags, the action may no longer be appropriate by the time its effects are fully realized. Expansionary policies may finally take effect just as the economy is already recovering, thereby encouraging inflation. Or contractionary policies designed to slow inflation might affect the economy just as it is starting to enter a recession, worsening the subsequent rise in unemployment.

Second, critics of strong interventionist policies argue that there are systematic political reasons why interventionists are often misguided. Politicians want the economy to expand before an election. They might boost government spending to overheat the economy, winning gains in employment before the election but incurring costs, in terms of higher inflation, that show up only after the election. In recent years, many countries have attempted to reduce the influence of elected politicians on monetary policy for just this reason.

Rules Versus Discretion Critics of intervention claim that historically, whether because of politically motivated decisions or simply because of the lags described earlier, government has actually exacerbated the economy's fluctuations. When the government attempts to dampen a boom, its policies aimed at reducing demand take effect just as the economy is weakening, reinforcing the downward movement. Conversely, when the government attempts to stimulate the economy, the increase in demand kicks in as the economy is strengthening on its own, thereby igniting inflation. Critics of government action such as Milton Friedman thus conclude that better outcomes would result if policies were based on simple **rules** rather than on the **discretion** of the government policymakers. Friedman proposed that the government should expand the money supply at a constant rate rather than actively tailor monetary policy to economic events in the hopes of stabilizing the economy. According to Friedman and others, by sticking to rules, the government would eliminate a major source of uncertainty and instability in the economy—uncertainty about future government policies.

A second argument for rules stresses the importance of commitment. A government might promise to keep inflation low. But as an election nears, politicians might be tempted to try to expand the economy a bit to improve their reelection chances, even though this action will lead to lower unemployment only temporarily while leaving the economy with higher inflation. Knowing that the government will face this temptation, individuals will not believe the initial promise to be steadfast; they will anticipate higher inflation in the future. As we learned in Chapter 37, a rise in inflation expectations increases current inflation. Lack of credible commitment to a low-inflation policy may result in higher-than-desired inflation without even a temporary gain of lower unemployment.

The uncertainty about whether a government will actually carry out a promised course of action is called the problem of **dynamic inconsistency.** This problem arises in many contexts. A city may promise to keep taxes low in order to attract a new shopping mall. Once the mall is built, however, the city may find it an irresistible source of tax revenues, despite earlier promises. Anticipating this change of course, the developers may decide not to build the mall in the first place.

For another example of dynamic inconsistency, consider the case of a final exam. Because its purpose is to provide students with an incentive to study the course material, teachers almost always think it good policy to announce a scheduled final exam. By the morning of the exam, it is too late to influence whether students have studied or not—the only thing a teacher has to look forward to is grading all those exams. So it makes sense to cancel the test. But if students anticipate this reprieve, they will not study, and announcing that there will be an exam will no longer have any effect. Few teachers cancel final exams, because they know that if they do it once, their future students will not prepare for an exam they expect to be canceled. The teacher has a *reputation* to protect. Similarly, the desire to maintain a reputation for doing what they promise can help governments fulfill their promises.

THE INTERVENTIONIST PERSPECTIVE

The case for intervention is based on two key beliefs. First, economic fluctuations are not simply the efficient response of the market to shifts in productivity, as the real business cycle theorists argue. Instead, wages do not adjust quickly enough to maintain a balance between labor supply and labor demand, and therefore declines in aggregate expenditures lead to cyclical unemployment. Second, the period of excessive unemployment can persist for a long time. In contrast, the underlying assumption of the noninterventionists is that markets adjust quickly, making cyclical unemployment a short-term affair at worst. While the process of wage and price adjustment alone may eventually bring the economy back to full employment, interventionists believe that this adjustment can be speeded up by appropriate policy interventions. They believe that macroeconomic policies can help stabilize the overall economy.

Today, the leading school of thought among economists who believe that government can and should design policies to stabilize the economy is called *New Keynesianism*. These economists share John Maynard Keynes's view that unemployment may be persistent and that though market forces may restore the economy to full employment, these forces often work so slowly that government action is required. The new Keynesian theorists differ from older Keynesian analysts in their emphasis on microeconomics—for instance, like many real business cycle and new classical economists, they believe that theories of aggregate behavior should be based on theories of the individual households and firms that make up the economy—and in their emphasis on the important role played by expectations about the future. But they also have identified a variety of reasons, such as costs of adjustment and imperfections of information, why markets do not adjust quickly to disturbances. Because markets may be slow to adjust, macroeconomic policies may be needed to help stabilize the economy in a timely fashion.

Wrap-Up

SCHOOLS OF THOUGHT ON MACROECONOMIC POLICY

Noninterventionists
Real business cycle theorists believe fluctuations in economic activity are due to external shocks and that markets respond quickly and efficiently. Government intervention has no useful role to play.

New classical economists think that the scope for government intervention is limited because wages and prices adjust quickly and because the private sector will adjust in anticipation of policies in ways that offset the impacts of the policies.

Others believe that even though markets adjust slowly, discretionary macroeconomic policies make matters worse rather than better because of the long and uncertain lags in determining the need for policy actions, in implementing policy changes, and in affecting the economy.

Interventionists
New Keynesian economists generally accept that policies can have no long-run effect on GDP or the natural rate of unemployment because wages, prices, and expectations eventually adjust, but they think markets respond slowly, so periods of cyclical unemployment can persist. Discretionary macroeconomic policy can be effective, and governments should design built-in stabilizers that can help make the economy less volatile.

Should the Federal Reserve Target Inflation?

Compared to our global financial system today, the financial structure of the country was vastly different in 1913, when the Federal Reserve was established. Its role has therefore evolved over time. The original intention of Congress, as laid out in the 1913 Federal Reserve Act, was that the Fed should prevent financial panics and bank runs. Only in the post–World War II era, after the experience of the Great Depression, have governments recognized that they bear a responsibility for preventing economic fluctuations. Accordingly, today the Fed's goal in conducting monetary policy is to promote low inflation, general economic stability, and sustainable economic growth.

An important lesson from the full-employment model examined in Part Six is that monetary policy is the chief determinant of inflation. Central banks, through their policies that affect reserve supply and the money supply, can control the *average* rate of inflation. This does not mean that inflation can be closely controlled month to month, or even year to year, but over longer time periods a central bank can exercise considerable control over the average level of inflation that the economy experiences. For this reason, in recent years most central banks have accepted that one of their primary responsibilities is to maintain low average inflation.

Monetary policy can also have important effects on two other macroeconomic goals—low (and stable) unemployment and economic growth. However, according to the full-employment model, neither the economy's potential GDP nor the unemployment rate at full employment depends on the money supply. They rest instead on household decisions about how much labor to supply in the marketplace, firms' decisions about how many workers to hire, and the economy's capital stock and technology—factors that do not vary with the absolute level of prices or the number of pieces of paper (green or any other color) that make up the money supply. Put in terms of our short-run model of Part Six, the level of potential GDP does not depend on the position of the central bank's policy rule.

This implication of the full-employment model is important. If full employment corresponds to an unemployment rate of, say, 5 percent, then the Fed cannot push the unemployment rate down to 4 percent and keep it there. It can do so temporarily, but as wages and prices adjust to restore labor market equilibrium, unemployment will return to 5 percent. The mechanisms that ensure this return to full employment are discussed in detail in Chapter 33. If monetary policy cannot succeed in keeping the unemployment rate below its full-employment level, then its appropriate goals are to contribute to economic stability by ensuring that full employment is maintained and by keeping inflation low. In this way, monetary policy ensures that the economy can experience sustainable economic growth.

To achieve the goals of full employment and low inflation, the Fed can pursue two types of policies. First, it can engage in **countercyclical policies**—policies designed to keep the economy at full employment by smoothing out fluctuations in the economy. If a recession begins, the Fed can try to stimulate the economy to move unemployment quickly back to its full-employment level. As we learned in Chapter 31, however, the economy can be stabilized around full employment with low inflation or with high inflation, since the full-employment output level does not depend on the average rate of inflation. Second, in addition to its countercyclical policies, the Fed must ensure that its actions are consistent with maintaining a low average rate of inflation. Central banks might try to stabilize the economy at full employment without keeping average inflation low. Alternatively, they might keep inflation low on average without helping to stabilize the economy at full employment. Most central banks, including the Fed, try to undertake policies that achieve both goals.

INFLATION TARGETING AND POLICY TRADE-OFFS

If the goal of monetary policy is to help stabilize the economy at full employment while still ensuring that inflation remains low, how should this policy actually be implemented? In recent years, central banks in many countries (including Canada, New Zealand, Mexico, England, Israel, and Sweden) have adopted **inflation targeting** as a framework for carrying out monetary policy. As might be expected of any approach used by such a diverse group of countries, its exact application has varied greatly. Inflation targeting generally involves the central bank publicly defining its policy goals solely in terms of keeping the inflation rate within a narrow range around a low average level. For example, New Zealand, which was the first to use inflation targeting to guide monetary policy, set a target for inflation of 0 to 2 percent. Under a law passed in 1989, the governor of the Reserve Bank of New Zealand (New Zealand's "Alan Greenspan") could be fired if inflation went above 2 percent.[1]

Many economists have called on the Federal Reserve to adopt a formal policy of inflation targeting. Among the most prominent advocates has been Ben Bernanke, chairman of President George W. Bush's Council of Economic Advisors and formerly a member of the Federal Reserve Board of Governors and professor of economics at Princeton University. Among the most prominent opponents of inflation targeting has been Alan Greenspan, chair of the Board of Governors. Supports of inflation targeting argue that the Fed, under Alan Greenspan, has behaved like an inflation targeter, so it might as well be honest and adopt a formal inflation target. Others worry that establishing a formal target for inflation on which the Fed's performance

---

[1]The target range has since been changed to 1 to 3 percent.

could be judged would reduce its flexibility to meet unforeseen future economic developments.

The Pros Supporters of inflation targeting cite three chief advantages.

Inflation targeting focuses on what the Fed can achieve Currently, the Fed has multiple goals. A 1977 congressional amendment to the Federal Reserve Act stipulated that they include promoting "maximum" sustainable output and employment and "stable" prices. The goal of stable prices is normally translated into a goal of low and stable inflation. The Fed's multiple aims concern both areas that it can control (such as average inflation) and matters that it can affect in the short run but not in the long run (such as output and employment). That it has multiple goals adds to the difficulty of holding the Fed accountable for its policy decisions. By establishing a formal target for inflation, the Fed would focus on an objective it can control and thereby increase its accountability. Opponents argue that by focusing only on inflation, the Fed would become less accountable for the effects of its policies on output and employment.

It enhances credibility Price- and wage-setting decisions depend on how much inflation individuals expect. If people begin to anticipate higher inflation, then actual inflation will start to increase, forcing the central bank to raise interest rates to lower aggregate demand and hold inflation in check. Inflation will remain low and stable only if individuals believe that the central bank is committed to keeping inflation low. Thus, the credibility of a central bank's policy is crucial, and it may be bolstered if a formal target for inflation is adopted. Opponents argue that credibility is earned by implementing policies that maintain low inflation—central banks cannot gain it by simply announcing an inflation target.

It institutionalizes good policy Many economists worry that U.S. monetary policy is too dependent on the abilities of whoever happens to be the chair of the Board of Governors. Policy under Alan Greenspan has been very successful, but other chairmen in the past have been less talented. Proponents of inflation targeting argue that its adoption would institutionalize good policy and help make policy less reliant on any one individual. By promoting continuity in policy, it would also serve to reduce the uncertainty that often accompanies a new chair's arrival. Formally targeting inflation would provide a framework for decisions that could guide future policymakers, thereby reducing the risk of policy mistakes that lead to inflation. Opponents also want to ensure the continuation of good policies, but they worry that inflation targeting will not necessarily achieve that aim.

The Cons Those who argue against inflation targeting cite three chief disadvantages.

Inflation targeting promotes one goal over other equally important goals of monetary policy The Federal Reserve is often described as now having a dual mandate: it should be concerned both with keeping inflation low *and* with helping to stabilize the economy at full employment. Achieving these two goals is viewed as consistent with promoting economic growth. Adopting a formal inflation target would elevate one goal at the expense of the other. While proponents argue that inflation targeting is consistent with actively stabilizing output around full employment, they argue that if the Fed is held accountable for achieving its inflation target, it will inevitably pay less attention to other goals.

Inflation targeting reduces flexibility Adopting a formal inflation target would reduce the Fed's flexibility in responding to new economic challenges. Supply shocks may require that the Fed allow inflation to increase temporarily in order to limit the economic contraction that would be needed to prevent its rise. A formal inflation target might limit the ability of the Fed to make such trade-offs, since its performance would be judged only on whether it maintained inflation at its target. Proponents of inflation targeting argue that in practice, most central banks with formal targets establish ranges for inflation—for example, the Riksbank, Sweden's central bank, has a target inflation rate of 2 percent, plus or minus 1 percentage point—which enable the central bank to let inflation rise temporarily if necessary to limit fluctuations in real output.

If it ain't broke, don't fix it Most commentators agree that the United States has enjoyed the benefits of good monetary policy over the past twenty years. Given this record of good performance, why change? Proponents of inflation targeting argue that its adoption would help ensure that these good policies continue into the future.

Case in Point

FED POLICY STATEMENTS—BALANCING POLICY GOALS

In 1999, the U.S. economy continued to expand and unemployment remained at historically low levels. The Fed was concerned that this strong growth would lead to higher inflation. The chief uncertainty was whether the low unemployment reflected a fall in the natural rate of unemployment. If it had fallen, then unemployment could remain low without a risk of inflation increasing; if not, then a continuation of actual unemployment below the natural rate would lead to a buildup in inflationary pressures over time. In the latter case, the Fed would want to raise interest rates to gradually slow the economy down.

During the summer, the Fed began to lean toward increasing interest rates. At their meeting on May 18, 1999, the FOMC members decided not to change interest rates, but they provided a clear signal that they were likely to raise rates soon. After the meeting, the Fed released the following statement:

> While the FOMC did not take action today to alter the stance of monetary policy, the Committee was concerned about the potential for a buildup of inflationary imbalances that could undermine the favorable performance of the economy and therefore adopted a directive that is tilted toward the possibility of a firming in the stance of monetary policy. Trend increases in costs and core prices have generally remained quite subdued. But domestic financial markets have recovered and foreign economic prospects have improved since the easing of monetary policy last fall. Against the

Internet Connection
BANKS AND INFLATION TARGETING

The Reserve Bank of New Zealand was one of the first central banks to use inflation targeting. Its Web site is www.rbnz.govt.nz. The Reserve Bank's target is defined as 1 to 3 percent inflation. The Bank of England is also an inflation targeter; its Web site is www.bankofengland.co.uk/Links/setframe.html, and its target is 2 percent inflation.

background of already-tight domestic labor markets and ongoing strength in demand in excess of productivity gains, the Committee recognizes the need to be alert to developments over coming months that might indicate that financial conditions may no longer be consistent with containing inflation.

By the time of their next meeting (on June 30), the FOMC members decided it was time to boost interest rates. After their meeting, they issued the following statement:

> The Federal Open Market Committee today voted to raise its target for the federal funds rate 25 basis points to 5 percent.[2] Last fall the Committee reduced interest rates to counter a significant seizing-up of financial markets in the United States. Since then much of the financial strain has eased, foreign economies have firmed, and economic activity in the United States has moved forward at a brisk pace. Accordingly, the full degree of adjustment is judged no longer necessary.
> Labor markets have continued to tighten over recent quarters, but strengthening productivity growth has contained inflationary pressures.
> Owing to the uncertain resolution of the balance of conflicting forces in the economy going forward, the FOMC has chosen to adopt a directive that included no predilection about near-term policy actions. The Committee, nonetheless, recognizes that in the current dynamic environment it must be especially alert to the emergence, or potential emergence, of inflationary forces that could undermine economic growth.

The Fed continued to increase the funds rate target through early 2000. By December 2000, there were signs the economy was slowing quickly, and a change in policy was needed to prevent it from heading into a recession. Acting between its normally scheduled meetings, the FOMC cut the funds rate target by half a percentage point on January 3, 2001. After the action, the FOMC released the following statement:

> The Federal Open Market Committee decided today to lower its target for the federal funds rate by 50 basis points to 6 percent. . . .

---

[2] A basis point is a hundreth of a percent, so a 25 basis point increase is a 0.25 percent increase—in this case, from 4.75 percent to 5 percent.

These actions were taken in light of further weakening of the sales and production, and in the context of lower consumer confidence, tight conditions in some segments of financial markets, and high energy prices sapping household and business purchasing power. Moreover, inflation pressures remain contained. . . .

CONSEQUENCES OF INFLATION TARGETING

Even a central bank that has adopted a formal inflation target still must make important policy choices. We can use the ADI framework to understand these policy trade-offs. Figure 38.3A shows two monetary policy rules. For both, the central bank's target for the inflation rate is π^T and the full-employment equilibrium real interest rate is r^*. When the economy is at full employment and inflation is on target, the nominal interest rate set by the central bank will be $i^* = r^* + \pi^T$. The policy rule labeled A is steeper than the one labeled B. If policy is set using rule A, a rise in inflation leads the central bank to boost interest rates by a larger amount than it would

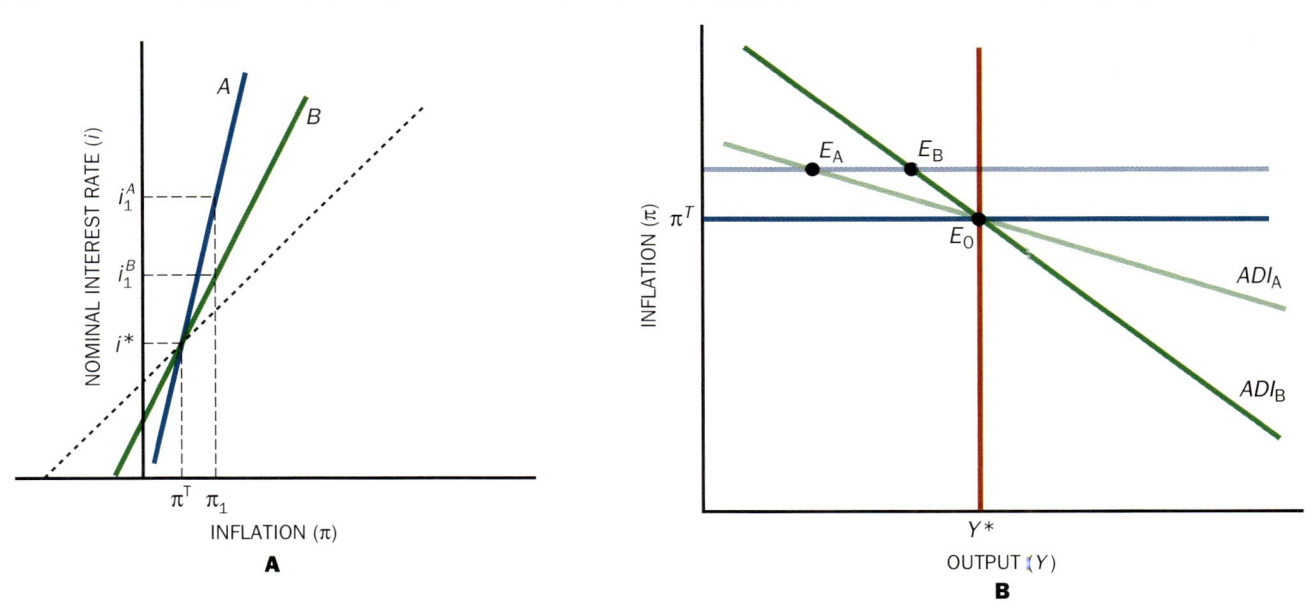

Figure 38.3

THE POLICY RULE AND FLUCTUATIONS

The way the central bank responds to inflation affects the slope of the ADI curve, and this in turn has important effects on how the economy responds to disturbances. Panel A shows two policy rules. Under rule A, changes in inflation lead to larger changes in the real interest rate than is the case under rule B. If inflation rises from π^T to π_1, the nominal interest rate is increased to i_1^A under rule A and only to i_1^B under rule B. Since as a result the real interest rate changes more under rule A, a change in inflation has a bigger impact on aggregate demand than with rule B. As a consequence, the ADI curve with rule A is flatter than the one under rule B (see panel B). An inflation shock, as in panel B, leads to a bigger fall in output under rule A. Output will vary more and inflation less with rule A than with rule B.

when using the rule given by B. Panel B shows the ADI curves under the two different policy rules, ADI_A and ADI_B. The full-employment equilibrium is at point E_0.

Suppose the economy is hit by a temporary inflation shock that increases inflation, as shown in panel B. An oil price increase or a rise in inflationary expectations would have this effect. If the central bank's behavior is described by the policy rule A, the economy moves to a new short-run equilibrium at point E_A. If the central bank's behavior is described by the policy rule B, the economy moves to a new short-run equilibrium at point E_B. Under policy rule A, output declines more than under policy rule B. The sharper decline in output will put greater downward pressure on inflation, leadng inflation to return to the target more quickly. In the face of inflation shocks, the economy will experience more stable inflation and less stable output and employment under policy rule A than under policy rule B. If the central bank responds less aggressively to inflation (as under rule B), it lets inflation fluctuate more but succeeds in keeping output and employment more stable. This is the trade-off between output stability and inflation stability that confronts the central bank.

In practice, because of the lags between a change in interest rates and their effects on the economy, central banks must be forward-looking, basing interest rate adjustments on expectations about future inflation. By responding aggressively to changes in expected inflation (a steep policy rule), monetary policy will limit inflation fluctuations, but the cost will be greater instability in real output and employment when the inflation adjustment curve shifts. By responding less aggressively, monetary policy will cause inflation to fluctuate more when the inflation adjustment curve shifts, but output and employment will be more stable.

Price Level Targeting The 1977 amendment to the Federal Reserve Act established "stable prices," not stable inflation, as one of the Fed's goals. Under a policy of keeping inflation at a low rate, say, 2 percent per year, the average level of prices continues to rise from year to year. If the price level rises more rapidly in one year, a policy of inflation targeting aims to reduce the inflation rate back to its target level. In contrast, a policy of **price level targeting** would try to cause prices to actually fall to bring the average level of prices back to its targeted level.

The difference between inflation targeting and price level targeting is illustrated in Figure 38.4. The figure assumes the target inflation rate is zero but that in period 2 a temporary shock pushes inflation up to 2 percent for one period, as depicted by the blue line in panel A. Under inflation targeting, the inflation rate is brought back to zero. For the sake of simplicity, it is assumed that this occurs in period 3. Panel B shows what happens to the price level: it jumps to a higher level in period 2 and then remains permanently higher. Policy brings inflation back to zero, but no attempt is made to return prices to their initial level.

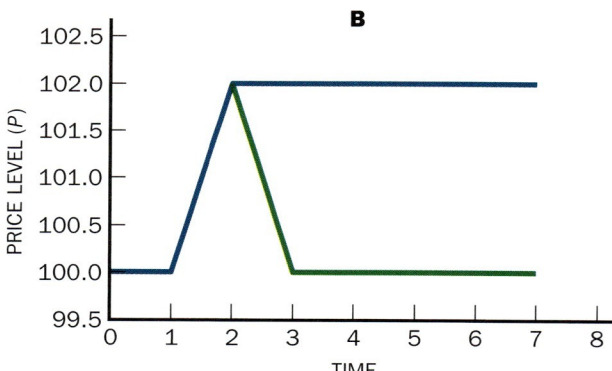

Figure 38.4

INFLATION TARGETING VERSUS PRICE LEVEL TARGETING

The blue line in panel A shows the rate of inflation as initially equal to zero. In period 2, there is a positive inflation disturbance, and inflation jumps to 2 percent. Under a policy of inflation targeting, the central bank tries to bring inflation back down to zero (shown in the figure as occurring in period 3). The behavior of the price level under this policy is shown in panel B. The temporary increase in inflation leaves the price level permanently higher than before.

Under a policy of price level targeting, the central bank would try to bring the price level back to its initial value, as shown by the green line in panel B. For the price level to fall, inflation must be negative, as shown in panel A by the green line.

International Perspective
CENTRAL BANK MANDATES

The formal policy goals of the Fed have evolved over time. In fact, the 1913 Federal Reserve Act that created the Federal Reserve System did not establish any specific macroeconomic goals. Instead, the chief hope was that the Fed would ensure an end to the financial crises that the United States had suffered periodically. The Great Depression of the 1930s and the high inflation rates experienced during the 1970s affected what we now consider to be the goals of monetary policy. A 1977 amendment to the Federal Reserve Act provides that the Fed "shall maintain long run growth of the monetary and credit aggregates commensurate with the economy's long run potential to increase production, so as to promote effectively the goals of maximum employment, stable prices, and moderate long-term interest rates." (See "The Goals of U.S. Monetary Policy," by John Judd and Glenn Rudebusch, *FRBSF Economic Letter,* January 29, 1999, at www.frbsf.org/econrsrch/wklyltr/wklyltr99/el99-04.html.) These goals involve measures of economic performance that are based both on the behavior of real economic activity (full employment, increased real income, growth, trade balance) and on the behavior of the general level of prices (stable prices).

Until recently, most other countries were similar to the United States in listing goals such as high employment, high growth, and low inflation or stable prices as the objectives to be pursued by monetary policy. But while there has been little debate in the United States over the legislated goals assigned to the Fed, the same has not been true elsewhere. The high inflation rates of the 1970s led many countries to rethink the goals of monetary policy. They have changed their laws to assign their central bank a more focused objective. Usually, this involves establishing low inflation or price stability as the primary, or in some cases the sole, objective of monetary policy. New Zealand was the first country to move in this direction. After the country suffered years of poor inflation performance, the legislation governing New Zealand's central bank (the Reserve Bank of New Zealand) was revised in 1989. The new legislation states, "The primary function of the Bank is to formulate and implement monetary policy directed to the economic objective of achieving and maintaining stability in the general level of prices." Other goals, such as high employment or growth, are not mentioned.

Monetary policy for the member countries of the European Economic and Monetary Union is conducted by the European Central Bank, which came into existence January 1, 1999. As in New Zealand, the governing legislation for the bank specifies that price stability is the primary objective of monetary policy. Again, unlike in the United States, unemployment considerations are not explicitly named among the policy objectives of the European Central Bank.

The full-employment model implies that monetary policy plays an important role in determining the average rate of inflation but can do little about the economy's average rate of unemployment. From this perspective, it is perhaps not surprising that many countries have established low inflation or stable prices as the central bank's primary policy objective. In the short run, however, monetary policy actions can have important effects on real economic activity and employment. In Chapter 33 we saw how the actions of the central bank help achieve the twin goals of maintaining low (and stable) inflation and maintaining full employment.

The green lines in the figure illustrate what happens under price level targeting. The inflation shock pushes the price level higher, but now policy acts to return the price level to its initial level. This requires *deflation*—prices must actually fall.

Few central banks have adopted price level targeting. The deflation needed to get the price level back on target after a positive inflation shock would require a costly recession and a period of high unemployment.[3]

---

[3] While no central bank has adopted price level targeting as a formal policy, the appendix to this chapter shows how our basic model can be modified to deal with the case of a price level target.

Deflation and a Zero Nominal Interest Rate During the 1970s and early 1980s, inflation seemed an intractable problem. Most countries succeeded in eventually reducing inflation, but only at the cost of significant increases in unemployment. Today, the situation is quite different. The average inflation rate in the United States was just over 3 percent in 2004.

In many countries, concern over inflation has been replaced by worries that prices will fall—deflation. In Japan, prices declined each year from 1999 to 2003. Japan also has been suffering a decade-long recession, its worst of the postwar era. The last significant deflation in the United States occurred in the 1930s during the Great Depression.

Monetary policy faces a new problem in stimulating the economy when prices are falling during a recession. To stimulate the economy, the central bank should lower interest rates. Suppose the real interest rate needed to restore full employment is 1 percent, and suppose falling prices lead people to expect deflation to continue at 2 percent. What nominal interest rate will the central bank need to target to achieve a real interest rate of 1 percent? The real rate is the nominal interest rate minus expected inflation, so

$$1 \text{ percent} = \text{required nominal interest rate} - (-2 \text{ percent}),$$

since the expected rate of inflation is –2 percent—that is, an expected deflation. If we rearrange this equation, the necessary nominal interest rate would be

$$\text{required nominal rate} = 1 \text{ percent} - 2 \text{ percent} = -1 \text{ percent!}$$

So a *negative* nominal interest rate would be necessary. But here is where the problem arises. Nominal interest rates cannot be less than zero. If the nominal interest rate were negative, you could borrow $100 today, pay back the $100 in a year, and receive an interest payment from the lender! If the nominal rate were –1 percent, after one year you would receive $1 from the lender. Given these conditions, everyone would try to borrow as much as they could. After all, if you could borrow $1 billion and just put it under your bed for a year, you would receive 1 percent, or $10 million, from the lender. Since everyone would try to borrow, and no one would want to lend, supply and demand would not balance in the capital market. A negative nominal interest rate cannot be an equilibrium.

The central bank can push the nominal interest rate down to zero but no lower. Thus, if the public expects a 2 percent deflation, the real interest rate cannot go below 2 percent—which might not be low enough to get the economy out of its recession. This is the situation the Bank of Japan faced at the end of the 1990s. Nominal interest rates were down to zero. Because the Bank of Japan continued to indicate that its real concern was ensuring that inflation did not reappear, people continued to expect falling prices, and the real interest rate remained too high.

Under these circumstances, what can a monetary authority do? One option is to announce a higher target for inflation. Suppose it announces that it will aim for 0 to 2 percent inflation. If as a result people start to expect some inflation, say, 1 percent, the real rate of interest falls from 2 percent to –1 percent (zero nominal rate–1 percent expected inflation). The promise to deliver some inflation helps stimulate the economy.

Deflations often have been associated with tough times, times of economic stagnation and high unemployment. When prices fall, the dollars a borrower must repay are worth more than the dollars that were borrowed. Much as unexpected inflation redistributes wealth from lenders to borrowers, so conversely, unexpected deflation benefits lenders at the expense of borrowers. During the 1870s and the 1930s, falling wages and prices for farm products hit borrowers hard, particularly farm families. Periods of deflation also have been associated with financial and banking crises. As the prices they receive for their products fall, many firms are unable to repay their loans. If they are forced into bankruptcy, the banks that have loaned money will not be repaid; they may also become bankrupt, leading to further disruptions in credit and economic activity.

Credibility Notions of credibility and reputation play a large role in discussions of monetary policy. It is easy to see why when we think about the problem of disinflation. As we have learned, policies to reduce inflation cause output to decline and unemployment to rise. Eventually, the economy returns to full employment with lower inflation, but the cost, in terms of cyclical unemployment, of reducing inflation can be quite significant. Many economists have argued that the cost of disinflation will be much smaller if the central bank announces in advance its plans to reduce inflation and if the central bank has credibility. If people expect lower inflation, the IA curve shifts down quickly, reducing the extent to which unemployment must exceed its natural rate to get inflation down.

Central banks with a reputation for delivering on their promises will have an easier time reducing inflation should it ever get too high. Many advocates of inflation targeting argue that setting explicit inflation goals, and meeting them, will build credibility for a central bank. It then will be better able to help stabilize the economy at full employment. Should unemployment fall below the natural rate, people will know that the monetary authority will keep inflation from getting out of control. Inflation expectations will remain stable, and actual inflation will not increase much. In contrast, if people are not sure about the monetary authority's commitment to low inflation, an economic expansion will raise concerns about higher future inflation. Inflation expectations will rise and actual inflation will start to increase more quickly.

DEMAND VERSUS SUPPLY DISTURBANCES AND POLICY TRADE-OFFS

Our discussion of inflation targeting and the interaction between fiscal and monetary policy illustrates an important insight. When the economy experiences disturbances that shift the inflation adjustment curve—such as oil price increases, temporary shifts in productivity, or shifts in inflation expectations—policymakers face a critical trade-off. They can try to keep output and employment stable, but doing so causes inflation to fluctuate more. Alternatively, policymakers can try to keep inflation stable,

e-Insight
e-TIME AND MACROECONOMIC POLICY

As the U.S. economy boomed during the late 1990s, economists speculated on how the business cycle would be affected. There has been less discussion of the impact the new information-based economy will have on macroeconomic policy. Policymakers will be affected if the economy now responds more rapidly to changing conditions.

Fluctuations in inventory investment, which have been a major factor in several previous business cycles, may in the future be limited by the new information technologies that enable firms to manage inventories better. In earlier business cycles, a slowdown in sales caused inventories to build up, as decisions about production could not be based on real-time sales information. The rising level of unsold inventories then triggered large cuts in production. Today, with access to almost instantaneous information on sales, production, and inventories, managers can fine-tune their production levels, avoiding the types of fluctuations seen in the past. By providing managers with information more rapidly, new technologies speed their responses to changing economic conditions.

Though businesses may benefit from being able to respond more quickly to changing economic conditions, policymakers may have less time to react and may therefore find themselves unable to anticipate economic developments in time to adjust policy. Because there is a lag between changes in policy and their effect on the economy, policymakers need to be forward-looking. In the case of monetary policy, the Federal Reserve would like to raise interest rates *before* inflation increases and lower rates *before* economic growth slows. If economic adjustments occur more quickly now, policymakers may be harder pressed to react in time. Thus, at the end of 2000, the sudden slowing of the U.S. economy caught policymakers by surprise. The Federal Reserve reacted with a half-point interest rate cut on January 3, 2001, *after* the slowdown began.

In the past, interest rate cuts by the Fed have taken twelve to eighteen months to have their peak impact on the economy. While the new economy may give the Fed less time to react, it remains to be seen whether it also shortens the lag between changes in policy and their impact on the economy.

Instantaneous computer tracking enables managers to avoid both inventory shortages and unnecessary inventory buildups.

but doing so leads to bigger swings in output and employment. Even though they would like to keep the economy stable at full employment and low inflation, policymakers must choose which goal to focus on—they cannot achieve both.

Policymakers do not face this same fundamental trade-off when the economy experiences disturbances that shift the ADI curve, such as shifts in fiscal policy, changes in spending decisions by households or firms, or economic fluctuations in other countries that affect net exports. If the ADI curve shifts to the left, threatening a recession, policymakers should engage in expansionary policies to offset the disturbance and keep the economy at full employment. In doing so, they also keep inflation stable. By offsetting disturbances that affect aggregate expenditures, policymakers can succeed in stabilizing both employment *and* inflation. It is not necessary to trade off one goal for another.

This is not to say that making policy decisions in response to demand disturbances is easy. The problem of lags and the difficulties of forecasting still apply. An example is provided by the Asian financial crisis of the late 1990s. It was widely predicted that this would reduce U.S. net exports and slow the U.S. economy down. The impact on U.S. output and inflation could be minimized if the Fed adopted a more expansionary policy. But the Fed had to decide how much more. Should the nominal interest rate be cut by 1 percent? 2 percent? And when? If fiscal policy should turn more contractionary, the full-employment real rate of interest would fall, but by how much? And how quickly would the fiscal contraction lead to a decline in spending? In principle, the central bank can offset the impacts of shifts in aggregate demand, such as fiscal policy, and keep both employment and inflation stable. In practice, policymakers are not able to fine-tune the economy to this extent. The key lesson, though, is that the choices between policy goals when supply shocks occur are much tougher than those faced when demand shocks occur.

Review and Practice

SUMMARY

1. The traditional view of government deficits argues that deficits reduce national saving, raise the equilibrium real interest rate, and crowd out private investment spending. The result is less capital and lower incomes in the future. The burden of government deficits falls on future generations.
2. Under Ricardian equivalence, individuals understand that deficits today mean higher taxes in the future. Those in the private sector increase their saving in anticipation of the higher future taxes. Thus, national saving does not fall and deficits do not matter.
3. Those who criticize active policy intervention to stabilize the economy argue that markets adjust quickly, making unemployment only short-lived. Attempts by government to intervene are not only unnecessary but largely ineffective, since they are offset by actions of the private sector. And to the extent that they do have effects, such policies often exacerbate fluctuations, because there are long lags, because the government has limited information, and because political pressures lead it to overheat the economy before elections.
4. Critics of discretionary policy believe that the government should tie its hands by using fixed rules. Discretionary policies may be inconsistent over time, leading to worse outcomes than occur when government follows predictable rules. Critics of fixed rules argue that by embracing them government gives up an important set of instruments and that fixed rules never work well because they fail to respond to the ever-changing structure of the economy.
5. The proponents of inflation targeting in the United States argue that it will make the Fed more accountable, increase the credibility of the Fed's low inflation policy, and institutionalize good policies.
6. Opponents of inflation targeting argue that it elevates one goal of monetary policy at the expense of other goals, limits Fed flexibility, and is unnecessary.
7. Aggregate supply shocks require policymakers to balance the goals of full employment and stable inflation. To achieve one goal, the other must be sacrificed. Aggregate demand shocks create no inherent conflict between these goals.
8. Disturbances such as oil price changes or shifts in inflationary expectations force policymakers to face a trade-off between stabilizing unemployment and stabilizing inflation. If the central bank adjusts interest rates more aggressively to changes in inflation, it can make inflation more stable, but output and employment will fluctuate more.

KEY TERMS

rules
discretion
dynamic inconsistency
countercyclical policies
inflation targeting
price level targeting

REVIEW QUESTIONS

1. Why might a government budget deficit reduce the economy's future stock of capital?
2. Suppose the government cuts taxes. If households save all of their tax cut, will the real interest rate and investment be affected? Explain.
3. What is meant by Ricardian equivalence?
4. How do inflation and unemployment affect different groups differently, and how do these differences affect views on macroeconomic policy?
5. Why do some economists argue that interventions to reduce economic fluctuations are either ineffective or counterproductive?
6. What is meant by dynamic inconsistency? Give at least two examples of policies that are dynamically inconsistent.
7. Why do some economists argue that interventions to reduce economic fluctuations are effective and productive?
8. What are the pros and cons of inflation targeting?
9. What trade-off between average unemployment and average inflation do policymakers face? What trade-off

between fluctuations in unemployment and fluctuations in inflation do policymakers face?
10. What is the difference between a policy of inflation targeting and a policy of price level targeting?

PROBLEMS

1. Suppose the government cuts taxes. Using a supply and demand analysis of the capital market, explain what the impact of the tax cut will be on the equilibrium real interest rate at full employment.
2. Suppose the government's budget is currently in balance but the government is projected to run a large deficit in the future because of large projected increases in spending. Assume Ricardian equivalence is true. How will these projected deficits affect current national saving if households expect that taxes will be raised in the future? How will the current equilibrium real interest rate and investment be affected?
3. Assume the economy is currently at full employment with an inflation rate of 2 percent. The government embarks on a major new expenditure program that increases aggregate expenditures (assume that full-employment output and the natural rate of unemployment are unaffected).
   (a) If the central bank's policy rule remains unchanged, what will be the short-run and long-run effects on output and inflation of this change in fiscal policy? What will be the long-run effects on the real interest rate at full employment?
   (b) Suppose the central bank's policy rule adjusts to reflect the change in the full-employment real interest rate. Will this alter the short-run or long-run effects of the fiscal expansion?
4. If you were in the position of the Fed in early 2001, with unemployment around 4 percent and inflation low but with signs the economy was starting to slow, would you have lowered interest rates? Why or why not? Does your answer depend on whether your estimate of the natural rate of unemployment is 4 percent or 6 percent?
5. "If expectations adjust quickly to changes in economic circumstances, including changes in economic policy, then it is easy to start an inflationary episode. But under the same conditions, it is also easy to stop inflation." Discuss. If true, what implications might this finding have for economic policy?
6. Assume that two members of the FOMC agree that the Fed's goals are to maintain full employment while ensuring low inflation, but one member (call this member W) believes that the costs of unemployment make it a much more pressing problem than inflation, while the other (member H) holds the opposite beliefs. For each of the following disturbances, will member W want the Fed to raise or lower interest rates? What about H? In which cases will the two agree? In which cases will they disagree?
   (a) An increase in business confidence
   (b) The development of new technologies that increase productivity
   (c) An increase in government purchases
   (d) An increase in inflation expectations
7. Suppose the economy is at full employment but inflation is viewed as too high. Consider the following two scenarios:
   (a) The central bank has great credibility. The central bank announces a policy of disinflation, and the public believes the announcement. Inflationary expectations fall immediately.
   (b) The central bank has no credibility. The central bank announces a policy of disinflation but the public is skeptical that the bank will actually follow through with it. The public's inflationary expectations fall only if they see actual inflation coming down.

   Discuss the likely unemployment consequences of reducing inflation in each of these two scenarios. In which case will the sacrifice ratio (the unemployment cost of reducing inflation) be higher? Explain why.

Appendix: Price Level Targeting

Almost all central banks focus on inflation, not the price level, and they implement monetary policy through their control of a nominal interest rate. Some economists have advocated forms of price level targeting in which the central bank would try to keep the price level constant rather than simply keep inflation low. Although this type of price level targeting is not practiced by any central bank, many traditional textbooks treat central banks as if their chief concern were the level of prices. The approach we have followed—one that focuses on inflation and the policy response to inflation—can easily be modified to deal with the case of a central bank that targets the price level.

Under a policy of targeting the price level, the central bank will increase the nominal interest rate whenever the price level rises and lower the nominal interest rate whenever the price level falls. The objective in either case is to affect the real interest rate and aggregate expenditures. Rather than leading to the negative relationship between inflation and aggregate expenditures represented by our ADI curve, a policy of price level targeting will lead to a negative relationship between the price level and aggregate expenditures. This relationship, shown in Figure 38.5, is usually called an *aggregate demand curve*.

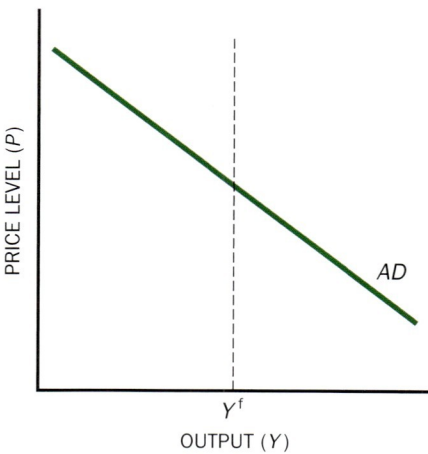

Figure 38.5

THE AGGREGATE DEMAND CURVE

If the central bank adjusts the interest rate whenever the price level deviates from its target level, the ADI curve is replaced with a relationship between the price level (P) and aggregate expenditures called the aggregate demand (AD) curve. If P increases, the central bank increases the interest rate, leading to a reduction in aggregate expenditures. Changes in fiscal policy or shocks to consumption, investment, or net exports shift the aggregate demand curve in the same way they would shift the ADI curve. An increase in government purchases, for instance, shifts the AD curve to the right.

Learning Goals

In this chapter, you will learn

1. About the principal investment alternatives available for your savings
2. The important characteristics of each of these investment options
3. Why some assets yield higher rates of return than others
4. Whether it is possible to "beat the market"
5. Some of the basic rules for intelligent investing

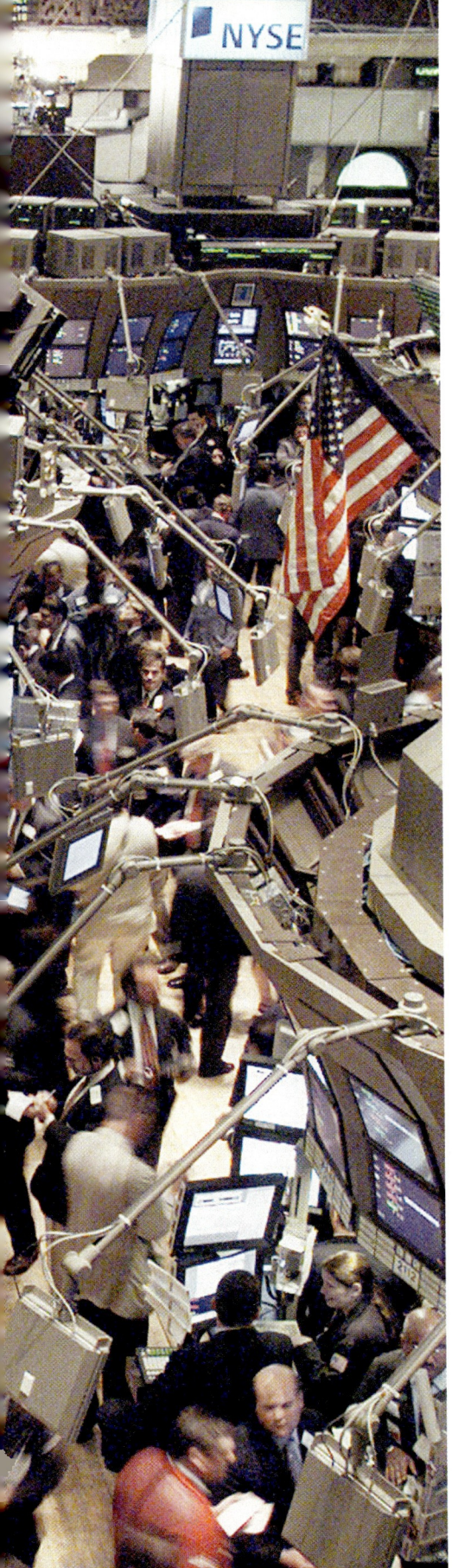

Chapter 39

A STUDENT'S GUIDE TO INVESTING

The 1990s saw a tremendous rise in the value of the stock market—it seemed as if almost every day some new company was selling shares to the public and creating new billionaires overnight. This picture all changed abruptly in 2000 when the stock market collapsed, causing millions to see their paper wealth disappear. The ups and downs of the stock market are often taken as key signals of the economy's health, and the swings of the financial market that we have seen during the past ten years are nothing new. When Alexander Hamilton, as the first U.S. secretary of the treasury under President George Washington, set up the first market for the new government's bonds in 1791, prices skyrocketed by more than 1,000 percent in the first month of trading before collapsing in value.

But what can economics tell us about the stock market and how it behaves? And what can economics tell us about how you should invest your money? Every decision to save is accompanied by a decision about what to do with the savings. They might go under the mattress, but usually savings are invested—most often in bank accounts, the stock or bond market, or the real estate market. These financial opportunities can be thought of as enticements to defer consumption—to save. Broadly speaking, an **investment** is the purchase of an asset in the expectation of receiving a return. For the economy as a whole, **real investment** must be distinguished from **financial investment**. Real investment includes the purchase of new factories and machines; it is the investment that is part of aggregate expenditures. Financial investment is the purchase of financial assets such as stocks and bonds that are expected to generate income or to appreciate in value.

This chapter examines financial investment. It first takes up the major alternatives available to savers and discusses the characteristics of those that are important to investors. From these characteristics, we can establish a simple theory to explain how the prices of financial assets such as stocks and bonds are determined. We can use what we learn about the characteristics of investment alternatives and the theory of asset prices to develop some strategies for intelligent investing.

Investment Alternatives

Savers wishing to invest are offered a range of possibilities. The choices they make depend on the amount of money they have to invest, their motivations to save, their willingness to bear risk, and such personal characteristics as age and health. Of the seemingly endless array of destinations for one's money, five are most important: bank deposits, including certificates of deposit (CDs); housing; bonds; stocks; and mutual funds. In making choices among them, investors focus on four characteristics: return, risk, tax liability, and liquidity.

BANK DEPOSITS

A *bank savings account* (or a similar account) offers three advantages: it pays interest, it allows easy access to the money in it, and it offers security. Even if the bank goes bankrupt, the federal government, through the Federal Deposit Insurance Corporation (FDIC), insures its deposits of up to $100,000.

As savings increase, the value of a higher interest rate also increases. A **certificate of deposit (CD),** which specifies an interest rate on money deposited in a bank for a preset length of time, is as safe as an ordinary bank account and yields a slightly higher return. The drawback of a CD is that withdrawals of money before the preset time has expired are subject to a penalty. The ease with which an investment can be turned into cash is called its **liquidity.** Perfectly liquid investments can be converted into cash speedily and without any loss in value. CDs are less liquid than standard saving accounts.

HOUSING

Two-thirds of American households invest by owning their own homes. Making this investment is far riskier than putting money into a savings account or a CD. Home prices usually increase over time, but not always, and recently the rate of increase has varied widely in different parts of the country. For example, over the past ten years, house prices have gone up almost 530 percent in Massachusetts but only 75 percent in Oklahoma. Prices may rise rapidly in one year, then remain flat or even fall in other years. Most families borrow most of the funds needed to purchase a house, and the owner bears the risk, since she is responsible for paying back the loan regardless of the market price of the house.

Housing as an investment has two other attributes—one attractive and one unattractive. On the positive side, property taxes and the interest on the loan used to purchase the house are generally tax deductible, and for most homeowners the capital gains escape taxation altogether. On the negative side, housing is usually fairly illiquid. If you try to sell your house quickly, on average you will receive less than if you have more time to make the sale. Moreover, the costs of selling a house are substantial, often more than 5 percent of the value of the house—in any case, more than the costs of selling stocks and bonds.

Internet Connection

CALCULATING INTEREST RATES

The Federal Reserve Banks of New York and Chicago have Web sites that explain how interest rates are calculated. Their addresses are www.ny.frb.org/education/calc.html#calc and www.chicagofed.org/consumer_information/abcs_of_figuring_interest.cfm.

BONDS

Bonds are a way for corporations and government to borrow. The borrower—whether a company, a state, a school district, or the U.S. government—promises to pay the lender (the purchaser of the bond, or investor) a fixed amount in a specified number of years. In addition, the borrower agrees to pay the lender each year a fixed return on the amount borrowed. Thus, if the interest rate on a ten-year bond is 10 percent, a $10,000 bond will pay the lender $1,000 every year, and $10,000 at the end of ten years. The date on which a loan or bond is to be paid in full is called its *maturity*. Bonds that mature within a few years are called *short-term bonds;* those that mature in more than ten years are called *long-term bonds*. A long-term government bond may have a maturity of twenty or even thirty years.

Bonds may seem relatively safe, because the investor knows what amounts will be paid. But consider a corporate bond that promises to pay $10,000 in ten years and pays $1,000 every year until then. Imagine that an investor buys the bond, collects interest for a couple of years, and then realizes that he needs cash and wants to sell the bond. There is no guarantee that he will get $10,000 for it. He may get more and he may get less. If the market interest rate has fallen to 5 percent since the original bond was issued, a new $10,000 bond now would pay only $500 a year. Clearly, the original bond, which pays $1,000 a year, is worth considerably more. Thus, a decline in the interest rate leads to a rise in the value of bonds; and by the same logic, a rise in the interest rate leads to a decline in the value of bonds. This uncertainty about market value is what makes long-term bonds risky.[1]

Even if the investor holds the bond to maturity, that is, until the date at which it pays the promised $10,000, there is still a risk, since he cannot know for sure what $10,000 will purchase ten years from now. If the general level of prices increases at

---

[1] The market price of the bond will equal the percent discounted value of what it pays. For instance, a 3-year bond that pays $10 per year each of 2 years and $110 at the end of the 3rd year has a value of

$$\frac{10}{1+r} + \frac{10}{(1+r)^2} + \frac{110}{(1+r)^3},$$

where r is the market rate of interest. We can see that as r goes up, the value of the bond goes down, and vice versa.

a rate of 7 percent over those ten years, the real value of the $10,000 will be just one-half what it would have been had prices remained stable during that decade.[2]

Because of the higher risk caused by these uncertainties, long-term bonds must compensate investors by paying higher returns, on average, than comparable short-term bonds. And because every corporation has at least a slight chance of going bankrupt, corporate bonds must compensate investors for that higher risk by paying higher returns than government bonds. These higher returns more than compensate for the additional bankruptcy risk, according to economic research. That is, if an investor purchases a very large number of good-quality corporate bonds, the likelihood that more than one or two will default is very small, and the overall return will be considerably higher than the return from purchasing government bonds of the same maturity (the same length of time until they come due).

Some corporate bonds are riskier than others—that is, there is a higher probability of default. These bonds must pay extremely high returns to induce investors to take a chance on them. When Chrysler appeared to be on the verge of bankruptcy in 1980, Chrysler bonds were yielding returns of 23 percent. Obviously, the greater a firm's debt, the more likely it is to be unable to meet its commitments, and the riskier are its bonds. Especially risky bonds are called *junk bonds;* the yields on such bonds are much higher than those from a financially solid firm, but the investor must take into account the high probability of default.

SHARES OF STOCK

Those with savings might also choose to invest in shares of corporate stock. When people buy shares in a firm, they literally own a fraction (a share) of the total firm. Thus, if the firm issues 1 million shares, an individual who owns 100 shares owns 0.01 percent of the firm. Investors choose stocks as investments for two reasons.

First, firms pay some fraction of their earnings—their receipts after paying workers, suppliers of materials, and all interest due on bank and other loans—directly to shareholders. These payments are called **dividends.** On average, firms distribute one-third of earnings as dividends; the remainder, called **retained earnings,** is kept for investment in the company. The amount of a dividend, unlike the return on a bond, depends on a firm's earnings and on what proportion of those earnings it chooses to distribute to shareholders.

In addition to receiving dividends, those who invest in stocks hope to make money by choosing stocks that will appreciate in value and that can then be sold at the higher price. The increase in the realized price of a share (or any other asset) is called a **capital gain.** (If the asset is sold at a price below that at which it was purchased, the investor realizes a *capital loss.*)

Shares of stock are risky for a number of reasons. First, the earnings of firms vary greatly. Even if firms' dividends are the same, differences in profits will lead to differences in retained earnings, and these will be reflected in the value of the shares. In addition, the stock price of a company depends on the beliefs of investors

---

[2] If prices rise at 7 percent a year, with compounding, the price level in 10 years is $(1.07)^{10}$ times the level it is today; $(1.07)^{10}$ is approximately equal to 2—thus prices have doubled.

regarding the prospects of the economy, the industry, and that particular firm. Loss of faith in any one of these could lead to a drop in the stock price. Thus, an individual who has to sell all his shares because of some medical emergency might find they have declined significantly in value. Even if the investor believes that the shares will eventually return to a higher value, he may be unable to wait.

Shares of stock are riskier than corporate bonds. When a firm goes bankrupt and must pay off its investors, the law requires bondholders to be paid off as fully as possible before shareholders receive any money at all. As a result, a bondholder in a bankrupt company is likely to be paid some share of her original investment, while a shareholder may receive nothing. But over the long run, shares of stock have yielded very high returns. While corporate bonds yielded on average an annual real rate of return of 2 percent in the period from 1926 to 2003, shares of stock in the same period yielded a real return of nearly 10 percent.

MUTUAL FUNDS

A **mutual fund** gathers funds from many different investors into a single large pool of funds, with which it can then purchase a large number of assets. A *money market* mutual fund invests its funds in CDs and comparably safe assets.

The advantage of a money market mutual fund is that it offers both higher rates of interest than bank accounts and high liquidity. The fund managers know that most individuals will leave their money in the account, and some will be adding money to the account as others pull money out. They are thus able to put a large proportion of the fund in certificates of deposits and still not have to pay the penalties for early withdrawal. In this way, money market mutual funds give investors the easy access to their funds associated with banks, while providing them the higher return associated with CDs.

Money market mutual funds may also invest their customers' money in short-term government bonds, called **Treasury bills,** or **T-bills.** Treasury bills are available only in large denominations ($10,000 or more). They promise to repay a certain amount (their face value, say, $10,000) in a relatively short period, less than 90 or 180 days, and investors buy them at less than their face value. The difference between the amount paid and the face value becomes the return to the purchaser.

With most money market mutual funds, you can even write a limited number of checks a month against your account. The major disadvantages of mutual funds are that they may require that you maintain a high minimum balance in your account and they may not be insured by the federal government. However, some money market funds invest only in government securities or government-insured securities, making them virtually as safe as bank accounts.

Other mutual funds invest in stocks and bonds. Typically, they buy stock or bonds in dozens, sometimes hundreds, of different companies. Investors recognize the advantage of **diversification**—of not putting all their eggs in the same basket. If you put all your savings into a single stock and that firm has a bad year, you'll suffer a large loss. If you own stock in two companies, losses in one company may offset gains in the other. Mutual funds, in effect, allow much broader diversification. Of course, if the whole stock market does badly, a stock mutual fund will suffer too. When stocks go down, bonds often go up, so some mutual funds invest in both stocks and bonds. Others invest in risky ventures that, if successful, promise high returns; these are sometimes referred to as "growth" funds. There are many other specially designed mutual funds, and together they are enormously popular. For most investors, the first foray into the bond or stock market is through the purchase of a mutual fund.

Desirable Attributes of Investments

Table 39.1 sets forth the various investment opportunities we have described, with a list of their most important attributes. In surveying the broad range of investment opportunities available, individuals must balance their personal needs against what the different investment options have to offer. The ideal investment would have a high rate of return, be low risk, and be exempt from tax. Unfortunately, as economists always like to point out, investors face trade-offs. You can only expect to get more of one desirable property—say a higher expected return—at the expense of another, such as safety. To understand what is entailed in these trade-offs, we need to take a closer look at each of the principal attributes of investments.

EXPECTED RETURNS

First on the list of desirable properties are high returns. As we have noted, returns have two components: the interest (on a bond), dividend payment (on a stock), or rent (on real estate) and the capital gain. For instance, if you buy some stock for $1,000, receive $150 in dividends during the year, and at the end of the year sell the stock for $1,200, your total return is $150 + $200 = $350 (a rate of return of 35 percent). If you sell the stock for only $900, your total return is $150 − $100 = $50 (a rate of return of 5 percent). If you sell it for $800, your total return is a *negative* $50 (a rate of return of −5 percent).

Internet Connection

INDEX FUNDS

Many mutual funds are designed to follow the return of a market index, such as the Standard and Poor's (S&P) 500 index. Standard and Poor's Web site at www.spglobal.com provides the latest information on the performance of their indexes. If you follow the links on the left side of the page, you will find a primer on the mathematics of calculating market indexes.

Table 39.1

ALTERNATIVE INVESTMENTS AND HOW THEY FARE

Investment	Expected returns	Risk	Tax advantages	Liquidity
Banking savings accounts	Low	Low	None	High
CDs (certificates of deposit)	Slightly higher than savings accounts	Low	None	Slightly less than savings accounts
Houses	High returns from mid-1970s to mid-1980s; in many areas, negative returns in late 1980s, early 1990s, high returns since late 1990s	Used to be thought safe; viewed to be somewhat riskier now	Many special tax advantages	Relatively illiquid; may take long time to find "good buyer"
Federal government long-term bonds	Normally slightly higher than T-bills	Uncertain market value next period; uncertain purchasing power in long run	Exempt from state income tax	Small charge for selling before maturity
Corporate Bonds	Higher return than federal bonds	Risks of long-term federal bonds plus risk of default	None	Slightly less liquid than federal bonds (depends on corporation issuing bond)
Stocks	High	High	Capital gains receive tax preference if stocks held for more than 1 year	Those listed on major exchange are highly liquid; others may be highly illiquid
Mutual Funds	Reflect assets in which funds are invested	Reflect assets in which funds are invested; reduced risk from diversification	Reflect assets in which funds are invested	High
T-bills	About same as CDs	Low	Exempt from state income tax	Small charge for selling before maturity

Few assets offer guaranteed returns. If the stock market booms, a stock share might yield 20 percent; but if the market drops, the total return might be zero or even negative. To compare two alternative investment options, we apply the concept of **expected returns.** The expected return on an asset is the single number that takes into account both the various possible returns per dollar invested and the chances that each of those possibilities will occur. If there is a one-in-four chance (a 25 percent probability) a stock will yield a 20 percent return over the next year,

e-Insight

INVESTING IN THE NEW ECONOMY

Investors worry about risk. Risk can be reduced by *diversification*, that is, by not putting all your eggs in one basket. Dividing investments among a large number of securities lowers the risk because the value of some may go up when the value of others goes down. In spite of the distinct advantages of risk diversification, many individuals own relatively few securities. One of the reasons is that it is costly to buy and sell different stocks. As a result, individuals have increasingly turned to mutual funds. Mutual funds are financial intermediaries that buy large numbers of securities. Transactions costs are lowered because the securities are bought in bulk. But nothing is free in life. Mutual fund managers have to make a living, and they too charge transaction fees. These costs are substantially lower than if the individual tried to buy an equally diversified portfolio on her own, but they can be considerable nonetheless. Mutual funds have significant tax disadvantages as well. For instance, say you buy shares in a mutual fund in January 2000. In February 2000, the mutual fund sells some shares that it purchased ten years ago, and records a large capital gain.

Then the value of the fund decreases—perhaps because it was a high-technology fund, and technology shares plummeted in April 2000. At the end of the year you may think you have incurred a loss. But the IRS will still insist you pay a tax as if you had a capital gain, because you owned shares in the mutual fund at the time the capital gain was realized. This may seem grossly unfair—you are worse off, yet you have to pay a tax as if you were better off—but that is the way the tax law works.

The new economy has opened up new possibilities for individuals to diversify without large transaction costs. At least one new economy firm (FOLIO*fn*) is offering to allow investors to trade large numbers of stock for a single monthly fee, *with no marginal costs*. This arrangement enables individuals to obtain a highly diversified portfolio, to avoid the transaction costs of mutual funds, and to avoid the tax disadvantages of mutual funds. Like all innovations, it will take time for it to penetrate throughout the economy; but if successful, it may revolutionize how individuals—especially small investors—invest their money.

a one-in-two chance (a 50 percent probability) the return will be 5 percent, and a one-in-four chance (a 25 percent probability) the return will be zero, the expected return on the stock is 7.5 percent (.25 × 20 percent + .5 × 5 percent + .25 × 0 percent).

Case in Point

PG&E EMPLOYEES LEARN WHY DIVERSIFICATION IS IMPORTANT

In January 2001, Pacific Gas & Electric Company (PG&E), a major supplier of electricity to northern California, quite suddenly found itself facing bankruptcy. Under California's utility deregulation statutes, PG&E was prohibited from raising its prices to consumers but had to pay market prices for the electricity it purchased to deliver to them. When skyrocketing demand and energy shortages in the West led to record energy prices, PG&E quickly ran out of cash. Wall Street was equally quick to respond. PG&E's stock price plummeted from $31.64 on September 11, 2000, to

A crowd protests rate hikes by the California utility PG&E, which were made in an effort to fend off bankruptcy.

$10.19 in January 2001. The utility's bonds were downgraded to the lowest echelons of the junk bond range, indicating that Wall Street thought there was little chance that bondholders would be repaid or receive interest. PG&E suspended dividends on its stock, laid off workers, and hired bankruptcy lawyers to assess its options.

For some PG&E employees, the energy crisis that put at risk the booming California economy carried a double threat. Workers were clearly in danger of losing jobs. But more than 80 percent of PG&E's workers were also shareholders who owned stock through the company's retirement plan. PG&E for years had contributed stock one-for-one when employees purchased company stock for their individual 401(k) retirement accounts. Employees had the option of selling the PG&E stock and replacing it with other assets, but not everyone took advantage of the chance to diversify. When PG&E stock lost two-thirds of its value, these workers' 401(k) retirement plans followed suit. Though their pensions and 401(k) could not be seized by a bankruptcy court, workers whose 401(k) plans were heavily invested in PG&E stock had no protection from the risk that stock prices would nosedive.

Longtime employees who failed to diversify out of PG&E stock to obtain a more balanced portfolio saw their dreams of early retirement and a secure old age vanish. When asked why so many employees were overinvested in PG&E stock, one employee replied that people believed in the company that had provided a good living for them (and in some cases, their parents) for most of their lives. The sudden collapse of PG&E underscores the importance of diversification to minimize (though not avoid entirely) the risk of holding individual stocks.[3]

An important first lesson in investment theory is as follows: *If there were no differences between assets other than the ways in which they produce returns (interest, dividends, etc.), then the expected returns to all assets would be the same.* Why? Suppose an asset offered an expected return of 10 percent while all others offered 6 percent. Investors, in trying to buy the higher-yielding asset, would bid more for it, thereby pushing up its price. As the price rose, the expected return would decline. The upward pressure would continue until the expected return declined to match the level of all other investments.

In fact, for different assets the expected returns per dollar invested differ markedly from one another, because return is affected by a number of other important attributes. These include risk, tax considerations, and liquidity (the ease with which an asset can be sold).

RISK

Most of us do not like the risk that accompanies most future-oriented economic activity. We might spend a few dollars on some lottery tickets or occasionally play the slot machines, but for the most part we try to avoid or minimize risks. Economists say that individuals are *risk averse* and their behavior displays **risk aversion.**

A prime consideration for any investor, therefore, is the riskiness of any investment alternative. Bank accounts, in this regard, are safe. Since government deposit insurance was instituted in the 1930s after the bank failures that occurred during the Great Depression, no one in the United States has lost money in an insured bank account. But investments in housing, stocks, and bonds and most other investments involve risk. The return may turn out to be substantially lower, or higher, than initially expected.

Historically, stocks have yielded a higher average return than bonds, but stocks are riskier—prices on the stock market fluctuate, and they can do so quite dramatically. On the single day of October 19, 1987, stock prices on the New York Stock Exchange fell by 508 points, a drop in value of 23 percent.

Panel A of Figure 39.1 shows the closing monthly value of the Dow Jones industrial average, an index of stock prices that is based on the prices of shares in major companies. Today, thirty companies are included in the index, which was revised in 1999 to include such firms as Microsoft and Intel. Because the index has grown so much since 1928, the 1929 stock market crash barely shows up in the figure. Though the index fell in value almost 13 percent on October 28, 1929, this was a decline of only 38 points—well within the typical range of daily fluctuations in the market today. The

---

[3]Based on an article by Jennifer Bjorhus, "PG&E's 'Family' Falling Apart," *San Jose Mercury News,* January 22, 2001, p. 1.

Figure 39.1

STOCK MARKET INDICES

Panel A shows the closing monthly value of the Dow Jones industrial average, an index of stock prices that is based on the prices of shares in major companies. Panel B plots the natural log of the Dow Jones index so that percentage changes in the level of stock prices can be seen more clearly.

largest one-day drop occurred on October 27, 1997, when the Dow Jones index lost 554 points.

The percentage change in the level of stock prices can be seen more clearly by plotting the natural log of the Dow Jones index (panel B). Here, the magnitude of the 1929 crash clearly stands out. The 1929 crash was not simply a one-day drop—three of the five biggest percentage daily declines over the 1900–2000 period occurred in late October and early November of 1929. The record for the largest percentage drop on a single day is held by December 12, 1914, when the market lost 24 percent of its value. Second is October 19, 1987, when the market fell 23 percent. The stock

Figure 39.2

EFFECTS OF DIFFERENCES IN RISK

Lowering risk shifts the demand curve for the asset to the right, increasing the equilibrium price and lowering the average return.

market decline between August 2000 and March 2001 shows up clearly in panel A.

While the New York Stock Exchange is by far the largest stock market in the world, there are others, and in recent years the Nasdaq market has grown in importance. The Nasdaq stock market, created in 1971, is heavily weighted toward the new technology companies. The stocks of Microsoft and Intel, for example, are traded on the Nasdaq market, not the New York Stock Exchange. The addition of Microsoft and Intel to the Dow Jones index in 1999 marked the first time that companies traded on the Nasdaq market, and not the New York Stock Exchange, were included in the index.

Both the Dow Jones index and the Nasdaq index show a tendency to rise over time—leading to capital gains for those who hold stock—but both also show the ups and downs that occur over shorter periods. It is these fluctuations in value that make investing in stocks risky.

Risk can never be avoided completely, and it has been said that financial markets are the places where risk is bought and sold. We can see the effects of changes in risk in Figure 39.2. A reduction in the riskiness of an asset makes it more desirable, thereby shifting the demand curve for the asset to the right. In the short run, the supply of an asset is inelastic. Even in the longer run, supply is likely not to be perfectly elastic. Accordingly, as illustrated in the figure, the price of the asset goes up, from p_0 to p_1. Accompanying the increase in price is a reduction in the return per dollar invested.

An asset that is less risky will have a higher demand. The higher demand will lead to a higher price and lower return. Therefore, the expected return will be lower on assets that are safer. Economists say such desirable assets sell at a *premium*, while assets that are riskier sell at a *discount*. Still, market forces ensure that assets of comparable risk must yield the same expected returns.

TAX CONSIDERATIONS

Since different assets are treated differently in the tax code, tax considerations are obviously important in choosing a portfolio. After all, individuals care about after-tax returns, not before-tax returns. Investments that face relatively low tax rates are said to be *tax-favored*.

State and municipal bonds illustrate this point. These bonds yield a lower return than do corporate bonds of comparable risk and liquidity. So why do people buy them? The answer is that the interest on bonds issued by states and municipalities is generally exempt from federal tax. The higher your income, the more valuable this tax exemption is, because your tax savings are greater the higher your tax *rate* (which tends to increase with income). The higher demand for these tax-exempt bonds from high-income investors drives up their price, thereby driving down the return received on the bonds. We can expect the return to decline to the point at which the after-tax return for high-income individuals is at most only slightly higher than for an ordinary taxable bond of comparable risk.

Investing in housing, particularly a house to live in, is another tax-favored form of investment enjoyed by most Americans. Most homeowners can deduct their real estate taxes and the interest payments on their mortgage when calculating their income for tax purposes. In addition, the capital gain from owning the house is not taxed until the house is sold. Even then, the capital gain (up to $500,000 for a married couple) from the sale is not taxed at all. If the tax advantages of home ownership were ever withdrawn, we could expect housing prices to decline precipitously in the short run (in which supply is inelastic), as illustrated in Figure 39.3. It is not likely that tax preferences for housing will be suddenly removed, however, because most voters own houses, and politicians are loathe to anger such a large number of their constituents.

LIQUIDITY

The fourth important attribute to consider is liquidity. An asset is liquid if the costs of selling it are very low. A bank account is completely liquid (unless the bank goes bankrupt), because you can turn it into cash at virtually no charge by writing a check. Corporate stock in a major company is fairly liquid, because the costs of selling at a well-defined market price are relatively small.

In the basic competitive model, all assets are assumed to be perfectly liquid. There is a well-defined price at which anything can be bought and sold; any household or

Figure 39.3

EFFECT OF REMOVING TAX PREFERENCES FOR HOUSING

Removing tax preferences for housing will shift the demand curve for housing down, and this will, in the short run (with an inelastic housing supply), cause marked decreases in the price of housing.

firm can buy or sell as much as it wants at that price; and the transaction is virtually without cost. But these assumptions are not always met: the costs of selling or buying an asset are often significant. As noted above, for instance, the costs of selling a house can be 5 percent or more of the house's value. At times, even municipal bonds have been fairly illiquid. The prices at which such bonds could be bought and sold have been known to differ by more than 20 percent.

Expectations and the Market for Assets

Gardeners today find shocking the price of tulip bulbs in early-seventeenth-century Holland, where one bulb sold for the equivalent of $16,000 in today's dollars. The golden age of tulips did not last long, however; and in 1637, prices of bulbs fell by more than 90 percent. Dramatic price swings for assets are not only curiosities of history. Between 1973 and 1980, the price of gold rose from $98 to $613, or by 525 percent; then, from 1980 to 1985, it fell to $318. Between 1977 and 1980, the price of farm land in Iowa increased by 40 percent, only to fall by more than 60 percent from 1980 to 1987. On October 19, 1987, stock values on the U.S. stock market fell by half a trillion dollars—almost 25 percent. Even a major war would be unlikely to destroy one-fourth of the U.S. capital stock in a single day. But there was no war or other external event to explain the 1987 drop.

How can the basic demand and supply model explain these huge price swings? If asset prices depend on the four basic attributes discussed above—expected return, risk, tax treatment, and liquidity—how can demand curves, or supply curves, shift so dramatically as to cause these large price movements?

The answer lies in the critical role that expectations play in the market for assets. Assets such as gold, land, or stocks are long-lived; they can be bought at one date and sold at another. For this reason, the price that individuals are willing to pay for them today depends not only on today's conditions—the immediate return or benefit—but also on some expectation of what tomorrow's conditions will be. In particular, the demand for an asset will depend on what the asset is expected to be worth in the future.

To see how expectations concerning future events affect *current* prices, consider a hypothetical example. People suddenly realize that new smog-control devices will, ten years from now, make certain parts of Los Angeles much more attractive places to live than they are today. As a result, future-oriented individuals will think that ten years from now the price of land in those areas will be much higher, say $1 million an acre. But, they also think, nine years from now it will already be widely recognized that in one short year an acre will be worth $1 million. Hence, nine years from now investors will be willing to pay almost $1 million for the land—even if, at that date (nine years from now), the smog has not yet been eliminated. In that case, these same individuals think, eight years from now investors will realize that in one short year the price will rise to almost $1 million and will pay close to that amount. Working backward like this makes it apparent that if people are confident land is going to be much more valuable in ten years, its price rises today.

Thinking Like an Economist

THE DISTRIBUTION OF WEALTH AND OWNERSHIP OF ASSETS

Although America is a very wealthy society, that wealth is distributed unevenly among American families. The chart shows median family net worth in 2001, classified by 2001 income percentiles. The median income of the 20 percent of families with the lowest incomes was $10,300, and the median net worth of these families was just $7,900. That means that half of the families in this income group had net worth less than $7,900. For families in the top 10 percent of income earners, median family income was $169,600, and median net worth was $833,600.

Not only is less wealth possessed by poor families than by high-income families, but the types of financial and nonfinancial assets held by families also differ by income. Wealthy families are more likely to own stocks and bonds, to hold mutual funds, and to have retirement accounts. The value of holdings of nonfinancial assets—cars, homes, nonresidential property, and businesses—varies widely by income as well. High-income families tend to have greater holdings in cars, residential property, and other property than do families with lower incomes, but the biggest difference across income categories is in the ownership of businesses. The median value of business equity held by the 10 percent of families with the highest 2001 income was $239,500, compared with holdings of $54,400 for the 10 percent of families with the next highest incomes.

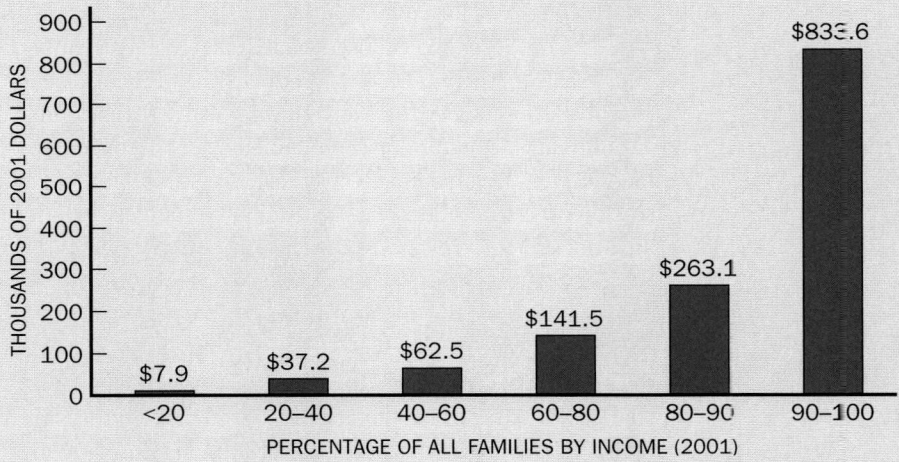

MEDIAN NET WORTH BY INCOME PERCENTILE

Thus, while changes in tastes or technology or incomes or the prices of other goods *today* could not account for some of the sharp changes in asset values described at the start of this section, changes in expectations concerning any of these variables in the future will have an effect *today* on the demand. Markets for assets are linked together over time. An event that is expected to happen in ten or fifteen or even fifty years can have a direct bearing on today's market.

To evaluate the effects of expected future prices on an asset's current price, the concept of present discounted value, introduced in Chapter 9, is important. By

Figure 39.4

HOW EXPECTATIONS CAN SHIFT DEMAND

Expectations that the price of an asset like gold will rise in the future can cause the demand curve to shift to the right, thereby raising the current price.

calculating the present discounted value, we can measure and compare returns anticipated in the future. Demand today for an asset will depend on the present discounted value that it is expected to fetch when sold in the future.

Present discounted values can change for two reasons. First, they can change because of a change in the expected price of an asset at the time one anticipates selling it. This type of change is illustrated in Figure 39.4. That such expectations of future prices can be quite volatile helps explain the volatility of asset prices. Investors in seventeenth-century Holland were willing to pay enormous prices for tulip bulbs because they expected to be able to sell the bulbs at even higher prices. Such price increases that are solely based on the expectation that prices will be higher in the future—and not based on increases in the actual returns yielded by the asset—are called **asset price bubbles.** Prices continue to rise as long as everyone expects them to rise. Once people believe that the rise will stop, the current price crashes. The tremendous increase in stock prices in the United States during the 1990s led many to worry that it was a bubble that would eventually crash. Others pointed to increased productivity that promised higher corporate profits in the future—an increase in the actual returns that stocks can pay.

Second, present discounted values can change because the interest rate changes. An increase in the interest rate reduces the present discounted value of the dollars that investors expect to receive in the future. This is one reason why increases in the interest rate are often accompanied by drops in share prices on the stock market, and vice versa. Smart investors therefore seek to forecast interest rates accurately. So-called Fed watchers try to anticipate changes in Federal Reserve policies that will affect the interest rate.

FORMING EXPECTATIONS

Changes in expectations about future returns or interest rates thus can be reflected in large changes in asset prices today. In part, individuals and firms form expectations by looking at past experience. If a company has steadily grown more valuable, investors may come to expect that pattern to continue. If the Federal Reserve acts to slow the economy by raising interest rates every time inflation rates increase, people come to expect inflation to be followed by higher interest rates.

Psychologists and economists have studied how individuals form expectations. Sometimes people are *myopic,* or short-sighted. They expect what is true today to be true tomorrow. The price of gold today is what it will be tomorrow. Sometimes they are *adaptive,* extrapolating events of the recent past into the future. If the price of gold today is 5 percent higher than it was last year, they expect its price next year to be 5 percent higher than it is today.

When people make full use of all relevant available data to form their expectations, economists say that their expectations are *rational.* The price of gold rises during an inflationary period, but the price of gold also goes down when inflation subsides. Thus, if a person knows that economic analysts are predicting lower inflation, she will not expect the gold price increases to continue. Even when individuals form their expectations rationally, they will not be right all the time. Sometimes they will be overly optimistic, sometimes overly pessimistic (although in making their decisions, they are aware of these possibilities). But the assumption of rational expectations is that on average they will judge correctly.

The 1970s was a decade when adaptive expectations reigned. Many investors came to expect prices of assets such as land and housing to continue to rise rapidly. The more they invested, the more money they made. The idea that the price of a house or of land might fall seemed beyond belief—even though history is full of episodes (most recently in Japan during the 1990s) when such prices fell dramatically. The weak real estate markets of the 1980s in many regions reminded investors of the importance of incorporating historical data in forming expectations.

But in this, as in all types of fortune-telling, history never repeats itself exactly. Since the situation today is never precisely like past experience, it is never completely clear which facts will be the relevant ones. Even the best-informed experts are likely to disagree. When it comes to predicting the future, everyone's crystal ball is cloudy.

Efficient Market Theory

The demand for any asset depends on all four of its basic attributes—average return, risk, tax treatment, and liquidity. In a well-functioning market, there are no bargains to be had: you get what you pay for. If some asset yields a higher average return than most other investments, it does so because that asset has a higher risk, is less liquid, or receives less favorable tax treatment.

That there are no bargains does not mean the investor's life is easy. He still must decide what he wants, just as he does when he goes into a grocery store. Figure 39.5 shows the kind of choices he faces. For the sake of simplicity, we ignore liquidity and tax considerations and focus only on average returns and risk. The figure shows the opportunity set in the way that is usual for this case. Because "risk" is bad, to get less risk we have to give up some average returns. That is why the trade-off has a positive slope. We can see that assets with greater risk have a higher average return. Point A represents a government T-bill—no risk but low return. Point B might represent a stock or mix of stocks of average riskiness; point C, a stock or mix of high risk. A very risk-averse person might choose A; a less risk-averse person, B; a still less risk-averse person, C.

The theory that prices perfectly reflect the characteristics of assets—there are no bargains—is called the **efficient market theory.** Since much of the work on efficient market theory has been done on publicly traded stocks, our discussion centers on them. The lessons can be applied to all asset prices, however.

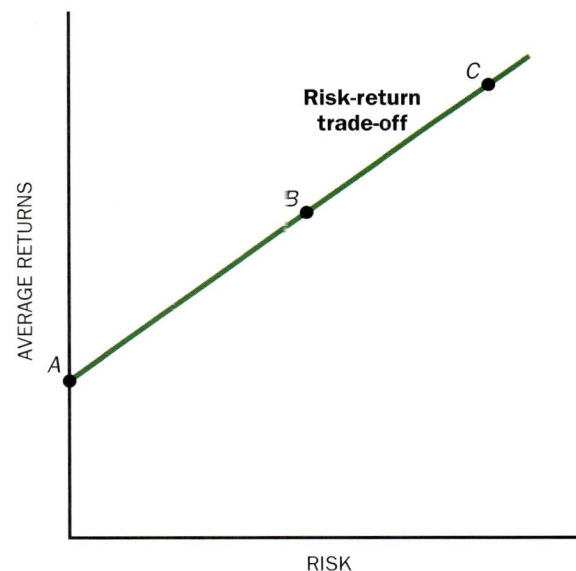

Figure 39.5

THE RISK-RETURN TRADE-OFF

To get a higher expected return, an investor must accept more risk.

EFFICIENCY AND THE STOCK MARKET

Most people do not think they can wander over to the racetrack and make a fortune. They are not so skeptical about the stock market. They believe that even if they themselves cannot sit down with the *Wall Street Journal* or browse an online broker's site and pick out all the best stocks, someone who studies the stock market for a living could do so. But economists startled the investment community in the early 1960s by pointing out that choosing successful stocks is no easier—and no harder—than choosing the fastest horses.

The efficient market theory explains this discrepancy in views. When economists speak of an efficient market, they are referring to one in which relevant information is widely known and quickly distributed to all participants. To oversimplify a bit, they envision a stock market where all investors have access to *Barron's* and *Fortune* magazines or to one of the many Internet sites devoted to providing good information about businesses, and where government requires businesses to disclose certain information to the public. Thus, each stock's expected return, its risk, its tax treatment, and so on will be fully known by all investors. Because participants have all the relevant information, asset prices will reflect that knowledge.

But it turns out that this broad dissemination of information is not only unrealistic but also unnecessary for the stock market to be efficient. Economists have shown that efficient markets do not require that *all* participants have information. If enough participants have information, prices will move as if the whole market had the information. All it takes is a few people knowledgeable enough to recognize a good deal (bad deal), and prices will quickly be bid up (or down) to levels that reflect complete information. And if prices reflect complete information, then even uninformed investors, purchasing at current prices, will reap the benefit; while they cannot "beat the market," neither do they have to worry about being "cheated" by an overpriced security.

You cannot beat an efficient market any more than you can beat the track. You can only get lucky in it. All the research done by the many big brokerage houses and individual investors adds up to a market that is in some respects like a casino. This is the irony of the view, held by most economists, that the stock market is an efficient one. If you are trying to make money in an efficient stock market, it is not enough to choose companies that you expect will be successful in the future. If you expect a company to be successful and everyone else also expects it to be successful, given the available information, then the price of the shares in that company will already be high. The only way to make abnormally high profits on stock purchases is to pick companies that will surprise the market by doing better than is generally expected. There are always such companies—the problem is to identify them before everyone else! When Microsoft shares first became available to the public in March 1968, they sold for 19 cents. By 2000, those shares were worth $58 dollars each. Early investors in technology stocks made enormous returns because technology firms did better than anyone had initially expected. Because of the success of many of these companies during the late 1990s, whenever a new one would "go public"—sells shares to the public for the first time—the price would often jump immediately to a very high level. The initial public offering of Google in 2004 exemplified this phenomenon. An investor buying the stock at high market prices can expect to earn only a normal level of profit. Of course, the trick is to know when to sell stocks before everyone else also decides it is time to sell. In 2000, the prices of technology stocks dropped dramatically. Today, shares of Microsoft trade for around $27 each.

The one exception is not really an exception because it involves trading with knowledge that other stock market participants do not have. *Inside traders* are individuals who buy and sell shares of companies for which they work. Studies show that their inside knowledge does in fact enable them to obtain above-average returns. Federal law requires inside traders to disclose when they buy and sell shares in their own company. People who may not have the inside knowledge but imitate the stock market behavior of the insiders also do slightly above average. The law also restricts the ability of insiders to share their information with outsiders and profit from their extra knowledge, and it exacts penalties for violations. After Ivan Boesky made untold millions trading on insider information in the 1980s, he paid large fines and even served time in jail. More recently, Martha Stewart spent five months in jail for obstructing an investigation into possible insider trading.

Because prices in an efficient market already reflect all available information, any price changes are a response to *unanticipated* news. If it was already known that something good was going to occur—for instance, that some new computer model better than all previous computers was going to be unveiled—the price of the firm's stock would reflect this knowledge (it would be high) before the computer actually hit the market. Investors might not know precisely how much better than its competitors the new computer was, and hence they could not predict precisely by how much future earnings were likely to rise. They would make an estimate. The market will reflect the average of these estimates. When the new computer is introduced, there is some chance that it will be better than this average, in which case the price will rise further. But there is also a chance that it will not be quite as good as this average estimate, in which case the price will fall, even though the computer is in fact better than anything else on the market. In the latter case, the "surprise" is that the computer is not as good as the market anticipated.

Since tomorrow's news is, by definition, unanticipated, no one can predict whether it will cause the stock price to rise or to fall. In an efficient stock market, prices will move unpredictably, depending on unexpected news. When a stock has an equal chance of rising or falling in value relative to the market as a whole, economists say that its price moves like a **random walk.** Figure 39.6 shows a computer-generated random walk, giving an idea of how unpredictable such a path is.

The phrase *random walk* conjures up the image of a drunk who rambles down the street with generally unstable—and unpredictable—movements. So too with the stock market. Although the level of all stock prices drifts upward, whether any particular stock will do better or worse than that average is unpredictable. If the stock market is indeed a random walk, it is virtually impossible for investors to beat the market. You can do just as well by throwing darts at the newspaper financial page as you can by carefully studying the prospects of each firm. The only way to do better than the market, on average, is to take greater risks; but taking greater risks also betters your chance of doing worse than the market.

The randomness of the market has one important consequence: *some* individuals are going to be successful. This is bad news for people who want to believe that their insights, rather than luck, are what has enabled them to beat the market.

EFFICIENT MARKETS OR RANDOM NOISE?

While most economists agree there is little evidence that individuals can consistently beat the market, even when they spend considerable money on information, they disagree over how to interpret this finding. Some see it as evidence of the efficiency of the market, as we have seen. But other economists view it as evidence of nothing more than the market's randomness. Those in the latter group point out that large changes in stock market prices often seem to occur in the absence of any "news" of sufficient magnitude to account for these changes. For example, there are usually ten or fifteen days in the year when the stock market changes by more than 2 percent—a very large change for a single day—without any obvious news-related explanation.

The famous economist John Maynard Keynes compared predictions of the stock market to predictions of the winner of a beauty contest in which what one had to decide was not who was most beautiful, but who the judges would think was the most beautiful. If investors suddenly "lose confidence" in a particular stock or in the whole stock market, or if they believe others are losing confidence, share prices may fall dramatically.

Figure 39.6

A COMPUTER-GENERATED RANDOM WALK

The series plotted here can be thought of as the closing price for a stock over 60 consecutive trading sessions. There is no predicting at the end of each day whether the stock will close higher or lower in the next day.

Strategies for Intelligent Investing

So far, we have investigated major investment alternatives available to those who save, some of the important attributes of each, and the ways in which their prices reflect these attributes. If you are lucky enough (have enough money) to be considering some of these alternatives, keep in mind the following four simple rules. These rules will not tell you how to make a million by the time you are twenty-five, but they will enable you to avoid the worst pitfalls of investing.

1. *Know the attributes of each asset, and relate them to your personal situation.* Each asset has characteristic returns, risk, tax treatment, and liquidity. In making choices among different assets, your attitude toward each of these attributes should be *compared with the average attitudes reflected in the marketplace.* Most individuals prefer safer, tax-favored, more liquid assets. That is why those assets sell at a premium (and produce a correspondingly lower average return). Are you willing to pay the amount required by the market for the extra safety or extra liquidity? If you are less risk averse than average, you will find riskier assets attractive. You will not be willing to pay the higher price—and accept the lower return—for a safer asset. And if you are confident that you are unlikely to need to sell an asset quickly, you will not be willing to pay the premium that more liquid assets require. If you are putting aside money for tuition next year, on the other hand, you probably will want to choose a relatively liquid asset.

2. *Give your financial portfolio a broad base.* In choosing among financial assets, you need to look not only at each asset separately but also at all of your assets together. A person's entire collection of assets is called her **portfolio.** (The portfolio also includes liabilities—what she owes—but consideration of these would take us beyond the scope of this chapter.) This rule is seen most clearly in the case of risk. One of the ways you reduce risk is by diversifying your investment portfolio. When a portfolio is well-diversified, it is extremely unlikely that something will go wrong with all the assets simultaneously. An investor with a diversified portfolio must still worry about events such as recessions or changes in the interest rate, which will tend to make all stocks go up or down. But events that primarily affect one firm will have a small impact on the overall holdings.

    Many mutual funds claim more than just diversification: they claim that their research and insight into markets enable them to pick winners. Our discussion of efficient markets casts doubt on these claims. Many other mutual funds do no research, claim no insights, and do nothing more than provide portfolio diversification. These are called *index funds.* There are several measures of the average price of stocks in the market. For instance, the Standard & Poor's (S&P) 500 index is the average price of 500 stocks chosen to be representative of the market as a whole. Other indexes track prices of various categories of stocks, such as transportation, utilities, or high technology. Index funds link their portfolio to these stock market indexes. Thus, there are a number of index funds that buy exactly the same mix of stocks that constitute the S&P 500 index. Naturally, these index funds do about as well as—no better and no worse than—the S&P 500 index, after a small charge for managing the fund is taken into account.

Because the index funds have low expenses, particularly in comparison with funds that are trying to outguess the market, they yield higher average returns to their investors than other funds with comparable risk.

3. *Look at* all *the risks you face, not just those in your financial portfolio.* Many people may be far less diversified than they believe. For example, consider someone who works for the one big company in town. She owns a house, has a good job, and has stock in the company, money in the bank, and a pension plan. But if that single company goes broke, she will lose her job, the value of her stock will fall, the price of her house is likely to decline as the local economy suffers, and even the pension plan may not pay as much as expected.

4. *Think twice before you think you can beat the market!* Efficient market theory delivers an important message to the personal investor. If an investment adviser tells you of an opportunity that beats the others on all counts, don't believe him. The bond that will produce a higher than average return carries with it more risk. The bank account that has a higher interest rate has less liquidity. The dream house at an unbelievable price probably has a leaky roof. The tax-favored bond will have a lower return—and so on. Efficient market theory, as we have seen, says that information about these characteristics is built into the price of assets, and hence built into the returns. Basically, investors can adjust the return to their portfolios only by adjusting the risk they face. Burton Malkiel, author of the best-selling book *A Random Walk Down Wall Street,* applies this theory to personal investment: "Every investor must decide the trade-off he or she is willing to make between eating well and sleeping well. The decision is up to you. High investment returns can be achieved only at the cost of substantial risk taking."[4]

---

[4]7th ed. (New York: Norton, 1999), p. 281.

Review and Practice

SUMMARY

1. Investment options for individuals include putting savings in a bank account of some kind or using them to buy real estate, bonds, or shares of stock or mutual funds.
2. Returns on investment can be received in four ways: as interest, dividends, rent, and capital gains.
3. Assets can differ in four ways: in their average returns, their riskiness, their treatment under tax law, and their liquidity.
4. By holding assets that are widely diversified, individuals can avoid many of the risks associated with specific assets, but not the risks associated with the market as a whole.
5. Today's price of an asset is influenced by expectations of the asset's price in the future. Expectation of a higher price in the future will cause the asset's price to rise today.
6. Asset prices can be very volatile because expectations about future returns can shift quickly.
7. The efficient market theory holds that all available information is fully reflected in the price of an asset. Accordingly, changes in price reflect only unanticipated events and, therefore, are random and unpredictable.
8. There are four rules for intelligent investors: (1) evaluate the characteristics of each asset and relate them to your personal situation; (2) give your financial portfolio a broad base; (3) look at all the risks you face, not just those in your financial portfolio; and (4) think twice before believing you can beat the market.

KEY TERMS

investment
real investment
financial investment
certificate of deposit (CD)
liquidity
dividends
retained earnings
capital gain
mutual fund
Treasury bills (T-bills)
diversification
expected returns
risk aversion
asset price bubbles
efficient market theory
random walk
portfolio

REVIEW QUESTIONS

1. Suppose an investor is considering two assets with identical expected rates of return. What three characteristics of the assets might help differentiate the choice between them?
2. List the principal alternative forms of investment that are available. What are the returns on each called? Rate them in terms of the characteristics described in Question 1.
3. True or false: "Two assets must have equal expected returns." If we modify the statement to read "Two assets that are equally risky must have equal expected returns," is the statement true? Explain your answer.
4. If you found out that several company presidents were buying or selling stock in their own companies, would you want to copy their behavior? Why or why not?
5. What is the efficient market theory? What implications does it have for whether you can beat the market? Does it imply that all stocks must yield the same expected return?
6. Why do economists expect the market to be efficient?
7. What alternative interpretations are given to the observation that individuals cannot, even by spending considerable money on information, consistently beat the market?
8. List and explain the four rules for intelligent investing.
9. True or false: "A single mutual fund may be a more diversified investment than a portfolio of a dozen stocks." Explain.

PROBLEMS

1. Imagine a lottery in which 1 million tickets are sold at $1 apiece, and the winning ticket receives a prize of $700,000. What is the expected return to buying a ticket in this lottery? Will a risk-averse person buy a ticket in this lottery?
2. Would you expect the rate of return on bonds to change with their length of maturity? Why or why not?
3. Why might a risk-averse investor put some money in junk bonds?
4. Would you predict that
   (a) the before-tax return on housing would be higher or lower than the before-tax return on other assets?
   (b) investors would be willing to pay more or less for a stock that has a high return when the economy is booming and a low return when the economy is in a slump than they would pay for a stock whose returns follow just the opposite pattern?
   (c) an investment with low liquidity would sell at a premium or at a discount compared with a similar investment with higher liquidity?
5. Imagine a short-term corporate $1,000 bond that promises to pay 8 percent interest over three years. This bond will pay $80 at the end of the first year and the second year, and $1,080 at the end of the third year. After one year, however, the market interest rate has increased to 12 percent. What will the bond be worth to an investor who is not too concerned about risk at that time? If the firm appears likely to go bankrupt, how will the expected return on this bond change?
6. The golfer Lee Trevino once said: "After losing two fortunes, I've learned. Now, when someone comes to me with a deal that's going to make me a million dollars, I say, 'Tell it to your mother.' Why would a stranger want to make me a million?" Explain how Trevino's perspective fits the efficient market theory.

GLOSSARY

absolute advantage: a country has an absolute advantage over another country in the production of a good if it can produce that good more efficiently (with fewer inputs)

adaptive expectations: expectations that respond or adapt to recent experience

adverse selection: the phenomenon that, as an insurance company raises its price, the best risks (those least likely to make a claim) drop out, so the mix of applicants changes adversely; now used more generally to refer to effects on the mix of workers, borrowers, products being sold, and so forth, resulting from a change in wages (interest rates, prices) or other variables

affirmative action: actions by employers to seek out actively minorities and women for jobs and to provide them with training and other opportunities for promotion

aggregate consumption function: the relationship between aggregate consumption and aggregate income

aggregate demand-inflation curve: the curve that shows the negative relationship between inflation and spending

aggregate expenditures: total spending on goods and services produced in the economy (consumption plus investment plus government purchases plus net exports)

aggregate expenditures schedule: the relationship between aggregate expenditures and national income for a given real rate of interest

aggregate saving: the sum of the savings of all individuals in society

antitrust laws: laws that discourage monopoly and restrictive practices and encourage greater competition

appreciation: a change in the exchange rate that enables a unit of currency to buy more units of foreign currencies

asset price bubbles: asset price increases that are based solely on the expectation that prices will be higher in the future, and not based on increases in the actual returns yielded by the asset

asymmetric information: a situation in which the parties to a transaction have different information, as when the seller of a used car has more information about its quality than the buyer

automatic stabilizer: expenditure that automatically increases or tax that automatically decreases when economic conditions worsen, and that, therefore, tends to stabilize the economy automatically

average cost: total costs divided by total output

average tax rate: the ratio of taxes to taxable income

average variable costs: total variable costs divided by total output

backward induction: approach of starting from the end of the game and working backward to determine the best strategy, often used for strategic interactions that occur a repeated but fixed number of times

balance of trade: a country's *imports* minus its *exports* (net exports)

basic competitive model: the model of the economy that pulls together the assumptions of self-interested consumers, profit-maximizing firms, and perfectly competitive markets

basic research: fundamental research; it often produces a wide range of applications, but the output of basic research itself usually is not of direct commercial value; the output is knowledge, rather than a product and it typically cannot be patented

basic trade identity: net exports plus capital inflows equals zero

beggar-thy-neighbor policies: restrictions on imports designed to increase a country's national output, so-called because they increase that country's output while simultaneously hurting the output of other countries

behavioral economics: a field of economics that rejects the basic model of consumer choice, drawing instead upon the findings of psychologists and economists who conduct laboratory experiments to study the ways people actually make choices

benefit taxes: taxes that are levied on a particular product, the revenues of which go for benefits to those who purchase the product

bilateral trade: trade between two parties

block grants: grants to states, which are given considerable discretion in how the money is spent

boom: a period of time when resources are being fully used and GDP is growing steadily

borrowed reserves: *reserves* borrowed from the discount window of the Federal Reserve

budget constraints: the limitations on consumption of different goods imposed by the fact that households have only a limited amount of money to spend (their budget); the budget constraint *defines* the opportunity set of individuals when the only constraint that they face is money

business cycle: fluctuations in real economic activity around the economy's average growth path

capital deepening: an increase in capital per worker

capital gain: the increase in the value of an asset between the time it is purchased and the time it is sold

capital goods investment: investment in machines and buildings (to be distinguished from investments in inventory, in research and development, or in training [human capital])

capital goods: the machines and buildings in which firms invest, with funds obtained in the *capital market*

capital inflows: money from abroad that is used to buy investments, to be deposited in U.S. banks, to buy U.S. government bonds, or to be lent in the United States for any reason

capital market: the various institutions concerned with raising funds and sharing and insuring risks, including banks, insurance markets, bond markets, and the stock market

capital outflows: money from the United States that is used to buy foreign investments or foreign government bonds, to be deposited in foreign banks or lent in foreign countries for any reason

cartel: a group of producers with an agreement to collude in setting prices and output

causation: the relationship that results when a change in one variable is not only correlated with but actually produces a change in another variable; the change in the second variable is a consequence of the change in the first variable, rather than both changes being a consequence of a change in a third variable

central bank: the government institution responsible for monetary policy

central planning: the system in which central government bureaucrats (as opposed to private entrepreneurs or even local government bureaucrats) determine what will be produced and how it will be produced

certificate of deposit (CD): an account in which money is deposited for a preset length of time and yields a slightly higher return to compensate for the reduced liquidity

circular flow: the way in which funds move through the capital, labor, and product markets between households, firms, the government, and the foreign sector

Coase's theorem: the assertion that, if property rights are properly defined, then people will be forced to pay for any negative externalities they impose on others and market transactions will produce efficient outcomes

collusion: when firms act jointly (more nearly as they would if there were a monopolist) to increase overall profits

command-and-control approach: the approach to controlling environmental externalities in which the government provides detailed regulations about what firms can and cannot do, including what technologies they can employ

commercial policies: policies directed at affecting either imports or exports

comparative advantage: a country has a comparative advantage over another country in one good as opposed to another good if its *relative* efficiency in the production of the first good is higher than the other country's

compensating wage differentials: differences in wages that can be traced to nonpecuniary attributes of a job, such as the degree of autonomy and risk

competition: rivalry between producers for customers or between consumers for goods and services

complements: two goods are complements if an increase in the price of one will reduce the demand for the other

constant, diminishing, or increasing returns to scale (economies of scale): when all inputs are increased by a certain proportion, output increases in equal, smaller, or greater proportion, respectively; increasing returns to scale are also called *economies of scale*

consumer price index: a price index in which the basket of goods is defined by what a typical consumer purchases

consumer protection legislation: laws aimed at protecting consumers, for instance by assuring that consumers have more complete information about items they are considering buying

consumer sovereignty: the idea that individuals are the best judges of what is in their own interests and promotes their well-being

consumer surplus: the difference between what a person would be willing to pay and what he actually has to pay to buy a certain amount of a good

corporation income taxes: taxes based on the income, or profit, received by a corporation

correlation: the relationship that results when a change in one variable is consistently associated with a change in another variable

countercyclical policies: policies designed to keep the economy at full employment by smoothing out fluctuations

countervailing duties: duties (tariffs) that are imposed by a country to counteract subsidies provided to a foreign producer

cross subsidization: the practice of charging higher prices to one group of consumers in order to subsidize lower prices for another group

crowding out: a decrease in private investment resulting from an increase in government expenditures

currency board: a system in which the exchange rate between the local currency and foreign currency is fixed by law

cyclical unemployment: the increase in unemployment that occurs as the economy goes into a slowdown or recession

deadweight loss: the difference between what producers gain and (the monetary value of) what consumers lose when output is restricted under imperfect competition; also, the difference between what the government gains and what consumers lose when taxes are imposed

deflation: a persistent decrease in the general level of prices

demand: the quantity of a good or service that a household or firm chooses to buy at a given price

demand curve: the relationship between the quantity demanded of a good and the price, whether for an individual or for the market (all individuals) as a whole

demand deposits: deposits that can be drawn upon instantly, like checking accounts

demographic effects: effects that arise from changes in characteristics of the population such as age, birthrates, and location

depreciation: (a) the decrease in the value of an asset; in particular, the amount that capital goods decrease in value as they are used and become old; (b) a change in the exchange rate that enables a unit of one currency to buy fewer units of foreign currencies

depression: a strong downward fluctuation in the economy that is more severe than a recession

devaluation: a reduction in the rate of exchange between one currency and other currencies under a fixed exchange-rate system

developed countries: the wealthiest nations in the world, including Western Europe, the United States, Canada, Japan, Australia, and New Zealand

diminishing marginal utility: the principle that says that as an individual consumes more and more of a good, each successive unit increases her utility, or enjoyment, less and less

diminishing returns (to scale): the principle that as one input increases, with other inputs fixed, the resulting increase in output tends to be smaller and smaller

discount rate: the interest rate charged on borrowed reserves

discretion: the ability to make explicit policy decisions in response to macroeconomic conditions

discretionary action: deliberate policy changes by the government, often used to indicate policy actions not constrained by past commitments

discretionary spending: government expenditures that are decided on an annual basis

disposable income: income after paying taxes

distribution: the allocation of goods and services produced by the economy

diversification: spreading one's wealth among a large number of different assets

dividends: that portion of corporate profits paid out to shareholders

dollarization: abandonment of the domestic currency in favor of the U.S. dollar

dominant strategy: strategy that works best no matter what the other player does in a game

dual economies: separations in many *less developed countries (LDCs)* between impoverished rural sectors and urban sectors that have higher wages and more advanced technology

dumping: the practice of selling a good abroad at a lower price than at home, or below costs of production

dynamic efficiency: an economy that appropriately balances short-run concerns (static efficiency) with long-run concerns (focusing on encouraging R & D)

dynamic inconsistency: the problem of whether a government will actually carry out a promised course of action

earned income tax credit: a reduction in taxes provided to low-income workers based on the amount of income they earn and the size of their family

economic rent: payments made to a factor of production that are in excess of what is required to elicit the supply of that factor

economies of scope: the situation that exists when it is less expensive to produce two products together than it would be to produce each one separately

efficiency wage: the wage at which total labor costs are minimized

efficiency wage theory: the theory that paying higher wages (up to a point) lowers total production costs, for instance by leading to a more productive labor force

efficient market theory: the theory that all available information is reflected in the current price of an asset

entitlement programs: programs that provide benefits automatically to individuals meeting certain criteria (such as age)

entry deterrence: the reduction of competition by preventing other firms from entering the market

entry-deterring practices: practices of incumbent firms designed to discourage the entry of rivals into the market

equilibrium price: the price at which demand equals supply

equilibrium quantity: the quantity demanded and supplied at the equilibrium price, where demand equals supply

equilibrium: a condition in which there are no forces (reasons) for change

European Union: an important regional trade bloc that now covers most of Europe

excess demand: the situation in which the quantity demanded at a given price exceeds the quantity supplied

excess reserves: *reserves* over and above the amount banks are legally required to hold (required reserves)

excess supply: the situation in which the quantity supplied at a given price exceeds the quantity demanded

exchange: the act of trading that forms the basis for markets

exchange efficiency: the condition in which whatever the economy produces is distributed among people in such a way that there are no gains to further trade

exchange rate the rate at which one currency (such as dollars) can be exchanged for another (such as euros, yen, or pounds)

excise taxes: taxes on a particular good or service

expansions: a period in which real GDP is growing

expected returns: the average return—a single number that combines the various possible returns per dollar invested with the chances that each of these returns will actually be paid

experimental economics: the branch of economics which analyzes certain aspects of economic behavior in a controlled, laboratory setting

export-led growth: the strategy that government should encourage exports in which the country has a comparative advantage to stimulate growth

exports: goods produced domestically but sold abroad

externality: a phenomenon that arises when an individual or firm takes an action but does not bear all the costs (negative externality) or receive all the benefits (positive externality)

factor demand: the amount of an input demanded by a firm, given the price of the input and the quantity of output being produced; in a competitive market, an input will be demanded up to the point where the value of the marginal product of that input equals the price of the input

federal funds market: the market through which banks borrow and lend reserves

federal funds rate: the interest rate on overnight interbank loans

Federal Open Market Committee (FOMC): the committee of the Federal Reserve System that sets monetary policy

final goods approach: measuring GDP by adding up all sales of final goods

financial investments: investments in stocks, bonds, or other financial instruments; these investments provide the funds that allow investments in *capital goods*

fiscal deficit: the gap between the government's expenditures and its revenues from sources other than additional borrowing

fiscal surplus: the amount by which government tax revenues exceed expenditures

fixed costs: the costs resulting from fixed inputs, sometimes called *overhead costs*

fixed exchange rate system: an exchange rate system in which the value of each currency is fixed in relationship to other currencies

flexible (or floating) exchange rate system: a system in which exchange rates are determined by market forces, the law of supply and demand, without government interference

flows: variables such as the output of the economy *per year;* stocks are in contrast to flows; flows measure the changes in stocks over a given period of time

four-firm concentration ratio: the fraction of output produced by the top four firms in an industry

fractional reserve system: the system of banking in which banks hold a fraction of the amount on deposit in reserves

free-rider: someone who enjoys the benefit of a (public) good without paying for it; because it is difficult to preclude anyone from using a pure public good, those who benefit from the goods have an incentive to avoid paying for them (that is, to be a free-rider)

free trade: trade among countries that occurs without barriers such as tariffs or quotas

frictional unemployment: unemployment associated with people moving from one job to another or moving into the labor force

fringe benefits: compensation that is not in the form of direct cash to a worker, such as health insurance, retirement pay, and life insurance

full employment: a situation in which the demand for labor equals the supply of labor

full-employment deficit: what the deficit would be if the economy were at full employment

full-employment level of output: the level of output that the economy can produce under normal circumstances with a given stock of plant and equipment and a given supply of labor

fully funded program: a pension program in which each worker pays into an individual retirement account that is invested until the worker retires

game table: table showing the payoffs to each player of a game

game theory: theory designed to understand strategic choices, that is, to understand how people or organizations behave when they expect their actions to influence the behavior of others

game tree: diagram used to represent sequential games

GDP deflator: a weighted average of the prices of different goods and services, where the weights represent the importance of each of the goods and services in *GDP*

General Agreement on Tariffs and Trade (GATT): the agreement among the major trading countries of the world that created the framework for lowering barriers to trade and resolving trade disputes; established after World War II, it has been succeeded by the World Trade Organization (WTO)

general equilibrium analysis: a simultaneous analysis of all capital, product, and labor markets throughout the economy; it shows, for instance, the impact on all prices and quantities of immigration or a change in taxes

general equilibrium: the full equilibrium of the economy, when all markets clear simultaneously

gift and estate taxes: taxes imposed on the transfers of wealth from one generation to another

globalization: the closer integration of the countries of the world—especially the increased level of trade and movements of capital—brought on by lower costs of transportation and communication

Great Depression: the prolonged, worldwide period of severe economic recession during the 1930s

green revolution: the invention and dissemination of new seeds and agricultural practices that led to vast increases in agricultural output in *less developed countries (LDCs)* during the 1960s and 1970s

gross domestic product (GDP): the total money value of all final goods and services produced within a nation's borders during a given period of time

horizontal equity: the principle that says that those who are in identical or similar circumstances should pay identical or similar amounts in taxes

horizontal merger: a merger between two firms that produce the same goods

human capital: the stock of accumulated skills and experience that makes workers productive

imperfect competition: any market structure in which there is some competition but firms face downward-sloping demand curves

imperfect information: a situation in which market participants lack information (such as information about prices or characteristics of goods and services) important for their decision making

imperfect substitutes: goods that can substitute for each other, but imperfectly so

implicit labor contract: an unwritten understanding between employer and employees that employees will receive a stable wage throughout fluctuating economic conditions

import function: the relationship between imports and national income

imports: goods produced abroad but bought domestically

incentives: benefits, or reduced costs, that motivate a decision maker in favor of a particular choice

income approach: the approach to calculating GDP that involves measuring the income generated to all of the participants in the economy

income effect: the reduced consumption of a good whose price has increased that is due to the reduction in a person's buying power, or "real" income; when a person's real income is lower, normally she will consume less of all goods, including the higher-priced good

income elasticity of demand: the percentage change in quantity demanded of a good as the result of a 1 percent change in income (the percentage change in quantity demanded divided by the percentage change in income)

income per capita: total income divided by the population

income-expenditure analysis: the analysis that determines equilibrium output by relating aggregate expenditures to income

individual income taxes: taxes based on the income received by an individual or household

industrial policies: government policies designed to promote particular sectors of the economy

industrialized countries: see *developed countries*

infant industry argument: the argument that industries must be protected from foreign competition while they are young, until they have a chance to acquire the skills to enable them to compete on equal terms

inferior good: a good the consumption of which falls as income rises

infinite elasticity: the situation that exists when any amount will be demanded (supplied) at a particular price, but nothing will be demanded (supplied) if the price increases (declines) even a small amount

inflation: the rate of increase of the general level of prices

inflation adjustment line: a line showing the current rate of inflation; used with the inflation-adjustment curve to determine the equilibrium level of output

inflation shocks: events that produce temporary shifts in the SRIA curve

inflation targeting: policies designed to stabilize the economy through countercyclical policies while ensuring that average inflation remains low

information: the basis of decision making that can affect the structure of markets and their ability to use society's scarce resources efficiently

inside lag: the time it takes to recognize there has been a chance in the economy and decide on the appropriate policy response; in the United States, the inside lag for fiscal policy is normally assumed to be longer than the outside lag for monetary policy

intellectual property: proprietary knowledge, such as that protected by patents and copyright

interest: the return a saver receives in addition to the original amount she deposited (loaned) and the amount a borrower must pay in addition to the original amount he borrowed

interest-rate parity condition: a condition assuming perfect capital mobility where expected returns are equal across countries in equilibrium

inventory investment: firms' investment in raw materials or output on hand

investment function: the relationship between the level of real investment and the value of the real interest rate; also called the *investment schedule*

investment: the purchase of an asset that will provide a return over a long period of time. From the national perspective, an increase in the stock of capital goods or any other expenditure designed to increase future output; from the perspective of the individual, any expenditure designed to increase an individual's future wealth, such as the purchase of a share in a company (Since some other individual is likely selling the share, that person is disinvesting, and the net investment for the economy is zero.)

job discrimination: discrimination in which disadvantaged groups have less access to better paying jobs

joint products: products that are naturally produced together, such as wool and mutton

labor force participation decision: the decision by an individual to seek work actively, that is, to participate in the labor market

labor force participation rate: the fraction of the working-age population that is employed or seeking employment

labor market: the market in which the services of workers are bought and sold

labor turnover rate: the rate at which a firm's workers quit to look for another job

land reform: the redistribution of land by the government to those who actually work the land

large open economy: an economy open to international trade and capital flows that is large enough, relative to the global economy, that its domestic conditions affect world levels of interest rates or incomes

law of supply and demand: the law in economics that holds that, in equilibrium, prices are determined so that demand equals supply; changes in prices thus reflect shifts in the demand or supply curves

learning by doing: the increase in productivity that occurs as a firm gains experience from producing and that results in a decrease in the firm's production costs

learning curve: the curve describing how costs of production decline as cumulative output increases over time

less-developed countries (LDCs): the poorest nations of the world, including much of Africa, Latin America, and Asia

life-cycle saving: saving that is motivated by a desire to smooth consumption over an individual's lifetime and to meet special needs that arise in various times of life; saving for retirement is the most important aspect of life-cycle saving

liquidity: the ease with which an investment can be turned into cash

loanable funds market: the market in which the supply of funds is allocated to those who wish to borrow; equilibrium requires that saving (the supply of funds) equals investment (the demand for funds)

long run: a length of time sufficient to allow wages and prices to adjust fully to equilibrate supply and demand

luxury taxes: excise taxes imposed on luxuries, goods typically consumed disproportionately by the wealthy

M1, M2, M3: measures of the money supply: M1 includes currency and checking accounts; M2 includes M1 plus savings deposits, CDs, and money market funds; M3 includes M2 plus large-denomination savings deposits and institutional money-market mutual funds.

macroeconomics: the top-down view of the economy, focusing on aggregate characteristics

managerial slack: the lack of managerial efficiency (for instance, in cutting costs) that occurs when firms are insulated from competition

marginal benefits: the extra benefits resulting, for instance, from the increased consumption of a commodity

marginal cost: the additional cost corresponding to an additional unit of output produced

marginal product: the amount output increases with the addition of one unit of an input

marginal propensity to consume: the amount by which consumption increases when income increases by a dollar

marginal propensity to import: the amount by which imports increase when income increases by a dollar

marginal propensity to save: the amount by which savings increase when income increases by a dollar

marginal rate of transformation: the amount of extra production of one good that one obtains from reducing the production of another good by one unit, moving along the production possibilities curve

marginal revenue: the extra revenue received by a firm for selling one additional unit of a good

marginal tax rate: the extra tax that will have to be paid as a result of an additional dollar of income

marginal utility: the extra utility, or enjoyment, a person receives from the consumption of one additional unit of a good

market clearing price: the price at which supply equals demand, so there is neither excess supply nor excess demand

market demand curve: the total amount of a particular good or service demanded in the economy at each price; it is calculated by "adding horizontally" the individual demand curves; that is, at any given price, it is the sum of the individual demands

market economy: an economy that allocates resources primarily through the interaction of individuals (households) and private firms

market failures: situations in which a market economy fails to attain economic efficiency

market structure: term used to describe the organization of the market, such as whether there is a high degree of *competition*, a *monopoly*, an *oligopoly*, or *monopolistic competition*

market supply curve: the total amount of a particular good or service that all the firms in the economy together would like to supply at each price; it is calculated by "adding horizontally" the individual firm's supply curves (that is, it is the sum of the amounts each firm is willing to supply at any given price)

marketable permits: a permit issued by the government, which can be bought and sold, that allows a firm to emit a certain amount of pollution

matching programs: programs in which federal outlays depend on state expenditures

medium of exchange: an item that can be commonly exchanged for goods and services throughout the economy

merit goods: goods that are determined by government to be good for people, regardless of whether people desire them for themselves or not

microeconomics: the bottom-up view of the economy, focusing on individual households and firms

monetary policy rule: the systematic relationship between the central bank's setting of policy and the variables that it reacts to, such as inflation, cyclical unemployment, or the output gap

money: any item that serves as a medium of exchange, a store of value, and a unit of account

money multiplier: the amount by which a new deposit into the banking system (from the outside) is multiplied as it is loaned out, redeposited, reloaned, etc., by banks

monopolistic competition: the form of imperfect competition in which the market has sufficiently few firms that each one faces a downward-sloping demand curve, but enough that each can ignore the reactions of rivals to what it does

monopoly rents: see *pure profit*

monopoly: a market consisting of only one firm

moral hazard: the principle that says that those who purchase insurance have a reduced incentive to avoid what they are insured against

multilateral trade: trade between more than two parties

multiplier: the amount equilibrium output increases when the aggregate expenditures schedule shifts by a dollar

mutual fund: a fund that gathers money from different investors and purchases a range of assets; each investor then owns a portion of the entire fund.

Nash equilibrium: game equilibrium when both players execute their dominant strategies (that is, neither player would change his strategy if offered the chance to do so at the end of the game)

national saving: the sum of private savings and government saving

natural monopoly: a monopoly that exists because average costs of production are declining beyond the level of output demanded in the market, thus making entry unprofitable and making it efficient for there to be a single firm

natural rate of unemployment: the unemployment rate when the economy is at potential GDP and cyclical unemployment is zero

net capital inflows: total capital inflows minus total capital outflows

neutrality of money: the idea that changing the money supply has no real effects on the economy, which is a basic implication of the full-employment model

newly industrialized countries (NICs): nations that have recently moved from being quite poor to being middle-income countries, including South Korea, Taiwan, Singapore, and Hong Kong

nominal GDP: the value of *gross domestic product* in a particular year measured in that year's prices

nominal rate of interest: the percentage return on a deposit, loan, or bond; the nominal rate of interest does not take into account the effects of inflation

nominal wage: the average wage not adjusted for changes in the prices of consumer goods

nondiscretionary spending: expenditures that are determined automatically, such as interest payments and expenditures on *entitlements*

nonborrowed reserves: the Federal Reserve affects the level of nonborrowed reserves through open-market operations

nonpecuniary attributes: aspects of a job other than the wage it pays

nonrivalrous goods: goods whose consumption or use by one person does not exclude consumption by another person

normal good: a good the consumption of which rises as income rises

normative economics: economics in which judgments about the desirability of various policies are made; the conclusions rest on value judgments as well as facts and theories

North American Free Trade Agreement (NAFTA): the agreement between Canada, the United States, and Mexico that lowered trade and other barriers among the countries

Okun's law: the relationship between the output gap and cyclical unemployment first identified by Arthur Okun; according to Okun's law, cyclical unemployment of 1 percent is associated with a negative output gap of approximately 2 percent

oligopoly: the form of imperfect competition in which the market has several firms, sufficiently few that each one must take into account the reactions of rivals to what it does

open economy: an economy that is actively engaged in international trade

Open Market Desk: the office at the New York Federal Reserve that undertakes open-market operations for the Federal Reserve System

open-market operations: central banks' purchase or sale of government bonds in the open market

operating procedures: the manner in which a central bank chooses to implement monetary policy

opportunity cost: the cost of a resource, measured by the value of the next-best alternative use of that resource

opportunity set: a summary of the choices available to individuals, as defined by budget constraints and time constraints

output gap: the percentage deviation of actual GDP from potential

outside lag: the time lag between when a policy action is undertaken and when the action has an impact on the economy; the outside lag for fiscal policy is normally assumed to be shorter than the outside lag for monetary policy

outsourcing: the move by U.S. firms to import goods and services these firms formerly produced in the United States

Pareto efficient: a resource allocation is said to be Pareto efficient if there is no rearrangement which can make anyone better off without making someone else worse off

partial equilibrium analysis: an analysis that focuses on only one or a few markets at a time

patent: a government decree giving an inventor the exclusive right to produce, use, or sell an invention for a period of time

pay-as-you-go program: pension programs such as Social Security in which the taxes paid by today's workers go to pay the benefits of today's retirees

payroll taxes: taxes based on payroll (wages) that is used to finance the Social Security and Medicare programs

peaks: the point in a business cycle where real output reaches its maximum level

perfect competition: a situation in which each firm is a price taker—it cannot influence the market price; at the market price, the firm can sell as much as it wishes, but if it raises its price, it loses all sales

perfectly mobile capital: capital that responds quickly to changes in returns in different countries

Phillips curve the trade-off between unemployment and inflation such that a lower level of unemployment is associated with a higher level of inflation

piece-rate system: a compensation system in which workers are paid specifically for each item produced

plant and equipment investment: purchases by firms of new capital goods

portfolio: an individual's entire collection of assets and liabilities

positive economics: economics that describes how the economy behaves and predicts how it might change—for instance, in response to some policy change

positive externalities: phenomena that occur when an individual or firm takes an action but does not receive all the benefits

potential GDP: a measure of what the value of GDP would be if the economy's resources were fully employed

present discounted value: how much an amount of money to be received in the future is worth right now

price: the price of a good or service is what must be given in exchange for the good

price ceiling: a maximum price above which market prices are not legally allowed to rise

price discrimination: the practice of a firm charging different prices to different customers or in different markets

price dispersion: a situation that occurs when the same item is sold for different prices by different firms

price elasticity of demand: the percentage change in quantity demanded of a good as the result of a 1 percent change in price (the percentage change in quantity demanded divided by the percentage change in price)

price elasticity of supply: the percentage change in quantity supplied of a good as the result of a 1 percent change in price (the percentage change in quantity supplied divided by the percentage change in price)

price floor: a minimum price below which market prices are not legally allowed to fall

price system: the economic system in which prices are used to allocate scarce resources

price taker: firms that take the price for the good or service they sell as given; the price is unaffected by their level of production.

price-level targeting: a rarely adopted policy designed to achieve a stable price level

principal: the original amount a saver deposits in a bank (lends) or a borrower borrows

prisoner's dilemma: a situation in which the noncooperative pursuit of self-interest by two parties makes them both worse off

private marginal cost: the marginal cost of production borne by the producer of a good; when there is a negative externality, such as air pollution, private marginal cost is less than social marginal cost.

private property: ownership of property (or other assets) by individuals or corporations; under a system of private property, owners have certain property rights, but there may also be legal restrictions on the use of property

privatization: the process whereby functions that were formerly undertaken by government are delegated instead to the private sector

producer price index: a price index that measures the average level of producers' prices

producer surplus: the difference between the price for which a producer would be willing to provide a good or service and the actual price at which the good or service is sold

product differentiation: the fact that similar products (like breakfast cereals or soft drinks) are perceived to differ from one another and thus are imperfect substitutes

product market: the market in which goods and services are bought and sold

production efficiency: the condition in which firms cannot produce more of some goods without producing less of other goods; the economy is on its production possibilities curve

production function: the relationship between the inputs used in production and the level of output

production possibilities curve: a curve that defines the opportunity set for a firm or an entire economy and gives the possible combination of goods (outputs) that can be produced from a given level of inputs

production possibilities: the combination of outputs of different goods that an economy can produce with given resources

product-mix efficiency: the condition in which the mix of goods produced by the economy reflects the preferences of consumers

profits: total revenues minus total costs

progressive tax system: describes a tax system in which the rich pay a larger fraction of their income than the poor

property rights: the rights of an owner of private property; these typically include the right to use the property as she sees fit (subject to certain restrictions, such as zoning) and the right to sell it when and to whom she sees fit

property taxes: taxes based on the value of property

protectionism: the policy of protecting domestic industries from the competition of foreign-made goods

public good: a good, such as national defense, that costs little or nothing for an extra individual to enjoy and the costs of preventing any individual from the enjoyment of which are high; public goods have the properties of nonrivalrous consumption and nonexcludability

pure profit: the profit earned by a monopolist that results from its reducing output and increasing the price from the level at which price equals marginal cost; also called *monopoly rents*

quantity equation of exchange: the equation $MV = PY$, which summarizes the relationship between the amount of money individuals wish to hold and the dollar value of transactions

quota rents: profits that result from the artificially created scarcity of quotas and accrue to firms that are allocated the rights to import

quotas: limits on the amount of foreign goods that can be imported

random walk: a term used to describe the way the prices of stocks move; the next movement cannot be predicted on the basis of previous movements

rational choice: a process in which individuals weigh the costs and benefits of each possibility and in which the choices made are those within the opportunity set that maximize net benefits

rationing systems: any system of allocating scarce resources, applied particularly to systems other than the price system; rationing systems include rationing by coupons and rationing by queues

real exchange rate: exchange rate adjusted for changes in the relative price levels in different countries

real GDP: the real value of all final goods and services produced in the economy, measured in dollars adjusted for inflation

real investment: the investment that is part of aggregate expenditures, such as the purchase of new factories and machines

real product wage: the wage divided by the price of the good being produced

real rate of interest: the real return to saving, equal to the nominal rate of interest minus the rate of inflation

real wage: the average wage adjusted for changes in the prices of consumer goods

recession: two consecutive quarters of a year during which GDP falls

regressive tax system: describes a tax system in which the poor pay a larger fraction of their income than the rich

regulatory capture: a term used to describe a situation in which regulators serve the interests of the regulated rather than the interests of consumers

relative elasticity: a good is said to be **relatively elastic** when the price elasticity of its demand is greater than unity; a good is said to be **relatively inelastic** when the price elasticity of its demand is less than unity

relative price: the ratio of any two prices; the relative price of CDs and DVDs is just the ratio of their prices

rent seeking: the name given to behavior that seeks to obtain benefits from favorable government decisions, such as protection from foreign competition

repeated games: games that are played many times over by the same players

repurchases (RPs): Federal Reserve open market transactions that involve a combined sale of a government security and an agreement to repurchase it at a future time, perhaps the next day

reputation: the "good will" of a firm resulting from its past performance; maintaining one's reputation provides an incentive to maintain quality

reservation wage: the wage below which an individual chooses not to participate in the labor market

reserves: funds held by banks in the form of vault cash or in deposits with the Federal Reserve

residential investment: households' purchases of new homes

restrictive practices: practices of oligopolists designed to restrict competition, including vertical restrictions like exclusive territories

retained earnings: that part of the net earnings of a firm that are not paid out to shareholders, but retained by the firm

revenue curve: the relationship between a firm's total output and its revenues

revenues: the amount a firm receives for selling its products, equal to the price received multiplied by the quantity sold

right-to-work laws: laws that prevent union membership from being a condition of employment

risk aversion: the avoidance of bearing risk

rivalrous goods: goods whose consumption or use by one person excludes consumption by another person

royalty: a fee charged by a patent holder that allows others to use its patent

rules: automatic adjustments of policy in response to macroeconomic conditions

sales tax: a tax imposed on the purchase of goods and services

scarcity: term used to describe the limited availability of resources, so that if no price were charged for a good or service, the demand for it would exceed its supply

search: the process by which consumers gather information about what is available in the market, including prices, or by which workers gather information about the jobs that are available, including wages

seasonal unemployment: unemployment that varies with the seasons, such as that associated with the decline in construction in winter

sequential game: a game in which players take turns and each can observe what choices were made in earlier moves

sharecropping: an arrangement, prevalent in many *less-developed countries (LDCs)* in which a worker works land, giving the landowner a fixed share of the output

short run: a length of time during which wages and prices do not fully adjust to equilibrate supply and demand

shortage: a situation in which demand exceeds supply at the current price

short-run aggregate production function: the relationship between output and employment in the short run, that is, with a given set of machines and buildings

short-run inflation adjustment curve: positively sloped curve that shows the rate of inflation at each level of output relative to potential GDP for a given expected rate of inflation

signal: to convey information, for example a prospective worker's earning a college degree to persuade an employer that he has desirable characteristics that will enhance his productivity

sin taxes: excise taxes on alcohol and tobacco

slope: the amount by which the value along the vertical axis increases as the result of a change in one unit along the horizontal axis; the slope is calculated by dividing the change in the vertical axis (the "rise") by the change in horizontal axis (the "run")

small open economy: an economy open to international trade and capital flows but whose domestic conditions are too small, relative to the global economy, to affect world levels of interest rates or incomes

social insurance: insurance provided by the government to individuals, for instance, against disabilities, unemployment, or health problems (for the aged)

social marginal cost: the marginal cost of production, including the cost of any negative externality, such as air pollution, borne by individuals in the economy other than the producer

stagflation: a situation with high inflation and high cyclical unemployment

static efficiency: the efficiency of the economy with given technology; taxes used to finance basic research and monopoly power resulting from patents cause a loss in static efficiency

statistical discrimination: differential treatment of individuals of different gender or race that is based on the use of observed correlations (statistics) between performance and some observable characteristics; it may even result from the use of variables like education in which there is a causal link to performance

stocks: variables like the capital stock or the money supply stock, that describe the state of the economy (such as its wealth) at a point of time; they are contrasted by *flows*

store of value: something that can be accepted as payment in the present and exchanged for items of value in the future

strategic behavior: decision making that takes into account the possible reactions of others

strategic trade theory: the theory that protection can give a country a strategic advantage over rivals, for instance by helping reduce domestic costs as a result of economies of scale

structural unemployment: long-term unemployment that results from structural factors in the economy, such as a mismatch between the skills required by newly created jobs and the skills possessed by those who have lost their jobs in declining industries

substitutes: two goods are substitutes if the demand for one increases when the price of the other increases

substitution effect: the reduced consumption of a good whose price has increased that is due to the changed trade-off, the fact that one has to give up more of other goods to get one more unit of the high-priced good; the substitution effect is associated with a change in the slope of the *budget constraint*

sunk costs: costs that have been incurred and cannot be recovered

supply curve: the relationship between the quantity supplied of a good and the price, whether for a single firm or the market (all firms) as a whole

supply shocks: unexpected shifts in the aggregate supply curve, such as an increase in the international price of oil or a major earthquake that destroys a substantial fraction of a country's capital stock

supply: the quantity of a good or service that a household or firm would like to sell at a particular price

surplus: the magnitude of the gain from trade, the difference between what an individual would have been willing to pay for a good and what she has to pay

surplus of labor: a great deal of unemployed or underemployed labor, readily available to potential employers

sustainable development: development that is based on sustainable principles; sustainable development pays particular concern to environmental degradation and the exploitation of natural resources

tariffs: taxes imposed on imports

tax expenditure: the revenue lost from a tax subsidy

tax subsidies: subsidies provided through the tax system to particular industries or to particular expenditures, in the form of favorable tax treatment

theory: a set of assumptions and the conclusions derived from those assumptions put forward as an explanation for some phenomena

thin (or incomplete) markets: markets with relatively few buyers and sellers

time constraints: the limitations on consumption of different goods imposed by the fact that households have only a limited amount of time to spend (twenty-four hours a day); the time constraint defines the opportunity set of individuals if the only constraint that they face is time

time inconsistency: a phenomenon that occurs when it is not in the best interest of a player to carry out a threat or promise that was initially designed to influence the other player's actions

time value of money: the fact that a dollar today is worth more than a dollar in the future

total costs: the sum of all fixed costs and variable costs

total factor productivity (TFP): the part of economic growth that cannot be explained by increases in capital or labor

total factor productivity analysis: the analysis of the relationship between output and the aggregate of all inputs; total factor productivity growth is calculated as the difference between the rate of growth of output and the weighted average rate of growth of inputs, where the weight associated with each input is its share in GDP

total reserves: *nonborrowed reserves* plus *borrowed reserves*

trade creation: new trade that is generated as a result of lowered tariff barriers

trade deficit: the excess of imports over exports

trade diversion: trade that is diverted away from outside countries as a result of lowering tariffs between the members of a trading bloc

trade secret: an innovation or knowledge of a production process that a firm does not disclose to others

trade-offs: the amount of one good (or one desirable objective) that must be given up to get more of another good (or to attain more of another desirable objective)

tragedy of the commons: an analogy used to describe the deletion of a common resource when individual users fail to take into account the impact of their actions on the common resource

transfer programs: programs directly concerned with redistribution, such as AFDC, TANF, and Medicaid, that move money from one group in society to another

Treasury bills (T-bills): short-term government bonds that are available only in large denominations

trough: the point during a recession at which real output reaches its lowest level

trusts: organizations that attempted to control certain markets in the late nineteenth century; they were designed to allow an individual or group owning a small fraction of the total industry to exercise control

unemployment rate: the ratio of the number of people seeking employment to the total labor force

union shops: unionized firms in which all workers are required to join the union as a condition of employment

unit of account: something that provides a way of measuring and comparing the relative values of different goods

unitary elasticity: a demand curve has unitary elasticity if the demand for the commodity decreases by 1 percent when the price increases by 1 percent. If demand has unitary elasticity, then expenditures on the good do not depend at all on price; a supply curve has unitary elasticity if the supply of the commodity increases by 1 percent when the price increases by 1 percent

utility: the level of enjoyment an individual attains from choosing a certain combination of goods

value added: the value added in each stage of production is the difference between the value of the output and the value of the inputs purchased from other firms

value of the marginal product of labor: the value of the extra output produced by an extra unit of labor; it is calculated by multiplying the marginal product of labor times the price of the good which is being produced

variable costs: the costs resulting from variable inputs

velocity: the speed with which money circulates in the economy, defined as the ratio of income to the money supply

vertical equity: the principle that people who are better off should pay more taxes

vertical merger: a merger between two firms, one of which is a supplier or distributor for the other

voting paradox: the fact that under some circumstances there may be no determinate outcome with majority voting: choice A wins a majority over B, B wins over C, and C wins over A

wage discrimination: paying lower wages to women or minorities

World Trade Organization (WTO): the organization established in 1995 as a result of the Uruguay round of trade negotiations; replacing GATT, it is designed to remove trade barriers and settle trade disputes

zero elasticity: the situation that exists when the quantity demanded (or supplied) will not change, regardless of changes in price

CREDITS

p. 2: Chuck Savage/Corbis; **p. 10**: (top) Kevin Fleming/Corbis; (bottom) eBay.com; **p. 24**: David Raymer/Corbis; **p. 39**: Brooks Kraft/Corbis; **p. 52**: Chip East/Reuters/Corbis; **p. 59**: Martyn Goddard/Corbis; **p. 74**: RF/Corbis; **p. 76**: Gideon Mendel/Corbis; **p. 83**: Reuters/Corbis; **p. 93**: RF/Corbis; **p. 100**: Keith Dannemiller/Corbis; **p. 108**: Steve Terrill/Corbis; **p. 130**: Christie & Cole/Corbis; **p. 149**: William Webber/Visuals Unlimited; **p. 154**: Rosenfeld/Zefa/Corbis; **p. 165**: AP/Wide World Photos; **p. 174**: RF/Corbis; **p. 180**: Warner Morgan/Corbis; **p. 197**: Peter Blakely/Corbis/SABA; **p. 204**: Roger Ressmeyer/Corbis; **p. 204**: Patrick Bennett/Corbis; **p. 214**: James Leynse/Corbis; **p. 228**: Ariel Skelley/Corbis; **p. 232**: Library of Congress; **p. 238**: Carter Smith/Corbis/Sygma; **p. 248**: Steve Raymer/Corbis; **p. 250**: Reuters/Corbis; **p. 253**: Kevin Fleming/Corbis; **p. 260**: AP/Wide World Photos; **p. 268**: Reuters/Corbis; **p. 276**: Reuters/Corbis; **p. 283**: Joe Raedle/Getty Images; **p. 288**: Reuters/Corbis; **p. 298**: Philip James Corwin/Corbis; **p. 310**: Gail Mooney/Corbis; **p. 322**: Bettmann/Corbis; **p. 332**: Owaki-Kulla/Corbis; **p. 341**: Richard T. Nowitz/Corbis; **p. 354**: AP/Wide World Photos; **p. 356**: AP/Wide World Photos; **p. 367**: AP/Wide World Photos; **p. 374**: Brooks Kraft/Corbis; **p. 379**: AP/Wide World Photos; **p. 397**: Kevin Lamarque/Reuters/Corbis; **p. 404**: Richard Bickel/Corbis; **p. 411**: Galen Rowell/Corbis; **p. 414**: Kevin R. Morris/Corbis; **p. 424**: Buddy Mays/Corbis; **p. 429**: Bill Varie/Corbis; **p. 433**: China Photos/Reuters/Corbis; **p. 438**: RF/Getty Images; **p. 446**: Reuters/Corbis; **p. 452**: Rick Friedman/Corbis; **p. 455**: Peter Kornicker/Corbis; **p. 460**: Bettmann/Corbis; **p. 472**: Morton Beebe/Corbis; **p. 479**: Joel Stettenheim/Corbis; **p. 481**: Corbis; **p. 484**: Hans Halberstadt/Photo Researchers; **p. 495**: Reuters/Corbis; **p. 508**: Lou Dematteis/Reuters/Corbis; **p. 512**: Bettmann/Corbis; **p. 524**: John Madere Photography/Corbis; **p. 542**: Najlah Feanny/Corbis; **p. 546**: Talaie/Corbis; **p. 552**: AP/Wide World Photos; **p. 556**: Joel W. Rogers/Corbis; **p. 576**: Bohemian Nomad Picturemakers/Corbis; **p. 584**: Mitch Kezar/Stone/Getty Images; **p. 593**: (top) Roger Ball/Corbis; (bottom) Sheldan Collins/Corbis; **p. 599**: Ed Bock/Corbis; **p. 604**: James Leynse/Corbis; **p. 623**: James Leynse/Corbis; **p. 636**: Walter Hodges/Corbis; **p. 646**: Henry Ford Museum; **p. 660**: LWA-Dann Tardif/Corbis; **p. 688**: Jim Watson/AFP/Getty Images; **p. 703**: Bob Krist/Corbis; **p. 714**: Lance Nelson/Corbis; **p. 726**: Brooks Kraft/Corbis; **p. 734**: Pfaffenbach/Reuters/Corbis; **p. 739**: AP/Wide World Photos; **p. 756**: Alan Schein Photography/Corbis; **p. 759**: Courtesy of Carl Walsh; **p. 771**: AP/Wide World Photos; **p. 773**: Reuters/Corbis; **p. 778**: Chor Sokunthea/Reuters/Corbis; **p. 792**: Keren Su/Corbis; **p. 806**: AP/Wide World Photos; **p. 818**: Joel Stettenheim/Corbis; **p. 828**: (top) Roger Ressmeyer/Corbis; (bottom) AP/Wide World Photos; **p. 836**: Alex Wong/Getty Images; **p. 858**: Walter Hodges/Corbis; **p. 864**: Reuters/Corbis; **p. 873**: AP/Wide World Photos.

INDEX

absolute advantage, 41, 426
accounting profits, 166–71
acid rain, 414–15
acquired endowments, 430, 431
acquisitions, see mergers
adaptive expectations, 825, 880–81
ADI curve, see aggregate demand-inflation curve
ADM (Archer Daniel Midland), 275, 411
adverse selection:
   in health care insurance, 340
   and market for lemons, 333–36
advertising, 347–49
   competition and, 348
   informative, 348
   persuasive, 348
   profits and, 348–49
AFDC (Aid to Families with Dependent Children), 387
affirmative action, 364
AFL (American Federation of Labor), 356
Africa, 808
   sub-Saharan, 796, 797
   see also LDCs
African Americans, 231–32
AFSCME (American Federation of State, County and Municipal Employees), 358
aggregate demand, 780
   inflation and, 689–712
   monetary policy and, 749–50, 751
   product market and, 534–35
   shifts in, 701–2
   supply and, 533–35
aggregate demand-inflation (ADI) curve, 691–704
   automatic stabilizers and, 729–31
   determinants of, 693–94
   inflation adjustment curves and, 704–7, 729–33, 832–33, 844
   macroeconomic policy and, 703–4
   monetary policy and, 736, 748–49, 783, 853–54
   open economy and, 779–83, 787
   output and, 698–701
   shifts in, 693–704, 781–83, 859
   slope of, 781, 783
   using, 697–701
aggregate expenditures:
   defining of, 661–62
   exchange rates and, 781–83
   government purchases and, 676, 695, 697
   international trade and, 676–80
aggregate expenditures schedule, 662–66, 672
   government purchases and, 676
   international trade and, 679–80, 683
   mathematical formulation of, 665–66
   real interest rate and, 683–84
   shifts in, 664–65, 675
   taxes and, 669–71
aggregate income, 493
aggregate labor market, 528–29
aggregate output, 493
aggregate price level, 606–7
aggregate spending, 653–56, 692–93, 696–97, 780, 783
   exchange rate and, 781–83
aggregate supply, 533–35
agriculture:
   in LDCs, 796
   productivity improvements in, 466
   subsidies for, 93–94
AIDS/HIV, 267
Aid to Families with Dependent Children (AFDC), 387
airline industry, 269
air safety, cost of, 228
Akerlof, George, 334
Alcoa Aluminum, 300
allowances, pollution, 414
Amazon.com, 293
American Airlines, 283
American Federation of Labor (AFL), 356
American Federation of State, County and Municipal Employees (AFSCME), 358
American Tobacco, 300, 301
Anheuser-Busch, 304
Antitrust Division, U.S. Department of Justice, 305
antitrust laws, 299–307
   enforcement of, 305
   Microsoft and, 243, 245, 272, 302–3
   relaxation of, 466–67
   soft drink companies and, 306–7
AOL, 9
Apple computers, 272

appreciation, 577, 761
Archer Daniel Midland (ADM), 275, 411
Argentina, 94, 748
Arrow, Kenneth, 394
assessed taxes, 90
asset demand curve, 876
asset price bubbles, 880
assets:
   attributes of, 885
   of banks, 621–22, 625
   prices and, 878–81
   see also investment, investments
asymmetric information, 335
AT&T:
   deregulation and, 305
   imperfect competition and, 291
   R&D in, 464
Atlanta, Ga., scrip issued in, 614–15
ATM cards, 623
auction sites, 11
Australia, 377
automatic stabilizer, 670, 729–36
automation, 147–48
automobile industry:
   concentration in, 302
   demand for SUVs in, 59–60
   gasoline prices and, 59–60
   imports and, 302
   oligopoly in, 243
   OPEC and, 59, 478
   unions and, 148, 361
average costs, 138–39, 145, 160–63
average tax rate, 384
average variable costs, 138, 161–62

Baazee.com, eBay's purchase of, 5
baby boomers, 829–30
backward-bending labor supply curve, 178
backward induction, 320
balanced budgets, 552–54
balance of trade, 677
balance sheets, 620–22, 625
Bangladesh, 796
bank deposits, 619, 866
bank holiday of 1933, 614
banking system, U.S., 612–32, 715–23
   stability of, 630–32
bank runs, 631–32
bankruptcy, 872–74

banks:
　　assets of, 621–22, 625
　　balance sheets of, 620–22, 625
　　central, 626–27, 653–55, 696, 722–23, 740–45, 748–49, 849–59
　　commercial, 613, 614
　　Federal Reserve, 626–28, 654, 716–17
　　history of, 205
　　liabilities of, 621–22, 625
　　money created by, 615–26
　　panics and, 322–24
　　regulation of, 614
　　reserves of, 621–26, 628–30, 715–21
barriers to entry, 281–84
Barro, Robert, 841–42
barter, 616, 620
basic competitive model, 25–29, 206, 226
　　imperfect markets and, 240–42
　　ingredients in, 29
basic model of economy, 25–29
basic research, as public good, 464–65
Beautiful Mind, A (Nasar), 314
beggar-thy-neighbor policies, 317, 441
behavioral economics, 119–21
Bell, Alexander Graham, 453, 454
Bell Laboratories, 291, 593–94
benefits:
　　compensation and, 365, 369
　　of economic interdependence, 423
　　marginal, 43–44, 104
　　costs and, *see* costs; marginal costs
benefit taxes, 383
Bentham, Jeremy, 113
Bernanke, Ben, 849
Berners-Lee, Tim, 454, 593
bilateral trade, 425
black markets, 33
block grants, 387
"Boggs Bills," 619–20
bonds, 867–68, 874, 876
boom, 495
borrowed reserves, 629, 718–19
borrowing, 511, 512, 762–63, 839–40, 842
Botswana, 796
brand names, 241
Brazil, 802
　　see also LDCs
breach of contract, 338
briberization, 296
BTU tax, 107
Buchanan, James, 394
budget, 824–27
　　balanced, 552–54
　　defense spending and, 562
　　discretionary spending and, 562
　　economic growth and, 840
　　factors affecting U.S., 561–62, 837, 838–39

　　federal taxes and, 562, 838–39
　　health care cost and, 562
　　and interest on the debt, 841
　　risk factors in, 562
　　and social spending on the elderly, 562
budget constraints, 34–35, 39
　　changes in, 105, 109–11
　　choices and, 34–35
　　consumption decision and, 102–5
　　demand curves and, 110
　　income and, 105–8
　　indifference curves and, 127–29
　　between leisure and income, 177
　　slope of, 103
　　trade-offs and, 103
　　two-period, 192
budget deficit, 481, 548–54, 556–62, 733–36, 838–42
　　future, 840, 841–42
　　growth of, 562, 837, 838–39
buildings, as factor of production, 132
Bureau of Economic Analysis, U.S., 488, 490, 491
Bureau of Labor Statistics, U.S., 485, 514
Bush, George W., 39, 149, 396–97, 408, 732, 838–39
business cycles, 494–96, 638–48, 650–51, 844–48
　　see also fluctuations, business

Cailliau, Robert, 454, 593
California, electricity market in, 94, 112, 298–99
Cambridge constant, $609n$
campaign contribution laws, 395
Canada, drug importation from, 399–400
capacity utilization, 496
capital:
　　human, 203–4, 592
　　international trade and, 448–49
　　in LDCs, 798
　　misallocation of, in LDCs, 798
　　perfectly mobile, 762–63
　　physical, 204
　　savings rates and, 569–70
capital deepening, 590–91, 592, 597
capital flows, 568–71, 572–74, 575
capital gains:
　　defined, 493, 868
　　income and, 493
　　tax rate for, 385
capital goods, 16, 200
　　as factor of production, 132
　　investment in, 537
capital investments, 537
capital markets, 15–16, 191–212, 536–39, 612
　　access to, 462
　　demand in, 200–201

　　equilibrium in, 534–35, 538–42, 691
　　in full-employment model, 540, 541
　　globalization and, 762–63, 771–74, 839–40
　　government and, 549–54
　　government borrowing in, 839–40
　　growth of, 536–37
　　interdependence in, 425
　　international, 480
　　investment in, 537–38
　　investors in, 16
　　liberalization and, 802–3
　　open economy and, 568–71
　　real interest rate and, 690–91
　　savings and, 536–39
capital requirements, 631–32
capital stock, 505, 533, 590–91
Carnegie, Andrew, 300
cartels, 275–77
　　OPEC, 59, 275
cash management accounts, 613
causation, correlation and, 19
CBO (Congressional Budget Office), 561–62, 838
CDs (certificates of deposit), 619, 866
Celler-Kefauver Antimerger Act of 1950, 300, 301
central bank, 626–27, 653–55, 696, 722–23, 740–45, 748–49, 849–59
centralization, *see* planned economies
centrally planned economy, 12
　　privatization in, 12, 296
Chamberlin, Edward, 273
China, 12, 91, 155, 797, 807
　　economic transition and, 812
　　future of, 813
　　market economy and, 793, 810
　　see also LDCs; planned economies
choices, 6
　　budget constraints and, 34–35
　　incentives and, 7
　　indifference curves and, 124–29
　　market economy and, 34, 118–19
　　opportunity set and, 34–37
　　scarcity and, 26
　　time constraints and, 34–35, 39
　　trade-offs and, 34–39, 103, 843–44, 845
　　see also decision making
cigarette tax, 220–21, 234
CIO (Congress of Industrial Organizations), 356
circular flows, 493, 534–35, 549–50, 554
cities, in LDCs, 798
Civil Rights Act of 1964, 364
Clayton Act of 1914, 300, 301
Clean Air Act Amendments of 1990, 414
Clinton, Bill:
　　economic policies of, 396
　　environmental regulations and, 149

fiscal expansion and, 732
Kyoto agreement and, 149, 408
Coase, Ronald, 409
Coase's theorem, 409
Coca-Cola Company, 306–7
coca leaf production and Colombian GDP, 495
collusion, 275–77, 314
tacit, 275
command and control approach, 410
Commerce Department, U.S., 6
commercial banks, 613, 614
commercial policies, 434–35
commitment, 327–28
communism, 808–10
failure of, 793, 808–10
see also centrally planned economy
comparative advantage, 41, 426–31
determinants of, 430–31
Internet and, 429
marginal rate of transformation and, 427–28
production possibilities and, 427–28
resource interactions and, 431
specialization and, 428–30
of U.S., 429
compensating wage differentials, 362
compensation:
benefits and, 365, 369
executive, 368
fringe benefits, 365, 369
incentives and, 364–70
as tied to performance, 31, 364–70
see also wage changes; wages
competition:
advertising and, 348
assessing degree of, 270–71
firms and, 155–71
government and, 289–307
imperfect, see imperfect competition
international trade and, 442–43
Internet resources on, 468
monopolistic, 243, 273–74
natural monopolies and, 299
perfect, 26–29, 242
Schumpeterian, 463
technological change and, 463–64
trade and, 246
vertical restrictions on, 279
competitive equilibrium, basic model of, 227–30
competitive firm, theory of, 155–71
competitive markets, 26–29
economic efficiency and, 215–34
income distribution and, 225–27
Pareto efficiency and, 225
competitive model, basic, 25–29, 206, 226, 240–42, 526–27

competitive supply, 158–60
complements, demand curves and, 57–58
compound interest, 195, 211
computer industry, 459, 540–42, 598–99, 708–9
aggregate supply and, 540–42
demand and, 62
Condorcet, Marquis de, 394
conglomerates, 301
Congress, U.S., fiscal policy and, 749–50
Congressional Budget Office (CBO), 561–62, 838
Congress of Industrial Organizations (CIO), 356
conservation, of natural resources, 407–18
constant returns, 134
constant returns to scale, 144
Constitution, U.S., 457
constraints:
budget, see budget constraints
incentives and, 392
time, 34–35
consumer choice, theory of, 118–19
Consumer Expenditure Survey, 514
consumer price index (CPI), 485, 514–17, 605–7, 784–85
consumer protection legislation, 250
consumers:
in product market, 16
rational, 26–29, 34, 44
surveys of, 109, 198
see also consumption; consumption decision
consumer sovereignty, principle of, 380, 418
consumer surplus, 117–18, 217–18, 220, 224, 435
consumption, 667–72, 696–97, 780, 782, 840
disposable income and, 667–71
expectations of future, 671
government purchases and, 670
use of term, 489
wealth and, 671–72
see also consumers; consumption decision
consumption decision:
budget constraints and, 102–5
education and, 206
income and, 105–8, 176–78, 667–71
indifference curves and, 124–29
leisure vs., 176–78
loss aversion and, 120
price changes and, 109–11
savings decision and, 192–93, 195–96
shifts in, 671
smoothing of, 193
see also consumers; consumption
consumption possibilities curve, 206
contestable markets, 269

contingency clauses, 338
contracts, implicit, 645–46
contract solutions to incentive problem, 338
copyrights, 595
corporate income tax, 383
corporations, see firms
correlation:
causation and, 19
variables and, 18–19
Costa Rica, 797
cost curves, 135–46, 156–60
input prices and, 139
long-run, 141–45
marginal, 136–39
short-run, 141–45
U-shaped, 138–39
cost minimization, 147
costs:
of air safety for children, 228
average, 138–39, 145, 160–63
average variable, 138, 161–62
benefits and, see benefits; marginal benefits; marginal costs
definition of, 132
of deflation, 512
as factor of production, 132
of firms, 131–50, 156–58
fixed, see fixed costs
of inflation, 509–11
marginal, see marginal costs
opportunity, 38–39, 140, 166–67, 504, 643
opportunity sets and, 37–44
price and, 70–71
of production, 147, 156–58
sticky prices and, 647, 648
sunk, 42–43, 161–62, 269
total, 135–36
as trade-offs within opportunity sets, 38–44
variable, 135
cotton gin, 460
Council of Economic Advisers, 476, 477
countercyclical policies, 849
countervailing duties, 439
coupons, rationing by, 33
CPI (consumer price index), 485, 514–17, 605–7, 784–85
credit:
lines of, 618
monetary policy and, 630
money and, 618–19
credit cards, 323
credit unions, 613
cross subsidization, 295
currency, 619
boards, 772–73
exchange rates and, 770–71, 772–74, 781

currency *(continued)*
   inflation and, 510–11, 512–13, 773–74
   curves, interpretation of, 49–50
   cycles, business, 494–96, 638–48, 650–51, 844–48
     see also fluctuations, business
cyclical unemployment, 502–3, 638, 641–43, 646, 648, 656, 821–22, 831

deadweight loss, 220, 221
debt, federal, 479, 480–81, 557, 560, 561, 840
   alternative perspectives on, 841
   "owe it to ourselves" argument and, 841
   relative to GDP, 555, 559, 560, 561
   Ricardian equivalence and, 841–42
   World War II and, 840
decision making:
   of government, 800–803
   households, 534–35
   see also choices
defense related research, 429
defense spending, 375, 376, 377, 558, 562, 595
deficit, federal, 548–54, 556–62, 837, 838–42
   consequences of, 839–40
   debt and, 479, 480–81, 555
   entitlements and, 558
   full-employment, 733–36
   future generations and, 556, 557–58, 840–41, 842
   Ricardian equivalence and, 841–42
   sources of, 838–39
   surpluses and, 557–61
   taxes and, 842
   traditional views of, 839–40
   see also budget deficit
deficit, federal budget, 395–96
deficit, foreign, 555
deflation, 480–81, 512, 520, 855–57
   costs of, 512
demand, 53–61, 67–69, 77–95
   aggregate, *see* aggregate demand
   capital market and, 200–201
   computers and, 62
   elasticity of, *see* elasticity of demand
   excess, 68
   factor, 182–84
   income elasticity of, 107
   for large cars, 60
   for money, 607–12
   pressures, 820–23
   price and, 53–61, 70–71; *see also* price elasticity of demand
   relative elasticity of, 79–80
   rent control and, 218–19
   for small cars, 59–60
   use of term, 54

   vs. supply, 857–59
   see also supply and demand, law of
demand curves, 53–61
   asset, 876
   budget constraints and, 110, 128
   and changes in expectations, 58
   and changes in taste, 58
   complements and, 57–58
   demographic effects and, 58
   derivation of, 109–11, 182–84
   elastic vs. inelastic, 79
   income and, 57–58
   for individuals, 54–55, 109–11
   for labor, 182–84
   linear, 98
   long-run vs. short-run adjustments to, 87
   market, 55–61, 67–69
   movements along, 60–61
   price changes and, 77–78, 109–11; *see also* price elasticity of demand
   for rent control, 92
   shifts in, 55–61, 644–46
   sources of shifts in, 57–58
   substitutes and, 57–58, 78, 110
   supply curves and, 86
demand deposits, 617, 619
demographic effects, demand curves and, 58
Denmark, 377
depreciation:
   capital stock and, 590
   exchange rates and, 577, 579, 762, 770–71
depression, 495
Depression, Great, *see* Great Depression
deregulation, 94, 298–99, 305
description of preferences, utility and, 113–18
developed countries, 795
   LDCs vs., 798–99
development, 794–98
   globalization and, 803–7
   in Soviet Union, 809
   sustainable, 601
   see also LDCs
Digital Economist, 219
digital economy, *see* new economy
diminishing marginal rate of substitution, 127
diminishing marginal utility, 114–16
diminishing returns, 533
   inputs and, 133–34
   principle of, 34
   production function and, 133
diminishing returns to scale, 144
direct expenditures, military and civilian, 595
discount rates, 629, 630, 718
discouraged workers, 501

discretionary expenditures, 562, 731–36
discrimination:
   in labor market, 363–64
   public policy toward, 364
   statistical, 363
   in wages, 363
disinflation, 700–701, 703
disinvestment, 675
disposable income, 536, 667–71
disruption and monetary policy, 743–45
dissaving, 199
distribution, 7, 14–15, 28, 432
   exchange and, 224
   see also income distribution; wealth distribution
distributional effects, 826
diversification, 869, 872–74, 885–86
dividends, 868
division of labor, *see* specialization
dollar:
   -euro exchange rate, 579, 758–62, 788–89
   exchange rates and, 579, 759–65, 772–74, 780–81, 783–85
   supply and demand and, 759–65
   trade deficit and, 577–80
dollarization, 772, 773–74
dominant strategies, 313, 316–18
dot-com bubble, 744–45
"dot-com" firms, 165
double-coincidence of wants, 616
Dow Jones Industrial Average, 874–76
drug industry, 268, 456
dual economy, 798
Dubner, Stephen, 343
dumping, 438–39
duopoly, 278
Du Pont Cellophane Case (1956), 300, 301, 303
duties, countervailing, 439
dynamic efficiency, 458
dynamic inconsistency, 846

earned-income tax credit, 385
East Asia miracle, 799–803
eBay, 5
e-commerce, 744–45
   see also new economy
economic analysis, rational consumers and, 26–29
economic expansion, 640–43
economic growth, *see* growth
economic profits, 166–71
economic rent, 168–69
   monopoly, 265, 292
economics:
   automobiles and, *see* automobile industry
   behavioral, 119–21

branches of, 17
definition of, 6–15
information in, 647, 882–84
laws of, *see specific laws and principles*
normative, 19–20
positive, 19
as social science, 18
economies, modern:
    creating money in, 615–26
    financial system in, 612–26
economies of scale, 145, 267–70
economies of scope, 148
economists:
    disagreement of, 19–20
    models used by, 18
    monetarists, 846
    new classical, *see* new classical economists
    new Keynesian, *see* new Keynesian economists
    on price determination, 70
    real business-cycle, 844
    thinking of, 25–44
economy:
    basic model of, 26–29
    centrally planned, *see* centrally planned economy
    changes in effects of, 541
    closed, 549, 570, 690
    dual, 798
    future of, 541
    market, *see* market economy
    mixed, 12
    planned, *see* planned economies
    stimulation of, 477, 479–81
    strategies for transition, 812–13
    in transition, 808–13
education:
    age and years of, 205
    consumption decision and, 206
    economic trade-offs and, 206
    federal funding for, 379
    human capital and, 203–4, 592
    income and, 203–4
    labor supply decision and, 203–4
    in LDCs, 798, 799
    opportunity costs and, 40
    state funding for, 390
    trade-offs and, 206
    in U.S., 592
    wage gap and, 230
    wealth distribution and, 226
efficiency, 220–25, 457–61
    basic competitive model and, 28
    competitive markets and, 215–34
    rent control and, 218–19, 226
    taxes and, 220–21
    trade-offs and, 380–81

see also Pareto efficiency
efficiency wage, 646
efficiency wage theory, 366
efficient market theory, 881–84
elasticity:
    infinite, 80
    of labor supply, 176–78
    relative, 79
    relative inelasticity vs., 80
    and slope, 98–99
    substitutes and, 110
    unitary, 79
    zero, 80
elasticity of demand:
    income, 105–7
    monopoly and, 263
    price, *see* price elasticity of demand
    relative, 79–80
elasticity of supply, price, *see* price elasticity of supply
elderly, social spending on, 562
electricity prices, 94, 112, 298–99
employment, full, *see* full employment
Employment Act of 1946, 474, 476, 477, 481, 641
employment-wage puzzle, 643–48
Endangered Species Act of 1973, 410–11
endowment effect, 120
endowments:
    acquired, 430, 431
    natural, 430, 431
energy prices, 71, 112, 704–5, 706, 710
    see also electricity prices; oil prices
Enron, 13
entitlements, 389–90, 548, 839–40
    deficit problem and, 558
    as property rights, 32
entry, entering the market, 160–61, 169–70
    barriers to, 281–84
    commitment and, 328
environment:
    economics of, 405–18
    externalities and, 405–18
    incentives and, 253
    information and, 418
    international trade and, 447
    natural resources in, 405–18
    pollution and, 390, 414–15
    supply curves and, 67
environmental degradation:
    command and control of, 410
    GDP and, 497–98
    as negative externality, 407–18
Equal Employment Opportunity Commission, 364
equality, incentives vs., 31
equilibrium:
    analysis of, 227–34

    analysis of partial, 234
    in capital markets, 534–35, 538–42, 691
    competitive, *see* competitive equilibrium
    exchange rates and, 578–80, 760–63, 774
    in federal funds market, 720–21
    general, 538–41
    gross domestic product and, 534–35, 663–64, 681–82, 683–84, 693–701, 832–33
    in labor markets, 527–32, 534–35, 540–41, 644–45, 646
    macroeconomics and, 526–27
    minimum wage and, 231–32
    with monopolistic competition, 273–74
    in product markets, 535, 540–42
    see also general equilibrium
equilibrium output, 160, 534–35, 663–65, 670–71, 676, 681–83, 684, 693–701, 832–33
equilibrium price, 67–68, 70, 87–90
equilibrium quantity, 67–68
equilibrium real interest rate, 551, 557–58, 745–48, 839
equilibrium wage, 184–85
equity:
    horizontal, 382
    and redistribution of income, 378–79
    vertical, 382
equity concerns, distribution of goods and, 15
equity-efficiency trade-off, 380–81
essential inputs, 282
estate taxes, 583
euro-dollar exchange rate, 758–62, 788–89
Eurodollars, 619
Europe, Eastern:
    alternative economic systems in, 810–11
    failure of socialist economies in, 793, 808–10
    future of, 843
European Central Bank, 734, 788–89, 855
European Monetary Union, 734, 770, 788–89, 855
European Union (EU), 447, 448, 734, 788–89, 805, 810
excess capacity, marketing strategies and, 282
excess demand, 68
excess reserves, 718–19
excess supply, 68
exchange, 7, 423
    distribution and, 224
    globalization and, 432–33
    voluntary, 117, 432
    see also international trade; trade
exchange efficiency, 223, 225
exchange rates:
    aggregate expenditures and, 781–83

exchange rates *(continued)*
   appreciation and, 577, 761
   borrowing and, 762–63
   changes in, 577–80
   currency and, 770–71, 772–74, 781
   definition of, 758
   depreciation and, 577, 579, 762, 770–71
   determining, 758–65
   dollar and, 579, 759–65, 772–74, 780–81, 783–85
   equilibrium, 578–80, 760–63, 774
   expectations and, 765
   exports and, 579, 760–62
   fiscal policies and, 787
   fixed system of, 766
   flexible, 758, 771–74, 787
   float, 771
   foreign borrowing and, 581–82, 762–63
   imports and, 760–62
   inflation and, 780–81, 783–85
   international cooperation and, 771–74
   management of, 766–74
   monetary policy and, 767–69, 785–87
   and price of goods, 678–80, 783–85
   real, 764, 771–72
   speculation and, 763–65
   stabilizing, 771–74
   supply and demand and, 759–65
   trade deficit and, 577–80
   trade-weighted, 577–78
   volatility and, 769–71, 772
excise taxes, 383
exclusionary practices, monopolies and, 272
executive compensation, 368
exit, exiting the market, 56, 160–62
expectations:
   adaptive, 825, 880–81
   change in, 60, 825–28
   demand curves and, 58
   exchange rates and, 765
   forming of, 880–81
   of future consumption, 671
   of inflation, 820, 824–27, 832
   rational, 880–81
expenditures:
   discretionary, 562, 731–36
   military and civilian, 595
experimental economics, 321
export-led growth, 801
exports, 424, 678, 680
   exchange rates and, 579, 760–62
   high-tech, 576–77
   income and, 678
   net, 490, 676–80, 683–84, 780, 781–82
   see also imports; international trade; trade
externalities:
   environment and, 405–18

imperfect markets and, 241, 252–54
negative, 405–18
network, 272
positive, 454
solving problem of, 416

FAA (Federal Aviation Administration), 228
facilitating practices, by oligopolies, 276
factor demand, 182–84
factors of production, 132
Fair Labor Standards Act of 1938, 231
"fair trade," 437–39
farm programs, 93–94
FASB (Federal Accounting Standards Board), 5–6
FDA (Food and Drug Administration), 13–14
Federal Accounting Standards Board (FASB), 5–6
Federal Aviation Administration (FAA), 228
Federal Deposit Insurance Corporation (FDIC), 632
federal funds interest rate, 628, 629, 630, 715–23, 737–40, 782
   target of, 717, 722, 737–38, 743, 852–53
federal funds market, 628–30, 715–21
   equilibrium in, 720–21
Federal Open Market Committee (FOMC), 628, 689–90, 709, 710, 715–18, 721, 736–39, 743, 845, 851–53
Federal Reserve Act of 1913, 627, 848, 850, 854, 855
Federal Reserve Bank of New York, 629, 716–17, 721, 738
   Trading Desk of, 716–17, 721
Federal Reserve Banks, 626–28, 654, 716–17
Federal Reserve Board (Fed), 481, 605–6, 609, 615, 621–22, 627, 654, 691–97, 715, 716, 736–51, 782, 849–51, 855, 858
   inflation and, 689–90, 700–701, 703, 708–9, 837–38, 843, 848–49
Federal Reserve System, 621–22, 624, 626–32, 715–23, 855
Federal Trade Commission (FTC), 245, 250, 300, 305, 306–7
Federal Trade Commission Act of 1914, 279, 304
fiat money, 617, 620
final outputs approach to GDP, 489–91, 493
   income approach vs., 493
financial intermediaries, 612–14
financial markets, 786
financial services, banking, 205, 322–24
financial system, in modern economies, 612–26
financial terms, glossary of, 619
firms, 534–35

   competitive, theory of, 155–71
   as consumers, *see* consumers
   costs of, 131–50, 156–58
   and demand for labor, 181–84
   displaced, 440
   production decision of, 155–71
   profit-maximizing, 26–29, 158–60
   supply curves of, 162–63
   supply decision of, 264
fiscal deficit, 549, 556–61, 574–75
fiscal policies, 695–97, 727, 729–36
   Congress and, 749–50
   discretionary, 731–36
   exchange rates and, 787
   expansionary, 732–33, 746–47
   lags in, 750–51
   monetary policies and, 749–51, 785–89
   open market operations and, 787
   recessions and, 732–33
fiscal surplus, 549, 556–61
fixed costs, 135, 161
   research and development as, 460–61
flows:
   capital, 568–71, 572–74, 575
   circular, 534–35, 549–50, 554
   and GDP measurement, 505
fluctuations, business, 638–48
   full employment and, 638
   in full-employment model, 643–44, 648–49
   new classical views of, 844
   reasons for, 643–48
   unemployment and, 637–38
   see also business cycles
Food and Drug Administration (FDA), 13–14
Ford, Henry, 454, 456, 459, 594, 646
foreign exchange market, 757–65, 771–74
Fortune 500, 3
four-firm concentration ratio, 271
fractional reserves, 622
fractional reserve system, 622
Freakonomics (Levitt and Dubner), 343
free-rider problem, 255
free trade, 434, 804, 807
frictional unemployment, 502, 503, 527, 822, 829
Friedman, Milton, 827–29, 846
fringe benefits, 365, 369
FTC (Federal Trade Commission), 245, 250, 300, 305, 306–7
full employment, 474–82, 503, 525–26, 533, 539–42, 605, 641–43, 649, 656
   business fluctuations and, 638
   inflation and, 689–90, 691, 698–701, 703, 820
Full Employment and Balanced Growth Act of 1978, 481, 641, 842–43

full-employment level of output, 533, 553, 554
full-employment model, 540–42
   business fluctuations in, 643–44, 648–49
   capital markets in, 540, 541
   government in, 547–48, 839
   government purchases in, 549–54
   inflation and, 843
   international trade and, 567–68
   investment in, 554
   labor markets in, 540, 541
   monetary policy in, 745–46, 848–49
   money supply in, 609–10, 611–12, 722–23
   productivity growth in, 585–86
   product markets in, 540, 541
   technological change in, 542
full-employment real interest rate, 551, 557–58, 745–48
fully funded program, Social Security as, 396–97
future-oriented consumption, 671

G-8 group, 789
games:
   repeated, 319–20
   zero sum, 319
game tables, 313
game theory, 277–79, 313
   see also strategic behavior
game trees, strategic behavior and, 325
Gary, Elbert H., 275
gasoline prices, 59
   and demand for small cars, 59
   taxes and, 108
GDP, *see* gross domestic product
General Agreement on Tariffs and Trade (GATT), 445–46, 447, 448
General Electric, 275
general equilibrium:
   analysis of, 227–34
   defining of, 215
   over time, 232–33
general equilibrium of the economy, 538–42
   model for, 540–42
general system of preferences (GSP), 805
Germany, hyperinflation in, 512–13
gift taxes, 383
glass ceiling, 363
globalization, 246, 423, 432–33, 475, 567–68, 779, 786, 789, 794, 839–40
   capital markets and, 762–63, 771–74, 839–40
   history of, 804
   LDCs and, 803–7
Global Trade Watch, 449
global warming, 148–49, 408
glossary of financial terms, 619
Gompers, Samuel, 356

goods:
   capital, 132, 200
   inferior, 110
   merit, 379–80, 418
   nonrival, 457
   public, *see* public goods
   rival, 457
   rivalrous vs. nonrivalrous, 593
goods market, *see* product market
government, 12, 375–400, 547–62
   and barriers to entry, 281–82
   borrowing by, 556, 557, 575, 842
   capital markets in, 549–54, 839–40
   competition policies of, 289–307
   decision making by, 800–803
   deregulation by, 94, 298–99
   economic role for, 609, 771–74
   expenditures of, *see* government expenditures
   in full-employment model, 547–48, 839
   health care and, 398–400
   imperfect competition and, 245–46
   imperfect information and, 250–51
   LDCs and, 800–803
   market economies and, 12
   market failures and, 378, 405
   market failures approach to role of, 405
   monopolies and, 245–46, 272, 289–307
   natural resources and, 416–18
   product markets and, 549, 554
   purchases by, *see* government purchases
   reasons for intervention by, 377–80
   size of, 377
   spending and revenue, 548, 549
   water rights and, 32
   wealth distribution and, 197
government expenditures, 375–76
   discretionary, 548, 562
   entitlement programs in, 548, 562, 839–40
   GDP and, 490
   nondiscretionary, 548, 562
government purchases, 780
   aggregate expenditures and, 676, 695, 697
   consumption and, 670
   equilibrium output and, 676
   in full-employment model, 549–54
   use of term, 490
gradualism vs. shock therapy, 811–12, 813
Grand Banks, 31
graphs, reading of, 47–50
Great Depression, 495, 519, 614, 727, 856
   international trade and, 317, 441
   money and, 614–15, 631
   unemployment and, 441, 473–77, 644
greenhouse gases, 148–49, 408
green revolution, 796

Greenspan, Alan, 481, 627, 689, 745, 849, 850
gross domestic product (GDP), 485, 486–98
   chain-weighted real, 488
   circular flow and, 493
   comparison of international, 495
   defined, 486
   deflator, 487–88, 518–19, 606–7, 784–85
   equilibrium, 534–35, 663–64, 681–82, 683–84, 693–701, 832–33
   final goods approach to, 489–91, 493
   flow and stocks and, 505
   green, 497–98, 601
   growth rates and, 586
   human development and, 497–98
   illegal activity and, 495
   income approach to, 492–93
   international trade and, 424
   nominal, 487–88, 608
   nonmarketed goods and, 497
   Okun's law and, 503–4
   per capita, 590
   potential, 494–96, 503–4, 533, 541–42, 553, 705–10, 830, 832
   problems in measurement of, 496–97
   quality changes and, 496
   real, 487–88, 494–96, 503–4, 586
   relative to federal debt, 555, 559, 560, 561
   standard of living and, 497
   value-added approach to, 492
   weaknesses in, 496–97
growth, 474, 481–82, 485–98
   budget and, 851
   of capital markets, 536–37
   costs of, 601
   export-led, 801
   limits to, 600–601
   output and, 586–89
   productivity and, *see* productivity growth
guns and butter trade-offs, 33, 49

Harberger, Arnold, 290
Hawley-Smoot Tariff Act of 1930, 317, 441
Head Start, 379
health care:
   cost of, 562
   cost of pharmaceuticals and, 399
   drugs from Canada and, 399–400
   government and, 398–400
   insurance for, 340–42
   as share of expenditures, 376, 377
health maintenance organizations (HMOs), 340, 399
Herfindahl-Hirschman Index (HHI), 306–7
HIV/AIDS, 267
Hong Kong, 796
horizontal equity, 382
horizontal mergers, 301

horizontal restrictions, oligopolies and, 279
hours worked, labor supply decision and, 175–81
households, decision making in, 534–35
housing:
    incentives and, 343
    information and, 343
    real estate agents and, 343
    subsidies, 388
human capital, 203–4, 592
human development, GDP and, 497–98
human rights, 447
Humphrey-Hawkins Act, 641, 842–43
hyperinflation in Germany, 512–13

ideas, production of, 594–95
Immigration and Naturalization Service (INS), 806–7
imperfect competition:
    and barriers to entry, 281–84
    government and, 245–46
    market structure and, 242–43
    monopolies and, 289–307
    price and quantity in, 244–45
    product differentiation and, 271–72
    restrictive practices in, 275, 279–80, 304–5
    search and, 345–46
    technological change and, 454–55
imperfect information, 241, 247–51, 333–50, 393
    consequences of, 349
    government and, 250–51
    health insurance and, 340
    incentive problem and, 337–42
    Internet and, 249
    market failures and, 242
imperfect labor mobility, 362
imperfect markets, 239–56
    externalities and, 241, 252–54
    information and, 247–51
    public goods and, 241–42, 254–55
    quantity in, 244–45
implicit contracts, 645–46
import function, 678–79, 680
imports, 424, 678–79, 680
    automobile industry and, 302
    costs of, 783–85
    exchange rates and, 760–62
    high-tech, 576–77
    marginal propensity for, 678, 679–80
    unemployment and, 432–34
    see also exports; international trade; trade
import substitution, 802
incentive problem, 337–42
    contract solutions to, 338
    market solutions to, 337–38
    reputation solutions to, 339
incentives, 8
    choices and, 7
    compensation and, 364–70
    compensation tied to performance as, 31, 364–70
    constraints and, 392
    environment and, 253
    equality vs., 31
    housing and, 343
    income as, 29–30
    income effects and, 112
    interest rate parity and, 784
    market economy as driven by, 33
    monopolies and, 302–3
    moral hazard and, 337
    piece rates and, 365–66
    in political process, 394
    prices as, 53
    profits as, 29–30
    property rights and, 29–30, 253
    real exchange rates and, 764
    tax, 90
    for workers, 364–70
income:
    aggregate, 493
    budget constraints and, 105–8
    capital gains and, 493
    circular flows of, 534–35, 549–50, 554
    consumption decision and, 105–8, 176–78, 667–71
    demand curves and, 57–58
    disposable, 536, 667–71
    and effect of taxation, see income redistribution
    exports and, 678
    future, 839–40
    household spending of, 106
    as incentive, 29–30
    individual vs. national, 493
    nominal value of, 608–9
    per capita, 586–89, 794–99
    vs. money, 608–9
income approach to GDP, 492–93
    final goods approach vs., 493
income distribution:
    competitive markets and, 225–27
    international trade and, 443
income effect:
    incentives and, 112
    indifference curves and, 129
    inferior goods and, 110
    savings decision and, 209–11
income elasticity of demand, 107
income-expenditure analysis, 661–66
    aggregate expenditure schedule and, 662–66
    equilibrium output and, 663–65
income-output identity, national, 663
income redistribution, equity and, 378–79
income tax:
    corporate, 383
    individual, 383
increasing returns, 134
increasing returns to scale, 145
index funds, 885–86
indexing, 510–11
India, 796, 797, 805–7
    Silicon Valley and, 806–7
    see also LDCs
indifference curves, 124–29
    budget constraints and, 127
    choices and, 124–29
    consumption decision and, 124–29
    income effect and, 129
    marginal rate of substitution and, 126–27
    savings decision and, 209–11
    substitution effect and, 130
individual demand curves, 54–55, 109–11
individual income, 493
individual income tax, 383
individual retirement accounts, and Social Security, 397
industrialized countries, 795
industrial policies, 466
industries:
    concentration in, 271
    number of firms in, 270–71
inelasticity, relative, 80
inequality:
    in LDCs, 798–99
    see also discrimination
infant industry argument, 443–45, 466, 802
inferior goods, 110
infinite elasticity, 80
inflation, 194, 477–79, 481–82, 509–20, 605, 606–12
    adjustment and, 652–53, 820–32
    aggregate demand and, 689–712
    alternative measures of, 517–19
    American experience with, 519–20
    central banks and, 742–45, 748–49
    changing expectations and, 825–27
    costs of, 509–11
    currency and, 510–11, 512–13, 773–74
    distributional effects and, 826
    exchange rates and, 780–81, 783–85
    expectations of, 820, 824–27, 832
    Fed and, 689–90, 700–701, 703, 708–9, 837–38, 843, 848–49
    full employment and, 689–90, 691, 698–701, 703, 820
    full-employment model and, 843
    government policies toward, 689–97, 843
    hyper-, 512–13
    indexing and, 510–11

industrialized economies and, 819–20
interest rates and, 739–49, 780–81
lenders and, 510
measurement of, 514–19
monetary policy and, 653–56, 691–97, 722–23, 848–59
overstatement of, 516
perceived costs of, 509–11
Phillips curve and, 821–23
quality improvements and, 517
rate of, 509, 652, 700–704, 707–10, 821
real costs of, 509–11
real rate of interest and, 739–41
sufferers from, 510–11
taxpayers and, 510
unanticipated, 843
uncertainty and, 511, 512–13
and unemployment trade-off, 477–78, 653, 656, 728–29, 819–35, 843–44, 845
variability, 819
Volcker victory over, 478, 700–701, 703
inflation adjustment curve, 704–10, 832–33
inflation adjustment line, 698–99, 710
inflation shocks, 705, 820, 830–31, 832
inflation stability-output stability trade-off, 729
inflation targeting, 654, 655, 747–48, 837–38, 848–59
consequences of, 853–57
pros and cons of, 850–51
inflation tax, 511
information, 7, 13–14
asymmetric, 335
and barriers to entry, 282
cost curves and, 142–43
economic, 647, 882–84
environment and, 418
housing and, 343
imperfect, *see* imperfect information
markets for, 249–50
perfect, 333
prices and, 248
real-time, 858
strategic behavior and, 326
technologies, 858
information-based wage differentials, 362
information economy, 249
information intermediaries, 346–47
information revolution, 429
see also new economy
information technology, 62, 344
see also computer industry; new economy
informative advertising, 348
injections, spending stream and, 535, 539, 554
innovation:
new economy and, 455

unions and, 360
inputs, 15
cost curves and, 139
diminishing returns and, 133
essential, single ownership of, 282
as factors of production, 132
variable, 132
inside lag, 750, 751
inside traders, 883
insourcing, 805–7
institutional infrastructure, 811–12
insurance:
adverse selection in, 340
health care, 340–42
moral hazards and, 340
social, 378, 389–90
Intel, 3, 155, 429
Itanium chips canceled by, 5
intellectual property, 303, 457
interdependence, international, 432–34
interest, 193
compound, 195, 211
simple, 211
interest rate parity, 784
interest rates:
changes in, 210–11
cut of January 3, 2001, 743
as discount rate, 629, 630, 718
foreign, 782–83
inflation and, 739–49, 780–81
investment and, 537–38, 673–74
monetary policies and, 481, 630, 691–97, 721–23, 736–51, 858
nominal, 195, 673, 692–95, 722–23, 739–41, 856–57
in open economy, 569–71
prices and, 880
prime, 737–38
real, 195; real interest rates
savings and, 196
savings decision and, 194–96, 200–201, 209–11, 536–39
wealth distribution and, 197
intermediate outputs, 489, 491, 492
international financial crisis, 480, 758, 770–71, 772–74, 803, 859
international financial system, 757–76
deficit in, 555
foreign exchange market and, 757–65, 771–74
International Monetary Fund, 555, 789, 803, 812
international trade, 423–49, 572–82
aggregate expenditures and, 676–80
balance of trade in, 677
beggar-thy-neighbor policies in, 317, 441
commercial policies and, 434–35
cooperation in, 445–49

countervailing duties in, 439
displaced workers and, 440
dumping in, 438–39
"fair trade" and, 437–39
in full-employment model, 567–68
GDP and, 424
globalization and, 423
Great Depression and, 317, 441
infant industry argument in, 443–45, 466
liberalization in, 443
and marginal propensity to import, 678, 679–80
nontariff barriers and, 435, 437
open economy and, 568–71, 789
protectionism and, 246, 432–34, 439–45
quotas and, 436
regional trading blocs in, 448–49
strategic trade theory in, 445
tariffs and, 317, 435–36, 437
see also exports; imports; trade; trade deficit
Internet, 3–6, 27
barter and, 620
comparative advantage and, 429
drug trade on, 5
information problem and, 249
labor market and, 532
labor markets and, 369
price discrimination and, 293
productivity and, 455
Internet connections:
banking information, 629
beige book, 738
Bureau of Economic Analysis, 489
business cycles, 642
consumer price index and, 516
economic growth, 590
Economic Report of the President, 732
Federal Open Market Committee, 710
foreign exchange rates, 785
index funds, 870
inflation calculator, 517
money facts, 610
Nobel Prize, 829
trade data, 573
World Bank's development goals, 796
interventionists, 847–48
inventories, 634
build up of, 675
investment and, 672, 674–75
production-facilitating function of, 674–75
investing, a student's guide, 865–88
alternatives, 866–70
desirable attributes of, 870–78
efficient market theory and, 881–84
expectations and, 878–81
strategies for intelligent, 885–86

investment, investments, 672–76, 696–97
    attributes of, 870–78
    bonds, 867–68, 874, 876
    in capital goods, 537
    in capital markets, 537–38
    determinants of, 537–38, 675
    diversification and, 869, 872–74, 885–86
    efficient market theory and, 881–84
    expected returns on, 537–38, 673, 870–74, 878–81
    financial, 537, 865
    foreign, 762–65, 784
    in full-employment model, 554
    government and crowding out, 551, 553
    India's Silicon Valley and, 806–7
    interest rates and, 537–38, 673–74
    in inventories, 672, 674–75
    liquidity of, 877–78
    market risks and, 674
    mutual funds, 613, 619, 869–70, 872, 885–86
    "new economy" and, 744–45, 872
    in open economy, 780, 782
    in plant and equipment, 672–73
    productivity growth and, 590–91
    real, 865
    residential, 672, 866, 877
    risks and, 673, 674, 676, 874–76, 886
    savings and, 536–39, 570–71, 575, 590–91, 839–40
    skepticism and, 886
    stock shares and, 868–69, 874–76, 882–84
    strategies for, 885–86
    tax-favored, 876–77
    use of term, 489–90
    variability and, 674–75
    see also assets; capital goods
investment function:
    and changes in real interest rate, 538, 551, 673, 675
    defined, 538
investment schedule, 674
investors, 16

Jackson, Thomas Penfield, 302–3
Japan, 91, 796, 800–801
    deficit in, 555
jobs:
    Internet resources on, 345
    nonpecuniary attributes of, 362
job security:
    unions and, 360, 361
    wage increases vs., 361
Johnson, Lyndon Baines, income tax surcharge of, 732
joint products, 148
Justice Department, U.S., 283, 301, 302–3, 305

Kennedy, John F., tax cut of, 701–2, 731
Kenya, 796
Kerry, John, 39
Keynes, John Maynard, 474, 513, 884
Korea, South, 796, 800
Kyoto agreement, 149, 408

labor:
    division of, see specialization
    as factor of production, 132
    outputs and, 134
    skilled vs. unskilled, 231, 381
    surplus, 799
    turnover rate of, 646
    value of the marginal product of, 183
    as variable input, 134
labor demand:
    equilibrium wage and, 184–85
    real wages and, 644–45
    for skilled and unskilled workers, 530–32
    technology investment and, 530–31
labor demand curves, 182–84
    shifts in, 529–32, 644–46
Labor Department, U.S., 499
labor force:
    data on, 176
    definition of, 499
    growth of, 597, 599
    human capital problem and, 592
    participation in, 179–81
    participation rate, 501, 541, 587–88
    quality of, 592, 597–99
    women in, 181, 541–42
    see also labor supply decision
labor markets, 16, 179–81, 527–32
    aggregate, 528–29
    equilibrium in, 527–32, 534–35, 540–41, 644–45, 646
    firms and, 181–84
    in full-employment model, 540, 541
    imperfections in, 355–70, 532
    interdependence in, 424–25
    Internet and, 369, 532
    minimum wage and, 367–68
    search and, 346
    unions and, 355–62
    wages and, 70, 230–31
labor supply, 175–85
    elasticity of, 176–78
    equilibrium wage and, 184–85
    in LDCs, 798–99
    population growth and, 798–99
    trade-offs and, 179
labor supply curve, 178
    backward-bending, 178
    shifts in, 529–32, 541–42, 644–46
labor supply decision:

education and, 203–4
hours worked and, 175–81
human capital and, 203–4
substitution effect and, 178
labor unions, see unions
land reforms, 797–98
LDCs (less developed countries), 793–808
    agriculture in, 796
    capital in, 798
    centralized planning and, 800–803
    developed vs., 798–99
    development strategies for, 802–8
    dual economy in, 798
    East Asia miracle and, 799–803
    education and, 798, 799
    equality in, 801
    export-led growth in, 801
    globalization and, 803–7
    government decision making in, 800–803
    import substitution in, 802
    inequality in, 798–99
    institutional failures in, 798
    labor intensive industries in, 798
    labor supply in, 798–99
    life in, 797–99
    NICs and, 796
    outsourcing and, 805–7
    population growth and labor supply in, 798–99
    savings in, 798, 799, 800
    stability in, 799
    technology in, 799–801
    technology lacking in, 798
    trade with, 803–7
leakage, spending stream and, 535, 539, 554
learning by doing, 461–62
learning curve, 461–62
legal criteria, for defining a market, 303–4
legal entitlements, 32
leisure vs. consumption decision, 176–78
lemons (defective cars), 333–36
lenders, 510, 512
less developed countries, see LDCs
Levine, David, 319
Levitt, Steven, 343
Lewis, Arthur, 799
liabilities of banks, 621–22, 625
liberalization, market economy and, 810, 812
life-cycle theory of savings, 193
life insurance companies, 613
linear demand curves, 98
lines of credit, 618
liquidity, 866, 877–78
loanable funds, market for, 191, 201, 536
loans, see credit
long run, 649, 654
long-run cost curves, 141–45

long-run supply curves, 164–66
loss, deadweight, 220, 221
loss aversion, 120
lotteries, rationing by, 33
Lucas, Robert, 827–29, 844
Ludd, Ned, 601
Luddites, 601
luxury tax, 383

M1, 617–18, 722
M2, 617–18
M3, 618
machines, as factor of production, 132
macroeconomic policies:
    ADI curve and, 703–4
    controversies in, 837–62
    on economic fluctuations, 637–58
    goals of, 842–48
    history of, 727
    international, 789
    interventionist, 847–48
    non-interventionist, 844–46, 847
    role of, 727–51
    stabilization and, 837, 842–44
macroeconomics, 473–97
    definition of, 17, 473
    dot-com bubble and, 744–45
    equilibrium and, 526–27
    history of, 473–74
    investment and, 675–76
    key concepts of, 648–56
    key goals of, 481–82
    LDCs and, 799, 803
    microeconomics vs., 527
    net exports and, 679–80
Malthus, Thomas, 454, 594, 600, 796
managed care, 340
managerial slack, 291
margin, 104
marginal benefits, 43–44, 104
marginal cost curves, 136–39
marginal costs, 43–44, 104, 136–41, 156–58, 872
    private, 407
    social, 407
marginal product, 133–34, 136
marginal propensity to consume, 667–68, 670–71
    multiplier and, 666, 670–71
marginal propensity to import, 678, 679–80
marginal propensity to save, 659–69
marginal rate of substitution, 126–27
marginal rate of transformation, 223, 427
marginal revenue, 156, 244
marginal tax rate, 380, 384
marginal value, 71
market, markets, 10, 11
    aggregate labor, 528–29

capital, see capital markets
clearing of, 88
competitive, see competitive markets
contestable, 269
defining of, 301
efficiency of, 881–84
exchange and, 27
exchange rate, see exchange rates
financial, 786
foreign exchange, 757–65, 771–74
for health insurance, 340–42
imperfect, see imperfect markets
for information, 249–50
labor, see labor markets; labor supply; labor supply decision
for lemons, 333–36
for loanable funds, 191
predatory pricing and, 282
product, see product market
thin or incomplete, 335
marketable permit response, 413
market clearing price, see equilibrium price
market demand curves, 55–61, 67–69
market economy, 11, 14, 808
    choices and, 34, 118–19
    as driven by incentives, 33
    failures of, see market failures
    move toward, 810–13
    as price system, 29–30
    profits and, 29–30
    property rights and, 29–30
    transition to, 793
market equilibrium, 169
market failures:
    government and, 378, 405
    imperfect information and, 242
    negative externalities as, 405–7
market failures approach to role of government, 405–7
market labor supply curve, 179–81
market power, 270
market risks, 673, 674
market solutions to incentive problems, 337–38
market structures, 242–46
market supply, 64–67, 71
market supply curves, 64–69, 163–64
matching programs, 387
materials, as factor of production, 132
MCI, 305
Medicaid, 398, 400
medical care:
    cost of, 562
    see health care
Medicare, 12, 121, 376, 383, 398, 399
medium of exchange, 616, 620
mergers:
    FTC and, 306–7

horizontal, 301
Oracle's hostile bid for PeopleSoft, 5–6
vertical, 301
merit bads, 379–80
merit goods, 379–80, 418
Mexico, 94, 433, 448–49, 797
microeconomics, 527
    definition of, 17
    macroeconomics vs., 527
Microsoft, 3, 155, 157, 297, 429
    monopoly case against, 243, 245, 272, 302–3
middle-class entitlement programs, 389–90
middlemen, information technology and, 334
migration, mass, 531–32
military and civilian expenditures, 595
minimum wage, 91
    general equilibrium and, 231–32
    labor markets and, 367–68
mixed economy, definition of, 12
models:
    basic, 26–29
    basic competitive, 25–29, 206, 226, 240–42
    basic competitive equilibrium, 227–30
    consumer choice, 118–19
    economists' use of, 18
    full-employment, see full-employment model
    general equilibrium, 540–42
    predictive power of, 28–29
    reality vs., 118–19
monetarists, on business fluctuations, 846
monetary policy, 609, 736–51
    aggregate demand and, 749–50, 751
    credibility and, 857
    credit channel of, 630
    designing of, 848–59
    discount rates and, 629, 630, 718
    discretion and, 846
    disruption and, 743–45
    exchange rates and, 767–69, 785–87
    fiscal policies and, 749–51, 785–89
    in full-employment model, 745–46, 848–49
    goals of, 837–38, 848–49, 850–51
    inflation and, 653–56, 691–97, 722–23, 849–59
    instruments of, 628–30, 715–21
    interest rates and, 481, 630, 691–97, 721–23, 736–51, 858
    lags and, 750–51
    open market operations and, 628–29, 630, 716–17, 719–20, 721–22, 787
    reserve requirements and, 628–30, 715–21
    role and mechanisms of, 727, 736–39

monetary policy (continued)
  trade-offs and, 849–59
monetary policy operating procedures, 721–23
  interest rate, 630, 721–23
  money supply, 721–23
monetary policy rule, 692, 695, 700–701, 740–49, 846, 853–54
  position of, 745–48
  and shifts in full-employment real interest rate, 746
  and shifts in inflation target, 747–48
  slope of, 748–49
money, 605–32, 715–23
  counterfeiting of, 619–20
  creation of, 615–26
  credit and, 618–19
  definitions of, 615–17, 619
  demand for, 607–12
  electronic cash and, 623
  fiat, 617, 620
  functions of, 615–17
  Great Depression and, 614–15, 631
  income vs., 608–9
  as medium of exchange, 616, 620
  printing of, 614–15
  as store of value, 617
  time value of, 193
  as unit of account, 616
  velocity of, 608–9
money market accounts, 613, 619, 869–70
money multiplier, 624–26
money supply, 609–12, 737–38
  banks and, 620–26
  control of, 626–30
  in full-employment model, 609–10, 611–12, 722–23
  measurement of, 617–18
  monetary policy and, 721–23
  neutrality of, 611–12
  price and, 609–12
monitoring workers, 366
monopolies, 243
  drawbacks of, 289–92
  and elasticity of demand, 263
  exclusionary practices and, 272
  government policies on, 272, 289–307
  imperfect competition and, 289–307
  Microsoft and, 243, 245, 272, 302–3
  natural, 246, 267–70, 293–99
  new economy and, 272
  oligopolies and, 261–84
  output of, 261–67, 289–92
  profits of, 265
  public ownership of, 294–95
  regulation of, 295–96
monopolistic competition, 243
  equilibrium with, 273–74

monopoly rents, 265
moral hazards, 340
  incentives and, 337
Morgan, J. P., 300
motivation:
  savings and, 192–99
  see also incentives
multilateral trade, 425–26
multinational corporations, 757, 804
multiplier, 666, 670–71, 680
  money, 624–26
music industry, oligopoly in, 281
mutual funds, 613, 619, 869–70, 872, 885–86

NAFTA (North American Free Trade Agreement), 433, 443, 448
Napster, 8–10, 595
Nasar, Sylvia, 314
Nasdaq, 876
Nash, John, 314
Nash equilibrium, 313–14, 318, 323
National Center for Environmental Economics, 430
National Cooperative Research Act of 1984, 467
national income, 493
National Income and Product Accounts, 490
national income-output identity, 663
National Labor Relations Board, 356
national saving, 551
natural endowments, 430, 431
natural monopolies, 267–70
  competition and, 299
  government and, 246, 293–99
  regulation of, 295–96
natural rate of unemployment, 502, 503, 643, 822–23, 829–30, 843, 851
natural resources:
  conservation of, 407–18
  government and, 416–18
negative externalities, 405–18
  environmental degradation as, 407–18
  marketable permit response to, 413
  as market failures, 405–7
  oversupply and, 405–7
  property rights responses to, 407–10
  regulatory measures response to, 407–10
  tax and subsidy response to, 412–13
  weighing alternative approaches to, 415
negative slope, 48
net exports, 490, 676–80, 683–84, 780, 781–82
Netscape, 272
network externalities, 272
new classical economists, 844
  on business fluctuations, 844
  new Keynesian economists vs., 847, 848

new economy, 3–4, 27, 650, 744–45, 872
  comparative advantage and, 429
  "dot com" firms and, 165
  financing of, 205
  inequality and, 381
  innovation and, 455
  monopoly power and, 272
  skills in, 381
new Keynesian economists:
  on business fluctuations, 847, 848
  new classical economists vs., 847, 848
news, unanticipated, 883
New York, N.Y., rent control in, 93
New York Stock Exchange, 13, 874–76
New Zealand, 246
NICs (newly industrialized countries), 796
nominal interest rates, 195, 673, 692–95, 722–23, 739–41, 856–57
nominal wage, 178
nonborrowed reserves, 719
non-interventionists, 844–46, 847
nonrivalrous goods, 457
nontariff barriers, 435, 437
normative economics, 19–20
North American Free Trade Agreement (NAFTA), 433, 443, 448

Occupational Safety and Health Administration (OSHA), 360
oil prices, 71, 83, 91, 232–33, 705, 706, 830–31
Okun's law, 503–4, 642–43
old boy networks, 363
oligopolies, 243, 274–84
  entry deterrence and, 281–84
  horizontal restrictions and, 279
  monopolies and, 261–84
  in music industry, 281
  strategic barriers to entry and, 281
  strategic behavior and, 312
  see also imperfect competition
online piracy, proposed legislation on, 4–5
OPEC (Organization of Petroleum Exporting Countries), 59, 275, 478, 705, 706, 830–31
open economy, 567–71
  ADI curve and, 779–83, 787
  budget surpluses and deficits in, 839–40
  capital markets and, 568–71
  components of, 780
  interest rates in, 569–71
  international coordination and, 789
  policy in, 779–91
  savings-investment identity for, 580–82
  small, 569–70
  U.S. as, 549, 570–71
Open Market Desk, 629

open market operations, 628–29, 630, 716–17, 719–20, 721–22, 787
opportunity costs, 38–39, 40, 140, 166–67, 504, 643
opportunity sets, 34–37
  choices and, 34–37
  costs and, 37–44
Oracle, 5
Organization of Petroleum Exporting Countries (OPEC), 59, 275, 478, 705, 706, 830–31
organizations, see firms
OSHA (Occupational Safety and Health Administration), 360
output, 15, 844
  ADI curve and, 698–701
  aggregate, 493
  alternative measures of, 496
  costs of recession, 504, 642–43
  equilibrium, 160, 534–35, 663–65, 670–71, 676, 681–83, 684, 693–701, 832–33
  final, 489–91, 493
  full employment level of, 533, 553, 554
  gap, 496, 503–4, 638–40, 642–43, 700, 702
  growth and, 586–89
  intermediate, 489, 491, 492
  labor and, 134
  level of, 133
  measurement of, 485–98, 505
  of monopolies, 261–67, 289–92
  per capita, 599
  potential, 533
  problems in measurement of, 496–97
  as production function, 134
  restricted, 289–92
  revenue and, 155–56
  value of, 489–93
output stability-inflation stability trade-off, 729
outside lag, 751
outsourcing, 805–7
oversupply, negative externalities and, 405–7

Pacific Gas & Electric Company (PG&E), 872–74
panics, bank, 322–24
Pareto, Vilfredo, 222
Pareto efficiency, 222–24
  competitive markets and, 225
  conditions for, 222–24
Pareto efficient, 226–27
partial equilibrium, analysis of, 227, 234
patents, 282, 457–59, 595
  efficiency and, 457–59
  idea production and, 455–57
  life of, 458

limitations to, 459
  protection of, 458–59
  trade secrets and, 459
paternalism, 418
pay-as-you-go, Social Security as, 396
payroll taxes, 383, 389
peak of cycle, 640–42
Pell grants, 379
Penn World Table, 495
PeopleSoft, 5
  economies of scope and, 148, 150
PepsiCo, Inc., 306–7
perfect competition, 26–29, 242
perfect information, 333
performance, compensation tied to, 31, 364–70
persuasive advertising, 348
pharmaceuticals, cost of, 399
Phillips, A. W., 821
Phillips curve, 828
  expectations-augmented, 822
  shifts in, 821–23
  unemployment-inflation trade-off and, 820–23
physical capital, 204
piece-rate system, 365–66
planned economies, socialist, 793, 808–10
planning, by government, see centrally planned economy
plant and equipment, investment in, 672–73
Poland, market economy and, 810
politics, unions and, 360
pollution, 390
  acid rain and, 414–15
population growth:
  labor supply and, 798–99
  in LDCs, 798–99
portfolio, diversification of, 885–86
positive economics, 19
positive externalities, 454
positive slope, 48
potential output, 533
poverty, 798, 826, 879
predatory pricing, marketing strategies and, 282
preferences, description of, 113–18
prejudice, see discrimination
Prescott, Ed, 844
present discounted value, 193–94, 211–12, 233, 879–80
price, prices, 8, 29–30, 53–71
  adjustments to, see price changes
  of assets, 878–81
  changes in, see price changes
  consensus on, 70
  cost and, 70–71
  definition of, 53, 70

demand and, 53–61, 70–71; see also price elasticity of demand
  determination of, 70–71
  energy, 704–5, 706
  entry and, 160
  equilibrium, 67–68, 70, 87–90
  exchange rates as, 578, 579
  of gasoline, 59–60, 108
  in imperfect markets, 244–45
  as incentive, 53
  income effect and, 112
  inflation and, 511, 652–53, 722–23, 820, 821
  information and, 248
  interest rates and, 880
  international trade and, 678–80, 783–85
  of oil, 71, 83, 91, 232–33
  predatory, 282
  quality and, 336
  relative, 38, 103, 758
  role of, 53–54
  sticky, see sticky prices
  supply and, 61, 63, 71; see also price elasticity of supply
  utility and, 117–18
  value and, 70–71
price ceilings, 91–92
price changes:
  consumption decision and, 109–11
  demand curves and, 77–78, 109–11; see also price elasticity of demand
  labor demand curves and, 183
  responses to, 111
  sensitivity to, 77–78
  small vs. large, 81
  wage changes as, 177
price discrimination, 266–67, 268
  Internet and, 293
price dispersion, 343
price elasticity of demand, 77–78, 81, 85
  short-run vs. long-run, 81–82
  small vs. large price changes and, 81–82
  use of, 78
price elasticity of supply, 82, 84–85
  short-run vs. long-run, 85, 164
  use of, 82, 84–85
price floors, 93–94, 118
price index:
  consumer, 514–17, 605–7
  "fixed basket problem" and, 516
  software and, 518
  use of term, 487–88, 514
price level, 605, 606–12, 652
  aggregate, 606–7
  money supply and demand and, 609–12
price level targeting, 854–55, 862
price makers, 244
price rigidities, see sticky prices
price system, market economy as, 29–30

price takers, 27, 131, 218
price wars, 269
prime interest rate, 737–38
principal, 193
prisoner's dilemma, 277–79, 312–16, 321, 326
private goods, 255
private marginal costs, 407
private property, rights of, *see* property rights
private sector, 12
privatization, 802–3, 810, 812–13
   in centrally planned economy, 12, 296
   in former Soviet Union, 296
   movement for, 295
producer price index, 517
producer surplus, 217–18, 220, 224
product, marginal, 133, 136
product differentiation:
   and defining markets, 302–3
   imperfect competition and, 271–72
production:
   costs of, 147, 156–58
   efficiency, 223
   factors of, 132
   multiple factors of, 146–49
   with single variable factor, 132
production decision:
   and basic conditions of competitive supply, 158–60
   costs and, 156–58
   entry and, 160, 169–70
   exit and, 161–62
   factor demand and, 182–84
   of firms, 155–71
   profits and, 166–71
   revenues and, 155–56
   supply and, 160, 163–64
   and theory of competitive firm, 169–70
production efficiency, 223, 225
production-facilitating function of inventories, 674–75
production function, 133–34
   short-run, 533
production input, 132–33
production possibilities curve, 35–37
   comparative advantage and, 427
   Pareto efficiency and, 223
productivity:
   Internet and, 455
   specialization and, 428–29
productivity growth, 585–603, 708–9
   and allocation of resources, 592–93
   explaining, 589–96
   in full-employment model, 585–86
   investment and, 590–91
   labor force growth and, 597, 599
   R & D spending and, 593–94, 595
   rate of, 586–89, 592

residual, 597
standard of living and, 585–90
structural, 650–51
technological change and, 589, 593–96, 708–9
total factor analysis of, 596–99
productivity wage differentials, 362
product market, 15–16, 532–35
   aggregate demand and supply in, 533–35
   aggregate supply in, 533–35
   consumers in, 16
   equilibrium in, 535, 540–42
   in full-employment model, 540, 541
   government and, 549, 554
   interdependence in, 424
product-mix efficiency, 223
products, joint, 148
profit-and-loss statement, 156
profit-maximizing firms, 26–29, 158–60
profits:
   accounting, 166–71
   advertising and, 348–49
   definition of, 132
   economic, 166–71
   entry and, 160–61
   as incentives, 29–30
   market economy and, 29–30
   of monopolies, 265
   pure, 265
progressive tax systems, 380
property rights:
   entitlement as, 32
   failure of, 31–32
   ideas and, 594–95
   ill-defined, 31
   incentives and, 29–30, 253
   intellectual, 303, 457
   intellectual property and, 595
   online piracy and, 4–5
   restricted, 32
   tragedy of the commons and, 31
property rights responses, 407–10
property taxes, 383
protectionism, 802
   displacement and, 674–75
   international trade and, 246, 432–34, 439–45
   political and economic rationale for, 439–45
   use of term, 432
public choice theory, 394
public goods:
   basic research as, 464–65
   free-rider problem of, 255
   imperfect markets and, 241–42, 254–55
   pure, 457
public ownership, 294–95
public sector, *see* government

publishing industry, 165
pure profit, 265
pure public goods, 457

quality:
   of labor force, 592
   measurement of changes in, 496
   price and, 336
quantity:
   equilibrium, 67–68
   in imperfect markets, 244–45
quantity equation of exchange, 608–9
queues, rationing by, 32–33
quota rents, 436

racial quotas, 364
random walk, 883–84
rational consumers, 26–29, 34, 44
rational expectations, 880–81
rationing, 32–33
   by coupons, 33
   by lotteries, 33
   by queues, 32–33
   in Soviet Union, 809
Reagan, Ronald, 395, 700
real business-cycle theory of business fluctuations, 844
real estate agents, housing and, 343
real exchange rates, 764, 771–72
real interest rates, 195, 673–74, 675, 740–41, 839
   aggregate expenditures schedule and, 683–84
   budget surpluses and, 839–40
   capital markets and, 690–91
   full-employment, 551, 557–58, 745–48
   inflation and, 739–41
   investment function and changes in, 538, 551, 673, 675
   monetary policy and, 691–97, 739–41, 745–48
   after tax, 684
reality, models vs., 118–19
real product wage, 182
real wage, 178
recession, 495–96, 638–43
   fiscal policy and, 732–33
   monetary policy in, 742–43
   of 1995–96, 782
   output costs of, 504, 642–43
   of 2001, 165, 480, 551, 558, 561
redistribution of income, *see* income redistribution
regional trading blocs, 448–49
regressive tax systems, 380
regulation, of natural monopolies, 295–96
regulatory capture, 296
regulatory measures response, 407–10

relative elasticity, 79
relative elasticity of demand, 79–80
relative inelasticity, 80
relative price, 38, 103
rent control, 92–93, 218–19, 226
rents, economic, 168–69
    monopoly, 265, 292
rent seeking, 292
repeated games, 319–20
replacement, threat of, 361
repurchases (RPs), 716–17
reputations, 321
reputation solutions, to incentive problem, 339
research and development (R & D), 291–92
    capital markets and, 462
    competition and, 463–64
    defense, 429
    as fixed cost, 460–61
    government support for, 464–67
    patents and, 455–57
    as public good, 464–65
    social benefits of, 464
    as source of technological progress, 593–94, 595
reservation wages, 180
reserve requirements, 628–30, 715–21
reserves, 621–26
    borrowed, 629, 718–19
    excess, 718–19
    fractional, 622
    nonborrowed, 719
residential investment, 672, 866, 877
resource interactions, comparative advantage and, 431
resources:
    allocation of, 592–93
    choices and, 26–29
restricted output, 289–92
restricted property rights, 32
restrictions, on trade, 432–34
restrictive practices, in imperfect competition, 275
    consequences of, 279–80
    curbing of, 304–5
retained earnings, 868
retirement plans, 872–74
returns, increasing, 134
Reuther, Walter, 356
revenue curves, 156–58
revenues, 132
    marginal, 156, 244
    output and, 155–56
    production decision and, 155–56
Ricardian equivalence, 841–42
Ricardo, David, 427, 430, 842
right-to-work laws, 357
risk, risks:
    budget, 562
    investments and, 673, 674, 676, 874–76, 886
    market, 673, 674
    technological, 674
    uncertainty and, 646, 647–48
rivalrous goods, 457
Robinson-Patman Act of 1936, 267, 300, 304
Rockefeller Foundation, 796
Roosevelt, Franklin D., 614
royalties, 457
Russia:
    economic transition and, 810–13
    failure of communism in, 793
    future of, 813
    market economy and, 810–11
    see also centrally planned economy; Soviet Union

sales tax, 383
S & L's (savings and loan associations), 613, 614
savings, savings decision, 536–39, 842
    aggregate, 199
    aging population and, 199
    capital markets and, 536–39
    consumption and, 192–93, 195–96
    demographics and, 199
    disposable income and, 536
    vs. dissavings, 199
    foreign, 571
    forms of, 199–200
    government deficits and, 548–61, 842
    households and, 192–93
    income effect and, 209–11
    indifference curves and, 209–11
    inflation and, 510, 511
    interest rates and, 194–96, 200–201, 209–11, 536–39
    investment and, 536–39, 570–71, 575, 590–91, 839–40
    in LDCs, 798, 799, 800
    life-cycle theory of, 193
    motivations for, 192–99
    personal rate of, 199
    Social Security and, 197
    substitution effect and, 209–11
    survey on, 198
    in U.S., 198–99, 570–71
savings deposits, 619, 866
savings-investment identity, for open economy, 580–82
savings rate, aggregate, 199
scarcity:
    choices and, 26
    trade-offs and, 7, 38
schools, see education
Schumpeter, Joseph, 463

Schumpeterian competition, 463
search:
    imperfect competition and, 345–46
    information intermediaries and, 346–47
    labor market and, 346
    use of term, 344
search problem, 342–47
seasonal unemployment, 502, 503, 527
Securities and Exchange Commission, 13, 250
Selden, George Baldwin, 459
selection, adverse, 333–36, 340
sensitivity to price changes, 77–78
September 11, 2001 terrorist attack, 743–45, 807, 839
sequential moves, 324–25
services, measurement of changes in, 496
Shapiro, Carl, 4
sharecropping, 797
Sherman Antitrust Act of 1890, 300–301
shock therapy vs. gradualism, 811–12, 813
shortages, surpluses and, 88–90
short run, 646–47, 649, 651, 654, 655, 656, 820–32
short-run cost curves, 141–45
short-run inflation adjustment curve (SRIA), 823–27, 830–31, 844
short-run production function, 533
short-run supply curves, 164–66
signaling, 335–36
Silicon Valley, 806–7
simple interest, 211
Singapore, 796, 800, 801
single ownership of an essential input, 282
sin taxes, 383
skilled vs. unskilled labor, 231, 381
slope, 48–49
    of budget constraints, 103
    elasticity and, 98–99
    negative, 48
    positive, 48
    of production function, 133–34
"smart cards," 623
Smith, Adam 4, 70, 216, 239, 474
smoothed consumption, 193
social insurance, 378
    burden of, 389
socialism, see centrally planned economy
social justice, 378
social marginal costs, 407
Social Security, 12, 383, 474
    age eligibility proposals for, 398
    as fully funded program, 396–97
    funding for, 396–98
    future of, 481
    indexed benefits in, 510, 516, 517
    individual retirement accounts and, 397
    low savings and, 197

Social Security *(continued)*
   as pay-as-you-go program, 396
   reduction in benefits proposed for, 398
   as share of expenditures, 375, 376, 377
   as support program, 389
   tax increases proposed for, 398
social spending on elderly, 562
software:
   economic characteristics of, 491
   price and quantity of, 518
South Africa, 268, 456
Soviet-style socialist economies:
   failure of, 793
   see also centrally planned economy
Soviet Union, 7, 296, 327, 408, 808–10
   see also Russia
specialization:
   comparative advantage and, 428–30
   limits of, 430
   productivity increased by, 428–29
speculation, 763–65
spending shocks, 730–31
spending stream, 535, 539
spotted owls, 410–11
stagflation, 477–78, 824
standard of living:
   in LDCs, 793–99
   measurement of, 497, 797
   productivity growth and, 585–90
   rising, 586–89
Standard Oil, 300–301
static efficiency, 457
statistical discrimination, 363
status quo bias, 121
steel industry:
   price-fixing in, 275
   unions and, 148
sticky prices, 646–48, 649–51, 652, 656
   costs and, 647, 648
   demand curves and, 646–47
   risk and uncertainty, 647–48
   sources of, 647–48
sticky wages, 645–46, 649, 652, 655
stock and GDP measurement, 505
stock markets, 13, 770–71, 868–69, 882–84
stock of capital, 505
stock options, expensing of, 6
stockpiles, agricultural, 94
stock shares, 868–69, 874–76, 882–84
store of value, 617
strategic behavior, 311–28
   commitment and, 327–28
   dominant strategies in, 313, 316–18
   in games without dominant strategies, 318
   game trees and, 325
   institutions in, 322
   Nash equilibrium and, 313–14, 318, 323

   oligopolies and, 312
   prisoner's dilemma and, 277–79, 312–16, 321, 326
   in repeated games, 319–20
   sequential moves in, 324–25
   time inconsistency and, 326–27
strategic trade theory, 445
strikes, 355
structural unemployment, 502, 503, 527, 822
sub-Saharan Africa, 796, 797
   see also LDCs
subsidies, 93–95, 385–86
   for agriculture, 93–94
   of housing, 388
   for technological change, 465–66
substitutes:
   demand curves and, 57–58, 77–78, 110
   elasticity and, 110
   price elasticity and, 81
substitution:
   and global warming, 148–49
   import, 802
   marginal rate of, 126–27
   principle of, 147–48
substitution effect, 110–13
   indifference curves and, 130
   labor supply decision and, 178
   savings decision and, 209–11
sunk costs, 42–43, 161–62, 269
superior knowledge, 430–31
supply, 61, 63–69, 77–95
   aggregate, 533–35
   competitive, 158–60
   elasticity of, 82, 84–85
   excess, 68
   market, 64–67, 71
   of money, *see* money supply
   pressures, 820–23
   price and, 61, 63, 71; *see also* price elasticity of supply
   production decision and, 160, 163–64
   rent control and, 218–19
   use of term, 61, 63
   vs. demand, 857–59
supply and demand, law of, 67–71, 77–95, 606–7, 652
   interfering with, 90–95
   shortages and surpluses and, 88–90
   tax policy and, 87–88, 220, 221
supply curves, 63–67
   aggregate, *see* aggregate supply curve
   and demand curves, 86
   environment and, 67
   of firms, 163–64
   for labor, 178
   long-run vs. short-run adjustments to, 87, 164–66

   market, 64–69, 163–64
   movements along, 67
   rent control and, 92
   shifts in, 65–67, 644–46
   sources of shifts in, 65–67
supply decision, *see* output
supply shocks, 705, 708
Supreme Court, U.S., 9, 10, 305–6
surpluses:
   budget, 396
   consumer, 117–18, 217–18, 220, 224, 435
   deficits and, 557–58, 561–62
   federal, consequences of, 839–40
   price floors and, 93–94, 118
   producer, 217–18, 220, 224
   shortages and, 88–90
   taxes and, 549–54, 555
surplus labor, 799
sustainable development, 601
Sweden, 377

tacit collusion, 275
Taft-Hartley Act of 1947, 356–57
Taiwan, 796, 800, 801
   see also LDCs
TANF (Temporary Assistance to Needy Families), 387, 388
tariffs, 317, 435–36, 437
   losses from, 435–36
tastes, change in, demand curves and, 58
tax and subsidy response, 412–13
tax credits, earned-income, 385
taxes:
   aggregate expenditures schedule and, 669–71
   assessed, 90
   benefit, 383
   on capital gains, 385
   on cigarettes, 220–21, 234
   on corporate income, 383
   deficits and, 549–54, 555, 557, 558, 561, 842
   distribution and, 226
   effects of changes in, 552–54
   efficiency and, 220–21
   excise, 383
   fiscal policy and, 731–36
   on gifts and estates, 383
   government revenues and, 548–54, 555
   importance of, 383
   on individual income, 383
   inefficiencies and, 111
   investments and, 876–77
   on luxuries, 383
   negative externalities and, 412
   as passed along to consumers, 87–88, 90
   on payrolls, 383, 389
   on property, 383

real returns and, 684
as redistribution of income, see income redistribution
revenue calculations, 108
sales, 383
sin, 383
and supply and demand, 87–88, 220, 221
U.S. budget and, 562, 838–39
window, 90
tax expenditures, 386
taxpayers, inflation and, 510
tax policy, and law of supply and demand, 87–88, 220, 221
tax rate:
  average, 384
  federal deficits and, 477, 479, 480–81
  indexing and, 510
  marginal, 380, 384
Tax Reform Act of 1986, 385
tax subsidies, 385–86
tax system:
  administrative simplicity of, 386
  characteristics of, 381–86
  efficiency of, 382, 385–86
  fairness of, 382, 383–86
  flexibility of, 382, 386
  progressive, 380
  regressive, 380
  scope of, 383
  transparency of, 382, 386
  in U.S., evaluation of, 381–86
Taylor, John, 729
technological change, 453–68, 479–80, 540–42
  competition and, 463–64
  and demand for capital, 201
  direct expenditures and, 595
  in full-employment model, 542
  ideas and, 593–96
  imperfect competition and, 454–55
  labor demand and, 530–31
  patents and, 457–59
  productivity growth and, 589, 593–96, 708–9
  subsidies for, 465–66
technological risks, 674
technology:
  computer, aggregate supply and, 540–42
  imports and exports of, 576–77
  information, 708–9, 786, 858
  in LDCs, 799–801
  sources of progress in, 593–96
telecommunications industry, 270, 272
Temporary Assistance to Needy Families (TANF), 387, 388
terrorism, 480, 555, 561, 562, 743–45, 807, 839
theorems, 226

theory, 18
thin or incomplete markets, 335
"thrifts," see S & L's
tie-ins, product, 280
time constraints, 34–35
time inconsistency, 326–27
time value of money, 193
tit for tat, 321
total costs, 135–36
total factor productivity analysis, 596–99
trade, 423
  balance of, 677
  bilateral, 425
  free, 804, 807
  globalization and, 803–7
  interstate sales, 304–5
  multilateral, 425–26
  mutually beneficial, 423
  restriction of, 432–34
  surplus in, 572
  see also international trade
trade creation, 448
trade deficit, 479, 572–82
  dollar and, 577–80
  exchange rate and, 577–80
  as problem, 580–82
  reversal of, 581–82
  savings-investment identity and, 580–82
trade diversion, 448
trade-offs:
  budget constraints and, 103
  choices and, 34–39, 103, 843–44, 845
  costs as, 38–44
  definition of, 6–7
  education and, 206
  employment and, 643
  environment and, 410–11
  equity and efficiency, 380–81
  growth vs. freedom, 809
  guns and butter, 33, 49
  incentives and equality, 31
  labor supply and, 179
  leisure and consumption, 176–78
  opportunity sets and, 38–44
  output stability-inflation stability, 729
  policy, 849–59
  predation and, 283
  real change and, 742
  scarcity and, 7, 38
  unemployment and inflation, 728–29, 825–27, 843–44, 845
  wage increases and job security, 361
  wheat and corn, 37
trade policies, 423–49
  changing of exchange rate, 577–80
  preferential treatment and, 805
trade secrets, 459

tragedy of the commons, property rights and, 31
transfer payments, 730, 734
transfer programs, 379, 386–89
traveler's checks, 619
treasury bills, 869
Treasury Department, U.S., 716, 812
trough of recession, 640–42
trusts, 300–301
Turing, Alan, 459
turnover of labor, 646
two-period budget constraints, 192

UAW (United Auto Workers), 356, 361
unemployment 481–82, 485, 498–505
  aggregate labor market and, 528–29
  baby boomers and, 829–30
  business fluctuations and, 637–38
  cyclical, 502–3, 638, 641–43, 646, 648, 656, 821–22, 831
  distributional effects and, 826
  forms of, 501–3
  frictional, 502, 503, 527, 822, 829
  full employment and, 533
  Great Depression and, 441, 473–77, 644
  and inflation trade-off, 477–78, 653, 656, 689–90 819–35, 843–44, 845
  international interdependence and, 432–34
  international trade and, 440
  "jobless recovery" and, 475, 480
  macroeconomic policies and, 728–29
  money wages and, 821
  natural rate of, 502, 503, 643, 822–23, 829–30 843, 851
  natural-rate proposition and, 822–23, 829–30
  Okun's law and, 503–4
  problems with statistics on, 501
  rate of, 485, 499–501, 505, 638–40, 643, 700–704, 708–9
  real wages and, 644–45
  seasonal, 502, 503, 527
  statistics on, 499–501
  structural, 502, 503, 527, 822
  threat of, 361
unions, 355–62
  decline of, 356–58
  economic effects of, 359–60
  and effect on nonunion workers, 359–60
  history of, 356–58
  innovation and, 360
  Internet resources on, 358
  job security and, 360, 361
  limits on power of, 360–61
  politics and, 360
  rise of, 356
  short-run gains vs. long-run losses of, 359

unions *(continued)*
    strikes by, 355
    substitution principle and, 148
union shops, 357
unitary elasticity, 79
United Auto Workers (UAW), 356, 361
United Kingdom, 377
United Nations (UN), 795
United States:
    comparative advantage of, 429
    as debtor nation, 581–82; *see also* trade deficit
    dollar, strength of, 788–89
    education in, 592
    equity in, 378
    expenditures in other countries vs., 377
    growth in, 485–98
    job loss and outsourcing, 805–7
    as mixed economy, 12
    1990s economy of, 707–10
    as open economy, 549, 570–71
    tax system of, 383–86
unit of account, 616
urbanization, in LDCs, 798
Uruguay Round, 804
U-shaped cost curves, 138–39
U.S. Steel Company, 275
utility, 113–18
    marginal, 114–16
    price and, 117–18

value:
    of the marginal product of labor, 182–84
    of output, 489–93
    present discounted, 193–94, 211–12
    price and, 70–71
    store of, 617
value-added approach to GDP, 492
variable costs, 135
    average, 138, 161–62
variable inputs, 132
variables, 18–19
Varian, Hal, 4

velocity of money, 608–9
venture capital, 205, 462
VERs (voluntary export restraints), 436
vertical equity, 382
vertical mergers, 301
vertical restrictions on competition, 279
Volcker, Paul, victory over inflation by, 478, 700–701, 703
voluntary exchange, 117, 432
voluntary export restraints (VERs), 436
voting paradox, 394

wage changes:
    job security vs., 361
    labor supply decision and, 179
wage differentials, 362–64
    imperfect labor mobility, 362
wage-employment puzzle, 643–48
wage gap, 230–31
wages:
    contracts and, 645–46
    efficiency, 366, 646
    equilibrium, 184–85
    high, 367–68
    indexed, 510
    inflation and, 510, 511, 652–53, 820–21
    international trade and, 442
    labor demand and, 644–45
    labor supply decision and, 180
    minimum, 231–32
    money, 821
    nominal, 178, 527–28, 645–46
    as price, 70
    real, 178, 527–29, 531–32, 540–41, 542, 644–45, 646
    real product, 182, 184
    reservation, 180
    risk and uncertainty, 646
    sticky, 645–46, 649, 652, 655
    unemployment and, 644–45, 821
    see also compensation; income; wage changes
Wagner Act of 1935, 356

Washington consensus, 803
water rights, 32
wealth:
    consumption and, 671–72
    distribution of, 879
wealth distribution, 7, 14
    interest rates and, 197
    taxes and, 226
Wealth of Nations, The (Smith), 4, 70, 216
welfare, as share of expenditures, 376, 377
Westinghouse, 275
wheat-corn trade-off, 37
Wheeler-Lea Act of 1938, 250
Whitney, Eli, 460
Wilson, Woodrow, 304
window tax, 90
wineries, 304–5
women, in labor force, 181, 541–42
workers:
    discouraged, 501
    displaced, 440
    monitoring of, 366
    motivation of, 364–70
    Silicon Valley and, 806–7
    see also labor markets; labor supply; labor supply decision; unions
World Bank, 789, 795, 803
World Trade Organization (WTO), 317, 322, 445–49, 456, 803
World War II, 475–76
    federal debt and, 840
World Wide Web, 454, 593, 786
Wright, Gavin, 232, 368
Wright Brothers, 453, 454
WTO (World Trade Organization), 317, 322, 445–49, 456

Yahoo, 744

zero elasticity, 80
zero sum games, 319
zoning laws, 410